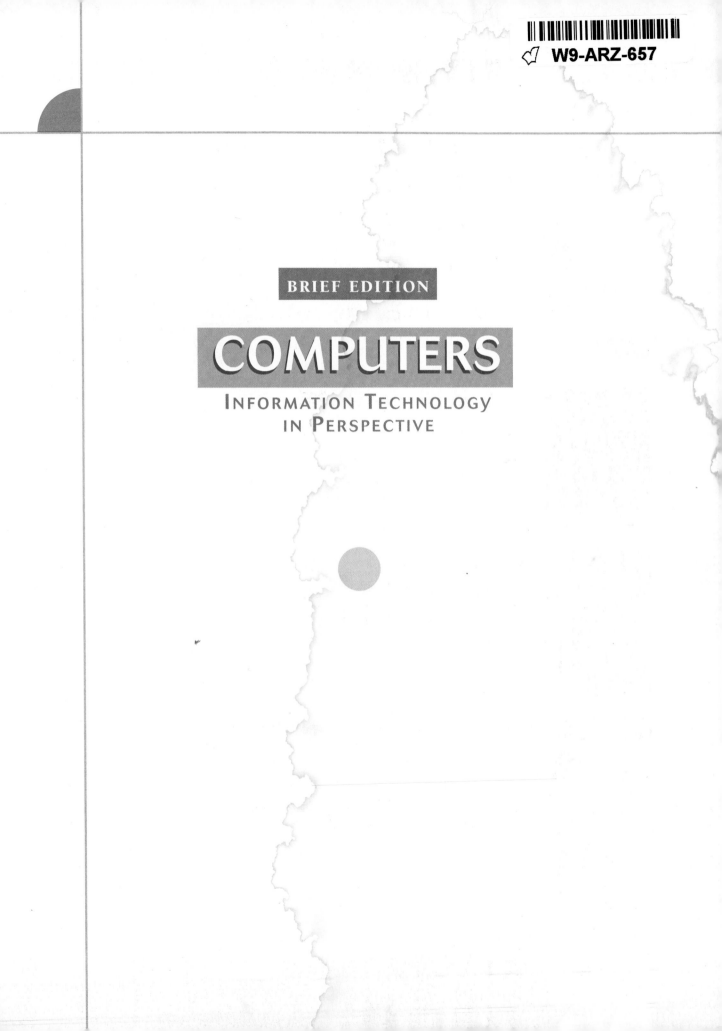

BRIEF EDITION

COMPUTERS

INFORMATION TECHNOLOGY
IN PERSPECTIVE

BRIEF EDITION

COMPUTERS

INFORMATION TECHNOLOGY IN PERSPECTIVE

ELEVENTH EDITION

Larry Long
and
Nancy Long

PEARSON

Prentice
Hall

Upper Saddle River, New Jersey 07458

Librabry of Congress Cataloging-in-Publication Data

Long, Larry E.
    Computers : information technology in perspective / Larry Long and Nancy Long.—11th ed., brief ed.
        p. cm.
    Includes index.
    ISBN 0-13-140581-0
    1. Computers. 2. Electronic data processing. I. Long, Nancy.   II. Title.

    QA76 .C576 2004
    004—dc21

                                                                    2003002581

Vice President/Publisher: Natalie Anderson
Executive Acquisitions Editor: Jodi McPherson
Senior Marketing Manager: Emily Williams Knight
Senior Editorial Project Manager: Kristine Lombardi Frankel
Assistant Editor: Melissa Edwards
Editorial Assistants: Jodi Bolognese and Jasmine Slowik
Marketing Assistant: Danielle Torio
Development Editor: Joyce Nielsen
Senior Media Project Manager: Cathi Profitko
Production Manager: Gail Steier de Acevedo
Senior Project Manager, Editorial Production: Tim Tate
Associate Director, Manufacturing: Vincent Scelta
Manufacturing Buyer: Tim Tate
Design Manager: Maria Lange
Art Director: Pat Smythe
Associate Director, Multimedia Production: Karen Goldsmith
Manager, Print Production: Christy Mahon
Print Production Liaison: Ashley Scattergood-Tooey
Interior Design: Ray Cruz
Cover Design: John Romer
Infographics: Kenneth Batelman
Illustrator (Interior): Black Dot Group
Full Service Composition: Black Dot Group/An AGT Company
Printer/Binder: Von Hoffmann Corporation
Cover Printer: Phoenix Color Corporation

Credits and acknowledgments borrowed from other sources and reproduced, with permission, in this textbook appear on appropriate page within text.

10 9 8 7 6 5 4 3 2 1
ISBN 0-13-140581-0

To our children,
Troy and Brady,
The motivation for all we do.

COVER CREDITS

CONTENTS OVERVIEW

CONTENTS

IT ILLUSTRATED

THE COMPUTER
ON A CHIP 200

IT ILLUSTRATED

PERSONAL COMPUTING
BUYER'S GUIDE 310

SPECIAL INTEREST SIDEBARS

PREFACE TO THE STUDENT

Welcome to the computer and information technology revolution. You've taken the first step toward information technology (IT) competency, the bridge to an amazing realm of adventure and discovery. Once you have read and understood the material in this text and have acquired some hands-on experience with computers, you will be poised to play an active role in this revolution.

- You'll be an intelligent consumer of PCs and related products.
- You'll be better prepared to travel the Internet and take advantage of its wealth of resources and services.
- You'll become a participant when conversations at work and school turn to computers and technology.
- You'll be better able to relate your computing and information processing needs to those who can help you.
- You'll know about a wide variety of software and services that can improve your productivity at work and at home; give you much needed information; expand your intellectual and cultural horizons; amaze you, your family, and your friends; and give you endless hours of enjoyment.

Achieving IT competency is the first step in a lifelong journey toward greater knowledge and interaction with more and better applications of IT. IT competency is your ticket to ride. Where you go, how fast you get there, and what you do when you arrive are up to you.

LEARNING AIDS

Each chapter contains several helpful learning aids that can help you understand and retain information technology concepts and terminology. The two-page chapter opening has two learning aids:

- *Learning Objectives*. The learning objectives give you a target for learning for each numbered section.
- *Why This Chapter Is Important to You*. This learning aid serves two purposes. First, it provides an overview of chapter content and, second, it offers compelling reasons why learning the material can help you achieve important life goals.

The body of the chapter has a learning aid at the beginning and end of each numbered section.

- *Why This Section Is Important to You*. Each section begins with a statement that answers the question, "Why do I need to know this?" There is a natural motivation to learn when you know the "Why?"
- *Section Self-Check*. These objective questions (multiple-choice and true-false) are designed to test and reinforce your knowledge of the section's content. Answers for these questions are provided at the back of the book.

The end-of-chapter material includes an extensive array of learning aids.

- *Chapter Summary*. Every boldface term is included in a section-by-section summary of the chapter.
- *Key Terms*. Key terms are listed in alphabetical order with cross-references to the pages where the terms are introduced.
- *Matching*. Here you match a word or a phrase to 15 terms or concepts from the chapter. Answers to this matching exercise are provided at the back of the book.
- *Chapter Self-Check*. The Chapter Self-Check, which is organized by numbered section, is an extension of the Section Self-Check; that is, it contains more of the same types of questions to assess your understanding of the material. Answers to these exercises are provided at the back of the book.

- *IT Ethics and Issues*. Several scenarios introduce important information technology ethical considerations and issues. Each scenario has discussion questions that encourage critical thinking and/or promote a lively in-class debate.
- *Discussion and Problem Solving*. These questions invite group discussion or individual/group problem solving related to concepts presented in the chapter.
- *Focus on Personal Computing*. Each chapter has exercises designed to expand your personal computing horizons, all within the context of chapter content.
- *Online Exercises*. The Long and Long Companion Website invites you to go online and explore the wonders of the Internet through a comprehensive set of Internet exercises. These entertaining exercises invite you to learn more about the topics in this book and to do some serendipitous (just-for-fun) surfing.

Computers is supported by a comprehensive mixed-media learning assistance package. The Long and Long Companion Website at **www.prenhall.com/long** includes *Online Exercises, Web Projects, Internet Links,* an *Interactive Study Guide,* and much more—all designed to help you learn about computers and information technology. Other online learning tools are described in the Preface to the Instructor.

YOU, COMPUTERS, AND THE FUTURE

Whether you are pursuing a career as an economist, a social worker, a politician, an attorney, a dancer, an accountant, a computer specialist, a sales manager, or virtually any other career, the knowledge you gain from this course ultimately will prove beneficial. Keep your course notes and your book; they will prove to be valuable references in other courses and in your career.

Even though computers are all around us, we are seeing only the tip of the information technology iceberg. You are entering the IT era in its infancy. Each class you attend and each page you turn offers a learning experience that takes you one step closer to an understanding of how computers and IT are making the world a better place in which to live and work.

PREFACE TO THE INSTRUCTOR

Everything seems to be changing—at home, at work, during leisure, and in education. The forces behind this change, computers and information technology (IT), are the reason we now live in an interconnected society. *Computers,* 11th edition, captures this paradigm shift in societal trends in a way that instills in students an urgent desire to learn and to play an active role in this technology revolution.

MEETING THE CHALLENGES OF TEACHING INTRODUCTORY IT COURSES

The introductory IT course has its teaching challenges. Throughout the term we are historians, scientists, and, on occasion, sociologists. In the same course we now toggle between lecture, lab, and, for some, distance learning via the Internet. If that's not enough, we teach an ever-increasing amount of material to students with a wide range of career objectives and technical abilities. *Computers* and its extensive teaching/learning system are written and designed to give you what you want and need to meet these challenges.

OBJECTIVES FOR THE ELEVENTH EDITION OF COMPUTERS

We had these primary objectives as we began writing this eleventh edition of *Computers.*

- *Make content relevant to the student.* Throughout the book, we make learning about IT a very personal experience. Each chapter begins with "Why This Chapter Is Important to You" and each major section begins with "Why This Section Is Important to You."

- *Motivate the student to learn.* The text and all supplements are written in a style that remains pedagogically sound while communicating the energy and excitement of IT to the student. We want the information in this book to be absorbed, retained, and enjoyed.

- *Present the right content at the right level for IT competency.* We cover only that material which is appropriate for *modern* IT competency. We feel an obligation to present topics at depths consistent with introductory learning. Our focus is on information that will have an impact on the student's ability to cope with the IT revolution.

- *Create content that reflects the state-of-the-art of the technology.* We are committed to maintaining our position as the most current IT concepts book available.

- *Streamline the presentation of material.* We have streamlined the presentation, eliminating those boxed items that may be interesting, but are not critical to chapter concepts or IT competency. This streamlining effort is in response to faculty and students who tell us they want a book that presents important material in a straightforward manner without extraneous clutter. The result is a cleaner, more easily absorbed presentation.

- *Present IT ethics in more depth.* An appreciation for IT ethics has emerged as a core topic for college graduates. A chapter is devoted to IT ethics. Each chapter has several *IT Ethics and Issues* scenarios with probing discussion questions designed to spur lively in-class discussions. Also, the *Discussion and Problem Solving* section has numerous engaging discussion questions on IT issues.

- *Cover the Internet in a way that reflects its true impact on society.* Chapters 3 and 9 are devoted to the Internet, and the Net is mentioned or discussed hundreds of times throughout the book. We are an interconnected society and it is our obligation to present the breadth of Internet applications, examine timely Internet issues, and gaze into the future of the Net.

- *Give professors plenty of flexibility.* The text and its mixed-media teaching/learning system are organized to permit maximum flexibility in course design and in the selection, assignment, and presentation of material.

- *Emphasize personal computing.* Students enjoy personal computing, so we take every opportunity to relate terms and concepts to their personal computing experiences.

- *Make this edition transition friendly. Computers,* 11th edition, was written to enable a smooth, seamless transition for those colleges moving from previous editions of *Computers.*

COMPUTERS IS AN ANNUAL EDITION

Computers is updated annually, and each year we make thousands of changes to bring *Computers* abreast with a rampaging technology. Just look at what has happened in one year since the last edition.

- Instant messaging emerged as a major communications tool in the corporate world.
- Open source software development is going mainstream.
- Broadband has reached critical mass in many geographic areas enabling the widespread implementation Net-based applications such as video-on-demand, grid computing, and videoconferencing.
- Chip technology has gone from microns to nanometers.
- De facto standards have emerged for rewritable DVD and short-range wireless communications.
- Home networking has become commonplace.
- Internet gaming has exploded.
- New IT ethics issues, such as the use of facial recognition systems, have emerged.
- People routinely check their e-mail and chat via cell phones.
- Hard disk storage capacities have doubled.
- The Internet is the conduit for most international calls.

CHANGES IN THE ELEVENTH EDITION

One reason that *Computers* has remained the choice of thousands of your colleagues through ten editions is because we try very hard to evolve with your needs and give you the features you need to teach successful courses. In that regard, this edition has several very visible changes.

- *Reorganized to meet emerging IT educational needs.* A number of changes have been made to the overall organization of the book. To provide a better fit for the semester format, the full book now has a Getting Started section and 12 chapters, one less than the 10th edition. "Going Online" is moved from Chapter 7 to Chapter 3. The Brief edition, which was previously the Getting Started plus 10 chapters, is now the Getting Started plus eight chapters.

- *Expanded "Getting Started" section.* Unique to introductory IT books, the very visual Getting Started section is expanded, to help jumpstart the student's personal computing experience and enable leveling of IT understanding. This popular section introduces the essential information students need to get them up and running—hardware basics, GUI/operating system concepts, file management, networking and Internet access concepts, and an introduction to using word processing, e-mail, Internet browser, and instant messaging software.

THE CRYSTAL BALL

- *Expanded end-of-chapter material.* The chapter review materials are significantly enhanced from previous editions. The *Chapter Summary* and *Discussion and Problem Solving* elements are continued and several new aids are added, including *Key Terms* (with page references), *Matching, Chapter Self-Check* (a supplement to *Section Self-Checks), IT Ethics and Issues* (scenarios and discussion), *Focus on Personal Computing* (hands-on PC exercises), and *Online Exercises* (references to the companion Web site).

PERSONAL COMPUTING

- *New margin elements: The Crystal Ball and Personal Computing.* These short, to-the-point sidebars give students some solid advice on how to prepare for the future and get the absolute most of their personal computing experience. Both are written in first person by author Larry Long. *The Crystal Ball* offers author predictions on information technology from 3 to 10 years into the future. The Crystal Ball looks to the future on many topics, such as health care and personal communications. *Personal Computing* contains tips, hints, and recommendations that can enhance the student's personal computing experience.

A COMPUTERS EDITION FOR EVERY COURSE

Computers comes in two editions.

- *The Brief Edition.* Eight *core chapters,* plus a *Getting Started* section at the beginning of the book, introduce students to the world of information technology: concepts relating to interaction with computers; fundamental hardware, software, and communications concepts; going online (the Internet and its applications); and IT ethics and issues. The brief book includes three colorful *IT Illustrated* modules: computer history, the making of integrated circuits, and a PC buyer's guide.

- *The Full Edition.* The full edition has four additional chapters. The student is introduced to the cyberworld, from e-commerce to Web site development. A *two-chapter* sequence introduces students to the various types of information systems and includes an overview of the latest approaches to system development. The focus of the last chapter is the future: IT careers, robotics, and future IT applications.

THE COMPUTERS TEACHING/LEARNING SYSTEM

Computers, 11th edition, continues the Long and Long tradition of having the most comprehensive, innovative, and effective support package on the market. The book is but one component of a comprehensive *mixed-media teaching/learning system* that is designed to give you maximum flexibility in course design and instruction. Use these resources to offer IT competency education in whatever formats meet your student and curriculum needs.

TOOLS FOR ONLINE LEARNING

A wealth of online learning tools are available to facilitate the teaching/learning process.

Long and Long Companion Website: www.prenhall.com/long

The Companion Website is customizable with real-time news, headlines, and current events and it offers a variety of activities and services, including downloadable supplements. These resources complement student learning.

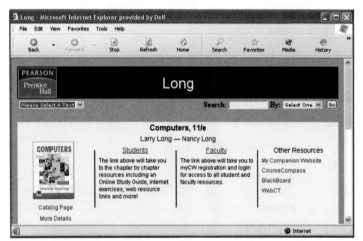

Long and Long Companion Website

- *Internet Exercises.* The Internet exercises encourage students to explore more fully IT competency topics while familiarizing themselves with the Internet. Each chapter has an Internet exercise for each of the special interest sidebars as well as an additional 2-4 exercises focusing on chapter specific topics and real-world issues.

- *Interactive Study Guide.* The Interactive Study Guide helps the student learn and retain concepts presented in the text. The student can choose from four skills quizzes: multiple choice, true or false, matching, or essay. A summary report is returned to the student within seconds. After completing a quiz, the student has the option of routing the answers to his or her e-mail address and/or to that of the instructor.

- *Online End-of-Chapter Materials.*

- *Web Resources.* Additional web resources include Careers in IT, Technology Updates, Technology Buying Guide, crossword puzzles, a Web Guide and much, much more.

- *Instructor Downloads.* The Companion Website includes many helpful password-protected faculty resources. These resources are dynamic, ever changing, and include supplementary exercises, the image library, videos, animations, the instructor's manual and Test Bank in Word and PDF format, and PowerPoint presentations.

The instructor's resources are also available on the instructor's one-stop CD-ROM called Present IT. The new IRCD/Present IT is a comprehensive, user-friendly, Instructor's Tool that is all you need to prepare and present powerful lectures to your students. You can easily customize your own lecture presentation selecting from dynamic PowerPoints, images, videos, animations, and more.

Image Library

- *Instructor's Manual (IM)*. The *Instructor's Manual* is available in Microsoft Word and PDF format and is available in hard copy, as well. The *Instructor's Manual* contains teaching hints, references to other resources, selected images, lecture notes, key terms with definitions, solutions to review exercises, and much more.

- *PowerPoint Slides*. Several hundred colorful and illustrative PowerPoint slides are available for use with Microsoft PowerPoint. The chapter-by-chapter PowerPoint slides can be customized easily to meet lecture needs.

- *Windows PH Test Gen and Test Item File*. *Windows PH Test Gen* is an integrated PC-compatible test-generation and classroom-management software package. The package permits instructors to design and create tests, to maintain student records, and to provide online practice testing for students. The accompanying *Test Item File* contains thousands of multiple-choice, true/false, matching, and essay questions.

Additional media resources include an image library, animations, and brand new TECH TV videos, giving motion and additional meaning to the student's learning experience.

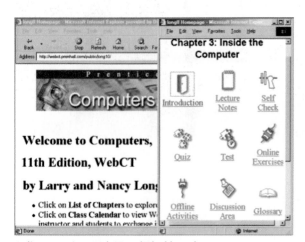

Online Learning: WebCT and Blackboard

Online Course Development and Management

Prentice Hall provides the content and support you need to create and manage your own online course in *WebCT, Blackboard,* or Prentice Hall's own *CourseCompass™*. These online course development tools, along with embedded Long and Long content, offer you and your colleagues all the advantages of a custom-built program, but without the hassle. If you are considering offering all or part of your course via distance learning, then these tools can help you create, implement, and deliver a high-quality online course or course component with relative ease. If you already offer an online course, then these tools can assist you in formalizing your course.

These Web-course tools give you the flexibility to customize your online course by integrating your custom material with content from *Computers,* 11th edition. Content includes lecture material, exercises, individual student projects, team projects, homework assignments, additional testing questions and all resources found on the Companion Website. Whether you are off and running or this is your first online course, these ready-to-go online course resources can save you countless hours of preparation and course administration time.

- *CourseCompass™ at* **www.coursecompass.com**. CourseCompass™ is a dynamic, interactive online course management tool powered by Blackboard. Best of all, Prentice Hall handles the hosting, the technical support, and the training so you can focus on your course by creating the best teaching and learning environment for both you and your students.

- *Blackboard at* **www.prenhall.com/blackboard**. Prentice Hall's abundant online content, combined with Blackboard's popular tools and interface, results in robust Web-based courses that are easy to implement, manage, and use—taking your courses to new heights in student interaction and learning.

- *WebCT at* **www.prenhall.com/webct**. Course-management tools within WebCT include page tracking, progress tracking, class and student management, gradebook, communication, calendar, reporting tools, and more.

Train and Assess IT

With Prentice Hall's *Train and Assess IT* software program, you can experience the more challenging computer topics anywhere you have access to a computer and/or the Internet. Delivered over the Web or on CD-ROM, the labs present an interactive, multimedia look into the world of computer concepts. The training component offers computer-based training that a student can use to preview, learn, and review computer concepts (Inside the Box, The Internet—Connecting from Home, PC Troubleshooting Basics, Working with Graphics, Security and Privacy, and many more), Windows concepts, and Microsoft Office applications (Word, Excel, PowerPoint, Access, and Outlook). Each lab takes about 20 minutes to complete. Built-in prescriptive testing suggests a study path based on student test results. The assessment component provides performance-based assessment to evaluate the students understanding of specific computer/IT skills.

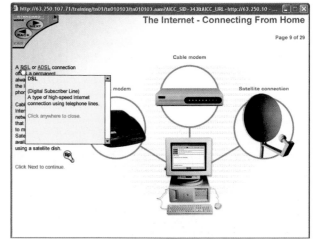

Train and Access IT

EXPLORE IT at www.prenhall.com/phit

A Web and CD-ROM-based training program for computer competency, *EXPLORE IT,* includes a variety of interactive multimedia training modules, including Troubleshooting, Programming Logic, Mouse and Keyboard Basics, Databases, Building a Web Page, Hardware, Software, Operating Systems, Building a Network, and more.

Finally, there is the author link. If you have questions regarding the book, resources, package, or course planning, contact us directly (Prentice Hall representatives can provide contact information).

LARRY LONG, PH.D.   NANCY LONG, PH.D.

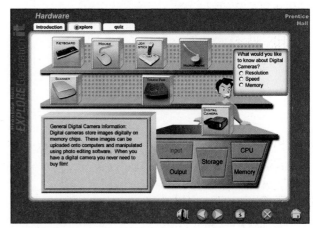

EXPLORE Generation IT Lab

ACKNOWLEDGMENTS

Any introductory book, especially this 11th edition of *Computers* and its many mixed-media ancillaries, is a major undertaking involving many talented people. Each year, my friends and colleagues at Prentice Hall do a magnificent job of articulating the focus of the book, supporting us during the writing process, and, ultimately, blending over a thousand separate elements of text and imagery into a beautiful and effective college textbook. These professionals should be very proud of *Computers,* for it is their book, too. Jodi McPherson, Natalie E. Anderson, Melissa Edwards, and Jasmine Slowik comprise a magnificent editorial team. The quality of the production is evident and for that we thank Kristine Lombardi Frankel, Gail Steier de Acevedo, Tim Tate, Vinnie Scelta, and their colleagues. Cathi Profitko, Karen Goldsmith, Christy Mahon, and their colleagues do wonders with our Web and mixed-media supplements. The art and design is beautiful, thanks to Pat Smythe, Maria Lange, Kenneth Batelman, Ray Cruz, and John Romer. Our book is made all the better with continuous feedback from Emily Knight and Daneille Torio in marketing. In addition, we would like to thank Joyce Nielsen, Sandy Reinhard, and Caryl Wenzel for their diligence in the development and production process.

We would like to thank those who created key ancillaries for *Computers*: *Delores Pusins* of Hillsborough Community College (Interactive Study Guide and Test Item File), *Frank Futyma* of Columbus Technical Institute (Instructor's Resource Manual), *Nancy Surynt* of Stetson University (PowerPoint slides), and *Sherry Thorup* of Middle Tennessee State University (content for WebCT and Blackboard online courses).

The feedback from numerous college professors, both invited and voluntary, has proven invaluable in refining this new edition to better serve their course needs. We would like to extend our heartfelt gratitude to these professors for their insight on this and previous editions of *Computers*.

Amir Afzal, Strayer College
Sally Anthony, San Diego State University
Gary R. Armstrong, Shippensburg University
Suzanne Baker, Lakeland Community College
Dr. David Bannon, Wake Technical Community College
Michael J. Belgard, Bryant and Stratton College
Harvey Blessing, Essex Community College
Amanda Bounds, Florida Community College at Jacksonville
Wayne Bowen, Black Hawk Community College
Jeanann Boyce, University of Maryland
Shira L. Broschat, Washington State University
Sandra Brown, Finger Lakes Community College
Michael Brown, DeVry Institute of Technology, Chicago
Roy Bunch, Chemeketa Community College
Don Cartlidge, New Mexico State University (emeritus)
Stephanie Chenault, The College of Charleston
Carl Clavadetscher, California Polytechnic State University, Pomona
Eli Cohen, Wichita State University
William Cornette, Southwest Missouri State University
Nancy Cosgrove, University of Central Florida
Cheryl Cunningham, Embry-Riddle Aeronautical University
Marvin Daugherty, Indiana Vocational Technical College
Joyce Derocher, Bay de Noc Community College
Wendell Dillard, Arkansas State University
Barbara Ellestad, Montana State University
Dan Everett, University of Georgia
Ray Fanselau, American River College
Shirley Fedorovich, Embry-Riddle Aeronautical University
J. Patrick Fenton, West Valley College
Dr. Diane Fischer, Dowling College
Barry Floyd, California Polytechnic State University, San Luis Obispo
Dr. Charles Foltz, East Carolina University
James Frost, Idaho State University

Jorge Gaytan, University of Texas, El Paso
Dr. Homa Ghajar, Oklahoma State University
Kirk L. Gibson, City College of San Francisco
Randy Goldberg, Marist College
Tom Gorecki, Charles County Community College
Timothy Gottlebeir, North Lake College
Nancy Grant, Community College of Allegheny County
Rob Murray, Ivy Tech State College
Nancy Grant, Community College of Allegheny County South Campus
Ken Griffin, University of Central Arkansas
Vernon Griffin, Austin Community College
Don Hall, Manatee Community College
Cindy Hanchey, Oklahoma Baptist University
Nancy Harrington, Trident Technical College
Wayne Headrick, New Mexico State University
Grace C. Hertlein, California State University
Shirley Hill, California State University
Seth Hock, Columbus State Community College
Fred Homeyer, Angelo State University
Peter Irwin, Richland College
James Johnson, Valencia Community College
Cynthia Kachik, Santa Fe Community College
Dr. M. B. Kahn, California State University at Long Beach
Dr. Adolph Katz, Fairfield University
Robert Keim, Arizona State University
Michael A. Kelly, City College of San Francisco
Helene Kershner, SUNY, Buffalo
Constance K. Knapp, Pace University
Suzanne Konieczny, Marshall University
Doug K. Lauffer, Community College of Beaver County
Sandra Lehmann, Moraine Park Technical College
Michael Lichtenstein, DeVry Institute of Technology, Chicago
Rajiv Malkan, Montgomery College
Ruth Malmstrom, Raritan Valley Community College
Dennis Martin, Kennebec Valley Vocational Technical Institute
LindaLee Massoud, Mott Community College
Gary Mattison, Strayer College
William McDaniel, Jr., Northern Virginia Community College at Alexandria
Michael A. McNeece, Strayer College
Dori McPherson, Schoolcraft College
William McTammany, Florida Community College at Jacksonville
Gloria Melara, California State University at Northridge
Mike Michaelson, Palomar College
Thomas H. Miller, University of Idaho
Domingo Molina, Texas Southmost College
Margaret J. Moore, Coastal Carolina Community College
Joseph Morrell, Metropolitan State College of Denver
Carol Mull, Asheville-Buncombe Technical Community College
Patricia Nettnin, Finger Lakes Community College
Edward Nock, DeVry Institute of Technology, Columbus
Lewis Noe, Ivy Technical Institute
Anthony Nowakowski, State University of New York College at Buffalo
Frank O'Brien, Milwaukee Technical College
Alvin Ollenburger, University of Minnesota
Anne L. Olsen, Wingate College
Dr. Emmanuel Opara, Prairie View A&M University
Beverly Oswalt, University of Central Arkansas
Michael Padbury, Arapahoe Community College

Rick Parker, College of Southern Idaho
Verale Phillips, Cincinnati Technical College
James Phillips, Lexington Community College
Nancy Roberts, Lesley College
Behrooz Saghafi, Chicago State University
Dr. John Sanford, Philadelphia College of Textiles and Science
Ruth Schmitz, University of Nebraska at Kearney
Judy Scholl, Austin Community College
Al Schroeder, Richland College
Marian Schwartz, North Central Technical College
Mark Seagroves, Wingate College
John F. Sharlow, Eastern Connecticut State University
Bari Siddique, Texas Southmost College
Richardson Siebert, Morton College
Robert Spear, Prince George's Community College
John Stocksen, Kansas City Kansas Community College
Carl Ubelacker, Cincinnati State Technical and Community College
Dr. Diane Visor, University of Central Oklahoma
Thomas Voight, Franklin University
Henry Wardak, Everett Community College
Lynn Wermers, North Shore Community College
Dr. Joseph Williams, University of Texas at Austin
Larry B. Wintermeyer, Chemeketa Community College
Floyd Jay Winters, Manatee Community College.

Finally, we wish to thank the professionals from over 100 companies who have contributed resources (information, photos, software, and images) to this book and its supplements.

Dr. Larry Long and **Dr. Nancy Long** have written more than 30 books, which have been used in hundreds of colleges throughout the world. Larry is a lecturer, author, consultant, and educator in the information technology fields. He has served as a strategic-level consultant to most major types of industries and has over 25 years of classroom experience at IBM, the University of Oklahoma, Lehigh University, and the University of Arkansas. Nancy, a reading specialist, has teaching and administrative experience at all levels of education.

COMPUTERS

INFORMATION TECHNOLOGY IN PERSPECTIVE

GETTING STARTED

This Getting Started section is designed to give you a quick start on your personal computing adventure. The emphasis here is on the essentials in the five areas listed below. Depending on your level of understanding and experience with computers and information technology, you may decide to carefully study this Getting Started section, skim it, or skip it altogether.

The Personal Computer (PC)

The Desktop and Notebook PC

A Typical PC System

The Microsoft Windows Operating System

The Boot Procedure

System Shut Down

Windows Wizards

Running an Application from the Windows Desktop

Data and File Management

Hierarchy of Data Organization

Working with Files

Going Online

Networks

The Internet and Internet Access

Common Internet Applications

Popular Applications

Word Processing

Gaming

THE PERSONAL COMPUTER (PC)

The personal computer (PC) is a bit of a mystery to the technology novice, but PCs aren't as complex as you might have thought. They have only four basic components: processor, input, output, and storage. Each PC can be outfitted with a variety of processors, many different types of input and output (I/O), and a wide array of storage devices. This section introduces common I/O and storage devices.

Desktop PC   Notebook PC

FIGURE GS-1
Personal Computers

THE DESKTOP AND NOTEBOOK PC

Most personal computers are either *desktop PCs* or *notebook PCs* (see Figure GS-1). The desktop PC can be found in every company and in most homes. The notebook PC, sometimes called a laptop PC, is a self-contained portable PC designed for use by mobile people. Reasonably powerful desktop PCs can be purchased for under $1,000. Expect to pay a premium for portability. A notebook PC might cost twice as much as a desktop PC with similar capabilities. Generally, desktop PCs outsell notebook PCs 2 to 1; however, that is changing, as more and more people are choosing notebook PCs. We can expect this trend to continue as the price of notebook PCs falls and notebook PC capabilities approach those of desktop PCs.

Microphone

Speakers
(Stereo Sound)

Video Camera

Image Scanner

Multimedia
All personal computers are equipped with a microphone for audio input and speakers for audio output. The inexpensive video camera is a common multimedia input peripheral on desktop PCs.

A TYPICAL PC SYSTEM

A wide range of peripheral devices (input/output and storage devices) can be attached to a PC's system unit. Figure GS-2 shows devices commonly configured with PCs.

Common Input Devices
The two most common input devices are the mouse and keyboard. All PCs have *keyboards* for entering text and commands. The most commonly used *point-and-draw device* is the *mouse*; however, other devices can aid you in navigating around the system, moving objects, and in drawing applications. For example, many notebook PCs come with touchpads. Generally, to select an item, move the cursor (a moveable pointer) over the item (perhaps an OK button or the name of a program) and click (tap) the left mouse button. To open (or choose) an item, double-click (two rapid taps) the left button. Right-clicking (tapping the right mouse button) causes a context-sensitive menu to be displayed.

FIGURE GS-2
PC Peripheral Devices

Monitor   Printer

Keyboard   Mouse

Common Output Devices
The results of processing are displayed on a *monitor*. The *printer* produces printed (hard copy) output, such as a report.

The System Unit
The *system unit* houses the *motherboard*, a single circuit board that includes the *processor*, *RAM* (memory for programs and data during processing), and *other electronic components*. The *electronic bus* on the motherboard provides the electronic path through which the processor communicates with memory/storage components and the various input/output peripheral devices. Permanent storage on *hard disk* and *interchangeable disks/discs* is encased in the system unit, too.

Modem

Hard disks   CD-ROM/DVD-ROM   DVD+RW/CD-RW Combination Drive   Floppy disk (diskette)

Communications
The *modem*, which may be internal (within the system unit) or external, provides a link to the Internet via a regular telephone line connection.

Storage
The typical PC will have three types of permanent storage. the permanently installed *hard disk* is housed in the system unit and contains data and programs which are read and transferred to RAM for processing. New programs are installed to hard disk and updated data are written to hard disk. The system unit will also have a floppy disk *drive* and either a *CD-ROM* or *DVD-ROM drive*. The *floppy disk (diskette)*, which can be either low or high capacity, can be inserted into the floppy disk drive as needed for read/write operations. High-capacity CD-ROM disks are inserted into their respective drives as needed for read-only operations. Most commercial programs are distributed on CD-ROM.

THE MICROSOFT WINDOWS OPERATING SYSTEM

Software refers to a collective set of instructions, called programs, which can be interpreted by a computer. The programs cause the computer to perform desired functions, such as word processing, the generation of business graphics, or flight simulation. At the center of the software action is the operating system. It controls everything that happens in a computer. We interact with the PC via its user-friendly, "point-and-click" graphical user interface (GUI). The operating system manages, maintains, and controls computer resources and is, therefore, considered system software. In contrast, applications software describes those programs that address a particular user application, such as word processing or e-mail. Microsoft Windows operating systems are installed on about 90% of the PCs in the world. The most widely used operating systems are Windows 95, Windows 98, Windows Me, Windows 2000, and Windows XP. Windows XP, the current version, is the basis for the examples used in this book. "Windows" is used as a collective reference to all Microsoft Windows operating systems, all of which are in common use.

FIGURE GS-3
System Start-up

THE BOOT PROCEDURE

The *system startup* procedure on almost any computer is straightforward—flip the on/off switch on the processor unit to *on*. It is good practice to turn on needed input/output devices before turning on the processor. When you *power up* you also *boot* the system. See Figure GS-3.

1. Turn on the PC to begin the boot process.

2. A program permanently stored in a ROM (read-only memory) chip is run automatically. The ROM-based start-up program performs a system check to verify that RAM, electronic complements, and input/output (I/O) devices are operational. During the system check, the PC manufacturer's name, the name of the college/company, or something else is displayed on a splash screen. If everything checks out, the program searches for the disk containing the operating system, usually the systems permanently installed hard disk. During the search process, you might hear the computer attempt to read from the diskette drive or the CD-ROM/DVD-ROM drive.

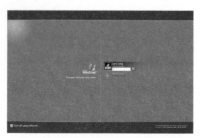

3. Upon finding the operating system (usually on the hard disk), the ROM program loads it from disk storage to RAM. Once loaded to RAM, the operating system takes control of the system.

4. Either the Windows welcome screen (shown here) or the classic Windows logon dialog box appears and requests that you choose a user account and enter a password. The logon procedure identifies you to the computer system and, possibly, a computer network and verifies that you are an authorized user. Modern PCs allow you to set up a computer with several user accounts, each of which can be personalized with regard to desktop appearance, favorite Internet sites, password-protected folders and files, and so on.

5. The Windows boot/logon procedure ends with the presentation of your personalized desktop. The Windows GUI is easily customized. Just click the right button on the mouse anywhere on the desktop and click *properties*.

THE SHUT DOWN PROCEDURE

Unlike electrical appliances, computers are not simply turned off when you're done using them. You must shut down your computer in an orderly manner. Shutting down involves a normal exit (click File, then Exit in the application menu) from all active applications programs before shutting off the power. All applications programs have an exit routine that, if bypassed, can result in loss of user data and problems during later sessions (see Figure GS-4).

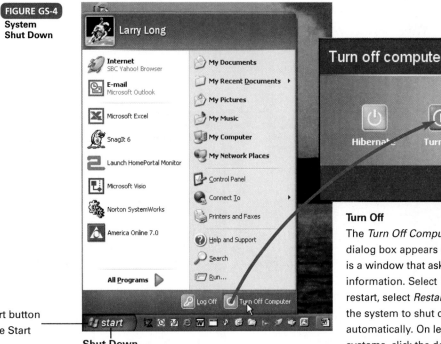
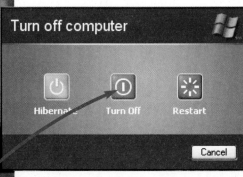

FIGURE GS-4
System Shut Down

Start
Click the Start button to display the Start Menu.

Shut Down
Select *Shut Down* from the *Start Menu*.

Turn Off
The *Turn Off Computer* (or *Shut Down Windows*) dialog box appears on the desktop. A *dialog box* is a window that asks you to enter further information. Select *Turn Off*, or, if you wish to restart, select *Restart*. Selecting *Restart* causes the system to shut down and then reboot automatically. On legacy Windows (9X and Me) systems, click the down arrow at the right of the drop-down list and select *Shut down*. Click the *OK* button to end your PC session.

FIGURE GS-5
The Add Hardware Wizard

WINDOWS WIZARDS

A utility called a wizard is one of the most helpful features of the Windows operating system (see Figure GS-5). A wizard is a series of interactive dialog boxes that guide you through a variety of system-related processes, such as setting up a network, adding hardware, or troubleshooting a problem. Wizards also are available to help you with numerous applications-related operations, such as sending a fax (via your PC), creating a Web site, publishing a Web site, preparing a resume, writing a newsletter, creating a bar graph, preparing a business plan presentation, setting up a database, and so on. The wizard may ask you to choose from available options or enter specific information at each step. Click Next to proceed through the steps and click Finish when the operation is completed.

RUNNING AN APPLICATION FROM THE WINDOWS DESKTOP

The foundation of the Windows graphical user interface is the Windows desktop. Any installed application can be launched (or run or started or opened) from the Windows desktop (see Figure GS-6).

Shortcut Icon
Click or double-click (tap left mouse button once or twice) on a shortcut icon (with embedded arrow) to run the program represented by the icon.

Desktop
The screen upon which Start button, icons, windows, and so on are displayed is known as the *desktop*.

Background
The desktop background can be a color or a user-selected image, such as this sunset image.

Paint
Select the desired program (Paint, in the example) and click on it to run the program.

Start
Click the *Start* button to display the *Start Menu*, run (or open) a *Program*, or find *Help and Support*.

Program Menu
Select a program or program group (the Accessories program group in the example).

Accessories Menu
This submenu lists the programs in the *Accessories submenu*.

Taskbar
The *taskbar* includes the Start button and shows what programs are running.

FIGURE GS-6
Starting a Program

Minimize Button, Maximize/Restore Button, Close Button
– Click the Minimize button to shrink the active window to a button in the taskbar.
☐ or ⊟ Click the Maximize/Restore button to fill the screen or restore the window to its previous size.
x Click the Close button to close (exit) the program.

Menu Bar
The *menu bar* lists the menus available for that application. Select *File*, then *Open* to open and display a particular file, in this case "Horseshoe at Niagara Falls with rainbow.jpg."

Title Bar
The title bar at the top of each window shows the name of the program and current document.

Pop-Out Menu
Choosing a menu option with an arrow () displays a pop-out menu.

Pull-Down Menu
A menu bar selection is pulled down.

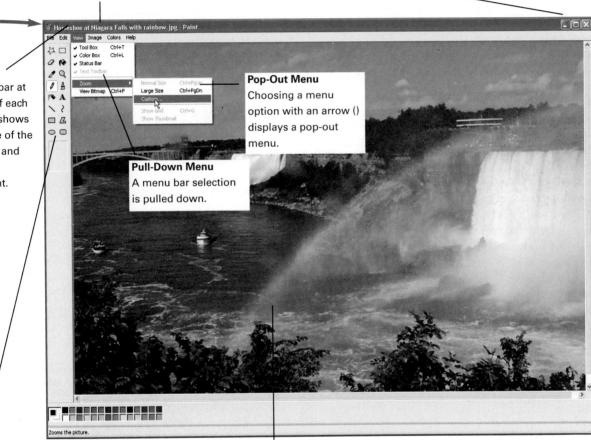

Toolbar
Most applications have one or more toolbars that contain a group of rectangular graphics, each of which represents a frequently used menu option or command. Generally, toolbars display related user options (for example, formatting or database) and can be displayed horizontally or vertically (shown here) on the perimeter of the work area, or it can float over the work area.

Application Window
Applications, such as Paint, are run in rectangular application windows.

DATA AND FILE MANAGEMENT

Data are the fuel for all information technology applications. Understanding these fundamental data and file management concepts will enable you to grasp the critical relationship between data, information, and computers. Data (the plural of datum) are just raw facts. Data are all around us. Every day we generate an enormous amount of data. Information is data that have been collected and processed into a meaningful form. Simply, information is the meaning we give to accumulated facts (data).

HIERARCHY OF DATA ORGANIZATION

Many types of software, including popular *spreadsheet* (shown here) and database software, let you assemble random pieces of data in a structured and useful manner. The principles of data management, which are new to most people taking this course, include the terms and concepts associated with the *hierarchy of data organization*. Each succeeding level in the hierarchy is the result of combining the elements of the preceding level (see Figure GS-7).

Records

A *record* is a description of an event (for example, a sale, a hotel reservation), an item (for example, a part or product), a person (for example, an employee or customer), and so on. Related fields describing an event or an item are logically grouped to form a record. These records contain fields that might be found in a typical employee record, as well as their values for Alvin Adams and other employees.

Bits and characters

In a computer system, a *character* (A, B, C, 1, 2, and so on) is represented by a group of *bits* (1s and 0s) that are configured according to an *encoding system*, such as *ASCII*. The combination of bits used to represent a character is called a byte. In ASCII, a C is represented inside a computer as 01000011, and a 5 is represented as 00110101. Audio, video, graphics, and all other types of data and information are stored as combinations of bits, as well.

Bits are configured to represent

Characters (bytes) are combined to form

Fields are logically grouped to form

Records containing related data elements are termed

Files are reorganized and logically integrated to achieve a

Database

0,1

11000001 = A

Alvin Adams

Alvin Adams, 820 Tioga Ave., NYC, etc.

Alvin Adams, etc.; Mary Birch, etc.; ...Zak Zakery, etc.

Employee master; Inventory master; Customer master; Supplier master, etc.

FIGURE GS-7
Levels in the Data Hierarchy

The database

The *database* is the integrated data resource for an *information system*. In essence, a database is a collection of files that are in some way logically related to one another. That is, one file might contain logical links that identify one or more files containing related information.

WORKING WITH FILES

In personal computing, the spreadsheet is the most popular software tool for organizing, storing, and manipulating data. After you enter data into this "Employee Master" Excel spreadsheet file, the file can be easily sorted, searched, and revised (fields edited, records added and deleted, and so on), copied, sent via the Internet, and manipulated to produce information and graphs. In the example shown in Figure GS-8, records are sorted by last name. This spreadsheet could just as easily be sorted by ID, zip code, job classification, or any other field (in either ascending or descending order). Note that the "Marital Status" field is *coded* for ease of data entry and to save storage space.

Fields Names

	A	B	C	D	E	F	G	H	I	J
1	FIRST NAME	LAST NAME	ID	STREET ADDRESS	CITY	STATE	ZIP	DATE HIRED	MARITAL STATUS	JOB CLASSIFICATION
2	Alvin	Adams	145687	820 Tioga Avenue	Bethlehem	PA	18015	2/9/1969	M	Senior Sales Rep
3	Mary	Birch	446392	134 E. Himes	Norman	OK	02101	7/8/1977	S	Sales Manager
4	Betty	Engler	830124	715 Stratton Road	Boston	MA	73069	11/22/2002	D	Sales Assistant
5	Kennan	Griffin	155578	2175 Orchard Drive	San Jose	CA	95106	3/3/1983	M	Sales Assistant
6	Nate	Phillips	485561	6 Blevoir Ln	Omaha	NE	68107	5/1/1995	M	Sales Associate
7	Sherry	Sherwood	564733	1101 Highland Blvd	Tupelo	MS	38802	12/28/1988	S	Senior Sales Rep
8	Zak	Zakery	286731	234 SW Morris Street	Flagstaff	AZ	86011	6/30/2000	S	Sales Associate

FIGURE GS-8
Spreadsheet with Employee Data

Fields

The *field* is the lowest level in the data hierarchy at which we can derive any meaning from the data. For example, a single character (such as *A*) has little meaning out of context. But when characters are combined to form a name (for example, *Alicia* or *Alvin*), they form a logical unit. A field is best described by example: name, employee ID, street address, job classification, and marital status. These are all fields, the basic subdivisions of a record.

Files

A *file* is a collection of related records. For example, the employee file contains a record for each employee, and an inventory file contains a record for each inventory item. Files are sorted, merged, and processed by a *key field*. For example, in an employee file, the key might be last name/first name or ID, and in an inventory file, the key might be part number. File is a common term in information technology and has a broader meaning. A file refers to any named area in a computer's permanent storage that may contain an image, a letter, a song, data, a report, and so on.

Not too many years ago, computers were simply number crunchers, printing payroll checks and processing accounts receivable. Today, they are that and much more, including tools for communication. Most existing computers are linked to a network of computers, often within an organization or a department, that share hardware/software resources and information. Home networks are becoming increasingly popular. Computer networks can be linked to one another, enabling the interchange of information between people in different companies or on different continents. Most personal computers are linked to a network and/or have ready access to the ultimate network, the Internet, which links millions of computers and networks and billions of people in every country in the world.

NETWORKS

A *local area network* (*LAN*) connects personal computers and other types of terminals and input/output devices in a suite of offices, a college laboratory, or a building (see Figure GS-9). Networks can be as small as a home network or large as an enterprise network serving thousands of knowledge workers. No two networks are the same.

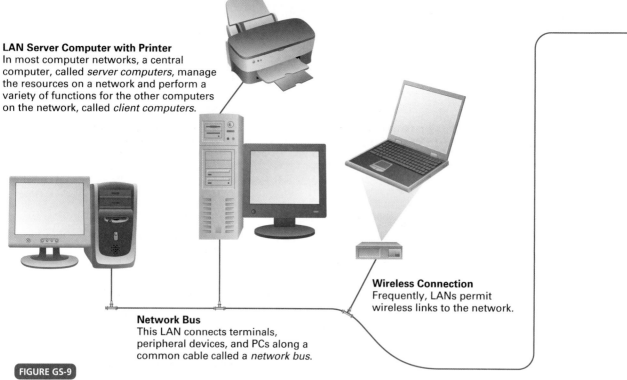

LAN Server Computer with Printer
In most computer networks, a central computer, called *server computers*, manage the resources on a network and perform a variety of functions for the other computers on the network, called *client computers*.

Wireless Connection
Frequently, LANs permit wireless links to the network.

Network Bus
This LAN connects terminals, peripheral devices, and PCs along a common cable called a *network bus*.

FIGURE GS-9
Local Area Networks and the Logon Procedure

Wiring Hub
Multiple PCs can be connected
to a hub, which is connected
to the network bus.

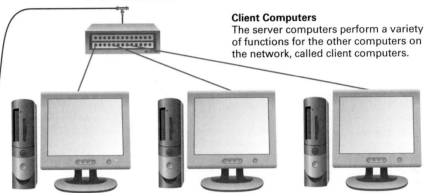

Client Computers
The server computers perform a variety
of functions for the other computers on
the network, called client computers.

Logon Procedure

Before you can "go online" and use network resources you must logon to the network. You
do this by opening the software that establishes the link to the Internet (see below) and
entering a *user ID* and *password*. the user ID (also called *user name*) is your electronic
identifier and may be known by your friends and colleagues. The password, however, is
yours alone to protect and use. The user ID identifies you for personal communications,
such as e-mail, and it identifies you to the server computer. The password lets you gain
access to the network and it's resources. Typically, the user ID is your name in a standard
format, often the first name or it's first initial in combination with the last name (jansmith,
jan_smith, jsmith, smithj). The password is any combination of contiguous characters
(gowildcats, fyhi2001), which may or may not be case sensitive. To help protect the
confidentiality of your password, an asterisk (*) is displayed for each character entered. It's
a good idea to change your password frequently

"Connect" Dialog Box

In Windows, use the "Connect" dialog
box to logon to an Internet service
provider (ISP) via a dialup connection.
Enter user name (user ID) and
password. You will need an ISP profile
(ArkansasUSA in the example) with
connection settings, including the
telephone number.

THE INTERNET AND INTERNET ACCESS

The Internet is a worldwide collection of interconnected networks. The Net actually comprises millions of independent networks at academic institutions, military installations, government agencies, commercial enterprises, Internet support companies, and just about every other type of organization.

Cyberspace is an amazing place. When you go online, you have access to literally billions of pages of information, from research materials to classic literature to reference material for almost anything to images of planets, people, and places. You can get a weather forecast for any place in the world, get real-time stock quotations, and listen to live radio broadcasts from Japan, Australia, Mexico, and most other countries. You can communicate directly with people from every country in the world via many communication applications, including e-mail, instant messaging, and videophone. You can tap the advice of experts in finance, health care, law, and many other fields. You will have no trouble finding a pick-up Internet-based video game. You can view live video broadcasts of important events. You can view the draws of any juniors tennis tournament, determine the progress of your UPS package, or read the news shortly after it happens. You can travel to almost anywhere via images, video, and inviting descriptions. Also, the Internet is the biggest market in the world, where you can buy and sell almost anything.

Typically, people connect to the Internet via a commercial information service, an ISP, or a local area network (LAN) with Internet access (see Figure GS-10).

Commercial Information Service
Millions of people go online by subscribing to a *commercial information service*, such as *America Online (AOL)*.

Connect via an Information Service

Local Area Network (LAN)

Communications-Ready PC
Most PCs are equipped with a *modem* that permits communication with remote computers, such as that of an ISP, via a telephone-line link.

Connect via a LAN with Internet Access

Connect via an ISP

FIGURE GS-10
Getting on the Internet

The Internet

Internet Server
Most companies and organizations maintain a presence on the internet. that presence is an *Internet Server*, (also *host*) that makes content available over the internet.

Information Service Provider (ISP)
An *ISP* is a company with an Internet account that, for a fee, provides individuals and organizations access to, or presence on, the Internet.

AMERICA ONLINE (AOL)

AOL and other commercial information services offer a wide range of online services via their own user interface software (AOL 8.0 shown here) over their proprietary network. Plus, AOL offers access to the worldwide Internet. When you *sign on* to AOL, you enter a *screen name*, the AOL user ID, and your *password*. AOL offers 20 "channels" (topic areas), such as music, travel, and news, plus myriad services such as real-time stock quotes.

Channel	Capacity	
Regular telephone lines	**POTS** **56K bps**	**DSL** **256 K bps to 9 M bps downstream (receiving information)** **256 K bps to 1.5 M bps upstream (sending information)**
Cable modem (Over Cable TV lines)	**400 K bps to 10 M bps**	
Digital Satellite (Requires satellite dish)	**400 k bps to 1.5 M bps downstream** **56 k bps to 1.5 M bps upstream**	

Communications Channel

A variety of communications channels carries digital signals between computers. The *channel capacity* (or *bandwidth*) is the number of bits (on/off electrical signals) a channel can transmit per second. Most people link to the Internet via *plain old telephone service* (POTS) at a maximum speed of 56 K bps (thousands of bits per second). This table shows the higher speed connections, some measured in M bps (millions of bps), being made available at reasonable prices. ISPs can tell you which channels are available in your city. Satellite service is available throughout the lower 48 states in the United States.

Internet Browser

You tap the resources of the Internet via Internet browser software, such as *Netscape* (shown here) or *Internet Explorer*. This National Park Service Web site provides information for people planning a visit to the Mount Rushmore National Memorial, including a map of the park (inset).

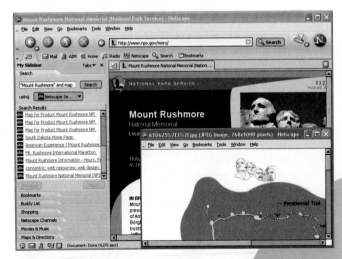

COMMON INTERNET APPLICATIONS

The Internet has many applications. Three of the most popular applications are browsing and searching the World Wide Web using an *Internet browser* and communicating with others via *e-mail* and *instant messaging*.

Internet Browser

Internet browsers let you retrieve and view the Internet's ever-growing resources as well as interact with Internet server computers. A browser runs on your PC and works with another program on an Internet server computer to let you "surf the Internet" (see Figure GS-11).

The Menu Bar

The menu bar at the top of the user command interface is used to select file options (print, save, and so on), to select edit options (including copy, cut, and paste), and to set and change a variety of options.

The Toolbar

Most of your interaction is with the buttons in the toolbar and the hyperlinks in the Web pages. These navigation buttons are common to browsers:

- **Back.** Go to the last site visited.
- **Forward.** Go forward to the next site in the string of sites you have viewed.
- **Stop.** Stop the transfer of information.
- **Refresh.** Reload the current page from the server.
- **Home.** Go to your default home page, usually your college or company.
- **Search.** Go to your default search site, usually a major portal.
- **Favorites/bookmarks.** A list of sites you visit frequently.

Hyperlinks

Hyperlinks in a form of hypertext (a colored, underlined word or phrase), hot images, or hot icons, permit navigation between Web pages on the Internet. Click on a hyperlink to jump (link) to another place in the same page or to another Web site. The cursor changes to a pointing hand 🖑 when positioned over a hyperlink.

Internet Portal

Often, Internet sessions begin at an Internet portal, such as Yahoo! (shown here). A *portal* is one of millions of Internet destinations, called a *Web site*. A portal offers a broad array of information and services, including a *menu tree* of categories and a *search engine* that lets you do keyword searches for specific information on the Internet.

FIGURE GS-11
Using a Browser

Browsing the Net

Poking around the Internet with no particular destination in mind is called browsing. An Internet portal with its menu tree of categories (see example) is always a good place to start. You may navigate through several levels of categories before reaching the pages you want. For example, if you select "Arts & Humanities," Yahoo! lists 26 categories from which to choose (in alphabetical order). Selecting "Humanities" under "Arts & Humanities" presents 17 subcategories and links to several general humanities sites. Selecting "Literature" gives you another set of subcategories and appropriate links, including "Electronic Literature." Drilling down into Electronic Literature presents you with numerous links to sites that contain Mark Twain's "Adventures of Huckleberry Finn" (with illustrations) and thousands of other online books.

Search Results

The typical search results in a list of hyperlinks to Web sites that meet your search criteria ("Great Wall of China"). If you don't get results, try other search criteria and/or another search engine (Google, Lycos, HotBot, Ask Jeeves, MSN, and so on).

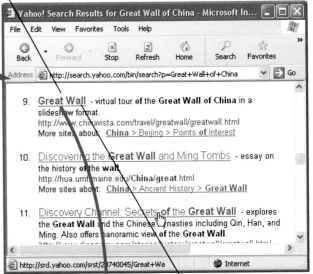

URL Bar

The current *URL* is displayed is this box. The URL is the Internet equivalent of an address. We use browsers to go to and view content at a particular address on the Internet. The home page address for Yahoo! (shown here) is

http://www.yahoo.com/

and for the White House the home page address is

http://www.whitehouse.gov/.

Each Web server's address begins with *http://* and is followed by a unique *domain name*, usually the name of the organization sponsoring the Internet server. The domain name is usually prefaced by www to designate a *World Wide Web* server. What follows the domain name is a *folder* or *path* containing the resources for a particular page. The White House tours URL is

http://www.whitehouse.gov/WH/Tours/visitors_center.html.

Key in an address and press Enter to go to a different Web site.

Click Hyperlink

Click on one or more of the resulting hyperlinks to go to a site (Discovery Channel, in the example).

Web Site Pages

Information on the Internet's *World Wide Web* (the Web) is viewed in *pages*. The Web is the Internet's main application for on-demand distribution of information. The first page you will normally view is the site's *home page*.

Searching the Net

The Internet has billions of pages. There are two basic approaches to finding something on the Internet: *searching* and *browsing*. Each major portal has a *search engine* to help you find the information or service you need. Enter one or more keywords that describes what you want, such as "Great Wall of China" in the example.

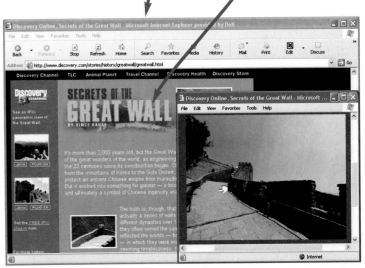

E-Mail

E-mail lets you send electronic mail to and receive it from anyone with an Internet e-mail address (see Figure GS-12). This is done with e-mail client software, such as Microsoft Outlook (shown here), or with Web-based e-mail via a browser.

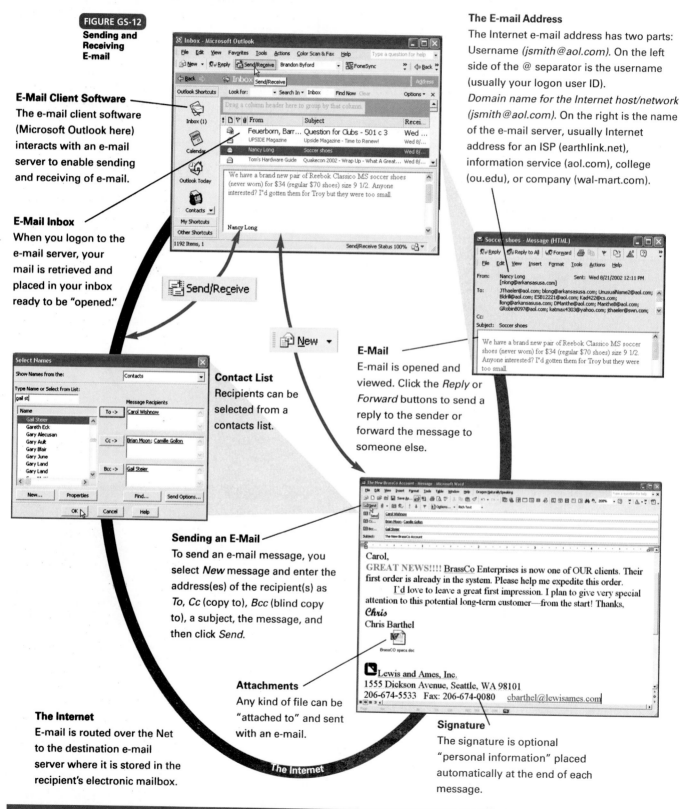

FIGURE GS-12
Sending and Receiving E-mail

E-Mail Client Software
The e-mail client software (Microsoft Outlook here) interacts with an e-mail server to enable sending and receiving of e-mail.

E-Mail Inbox
When you logon to the e-mail server, your mail is retrieved and placed in your inbox ready to be "opened."

Send/Receive

New

Contact List
Recipients can be selected from a contacts list.

Sending an E-Mail
To send an e-mail message, you select *New* message and enter the address(es) of the recipient(s) as *To*, *Cc* (copy to), *Bcc* (blind copy to), a subject, the message, and then click *Send*.

The Internet
E-mail is routed over the Net to the destination e-mail server where it is stored in the recipient's electronic mailbox.

Attachments
Any kind of file can be "attached to" and sent with an e-mail.

The E-mail Address
The Internet e-mail address has two parts: Username (*jsmith@aol.com*). On the left side of the @ separator is the username (usually your logon user ID).
Domain name for the Internet host/network (*jsmith@aol.com*). On the right is the name of the e-mail server, usually Internet address for an ISP (earthlink.net), information service (aol.com), college (ou.edu), or company (wal-mart.com).

E-Mail
E-mail is opened and viewed. Click the *Reply* or *Forward* buttons to send a reply to the sender or forward the message to someone else.

Signature
The signature is optional "personal information" placed automatically at the end of each message.

Instant Messaging

Both instant messaging (IM) and e-mail enable personal communication via the Internet but they have significant differences. Instant messaging allows messages to be sent and displayed in real-time (instantly), where e-mail is stored until retrieved by the recipient. Instant messaging allows text-based conversations with several friends, plus you can talk to them or have video conversations. IM is used extensively in the business world, as well, because workers are informed immediately when their colleagues go online and are available.

The Windows Messenger client software (shown in Figure GS-13) works with the .NET Messenger Service to deliver a variety of services, including file sharing, setting up online meetings or Internet games, sending text messages to cell phones, viewing programs simultaneously, and doing whiteboarding. To participate in instant messaging, you must sign up with one of the instant messaging services and install its client software. Yahoo! and AOL offer popular messaging services. Instant messaging conversations can be between people on opposite ends of the world or between a father at the office and his son at home (illustrated here).

Sign In/Sign Out

Choose Sign In (in the File menu) to inform others who have you on their contact list that you are online. Choose Sign Out to end a session.

Online/Not Online

This area shows which of your contacts are online and which are not. Click on a contact to send a request to begin a conversation. A Windows Wizard guides you through the steps for adding contacts to your list.

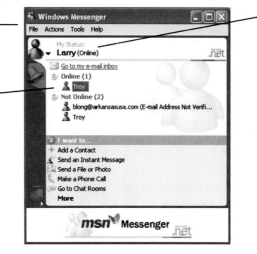

Status

The status area indicates whether you are online (signed in) or offline (signed out).

Video Conversation

If your system is configured with a video camera, the person on the other end of the conversation can view the video in real-time. The picture-in-picture option lets you see both the send and receive images. Click start/stop talking or start/stop camera to add/end audio and/or video in the conversation.

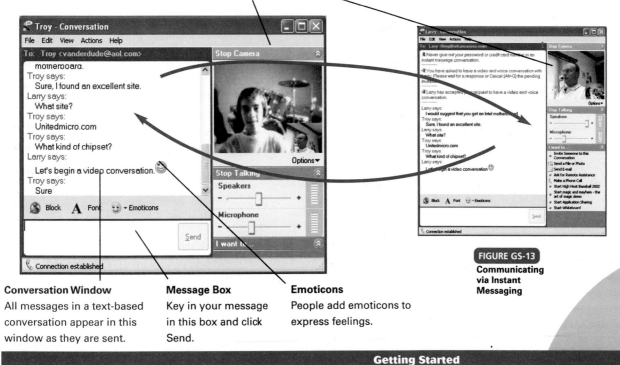

FIGURE GS-13

Communicating via Instant Messaging

Conversation Window

All messages in a text-based conversation appear in this window as they are sent.

Message Box

Key in your message in this box and click Send.

Emoticons

People add emoticons to express feelings.

POPULAR APPLICATIONS

The four most popular applications of personal computing are word processing, gaming, Internet-based personal communications (e-mail and instant messaging), and Internet browsers. Word processing and gaming are the focus of this section.

Save Document
If you wish to work with the document later, you will need to save it to disk storage for later recall (File, Save).

OPEN DOCUMENT
To recall a document from disk storage, click *File*, *Open*, and then go to the desired folder.

Format Document
Click Format to pull down a menu with a variety of formatting options, including Font (typeface, size, and attribute) and Paragraph presentation.

Text Cursor
Move the text cursor with the mouse and then click to reposition the blinking text entry cursor.

Insert Images
You can insert images (*Insert*, *Picture*, *Clip Art*, or *From File*), such as the barn, and then resize and/or reposition them anywhere within the document.

Help
Click on *Help* to learn more about word processing and its features.

The Document
One or more word processing documents can be opened and displayed (at least, in part) in the work area.

Entering Text
The newsletter shown here demonstrates many of word processing's features (columns, integration of images, text boxes, footers, varying style, size, and color of fonts, and so on). However, to create a simple document, you simply open a new document (*File, New* in the main menu) and begin entering text from the keyboard at the text cursor position.

WORD PROCESSING

Word processing software, such as Microsoft Word (shown in Figure GS-14), lets you create, edit (revise), and format documents, which can be printed, displayed, posted to the Internet as Web pages, e-mailed as Microsoft Word attachments, faxed, and so on. The term document is a generic term that refers to whatever is currently displayed in a software package's extended work area (the area in a window below the title bar or toolbar and all that can be viewed by scrolling vertically and horizontally in the same work area). Once you create a document, you give it a name and save it to disk storage as a file, for example, "Newsletter.doc" (see the document name in the title bar).

Print Document
Click *File* then *Print* to print the document.

FIGURE GS-14
Using Word Processing

GAMING CATEGORIES

Gaming is so pervasive in personal computing that you should be aware of the scope and types of games. Computer games are rated by the Entertainment Software Rating Board and given one of six ratings, ranging from "early childhood" to "adults only." Games can be placed in the nine categories and all but the puzzle category are shown in Figure GS-15.

FIGURE GS-15 Gaming Catagories

Strategy

In strategy games, such as *Warcraft III-Reign of Chaos* from Blizzard, players become leaders who must collect and use their resources wisely to overcome their opponent, sometimes alien invaders.

Simulation

In simulation games, the game scenario allows players to operate in a simulated environment, such as piloting an airplane, or be a part of a life-like situation, such as living in and working in a simulated city.

Edutainment

These games combine gaming and learning. In their quest to find the international sleuth, Carmen Sandiego, players learn about history, geography, and other topics.

Sports and Recreation

In this category of games, players play video versions of almost any type of sport or recreational game, from hockey (*NHL 2001* from EA Sports shown here) and baseball to darts and fishing. Players become batters, quarterbacks, and so on and swing the bat or throw the ball.

Action/Adventure

A large group of games place players in a fantasy world such as in *Jedi Knight II: Jedi Outcast* from Lucas Arts. In this genre, players run, leap, or climb to find entryways that let them progress to the next level. Along the way, they unlock mysteries so they can continue their journey and overcome evil people to reach an objective.

RPG (Role Playing Game)

In RPG games, players take on a specific role, where they are at the epicenter of a fantasy that may involve war, betrayal, and faith, such as in *Neverwinter Nights* from BioWare. In their journey, players attain new skills and abilities by winning battles.

Racing

In racing games, such as *NASCAR 4* by Sierra, players "drive" cars, motorcycles, spaceships, jet skis, snowmobiles, and so on to win races in a variety of venues.

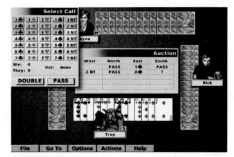

Traditional

Many traditional board, card, and casino-type games are now available in video-game formats. Shown here is Bridge, one of many card games in *Hoyle Card Games* from Sierra.

Chapter 1

Learning Objectives

Once you have read and studied this chapter, you will have learned:

- How information technology influences our society and you at work, at home, and at play (Section 1-1).

- What it means to achieve IT competency and become an active participant in our information society (Section 1-2).

- How local and worldwide computer networks impact businesses and society (Section 1-3).

- Essential hardware, software, and computer system terminology that will enable you to begin your information technology learning adventure with confidence (Section 1-4).

- The relative size, scope, uses, and variety of available computer systems (Section 1-5).

- The fundamental components and capabilities of an IT system (Section 1-6).

- A variety of enterprise computing and personal computing applications (Section 1-7).

THE TECHNOLOGY REVOLUTION

Why this chapter is important to you

Welcome! To the computer revolution, that is. We'll be using this "Why This Chapter is Important to You" space to make this book very personal—to show you why studying computers, information technology, and personal computing is important to you, now and in the future. We're all members of a rapidly maturing information society. In this dynamic new society, people at home and in schools, institutions, and businesses are engaged in an ever-growing partnership with computers and information technology, called *IT*. Whether we like it or not, for good or bad, computers and technology are part of just about everything we do, during both work and play. And the fact is, computers will play an even greater role in our lives next month and in years to come.

In the 1960s, mainstreamers considered people who had anything to do with computers, especially the techies who actually touched them, to be different, even a little weird. Through the 1970s, computer-illiterate people led happy and productive lives, not knowing the difference between a system bug and a byte. Well, those days are gone.

Today we're all part of an exploding information society—you, us, and the rest of the world. Computer-knowledgeable people are considered mainstream, even cool in some circles. The rest are on the outside looking in. By reading this book and taking this course, you're telling your family, friends, and, perhaps, your colleagues at work that you want to participate—to be an insider.

It's amazing how achieving information technology competency can help you keep in touch, help you learn, help make many of life's little chores easier and more fun, and help you earn more money. Upon successful completion of this course, you will be information technology competent. In most fields, this competency is considered critical to *getting* and *keeping* a good job. Your adventure into this amazing world of technology begins right here. Have fun!

WHY THIS SECTION
IS IMPORTANT
TO YOU

We now live in an information
society where most adults are
considered knowledge workers.
Your contribution to society is
only enhanced when you appreciate the scope and influence
that information technology has
on our society.

1-1   Our Information Society

Where will you be and what will you be doing in the year 2010? This is a tough question even for IT futurists, who are reluctant to speculate more than a year or so into the future. Things are changing too quickly. A stream of exciting new innovations in **information technology** (**IT**) continues to change what we do and how we think. We use the term *IT* to refer to the integration of computing technology and information processing.

Most of us are doing what we can to adapt to this new **information society** where **knowledge workers** channel their energies to provide a wealth of computer-based information services. A knowledge worker's job function revolves around the use, manipulation, and broadcasting of information. Your knowledge of computers will help you cope with and understand today's technology so you can take your place in the information society—at work, in the home, and during your leisure time.

THE TECHNOLOGY REVOLUTION: TODAY

In an information society, the focus of commerce becomes the generation and distribution of information. This technological revolution is changing our way of life: the way we live, work, and play. The cornerstone of this revolution, the *computer*, is transforming the way we communicate, do business, and learn.

Personal computers, or **PCs,** offer a vast array of *enabling technologies* that help us do all kinds of things, many of which you may never have imagined or dreamed possible (see Figure 1-1).

FIGURE 1–1

PORTABLE SHOPPING SYSTEM
Information technology is changing our lives in many ways. For example, many retail establishments give customers access to a Portable Shopping System that lets shoppers save time by scanning the bar codes of goods as they shop rather than queuing at checkouts. Before starting purchases, customers take a hand-held bar code scanner out of a dispenser rack. The customer scans goods as they are placed in the basket, and the corresponding price appears on the portable scanner's screen. The system gives the customer a running total of the amount of the purchase. After shopping, the customer puts the scanner in the rack and gets a bar-coded ticket detailing the items purchased. This ticket is scanned at the check out. Customers pay as usual, receive their receipt, and are on their way.

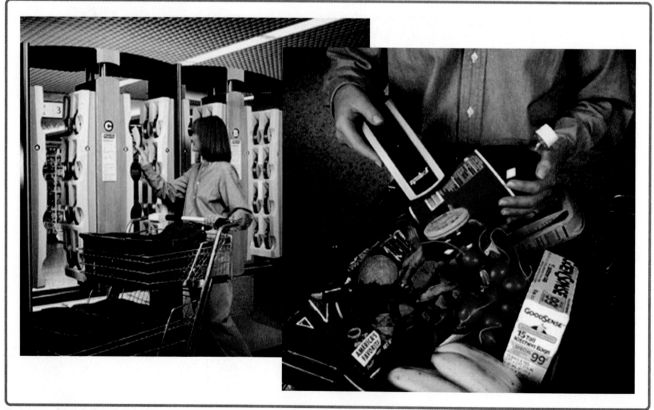

Courtesy of Symbol Technologies, Inc.

At Work

Millions of people can be "at work" wherever they are as long as they have their portable personal computers—at a client's office, in an airplane, or at home (see Figure 1-2). The *mobile worker's* personal computer provides electronic links to a vast array of information and to clients and corporate colleagues, across town or across the country. It even has maps that pinpoint your location to help you navigate the streets of the world.

Tasks that used to take hours, even days, now can be completed in minutes with the aid of IT. Rather than dictating to a machine for transcription by a secretary, managers can simply dictate messages *directly* to their computers. The managers can then send them electronically to their colleagues in a fraction of a second. Marketing reps can prepare convincing presentations, complete with sound, video, and visual effects, in a tenth the time it took a generation ago. Attorneys who used to spend days combing through legal documentation in preparation for trial now use keyword searches to identify applicable books, documents, and cases in a matter of minutes. The managers' messages are timelier, the marketing reps' presentations are more effective, and attorneys can be confident that they haven't missed anything.

At Home

The typical home has at least one personal computer and often several. Millions of people now depend on their PCs to help them with all kinds of tasks: communicating with relatives, preparing the annual Christmas newsletter, doing homework, managing the family investment portfolio, sending greeting cards, and much, much more. The home PC is a family's link to the **Internet,** a worldwide network of computers, with its marvelous resources and applications. People link to the Internet to learn which bank offers the best mortgage rate, to send their congressperson a message, to order tickets to the theater, to learn about the Renaissance period, to visit the virtual Smithsonian Museum, to get a good deal on a new car, to shop for new shoes, to order a pizza, or simply to browse the day away.

Already, a third of the population is looking to the Internet first for their news. The British have introduced *Ananova,* a very likable virtual newscaster, who reads the news as any human newscaster

FIGURE 1–2	**TECHNOLOGY IN OUR JOBS** Twenty-five years ago, college curricula in architecture, accounting, nursing, and, even, engineering included relatively little study in the area of computers and information technology. Today, knowledge workers in the office and on the shop floor rely on information technology for everything from product inspection to cost analysis. The computer has dramatically changed the way people in hundreds of professions do their jobs.

Courtesy of Sun Microsystems, Inc.

would, except she does so in English, French, German, or Italian—your choice. She is a bit unusual having the characteristics of an animated character, green tinted hair, and big eyes. Ananova's voice is synthesized speech created from scanning electronic text for the various stories she "reads."

A home may not only have several PCs, but it may have a variety of special-function computers. Many of these can be programmed by you to perform specific tasks, such as recording a movie on a VCR. We have small computers, called **microprocessors**, in VCRs, automobiles, air-conditioning systems, dishwashers, telephone answering systems, and in many more devices and appliances, including pet food dispensing devices. Computers are all around us—all the time.

At Play

The computer and information technology have had a dramatic impact on our leisure activities. Sure, we still have fun, as we always have, but it's different now. Increasingly, we communicate with our friends and relatives via the Internet through **electronic mail** (**e-mail**) and **instant messaging** (**IM**). Both electronic mail and instant messaging (see "Getting Started" for an overview) allow us to send and receive information (text, audio, and video) via computer-to-computer hookups. Millions of people spend hours "chatting" with other people from around the globe on just about any subject from Elvis sightings to romance, often people they don't know and may never hear from again. **Chat** is an Internet application that allows you to enter a virtual chat room and converse in real time (at the present) with people who are linked to the Internet. You can chat by keying in and/or speaking what you want to say.

Gaming is another major application of computers (see "Getting Started" for an overview). The software enables virtual worlds to be created within computers where gamers engage in mortal combat, immerse themselves in a virtual city, or work through a labyrinth for clues to save the world. Gamers can compete alone, with others on the same computer, or with others around the world. A gamer can play solitaire or play chess with a grand master in Russia.

Today's personal computers have sophisticated audiovisual systems that allow you to listen to CDs or play the latest hit song retrieved from the Internet. If listening to the music isn't enough, you can view the music video, as well. People routinely watch DVD movies on their PCs.

Sports fanatics have found a home on the Internet. The Internet is filled with information and statistics on literally thousands of teams from junior soccer to major league baseball. Avid fans enjoy viewing real-time statistics and analysis on their PC while watching the game on television. The really serious fan may be involved in a running chat session before, during, and after the game. No longer is the true fan cut off from the game because it's not televised or played on local radio stations. Most major radio stations are broadcasting over the Internet as well as the airwaves, making their signal available worldwide. Generally, if an important game is on the radio, you can listen to it from wherever you are.

FIGURE 1-3 The Internet Appliance
The Compaq iPAQ Home Internet Appliance is representative of the many products being developed for the technology revolution. The iPAQ is especially designed to let you surf the Internet. You can use it to do online shopping, send/receive electronic mail (e-mail), perform banking transactions, or make a telephone call. Most Internet appliances are designed to run right out of the box. Simply plug in the power and telephone cord and you are ready to communicate.

THE TECHNOLOGY REVOLUTION: TOMORROW

Tomorrow, the next wave of enabling technologies will continue to cause radical changes in our lives (see Figure 1-3). For example, if you're in the market for a new home, you will be able to "visit" any home for sale in the country from the comfort of your own home or office via computer. All you will need to do is tell the computer what city to look in and then enter your search criteria (price range, house style, and so on). The electronic realtor will then list those houses that meet your criteria, provide you with detailed information on the house and surrounding area, and then offer to take you on a tour of the house—inside and out. After the virtual tour, you will be able to "drive" through the neighborhood, looking left and right as you would in your automobile. Such systems may seem a bit futuristic, but much of the available real estate in the United States can be viewed on your computer. Systems that permit neighborhood drive-throughs are under active development!

Each day new applications, such as a national multilist for real estate, are being created. Already, votes are being cast online. How long will it be before our PC is the voting booth? Doctors are beginning to make house calls via telemedicine. We continue to march toward a cashless society. It may be inevitable that the stock markets of the world will be open continuously, enabling individuals to buy and sell securities directly. The infrastructure that supports these applications is sometimes called the **information superhighway**. It encompasses a network of electronic links that eventually will connect virtually every facet of our society, both public (perhaps the local supermarket) and private (perhaps Aunt Minnie's recipes).

LOOKING BACK A FEW YEARS

To put the emerging information society into perspective, let's flash back a half century and look *briefly* at the evolution of computing (see Figure 1-4).

- A little over 50 years ago, our parents and grandparents built ships, kept financial records, and performed surgery, all without the aid of computers. Indeed, everything they did was without computers. There were no computers!

- In the 1960s, mammoth multimillion-dollar computers processed data for those large companies that could afford them. These computers, the domain of highly specialized technical gurus, remained behind locked doors. In "the old days," business computer systems were designed so a computer professional served as an intermediary between the **user**—someone who uses a computer—and the computer system.

FIGURE 1–4

A WORLD WITHOUT COMPUTERS
The industrial society evolved in a world without computers. The advent of computers and automation has changed and will continue to change the way we do our jobs. In the automobile industry, those assembly-line workers who used to perform repetitive and hazardous jobs now program and maintain industrial robots to do these jobs.

GM Assembly Division, Warren, Michigan
Courtesy of Ford Motor Company

- In the mid-1970s, computers became smaller, less expensive, and more accessible to smaller companies and even individuals. This trend resulted in the introduction of personal computers. During the 1980s, millions of people from all walks of life purchased these miniature miracles. Suddenly, computers were for everyone!

- Today, most Americans have at least one computer at home or work that is more powerful than those that processed data for multinational companies during the 1960s. The widespread availability of computers has prompted an explosion of applications. At the individual level, we can use our PCs to go on an electronic fantasy adventure or hold an electronic reunion with our scattered family. At the corporate level, virtually every business has embraced information technology. Companies in every area of business are using IT to offer better services and gain a competitive advantage.

THIS COURSE: YOUR TICKET TO ADVENTURE

You are about to embark on a journey that will stimulate your imagination, challenge your every resource, from physical dexterity to intellect, and alter your sense of perspective on technology. Learning about computers is more than just education. It's an adventure!

Gaining a solid understanding of information technology, computers, and personal computing is just the beginning—your IT adventure lasts a lifetime. Information technology is changing every minute of the day. Every year, hundreds of new IT-related buzzwords, concepts, applications, and computing devices will confront you. Fortunately, you will have established a base of IT knowledge (information technology competency) upon which you can build and continue your learning adventure.

1-1.1 The term used to describe the integration of computing technology and information processing is: (a) information technology, (b) information handling, (c) software, or (d) data tech.

1-1.2 A person whose job revolves around the use, manipulation, and dissemination of information is called: (a) an office wunderkind, (b) a knowledge worker, (c) a data expert, or (d) an info being.

1-1.3 Mail sent electronically is called: (a) snail mail, (b) quick mail, (c) e-mail, or (d) e-news.

THE CRYSTAL BALL:
One Computer Per House Home networking in the multi-PC home is becoming increasingly common. Will PCs proliferate throughout the house like telephones and TVs? Probably not—it would be too expensive to maintain the hardware and software for this many PCs. Within the near future, the typical household will have a single multiprocessor computer system that serves a variety of networked workstations throughout the home and, possibly, controls some processes, such as heating/cooling and lighting. Each workstation will be configured to fit its applications and/or users. For example, the workstation in the bedroom might include a large wall-mounted monitor for on-demand movie/TV viewing and the kitchen might have a touch-screen monitor.

1-2 R$_x$ for Cyberphobia: Information Technology Competency

Not too long ago, people who pursued careers in almost any facet of business, education, or government were content to leave computers to computer professionals. Today these people are knowledge workers and computers are an integral part of what they do. In less than a generation, **information technology competency** (**IT competency**) has emerged in virtually any career from a *nice-to-have skill* to a *job-critical skill*.

WHAT IS INFORMATION TECHNOLOGY COMPETENCY?

If you're afraid of computers, information technology competency is a sure cure. IT competency will allow you to be an active and effective participant in the emerging information society. You and other IT-competent people will:

- *Feel comfortable using and operating a computer system.*
- *Be able to make the computer work for you.* The IT-competent person can use the computer to solve an endless stream of life's problems, from how to pass away a couple of idle hours to how to increase company revenues.
- *Be able to interact with the computer—that is, generate input to the computer and interpret output from it.* **Input** is data entered to a computer system for processing. **Output** is the presentation of the results of processing (for example, a printed résumé or a tax return).
- *Be comfortable in cyberspace.* Cyberspace is a nonphysical world made possible by a worldwide network of computer systems. Once in cyberspace, you can communicate with one another and literally travel the virtual world, visiting Walt Disney World in Florida, the Louvre Museum in Paris, and a million other interesting places.
- *Understand the impact of computers on society, now and in the future.* Automation is having such a profound impact on society that we must position ourselves to act responsibly to ensure that these changes are in the right direction.
- *Be an intelligent consumer of computers and computer equipment, collectively called* **hardware.** Smart computer shoppers save a lot of money, usually getting what they need, not what someone else says they need.
- *Be an intelligent consumer of software and other nonhardware-related computer products and services.* **Software** refers to a collective set of instructions, called **programs**, which can be interpreted by a computer. The programs cause the computer to perform desired functions, such as flight simulation (a computer game), the generation of business graphics, or word processing.

- *Be conversant in the language of computers and information technology.* In this book, you will learn those terms and phrases that not only are the foundation of computer terminology but also are very much a part of everyday conversation at school, home, and work.

Anyone who has achieved information technology competence is quick to tell you what a difference this IT knowledge has made in his or her life. Often it is the difference between getting a job or a promotion. It may open new lines of communication. It may help you save thousands of dollars each year in your purchases.

Businesses know about the importance of computer competency, too. A common complaint among management is that workers are all falling behind the technology. With only 15% of the workforce considered to be IT-competent, management is looking for ways to increase the competency of workers and therefore the overall productivity of companies. For example, several companies provide personal computers and Internet service to all employees—for their homes. Company management hopes that employees will embrace the technology in their homes and carry that understanding to the workplace.

This book is about building IT competency. Once you have completed this course you will join the ranks of those who have no fear of working, living, and playing in the information society. There is one catch, however, in that your information technology competency is valid only for one point in time. The pursuit of IT competency is a never-ending one because IT is always changing (see Figure 1-5).

FIGURE 1–5 Getting Smaller
The circuitry on this relatively recent network card is now contained in a single chip on the right. The world of electronics is getting smaller. We now carry our computers. Some people wear them around their waist. It's inevitable that even greater power and capability will be contained in a wristwatch-type computer that will listen and speak to us.

Photo courtesy of Hewlett-Packard Company

REASONS TO BECOME IT-COMPETENT

There are many reasons that people opt to become IT-competent. These motivations to learn can be grouped into five broad categories.

- *Personal.* Much of the world's information is now in digital format and made available to those with IT knowledge and access to a PC and the Internet. Whether it is reviewing the London bus routes for vacation planning or studying horticulture via distance learning, people are finding that information technology is enhancing their lives. It can help us pursue our hobbies, like genealogy and gardening, provide us with critical medical information, help us learn more about political candidates, and help us organize our family finances. Generally, people are aware of impressive claims for the potential benefits of IT, and they want to enjoy those benefits, both at home and at work.

- *Workplace.* Each day information technology is becoming an increasingly important part of what we do in the workplace. Strategic use of information technology has emerged as a competitive weapon for those companies whose employees recognize and use the potential of IT. There are relatively few jobs that do not require some level of IT understanding. For example, only a few years ago the retail clerk simply learned how to use the cash register. Now that cash register is a point-of-sale (POS) terminal that links the salesperson to inventory systems, order tracking, and other business systems. Every company has problems. Computers along with their software have emerged as the solution tools of the new century. The greater the percentage of employees that can use these tools, the more effective and profitable the company can be.

- *Education.* Information technology opens new doors for education. Millions of people are now learning everything from agriculture to zoology via self-based, interactive, computer-based courses—both stand-alone and Internet-based. The computer is proving to be an effective teaching tool in enhancing traditional methods in kindergarten through higher education to continuing education for professionals. Many colleges now offer degrees whereby the student never sets foot on a physical college campus. This alternative to traditional education is blending well in the information society because it gives people the flexibility to pursue education at their own pace on their own schedule. However, to be an effective learner in this new era of education, IT competency is required.

- *Societal.* Many of the most prominent public issues being debated revolve around the use and implementation of technology. IT competency is necessary to fully understand the ethical issues being debated, such as a national database, electronic money, computer viruses, privacy of personal information, computer monitoring, **spam** (unsolicited e-mail), censorship on the Internet, biometric identification via scanning at public venues, and so on. It is critical that we be informed so that we better understand the potential risks posed by IT-related changes to our social values, freedoms, and economic interests.

- *Curiosity.* Naturally, there is simple curiosity about how this powerful and pervasive technology works.

THE COMPUTER PROFICIENCY DIGITAL DIVIDE

In the United States an estimated 120 million people are considered knowledge workers because they routinely work with computers. However, the vast majority of these people, over 100 million, would not be considered information technology competent! The fact that these people routinely use computers but are not IT-competent is referred to as the "computer proficiency digital divide." Most people use their PCs for only one or two applications, such as word processing or e-mail, or they are trained to work with a specific system, such as accounting, airline reservations, or inventory management. Many of the latter become quite good at the specialized systems but may find no need or time to learn personal computing applications that would let them help their children with their homework, do research, or scan a child's image for grandmother.

Many people believe themselves to be IT competent because they are personal computing veterans or use computers at work. Some are and some are not, mostly because their realm of exposure to IT is limited. Here is a simple test you can use to assess your level of IT competence. Can you describe five critical IT ethics issues facing our information society? Which port is faster, the USB or the 1394? Why is it necessary to run a disk defragmenter? What type of wiring is used in a typical home network? Name three top-level domain Ids other than .com and .edu. In cybertalk, BRB means what? What do TIF, PNG, and JPG files have in common? Describe five time- and/or money-saving personal computing applications for the home other than gaming, word processing, and Internet-based applications. Why would you filter information in an enterprise information system? How might an intelligent agent make your life a little easier? Given your circumstances, which broadband solution would be best for you—DSL, cable, or satellite? These are just a few of the hundreds of points of knowledge that come with IT competency. If you fell short on a few of these, don't worry, because IT competency is a clear objective of this book and this course.

SECTION SELF-CHECK

1-2.1 To be IT-competent, you must be able to write computer programs. (T/F)
1-2.2 Generally, what is the presentation of the results of processing called: (a) output, (b) printout, (c) outcome, or (d) download?
1-2.3 Hardware refers collectively to computers and computer equipment. (T/F)

1-3 The Net Connection

Through the 1980s, computers were known for their ability to bring data together to produce information. Today, computers also bring people together, from all over the world, opening the door for improved communication and cooperation.

OUR GLOBAL VILLAGE

In 1967 Marshall McLuhan said, "The new electronic interdependence recreates the world in the image of a global village." His insightful declaration is now clearly a matter of fact. At present, we live in a *global village* in which computers and people are linked within companies and between countries (see Figure 1-6). Over 80% of all classrooms and 98% of all libraries in United States are linked to the Internet and, therefore, the world. To put this in perspective, consider that it took decades for this kind of acceptance for the telephone.

The global village is an outgrowth of the **computer network.** Most existing computers are linked electronically to a network of one or more computers to share hardware/software resources and information. When we tap into a network of computers, we can hold electronic meetings with widely dispersed colleagues, retrieve information from the corporate database, and even work simultaneously on the same design project.

On a more global scale, computer networks enable worldwide airline reservation data to be entered in the Bahamas and American insurance claims to be processed in Ireland. People in Hong Kong, Los Angeles, and Berlin can trade securities simultaneously on the New York Stock Exchange and other exchanges around the world. Computer networks can coordinate the purchases of Korean electronics, American steel, and Indonesian glass to make cars in Japan, and can then be used to track sales of those cars worldwide. Lotteries are no longer confined to a state, or even the nation. Internet-based lotteries draw players from the entire world, paying huge pots to the winners. We can track every point in every match at the U.S. Open Tennis Tournament as they are played.

Thanks to computer networks, we are all part of a global economy, in which businesses find partners, customers, suppliers, and competitors around the world. The advent of this global economy is

FIGURE 1-6

THE GLOBAL VILLAGE
Computer-based communication is turning the world into a global village. We can communicate electronically with people on the other side of the world as easily as we might have a conversation with a neighbor.

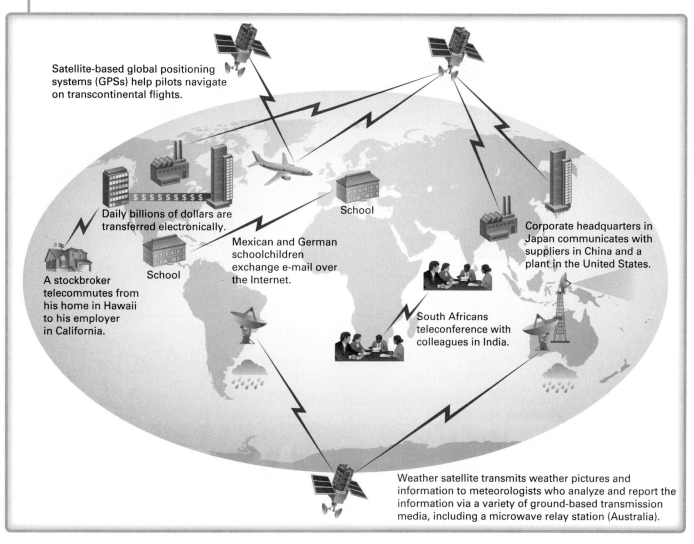

- Satellite-based global positioning systems (GPSs) help pilots navigate on transcontinental flights.
- Daily billions of dollars are transferred electronically.
- $ $ $ $ $ $ $ $
- School
- Mexican and German schoolchildren exchange e-mail over the Internet.
- School
- A stockbroker telecommutes from his home in Hawaii to his employer in California.
- Corporate headquarters in Japan communicates with suppliers in China and a plant in the United States.
- South Africans teleconference with colleagues in India.
- Weather satellite transmits weather pictures and information to meteorologists who analyze and report the information via a variety of ground-based transmission media, including a microwave relay station (Australia).

changing society across the board, often in subtle ways. For example, customer service may continue to improve as companies realize how quickly a single irate customer can use the Internet to broadcast messages vilifying a company or a particular product to millions of potential customers. Computers, related hardware, and software products are especially vulnerable to such customer attacks. If a product does not stand up to advertised capabilities, the computing community will quickly expose its shortcomings to potential buyers. This same level of scrutiny will ultimately be applied to other products and services. For example, there are hundreds of **newsgroups**, essentially interactive electronic bulletin boards, devoted exclusively to discussions of restaurants in various cities and countries. In these cities and countries, you can be sure that frequent diners know which restaurants offer good food and value and which ones do not. These and thousands of other special-topic newsgroups can be found on the Internet.

THE INTERNET: MILLIONS OF INTERCONNECTED NETWORKS

The Internet, also known simply as **the Net,** is a worldwide network of computers that has emerged as *the* enabling technology in our migration to a global village. It connects millions of computers in millions of networks in every country in the world. All colleges are on the Net; that is, they have an Internet account. The same is true of the vast majority of businesses. Because these organizations have established links to the Internet, people in these organizations can access the Internet. Individuals with PCs can access the Internet, too. If you have access to a computer at a college computer lab or at work, the PCs are probably "on the Net."

FIGURE 1–7   THE INTERNET AND AOL

INTERNET SHOPPING
Most people subscribe to an internet service provider (ISP) to get on the Internet. Once online, you can shop the electronic malls of the information superhighway to find exactly what you want, whether it's an 11-in-1 electronic survival kit or a home.

VIRTUAL NEWS
You also can listen to the news read by Ananova, a virtual newscaster, who reads the news in four different languages.

AOL
Most of the rest join America Online (AOL), the most popular online information service. AOL lets you go on the Internet, plus it has 20 interest areas from which to choose, and a variety of other services. Shown here is the Welcome screen, which usually announces "You've got mail" when you "sign on," the weather forecast for the Virgin Islands, the e-mail list and an e-mail, the buddy list (which alerts you when one of your buddies signs on so you can chat), and Internet Radio.

Getting Connected

Typically, individuals gain access to the Internet by subscribing to an **Internet service provider** (**ISP**) (see Figure 1-7). For a monthly fee, you can link your PC to the ISP's computer, thus gaining access to the Net. The monthly cost ranges from $20 to $100, depending on the speed of the connection. An ISP is a company with an Internet account that provides individuals and organizations access to, or presence on, the Internet. Another way to get on the Net is to subscribe to a commercial **information service,** such as **America Online** (see Figure 1-7). **AOL** has over 30 million subscribers. AOL and other commercial information services have one or several large computer systems that offer a wide range of information services over their proprietary network, which, of course, is linked to the worldwide Net. AOL services include up-to-the-minute news and weather, electronic shopping, e-mail, chat rooms, and much more. Most types of services provided by AOL are available to people who go online via an ISP. However, AOL packages them with an easy-to-use interface. AOL is sometimes referred to as an "ISP with training wheels."

The services and information provided by the Net and information services are **online**; that is, once the user has established a communications link between his or her PC, the user becomes part of the network. Most individuals at home use a regular telephone line in conjunction with a device called a modem to link to the Internet. A **modem** permits communication with remote computers via a telephone-line link. When online, the user interacts directly with the computers in the information network to access desired information and services. Other ways to link with the Internet are presented in Chapter 7, "Networks and Networking." When the user terminates the link, the user goes **offline.**

The Internet emerged from a government-sponsored project to promote the interchange of scientific information. This spirit of sharing continues as the overriding theme over the Internet. For example, aspiring writers having difficulty getting read or published can make their writing available to millions of readers, including agents and publishers, in a matter of minutes. Unknown musicians also use the Internet to gain recognition. *Surfers* on the Internet (Internet users) wanting to read a story or listen to a song, **download** the text or a digitized version of a song (like those on CDs) to their personal computer, then read it or play it through their personal computer. Popular **MP3 players,** the next generation Walkmans, can store and play digital music in MP3 format, a method of storing CD-quality music using relatively little memory (see Figure 1-8). Downloading is simply transmitting information from a remote computer (in this case, an Internet-based computer) to a local computer (in most cases, a PC). Information (perhaps a story or a song) going the other way, from a local computer to a remote computer, is said to be **uploaded.**

This spirit of sharing has prompted individuals and organizations all over the world to make available information and databases on a wide variety of topics. This wonderful distribution and information-sharing vehicle is, of course, a boon for businesses. Thousands of publishers, corporations, government agencies, colleges, and database services give Internet users access to their information—some provide information gratis and some charge a fee. Each year, more and more businesses are looking to the Internet as a vehicle to generate revenue.

The Web and Other Internet Applications

The Internet and the World Wide Web (the Web) are used interchangeably, as are the Net and the Web, but they are not the same. The Internet is a global network of computers and transmission facilities. It is the tool that enables a variety of amazing applications. E-mail, instant messaging, and newsgroups are a few of the many applications supported on the Internet. Perhaps the most important Internet application is the **World Wide Web** because it is this application, often called **the Web,** that lets us view the information on the Internet. The information, which may be graphics, audio, video, animation, and text, is viewed in **Web pages.** Other Internet applications, such as chat, videophone (see Figure 1-9), and gaming, are presented and illustrated in Chapter 3, "Going Online."

Services and capabilities of the Internet and commercial information services are growing daily. For example, a hungry traveler on the Internet can now order a pizza via the Net from a large number

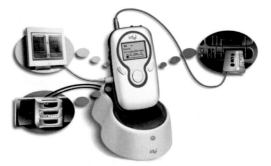

FIGURE 1–8 MP3 Player
There is a revolution under way in the way music is packaged, delivered, and played. Millions of MP3 songs are downloaded each day over the Internet and played on PCs or on MP3 players, like this Intel Pocket Concert Audio Player. You can load it up with four hours of music and take it anywhere. The unit is easily connected to your PC, home stereo, or auto stereo.

Photo courtesy of Intel Corporation

FIGURE 1–9 The Videophone Now a Reality
These schoolchildren in India are videoconferencing with children in the United States. This type of videophone link lets you check out a blind date, attend a virtual family reunion, speak with your business associate in another city, or say good night to your kids "in person" while away on a business trip. To make videophone calls, you need videophone software, an analog or digital camera, a PC, Internet access, and a link to a standard telephone line.

Photo courtesy of Intel Corporation

of online pizza delivery services. It works pretty much like a telephone order, except you enter the information on your PC, and it is routed immediately to the pizza shop nearest you. Usually, the order is displayed for the pizza chef within seconds. Of course, you can't download a pizza—it has to be delivered in the traditional manner. Already you can order almost any consumer item from tulips to trucks through the electronic malls.

Services available from the publicly available Internet and the subscription-based information services play a major role in shaping our information society. We'll discuss both in considerable detail throughout the book. Figure 1-10 presents an overview of popular Internet applications in seven dif-

---

FIGURE 1–10 OVERVIEW OF POPULAR INTERNET APPLICATIONS

PERSONAL COMMUNICATIONS

E-mail	Sand/receive personal and work-related electronic mail
Instant messaging	Real-time text, audio, and/or video communication
Chat	Normally, text-based interaction among groups of people in virtual chat rooms

BROWSING AND SEARCHING FOR INFORMATION

News	Newspapers, television stations, magazines, Internet portals, and other sites offer up-to-the-minute state, local, national, and international news, as well as topic-specific news, such as the stock market analysis and results
Sports	All professional leagues and teams, as well as all colleges, provide continuously-updated sports information and statistics to complement major sports news organizations, such as ESPN
Weather	Up-to-the-minute weather and weather forecasting is available for any city or region
Research for school or job	Billions of pages of information are available on almost any subject
Travel information	A breadth of information is available for tens of thousands of destinations, including cities, specific sites, resorts, and so on, including how to get there
Medical information	The Net has a plethora of medical data, advice, and information

DOWNLOADING AND FILE SHARING

Images and video	These include any kind of still image, from NASA space shots to family baby photos and a variety of brief videos from music videos to family clips
Music	Millions of songs are downloaded and shared, both legally and illegally, each day
Movies	That legal and illegal downloading/sharing of commercial and private movies is growing

STREAMING MEDIA

Video clips	News events, movie trailers, sports highlights, and so on
Audio	Speeches, radio station broadcasts, electronic greeting-card songs, and so on, are streamed over the Net
Movies	On-demand movies may someday threaten the existence of the video store

ONLINE TRANSACTIONS

Online shopping	Shop and buy almost anything on Internet, from groceries to automobiles
Online auctions	Bid on any of thousands of new and used items on the virtual auction block or place your own items up for auction
Online banking	Most bricks-and-mortar banking transactions can be down be done online
Making reservations	All types of travel reservations, including airline, train, hotel, auto rental, and so on, can be made online
Stock trading	Stocks can be bought and sold online
Gambling	Place real bets on virtual casino games and win/lose real money

ENTERTAINMENT

Multiplayer gaming	Play bridge or fight galactic battles with other Net-based gamers
Serendipitous browsing	Surf the Net just for fun to see where it leads you
Adult content	Adult entertainment is a major dot.com industry
Hobbyist	All popular hobbies are supported by sites that contain information and related activities

ferent categories: personal communications, browsing and searching for information, downloading and file sharing, streaming media, online transactions, and entertainment.

1-3.1 A global network called the Internet links millions of computers throughout the world. (T/F)

1-3.2 A computer network links computers to enable the: (a) linking of terminals and HDTV hookups, (b) sharing of resources and information, (c) distribution of excess processor capabilities, or (d) expansion of processing capabilities.

1-3.3 When the user terminates the link with a commercial information service, the user goes: (a) offline, (b) on-log, (c) out-of-site, or (d) online.

SECTION SELF-CHECK

1-4 The Basics: Hardware, Software, and Computer Systems

Almost everyone in our information society has a basic understanding of what a computer is and what it can do. This book is designed to add depth to what you already know.

HARDWARE BASICS

At the heart of any **computer** is its **processor,** *an electronic device that can interpret and execute programmed commands for input, output, computation, and logic operations.* The size of an actual PC processor, a computer's main piece of hardware, is about the size of a matchbook. Smaller ones like those used in VCRs and automobile ignition systems are about the size of your fingernail. Because of their size, processors frequently are referred to as microprocessors. Generally, the terms *processor* and *microprocessor* are used interchangeably.

To many people, computers are somewhat mystical, out of their range of comprehension. But computers aren't as complicated as you might have been led to believe. A **computer system** has only four basic components: *input, processor, output,* and *storage* (see Figure 1-11). Note that the processor, or computer, is just one component in a computer system. It gives the computer system its intelligence, performing all *computation* and *logic* operations. In everyday conversation, people simply say "computer" when they talk about a computer system. We'll do this as well throughout this book.

Each of the components in a computer system can take on a variety of forms. For example, *output* (the results of processing) can be routed to a televisionlike **monitor,** audio speakers (like those on your stereo system), or a **printer** (see Figure 1-11). The output on a monitor or the sounds from the speakers, which are temporary, are called **soft copy.** Printers produce **hard copy,** or printed output that can be physically handled, folded, and so on. Data can be entered to a computer system for processing (input) via a **keyboard** (for keyed input), a microphone (for voice and sound input), or a **point-and-draw device,** such as a **mouse** (see Figure 1-11).

Storage of data and software in a computer system is either *temporary* or *permanent.* **Random-access memory** (RAM, rhymes with "*ham*") provides temporary storage of data and programs during processing within solid-state **integrated circuits.** Integrated circuits, or **chips,** are tiny (about .5 inch square) silicon chips into which thousands of electronic components are etched. The processor is also a chip. Permanently installed and interchangeable **magnetic disks** provide permanent storage for data and programs (see Figure 1-11). Because the surface of circular, spinning disks is coated with easily magnetized elements for read/write operation, such as nickel, they sometimes are called *magnetic disks.* Information is read from and written to a variety of disks. **Optical disc** storage media that looks like audio CDs is either read only or read/write. Note the difference in spelling between magnetic *disks* and optical *discs.* A computer system is comprised of its internal components (for example, RAM and special features), the various storage devices, and its input and output **peripheral devices** (printer, monitor, mouse, and so on).

SOFTWARE BASICS

Software refers to any program that tells the computer system what to do. Of course, there are many different types of software. The more you understand about the scope and variety of available software, the more effective you will be as a user. Actually, understanding software is a lot like being in a big house—once you know its layout, you're able to move about the house much easier.

Once but a cottage, this house of software is almost a mansion. Software falls into two categories, system and applications software.

FIGURE 1–11

THE FOUR FUNDAMENTAL COMPONENTS OF A PERSONAL COMPUTER SYSTEM
In a personal computer system, the storage and processing components are often contained in the same physical unit. In the illustration, the interchangeable disk/discs-storage medium is inserted into the unit that contains the processor.

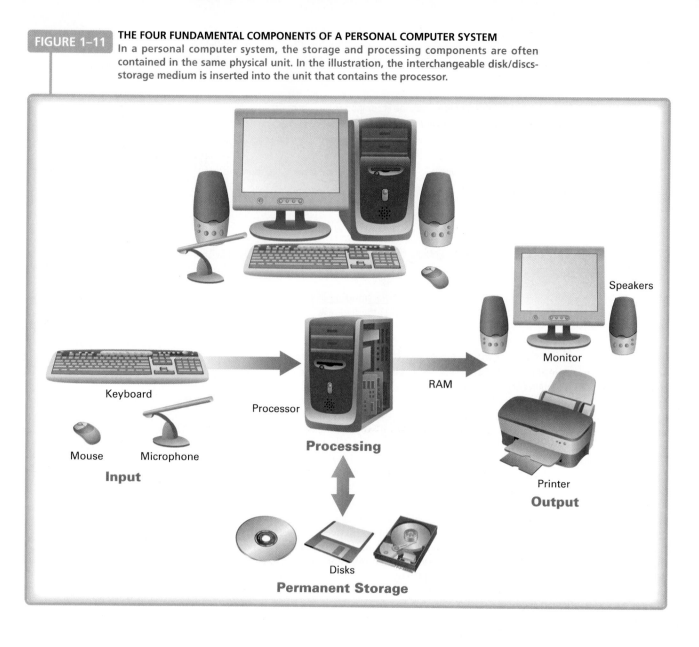

- *System software*. When you turn on the computer, the first actions you see are directed by system software. **System software** programs take control of the PC on start-up, and then play a central role in everything that happens within a computer system by managing, maintaining, and controlling computer resources.

- *Applications software*. **Applications software** is designed and created to perform specific personal, business, or scientific processing tasks, such as word processing, tax planning, or interactive gaming. We'll visit every room in the house by the time you finish this book.

COMPUTER SYSTEMS BASICS

General-purpose computers capable of handling a variety of tasks can be found in a range of shapes, from cube-shaped to U-shaped to cylindrical to notebook-shaped. However, the most distinguishing characteristic of any computer system is its *size*—not its physical size, but its *computing power*. Loosely speaking, size, or computing power, is the amount of processing that can be accomplished by a computer system in a certain amount of time, usually a second.

At one end of the power spectrum is the low-end personal computer that costs less than $500 and at the other is the powerful **supercomputer** that may cost more than an office building. The personal computer, as the name implies, serves one person at a time. In contrast, a super-computer can handle the processing needs of thousands of users at a time or perform processing that would take thousands of PCs.

Over the past five decades computers have taken on as many handles as there were niche needs. Terms like *mainframe computer* and *minicomputer* were popular in the 1970s and 1980s. Today, computers are generally grouped in these categories: notebook PCs, desktop PCs, wearable PCs, handheld computers, thin clients, workstations, server computers, and supercomputers. Give desktop PCs a slight edge in power over notebook PCs, but, generally, the two types offer similar computing capabilities. Wearable PCs are worn by the user, about the waist, head, or on the arm, providing the ultimate in mobile processing. The workstation is a notch above the top desktop PCs, offering individuals the performance they need for demanding scientific and graphics applications. In most computer networks, one or more central computers, called **server computers,** manage the resources on a network and perform a variety of functions for the other computers on the network, called **client computers,** which usually are PCs or workstations. PCs, workstations, and thin clients are linked to the server computer to form the network. **Thin clients** are somewhat less than full-featured PCs (thin) and they are clients of (dependent on) server computers for certain resources, such as storage and some processing.

Any general-purpose computer, a notebook PC to a supercomputer, can be a server computer. But manufacturers build a special class of computers, called server computers, which are designed specifically for the server function. There are small ones for small businesses and larger ones to handle network needs for multinational companies. We should emphasize that these categories of computers are relative. What people call a personal computer system today may look like a workstation at some time in the future and be called by an entirely different name.

PCs, workstations, "servers," and supercomputers are computer systems. Each offers many **input/output,** or **I/O,** alternatives—ways to enter data into the system and to present information generated by the system. All computer systems, no matter how small or large, have the same fundamental capabilities—*input, processing, output,* and *storage.* Keep this in mind as you encounter the computer systems shown in Figure 1-12. In keeping with conversational computerese, we will drop the word *system* when discussing the categories of computer systems. Remember, however, that a reference to any of these categories (for example, supercomputer) implies a reference to the entire computer system.

The differences in the various categories of computers are very much a matter of scale. Try thinking of a *supercomputer* as a *wide-body jet* and a *personal computer* as a *commuter plane.* Both types of airplanes have the same fundamental capability—they carry passengers from one location to another. Wide-bodies, which fly at close to the speed of sound, can carry hundreds of passengers. In contrast, commuter planes travel much slower and carry fewer than 50 passengers. Wide-bodies travel between large international airports, across countries, and between continents. Commuter planes travel short distances between regional airports. The commuter plane, with its small crew, can land, unload, load, and be on its way to another destination in 15 to 20 minutes. The wide-body may take 30 minutes just to unload. A PC is much like the commuter plane in that one person can get it up and running in just a few minutes. One person controls all aspects of the PC. The supercomputer is like the wide-body in that a number of specialists are needed to keep it operational. No matter what their size, airplanes fly and carry passengers and computers process data and produce information. Besides obvious differences in size, the various types of computers differ mostly in how they are used. Section 1-5 should give you insight into when and where a particular system might be used.

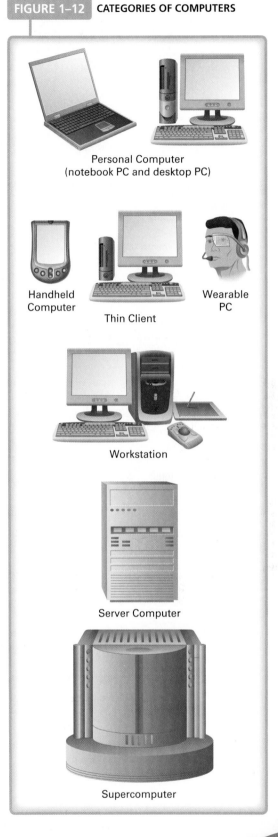

FIGURE 1–12   CATEGORIES OF COMPUTERS

Personal Computer
(notebook PC and desktop PC)

Handheld
Computer

Thin Client

Wearable
PC

Workstation

Server Computer

Supercomputer

1-4.1 Supercomputers have greater computing capacity than personal computers. (T/F)

1-4.2 A printer is an example of which of the four computer system components: (a) input, (b) output, (c) processor, or (d) storage?

1-4.3 Which component of a computer system executes the program: (a) input, (b) output, (c) processor, or (d) storage?

1-5 Personal Computers to Supercomputers

Every day, more computers are sold than existed in the entire world 35 years ago. Back then, most medium to large companies had a computer, but they came in only one size—big. They filled large rooms, even buildings. Today, computers come in a variety of sizes. In this section we take a closer look at these popular categories of computers: personal computers (notebook PCs, desktop PCs, and wearable PCs), handheld computers, thin clients, workstations, server computers, and supercomputers.

PERSONAL COMPUTERS: UP CLOSE AND PERSONAL

In 1981, IBM introduced its **IBM PC** and it legitimized the personal computer as a business tool. Shortly after that, other manufacturers began making PCs that were 100% compatible with the IBM PC; that is, they basically worked like an IBM PC. Most of today's personal computers (over 80%) evolved from these original PC-compatibles. Long removed from the IBM PC, they are also called **Wintel PCs** because they use the Microsoft *Windows 9x/Me/2000/XP* (a collective reference to Microsoft *Windows 95*, *Windows 98*, *Windows Millennium (Me)*, *Windows 2000*, or *Windows XP*) control software and an Intel Corporation or Intel-compatible processor. Each of the Microsoft Windows family of **operating systems** controls all hardware and software activities on Wintel PCs. Operating systems form the foundation of the system software category of software.

The Wintel PC represents the dominant PC platform. A **platform** defines a standard for which software is developed. Specifically, a platform is defined by two key elements:

- The processor (for example, Intel® Pentium III®, Intel® Celeron™, Intel Pentium 4®, Intel Itanium™, Intel McKinley™, Motorola® PowerPC®, AMD Athlon, and so on)
- The operating system (for example, Windows® XP, Windows Me, Mac® OS X, Unix®, Linux, Lindows, and so on)

Generally, software created to run on one platform is not compatible with any other platform. Most of the remaining personal computers are part of the Apple *Power Mac®*, *PowerBook®*, or *iMac™* line of computers. These systems use the *Mac® OS X* operating system and are powered by Motorola® *PowerPC®* processors.

One person at a time uses a PC. The user turns on the PC, selects the software to be run, enters the data, and requests the information. The PC, like other computers, is very versatile and has been used for everything from communicating with business colleagues to controlling household appliances. The personal computer is actually a family of computers, some are small and portable and some are not meant to be moved. The most common PCs, the notebook and desktop, have a full keyboard, a monitor, and can function as stand-alone systems (see Figure 1-13).

Notebook PCs

Until recently, people in the business world often purchased two PCs, a **notebook PC** for its portability and a **desktop PC** for its power and extended features. Early notebook PCs simply didn't have the power or the capabilities of their desktop cousins. That has changed. Now, notebook PCs offer desktop-level performance. These powerful notebook PCs let people take their "main" computer with them wherever they are, at work, at home, or on vacation. Each year, an increasing percentage of people choose to buy notebook PCs as their only PC. Today, close to half of all personal computers purchased for use in businesses are notebooks. That percentage continues to increase.

Notebook PCs are light (a few pounds up to about eight pounds), compact, and portable. It's easy to fold them up and take them with you. Notebook PCs, which also are called **laptop PCs,** are about the size of a one-inch-thick notebook. They have batteries and can operate with or without an external power source, on an airplane or a wilderness trail.

High-end notebook PCs can run circles around some desktop PCs. Some user conveniences, however, must be sacrificed to achieve portability. For instance, input devices, such as keyboards and point-and-draw devices, are given less space in portable PCs and may be more cumbersome to use.

FIGURE 1–13   PERSONAL COMPUTERS: DESKTOPS AND NOTEBOOKS

THE IMAC DESKTOP

Apple computer pioneered the all-in-one concept with its original see-though iMac in 1998. This iMac, which has a 10.6-inch footprint, was completely redesigned in 2002 with a flat screen that "floats" in mid-air, allowing for ease of adjustment. The new iMacs, which are designed to be the center of our emerging digital lifestyle, have a SuperDrive™ that permits playing and creating custom CDs and playing DVDs. Under the hood, the iMac sports an impressive list of features, including a powerful processor, plenty of memory, stereo sound, and network and Internet capabilities.

Courtesy of Apple Computer, Inc.

DESKTOP PC

This Dell Dimension tower system can sit under, beside, or on top of a desk. This home office system is configured with a large-screen monitor, an ink jet printer, a flatbed scanner, a digital video camera, and a satellite modem (atop the system unit) for high-speed Internet. The system has five speakers, including a woofer, and an uninterruptible power source (UPS) for backup if power is interrupted.

Long and Associates

NOTEBOOK PC

When searching for a personal computer, this executive identified portability and flexibility as her primary criteria, so she chose a laptop PC. Laptop users can now ask for SuperDisk drives (shown here) to be built into new notebooks for convenient, interchangeable, and high-capacity storage (over 100 million characters of data on a SuperDisk the size of a traditional floppy disk).

Photo courtesy of Imation Corporation

FUTURISTIC CONCEPT PCS

Intel Corporation is working with PC manufacturers to build better, simpler, and more effective personal computers. Shown here are several Intel Concept PCs that showcase the possibilities and benefits of drastically redesigned, legacy-free, easily upgradeable personal computers. These concept PCs provide a glimpse into the future of mobile PCs. The concept PCs include features that enable the always on, always connected vision, include seamless wireless connectivity capabilities, enhanced security, ease of use, as well as Tablet PC/notebook PC functionality. The futuristic concept PCs have small external displays that can show a calendar, phone numbers, or incoming e-mail so the user does not have to open and boot up the system to obtain this information. The systems have fingerprint recognition biometrics to ensure they are truly personal.

Photo courtesy of Intel Corporation

Generally, notebook PCs take up less space and, therefore, have a smaller capacity for permanent storage of data and programs. Laptop battery life can be as little as a few hours for older models to 20 hours for state-of-the-art rechargeable lithium batteries.

Many notebook PC buyers purchase a **port replicator,** too. Also called a **docking station,** the port replicator lets you enjoy the best of both worlds—portability plus the expanded features of a desktop PC. The notebook PC, which supplies the processor and storage, is simply inserted into or removed from the port replicator, as needed. The process takes only a few seconds. The port replicator can be *configured* to give the "docked" notebook PC the look and feel of a desktop PC. Once inserted, the notebook can use the port replicator *ports* and whatever is connected to them. **Ports** are electronic interfaces through which devices like the keyboard, monitor, mouse, printer, image scanner (to enter images to the system), and so on are connected. Port replicators also provide bigger speakers and an AC power source. Some provide a direct link to the corporate network.

Desktop PCs

The ubiquitous desktop PCs are not considered portable because they rely on an outside power source and are not designed for frequent movement. The desktop PC's **system unit,** which contains the processor, disk storage, and other components, may be placed in any convenient location (on a nearby shelf, on the desk, or on the floor). The system unit for early desktop PCs was designed to lay flat on a desk to provide a platform for the monitor. Today's *tower* system unit with its smaller *footprint* (the surface space used by the unit) has made the early models obsolete. The desktop PC's footprint continues to dwindle as the tower shrinks and more users opt for the space-saving flat-panel monitors.

Configuring a PC: Selecting the PC's Components

PC users often select, configure, and install their own system. The configuration of a PC or what you put into and attach to your computer can vary enormously. Common configuration options are shown in Figure 1-14.

Nowadays, the typical off-the-shelf PC is configured to run multimedia applications. **Multimedia applications** integrate text, sound, graphics, motion video, and/or animation. Computer-based encyclopedias, such as *Grolier Multimedia Encyclopedia,* and games, such as Broderbund's Carmen Sandiego series, provide a good example of multimedia applications. The encyclopedia can take you back to July 20, 1969, and let you see motion video of the *Apollo 11* lunar module *Eagle* landing on the moon at the Sea of Tranquility. If you wish, you can listen to Commander Neil Armstrong proclaim, "That's one small step for [a] man, one giant leap for mankind" as he steps on the moon. Of course, the electronic encyclopedia contains supporting text that explains that he intended to say "a man." The typical PC includes the following components.

- *Motherboard.* The **motherboard** is a single circuit board that includes the processor and other electronic components. It provides the path through which the processor communicates with memory components and the various I/O peripheral devices. The motherboard is housed in the system unit.

- *Keyboard.* The keyboard is the primary text input device.

- *Point-and-draw device.* The point-and-draw device, which is usually a mouse on desktop PCs, aids in navigation around the system, in moving screen objects, and in drawing applications.

- *Monitor.* The monitor is the display that provides *soft copy* (temporary) output.

- *Printer.* The printer lets the system produce *hard copy* (printed) output.

- *Hard disk.* PCs have a permanently installed high-capacity **hard-disk drive** for permanent storage of data and programs.

- *Floppy disk drive.* PCs usually have a traditional **floppy disk drive** into which an interchangeable **diskette,** or **floppy disk,** is inserted. The system may be configured with an additional higher-capacity interchangeable disk drive, as well.

- *CD-ROM or DVD-ROM drive.* Typically, the PC will have either a read-only **CD-ROM drive** or the newer **DVD-ROM drive** into which an interchangeable **CD-ROM,** which looks like an audio CD, is inserted. The DVD-ROM drive accepts all DVD format discs, as well, including **DVD-Video** for playing movies. Some models are configured with a rewritable option, either **CD-RW** and/or **DVD+RW.**

- *Microphone.* The microphone allows audio input to the system.

- *Speakers.* The speakers provide audio output.

Virtually all PCs, both desktop and notebook, give users the flexibility to configure the system with a variety of storage and I/O peripheral devices. Of course, most or all extra peripherals are left at the office/home when a notebook goes mobile. A PC system is configured by linking any of a wide variety

FIGURE 1–14

THE PERSONAL COMPUTER AND COMMON PERIPHERAL DEVICES
A wide range of peripheral devices can be connected to a PC. Those shown here and others are discussed in detail in later chapters.

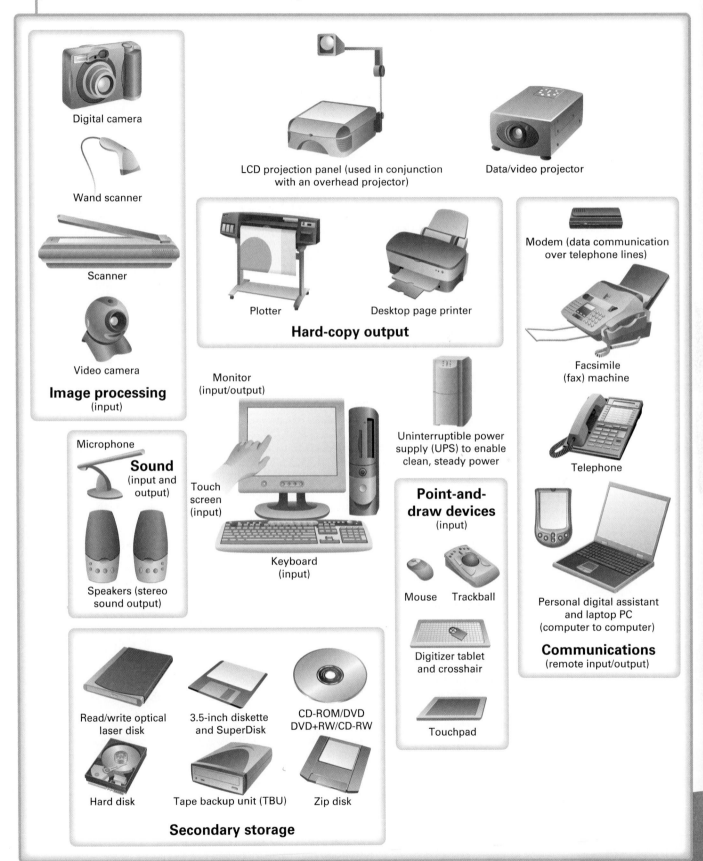

Digital camera

Wand scanner

Scanner

Video camera

Image processing
(input)

LCD projection panel (used in conjunction with an overhead projector)

Data/video projector

Plotter

Desktop page printer

Hard-copy output

Modem (data communication over telephone lines)

Facsimile (fax) machine

Telephone

Microphone

Sound
(input and output)

Speakers (stereo sound output)

Monitor
(input/output)

Touch screen
(input)

Keyboard
(input)

Uninterruptible power supply (UPS) to enable clean, steady power

Point-and-draw devices
(input)

Mouse   Trackball

Digitizer tablet and crosshair

Touchpad

Personal digital assistant and laptop PC
(computer to computer)

Communications
(remote input/output)

Read/write optical laser disk

3.5-inch diskette and SuperDisk

CD-ROM/DVD DVD+RW/CD-RW

Hard disk

Tape backup unit (TBU)

Zip disk

Secondary storage

of peripheral devices to the processor component. Figure 1-14 shows the more common storage and peripheral devices that can be configured with a PC. Many other peripherals can be linked to the "typical" PC, including video cameras, telephones, image scanners, other computers, security devices, and even a device that will enable you to watch your favorite television show on the PC's monitor.

Wearable PCs

Thousands of mobile workers could benefit from using a computer if only the computer were lighter, freed their hands, and didn't tether them to a desk or a power outlet. Now a new generation of **wearable PCs** promises to extend the trend begun by notebook and handheld computers.

Wearable computers, long a staple of science fiction, are here. In an effort to create truly personal computers that meld a computer and its user, designers have divided the wearable PC's components into cable-connected modules that fit into headsets, drape across shoulders, hang around the neck, and fasten around the waist, forearm, or wrist. Lightweight (two pounds or less), the components are covered in soft plastic and strapped on with Velcro.

Manufacturers of these wearable PCs combine existing or emerging technologies to create customized PCs for specific types of workers. The TLC (Tender Loving Care) PC for paramedics is a good example. At an accident scene, speech-recognition software lets the paramedic dictate symptoms and vital signs into a slender microphone hanging from a headset. The computer, draped across the medic's shoulders like a shawl, compares this data to a CD-ROM medical directory in the shoulder unit. The computer then projects possible diagnoses and suggested treatments onto the headset's miniature display. The TLC unit improves upon the two-way radio medics now use to communicate with emergency-room doctors. Instead of describing symptoms over a two-way radio, medics could use a trackball-operated video camera and body sensor strapped to their palm to *show* doctors the patient's condition. The video and additional data would be beamed to the doctors by a satellite link. Headphones would let the medics get feedback and additional advice from the waiting doctors.

Certainly, the trend is toward increasingly smaller PCs. Some say that an emerging trend is toward increasingly wearable PCs. If this trend holds, it's inevitable that vendors will be as concerned with fashion as they are with functionality. Power and size have always been critical elements of PCs, but now design is of growing importance. We may be entering an era of fashion wars where we may have to upgrade our PC to keep up with the latest fashion fad! With everyone drawing from essentially the same pool of microprocessors, is it possible that technical innovation may someday take a back seat to fashion?

Perhaps the most intriguing concept in wearable computers is the Body Net. The Body Net will be a network of wearable computers strategically located over the body. For example, the shoe-based computer might detect your location, and then transmit appropriate location-specific information for viewing on your eyeglasses computer. Perhaps within the decade, the PC will become as much an essential part of one's wardrobe as an indispensable business tool.

HANDHELD COMPUTERS: A COMPUTER IN HAND IS BETTER THAN . . .

Handheld computers are just that, computers that can be held in your hand. Handheld computers come in various form factors to address a variety of functions. The term **form factor** refers to a computer's physical shape and size. Computers, especially handheld computers and notebook PCs, continue to take on new form factors, often with unique features and capabilities. For example, one form factor integrates a cellular phone with a handheld computer. Another enables a notebook to be converted to a pen-based computer with handheld-like functionality.

Palmtop PC, personal digital assistant (PDA), connected organizer, personal communicator, mobile business center, and Web phone are just a few of the many names for handheld computers. Handheld computers weigh only a few ounces, can operate for days on their batteries, and can fit in a coat pocket or a handbag. As with notebooks, handheld computers must sacrifice some user convenience to achieve portability. The keyboards on those that have keyboards are miniaturized, making data entry and interaction with the computer difficult and slow. The display screen on some pocket PCs is monochrome (as opposed to color) and may be difficult to read under certain lighting situations.

Handheld computers are becoming increasingly important as the nature of information technology applications becomes ever more mobile. The increase in the number of handheld computers in use is a by-product of our information society's transformation to a mobile, geographically dispersed workforce that needs fast, easy, remote access to networked resources, including e-mail. Some handheld computers have built-in wireless communications capabilities that give their users immediate access to the Internet, colleagues, and clients, and needed information, virtually anytime, anywhere. Interaction with handheld computers can be via an electronic pen (handwritten text and graphics), by touching the keys on an on-screen keyboard, by keying on a reduced-key keyboard, or by speech (see Figure 1-15).

FIGURE 1–15 HANDHELD AND WEARABLE COMPUTERS

POCKET PC WITH KEYBOARD

This HP Pocket PC delivers the power, speed, and flexibility needed by people on the go. This miniature computer, which can fit in a purse or a coat pocket, can run the same applications as its notebook and desktop cousins. This handheld computer is shown with the HP e-copier, which can be moved over any hard copy document to produce an electronic copy (image) of anything from a business card to a flip chart.

Photo courtesy of Hewlett-Packard Company

HANDHELD COMPUTER

The Compaq iPAQ Pocket PC and its accessories give people access to the Internet and important business and personal information at any given time, in any given place. This palm-sized computer can store thousands of addresses, years of appointments, to-do items, memos, and e-mail messages. The executive can use a stylus or a screen-based keyboard to enter data. Also, it's easy to exchange information with a desktop or notebook PC.

WEARABLE PC

This communications maintenance man uses a hands-free, paperless computer system while performing his duties. Xybernaut's wearable PC, the Mobile Assistant, is worn on a belt or shoulder strap and includes a display worn on the head like a headset. The wearable PC is a voice-controlled personal computer that frees workers from bulky manuals. This man simply navigates to needed information by voice interface, and then glances at the display.

Courtesy of Xybernaut

PCS IN MUSEUMS

People visiting the Whitney Museum of American Art can take a self-guided interactive gallery tour with the assistance of a handheld PC. The pen-based PCs are loaded with multimedia information keyed to the artworks. Viewers of this 1916 portrait of Gertrude Vanderbilt Whitney, by Robert Henri, can hear the artist's letter written to Gertrude Whitney to arrange the sitting, listen to period chamber music, and look at photographs of Gertrude Whitney's palatial childhood home.

Photo courtesy of Intel Corporation

Mobile workers have found handheld computers that use an electronic pen, also called a **stylus**, in conjunction with a combination monitor/drawing pad to be very useful. These types of handheld computers, which are sometimes called **pen-based computers,** may or may not have a small keyboard. Users can select options, enter data via the on-screen keyboard, and draw with the pen. Pen-based computers often are designed for a particular application. For example, United Parcel Service (UPS) couriers use pen-based handhelds when they ask you to sign for packages on a touch-sensitive display screen with an electronic stylus. Coca-Cola and Pepsi-Cola distributors equip their salespeople with handheld computers, which enable them to manage their territories better.

Handheld computers with their improved input technology are making a big splash, as mobility and being connected become requirements for knowledge workers. Handhelds are improving each year in their ability to interpret handwritten text. Current technology demands that the user enter the alphanumeric information according to some basic rules. One rule might be that each letter has a particular starting point. For example, the user begins at the top to enter an "i" (see Figure 1-16). Handwritten characters are interpreted by handwriting-recognition software and then entered into the system. Insurance agents and claims adjusters who need to work at accident or disaster scenes have found handheld computers more suitable to their input needs, which may include entering both text and drawings. **Speech-recognition software**, which allows the user to enter spoken words into the system, is being integrated into high-end handheld computers. Speech recognition can be much faster than handwritten input, but it's impolite to talk to your computer during a meeting.

Generally, handheld computers support a variety of **personal information management (PIM)** systems. A PIM might include appointment scheduling and calendar, e-mail, fax, phone-number administration, to-do lists, tickler files, "Post-it" notes, diaries, and so on. Some handhelds can support a variety of PC-type applications, such as spreadsheets and personal financial management. Also, handhelds are designed to be easily connected to other computers and printers for data transfer, network access, and printing. Accessories for handhelds include a full-sized keyboard.

There are as many applications for handheld computers as there are organizations and functions. For example, a growing application for handhelds is emerging in the doctor's office, where the handheld may make the doctor's prescription pad a thing of the past. Thousands of doctors are using handheld computers to help them when they prescribe drugs. The doctor can ask the system to list applicable drugs for a particular medical condition. After selecting a drug, the system checks for possible drug interactions with other drugs the patient might be taking and it lists possible side effects. The system even makes recommendations relative to the patient's insurance coverage. Upon completion of the *e-prescribing* process, the prescription is e-mailed directly to the druggist. The automation of the prescribing process is expected to give a boost to health-care quality considering that over 100,000 people die and 2 million people are hospitalized because of drug side effects and prescription errors.

Handhelds, though, are not all business. You can use them to play interactive games, chat with friends on the Internet, listen to downloaded MP3 music (as you would on a Walkman), or read a good **electronic-book (e-book)**. Or, if you prefer, you can kick back, don your head set, and let the computer's **text-to-speech software** read the e-book to you!

HANDWRITTEN INPUT
These Graffiti characters, which are similar to capital letters, are the basis for entering handwritten data into Palm handheld computers. All characters are entered with a single stroke and most people learn the strokes in minutes. The dot indicates where to begin the stroke for a particular character. Numbers and letters are entered in separate areas.

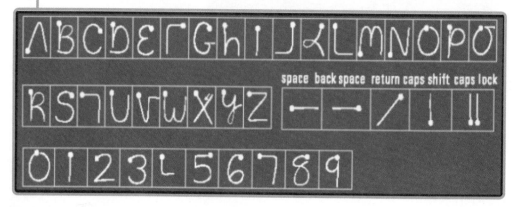

THIN CLIENTS: IN NETWORKS, THIN IS IN

In contrast to the conventional PC, the *thin client* is designed to function only when it is linked to a server computer (normally part of an organization's internal network of computers). The thin client looks similar to a PC (see Figure 1-17) but has several major differences. First, it has a relatively small processor and considerably less RAM (internal storage) than modern personal computers. Second, it does not have a permanently installed disk. And, it is less expensive than a stand-alone PC.

The thin client depends on a central network server computer to do much of its processing and for permanent storage of data and information. Here is the way a thin client works: The network computer user has access to a wide range of applications. However, the software applications and data are downloaded as they are needed to the thin client from a network's central computer. Whether or not to buy into the thin client concept is one of the major debates in the information technology community. Exchanging PCs for thin clients will eliminate the expensive and time-consuming task of installing and maintaining PC-based software, but it will make all thin clients dependent on the server computer. If the server goes down, all thin clients depending on it go down.

FIGURE 1–17 Thin Clients
In some companies, thin clients, such as this Sun Ray 1 Appliance, have replaced PCs in the workplace. Thin clients are so named because they are somewhat less than full-featured PCs (thin) and they are clients of (dependent on) server computers for certain resources.

Courtesy of Sun Microsystems, Inc.

WORKSTATIONS: HOT RODS

What looks somewhat like a desktop PC but isn't? It's a *workstation*, and it's very fast (see Figure 1-18). Speed is one of the characteristics that distinguish workstations from PCs. In fact, some people talk of workstations as "souped-up" PCs, the hot rods of computing. The workstation is for "power users"—engineers doing design work, scientists and researchers who do "number crunching," graphics designers, creators of special effects for movies, and so on. Although high-end desktop PCs may not perform as well as workstations, they are used for these applications, as well.

The workstation's input/output devices also set it apart from a PC. A typical workstation will sport a large-screen color monitor capable of displaying graphics at very high-resolutions. **Resolution** refers to the clarity of the image on the monitor's display. For pointing and drawing, the workstation user can call on a variety of specialized point-and-draw devices that combine the precision of a gun sight with the convenience of a mouse. Add-on keypads can expand the number of specialized *function keys* available to the user.

FIGURE 1–18 Workstation
This high-powered workstation is used for video editing and adding visual effects and animation for television programming and for films.

Courtesy of Autodesk, Inc.

The capabilities of today's high-end PCs are very similar to those of low-end workstations. In a few years, the average PC will have the capabilities of today's workstation. Eventually the distinctions between the two will disappear, and we will be left with a computer category that is a cross between a PC and a workstation. Time will tell whether we call it a PC, a workstation, or something else.

SERVER COMPUTERS: CORPORATE WORKHORSES

Most computers, including PCs and workstations, exist as part of a network of computers. At the center of most networks is one or more server computers (see Figure 1-19). In this section, we discuss the relationship between the server and its client computers. First, however, let's get some historical perspective.

Centralized Computing: A Bygone Era

Through the 1980s, huge mainframe computers performed most of the processing activity within a computer network. Back then, the shared use of a centralized mainframe offered the greatest return for the hardware/software dollar. Today, PCs and workstations offer more computing capacity per dollar than do mainframe computers. This reversal of hardware economics has caused IT professionals to rethink the way they design and use computer networks.

During the era of centralized mainframe computers, users communicated with a centralized host computer through dumb terminals that had little or no processing capability. The mainframe performed the processing for all users, sometimes numbering in the thousands. Now, the trend in the design of computer networks is toward *client/server computing.*

Client/Server Computing: Computers Working Together

In **client/server computing,** processing capabilities are distributed throughout the network, closer to the people who need and use them. A *server computer* supports many *client computers.*

- A *server computer,* which can be anything from a PC to a supercomputer, performs a variety of functions for its client computers, including the storage of data and applications software.

- The *client computer,* which is typically a PC, a workstation, or a thin client, requests processing support or another type of service (perhaps printing or remote communication) from one or more server computers.

In the client/server environment, both client and server computers perform processing to optimize application efficiency. For example, the client computer system might run a database application *locally* (on the client computer) and access data on a *remote* (not local) server computer system. In client/server computing, applications software has two parts—*the front end* and *the back end.*

- The client computer runs **front-end applications software,** which performs processing associated with the user interface and applications processing that can be done locally (for example, database and word processing).

- The server computer's **back-end applications software** performs processing tasks in support of its client computers. For example, the server might accomplish those tasks associated with storage and maintenance of a centralized corporate database.

FIGURE 1–19 Server Computer
This Sun server computer system includes disk storage in the unit, a backup fault-tolerant server, and several rack-mounted server computers. The system is capable of serving hundreds of client computers.

Courtesy of Sun Microsystems, Inc.

In a client/server database application (see Figure 1-20), users at client PCs run front-end software to *download* (server-to-client) parts of the database from the server for processing. Upon receiving the requested data, perhaps sales data on customers in the mid-Atlantic region, the client user runs front-end software to work with the data. After local processing, the client computer may *upload* (client-to-server) updated data to the server's back-end software for processing. The server then updates the customer database. The database application is popular in client/server computing, but the scope and variety of applications are growing daily.

Many people share the server computer's processing capabilities and computing resources. Server computers are usually associated with **enterprise systems**—that is, computer-based systems that service departments, plants, warehouses, and other entities throughout an organization. For example, human resource management, accounting, and inventory management tasks may be enterprise systems handled by a central server computer. Typically, users communicate with one or more server computers through a PC, a workstation, a thin client, or a **terminal.** A terminal has a keyboard for input and a monitor for output. Terminals are standard equipment at airline ticket counters. The traditional terminals that have no onboard intelligence, that is, no processor, are being replaced with thin clients. Depending on the size of the organization, a dozen people or 10,000 people can share system resources (for example, information, software, and access to the Internet) by interacting with their PCs, terminals, workstations, thin clients, handheld computers, and other communications devices.

Client/server environments with heavy traffic, such as America Online or a large company, might use a **proxy server computer.** This computer sits between the client PC and a normal server, handling many client requests and routing only those requests that it cannot handle to the real server. The proxy server improves overall performance by reducing the number of tasks handled by the real server. Proxy servers also are used as filters to limit outside access to the server and to limit employee

FIGURE 1–20 A WALKTHROUGH OF A CLIENT/SERVER DATABASE APPLICATION

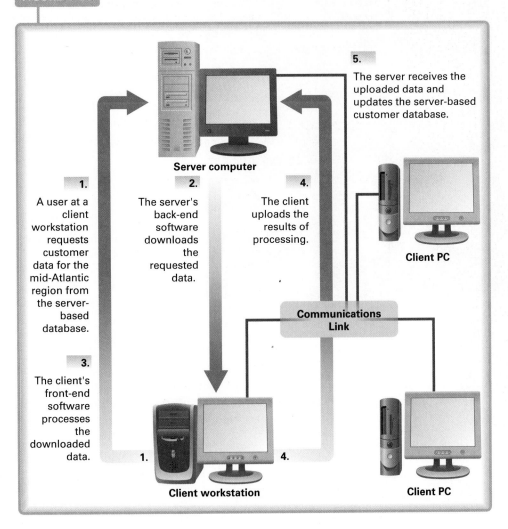

5.
The server receives the uploaded data and updates the server-based customer database.

Server computer

1.
A user at a client workstation requests customer data for the mid-Atlantic region from the server-based database.

2.
The server's back-end software downloads the requested data.

4.
The client uploads the results of processing.

Client PC

Communications Link

3.
The client's front-end software processes the downloaded data.

1. **4.**

Client workstation

Client PC

access to specific Web sites. In Chapter 7, "Networks and Networking," we'll introduce several other special-purpose server computers that can be used to improve overall system efficiency.

SUPERCOMPUTERS: PROCESSING GIANTS

During the early 1970s, administrative data processing dominated computer applications. Bankers, college administrators, and advertising executives were amazed by the blinding speed at which million-dollar mainframe computers processed their data. Engineers and scientists were grateful for this tremendous technological achievement, but they were far from satisfied. When business executives talked about unlimited capability, engineers and scientists knew they would have to wait for future enhancements before they could use computers to address truly complex problems. Automotive engineers were still not able to create three-dimensional prototypes of automobiles inside a computer. Physicists could not explore the activities of an atom during a nuclear explosion. A typical scientific job involves the manipulation of a complex mathematical model, often requiring trillions of operations to resolve. During the early 1970s, some complex scientific processing jobs would tie up large mainframe computers at major universities for days at a time. This, of course, was unacceptable. The engineering and scientific communities had a desperate need for more powerful computers. In response to that need, computer designers began work on what are now known as supercomputers (see Figure 1-21).

Supercomputers primarily address **processor-bound applications**, which require little in the way of input or output. In processor-bound applications, the amount of work that can be done by the computer system is limited primarily by the speed of the computer. Such applications involve highly complex or vastly numerous calculations, all of which require processor, not I/O, work.

M E M O R Y

Categories of Computer Systems

- Personal computer (PC)
  - Notebook PC
  - Desktop PC
  - Wearable PC
- Handheld computer
- Thin client (works with server computer)
- Workstation
- Server computer
- Supercomputer

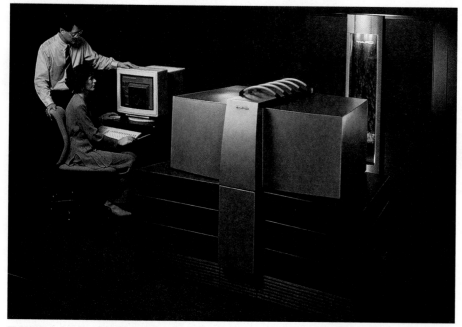

FIGURE 1–21 Supercomputer
The CRAY T90™ supercomputer is one of the most powerful general-purpose computers. General-purpose computers are capable of handling a wide range of applications.

Courtesy of E-Systems, Inc.

Supercomputers are known as much for their applications as they are for their speed or computing capacity, which may be 100 times that of a typical corporate server computer (see Figure 1-22). IBM is just finishing up work on Blue Gene, a supercomputer with over a million processors that will perform 1 million billion (10^{15}) math operations per second. These are representative supercomputer applications:

- Supercomputers enable the simulation of airflow around an airplane at different speeds and altitudes.

- Auto manufacturers use supercomputers to simulate auto accidents on video screens. (It is less expensive, more revealing, and safer than crashing the real thing.)

- Meteorologists employ supercomputers to study how oceans and the atmosphere interact to produce weather phenomena such as El Niño. It is hoped that eventually supercomputers will help meteorologists make earlier and better forecasts, especially concerning the paths of hurricanes and tornadoes and for flash floods and snowstorms.

- Supercomputers are being used to solve how the proteins are formed in the human body. IBM's Blue Gene is expected to take one year to calculate how a typical protein folds itself into a specific shape that determines its function in the body.

- Hollywood production studios use supercomputers to create the advanced graphics used to create special effects for movies such as *Star Wars Episode II: Attack of the Clones* and for TV commercials.

- Supercomputers sort through and analyze mountains of seismic data gathered during oil-seeking explorations.

- Medical researchers use supercomputers to simulate the delivery of babies.

SECTION SELF-CHECK

1-5.1 The power of a PC is directly proportional to its physical size. (T/F)

1-5.2 Workstation capabilities are similar to those of a low-end PC. (T/F)

1-5.3 What has I/O capabilities and is designed to be linked remotely to a host computer: (a) terminal, (b) printer, (c) port, or (d) mouse?

1-5.4 A notebook PC can be inserted into which of these to enable functionality similar to a desktop PC: (a) slate, (b) port hole, (c) runway, or (d) port replicator?

1-5.5 Spoken words are entered directly into a computer system via: (a) key entry, (b) OCR, (c) Morse code, or (d) speech recognition.

1-5.6 A client computer requests processing support or another type of service from one or more: (a) sister computers, (b) server computers, (c) customer computers, or (d) IT managers.

1-6   Computer System Capabilities

Now that we know a little about the basic types of computer systems, let's examine what a computer can and cannot do. First, let's talk about one of the computer's most significant capabilities—manipulating data to produce information.

PROCESSING DATA AND PRODUCING INFORMATION

Information as we now know it is a relatively new concept. Just 50 short years ago, *information* was the telephone operator who provided directory assistance. Around 1950, people began to view information as something that could be collected, sorted, summarized, exchanged, and processed. But only during the last two decades have computers allowed us to begin tapping the potential of information (see Figure 1-23).

Computers are very good at digesting data and producing information. For example, when you order a cross-country bicycle from an Internet-based *e-tailer*, an online retailer, the data you enter to the system (name, address, product ID) are entered directly into the e-tailer's computer. When you run short of cash and stop at an automatic teller machine, all data you enter, including that on the magnetic stripe of your bankcard, are processed immediately by the bank's computer system. A computer system eventually manipulates your **data** to produce **information.** The information could be an invoice sent to you via e-mail for the bicycle or a statement from the bank reflecting your withdrawal.

Traditionally, we have thought of data in terms of numbers (account balance) and letters (customer name), but recent advances in information technology have opened the door to data in other formats, such as visual images. For example, dermatologists (physicians who specialize in skin disorders) use digital cameras to take close-up pictures of patients' skin conditions. Each patient's record (information about the patient) on the computer-based **master file** (all patient records) is then updated to include the digital image. During each visit, the dermatologist recalls the patient record, which includes color images of the skin during previous visits. Data can also be found in the form of sound. For example, data collected during noise-level testing of automobiles include digitized versions of the actual sounds heard within the car.

FIGURE 1–22 Supercomputer Application
At Phillips Petroleum Company this Cray Research supercomputer is used to analyze huge amounts of seismic/geological data gathered during oil-seeking explorations. The company uses the computer for many other processor-intensive applications.

Photo courtesy of Phillips Petroleum Company

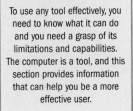

> **WHY THIS SECTION IS IMPORTANT TO YOU**
>
> To use any tool effectively, you need to know what it can do and you need a grasp of its limitations and capabilities. The computer is a tool, and this section provides information that can help you be a more effective user.

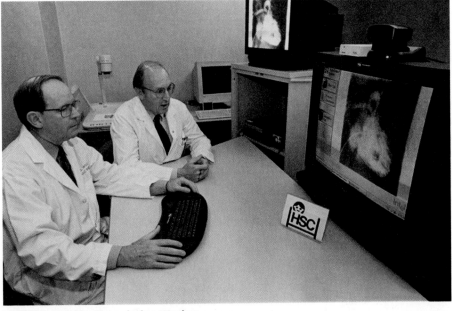

FIGURE 1–23 The Knowledge Worker
Today, we belong to an information society where we are "knowledge workers." For example, doctors are knowledge workers. These doctors use computers and communications technology to practice telemedicine, that is, providing health care remotely over communications links.

Photo courtesy of Intel Corporation

The relationship of data to a computer system is much like the relationship of gasoline to an automobile. Data provide the fuel for a computer system. Your car won't get you anywhere without gas, and your computer won't produce any information without data. It's all about data.

COMPUTERS IN ACTION: A PAYROLL SYSTEM

To get a better idea of how a computer system actually works, let's look at how it might do the processing of a *payroll system*. Just about every organization that has employees and a computer maintains a computer-based payroll system. The payroll system enables input and processing of pertinent payroll-related data to produce payroll checks and a variety of reports. The payroll system walkthrough in Figure 1-24 illustrates how data are entered into a network of personal computer systems

FIGURE 1–24 **A WALKTHROUGH OF A LAN-BASED PAYROLL SYSTEM**
This step-by-step walkthrough of parts of a LAN-based payroll system (three client PCs and a server) illustrates input, storage, processing, and output.

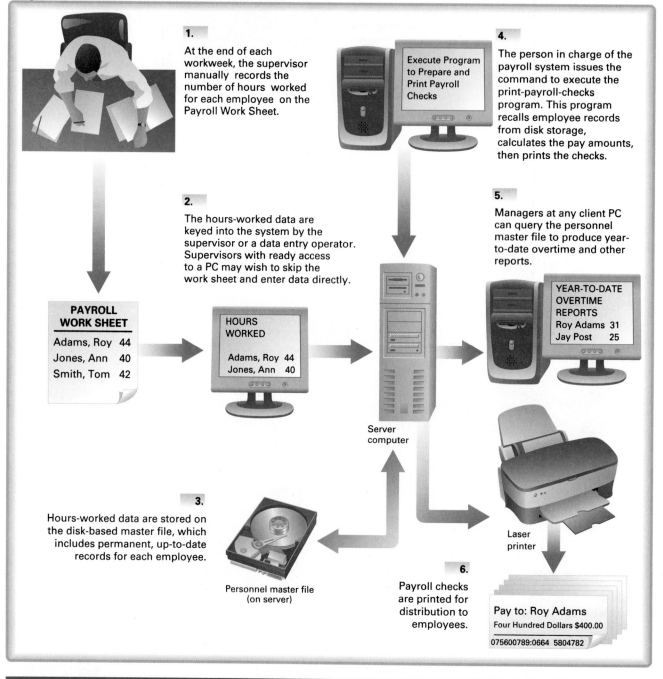

1. At the end of each workweek, the supervisor manually records the number of hours worked for each employee on the Payroll Work Sheet.

2. The hours-worked data are keyed into the system by the supervisor or a data entry operator. Supervisors with ready access to a PC may wish to skip the work sheet and enter data directly.

3. Hours-worked data are stored on the disk-based master file, which includes permanent, up-to-date records for each employee.

4. The person in charge of the payroll system issues the command to execute the print-payroll-checks program. This program recalls employee records from disk storage, calculates the pay amounts, then prints the checks.

5. Managers at any client PC can query the personnel master file to produce year-to-date overtime and other reports.

6. Payroll checks are printed for distribution to employees.

PAYROLL WORK SHEET
Adams, Roy 44
Jones, Ann 40
Smith, Tom 42

Execute Program to Prepare and Print Payroll Checks

HOURS WORKED
Adams, Roy 44
Jones, Ann 40

YEAR-TO-DATE OVERTIME REPORTS
Roy Adams 31
Jay Post 25

Server computer

Personnel master file (on server)

Laser printer

Pay to: Roy Adams
Four Hundred Dollars $400.00
075600789:0664 5804782

and how the four system components (input, processing, output, and storage) interact to produce payroll checks and information (in our example, a year-to-date overtime report).

In the walkthrough of Figure 1-24, the payroll system and other company systems are supported on a **local area network** (**LAN**). A LAN connects PCs or workstations that are relatively near one another, such as in a suite of offices or a building. The typical LAN employs client/server computing where data and applications software are on the server. In Figure 1-24, client PCs throughout the company are linked to a server computer.

WHAT CAN A COMPUTER DO?

Computers perform two operations: input/output operations and processing operations.

Input/Output Operations: Read and Write

Within a computer system, information is continuously moved from one part of the system to another. The processor controls this movement. It interprets information from the keyboard (a tapped key), moves it to memory and eventually to the monitor's display, the printer, or perhaps a stored file. This movement is referred to as input/output, or I/O for short. In performing input/output operations, the computer *reads* from input and storage devices, and then *writes* to output and storage devices.

Before processing begins, *commands* and/or *data* must be "read" from an input device and/or storage device. Typically, user commands and data are entered on a *keyboard* or via *speech recognition* (spoken words entered to the computer system), or they are retrieved from storage, such as a magnetic disk. Once commands and data have been processed, they are "written" to a magnetic disk or to an output device, such as a monitor or printer.

Input/output (I/O) operations are shown in the payroll-system walkthrough example in Figure 1-24. Hours-worked data are entered by a supervisor, or "read," into the computer system (Activity 2). These data are "written" to magnetic disk storage for recall later (Activity 3). Data are "read" from the personnel master file on magnetic disk, processed (Activity 4), and "written" to the printer to produce the payroll checks (Activity 6).

Processing Operations: Doing the Math and Making the Decisions

Any two computers instructed to perform the same operation will arrive at the same result because the computer is totally objective. Computers can't have opinions. They can perform only *computation* and *logic operations programmed by human beings*.

Computation Operations

Computers can add (+), subtract (−), multiply (*), divide (/), and do exponentiation (^). In the payroll system example of Figure 1-24, an instruction in a computer program tells the computer to calculate the gross pay for each employee in a computation operation. For example, these calculations would be needed to compute gross pay for Ann Jones, who worked 40 hours this week and makes $15 per hour:

Pay = 40 hours worked * $15/hour = $600

The actual program instruction that performs the above calculation might look like this:

PAY = HOURS_WORKED * PAY_RATE

The computer would then recall values for HOURS_WORKED and PAY_RATE from the personnel master file and calculate PAY.

Logic Operations

The computer's logic capability enables comparisons between numbers and between words. Based on the result of a comparison, the computer performs appropriate functions. In the example of Figure 1-24, Tom Smith and Roy Adams had overtime hours because they each worked more than 40 hours (the normal workweek). The computer must use its *logic capability* to decide if an employee is due overtime pay. To do this, hours worked are compared to 40.

Are hours worked > (greater than) 40?

For Roy Adams, who worked 44 hours, the comparison is true (44 is greater than 40). A comparison that is true causes the difference (4 hours) to be credited as overtime and paid at time and a half. The actual instruction that would perform the logical operation might look like this.

IF HOURS_WORKED > 40 THEN PAY_OVERTIME

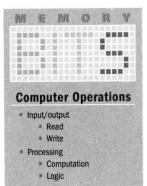

Computer Operations

- Input/output
  - Read
  - Write
- Processing
  - Computation
  - Logic

THE COMPUTER'S STRENGTHS

In a nutshell, computers are fast, accurate, consistent, and reliable; plus, they aid in communications and can store huge amounts of data. They don't forget anything, and they don't complain.

Speed

Computers perform various activities by executing instructions, such as those discussed in the previous section. These operations are measured in **milliseconds, microseconds, nanoseconds,** and **picoseconds** (one thousandth—*milli,* one millionth—*micro,* one billionth—*nano,* and one trillionth—*pico* of a second, respectively). To place computer speeds in perspective, consider that a beam of light travels down the length of this page in about one nanosecond. During that time a large server computer can perform the computations needed to complete a complex tax return.

Accuracy

Computers are amazingly accurate, and their accuracy reflects great *precision.* Computations are accurate within a penny (see Figure 1-25), a micron (a millionth of a meter), a picosecond, or whatever level of precision is required. Errors do occur in computer-based systems, but precious few can be directly attributed to the computer system itself. Most can be traced to a program logic error, a procedural error, or erroneous data. These are *human errors.*

FIGURE 1–25

TRILLIONS OF DOLLARS TRADED WITHOUT ERROR
At the New York Stock Exchange, literally trillions of dollars' worth of securities are routinely bought and sold with nary a penny lost, a testament to the accuracy of computers. Visitors to its Internet Web site can learn about trading and view the trading floor via continuous 360 degree scans from different perspectives. Shown here is a pan of the floor from the famous bell platform where trading is signaled to be open and closed.

Courtesy of the New York Stock Exchange

Consistency

Baseball pitchers try to throw strikes, but often end up throwing balls. Computers always do what they are programmed to do—nothing more, nothing less. If we ask them to throw strikes, they throw nothing but strikes. This ability to produce the consistent results gives us the confidence we need to allow computers to process *mission-critical* information (information that is necessary for continued operation of an organization, a space shuttle, and so on).

Reliability

Computer systems are the most reliable workers in any company, especially when it comes to repetitive tasks. They don't take sick days or coffee breaks, and they seldom complain. Anything below 99.9% *uptime,* the time when the computer system is in operation, is usually unacceptable. For some companies, any *downtime* is unacceptable. These companies provide **backup computers** that take over automatically should the main computers fail.

Communications

Computers can communicate with other computers, and, by extension, with us. Using physical and wireless links, computers are able to share resources, including processing capabilities, all forms of data and information, and various peripheral devices (printers, scanners). This communications capability has enabled the formation of computer networks within an organization and the emergence of the worldwide Internet network. These networks have certainly made communications between people easier and timelier.

Memory Capability

Computer systems have total and instant recall of data and an almost unlimited capacity to store these data, images, audio, video, or whatever can be digitized. A typical server computer system may have trillions of characters and millions of images stored and available for instant recall. A typical PC may have immediate access to billions of characters of data and thousands of images. To give you a benchmark for comparison, this book contains approximately 2 million characters and about 500 images.

Comparing Computer and Human Capabilities

The capabilities of computers and human beings are often compared because our information society is continually making decisions about whether a particular task is best done by a computer or a human. It's not always an obvious decision.

Human output (speech) is slow, maybe 120 words per minute for fast talkers, where computers talk in gigabytes per second. We recognize images (pattern recognition) more quickly than the fastest supercomputers. Computers struggle with pattern recognition. It's estimated that our memory is measured in terabytes (trillions of bytes), right up there with the best of computers. Computers do a much better job, however, of recalling stored information. They are 100% accurate in presenting stored information, which is seldom the case with humans. Computers can learn. So can we, but we do a much better job of applying what we learn to life situations.

The most significant difference between computers and humans is that we think. Computers do only what we tell them to do. And, at least for the foreseeable future, we remain in control.

1-6.1	The operational capabilities of a computer system include the ability to do both logic and computation operations. (T/F)
1-6.2	Downtime is unacceptable in some companies so they have backup computers. (T/F)
1-6.3	Which of the following would be a logic operation: (a) TODAY<BIRTHDATE, (b) GROSS-TAX-DEDUCT, (c) HOURS*WAGE, or (d) SALARY/12?

SECTION SELF-CHECK

1-7   How Do We Use Computers?

This section provides an overview of potential computer applications, which should give you a feel for how computers are affecting your life. These applications are presented in two parts, *enterprise computing* and *personal computing*. These applications, however, are but a few of the many applications presented throughout the book.

ENTERPRISE COMPUTING

Enterprise computing comprises all computing activities designed to support any type of organization: a company, a government entity, a university, and so on. Enterprise applications are in three groups: *information systems, process/device control,* and *science, research, and engineering.*

Information Systems

The bulk of existing computer power is dedicated to **information systems.** This includes all uses of computers that support the administrative aspects of an organization, such as airline reservation systems, student registration systems, hospital patient-billing systems, and countless others (see Figure 1-26). We combine *hardware, software, people, procedures,* and *data* to create an information system. A computer-based information system provides an organization with *data processing* capabilities and the knowledge workers in the organization with the *information* they need to make better, more informed decisions.

During any given day we are likely to interact with and/or cause activity within a variety of information systems. You interact directly with a bank's information system when you withdraw money from an ATM (automatic teller machine). When you purchase an item, the retail store updates its inventory and records the sale data. The credit card company updates its records to reflect the purchase and, possibly, debits that amount from your bank account. Each time you use your cellular phone, data are collected and passed around to information systems of cooperating phone companies, as needed. The first stop on a trip to the library is usually the PC linked to the library's information system.

Information systems process personal data on an ongoing basis, often without our knowledge. As you read this, some organization's information system has identified you as a target of commerce and will be sending you an unsolicited e-mail, called spam, or a printed brochure in the near future. A utility company may be processing your monthly invoice. Another information system might have determined that you are due a rebate on your city income taxes. Take a look around you today and be mindful of when you (or your personal information) are part of information systems.

Process/Device Control

Within an enterprise, the number of applications for computer-based **process/device control** is growing rapidly. For example, computers control every step in the oil-refining process and they control thousands of devices from air conditioners to theme park rides (see Figure 1-27). Computers that control processes accept data in a continuous **feedback loop.** In a feedback loop, the process itself generates data that become input to the computer. As the data are received and interpreted by the computer, the computer initiates action to control the ongoing process. An automated traffic-control system is a good example of the continuous feedback loop in a computerized process-control system. Have you ever driven an automobile through a city with an automated traffic-control system? If so, you would soon notice how the traffic signals are coordinated to minimize delays and optimize traffic flow. Traffic sensors are strategically placed throughout the city to feed data continuously to a central computer on the volume and direction of traffic flow (see Figure 1-28). The computer-based control system that activates the traffic signals is programmed to plan ahead. That is, if the sensors locate a group of cars traveling together, traffic signals are then timed accordingly.

S88E5107 1998:12:10 09:33:22

FIGURE 1–26 NASA Information System
Each launch of the space shuttle creates enormous activity in the NASA-based information system that supports the shuttle and the International Space Station. Astronauts, like this one, have ready access to onboard computers, which are linked to the NASA computers. The onboard systems provide ongoing feedback to ground-based scientists during space experiments. The information system encompasses everything from monitoring space resources (fuel, oxygen, and so on) to more earth-based concerns such as inventory and logistics.

Courtesy NASA

Server-sized process-control computers monitor and control the environment (temperature, humidity, lighting, security) inside skyscrapers. These computer-controlled skyscrapers are often referred to as "smart" buildings. At the other end of the process-control spectrum, tiny "computers on a chip" are being embedded in artificial hearts and other organs. Once the organs are implanted in the body, the computer monitors critical inputs, such as blood pressure and flow, and then takes corrective action to ensure stability of operation in a continuous feedback loop.

Computers control **industrial robots** that perform the materials handling duties in huge warehouses. These robots, which navigate about the warehouse without human intervention, pick and place inventory items in bins under computer control. In automobile assembly facilities, computer-controlled robots do the welding and the painting, and they keep the assembly line moving.

FIGURE 1–27 Jurassic Technology
The entertainment industry relies on computers and information technology to enliven experiences, often by using computers to control process and devices. Technology makes it possible for us to go back in time and experience the Jurassic period. At Universal Studios Hollywood theme park, the Jurassic Park River Adventure ride is completely automated.

Photo courtesy of Intel Corporation: Photo by Dana Fineman-Appel, Hollywood, California

Science, Research, and Engineering

Engineers and scientists routinely use the computer as a tool in *experimentation*, *design*, and *development*. There are at least as many science and research applications for the computer as there are scientists and engineers. One of these applications is **computer-aided design** (**CAD**), which involves

FIGURE 1–28   **AN AUTOMATED TRAFFIC-CONTROL SYSTEM**
In a continuous feedback loop, street sensors provide input to a process-control computer system about the direction and volume of traffic flow. Based on their feedback, the system controls the traffic lights to optimize the flow of traffic.

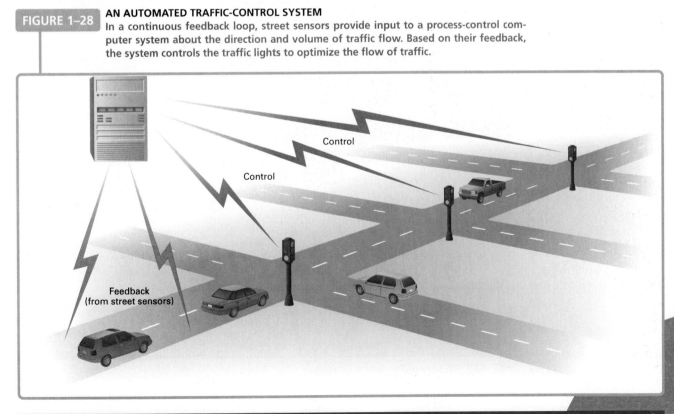

using the computer in the design process (see Figure 1-29). CAD systems enable the creation and manipulation of an on-screen graphic image. CAD systems provide a sophisticated array of tools, enabling designers to create three-dimensional objects that can be flipped, rotated, resized, viewed in detail, examined internally or externally, and much more. Photographs in this chapter and throughout the book illustrate a variety of CAD applications, such as automobile design and architectural design.

PERSONAL COMPUTING

Personal computing, an environment in which one person controls the PC, takes in everything from 3-D games, to going online, to computer-based education, to music composition. A seemingly endless number of software packages add variety to the personal computing experience (see Figure 1-30). The growth of personal computing has surpassed even the most adventurous forecasts of a decade ago. It's not uncommon for companies to have more personal computers than they do telephones. At home, each family member wants his or her own PC. With most PCs now part of a network or linked to the Internet, the reach of personal computing applications is virtually unlimited.

Buying a PC: The PC Investment

The personal computing adventure begins when you acquire a PC. Let's put this purchase into perspective. The typical home PC is used 10 to 50 hours a week. It's not passive like a TV. We interact with it to have fun, be informed, and do the chores of life. As any PC owner will tell you, the PC quickly becomes a major part of what you do. The cost of a PC reflects its importance in your life and home. PCs have emerged as the third most expensive item for the typical family—right behind homes and automobiles. For those families that do not own a home or an automobile, their PC(s) may be their biggest expense.

Living the personal computing adventure can run into serious money—quickly. But you need to weigh that cost against the enormous benefits of having one PC or, perhaps, a few PCs around the house. Given the potential of the PC and the impact it can have on your life and those around you, the PC remains one of the best investments you can make.

Most of the things we own are single-function items. Our automobiles take us from point A to point B. The only variation in functionality is the level of comfort the rider experiences. The dish-

FIGURE 1–29 Computer-Aided Design
This engineer uses computer-aided design (CAD) software to design automobiles.

Courtesy of Sun Microsystems, Inc.

washer washes dishes. Some of our household items are multifunction, like the kitchen sink, a Swiss Army knife, and the umbrella. The PC, however, is a general-purpose device capable of performing an almost endless variety of tasks. Any PC purchased with purpose and invigorated with imagination is well worth its cost—and then some.

PC Applications Galore

A variety of domestic and business applications form the foundation of personal computing. Domestic applications include everything from personal finance to education to entertainment to reference (see Figure 1-31). PC software is available to support thousands of common and not-so-common personal and business applications.

The Software Suite

Software suites are bundles of complementary software that include, to varying degrees, several or all of the productivity software mentioned in this section. The various programs within a given software suite have a common interface and are integrated for easy transfer of information among programs. Examples in the book are from Microsoft Office, the most widely used software suite (see Figure 1-32). Corel WordPerfect Office and Lotus SmartSuite are the other major suites. Most new PCs are sold with a software suite installed on the system.

FIGURE 1–30 The Personal Computing Experience
Personal computing provides a much richer experience than just a few years ago. After receiving a box of chocolates for Valentine's Day, this man immediately called his fiancée to show his appreciation. Through a videophone Internet hookup, she is able to see and hear his expression of joy. She sent him a digital image of her with the roses she received from him.

Photo courtesy of Intel Corporation

Over the history of personal computing, these software suite applications have formed the foundation for personal computing in the home and in the business world.

- *Word processing.* **Word processing software** enables users to create, edit (revise), and format documents in preparation for output (for example, printing, displaying locally or over the Internet, faxing, or sending via e-mail).

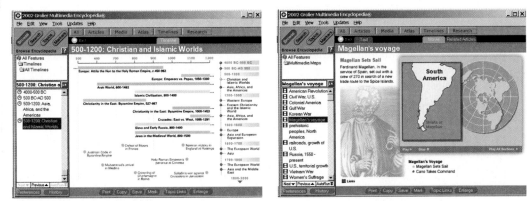

FIGURE 1–31 The Multimedia Encyclopedia
The multimedia encyclopedia is a good place to start your multimedia PC adventure. The *Grolier Year 2002 Multimedia Encyclopedia* (shown here) contains timelines (see illustration), millions of words, thousands of images, almost hundreds of videos, and hours of audio telling and showing us about thousands of persons, places, and things. The CD-ROM encyclopedia uses the full capabilities of multimedia to enrich the presentation of information. "Thumbing" through an encyclopedia will never be the same.

The Grolier Multimedia Encyclopedia copyright © 2002 by Grolier Interactive Inc.

FIGURE 1–32

MICROSOFT OFFICE
The Microsoft Office software suite includes (clockwise from top left) PowerPoint (presentation), Word (word processing), Excel (spreadsheet), Access (database), and, in the center, Outlook (personal information management).

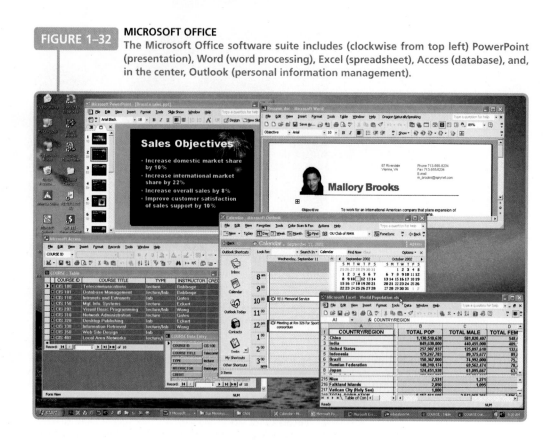

- *Presentation.* **Presentation software** lets you create professional-looking images for group presentations, self-running slide shows, reports, and for other situations that require the presentation of organized, visual information. The electronic images may include multimedia elements, such as sound, special effects, animation, and video.

- *Spreadsheet.* A **spreadsheet** is simply a table of values, numbers, names, and so on. **Spreadsheet software** lets you work with the rows and columns of data in a spreadsheet. Spreadsheet software can summarize columns of data and perform a variety of statistical and financial operations on data. When values change, all other affected values are changed automatically.

- *Database.* **Database software** permits you to create and maintain a database and to extract information from the database. In a database, data are organized for ease of manipulation and retrieval.

- *Desktop publishing.* **Desktop publishing software** allows you to produce camera-ready documents (ready to be printed professionally) from the confines of a desktop. People routinely use desktop publishing software to create newsletters, advertisements, procedures manuals, and many other printing needs.

- *Communications.* **Communications software** is a family of software applications that enables you to send e-mail and faxes, tap the resources of the Internet via **Internet browsers,** and link your PC with a remote computer.

- *Personal information management.* **PIM software,** mentioned earlier in the chapter, is an umbrella term that encompasses a variety of personal management and contact information programs. A particular PIM package might include calendar applications (appointment scheduling and reminders), communications applications (e-mail and fax), and databases that help you organize your phone numbers, e-mail addresses, to-do lists, notes, diary entries, and so on.

These software packages have demonstrated millions of times that they can save you time and money and, generally, make life more convenient.

Building a Software Portfolio

A **software portfolio** is simply the mix of software that you have on your computer. The software suite and other software that might be installed on your computer at the time of purchase provide a good start to growing your portfolio to meet your personal computing needs and goals. With over a

THE CRYSTAL BALL:

PC Prices In the early 1970s, an "electronic" calculator that performed only the basic arithmetic functions cost between $300 and $500, about the price of today's desktop PC. Most people have at least one. I paid $12,000 for my first PC in 1978, roughly the cost of a BMW at the time. Today, a good calculator is a ubiquitous consumer item and can be purchased for under $20. By 2010, the PC (or whatever its emergent form factor will be called) will be an inexpensive consumer item priced at less than a quarter of its current inflation-adjusted cost. Plus, you can bet that they will be continuously online and small enough such that we carry them with us wherever we go.

half-million free and commercial software packages on the market, there is personal computing support for just about any application and the boldest imagination.

One of the hottest areas of personal computing growth is in the area of graphics and multimedia. This growth has been spurred by the availability of inexpensive support hardware, such as digital cameras and image scanners. People are finding a plethora of home and family software that can help them create their own calendars, greeting cards, and banners, help them prepare and file their tax returns, help them design a room or a house, help them manage their finances, and much more. Personal computing has opened a new world in personal communication, enabling video phone conversations between neighbors and friends on the other side of the world. Personal computing has redefined reference materials. We now find encyclopedias and comprehensive dictionaries on CD-ROM or the Internet. The easily accessible Internet has white pages and Yellow Pages for the entire United States. The road atlas is now electronic and dynamic, highlighting for us the best route to our destination.

Students at all levels, from kindergarten to professional adult education, are embracing personal computing as a new approach to learning. Computer-based education and online classes will not replace teachers any time soon, but educators agree that CD-ROM-based *computer-based training* (*CBT*) and *Internet-based distance learning* are having a profound impact on traditional modes of education. Available programs and online courses can help you learn keyboarding skills, increase your vocabulary, study algebra, learn about the makeup of the atom, practice your Russian, learn about computers, and much more. Colleges and even high schools offer thousands of courses online via distance learning. You can now get an MBA, a law degree, and a bachelor's degree in most disciplines without attending a single traditional classroom lecture.

There are thousands of commercial applications created specifically to tickle our fancy and entertain us. You can play electronic golf. You can buy a computer chess opponent in the form of a board, chess pieces, and a miniature robotic arm that moves the pieces (you have to move your own pieces). You can "pilot" an airplane to Paris and battle Zorbitrons in cyberspace.

The amount of computing capacity in the world is doubling every two years. The number and sophistication of personal computing applications are growing at a similar pace. Tomorrow, there will be applications that are unheard of today.

1-7.1	More computing capacity is dedicated to information systems than to CBT. (T/F)	
1-7.2	The foundation of personal computing over the last decade has been 3-D computing games. (T/F)	
1-7.3	Which of the following is not a software suite: (a) Borland's Business Suite, (b) Corel WordPerfect Office, (c) Lotus SmartSuite, or (d) Microsoft Office?	
1-7.4	The PC is considered to be what type of device: (a) single function, (b) multifunction, (c) special-purpose, or (d) general-purpose?	

SECTION SELF-CHECK

1-1 OUR INFORMATION SOCIETY

In an **information society**, **knowledge workers** focus their energies on providing myriad information services. The knowledge worker's job function revolves around the use, manipulation, and dissemination of information. Learning about computers is an adventure that will last a lifetime because **information technology** (**IT**), the integration of computing technology and information processing, is changing daily.

The computer revolution is transforming the way we communicate, do business, and learn. This technological revolution is having a profound impact on the business community and on our private and professional lives. For example, increasingly, we communicate with our colleagues at work through **electronic mail** (**e-mail**) or with our friends through **instant messaging** (**IM**) and **chat** rooms. Sometimes you may get unsolicited e-mail, called **spam**.

In this century we can anticipate traveling an **information superhighway**, a network of high-speed data communications links, that eventually will connect virtually every facet of our society. Today, millions of people have a **personal computer** (**PC**). This widespread availability has resulted in an explosion of applications for computers. At home, people may connect to the **Internet**, a worldwide network of computers. Home appliances may also include **microprocessors**.

Through the 1970s, **users** related their information needs to computer professionals who would then work with the computer system to generate the necessary information. Today, users work directly with their PCs to obtain the information they need.

1-2 R$_x$ FOR CYBERPHOBIA: INFORMATION TECHNOLOGY COMPETENCY

Information technology competency (**IT competency**) is emerging as a universal goal in our information society. IT-competent people know how to purchase, set up, and operate a computer system, and how to make it work for them. The IT-competent person is also aware of the computer's impact on society and is conversant the language of technology.

Software refers collectively to a set of machine-readable instructions, called **programs**, that cause the computer to perform desired functions. Computers and computer equipment, which accept **input** and provide **output**, are called **hardware**.

The fact that many people routinely use computers but are not IT-competent is referred to as the "computer proficiency digital divide."

1-3 THE NET CONNECTION

We now live in a global village in which computers and people are linked within companies and between countries. Most existing computers are part of a **computer network** that shares resources and information.

The Internet links almost a billion users in a global network. **The Net** can be accessed by people in organizations with established links to the Internet and by individuals with PCs, often via **Internet service providers** (**ISPs**). Often this is done with a **modem**, a device that permits communication with remote computers via a telephone-line link. Commercial **information services**, such as **America Online** (**AOL**), offer a wide range of information services, including up-to-the-minute news and weather, electronic shopping, e-mail, and much more. When the user terminates this **online** link, the user goes **offline**. Internet users can **download** text or a digitized version of a song directly to their PC, then read it or play it through their PC. **MP3 players** can store and play digital music recorded in MP3 format. Information is **uploaded** from a local computer to a remote computer. The **World Wide Web**, or **the Web**, is an Internet application that lets us view Internet **Web pages**. Another application, **newsgroups**, provides electronic bulletin boards. Generally, Internet applications can be placed into these categories: personal communications, browsing and searching for information, downloading and file sharing, streaming media, online transactions, and entertainment.

1-4 THE BASICS: HARDWARE, SOFTWARE, AND COMPUTER SYSTEMS

At the heart of any **computer** is its **processor**, an electronic device capable of interpreting and executing programmed commands for input, output, computation, and logic operations.

Output on a computer can be routed to a **monitor** or a **printer**. The output on a monitor is temporary and is called **soft copy**. Printers produce **hard copy** output. Data can be entered via a **keyboard** or a **mouse**, a **point-and-draw device**.

System software plays a central role in everything that happens within a computer system from start-up to shutdown. **Applications software** performs specific personal, business, or scientific processing tasks.

Random-access memory (**RAM**) provides temporary storage of data and programs during processing within solid-state **integrated circuits**, or **chips**. Permanently installed and interchangeable **magnetic disks** and **optical discs** provide permanent storage for data and programs. A computer system can include a variety of **peripheral devices**.

The differences in the various categories of computers are a matter of computing power, not its physical size. Today, computers are generally grouped in these categories: notebook PCs, desktop PCs, handheld computers, **thin clients**, workstations, **server computers**, and **supercomputers**. Server computers manage the resources on a network and perform a variety of functions for **client computers**. All **computer systems**, no matter how small or large, have the same fundamental capabilities—*input, processing, output,* and *storage.* Each offers many **input/output**, or **I/O**, alternatives.

1-5 PERSONAL COMPUTERS TO SUPERCOMPUTERS

In 1981, IBM introduced its **IBM PC**, defining the original PC-compatible machine, now also called a **Wintel PC** because of its use of Microsoft Windows **operating systems** and the Intel processors. The Apple iMac and Power Mac, with their Mac OS X and Motorola PowerPC processors, is the other major **platform**. Computers come in a variety of physical and computing sizes. Most personal computers are either **notebook PCs** (also called **laptops**) or **desktop PCs**. Many notebook PC buyers purchase a **port replicator**, called a **docking station**, for portability plus the expanded features of a desktop PC. **Ports** are electronic interfaces through which devices like the keyboard, monitor, mouse, printer, image scanner, and so on are connected. The desktop PC's **system unit** contains the processor, disk storage, and other components. Many mobile workers are benefiting from using a **wearable PC**.

The typical off-the-shelf PC is configured to run multimedia applications. **Multimedia applications** combine text, sound, graphics, motion video, and/or animation. The typical multimedia-configured PC includes a **motherboard**; a keyboard and a point-and-draw device for input; a monitor and a printer for output; a **hard-disk drive** and a **floppy disk drive** into which an interchangeable **diskette**, or **floppy disk**, is inserted; a **CD-ROM drive** into which an interchangeable **CD-ROM** is inserted; a **DVD-ROM** drive that accepts all DVD format discs, such as **DVD-Video** for playing movies; and a microphone and a set of speakers for audio I/O. Some models have rewritable **CD-RW** and/or **DVD+RW**.

Palmtop PC, personal digital assistant (PDA), connected organizer, personal communicator, mobile business center, and Web phone are just some of the names for **handheld computers**. A handheld can have a variety of physical shapes and sizes, referred to as its **form factor**. **Pen-based computers** which may or may not have small keyboards, make use of an electronic pen, call a **stylus**, to do such tasks as selecting options, entering data (via handwritten characters), and drawing. Keying can also be accomplished via an onscreen keyboard. **Speech-recognition** software, which allows the user to enter spoken words into the system, is being integrated into high-end handheld computers. Handheld computers support a variety of **personal information management** (**PIM**) systems, including appointment scheduling and to-do lists. You may also be using handhelds to read a good **electronic-book** (**e-book**) via the computer's **text-to-speech software**.

The thin client computer is designed to function only when it is linked to a server computer.

The workstation's speed and input/output devices set it apart from a PC. A typical workstation will have a high-**resolution** monitor and a variety of specialized point-and-draw devices. A common use of workstations is for engineering design.

In **client/server computing**, processing is distributed throughout the network. The client computer requests processing or some other type of service from the server computer. Both client and server computers perform processing. The **proxy server computer** sits between the client and server, intercepting client requests to improve overall system performance. The client computer runs **front-end applications software**, and the server computer runs the **back-end applications software**.

Server computers are usually associated with **enterprise systems**; that is, computer-based systems that service entities throughout the company. Typically, users communicate with one or more server computers through a PC, a workstation, a thin client, or a **terminal**. Supercomputers primarily address **processor-bound applications**.

A computer system manipulates your **data** to produce **information**. The permanent source of data for a particular computer application area is sometimes called a **master file**.

1-6 COMPUTER SYSTEM CAPABILITIES

A **local area network** (**LAN**) connects PCs or workstations in close proximity. The LAN's server computer performs a variety of functions for other client computers on the LAN.

Computer system capabilities are either input/output or processing. Processing capabilities are subdivided into computation and logic operations.

Computers perform input/output (I/O) operations by reading from input and storage devices and writing to output devices.

The computer is fast, accurate, consistent, and reliable, and aids in communications and has an enormous memory capacity. Computer operations are measured in **milliseconds, microseconds, nanoseconds,** and **picoseconds.** When downtime is unacceptable, companies provide **backup** computers that take over automatically should the main computers fail.

1-7 HOW DO WE USE COMPUTERS?

Enterprise computing comprises all computing activities designed to support any type of organization: a company, a government entity, a university, and so on. Enterprise applications are in three groups: information systems, process/device control and science, research, and engineering.

- *Information systems.* The computer is used to process data and produce business information. Hardware, software, people, procedures, and data are combined to create an **information system.**

- *Process/Device Control.* In computer-based **process/device control**, processes accept data in a continuous **feedback loop. Industrial robots** perform many jobs from materials handling to painting without human intervention.

- *Science, research, and engineering.* The computer is used as a tool in experimentation, design, and development. **Computer-aided design** (**CAD**) involves using the computer in the design process.

The PC is used for **personal computing** by individuals for a variety of business and domestic applications, including such productivity tools as **word processing software, presentation software, spreadsheet software, database software, desktop publishing software, communications software,** including **Internet browsers,** and personal information management software. **Software suites** are bundles of complementary software that may include several or all of these common productivity software packages. A **spreadsheet** is a table of values, numbers, names, and so on. A **software portfolio** is the mix of software that you have on your computer.

KEY TERMS

America Online (p. 31)
AOL (p. 31)
applications software (p. 34)
back-end applications software (p. 44)
backup computer (p. 51)
CD-ROM (p. 38)
CD-ROM drive (p. 38)
CD-RW (p. 38)
chat (p. 24)
chip (p. 33)
client computer (p. 35)

client/server computing (p. 44)
communications software (p. 56)
computer (p. 33)
computer network (p. 28)
computer system (p. 33)
computer-aided design (CAD) (p. 53)
data (p. 47)
database software (p. 56)
desktop PC (p. 36)
desktop publishing software (p. 56)
diskette (floppy disk) (p. 38)

docking station (p. 38)
download (p. 31)
DVD+RW (p. 38)
DVD-ROM (p. 38)
DVD-Video (p. 38)
electronic mail (e-mail) (p. 24)
electronic-book (e-book) (p. 42)
enterprise computing (p. 52)
enterprise systems (p. 44)
feedback loop (p. 52)
floppy disk drive (p. 38)

form factor (p. 40)
front-end applications software (p. 44)
handheld computer (p. 40)
hard copy (p. 33)
hard-disk drive (p. 38)
hardware (p. 26)
IBM PC (p. 36)
industrial robot (p. 53)
information (p. 47)
information service (p. 31)
information society (p. 22)
information superhighway (p. 25)
information system (p. 52)
information technology (IT) (p. 22)
information technology competency (IT
    competency) (p. 26)
input (p. 26)
input/output (I/O) (p. 35)
instant messaging (IM) (p. 24)
integrated circuit (p. 33)
Internet (p. 23)
Internet browser (p. 56)
Internet service provider (ISP) (p. 31)
keyboard (p. 33)
knowledge worker (p. 22)
laptop PC (p. 36)
local area network (LAN) (p. 49)
magnetic disk (p. 33)
master file (p. 47)
microprocessor (p. 24)

microsecond (p. 50)
millisecond (p. 50)
modem (p. 31)
monitor (p. 33)
motherboard (p. 38)
mouse (p. 33)
MP3 player (p. 31)
multimedia application (p. 38)
nanosecond (p. 50)
newsgroup (p. 29)
notebook PC (p. 36)
offline (p. 31)
online (p. 31)
operating system (p. 36)
optical disc (p. 33)
output (p. 26)
pen-based computer (p. 42)
peripheral device (p. 33)
personal computer (PC) (p. 22)
personal computing (p. 54)
personal information management (PIM)
    (p. 42)
picosecond (p. 50)
platform (p. 36)
point-and-draw device (p. 33)
port (p. 38)
port replicator (p. 38)
presentation software (p. 56)
printer (p. 33)
process/device control (p. 52)

processor (p. 33)
processor-bound application (p. 45)
programs (p. 26)
proxy server computer (p. 44)
random-access memory (RAM) (p. 33)
resolution (p. 43)
server computer (p. 35)
soft copy (p. 33)
software (p. 26)
software portfolio (p. 56)
software suite (p. 55)
spam (p. 27)
speech-recognition software (p. 42)
spreadsheet (p. 56)
spreadsheet software (p. 56)
stylus (p. 42)
supercomputer (p. 34)
system software (p. 34)
system unit (p. 38)
terminal (p. 44)
text-to-speech software (p. 42)
the Net (p. 29)
thin client (p. 35)
uploaded (p. 31)
user (p. 25)
wearable PC (p. 40)
Web page (p. 31)
Wintel PC (p. 36)
word processing software (p. 55)
World Wide Web (the Web) (p. 31)

MATCHING

1. Modem
2. Industrial robots
3. Text-to-speech
4. Newsgroups
5. Hardware
6. Software
7. Peripheral devices
8. MP3
9. Backup computers
10. Stylus
11. 1000 nanoseconds
12. Form factor
13. Hard copy
14. Processing operations
15. Master file

a. electronic pen
b. printed output
c. reading e-books
d. size and shape
e. all patient records
f. music file
g. take over when computers fail
h. monitor and printer
i. computation and logic operations
j. 1 microsecond
k. programs
l. computing equipment
m. interactive electronic bulletin boards
n. telephone-line link
o. welding and painting

CHAPTER SELF-CHECK

1-1.1   A person who uses a computer is called a: (a) user, (b) client, (c) software consumer, or (d) utilizer.

1-1.2   Which of these is not a means of personal communication on the Internet: (a) electronic mail, (b) instant messaging, (c) instanotes, or (d) chat?

1-1.3   Because of incompatible video formats, it is not yet possible to view DVD movies on a PC. (T/F)

1-2.1   What causes computers to perform desired functions: (a) programs, (b) soft copy, (c) instruction lists, or (d) procedures?

1-2.2   Data entered to a computer system for processing would be: (a) output, (b) throughput, (c) input, or (d) dataput.

1-2.3   Unsolicited e-mail is knows as: (a) ham, (b) bologna, (c) RAM JAM, or (d) spam.

1-3.1   Uploading on the Internet is transmitting information from an Internet-based host computer to a local PC. (T/F)

1-3.2   The Internet is also known as: (a) the Bucket, (b) the Global Interface, (c) the Net, or (d) Cybernet.

1-3.3 Individuals gain access to the Internet by subscribing to a(n): (a) PSI, (b) ISP, (c) IPS, or (d) SPI.

1-4.1 Output on a monitor is soft copy and output on a printer is hard copy. (T/F)

1-4.2 Of the different types of computers, only personal computers offer a variety of I/O alternatives. (T/F)

1-4.3 Applications software takes control of a PC on start-up and then controls all system software activities during the computing session. (T/F)

1-4.4 Integrated circuits are also called: (a) slivers, (b) chips, (c) flakes, or (d) electronic sandwiches.

1-4.5 Thin clients are like PCs but with more features. (T/F)

1-5.1 The four size categories of conventional personal computers are miniature, portable, notebook, and business. (T/F)

1-5.2 Server computers usually are associated with enterprise systems. (T/F)

1-5.3 Supercomputers are oriented to what type of applications: (a) I/O-bound, (b) processor-bound, (c) inventory management, or (d) word processing?

1-5.4 What is the name given those applications that combine text, sound, graphics, motion video, and/or animation: (a) videoscapes, (b) motionware, (c) multimedia, or (d) anigraphics?

1-5.5 The trend in the design of computer networks is toward: (a) distributed transmission, (b) client/server computing, (c) CANs, or (d) centralized mainframe computers.

1-6.1 On a LAN, the client computer stores all data and applications software used by the server computer. (T/F)

1-6.2 A microsecond is 1000 times longer than a nanosecond. (T/F)

1-6.3 In a LAN, a server computer performs a variety of functions for its: (a) client computers, (b) subcomputers, (c) LAN entity PC, or (d) work units.

1-6.4 An Internet-based online retailer is called a(n): (a) online tailer, (b) net-tailer, (c) e-tailer, or (d) cybertailer.

1-6.5 Supercomputers outperform humans when it comes to pattern recognition. (T/F)

1-7.1 Desktop publishing refers to the capability of producing camera-ready documents from the confines of a desktop. (T/F)

1-7.2 What type of computing comprises all computing activities designed to support an organization: (a) personal, (b) enterprise, (c) industrial, or (d) professional?

1-7.3 Computers that control processes accept data in a continuous: (a) infinite loop, (b) data highway, (c) data traffic pattern, or (d) feedback loop.

1-7.4 The PC productivity tool that manipulates data organized in rows and columns is called a: (a) database record manager, (b) presentation mechanism, (c) word processing document, or (d) spreadsheet.

1-7.5 The typical home PC is used 10 to 50 hours a week. (T/F)

1-7.6 Which PC productivity tool would be helpful in writing a term paper: (a) word processing, (b) presentation, (c) spreadsheet, or (d) communications?

1-7.7 Various programs within a given software suite have a common interface. (T/F)

IT ETHICS AND ISSUES

THE SPAM DILEMMA

As we all know, Spam is a popular Hormel meat product. By some unlucky quirk of fate unsolicited e-mail was given the same name—spam. To Netizens, citizens of the Internet, spam is the Internet equivalent of junk mail and those dreaded telemarketing calls. To the senders of junk e-mail, spam is simply bulk e-mail, usually some kind of advertisement and/or an invitation to try some service or product. Spam may be unsolicited religious, racial, or sexual messages, as well. Such messages can be especially irritating. Generally, Internet users loathe spamming because spammers (those who send spam) use the shotgun approach, broadcasting their message to large numbers of people. Inevitably, enough of these messages find a welcome audience, prompting spammers to send more spam.

Those who receive e-mail consider their e-mail boxes a personal and costly resource. They feel that spam wastes their time, violates their electronic mailbox, and in some cases insults their integrity. On the other hand, spammers cite free speech and the tradition of a free flow of information over the Internet as justification for broadcasting their messages. Spam renews the conflict between free speech and the individual's right to privacy.

Discussion: *Currently, laws favor the spammers; that is, there is little an individual can do to thwart the barrage of junk mail, other than ask his or her ISP to filter spam whenever possible. Do you believe legislation should be enacted to control unsolicited e-mail over the Internet or do you favor industry self-regulation? Explain.*

Discussion: *What are the costs associated with spam? Who pays for spam?*

Discussion: *What are the benefits associated with spam? Who derives the most benefit from spam?*

SHOULD PC OWNERSHIP BE AN ENTRANCE REQUIREMENT FOR COLLEGES?

As the job market tightens, colleges are looking to give their students a competitive edge. With computer knowledge becoming a job prerequisite for many positions, hundreds of colleges have made the purchase of a personal computer a prerequisite for admission (see Figure 1-33). Personal computers are versatile in that they can be used as stand-alone computers or they can be linked to the college's network, the Internet, or other personal computers in a classroom. At these colleges, PCs are everywhere—in classrooms, lounges, libraries, and other common areas.

Wouldn't it be great to run a bibliographic search from your dorm room or home? Make changes to a report without retyping it? Run a case search for a law class? Use the computer for math homework calculations?

Instead of making hard copies of class assignments, some instructors key in their assignments, which are then "delivered" to each student's electronic mailbox. At some colleges, student PCs are networked during class, enabling immediate distribution of class materials. Students can correspond with their instructors through their computer to get help with assignments. They can even "talk" to other students at connected colleges.

Discussion: *If your college does not require PC ownership for admission, should it? If it does, should the policy be continued?*

FIGURE 1–33 The Interactive Networked Classroom
Owning a PC is a prerequisite for admission to the University of Oklahoma's College of Engineering. OU students shown here use PCs with wireless technology that lets them connect to the Internet anywhere within the engineering complex. During class, students and the instructor can easily create a wireless local area network to link all PCs. Students can do the same for a linked study group.

Discussion: *What could students, professors, and college administrators do that they are not doing now (without a PC ownership requirement) if the entire campus were networked and every student were required to have a notebook PC?*

HATE SITES ON THE INTERNET

How do some consumers voice grievances about companies, products, and services? How do some people voice their disgust over a rock group, a political organization, or even a university? They publish their thoughts, warts and all, on the Internet, usually on their own Web page. Just enter the keyword *hate* or *sucks* into an Internet search facility and see how many hits it gets. Anyone or anything is a potential target.

Some of this hate venom may be deserved, but perhaps it isn't. The Internet is a powerful voice that can be used to call attention to flaws in a company's products or services. It can also be used to vilify individuals who may simply be doing their jobs, effectively and legally.

Discussion: *Some experts in the field of Internet monitoring say that the best response to hate site venom is no response. How would you respond if one or more Internet sites mounted an unjustified attack on your company's products? How would you respond to an unjustified personal attack?*

Discussion: *Visit a Web site that is dedicated to denouncing someone, something, an idea, or an organization. Is the content fair and is it appropriate for the Internet? Explain.*

DISCUSSION AND PROBLEM SOLVING

1-1.1 Information technology has had far-reaching effects on our lives. How have the computer and IT affected your life?

1-1.2 Discuss how the complexion of jobs will change as we evolve from an industrial society into an information society. Give several examples.

1-1.3 Contrast these Internet applications: e-mail, instant messaging, and chat.

1-1.4 Think back and discuss your earliest remembrances of computers. Compare those computers to today's.

1-2.1 What is your concept of information technology competency? In what ways do you think achieving information technology competency will affect your domestic life? Your business life?

1-2.2 At what age should information technology competency education begin? Is society prepared to provide IT education at this age? If not, why?

1-2.3 What would be your number one reason to become IT competent?

1-2.4 Do you consider yourself IT competent? Why or why not?

1-3.1 Comment on how information technology is changing our traditional patterns of personal communication.

1-3.2 If you are a current user of the Internet, describe four Internet services that have been of value to you. If not, in what ways do you think the Internet might be a benefit to you?

1-3.3 What might you want to download over the Internet?

1-3.4 Which three Internet applications listed in Figure 1-10 are most appealing to you? Why?

1-4.1 List as many computer and information technology terms as you can (up to 30) that are used in everyday conversations at the office and at school.

1-4.2 Describe an ideal applications software package that might help you meet your personal or business information processing needs.

1-4.3 RAM, magnetic disks, and optical discs enable storage of data on a computer system. Why don't we simplify and have just one of these options?

1-5.1 If you could purchase only one personal computer, which would you buy, a notebook PC or a desktop PC? Why?

1-5.2 Explain circumstances that would cause you to order a port replicator with a notebook PC.

1-5.3 Speculate on how one of these professionals would use a handheld computer: a police officer, an insurance adjuster, a delivery person for a courier service, or a newspaper reporter.

1-5.4 Management at a large company with 1000 three-year-old PCs, all on a network, is debating whether to replace the PCs with thin clients or with new PCs. Each has its advantages. What would you consider to be the single most important advantage for each option?

1-5.5 Give at least two reasons why a regional bank might opt to buy six server computers rather than one supercomputer.

1-5.6 Lots of people wear their PCs. Speculate on why they wear them.

1-5.7 What would be your ideal form factor for a handheld computer?

1-5.8 Speculate on two supercomputer applications not mentioned in the book.

1-5.9 Discuss the relationship between the server computer and its client computers.

1-6.1 Compare the information processing capabilities of human beings to those of computers with respect to speed, accuracy, reliability, consistency, communications, and memory capability.

1-6.2 Within the context of a computer system, what is meant by *read* and *write*?

1-6.3 Identify and briefly describe five computation and five logic operations that might be performed by a computer during the processing of college students throughout the academic year.

1-6.4 Every company has records on computer-based master files or in a database. Describe three types of master files.

1-7.1 The use of computers tends to stifle creativity. Argue for or against this statement.

1-7.2 Comment on how computers are changing our traditional patterns of recreation.

1-7.3 Of the productivity software described in this chapter, choose the two that will have (or currently have) the most impact on your productivity. Explain why you chose these two.

1-7.4 Explain why software packages in a software suite are complementary.

1-7.5 The dominant software suite is Microsoft Office, in its various versions. However, some analysts claim that alternative software suites are as good as or better than it is. Under what circumstances would a company with 5000 PCs opt to go with a Microsoft competitor?

1-7.6 Pick an enterprise you know and list as many of its computing activities as you can, categorizing them as an information system, a process/device control application, or a science, research, and engineering application.

FOCUS ON PERSONAL COMPUTING

1. Go exploring and find out more about your PC (or the one in your college lab). Go to the "Accessories" group on the programs listing (click *Start, All Programs,* and highlight *Accessories*). Every Windows-based PC comes with some interesting and helpful programs. Open at least six Accessories group programs. Give a brief explanation of each and include your assessment of its applicability to your personal computing needs. The Accessories group includes a calculator, a graphics application, a sound recorder, and many more programs.

2. Continue your discovery adventure and run at least three more programs that are not in the Accessories group or a Microsoft Office program (Word, Excel, PowerPoint, and so on). Give a brief explanation of each program and include your assessment of its applicability to your personal computing needs.

INTERNET EXERCISES @ www.prenhall.com/long

1. The Online Study Guide (multiple choice, true/false, matching, and essay questions)

2. Internet Learning Activities
- The Global Village
- Personal Computers
- Handheld Computers
- Workstations
- Server Computers
- Supercomputers
- Computer History

3. Serendipitous Internet Activities
- At the Movies

THE HISTORY OF COMPUTING

The history of computers and computing is of special significance to us, because many of its most important events have occurred within our lifetime. Historians divide the history of the modern computer into generations, beginning with the introduction of the UNIVAC I, the first commercially viable computer, in 1951. But the quest for a mechanical servant—one that could free people from the more boring aspects of thinking—is centuries old.

Why did it take so long to develop the computer? Some of the "credit" goes to human foibles. Too often brilliant insights were not recognized or given adequate support during an inventor's lifetime. Instead, these insights would lay dormant for as long as 100 years until someone else rediscovered—or reinvented—them. Some of the "credit" has to go to workers, too, who sabotaged labor-saving devices that threatened to put them out of work. The rest of the "credit" goes to technology; some insights were simply ahead of their time's technology. Figure 1-34 illustrates an abbreviated history of the stops and starts that have given us this marvel of the modern age, the computer.

Figure 1–34 — JOURNEY THROUGH THE HISTORY OF COMPUTING

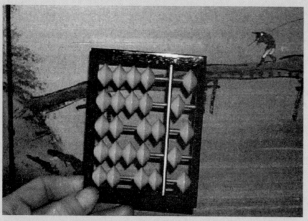

3000 B.C.: THE ABACUS
The abacus is probably considered the original mechanical counting device (it has been traced back 5000 years). It is still used in education to demonstrate the principles of counting and arithmetic and in business for speedy calculations.

Long and Associates

1623–1662: BLAISE PASCAL
Although inventor, painter, and sculptor Leonardo da Vinci (1425–1519) sketched ideas for a mechanical adding machine, it was another 150 years before French mathematician and philosopher Blaise Pascal (1623–1662) finally invented and built the "Pascaline" in 1642 to help his father, a tax collector. Although Pascal was praised throughout Europe, his invention was a financial failure. The hand-built machines were expensive and delicate; moreover, Pascal was the only person who could repair them. Because human labor was actually cheaper, the Pascaline was abandoned as impractical.

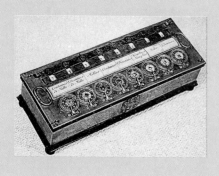

1642: THE PASCALINE
The Pascaline used a counting-wheel design: Numbers for each digit were arranged on wheels so that a single revolution of one wheel would engage gears that turned the wheel one tenth of a revolution to its immediate left. Although the Pascaline was abandoned as impractical, its counting-wheel design was used by all mechanical calculators until the mid-1960s, when they were made obsolete by electronic calculators.

3000 • B.C. City of Troy first inhabited   1639 • First North American printing press

1801: JACQUARD'S LOOM

A practicing weaver, Frenchman Joseph-Marie Jacquard (1753–1871) spent what little spare time he had trying to improve the lot of his fellow weavers. (They worked 16–hour days, with no days off!) His solution, the Jacquard loom, was created in 1801. Holes strategically punched in a card directed the movement of needles, thread, and fabric, creating the elaborate patterns still known as Jacquard weaves. Jacquard's weaving loom is considered the first significant use of binary automation. The loom was an immediate success with mill owners because they could hire cheaper and less skilled workers. But weavers, fearing unemployment, rioted and called Jacquard a traitor.

Courtesy of International Business Machines Corporation. Unauthorized use not permitted.

1793–1871: CHARLES BABBAGE

Everyone, from bankers to navigators, depended on mathematical tables during the bustling Industrial Revolution. However, these hand-calculated tables were usually full of errors. After discovering that his own tables were riddled with mistakes, Charles Babbage (1793–1871) envisioned a steam-powered "difference engine" and then an "analytical engine" that would perform tedious calculations accurately. Although Babbage never perfected his devices, they introduced many of the concepts used in today's general-purpose computer.

Courtesy of International Business Machines Corporation. Unauthorized use not permitted.

1842: BABBAGE'S DIFFERENCE ENGINE AND THE ANALYTICAL ENGINE

Convinced his machine would benefit England, Babbage applied for—and received—one of the first government grants to build the difference engine. Hampered by nineteenth-century machine technology, cost overruns, and the possibility his chief engineer was padding the bills, Babbage completed only a portion of the difference engine (shown here) before the government withdrew its support in 1842, deeming the project "worthless to science." Meanwhile, Babbage had conceived of the idea of a more advanced "analytical engine." In essence, this was a general-purpose computer that could add, subtract, multiply, and divide in automatic sequence at a rate of 60 additions per second. His 1833 design, which called for thousands of gears and drives, would cover the area of a football field and be powered by a locomotive engine. Babbage worked on this project until his death. In 1991 London's Science Museum spent $600,000 to build a working model of the difference engine, using Babbage's original plans. The result stands 6 feet high, 10 feet long, contains 4000 parts, and weighs 3 tons.

New York Public Library Picture Collection

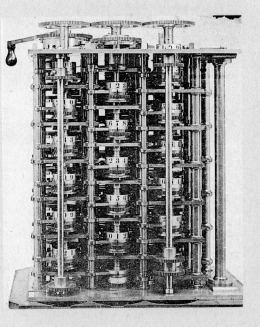

1801 • Thomas Jefferson elected President

1838 • Samuel F. B. Morse develops Morse Code

1816–1852: LADY ADA AUGUSTA LOVELACE

The daughter of poet Lord Byron, Lady Ada Augusta Lovelace (1816–1852) became a mentor to Babbage and translated his works, adding her own extensive footnotes. Her suggestion that punched cards could be prepared to instruct Babbage's engine to repeat certain operations has led some people to call her the first programmer. Ada, the programming language adopted by Department of Defense as a standard, is named for Lady Ada Lovelace.

The Bettmann Archive/BBC Hulton

1860–1929: HERMAN HOLLERITH

With the help of a professor, Herman Hollerith (1860–1929) got a job as a special agent helping the U.S. Bureau of the Census tabulate the head count for the 1880 census—a process that took almost eight years. To speed up the 1890 census, Hollerith devised a punched-card tabulating machine. When his machine outperformed two other systems, Hollerith won a contract to tabulate the 1890 census. Hollerith earned a handsome income leasing his machinery to the governments of the United States, Canada, Austria, Russia, and others; he charged 65 cents for every 1000 people counted. (During the 1890 U.S. census alone, he earned more than $40,000—a fortune in those days.) Hollerith may have earned even more selling the single-use punched cards. But the price was worth it. The bureau completed the census in just 22 years and saved more than $5 million.

Courtesy of International Business Machines Corporation. Unauthorized use not permitted.

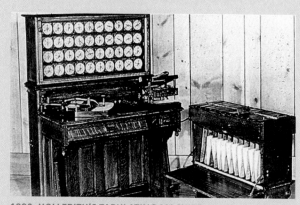

1890: HOLLERITH'S TABULATING MACHINE

Hollerith's *punched-card tabulating machine* had three parts. Clerks at the U.S. Bureau of the Census used a hand punch to enter data onto cards a little larger than a dollar bill. Cards were then read and sorted by a 24-bin sorter box (right) and summarized on numbered tabulating dials (left), which were connected electrically to the sorter box. Ironically, Hollerith's idea for the punched card came not from Jacquard or Babbage but from "punch photography." Railroads of the day issued tickets with physical descriptions of a passenger's hair and eye color. Conductors punched holes in the ticket to indicate that a passenger's hair and eye color matched those of the ticket owner. From this, Hollerith got the idea of making a punched "photograph" of every person to be tabulated.

Courtesy of International Business Machines Corporation. Unauthorized use not permitted.

1924: IBM'S FIRST HEADQUARTERS BUILDING

In 1896 Herman Hollerith founded the Tabulating Machine Company, which merged in 1911 with several other companies to form the Computing-Tabulating-Recording Company. In 1924 the company's general manager, Thomas J. Watson, changed its name to International Business Machines Corporation and moved into this building. Watson ran IBM until a few months before his death at age 82 in 1956. His son, Thomas J. Watson, Jr., lead IBM into the age of computers.

Courtesy of International Business Machines Corporation. Unauthorized use not permitted.

1883 • Brooklyn Bridge completed in New York City   1923 • Vladimir Zworykin patents first television transmission tube

1920s–1950s: THE EAM ERA

From the 1920s throughout the mid-1950s, punched-card technology improved with the addition of more punched-card devices and more sophisticated capabilities. The *electromechanical accounting machine (EAM)* family of punched-card devices includes the card punch, verifier, reproducer, summary punch, interpreter, sorter, collator, and accounting machine. Most of the devices in the 1940s machine room were "programmed" to perform a particular operation by the insertion of a prewired control panel. A machine-room operator in a punched-card installation had the physically challenging job of moving heavy boxes of punched cards and printed output from one device to the next on hand trucks.

1903–1995: DR. JOHN V. ATANASOFF AND HIS ABC COMPUTER

In 1939 Dr. John V. Atanasoff, a professor at Iowa State University, and graduate student Clifford E. Berry assembled a prototype of the *ABC* (for *Atanasoff Berry Computer*) to cut the time physics students spent making complicated calculations. A working model was finished in 1942. Atanasoff's decisions—to use an electronic medium with vacuum tubes, the base-2 numbering system, and memory and logic circuits—set the direction for the modern computer. Ironically, Iowa State failed to patent the device and IBM, when contacted about the ABC, airily responded, "IBM will never be interested in an electronic computing machine."

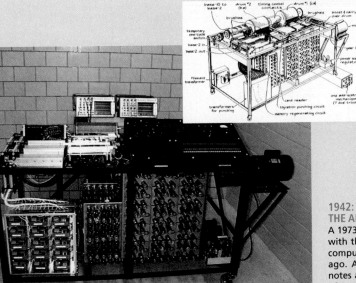

1942: THE FIRST ELECTRONIC DIGITAL COMPUTER: THE ABC

A 1973 federal court ruling officially credited Atanasoff with the invention of the automatic electronic digital computer. The original ABC was dismantled decades ago. Ames Laboratory at Iowa State University used notes and drawings to reconstruct this working replica of Atanasoff and Berry's history-making invention.

1939–1945 • World War II

1944: THE ELECTROMECHANICAL MARK I COMPUTER

The first electromechanical computer, the *Mark I,* was completed by Harvard University professor Howard Aiken in 1944 under the sponsorship of IBM. A monstrous 51 feet long and 8 feet high, the Mark I was essentially a serial collection of electromechanical calculators and was in many ways similar to Babbage's analytical machine. (Aiken was unaware of Babbage's work, though.) The Mark I was a significant improvement, but IBM's management still felt electromechanical computers would never replace punched-card equipment.

Courtesy of International Business Machines Corporation. Unauthorized use not permitted.

1946: THE ELECTRONIC ENIAC COMPUTER

Dr. John W. Mauchly (middle) collaborated with J. Presper Eckert, Jr. (foreground) at the University of Pennsylvania to develop a machine that would compute trajectory tables for the U.S. Army. (This was sorely needed; during World War II, only 20% of all bombs came within *1000 feet* of their targets.) The end product, the first fully operational electronic computer, was completed in 1946 and named the *ENIAC* (Electronic Numerical Integrator and Computer). A thousand times faster than its electromechanical predecessors, it occupied 15,000 square feet of floor space and weighed 30 tons. The ENIAC could do 5000 additions per minute and 500 multiplications per minute. Unlike computers of today that operate in binary, it operated in decimal and required 10 vacuum tubes to represent one decimal digit.

The ENIAC's use of vacuum tubes signaled a major breakthrough. (Legend has it that the ENIAC's 18,000 vacuum tubes dimmed the lights of Philadelphia whenever it was activated.) Even before the ENIAC was finished, it was used in the secret research that went into building the first atomic bomb at Los Alamos.

U.S. Army

1951: THE UNIVAC I AND THE FIRST GENERATION OF COMPUTERS

The first generation of computers (1951–1959), characterized by the use of vacuum tubes, is generally thought to have begun with the introduction of the first commercially viable electronic digital computer. The Universal Automatic Computer (*UNIVAC I* for short), developed by Mauchly and Eckert for the Remington-Rand Corporation, was installed in the U.S. Bureau of the Census in 1951. Later that year, CBS News gave the UNIVAC I national exposure when it correctly predicted Dwight Eisenhower's victory over Adlai Stevenson in the presidential election with only 5% of the votes counted. Mr. Eckert is shown here instructing news anchor Walter Cronkite in the use of the UNIVAC I.

The UNIVAC I just celebrated its golden anniversary (50 years). Forty-six companies and government agencies, including General Electric, DuPont, and the Internal Revenue Service, paid over $1 million for the UNIVAC I, a "walk-in" computer. The maintenance crew had to go inside the computer regularly to change burnt out vacuum tubes (the system had over 5000 of them). The 30-ton system's internal memory was a little more than 10Kb, less than a printed page worth of characters.

Courtesy of Unisys Corporation

1954: THE IBM 650

Not until the success of the UNIVAC I did IBM make a commitment to develop and market computers. IBM's first entry into the commercial computer market was the *IBM 701* in 1953. However, the *IBM 650* (shown here), introduced in 1954, is probably the reason IBM enjoys such a healthy share of today's computer market. Unlike some of its competitors, the IBM 650 was designed as a logical upgrade to existing punched-card machines. IBM management went out on a limb and estimated sales of 50—a figure greater than the number of installed computers in the entire nation at that time. IBM actually installed 1000. The rest is history.

Courtesy of International Business Machines Corporation. Unauthorized use not permitted.

1947 • Chuck Yeager breaks sound barrier   **1953 • Hillary and Norgay climb Mt. Everest**

1907–1992: "AMAZING" GRACE MURRAY HOPPER

Dubbed "Amazing Grace" by her many admirers, Dr. Grace Hopper was widely respected as the driving force behind COBOL, the most popular programming language, and a champion of standardized programming languages that are hardware-independent. In 1959, Dr. Hopper led an effort that laid the foundation for the development of COBOL. She also helped to create a compiler that enabled COBOL to run on many types of computers. Her reason: "Why start from scratch with every program you write when a computer could be developed to do a lot of the basic work for you over and over again?"

To Dr. Hopper's long list of honors, awards, and accomplishments, add the fact that she found the first "bug" in a computer—a real one. She repaired the Mark II by removing a moth that was caught in Relay Number II. From that day on, every programmer has *debugged* software by ferreting out its *bugs,* or errors, in programming syntax or logic.

The late Rear Admiral Hopper USN (ret) served the United States Navy and its computer and communications communities for many years. It's only fitting that a Navy destroyer is named in her honor.

Official U.S. Navy Photo

1958: THE FIRST INTEGRATED CIRCUIT

If you believe that great inventions revolutionize society by altering one's lifestyle or by changing the way people perceive themselves and their world, then the integrated circuit is a great invention. The integrated circuit is at the heart of all electronic equipment today. Shown here is the first integrated circuit, a phase-shift oscillator, invented in 1958 by Jack S. Kilby of Texas Instruments. Kilby (shown here in 1997 with his original notebook) can truly say to himself, "I changed how the world functions."

Texas Instruments Incorporated

1959: THE HONEYWELL 400 AND THE SECOND GENERATION OF COMPUTERS

The invention of the transistor signaled the start of the second generation of computers (1954–1964). Transistorized computers were more powerful, more reliable, less expensive, and cooler to operate than their vacuum-tubed predecessors. Honeywell (its *Honeywell 400* is shown here) established itself as a major player in the second generation of computers. Burroughs, UNIVAC, NCR, CDC, and Honeywell—IBM's biggest competitors during the 1960s and early 1970s—became known as the BUNCH (the first initial of each name).

Courtesy of Honeywell, Inc.

1957 • *Sputnik* launched

1963: THE PDP-8 MINICOMPUTER

During the 1950s and early 1960s, only the largest companies could afford the six- and seven-digit price tags of *mainframe* computers. In 1963 Digital Equipment Corporation introduced the *PDP-8* (shown here). It is generally considered the first successful *minicomputer* (a nod, some claim, to the playful spirit behind the 1960s miniskirt). At a mere $18,000, the transistor-based PDP-8 was an instant hit. It confirmed the tremendous demand for small computers for business and scientific applications. By 1971, more than 25 firms were manufacturing minicomputers, although Digital and Data General Corporation took an early lead in their sale and manufacture.

Reprinted with permission of Compaq Computer Corporation. All Rights Reserved.

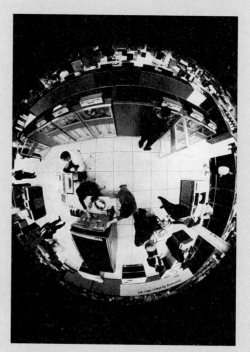

1964: THE IBM SYSTEM/360 AND THE THIRD GENERATION OF COMPUTERS

The third generation was characterized by computers built around integrated circuits. Of these, some historians consider IBM's *System/360* line of computers, introduced in 1964, the single most important innovation in the history of computers. System/360 was conceived as a family of computers with *upward compatibility;* when a company outgrew one model it could move up to the next model without worrying about converting its data. System/360 and other lines built around integrated circuits made all previous computers obsolete, but the advantages were so great that most users wrote the costs of conversion off as the price of progress.

Courtesy of International Business Machines Corporation. Unauthorized use not permitted.

1964: BASIC—MORE THAN A BEGINNER'S PROGRAMMING LANGUAGE

In the early 1960s, Dr. Thomas Kurtz and Dr. John Kemeny of Dartmouth College began developing a programming language that a beginner could learn and use quickly. Their work culminated in 1964 with BASIC. Over the years, BASIC gained widespread popularity and evolved from a teaching language into a versatile and powerful language for both business and scientific applications. True BASIC is the commercial version created by Kemeny and Kurtz which now runs without change on nine popular operating systems.

Courtesy of True BASIC, Inc.

1964 • Beatlemania develops in the U.S.

1969: ARPANET AND THE UNBUNDLING OF HARDWARE AND SOFTWARE

The year 1969 was a big one for important technological achievements. Astronaut Neil A. Armstrong descended the ladder of the *Apollo 11* lunar module making the first step by man on another celestial body. Also in 1969, a U.S. Department of Defense's Advanced Research Project Agency (ARPA) sponsorship of a project, named ARPANET, was underway to unite a community of geographically dispersed scientists by technology. The first official demonstration linked UCLA with Stanford University, both in California. Unlike the moon landing, which had live TV coverage throughout the world, this birth of the Internet, had no reporters, no photographers, and no records. No one remembered the first message, only that it worked. By 1971, the ARPANET included more than 20 sites. Ten years later, the ARPANET had 200 sites. In 1990, ARPANET evolved into what we now know as the Internet.

Also in 1969, International Business Machines (IBM) literally created the software industry overnight when it *unbundled* its products. At the time, IBM had the lion's share of the world market for computers. Software, maintenance, and educational services were included (bundled) with the price of the hardware. When IBM unbundled and sold software separately, the software industry began to flourish.

Courtesy of NASA

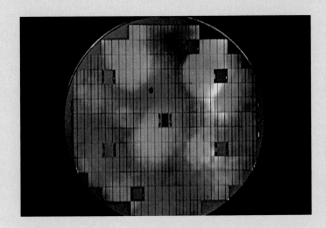

1971: INTEGRATED CIRCUITS AND THE FOURTH GENERATION OF COMPUTERS

Although most computer vendors would classify their computers as fourth generation, most people pinpoint 1971 as the generation's beginning. That was the year large-scale integration of circuitry (more circuits per unit of space) was introduced. The base technology, though, is still the integrated circuit. This is not to say that two decades have passed without significant innovations. In truth, the computer industry has experienced a mind-boggling succession of advances in the further miniaturization of circuitry, data communications, and the design of computer hardware and software.

Courtesy of International Business Machines Corporation. Unauthorized use not permitted.

1969 • *Apollo 11* lands on moon

1975: MICROSOFT AND BILL GATES

In 1968, seventh grader Bill Gates and ninth grader Paul Allen were teaching the computer to play monopoly and commanding it to play millions of games to discover gaming strategies. Seven years later, in 1975, they were to set a course that would revolutionize the computer industry. While at Harvard, Gates and Allen developed a BASIC programming language for the first commercially available microcomputer, the MITS Altair. After successful completion of the project, the two formed Microsoft Corporation, now the largest and most influential software company in the world. Microsoft was given enormous boost when its operating system software, MS-DOS, was selected for use by the IBM PC. Gates, now the richest man in America, provides the company's vision on new product ideas and technologies.

Courtesy of Microsoft Corporation

1981: THE IBM PC

In 1981, IBM tossed its hat into the personal computer ring with its announcement of the IBM Personal Computer, or IBM PC. By the end of 1982, 835,000 had been sold. When software vendors began to orient their products to the IBM PC, many companies began offering *IBMPC compatibles* or *clones*. Today, the IBM PC and its clones have become a powerful standard for the personal computer industry.

Courtesy of International Business Machines Corporation. Unauthorized use not permitted.

1977: THE APPLE II

Not until 1975 and the introduction of the *Altair 8800* personal computer was computing made available to individuals and very small companies. This event has forever changed how society perceives computers. One prominent entrepreneurial venture during the early years of personal computers was the Apple II computer (shown here). Two young computer enthusiasts, Steven Jobs and Steve Wozniak (then 21 and 26 years of age, respectively), collaborated to create and build their Apple II computer on a makeshift production line in Jobs' garage. Seven years later, Apple Computer earned a spot on the Fortune 500, a list of the 500 largest corporations in the United States.

Courtesy of Apple Computer, Inc.

1982: MITCHELL KAPOR DESIGNS LOTUS 1-2-3

Mitchell Kapor is one of the major forces behind the microcomputer boom in the 1980s. In 1982, Kapor founded Lotus Development Company, now one of the largest applications software companies in the world. Kapor and the company introduced an electronic spreadsheet product that gave IBM's recently introduced IBM PC (1981) credibility in the business marketplace. Sales of the IBM PC and the electronic spreadsheet, Lotus 1-2-3, soared.

1976 • United States 200th birthday   1983 • Compact disc (CD) introduced for recorded music

1984: THE MACINTOSH AND GRAPHICAL USER INTERFACES

In 1984 Apple Computer introduced the Macintosh desktop computer with a very "friendly" graphical user interface—proof that computers can be easy and fun to use. Graphical user interfaces (GUIs) began to change the complexion of the software industry. They have changed the interaction between human and computer from a short, character-oriented exchange modeled on the teletypewriter to the now familiar WIMP interface—Windows, Icons, Menus, and Pointing devices.

Courtesy of Apple Computer, Inc.

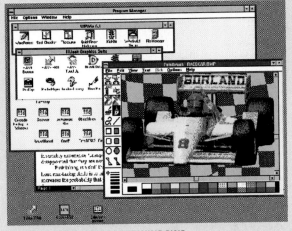

1985–PRESENT: MICROSOFT WINDOWS

Microsoft introduced Windows, a GUI for IBMPC-compatible computers in 1985; however, Windows did not enjoy widespread acceptance until 1990 with the release of Windows 3.0. Windows 3.0 gave a huge boost to the software industry because larger, more complex programs could now be run on IBMPC compatibles. Subsequent releases, including Windows 95, Windows 98, Windows 2000, and Windows XP made personal computers even easier to use, fueling the PC explosion of the 1990s.

1993: THE PENTIUM PROCESSOR AND MULTIMEDIA

The IBM PC-compatible PCs started out using the Intel 8088 microprocessor chip, then a succession of ever more powerful chips, including the Intel 80286, 80386, or 80486 chips. But not until the Intel Pentium (shown here) and its successors, the Pentium Pro and Pentium II, did PCs do much with multimedia, the integration of motion video, animation, graphics, sound, and so on. The emergence of the high-powered Pentium processors and their ability to handle multimedia applications changed the way we view and use PCs.

Photo courtesy of Intel Corporation

1989: THE WORLD WIDE WEB

Former Swiss physicist Tim Berners-Lee invented the World Wide Web, an Internet application that allows us to view multimedia Web pages on the Internet. Berners-Lee and a small team of scientists conceived HTML (the language of the Internet), URLs (Internet addresses), and put up the first server supporting the new World Wide Web format. The World Wide Web, one of several Internet-based applications, came of age as Web traffic grew 341,634% in its third year, 1993. The "Web" was unique and inviting in that it enabled "Web pages" to be linked across the Internet. Today, the World Wide Web is the foundation for most Internet communications and services.

Courtesy of CERN

1989 • Berlin Wall falls

1993: THE INTERNET BROWSER

The 1995 bombing of the Murrah Federal Building in Oklahoma City stirred the emotions of the people throughout the world. This picture by Liz Dabrowski, staff photographer for The Oklahoma Daily (the student voice of the University of Oklahoma in Norman), speaks volumes about what happened and reminds us that we must never forget. In retrospect, we now view 1993 through 1995 as turnaround years for the Internet when millions of people began to tune into it for news of the bombing and other events and for a wealth of other information and services. A number of Internet browsers were introduced during this time, including the Prodigy (a commercial information service) browser shown here and Netscape Navigator. These browsers enabled users to navigate the World Wide Web with ease.

1996: THE HANDHELD COMPUTER

The PalmPilot handheld computer was introduced and signaled to the world that you could place tremendous computing power in the palm of your hand. Now millions of people rely on PalmPilots and other similar handhelds for a variety of personal information management applications, including e-mail.

3Com and the 3Com logo are registered trademarks. PalmIII™ and the PalmIII™ logo are trademarks of Palm Computing, Inc., 3Com Corporation, or its subsidiaries.

1996: U.S. STAMP COMMEMORATES HALF CENTURY OF COMPUTING

The dedication of this U.S. Postal Service stamp was unique in that it was the first to be broadcast live over the Internet so that stamp collectors throughout the world could see and hear the ceremony. The USPS issued the stamp to commemorate the 50th anniversary of the ENIAC (the first full-scale electronic computer) and the 50 years of computer technology that followed. The dedication was held at Aberdeen Proving Ground, Maryland, the home of the ENIAC. In 1999, the U.S. Postal Service granted permission to E-stamp Corporation to issue electronic stamps, stamps sold over the Internet that can be printed along with the name and address on an envelope (shown here). This entrepreneurial effort reminds us that in the new millennium, anything that can be digitized will eventually be distributed over the Internet.

Courtesy of E-Stamp Corporation

1995 • Bombing of the Murrah Federal Building in Oklahoma City   2001 • September 11 terrorist attack on the United States

1. Lady Ada Lovelace suggested the use of punched cards to Charles Babbage during the 19th century. (T/F)

2. According to a federal court ruling, John Atanasoff is credited with the invention of the automatic electronic digital computer. (T/F)

3. The first significant use of binary automation was Blaise Pascal's Pascaline. (T/F)

4. The first family of computers with upward compatibility was introduced in 1964 by IBM. (T/F)

5. The Internet evolved from ARPANET, a U.S. government sponsored project. (T/F)

6. The first commercially viable computer was introduced in: (a) 1937, (b) 1951, (c) 1978, or (d) 1984.

7. The punched card tabulating machine used in the 1890 census was invented by: (a) Babbage, (b) Gates, (c) Hollerith, or (d) Kapor.

8. The first operational electronic computer was named the: (a) ENIAC, (b) UNIVAC III, (c) IBM 650, or (d) Monrobot.

9. The first integrated circuit was invented in what decade: (a) 1940s, (b) 1950s, (c) 1960s, or (d) 1970s?

10. Apple Computer was started by two young computer enthusiasts in what decade: (a) 1940s, (b) 1950s, (c) 1960s, or (d) 1970s?

SECTION
SELF-CHECK

Chapter 2

Learning Objectives

Once you have read and studied this chapter, you will have learned:

- The purpose and objectives of an operating system, the program that controls all activities within a computer system, plus common operating system platforms (Section 2-1).

- The fundamental concepts and terminology associated with the Windows operating environment (Section 2-2).

- The function and uses of software suite applications (word processing, presentation, spreadsheet, database, and personal information management) (Section 2-3).

- An overview of popular personal computing software including graphics, home and family, education and edutainment, reference, and business and financial (Section 2-4).

SOFTWARE

Why this chapter is important to you

Computing has a language all its own—*computerese*. Operating system terms and concepts contribute mightily to computerese. Fortunately, many of the words and phrases are simply old words being applied to software concepts (for example, *menus, background,* and *help*). Some terms evolved out of the need to abbreviate verbal and written communication (for example, *GUI* and *plug-and-play*). When you consider that the sum total of computing knowledge is doubling every two years, it is no wonder that its language is filled with buzzwords, acronyms, and the like. Even with its shortcomings, computerese provides a surprisingly efficient way to communicate. Our challenge is to learn these terms, then to keep up with the inevitable changes.

To be conversant with a personal computer, you must know your way around its operating system, such as the popular Microsoft Windows operating systems. Once you have read and studied this chapter, you'll be better prepared to interact effectively with the Windows environment, something that most knowledge workers do for several hours each day.

Also in this chapter is an introduction to applications software that is commonly used in business and the home, including software associated with software suites and a variety of popular personal computing applications. In this chapter you will learn that almost anything involving the manipulation of text and images can be done more easily and professionally with word processing software. You'll learn that you can prepare professional-looking visual aids that can bolster the effectiveness of any presentation. You'll learn how spreadsheet and database software can help you organize, analyze, and present all kinds of information. Perhaps, most importantly, you will learn that many personal computing tools exist for work and home that can save you lots of time, make you more productive, and help you present yourself in a more professional manner.

2-1 The Operating System

When we go out to a movie we see only a few of those responsible for making the film—the actors. We don't see the director, the producers, the writers, the editors, and many others. Perhaps it's because of this visual link that we, the audience, tend to become adoring fans of glamorous actors. We tend to forget the others involved in the film, even the director who is the person who ties it all together and makes it happen. It's much the same with software. As software users, we tend to shower our praise on that which we see most often—the *applications software.* However, *system software,* like the film director, stays in the background and ties it all together. The most prominent of these behind-the-scenes players is the operating system.

The *operating system* and its **graphical user interface (GUI)**, both system software, are at the heart of the software action (see Figure 2-1). All other software depends on and interacts with the operating system, the software that controls everything that happens in a computer. Its graphical user interface provides a user-friendly interface to the operating system. *System software* takes in those programs that manage, maintain, and control computer system resources. That includes a variety of **utility programs** that are available to help you with the day-to-day chores associated with personal computing (such as disk and file maintenance) and to keep your system running at peak performance. *Applications software* describes those programs used by the end user for a particular application, such as word processing or tax planning. Figure 2-1 illustrates examples of and the relationship between system and applications software.

Just as the processor is the nucleus of the computer system, the *operating system* is the nucleus of all software activity (see Figure 2-1). Microsoft Windows, Mac OS X, UNIX, Linux, and LindowsOS are popular operating systems for PCs and workstations. The operating system is actually a family of *system software* programs that monitor and control all I/O and processing activities within a computer system. One of the operating system programs, often called the **kernel,** loads other operating system and applications programs to RAM, the PC's main internal memory, as they are needed. The kernel is loaded to RAM on system start-up and remains *resident*—available in RAM—until the system is turned off. Typically, the kernel is responsible for task/process management and for memory/disk management.

If you purchase a PC off-the-shelf, you get whatever operating system is installed. Upgrading an operating system to a new version is not difficult and existing user files remain compatible. However, changing to an entirely different operating system can be cumbersome. When you order a PC, you may have several operating systems from which to choose. One might be business-oriented (set up for business networking) and one might be less expensive and more appropriate for home computing.

All hardware and software are under the control of the operating system. Among other things, the operating system:

- Determines how valuable RAM is allotted to programs
- Performs tasks related to disk and file management
- Sets priorities for handling tasks
- Manages the flow of instructions, data, and information to and from the processor

OPERATING SYSTEM OBJECTIVES

The operating system is what gives a *general-purpose computer,* such as a PC or a company's Internet server computer, its flexibility to tackle a variety of jobs. Most *dedicated computers,* such as those that control devices (dishwashers, car ignition systems, and so on) and arcade games, are controlled by a single-function program and do not need a separate operating system.

One of the best ways to understand an operating system is to understand its objectives. These objectives are listed and explained in Figure 2-2. All operating systems are designed with the same basic objectives in mind. However, server and PC operating systems differ markedly in complexity and orientation. On the server, *multiuser operating systems* coordinate a number of special-function processors and monitor interaction with hundreds, even thousands, of terminals and PCs in a network. Most PC operating systems are designed to support a *single user on a single PC* and enable optional *networking with other computers.*

FIGURE 2-1 **RELATIONSHIP BETWEEN THE OPERATING SYSTEM, THE GUI, AND APPLICATIONS SOFTWARE**
The operating system coordinates all software activity within a computer system. Our interaction with the operating system is through the graphical user interface, the GUI. Utility programs help you and the operating system manage system resources. With applications software packages, such as spreadsheet and expert systems, we can address a variety of problems. For example, a manager can use spreadsheet software to create *templates* (models) for summarizing sales and maintaining the office's fixed inventory. A knowledge engineer can use expert system software to create a loan evaluation system to assist a bank's loan officers in making better, more consistent decisions.

FIGURE 2–2 OBJECTIVES OF AN OPERATING SYSTEM

OPERATING SYSTEM OBJECTIVES

1. *To facilitate communication between the computer system and its users.*	Users issue system-related commands via the graphical user interface (GUI).
2. *To facilitate communication among computer system components.*	The operating system controls the movement of internal instructions and data between I/O peripheral devices, the processor, programs, and storage.
3. *To facilitate communication between linked computer systems.*	The operating system enables linked computers to communicate.
4. *To maximize throughput.*	System resources are employed to maximize throughput.
5. *To optimize the use of computer system resources.*	The operating system is continually looking at what tasks need to be done and what resources are available to accomplish these tasks; then it makes decisions about what resources to assign to which tasks.
6. *To keep track of all files in disk storage.*	The operating system enables users to perform such tasks as making backup copies of disks, erasing disk files, making inquiries about files on a particular disk, and preparing new disks for use. The operating system also handles many file- and disk-oriented tasks that are transparent (invisible) to the end user (for example, keeping track of the physical location of disk files).
7. *To provide an envelope of security for the computer system.*	The operating system can allow or deny user access to the system as a whole or to individual files.
8. *To monitor all systems capabilities and alert the user of system failure or potential problems.*	The operating system is continually checking system components for proper operation.

ALLOCATING SYSTEM RESOURCES

We all must live within our means, and the same goes for computers. A conscientious shopper can stretch the value of a dollar, and a good operating system can get the most from its limited resources, especially its processor. Operating systems get the most from their processors through **multitasking,** the *concurrent execution of more than one program at a time.* Actually, a single computer can execute only one program at a time. However, its internal processing speed is so fast that several programs can be allocated "slices" of computer time in rotation, making it appear that several programs are being executed at once.

The great difference in processor speed and the speeds of the peripheral devices makes multitasking possible. The speed of a 22-page-per-minute printer doesn't come close to pushing the processor of a low-end PC. The computer's processor is continually waiting for peripheral devices to complete such tasks as retrieving a record from disk storage or printing a report. During these waiting periods, the processor just continues processing other programs. The operating system ensures that the most appropriate resources are allocated to competing tasks in the most efficient manner.

Modern personal computing is done in a multitasking environment, where one or more programs run concurrently and are controlled and assigned priorities by the operating system. For example, you can prepare a graphics presentation in PowerPoint while downloading a new MP3 song via the Internet. The **foreground** is that part of RAM containing the active or current program (PowerPoint in this example) and is usually given priority by the operating system. Other lower-priority programs, such as the MP3 download in the example, are run in the **background** part of RAM. The operating system rotates allocation of the processor resource between foreground and background programs, with the foreground programs receiving the lion's share of the processor's attention.

THE USER INTERFACE

To appreciate the impact of graphical user interfaces (GUIs), it helps if you know what preceded them.

Text-Based Software

Through the 1980s, the most popular microcomputer operating system was **MS-DOS.** The *MS* is short for *Microsoft* and *DOS* is an abbreviation for *disk operating system,* meaning that it is loaded from disk. MS-DOS was strictly *text-based, command-driven* software. That is, we issued commands directly to DOS (the MS-DOS nickname) by entering them on the keyboard, one character at a time. For example, if you wished to issue a command to copy a word processing document from a hard disk to a floppy disk for your friend, you might have entered the following command via the keyboard at the DOS prompt (C:\>).

copy c:\myfile.txt a:\yourfile.txt

Command-driven DOS, in particular, demanded strict adherence to command **syntax,** which are the rules for entering commands, such as word spacing, punctuation, and so on (see Figure 2-3).

GUI-Based Software

Operating systems let you key in text commands or select commands by "pointing and clicking" with a mouse. Most people prefer the user-friendly, graphics-oriented environment—the graphical user interface (see Figure 2-3), or GUI (pronounced "*G-U-I*" or "*gooey*").

GUI users interact with their computers by using a pointing device (perhaps a *mouse* on desktop PCs or a *touchpad* on notebook PCs) and a keyboard to issue commands. Rather than enter a command directly, you choose from options displayed on the screen. The equivalent of a syntax-sensitive operating system command is entered by pointing to and choosing one or more options from menus or by pointing to and choosing a graphics image, called an **icon.** An icon is a picture that represents a processing activity or a file. For example, the file folder icon represents processing activities associated with file management. Users might drag an item to the "trash can" icon to delete a file from disk storage.

GUIs have eliminated the need for us to memorize and enter cumbersome commands. For example, in GUIs all we have to do to copy a file from one disk to another disk is to reposition the file's icon from one area on the screen to another.

PC OPERATING SYSTEMS AND PLATFORMS

In Chapter 1, we learned that the *processor* and an *operating system* define a *platform.* Software created to run on a specific platform will not run on other platforms. The typical computer system, large or

FIGURE 2–3 **TEXT-BASED AND GRAPHICS-BASED INTERFACES**
MS-DOS (shown here), the primary PC operating system for the first 15 years of personal computing, has a text-based, command-driven interface. Windows XP has a graphical user interface (GUI) in which files can be dragged with a mouse between disk icons. Each has its pros and cons. For example, MS-DOS demands knowledge of syntax, but the GUI may require more operations (myfile.txt would need to be renamed to yourfile.txt after the drag operation to accomplish the same operation as shown in MS-DOS).

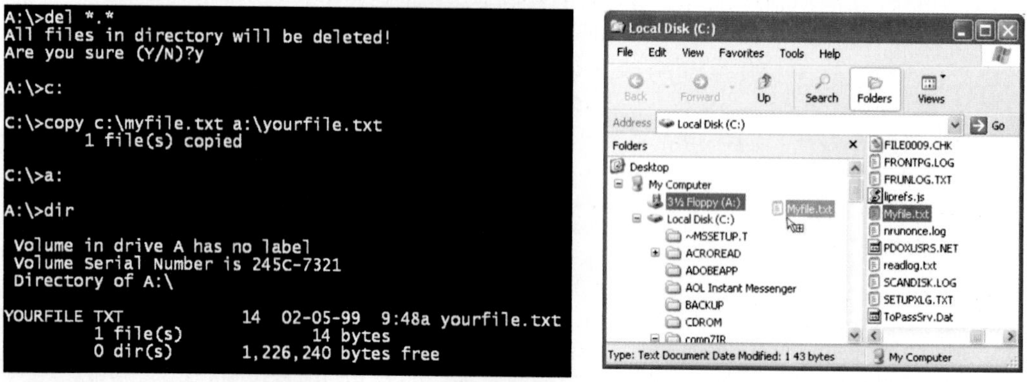

small, runs under a single platform. However, some can run several platforms. A *multiplatform computer* runs its *native* platform and *emulates* other platforms.

The selection of a platform is important because it sets boundaries for what you can and cannot do with your computer system.

PC Platforms Overview

In the server computer environment, choosing a platform is the responsibility of IT specialists. Typically, in the PC environment, you—the individual user—are responsible for selecting the platform. The following discussion focuses on the most common personal computing environments—those developed for PC-compatible computers.

The PC/Windows Platforms: 95, 98, Me, NT, 2000, XP, and CE.

Most personal computer users choose the *Wintel* platform, which combines one of the Microsoft Windows operating systems with an Intel-compatible processor. Windows 95, 98, Me, NT, 2000, XP, and CE are installed on millions of PCs. A major advantage of the Windows 9x/Me/2000/XP family is its ability to run 32-bit programs, that is, programs that use the full 32-bit data paths in the processor. (MS-DOS and the original Windows are 16-bit operating systems.) All members of the Windows family have a similar look and feel.

- *Legacy Versions of Windows: Windows 95, Windows 98, Windows Me, Windows NT, and Windows 2000.* **Windows 95, Windows 98,** and **Windows Me** (Millennium Edition) operating systems are older version of Windows, but are still widely used in the home and in both small and large business. These legacy Windows operating systems emerged from MS-DOS, the original text-based Microsoft operating system, which ruled the PC-compatible environment for the first decade of personal computing. **Windows NT** was the first Windows operating system to divorce itself from the limitations of MS-DOS, thus beginning a new era for PCs. **Windows 2000** was the successor to Windows NT.

- *Modern PC Operating Systems: Windows XP.* **Windows XP** is the version of Windows beyond Windows Me and Windows 2000. In developing Windows XP, Microsoft merged the strengths of Windows 2000 (standards-based security, manageability, and reliability) with the best features of Windows Me (Plug and Play and easy-to-use user interface). Windows XP is the future of the PC/Windows family of operating systems and reflects a push by Microsoft for all Windows users to migrate to Windows XP.

  Windows XP is a powerful client operating system that is emerging as the choice for businesses doing client/server computing. Windows XP, the client-side operating system, works with **Windows 2000 Server** or the newer **Windows .Net Server,** the server-side portion of the operating system (which runs on the server computer) to make client/server computing possible. Windows XP comes in two versions: **Windows XP Professional,** for businesses requiring local area networking capabilities and a high level of security, and **Windows XP Home Edition,** for home and small business users. Microsoft offers **Windows XP 64-Bit Edition** for use on high performance 64-bit workstations.

  Windows operating systems have many features, such as **plug-and-play,** which permits users to plug in a peripheral device or an add-on circuit board into an external port or into a slot on the motherboard, even when the PC is running. The operating system also permits **home networking,** the linking of PCs in a home or small office to share information and resources.

  Wintel platforms are *mostly* **backward compatible,** that is, they allow programs written for earlier Microsoft platforms to be run on modern systems. Because Windows XP is so radically different from earlier operating systems, however, a considerable number of programs designed for older platforms will not run under Windows XP.

  Windows XP is among the new wave of client/server platforms supporting LAN-based *workgroup computing.* Workgroup computing allows people on a network to use the network to foster cooperation and the sharing of ideas and resources. Groupware, such as instant messaging, calendars, brainstorming, and scheduling, is developed to run under workgroup platforms.

- *Windows CE.* The **Windows CE** operating system is designed for handheld and pocket PCs (see Figure 2-4). Its look and feel are similar to those of the other members of the family. Windows CE users can share information with other Windows-based PCs and they can connect to the Internet.

FIGURE 2–4 The Windows CE Platform
This pocket PC runs the Windows CE operating system and has full Internet connectivity. You can check stock quotes from the airport, send an e-mail from a taxi, or read the news from almost anywhere, anytime.

The Macintosh/Mac OS X Platform

The Apple family of microcomputers (including the Macintosh, PowerBook, iMac, eMac, and iBook computers) and its operating system, **Mac OS X** (see Figure 2-5), define another major platform. About one in every 10 PCs runs under this platform. The Apple line of microcomputers is based on the Motorola family of microprocessors. One inviting feature of Apple's Mac OS X is that it can be adjusted to fit the user's level of expertise.

Linux, UNIX, and LindowsOS

Linux is a spin-off of the popular **UNIX** multiuser operating system that has been around for decades (see Figure 2-5). The open source operating system was developed over the last decade via a worldwide consortium of developers, all working on the same code. **Open source software** is software for which the actual source programming code (the instructions) is made available to users for review and modification. Linux runs on a number of hardware platforms, including those using Intel and Motorola processors. Because Linux is made available for free over the Internet and is generally regarded to be an excellent operating system, it continues to grow in popularity. Web servers and e-mail servers throughout the world rely on Linux. The significance of the amazing growth of this operating system is that it has the potential to become a competitor to Microsoft Windows client and server programs. With a price tag close to zero and many devoted developers throughout the world, we can expect it to continue to grow in worldwide acceptance. Also, the fact that major technology companies, such as IBM, are creating products that use and can work with Linux helps fuel Linux acceptance. Linux runs on handheld computers, too.

FIGURE 2–5

OPERATING SYSTEMS: WINDOWS XP, LINUX, AND MAC OS X
The interfaces for three popular PC operating systems are shown here. Windows XP represents the Windows family of operating systems. Linux is the open source operating system and Mac OS X is used with Apple computers.

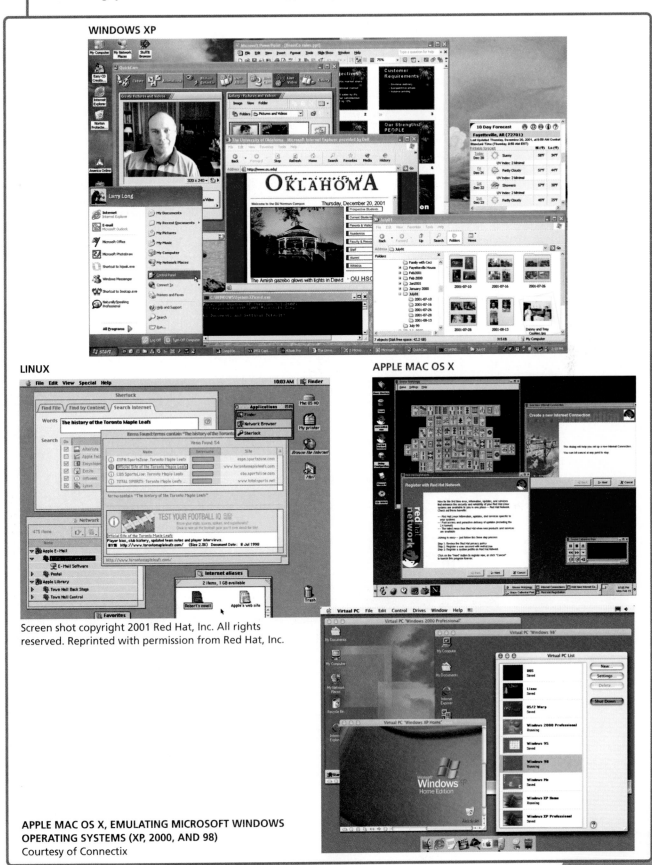

WINDOWS XP

LINUX

Screen shot copyright 2001 Red Hat, Inc. All rights reserved. Reprinted with permission from Red Hat, Inc.

APPLE MAC OS X

APPLE MAC OS X, EMULATING MICROSOFT WINDOWS OPERATING SYSTEMS (XP, 2000, AND 98)
Courtesy of Connectix

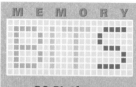

PC Platforms

- Legacy PC-Compatible
  - MS-DOS
  - MS-DOS with Windows
  - Windows 95 and Windows 98
  - Windows Me (Millennium Edition)
  - Windows 2000
- Current PC-compatible
  - Windows XP (Home and Professional versions)
  - Windows CE (handheld and pocket PC)
- Apple Mac OS X
- UNIX, Linux, and LindowsOS

LindowsOS, a commercial Linux-based operating system for PCs, has a Windows-like interface and offers file-level compatibility with many popular Windows-based applications, such as Word and Excel. These selling points and its inviting price tag have prompted industry analysts to predict that LindowsOS may soon surpass Mac OS X to become the second most installed commercial PC operating system.

Platform Problems

Many companies purchase and maintain a fleet of automobiles for use by employees. Companies routinely exchange entire fleets of Chevrolets for Fords (and vice versa) without any loss of functionality. Employees simply come to work in a Chevy and drive away in a Ford. The fleet decision doesn't commit a company over the long term. The choice of a computer platform, however, does.

When you decide on a particular platform, you begin to purchase and create resources for that platform. The investment required in selecting a platform demands a long-term commitment—at least five years. This type of commitment makes choosing a platform at the individual or company level a very important decision (see Figure 2-6).

All companies have platform problems, although some have fewer problems than others. Those that standardize on platforms can enjoy the benefits of easily shared resources (from data to printers). Those that do not must do some work to achieve interoperability. **Interoperability** refers to the ability to run software and exchange information in a **multiplatform environment** (a computing environment of more than one platform). *Enabling technologies* that allow communication and the sharing of resources between different platforms are called **cross-platform technologies.** Multiplatform organizations use cross-platform technologies, both hardware and software, to link PCs, workstations, networks, and so on. Multiplatform environments are more the rule than the exception in medium-sized and large organizations. Whenever possible, companies try to minimize the number of platforms used in the company. The fewer the number of platforms, the less the hassle and expense associated with installing and maintaining cross-platform technologies.

FIGURE 2–6 Installing the Operating System
At this Gateway Corporation assembly plant, workers install the operating system, then test all facets of system operation. Most of Gateway's PCs are custom-built to user specifications, with the user often selecting from several operating system options.

Courtesy of Gateway, Inc.

UTILITY PROGRAMS

System software, which includes the operating system and its GUI, is applicationsindependent. Generally, system software supports the operation and maintenance of the PC's hardware, software, and files. A wide variety of system software *utilities* are available to help you with the day-to-day chores associated with personal computing (disk and file maintenance, system recovery, security, backup, virus protection, and so on) and to keep your system running at peak performance. Figure 2-7 gives you a sampling of common utilities programs you might use to enhance your personal computing environment.

SECTION SELF-CHECK

2-1.1	The kernel is loaded to RAM on system start-up. (T/F)
2-1.2	The concurrent execution of more than one program at a time is called: (a) double duty, (b) multitasking, (c) multilayering, or (d) multiple kerneling.
2-1.3	Programs designed to be used by the end user are: (a) system software, (b) systemware, (c) personware, or (d) applications software.
2-1.4	Cross-platform technologies enable communication and the sharing of resources between different platforms. (T/F)
2-1.5	Making an input device immediately operational by simply plugging it into a port is referred to as: (a) plug-and-play, (b) cap-and-cork, (c) pop-and-go, or (d) plug-and-go.
2-1.6	Which of the following is not in the PC/Windows platform family: (a) Windows 98, (b) Windows TN, (c) Windows XP, or (d) Windows 2000?
2-1.7	Software that provides detailed information with regard to available memory and disk space would be considered utility software. (T/F)
2-1.8	Utility software would be considered: (a) applications software, (b) system software, (c) utilitarian software, or (d) operating system software.

2-2 Windows Concepts and Terminology

The Microsoft Windows family of operating systems dominates the PC-compatible environment throughout the world. The Microsoft master plan has all Windows users eventually migrating to Windows XP so that we can partake of the Windows "experience" (XP stands for "experience"). Most new PCs come with a Windows XP operating system installed on the hard disk. Windows XP Home Edition works well in the home or a small business, but Windows XP Professional, with its security and networking capabilities, is better suited for businesses with networking on a local area network (LAN). All PC/Windows platforms have a similar look and feel.

The terms, concepts, and features discussed in this section generally apply to Windows 9x/Me/2000/XP; however, the examples are based on Windows XP. The name *Windows* describes basically how the software functions. The GUI-based Windows series runs one or more applications in **windows**—rectangular areas displayed on the screen. The Windows operating system series has introduced a number of concepts and terms, all of which apply to the thousands of software packages that have been and are being developed to run on the Windows platforms.

HELP: F1

Books, like this one, and tutorial software are complementary learning tools. Hands-on activities with Windows or any other software package are essential to learning. The explanations in the following sections will make more sense once you begin working with Windows. We recommend that you visit your college's PC lab and run Help to learn more about your Windows operating system.

Help is readily available.

- *Help for Windows.* All you have to do is click *Start*, then *Help and Support* for operating system help (Figure 2-8). This feature provides online access to comprehensive, continually updated support information, including FAQs (frequently asked questions) and solutions to common problems. The Windows Help capabilities include step-by-step tutorials that lead you through numerous common Windows procedures, such as how to set up home networking or how to use the mouse. Help also includes troubleshooters.

- *Help for any applications program.* Click on *Help* in the main menu at the top of the application window.

WHY THIS SECTION IS IMPORTANT TO YOU

The thesaurus lists these synonyms for the word *interact*: *blend, associate, hobnob, mingle, combine, mix, stir,* and *socialize.* To some extent, we do all of these, even socialize, when we interact with PCs and their software. The concepts and terms introduced in this section are applicable to thousands of software packages written for the Windows environment. Once you understand them, you will feel comfortable with the user interfaces of all PC software.

FIGURE 2–7 UTILITY SOFTWARE

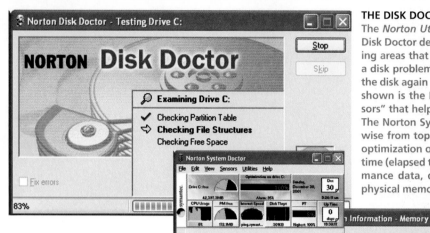

THE DISK DOCTOR

The *Norton Utilities* (a Symantec Corporation product) Disk Doctor determines the health of your disks, checking areas that could cause problems. After diagnosing a disk problem, the "doctor" corrects it so you can use the disk again and get to your programs and data. Also shown is the Norton System Doctor, which has "sensors" that help optimize the PC for peak performance. The Norton System Doctor is set up to monitor (clockwise from top left) disk drive space available, level of optimization of disk drive, date and time, Windows up time (elapsed time since Windows was started), performance data, disk drive throughput, Internet speed, physical memory (RAM), and CPU (processor) usage.

SYSTEM INFORMATION

The *Norton Utilities* System Information tool gives you detailed information about your PC, its peripherals, and any Internet or network connection. The Memory tab information shown here graphically depicts available memory and lists how much RAM each program in memory is using. The Windows XP operating system, the selected program (Windows32), occupies 53.3 MB of memory.

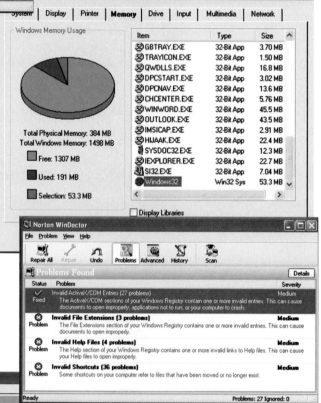

DEFRAGGING

The *Norton Utilities* Speed Disk optimizes your hard disks by rearranging file fragments into contiguous files in a process called *defragmentation* (discussed in Chapter 5). The example shows a map of a recently defragmented disk. Frequently accessed files are grouped in one area of the disk to minimize movement of the disk-access arm.

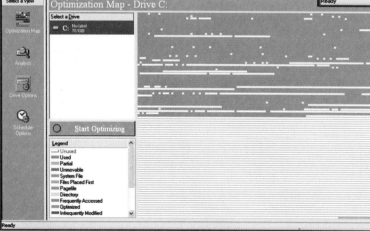

THE WINDOWS DOCTOR

The *Norton Utilities* WinDoctor diagnoses your Windows environment, and then fixes most common types of Windows problems, thereby keeping your Windows environment running at peak efficiency.

FIGURE 2-7 continued

VIRUS PROTECTION
Norton AntiVirus, a popular virus vaccine, scans your disk drive(s) for viruses at system startup. Also, it monitors your PC for any activity that might indicate that a virus is at work in your system. It alerts you to problems, and then removes the virus. Each month, more viruses are added to a list of thousands that float around cyberspace. The LiveUpdate feature lets you periodically download protection from new viruses.

INTERNET PRIVACY PROTECTION
Internet Explorer gives users the option to set the level of Internet privacy protection. Sliding the selector up increases the level of privacy protection and sliding it down minimizes privacy protection to the point that all cookies are accepted. A cookie is personal information given to your Internet browser by a Web server. The cookie is stored on your disk and sent back to the server each time you access the Web site.

SCREEN SAVERS
A screen saver program takes over the display screen when there is no key or mouse input for a specified time, say 10 minutes. Originally, screen savers were designed to eliminate ghosting, the permanent etching of a pattern on a display screen. The newer monitors do not have this problem, but people love screen savers for their visual appeal, and they hide their work from snoopers when they leave the work area. As shown here, there is a screen saver for everyone and every mood. Screen savers fill the display with constantly moving images or animation until you tap a key or move the mouse.

FIGURE 2–8

THE WINDOWS HELP FEATURE
The Help and Support feature lets you find help by scanning a *hierarchical list by topic.* Click on the *Index* button to search an index similar to one you would find in a book (but without page references). Enter a topic in the *Search* box to search the help files by keyword. Click on the *Support* button for Internet-based Windows XP help and technical support and other valuable help resources.

- *Context-sensitive help.* Tap the *F1* key to get *context-sensitive help;* that is, help that relates to the window, object, or whatever is active at the time.

Generally, Help offers you several ways to find the information you need. Most Windows and applications help features will offer these options.

- *Contents.* Use the *Contents* list when you want to look through categories.

- *Search.* You can search for a word or phrase (for example, type "printer").

- *Index.* If you prefer, you can scroll through a book-style alphabetical *Index* to locate the item of interest.

NON-WINDOWS AND WINDOWS APPLICATIONS

Any software application that does not adhere to the Microsoft Windows standard is a **non-Windows application.** Most non-Windows applications will run under Windows, but these software packages do not take advantage of the many helpful Windows features. Generally, non-Windows programs are older software created for MS-DOS.

Programs that adhere to Windows conventions are **Windows applications.** These conventions describe:

- Type and style of window

- Arrangement and style of menus

- Use of the keyboard and mouse

- Format for screen image display

Virtually all new software for the PC environment is designed to run on the Windows platform. The GUI for Windows versions of Word, Quicken, Adobe Illustrator, and all other Windows applications have the same look and feel. *When you learn the Windows GUI, you also learn the GUI for all Windows-based software packages.*

CLICKING, DOUBLE-CLICKING, AND DRAGGING

The Windows GUI uses both a keyboard and a point-and-draw device for input. The point-and-draw device is often a mouse, but with so many notebooks being purchased, it is increasingly a touchpad or some other such device.

When performing operating system functions in Windows, you can opt for the *single-click mode* or the traditional *double-click mode* of Windows 95. Single-click mode is primarily for general Windows operations and may not be available in many applications. Figure 2-9 summarizes the differences between the two modes of clicking.

Right-clicking (tapping the right button on a mouse set up for right-handed use) causes a *context-sensitive menu* to be displayed. The resulting menu relates to the window, object, or whatever the mouse pointer is on at the time of the right-click.

Press and hold the left button to **drag** across the screen. When using a graphics software program, you specify the type of object you want to draw, then drag the mouse pointer across the screen to create the object. When using a word processing program, you highlight a block of text by dragging the mouse pointer from the beginning to the end of the text block. In a GUI, you can point to an object, perhaps an icon, then drag (move) it to a new position. Click and drag operations in a graphics software package are demonstrated in Figure 2-10.

THE DESKTOP

The Windows screen upon which icons, windows, and so on are displayed is known as the **desktop.** The Windows desktop, which is introduced in *Getting Started,* may contain these items (see Figure 2-11).

- *Background.* The background can be anything from a single-color screen to an elaborate image, such as the shoreline in Figures 2-11.

- *One active window.* The **active window** displays the application being currently used by the user.

FIGURE 2–9   CLICKING AND RIGHT-CLICKING FOR WINDOWS OPERATING SYSTEMS

Windows Task	Double-Click Mode (tap the primary button, the left button for right handers, in rapid succession)	Single-Click Mode (tap the primary button)
Select an item	Point and click on item (an icon, a file-name, a taskbar program, and so on).	Point to item.
Open (or choose) an item	Double-click on the item.	Click on the item.
Select a range of items	Click the first item in a group of items, press and hold the Shift key, then **click** the last item (for example, files or words in a paragraph).	Point to the first item in a group of items, press and hold the Shift key, and then **point to** the last item in the group.
Select multiple individual items	Click any item in a group, press and hold the Ctrl key, and then **click** other individual items in the group.	Point to any item in a group, press and hold the Ctrl key, and then **point to** other individual items in the group.
Drag-and-drop item	Point to an item, press and hold the mouse button, and drag the item to new location.	Same as double-click mode.
Display a context-sensitive menu of tasks or options	Point to Item and Right-Click (tap the secondary button, the right one for right handers)	

FIGURE 2–10   **THE MOUSE AND THE MOUSE POINTER**
In the example, a computer artist repositions the mouse pointer on the sun, and then moves the sun image from the left to the right side of the screen.

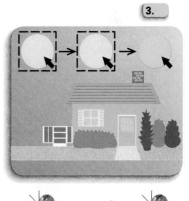

1. The graphics cursor, or pointer, is initially at Position 1 on the display screen. The artist moves the mouse up (toward monitor) to position the pointer over the image to be moved (Position 2).

The artist clicks (taps the left mouse button) on the sun image to highlight the area containing the sun image (rectangular box).

The artist drags the image to the desired location (Position 3) by pressing and holding the mouse's left button and moving the mouse. The artist releases the button to complete the drag operation.

FIGURE 2–11

THE WINDOWS DESKTOP
The appearance of this Windows XP desktop depends on the user's application mix and visual wishes at a particular time. Windows enables sophisticated multitasking, that is, running several programs at one time. This feature allows you to work on a word processing document while backing up files and checking e-mail on the Internet. The taskbar lists all open applications. To personalize the desktop, right-click anywhere on the desktop, select Properties, and then change the color scheme, the background, the resolution, or other desktop features.

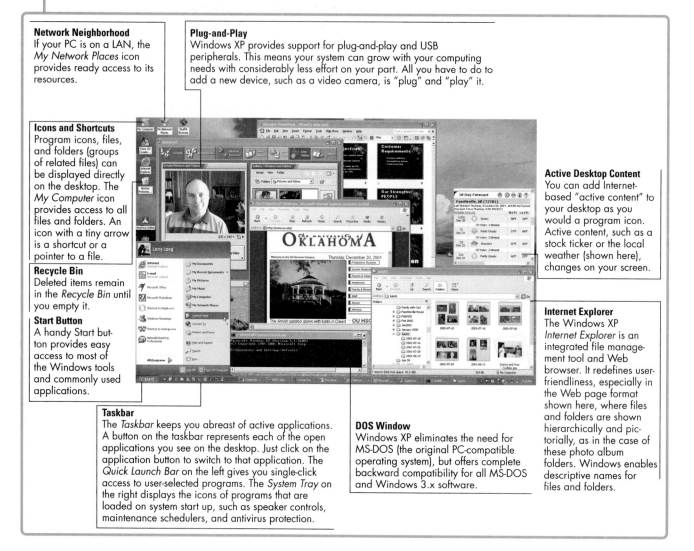

Network Neighborhood
If your PC is on a LAN, the *My Network Places* icon provides ready access to its resources.

Plug-and-Play
Windows XP provides support for plug-and-play and USB peripherals. This means your system can grow with your computing needs with considerably less effort on your part. All you have to do to add a new device, such as a video camera, is "plug" and "play" it.

Icons and Shortcuts
Program icons, files, and folders (groups of related files) can be displayed directly on the desktop. The *My Computer* icon provides access to all files and folders. An icon with a tiny arrow is a shortcut or a pointer to a file.

Recycle Bin
Deleted items remain in the *Recycle Bin* until you empty it.

Start Button
A handy Start button provides easy access to most of the Windows tools and commonly used applications.

Active Desktop Content
You can add Internet-based "active content" to your desktop as you would a program icon. Active content, such as a stock ticker or the local weather (shown here), changes on your screen.

Internet Explorer
The Windows XP *Internet Explorer* is an integrated file management tool and Web browser. It redefines user-friendliness, especially in the Web page format shown here, where files and folders are shown hierarchically and pictorially, as in the case of these photo album folders. Windows enables descriptive names for files and folders.

Taskbar
The *Taskbar* keeps you abreast of active applications. A button on the taskbar represents each of the open applications you see on the desktop. Just click on the application button to switch to that application. The *Quick Launch Bar* on the left gives you single-click access to user-selected programs. The *System Tray* on the right displays the icons of programs that are loaded on system start up, such as speaker controls, maintenance schedulers, and antivirus protection.

DOS Window
Windows XP eliminates the need for MS-DOS (the original PC-compatible operating system), but offers complete backward compatibility for all MS-DOS and Windows 3.x software.

- *One or more inactive windows.* **Inactive windows** display applications that are running but not being used by the user.
- *Icons.* These small pictures represent programs and other Windows elements.
- *Internet-based active content.* The desktop can display real-time Internet content, such as the weather or stock prices.
- *Various bars showing processing options.* These bars make it easier for you to navigate between applications.

People usually customize their desktops to reflect their personalities as well as their processing and information needs, so no two desktops are the same.

The Taskbar

Typically, a Windows session begins with the **Start button** in the taskbar. The **taskbar,** which can be displayed all the time or hidden, as desired, shows what programs are running and available for use. Click the *Start* button in the taskbar to display the Start menu and open the door to the resources on your PC. An application window can be opened in several ways, but usually people point and click on the desired application icon in the *Programs* option on the Start menu (see Figure 2-12). Highlighting the Programs option presents a pop-out menu with either application options or folders containing other options. A Windows **folder** is a logical grouping of related files and/or subordinate folders.

The Window

Figure 2-13 shows a typical rectangular Windows **application window.** An application window contains an **open application** (a running application), such as Paint or Word. Several applications can be open or running simultaneously, but there is only one *active window* at any given time. Application commands issued via the keyboard or the mouse apply to the active window. The active window's title bar (at the top of each application) is highlighted. There is no active window in Figure 2-11 because the user has clicked on the Start button to open another program. The elements of an application window are: the workspace, the scroll bars, the title bar, the menu bar, the toolbar, the ruler bar, and the corners and borders. Each is described in the following sections and illustrated in Figure 2-13.

Workspace

The application **workspace** is the area in a window below the title bar, menu bar or toolbar. Everything that relates to the application noted in the title bar is displayed in the workspace. In the

FIGURE 2–12

THE START MENU WITH POP-OUT MENUS
The *Start* menu *All Programs* option is selected, prompting a display of available programs. The *Norton SystemWorks* folder and then the *Norton Utilities* subfolder are highlighted, causing its contents (11 applications) to be displayed. Note that recently accessed programs/folders are highlighted.

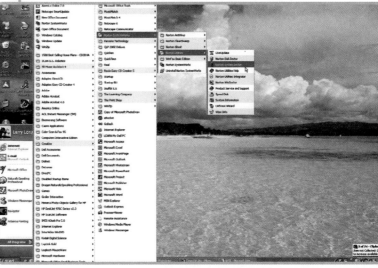

FIGURE 2–13

ELEMENTS OF AN APPLICATION WINDOW
In this example display, the workspace in this *Microsoft PhotoDraw* application has two open document windows, both showing processor chips. The top window, which is the active document window, contains an image of the Intel 8088 processor— the one used in the original 1981 IBM PC. A pan and zoom thumbnail of this image (bottom left) outlines what portion of the image is visible in the document window. The bottom document window shows a state-of-the-art Intel chip.

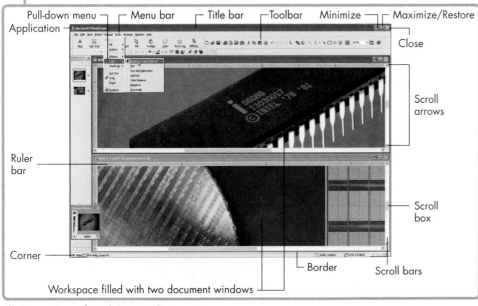

Photo courtesy of Intel Corporation

example in Figure 2-13, two **document windows** are displayed in the parent application window's workspace. Both are photo images and each is shown in a document window. The workspace of a word processing program might contain one or more word processing documents. If only one file/document is displayed in the workspace, then its filename appears in the title bar. If multiple files/documents are displayed, then filenames appear in the title bars of their windows.

When document content is more than can be displayed in a window, the window is outfitted with **vertical** and/or **horizontal scroll bars** (see Figure 2-13). Each bar contains a **scroll box** and two **scroll arrows.** Use the mouse or keyboard to move a box up/down or left/right on a scroll bar to display other parts of the application. This movement is known as **scrolling.**

Title Bar

The horizontal **title bar** at the top of each window runs the width of the window from left to right (see Figure 2-13). The elements of the title bar include the *application icon, window title, Minimize button, Maximize/Restore button, Close button,* and the *title area.* Point and click (or drag) on these elements to change the presentation of the window.

- *Application icon in title bar.* The application icon is a miniature visual representation of the application and is displayed on the left end of the title bar.

- *Window title.* The title bar displays the title of the application ("Microsoft PhotoDraw" in Figure 2-13).

- *Minimize, Maximize/Restore, and Close buttons.* Point and click on the Minimize button (▬), the Maximize (to full screen) or Restore (to a window) button (□ or ⧉), or the Close button (✖) at the right end of the title bar in Figure 2-13.

- *Title area.* To *move* a window, the user simply points to the window title bar and drags the window to the desired location.

Menu Bar

The menu bar for an application window runs the width of the window just below the title bar (see Figure 2-13). The menu bar lists the menus available for that application. Choosing an option from the menu bar results in a pull-down menu. The *File, Edit, View,* and *Help* menus are available for most applications. Other menu options depend on the application. When you select an item from the menu bar, a subordinate **pull-down menu** (see Figure 2-13) is "pulled down" from the selected menu bar option and displayed as a vertical list of menu options.

Certain conventions apply to user interactions with any menu.

- *Only the undimmed options can be chosen.* Dimmed options are not available for the current circumstances. For example, the *Copy* option would not be available in an *Edit* menu if nothing had been selected to be copied.

- *Corresponding shortcut keys are presented next to many options in Windows menus.* The **shortcut key** is a key combination (for example, Alt+F4 to *Exit* and Ctrl+C to *Copy*), to issue commands within a particular application without activating a menu.

- *Choosing a menu option followed by an arrow (▶) results in a pop-out menu.* The *Color* menu option on Figure 2-13 demonstrates the resulting **pop-out menu.**

- *A user-recorded check mark (✓) to the left of the menu option indicates that the option is active and applies to any related commands.* For example, many programs have a toolbar, a ruler, and a status bar that are hidden or displayed depending on whether or not these items are checked in the *View* menu.

- *There are three ways to choose a menu option.*

  1. Point and click the mouse on the option.

  2. Tap the Alt key to activate the current menu bar. This lets you select an option via keyboard. Enter the underlined letter key, called a **mnemonic** (pronounced *"neh MON ik"*), of the menu option in combination with the Alt key on a keyboard (Alt+o for the *Format* menu in Figure 2-13). Press the underlined letter of a pull-down menu option to choose that option (*l* for *Color* in Figure 2-13).

  3. Once the menu is activated (by mouse click or keyboard), you can use the keyboard arrow keys to select (highlight) the desired option and press the Enter key to choose it.

- *Choosing a menu option followed by an ellipsis (. . .) results in a dialog box.* A pop-up **dialog box** typically asks the user to make further choices or enter additional information.

You'll encounter a variety of menus, including the pop-up and floating menus. The context-sensitive **pop-up menu** is displayed when you right-click the mouse. The pop-up menu gives you options appropriate for whatever you're doing at the time. The **floating menu** "floats" over the display and can be dragged with a mouse to any position on the work area.

You can use a hotkey to issue a few special commands without going through a menu. Tapping the **hotkey,** which is typically a key combination, causes some function to happen in the computer, no matter what the active menu or application (Alt+PrintScreen captures the image of the active window so you can save, display, or print it).

Toolbar

A software package's menu bar is but the tip of a hierarchy of menus that may contain as many as 200 menu item options. You might work with a software package for years and not choose some of these options. You might use others every day. **Toolbars** have been created to give you ready access to these frequently used menu items. Toolbars contain multiple buttons with graphics that represent related menu options or commands (see Figure 2-13). To execute a particular command, simply click on the button. The graphics on the buttons are designed to represent actions of the command. You can customize your toolbars to meet your processing needs.

Ruler Bar

Typically, the **ruler bar** shows the document window's content relative to the printed page. The default usually is inches and standard letter-sized paper (see Figure 2-13).

Corners and Borders

To resize a window, use a mouse and point to a window's border or corner. The mouse pointer changes to a double arrow when positioned over a border or corner. Drag the border or corner in the directions indicated by the double arrow to the desired shape.

The Dialog Box

You will encounter scores of dialog boxes in Windows (such as the Display Properties dialog box) and in user applications. Often, you, the user, must okay or revise entries in the *dialog box* before you can continue with a particular operation. The dialog box may contain any of these elements (see Figure 2-14).

- *Tabs*. The tabs enable similar properties to be grouped within a dialog box (for example, *Appearance* and *Screen Saver*).
- *Text box*. Enter text information in the text box or accept the displayed default entry.
- *Command buttons*. Point and click on the OK command button to carry out the command with the information provided in the dialog box.

FIGURE 2–14 **ELEMENTS OF A DIALOG BOX**
Many common dialog box elements are shown in the Display Properties dialog box. Not shown are the option button and scroll bar adjustment elements.

- *List boxes*. A list box displays a list of available choices for a particular option.
- *Drop-down list boxes*. The drop-down list box is an alternative to the list box when the dialog box is too small for a list box to be displayed.
- *Drop-down palette*. The drop-down palette displays a matrix of available font, line, or fill colors.
- *Option buttons*. Circular buttons, called option buttons, preface each item in a list of mutually exclusive items (only one can be activated). Point and click a button to insert a black dot in the button and activate the option.
- *Scroll bar adjustment*. The scroll bar adjustment enables users to change options, such as the speed at which the cursor blinks or speaker volume.
- *Spin box*. The spin box lets you adjust a numerical setting by keying in the desired number or clicking the up or down arrow to "spin" to the desired number.

Icons

Icons, the graphical representation of a Windows element, play a major role in the Windows GUI. Commonly used icons include *application icons*, *shortcut icons*, *document icons*, and *disk drive icons*. The **Explorer** window in Figure 2-15 shows the use of these icons. Use the Explorer to perform file management tasks such as creating folders, copying files, moving files, deleting files, and other tasks related to folder and file management. In Windows, named folders are created to hold document and program files.

Application Icons

The **application icon** is included on a minimized application button in the taskbar and on the title bar in a window. It is usually a graphic rendering of the software package's logo.

Shortcut Icons

A **shortcut icon** to any application, document, or printer can be positioned on the desktop, in a folder, or in several other places. The shortcut icon has an arrow in its lower left corner. Shortcuts are clicked (or double-clicked) to begin an application.

FIGURE 2–15

THE WINDOWS EXPLORER
The Windows Explorer makes resources on the computer readily accessible to the user. The plus sign to the left of the icon indicates that the item has subordinate folders. Click the disk or folder icon to show its content or double-click on an application icon to open the application. Positioning the mouse pointer over an applications icon (as shown here) highlights the icon and causes a hint, details, or explanation to be displayed in the status bar at the bottom of the window.

Document Icons

The active document window, which is a window within an application window, can be minimized to a **document icon** within an application's workspace.

Disk Drive Icons

The **disk drive icons** graphically represent several disk drive options: floppy, hard, network (hard), removable disk (for example, Zip disk drive), and CD-ROM (including DVD and CD-RW). The floppy (A), hard disk (C), Zip disk (D), and CD-ROMs (E, a DVD and F, a CD-RW) icons shown in Figure 2-15 resemble the faceplates of the disk drives or show the type of storage media.

Viewing Windows

The Windows environment lets you view multiple applications in windows on the desktop display. Once open, a window can be resized, minimized (and restored), maximized (and restored), and closed.

Essentially, any applications software for the Windows environment can be:

- Viewed and run in a window, the shape and size of which is determined by you, the user
- Run full-screen (maximized), that is, filling the entire screen, with no other application windows or icons showing

When multiple applications are running, the user can use the *Move* and *Resize* capabilities to arrange and size the windows to meet viewing needs.

Within a given application window, such as Microsoft Excel, multiple document windows can be sized, shrunk, and arranged by the user within the workspace. As an alternative, the user can request that the document windows be automatically presented as **cascading windows** or **tiled windows**, which are illustrated in Figure 2-16.

Switching Between Windows

In the Windows environment, users can open as many applications as available RAM will permit. The active window is always highlighted in the **foreground**. When located in the foreground all parts of the window are visible. Other open windows are in the **background**, or behind the foreground (see Figure 2-11). These terms describe RAM concepts, too. To switch between open applications, point and click anywhere on the desired inactive window or on the desired application button in the taskbar. You can also use the Alt+Tab shortcut key to toggle between application windows.

Terminating an Application and a Windows Session

Perform three operations before ending a Windows session.

1. *Save your work.* The *Save* option in the *File* menu updates the existing file to reflect the changes made during the session. The *Save As* option allows users to save the current file under another filename.

2. *Close all open windows.* After saving your work, exit a Windows application through its menu bar (*File* then *Exit*) or by pointing and clicking the Close button in the title bar.

FIGURE 2–16

ARRANGEMENT OF WINDOWS
Here, four open applications are tiled on the Windows XP desktop (clockwise from top left: *Microsoft PhotoDraw, Outlook, Internet Explorer,* and *Microsoft Visio*). The applications, as well as documents within an application's workspace, can be presented as tiled documents (in top left Microsoft PhotoDraw images) or cascading (bottom left Visio documents are overlapped such that all title bars are visible).

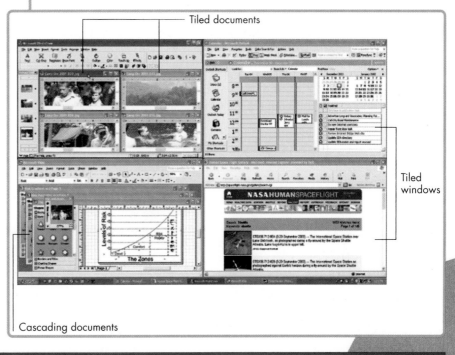

Tiled documents

Tiled windows

Cascading documents

3. *Shut down Windows.* Click *Start* in the taskbar, and then select *Turn Off Computer* (or *Shut Down*). The shut down process is illustrated in Getting Started.

SHARING INFORMATION AMONG APPLICATIONS

The Windows environment offers several methods for sharing information: the Clipboard, and object linking, and object embedding.

The Clipboard: Copy, Cut, and Paste

One of the most inviting aspects of the Windows environment is the ability to copy and move information (text, graphics, sound clips, video clips, or a combination) within and between applications. The most common method of sharing information among applications is to use the Windows **Clipboard** and the *Edit* option in the menu bar. Think of the Clipboard as a holding area for information. The information in the Clipboard can be en route to another application, or it can be copied anywhere in the current document. *Edit* is an option in the menu bar of most Windows applications. Choosing *Edit* results in a pull-down menu from the menu bar. Options common to most Edit menus are *Cut, Copy, Paste,* and *Delete.* The **source application** and **destination application** can be the same, or they can be entirely different applications.

The procedure for transferring information via the Clipboard is demonstrated in Figure 2-17. This example illustrates the *Copy* procedure. Choosing the *Cut* option causes the specified information to be removed from the source application and placed on the Windows Clipboard. Whether *Copy* or *Cut* is chosen, the Clipboard contents remain unchanged until the next copy/cut operation, so you can paste the Clipboard contents as many times as needed.

Object Linking and Embedding: OLE

Another way to link applications is through **object linking and embedding,** or **OLE.** Loosely, an **object** is an item within a Windows application that can be individually selected. The object can be a block of text, all or part of a graphic image, or even a sound or video clip. OLE gives us the capability to create a **compound document** that contains one or more objects from other applications. A document can be a word processing newsletter, a *Microsoft Visio* drawing, a spreadsheet, and so on. The object originates in a **server application** and is linked to a destination document of a **client application.** For example, when a Visio (server application) drawing (object) is linked to a Word (client) note (destination document), the result is a compound document (see Figure 2-18).

OLE Object Linking

OLE lets you *link* or *embed* information. When you link information, the link between source and destination documents is *dynamic*; that is, any change you make in the source document is reflected in the destination document. To link an object, follow the copy/paste procedure, except select *Paste Special* in the *Edit* menu, then choose the *Paste Link* option button in the dialog box.

The capabilities of object linking are demonstrated in Figure 2-18. Linking doesn't actually place the object into the destination document—it places a pointer to the source document (a disk-based file). In linking, the object is saved as a separate file from the source document. Linking is helpful when the object is used in several destination documents because when you change the source, it is updated in all documents to which it is linked.

OLE Object Embedding

When you embed information, you insert the actual object, not just a pointer. Whereas linking is dynamic, embedding is not. To embed an object, choose the *Paste* option button in the *Paste Special* dialog box. You can change the source within the destination document, but the original (if there is one) is unchanged. A source document is not required in object embedding.

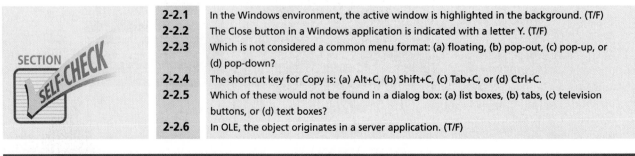

2-2.1	In the Windows environment, the active window is highlighted in the background. (T/F)	
2-2.2	The Close button in a Windows application is indicated with a letter Y. (T/F)	
2-2.3	Which is not considered a common menu format: (a) floating, (b) pop-out, (c) pop-up, or (d) pop-down?	
2-2.4	The shortcut key for Copy is: (a) Alt+C, (b) Shift+C, (c) Tab+C, or (d) Ctrl+C.	
2-2.5	Which of these would not be found in a dialog box: (a) list boxes, (b) tabs, (c) television buttons, or (d) text boxes?	
2-2.6	In OLE, the object originates in a server application. (T/F)	

FIGURE 2–17

COPY AND PASTE VIA THE CLIPBOARD
This walkthrough demonstrates the procedure for transferring information among multiple Windows applications: Paint (a paint program), Word (a word processing program), and an Internet-based encyclopedia. In the example, the Eiffel Tower image in a Paint document is marked and copied (to the Clipboard), then pasted to a Word document. Supporting text in the online *Encarta Encyclopedia* is marked and copied to the same Word document via the Clipboard.

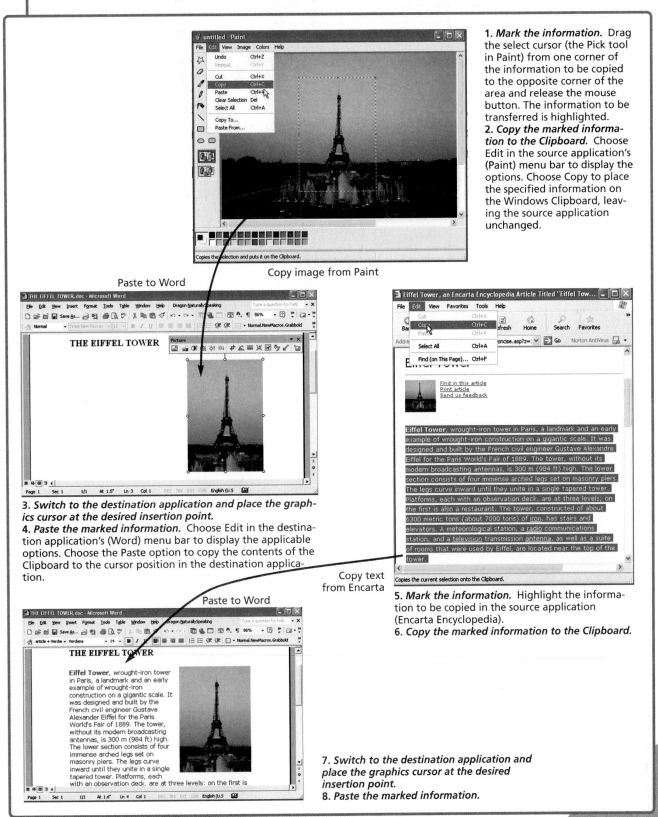

1. *Mark the information.* Drag the select cursor (the Pick tool in Paint) from one corner of the information to be copied to the opposite corner of the area and release the mouse button. The information to be transferred is highlighted.
2. *Copy the marked information to the Clipboard.* Choose Edit in the source application's (Paint) menu bar to display the options. Choose Copy to place the specified information on the Windows Clipboard, leaving the source application unchanged.

Copy image from Paint

Paste to Word

3. *Switch to the destination application and place the graphics cursor at the desired insertion point.*
4. *Paste the marked information.* Choose Edit in the destination application's (Word) menu bar to display the applicable options. Choose the Paste option to copy the contents of the Clipboard to the cursor position in the destination application.

Copy text from Encarta

5. *Mark the information.* Highlight the information to be copied in the source application (Encarta Encyclopedia).
6. *Copy the marked information to the Clipboard.*

Paste to Word

7. *Switch to the destination application and place the graphics cursor at the desired insertion point.*
8. *Paste the marked information.*

FIGURE 2-18 **OBJECT LINKING**
The map image is linked to a Word document (left) to create a compound document.
The original object did not include the school image or the stop sign image. The image
was modified in *Microsoft Visio* (middle) within the context of the Word document, and
the linked object was updated automatically in Word (right).

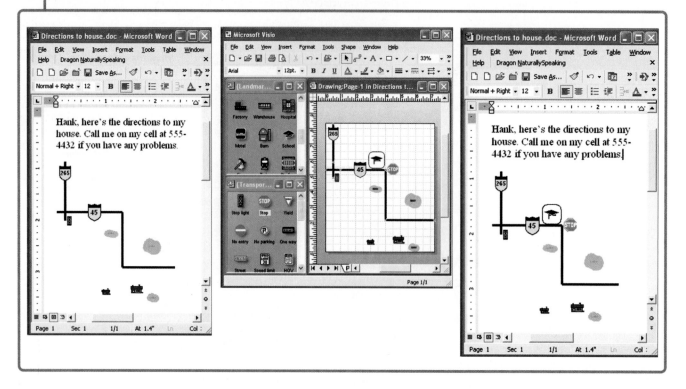

2-3 Productivity Software: The Software Suite

Software suites, such as Microsoft Office, Corel WordPerfect Office, and Lotus SmartSuite, are introduced in Chapter 1. These suites are made up of several complementary applications that can
include word processing, presentation, spreadsheet, database, personal information management,
desktop publishing, and communications (Internet-related) software. Most new PCs are sold with a
full or partial software suite installed on the system. This section is designed to give you an overview
of the general functionality and capabilities of the first five on this list.

WORD PROCESSING: THE MOST POPULAR PRODUCTIVITY APPLICATION

At work, at home, at school, and even during leisure activities, we spend much of our time writing.
Whether an e-mail, a party announcement, a report, a diary entry, or a newsletter, all can be made easier and more presentable through the use of word processing software.

Word Processing Concepts and Features

Word processing software lets us create, edit (revise), and format documents in preparation for output. Output can be a document that is printed, displayed on a monitor, faxed, e-mailed, or, perhaps,
posted to the Internet for worldwide access.

Word processing is the perfect example of how automation can be used to increase productivity
and foster creativity. It reduces the effort you must devote to the routine aspects of writing so you can
focus your attention on its creative aspects. For example, a *spelling checker* checks your grammar and
spelling, an *online thesaurus* helps you find the right word, and a *grammar and style checker* highlights
grammatical concerns.

Creating a Document

You'll probably learn the process and techniques of preparing a word processing document in a lab or,
perhaps, via interactive computer-based training. To create an original document, such as a résumé

(see Figure 2-19), you simply begin entering text from the keyboard and, as needed, enter formatting commands that enhance the appearance of the document when it is printed or displayed (spacing, italics, and so on). You can insert images, such as the photo in Figure 2-19, then resize and/or reposition them anywhere within the word processing document. Once you are satisfied with the content and appearance of the document, you are ready to print, send, or display it.

Formatting a Document

You format a word processing document by specifying what you wish the general appearance of the document to be when it is printed. Typically, the preset format, or *default settings,* fit most word processing applications. For example, the size of the output document is set at letter size ($8\frac{1}{2}$ by 11 inches); the left, right, top, and bottom margins are set at 1 inch; tabs are set every $\frac{1}{2}$ inch; and line spacing is set at 6 lines per inch. The default font might be 12 point Times New Roman. Times New Roman is one of dozens of available **typefaces** you can use in documents. A typeface refers to a set of characters of a particular design (Courier, Futura Book, Old English, and so on are typefaces). A **font** is described by its typeface, its height in points (8, 10, 14, 24, and so on; there are 72 points to the inch), and its presentation attribute (regular, **bold**, *italic,* underline, and so on).

What You Can Do with Word Processing: The Features Package

Typically, text is entered in a word processing or other type of document via *keyboard* or *speech recognition.* In speech recognition, you simply speak into a microphone and the words are interpreted by speech-recognition software and entered in the document. Word processing packages are **WYSIWYG** (pronounced "*WIZ e wig*"), an acronym for "What you see is what you get." This means that what you do to a document, whether entering text or inserting an image, is reflected on the screen showing you what the document will look like when it is printed. Word processing software has many features that help you create exactly what you want. The specifics of these features are left to the hands-on lab, but Figure 2-20 gives you a good visual summary of word processing features and capabilities. All word processing programs come with a healthy supply of prepackaged electronic images called **clip art.**

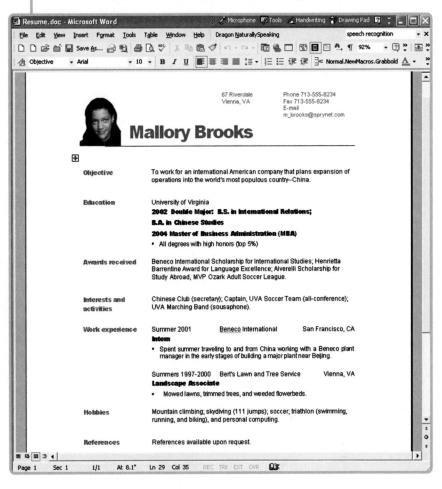

Putting Word Processing to Work

Word processing is extremely versatile, offering you a wide range of capabilities. Here are a few more applications for word processing. You will find many more as you gain experience with this, the most used of all software applications.

- *Merging documents with a database.* Word processing software allows you to merge data in a database with the text of a document. The most common use of this capability is the *mail-merge* feature. The mail-merge example is a good illustration of the use of **boilerplate** text. Boilerplate is existing text that can be reused and customized for a variety of word processing applications.

- *Electronic documents.* Many companies are opting to put their reference materials in electronic, rather than printed, documents. Electronic versions of product catalogs, procedures manuals, personnel handbooks, and so on are now common in the business community. They are easier to create, maintain, and distribute.
- *Creating Web pages.* If you can create a word processing document, you can create a Web page on the Internet. Any word processing document can be saved in Web page format.

FIGURE 2–20

WORD PROCESSING FEATURES OVERVIEW

This word processing document illustrates features common to most word processing software. Note that you can create special effects with the *drawing tool* and *border* features. The *watermark* feature lets you add a drawing, a company logo, headline-sized text (such as the "PRIORITY" in this example), or any image behind the printed document text. In the electronic world, documents are "networked" with hyperlinks (references to different sections of an electronic document or to other related electronic documents on the local computer or on the Internet). Even the *callouts,* which label the features, are a word processing feature. Not shown is the *editing* feature that lets you add editorial remarks and make corrections to an original document. This feature is helpful when several people review a document prior to publication.

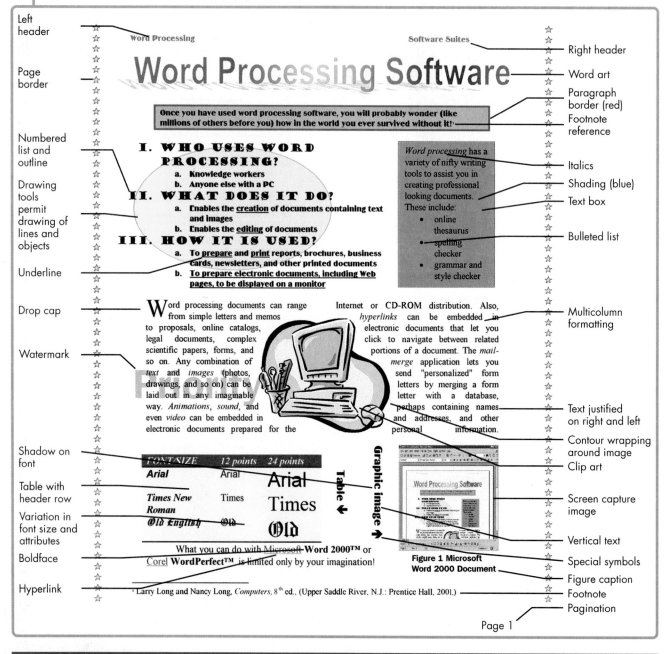

Word Processing versus Desktop Publishing Software

Word processing can handle most document generation tasks, but those organizations that need to produce complicated documents to be printed professionally use desktop publishing software. With desktop publishing software you can create *camera-ready documents* (ready to be printed professionally) such as newsletters, brochures, user manuals, pamphlets, flyers, restaurant menus, periodicals, greeting cards, graduation certificates, and thousands of other printed and published items. The flyer for a school fund-raiser in Figure 2-21 was produced with Microsoft Publisher. The image highlighting the various objects illustrates how desktop publishing documents are composed of rectangular *frames*, text, and images that can be resized and repositioned to meet layout needs. In contrast to word processing, wherein the emphasis is on inserted objects within the running text, desktop publishing emphasizes the overall *document composition*. Various types of *frames* (objects) are pulled together and laid out on a page.

PRESENTATION SOFTWARE: PUTTING ON THE SHOW

Many studies confirm that people who use *presentation software* to create presentations are perceived as being better prepared and more professional than those who do not. Judicious use of this software can help you persuade people to adopt a particular point of view, whether at the lectern or the pulpit. Typically, presentation software is used in conjunction with an LCD projector that projects images onto a screen for all to see.

Presentation software lets you create highly stylized images for group presentations of any kind, to create self-running slide shows for PC-based information displays at trade shows, for class lectures (offline or online), and any other situation that requires the presentation of organized, visual information (see Figure 2-22). The software, such as Microsoft PowerPoint, gives you a rich assortment of tools to help you create a variety of charts, graphs, and images and to help you make the presentation.

Follow these steps to prepare a presentation using presentation software.

1. *Select a template.* Presentation software comes with many handy **templates.** Generically, a template is a form, mold, or pattern used as a guide to making something. All productivity software packages have templates to give us a leg up when creating documents. Templates

FIGURE 2–21 **DESKTOP PUBLISHING**
Word processing software is sufficient for most home and business document preparation tasks, but desktop publishing software may be needed for the more sophisticated tasks that require camera-ready copy for professional printing jobs.

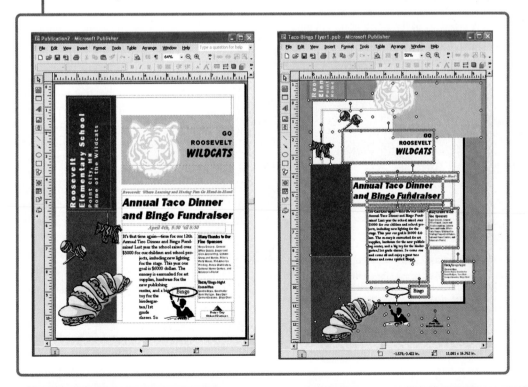

FIGURE 2-22 **POWERPOINT SLIDE SORTER VIEW**
Microsoft PowerPoint helps you prepare and present slides for presentations. PowerPoint has a variety of slide templates from which you can choose. You can work with the entire presentation or with a single chart (see Figure 2-23). Slides are easily rearranged by simply dragging a slide to a new position.

FIGURE 2-23 **POWERPOINT TRI-PANE VIEW**
The PowerPoint tri-pane view shows the *slide, outline,* and *notes* so you can work with all the elements of the presentation at once.

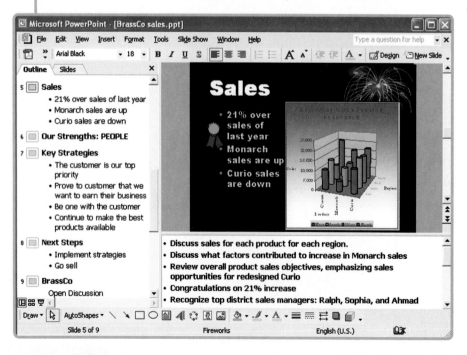

can be real time-savers. (In word processing, there are templates for business letters, faxes, memos, reports, and so on.) PowerPoint, the industry standard for presentation software, has two types of templates: *design templates* and *content templates.* Design templates are predesigned formats and complementary color schemes with preselected background images you can apply to any content material (the outline) to give your slides a professional, customized appearance. A **slide** is one of the images to be displayed. A design template was used to create the presentation "look" shown in Figure 2-22. Content templates go one step further and suggest content for specific subjects (for example, business plan, project overview, employee orientation, and many others).

2. *Create an outline for the presentation.* PowerPoint's tri-pane view lets you view the *slide, outline,* and *notes* at the same time (see Figure 2-23). This view makes it easy to add new slides, edit text, and enter notes while creating a presentation. The outline feature helps you organize your presentation material into a multilevel outline. What you include in the outline is automatically formatted into slides based on the selected design template. In the slides, the main points (first-level headings in the outline) become slide titles and their subordinate items become subheadings and subpoints. Each software package produces its own unique files. However, with so much overlap in functionality between popular productivity software, files can be imported from one type of software to another. When we **import** a file, we convert it from its foreign format to a format that is compatible with the current program. For example, people frequently import Microsoft Word outlines into the PowerPoint outline feature. Microsoft Excel spreadsheets can be imported directly into the PowerPoint chart feature. When we **export** a file, we convert a file in the current program to a format that can be read directly by another program.

3. *Compile and create other nontext resources.* Text alone, no matter how well formatted, may fall short of what is needed for a quality presentation. A good slide presentation will include

some or all of the following: *photo images, charts* and *graphs,* original *drawings,* a variety of eye-catching *clip art, audio clips,* and even *full-motion video* captured with a digital camera. Obviously, not all presentations will comprise every capability, but at a minimum, there is clip art available for every presentation situation (for example, the blue ribbon in Figure 2-23). It's a good idea to use audio to introduce or highlight critical points. For example, a slide on a new employee bonus plan can be introduced with the *ka-ching* sound of a cash register.

With presentation software, you can create a variety of charts from data imported from a spreadsheet or a database, or you can enter the data into a PowerPoint table. Usually the data needed to produce a graph already exist in a spreadsheet or a database. Among the most popular charts are *pie charts* and *bar charts.* You have many other charting options, including *line charts, bubble charts, range charts, doughnut charts,* and *area charts,* each of which can be presented in two or three dimensions and annotated with *titles, labels,* and *legends.*

Besides traditional business charts, presentation software allows you to prepare *organization charts* showing the hierarchical structure of an organization (see Figure 2-24) and *maps* showing demographic information in context with geographic location.

4. *Integrate resources.* Once all text and visual resources have been compiled, it is time to integrate them into a visually appealing presentation. Typically, people work from the slides generated from the outline, inserting clip art, charts, and so on as needed. Some slides may include only a title and images, such as the sixth slide in Figure 2-22. The PowerPoint *slide sorter* view gives you an overview of the presentation. The slide sorter shows thumbnail images to enable the viewing of all or much of a presentation in sequence on a single screen. A **thumbnail** is a miniature display of an image or perhaps a page (document or Web). The slide sorter makes it easy to add or delete slides and to rearrange them to meet presentation needs.

5. *Add special effects.* With PowerPoint, you can give the audience a little candy for the eyes and ears. For example, the current graph or image can be made to *fade out* (dissolve to a blank screen) while the text is fading in. An applause sound can be played when a particular image or element is displayed. PowerPoint offers a variety of transitions and sounds, each of which adds an aura of professionalism while helping to hold the audience's attention. Also, text and objects can be animated. For example, text and objects can be made to fly in from the perimeter of the screen a word or a letter at a time.

6. *Add notes.* Each slide in a presentation can have corresponding notes (see Figure 2-23). Frequently, people make notes for themselves to help them remember to make key points during a presentation.

7. *Deliver the presentation.* A PC-based presentation can be made to an individual or a small group on a single PC, or it can be projected onto a large screen. Or, it can be fashioned as a self-running information center where screens are preset to display in a timed sequence. Or, the entire presentation can be saved as Web pages and posted to the Internet.

FIGURE 2-24

POWERPOINT ORGANIZATION CHART
PowerPoint 2002, shown here, has new collaboration and animation features that PowerPoint users will find inviting.

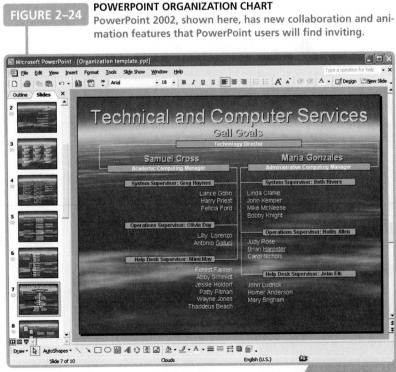

Whether you're preparing a report, a speech, a newsletter, or any other form of business, academic, or personal communication, it pays—immediately and over the long term—to take full advantage of presentation software.

SPREADSHEET SOFTWARE: THE MAGIC MATRIX

A spreadsheet is simply a grid for entering rows and columns of data. The typical home or office has scores of applications for organizing tabular information. Instructors' grade books are good uses for spreadsheet software, with student names labeling the rows, quizzes labeling the columns,

FIGURE 2–25 Spreadsheet in Space
On this space walk, Astronauts Steven L. Smith and John M. Grunsfeld are replacing gyroscopes contained inside the Hubble Space Telescope. The typical space shuttle is filled with notebook PCs. Astronauts rely heavily on spreadsheet software to organize and analyze data collected from a variety of activities.

Courtesy of NASA

and scores being the entries. Think of anything that has rows and columns of data and you have identified an application for spreadsheet software: income (profit-and-loss) statements, personnel profiles, demographic data, home inventories, and budget summaries, just to mention a few (see Figure 2-25).

Spreadsheet Concepts and Features

We will use the March sales summary, shown in Figure 2-26, to demonstrate spreadsheet concepts. The national sales manager for BrassCo Enterprises, a manufacturer of an upscale line of brass coat hanger products (the Crown, the Monarch, and the Curio), compiles monthly sales summaries using a spreadsheet software template. The template, simply a spreadsheet model, contains the layout and formulas needed to produce the summary illustrated in Figure 2-26. The manager entered only the data for the current month (the sales amounts for each salesperson for March) and the spreadsheet template performed all of the necessary calculations (the totals and the commissions).

Organization: Rows and Columns

Spreadsheets are organized in a tabular structure with rows and columns. The intersection of a particular row and column designates a **cell**. As you can see in Figure 2-26, the rows are numbered, and the columns are lettered.

Data are entered and stored in a cell. During operations, data are referred to by their **cell address**, which identifies the location of a cell in the spreadsheet by its column and row, with the column designator first. For example, in the monthly sales summary of Figure 2-26, C4 is the address of the column heading for product Crown, and D5 is the address of the total amount of Monarch sales for R. Rosco ($30,400).

In the spreadsheet work area (the rows and columns), sometimes called a *worksheet*, a movable highlighted area "points" to the *current cell*. The current cell is highlighted with either a different background color or a dark border (see the dark border around cell A1, the current cell, in the first example in Figure 2-26). This highlighted area, called the **pointer,** can be moved around the spreadsheet with the arrow keys or the mouse. The address and content of the current cell are displayed in the cell content portion of the spreadsheet above the work area (sometimes called the *formula bar*). The content or value resulting from a formula of each cell is shown in the spreadsheet work area.

Spreadsheets can be large, sometimes thousands of rows and hundreds of columns. When document content is more than can be displayed in a window, you can simply scroll vertically or horizontally through the spreadsheet.

Ranges: Groups of Cells

Many spreadsheet operations ask you to designate a **range** of cells. These are highlighted in Figure 2-26: *cell range* (a single cell); *column range* (all or part of a column of adjacent cells); *row range;* and *block range* (a rectangular group of cells). A particular range is indicated by the addresses of the endpoint cells separated by a colon, such as the row range C14:E14.

Cell Entries

To make an entry in the spreadsheet, simply move the pointer to the appropriate cell, and key in the data. The major types of entries are *label* entry, *numeric* entry, and *formula* entry shown in Figure 2-26. A label entry may be a word or a phrase that occupies a particular cell. In Figure 2-26, "NAME" in cell A4 is a label entry, as is "COMMISSION" in G4.

In Figure 2-26, the dollar sales values in the range C5:E10 are *numeric*. The dollar sales values in the ranges F5:G10 and C12:G12 are results of *formulas*. Cell F5 contains a formula, but it is the numeric result (for example, 61150 in Figure 2-26) that is displayed in the spreadsheet work area. With the pointer positioned at F5, the formula appears in the cell contents box. The formula value in F5 computes the total sales made by the salesperson in row 5 for all three products (that is, total sales is =C5+D5+E5). The actual numeric value appears in the spreadsheet work area (see Figure 2-26).

Spreadsheet formulas use standard notation for **arithmetic operators:** + (add), − (subtract), * (multiply), / (divide), ^ (raise to a power, or *exponentiation*). In Microsoft Excel, formulas begin with an equals sign (=). The formula in F5 computes the total sales for R. Rosco. The range F6:F10 contains similar formulas that apply to their respective rows (=C6+D6+E6, =C7+D7+E7, and so on). For example, the formula in F6 computes the total sales for G. Mann. The last image in Figure 2-26 provides a summary of the actual unformatted cell contents for all cells.

FIGURE 2-26   SPREADSHEET TEMPLATE SHOWING A MONTHLY SALES SUMMARY

Spreadsheets can be formatted to better portray the information (for example, the use of color, font size, and shading). Also, note that the spreadsheet drawing tool lets you draw lines and highlight elements of the spreadsheet. The red markings are included here to help illustrate spreadsheet concepts.

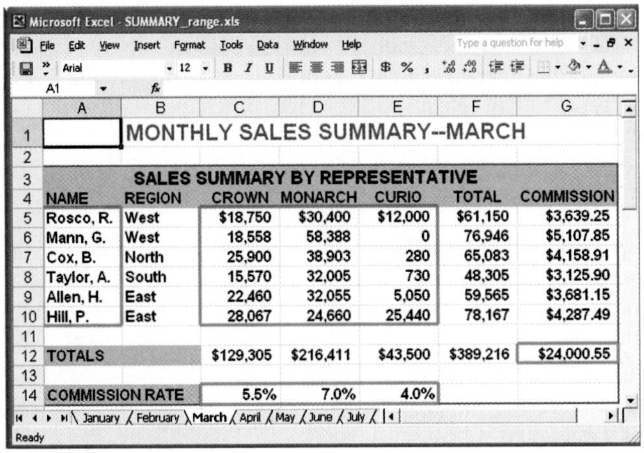

SPREADSHEET RANGES

The highlighted cells in this spreadsheet illustrate the four types of ranges: cell (G12), column (A5:A10), row (C14:E14), and block (C5:E10).

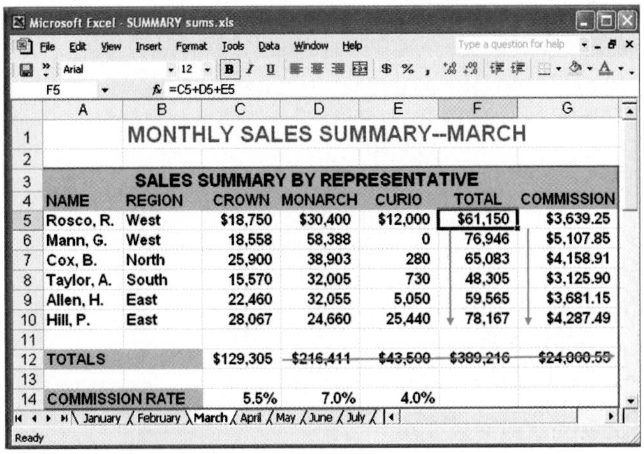

COPYING FORMULAS

The actual content of F5 is the formula in the cell contents box (=C5+D5+E5). The result of the formula (61150) appears in the spreadsheet at F5, formatted as currency ($61,150). In creating the spreadsheet template for the monthly sales summary, the national sales manager for BrassCo entered only three formulas (see cell contents summary below).

- The formula in F5 to sum the product sales for each salesperson was copied to the range F6:F10.
- The formula in G5: =$C$14*C5+$D$14*D5+$E$14*E5 to compute the commission for each salesperson was copied to the range G6:G10.
- The formula in C12: =SUM(C5:C10) to sum the sales for each product was copied to the range D12:G12.

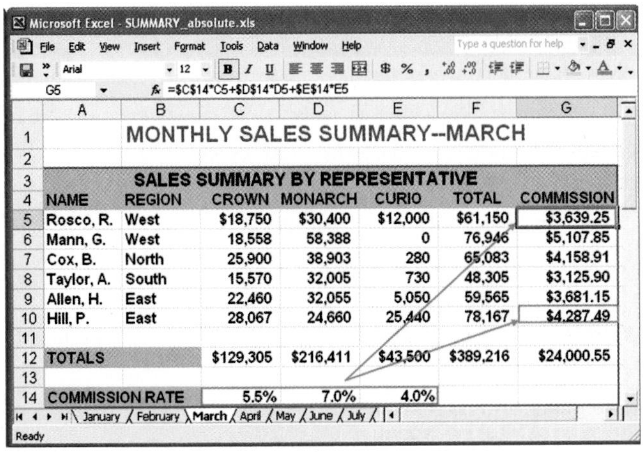

COPYING FORMULAS THAT INCLUDE ABSOLUTE CELL ADDRESSES

Each of the commission computation formulas in the range G5:G10 has the same multipliers—the commission rates in the range C14:E14. Because the *relative* positions between the commission formulas in G5:G10 and the commission rates in C14:E14 vary from row to row, the commission rates are entered as *absolute* cell addresses. If the contents of a cell containing a formula are copied to another cell, the relative cell addresses in the copied formula are revised to reflect the new position (perhaps a new row), but the absolute cell addresses are unchanged. Notice in the cell contents summary below how the absolute addresses ($C$14, $D$14, and $E$14) in the copied formulas (G6:G10) remained the same in each formula and the relative addresses were revised to reflect the applicable row. If a dollar sign precedes the letter and/or number in a cell address, such as $C$14, the column and/or row reference is absolute.

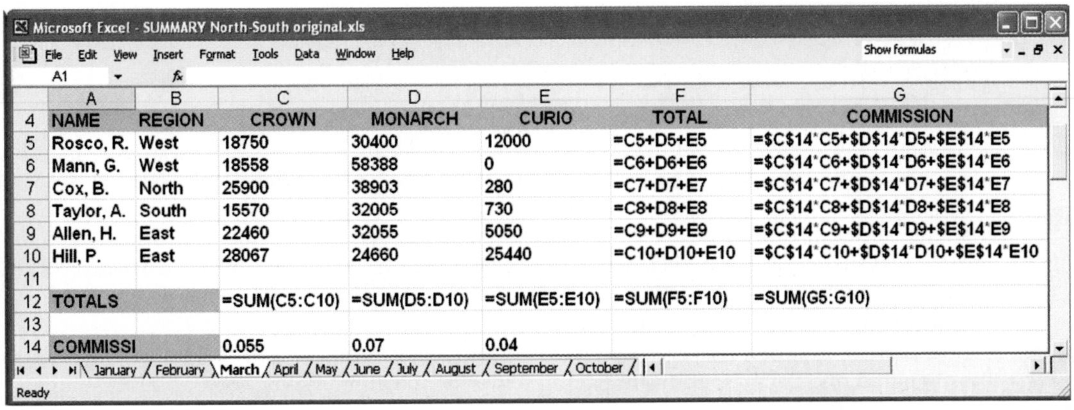

CELL CONTENTS SUMMARY

This cell contents summary illustrates the actual content of the cells in the above spreadsheet. To switch between displaying formulas and their values, press Ctrl+` (grave accent).

2-3: Productivity Software: The Software Suite   105

FIGURE 2-27

SPREADSHEET GRAPHS
Microsoft Excel, shown here, makes it easier to link data to Internet-based applications. Regional income for each of the three products (range C4:E7) are graphically illustrated in this three-dimensional bar chart.

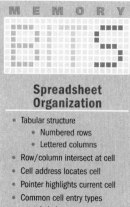

Microsoft Excel - Income Summary.xls

F4 ▼ =SUM(C4:E4)

BRASSCO INCOME SUMMARY BY PRODUCT AND REGION

		Crown	Monarch	Curio	TOTAL
	East	10,200	5,350	12,440	$27,990
	South	13,235	9,855	15,786	$38,876
	West	8,140	10,202	14,915	$66,866
	North	20,500	15,405	16,972	$52,877
	TOTAL	$52,075	$40,812	$60,113	$153,000

BRASSCO INCOME BY REGION BY PRODUCT

2002 / 2003 / 2004

Ready

Spreadsheets offer users a variety of predefined operations called **functions.** To use a function, simply enter the desired function name and enter one or more arguments. The **argument,** which is placed in parentheses, identifies the data to be operated on. The "compute the sum" function, SUM, in C12 in Figure 2-26 (see cell contents summary) adds the numbers in the range C5:C10 and displays the result in C12. Other spreadsheet functions include trigonometric functions, square roots, comparisons of values, manipulations of strings of data, computation of net present value and internal rate of return, and a variety of techniques for statistical analysis.

Spreadsheet Graphics

Spreadsheet packages let you generate a variety of charts from spreadsheet data. The spreadsheet template in Figure 2-27 presents an Income Summary by Product and Region for BrassCo. The income figures for each region (the range C4:E7) are plotted by product in a three-dimensional bar chart. To put spreadsheet data into a chart, the BrassCo VP needed only to respond to a series of prompts from the spreadsheet program. The first prompt asked him to select the type of graph to be generated. He then identified the source of the data, entered labels and titles, and so on. The resulting graph permits him to better understand the regional distribution of income by product.

DATABASE SOFTWARE: A DYNAMIC DATA TOOL

Hundreds and maybe even thousands of databases contain information about you. The typical knowledge worker interacts with databases all day long. These are good reasons to learn more about databases. Database software lets you enter, organize, and retrieve stored data. With Microsoft Access, featured here, and other database software packages you can:

- Create and maintain a database (add, delete, and revise records)

- Extract and list information that meets certain conditions

- Make inquiries (for example, "What is the total amount owed by all customers in Alabama?")

- Sort records in ascending or descending sequence by key fields (for example, alphabetical by last name)

- Generate formatted reports with subtotals and totals

These are the basic features. They have other features as well, including spreadsheet-type computations, presentation graphics, and programming.

Database Software and Spreadsheet Software: What's the Difference?

Both database and spreadsheet software packages let you work with data as rows and columns in a spreadsheet and as records in a database. Spreadsheet software gives you greater flexibility in the manipulation of rows and columns of data. Everything relating to spreadsheet-based data is easier with spreadsheet software—creating formulas, generating charts, what-if analysis (for example, "What if revenue increases by 10% next year?"), and so on. Database software offers greater flexibility in the organization and management of records within a database. Everything relating to a database is easier with database software—queries (requests for information), data entry, linking databases, report generation, programming to create information systems, and so on.

In short, spreadsheet packages are great number crunchers and are very helpful for small database applications. Database software packages may be too cumbersome for any serious number crunching, but they are terrific for creating any kind of personal or business information system.

MEMORY

Spreadsheet Organization

- Tabular structure
  - Numbered rows
  - Lettered columns
- Row/column intersect at cell
- Cell address locates cell
- Pointer highlights current cell
- Common cell entry types
  - Label
  - Numeric
  - Formula

Database Concepts and Features

The concepts and features of database software packages are very similar. The Microsoft Access example in this section is generally applicable to all database software.

Creating a Database with Database Software

In a database, related *fields,* such as student, course ID, and major, are grouped to form *records* (for example, a student record in the STUDENTS table in Figure 2-28). PC-based database packages use the *relational* approach to database management, which organizes data into *tables* in which a *row* is equivalent to a *record* that contains *fields* (set apart by columns). As you can see, the database *table* is conceptually the same as a *file*. One or more tables comprise a **relational database,** which refers to all of the tables in the database and the relationships between them.

The best way to explain the concepts of database software is by example. The chairperson of the Computer Information Systems (CIS) department uses Microsoft Access to help her with record-keeping tasks and to provide valuable information. She has created an education database with two tables: COURSE and STUDENT (see Figure 2-28). The COURSE table contains a record for each course offered in the CIS Department. Each record (row) in the COURSE table contains the following fields:

- COURSE ID
- COURSE TITLE
- TYPE of course (lecture, lab, or lecture/lab)
- INSTRUCTOR name
- CREDIT hours awarded for completion of course

The STUDENT table contains a record for each student who is enrolled in or has taken a CIS course. The table has only a few students to enable ease of demonstration of concepts, but it works just the same with hundreds of students. Each record contains the following fields:

- STUDENT (name of student; last name first)
- COURSE ID (provides a link to the COURSE table)
- MAJOR
- DATE ENROLLED
- STATUS (course status: incomplete [I], withdrew [W], or a grade [A, B, C, D, E, or F])

No single field in the STUDENT table uniquely identifies each record. However, the combined STUDENT and COURSE ID fields do identify each record. Therefore, to access a particular record in the STUDENT table, the chairperson must specify both the STUDENT and COURSE ID (for example, Targa, Phil, CIS 330). The COURSE and STUDENT tables can be linked because they have the COURSE ID field in common.

The first thing you do to set up a database table is to specify its structure by identifying the characteristics of each field in it. This structuring is done interactively, with the system prompting you to enter the field name, the field type, and so on. For example, in the first row of Figure 2-29

FIGURE 2–28

EDUCATION DATABASE: COURSE TABLE AND STUDENT TABLE
The Microsoft Access Education database is comprised of these two tables. The COURSE table contains a record for each course offered by the Computer Information Systems Department. The STUDENT table contains a record for each student who is enrolled in or has taken a course. The COURSE ID field links the two tables.

COURSE : Table

	COURSE ID	COURSE TITLE	TYPE	INSTRUCTOR	CREDIT
▶	CIS 100	Telecommunications	lecture	Babbage	3
	CIS 101	Database Management	lecture/lab	Babbage	2
	CIS 110	Intranets and Extranets	lab	Gates	3
	CIS 150	Mgt. Info. Systems	lecture	Eckert	3
	CIS 202	Visual Basic Programming	lecture/lab	Wang	4
	CIS 310	Network Administration	lecture	Gates	4
	CIS 320	Desktop Publishing	lab	Eckert	3
	CIS 330	Information Retrieval	lecture/lab	Wang	3
	CIS 350	Web Site Design	lab	Gates	1
	CIS 401	Local Area Networks	lecture/lab	Wang	3

Record: 1 of 10

	STUDENT	COURSE ID	MAJOR	DATE ENROLLED	STATUS
▶	Adler, Phyllis	CIS 401	Marketing	2/10/2004	W
	Austin, Jill	CIS 330	Finance	1/12/2003	I
	Austin, Jill	CIS 401	Finance	1/12/2004	C
	Bell, Jim	CIS 330	Marketing	1/12/2004	A
	Day, Elizabeth	CIS 310	Accounting	3/18/2003	B
	Fitz, Paula	CIS 310	Finance	4/4/2003	A
	Johnson, Charles	CIS 100	Marketing	1/10/2003	W
	Klein, Ellen	CIS 100	Accounting	1/10/2003	C
	Massey, Rose	CIS 101	Management	2/14/2003	I
	Mendez, Carlos	CIS 310	Accounting	1/20/2004	A
	Mendez, Carlos	CIS 150	Accounting	1/15/2003	I
	Targa, Phil	CIS 330	Finance	1/12/2004	B
	Targa, Phil	CIS 100	Finance	1/4/2003	B

Record: 1 of 13

FIGURE 2–29

STRUCTURE OF THE EDUCATION DATABASE
This display shows the structure of the COURSE and STUDENT tables of the education database of Figure 2-28. The COURSE record (left) has four text fields and one number field. The STUDENT record has four text fields and one date/time field.

COURSE : Table

Field Name	Data Type
COURSE ID	Text
COURSE TITLE	Text
TYPE	Text
INSTRUCTOR	Text
CREDIT	Number

Field Properties

General | Lookup

Field Size   7

STUDENT : Table

Field Name	Data Type
COURSE ID	Text
STUDENT	Text
MAJOR	Text
DATE ENROLLED	Date/Time
STATUS	Text

Field Properties

General | Lookup

Field Size   7

FIGURE 2–30

**DATA ENTRY
SCREEN FORMAT**
The screen format for entering, editing, and adding records to the COURSE table is illustrated.

the *field name* is COURSE ID; the *data type* is "text"; and the *field size,* or field length, is seven positions. The field names for the COURSE and STUDENT tables are listed at the top of each table in Figure 2-28 (COURSE ID, COURSE TITLE, TYPE, and so on). Content for a *text* field can be a single word or any **alphanumeric** (numbers, letters, and special characters) phrase. For *number* field types, you can specify the number of decimal positions that you wish to have displayed (none in the example because credit hours are whole numbers).

Once you have defined the structure of the database table, you are ready to enter the data. The best way to enter data is to create a *screen format* that allows convenient data entry. The data entry screen format is analogous to a hard-copy form that contains labels and blank lines for you to fill in (for example, a medical questionnaire). Data are entered and edited (added, deleted, or revised) one record at a time with database software, just as they are on hard-copy forms. Figure 2-30 shows the data entry screen format for the COURSE table.

COURSE Data Entry

COURSE ID	CIS 100
COURSE TITLE	Telecommunications
TYPE	lecture
INSTRUCTOR	Babbage
CREDIT	3

Record: 1 of 10

FIGURE 2–31 QUERY BY EXAMPLE

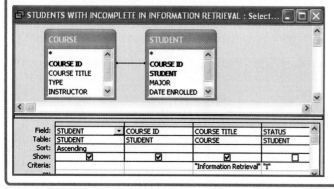

QBE: ONE CONDITION
The department chairperson wanted a listing of all students taking courses from Professor Wang. She requested a list of all courses that meet the condition INSTRUCTOR=*Wang* (see Figure 2-28). All records that meet this condition (see criteria query box shown here) are displayed in the answer window in ascending alphabetical order by student name. She selected only three fields to be included in the results display (checked boxes in figure). Notice that the query needed information from both tables.

QBE: USING LOGICAL OPERATORS
To produce the results shown here, the department chairperson set up her query by example to select only those courses that include a lab; that is, the criteria is (course) TYPE=*lab* OR *lecture/lab* (see Figure 2-28). The OR operator can be applied between fields (see example) or within fields. Only the COURSE table is needed for the query.

QBE: TWO CONDITIONS
The query in this example is set up to list those students who have an incomplete (STATUS=*I*) in the course entitled Information Retrieval (COURSE ID=*Information Retrieval*). The query requires the use of both tables in the database.

Query by Example

Database software also lets you retrieve, view, and print records based on **query by example.** In query by example, you set conditions for the selection of records by composing one or more example *relational expressions.* A relational expression normally compares one or more field names to numbers or character strings using the **relational operators** (= [equal to], > [greater than], < [less than], and combinations of these operators). Several conditions can be combined with **logical operators** (*AND, OR,* and *NOT*). Figure 2-31 demonstrates three types of query by example—one condition, using logical operators, and two conditions.

Sorting: Rearranging Records

The records in a database table also can be sorted for display in a variety of formats. For example, the COURSE table in Figure 2-28 has been sorted and is displayed in ascending order by COURSE ID. To obtain this sequencing of the database records, the department chairperson selected COURSE ID as the *key field* and *ascending* (versus descending) as the sort order. To get a presentation of the COURSE table sorted by COURSE ID within INSTRUCTOR, she needs to identify a *primary sort field* and a *secondary sort field.* Secondary sort fields are helpful when duplicates exist in the primary sort field (for example, there are three records for INSTRUCTOR=Gates). She selects INSTRUCTOR as the primary sort field, but she wants the courses offered by each INSTRUCTOR to be listed in ascending order by COURSE ID (see Figure 2-32).

FIGURE 2-32

COURSE TABLE SORTED BY COURSE ID WITHIN INSTRUCTOR
This display is the result of a sort operation on the COURSE table with the INSTRUCTOR field as the primary sort field and the COURSE ID field as the secondary sort field. Notice that the COURSE ID field entries are in alphabetical order by instructor; that is, the three "Gates" records are in sequence by COURSE ID (CIS 110, CIS 310, and CIS 350).

INSTRUCTOR	COURSE ID	COURSE TITLE	TYPE	CREDIT
Babbage	CIS 100	Telecommunications	lecture	3
Babbage	CIS 101	Database Management	lecture/lab	2
Eckert	CIS 150	Mgt. Info. Systems	lecture	3
Eckert	CIS 320	Desktop Publishing	lab	3
Gates	CIS 110	Intranets and Extranets	lab	3
Gates	CIS 310	Network Administration	lecture	4
Gates	CIS 350	Web Site Design	lab	1
Wang	CIS 202	Visual Basic Programming	lecture/lab	4
Wang	CIS 330	Information Retrieval	lecture/lab	3
Wang	CIS 401	Local Area Networks	lecture/lab	3

Generating Reports

A database is a source of information, and database software helps you get the information you need. A *report* is the presentation of information derived from one or more databases. The simple listings of selected and ordered records in Figure 2-31 are "quick and dirty" reports. Such reports are the bread and butter of database capabilities and can be easily copied or imported into word processing or desktop publishing documents.

Database software allows you to create customized reports and to design their *layout.* This design capability allows you to change spacing and to include titles, subtitles, column headings, separation lines, and other elements that make a report more readable. Managers often use this capability to generate periodic reports, such as the Course Status Summary report shown in Figure 2-33.

Database: The Next Step

The database capabilities illustrated and discussed in this section merely "scratch the surface" of the potential

FIGURE 2-33

CUSTOMIZED REPORT
To obtain this Course Status Summary report, the CIS Department chairperson needed both the COURSE and STUDENT tables of Figure 2-28 from the education database.

COURSE STATUS SUMMARY

INSTRUCTOR	STUDENT	COURSE ID	COURSE TITLE	STATUS
Babbage				
	Johnson, Charles	CIS 100	Telecommunications	W
	Klein, Ellen	CIS 100	Telecommunications	C
	Targa, Phil	CIS 100	Telecommunications	B
	Massey, Rose	CIS 101	Database Management	I
Eckert				
	Mendez, Carlos	CIS 150	Mgt. Info. Systems	I
Gates				
	Day, Elizabeth	CIS 310	Network Administration	B
	Fitz, Paula	CIS 310	Network Administration	A
	Mendez, Carlos	CIS 310	Network Administration	A
Wang				
	Austin, Jill	CIS 330	Information Retrieval	I
	Bell, Jim	CIS 330	Information Retrieval	A
	Targa, Phil	CIS 330	Information Retrieval	B
	Adler, Phyllis	CIS 401	Local Area Networks	W
	Austin, Jill	CIS 401	Local Area Networks	C

of database software. For example, with relative ease, you can generate sophisticated reports that involve subtotals, calculations, and programming. In addition, data can be presented as a graph. You can even change the structure of a database (for example, add another field). Database software's programming capability has enabled users to create thousands of useful information systems, including student information systems, inventory management systems, hospital patient accounting systems (see Figure 2-34), and cinema management systems.

PERSONAL INFORMATION MANAGEMENT SOFTWARE

Personal information management or *PIM* software is a catch-all phrase that generally refers to messaging and personal information management software that helps you manage your messages, appointments, contacts, and tasks. PIM software, such as Microsoft® Outlook®, may include *calendar* applications for appointment scheduling and reminders; communications applications such as *e-mail, phone dialer,* and *fax;* and *databases* for organizing telephone numbers, e-mail addresses, to-do lists, notes, diary entries, and so on. Figure 2-35 gives you an overview of Microsoft Outlook personal information management software.

TEMPLATES: GETTING HELP WITH GETTING STARTED

Just as there is no reason to reinvent the wheel, there are relatively few circumstances where we must start from scratch to create a document, database, or presentation. Much of what we want to do has already been done before, whether it's an expense statement spreadsheet, a fax form, or an important market report presentation. Each of the major productivity software packages offers a variety of templates to help you get a head start on your projects. A template is simply a document or file that is already formatted or designed for a particular task. You add the content.

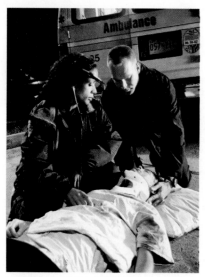

FIGURE 2–34 Databases Part of Our Daily Routine
Data management is part of our daily lives at home and at work, whether we use computers or not. This paramedic dons a Xybernaut wearable PC during emergencies, giving her immediate access to a comprehensive medical troubleshooting database.

Courtesy of Xybernaut

FIGURE 2–35 **MICROSOFT OUTLOOK: PERSONAL INFORMATION MANAGEMENT SOFTWARE**
Microsoft® Outlook® is a handy time-management tool that you can use on your own or as part of a group.

STARTING THE DAY
Microsoft Outlook's *Outlook Today* gives you a snapshot of your day. It lists how many new e-mail messages you have, your appointments for the week, and your tasks. It is the best place to get an overview of your day and the week ahead.

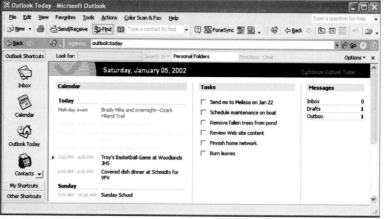

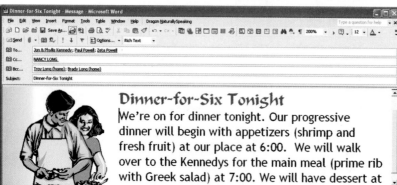

CREATE AND SHARE INFORMATION
The foundation application of PIM software is e-mail. Outlook offers a variety of ways to make your e-mail messages stand out. You can get fancy and write your e-mail on "Stationery" (shown here). You can also add pictures, fonts, and colors to add emphasis to your message. Instant messaging is integrated within the Office XP version of Microsoft Outlook, but not in previous versions of Office.

FIGURE 2–35 continued

KEEPING YOUR APPOINTMENTS

Microsoft Outlook gives you a variety of views for your appointments, including a monthly overview and a daily hour-by-hour listing of appointments (both shown here). It also reminds you of your scheduled appointments and meetings. Appointments can be color coded to indicate the type of appointment, such as important (red), personal (green), or telephone call (yellow). When used on a LAN, Microsoft Outlook helps you schedule meetings by checking the calendars of other participants. People in a workgroup can view nonprivate portions of each other's schedule for the purpose of scheduling meetings. And with PIM software, you will never miss another birthday or anniversary because it keeps track of annual events and recurring events (weekly, monthly, and annual).

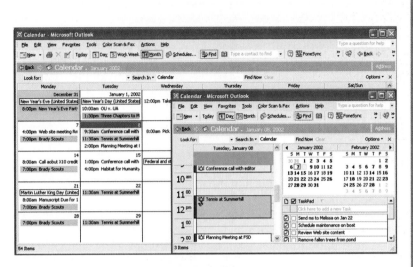

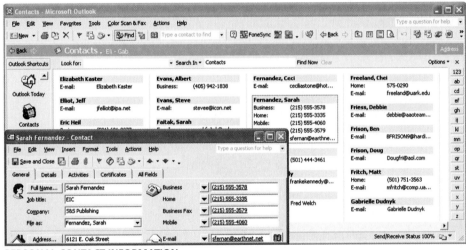

PERSONAL CONTACT INFORMATION

Use PIM software to store the names, phone numbers, and addresses of friends and business colleagues, and any other information that relates to the contact (birthday or anniversary date) in a contacts folder. Just click a button to address a meeting request, e-mail message, or task request to the contact. You can also have Outlook dial the contact's phone number. Outlook will time the call and keep a record in the Journal, complete with the notes you take during the conversation.

THE TO-DO LIST

You can use Microsoft Outlook to manage what you have to do each day. Use it to prioritize your tasks, set reminders for deadlines, and update your progress. Outlook also tracks repeating tasks. When used in a LAN workgroup, use this feature to assign tasks to others and monitor their progress.

FIGURE 2–36

TEMPLATES FOR EVERY OCCASION
Microsoft Office (shown here) offers a wide variety of templates, including forms for articles of incorporation (Word) and a "motivating a team" presentation (PowerPoint).

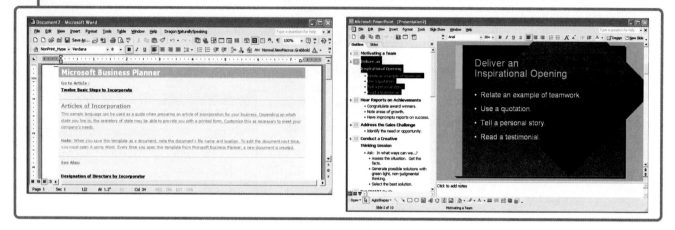

Database Inquiries

- Query by example (create relational expressions with)
  - Relational operators (=, >, <)
  - Logical operators (AND, OR, NOT)
- Sorts (identify)
  - Primary sort field
  - Secondary sort field (if needed)

- *Word processing templates.* Word processing software may come with templates for brochures, e-mail messages, letters, Web pages, faxes, articles of incorporation (see Figure 2-36), memos, calendars, résumés, directories, manuals, and even academic theses.

- *Spreadsheet templates.* In spreadsheets, you have templates for expense statements, purchase orders, grade books, and for many other row-and-column documents.

- *Database software.* Database software includes templates for many database applications such as asset tracking, contract management, inventory control, order entry, resource scheduling, students and classes, video collections, wine lists, and so on.

- *Presentation software templates.* Presentation software offers templates for a presentation on motivating a team (see Figure 2-36), business plan, financial overview, employee orientation, project overview, marketing plan, training program, and even one for communicating bad news.

Judicious use of templates and other canned and automated resources can save you a lot of valuable time.

SECTION SELF-CHECK

2-3.1	Preset format specifications are referred to as concrete settings. (T/F)
2-3.2	Which of these terms is not normally associated with the default settings on word processing software: (a) merge sequence, (b) document size, (c) margins, or (d) font?
2-3.3	Word processing packages are WYSIWYG. (T/F)
2-3.4	An image to be displayed in a PC-based presentation is called a slide. (T/F)
2-3.5	A pattern used to facilitate the creation of a slide presentation is called a: (a) guide word, (b) demographic datum link, (c) template, or (d) hyperlink.
2-3.6	When we convert a file from its foreign format to a format that is compatible with the current program, we: (a) import the file, (b) export the file, (c) bypass the file, or (d) link the file.
2-3.7	D20:Z40 and Z20:D40 define the same spreadsheet range. (T/F)
2-3.8	Panning a spreadsheet to view different parts of the document is called: (a) slipping, (b) scrolling, (c) rolling, or (d) grid pasting.
2-3.9	If the formula =B1+B2-B3 in cell B4 was copied to cell C4, the formula in C4 would be: (a) =B1+B2-B3, (b) =C1+C2-C3, (c) =A1+A2-A3, or (d) =-B1-B2+B3.
2-3.10	If the COURSE database table in Figure 2-28 is sorted in descending order by COURSE ID, the third course record would be Local Area Networks. (T/F)
2-3.11	Database files are sorted, merged, and processed by: (a) a key field, (b) an ISBN, (c) columnar index, or (d) a lock entry.
2-3.12	Which record(s) would be selected from the COURSE table in Figure 2-28 for the condition TYPE=lecture/lab: (a) 100, 330, 110, 401, (b) 101, 202, 330, 401, (c) 202, 150, 320, 350, or (d) 110, 150, 320, 350?
2-3.13	PIM software includes all but which of the following: (a) to-do lists, (b) virus list, (c) notes, or (d) diary entries?

Word processing software, presentation software, spreadsheet software, browser, e-mail, and gaming software are wonderful applications for PCs. Indeed, you could become a happy PC user and never venture far from the capabilities of these high-use applications. However, there is a lot more to personal computing than these applications. Indeed, there are over a half-million commercial software packages and downloadable shareware (copyright software for which the author requests a small fee for its use), freeware, and public-domain software. **Shareware** is copyright software that can be downloaded for free, but its use is based on an honor system where users pay a small fee to the author(s) for using it. **Freeware** is copyright software that can be downloaded and used free of charge. **Public-domain software** is not copyrighted and can be used without restriction.

GRAPHICS SOFTWARE

A dollar may not buy what it used to, but a picture is still worth a thousand words. *Graphics software* enables the creation, manipulation, and management of computer-based images. With graphics software you can issue a command to draw a blue square. Issue another command and suddenly the square is bigger, smaller, rotated, squeezed, stretched, or even "painted" with different colors and textures. Graphics software helps you create line drawings, company logos, maps, clip art, blueprints, flowcharts, or just about any image you can visualize. You can even touch up red eyes in photographs.

Graphic images can be maintained as **bit-mapped graphics**, **vector graphics**, or in a **metafile** format. In bit-mapped graphics, the image is composed of patterns of dots called *picture elements*, or **pixels**. The term **raster graphics** is also used to describe *bit-mapped* images. In vector graphics, the image is composed of patterns of lines, points, and other geometric shapes (vectors). The metafile format is a class of graphics that combines the components of bit-mapped and vector graphics formats. The naked eye cannot distinguish one method of graphics display from another; however, the differences are quite apparent when you try to manipulate images in the various formats.

Bit-Mapped Graphics

Bit-mapped graphics, displayed as dot patterns, are created by graphics paint software (see Figure 2-37), digital cameras, fax machines, scanners, and when you capture an image on a screen. The term *bit-mapped* is used because the image is projected, or "mapped," onto the screen based on binary bits. Dots, or pixels, on the screen are arranged in rows and columns. The typical PC monitor displays over a million pixels in rows and columns (for example, in 1024 rows and 1280 columns). Each dot or pixel on a monitor is assigned a number that denotes its position on the screen grid (120th row and 323rd column) and its color.

As with all internal numbers in a computer system, the numbers that describe the pixel attributes (position and color) are binary bits (1s and 0s). The number of bits needed to describe a pixel increases with the monitor's resolution and the number of colors that can be presented (from 256 colors in 8-bit color mode to 32-bit true color mode with millions of colors). Images are stored according to a **file format** that specifies how the information is organized in the file. Most of the popular programs that create graphic images have their own file formats. The bit-mapped file format for a specific file is noted by its filename extension (for example, AuntBertha.bmp or CompanyLogo.gif). These are a few of the many commonly used graphics formats.

- *BMP.* **BMP** is the most common format used in the Microsoft Windows environment.
- *GIF.* **GIF**, a patented format, is used in Web pages and for downloadable online images.
- *TIFF and TIF.* **TIFF**, or **TIF**, is the industry standard for high-resolution bit-mapped images used in print publishing.
- *PCX.* **PCX** was introduced for PC Paintbrush (distributed with Windows) but is supported by many graphics packages and by scanners and faxes.
- *PNG.* **PNG** provides a patent-free replacement for GIF.
- *JPEG or JPG.* **JPEG**, or **JPG**, is commonly used on Web pages and in digital photography.

Vector Graphics

Vectors, which are lines, points, and other geometric shapes, are configured to create the vector graphics image. The vector graphics display, in contrast to the bit-mapped graphics display, permits the user to work with objects, such as a drawing of a computer. Computer-aided design (CAD) software, which is used by engineers and scientists, uses vector graphics to meet the need to manipulate individual objects on the screen. Figure 2-38 illustrates a vector graphics image. Notice how the

FIGURE 2–37

PAINT: A PAINT PROGRAM
Paint software provides you with a sophisticated electronic canvas for the creation of bit-mapped images. Because the canvas is a bit map, you must erase or draw over any individual part with which you are dissatisfied.

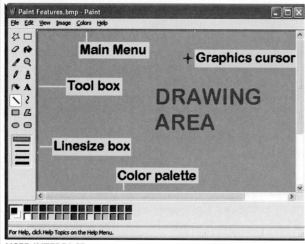

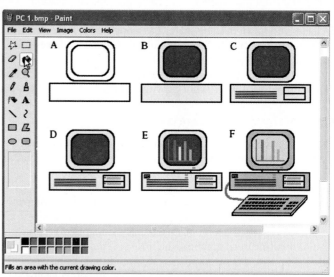

USER INTERFACE

The user interface for Paint, which is distributed with Windows, is representative of paint programs. The parts of the interface include:

- *Drawing area.* The image is created in this area.

- *Graphics cursor.* A point-and-draw device, such as a mouse, is used to move the graphics cursor to draw images and to select options. When positioned in the drawing area, the graphics cursor takes on a variety of shapes, depending on the tool selected.

- *Main menu.* Pull-down menus appear when any of the items in the main menu bar are selected.

- *Tool box.* One of the tools in the tool box is active at any given time. Use the tools to draw; to move, copy, or delete parts of the screen; to create geometric shapes; to fill defined areas with colors; to add text; and to erase.

- *Linesize box.* This box contains the width options for the drawing line.

- *Color palette.* This box contains colors and patterns used with the drawing tools.

CREATING AN IMAGE

This screen shows the steps in creating an image of a PC.

- *Step A.* The *box* and *rounded box tools* are used to create the outlines for the monitor and the processor unit. Notice that the *text tool* (denoted by "A" in the tool box) is used to label the steps.

- *Step B.* The area containing the bit-mapped image created in Step A was *copied* to position B, and then the *paint fill tool* was used to fill in *background colors.* The image in each of the following steps was created from a copy of the image of the preceding step.

- *Step C.* The *line tool* is used to draw the vents on the front of the processor unit. Drag the graphics cursor from one point to another and release the mouse button to draw the line. The two box areas for the disks were created with the box and line tools.

- *Step D.* When the *brush tool* is active, the *foreground color* is drawn at the graphics cursor position. Use the brush tool for freehand drawing, such as the addition of the pedestal for the monitor. The disk slots and the disk-active lights were drawn with the line tool.

---

screen portion of the overall image is actually made up of many objects. Think of a vector graphics screen image as a collage of one or more objects.

Vector graphics images take up less storage space than do bit-mapped images because vector graphics are defined in geometric shapes, each of which can define the attributes of many pixels. Vector graphics images provide more flexibility in that individual objects within the drawing can be resized, moved, stretched, and generally manipulated without affecting the rest of the drawing. **CGM** and **EPS** are widely supported vector graphics file formats. A popular metafile format, **WMF,** is used for exchanging graphics between Windows applications.

HOME AND FAMILY SOFTWARE

Over half the homes in America have at least one PC. Many have one for the parent's home office and one for the kids. Some have home networks, linking all home computers. Today, a wide range of software is available for these home PCs that can help us with the many activities of day-to-day living, as well as some of the chores of life. Figure 2-39 illustrates but a few of the thousands of software applications that you might find around the home. For example, home *legal advisers* assist you with the creation of a variety of legal documents, from wills to lease agreements. Trip planning software has detailed information on thousands of stops along the route to any destination in the United States. Medical software is a staple around the home PC. Software is available that is specifically designed for personal advocacy; that is,

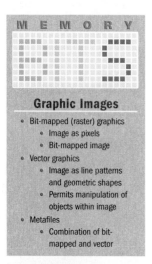

MEMORY

Graphic Images

- Bit-mapped (raster) graphics
  - Image as pixels
  - Bit-mapped image
- Vector graphics
  - Image as line patterns and geometric shapes
  - Permits manipulation of objects within image
- Metafiles
  - Combination of bit-mapped and vector

FIGURE 2–37 continued

- *Step E.* A logo (upper-left corner of processor box) and a bar graph are added. The *PC* in the black logo box was drawn one pixel at a time. The *zoom* feature explodes a small segment of the draw area to enable the user to draw one pixel at a time (see the next screen).
- *Step F.* In this final step, the yellow color is *erased* to gray. Paint software permits the user to selectively switch one color for another within a user-defined area or in the entire drawing area. The keyboard was *tilted* for a three-dimensional look.

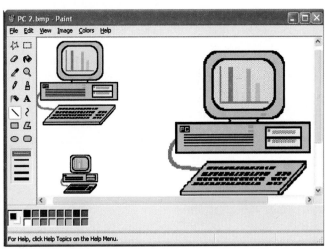

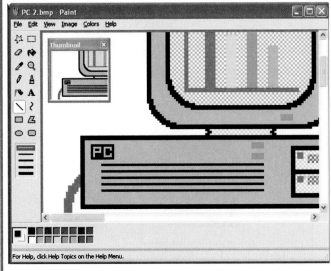

THE SHRINK/GROW FEATURE

The PC image in the upper left corner was copied from Step F above. The original image was selected with the *pick tool,* and then copied to the Clipboard. The Clipboard contents were then loaded to a clean drawing area. The PC image in Step F is reduced and enlarged with the shrink/grow feature of paint software. Notice that image resolution suffers when the image is shrunk or enlarged (for example, the disk slots).

ZOOM FEATURE

In the illustration, the paint software user has zoomed in on the upper-left corner of the processor box in the completed PC image (Step F). Each square is a pixel.

FIGURE 2–38

ADOBE ILLUSTRATOR: A DRAW PROGRAM
Adobe® Illustrator®, shown here, is a vector graphics program. The user draws, then integrates objects to create the drawing. This drawing is made up of several vector objects. Some of the many objects that make up the drawing are moved and highlighted to demonstrate what makes up a vector graphics drawing. In the exploded example, each object is highlighted in blue. Adobe Illustrator's interface is similar to Paint's (see Figure 2-37); however, its drawing features are much more sophisticated.

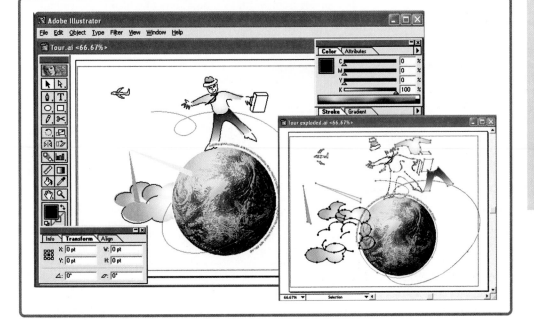

PERSONAL COMPUTING:
The Worth of the Software Bundle
One of the greatest challenges in choosing between alternative PCs is appraising the worth of the preinstalled software. PC vendors want the quality or variety of their software bundle(s) to either confuse the buyer or be the difference maker, depending on the quality of their offerings. The bundled software frequently is the biggest variable in the PC-purchase decision process. A PC vendor may advertise the worth of their software as $800, but the real value is its "street price," which is probably no more than $50 or $60.

it helps you make your point to government agencies, political action groups, politicians, and any other organization or individual you wish to influence. There are software packages designed to help college-bound students and their parents find and secure financial aid. And when they graduate, résumé creation software packages can help them put their best foot forward when looking for a job.

Of course, a plethora of software packages has emerged for hobbyists. No matter what your hobby, you are sure to find software that helps you with some aspect of your hobby. For example, tennis software helps you match statistics, create tournament draws, and figure rankings. There are packages for gardeners/landscapers, astronomers, astrologists, bicycling enthusiasts, UFO watchers, golfers, fishing fans, and for many more.

FIGURE 2–39   **HOME AND PERSONAL SOFTWARE**

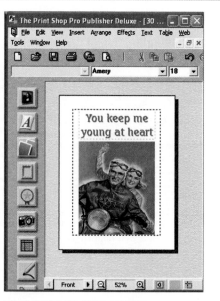

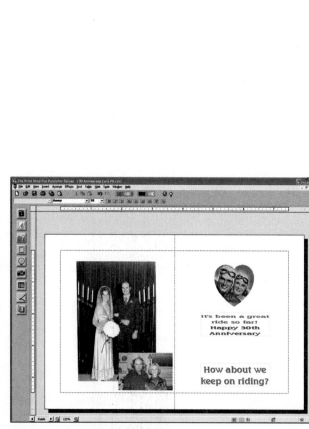

BECOME YOUR OWN PRINTER

All too often, the local greeting card store has cards and announcements for everyone except you. When you want something special, try doing it yourself with *The Print Shop 12* (a product of Broderbund). This software helps you create personalized greeting cards (shown here), banners, business cards, letterheads, certificates, calendars, announcements, invitations, and more. The software offers hundreds of templates from which to choose, one of which is shown here. Only the picture images on the inside were added. If you wish, you can easily create your own from scratch.

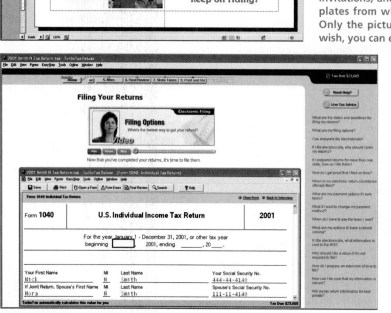

HELP WITH TAXES

Millions of people now prepare their own taxes with tax preparation software, such as *Quicken® TurboTax* (shown here). The interactive software guides you, step-by-step, through the process, answering your questions and making suggestions as needed. Upon completion, you are given the option of filing your return the traditional way (via the postal service) or electronically.

FIGURE 2–39 continued

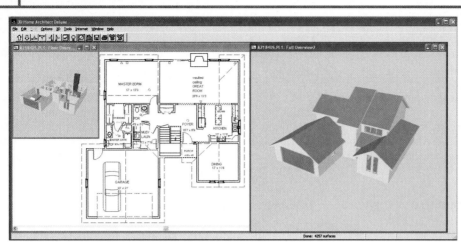

BUILDING A HOUSE?
Are you considering remodeling your current home or building a new one? Then perhaps your first stop should be *3D Home Architect*™ (a product of Broderbund). With this software you can create a floor plan and even see what it might look like by requesting a 3-D external view. You can create a three-dimensional design of your kitchen, play with decorating ideas throughout the house, and even "walk through" the inside of the house to see if the design is what you want.

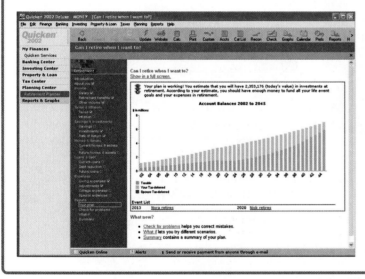

FINANCIAL PLANNING FOR THE FUTURE
Quicken® Retirement Planner guides you step-by-step through the creation of a personalized retirement plan. Use it to plan for retirement, college expenses, buying a vacation home, and much more. The program assists you in deciding how much you should save and where to invest your savings. It also tracks your progress and can generate a variety of helpful reports and graphs.

EDUCATION AND EDUTAINMENT SOFTWARE

Emerging technologies are prompting fundamental changes in education. The *static, sequential* presentation of books has been the foundation for learning since Gutenberg. Now, however, we are beginning to see *dynamic, linked,* and *interactive technology-based* resources in virtually every discipline. When coupled with online distance learning and personal interaction of the traditional classroom environment, such resources offer a richer learning environment. We need to restate that computer-based education will not replace the classroom or teachers anytime soon, but those who have tried it agree that CBT (computer-based training) will have a dramatic impact on the way we learn.

Educational software is experiencing an explosion of acceptance in our homes and schools. Computer-based educational resources take many forms and are being embraced by young and old alike. Students can learn anatomy by taking virtual tours of the body. Students can travel through the Milky Way to Cassiopeia and other constellations while an electronic teacher explains the mysteries of the universe. Millions of elementary age students are getting one-on-one instruction on keyboarding skills. Chemistry students are doing lab exercises with bits and bytes rather than dangerous chemicals. Some innovative software packages tease the mind by inviting students to learn the power of logic and creativity.

It did not take long for education software developers to combine *education* and ent*ertainment* into a single learning resource. This *edutainment software* gives students an opportunity to play while learning. Figure 2-40 provides a few examples of education and edutainment software.

REFERENCE SOFTWARE

As soon as the technology gurus figured out that audio CDs could hold 650 MB of digital data, the CD-ROM was born. Almost immediately after the introduction of the CD-ROM, books, dictionaries, encyclopedias, newspapers, corporate manuals, and thousands of other printed materials were being translated to digital media, namely the CD-ROM. Now that CD-RW (rewritable) is reasonably priced, we at home and in small offices can create our own CD-ROM-based reference material, too.

Computer-based reference material is much more than simply text on a disk. It is searchable and interactive. Attorneys no longer spend days pouring over scores of cases to prepare for trials. Keyword searches can result in a display of applicable cases within seconds.

FIGURE 2–40 EDUCATION AND EDUTAINMENT SOFTWARE

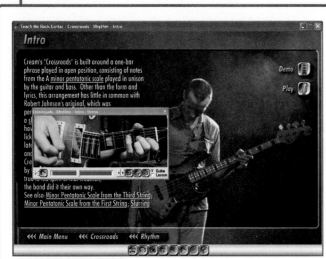

PLAYING ROCK GUITAR
Voyetra's Teach Me Rock Guitar™ provides an easy, step-by-step method for learning rock guitar. The Animated Fretboard shows you the fingerings on the guitar neck in real time as you play. You can even jam with the band!

LEARN TO SPEAK SPANISH
Computers and their software have proven to be effective teachers of languages. The Spanish software gives instruction and practice in real-world conversations.

THE eBOOK
This device, the Rocket eBook™ holds the equivalent of a semester's worth of college textbooks (about 4000 pages of text and images). You can read or study it as you would a print book, making margin notes, underlining special passages, and bookmarking pages. The eBook is searchable, too.

Courtesy of NuvoMedia, Inc.

Just about any frequently used printed reference material is available on CD-ROM, or it is being considered for CD-ROM publication. We can get detailed geographic information, multilingual dictionaries, state, and federal census information, specific entrance requirements for thousands of colleges, Fortune 500 financial information, and much more. Figure 2-41 illustrates a variety of CD-ROM-based reference materials.

FIGURE 2–41 REFERENCE SOFTWARE

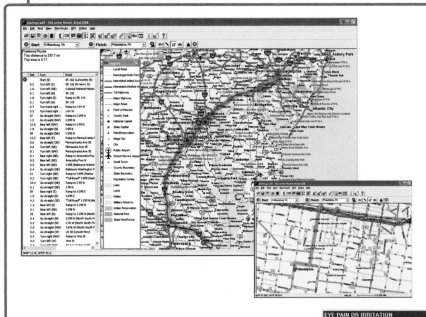

NEVER BE LOST AGAIN

With *Street Atlas USA®* 9.0 by DeLorme you will never be lost again. Incredibly detailed maps help you take the effort out of trip planning. Street Atlas USA 9.0 is a seamless map of the entire country. It offers detail, street address search power, and door-to-door routing. Just identify your start (Williamsburg, Virginia) and finish (Philadelphia, Pennsylvania) points and the software calculates and then displays the best route (in purple). You can zoom in for street-level maps (downtown Philadelphia in the example) that can include as much or little information as you wish, from specific types of restaurants to historical sites. The program also interfaces with global positioning systems (GPSs) to pinpoint your location on the map display and to guide you to your destination, prompting you visually and verbally as to when and where to turn.

HOME MEDICAL ADVISOR

Home Medical Advisor™ is a practical guide to symptom diagnosis and preventive care. You can even talk to a "video" doctor to get answers to detailed questions (shown here) and then receive possible diagnoses and treatments. Hundreds of videos show you exactly what to expect if you are scheduling an eye exam, planning surgery, or having a baby. You can analyze potentially harmful interactions of more than 8000 over-the-counter and prescription drugs. Find expert emergency advice and video demonstrations right when you need them—instantly!

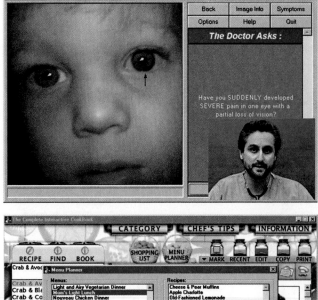

INTERACTIVE COOKBOOK

All the ingredients for planning and preparing perfect recipes and meals are mixed into one program, Compton's® *Complete Cookbook*™. All of the 2000 plus recipes come with step-by-step instructions, color pictures, detailed nutritional facts, and tips from top chefs. To make planning a snap, the software provides a "smart shopping" list and a menu planner.

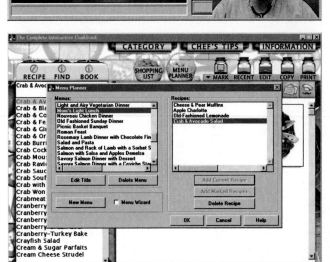

BUSINESS AND FINANCIAL SOFTWARE

There are literally thousands of PC-based business and financial-oriented software packages for the home and small office. In the business community, there are software packages specifically designed for physicians' clinics, construction contractors, CPAs, churches, motels, law offices, nonprofit organizations, real estate companies, recreation and fitness centers, restaurants, and just about any other organization that has administrative information processing needs. Some business-oriented software for smaller companies can run on a single PC, and other packages are designed for the LAN client/server environment so information can be shared among workers. At home, millions of people now keep family financial records on a PC. Figure 2-42 shows several business/financial software examples.

SECTION SELF-CHECK

2-4.1	Another term for bit-mapped graphics is: (a) raster, (b) vector, (c) faster, or (d) geometric.
2-4.2	Which of these software applications would not be considered a common application for home use: (a) greeting cards, (b) tax preparation, (c) morphing, or (d) trip planning?
2-4.3	It is technologically possible for people at home to put their own reference material on CD-ROM by using what technology: (a) CD-RW, (b) audio CD, (c) VHS, or (d) PCMCIA.
2-4.4	Tax preparation software lets you file taxes electronically. (T/F)
2-4.5	Mapping systems can interface with global positioning systems to pinpoint your location on a map. (T/F)

FIGURE 2–42   **BUSINESS SOFTWARE**

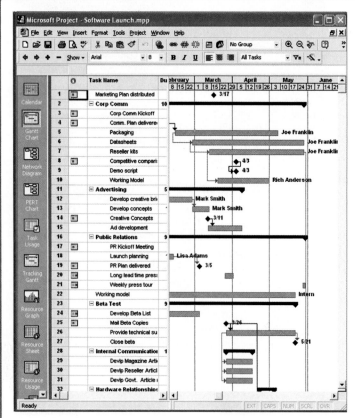

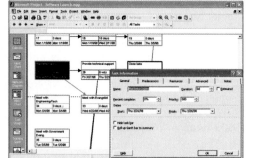

PROJECT MANAGEMENT

Microsoft's *Project* is a great tool for anyone who oversees a team, plans a budget, juggles schedules, or has deadlines to meet. Project management software helps you plan and track your projects more effectively so you can identify and respond to conflicts before they happen.

FIGURE 2–42 continued

BUSINESS AND HOME FINANCES

Anyone who has attempted to balance a sadly out-of-kilter checkbook or consolidate tax information will appreciate *Quicken*® (Quicken software is made and owned by Intuit). Industry analysts refer to Quicken as a "killer app," an application with such useful capabilities that it alone can justify the expense of a computer. This financial management system helps you, personally, or it can help a company manage bills, bank accounts, investments, tax records, assets and liabilities, and much more. You can even write your checks online and all the details are automatically entered into your checkbook register (see example), thereby eliminating duplicate entries. Just print on check stock (see example) designed for your printer, sign, and send. Many avid Quicken users keep track of everything from credit-card purchases to stock transactions. The money trail summarized by Quicken gives these people and companies some insight into what is happening at home and in its businesses. Quicken offers users a variety of reports and graphs (see itemized categories report).

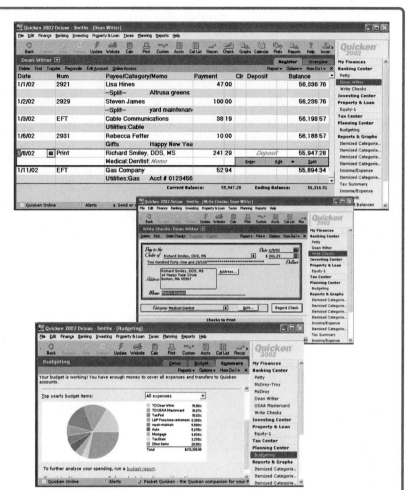

APPLICATION-SPECIFIC SOFTWARE: DENTISTRY

For those in almost any business, information technology plays a role in its operation. With Dr. Richard Roblee, an expert in aesthetic dentistry and orthodontic techniques and interdisciplinary therapy, it is critical to his practice and philosophy of treatment. Dr. Roblee relies on several patient information systems to help him, his staff, and his patients track progress, sometimes for years. The client database houses all critical client information, including dental history (both descriptive and visual) and treatment plan.

Courtesy of Dr. Richard Roblee,
D.D.S., M.S.; IDT Systems, Inc.
roblee@idt-network.com

2-1 THE OPERATING SYSTEM

The operating system and its **graphical user interface (GUI)** are the nucleus of all software activity. One of the operating system programs, called the **kernel**, loads other operating system and applications programs to RAM as they are needed. **Utility programs** are a type of system software.

All operating systems are designed with the same basic objectives in mind. Perhaps the most important objectives are to facilitate communication between the computer system and the people who run it and to optimize the use of computer system resources.

Operating systems get the most from their processors through **multitasking**—the concurrent execution of more than one program at a time. High-priority programs run in the **foreground** part of RAM and the rest run in the **background**.

Through the 1980s, the most popular microcomputer operating system, **MS-DOS**, was strictly *text-based, command-driven* software that required strict adherence to command **syntax**. The trend now is toward GUIs that use graphical **icons**. All modern operating systems have adopted the GUI concept.

A processor and an operating system define a platform, a standard for which software packages are developed. The modern PC/Windows platforms include PC-compatible computers with **Windows 95, Windows 98, Windows Me** (Millennium Edition), **Windows NT, Windows 2000, Windows XP**, or **Windows CE** (for handheld and pocket PCs). Windows XP, the client-side operating system, works with **Windows 2000 Server** or the newer **Windows .Net Server**, the server-side portion of the operating system to make client/server computing possible. Windows XP comes in two versions—**Windows XP Professional** and **Windows XP Home. Windows XP 64-Bit Edition** is designed for high-performance 64-bit workstations. Windows operating systems have many features, such as **plug-and-play** and **home networking**. Wintel platforms are *mostly* **backward compatible.**

The Apple family of microcomputers and **Mac OS X** define another major platform.

Linux, a spin-off of the popular **UNIX** operating system, is a popular operating system for a variety of computers. Linux is **open source software.** The Linux-based **LindowsOS** has file-level compatibility with many Windows-based applications.

System software, which includes the operating system and utility software, is applications-independent. Utility software is available to help you with disk and file maintenance, system recovery, security, backup, virus protection, and other system-related tasks.

Those companies that do not standardize on a platform must work to achieve **interoperability,** which refers to the ability to run software and exchange information in a **multiplatform environment.** Enabling technologies that allow communication and the sharing of resources between different platforms are called **cross-platform technologies.**

A wide variety of system software *utilities* can help with personal computing tasks, such as disk and file maintenance, system recovery, security, backup, and virus protection.

2-2 WINDOWS CONCEPTS AND TERMINOLOGY

The Windows *Help and Support* capabilities include step-by-step tutorials that lead you through numerous common procedures.

The GUI-based Windows series runs one or more applications in **windows**—rectangular areas displayed on the screen.

Any software application that does not adhere to the Microsoft Windows standard is a **non-Windows application.** Programs that adhere to Windows conventions are **Windows applications.**

The Windows GUI relies on a point-and-draw device, such as a mouse, to click and **drag.**

The screen upon which icons, windows, and so on are displayed is known as the **desktop. The active window** displays the application being currently used by the user. **Inactive windows** display applications that are running but not being used by the user.

Typically, a Windows session begins with the **Start button** in the **taskbar.** An active application window can be minimized to a button in the taskbar. You may open a Windows **folder,** which contains a logical grouping of related files and/or subordinated folders, to obtain a work file.

A rectangular **application window** contains an **open application** (a running application). Several applications can be open, but there is only one active window at any given time.

Everything that relates to the application noted in the title bar is displayed in the **workspace.** Several **document windows** can be displayed in the parent application window's workspace.

When document content is more than can be displayed in a window, the window is outfitted with **vertical** and/or **horizontal scroll bars,** each with a **scroll box** and two **scroll arrows** to enable **scrolling.**

The horizontal **title bar** at the top of each window has these elements: application icon, window title, Minimize button, Maximize/Restore button, Close button, and the title area.

When you select an item from the menu bar, a subordinate **pull-down menu** is "pulled down." Use the left/right or up/down arrow keys to enter the **mnemonic,** or use the mouse to position the mouse pointer at the desired option. Further selection may result in a menu or a pop-up **dialog box.** A **pop-out** menu results when you choose a menu option followed by a right-pointing arrow. The context-sensitive **pop-up menu** is displayed when you right-click the mouse. The **floating menu** "floats" over the display. The **shortcut key** and the **hotkey** help speed up interaction on the keyboard.

Toolbars, containing rectangular graphics, give you ready access to frequently used menu items. The **ruler bar** shows the document window's content relative to the printed page.

The Windows **Explorer,** which can include commonly used icons such as **application icons, shortcut icons, document icons,** and **disk drive icons,** performs file management tasks such as creating folders, copying files, moving files, deleting files, and other folder/file-related tasks.

The Windows environment lets you view multiple applications that can be resized, shrunk, and arranged by the user within the workspace. Or, they can be arranged as **cascading windows** or **tiled windows.**

The active window is always highlighted in the **foreground.** Other open windows are in the **background.** These terms describe RAM concepts, too.

The most common method of sharing information among applications is to use the Windows **Clipboard** and the *Edit* option in the menu bar. The **source application** and **destination application** for a copy or move operation can be one and the same or they can be entirely different applications.

Applications can be linked through **object linking and embedding,** or **OLE.** An **object** is an item within any Windows application that can be individually selected. We can create **compound documents** that contain one or more objects from other applications. The object originates in a **server application** and is linked to a destination document of a **client application.**

OLE lets you *link* or *embed* information. When you link information, the link between source and destination documents is dynamic. When you embed information, you insert the actual object, not just a pointer.

2-3 PRODUCTIVITY SOFTWARE: THE SOFTWARE SUITE

Word processing lets you create text-based documents into which you can integrate images. When you format a document, you are specifying the size of the page to be printed and how you want the document to look when printed. The preset format, or *default settings,* may fit your word processing application. A **font,** which refers to the style, appearance, and size of print, is described by its **typeface.** Most word processing packages are considered **WYSIWYG,** short for "What you see is what you get." The find and replace features make all word processing documents searchable. **Clip art** is prepackaged electronic images stored on disk to be used as needed.

Word processing has a variety of features that enable users to enhance the appearance and readability of their documents, including footnoting, numbered and bulleted lists, outline, drawing tools, borders, integration of images, multicolumn text, and more. Word processing software provides the capability of merging data in a database with the text of a document. The *mail-merge* application is an example. Here you merge a *database file* with a *form file.* **Boilerplate** text is existing text that can in some way be reused and customized for a variety of word processing applications.

You can convert word processing documents to create Web pages on the World Wide Web (the Web), the primary application used for viewing information on the Internet.

Word processing can handle most document generation tasks, but those organizations that need to produce complicated documents to be printed professionally use desktop publishing software to create *camera-ready documents.*

Presentation software enables you to create a wide variety of visually appealing and informative presentation graphics. These steps are used with presentation software: (1) *Select a* **template.** Microsoft's PowerPoint offers both *design templates* and *content templates.* (2) *Create an outline for the presentation.* PowerPoint's tri-pane view lets you view the *slide, outline,* and *notes* at the same time. **Import** content from other programs directly into PowerPoint slides. **Export** PowerPoint slides to other programs. (3) *Compile and create other nontext resources.* A slide presentation may include text, photo images, charts and graphs, original drawings, clip art, audio clips, and even full-motion video. Among the most popular charts are the pie and bar charts. Presentation software also permits the preparation of organization charts and maps. (4) *Integrate resources.* The PowerPoint *slide sorter* view gives you an overview of the presentation via **thumbnail** images. (5) *Add special effects.* With PowerPoint you can have an image

fade out, be wiped away, show animation, or add sound, to name a few. (6) *Add notes.* (7) *Deliver the presentation.*

Spreadsheet software provides an electronic alternative to thousands of traditionally manual tasks that involve rows and columns of data. The intersection of a particular row and column in a spreadsheet designates a **cell.** During operations, data are referred to by their **cell addresses.** The **pointer** can be moved around the spreadsheet to any cell address. To make an entry, to edit, or to replace an entry in a spreadsheet, move the pointer to the appropriate cell.

The four types of **ranges** are a single cell, all or part of a column of adjacent cells, all or part of a row of adjacent cells, and a rectangular block of cells. A particular range is depicted by the addresses of the endpoint cells (for example, C5:E10).

Three major types of entries to a cell are label, numeric, and formula. Spreadsheet formulas use standard programming notation for **arithmetic operators.** Spreadsheets offer predefined operations called **functions.** Each function includes one or more **arguments** that identify the data for the operation.

Different people can use a spreadsheet template over and over for different purposes. If you change the value of a cell in a spreadsheet, all other affected cells are revised accordingly. Spreadsheet packages also can let you generate a variety of charts from spreadsheet data.

Database software lets you enter, organize, and retrieve stored data. Both database and spreadsheet software packages enable us to work with tabular data and records in a database. Database software uses the **relational database** approach to data management. Relational databases are organized in tables in which a row is a record and a column is a field.

In database software, the user-defined structure of a database table identifies the characteristics of each field in it. Related fields are grouped to form records. Content for a *text* field can be a single word or it can be any **alphanumeric** (numbers, letters, and special characters) phrase.

Database software also permits you to retrieve, view, and print records based on **query by example.** To make a query by example, users set conditions for the selection of records by composing a relational expression containing **relational operators** that reflects the desired conditions. Several expressions can be combined into a single condition with **logical operators.**

Records in a database can be sorted for display in a variety of formats. To sort the records in a database, select a primary sort field and, if needed, a secondary sort field. Database software can create customized, or formatted, reports.

Personal information management, or PIM, refers to messaging and personal information management software. PIM software helps you manage your messages, appointments, contacts, and tasks.

Each of the major productivity software packages offers a variety of templates to help you get a head start on your projects. A template is simply a document or file that is already formatted or designed for a particular task.

2-4 APPLICATIONS SOFTWARE FOR YOUR PC

There are over a half-million commercial software packages and downloadable **shareware, freeware,** and **public-domain software.**

Graphics software facilitates the creation, manipulation, and management of computer-based images. Graphic images are presented as **bit-mapped graphics** (file formats include **BMP, GIF, TIFF** or **TIF, PCX, PNG,** and **JPEG** or **JPG**), **vector graphics** (**CGM** and **EPS**), and **metafiles** (**WMF**). In bit-mapped graphics, or **raster graphics,** the image is composed of patterns of dots (pixels). In vector graphics, the image is composed of patterns of lines, points, and other geometric shapes (vectors). The metafile is a class of graphics that combines the components of bit-mapped and vector graphics formats. Paint software, which works with bit-mapped images, provides the user with an electronic canvas.

A wide range of software is available for home PCs that can help us with the many activities of day-to-day living. Popular home applications include greeting cards and banners, tax preparation, and edutainment. Edutainment software combines education and entertainment into a single software package. Most of the reference material distributed on CD-ROM is commercial (for example, encyclopedias) or proprietary; however, with CD-RW we can create our own CD-ROM-based reference material. A wide variety of PC-based business and financial-oriented software packages are available for the home and small office.

KEY TERMS

active window (p. 88)
alphanumeric (p. 108)
application icon (p. 94)
application window (p. 91)
argument (p. 106)
arithmetic operator (p. 104)
background (program/window) (p. 95)
background (RAM) (p. 79)
backward compatible (p. 81)
bit-mapped graphics (p. 113)
BMP (p. 113)
boilerplate (p. 99)
cascading windows (p. 95)
cell (p. 104)
cell address (p. 104)
CGM (p. 114)
client application (p. 96)
clip art (p. 99)
Clipboard (p. 96)
compound document (p. 96)
cross-platform technology (p. 84)
desktop (p. 88)
destination application (p. 96)
dialog box (p. 92)
disk drive icon (p. 95)
document icon (p. 95)
document window (p. 92)
drag (p. 88)
EPS (p. 114)
Explorer (p. 94)
export (p. 102)
file format (p. 113)
floating menu (p. 93)
folder (p. 91)
font (p. 99)
foreground (program/window) (p. 95)
foreground (RAM) (p. 79)
freeware (p. 113)
function (p. 106)
GIF (p. 113)

graphical user interface (GUI) (p. 78)
home networking (p. 81)
horizontal scroll bar (p. 92)
hotkey (p. 93)
icon (p. 80)
import (p. 102)
inactive window (p. 90)
interoperability (p. 84)
JPEG (JPG) (p. 113)
kernel (p. 78)
LindowsOS (p. 84)
Linux (p. 82)
logical operator (p. 109)
Mac OS X (p. 82)
metafile (p. 113)
mnemonic (p. 92)
MS-DOS (p. 80)
multiplatform environment (p. 84)
multitasking (p. 79)
non-Windows application (p. 88)
object (p. 96)
object linking and embedding (OLE) (p. 96)
open application (p. 91)
open source software (p. 82)
PCX (p. 113)
pixels (p. 113)
plug-and-play (p. 81)
PNG (p. 113)
pointer (p. 104)
pop-out menu (p. 92)
pop-up menu (p. 92)
public-domain software (p. 113)
pull-down menu (p. 92)
query by example (p. 109)
range (p. 104)
raster graphics (p. 113)
relational database (p. 107)
relational operator (p. 109)
ruler bar (p. 93)

scroll arrow (p. 92)
scroll box (p. 92)
scrolling (p. 92)
server application (p. 96)
shareware (p. 113)
shortcut icon (p. 94)
shortcut key (p. 92)
slide (p. 102)
source application (p. 96)
Start button (p. 90)
syntax (p. 80)
taskbar (p. 90)
template (p. 101)
thumbnail (p. 103)
TIFF (TIF) (p. 113)
tiled windows (p. 95)
title bar (p. 92)
toolbar (p. 93)
typeface (p. 99)
UNIX (p. 82)
utility program (p. 78)
vector graphics (p. 113)
vertical scroll bar (p. 92)
window (p. 85)
Windows .Net Server (p. 81)
Windows 2000 (p. 81)
Windows 2000 Server (p. 81)
Windows 95 (p. 81)
Windows 98 (p. 81)
Windows applications (p. 88)
Windows CE (p. 81)
Windows Me (p. 81)
Windows NT (p. 81)
Windows XP (p. 81)
Windows XP 64-Bit Edition (p. 81)
Windows XP Home Edition (p. 81)
Windows XP Professional (p. 81)
WMF (p. 114)
workspace (p. 91)
WYSIWYG (p. 99)

MATCHING

1. Windows CE	**a.** move object with mouse
2. alphanumeric	**b.** Alt+F4
3. a spinoff of UNIX	**c.** copyrighted software
4. arithmetic operator	**d.** operating system for handhelds
5. relational database	**e.** tables in a database
6. freeware	**f.** Linux
7. JPG	**g.** described by typeface
8. graphical user interface	**h.** contains object from another application
9. range	**i.** common Web file format
10. background (windows)	**j.** grouping of related files
11. drag	**k.** numbers and letters
12. compound document	**l.** add (+) and subtract (–)
13. font	**m.** defined area in a spreadsheet
14. folder	**n.** GUI
15. shortcut key	**o.** location of inactive windows

CHAPTER SELF-CHECK

2-1.1 MS-DOS is a state-of-the-art operating system. (T/F)

2-1.2 All computers, including computers dedicated to a particular application, have operating systems. (T/F)

2-1.3 A GUI is: (a) text-based, (b) graphics-based, (c) label-based, or (d) paste-based.

2-1.4 The Macintosh family of PCs is unique in that it does not need an operating system. (T/F)

2-1.5 A computing environment that runs more than one platform is what type of environment: (a) high platform, (b) low platform, (c) multiplatform, or (d) cross-platform?

2-1.6 UNIX is a subset of Windows 2000 Server, a more sophisticated operating system. (T/F)

2-1.7 The future of the PC/Windows family of operating systems is: (a) Windows Me, (b) Windows 98, (c) Windows XP, or (d) Windows NEXT.

2-1.8 The operating system for the Apple iMac is: (a) OS Mac, (b) iMac OS, (c) Mac OS X, or (d) The Mac BOSS.

2-1.9 Which of these is a spin-off of the popular UNIX multiuser operating system: (a) Bendix, (b) Linux, (c) Linus, or (d) Lucy?

2-1.10 The proper use of utility software can help keep a PC running at peak efficiency. (T/F)

2-1.11 The universal use of virus vaccine software over the past decade has done away with the threat of computer viruses. (T/F)

2-1.12 To eliminate the possibility of ghosting on modern monitors, the use of screen savers is essential. (T/F)

2-1.13 Which of the following would not be considered utility software: (a) virus protection, (b) backup, (c) file maintenance, or (d) gaming?

2-1.14 The process that rearranges file fragments into contiguous files is called: (a) unfragging, (b) file filling, (c) folder folding, or (d) defragmentation.

2-2.1 Any software application that does not adhere to the Microsoft Windows standard is a non-Windows application. (T/F)

2-2.2 The cascading windows option fills the workspace in such a way that no document window overlaps another. (T/F)

2-2.3 A Windows folder can contain either files or subordinated folders, but not both. (T/F)

2-2.4 Which of these is a point-and-draw device: (a) printer, (b) CD-ROM, (c) mouse, or (d) scanner?

2-2.5 Document windows are displayed in the parent application window's: (a) system window, (b) title bar, (c) scroll area, or (d) workspace.

2-2.6 Object linking does not actually place the object into the destination document. (T/F)

2-2.7 What kind of document contains one or more objects from other applications: (a) hyperlinked, (b) composite, (c) complex, or (d) compound?

2-2.8 To embed an object, choose the Paste Link option button in the Paste Special dialog box. (T/F)

2-3.1 An online thesaurus can be used to suggest synonyms for a word in a word processing document. (T/F)

2-3.2 Boilerplate text is existing text that can in some way be reused and customized for a variety of word processing applications. (T/F)

2-3.3 Desktop publishing documents are composed of rectangular: (a) windows, (b) boxes, (c) doors, or (d) frames.

2-3.4 What refers to a set of characters of a particular design: (a) calligraph, (b) stencil, (c) typeface, or (d) keyface?

2-3.5 The height of a 36-point letter is: (a) one-fourth inch, (b) one-half inch, (c) 1 inch, or (d) 2 inches.

2-3.6 In desktop publishing, the emphasis is on overall document composition, not the running text as in word processing. (T/F)

2-3.7 Presentation software allows users to create charts, graphs, and images for use during presentations. (T/F)

2-3.8 The presentation software slide sorter view lets users add or delete slides and rearrange them to meet presentation needs. (T/F)

2-3.9 Audio clips are an example of a nontext resource for presentation software. (T/F)

2-3.10 A typical slide in a slide presentation would not include: (a) photo images, charts, and graphs, (b) clip art and audio clips, (c) content templates, or (d) full-motion video.

2-3.11 Which of these is a presentation software special effect: (a) fade out, (b) thumbnail, (c) notes, or (d) export file?

2-3.12 The term spreadsheet was coined at the beginning of the personal computer boom. (T/F)

2-3.13 The intersection of a particular row and column in a spreadsheet designates a cell. (T/F)

2-3.14 Spreadsheet software works only with numbers and does not generate charts. (T/F)

2-3.15 A model of a spreadsheet designed for a particular application is sometimes called a template. (T/F)

2-3.16 The spreadsheet pointer highlights the: (a) relative cell, (b) status cell, (c) current cell, or (d) merge cell.

2-3.17 Data in a spreadsheet are referred to by their cell: (a) box, (b) number, (c) address, or (d) code.

2-3.18 Which of these is not a range in a spreadsheet: (a) block range, (b) row range, (c) column range, or (d) grazing range?

2-3.19 Database software gives you greater flexibility in the manipulation of rows and columns of data than does spreadsheet software. (T/F)

2-3.20 AND and OR are relational operators. (T/F)

2-3.21 In a database, related fields are grouped to form records. (T/F)

2-3.22 The definition of the structure of a database table would not include which of the following: (a) field names, (b) field sizes, (c) data types, or (d) pointer cell.

2-3.23 The relational operator for greater than or equal to is: (a) > OR =, (b) < AND = , (c) < NOT = , or (d) < OR =.

2-3.24 Which record(s) would be selected from the COURSE table in Figure 2-28 for the condition TYPE=lecture/lab: (a) 100, 330, 110, 401, (b) 101, 202, 330, 401, (c) 202, 150, 320, 350, or (d) 110, 150, 320, 350?

2-3.25 Which record(s) would be selected from the STUDENT table in Figure 2-28 for the condition STATUS=complete AND MAJOR=marketing: (a) Targa, Phil/330, (b) Targa, Phil/100, (c) Johnson, Charles/100, (d) Bell, Jim/330?

2-3.26 Which of these is normally not associated specifically with database terminology: (a) table, (b) query by example, (c) relational, (d) audio clip?

2-3.27 Personal information management is concerned with messages, appointments, contacts, and tasks. (T/F)

2-3.28 Which of these is messaging and personal information management software: (a) IMP, (b) PIM, (c) MIP, or (d) IPM?

2-3.29 A template is simply a document or file that is already formatted or designed for a particular task. (T.F)

2-4.1 In bit-mapped graphics, the image is composed of patterns of: (a) vectors, (b) pictures, (c) dots, or (d) objects.

2-4.2 Which type of graphics software package provides a computer-based version of the painter's canvas: (a) draw, (b) paint, (c) illustrator, or (d) sketch?

2-4.3 What class of graphics combines the components of bit-mapped and vector graphics formats: (a) metafiles, (b) raster files, (c) text files, or (d) MIDI files?

2-4.4 Which of the following pairs of file formats are used in Web page design: (a) JPG and BMP, (b) TIF and PCX, (c) JPG and GIF, or (d) TIF and PNG?

2-4.5 Which of the following is not a characteristic of education software: (a) linked, (b) sequential, (c) interactive, or (d) dynamic?

2-4.6 Which type of software gives the student an opportunity to play while learning: (a) education, (b) entertainment, (c) edutainment, or (d) fun-and-learn?

2-4.7 In the interactive learning environment, we learn: (a) primarily within workgroups, (b) at our own pace, (c) by the schedule in a syllabus, or (d) only at night.

2-4.8 Which of the following is not a characteristic of reference material on CD-ROM: (a) searchable, (b) interactive, (c) multimedia, or (d) limited to public domain content?

2-4.9 Which of these software packages would not be considered a business-specific application: (a) physician's clinic, (b) fitness center, (c) real estate, or (d) nationwide telephone directory?

2-4.10 Project management software helps you plan and track your projects more effectively. (T/F)

IT ETHICS AND ISSUES

THE QUALITY OF SOFTWARE

The software market is highly competitive even though Microsoft dominates the operating system and productivity software markets. Competition and other market pressures have forced software vendors, including Microsoft, into rushing their products to market, bugs and all. Some industry observers have argued that the quality of software is declining with an increasingly higher percentage of bugs being left intact within commercial software. The end result of this rush to market is that customers lose time and money coping with annoying bugs. Information technology and those who make software decisions are putting pressure on software vendors to raise the quality of their software. Generally, they want a clean product, even if they have to wait for it.

Discussion: *What can software vendors do within the context of competition and economic reality to improve software quality?*

Discussion: *What can those who buy commercial software do to improve software quality?*

COUNTERFEIT SOFTWARE

In some countries, counterfeit software far outnumbers legitimate proprietary software. Counterfeit software is software that is illegally mass produced from copies of the original manufacturer's software and packaged for retail sales. Counterfeit software may look very much, or exactly, like that distributed by the product's manufacturer. Until recently it was believed that most of this activity was offshore (outside the United States); however, a counterfeit ring that had produced and sold millions of dollars worth of counterfeit Microsoft was uncovered in California. The sophisticated operation included commercial CD-ROM duplicators, color printing presses, packaging machines, and everything else needed to create the illusion of a legitimate software package worthy of a certificate of authenticity.

Discussion: *What would be appropriate punishment for the owner of a company that produced and sold over $50 million worth of counterfeit copyright software? For someone who knowingly sold the counterfeit products to legitimate retail outlets? For someone who worked on the counterfeit company's production line?*

Discussion: *What can be done to protect intellectual property from counterfeit operations that is not already being done?*

Discussion: *What, if any, punishment should be given a student who uses CD-RW capability to make a duplicate copy of Microsoft Office, and then gives it to his or her friend. What about the friend who installs and uses the pirated copy of Microsoft Office?*

Discussion: *Does widespread abuse of copyright laws have any impact on incentives for creating intellectual property, such as software? Explain.*

DISCUSSION AND PROBLEM SOLVING

2-1.1 Some people contend that the traditional text-based, command-driven operating system interface has some advantages over the modern graphical user interface. Speculate on what these advantages might be.

2-1.2 Multitasking allows PC users to run several programs at a time. Describe a PC session in which you would have at least two applications running at the same time.

2-1.3 Why is the selection of a platform such an important decision to an organization?

2-1.4 A popular platform for the handheld and pocket PCs is Windows CE. Why don't these devices use Windows 98/Me/2000/XP like other personal computers?

2-1.5 How often should you run virus vaccine software to scan your PC system for viruses?

2-1.6 Discuss the consequences of not performing routine disk maintenance with utility software.

2-2.1 Describe the Windows desktop. Where would you put the taskbar—at the top, at the bottom, or on one of the sides? What else would you do to personalize your desktop?

2-2.2 List and briefly describe four elements of the Windows application window.

2-2.3 In the Windows environment, how is an item, such as an application program or a menu option, selected with a mouse? How is the item opened?

2-2.4 Describe the relationship between a Windows menu bar, a pop-out menu, and a menu item followed by an ellipsis (. . .).

2-2.5 There are two camps when it comes to learning a software package. Some prefer to read the instructions carefully before attempting to create a document. Others prefer to begin using the software, tapping context-sensitive help as needed. In which camp would you feel most comfortable? Why?

2-2.6 Describe three situations in which you might use the Clipboard to copy or move information within or between applications.

2-2.7 Some organizations may delay their migration from an earlier version of Windows to the most recent version of Windows for several years. What do they lose and what do they gain by delaying this decision?

2-2.8 Software vendors list minimum system requirements (processor speed, amount of RAM, etc.) to run their software. Frequently, however, a minimal PC may not permit any real user interaction with the software (too slow, poor graphics, and so on). Why don't vendors publish more realistic system requirements for their software?

2-2.9 Briefly describe at least one advantage gained by dynamically linking information via OLE. Give an example of when object linking might be appropriate.

2-3.1 List five ways that you might use word processing software at school or work. And five more ways at home.

2-3.2 Name five format considerations for a word processing document.

2-3.3 What is meant when a document is formatted to be justified on the right and on the left? Give three examples where type of justification is used.

2-3.4 Customer-service representatives at BrassCo Enterprises spend almost 70% of their day interacting directly with customers. Approximately one hour each day is spent preparing courtesy follow-up letters based on boilerplate text, primarily to enhance goodwill between BrassCo and its customers. Do you think the "personalized" letters are a worthwhile effort? Why or why not?

2-3.5 Identify at least one print document in each of the following environments that would be more effective if distributed as an electronic document: federal government, your college, and any commercial organization. Name five types of charts that can be created with presentation software and illustrate three of them. Describe a situation in which you may need to export a presentation software file to a different type of document (for example, word processing). Do the same for importing a file into a presentation software file.

2-3.6 Create a series of bulleted text charts (manually or with presentation software) that you might use to make a presentation to the class on the capabilities and benefits of presentation software.

2-3.7 Identify three applications for spreadsheet software. Then for each application describe the layout specifying at least three column entries and, generally, what would be contained in the rows.

2-3.8 Use the examples in this section as your guide, and create a formula that might be used in one of the spreadsheet applications you identified in the above question (or another of your choosing). Briefly describe the entries in the formula.

2-3.9 Give an example of four types of ranges. Also, list an alternative way to define the range A4:P12.

2-3.10 Describe the relationship between a field, a record, and the structure of a database table.

2-3.11 If you were asked to create a PC-based inventory management system for a privately owned retail shoe store, would you use spreadsheet software, database software, or both? Why?

2-3.12 Describe two types of inquiries to a student database that involve calculations.

2-3.13 Under what circumstances is a graphic representation of data more effective than a tabular presentation of the same data?

2-3.14 Give examples and descriptions of at least two other fields that might be added to the record for the STUDENT table (Figure 2-28).

2-3.15 Name two possible key fields for an employee file. Name two for an inventory file.

2-3.16 Use appropriate relational and logical operators to set conditions for displaying STUDENT, COURSE TITLE, and MAJOR for all courses completed by marketing or accounting majors that include a lecture. Illustrate the results showing column headings and the appropriate entries sorted by student.

2-3.17 Describe how you might use personal information management software at home.

2-3.18 Describe how you might use personal information management software at work. Which PIM component would be most helpful to you?

2-4.1 Why do you suppose there are so many different graphics file formats? Why doesn't the graphics industry standardize a single format for bit-mapped graphics and a single format for vector graphics?

2-4.2 If you have a PC, list the three home and family software packages in your software portfolio that are most important to you. What home and family packages would you like to add to your portfolio?

2-4.3 What home and family software packages would you like to add to your software portfolio during your first year of PC ownership?

2-4.4 Would you feel comfortable creating common legal documents, such as wills and bills of sale, with legal software without input from an attorney? Explain.

2-4.5 Some children spend more time playing computer-based games than they do attending school. Would you limit your child's time at playing games? If so, how much time each day would be appropriate?

2-4.6 For centuries, the book has been the primary resource for learning. How do you feel about exchanging that tradition for computer-based learning resources that are dynamic, linked, and interactive?

2-4.7 What do you think about integrating entertainment with education software for elementary age children? How about doing this with education software for adults?

2-4.8 Identify at least three printed reference documents you have used in the past that might be improved if made available as CD-ROM-based reference software. Explain why each would be better in electronic format.

2-4.9 A diminishing number of attorneys choose to use printed law books. Would you prefer to retain the services of an attorney who prefers books or one who prefers using electronic media? Explain.

2-4.10 If you work in a business, briefly describe the personal computing software (other than office suite software) that is most useful to you in your job.

FOCUS ON PERSONAL COMPUTING

1. Begin a personal computing session. In Windows, click on *Start* then *Help and Support* in any version of Windows, and then choose options that tell you more about the Windows operating system. For example, Windows XP has "Windows Basics" which tells you how to perform core Windows tasks, search for information, protect your computer, and keep Windows up-to-date. Spend a few minutes learning more about Windows and list four things you learned that you did not know before.

2. Use paint software, such as Paint or Paintbrush (in legacy versions of Windows), to create an image of your choice. Use at least five different paint software features in the creation of the image. Discuss the capabilities and limitations of Paint.

3. Go to a local PC software store, or, if you have access to the Internet, go online and navigate to a software e-tailer, such as Amazon.com (www.amazon.com). Identify at least one commercial software package in each of these categories: graphics, home and family, education, and reference. Which would you purchase first to begin building your software portfolio? Why? How about second? Why?

1. The Online Study Guide (multiple choice, true/false, matching, and essay questions)
2. Internet Learning Activities
   - Operating Systems
   - The Windows Environment
   - Word Processing
   - Spreadsheet/Database
   - Graphics
3. Serendipitous Internet Activities
   - Humor
   - Hotels and Restaurants
   - Money Management

chapter 3

Learning Objectives

Once you have read and studied this chapter, you will have learned:

- The scope of the online world and some of its many opportunities, plus Internet concepts, including how to go online and the makeup of an Internet address (Section 3-1).

- How you can use Internet browsers to access a wealth of information on the Internet (Section 3-2).

- The scope of Internet resources and the various types of Internet applications, including the World Wide Web, FTP, e-mail, instant messaging, newsgroups, and videoconferencing (Section 3-3).

GOING ONLINE:

Why this chapter is important to you

The Internet is a new door in our lives that was simply not there a few years ago. In this chapter you'll learn about online information services and the Internet, what you'll need to do to get on, what you'll find when you get there, and how you travel to what seems to be an endless variety of cybersites.

To say that the Internet has had a profound impact on our lives is truly an understatement. What we do at work, how we work, how we learn, and what we do during leisure time have changed dramatically during the short-lived public Internet era. The virtual classroom, where students can attend classes online, is remaking our college and university system. Each year millions more people choose to telecommute to work from their homes. Many more people make their résumé available to millions by posting it to the Internet, then using searchable jobs databases to find employment throughout the world. Many people stay connected to the Internet all day long, taking advantage of its latest resources to get help with many daily activities—planning a vacation, getting the best deal on an airline ticket, communicating with friends via e-mail or instant messaging, and so on. More and more, we rely on the Internet to get our news and weather, and even to play games with other cybersurfers.

For those of you who have not had an opportunity to browse the Internet, this chapter should unlock the door to information and services that can stagger your imagination. The typical response from a first-time visitor to the Internet, called a newbie, is something like "Wow, I had no idea!"

3-1 The Internet

E-mail, which is now familiar to most people, is one of the bright stars shining in cyberspace (see Figure 3-1). Now imagine being able to explore an entire universe with millions of interesting stars offering thousands of helpful databases, forums for discussions on everything from autos to Zimbabwe, online chat, free downloadable files of every conceivable type, countless free and pay-for-use information services, real-time (as it happens) statistics on sporting events, the latest music videos, college courses and degrees, real-time stock quotes, new and classic electronic books (e-books), the biggest mall in the world, and so much more (see Figure 3-2). That's *the Internet*.

INTERCONNECTED NETWORKS

The Internet is a worldwide collection of *inter*connected *networks*. It's actually composed of millions of independent networks at academic institutions, military installations, government agencies, commercial enterprises, Internet support companies, and just about every other type of organization. Many individuals and families maintain a presence on the Internet, too. Indeed, just about every company and organization has a presence on the Internet. If not, they are in the process of creating a presence.

Just how big is the Internet? The Net links over a million networks with Internet host server computers in every country in the world. Each host computer, an Internet server computer, is connected to the Internet 24 hours a day. Thousands more link up to this global network each month.

The number of people using the Internet is now in the billions. Within the decade, the whole world may be wired, as every country has made access to the Internet a priority, including third world countries. Developed countries are moving toward universal access where every citizen will have ready access to the Net. In America, over 99% of the schools have Internet access that is made available to students. The Internet has created this global village, for we now live in a community of the world.

ARPANET TO THE INTERNET

A lot happened in 1969, including the first landing on the moon, and Woodstock, the culture-defining three-day rock festival. Amidst all of this activity, the birth of what we now know as the Internet went virtually unnoticed. A small group of computer scientists on both coasts of the United States were busy creating a national network that would enable the scientific community to share ideas over communications links. The government-sponsored project, named ARPANET, was to unite a community of geographically dispersed scientists by technology. By 1981, the ARPANET linked 200 sites. A few years later, this grand idea of interconnected networks caught on like an uncontrolled forest fire, spreading from site to site throughout the United States. Other countries wanted in on it, too. In 1990, ARPANET was eliminated, leaving behind a legacy of networks that evolved into the Internet. At that time, commercial accounts were permitted access to what had been a network of military and academic organizations.

What we now know as the Internet is one of the federal government's success stories. Although the Internet, along with its policies and technologies, is now pushed along by market forces, the United States government remains active in promoting cooperation between communications, software, and computer companies.

WHO GOVERNS THE INTERNET?

When the ARPANET was conceived, one objective of its founders was to create a network in which communications could continue even if parts of the network crashed. To do this, it was designed with no central computer or network. This is still true today. The U.S. Internet *backbone*, the major communications lines and nodes to which thousands of host computers are connected, crisscrosses the United States with no node being the central focus of communications.

Unlike AOL, CompuServe, and other information services, the Internet is coordinated (not governed) by volunteers from many nations serving on various advisory boards, task groups, steering committees, and so on. There is no single authoritative organization. The volunteer organizations set standards for and help coordinate the global operation of the Internet. Each autonomous network on the Internet makes its own rules, regulations, and decisions about which resources to make publicly available. Consequently, the people who run these independent networks are reinventing the Internet almost daily.

FIGURE 3–1 The Internet Is Changing Our Way of Life
Ten years ago, virtually all U.S. mail was processed by the U.S. Postal Service (shown here at the San Diego Post Office). Today, several hundred e-mails (see inset) are sent via the Internet for each letter processed by the Postal Service. That ratio has increased dramatically since the events of September 11, 2001. Many organizations changed their policies to encourage more extensive use of electronic communications when terrorist began mailing letters and packages containing the bacterium that causes anthrax.

Courtesy of Lockheed Martin Corporation

FIGURE 3–2 Videoconferencing
Others throughout the world were able to "attend" this presentation at the annual Intel Developer Forum via Internet-based videoconferencing.

Courtesy of Intel Corporation

Any person or organization desiring to connect a computer to the Net must register its **domain name** (for example, ibm.com, yahoo.com, and so on) and computer. The domain name is usually the name of the organization, an abbreviation of the name, or a something similar. The Internet is transitioning to a privatization of the domain name registration process. Now, if you or your company would like to secure a domain name, you would contact any of a number of domain name registration service providers from around the world. In the past, InterNIC, a government-funded organization, provided registration services for the Internet community. Collectively, these organizations keep track of the computers connected to the Net (site names and addresses). They also provide assistance to users concerning policy and the status of their existing registrations. Registered Internet hosts must pay an amount based on Internet usage to support the Internet's backbone.

CONNECTING TO THE INTERNET: NARROWBAND AND BROADBAND

A variety of communication channels, some made up of wires and some without wires, carry digital signals between computers and over the Internet. Each is rated by its *channel capacity* or **bandwidth**, which refers to the amount of digital information that can be pushed through the channel. Bandwidth or channel capacity is the number of bits a line can transmit per second. Domestic channel capacities vary from 56,000 **bits per second** (**bps**), or 56 K bps (thousands of bits, or kilobits, per second), to 9 M bps (millions of bits, or megabits, per second). Commercial channels carry up to 622 M bps.

Channels with high bandwidth are called *broadband*. A channel with a low bandwidth is called *narrowband*. Broadband and narrowband channels are analogous to interstate highways and county roads, respectively. The former carry considerably more traffic, bits, or automobiles, than the latter. The generic term for high-speed Internet access is **broadband access.**

Narrowband: Dialup Service

A dialup link is a temporary connection established by using a modem to dial up the number of the Internet service provider's (ISP's) remote computer (over a regular telephone line). Dialup access is available to anyone with **POTS**—plain old telephone services. When you call the telephone company and request a telephone line, it installs POTS. This narrowband service is in just about every home and business in the United States. This analog line permits voice conversations and digital transmissions with the aid of a modem. Traditional modem technology permits data transmission up to 56 K bps (thousands of bits per second).

PERSONAL COMPUTING:
Broadband vs. Narrowband For about double the monthly subscription cost of dialup Internet access you can have broadband access at 20 to 30 times the speed. The click-and-view Internet (broadband) is a different world than the click-and-wait Internet (at 56 K bps). Broadband changes your perspective on what you can do on the Internet. When you can go more places in less time, you become a cyberexplorer. You don't hesitate to download a 3 MB demo song from a new album. You can enjoy streaming video at broadband resolutions (near TV quality). You tend to take advantage of more online services. Plus, broadband access can be enjoyed by everyone in the family via home networking. If your pocketbook will allow, broadband offers a truly different Net experience.

Broadband: Fast Internet Service

For most of the public Internet era, dialup service was the only option. Now millions are enjoying broadband access, which is 15 to 30 times faster than narrowband access. As anyone who is familiar with click-and-wait narrowband access can attest, Internet access via broadband offers an entirely different experience. A Web page that might take one minute to load at narrowband speeds takes only three seconds on a broadband line.

Broadband opens the door for some amazing applications. Applications include support for full-motion video, videoconferencing, high-speed transfer of graphics, and real-time applications involving a group of online participants. Broadband has become popular for telecommuters who work at home but need to be networked to their office's computer system.

Broadband is "always on," so there is no need to dial up and logon. Generally, the broadband access fee is about double that of narrowband. The most common broadband options are, in order of popularity, cable, DSL, satellite, and wireless.

- *Cable.* Cable television systems originally were designed to deliver television signals to subscribers' homes. However, cable companies everywhere are updating their analog cable infrastructure to enable delivery of digital service that offers crystal-clear television signals and high-speed Internet access. Initially, cable Internet access companies are offering 1 M bps (megabits per second) up to 10 M bps service, significantly faster than POTS service and only slightly more expensive. A 1 M bps channel capacity is very inviting to the millions of people who are chugging along at 56 K bps over POTS lines. Linking to cable TV for Internet access requires that you be a cable subscriber and have a *cable modem*.

- *DSL.* Another technology, **DSL (Digital Subscriber Line)**, has made it possible to receive data over POTS lines at 1.5 to 9 M bps (the **downstream rate**). In a few years, the downstream rate will be 52 M bps. The **upstream rate** (sending) is 128 K bps to 1.5 M bps. Like cable, DSL requires a special *DSL modem;* however, it can share an existing telephone line such that voice conversations and digital transmission can occur at the same time. Cable access was the first widely available broadband service and is leading the way, but DSL is rapidly closing the gap as it is made available to new markets.

- *Satellite.* Broadband Internet access via cable or DSL is not universally available, even for people living in some metropolitan areas. However, satellite service is available to anyone in America with a southern exposure to the sky and the necessary equipment, a digital *satellite dish* and a *satellite modem.* Digital satellite access offers downstream speeds of 400 K bps to 1.5 M bps and upstream rates of 56 K bps to 1.5 M bps.

  Satellite has a built-in lag in response time of about a quarter of a second, because of the time it takes the signal to travel to the satellite and back (about 47,000 miles). For most Internet activities, this latency is not a problem, but it can cause problems for real-time interaction, such as in online multiplayer gaming. Also, satellite access may not be available when the cloud cover is dense (thunderstorms). The latency problem and its dependence on weather make satellite Internet access a good choice only when cable and DSL Internet service are not available.

- *Wireless.* Wireless communication lets users take their PC and a link to a LAN (and therefore the Internet) with them to the classroom, conference room, the boss's office, poolside, or wherever they want to go within the limited range of the wireless link. For example, hundreds of colleges make wireless LANs available to students and professors from wherever they might be on campus. Access points, which are hardwired to a central server computer, are scattered throughout campus to extend the reach of the wireless LAN. The **access points** are communications hubs that enable users of PCs and other devices with wireless capabilities to link with the campus LAN via short-range radio waves. The most popular standard used for short-range wireless communication is **Wi-Fi** (*wireless fidelity*), a name given to the **IEEE 802.11b** communications standard. Wi-Fi permits wireless transmission at 11 M bps up to about 300 feet from an access point. The **IEEE 802.11a** communications standard permits a transmission rate of 54 M bps, but more access points are needed since the effective range is only 50 feet. Each wireless device must be equipped with a **wireless LAN PC card** or equivalent device to transmit and receive radio signals.

THE LINK TO THE INTERNET

The online world offers a vast network of resources, services, and capabilities. To go online, people at home with PCs generally subscribe to a commercial information service, such as America Online (AOL), or open an account with a company that will provide access to the Internet, an ISP. When at the office or school, people usually go online via a direct link on the organization's local area network or LAN.

Making the Internet Connection

The three most popular ways to connect your PC to the Internet are introduced in Getting Started and discussed in detail in this section. To go online, you will need to connect your PC to the global network we call the Internet.

Connect via an Information Service Gateway

One way to gain access to the Internet is to subscribe to a commercial information service, such as America Online. This connection method is a popular choice for people working from their home or small business and for those who wish to link their home PC to the Internet. AOL and the other major information services are themselves large self-contained networks. Each provides an electronic *gateway* to the Net; that is, you are linked to the information services network that, in turn, links you to the Internet.

Commercial information services have an array of powerful server computer systems that offer a variety of online services, from hotel reservations to daily horoscopes. About one-third of the American households with PCs subscribe to America Online (AOL) and other major information services, such as CompuServe, an AOL subsidiary, or MSN (Microsoft Network), a Microsoft service. Generally, other information services such as LEXIS-NEXIS, Dow Jones Business Information Service, and DialogWeb cater to niche markets, providing specific services to customers with special information needs (legal, financial, and so on). Information services have grown at a rate of 30% per year since 1990 and there is still plenty of room to grow.

To take advantage of information services, you need a communications-equipped PC (that is, one with a modem and communications software) and a few dollars. Most services have a *monthly service charge*. The monthly service charge for the most popular services is usually a flat rate of $20 to $30 for unlimited usage. Initially, you get:

● *Communications software*. Some information services, such as AOL, give you communications software packages designed specifically to interface with their information service network. Others rely on Internet browsers to deliver the service.

● *A user ID and password*. To obtain authorization to connect with the online information service, you need to enter your user ID and a password to **logon**, or make the connection with the server computer. The **user ID**, sometimes called a **screen name** for AOL users, identifies the user during personal communications and it identifies the user to the server computer. The **password** is a word or phrase known only to the user. When entered, it permits the user to gain access to the network or to the Internet.

● *A user's guide*. A user's guide provides an overview of services and includes telephone numbers that can be dialed to access the information service's private network.

Figure 3-3 takes you on a brief visual tour of America Online, the most popular information service. This walkthrough figure shows you a few of the well-traveled roads on this stretch of the information highway, but it does not begin to show the true breadth and scope of America Online (or any other major information service). Existing services are updated and new services are added on AOL and all of the other information services every day.

AOL is often the choice of Internet newbies. **Newbies** are what seasoned Internet surfers (those who regularly travel or "surf" from Internet site to Internet site) call novice Internet users. Newbies like AOL because it offers a user-friendly interface to a wealth of AOL and Internet services and information. In contrast, an ISP simply offers Internet access. Finding and retrieving Internet resources is up to the subscriber.

Connect via an Internet Service Provider

Most Internet users make the connection via a low-speed **dialup connection** or a high-speed **broadband connection** (via cable, DSL, satellite, or wireless) through an Internet service provider. Satellite service is widely available, but DSL and digital cable may or may not be available in your area; however, these high-demand services are being installed at a breakneck pace throughout America and in many other countries. An *ISP* is an organization that provides individuals and other organizations with access to, or presence on, the Internet. ISPs usually are commercial enterprises, but they can be colleges, churches, or any organization with an Internet account and willingness to share or sell access to the Internet. There are thousands of Internet service providers, ranging from local elementary schools making unused line capacity available to students and parents to major international communications companies, such as AT&T and Sprint.

ISPs do not offer the extended services made available by commercial information services, such as CompuServe and AOL, to their customers. What you get is access to the Internet. Services similar to what AOL offers its members are readily available to anyone with Internet access; however, those services and information are not as conveniently packaged.

FIGURE 3–3 TOURING AMERICA ONLINE

COMPUTER CENTER

The AOL Computer Center is among the most active areas. PC enthusiasts can chat for hours about any subject relating to hardware or software. This AOL channel lets you download any of thousands of programs.

SIGN ON TO AMERICA ONLINE

American Online 8.0 software, shown here, provides the interface for over 30 million AOL users. When you sign on to America Online you enter a screen name, usually an alias, like SkyJockey or PrincessLea, and a password. The software dials the AOL number, makes the connection, and displays the AOL main menu (see example), which is divided into 20 channels. You can also sign on to AOL via an ISP/LAN Internet connection.

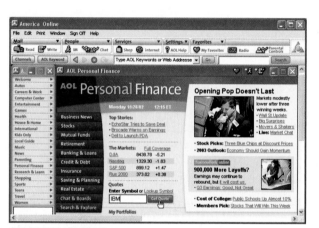

PERSONAL FINANCE

Get up-to-the-minute quotes on stocks, securities, bonds, options, and commodities. A wealth of financial information and services are available for the asking.

Direct via Network Connection

A direct connection to the Internet via a local area network generally is preferable to a dialup link because it normally gives you faster interaction with the Internet. With a direct LAN connection, your PC is linked directly to the Internet via a local area network. A LAN will normally have a broadband link to the Internet, which is shared by the users on the LAN. Depending on the size of the LAN and the extent of Internet usage, the LAN may be connected to a DSL line (up to 9 M bps), a **T-1 line** (1.544 M bps), or a **T-3 line** (44.736 M bps). A faster connection means shorter waits between Internet interactions and the responses. A dialup connection can take from 15 seconds to about 45 seconds to establish, whereas a direct connection via a LAN is "always on." To have a direct connection, your PC must be connected to a LAN that has a link to an Internet host. This is the case with most businesses and college computer labs.

There is a good chance that your college or company's computer network is linked to the Internet. Obtaining access may be as easy as asking your boss, instructor, or the network administrator to assign you an Internet address (user ID) and password.

TCP/IP and Packets

The *Transmission Control Protocol/Internet Protocol* (*TCP/IP*) is the communications protocol that permits data transmission over the Internet. Any operating system (for example, Window or Mac OS) comes with the software needed to handle TCP/IP communications. Communications over the Net are built around this two-layer protocol. A *protocol* is a set of rules computers use to talk to each other.

FIGURE 3–3 continued

PEOPLE CONNECTION
People "enter" AOL chat rooms, the most popular service on AOL, and talk with real people in real time. It's like having a conference call, except the people involved key in their responses. You can "listen in" or be an active part of the electronic conversation. The scrolling conversation on the left is for "The Coffee House," one of the many "Friends" rooms. Also, you can send an instant message to "buddies" who happen to be online, too. Of course, you can send e-mail to anyone in the world who has an e-mail address.

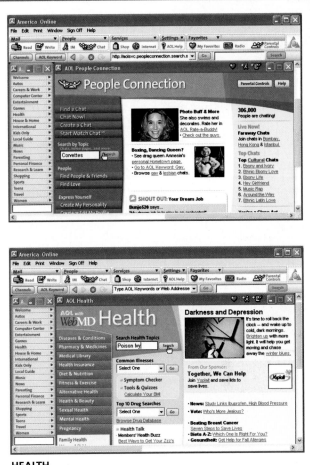

ENTERTAINMENT
The Entertainment channel offers movie reviews, TV guide listings, photos of celebrities, and songs from any style of music, and much more.

HEALTH
You can learn about nutrition and dieting, health and beauty, alternative medicine, HMOs, treatments for various illnesses, treatments for common health problems, and much more at the Health channel.

The *Transmission Control Protocol* (the TCP of the TCP/IP) sets the rules for the packaging of information into **packets.** Each message, file, and so on to be sent over the Internet is disassembled and placed into packets for routing over the Internet. The *Internet Protocol* (the IP of the TCP/IP) handles the address, such that each packet is routed to its proper destination. Here is how it works. When you request a file from an Internet server computer, the TCP layer divides the file into one or more packets, associates a number with each packet, and then routes them one-by-one through the IP layer. Each packet has the same destination *IP address,* but the packets are independent of one another as they travel through the Internet and may take different paths to their destination. A packet may pass through a number of servers and routers before reaching its destination. At the destination, the TCP layer waits until all the packets arrive, reassembles them, and then forwards them to users as a single file.

Each **point-of-presence** (**POP**) on the Internet, such as an Internet service provider, has a unique **IP address** that consists of four numbers (0 to 255) separated by periods (for example, 206.28.104.10). A POP is an access point to the Internet. An ISP may have many POPs for use by their subscribers. Typically, when a user logs on to an ISP, the user's computer is assigned a temporary IP address, called a **dynamic IP address.** By assigning IP addresses as they are needed, the number of IP addresses needed to serve customers is minimized since not all customers are online at any given time.

When you dial up an ISP's local POP, your dialup connection generally is made through a **PPP** (**Point-to-Point Protocol**) connection to an Internet host. Once a TCP/IP connection is established, you are on the Internet, not an information service gateway. The TCP/IP protocol is different from the protocol used within the AOL and CompuServe networks. Their Internet gateways enable communication between the information services' native communications protocols and TCP/IP.

Going Online without a PC

FIGURE 3–4 The Internet on a Phone

The Internet is now available via a variety of devices, including the telephone. This woman is using her Nokia cellular phone to access services and text information over the Internet. The data phone even lets you check and send e-mail. Communication is at 14.4 K bps, relatively slow for graphics, but fast for text on its small display (96 × 65 pixels).

Courtesy of Nokia

You don't have to have a PC to connect to the Internet. Access to the Internet is becoming so much a part of our lives that engineers are finding new ways to give us Internet access. Cyberphobics and those who don't want to purchase a PC can gain access in other ways. The most popular devices are those associated with TV. Some new TVs have built-in modems, Web browsers, and e-mail software. Or, if you don't need a new TV, these capabilities can be purchased in the form of a set-top box and linked to existing TVs. Each TV option comes with a remote keyboard for input.

Entrepreneurs are becoming very imaginative about delivery of Internet service. There's even a plug-in cartridge that turns a Sega video game into a Web browser. The telephone Internet appliance is another path to Internet access. Such devices are used primarily for checking e-mail. Some cellular phones with small embedded displays, called data phones, let you tap into the Internet (see Figure 3-4). Some ISPs offer an **Internet appliance,** such as Intel Corporation's Dot.Station, with subscription to the service. An Internet appliance is an inexpensive communications device with a monitor and keyboard that is primarily for families that do not have a PC. The typical Internet appliance integrates access to the Internet, e-mail, a built-in telephone, and home organization applications.

RETRIEVING AND VIEWING INFORMATION ON THE INTERNET

Once you have established an Internet connection, you're ready to explore the wonders of the Internet—almost. To do so, you need to open a *client program* that will let you retrieve and view Internet resources. A **client program** runs on your PC and works in conjunction with a companion **server program** that runs on the Internet host computer. The client program contacts the server program, and they work together to give you access to the resources on the Internet server. Client programs are designed to work with one or more specific kinds of server programs (for example, the Microsoft Internet Explorer client software works with the companion Internet Explorer server software). A single server computer might have several different server programs running on it, so that it works with multiple clients.

An *Internet browser* is one kind of client. Browsers are application software that present you with a graphical user interface (GUI) for searching, finding, viewing, and managing information over any network. Microsoft Internet Explorer and Netscape are the two most popular browsers. Both are used in the examples throughout this book. Most information on the Internet is accessed and viewed in the workspace of browser client programs. You give the browser an Internet address, called the **URL,** and it goes out over your Internet connection, finds the server site identified in the URL, then downloads the requested file(s) for viewing on your browser. The operation of browsers is discussed later in this chapter.

THE INTERNET ADDRESS: URL

The URL, or **uniform resource locator** (pronounced "*U-R-L*" or sometimes "*earl*") is the Internet equivalent of a postal service street address. Just as postal addresses are interpreted from general to specific (country, state, city, to street address), URLs are interpreted in the same manner. The URL gives those who make information available over the Internet a standard way to designate where Internet elements, such as server sites, documents, files, newsgroups, and so on, can be found. Let's break down one of the following URLs from a proposed companion Internet site for this book (see Figure 3-5).

FIGURE 3–5

THE URL WEB ADDRESS
A Web page is accessed by its URL or Uniform Resource Locator.

http://www.prenhall.com/long/11e/main.html

http:	www.prenhall.com	long/11e	main.html
World Wide Web access method or protocol.	Address, or the domain name, of server at the Internet host site. It will always have at least two parts, separated by dots.	The name of the folder (Long) and, if needed, the subordinate folder (11e) on the server computer's disk that contains the html (Web) document or file to be retrieved.	The name of the document to be retrieved and displayed, in this case an html Web page. This could be a jpg file, pdf file, or some other type of file.

- *Access method or protocol—**http:**//www.prenhall.com/long/11e/main.html*. That portion of the URL before the first colon (*http* in the example) specifies the access method or protocol. This indicator tells your client software, your Internet browser, how to access that particular file. The *http* tells the software to expect an **http (HyperText Transport Protocol)** file. Http is the primary access method for interacting with the Internet. Other common access methods include *ftp* (File Transfer Protocol) for transferring files, and *news* for newsgroups. When on the Internet, you will encounter URLs like these.

ftp://ftp.prenhall.com (Prentice Hall ftp site)

http://www.yahoo.com (Internet portal and search engine)

news://alt.tennis (tennis newsgroup)

- *Domain name—http://**www.prenhall.com/**long/11e/main.html*. That portion following the double forward slashes (//), *www.prenhall.com*, is the server address, or the domain name. The *domain name*, which is a unique name that identifies an Internet host site, will always have at least two parts, separated by dots (periods). This host/network identifier adheres to rules for the domain hierarchy. At the top of the domain hierarchy (the part on the right) is the country code for all countries except the United States. For example, the address for the Canadian Tourism Commission is *info.ic.gc.**ca***. Other common country codes are *au* (Australia), *dk* (Denmark), *fr* (France), and *jp* (Japan). The United States is implied when the country code is missing. The **top-level domains** or **TLDs,** such as *com,* denote affiliations. Colleges are in the *edu* TLD. Other TLDs are shown in Figure 3-6. The next level of the domain hierarchy identifies the host network or host provider, which might be the name of a business or college (*prenhall* or *stateuniv*). Large organizations might have networks within a network and need subordinate identifiers. The example Internet address *cis.stateuniv.edu* identifies the *cis* local area network at *stateuniv*. The Physics Department LAN at State University might be identified as *physics.stateuniv.edu*. An optional *www* prefaces most World Wide Web domain names.

- *Folder—http://www.prenhall.com/**long/11e**/main.html*. What follows the domain name is a folder or path containing the resources for a particular topic. The resource folder, */long* in this example, refers to the proposed Long and Long companion Internet site for all Prentice Hall books by Larry and Nancy Long. Several books are covered within this resource, so subordinate directories are needed to reference a specific book (*long/11e,* implying *Computers,* eleventh edition, folder within the */long* folder).

- *Filename—http://www.prenhall.com/long/11e/**main.html***. At the end of most URLs is the specific filename of the file that is retrieved from the server (the server named *www.prenhall.com* in this example) and sent to your PC over the Internet. The *html* (or *htm*) extension (after the dot) in the filename *main.html* indicates that this is an html file. **HTML (HyperText Markup Language)** is the language used to compose and format most of the content you see when cruising the Net. Some Web files have an *shtml* extension and refer to a type of html file that has nonstandard commands. Of course, the retrieved file can be an image file, an audio file, a video file, or some other type of file. Entering a URL domain name (*www.prenhall.com*) without the *http://* access method identifier or without a filename causes the site's home page to be displayed.

HTML: PUTTING THE PAGE TOGETHER

HTML is a **scripting language,** that is, the programmed tasks to be performed are described in script. A scripting language is interpreted within another program. An Internet browser such as Internet Explorer, the *client program* on your PC, interprets the HTML instructions and then interacts with the server program in accordance with those instructions to download the necessary elements (text, graphics, and so on) and display the Web page. Figure 3-7 shows an HTML source document and the resulting Web page. HTML documents are text (ASCII) files that can be created with any text editor or word processing package. In HTML, each element in the electronic

FIGURE 3–6

TOP-LEVEL DOMAINS
The domain name that comes before these top-level domains can contain only letters, numbers, and hyphens (but not consecutive hyphens or hyphens at the beginning or end) and have at least 3 but no more than 63 characters (for example, www.3-to-63-letters-or-numbers.com).

U.S. Top-Level Domain Affiliation ID	Affiliation
aero	Airline groups
biz	Businesses
com	Commercial
coop	Business cooperatives
edu	Education
gov	Government
info	Purveyors of information
mil	Military
name	Personal Web sites
net	Network resources
org	Usually nonprofit organizations
museum	Museums
pro	Professional

FIGURE 3–7 A WEB PAGE AND ITS HTML SOURCE DOCUMENT

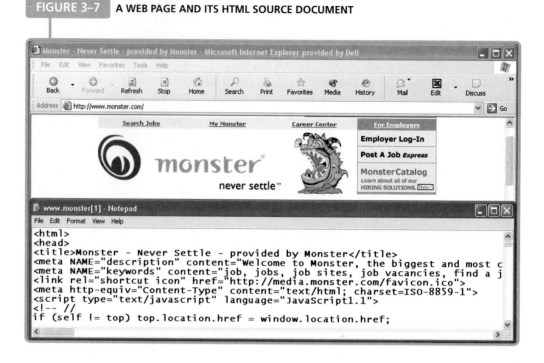

document is tagged and described (for example, justification). Elements include title, headings, tables, paragraphs, lists, and so on. In this example, the title and a paragraph are tagged.

<TITLE ALIGN=CENTER>A Centered Title of an Electronic Document</TITLE>

<P>This paragraph is displayed in standard paragraph format.</P>

Tags always come in pairs, with the last one including a forward slash (/). Tags can include attributes, which further describe the presentation of the element. For example, the title in the example is to be centered on the screen (ALIGN=CENTER). The HTML language also permits the identification of inline (inline with the text) graphic images to be inserted in the document. Inline images are retrieved from the server and inserted as per the HTML instructions (position and size).

For those people who are not used to programming, HTML can be rather cryptic. Fortunately, there are a number of good WYSIWYG development tools that allow you to generate HTML documents using drag-and-drop techniques along with fill-in-the-blank dialog boxes. The tags are inserted automatically for you. For example, you can create a word processing document in Microsoft Word, then save it as an html file, which can be posted to a Web server computer and made available over the Internet.

Over the last decade, billions of Web pages have been created with HTML. Recently, the World Wide Web Consortium announced that the more feature-rich **XHTML** would be the new standard. Effectively, this retires the now somewhat limited HTML. Although HTML is currently the official standard, it will take a while for XHTML to be accepted and used by Web developers.

3-1.1 The monthly service charge for Internet access for most commercial information services is set by law at $10 per month for unlimited usage. (T/F)

3-1.2 These communications channels are listed by capacity (from least to most): dialup, T-1, and T-3. (T/F)

3-1.3 In an Internet address, levels in the host/network identifier are separated by a(n): (a) period, (b) comma, (c) @ symbol, or (d) colon.

3-1.4 TCP/IP is the communications protocol for: (a) the Net, (b) sending faxes, (c) all internal e-mail, or (d) spherical LANs.

3-1.5 The Internet is short for (a) International Network, (b) interconnected networks, (c) internal net e-mail terminal, or (d) inner net.

3-1.6 Which of these communications services is distributed over POTS: (a) cable, (b) Wi-Fi, (c) 802.11b, or (d) DSL?

3-1.7 A dialup connection to the Internet is considered broadband access. (T/F)

3-2 | Internet Browsers

The Internet browser, or *Web browser,* is a software tool that makes it possible for you to tap the information resources of the electronic world and to communicate with others frequenting the electronic world. All new PCs come with browser software already installed, usually Internet Explorer and/or Netscape. Browsers have several main functions.

- *Retrieve and view Internet-based information.* They enable us to retrieve and view information from World Wide Web and FTP server computers on the Internet, on internal (within an organization) intranets, and on any disk medium with HTML-based content (for example, some books, magazines, and company manuals are distributed as electronic versions in HTML format on CD-ROM).

- *Interact with servers.* They allow us to interact with server-based systems and to submit information to these systems.

- *View electronic documents.* They are the foundation tool for viewing electronic documents.

- *Download and upload information.* They let us download digital information, then view and/or hear the downloaded video, images, music, and so on. They let us upload information, as well.

- *E-mail.* They allow us to send and receive e-mail.

- *Newsgroups.* They allow us to participate with online newsgroups.

Here, we focus on the basic elements of browser software. E-mail and newsgroups are covered later.

The viewing area of a browser can be filled with documents containing any combination of text, images, motion video, and animation. The visual information can be enhanced with real-time audio. These various forms of communication are presented within HTML/XHTML documents. The browser opens an HTML/XHTML document and displays the information according to HTML/XHTML instructions embedded in the document. The HTML/XHTML document pulls together all the necessary elements, including image files, audio streams, and small programs. The browser accepts the program in the form of **applets** or **ActiveX controls,** then interprets and executes them. These applets or ActiveX controls give Web developers added flexibility to create imaginative animation sequences or interactive multimedia displays. Browsers can be used with or without an Internet connection; however, an Internet link is needed to access files other than those on your PC or your local area network. Here a few of the many things you can do with browsers:

- Visit the museums of the world.
- Listen to the very latest song from your favorite group.
- Do your grocery shopping.
- Track the progress of the space shuttle.
- Tune in to a radio station in Australia.
- Send and receive holiday greetings to/from friends and family.
- Make an inquiry regarding the status of an order.
- Study from an interactive book in preparation for an exam.
- Send digital business materials, such as contracts and portable documents.
- Participate in ongoing discussions about, and even with, your favorite celebrity.
- Learn more about Greek mythology, kangaroos, or almost anything else.

CONCEPTS AND FEATURES

We interact with word processing, desktop publishing, presentation, spreadsheet, and database software to create some kind of a document. Browser software is different in that there is no resulting document. Browsers let you retrieve and view information as well as interact with server computers. Compared to the other productivity tools, browsers are easy to use, almost intuitive. It's not unusual for non-IT-competent people, unfamiliar with browsers, to be cruising the Internet within minutes after their first exposure to the software.

To use browsers effectively, it helps to understand the basic makeup of the Internet and the browser's navigational tools.

Internet Organization

The vast majority of the Internet resources made available by millions of participating networks can be accessed by anyone, from anywhere. All that is needed is a browser and an Internet connection.

Most knowledge workers now have access to the Internet at work. Families and individuals get online by subscribing to an Internet service provider (ISP) or commercial information service.

The Web Site

At the top of the Internet's organization are the Internet servers, the computers that provide on-demand distribution of information. When you navigate to a particular Web site (perhaps that of your college), the first page you will normally view is the site's **home page.** Information on the Web, which may be graphics, audio, video, animation, and text, is viewed in **pages.** A Web page can contain text plus any or all of these multimedia elements.

Think of a Web page as a page in an alternative type of book, one with nonsequential linked documents at a Web site. The home page is the table of contents for the resources at a server site. A home page will have links to many other pages, some associated with the home page and located on the same server computer and others that may be elsewhere on the Internet. The home page for this book *<http://www.prenhall.com/long>* has hundreds of pages and links to other pages. The home page for Prentice Hall *<http://www.prenhall.com>*, the publisher of this book, has thousands of pages and links to other pages. A page has no set length and can be a few lines of text, or it can be thousands of lines with many graphic images. **Hyperlinks,** in a form of *hypertext* (usually a colored, underlined word or phrase), *hot images,* or *hot icons,* permit navigation between pages and between other resources on the Internet. Click on a hyperlink to jump (link) to another place in the same page or to another Web site on the Internet. All hyperlinks are hot; that is, when you click on one with your mouse, the linked page is retrieved for viewing. An image or icon is hot if the cursor pointer turns into a hand image when positioned over it. Hyperlinks make it easy to skip around within or between Web pages to find what you want.

Each Web page is actually a file with its own URL. Typically, you will start at a Web site's home page, but not always. A college's home page might be at URL http://stateuniv.edu, but each college or department might have a home page as well (for example, *http://stateuniv.edu/cis* for the Computer Information Systems Department's home page). A page is a scrollable file; that is, when it is too large for the viewing area, you can scroll up or down to view other parts of the page.

Internet Servers and Addresses

The World Wide Web (WWW), or Web server, with its multimedia capability, has emerged as the dominant server type on the Internet. The FTP server provides a storehouse for information (in downloadable files) and a convenient way to transfer files between computers. Browsers accommodate information retrieval for any type of Internet server.

We navigate to an address on the Internet just as we drive to a city street. These Internet addresses are called URLs. URLs must begin with *http://* (WWW site), *ftp://* (FTP site), *mail:,* or *news:.* The domain name is usually prefaced by *www* to designate a World Wide Web server (for example, *www.ford.com*).

The pages at a server site are set up within a hierarchy of URLs. At the top in the following example is the company URL, for example, Prentice Hall. Special-topic directories, such as home pages for various Prentice Hall authors (Kotler, Long, Macionis, and Morris in the following example), are subordinate to the company URL but have their own URLs. These directories have subdirectories, which may also have subdirectories, and so on, each of which has its own unique URL. This subset of some of the URLs at the Prentice Hall server site illustrates one hierarchy of URLs.

HOME PAGE *http://www.prenhall.com* (Prentice Hall home page URL)

■ *http://www.prenhall.com/kotler* (home page URL for Kotler books)

■ *http://www.prenhall.com/long* (the Internet Bridge, home page URL for all Long books)

   ● *http://www.prenhall.com/long/computers10e/index.html* (the opening page for a Long book)

      ▲ http:// . . . (other pages associated with the above book)

   ● *http://www.prenhall.com/long/computers11e/index.html* (the opening page for another Long book)

      ▲ http:// . . . (other pages associated with the above book)

■ *http://www.prenhall.com/macionis* (home page URL for Macionis books)

■ *http://www.prenhall.com/morris* (home page URL for Morris books)

Here's the good news. For most of your navigation around the Internet, you'll simply click on a named hyperlink to go to a URL. Occasionally, you will need to enter a URL, usually a home page. This hierarchy of URLs is illustrated in Figure 3-8.

Navigating the Internet

Microsoft Internet Explorer and Netscape, the dominant browsers, are shown in Figure 3-9. Internet Explorer is the Internet client of choice for four of every five users in the world.

The Menu Bar

The menu bar at the top of the user command interface is used to select File options (Print, Save, and so on), to select Edit options (including Copy, Cut, and Paste), and to set and change a variety of options (for example, how buttons are displayed, color options, font choices, and so on). As with most menu bars, the Help pull-down menu is the last option.

The Toolbar

In a typical browser session, most of your interaction is with the toolbar and the hot links in the Web pages. These are the navigation buttons on the Internet Explorer toolbar (Netscape's toolbar has similar functions).

- *Back*. During the course of a browser session you will normally view several pages, one after another. This button takes you back to the last site (or page) that you visited.

- *Forward*. Use this button if you clicked on the Back button and would like to go forward to the next site in the string of sites (or pages) you have viewed.

- *Stop*. Use the Stop button to abort any transfer of information to/from the server. The browser displays the last fully viewed site.

- *Refresh*. This button refreshes (reloads) the current document into the browser. Information on some pages is volatile and may need to be updated.

- *Home*. This button takes you to the URL that you have selected as your default home page, perhaps that of your college or company.

- *Search*. This button calls up the Internet portal that you have selected as your default search site. A **portal** is a Web site that offers a broad array of information and services, including a menu tree of categories, a tool that lets you search for specific information on the Internet, and a variety of services from up-to-the-minute stock quotes to horoscopes. Infoseek, Excite, and Yahoo! are portals.

- *Favorites*. Click on the Favorites button (in Internet Explorer) or Bookmarks button (Netscape) to view a list of sites that you placed in your Favorites or Bookmarks folder. Typically, these are the sites that you visit frequently.

   The browser logo symbol to the right of the toolbar is animated when your browser is transferring or waiting on the information from the server.

The URL/Search Bar

The URL/Search bar, sometimes called the location bar, serves several purposes.

- It allows you to key in (or paste in) the URL (the address or "location") of the desired Web site.

- It displays the URL of the page being displayed in the workspace.

- It includes a drop-down box with a list of previously visited URLs. To return to one of these sites, simply select it from the list.

- It permits keyword searches of Internet resources.

THE HIERARCHY OF URLS AT A SERVER SITE
This figure shows three levels of URLs at the United States Air Force site. In the background is the Air Force Link home page <www.af.mil>. Selecting the "Photos" option (in black menu bar) displays the photos page <www.af.mil/photos>. Selecting the "Fighters" hyperlink takes you to Photos-Fighters page <www.af.mil/photos/fighters.shtml>. Choosing a particular photo (each is a hyperlink) takes you to the next level that displays caption information and a larger image.

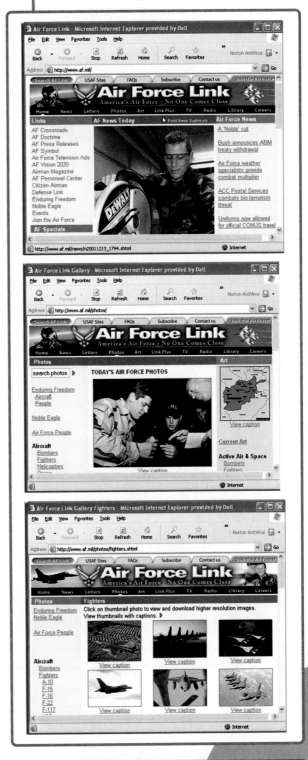

FIGURE 3–9

MICROSOFT INTERNET EXPLORER AND NETSCAPE BROWSERS
The functionality and appearance of these two browsers is similar and they have the same basic elements.

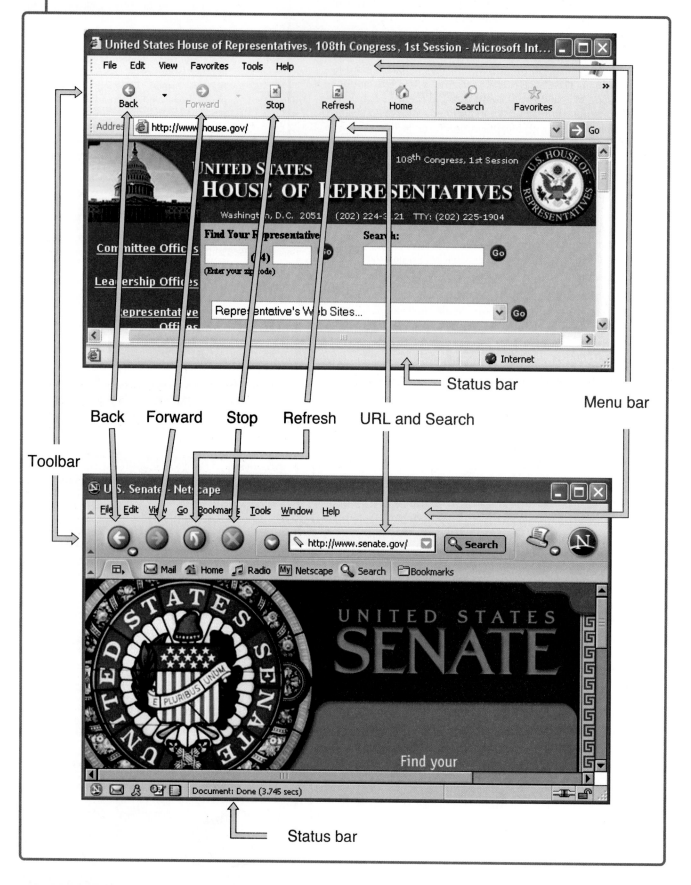

Status bar

Menu bar

Back   Forward   Stop   Refresh   URL and Search

Toolbar

Status bar

The Workspace

The workspace is that area in which the document is displayed. You can view documents by scrolling or by using the Page Up and Page Down keys. Left click on a hyperlink, a hot image, or a hot icon to navigate to and view another Web page. Right click to call up a menu that includes such options as adding the site to your Favorites list, saving the current document, downloading the image, and so on.

The Status Bar

The status bar is found below the workspace. This area displays the status of transmissions to and from Internet servers ("Finding site: *www.prenhall.com*," "Connecting to site," "Web site found. Waiting for reply," "Opening picture: *logo.gif* at *www.prenhall.com*," and so on). When transmission is complete, the status bar may display other information or instructions relating to the use of the browser. The transmission status box gives you a visual reference of transmission progress.

BROWSER PLUGINS

The function and use of Internet browsers are changing as quickly as the applications on the Internet. At this writing, there are a number of complementary applications, called **plugins,** which can enhance the functionality of browsers. Here are a few of the more popular plugins. Download sites are listed in parentheses.

- *Shockwave Player (www.macromedia.com).* Macromedia Shockwave Player displays Web content created with Macromedia Shockwave software, such as interactive multimedia product demos, e-commerce presentations, animations, and multiuser games.

- *Flash Player (www.macromedia.com).* Macromedia Flash Player lets Web surfers view content created with Macromedia Flash, including dynamic graphics and animations.

- *RealJukebox (www.real.com).* The RealJukebox plugin gives you everything you need to play and record MP3 music.

- *Liquid Player (www.liquidaudio.com).* The Liquid Player plugin lets you play and record MP3 music, plus you can read lyrics and liner notes, organize your music, view album art, and create your own CDs.

- *RealPlayer (www.real.com).* RealPlayer lets you listen to streaming audio and view streaming video. **Streaming audio** and **streaming video** are different from downloading in that a file is not saved on your computer for replay.

- *QuickTime (www.apple.com).* QuickTime lets you view QuickTime videos, listen to music, and view panoramas.

- *iPIX® Movies (www.ipix.com).* This unique plugin lets you view an image from every direction. You can look up, down, and all around by simply pointing where you wish to view. The only way to understand fully this plugin is to view an iPIX movie (see Figure 3-10).

- *Acrobat Reader (www.adobe.com).* Adobe Acrobat Reader reads and displays PDF-format electronic documents.

It may be inevitable that these and other capabilities will be integrated into future releases of major browsers. Browsers will continue to change with the technology, but most industry observers feel that browsers will remain intuitive and, perhaps, become even easier to use.

FIGURE 3–10

BROWSER PLUGINS: IPIX® MOVIES The iPIX browser plugin is one of several Internet browser plugins. This one lets Net surfers view an image from every direction. Simply move a pointing hand to the edge of the image to look up, down, and all around. You can even zoom in for a closer look. Real estate companies can give prospective buyers a panoramic view of every room in a house. Colleges use these "bubble" or "360" images to make their Web sites stand out for students looking for a place to study.

3-2.1 The Internet browser is also called a Web browser. (T/F)

3-2.2 Small programs embedded in HTML documents are called: (a) apples, (b) applets, (c) applications, or (d) omelets.

3-2.3 Internet-based capabilities that help you find information on the Internet are: (a) seek portals, (b) find files, (c) search motors, or (d) search engines.

3-2.4 A URL that begins with http:// begins the address for what type of Internet server: (a) Web, (b) e-mail, (c) file transfer protocol, or (d) news?

3-2.5 To eliminate the spread of viruses, the uploading of files is no longer permitted on the Internet. (T/F)

3-3 Internet Resources and Applications

The Internet offers a broad spectrum of resources, applications, and capabilities. In this section, we'll discuss how to find what you need, the major Internet applications, and ways you can use the Internet to communicate with people.

FINDING RESOURCES AND INFORMATION ON THE NET

The Internet has thousands of databases, such as the *Congressional Record,* NIH clinical information, a list of job openings for the entire United States, and the lyrics to "Yesterday" by the Beatles. You name it and, if it can be digitized, there is a good chance that it is on the Net. The information on the Internet is out there, but getting to it can be challenging—and a lot of fun. We can search for it or just wander around the Internet until we find it. Or, we can be passive about it and let the information come to us.

There are three ways to search the Internet: *browse, search*, and *ask someone*. The function of a browser is to take you somewhere in the electronic world. Where you go and how you get there is entirely up to you. There are two basic approaches to using a browser: *browsing* and *searching*. The difference between browsing and searching is best explained through an analogy to a print book. When you leaf through a book, you're browsing. When you select a topic from the index and open the book to the indicated page, you're searching.

Browsing the Net

Browsers let you poke around the Internet with no particular destination in mind—this is browsing. Some people just get on the Internet and travel to wherever their heart leads them. All the popular portals on the Net offer a menu tree of categories. An Internet portal is always a good place to start. These portal sites divide the wealth of resources on the Internet into major categories. The categories for Yahoo!, one of the most popular portals, are representative.

Arts & Humanities	Entertainment	Recreation & Sports	Social Science
Business & Economy	Government	Reference	Society & Culture
Computers & Internet	Health	Regional	
Education	News & Media	Science	

Click on one of these main categories, each a hyperlink, to view subcategories. For example, clicking on Yahoo!'s "Arts & Humanities" displays subcategories: Art History, Artists, Arts Therapy, and so on. You may navigate through several levels of categories before reaching the pages you want. The typical portal will have a variety of service options as well, such as shopping, news and sports, new/used automobile research, job search, classified ads, games, horoscopes, people search, yellow pages, stock quotes, chat rooms, television listings, map search (maps and driving instructions), personals, and more.

Most of us have at least one general interest area in mind, even when browsing. For example, let's say you want to go shopping for holiday gifts. You can do this by going to the various "shop" categories, moving from virtual store to virtual store. Whether shopping or just surfing the Internet, browsing is always fun because you never know what you will find or where you will end up. Many pages have *banner ads* or *skyscraper ads* that entice us to click on them and travel to a totally unrelated site. With increasing frequency, Net surfers are experiencing *pop-under ads* (ads that open in a separate browser window "under" the requested page) and *floating ads* (an ad that "floats" over the requested pages for a few seconds). These ads often are context sensitive based on your preferences that may have been saved from previous sessions. For example, if you indicated an interest in skiing, a pop-under ad might present you with a special promotion package for a skiing vacation. Sometimes the ads appear based on your menu selection or search item. If you choose "skiing," up pops a related ad in a separate browser window. Such ads are becoming increasingly controversial.

Using Search Engines to Search the Net

You can browse the Net or you can search it. If you knew that you wanted to buy your parents sterling silver candlesticks for their twenty-fifth anniversary, then you would want to go directly to a site that sells them—the quicker the better.

The Net helps those who help themselves. Each major portal, such as Excite, provides a resource discovery tool, called a **search engine,** to help you find the information or service your need. Most of them let you find information by keyword(s) searches. You can search the Net by keying in one or more keywords, or perhaps a phrase, that best describes what you want (perhaps, information on "Julia Roberts" or who might offer a "masters degree biomedical engineering"). The rules by which you enter the keywords and phrases vary slightly between the search engines (see Figure 3-11). These hints may reduce your search time.

FIGURE 3-11 **AN INTERNET SEARCH ENGINE**
Yahoo!, shown here, is a popular Internet portal and search engine. Internet users can enter keywords or phrases (such as "bed and breakfast and Berkshires" in search box in the background window), and the search engine scans its database, and then lists applicable pages (see middle window). Clicking on the "Bed and Breakfast in the Berkshires" hyperlink took the user to the linked Web site (foreground window). Yahoo! also allows users to navigate to desired sites through a menu tree of categories and subcategories (see lower left of Yahoo! home page).

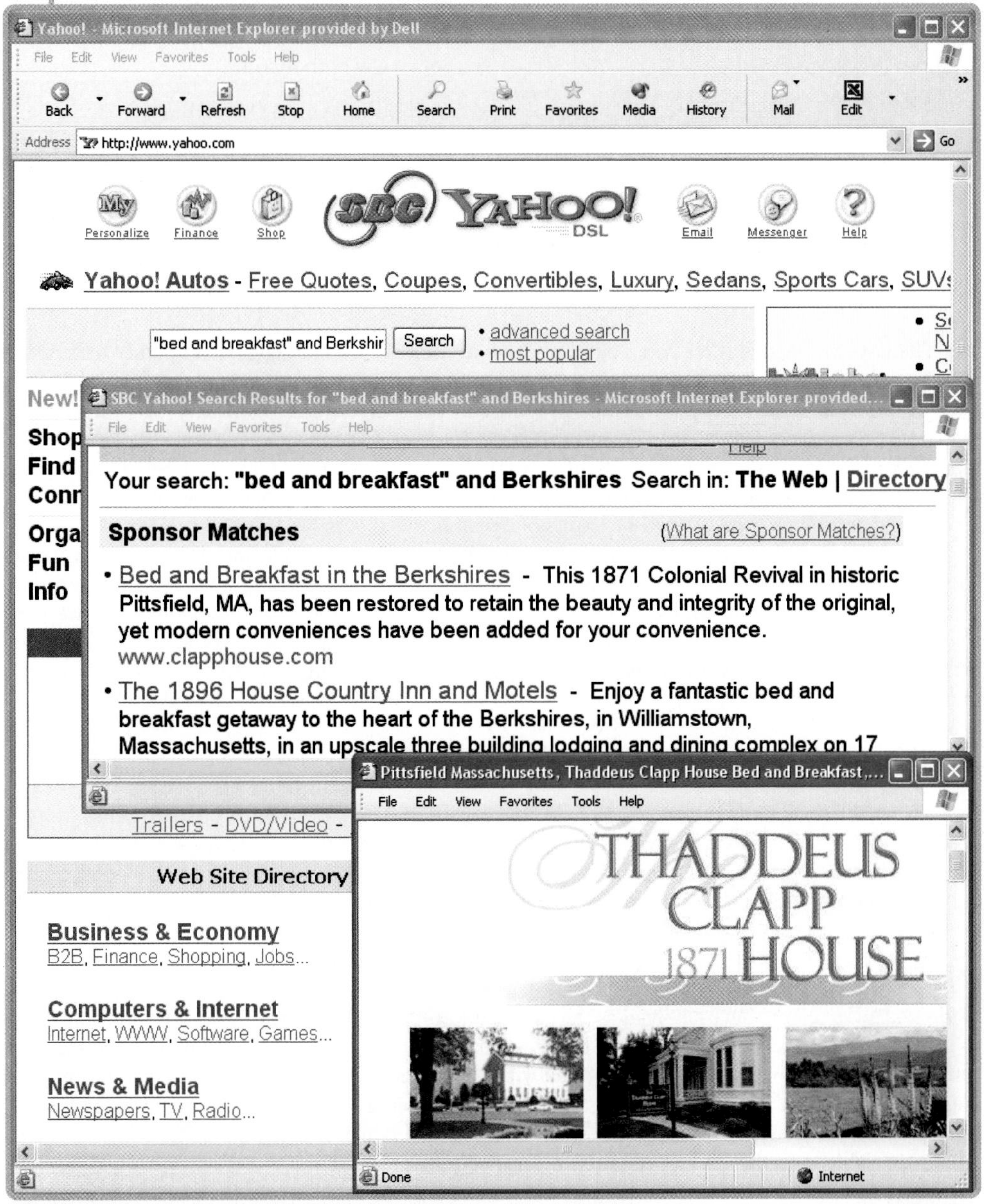

- *Read the search rules.* Each search engine has different rules for formulating the inquiry. Click on "help" and read the instructions first.

- *If you don't get results with one search engine, try another.* The results vary significantly between search engines, because their databases are compiled in completely different manners. For example, Yahoo!'s database is organized by category, encouraging topical searches such as "White House AND press room." Google's database is created from actual content on the Web, enabling searches for specific phrases, such as "Penn State Nitany Lions."

- *The results of the search are seldom exhaustive.* You may need to go to one of the listed sites, and then follow the hyperlinks to find the information you need.

- *Choose search words carefully.* The keywords and phrases you enter are critical to the success of your search. Try to be as specific as you can. You may wish to try the portal's advanced search options which enable you to narrow your search. For example, Yahoo! lets you limit your search to a particular language or country, or to a particular time frame (for example, past 3 months). You can identify words to be included or excluded.

- *Be persistent.* Many of your searches will result in something like "Search item not found." This doesn't mean that the information you need is not on the Internet. It means only that you need to extend your search to other search criteria and/or other search engines.

The Internet has hundreds of search tools, some of which focus on a particular area, such as technology or medicine. These are among the more popular search tools.

Yahoo! (www.yahoo.com)	HotBot (www.hotbot.com)
Infoseek (www.infoseek.com)	Ask Jeeves (www.askjeeves.com)
Google (www.google.com)	MSN Internet Search (search.msn.com)
AltaVista (www.altavista.com)	Netscape Search (search.netscape.com)
Search.com (www.search.com)	Metacrawler (www.metacrawler.com)
Excite (www.excite.com)	Dogpile (www.dogpile.com)
Northern Light (www.northernlight.com)	

The last two, Metacrawler and Dogpile, search a number of search engines in parallel, then display the result for each search tool.

Search tools search only a fraction of Web content. Search engines index (include in their searches) only a small percentage of Web sites on the Internet. For most tools, searches cover no more than 20% of the Web. Most search less than 10%. Search engines tend to index the more popular sites, that is, those sites with the most **hits** and links to them. A hit is either when a Web page is retrieved for viewing or when a page is listed in results of a search.

Generally, portals with search engines are business ventures. Keep in mind that the companies sponsoring these widely used portals make money by selling advertising and by selling priority rights to a particular word or phrase. For example, if you enter the keywords "long-distance telephone," the company that purchased the rights to these words or this phrase would be listed in a priority position (first or possibly alone). It pays to tap into several portals to get the best deal or most impartial information.

Asking Someone

People on the Net are a family, ready to help those in need. Don't hesitate to post an inquiry to the people in the cyberworld via a topical newsgroup when you need help. Also, the Net is full of **FAQs (frequently asked questions)** pages and files that you can view or download. There is a good chance that your question has probably been asked and answered before.

INTERNET APPLICATIONS

World Wide Web servers have emerged as the choice for cruising the Internet; however, traditional not-as-user-friendly types of servers contain useful information still not available from World Wide Web sources. FTP, which predates the World Wide Web, is the most widely used resource for information outside of the Web. Critical resources on these servers are being reformatted and modernized for distribution via World Wide Web servers, but this may take a while. In the meantime, these resources remain available from these effective but old-fashioned servers.

Web Servers

The World Wide Web, affectionately called *the Web,* is an Internet system that permits linking of multimedia documents among servers on the Internet. By establishing a linked relationship between Web documents, related information becomes easily accessible. These linked relationships are completely independent of physical location. These attributes set Web servers apart from other Internet servers.

- *User-friendly*. Prior to the World Wide Web, most Internet users were techies and IT professionals. With Internet browsers, we can point-and-click our way around the Web.

- *Multimedia documents*. A Web page is much more than a page in a book. It can contain all of these multimedia elements: graphics, audio, video, animation, and text.

- *Hyperlinks*. Multimedia resources on the Web are linked via hyperlinks. Words, phrases, and graphics can be marked to create interactive links to related text or multimedia information.

- *Interactive*. The Web system, with its pages, enables interactivity between users and servers. There are many ways to interact with the Web. The most common form of interactivity is clicking on hyperlinks to navigate around the Internet. Some pages have input boxes into which you can enter textual information. You can click on option buttons to select desired options. **Option buttons** are circle bullets in front of user options that when selected include a dot in the middle of the circle. Each time you enter information in a text box or make selections, you will normally have to click on a submit button to transmit the information to the server computer. Also, the various browser plugins offer a variety of interactivity.

- *Frames*. Some Web sites present some or all of their information in **frames.** The frames feature enables the display of more than one independently controllable section on a single Web page (see Figure 3-12). When you link to a Web page that uses frames, the URL of that page is that of

FIGURE 3–12

A WEB PAGE WITH FRAMES
The home page for Slate, an e-zine (online magazine), uses frames to list the e-zine's departments (the vertical frame on the left) and the options for their affiliate MSN (the vertical frame on the right). A pop-out menu appears when the hand is positioned over a Slate department, showing hyperlinks to related articles. Slate articles (the Web site content) are displayed between the two always-available options frames.

a master HTML file that defines the size, position, and content of the frames. Ultimately, your request for a frames page results in multiple HTML files being returned from the Web server. The frames capability may be used to display the main site options in one small frame and the primary information page in another larger frame. Sometimes a third frame displays context-sensitive instructions.

FTP Servers

The **File Transfer Protocol** (**FTP**) allows you to download and upload files on the Internet, in much the same way you might manipulate files in folders on your PC. FTP has been around for a long time, so thousands of FTP sites offer millions of useful files—most are free for the asking. FTPing is a popular activity on the Net. You can download exciting games, colorful art, music from up-and-coming artists, statistics, published and unpublished books, maps, photos, utility and applications programs—basically anything that can be stored digitally. Many FTP sites invite users to contribute (upload) files of their own.

You must be an authorized user (know the password) to access protected FTP sites. Most, however, are anonymous FTP sites that maintain public archives. **Anonymous FTP** sites allow anyone on the Net to transfer files without prior permission. If you are asked to enter a user ID and a password, don't panic. Just enter "anonymous" or "ftp" at the user ID prompt and enter your e-mail address (or just tap the Enter key) at the password prompt. Although most files on an FTP server might be restricted to the server computer and its users, often there is a public or "pub" directory that contains files accessible to all Internet users.

The trick to successful FTPing is knowing where to look. Fortunately, you can connect to FTP sites using a Web browser. Figure 3-13 demonstrates the hierarchical organization of FTP files.

WEBCASTING

Until recently, all Internet sites were more or less passive, waiting for Net surfers to find them. It's now apparent that the Internet can be a broadcast medium as well. For example, thousands of radio stations now **webcast** their audio signals over the Internet (see Figure 3-14). If you have an Internet con-

FIGURE 3–13   **FTPING ON THE INTERNET**
The browser image illustrates how you might navigate through the directories of an anonymous FTP site. The user proceeded from the /graphics/ directory to the /graphics/train/ directory to the /graphics/train/diesel/ directory to the 1189-1.GIF file (the train engine). The FTP site shown here, however, has been converted to a user-friendlier World Wide Web format (right). Other major FTP sites have undergone or are undergoing a similar transformation.

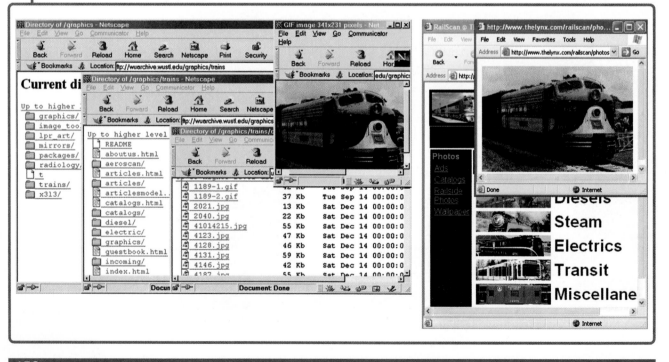

nection and a multimedia PC, there is no reason for you to miss the radio broadcast of any of your favorite team's games. To tune in to the game, simply use your browser to navigate to the webcasting radio station's Internet site, then request a *real-time audio stream* of the game. You may need a streaming audio browser plugin to receive and play the audio or video stream. The audio player plugins let you preset "stations" and scan them, much as you would in a car radio. Can TV broadcasting be far behind?

Generally, Internet applications are based on **pull technology** whereby the user requests information via a browser. Broadcast applications employ **push technology**, whereby information is sent automatically to a user. Several companies, including USA Today, broadcast news and other information in real time that can be customized to your information needs. For example, you can request news on a particular topic (personal computing, politics) or from a particular country, weather for a particular region, stock quotes for selected companies, business news for selected industries, sports news relating to a particular sport (even to your teams), and so on. The company periodically scans available Net sources then automatically delivers information to you via push technology for viewing (see Figure 3-15).

FIGURE 3–14 WEBCASTING ON THE INTERNET
This figure shows a real-time audio stream from BluegrassCountry.org, a webcasting Internet radio station. Windows Media Player plays real-time streaming audio in stereo. A built-in equalizer and a variety of "visualization" options, which can be made full-screen, enhance your listening enjoyment. You can listen while surfing the Internet.

THE JUKEBOX

A major new Internet application is the **digital jukebox.** Now that virtually all music is digital, the Internet may be emerging as the primary delivery system for music in the near future. Jukebox software (see Figure 3-16), which is offered by Microsoft, Real Networks, and others records, stores, and plays music on the PC. The software can also download stored music to portable players. The Internet is truly alive with music, with lots of MP3 music files, and thousands of radio stations and other sites offering online music. The digital jukebox can help you gather MP3 and other audio files from Internet music resources. Use it to play stored music or real-time music from the Internet or CDs based on user-defined playlists. Jukebox software also has a capability to play popular videos along with the music. It also lets you visualize the music through abstract digital art that is constantly changing with the rhythm and sound of the music.

COMMUNICATING WITH PEOPLE OVER THE NET

The Internet is not just a resource for information and services; it is also an aid to better communication. There are several ways for people to communicate over the Internet, including e-mail, audio mail, newsgroups, mailing lists, chat rooms, instant messaging (IM), Internet telephone, and videophone.

E-mail

You can send e-mail to and receive it from anyone with an Internet e-mail address, which is just about everyone who uses the Internet. Each Internet user has an electronic mailbox to which e-mail is sent. E-mail sent to a particular person can be "opened" and read by that person. To send an e-mail message, the user simply enters the address (for example, *TroyBoy@mindspring.com*) of the recipient, keys in a message, adds a subject in the subject line, and clicks the send icon to place the message in the recipient's electronic mailbox. When you send an e-mail, it is routed over the Net to the destination server where it is stored on disk in the recipient's electronic mailbox. The e-mail remains there until the recipient logs on to the server and retrieves his or her e-mail. All e-mail to that address is then routed to the recipient's PC and e-mail client software for viewing.

You can send an e-mail message to anyone on the Net, even the President of the United States (*president@whitehouse.gov*). You can even use Internet e-mail to give your congressperson a few political hints.

FIGURE 3–15

PUSH TECHNOLOGY

The USA Today NewsTracker gathers news, weather, sports, and financial information according to preset user specifications and then delivers it in real-time via the Internet via push technology. The NewsTracker banner (top) can remain active at the top of the screen and other applications. The NewsTracker screen saver (bottom) presents current news on user-selected topics. Just click on a heading in the banner or screen saver to get the complete story or click on the "alerts" button to get personalized news, sports, and so on.

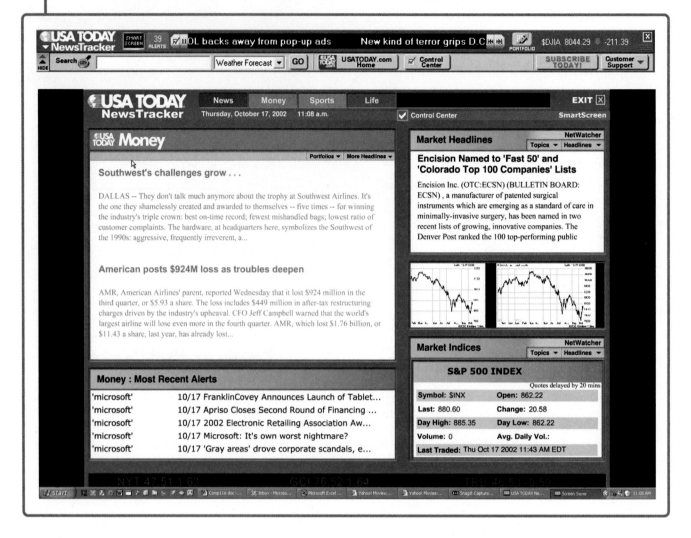

There are two ways to send/receive e-mail—via *e-mail client software* or via *Web-based e-mail*. E-mail client software, such as Microsoft Outlook, enables e-mail through a program running on your computer (see Figure 3-17). Web-based email is handled through interaction with a Web site, such as Yahoo! (see Figure 3-18). Each method has its advantages. The main advantages of the e-mail client approach are that e-mail can be integrated with other applications such as a calendar and task list, and all of these related applications can be incorporated with other e-mail client users on an organization's local area network. Web-based e-mail is easily accessible from any Internet-connected computer in the world—at a coffee house in Tokyo, a public library, a friend's house, and so on.

Your Internet e-mail address is your online identification. Once you get on the Internet, you will need to let other users and other computers know how to find you. All of your interaction will be done using your Internet address. Think of an Internet address as you would your mailing address. Each has several parts with the most encompassing part at the end. When you send mail outside the country, you note the country at the end of the address. The Internet address has two parts and is separated by an @ symbol. Consider this example Internet address for Kay Spencer at State University in CIS:

kay_spencer@cis.stateuniv.edu

- *Username—**kay_spencer**@cis.stateuniv.edu.* On the left side of the @ separator is the username (usually all or part of the user's name). Organizations often standardize the format of the username so users don't have to memorize so many usernames. One of the most popular formats is simply the

FIGURE 3–16

DIGITAL JUKEBOXES
Millions of songs flow throughout the Internet everyday. Digital Jukeboxes, such as RealJukebox shown here in full and "skin" (not within a window) views, enable downloading, cataloging, playing, and visualization of songs, along with artist information and Internet links to related sites.

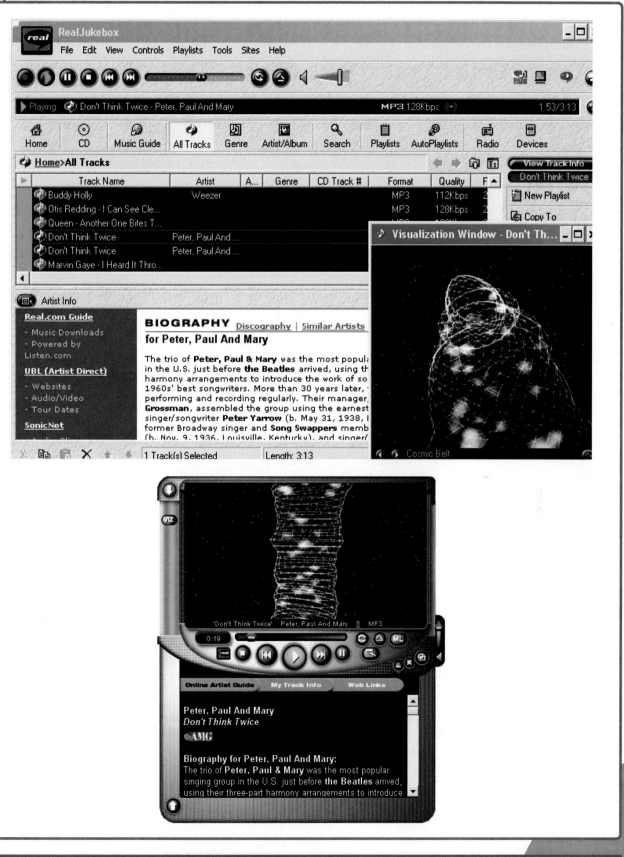

FIGURE 3–17

E-MAIL VIA E-MAIL CLIENT SOFTWARE

Microsoft Outlook (shown here) is representative of e-mail client software and the presentation is representative of e-mail in general: to, cc (copy to), bcc (blind copy to), subject, text of message, and an attached file. The attached file is sent with the message. This e-mail client software (the software you use to receive and send e-mail) permits messages to be sent and viewed in rich text format, that is, with variations in font attributes and embedded graphics. The optional "personal information" placed automatically at the end of each message is called a signature. People usually include name, address, company (if appropriate), and communications information into the signature.

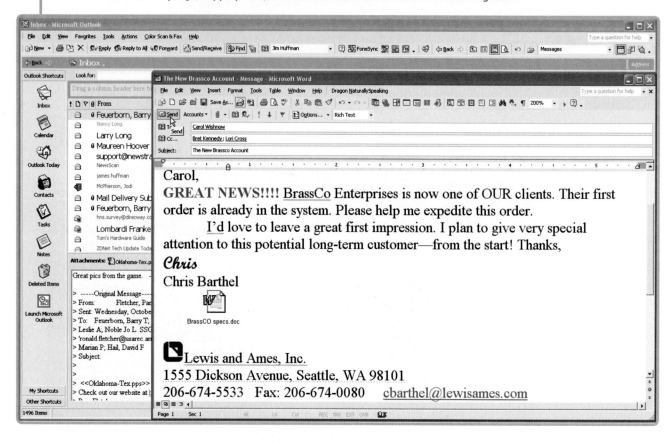

first and last name separated by an underscore (kay_spencer). Some organizations prefer an abbreviated format to help minimize keystrokes. For example, some have adopted a username format in which the first five letters of the last name are prefaced by the first letter of the first name (kspenc).

● *Domain name for the host/network—kay_spencer@**cis.stateuniv.edu.*** That portion to the right of the @ identifies the host or network that services your e-mail, sometimes called the **e-mail server.** This is normally the Internet address for your Internet service provider (for example, sbcglobal.net), your information service (for example, aol.com), your college (for example, stateuniv.edu), or your company (for example, wal-mart.com).

The e-mail client software is the software that interacts with the e-mail server to enable sending and receiving of e-mail. Early e-mail client software packages limited messages to simple ASCII text. However, most modern e-mail client software and Web-based e-mail let you embed graphics and do fancy formatting as you might in a word processing document. Also, you can attach files to an e-mail message. For example, you might wish to send a program or a digitized image along with your message. The **attached file** is routed to the recipient's e-mail server computer along with the message. It and the message are downloaded to your PC when you ask for your e-mail.

The typical e-mail client software has some handy features. For example, you can send copies of your e-mail to interested persons. Or, you can forward to another person(s) e-mail messages that you received. Another feature lets you send a single e-mail to everyone on a particular distribution list (for example, workers in a particular department or players on a soccer team). You can even send your e-mail to a fax machine. E-mail features and services continue to grow (see Figure 3-19). One of the information services translates e-mail messages posted in French and German into English, and vice versa.

FIGURE 3–18

WEB-BASED E-MAIL
The interaction through Yahoo! Mail is via a Web site. Web-based e-mail is sent and delivered via a Web site versus an e-mail client. An advantage of this type of e-mail is that it provides seamless integration of your e-mail and the World Wide Web. With Web-based e-mail, folders containing your e-mail (inbox, sent, and so on) are maintained at the server site (for example, Yahoo!). This allows you to send and receive e-mail from any PC with an Internet connection and a browser.

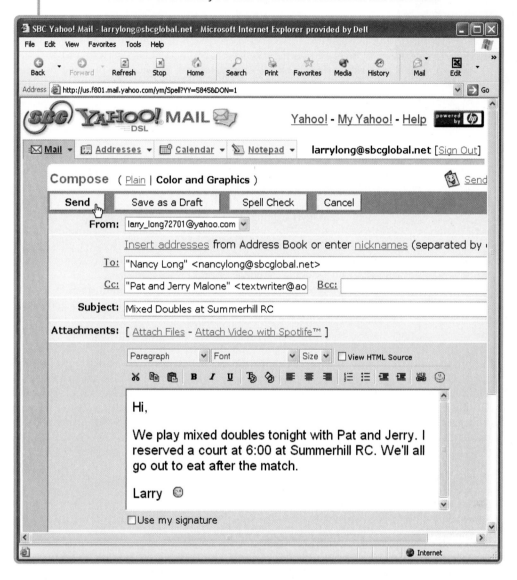

POP stands for both point-of-presence on the Internet (discussed earlier in this chapter) and **Post Office Protocol.** Post Office Protocol refers to the way your e-mail client software gets your e-mail from the server. When you get access from an Internet service provider, you also get a Post Office Protocol account. When you set up your e-mail client software, you will need to specify this account name to get your mail (usually your username).

The United States Postal Service is losing ground to electronic communications. As more people send birthday invitations and greeting cards via e-mail and business communications continues its trend away from "snail mail" to e-mail, look for substantial increases in e-mail volume and commensurate decreases in traditional mail. E-mail has resulted in tremendous changes in the business world, as did the invention of the telephone. The telephone, however, is essentially one-to-one communication, but e-mail can be one-to-one, one-to-many, or many-to-many—and it's written, documented information.

Audio Mail

E-mail is just text. But with audio mail software you speak your message instead of typing it. Users send sound files over the Internet (rather than e-mail), thus producing a form of worldwide audio

FIGURE 3–19 Wireless Inter-tainment Computer
With new Cybiko portable wireless inter-tainment system kids can chat with friends, play interactive games, send and receive emails, and enjoy hundreds of applications. The manufacturer has teamed with a number of shopping malls so that youth shoppers can receive and send your email wirelessly.

Courtesy of Cybiko, Inc.

messaging. Proponents of **audio mail** tout it as a faster and more effective way to communicate over the Internet. It eliminates the need to key in, edit, and spell-check text before sending a message, a time-consuming task for many of us. Also, audio mail conveys humor and other emotions that may be lost in e-mail messages. Audio mail is just evolving, but it's inevitable that this system of worldwide audio messaging will continue to grow and mature.

Newsgroups

A **newsgroup** is the cyberspace version of a bulletin board. A newsgroup can be hosted on Internet servers and on USENET servers. **USENET** is a worldwide network of servers that can be accessed over the Internet. "Newsgroups" is a misnomer in that you seldom find any real news. They are mostly electronic discussion groups. Tens of thousands of newsgroups entertain global discussions on thousands of topics, including your favorite celebrities or professional teams. If you're unable to reach celebrities via e-mail, you can talk about them on an Internet newsgroup. For example, *alt.fan.letterman* (the newsgroup's name) is one of the David Letterman newsgroups. Sometimes the talk show host joins the fun. If Letterman is not your cup of tea, you can join another newsgroup and talk about Madonna (*alt.fan.madonna*) or Elvis (*alt.fan.elvis-presley*). Real Elvis fans can learn about recent Elvis sightings on the *alt.elvis.sighting* newsgroup.

Newsgroups are organized by topic. The topic, and sometimes subtopics, is embedded in the newsgroup name. Several major topic areas include news, *rec* (recreation), *soc* (society), *sci* (science), and *comp* (computers). For example, *rec.music.folk* is the name of a music-oriented newsgroup in the recreation topic area whose focus is folk music. Another example is *rec.sport.tennis*.

You need *newsreader client software* or similar software that is built into most Internet browser clients. Generally, newsgroups are public, but if you wish to keep up with the latest posting in a particular newsgroup, you will want to subscribe to it (at no charge). The newsreader software lets you read previous postings (messages), add your own messages to the newsgroup, respond to previous postings, and even create new newsgroups. Figure 3-20 illustrates interaction with a newsgroup.

People who frequent newsgroups refer to the original message and any posted replies to that message as a **thread.** The newsreader sorts and groups threads according to the original title. For example, a thread that begins with a message titled "Pete Sampras' forehand" includes all of the replies titled "RE: Pete Sampras' forehand." If you post a message with an original title or reply to a message and change the title, you start a new thread. For example, posting a reply titled "Pete Sampras' backhand" begins a new thread.

FIGURE 3–20

NEWSGROUPS ON THE INTERNET
People frequenting the highlighted newsgroup (rec.music.fold) post messages related to aerobic fitness. This person has subscribed to this and eight other newsgroups (see list in folders window). In the example, a newsgroup subscriber was viewing a thread dealing with the subject "George—exceptionally talented, and Way under-credited and under-appreciated. . ." This user can reply as well and have his reply added to this thread for all subscribers to see.

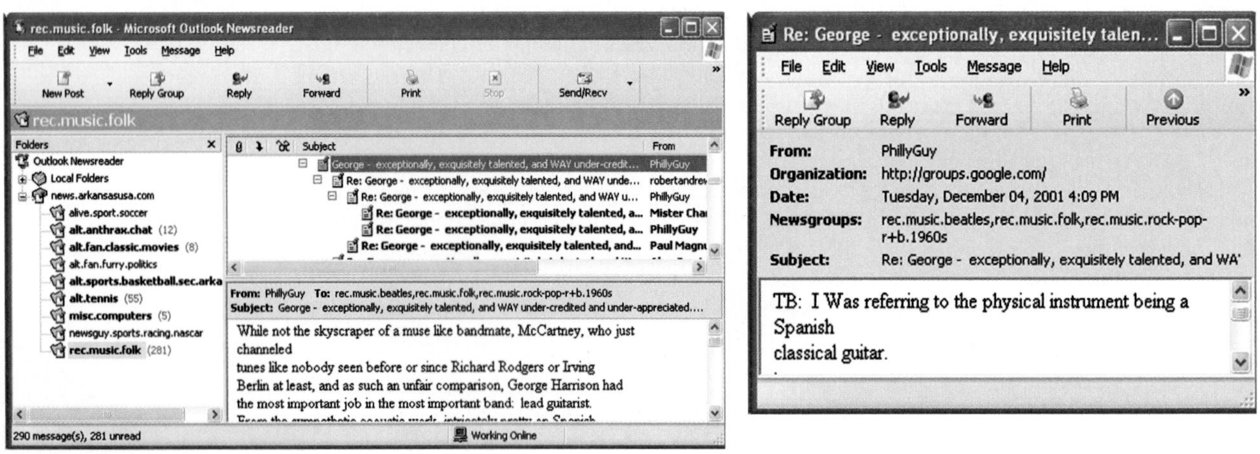

Mailing Lists: Listservs

The Internet **mailing list** is a cross between a newsgroup and e-mail. Mailing lists, which are also called *listserv's,* are like newsgroups in that they allow people to discuss issues of common interest. However, newsgroups are *pull technology* and mailing lists are *push technology;* that is, mailing list content is delivered automatically to your e-mail address.

There are mailing lists for most, if not all, of your personal interest areas. To find one of the interest areas, you scan or search available mailing lists from any of a number of sources. Portals, such as Infoseek, summarize and describe thousands of listserv's by description, name, and subject (just search on "mailing list"). When you find one you like, you simply send an e-mail message containing the word *subscribe* plus your name to the mailing list sponsor, and the sponsor puts you on the list. Mailing lists have two addresses, one to send instructions like subscribe (and unsubscribe) to the list, usually listserv@someplace.com. For example, you can subscribe to the Women's History mailing list at listserv@h-net.msu.edu. The other address is where you send e-mail messages to be distributed to others on the list. Most mailing lists are administered automatically at the server site.

Generally, there is no subscription fee. Once on the list, you receive every e-mail message sent out by the sponsor of the mailing list. Some mailing lists are one-way from the list's sponsor. Others accept and redistribute all e-mail received from subscribers. Sending mail to the list is as easy as sending an e-mail message to its mailing list address.

Subscribing to a mailing list can be stimulating and, possibly, overwhelming. Remember, each message posted is broadcast to all on the list. If you subscribe to a couple of active mailing lists, your Internet mailbox could be filled with dozens if not hundreds of messages—each day! So, if you can't get enough of David Letterman through a newsgroup, you can subscribe to a mailing list whose theme is Letterman.

Internet Relay Chat: IRC

At any given time, the Internet is filled with virtual chat sessions where people talk about anything from vintage muscle cars to yoga. They do this using the **Internet Relay Chat (IRC)** protocol, which allows users to join and participate in group chat sessions. A chat session is when two or more Internet users carry on a typed, real-time, online conversation. Chatting is a favorite pastime of million of cybernauts. They do this by establishing a link with a chat server; that is, an Internet server that runs the IRC protocol.

Chat servers let users join chat sessions called *channels.* A single chat server can have dozens, even thousands, of chat channels open at the same time. The name of the channel will usually reflect the general nature of the discussion. Usually channel names are unchanged, but topics on the channels are continuously changing. For example, in a channel called "Personal Computing," the topic might be "iMac tips" one day and "Windows XP troubleshooting" the next day.

The channel operator creates or moderates the channel and sets the topic. This way, chat participants can exchange ideas about common interests. Chats are ideal for group discussions. For example, many organizations schedule chat sessions as a way to exchange information between employees and customers. Universities schedule chat sessions to exchange technical information and advice. When you log into a chat session, you can "talk" by keying in messages that are immediately displayed on the screens of other chat participants (see Figure 3-21). Any number of people can join a channel discussion. The rate at which you communicate is, of course, limited by your keyboarding skills.

The natural evolution is from keyed-in chat to voice chat where the person's actual voice is heard in the chat room. Some people say that the inevitable emergence of voice chat signals the end of traditional chat. Others, however, cite the advantages of anonymity in text-based chat rooms and feel keyed-in chat will be around for some time to come.

Instant Messaging

Instant messaging (IM) is a logical outgrowth of e-mail. It is a convenient way for you to know when your friends, family, and colleagues are online so you can communicate with them in real-time. America Online popularized instant messaging, but now several Internet companies, including Yahoo! and Microsoft, provide instant messaging services.

To participate in instant messaging, you must first sign up with one of the instant messaging services and install its client software. Then you must create a contact list that contains the online identities of the people you wish to track for instant messaging. Typically, the people on your list will have you on their list. When you go online and sign in to the IM service, you are notified when your "buddies" are online and they are notified that you are online. You can then send instant messages, and even images, to those "buddies" currently online. Also, instant messaging software lets you initiate a telephone-type conversation with people on the contact list, if you wish to talk, rather than key in the words. Some instant messaging programs permit video conversations (see Figure 3-22).

THE CRYSTAL BALL:
Expanding Online Services Face-to-face services may dwindle as we find better ways to deliver services online. For example, many states let their citizens renew licenses (car, hunting, and so on) online without human intervention, thus saving states and their citizens time and money. To some extent, these services already are online: telemedicine, interactive artificial-intelligence-based technical support, elections and voting, religious confessionals, weddings, loan processing, college applications, the daily newspaper, most common legal services, courses at all levels of education, and remote participation in virtually any public meeting. Whether it is signing up for youth league soccer, ordering a pizza, or buying a house, our lives will be made less complex via this growing base of online services.

FIGURE 3–21

AN AOL CHAT SESSION
One of the most popular destinations on AOL is the thousands of chat rooms. AOL and other Chat programs let you "enter" a chat room and have real-time conversations with other people from all over the world.

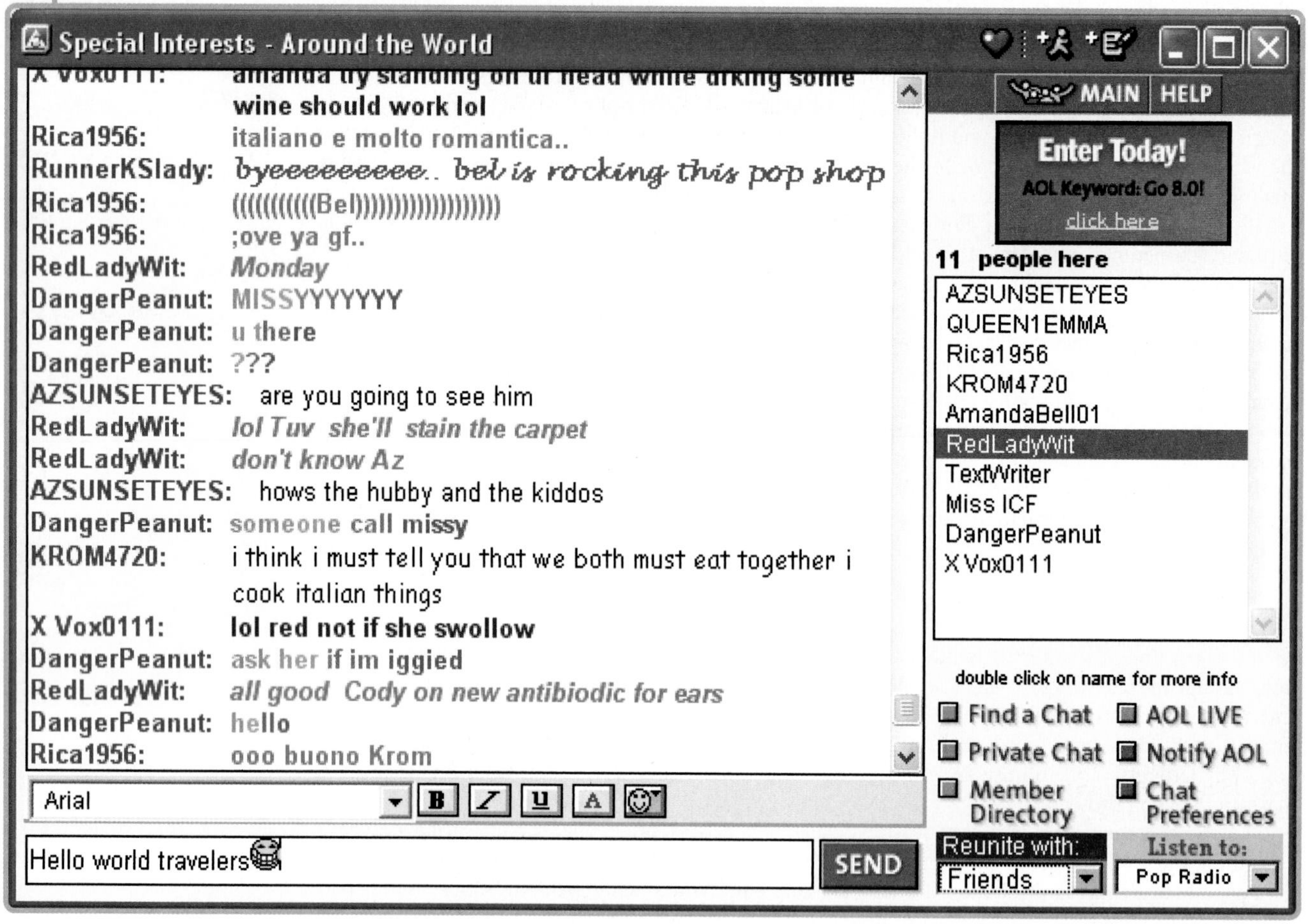

Originally designed to enable casual online interaction, instant messaging is rapidly becoming a viable business tool (see Figure 3-23). People in the business community have the same problem getting hold of their colleagues as the rest of us do communicating with our friends and neighbors. In fact, telephone tag may be the most played game in the corporate world. Instant messaging offers a new level of connectivity not available in e-mail or telephone exchanges. What instant messaging offers is a real-time link between people who routinely interact with one another in a business environment. IM immediately informs the others when one of their colleagues is available. Also, the most recent versions of instant messaging software permit sophisticated communication that includes file/application sharing, whiteboarding, and the ability to have audio and video conferencing. **Whiteboarding** enables participants to sketch and illustrate ideas. When one person runs the whiteboard option, it automatically appears on everyone's screen. Everything that is drawn on the whiteboard is displayed for all to see.

One side benefit that could have a major impact on how and where we work is that instant messaging provides managers with greater control over workers who may be telecommuting. The net effect is that companies are becoming more receptive to telecommuting arrangements.

The Internet Telephone

To make a traditional phone call we simply pick up a telephone, which is linked to a worldwide communications network, and speak into its microphone and listen through its speaker. Guess what? Millions of Internet users with multimedia PCs have these same capabilities: access to a worldwide network (the Internet), a mike, and a speaker. The Internet telephone application is becoming so popular that is being bundled with other popular Internet communications software, such as instant messaging (see Figure 3-22). Internet phone software capability lets you call people at other computers on

FIGURE 3–22

INSTANT MESSAGING: VIDEO CONVERSATION
The Windows Messenger instant messaging software permits text, audio, and video conversations (shown here).

FIGURE 3–23 Instant Messaging at the Office
The use of instant messaging is growing at the office. Employees "sign-in" and "sign-out" depending on their availability for electronic interaction.

On the Internet

- Accessing Information and Services
  - World Wide Web (the Web)
  - FTP
  - Webcasting
  - Digital jukebox
- Communicating with People
  - E-mail
  - Audio mail
  - Newsgroups
  - Mailing list (listserv)
  - IRC (chat)
  - Instant messaging
  - Internet telephone

the Internet. These computers must have the same capabilities. By now, you are probably wondering about cost. There is no added cost over the cost of your PC and your Internet connection. People routinely use this capability to talk for hours on international calls!

Here is how the Internet telephones work. First, you establish a connection with the Internet, then open your Internet telephone software. The software automatically notifies the host server that you are available for calls. If you and your brother, who lives in Germany, wanted to talk via Internet telephone, you would both have to be online with Internet telephone software running and be registered with the same server. Internet telephone service is available that will let you call any traditional telephone in the world via your PC and the Internet, but there is a per-minute fee, which is usually less that the charges for traditional long-distance telephone service.

Cybertalk and Netiquette

Typically, we key in, rather than speak, our words and emotions when we communicate online. People who frequent chat rooms, do instant messaging, send e-mail, and participate in newsgroups have invented keyboard shortcuts and **emoticons** (emotion icons), which are sometimes called smileys, to speed up the written interaction and convey emotions. Some of the most frequently used keyboard shortcuts and smileys are illustrated in Figure 3-24.

In cyberspace there is no eye contact or voice inflection, so cybernauts use smileys to express emotions. They must be effective because many couples who meet on the information highway are eventually married. Their courtship may have involved some of the smileys in Figure 3-24.

There are some basic rules of **netiquette,** Internet etiquette.

- Avoid using all capital letters, unless you wish to shout.
- Never send spam, unsolicited e-mail, as this is the ultimate Internet faux pas.

FIGURE 3–24   **CYBERTALK: KEYBOARD SHORTCUTS AND EMOTICONS**

INTERNET SHORTHAND

AFJ	April fool's joke	**LOL**	Laughing out loud
<–AFK	Away from keyboard	**ROFL**	Rolling on the floor laughing
BRB	Be right back	**TPTB**	The powers that be
BTW	By the way...	**TTYL**	Talk to you later
F2F	Face-to-face	**<VBG>**	Very big grin
FAQs	Frequently asked questions	**WAG**	A guess
<GG>	Grin	**Wizard**	A gifted or experienced user
IMHO	In my humble opinion...	**YKYBHTLW**	You know you've been hacking too long when
IRL	In real life		

EMOTICONS: EMOTION ICONS

*	Kiss	:-~)	User with a cold
:-)	Smiling	:-@	Screaming
:'-(	Crying (sad)	:-&	Tongue tied
:'-)	Crying (happy)	:-Q	Smoker
:-(	Sad	:-D	Laughing
<:(	Dunce	:-/	Skeptical
:-o	Amazed	O :-)	Angel
:-|	Bored	;-)	Wink
:-I	Indifferent	:c)	Pigheaded
8-)	Wearing sunglasses	@–>–>–	A rose
::-)	Wearing glasses	[[[***]]]	Hugs and kisses

EMOTICONS: POP ART

+-(:-)	The Pope
==:-D	Don King
[8-]	Frankenstein
= =):-)=	Abe Lincoln
@@@@@@@@:)	Marge Simpson
/:-)	Gumby
7:-)	Ronald Reagan
\	
8-]	FDR
*<(:')	Frosty the Snowman
(8-o	Mr. Bill
~8-)	Alfalfa
@;^D	Elvis

- Be sensitive to the moral compass of your recipients when forwarding Internet content, especially jokes.
- Never send e-mail containing the personal information of others without their permission.
- Use the "returned receipt requested" option sparingly.
- Be patient with newbies and recognize that they are working up the learning curve.
- Some people prefer a casual style of communication, so avoid making comments about keyboarding style, spelling, or grammar.
- Honor someone's private communication with you and keep it private.
- Think twice before attaching a large file to an e-mail going to someone with a slow dialup service.
- Never forward a virus warning without confirming it with reliable sources because most virus warnings are hoaxes.
- Use antivirus software to maintain a virus free environment, as most viruses are passed via e-mail.

CRUISING THE NET

Vast, enormous, huge, immense, massive—none of these words is adequate to describe the scope of the Internet. Perhaps *the Internet* may someday emerge as a euphemism for anything that is almost unlimited in size and potential. There are at least as many applications on the Internet as there are streets in Moscow. To truly appreciate Moscow, you would need to learn a little of the Russian language and the layout of the city. Navigating the Internet also requires a little bit of knowledge. Gaining this knowledge takes time and practice. In this brief space, we can hope to expose you to only some of the thoroughfares.

As you gain experience and confidence, you can veer off onto the Internet's side streets. For example, the Internet is a romance connection. Many married couples met and courted over the Net. Of course, where there is marriage there is divorce. Some couples prefer to negotiate their divorce settlement over Internet e-mail. This written approach to arbitration allows parties to choose their words more carefully and to keep records of exactly what has been said. In the religious arena, some people confess their sins over the Internet. To do so, they choose a sin from a menu, enter the date of their last confession, and then receive their penance.

As you can see, the Internet offers a vast treasure trove of information and services. Emotions of newbies (those new to the Internet) run high when they enter the Net for the first time. They simultaneously are shocked, amazed, overwhelmed, appalled, and enlightened. The Internet is so vast that seasoned users experience these same emotions. Figure 3-25 includes examples of a few of the millions of stops along the Internet.

FIGURE 3–25   **SURFING THE WORLD WIDE WEB**

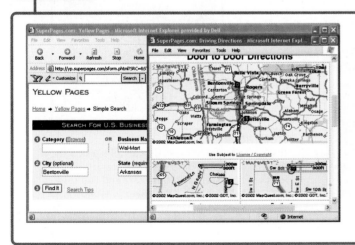

THE YELLOW PAGES
Use the "Yellow Pages" tab at SuperPages.com <www. SuperPages.com> on the Net to find quickly any business in the United States. A search for "Wal-Mart" in "Bentonville," "AR" listed the addresses and phones of area Wal-Mart stores and of the home office. The user can also request a map (inset) of a door-to-door or city-to-city street map from specific addresses. The SuperPage site lets you search for individuals, as well.

FIGURE 3–25 continued

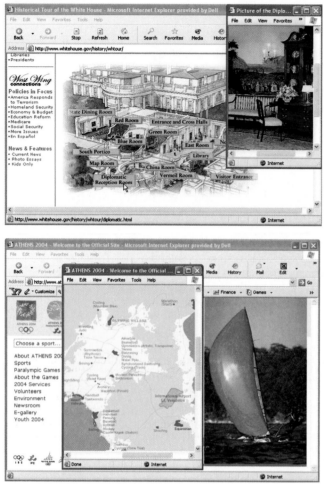

WHITE HOUSE TOUR

When you take your cybertour of the White House <www.whitehouse.gov> be sure to sign the guest book. During the tour, you can listen to the comments of President Bush and Vice President Cheney, meet the first family, and see the White House. In the breakout of the White House, you just click on a room to learn more about it. Shown here in the inset is the diplomatic reception room.

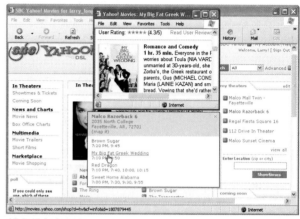

AT THE MOVIES

The Internet has just about everything but the movie (and that will change someday soon). You can even get show times at your local theaters (shown here). Click on a movie to read and view in-depth information about the movie, including reviews by professionals and people who just like movies.

THE ULTIMATE TRAVEL BROCHURE

The Internet has emerged as "the" source for travel information. It's easy to get information about any destination or event, including the 2004 Olympics in Athens, Greece.

STORY HOUR

There is something for children of all ages on the Net. The Wired for Books site offers many wonderful illustrated stories, in both text and audio formats, including *Alice's Adventures in Wonderland* by Lewis Carroll (shown here). Many stories at the site can be read from the Web pages or it can be viewed and heard as a streaming audio slide show, where the "pages" are turned automatically.

SPECIAL-INTEREST PAGES

No matter what your interests or hobbies, whether whitewater rafting, bungee jumping, or ballooning, there is a wealth of information, including images, about it (or them) on the Internet.

FIGURE 3–25 continued

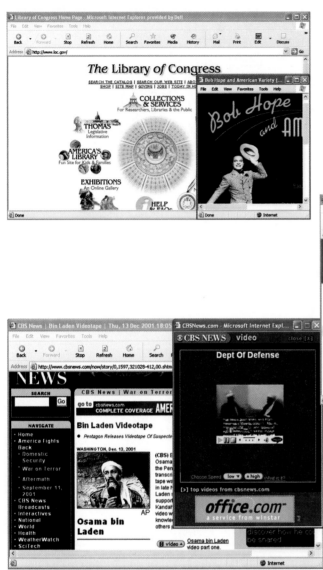

THE LIBRARY OF CONGRESS
Washington, D. C., has much to see, including the exhibits at the Library of Congress <www.loc.gov>. The electronic versions of many exhibits are posted to the Internet for people from all over the world to enjoy. Shown here in the inset is the Bob Hope and American Variety exhibit.

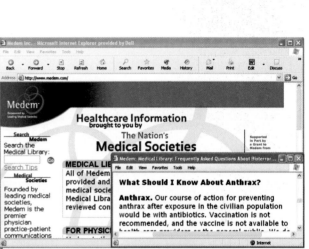

HEALTH INFORMATION ON THE INTERNET
More than half of all Internet users have sought out health-related information on the Internet, some from this Medem site <www.medem.com>.

STREAMING VIDEO
Internet surfers can view streaming video with audio at many Web sites. Here, CBS News has made an Osama bin Laden videotape available for viewing over the Internet. The U.S. Department of Defense released the tape that reveals bin Laden's role in the events of September 11, 2001. You can see thousands of live and taped videos of movies, sporting events, news broadcasts, speeches, interviews, walkthroughs of homes for sale, and so on.

ENCYCLOPEDIA BRITANNICA
For decades, the 30-volume Encyclopedia Britannica <www.britannica.com> was a fixture in homes all over the world. Now it's online, available to anyone with Internet access. Just enter "Milky Way Galaxy" or any other topic to view Britannica content plus Web links to more related information.

FIGURE 3–25 continued

SHOPPER'S PARADISE

The Internet is becoming a shopper's paradise, whether for retail or the excitement of an auction. Online auctions at eBay <www.ebay.com> are going on 24 hours a day with thousands of items up for bid, including this pool table. Auctions take place over a few minutes or in as many as several days.

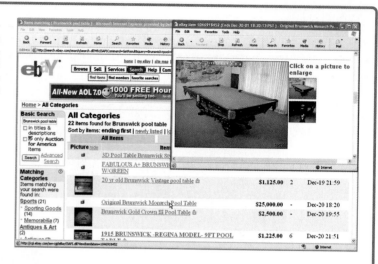

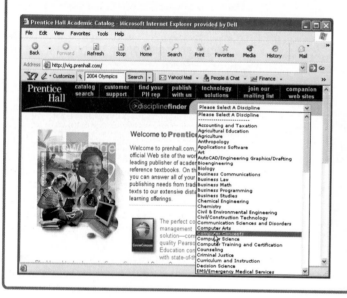

COMMERCIAL WEB PRESENCE

Most businesses, including the publisher of this book, Prentice Hall, have a presence on the Internet. Prentice Hall <www.prenhall.com> has a comprehensive Web site over which students and professors can communicate with one another and download important class materials. Users can thumb through the Prentice Hall College Division's catalog to obtain information about any book it offers. Many Prentice Hall books, including this one, have a companion Web site.

SECTION SELF-CHECK

3-3.1 The IRC protocol enables users to join and participate in group chat sessions. (T/F)

3-3.2 All Internet search engines have the same rules for formulating the inquiry. (T/F)

3-3.3 Which of these would not be considered an Internet portal: (a) Yahoo!, (b) Google, (c) Webcast, or (d) Excite?

3-3.4 What FTP feature allows anyone on the Net to use FTP sites without prior permission: (a) unsigned FTP, (b) secret FTP, (c) unnamed FTP, or (d) anonymous FTP?

3-3.5 Which of these applications is associated with text chat: (a) Internet telephone, (b) IRC, (c) e-mail, or (d) newsgroups?

3-3.6 The two ways e-mail is delivered are: (a) client and FTP, (b) Web-based and FTP, (c) Web-based and client, or (d) client and consumer.

3-1 THE INTERNET

The Internet (a worldwide collection of *inter*connected *net*works) is composed of thousands of independent networks in virtually every type of organization. The Department of Defense's ARPANET project was the genesis of the Internet. Volunteers from many nations coordinate the Internet. The Internet is transitioning to a privatization of the domain name registration process.

Communication channels are rated by their **bandwidth.** Channel capacities range from 56,000 **bits per second (bps)** for dialup service to high-speed **broadband access** at 622 M bps for commercial service. Narrowband dialup access is available to anyone with **POTS**—plain old telephone services. Common broadband options, which are up to 30 times faster than narrowband access, include cable, DSL, satellite, and wireless. A cable modem is required for cable access. **DSL (Digital Subscriber Line)** shares an existing telephone line and can provide access speed up to 9 M bps (the **downstream rate**) with an **upstream rate** (sending) of up to 1.5 M bps. The advantage of satellite service is that anyone in America with a southern exposure to the sky and the necessary equipment can have it. Wireless communication lets users take their PC anywhere within the range of a wireless signal and a link to a LAN via an **access point**, a wireless communications hub. The most popular standard used for short-range wireless communication is **Wi-Fi**, based on the **IEEE 802.11b** communications standard. The **IEEE 802.11a** communications standard permits a higher transmission rate but the effective range is less. Wireless devices must be equipped with a **wireless LAN PC card.**

The online world offers a vast network of resources, services, and capabilities. Most of us enter it simply by plugging the phone line into our PC's modem and running our communications software. **Newbies** are novice Internet users.

There are three levels at which you can connect your PC to the Internet. The easiest way to gain access is through a commercial information service's gateway. When you subscribe to a commercial information service such as America Online or CompuServe, you get communications software, a **user ID** (sometimes called a **screen name**), a **password** (required for **logon**), and a user's guide. Or you can make the connection via a **dialup connection** or a broadband connection through an *Internet service provider (ISP)*. At the third level, there is direct connection to the Internet whereby your PC is wired directly into the Internet. Such connections often use a DSL line (up to 9 M bps), a **T-1 line** (1.544 M bps), or a **T-3 line** (44.736 M bps).

The Transmission Control Protocol/Internet Protocol (TCP/IP) is the communications protocol that permits data transmission over the Internet. The *Transmission Control Protocol* sets the rules for the packaging of information into **packets.** The *Internet Protocol* handles the address, such that each packet is routed to its proper destination. When you dial up an ISP's local **POP** (**point-of-presence**), each of which has a unique **IP address,** your dialup connection is made through a **PPP (Point-to-Point Protocol)** connection to an Internet host.

The typical **Internet appliance** integrates access to the Internet, e-mail, a built-in telephone, and home organization applications.

A **client program** runs on your PC and works in conjunction with a companion **server program** that runs on the Internet host computer. The client program contacts the server program, and they work together to give you access to the resources on the Internet server. An *Internet browser* is one kind of client. The dominant browsers are Microsoft Internet Explorer and Netscape.

The **URL** (**uniform resource locator**), which is the Internet equivalent of an address, progresses from general to specific. That portion of the URL before the first colon (usually *http*) specifies the access method. The *http* tells the software to expect an **http (HyperText Transport Protocol)** file. That portion following the double forward slashes (*//*) is the server address, or the **domain name**. It has at least two parts, separated by dots (periods). The **top-level domains** or **TLDs,** such as *com* and *org*, denote affiliations. What follows the domain name is a folder or path containing the resources for a particular topic. At the end of the URL is the specific filename of the file that is retrieved from the server. **HTML (HyperText Markup Language)** is a **scripting language** used to compose and format most files on the Net. A more feature-rich **XHTML** is to become the new standard.

3-2 INTERNET BROWSERS

Internet browser, or Web browser, software lets us tap the information resources of the electronic world. It enables us to retrieve and view Internet-based information, interact with server-based systems, view electronic documents, pass digital information between computers, send and receive e-mail, and join newsgroups. The browser opens an HTML/XHTML document and displays the information according to HTML/XHTML instructions embedded in the document. The HTML/XHTML documents may reference **applets** or **ActiveX controls** which are small programs.

At the top of the Internet organization scheme are the Internet servers. Each World Wide Web server has one or more **home pages,** the first page you will normally view when traveling to a particular site. Web resources, which may be graphics, audio, video, animation, and text, are viewed in **pages.**

Each Web page is actually a file with its own URL. We navigate to an address on the Internet just as we drive to a street address. **Hyperlinks,** in a form of *hypertext, hot images,* or *hot icons*, permit navigation between pages and between other resources on the Internet. The pages at a server site are set up within a hierarchy of URLs.

The basic elements used for server navigation and viewing include the menu bar, the toolbar, the URL/search bar, the workspace, and the status bar. The toolbar has several navigational buttons, including the Search button. This button calls up the Internet portal that you have selected as your default search site. **Portals** are Web sites that offer a broad array of information and services, including a menu tree of categories and a capability that helps us find online resources.

There are a number of complementary applications, called **plugins,** that can enhance the functionality of browsers. Examples include *Shockwave Player, QuickTime,* and *RealPlayer,* which let you listen to **streaming audio** and view **streaming video.**

3-3 INTERNET RESOURCES AND APPLICATIONS

There are three ways to search the Internet: *browse*, *search*, and *ask someone*. You can browse through menu trees of *categories* or you can search using a variety of resource discovery tools, including **search engines.** People on the Net are ready to help those in need. There are also **FAQ (frequently asked questions)** pages and files.

The World Wide Web is an Internet application that permits linking of multimedia documents among Web servers on the Internet. By establishing a linked relationship between Web documents, related information becomes easily accessible. Web resources are designed to be accessed with easy-to-use browsers.

Web pages are linked via hyperlinks. The Web enables interactivity between users and servers. For example, you can click on **option buttons** to select desired options. Some Web sites present some or all of their information in **frames.**

The **File Transfer Protocol (FTP)** allows you to download and upload files on the Internet. Most are **anonymous FTP** sites. **Webcasting** (Internet broadcasting) has emerged as a popular Internet application. With **pull technology** the user requests information via a browser. With **push technology** information is sent automatically to a user.

Digital jukebox software records, stores, and plays music on the PC. It can help you gather MP3 and other audio files from Internet music resources.

The Internet is an aid to better communication. You can send e-mail to and receive it from anyone with an Internet e-mail address. The two ways to send/receive e-mail are via e-mail client software or via Web-based e-mail, which is handled through interaction with a Web site.

The Internet e-mail address has two parts, the username and the domain name, and is separated by an @ symbol. The domain name identifies the **e-mail server.** An **attached file** can be sent with an e-mail message. **Post Office Protocol** refers to the way your e-mail client software gets your e-mail from the server.

Audio mail lets you speak your Internet message instead of typing it.

A **newsgroup** can be hosted on Internet servers and on USENET servers. People who frequent newsgroups refer to the original message and any posted replies to that message as a **thread.** The Internet **mailing list** (listserv) is a cross between a newsgroup and e-mail.

The **Internet Relay Chat (IRC)** protocol allows users to participate in group chat sessions. A chat session is when two or more Internet users carry on a typed, real-time, online conversation.

Instant messaging is a convenient way for you to know when your friends are online so you can communicate with them in real time. Some versions of instant messaging software permit file/application sharing, **whiteboarding,** and the ability to have audio and video conferencing.

The Internet phone capability lets you call people at other computers on the Internet. Internet telephone service is available that will let you call any traditional telephone in the world via your PC and the Internet. People who communicate online have invented keyboard shortcuts and **emoticons** to speed up the written interaction and convey emotions. Rules of **netiquette,** Internet etiquette, demand sensitivity and concern for others in cyberspace.

The Internet offers a vast treasure trove of information and services.

KEY TERMS

access point (p. 134)
ActiveX controls (p. 141)
Anonymous FTP (p. 150)
applets (p. 141)
attached file (p. 154)
audio mail (p. 156)
bandwidth (p. 133)
bits per second (bps) (p. 133)
broadband access (p. 133)
broadband connection (p. 135)
client program (p. 138)
dialup connection (p. 135)
digital jukebox (p. 151)
domain name (p. 133)
downstream rate (p. 134)
DSL (Digital Subscriber Line) (p. 134)
dynamic IP address (p. 137)
e-mail server (p. 154)
emoticon (p. 160)
FAQ (frequently asked question) (p. 148)
frames (p. 149)
FTP (File Transfer Protocol) (p. 150)
hits (p. 148)

home page (p. 142)
HTML (HyperText Markup Language) (p. 139)
http (HyperText Transport Protocol) (p. 139)
hyperlink (p. 142)
IEEE 802.11a (p. 134)
IEEE 802.11b (p. 134)
Internet appliance (p. 138)
Internet Relay Chat (IRC) (p. 157)
IP address (p. 137)
logon (p. 135)
mailing list (p. 157)
netiquette (p. 160)
newbie (p. 135)
newsgroup (p. 156)
option button (p. 149)
packets (p. 137)
page (p. 142)
password (p. 135)
plugin (p. 145)
point-of-presence (POP) (p. 137)
portal (p. 143)
Post Office Protocol (p. 155)

POTS (p. 133)
PPP (Point-to-Point Protocol) (p. 137)
pull technology (p. 151)
push technology (p. 151)
screen name (p. 135)
scripting language (p. 139)
search engine (p. 147)
server program (p. 138)
streaming audio (p. 145)
streaming video (p. 145)
T-1 line (p. 136)
T-3 line (p. 136)
thread (p. 156)
top-level domain (TLD) (p. 139)
upstream rate (p. 134)
URL (uniform resource locator) (p. 138)
USENET (p. 156)
user ID (p. 135)
webcast (p. 150)
whiteboarding (p. 158)
Wi-Fi (p. 134)
wireless LAN PC card (p. 134)
XHTML (p. 140)

MATCHING

<table>
<tr><td>1. netiquette</td><td>a. Net resource discovery tool</td></tr>
<tr><td>2. newsgroup</td><td>b. high-speed Internet</td></tr>
<tr><td>3. broadband access</td><td>c. enhances browser functionality</td></tr>
<tr><td>4. search engine</td><td>d. linking people in real-time</td></tr>
<tr><td>5. POP</td><td>e. IEEE 802.11b</td></tr>
<tr><td>6. TCP/IP</td><td>f. Internet etiquette</td></tr>
<tr><td>7. ARPANET</td><td>g. PPP</td></tr>
<tr><td>8. instant messaging</td><td>h. USENET</td></tr>
<tr><td>9. plugin</td><td>i. scripting language</td></tr>
<tr><td>10. megabits</td><td>j. satellite</td></tr>
<tr><td>11. bandwidth</td><td>k. rules for Internet packets</td></tr>
<tr><td>12. universally available Net access</td><td>l. access point to the Net</td></tr>
<tr><td>13. dialup connection</td><td>m. channel capacity</td></tr>
<tr><td>14. HTML</td><td>n. millions of bits</td></tr>
<tr><td>15. Wi-Fi</td><td>o. early Internet</td></tr>
</table>

CHAPTER SELF-CHECK

3-1.1 One way to go online is to subscribe to a commercial information service. (T/F)

3-1.2 America Online has a self-contained network. (T/F)

3-1.3 The Internet is like AOL, a commercial information service. (T/F)

3-1.4 ARPANET was the first commercially available communications software package. (T/F)

3-1.5 A newbie is anyone with a fear of cyberspace. (T/F)

3-1.6 Which of the following is not a link to the Internet: (a) interstate bonds, (b) DSL, (c) cable, or (d) wireless satellite?

3-1.7 Which of the following is not included with a subscription to an information service: (a) communications software, (b) a user ID, (c) speech-recognition software, or (d) a password?

3-1.8 Which of the following is not an online commercial information service: (a) Dow Jones Business Information Service, (b) the Web, (c) AOL, or (d) CompuServe?

3-1.9 Which of these is not a U.S. top-level domain affiliation ID: (a) moc, (b) edu, (c) gov, or (d) org?

3-1.10 In the URL, *http://www.abccorp.com/pr/main.htm*, the domain is: (a) *http*, (b) *www.abccorp.com,* (c) *pr/main.htm,* or (d) *www.*

3-1.11 What type of company provides people with access to the Internet: (a) PSI, (b) ISP, (c) SPI, or (d) IPS?

3-1.12 In the e-mail address, *mickey_mouse@disney.com*, the user ID is: (a) *mickey_mouse,* (b) *mouse,* (c) *disney.com,* or (d) *@.*

3-1.13 A 56,000 bits-per-second channel is the same as a: (a) 56 kps pipe, (b) 56 K bps line, (c) dual 28000X2 K bps line, or (d) single-channel DSL.

3-1.14 A communication channel is rated by its: (a) channel aptitude, (b) bandwidth, (c) flow, or (d) datastream.

3-1.15 Narrowband has slightly more capacity than broadband. (T/F)

3-1.16 Which broadband service has a built-in lag in response time: (a) DSL, (b) satellite, (c) cable, or (d) Wi-Fi?

3-1.17 Which of these would not be associated with a wireless local area network: (a) access points, (b) Wi-Fi, (c) IEEE 802.11b, or (d) DSL?

3-1.18 Every home user is assigned a permanent IP address on the Internet. (T/F)

3-2.1 Internet portals are designed to permit searches by category or by keyword, but never both. (T/F)

3-2.2 On the Internet, only hypertext hyperlinks are hot. (T/F)

3-2.3 Which of the following labels might be included with an Internet address: (a) <bps>, (b) ULS, (c) http://, or (d) fpt://?

3-2.4 The opening page for a particular Web site normally is the: (a) opener page, (b) home page, (c) flip-flop page, or (d) master page.

3-2.5 Which of the following buttons is not one of the main buttons on a browser toolbar: (a) Back, (b) Forward, (c) Refresh, or (d) House?

3-2.6 Web pages can be tied together by: (a) cybertext links, (b) hydratext links, (c) hydrolinks, or (d) hyperlinks.

3-3.1 Yahoo! is a site on the Internet that can be used to browse the Net by content category. (T/F)

3-3.2 Subscribing to a popular mailing list would result in more Internet e-mail than posting a message to a newsgroup. (T/F)

3-3.3 A file attached to an e-mail is routed to the recipient's e-mail server computer along with the message. (T/F)

3-3.4 Which server on the Internet offers hypertext links: (a) QOQ, (b) Web, (c) Gopher, or (d) ftp?

3-3.5 All but which one of these would be a common way to search for information on the Internet: (a) browse, (b) search, (c) push/pull, or (d) ask someone on the Net?

3-3.6 What Web features enable the display of more than one page on a screen: (a) borders, (b) windows, (c) frames, or (d) structures?

3-3.7 Generally, today's Internet applications are based on what technology: (a) push, (b) pull, (c) place, or (d) draw?

3-3.8 On a newsgroup, the original message and any posted replies to that message are a: (a) needle, (b) thread, (c) pinpoint, or (d) tapestry?

E-MAIL ETIQUETTE

As a knowledge worker, you may spend an hour or more each day composing or responding to e-mail. E-mail is now as much a part of the business world as the paycheck. How we present ourselves in our e-mails can play a role in how effective we are in business and in what people think of us. You can leave a good or bad impression with your correspondents depending on your understanding of netiquette, a slang term for Internet etiquette, that is, *what you say* in your message and *how you say it*. During face-to-face conversations we use vocal inflections or body movements that clarify words or phrases. E-mail is just words, leaving the door open for misinterpretation of our intended message. Anyone composing e-mail should be aware that it's electronic and could be easily forwarded, printed, and even broadcast to others. Broadcasting sensitive information could be very embarrassing to you and to others. Every e-mailer should be careful what he or she writes and follow the basic tenets of e-mail etiquette. For example, you should inform senders when you forward their e-mail. A good e-mail message includes a subject, has a logical flow, and concludes with a signature (name, association, and contact information).

Discussion: *What would be considered good netiquette?*

Discussion: *Describe e-mails that you have received (or seen) that you feel are in poor taste and out of step with good e-mail etiquette. What could the sender have done to modify the e-mail while retaining the essential message?*

THE UNWANTED CHAT ROOM GUEST

The Internet and information services, such as America Online, sponsor hundreds of topical chat rooms where participants chat (via text input) with one another about a specific topic. Topics range from auto repair to Little League baseball to "over 60" to Harley-Davidson motorcycles. However, it's not unusual for at least one of the participants to be an unwanted guest. Unwanted guests make rude or obnoxious comments that have nothing to do with the focus of the chat room. Sometimes these comments become inappropriately profane and personal, causing well-meaning participants to leave the chat room.

Discussion: *Should those who enter a public chat room have the right to talk about whatever they wish, disregarding the stated topic of the chat rooms?*

Discussion: *What, if anything, should be done to stop these unwanted guests from wasting the time of the other participants and violating the purpose of the chat room?*

ADS IN PERSONAL E-MAIL

The search continues by marketing people for better ways to reach customers via Internet advertising. One company has introduced a technology that marketing people can use to advertise their products and services within your personal e-mail messages. It works like this: your e-mails are intercepted at the mail server and then wrapped with advertising content. In theory, the advertising will be tailored to the individual receiving the e-mail based on his/her demographic profile. Marketers are hoping that e-mail recipients will continue to open personal mail and, whether they like it or not, read the advertisements, as well.

Discussion: *Internet companies have found it necessary to integrate advertising within their services. Is this approach to Net advertising justified given the current economic climate of Internet commerce?*

Discussion: *Is this approach more or less palatable than spam to the e-mail community? Why?*

DISCUSSION AND PROBLEM SOLVING

3-1.1 Describe at least three things you do now without the aid of online communications that may be done in the online environment in the near future.

3-1.2 The federal government is calling for "universal service" such that everyone has access to the "information superhighway." Is this an achievable goal? Explain.

3-1.3 Discuss how you would justify spending $15 to $25 a month to subscribe to an ISP for dialup Internet access. How would you justify spending $40 to $60 a month for broadband Internet access?

3-1.4 Speculate on how Internet appliances might change your life during the next decade.

3-1.5 Which two America Online channels would be of most interest to you? Explain.

3-1.6 What is the organizational affiliation of these Internet addresses: smith_jo@mkt.bigco.com; politics@washington.senate.gov; and hugh_roman@anthropology.stuniv.edu?

3-1.7 Expand and discuss the meaning of the following acronyms: TCP/IP, ISP, http, and URL.

3-1.8 Briefly describe one of the three levels at which you can connect your PC to the Internet.

3-2.1 The Microsoft Internet Explorer browser is now the most used browser in the world. A few years ago, the Netscape browser was the dominant browser. Some will argue that Netscape still makes the best browser. Speculate on what might have caused the turnaround.

3-2.2 The Internet has over 2 billion pages of information, some of which are placed online and not updated for years. Should there an effort to purge inactive information on the Internet? Explain.

3-2.3 What is your favorite portal on the Internet and why?

3-2.4 Why are there so many plugins for Internet browsers and why are they not built into the original browser software?

3-3.1 In what ways is the World Wide Web different from other servers on the Internet?

3-3.2 Describe circumstances for which you would prefer browsing the Net to using a search engine.

3-3.3 Discuss the pros and cons of FTPing on the Internet.

3-3.4 Videophones are available on the Internet now. Is this innovation in personal communications something you are looking forward to or dreading? Explain.

3-3.5   Would you prefer to receive traditional e-mail or audio mail? Explain.

3-3.6   Discuss the advantages and disadvantages of e-mail and instant messaging in a domestic setting, and in a business setting.

3-3.7   What type of information would you like to be sent to you automatically via Internet push technology?

3-3.8   Describe five things you would like to do on the Internet.

3-3.9   What is your favorite Internet application and why?

FOCUS ON PERSONAL COMPUTING

1. If you have not already done so, spend a few minutes doing some serendipitous surfing on the Internet via a dialup, narrowband Internet link. Do the same on a system with a broadband connection. Briefly describe how your perspective, what you did, and where you went changed when you began the broadband session.

2. On an Internet-enabled PC, do at least two of the following tasks. Search for and play the signal from an Internet radio station based in a country other than your own. Find, download, and play a hit song. Find a long-lost friend (where they live or work). Plan your dream vacation (flight schedules and lodging). Describe your activities.

3. Send an e-mail. Find and visit a newsgroup of interest to you. Set up instant messaging with several of your friends. Be a participant in an Internet chat room. If possible, hold a voice conversation over the Internet. Which of these means of Internet communications is of the greatest interest to you? Explain.

INTERNET EXERCISES @ www.prenhall.com/long

1. The Online Study Guide (multiple choice, true/false, matching, and essay questions)

2. Internet Learning Activities
  • The Internet
  • Going Online

3. Serendipitous Internet Activities
  • Magazines

Chapter

4

Learning Objectives

Once you have read and studied this chapter, you will have learned:

- How data are stored and represented in a computer system (Section 4-1).

- The function of and relationships between the internal components of a personal computer, including the motherboard, processor, random-access memory (RAM) and other memories, ports, buses, expansion boards, and PC cards (Section 4-2).

- How to distinguish processors by their word size, speed, and memory capacity (Section 4-3).

- Several approaches to processor design (Section 4-4).

INSIDE THE COMPUTER

Why this chapter is important to you

A PC card here, a DVD drive there, a few GHz, and all of a sudden you're talking big bucks. A modern midlevel, communications-ready PC configured with a "standard" set of peripheral devices will run you about two grand. Hang on a few extras and add more power and you're over $3,000. And that's just the hardware! With Mom, Dad, and the kids all wanting their own PC, it's not unusual for expenditures on hardware to top that of the family car. With a significant portion of your budget at stake, you want to make informed decisions when purchasing PCs.

When you purchase a car, you know that it will perform its basic function—to carry people over roadways from point to point. Not so with PCs. PCs have thousands of functions, and when you purchase one, you want to be sure that it will do what you want it to do. Most of us can easily grasp the variables involved in buying a house or a car. The average car buyer can assess functionality and style relative to his or her budget constraints and aesthetic tastes, then make a reasonably informed decision. However, to get what you want and need in a PC, and to get the most for your money, you need to have an overall understanding of the essential elements of a computer.

One desktop PC looks about like another, with perhaps a little variation in color, style, and size. The same can be said of notebooks. Look inside, however, and they can be vastly different. Similar-looking PC boxes can be mansions or efficiency apartments on the inside. One might have a 2.8-GHz processor and another a much slower 1.2-GHz processor. Differences in processor speed, cache and RAM capacity, type of RAM, speed of the modem, what's embedded on the motherboard, the type of bus, and so on, dictate overall system performance and ability to enhance the system. If you understand these essential elements, you'll be able to make informed decisions when purchasing PCs—and that may be as often as once or twice a year for work and family. Those people who depend on advice from the PC salesperson may end up spending far more than necessary and still not get what they need to do the job.

WHY THIS SECTION
IS IMPORTANT
TO YOU

Much of what we see, hear, and do is going digital: music, cell phones, photographs, books, movies, catalogues, and much more. This section will help prepare you for immersion into an increasingly digital world.

4-1 Going Digital

A computer is an entertainment center with hundreds of interactive games. It's a virtual university providing interactive instruction and testing. It's a painter's canvas. It's a video telephone. It's a CD player. It's a home or office library. It's a television. It's the biggest marketplace in the world. It's the family photo album. It's a print shop. It's a wind tunnel that can test experimental airplane designs. It's a recorder. It's an alarm clock that can remind you to keep an appointment. It's an encyclopedia. It can perform thousands of specialty functions that require specialized skills, such as preparing taxes, drafting legal documents, counseling suicidal patients, and much more.

In all of these applications, the computer deals with everything as electronic signals. Electronic signals come in two flavors—**analog** and **digital**. Analog signals are *continuous* waveforms in which variations in frequency and amplitude can be used to represent information from sound and numerical data. Traditionally, the sound of our voice has been carried by analog signals when we talk on the telephone. That, however, is changing. Just about everything in the world of electronics and communication is *going digital* because computers are digital. Computers use digital signals where everything is described in two states: The circuit is either *on* or *off*. Generally, the *on* state is expressed or represented by the number 1 and the *off* state by the number 0.

So how do you go digital? You simply need to **digitize** your material. To digitize means to convert data, analog signals, and images into the discrete format (1s and 0s) that can be interpreted by computers. For example, Figure 4-1 shows how music can be digitized. Once digitized, you can use a computer to work with (revise and copy, among other things) the music recording, data, image, shape, and so on. Old recordings of artists from Enrico Caruso to the Beatles have been digitized and then digitally reconstructed on computers to eliminate unwanted distortion and static. Some of these reconstructed CDs are actually better than the originals!

BINARY DIGITS: 1 AND 0

The electronic nature of the computer makes it possible to combine the two digital states—*on* and *off*—to represent letters, numbers, colors, sounds, images, shapes, and even odors. An "on" or "off" electronic state is represented by a *bit,* short for binary digit. In the **binary** numbering system (base 2), the *on-bit* is a 1 and the *off-bit* is a 0. Physically, these states are achieved in a variety of ways.

- In RAM (temporary storage), the two electronic states often are represented by the presence or absence of an electrical charge in an integrated circuit—a computer chip (see Figure 4-2).

- In disk storage (permanent storage), the two states are made possible by the magnetic arrangement of the surface coating on magnetic disks (see Figure 4-3).

- In CDs and CD-ROMs, digital data are stored permanently as microscopic pits.

- In fiber optic cable, binary data flow through as pulses of light.

Bits may be fine for computers, but human beings are more comfortable with letters and decimal numbers (the base-10 numerals 0 through 9). We like to see colors and hear sounds. Therefore, the letters, decimal numbers, colors, and sounds we input into a computer system while doing word pro-

FIGURE 4–1

GOING DIGITAL WITH COMPACT DISCS
The recording industry has gone digital. To create a master CD, analog signals are converted to digital signals that can be manipulated by a computer and written to a master CD. The master is duplicated and the copies are sold through retail channels.

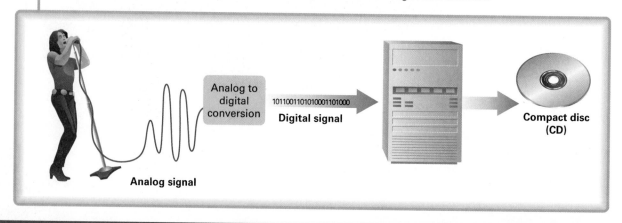

Analog to digital conversion

1011001101010001101000

Digital signal

Compact disc (CD)

Analog signal

cessing, graphics, and other applications must be translated into 1s and 0s for processing and storage. The computer translates the bits back into letters, decimal numbers, colors, and sounds for output on monitors, printers, speakers, and so on.

ENCODING SYSTEMS: BITS AND BYTES

Computers don't speak to one another in English, Spanish, or French. They have their own languages, which are better suited to electronic communication. In these languages, bits are combined according to an *encoding system* to represent letters, numbers, and special characters (such as *, $, +, and &), collectively referred to as *alphanumeric* characters.

ASCII and ANSI

ASCII (American Standard Code for Information Interchange—pronounced "*AS-key*") is the most popular encoding system for PCs and data communication. In ASCII, alphanumeric characters are *encoded* into a bit configuration on input so that the computer can interpret them. This coding equates a unique series of 1s and 0s with a specific character. Figure 4-4 shows the ASCII bit string of commonly used characters. Just as the words *mother* and *father* are arbitrary English-language character strings that refer to our parents, 01000010 is an arbitrary ASCII code that refers to the letter *B*. When you tap the letter *B* on a keyboard, the *B* is sent to the processor as a coded string of binary digits (01000010 in ASCII) as shown in Figure 4-5. The characters are *decoded* on output so we can interpret them. The combination of bits used to represent a character is called a *byte* (pronounced "*bite*").

FIGURE 4–2 Microminiaturization of the Chip's Bit
During the first generation of computers a bit was represented by a vacuum tube. This silicon wafer contains a number of thumbnail-sized Pentium 4 processor chips, each with the capability to process and store billions of bits.

Photo courtesy of Intel Corporation

Courtesy of International Business Machines Corporation. Unauthorized use not permitted.

FIGURE 4–3 Temporary and Permanent Storage
Digital video output is stored temporarily in the RAM chips on this circuit board (left), which enables displayed output from a PC. Video information can be stored permanently on magnetic disk (right). The time it takes to access information from this high-capacity Seagate disk drive is incredibly fast at around 5 milliseconds; however, accessing information stored in RAM is virtually instantaneous.

Courtesy of Sun Microsystems, Inc.

Courtesy of © Seagate Technology, Inc.

FIGURE 4–4

ASCII CODES

This figure shows the binary (base 2) ASCII codes, along with their decimal (base 10) and hexadecimal (hex, base 16) equivalents, for uppercase letters, numbers, and several special characters. The binary ASCII codes for uppercase and lowercase letters are similar. Replace the third binary digit with a 1 to get the lowercase equivalent of a capital letter (*B* is 01000010 and *b* is 01100010).

Character	ASCII Codes		
	Binary	Decimal	Hex
Space	00100000	32	20
!	00100001	33	21
"	00100010	34	22
#	00100011	35	23
$	00100100	36	24
%	00100101	37	25
&	00100110	38	26
'	00100111	39	27
(	00101000	40	28
)	00101001	41	29
*	00101010	42	2A
+	00101011	43	2B
,	00101100	44	2C
-	00101101	45	2D
.	00101110	46	2E
/	00101111	47	2F
0	00110000	48	30
1	00110001	49	31
2	00110010	50	32
3	00110011	51	33
4	00110100	52	34
5	00110101	53	35
6	00110110	54	36
7	00110111	55	37
8	00111000	56	38
9	00111001	57	39
A	01000001	65	41
B	01000010	66	42
C	01000011	67	43
D	01000100	68	44
E	01000101	69	45
F	01000110	70	46
G	01000111	71	47
H	01001000	72	48
I	01001001	73	49
J	01001010	74	4A
K	01001011	75	4B
L	01001100	76	4C
M	01001101	77	4D
N	01001110	78	4E
O	01001111	79	4F
P	01010000	80	50
Q	01010001	81	51
R	01010010	82	52
S	01010011	83	53
T	01010100	84	54
U	01010101	85	55
V	01010110	86	56
W	01010111	87	57
X	01011000	88	58
Y	01011001	89	59
Z	01011010	90	5A

The 7-bit ASCII code can represent up to 128 characters (2^7), but the PC byte is 8 bits. There are 256 (2^8) possible bit configurations in an 8-bit byte. Hardware and software vendors accept the 128 standard ASCII codes and use the extra 128 bit configurations to represent control characters (such as ringing a bell) or noncharacter images to complement their hardware or software product. Microsoft Windows uses the 8-bit **ANSI** encoding system (developed by the American National Standards Institute) to enable the sharing of text between Windows applications. The first 128 ANSI codes are the same as the ASCII codes, but the next 128 are defined to meet the specific needs of Windows applications.

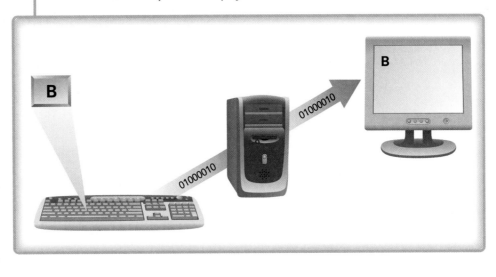

FIGURE 4–5

ENCODING
When you tap the B key on the keyboard, a binary representation of the letter *B* is sent to the processor. The processor sends the encoded *B* to the monitor, which interprets and displays a **B.**

Although the English language has considerably fewer than 128 printable characters, the extra bit configurations are needed to represent additional common and not-so-common special characters (such as - [hyphen]; @ [at]; | [a vertical bar]; and ~ [tilde]) and to signal a variety of activities to the computer (such as ringing a bell or telling the computer to accept a piece of datum).

Unicode

ASCII, with 128 character codes, is sufficient for the English language but we're now a global economy and ASCII falls far short of the Japanese language requirements (see Figure 4-6). The relatively new **Unicode**, a 16-bit encoding system, will enable computers and applications to talk to one another more easily and will handle most languages of the world (including Hebrew, Japanese, and Greek). Unicode's 16-bit code allows for 65,536 characters (2^{16}). Eventually, Unicode may be adopted as a standard for information interchange throughout the global computer community. Universal acceptance of the Unicode standard would make international communication in all areas easier, from monetary transfers between banks to e-mail.

FIGURE 4–6

THE NEED FOR 16-BIT ENCODING
An 8-bit encoding system, with its 256 unique bit configurations, is more than adequate to represent all of the alphanumeric characters used in the English language. The Japanese, however, need a 16-bit encoding system, like Unicode, to represent thousands of characters, some of which are shown on this Toyota Museum Web page. English has evolved as the language of the Internet, so many international sites give viewers an "English" option (see button at bottom).

Hexadecimal

Perhaps the biggest drawback to using the binary numbering system for computer operations is that we occasionally must deal with long and confusing strings of 1s and 0s. To reduce the confusion, the **hexadecimal,** or base-16, numbering system is used as shorthand to display the binary contents of RAM and disk storage.

Notice that the bases of the binary and hexadecimal numbering systems are multiples of 2—2 and 2^4, respectively. Because of this, there is a convenient relationship between these numbering systems. The table in Figure 4-7 illustrates that a single hexadecimal digit represents

FIGURE 4–7 NUMBERING SYSTEM EQUIVALENCE TABLE

Binary (Base 2)	Decimal (Base 10)	Hexadecimal (Base 16)
00	0	0
01	1	1
10	2	2
11	3	3
100	4	4
101	5	5
110	6	6
111	7	7
1000	8	8
1001	9	9
1010	10	A
1011	11	B
1100	12	C
1101	13	D
1110	14	E
1111	15	F
10000	16	10

four binary digits ($0111_2 = 7_{16}$, $1101_2 = D_{16}$, 1010_2, $= A_{16}$ where subscripts are used to indicate the base of the numbering system). Notice that in hexadecimal, or "hex," *letters* are used to represent the six higher-order digits.

Two hexadecimal digits can be used to represent an eight-bit byte. The binary and hex ASCII representations of the letter Z are 01011010_2 and $5A_{16}$, respectively. Figure 4-4 shows the binary, decimal, and "hex" equivalents for common characters.

4-1.1	Data are stored permanently on magnetic storage devices, such as magnetic disk. (T/F)
4-1.2	Binary data flow through fiber optic cable as pulses of light. (T/F)
4-1.3	What are the two kinds of electronic signals: (a) analog and digital, (b) binary and octal, (c) alpha and numeric, or (d) bit and byte?
4-1.4	The combination of bits used to represent a character is called a: (a) bits on/off, (b) binary config, (c) 0-1 string, or (d) byte.
4-1.5	The 16-bit encoding system is called: (a) Unicorn, (b) Unicode, (c) Hexacode, or (d) 10 plus 6 code.

4-2   The PC System Unit

The processor, RAM, and a variety of other electronic components are housed in the *system unit,* usually a metal and plastic upright box (the tower), or inside the notebook's shell. As components get smaller, the system unit is being redefined with the integration of system unit components and the monitor into a single unit. In this section, we'll look inside the box at the major components of a computer system. Figure 4-8 gives you a peek inside the system unit of a PC.

Someday we won't have to worry about what's inside a PC. That day, however, will not be any time soon. So, let's start with the component that ties it all together, the *motherboard.*

THE MOTHERBOARD: THE CENTRAL NERVOUS SYSTEM

The *motherboard,* a single circuit board, provides the path through which the processor communicates with memory components and peripheral devices. Think of the processor as the PC's brain and the motherboard as the PC's central nervous system. Continuing the analogy, think of the motherboard's **chipset** as the heart of the system, controlling the flow of information between system components

FIGURE 4–8

SYSTEM UNIT AND MOTHERBOARD
The system unit is this box and its contents—the computer system's electronic circuitry, including the motherboard with the processor and various expansion boards (added capabilities discussed later in this chapter), and various storage devices.

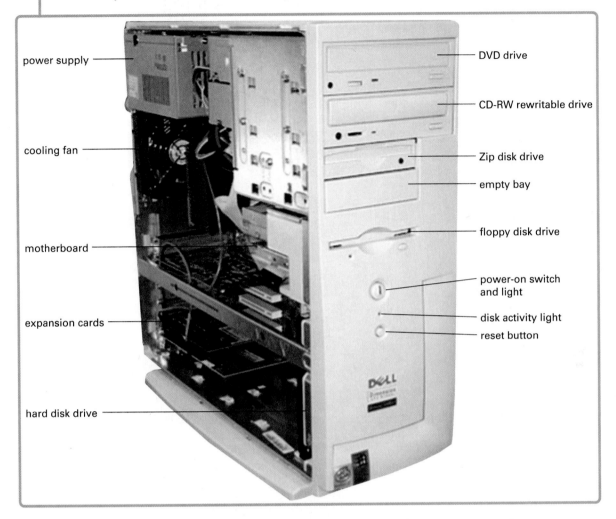

- power supply
- cooling fan
- motherboard
- expansion cards
- hard disk drive
- DVD drive
- CD-RW rewritable drive
- Zip disk drive
- empty bay
- floppy disk drive
- power-on switch and light
- disk activity light
- reset button

connected to the board. The chipset is important because it determines what features are supported on the system (including types of processors and memory). In a personal computer, the following are attached to the motherboard (see Figure 4-9):

- Processor (main processor)
- Support electronic circuitry, such as the chipset
- Memory chips (for example, RAM and other types of memory)
- Expansion boards (optional circuit boards, such as a fax/modem)

The various chips have standard-sized pin connectors that allow them to be attached to the motherboard and, therefore, to a common electrical **bus** that permits data flow between the various system components.

Just as big cities have mass transit systems that move large numbers of people, the computer has a similar system that moves billions of bits a second. Both transit systems use buses, although the one in the computer doesn't have wheels. All electrical signals travel on a common electrical bus. The term *bus* was derived from its wheeled cousin because passengers on both buses (people and bits) can get off at any stop. In a computer, the bus stops are the processor's control unit and its arithmetic and logic unit, RAM and other types of internal memory, and the **device controllers** (small computers) that control the operation of the peripheral devices.

Ultimately, the type of processor and the amount of RAM placed on the motherboard define the PC's speed and capacity. The central component of the motherboard, the processor, is generally not made by the manufacturers of PCs. Companies that specialize in the development and manufacture of processors make it. A number of companies make PC processors, including Intel, Motorola, Advanced Micro Devices (AMD), and IBM.

FIGURE 4–9

MOTHERBOARD
Shown here is a motherboard ready to be installed to a PC (top) and the same motherboard installed in a system unit (bottom) and configured with a 2.8-GHz (gigahertz) Intel Pentium 4 processor (under the cooling fan) and 1 GB of RAM in two DIMMs.

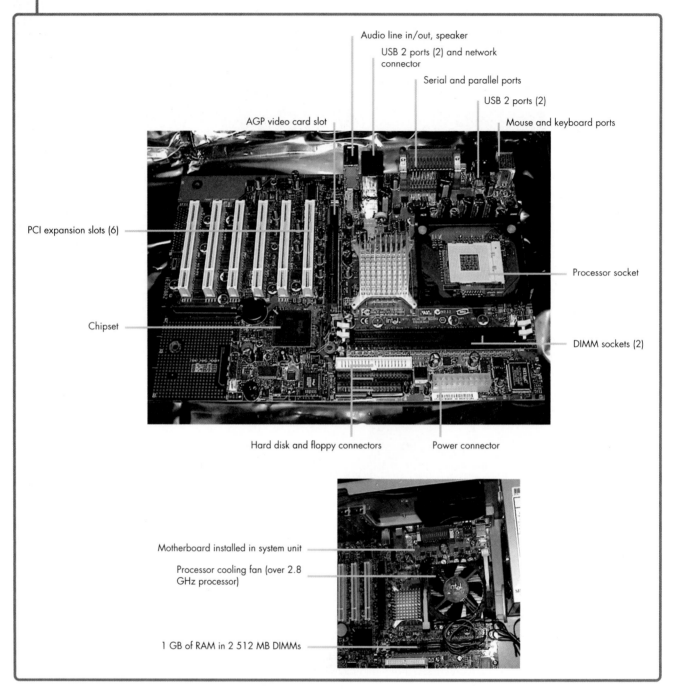

Audio line in/out, speaker

USB 2 ports (2) and network connector

Serial and parallel ports

USB 2 ports (2)

AGP video card slot

Mouse and keyboard ports

PCI expansion slots (6)

Processor socket

Chipset

DIMM sockets (2)

Hard disk and floppy connectors

Power connector

Motherboard installed in system unit

Processor cooling fan (over 2.8 GHz processor)

1 GB of RAM in 2 512 MB DIMMs

THE PROCESSOR: COMPUTER ON A CHIP

What is smaller than a postage stamp and found in wristwatches, sewing machines, and CD players? The answer is a *processor*. The processor is literally a "computer on a chip." We use the term *chip* to refer to any self-contained integrated circuit. The size of chips varies from fingernail size to postage-stamp size (about 1-inch square). Processors and small processors, called microprocessors, have been integrated into thousands of mechanical and electronic devices—even elevators, band saws, and ski-boot bindings. In a few years, virtually everything mechanical or electronic will incorporate processor technology into its design (see Figure 4-10).

The motherboard for the original (1981) and most of the *IBM PC-compatible* computers manufactured through 1984 used the Intel 8088 microprocessor chip. Since then, Intel has introduced a succession of increasingly more advanced processors to power the IBM PC-compatible PCs, called *PC compati-*

bles or, simply, *PCs*. The Intel "286" (Intel 80286), "386," and "486" processors took us into the 1990s followed by the Intel **Pentium®**, **Pentium® Pro**, **Pentium® II**, and **Pentium® III** series. Most new system units have an Intel **Pentium 4®** (see Figure 4-11), **Celeron®**, or **Itanium™** processor inside. The more expensive Pentium 4 or Itanium-based PCs offer the greatest performance, whereas the less expensive Celeron-based PCs offer good value with reduced performance.

Gordon Moore, cofounder of Intel Corporation, made a prediction in 1965 that has proven to be remarkably accurate. Moore's Law states that *the density of transistors on a chip doubles every 18 months.* Often Moore's Law is stated in terms of *processing power,* which is directly related to the density of a chip's transistors. Dr. Andy Grove, the other cofounder of Intel, has said that Moore's Law has become a self-fulfilling prophecy at Intel because no engineer wants to design a chip that would fall below this implied standard. Some experts say that chip designers will begin to bump up against the laws of physics around 2005 and the pace of chip evolution may slow.

FIGURE 4–10 Microprocessors Everywhere
Microprocessors are present in almost every aspect of our lives. The electrical and mechanical appliances plus a variety of personal computers are networked throughout this Portland, Oregon home. Microprocessors and structured wiring allows audio, video, computer and Internet signals to be routed anywhere in the home. Several wireless Tablet PCs allow home owners to surf the Web and control the connected products around their home from anywhere in the house.

Photo courtesy of Intel Corporation

FIGURE 4–11 Intel Pentium 4 Processor
About the size of four keys on a keyboard, this 1.8-GHz Mobile Pentium 4 processor provides the processing capability for this notebook PC.

Photo courtesy of Intel Corporation

Inside the Processor

The processor runs the show and is the nucleus of any computer system. Regardless of the complexity of a processor, sometimes called the **central processing unit** or **CPU**, it has only two fundamental sections: the *control unit* and the *arithmetic and logic unit*. These units work together with RAM and other internal memories to make the processor, and the computer system, go. Figure 4-12 illustrates the interaction between computer system components.

The Control Unit

The **control unit** is the command center of the processor. It has three primary functions:

- To read and interpret program instructions
- To direct the operation of internal processor components
- To control the flow of programs and data in and out of RAM

During program execution, the first in a sequence of program instructions is moved from RAM to the control unit, where it is decoded and interpreted by the **decoder**. The control unit then directs other processor components to carry out the operations necessary to execute the instruction.

The processor contains high-speed working storage areas called **registers** that can store no more than a few bytes (see Figure 4-12). Because registers reside on the processor chip, they handle instructions and data at very high speeds and are used for a variety of processing functions. One register, called the **instruction register**, contains the instruction being executed. Other general-purpose registers store data needed for immediate processing. Registers also store status information. For example, the **program register** contains the location in RAM of the next instruction to be executed. Registers facilitate the processing and movement of data and instructions between RAM, the control unit, and the arithmetic and logic unit.

FIGURE 4–12 **INTERACTION BETWEEN COMPUTER SYSTEM COMPONENTS**
During processing, instructions and data are passed between the various types of internal memories, the processor's control unit and arithmetic and logic unit, and the peripheral devices over the common electrical bus. A system clock paces the speed of operation within the processor and ensures that everything takes place in timed intervals.

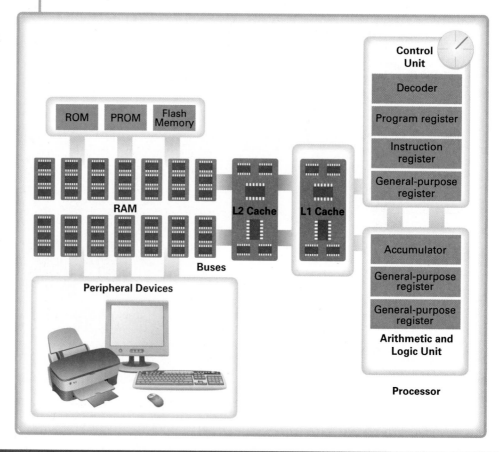

The Arithmetic and Logic Unit

The **arithmetic and logic unit** performs all computations (addition, subtraction, multiplication, and division) and all logic operations (comparisons). The results are placed in a register called the **accumulator.** Examples of *computations* include the payroll deduction for social security, the day-end inventory level, and the balance on a bank statement. A *logic* operation compares two pieces of data, either alphabetic or numeric. Based on the result of the comparison, the program "branches" to one of several alternative sets of program instructions. For example, in an inventory system each item in stock is compared to a reorder point at the end of each day. If the inventory level falls below the reorder point, a sequence of program instructions is executed that produces a purchase order.

RAM: Digital Warehouse

RAM enables data to be both read and written to *solid-state* memory. It is **volatile memory** because when the electrical current is turned off or interrupted, the data are lost. In contrast to permanent storage on disk, RAM provides the processor with only *temporary* storage for programs and data. All programs and data must be transferred to RAM from an input device (such as a keyboard) or from disk before programs can be executed and data can be processed. Once a program is no longer in use, the storage space it occupied is assigned to another program awaiting execution. Programs and data are loaded to RAM from disk storage because the time required to access a program instruction or piece of datum from RAM is significantly less than from disk storage. RAM is essentially a high-speed holding area for data and programs. In fact, *nothing really happens in a computer system until the program instructions and data are moved from RAM to the processor.*

The processor, according to program instructions, manipulates the data in RAM. A program instruction or a piece of datum is stored in a specific RAM location called an **address.** RAM is analogous to the rows of boxes you see in post offices. Just as each Post Office box has a number, each byte in RAM has an address. Addresses permit program instructions and data to be located, accessed, and processed. The content of each address changes frequently as different programs are executed and new data are processed.

The transfer of data to and from RAM is very fast because solid-state electronic circuitry has no moving parts. Electrically charged points in the RAM chips represent the bits (1s and 0s) that comprise the data and other information stored in RAM. RAM is attached to the motherboard, like the processor, and therefore to the electronic bus. Over the past two decades, researchers have given us a succession of RAM technologies, each designed to keep pace with ever-faster processors. Most new PCs are being equipped with **synchronous dynamic RAM (SDRAM)**, **DDR SDRAM** (a newer "double data rate" SDRAM), or **Rambus DRAM (RDRAM)**.

A state-of-the-art memory chip, smaller than a postage stamp, can store about 128,000,000 bits, or more than 12,000,000 characters of data! Physically, memory chips are installed on **single in-line memory modules,** or **SIMMs,** and on the newer **dual in-line memory modules,** or **DIMMs.** SIMMs are less expensive but have only a 32-bit data path to the processor, whereas DIMMs have a 64-bit data path. The RDRAM chips are installed on **rambus in-line memory modules (RIMMs)**. The modules are about an inch high and four to six inches long (see Figure 4-9).

THE CRYSTAL BALL: Will Solid-State Memory Replace Rotating Memory? Many mainframe computers of the 1960s had only 512 KB of RAM. That amount of RAM was housed in refrigerator-size cabinets and could cost up to a million dollars. Today, digital cameras have thumbnail-size memory cards with 1,000 times that amount of RAM (512 MB of RAM) at a millionth the cost per byte. At an internal seminar in 1968, an IBM researcher told IBMers that all memory (RAM) in all the computers in the world at that time would fit into a brandy snifter by the turn of the century. Well, he was right. Indications are that we are in a transition from the relatively slow rotating disk storage to high-speed solid-state memory.

Cache and Other High-Speed Memories

Data and programs are being continually moved in and out of RAM at electronic speeds. But that's not fast enough. To achieve even faster transfer of instructions and data to the processor, computers are designed with **cache memory** (see Figure 4-12). Computer designers use cache memory to increase computer system throughput. **Throughput** refers to the rate at which work can be performed by a computer system.

Like RAM, cache is a high-speed holding area for program instructions and data. However, cache memory uses internal storage technologies that are much faster (and much more expensive) than conventional RAM. With only a fraction of the capacity of RAM, cache memory holds only those instructions and data that are *likely* to be needed next by the processor. Cache memory is effective because, in a typical session, the same data or instructions are accessed over and over. The processor first checks cache memory for needed data and instructions, thereby reducing the number of accesses to the slower RAM. When you purchase a PC, you will see references to level 1 (L1) and level 2 (L2) cache. *Level 1 cache* is built into the processor, whereas *level 2 cache* is on another chip, sitting between the processor and RAM (see Figure 4-12). L2 cache is ultra-fast memory that buffers the transfer of information between the processor and RAM, thereby accelerating internal data movement.

The user cannot alter another special type of internal memory, called *read-only memory* (ROM) (see Figure 4-7). The contents of **ROM** (rhymes with "*mom*") are "hard-wired" (designed into the logic of the memory chip) by the manufacturer and can be "read only." When you turn on a microcomputer system, a program in ROM automatically readies the computer system for use and produces the initial display-screen prompt. A variation of ROM is **programmable read-only memory (PROM)**. PROM is ROM into which you, the user, can load read-only programs and data.

FIGURE 4–13 The Flash Memory Card
Nonvolatile flash memory cards are being used in many consumer products, such as digital cameras (shown here) and MP3 players. The flash cards hold images in the digital camera until the content can be uploaded to a personal computer. The memory card can be inserted directly into some PCs.

Photo courtesy of Intel Corporation

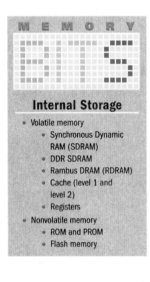

Internal Storage

- Volatile memory
  - Synchronous Dynamic RAM (SDRAM)
  - DDR SDRAM
  - Rambus DRAM (RDRAM)
  - Cache (level 1 and level 2)
  - Registers
- Nonvolatile memory
  - ROM and PROM
  - Flash memory

Flash memory (see Figure 4-13) is a type of PROM that can be altered easily by the user. Flash memory can be found on all new PCs, I/O devices, and storage devices. It is **nonvolatile memory** that retains its contents after an electrical interruption. The logic capabilities of these devices can be upgraded by simply downloading new software from the Internet or a vendor-supplied disk to flash memory. Upgrades to early PCs and peripheral devices required the user to replace the old circuit board or chip with a new one. The emergence of flash memory has eliminated this time-consuming and costly method of upgrade. The PC's **BIOS** (Basic Input Output System) is stored in flash memory. The built-in BIOS software contains the instructions needed to boot (start up) the PC and load the operating system. It also contains specific instructions on the operation of the keyboard, monitor, disk drives, and other devices. A PC's BIOS software should be periodically upgraded to the most recent version so that the PC can recognize new innovations in I/O and disk/disc storage.

What Happens Inside: Unraveling the Mystery

BASIC is a popular programming language. The simple BASIC program in Figure 4-14 computes and displays the sum of any two numbers (22 and 44 in the example). The instructions in this example program are intuitive; that is, you don't really need to know BASIC to understand what is happening. Figure 4-14 gives you insight into how a processor works by showing the interaction between RAM, the control unit, and the arithmetic and logic unit during the execution of this program. There is actually more going on in the processor, but this example captures the essence of what's happening. Figure 4-14 uses only 10 RAM locations and only for data. In practice, both programs and data would be stored in RAM, which usually has a minimum of 64 million storage locations.

The statement-by-statement walkthrough in Figure 4-14 illustrates generally what happens as each BASIC instruction is executed. More complex arithmetic and input/output tasks involve further repetitions of these fundamental operations. Logic operations (greater than, less than, equal to, and so on) are similar, with values being compared between RAM locations, the accumulator, and the various registers (see Figure 4-12).

The Instruction Cycle

We communicate with computers by telling them what to do in their native tongue—the machine language. You may have heard of computer programming languages such as BASIC (in Figure 4-14) and C++. Dozens of these languages are in common usage, but all need to be translated into the only language that a computer understands—its own **machine language.** Typically, each instruction in a human-oriented language, like BASIC, is translated into several machine language instructions. As you might expect, machine language instructions are represented inside the computer as strings of binary digits.

These instructions are executed within the framework of an **instruction cycle.** The speed of a processor is sometimes measured by how long it takes to complete an instruction cycle. The timed interval that comprises the instruction cycle is the total of the *instruction time,* or *I-time,* and the *execution time,* or *E-time.* The actions that take place during the instruction cycle are shown in Figure 4-15.

Most modern processors are capable of **pipelining;** that is, they can begin executing another instruction before the current instruction is completed. In fact, several instructions can be pipelined simultaneously, each at a different part of the instruction cycle. Pipelining improves system throughput significantly.

PUTTING IT ALL TOGETHER

The motherboard, with its processor and memory, is ready for work. Alone, though, a motherboard is like a college with no students. The motherboard must be linked to I/O, storage, and communication devices to receive data and return the results of processing.

A Fleet of Buses

The typical desktop motherboard includes several empty **expansion slots** (see Figure 4-9) that provide direct connections to the common electrical bus. These slots let you expand the capabilities of a PC by plugging in a wide variety of special-function **expansion boards,** also called **expansion cards.** These add-on circuit boards contain the electronic circuitry for many supplemental capabilities, such as extra ports, a modem, or video capture capability. Expansion boards are made to fit a particular type of bus. These are the more popular types of buses for PC compatibles:

- *PCI local bus.* The **PCI** (**Peripheral Component Interconnect**) **local bus** enables expansion boards to be linked directly to the system's common bus. Modern motherboards normally include several PCI local bus slots for expansion boards.

FIGURE 4–14

WHAT HAPPENS INSIDE THE PROCESSOR
Illustrated here is the essence of what happens inside a computer when the five-instruction BASIC program shown here is executed. The RAM in this example has 10 numbered storage locations. The accumulator is part of the arithmetic and logic unit.

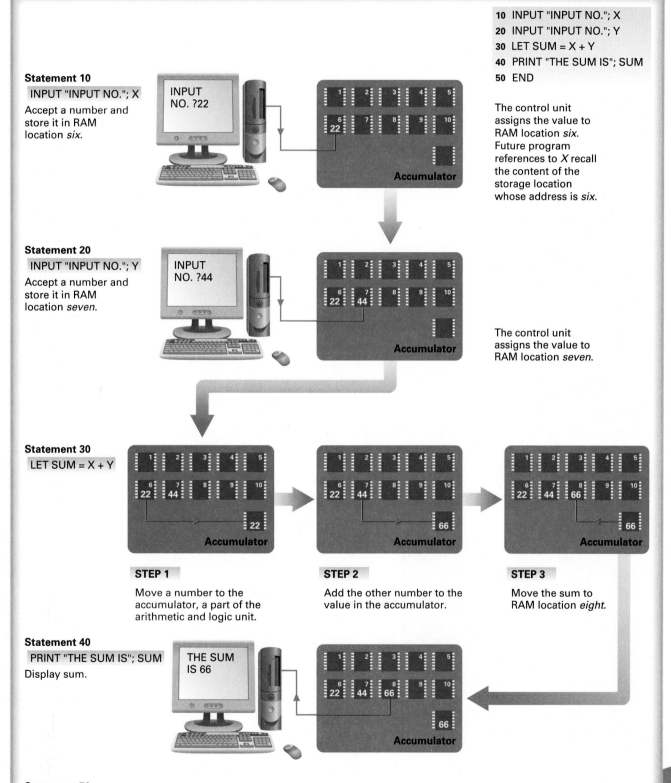

10 INPUT "INPUT NO."; X
20 INPUT "INPUT NO."; Y
30 LET SUM = X + Y
40 PRINT "THE SUM IS"; SUM
50 END

Statement 10
INPUT "INPUT NO."; X
Accept a number and store it in RAM location *six*.

INPUT NO. ?22

The control unit assigns the value to RAM location *six*. Future program references to *X* recall the content of the storage location whose address is *six*.

Statement 20
INPUT "INPUT NO."; Y
Accept a number and store it in RAM location *seven*.

INPUT NO. ?44

The control unit assigns the value to RAM location *seven*.

Statement 30
LET SUM = X + Y

STEP 1
Move a number to the accumulator, a part of the arithmetic and logic unit.

STEP 2
Add the other number to the value in the accumulator.

STEP 3
Move the sum to RAM location *eight*.

Statement 40
PRINT "THE SUM IS"; SUM
Display sum.

THE SUM IS 66

Statement 50
END
Terminate execution.

FIGURE 4–15 **THE INSTRUCTION CYCLE**

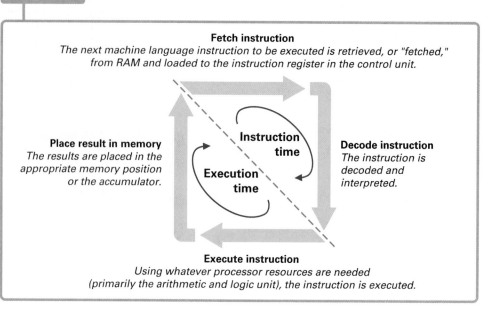

Fetch instruction
The next machine language instruction to be executed is retrieved, or "fetched," from RAM and loaded to the instruction register in the control unit.

Place result in memory
The results are placed in the appropriate memory position or the accumulator.

Instruction time

Execution time

Decode instruction
The instruction is decoded and interpreted.

Execute instruction
Using whatever processor resources are needed (primarily the arithmetic and logic unit), the instruction is executed.

PERSONAL COMPUTING:
Planning for USB USB (universal serial bus) 2.0 offers transmission speeds 40 times faster than the original USB standard. The new USB standard, which is available with new PCs, is backwards compatible, so you can continue to use early USB devices. When purchasing peripheral devices, look for the high-speed USB logo to ensure that they meet the emerging de facto standard, USB 2.0. Also, be aware that each USB port is considered an independent path which can transmit information no faster than the lowest performing element on the USB connection (USB devices can be daisy-chained). Avoid mixing and matching USB standards and either select a PC with plenty of USB 2.0 ports (six is usually sufficient) or choose a USB 2.0 hub.

- *Universal Serial Bus.* The **Universal Serial Bus** (**USB**) permits up to 127 peripheral devices to be connected to a single USB port (see Figure 4-16). The USB port eliminates the hassle of installing expansion cards. PC peripheral devices are designed to connect to the USB port on the motherboard. The USB **hot plug** feature allows peripheral devices to be connected to or removed from the USB port while the PC is running. This is especially helpful to gamers who like to switch game controllers when they begin a new game. Newer hardware is based on **USB 2.0,** a standard that permits data transfer at 480 M bps, about 40 times faster than the original USB standard.

- *1394 bus.* The **1394 bus** is a recent bus standard that supports data transfer rates of up to 400M bps, over 30 times faster than the USB bus. In the Apple world, this type of bus is called **FireWire.** The consumer electronics industry is very excited about the 1394 bus because it is ideal for devices that need to transfer data at very high speed in real time, such as audio/video (A/V) appliances. Up to 63 external devices can be daisy-chained to a 1394 port. Like USB, 1394 supports hot plugging.

- *SCSI bus.* The **SCSI** (**Small Computer System Interface**) **bus,** or "scuzzy" bus, provides an alternative to the expansion bus. Up to 15 SCSI peripheral devices can be daisy-chained to a SCSI interface expansion card via the SCSI port. That is, the devices are connected along a single cable, both internal and external, with multiple SCSI connectors (see Figure 4-17).

- *AGP bus.* The **AGP** (**Accelerated Graphics Port**) **bus** is a special-function bus designed to accommodate the throughput demands of high-resolution 3-D graphics. This special bus provides a direct link between the graphics adapter, which feeds video data to the monitor, and RAM.

  In time, most of the peripheral devices will be designed for the easy-to-use USB and/or 1394 buses. Most new PCs come with at least one FireWire (1394) port and at least a couple of USB ports. FireWire is used mostly for devices that require high data transfer rates, such as digital video cameras and auxiliary hard disks.

FIGURE 4–16 Peripherals World Record
Television personality Bill Nye, "The Science Guy," helped connect 111 peripheral devices to a single PC via a USB port, setting a new world record. Peripherals ranged from mice, joysticks, and keyboards to digital speakers and video conferencing systems.

Photo courtesy of Intel Corporation

Ports: Digital Entry/Exit Points on a PC

In a PC, external peripheral devices (such as a printer and a mouse) usually come with a cable and a multipin connector. To link a device to the PC, you plug its connector into a socket in much the same way you plug a lamp cord into an electrical outlet. The socket, called a *port*, provides a direct link to the PC's common electrical bus on the motherboard via a particular type of bus, such as the USB or PCI. Ports on a typical PC are shown in Figure 4-18.

External peripheral devices and other computers can be linked to the processor via cables or a wireless connection. The motherboard is designed with several port options, including at least one serial port and parallel port each, a keyboard port, a mouse port, plus a couple of USB ports.

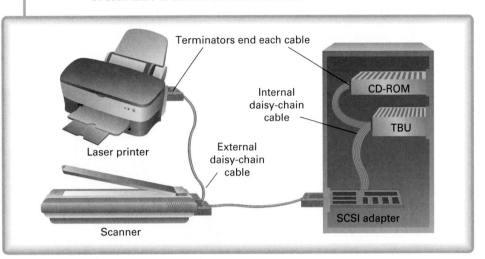

FIGURE 4–17

SCSI BUS
Two external devices, a printer and a scanner, are daisy-chained on the SCSI's external cable. Two internal devices, the CD-ROM and the tape backup unit, are daisy-chained on the SCSI's internal cable. Terminators are attached at the end of each cable to denote the end of the chain.

- *Serial port.* The **serial port** allows the serial transmission of data, one bit at a time (see Figure 4-19). Imagine a line of fans going single-file through a turnstile at a high school football game. An external modem might be connected to a serial port. The standard for PC serial ports is the 9-pin or 25-pin (male or female) **RS-232C connector.** One of the 9 or 25 lines carries the serial signal to the peripheral device, and another line carries the signal from the device. The other lines carry control signals.

- *Parallel port.* The **parallel port** allows the parallel transmission of data; that is, several bits are transmitted simultaneously. Figure 4-19 illustrates how 8-bit bytes travel in parallel over 8 separate lines. Imagine 8 lines of fans going through 8 adjacent turnstiles at an NFL football game. Extra lines carry control signals. Parallel ports use the same 25-pin RS-232C connector or the 36-pin **Centronics connector.** These ports provide the interface for such devices as printers, external magnetic tape or disk backup units, and other computers.

- *SCSI port.* The **SCSI port** provides a parallel interface to the SCSI bus that enables faster data transmission than with serial and parallel ports. Also, up to 15 peripheral devices can be daisy-chained to a single SCSI port; that is, they are connected along a single cable. The typical off-the-shelf PC compatible may not come with a SCSI bus, the add-on circuitry needed for a SCSI port.

- *USB port.* The **USB port** is a relatively recent innovation in high-speed device interfaces. Most new PCs have up to six USB ports. Most new peripherals are set up to use USB ports; however, the USB cable may not be included with the new product. It is purchased as an accessory item.

- *1394 port.* The **1394 port** is the newest and fastest port. The 1394 bus is still a little pricey and is not included on all new PCs. Many people use their 1394 port to connect an external hard drive, a device that demands very fast data transfer rates.

- *Dedicated keyboard and mouse ports.* These two ports have a round 6-pin connector.

- *IrDA port.* The **IrDA port,** or **infrared port,** transmits data via infrared light waves. Many PCs and devices, such as printers, come with IrDA ports. As long as the devices are within a few feet, data can be transferred without the use of cables.

A variety of ports shown in Figure 4-18 enable system links with a joystick or MIDI music device (via the *game port*), cable television, a local area network, a telephone line, the monitor, and other devices.

PC GROWTH: ADDING CAPABILITIES

Today's PCs are designed such that they can grow with your personal computing needs. Initially you purchase what you need and/or can afford, then purchase and install optional capabilities as required.

Expansion Boards

The *expansion slots* associated with expansion buses (PCI, SCSI, AGP, etc.) let you add features to your PC by adding *expansion boards.* The number of available expansion slots varies from computer to computer (see Figure 4-9). Keep in mind that an expansion board and/or peripheral device is designed for use with

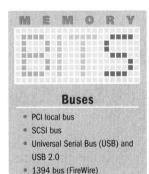

M E M O R Y

Buses

- PCI local bus
- SCSI bus
- Universal Serial Bus (USB) and USB 2.0
- 1394 bus (FireWire)
- AGP bus

FIGURE 4–18

MAKING THE CONNECTION TO THE SYSTEM UNIT
Typically, external connections to the motherboard and expansion cards are made to
the ports at the rear of the system unit. The various ports are labeled in the first illustration. Several of the many possible cables that can be connected to the ports are
shown left to right (SCSI to scanner and parallel to printer in inset, SCSI to adapter, USB,
coaxial network cable, keyboard, mouse, video, parallel, L and R speakers, microphone,
headset, serial). Also shown is the hodgepodge of wires that result when devices are
linked to the system unit. As you can see, a large number of devices using a variety of
connectors and cables can be linked to a PC.

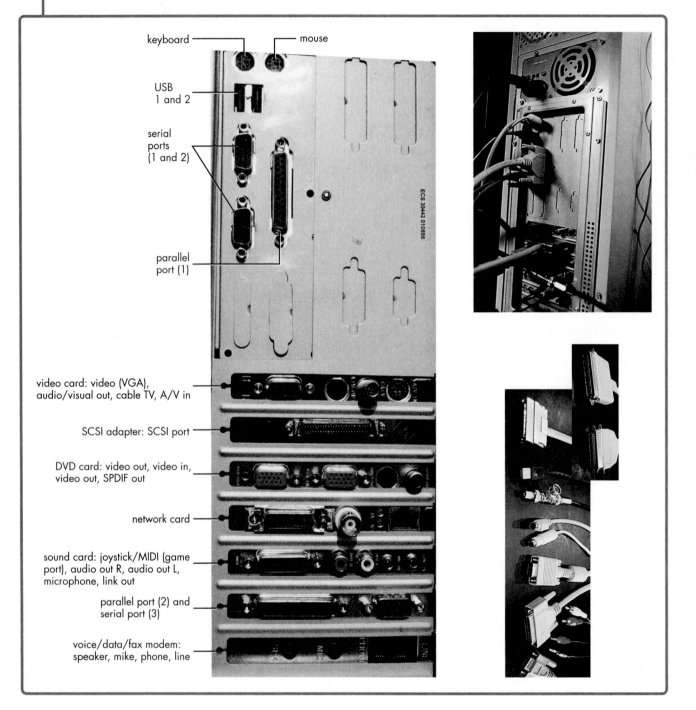

keyboard

mouse

USB
1 and 2

serial
ports
(1 and 2)

parallel
port (1)

ECS 3D442 010898

video card: video (VGA),
audio/visual out, cable TV, A/V in

SCSI adapter: SCSI port

DVD card: video out, video in,
video out, SPDIF out

network card

sound card: joystick/MIDI (game
port), audio out R, audio out L,
microphone, link out

parallel port (2) and
serial port (3)

voice/data/fax modem:
speaker, mike, phone, line

a particular type of expansion bus (PCI, SCSI, and so on). There are literally hundreds of expansion boards from which to choose. You will find these on most PCs:

- *Graphics adapter.* These adapters permit interfacing with video monitors. The VGA (video graphics array) board and the newer **AGP board** enable the interfacing of high-resolution monitors with the processor.

- *Sound.* The sound card, which is included on most new PCs, makes two basic functions possible. First, it enables sounds to be captured and stored on disk. Second, it enables sounds, including music and spoken words, to be played through external speakers. The sound card can add realism to computer games with stereo music and sound effects. It also allows us to speak commands and enter words to our PCs via speech recognition. The typical sound card will have receptacles for a microphone, a headset, an audio output, and a joystick. Basic sound card functionality is built into some motherboards; however, if you wish to have top-quality audio, you might want to upgrade to a sound card.

- *Data/voice/fax modem.* A *modem* permits communication with remote computers via a telephone-line link. The **data/voice/fax modem** performs the same function as a regular modem, plus it has added capability. It enables you to receive and make telephone calls, and it enables your PC to emulate a **fax** machine. Fax machines transfer images of documents via telephone lines to another location.

Depending on your applications needs, you might wish to enhance your system with some of these capabilities:

- *USB hub.* Plug a **USB hub** into a single USB port to expand the number of available USB ports (usually to either three, four, or five extra USB ports). The typical PC will need from 2 to 10 USB ports.

- *Network interface card.* The **network interface card** (**NIC**) enables and controls the exchange of data between the PCs in a local area network or a home network. Each PC in a network must be equipped with an NIC.

- *SCSI interface card.* The SCSI bus can be built into the motherboard or installed as an expansion board.

- *Video capture card.* This card enables full-motion color video with audio to be captured and played on a monitor or stored on disk. To capture video and convert it to digital format, simply plug the standard cable from the video camera or VCR into the video capture card and play the video. Once on disk storage, video information can be edited; that is, the content can be rearranged and integrated with text, graphics, special effects, and other forms of presentation, as desired. Some all-in-one AGP graphics cards include video capture card functionality, eliminating the need for a separate graphics card.

Personal computers are composed of components that are assembled in a case—the motherboard, the processor, several disks/discs, expansion boards as needed, and so on. Each year thousands of people order the components and build their own desktop PCs. Once you have the components in hand (see Figure 4-20), the assembly takes from one to three hours.

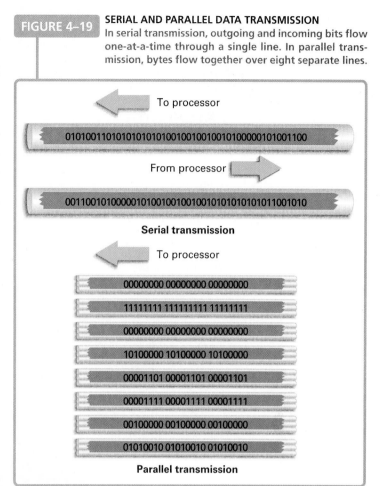

FIGURE 4–19 SERIAL AND PARALLEL DATA TRANSMISSION
In serial transmission, outgoing and incoming bits flow one-at-a-time through a single line. In parallel transmission, bytes flow together over eight separate lines.

FIGURE 4–20 Build Your Own PC
Many people of all ages and backgrounds build their own desktop PCs. A junior high school student ordered these components and built his own high-end custom PC. All that is needed to assemble the components and load the operating system is a screwdriver. The components for this high-end PC include: (in the front) a 120-GB hard disk, a DVD drive, a PCI sound card, a 2.8-GHz Intel Pentium 4 processor and processor cooling fan, and two 512-MB DIMMs of DDR SDRAM; (in middle) a tower case with a 400-watt power supply and three cooling fans, a Zip disk drive, a DVD/CD read/write drive, and an Intel motherboard; and (on top) the Windows XP operating system and an AGP video card with 128 MB of video RAM. The PC was not configured with a modem because it would be linked to an Internet-enabled home network via the network interface card that is embedded in the motherboard.

Long and Associates

PC Cards: PCMCIA Technology

The **PCMCIA card**, sometimes called a **PC card**, is a credit card-sized removable expansion module that is plugged into an external PCMCIA expansion slot on a PC, usually a notebook (see Figure 4-21). The PC card functions like an expansion board in that it offers a wide variety of capabilities. PC cards can be expanded RAM, programmable nonvolatile flash memory, network interface cards (wireless and wired), data/voice/fax modems, hard-disk cards, and much more. For example, one PC card comes in the form of a mobile **GPS** (**global positioning system**). The mobile GPS card can be used to pinpoint the latitude and longitude of the user within a few feet, anywhere on or near earth. Business travelers use GPS cards in conjunction with computer-based road maps to help them get around in unfamiliar cities.

Notebook computers are equipped with at least one PCMCIA-compliant interface. PDAs (personal digital assistants) and notebook PCs do not have enough space for as many expansion slots as do their desktop cousins. Interchangeable PC cards let laptop users insert capabilities as they are needed. For example, a user can insert a data/voice/fax modem PC card to send e-mail, then do a *hot swap* (PC remains running) with a hard disk card to access corporate maintenance manuals.

FIGURE 4–21 PC Cards for Notebooks
Notebook PCs, because of their compact size, have fewer expansion slots than desktop PCs. For this reason, notebook PCs are designed with PCMCIA expansion slots. PC cards are plugged into PCMCIA expansion slots to give the system added capability. This PC Card, which is shown with its PCI card counterpart, serves as a wireless network interface card (NIC) or a wireless voice/data/fax modem.

Courtesy of Symbol Technologies, Inc.

SECTION SELF-CHECK

4-2.1	The arithmetic and logic unit controls the flow of programs and data in and out of main memory. (T/F)
4-2.2	The RS-232C connector provides the interface to a port. (T/F)
4-2.3	The rate at which work can be performed by a computer system is called: (a) system spray, (b) throughput, (c) push through, or (d) volume load.
4-2.4	The timed interval that comprises the instruction cycle is the total of the instruction time and: (a) execution time, (b) I-time, (c) X-time, or (d) delivery time.
4-2.5	PC components are linked via a common electrical: (a) train, (b) bus, (c) car, or (d) plane.

4-3   Describing the Processor and Its Performance

How do we distinguish one computer from the other? Much the same way we'd distinguish one person from the other. When describing someone we generally note gender, height, weight, and age. When describing computers or processors, we talk about *word size, core speed, bus speed,* and the *memory capacity* because it is these elements that make the biggest contribution to system performance. For example, a computer might be described as a 64-bit, 3.4-GHz, 1-GB PC with a 533 MHz bus. Let's see what this means.

WORD SIZE: BUS WIDTH

Just as the brain sends and receives signals through the central nervous system, the processor sends and receives electrical signals through its common electrical bus a word at a time. A **word**, or *bus width,* describes the number of bits that are handled as a unit within a particular computer system's bus or during internal processing. Internal processing involves the movement of data and commands between registers, the control unit, and the arithmetic and logic unit (see Figure 4-12). Many popular computers have 64-bit internal processing but only a 32-bit path through the bus. The word size for internal processing for most modern PCs is 64 bits (eight 8-bit bytes). Workstations, mainframes, and supercomputers have 64-bit word sizes and up.

CORE SPEED: GHZ, MIPS, AND FLOPS

A tractor can go 22 miles per hour (mph), a minivan can go 90 mph, and a slingshot drag racer can go 300 mph. These speeds, however, provide little insight into the relative capabilities of these vehicles. What good is a 300-mph tractor or a 22-mph minivan? Similarly, you have to place the speed of computers within the context of their design and application. Generally, PCs are measured in *GHz,* workstations and some server computers are measured in *MIPS,* and supercomputers are measured in *FLOPS.*

- *Gigahertz: GHz.* The PC's heart is its *crystal oscillator* and its heartbeat is the *clock cycle.* The crystal oscillator paces the execution of instructions within the processor. A PC's processor speed, or *core speed,* is rated by its frequency of oscillation, or the number of clock cycles per second. Legacy PCs are rated in **megahertz,** or **MHz** (millions of clock cycles per second), but modern PCs are measured in **gigahertz,** or **GHz** (billions of clock cycles per second), with high-end PCs running in excess of 3 GHz. The elapsed time for one clock cycle is 1 divided by the frequency. For example, the time it takes to complete one cycle on an 4-GHz processor is 1/4,000,000,000, or 0.00000000025 seconds, or .25 nanoseconds (.25 billionths of a second). Normally several clock cycles are required to fetch, decode, and execute a single program instruction. The shorter the clock cycle, the faster the processor.

- *MIPS.* Processing speed may also be measured in **MIPS,** or millions of instructions per second. Although frequently associated with workstations and some server computers, MIPS is also applied to PCs. Computers can operate up to several thousand MIPS. Figure 4-22 illustrates relative performance (speed) of past and present Intel processors in MIPS. The MIPS measurement is not as accurate as MHz and FLOPS.

- *FLOPS.* Supercomputer speed is measured in **FLOPS**—floating point operations per second (see Figure 4-23). Supercomputer applications, which are often scientific, frequently involve floating point operations. Floating point operations accommodate very small or very large numbers. State-of-the-art supercomputers operate at speeds in excess of a trillion FLOPS.

BUS SPEED: THE PC BOTTLENECK

Modern processors are thousands of times faster than they were 25 years ago. The technology of the electronic bus which handles the movement of data between the various components on the motherboard has not kept pace with processor speed. This lag in speed has made the bus the chief bottleneck to processing efficiency within the PC. Like processors, bus speed is measured in cycles per second, but most processors operate at GHz speeds and buses operate at MHz speeds, usually around 250 to 600 MHz for modern PC processors.

FIGURE 4–22   **THE INTEL® FAMILY OF PROCESSORS**
The Intel family of processors has been installed in 9 of every 10 PCs in use today. This chart is an approximation of the relative speeds of popular Intel processors. The state-of-the-art processor has about 20,000 times the speed of the Intel 8088 (2000 MIPs to .2 MIPs), the processor that ushered in the age of personal computing. Note that this chart is logarithmic, so the MIP value increases by a factor of 10 at each labeled interval.

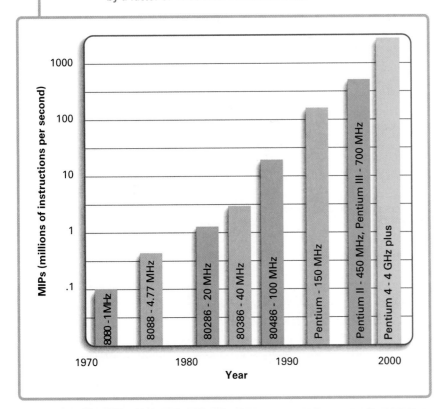

MEMORY

Processor Description
- Word size: Bits handled as a unit
  - 32 bits
  - 64 bits
- Core Speed
  - PCs: MHz and GHz (clock cycles)
  - PCs, workstations, and server computers: MIPS
  - Supercomputers: FLOPS
- Bus Speed
  - MHz and GHz (clock cycles)
- Memory Capacity
  - Kilobyte (KB), kilobit (Kb)
  - Megabyte (MB), megabit (Mb)
  - Gigabyte (GB)
  - Terabyte (TB)

FIGURE 4-24 HOW MUCH IS A KB, AN MB, A GB, AND A TB?

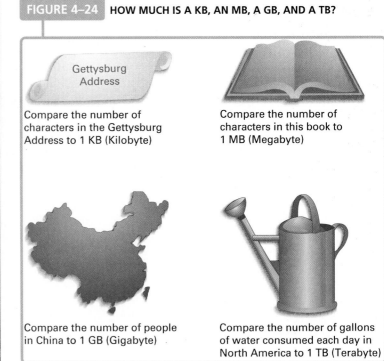

Compare the number of characters in the Gettysburg Address to 1 KB (Kilobyte)

Compare the number of characters in this book to 1 MB (Megabyte)

Compare the number of people in China to 1 GB (Gigabyte)

Compare the number of gallons of water consumed each day in North America to 1 TB (Terabyte)

FIGURE 4-23 World Speed Record for Computers
This engineer at Sandia National Labs is inspecting a connection in one of the 86 cabinets that house the 9,200 processors. The collective power of thousands of processors enables this supercomputer to perform at more than one trillion operations-per-second (1 trillion FLOPS or TERAFLOPS). This record-setting supercomputer is used to ensure the safety, reliability, and effectiveness of the U.S. nuclear stockpile through computer simulation instead of nuclear testing.

Photo courtesy of Intel Corporation

MEMORY CAPACITY: MB, GB, AND TB

The capacities of RAM, cache, and other memories are stated in terms of the number of bytes they can store. Memory capacity for most computers is stated in terms of **megabytes (MB)** and **gigabytes (GB)**. One megabyte equals 1,048,576 (2^{20}) bytes, about a million bytes. One gigabyte (2^{30} bytes) is about one billion bytes. Memory capacities of modern PCs range from 128 MB to 2 GB. High-speed cache memory capacities usually are measured in **kilobytes (KB)**, the most common being 512 KB of cache. One kilobyte is 1024 (2^{10}) bytes of storage.

Some high-end server computers and supercomputers have more than 1000 GB of RAM. It's only a matter of time before we state RAM in terms of **terabytes (TB)**, about one trillion bytes. GB and TB are frequently used in reference to high-capacity disk storage. Occasionally you will see memory capacities of individual chips stated in terms of **kilobits (Kb)** and **megabits (Mb)**. Figure 4-24 should give you a feel for KBs, MBs, GBs, and TBs.

DIFFERENCES IN PROCESSOR PERSONALITY

Word size, core and bus speed, and *memory capacity* are the primary descriptors of processors and processor performance. However, computers, like people, have their own "personalities." That is, two similarly described computers might possess attributes that give one more capability than the other. For example, one 64-bit, 3.4-GHz, 1-GB PC with a 533-MHz bus might have 1 MB of cache memory and another with the same specs might have only 512 KB of cache. Remember this: When you buy a PC, the basic descriptors tell most but not the entire story.

SECTION SELF-CHECK

4-3.1	*MIPS* is an acronym for "millions of instructions per second." (T/F)
4-3.2	A common bus width for modern PCs is 16 bits. (T/F)
4-3.3	Which has the most bytes: (a) a kilobyte, (b) a gigabyte, (c) a megabyte, or (d) a big byte?
4-3.4	The time it takes to complete one cycle on a 2-GHz processor is: (a) 1/2,000,000,000 second, (b) .000000005 second, (c) .5 microseconds, or (d) .5 thousandths of a second?
4-3.5	Word size is the same as: (a) bus speed, (b) bus width, (c) bus stop, or (d) bus capacity.

4-4 Processor Design

Researchers in IT are continually working to create new technologies and processes that will make processors faster and better utilize resources, thereby improving system throughput. The design process extends to creating processors for use in different environments (see Figure 4-25).

PARALLEL PROCESSING: COMPUTERS WORKING TOGETHER

In a single processor environment, the processor addresses the programming problem sequentially, from beginning to end. Today, designers are building computers that break a programming problem into pieces. Work on each of these pieces is then executed simultaneously in separate processors, all of which are part of the same computer system. The concept of using multiple processors in the same computer system is known as **parallel processing.** In parallel processing, one main processor examines the programming problem and determines what portions, if any, of the problem can be solved in pieces (see Figure 4-26). Those pieces that can be addressed separately are routed to other processors and solved. The individual pieces are then reassembled in the main processor for further computation, output, or storage. The net result of parallel processing is better throughput.

Computer designers are creating server computers and supercomputers with thousands of integrated microprocessors. Parallel processing on such a large scale is referred to as **massively parallel processing** (**MPP**). These superfast supercomputers have sufficient computing capacity to attack applications that have been beyond that of computers with traditional computer designs. For example, researchers can now simulate global warming with these computers.

Neural Networks: Wave of the Future?

Most of us interact with digital computers. Digital computers are great at solving structured problems involving computations and logic operations. However, most of the challenges we face from day to day can't be solved with these capabilities. For example, several times each year we are confronted with this problem: to find a pair of shoes that fits. This is a very human problem, better suited to the workings

FIGURE 4–25

PC PROCESSOR DESIGN CONSIDERATIONS
Design considerations for processors used in desktop PCs, such as the Pentium 4 (the microscopic view), and notebook PCs are different. For example, the mobile Intel Celeron processor has a feature that drops the processor power consumption when the laptop is idle or inactive to preserve battery life. Laptop processors must also be designed to dissipate heat within smaller enclosures.

Photos courtesy of Intel Corporation

FIGURE 4–26
PARALLEL PROCESSING
In parallel processing, auxiliary processors solve pieces of a problem to enhance system throughput.

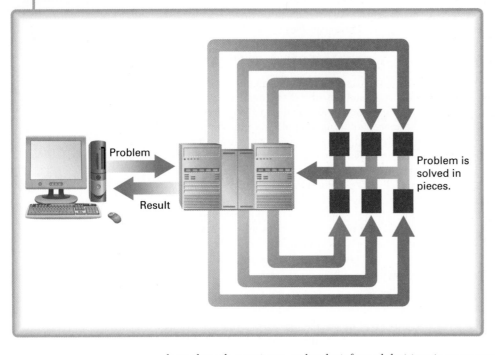

Problem

Result

Problem is solved in pieces.

of the human brain than for digital computers. Such problems involve unstructured input and outcomes that are unclear, so we use the best available processor—our brain. Scientists are studying the way the human brain works and are attempting to build computers that mimic the incredible human mind. The base technology for these computers is **neural networks.**

The neural network computer employs hundreds, even thousands, of small, interconnected processors, called *processing units*. The neural network works by creating connections and maintaining relationships between these processing units, the computer equivalent of neurons in the brain. Working within a specific sphere of knowledge (for example, worldwide agriculture strategies), the neural network computer can draw from its human-supplied knowledge base, learn through experience, and make informed decisions in an unstructured environment. Here are but a few of an increasing number of neural network applications: playing chess, improving automobile engine efficiency, enabling improved vision technology, planning crop rotation strategies, and forecasting financial market fluctuations.

The primary difference between traditional digital computers and neural networks is that digital computers process *structured data sequentially* whereas neural networks process *unstructured information simultaneously*. Digital computers will always be able to outperform neural networked computers and the human brain when it comes to fast, accurate numeric computation. However, if neural networks live up to their potential, they will be able to handle tasks that are currently very time-consuming or impossible for conventional computers, such as recognizing a face in the crowd.

GRID COMPUTING: SHARING COMPUTING POWER

During the past few years, the potential of **grid computing** has been compared to that of the Internet. The basic premise of grid computing is to use available computing resources more effectively. The typical PC user has a computer that is more powerful than the behemoth mainframe computers of the 1960s and 1970s but these users use less than 1 percent of their PCs' processing capabilities. Now that the world is networked via the Internet and an increasing number of users are linked to the Net via broadband, it is now possible to share vast amounts of unused processing resources via grid computing. Grid computing takes advantage of the unused processing capabilities of hundreds, even thousands of personal computers, to address a single programming problem.

In terms of evolution, grid computing is about where the Internet was in the 1970s. It has devoted fans who expect it to define a new era in information technology; but grid computing may be several years away from widespread acceptance and use. Here is how it works. People who are willing to share unused computing capacity via a network to solve a large processor-oriented problem, perhaps the analysis of extraterrestrial data, download and install a program. The program enables an interface with the server computer that coordinates the grid computing effort. PCs in the grid system work on a piece of the problem, but only when the PC is not in use. In this way, grid systems can combine unused resources with processing potential greater than some supercomputers. Supercomputers can cost millions of dollars, but grid systems composed entirely of volunteer participants who willingly share their computing resources are routinely performing supercomputer-level processing for virtually nothing.

IBM, Oracle, and other major technology companies are beginning to employ grid computing. The word is out; grid computing works. It offers a way for companies to greatly expanding their computing capacity while saving significant amounts of money. If grid computing continues to grow at the same pace of acceptance and use, introductory information technology books will soon be devoting an entire chapter to this important new technology.

4-4.1 In a single processor environment, the processor addresses the programming problem sequentially. (T/F)

4-4.2 Parallel processing on a large scale is referred to as massively trapezoidal processing. (T/F)

4-4.3 The base technology for computers that mimic the human mind is called: (a) HAL, (b) neural network, (c) human brain focus, or (d) interconnected processing.

4-4.4 Which of the following would not be representative of a neural network application: (a) playing chess, (b) planning crop rotation strategies, (c) processing payroll, or (d) enabling improved vision technology?

4-1 GOING DIGITAL

The two kinds of electronic signals are **analog** and **digital**. To make the most effective use of computers and automation, the electronics world is going digital. The music industry **digitizes** the natural analog signals that result from recording sessions, then stores the digital version on CDs. Computers are digital and, therefore, work better with digital data.

The two digital states of the computer—on and off—are represented by a *bit,* short for binary digit. These electronic states are compatible with the **binary** numbering system. Letters and decimal numbers are translated into bits for storage and processing on computer systems.

Data are stored temporarily during processing in RAM and permanently on devices such as disk drives.

Alphanumeric (*alpha* and *numeric*) characters are represented in computer storage by unique bit configurations. Characters are translated into these bit configurations, also called *bytes,* according to a particular coding scheme, called an *encoding system*.

The 7-bit *ASCII* encoding system is the most popular encoding system for PCs and data communication. An extended version of ASCII, an 8-bit encoding system, offers 128 more codes. Microsoft Windows uses the 8-bit **ANSI** encoding system.

Unicode, a uniform 16-bit encoding system, will enable computers and applications to talk to one another more easily and will accommodate most of the world's languages.

The **hexadecimal,** or base-16, numbering system is used as shorthand to display the binary contents of RAM and disk storage.

4-2 THE PC SYSTEM UNIT

The processor, RAM, and other electronic components are housed in the *system unit*. The *processor* is literally a computer on a chip. This processor, the electronic circuitry for handling input/output signals from the peripheral devices, and the memory chips are mounted on a single circuit board called a *motherboard*. The motherboard's **chipset** controls the flow of information between system components.

The **bus** is the common pathway through which the processor sends/receives data and commands to/from RAM and disk storage and all I/O peripheral devices. Like the wheeled bus, the bus provides data transportation to all processor components, memory, and **device controllers.**

Most new system units have an Intel **Pentium®** 4, **Celeron®,** or **Itanium™** processor inside, but many older systems with **Pentium®, Pentium® Pro, Pentium® II,** and **Pentium® III** processors continue to be workhorses.

The processor is the nucleus of any computer system. A processor, which is also called the **central processing unit** or **CPU,** has only two fundamental sections, the **control unit** and the **arithmetic and logic unit,** which work together with RAM to execute programs. The control unit's **decoder** interprets

instructions, then the control unit directs the arithmetic and logic unit to perform computation and logic operations. During execution, instructions and data are passed between very high-speed **registers** (for example, the **instruction register,** the **program register,** and the **accumulator**) in the control unit and the arithmetic and logic unit.

RAM, or random-access memory, provides the processor with temporary storage for programs and data. Physically, memory chips are installed on **single in-line memory modules (SIMMs), dual in-line memory modules (DIMMs),** and **rambus in-line memory modules (RIMMs).** Most new PCs are being equipped with **synchronous dynamic RAM (SDRAM), DDR SDRAM,** or **Rambus DRAM (RDRAM).**

In RAM, each datum is stored at a specific **address.** RAM is **volatile memory** (contrast with **nonvolatile memory**); that is, the data are lost when the electrical current is turned off or interrupted. All input/output, including programs, must enter and exit RAM. Other variations of internal storage are **ROM, programmable read-only memory (PROM),** and **flash memory,** a nonvolatile memory. The **BIOS** software is stored in flash memory.

Some computers employ **cache memory** (level 1 and level 2) to increase **throughput** (the rate at which work can be performed by a computer system). Like RAM, cache is a high-speed holding area for program instructions and data. However, cache memory holds only those instructions and data likely to be needed next by the processor.

Every **machine language** has a predefined format for each type of instruction. During one **instruction cycle,** an instruction is "fetched" from RAM, decoded in the control unit, and executed, and the results are placed in memory. The instruction cycle time is the total of the instruction time (I-time) and the execution time (E-time). Most modern processors are capable of **pipelining** to speed up processing.

The motherboard includes several empty **expansion slots** so you can purchase and plug in optional capabilities in the form of **expansion boards** or **expansion cards.** The most common expansion boards plug into a **PCI local bus.** The **SCSI bus,** or "scuzzy" bus, allows up to 15 SCSI peripheral devices to be daisy-chained to a SCSI interface expansion card. The **Universal Serial Bus (USB)** permits up to 127 USB peripheral devices to be **hot plugged** to the PC. The **USB 2.0** standard is 40 times faster than the original USB standard. The **1394 bus** (**FireWire** in the Apple world) is a bus standard that supports data transfer rates of up to 400M bps. The **AGP bus** is a special-function bus for high-resolution 3-D graphics.

In a PC, external peripheral devices come with a cable and a multipin connector. A port provides a direct link to the PC's common electrical bus. External peripheral devices can be linked to the processor via cables through a **serial port, parallel port, SCSI port, USB port, 1394 port,** or **IrDA (infrared)**

port. The standard for PC serial ports is the **RS-232C connector.** The RS-232C and **Centronics connectors** are used with parallel ports.

Popular expansion boards include graphics adapters such as the **AGP** or **accelerated graphics port board**, sound, **data/voice/fax modem** (enables emulation of a **fax** machine), **network interface card (NIC)**, and video capture card.

The **PCMCIA card,** sometimes called a **PC card,** provides a variety of interchangeable add-on capabilities in the form of credit-card-sized modules. The PC card is especially handy for the portable environment. A mobile **GPS (global positioning system)** can be a PC card.

4-3 DESCRIBING THE PROCESSOR AND ITS PERFORMANCE

A processor is described in terms of its word size (bus width), core speed, bus speed, and memory capacity.

A **word** is the number of bits handled as a unit within a particular computer system's common electrical bus or during internal processing.

Personal computer speed, called the core speed, is measured in **megahertz (MHz)** and **gigahertz (GHz).** High-end PC, workstation, and server computer speed is measured in **MIPS.** Supercomputer speed is measured in **FLOPS.**

Bus speed, which is less than core speed, is measured in cycles per second. Bus speed can be a bottleneck in processing performance.

Memory capacity is measured in **kilobytes (KB), megabytes (MB), gigabytes (GB),** and **terabytes (TB).** Chip capacity is sometimes stated in **kilobits (Kb)** and **megabits (Mb).**

4-4 PROCESSOR DESIGN

In **parallel processing,** one main processor examines the programming problem and determines what portions, if any, of the problem can be solved in pieces. Those pieces that can be addressed separately are routed to other processors, solved, then recombined in the main processor to produce the result. Parallel processing on a large scale is referred to as **massively parallel processing (MPP).**

Neural networks mimic the way the human brain works. The neural network computer uses many small, interconnected processors to address problems that involve *unstructured information.*

The basic premise of **grid computing** is to use available computing resources more effectively. Grid computing addresses a single programming problem by tapping the unused processing capabilities of many PCs via a network.

KEY TERMS

1394 bus (p. 184)
1394 port (p. 185)
accumulator (p. 181)
address (p. 181)
AGP board (p. 187)
AGP bus (p. 184)
analog (p. 172)
ANSI (p. 175)
arithmetic and logic unit (p. 181)
binary (p. 172)
BIOS (p. 182)
bus (p. 177)
cache memory (p. 181)
Celeron® (p. 179)
central processing unit (CPU) (p. 180)
Centronics connector (p. 185)
chipset (p. 176)
control unit (p. 180)
data/voice/fax modem (p. 187)
DDR SDRAM (p. 181)
decoder (p. 180)
device controller (p. 177)

digital (p. 172)
digitize (p. 172)
dual in-line memory module (DIMM)
  (p. 181)
expansion board (p. 182)
expansion card (p. 182)
expansion slot (p. 182)
fax (p. 187)
FireWire (p. 184)
flash memory (p. 182)
FLOPS (p. 189)
gigabyte (GB) (p. 190)
gigahertz (GHz) (p. 189)
GPS (global positioning system) (p. 188)
grid computing (p. 192)
hexadecimal (p. 175)
hot plug (p. 184)
infrared port (p. 185)
instruction cycle (p. 182)
instruction register (p. 180)
IrDA port (p. 185)
Itanium™ (p. 179)

kilobit (Kb) (p. 190)
kilobyte (KB) (p. 190)
machine language (p. 182)
massively parallel processing (MPP)
  (p. 191)
megabit (Mb) (p. 190)
megabyte (MB) (p. 190)
megahertz (MHz) (p. 189)
MIPS (p. 189)
network interface card (NIC) (p. 187)
neural network (p. 192)
nonvolatile memory (p. 182)
parallel port (p. 185)
parallel processing (p. 191)
PCI local bus (p. 182)
PCMCIA card (PC card) (p. 188)
Pentium 4® (p. 179)
Pentium® (p. 179)
Pentium® II (p. 179)
Pentium® III (p. 179)
Pentium® Pro (p. 179)
pipelining (p. 182)

program register (p. 180)
programmable read-only memory
    (PROM) (p. 181)
Rambus DRAM (RDRAM) (p. 181)
rambus in-line memory module (RIMM)
    (p. 181)
registers (p. 180)
ROM (p. 181)
RS-232C connector (p. 185)

SCSI bus (p. 184)
SCSI port (p. 185)
serial port (p. 185)
single in-line memory module (SIMM)
    (p. 181)
synchronous dynamic RAM (SDRAM)
    (p. 181)
terabyte (TB) (p. 190)

throughput (p. 181)
Unicode (p. 175)
Universal Serial Bus (USB) (p. 184)
USB 2.0 (p. 184)
USB hub (p. 187)
USB port (p. 185)
volatile memory (p. 181)
word (p. 188)

MATCHING

1. 1394 bus
2. DDR SDRAM
3. pipelining
4. binary
5. Pentium 4
6. chipset
7. Moore's Law
8. BIOS
9. grid computing
10. registers
11. ASCII
12. machine language
13. throughput
14. hexadecimal
15. AGP

a. doubling of transistors each 1.5 years
b. graphics adapter
c. stored in flash
d. encoding
e. in processor control unit
f. rate of work by a CPU
g. language of computers
h. base 16
i. motherboard flow control
j. type of memory
k. 1, 0
l. networking of unused computing capacity
m. Intel processor
n. FireWire
o. overlapping instruction execution

CHAPTER SELF-CHECK

4-1.1   Bit is the singular of byte. (T/F)

4-1.2   The hexadecimal numbering system has 26 unique numbers. (T/F)

4-1.3   Stereo music cannot be digitized. (T/F)

4-1.4   The base of the binary number system is: (a) 2, (b) 8, (c) 16, or (d) 32.

4-1.5   How many ANSI bytes can be stored in a 32-bit word: (a) 2, (b) 4, (c) 6, or (d) 8?

4-1.6   What is the ASCII code for Q if the code for P is 01010000: (a) 01010011, (b) 01010010, (c) 01010001, or (d) 01011111?

4-1.7   A hexadecimal A3 is what in binary: (a) 10100011, (b) 01010011, (c) 00111010, or (d) 11110011?

4-2.1   The control unit is that part of the processor that reads and interprets program instructions. (T/F)

4-2.2   PC cards can be hot swapped while the PC is running. (T/F)

4-2.3   The 1394 bus transfers data at a slower rate than the USB bus. (T/F)

4-2.4   Which of the following memory groups are in order based on speed (slowest to fastest): (a) registers, cache, RAM, (b) cache, RAM, registers, (c) cache, registers, RAM, or (d) RAM, cache, registers?

4-2.5   BIOS software is stored permanently: (a) in flash memory, (b) in DDR SDRAM, (c) on hard disk, or (d) on DVD-ROM.

4-2.6 Which one of the following would not be attached to a motherboard: (a) RAM, (b) processor, (c) FLOP, or (d) expansion board?

4-2.7 Which port enables the parallel transmission of data within a computer system: (a) serial, (b) parallel, (c) Centronics, or (d) speaker?

4-2.8 Which two buses enable the daisy-chaining of peripheral devices: (a) USB and SCSI, (b) SCSI and infrared, (c) USB and PCI local bus, or (d) PCI local bus and ISA?

4-3.1 The word size of all PCs is 32 bits. (T/F)

4-3.2 Bus speed is always the same as core speed. (T/F)

4-3.3 A gigabyte of RAM has more storage capacity than a megabit of RAM. (T/F)

4-3.4 Which of these would not be a major factor in processor performance: (a) core speed, (b) bus width, (c) size of RAM, or (d) bus length?

4-3.5 A high-capacity hard disk would be measured in: (a) GB or TB, (b) KB or TB, (c) kilobits or megabits, or (d) MB or GB.

4-3.6 Supercomputer speed is measured in: (a) LOPS, (b) MOPS, (c) FLOPS, or (d) POPS.

4-4.1 In parallel processing, two main processors examine the programming problem and determine what portions, if any, of the problem can be solved in pieces. (T/F)

4-4.2 In grid computing, all PCs on the grid must commit their resources until processing is complete. (T/F)

4-4.3 Grid computing is well ahead of the Internet in technological evolution. (T/F)

4-4.4 The concept of using multiple processors in the same computer system is known as: (a) massive processing, (b) acute processing, (c) parallel processing, or (d) perpendicular processing.

4-4.5 Neural networks process unstructured information: (a) intermittently, (b) sequentially, (c) simultaneously, or (d) as time permits.

4-4.6 The neural network computer employs many small, interconnected processors, called: (a) brain units, (b) neural nets, (c) mini PCs, or (d) processing units.

4-4.7 Grid computing takes advantage of what capabilities in remote PCs: (a) printing, (b) Net search, (c) unused processing, or (d) lattice uploading?

IT ETHICS AND ISSUES

MONITORING OF E-MAIL

Many organizations monitor both e-mail and telephone conversations of their employees. These organizations cite productivity and quality control as justification. People who used to chat at the water cooler or snack counter do so now over office e-mail or instant messaging. Monitored e-mail is just as likely to surface "meet you at the gym after work" as "meet you in the conference room."

Realistically, e-mail is monitored to discourage nonbusiness messages and to keep employees focused on job-related activities. We now know that e-mail, when used responsibly, can boost productivity. We also know that, if abused, e-mail can be counterproductive.

Once an organization decides to monitor e-mail, it can do so in several ways. Individuals can scan e-mail archives for inappropriate transmissions, often a time-consuming process. In large organizations, computers scan e-mail archives for keywords (baseball, party, boss, and so on) and kick out messages with questionable content. Already many employees have been fired or disciplined for abusing e-mail.

Employees feel that monitoring of e-mail is an invasion of personal privacy. Many workers view e-mail as just another tool, such as a telephone, and that they should be allowed some reasonable personal use. The issue is being argued in the courts.

Discussion: *Does an employer's right to know outweigh the employee's right to privacy?*

Discussion: *What statements do you feel should be included in a corporate policy on e-mail usage?*

Discussion: *Which do you feel is more invasive, the monitoring of voice mail and inspection of lockers or the monitoring of e-mail? Why?*

Discussion: *The use of instant messaging is growing in the corporate world, but companies that monitor e-mail seldom monitor instant messaging. To be consistent, should they monitor instant messaging, too? Why or why not?*

TERM-PAPER FRAUD

Plagiarism, more specifically term-paper fraud, has been a problem in higher education throughout this century. However, only during the past few years have for-sale term papers on every common subject been showcased to the world and made readily available over the Internet. Students purchase these papers hoping to pass them off as originals. Typically, they will use a variety of software tools to add a personal touch to these recycled papers.

Many sites on the Internet offer "term-paper assistance" in a variety of topic areas. One site has both off-the-shelf and custom term-paper services, inviting students to "Get a brand-new paper written from scratch according to your exact specifications. Click here." Some states have passed laws prohibiting the sale of prefabricated term papers. However, term-paper mills circumvent these laws by stating that the intended purpose of their term papers is that they be used as models that students can use during the preparation of their own term papers.

Discussion: *Is plagiarism a problem on your campus? If so, how big a problem?*

Discussion: *What can students do to help deter plagiarism and encourage academic honesty? What can college administrators do? What can professors do? What can government do?*

Discussion: *Do students who plagiarize the work of others rob themselves of the knowledge and experience they gain from writing a well-developed paper? Explain.*

DISCUSSION AND PROBLEM SOLVING

4-1.1 Generally, computers are digital and human beings are analog, so what we say, hear, and see must be converted, or digitized, for processing on a computer. Speculate on how a family photograph might be digitized for storage and processing on a computer system.

4-1.2 Create a 5-bit encoding system to be used for storing uppercase alpha characters, punctuation symbols, and the apostrophe. Discuss the advantages and disadvantages of your encoding system in relation to the ASCII encoding system.

4-1.3 How many characters can be represented with a 12-bit encoding system?

4-1.4 Write your first name as an ASCII bit configuration.

4-2.1 List at least 10 products that are smaller than a toaster oven and use microprocessors. Select one and describe the function of its microprocessor.

4-2.2 Describe the advantages of a USB port over a parallel port. Also, describe the advantages of a parallel port over a serial port.

4-2.3 Distinguish between RAM and flash memory. Be specific.

4-2.4 Which two functions does the arithmetic and logic unit perform? Give a real-life example for each function.

4-2.5 Explain the relationship between a processor, a motherboard, and a PC.

4-2.6 Generally describe the interaction between the processor's control unit, registers, and RAM.

4-2.7 Give one example of where each of the memory technologies in question 4-2.6 might be used in a personal computer system.

4-2.8 Illustrate the interaction between the user RAM and the accumulator in the arithmetic and logic unit for the following basic program. Use the model shown in Figure 4-14.

```
INPUT "Enter ages for 3 children"; A, B, C
LET AVGAGE=(A+B+C)/3
PRINT "The average age is"; AVGAGE
END
```

4-2.9 List three expansion boards you would like to have on your own PC. How would you use these added capabilities?

4-2.10 Describe a hot swap as it relates to a PCMCIA-compliant interface.

4-2.11 Why do you suppose PC motherboards are designed to accommodate several types of buses?

4-2.12 Would you consider building your own computer? Why or why not?

4-3.1 Assume a move data instruction requires five clock cycles. Compute the time it takes, in nanoseconds, to execute a move data instruction on a 3-GHz processor.

4-3.2 Convert 5 MB to KB, Mb, and Kb. Assume a byte contains eight bits.

1. Explore the inside of a PC (yours or a lab computer made available to students for this exercise). Remove the cover on a tower PC to expose the motherboard. Usually, this is no more difficult than loosening a couple of thumbscrews and removing a side panel. Do not touch any electronic components since they are sensitive to static electricity. Identify as many of the motherboard components shown in Figure 4-9 as you can. Look inside and on the back of the computer to identify the number of PCI expansion slots and DIMM sockets on the motherboard. Also, count the number of USB ports.

2. Use available system monitoring software and/or system documentation to determine the following information for a particular PC (yours or a lab PC): processor speed, amount and type of RAM, and amount of L1 and L2 cache.

INTERNET EXERCISES @ www.prenhall.com/long

1. The Online Study Guide (multiple choice, true/false, matching, and essay questions)
2. Internet Learning Activities
   - Encoding
   - Processors, Chips, and RAM
3. Serendipitous Internet Activities
   - Popular Culture
   - Online Shopping

IT ILLUSTRATED

THE COMPUTER ON A CHIP

The invention of the light bulb in 1879 symbolized the beginning of electronics. Electronics then evolved into the use of vacuum tubes, then transistors, and now integrated circuits. Today's microminiaturization of electronic circuitry is continuing to have a profound effect on the way we live and work. The increased speed and capability of computers influence all the many services we may take for granted. Where would telecommunications, speech recognition, advanced software applications, and the Internet be without this technology?

Current chip technology permits the placement of hundreds of thousands of transistors and electronic switches on a single chip. Chips already fit into wristwatches and credit cards, but electrical and computer engineers want them even smaller. In electronics, smaller is better. The ENIAC, the first full-scale digital electronic computer, weighed 50 tons and occupied an entire room. Today, a computer far more powerful than the ENIAC can be fabricated within a single piece of silicon the size of a child's fingernail.

Chip designers think in terms of nanoseconds (one billionth of a second) and microns (one millionth of a meter). They want to pack as many circuit elements as they can into the structure of a chip. This is called *scaling,* or making the transistor, and the technology that connects it, smaller. High-density packing reduces the time required for an electrical signal to travel from one circuit element to the next— resulting in faster computers. Circuit lines on early 1980s PC processors were 10 microns wide. Today's circuit lines are .09 microns or 90 nanometers (one billionth of a meter). The reduced size of the circuit lines enables chips to hold over 100 million transistors and provide thousands of times the power of earlier processors.

As transistors become smaller, the chip becomes faster, conducts more electricity, and uses less power. Also, it costs less to produce as more transistors are packed on a chip.

The computer revolution will continue to grow rapidly into the twenty-first century as long as researchers find ways to make transistors faster and smaller, make wiring that links them less resistive to electrical current, and increase chip density. Each year, researchers have developed radically new techniques for manufacturing chips. For example, IBM recently began developing a logic chip and processor using silicon-on-insulator (SOI) technology, an innovative approach to the chip-making process. The process presented here provides a general overview that is representative of the various techniques used by chip manufacturers (see Figure 4-27).

Chips are designed and manufactured to perform a particular function. One chip might be a microprocessor, or the "brains," for a personal computer. Another, such as a memory chip, might be for temporary random-access storage (RAM). Logic chips are used in beverage vending machines, televisions, refrigerators, cell phones, and thousands more devices. Microprocessors, memory, and logic chips are three of the most common kinds of chips.

The development of integrated circuits starts with a project review team made up of representatives from design, manufacturing, and marketing. This group works together to design a product the customer needs. Next, they go through prototype wafer manufacturing to resolve potential manufacturing problems. Once a working prototype is produced, chips are manufactured in quantity and sent to computer, peripheral, telecommunications, and other customers.

The manufacturing of integrated circuits involves a multistep process using various photochemical etching and metallurgical techniques. This complex and interesting process is illustrated here with photos, from silicon to the finished product. The process is presented in five steps: design, fabrication, packaging, testing, and installation.

SECTION SELF-CHECK

Design

1. Using Cad For Chip Design

Chip designers use computer-aided design (CAD) systems to create the logic for individual circuits. Although a chip can contain up to 30 layers, typically there are 10 to 20 patterned layers of varying material, with each layer performing a different purpose. In this multilayer circuit design, each layer is color-coded so the designer can distinguish between the various layers. Some of the layers lie within the silicon wafer and others are stacked on top.

Courtesy of Micron Technology, Inc.

2. Creating a Mask

The product designer's computerized drawing of each circuit layer is transformed into a *mask,* or *reticle,* a glass or quartz plate with an opaque material (such as chrome) formed to create the pattern. The process used to transfer a pattern or image from the masks to a wafer is called *photolithography.* The number of layers depends on the complexity of the chip's logic. The Intel Pentium processor, for example, contains 20 layers. When all these unique layers are combined, they create the millions of transistors and circuits that make up the architecture of the processor. Needless to say, the manufacturing process forming this sequence of layers is a very precise one!

Courtesy of Micron Technology, Inc.

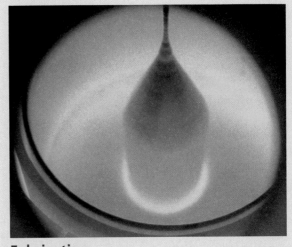

Fabrication

3. Creating Silicon Ingots

Molten silicon is spun into cylindrical ingots, usually from six to eight inches in diameter. Because silicon, the second most abundant substance, is used in the fabrication of integrated circuits, chips are sometimes referred to as "intelligent grains of sand."

M/A-COM, Inc.

4. Cutting the Silicon Wafers

The ingot is shaped and prepared prior to being cut into silicon wafers. Once the wafers are cut to about the thickness of a credit card, they are polished to a perfect finish.

M/A-COM, Inc.

5. Wearing Bunny Suits

To help keep a clean environment, workers wear semi-custom-fitted Gortex® suits. They follow a 100-step procedure when putting the suits on.

Courtesy of Intel Corporation

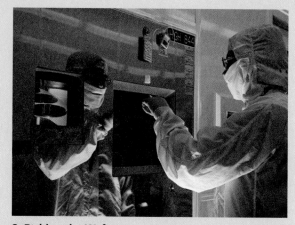

6. Keeping a Clean House

Clean air continuously flows from every pore of the ceiling and through the holes in the floor into a filtering system at the manufacturing plant. A normal room contains some 15 million dust particles per cubic foot. A clean, modern hospital has about 10,000 dust particles per cubic foot. A class-1 clean room (the lower the rating, the cleaner the facility) contains less than one dust particle per cubic foot. All of the air in a "clean room" is replaced seven times every minute.

Portions of the microchip manufacturing process are performed in yellow light because the wafers are coated with a light-sensitive material called "photoresist" before the next chip pattern is imprinted onto the surface of the silicon wafer.

Courtesy of AMD

8. Etching the Wafers

A photoresist is deposited onto the wafer surface creating a film-like substance to accept the patterned image. The mask is placed over the wafer and both are exposed to ultraviolet light. In this way the circuit pattern is transferred onto the wafer. The photoresist is developed, washing away the unwanted resist and leaving the exact image of the transferred pattern. Plasma (superhot gases) technology is used to etch the circuit pattern permanently into the wafer. This is one of several techniques used in the etching process. The wafer is returned to the furnace and given another coating on which to etch another circuit layer. The procedure is repeated for each circuit layer until the wafer is complete.

Some of the layers include aluminum or copper interconnects, which leave a fine network of thin metal connections or wires for these semiconductor chips. The wires are used to link the transistors. Aluminum has long been the standard for semiconductor wiring, but recent innovations with the use of copper wiring, a better conductor of electricity, will help create the next generation of semiconductors.

Courtesy of Micron Technology, Inc.

7. Coating the Wafers

Silicon wafers that eventually will contain several hundred chips are placed in an oxygen furnace at 1200 degrees Celsius. In the furnace, the wafer is coated with other minerals to create the physical properties needed to produce transistors and other electronic components on the surface of the wafer.

Photo courtesy of National Semiconductor Corporation

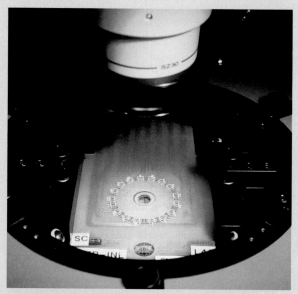

9. Tracking the Wafers

Fabrication production control tracks wafers through the fabricating process and measures layers at certain manufacturing stages to determine layer depth and chemical structure. These measurements assess process accuracy and facilitate real-time modifications.

Courtesy of Micron Technology, Inc.

10. Drilling the Wafers
It takes only a second for this instrument to drill 1440 tiny holes in a wafer. The holes enable the interconnection of the layers of circuits. Each layer must be perfectly aligned (within a millionth of a meter) with the others.

Courtesy of International Business Machines Corporation

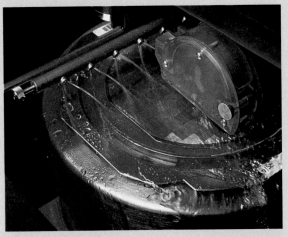

13. Dicing the Wafers
A diamond-edged saw, with a thickness of a human hair, separates the wafer into individual processors, known as die, in a process called *dicing*. Water spray keeps the surface temperature low. After cutting, high-pressure water rinses the wafer clean. In some situations, special lasers are used to cut the wafers.

Courtesy of Micron Technology, Inc.

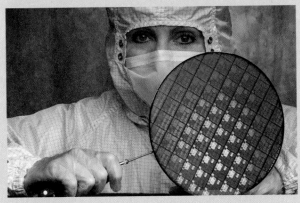

Packaging

11. Removing the Etched Wafers
The result of the coating/etching process is a silicon wafer that contains from 100 to 400 integrated circuits, each of which includes millions of transistors.

Courtesy of International Business Machines Corporation

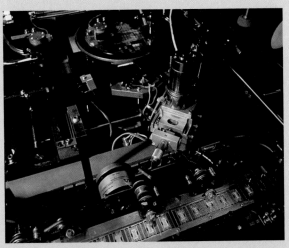

14. Attaching the Die
Individual die are attached to silver epoxy on the center area of a lead frame. Each die is removed from the tape with needles plunging up from underneath to push the die while a vacuum tip lifts the die from the tape. Lead frames are then heated in an oven to cure the epoxy. The wafer map created in probe tells the die-attach equipment which die to place on the lead frame.

Courtesy of Micron Technology, Inc.

12. Mounting the Wafer
Each wafer is vacuum mounted onto a metal-framed sticky film tape. The wafer and metal frame are placed near the tape, then all three pieces are loaded into a vacuum chamber. A vacuum forces the tape smoothly onto the back of the wafer and metal frame.

Courtesy of Micron Technology, Inc.

15. Packaging the Chips

The chips are packaged in protective ceramic or metal carriers. The carriers have standard-sized electrical pin connectors that allow the chip to be plugged conveniently into circuit boards. Because the pins tend to corrode, the pin connectors are the most vulnerable part of a computer system. To avoid corrosion and a bad connection, the pins on some carriers are made of gold.

Courtesy of International Business Machines Corporation

Testing

16. Testing the Chips

Each chip is tested to assess functionality and to see how fast it can store or retrieve information. Chip speed (or access time) is measured in nanoseconds (a billionth, 1/1,000,000,000th of a second). The precision demands are so great that as many as half the chips are found to be defective. A drop of ink is deposited on defective chips.

Courtesy of Micron Technology, Inc.

17. Burning In

This burn-in oven runs performance tests on every chip, simulating actual usage conditions. Each chip is tested by feeding information to the chip and querying for the information to ensure the chip is receiving, storing, and sending the correct data.

Courtesy of Micron Technology, Inc.

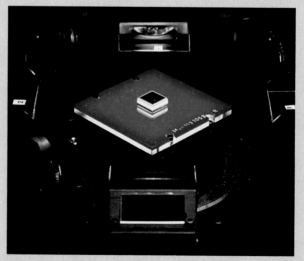

18. Scanning

All chips are scanned, using optics or lasers, to discover any bent, missing, or incorrectly formed leads.

Courtesy of Micron Technology, Inc.

Installation

19. Creating Circuit Boards

Pick and place equipment precisely positions various chips on the solder and contacts. Completed boards are then heated in the reflow ovens, allowing the lead coating and solder to melt together, affixing the chip to the printed circuit board.

Courtesy of Micron Technology, Inc.

20. Installing the Finished Chips

The completed circuit boards are installed in computers and thousands of other computer-controlled devices.

Photo courtesy of Intel Corporation

Chapter 5

5

Learning Objectives

Once you have read and studied this chapter, you will have learned:

● The relationship between mass storage and the various types of files (Section 5-1).

● The various types of magnetic disk devices and media, including organization, principles of operation, maintenance, performance considerations, and security concerns (Section 5-2).

● The operational capabilities and applications for the various types of optical laser disc storage (Section 5-3).

● The sources of computer viruses and approaches to protecting your system from these viruses (Section 5-4).

● Methods and procedures for backing up disk files (Section 5-5).

STORING AND RETRIEVING INFORMATION

Why this chapter is important to you

Not too long ago, we stored things in file drawers, hall closets, family photo albums, notebooks, recipe boxes, keepsake boxes, calendars, Rolodex name and address files, and many other places. We also had bookshelves filled with all kinds of reference books, from the phone books to encyclopedias. We had wire frame holders to store long-play record albums (LPs). Most of us still store things in these same places, but to a far lesser extent. The family photo album may be scanned and stored on a rewritable CD-ROM. Personal information software is rapidly replacing the Rolodex file. Young families are opting to buy an interactive encyclopedia on CD-ROM rather than an expensive, space-consuming 20-volume set. Music is now available from many electronic sources. You get the idea. Much of what used to be physical and tangible is now stored permanently in electronic form on various storage media.

This chapter gives you an overview of electronic storage media and devices. In a nutshell, media used for storage of data and various forms of information can be classified as disk, tape, or optical (such as a CD-ROM). Each has its advantages and disadvantages. For example, the functionality of the removable Zip disks and SuperDisks is similar, but speed and compatibility considerations may sway you toward one or the other. After studying this chapter, you'll be better prepared to answer the always popular question "How much hard disk space do I need?" Pointers throughout the chapter will help you protect your valuable data and information from electronic vandals and accidental loss.

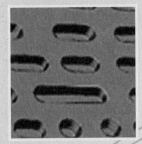

The somewhat confusing array of storage options makes us all vulnerable to making big mistakes when purchasing and using computer systems. This chapter should help you sort out the options and give you some insight as to what (and how much) to buy. Plus, it will help you to know when and how to use the various storage alternatives.

WHY THIS SECTION
IS IMPORTANT
TO YOU

During the past few decades,
contents of our file cabinets,
photo albums, day planners,
calendars, and so on have been
slowly migrating to electronic
files on mass storage devices,
such as disk. Read on to better
prepare yourself to work with
scores, if not hundreds, of files
each day.

5-1 Mass Storage, Files, and File Management

Did you ever stop to think about what happens behind the scenes when you. . .

- Request a telephone number through directory assistance?
- Draw money from your checking account at an ATM?
- Check out at a supermarket?
- Download a file on the Internet?

Needed information—such as telephone numbers, account balances, item prices, or stock summary files on the Internet—is retrieved from rapidly rotating disk-storage media and loaded to random-access memory (RAM) for processing. Untold terabytes (trillions of bytes) of information, representing millions of applications, are stored *permanently* for periodic retrieval in magnetic (such as hard disk) and optical (such as DVD+RW) storage media. There they can be retrieved in milliseconds. For example, as soon as the directory assistance operator keys in the desired name, the full name and number are retrieved from disk storage and displayed. Moments later, a digitized version of voice recordings of numbers is accessed from disk storage and played in response to the caller's request: "The number is five, zero, one, five, five, five, two, two, four, nine."

STORAGE TECHNOLOGIES

Within a computer system, programs and information in all forms (text, image, audio, and video) are stored in both *RAM* and permanent **mass storage**, such as *magnetic disk and tape* (see Figure 5-1). Programs and information are retrieved from mass storage and stored *temporarily* in high-speed RAM for processing. In this section, we examine two common types of mass storage—magnetic disk and magnetic tape.

Over the years, manufacturers have developed a variety of permanent mass storage devices and media. Today the various types of **magnetic disk drives** and their respective storage media are the state of the art for permanent storage. **Optical laser disc** continues to emerge as an means of mass storage. Note that *disk* is spelled with a "k" for magnetic disk media and with a "c" for optical disc media. **Magnetic tape drives** complement magnetic disk storage by providing inexpensive *backup* capability and *archival* storage. First, let's take a look at the files stored on magnetic disk drives.

THE MANY FACES OF FILES

We have talked in general about the *file* in previous chapters. The file is simply a recording of information. It is the foundation of permanent storage on a computer system. To a computer, a file is a string of 0s and 1s (digitized data) that are stored and retrieved as a single unit. Each file has a user-supplied filename by which it is stored and retrieved.

Types of Files: ASCII to Video

There are many types of files (see Figure 5-2), most of which are defined by the software that created them (for example, a word processing document, graphics, or a spreadsheet). The following are among the more popular types of files.

- *ASCII file.* An **ASCII file** is a text-only file that can be read or created by any word processing program or text editor.

- *Data file.* A **data file** contains data in any format.

- *Document file.* All word processing and desktop publishing **document files** contain text and, often, embedded images.

- *Spreadsheet file.* A **spreadsheet file** contains rows and columns of data.

- *Web page file.* A **Web page file** is compatible with the World Wide Web and Internet browsers.

FIGURE 5–1

RAM AND MASS STORAGE
Programs and data are stored permanently in mass storage and temporarily in RAM.

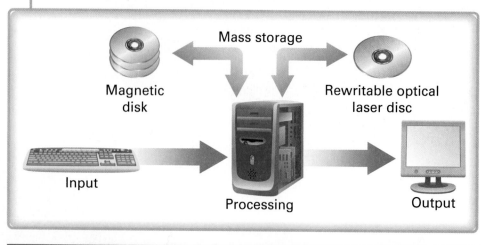

Mass storage

Magnetic disk

Rewritable optical laser disc

Input

Processing

Output

FIGURE 5-2

STORING DIGITIZED RESOURCES

Anything we digitize and store permanently takes up space on a disk or disc. This clip art (hot air balloon) is representative of thousands available for use in documents—the disk/disc storage requirement is 18 KB. A 4.88-second digital recording of an audio greeting (Sound Recorder software) can be attached to and sent with an e-mail message—the disk/disc storage requirement is 94 KB. This surreal art exhibit is all the more remarkable for the way the computer artist has used graphics techniques to model light, shadow, and reflections, mimicking a photograph's realism—the disk/disc storage requirement is 7.127 MB.

Photo courtesy of Intel Corporation

- *Source program file.* A **source program file** contains user-written instructions to the computer. These instructions must be translated to machine language prior to program execution.
- *Executable program file.* An **executable program file** contains executable machine language code.
- *Graphics file.* A **graphics file** contains digitized images.
- *Audio file.* An **audio file** contains digitized sound.
- *Video file.* A **video file** contains digitized video frames that when played rapidly (for example, 30 frames per second) produce motion video.

Files and Parking Lots

Mass storage is much like a parking lot for files. In a parking lot, a variety of vehicles—cars, buses, trucks, motorcycles, and so on—are put in parking places to be picked up later. Similarly, all sorts of files are "parked" in individual spots in mass storage, waiting to be retrieved later. To help you find your vehicle, large parking lots are organized with numbered parking places in lettered zones. The same is true with files and mass storage. Files are stored in numbered "parking places" on disk for retrieval. Fortunately, we do not have to remember the exact location of the file. The operating system does that for us. All we have to know is the name of the file. We assign user names to files, then recall or store them by name. Filenames in the Windows environment can include spaces, but some special characters, such as the slash (/) and colon (:), are not permitted. Your system will alert you if you include one of these special characters and give you an opportunity to rename the file. An optional three-character extension identifies the type of file and associates it with a program.

- *Readme.txt* is an ASCII file.
- *Student-Course.mdb* is a file containing a Microsoft Access database.
- *Letter.doc* is a Microsoft Word document file.
- *Income Statement.xls* is a Microsoft Excel spreadsheet file.
- *Adams School Home Page.htm* is a Web page file.
- *Module 1-1.vbp* is a Visual Basic source program file.
- *Play Game.exe* is an executable program file.
- *Family album.gif, Vacation Banff.bmp, Logo.jpg, Sarah.tif, Project A.pcx* are graphic files.
- *My_song.wav* is an audio file.
- *Introduction Sequence.mov* is a video file.

Figure 5-3 lists the common types of files and their associated programs. Many applications can work with a variety of file formats. For example, photo illustration programs can load *jpg, gif, tif,* and other graphics file formats. However, most popular applications programs have at least one **native file format** that is associated with that program—Microsoft Word is *doc,* Microsoft Excel is *xls,* and Adobe Acrobat is *pdf.*

What to Do with a File

Everything we do on a computer involves a file and, therefore, mass storage. But what do we do with files?

- *We create, name, and save files.* We create files when we name and save a letter, a drawing, a program, or some digital entity (an audio clip) to mass storage.
- *We copy files, move, and delete files.* We copy files from CD-ROMs to a hard disk to install software. We move files during routine file management activities. When we no longer need a file, we delete it.
- *We retrieve and update files.* We continuously retrieve and update our files (such as when we update the entries in a spreadsheet or revise a memo).
- *We display, print, or play files.* Most user files that involve text and graphics can be *displayed* and *printed.* Audio and video files are *played.*
- *We execute files.* We execute program files to run our software. In the Windows environment, executable filenames end in EXE, COM, BAT, and PIF.
- *We download and upload fZiles.* We download useful files from the Internet to our PCs. We sometimes work on, and then upload updated files to our company's server computer.

- We export/import files. The *file format*, or the manner in which a file is stored, is unique for each type of software package. When we import a file, we convert it from its foreign format (perhaps WordPerfect, a word processing program) to a format that is compatible with the current program (perhaps Microsoft Word, also a word processing program). We export files when we want to convert a file in the current program to a format needed by another program.

- *We compress files.* When the air is squeezed out of a sponge, it becomes much smaller. When you release it, the sponge returns to its original shape—nothing changes. **File compression** works in a similar fashion. File formats for most software packages are inefficient, resulting in wasted space on mass storage when you save files. Using file compression, a repeated pattern, such as the word *and* in text documents, might be replaced by a one-byte descriptor in a compressed file, saving two bytes for each occurrence of *and*. For example, "A band of sand stands grand in this land" might be compressed to "A bδ of sδ stδs grδ in this lδ," where the symbol "δ" replaces "and" in the stored file. One technique used when compressing graphics files replaces those portions of an image that are the same color with a brief descriptor that identifies the color only once and the area to be colored. Depending on the type and content of the file, file compression can create a compressed file that takes 10% to 90% less mass storage (the average is about 50%). The most popular file compression format is the zip format, which is supported by a variety of programs and results in a **zip file.** A zipped file, which usually has a zip extension (such as longfile.zip), is compressed and must be unzipped before it can be used. A group of files can be compressed together as a single convenient zip file. When the zip file is unzipped, the individual files are restored. Zipped files take up less storage space and they take less time to download/upload on the Net. A special version of the zip file is the executable **self-extracting zip file.** These have an *exe* extension (longfile.exe) and must be executed (run) to unzip the file(s). The only relationship between zip files and Zip disks is that you can store a zip file on a Zip disk.

- *We protect files.* We can protect sensitive files by limiting access to authorized persons. For example, a human resources manager might want to limit access to the company's personnel file that might contain salary, health, and other sensitive information.

FIGURE 5–3 COMMON FILE EXTENSIONS AND THEIR ASSOCIATED PROGRAMS

Word Processing and Text Documents
.DOC	Microsoft Word and WordPad
.WPD	WordPerfect
.WKS	Microsoft Works
.TXT	Plain ASCII text/unformatted
.PDF	Adobe Acrobat

Spreadsheets
.XLS	Microsoft Excel
.WQ1	Corel Quattro Pro
.WK1	Lotus 1-2-3
.WK3	
.WK4	

Database
.MDB	Microsoft Access

Presentation Graphics
.PPT	Microsoft PowerPoint

Graphics Formats (graphics programs typically open a variety of file types)
.GIF	CompuServe graphics interchange format
.JPG	JPEG compressed graphics format
.BMP	Windows bitmap
.PCT	PICT format
.TIF	Tagged image format (TIFF)
.PCX	PCX format
.WMF	Windows Meta File
.EPS	Encapsulated PostScript
.CGM	Computer Graphics MetaFile

Sound & Video Formats
.WAV	Windows WAV sound
.AIF	Macintosh AIFF sound
.RA	RealAudio sound
.AVI	Windows Video File
.MOV	Macintosh Quicktime video
.MPG	MPEG video format

Compressed Formats
.ZIP	PKzip/WinZIP compression
.HQX	BinHex compression (Macintosh)
.BHX	

System and Miscellaneous Files
.HTM	HTML code (Web pages)
.EXE	Executable file
.COM	
.BAT	MS-DOS batch file
.INI	Windows initialization file
.SYS	System file
.VBP	Visual Basic program file

FILE MANAGEMENT

In the Windows environment, the *Windows Explorer* (the folder program icon) utility program is an integrated Web browser (Internet Explorer or the "e" program icon) and file management tool. The explorer becomes a Windows Explorer for file management when you enter or select a disk (for example, C:) in the address bar, or a Web browser if you enter a URL Internet address (for example, *http://www.wal-mart.com*). The Windows Explorer, which opens when you choose the *My Computer* icon on the desktop, lets you view files in several formats (see Figure 5-4). With the Explorer, you can do all of your file management tasks such as creating, copying, moving, and deleting folders and files, as well as other folder/file-related tasks. Folders are created for a specific disk drive. The PC used to capture the screen in Figure 5-4 has a hard disk (C:) and four interchangeable disk drives: a floppy drive (A:), a Zip disk drive (D:), a DVD/CD-ROM drive (E:), and a CD-RW drive (F:).

In Windows, a *folder* is a named grouping of related files and/or subordinate folders. We create folders to hold documents, programs, images, music, and other types of files. File types can be mixed within a folder; that is, the folder can hold any type of file. Some folders, such as the *Windows* and *Program Files* folders, are created by the Windows operating system during system installation; however, most folders are created by the user. Most people choose to create their folders in a hierarchical manner to provide a logical structure for their files. For example, the file structure on disk drive D: in Figure 5-5 has two main folders, *Family Photo Album* and *Personal*. In the *Family Photo Album* folder, photos are grouped in four subordinate folders: *Boy Scout Camp, Boys School Photos, Family Reunions,* and *Sports.* The *Sports* folder has four subordinate folders to enable sports images to be grouped by

FIGURE 5-4

MY COMPUTER
Double-clicking on the *My Computer* icon on the desktop opens an Explorer window that shows active storage devices. As illustrated in the Icons view, this PC has a hard disk, referred to as Local Disk (C:), and four interchangeable disk drives: 3½ Floppy (A:), Removable Disk (D:), CD Drive (E:), and CD Drive (F:). Right-click on a disk icon and choose Properties to view disk usage information. The Properties dialog box for the hard disk (drive C:) shows 29.1 GB of used space and 40.9 GB of free space.

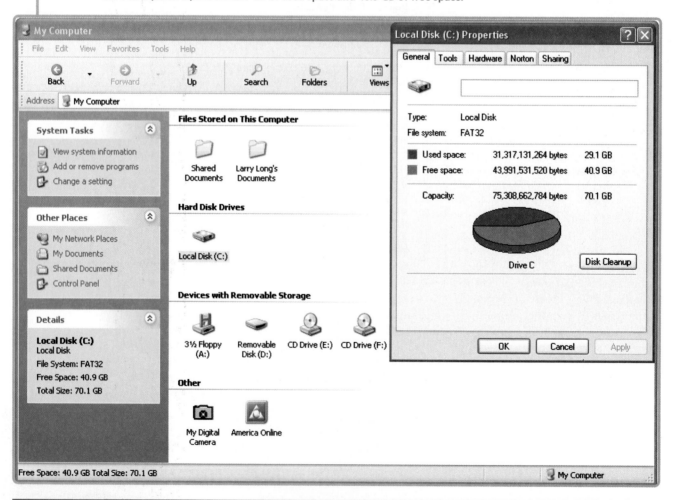

FIGURE 5–5

DISK DRIVES AND MEDIA
The Windows Explorer is a versatile utility program that lets you manipulate files and folders. Click on a disk or a folder in the Folders pane (left) and see the contents on the right. Click on the "+" to expand and list subordinate folders. Click on the "-" to hide subordinate folders. In this example, the files for the "Family Photo Album\Sports\Soccer\2003" folder are displayed, both in Thumbnails view (foreground window) and Details view (background window).

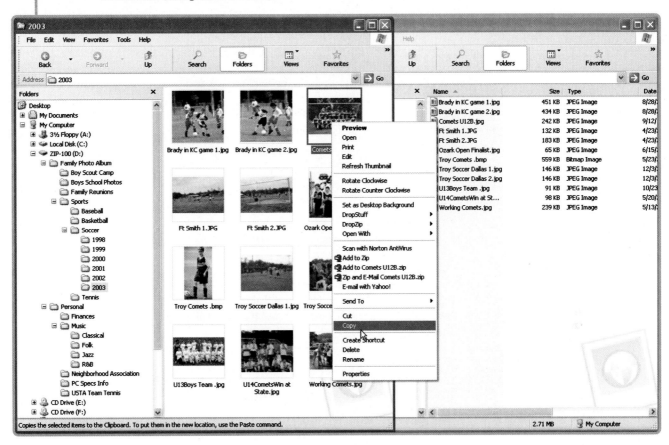

sport. The *Soccer* folder has six subordinate folders so soccer photos can be organized by year. The *Personal* folder at the top of the hierarchy has five subordinate folders, one of which is *Music*. The *Music* folder has four subordinate folders: *Classical, Folk, Jazz,* and *R&B*.

You can store a specific file within a particular folder at any level in the hierarchy. For example, Sports photo images in Figure 5-5 are stored at the bottom of the hierarchy (for example, in the 2003 folder). Since files are stored within a hierarchical structure of folders, you must give the operating system the **path** to follow to store or retrieve a particular file. In Figure 5-5, for example, the image *Brady in KC game 1.jpg* has the following path:

Family Photo Album\Sports\Soccer\2003\Brady in KC game 1.jpg

The audio file for Beethoven's 5th Symphony (not shown in the figure) is stored in this path:

Personal\Music\Classical\Beethovens 5th.mp3

In the Mac OS X environment, a colon (:) is used in place of the backslash (\). In UNIX/Linux, it is a forward slash (/).

As mentioned previously, common file management activities include saving, opening, copying, moving, deleting, and renaming files. The commands used to perform these activities are described below.

● *Save/Save As*. Files are created and saved to a particular folder via the *Save* or *Save As* option in the *File* menu of an applications program. For an unsaved document, either save option lets you choose a disk, a folder, and a filename for the file. Choose *Save As* if you want to store the content of the current document, which has already been saved, in a new file with a new filename and/or a different disk/folder.

● *Open*. In the Explorer, navigate through the path to the filename, then double-click on the filename to open the file in the associated application program or to execute a program file. Or, you can choose *Open* in the *File* menu or the right-click shortcut menu (see Figure 5-5). For example, when you double-click on a Microsoft Word document, the Word application starts and the file is retrieved and displayed in the Word work area. Double-clicking a program file causes the program to open and run.

- *Copy*. The *Copy* command option in the Explorer lets you create a duplicate of one or more files or folders. Highlight what you want to duplicate and choose the *Copy* command from the *Edit* menu or from the shortcut menu. To highlight multiple files, press and hold the Ctrl key, and then click on each of the desired files or folders. To complete the copy operation, navigate to where you want to save the copy (the path), then choose the *Paste* option from the *Edit* menu or the shortcut menu. Or, if you prefer, you can press and hold the Ctrl key, and then use the mouse to drag the high-lighted file(s)/folder(s) to their new location.

- *Cut (Move)*. The *Cut* command option in the Explorer lets you move one or more files or folders. The *Cut* command (in the *Edit* menu or the shortcut menu) works like the *Copy* command, except that a cut operation deletes the highlight item(s) from its original folder. You also can use the mouse to drag item(s) to their new location (without pressing any additional keys).

- *Delete*. Tap the Delete key or choose *Delete* in the *Edit* menu or the shortcut menu to delete whatever files/folders are highlighted.

- *Rename*. To rename the file or folder, highlight the desired file or folder, then choose *Rename* from the shortcut menu.

Copy and cut operations place whatever has been copied or cut on the Clipboard; therefore, you can paste the Clipboard contents as many times as you want.

5-1.1 Data are retrieved from temporary mass storage and stored permanently in RAM. (T/F)

5-1.2 A file is to mass storage as a vehicle is to a parking lot. (T/F)

5-1.3 When we import a file, we convert a file in the current program to a format needed by another program. (T/F)

5-1.4 One way to reduce the size of a file is called file: (a) deflation, (b) compression, (c) down-sizing, or (d) decreasing.

5-1.5 Magnetic tape storage provides inexpensive: (a) archival storage, (b) random-access storage, (c) direct-access storage, or (d) cache storage.

WHY THIS SECTION IS IMPORTANT TO YOU

We buy them; we entrust our precious documents, images, and information to them; we protect them from harm's way; and we attend to their every need to ensure the integrity of their valuable content. Pound for pound, magnetic disks may be among your most important material possessions.

5-2 Magnetic Disks

Magnetic disks have *random-* or *direct-access* capabilities. You are quite familiar with these access concepts, but you may not realize it. Suppose you have Paul Simon's classic album, *The Rhythm of the Saints*, on CD. The first four songs on this CD are (1) "The Obvious Child," (2) "Can't Run But," (3) "The Coast," and (4) "Proof." Now suppose you also have this album on a cassette tape. To play the third song on the cassette, "The Coast," you would have to wind the tape forward and search for it sequentially. To play "The Coast" on the CD, all you would have to do is select track number 3. This simple analogy demonstrates the two fundamental methods of storing and accessing data—*sequential* and *random*.

For a mechanical device, magnetic disks are very fast, able to seek and retrieve information quicker than a blink of an eye (in milliseconds). This direct-access flexibility and speed have made magnetic disk storage the overwhelming choice of computer users, for all types of computers and all types of applications (see Figure 5-6). A variety of magnetic disk drives, the *hardware device,* and magnetic disks, the *medium* (the actual surface on which the information is stored), are manufactured for different business requirements.

HARDWARE AND STORAGE MEDIA

There are two fundamental types of magnetic disks: interchangeable and fixed.

- *Interchangeable magnetic disks.* **Interchangeable magnetic disks** can be stored offline and loaded to the magnetic disk drives as they are needed.

- *Fixed magnetic disks.* **Fixed magnetic disks,** also called hard disks, are permanently installed, or fixed. All hard disks are rigid and are usually made of aluminum with a surface coating of easily magnetized elements, such as iron, cobalt, chromium, and nickel. Today's integrated systems and databases are stored on hard disk, especially those used in workgroup computing. Such systems and databases require all data and programs to be online (accessible to the computer for processing) at all times.

Figure 5-7 shows some of the different types of interchangeable magnetic disks and fixed disks. As you can see, the drives for the various magnetic disk media are available in a wide variety of shapes and storage capacities. The type you (or a company) should use depends on the volume of data you have and the frequency with which those data are accessed.

MAGNETIC DISK DRIVES AND MEDIA

Virtually all PCs sold today are configured with at least one hard-disk drive and most have at least one interchangeable magnetic disk drive. The interchangeable disk drive pro-

FIGURE 5–6 Information on Magnetic Disk
Today, most readily accessible information is stored on hard disk. The information provided by these interactive ATMs and kiosks is stored on disk and all transactions are recorded on disk.

Courtesy of Diebold, Incorporated

vides a means for the distribution of data and software, and for backup and archival storage. The high-capacity hard-disk storage has made it possible for today's PC users to enjoy the convenience of having their data and software readily accessible at all times.

The Diskette

Four types of interchangeable disk drives are commonly used on PCs. These disk drives accept interchangeable magnetic disks, such as the traditional *diskette* and the newer high-capacity *SuperDisk, HiFD disk,* and *Zip disk.*

- *Diskette, SuperDisk, and HiFD disk.* The traditional 3.5-inch diskette, or *floppy disk,* is a thin, Mylar disk that is permanently enclosed in a rigid plastic jacket. The widely used standard for traditional diskettes permits only 1.44 MB of storage, not much in the modern era in which 4-MB images and 30-MB programs are commonplace. State-of-the-art versions, called **SuperDisk** and **HiFD disk,** can store 120 and 200 MB of information, respectively. The diskette, the SuperDisk, and the HiFD disk are the same size but have different disk densities. **Disk density** refers to the number of bits that can be stored per unit of area on the disk-face surface. In contrast to a hard disk, the diskette, the SuperDisk, and the HiFD disk are set in motion only when a command is issued to read from or write to the disk. The 120-MB SuperDisk and 200-MB HiFD disk combine floppy and hard disk technology to read from and write to specially formatted floppy-size disks. Both high-density drives read from and write to the traditional diskette as well.

- *Zip disk.* The original **Zip® drive** reads and writes to 100-MB **Zip® disks.** The most recent innovation, a 750-MB Zip drive, handles all versions of Zip disks (100, 250, and 750 MB). The SuperDisk, HiFD disk, and 750-MB Zip disk have storage capacities of 70, 139, and 521 floppy diskettes, respectively.

The diskette-based floppy disk drive is still standard equipment on most PCs; however, many PC buyers opt to upgrade to a SuperDisk or a HiFD disk, which can handle the floppy disk, too. Soon, the 3.5-inch floppy may become a historical artifact. The iMac™ from Apple Computer doesn't come with a floppy disk drive, relying instead on DVD-ROM/CD-RW combination drives, local area networks, and the Internet as vehicles for the transfer of information and programs.

FIGURE 5–7   DISK DRIVES AND MEDIA

SUPERDISK

This illustration compares the capacity of a 120-MB SuperDisk (right) to the traditional floppy disk. The SuperDisk drive is compatible with the traditional 1.44-MB diskette.

Courtesy of Imation Corporation

ZIP DISK

An alternative high-capacity inter-changeable disk is the 100-, 250-, or 750-MB Zip disk (shown here) with an external Zip drive.

Courtesy of Iomega Corporation

HARD DRIVE

This 50-GB hard drive is pictured as it is delivered to the manufacturer (in a sealed enclosure) and exposed to show its inner workings (12 platters with 24 read/write heads).

Courtesy of Seagate Technology

MICRODRIVE

IBM unveiled the world's smallest and lightest hard-disk drive with a disk platter that will fit into an egg. The IBM Microdrive weighs less than an AA battery and holds 340 MB. The device is designed for use in PDAs and palmtop PCs.

Courtesy of International Business Machines Corporation.
Unauthorized use not permitted.

PORTABLE HARD DISK

The external portable hard disk lets you take your files with you and access them on any PC with a USB port.

Courtesy of Iomega Corporation

A blank interchangeable disk has a very modest value. But once you save your files on it, its value, at least to you, increases greatly. Such a valuable piece of property should be handled with great care. Here are a few commonsense guidelines for handling interchangeable disks.

- Avoid temperature extremes.
- Store disks in a protected location, preferably in a storage tray away from direct sunlight and magnetic fields (for example, magnetic paperclip holders).
- Remove disks from disk drives before you turn off the computer, but only when the "drive active" light is off.
- Use an interchangeable drive cleaning kit periodically.
- Avoid force when inserting or removing a disk, as there should be little or no resistance.
- Don't touch the disk surface.

The Hard Disk

Hard disk manufacturers are working continuously to achieve two objectives: (1) to put more information in less disk space and (2) to enable a more rapid transfer of that information to/from RAM. Consequently, hard-disk storage technology is forever changing. There are three types of hard disks—those that are permanently installed, those that are portable, and those that are interchangeable between like systems.

- *Permanently installed hard disks.* Generally, the 1- to 5.25-inch (diameter of disk) permanent hard disks have storage capacities from about 20 GB (gigabytes) to over 200 GB. A 200-GB hard disk stores about the same amount of data as 42 DVDs or 308 CD-ROMs.

A hard disk contains up to 12 disk platters stacked on a single rotating spindle. PC-based hard disks will normally have from one to four platters. Data are stored on all *recording surfaces*. For a disk with four platters, there are eight *recording surfaces* on which data can be stored (see Figure 5-8). The disks spin continuously at a high speed (from 7,200 to 15,000 revolutions per minute) within a sealed enclosure. The enclosure keeps the disk-face surfaces free from contaminants (see Figure 5-9), such as dust and cigarette smoke. This contaminant-free environment allows hard disks to have greater density of data storage than the interchangeable diskettes.

The rotation of a magnetic disk passes all data under or over a **read/write head,** thereby making all data available for access on each revolution of the disk (see Figure 5-8). A fixed disk will have at least one read/write head for each recording surface. The heads are mounted on **access arms** that move together and literally float on a cushion of air over (or under) the spinning recording surfaces. The tolerance is so close that a particle of smoke from a cigarette will not fit between these "flying" heads and the recording surface!

- *Portable hard disk.* The **portable hard disk** is an external device that is easily connected to any personal computer via a USB port or FireWire port. All new PCs are configured with multiple high-speed USB 2.0 ports and many have at least one FireWire port. Port technology has finally caught up with portable hard disks enabling high-speed transfer of data (up to 480-M bps). Portable hard disks are popular in the business world where knowledge workers can take their user files with them to their home office or to a PowerPoint presentation in San Francisco. Portable hard disk capacities are similar to those of fixed hard disks and they weigh from .5 to 2 pounds.

- *Interchangeable hard disks.* Some systems are configured with interchangeable hard disks which are inserted and removed as easily as a CD-ROM disc. Systems that use interchangeable hard disks must be configured with the necessary disk drive hardware. Interchangeable hard disks are still in use, but customers now prefer portable hard disks because they can be connected to any PC.

FIGURE 5–8   **FIXED HARD DISK WITH FOUR PLATTERS AND EIGHT RECORDING SURFACES**

A cylinder refers to similarly numbered concentric tracks on the disk-face surfaces. In the illustration, the read/write heads are positioned over Cylinder 0012. At this position, the data on any one of the eight tracks numbered 0012 are accessible to the computer on each revolution of the disk. The read/write heads must be moved to access data on other tracks/cylinders.

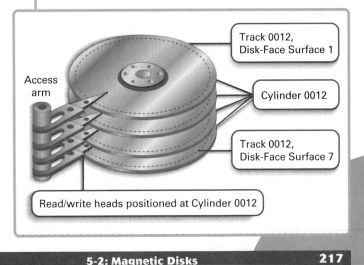

Track 0012, Disk-Face Surface 1

Cylinder 0012

Track 0012, Disk-Face Surface 7

Access arm

Read/write heads positioned at Cylinder 0012

DISK READ/WRITE HEAD FLYING DISTANCE
When the disk is spinning at 7200 rpm, the surface of the disk travels across the read/write head at approximately 100 mph.

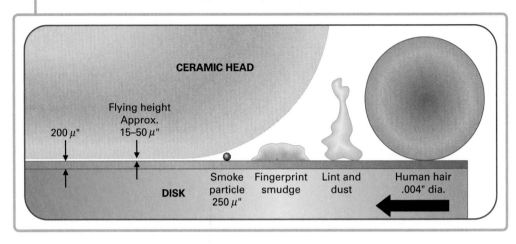

One of the most frequently asked questions is "How much hard drive capacity do I need?" The answer you hear most is "As much as you can afford." Disk space is like closet space—you never seem to have enough. If it's there, you tend to fill it with something. Software vendors are well aware of a rule of thumb that hard disk storage on new PCs doubles every year, so they keep building software to use our expanding hard drive space. For example, the original MS-DOS operating system was 160 KB, Windows 3.1 was 10 MB, and Windows XP is over 100 MB—over 600 times the size of DOS.

MAGNETIC DISK ORGANIZATION

The way in which data and programs are stored and accessed is similar for all hard disks. Conceptually, a floppy disk looks like a hard disk with a single platter. Both media have a thin film coating of one of the easily magnetized elements (cobalt, for example). The thin film coating on the disk can be magnetized electronically (see Figure 5-10) by the read/write head to represent the absence or presence of a bit (0 or 1).

Tracks, Sectors, and Clusters

Data are stored in concentric **tracks** by magnetizing the surface to represent bit configurations (see Figure 5-11). Bits are recorded using *serial representation;* that is, bits are aligned in a row in the track. The number of tracks varies greatly between disks, from as few as 80 on a diskette to thousands on high-capacity hard disks. The spacing of tracks is measured in **tracks per inch,** or **TPI.** The 3.5-inch diskettes are rated at 135 TPI. The TPI for hard disks can be in the thousands. The *track density* (TPI) tells only part of the story. The *recording density* tells the rest. Recording density, which is measured in *megabits per inch,* refers to the number of bits (1s and 0s) that can be stored per inch of track. High-density hard disks have densities in excess of 3 megabits per inch.

PC disks use **sector organization** to store and retrieve data. In sector organization, the recording surface is divided into pie-shaped **sectors** (see Figure 5-11). The number of sectors depends on the density of the disk. A hard disk may have hundreds of sectors. Typically, the storage capacity of each sector on a particular track is 512 bytes, regardless of the number of sectors per track. Adjacent sectors are combined to form **clusters,** the capacity of which is a multiple of 512. Typically, clusters range in size from 4,096 bytes up to 32,768 bytes (that's 8 up to 64 sectors). The cluster is the smallest unit of disk space that can be allocated to a file, so every file saved to disk takes up one or more clusters.

Each disk cluster is numbered, and the number of the first cluster in a file comprises the **disk address** on a particular file. The disk address represents the physical location of a particular file or set of data on a disk. To read from or write to a disk, an access arm containing the read/write head is moved, under program control, to the appropriate *track* or *cylinder* (see

FIGURE 5–10 Bits on the Surface of a Magnetic Disk
This highly magnified area of a magnetic disk-face surface shows elongated information bits recorded serially along 8 of the disk's 1774 concentric tracks. One square inch of this disk's surface can hold 22 million bits of information.

Courtesy of International Business Machines Corporation. Unauthorized use not permitted.

FIGURE 5–11

CUTAWAY OF A DISKETTE
The access arm on this 3.5-inch disk drive is positioned at a particular track (Track 2 in the example). Data are read or written serially in tracks within a given sector. On the right, the flexible 3.5-inch recording disk spins between two soft liners when accessed. The recording surface is sandwiched in a rigid plastic jacket for protection. When inserted, the metal shutter slides to reveal the recording window.

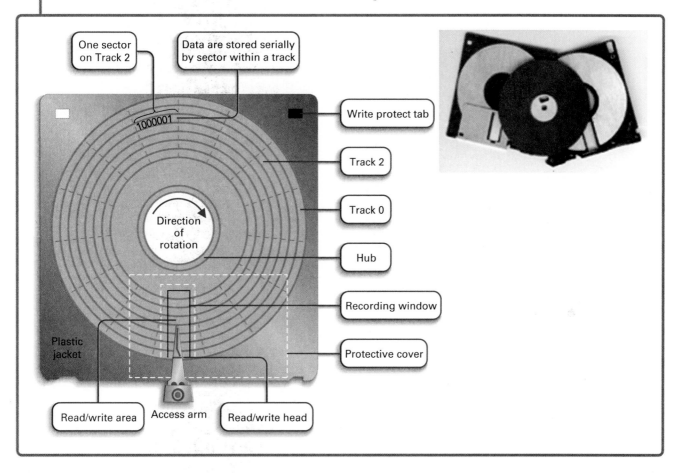

Figures 5-8 and 5-11). A particular **cylinder** refers to the same-numbered tracks on each recording surface (for example, Track 0012 on each recording surface; see Figure 5-8). When reading from or writing to a hard disk, all access arms are moved to the appropriate *cylinder*. For example, each recording surface has a track numbered 0012, so the disk has a cylinder numbered 0012. If the data to be accessed are on Recording Surface 01, Track 0012, then the access arms and the read/write heads for all eight recording surfaces are moved to Cylinder 0012. When the cluster containing the desired data passes under or over the read/write head, the data are read or written. Fortunately, software automatically monitors the location, or address, of our files and programs. We need only enter the name of the file to retrieve it for processing.

One of the major limitations of traditional sector organization is that recording space is wasted on the outer tracks. To overcome this limitation, some high-performance disk manufacturers employ a technique called **zoned recording.** In zoned recording, tracks are grouped into zones and all tracks in a particular zone have the same number of sectors (see Figure 5-12). A zone contains a greater number of sectors per track as you move from the innermost zone to the outermost zone. This approach to disk organization enables a more efficient use of available disk space.

The File Allocation Table

Each disk used in the Windows environment has a **Virtual File Allocation Table** (**VFAT**) in which information about the clusters is stored (it was a FAT in early operating systems). The table includes an entry for each cluster that describes where on the disk it can be found and how it is used (for example, whether the file is open or not). Clusters are *chained* together to store information larger than the capacity of a single cluster. Here's what happens when you or a program on your PC makes a request for a particular file.

FIGURE 5–12

ZONED RECORDING ON A HARD DISK
Zoned recording groups tracks into concentric zones such that the number of sectors in each track increases as the zones spread to the outer edge of the disk, thus enabling a more efficient use of storage space on the disk face surface.

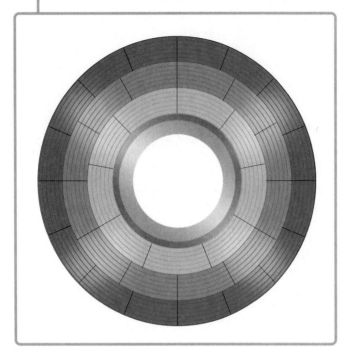

1. The operating system searches the VFAT to find the physical address of the first cluster of the file.

2. The read/write heads are moved over the track/cylinder containing the first cluster.

3. The rapidly rotating disk passes the cluster under/over the read/write head, and the information in the first cluster is read and transmitted to RAM for processing.

4. The operating system checks an entry within the initial cluster that indicates whether the file consists of further clusters, and if so, where on the disk they are located.

5. The operating system directs that clusters continue to be read and their information transmitted to RAM until the last cluster in the chain is read (no further chaining is indicated).

A 100-KB file being stored on a disk with 32,768 byte clusters would require four clusters (three clusters will store only 98,304 bytes). Most of the space in the fourth cluster is wasted disk space. Large clusters may improve overall system performance, but they tend to make more space inaccessible. The trade-off between system performance and efficient use of disk space is a major consideration during the disk design process.

Eventually your PC will give you a "lost clusters found" message, indicating that the hard disk has orphan clusters that don't belong to a file. Typically, lost clusters are the result of an unexpected interruption of file activity, perhaps a system crash or loss of power. Windows users should run the **ScanDisk** utility program periodically to "scan" the disk for lost clusters and, if any are found, let you return them to the available pool of usable clusters.

Defragmenting the Disk to Enhance Performance

The easiest and least expensive way to get a performance boost out of your PC (make it run faster) is to run a utility program called **Disk Defragmenter** in the Windows environment (see Figure 5–13). The program consolidates files into contiguous clusters; that is, the clusters for each file are chained together on the same or adjacent tracks (see Figure 5–14), thereby minimizing the movement of the read/write head. After running the program, each file stored on a disk is a single cluster or a chain of clusters. A 5-MB file may require hundreds of linked clusters. Ideally, all files would be stored on disk in contiguous clusters, but such is not the case with computing. Over time, files are added, deleted, and modified such that, eventually, files must be stored in noncontiguous clusters. When clusters are scattered, the read/write heads must move many times across the surface of a disk to access a single file. This excess mechanical movement slows down the PC because it takes longer to load a file to RAM for processing.

FIGURE 5–13

DEFRAG SUMMARY
The Speed Disk utility program within Symantec's Norton SystemWorks optimizes the disk by performing the defragmentation process. During the process, the Speed Disk program gives a visual overview of the status of each cluster on the hard drive. The colors indicate cluster status: used, bad, frequent access, applications, and so on.

FIGURE 5-14

DISK DEFRAGMENTATION
(a) Initially, five files are stored ideally in contiguous clusters. (b) The user adds a few objects to a graphics file (blue), increasing its size and the number of clusters needed to store it. Note that file clusters are no longer contiguous. Then, a file (green) is deleted. (c) A new file (orange) is stored in noncontiguous clusters. (d) The disk is defragmented, resaving all files in contiguous clusters.

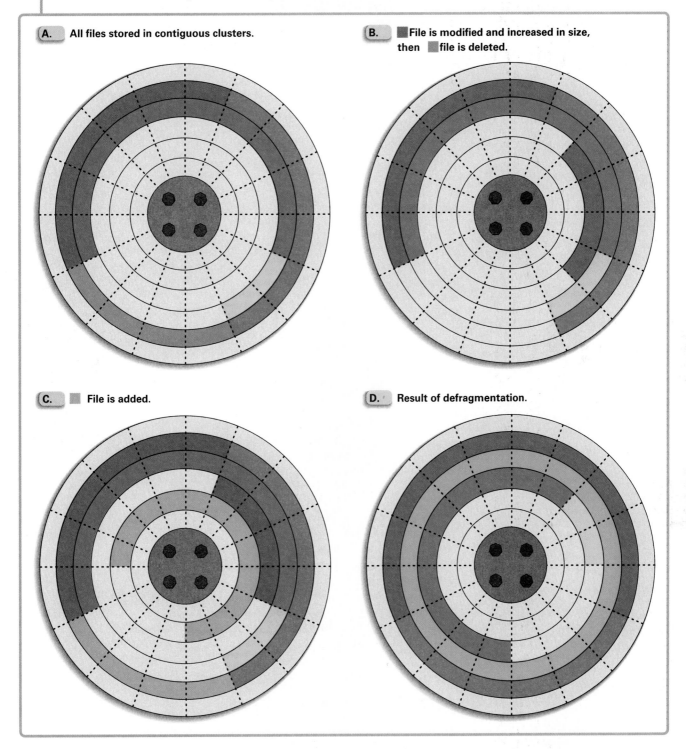

A. All files stored in contiguous clusters.

B. █ File is modified and increased in size, then █ file is deleted.

C. █ File is added.

D. Result of defragmentation.

The mechanical movement of the disk read/write heads is the most vulnerable part of a PC system—the greater the fragmentation of files, the slower the PC. Fortunately, we can periodically reorganize the disk such that files are stored in contiguous clusters. This process, appropriately called **defragmentation**, is done with a handy utility program (see Figure 5-13). How often you run a "defrag" program depends on how much you use your PC. The fragmentation problem and the defragmentation solution are illustrated in Figure 5-14. In the example, five files are loaded to a disk,

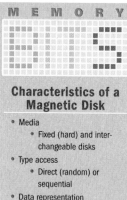

Characteristics of a Magnetic Disk

- Media
  - Fixed (hard) and interchangeable disks
- Type access
  - Direct (random) or sequential
- Data representation
  - Serial
- Storage scheme
  - Clusters on tracks

each in contiguous clusters. A file is modified, another is deleted, and another is added, resulting in fragmentation of several files and a need for defragmentation. The defragmentation process rewrites fragmented files into contiguous clusters (see Figure 5-14).

Formatting: Preparing a Disk for Use

A new disk is coated with a surface that can be magnetized easily to represent data. However, before the disk can be used, it must be **formatted.** The formatting procedure causes the disk to be initialized with a recording format for your operating system. Specifically, it

- Creates sectors and tracks into which data are stored.
- Sets up an area for the virtual file allocation table.

If you purchased a PC today, the hard disk probably would be formatted and ready for use. However, if you added a hard disk or upgraded your existing hard disk, the new disk would need to be formatted.

DISK SPEED

Data access from RAM is performed at electronic speeds—approximately the speed of light. But the access of data from disk storage depends on the movement of mechanical apparatus (read/write heads and spinning disks) and can take from 4 to 8 milliseconds—still very slow when compared with the microsecond-to-nanosecond internal processing speeds of computers. Disk engineers want to reduce *access time* and increase the *data transfer rate.*

Access time is the interval between the instant a computer makes a request for the transfer of data from a disk-storage device to RAM and the instant this operation is completed. The read/write heads on the access arm in the illustration of Figure 5-8 move together. Some hard disks have multiple access arms, some with two read/write heads per disk-face surface. Having multiple access arms and read/write heads results in less mechanical movement and faster access times.

The **data transfer rate** is the rate at which data are read from mass storage to RAM or written to mass storage from RAM. Even though the data transfer rate from magnetic disk to RAM may be 400 million bytes per second, the rate of transfer from one part of RAM to another is much faster. **Disk caching** (pronounced *"cashing"*) is a technique that improves system speed by taking advantage of the greater transfer rate of data within RAM. With disk caching, programs and data that are *likely* to be called into use are moved from a disk into a separate disk caching area of RAM. When an application program calls for the data or programs in the disk cache area, the data are transferred directly from RAM rather than from the slower magnetic disk. Updated data or programs in the disk cache area eventually must be transferred to a disk for permanent storage. All modern PCs take full advantage of disk caching to improve overall system performance.

SECTION SELF-CHECK

5-2.1	Virtually all PCs sold today are configured with at least one DVD drive and one portable hard disk drive. (T/F)
5-2.2	The capacity of portable hard disks is about that of 100 floppy disks. (T/F)
5-2.3	Which has the greatest storage capacity: (a) the traditional floppy, (b) the latest Zip disk, (c) the SuperDisk, or (d) the HiFD disk?
5-2.4	The defragmentation process rewrites fragmented files into: (a) contiguous clusters, (b) continuous clusters, (c) circular clusters, or (d) Cretan clusters.
5-2.5	The rate at which data are read from disk to RAM is the: (a) TPI, (b) caching rate, (c) data transfer rate, or (d) streaming velocity.

5-3 Optical Laser Discs

Some industry analysts have predicted that *optical laser disc* technology eventually may make magnetic disk and tape storage obsolete. With this technology, two lasers replace the read/write head used in magnetic storage. One laser beam writes to the recording surface by scoring microscopic *pits* in the disc, and another laser reads the data from the light-sensitive recording surface. A light beam is easily deflected to the desired place on the optical disc, so a mechanical access arm is not needed.

Optical technology opens the door to new and exciting applications. Already this technology is leading the way to the library of the future. Because the world's output of knowledge is doubling every four years, the typical library is bursting at the seams with books and other printed materials. With library budgets declining, it may be impractical to continue to build structures to warehouse printed materials. Perhaps the only long-term solution for libraries is to move away from storing printed materials and toward storing information in electronic format—possibly some form of optical disc. Perhaps in the not-too-distant future we will check out electronic "books" by downloading them from a library's optical disc to our personal optical disc. In such a library of the future, knowledge will be more readily available and complete. In theory, the library of the future could have every book and periodical ever written. And, a "book" would never be out on loan.

Optical laser discs are becoming a very inviting option for users. These discs are less sensitive to environmental fluctuations, and they provide more direct-access storage at a much lower cost than does the magnetic disk alternative. Optical laser disc technology continues to emerge and has yet to stabilize. Common disc technologies are introduced in this section: *CD, CD-ROM, CD-R, CD-RW, DVD, DVD-ROM, DVD-R, DVD-RAM, DVD+RW, DVD-RW,* and *FMD-ROM*.

CD-ROM AND DVD-ROM

CD-ROM and DVD-ROM technologies have had a dramatic impact on personal computing and IT during the past decade because these technologies continue to provide ever-increasing storage capacity and ever-decreasing cost.

CD-ROM History

Introduced in 1980 for stereo buffs, the extraordinarily successful *CD,* or *compact disc,* is an optical laser disc designed to enhance the reproduction of recorded music. To make a CD recording, the analog sounds of music are digitized and stored on a 4.72-inch optical laser disc. Seventy-four minutes of music can be recorded on each disc in digital format in 2 billion bits. A bit is represented by the presence or absence of a pit on the optical disc. With its tremendous storage capacity per square inch, computer industry entrepreneurs immediately recognized the potential of optical laser disc technology. In effect, anything that can be digitized can be stored on optical laser disc: data, text, voice, still pictures, music, graphics, and motion video (see Figure 5-15).

CD-ROM and DVD-ROM Technology

CD-ROM, a spin off of audio CD technology, stands for *compact disc–read-only memory.* The name implies its application. Once inserted into the *CD-ROM drive,* the text, video images, and so on can be read into RAM for processing or display. However, the data on the disc are fixed—*they cannot be altered.* This is in contrast, of course, to the read/write capability of magnetic disks.

What makes CD-ROM so inviting is its vast capacity to store data and programs. The capacity of a single CD-ROM is up to 650 MB—about that of 450 diskettes. To put the density of CD-ROM into perspective, the words in every book ever written could be stored on a hypothetical CD-ROM that is 8 feet in diameter.

Magnetic disks store data in concentric tracks, each of which is divided into sectors (see Figure 5-11). The sectors on the inside tracks hold the same amount of information as those on the outside tracks, even though the sectors on the outside tracks take up more space. In contrast, CD-ROMs store data in a single track that spirals from the center to the outside edge (see Figure 5-16). The ultra thin track spirals around the disc thousands of times.

Data are recorded on the CD-ROM's reflective surface in the form of *pits* and *lands.* The pits are tiny reflective bumps that have been burned in with a laser. The lands are flat areas separating the pits. Together they record read-only binary (1s and 0s) information that can be interpreted by the computer as text, audio, images, and so on. Once the data have been recorded, a protective coating is applied to the reflective surface (the nonlabel side of a CD-ROM).

The pits and lands are more densely packed on the newer *DVD-ROM,* enabling 4.7 GB of storage. DVD-ROM comes in several versions. *Layering* the pits and lands increases the capacity to 8.5 GB. A *double-sided* DVD-ROM has either a 9.4 GB capacity (twice 4.7 GB) or 17 GB capacity (twice 8.5 GB or the capacity of 11,800 diskettes).

Popular CD-ROM drives are classified simply as 32X, 40X, or 75X. These spin at 32, 40, and 75 times the speed of the original CD standard. The faster the spin rate, the faster data are transferred to RAM for processing.

FIGURE 5–15 Sampling of CDs, CD-ROMs and DVDs
High-capacity CD-ROMs and DVDs, which evolved from the audio CD, have opened the door to exciting multi media applications with audio, video, graphics, and more. Also, they have become the standard for distribution of software and have replaced tape as the standard for the distribution of movies.

FIGURE 5–16

OPTICAL LASER DISC ORGANIZATION
A laser beam detector interprets pits and lands, which represent bits (1s and 0s), located within the sectors in the spiraling track on the CD-ROM reflective surface. Next to the illustration is a microscopic view of the pits and lands on the surface of a CD-ROM.

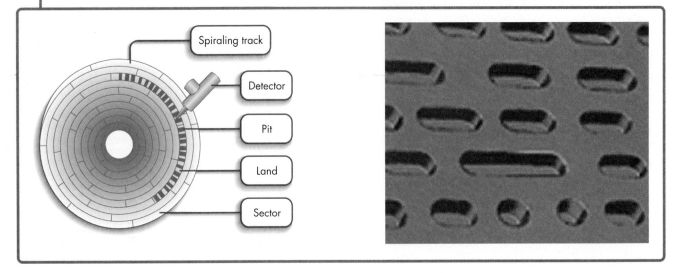

The slower speeds may cause program/image load delays and video to be choppy, especially when gaming. The original 1X CD-ROM data transfer rate was 150 KB per second, so the 75X CD-ROM data transfer rate is 75 times that, or 11.25 MB per second. The speed at which a given CD-ROM spins depends on the physical location of the data being read. The data pass over the movable laser detector at the same rate, no matter where the data are read. Therefore, the CD-ROM must spin more quickly when accessing data near the center.

Because data are more densely packed on a DVD-ROM, the data transfer rate is nine times that of a CD-ROM spinning at the same rate. For example, an 8X DVD-ROM drive transfers data at about the same rate as a 75X CD-ROM.

The laser detector is analogous to the magnetic disk's read/write head. The relatively slow spin rates make the CD-ROM access time much slower than that of its magnetic cousins. A CD-ROM drive may take 10 to 50 times longer to ready itself to read the information. Once ready to read, the transfer rate also is much slower.

The introduction of *multidisc CD-ROM player/changers* enables ready access to vast amounts of online data. This device is like a CD audio player/changer in that the desired CD-ROM can be loaded automatically to the CD-ROM disc drive under the control of a computer program. These CD-ROM player/changers, sometimes called **jukeboxes,** can hold from 6 to more than 500 CD-ROMs. The larger jukeboxes have multiple drives so that network users can have simultaneous access to different CD-ROM resources.

Just as CD-ROMs have become mainstream equipment, DVD-ROMs with much greater capacities are poised to replace them. The DVD-ROM has the same physical dimensions as the CD and the CD-ROM, but it can store from 7 to 25 times as much information. DVD-ROM drives are *backward compatible;* that is, they can play all of your CD-ROMs and CDs. They can read or play other DVD formats, too, including *DVD-video* and *DVD-audio.* DVD-video and DVD-audio are expected to replace videotapes and CDs in a few years. In 2002, the rental of DVD-video movies surpassed video tape rentals, signaling the inevitable replacement of VHS video tape with DVD-video format movies as the format of choice by video customers. This home entertainment version is usually shortened to simply DVD.

CD-ROM and DVD-ROM Applications

The tremendous amount of low-cost direct-access storage made possible by optical laser discs has opened the door to many new applications. The most visible application for CD-ROM is that it has emerged as the media-of-choice for the distribution of software. CD-ROM has the capacity to store massive sound, graphics, motion video, and animation files needed for multimedia applications. Many of the thousands of commercially produced CD-ROM discs contain reference material. The following is a sampling of available CD-ROM discs.

● Multimedia encyclopedias (including full text, thousands of still photos, motion video sequences, and sounds)

- Comprehensive reference materials (dictionary, thesaurus, almanac, atlas, book of facts, and more)
- The results of the 2000 U.S. Census at the county level
- The text of thousands of books, such as *Moby Dick,* the King James version of the *Bible, Beowulf, The Odyssey,* and many more
- Reviews and information on thousands of movies
- Street maps of the entire United States
- Games
- Sound effects (thousands of sound clips)
- Legal proceedings and cases for each state

The consumer cost of commercially produced CD-ROMs varies considerably from as little as a couple of dollars to several thousand dollars. All of these applications apply to DVD-ROM, too. DVD-ROM with its substantially greater capacities enables the distribution of bigger and better games on a single disc, larger databases (for example, huge clip-art libraries), feature-length movies, the telephone listings of everyone in the United States, and so on.

Creating CD-ROMs and DVD-ROMs for Mass Distribution

Most CD-ROMs and DVD-ROMs are created by commercial enterprises and sold to the public for multimedia applications and reference. Application developers gather and create source material, then write the programs needed to integrate the material into a meaningful application. The resulting files are then sent to a mastering facility. The master copy is duplicated, or "pressed," at the factory, and the copies are distributed with their prerecorded contents (for example, the complete works of Shakespeare or *Gone with the Wind*). Depending on the run quantity, the cost of producing and packaging a CD-ROM or DVD-ROM for sale can be less than a dollar apiece! These media provide a very inexpensive way to distribute applications and information.

REWRITABLE OPTICAL LASER DISC OPTIONS

Optical laser technologies are now in transition from write-only technologies, such as CD-ROM and DVD-ROM, to read and write technologies. This means that we, the end users, can make our own CD-ROMs and DVD-ROMs.

CD-R and CD-RW

Most of the world's PCs have CD-ROM or DVD-ROM drives. This rapid and universal acceptance of CD-ROM gave rise to another technology—**CD-R, compact disc-recordable.** A few years ago, the capability to record on CD-ROM media cost over $100,000. CD-R drives, at less than $100, brought that capability to any PC owner. While people were celebrating the arrival of CD-R, another more flexible CD technology was introduced—**CD-RW (CD-ReWritable).** This technology goes one step further, allowing users to rewrite to the CD-sized media, just as is done on magnetic disk media. With the cost of CD-R and CD-RW technologies converging, CD-R drives have disappeared from the optical drive landscape. CD-RW discs can be inserted and read on modern CD-ROM drives, but they will not work with the older models.

DVD+RW, DVD-RW, and DVD-RAM

As you might expect, DVD (digital video disc) technology is emerging like CD-ROM technology with recordable and read/write capabilities. **DVD-R** is like CD-R but with the recording density of DVD-ROM. **DVD+RW, DVD-RW,** and **DVD-RAM**, are like CD-RW, giving us rewritable capabilities for high-capacity DVD technology. DVD-RAM, DVD-RW, and DVD+RW are competing technologies, with the most recent technology, DVD+RW, appearing to emerge as the technology of choice for PC vendors. DVD rewritable alternatives are more costly than CD-RW, but as the price drops DVD rewritable drives might become a standard peripheral on new PCs. State-of-the-art DVD rewritable drives can read all DVD and CD-ROM formats. You can rewrite to rewritable discs thousands of times.

With **FMD-ROM** technology looming on the horizon, it won't be long before DVD technology is old hat. FMD-ROM, a very high-density, multilayer disc, holds up to 140 GB of data, 215 times that of CD-ROM and 30 times that of the 4.7 GB DVD-ROM (see Figure 5-17). FMD-ROM drives are backward compatible, able to read CD and DVD discs.

FIGURE 5–17 High-Capacity FMD-ROM
A single FMD-ROM disc can store printed documentation that, if stacked, would stretch almost two miles into the sky.

Courtesy of Constellation 3D

FIGURE 5–18 The Mini USB Drive
About the size of a Car key, the solid-state, flash memory Iomega® Mini USB drive is a portable solution for transporting and sharing data. Plug it into any computer's USB port and it is immediately recognized as an active drive, enabling applications to be launched and run directly from the drive. The miniature drive requires no cables, adapters, or batteries.

Courtesy of Iomega Corporation

FIGURE 5–19 Solid-State Storage Applications
This RCA eBook uses solid state random access memory, rather than disk, to hold more than 5,000 pages of material. Popular magazines, novels, and periodicals are readily available for downloading and viewing on the eBook.

Photo courtesy of RCA Corporation

OPTICAL DISCS IN YOUR PC

The typical PC will have one or two optical drives. At a minimum, users want a PC with a DVD-ROM drive so they have full optical read capability and can enjoy all CD-ROM and DVD applications, including playing DVD movies. Increasingly, however, PC users are "burning" their own CDs and CD-ROMs, so they want rewritable capability, too. One of the most popular options is the *DVD-ROM/CD-RW combination drive* which gives users the flexibility to read CD-ROM and DVD-ROM format discs (including audio CDs and DVD movies) and to burn their own audio and video CDs, to burn discs for data transfer, and to provide read/write backup of user files. Some people choose to configure their PCs with both a DVD-ROM drive and a DVD-ROM/CD-RW combination drive to enable easy duplication of optical media.

Those users with a few extra dollars to spend and expanded application needs are choosing a *DVD+RW/CD-RW combination drive*. You can use it to store original videos on DVD disc or archive up to 4.7 GB of data to a DVD+RW disc. People who spend the money on this high-end rewritable disk combo drive will usually add a DVD-ROM drive, as well, to facilitate duplication tasks.

WHAT'S THE BEST MIX OF STORAGE OPTIONS?

The choice of which technologies to choose for a system or an application is often a trade-off between storage capacity, cost (dollars per megabyte), and speed (access time). You can never really compare apples to apples when comparing storage media because one might have an advantage in access time, portability, random access, nonvolatility, and so on. Solid-state storage (RAM) is the fastest and most expensive (about $0.20 per MB), but it's volatile. Hard disk offers fast, permanent storage for less than a half penny per MB. You can get 1 MB of interchangeable DVD-RW storage for about a quarter the cost of hard disk storage and about a hundredth the cost of RAM, but it is relatively slow. A well-designed system will have a mix of storage options. Each time you purchase a PC, you should spend a little extra time assessing your application and backup needs so you can configure your system with an optimum mix of storage options.

Storage is like money: No matter how much you have, you always want more. Each year, improvements are made in existing mass storage devices as the storage industry strives to meet our craving for more storage.

Rotating storage media may go the way of the steam engine when low-cost solid-state memory (RAM) can store as much in less space. Already, nonvolatile flash memory chips, such as the Mini USB drive, are being developed that will have many times more storage capacity than the largest flash chips currently available (see Figure 5-18). Flash memory already is the basis for e-book (electronic book) readers that hold many books, magazines, and so on (see Figure 5-19). Perhaps someday the only moving part on PCs will be the cooling fan.

What does being able to store more information in less space mean to you? It means videophones that can be worn like wristwatches. It means that you can carry a diskette-sized reader and all your college "textbooks" in your front pocket. Each new leap in storage technology seems to change much of what we do and how we do it.

It was inevitable that the dark side would spread evil to the cyberworld. This evil comes in the form of computer viruses. Computers can get sick just like people. A variety of highly contagious viruses can spread from computer to computer, much the way biological viruses do among human beings. Just as a virus can infect human organs, a **computer virus** can infect programs, documents, and databases. It can also hide duplicates of itself within legitimate programs, such as an operating system or a word processing program. A computer virus is a man-made program or portion of a program that causes an unexpected event, usually a negative one, to occur. Viruses reside on and are passed between magnetic disks.

It is estimated that computer viruses cost businesses and individuals worldwide up to $20 billion a year. There are many viruses—over 50,000, to date. Some act quickly by erasing user programs and files on disk. Others grow like a cancer, destroying small parts of a file each day. Some act like a time bomb. They lay dormant for days or months but eventually are activated and wreak havoc on any software on the system. Several *denial of service* viruses cause the Internet to be flooded with e-mail, each with an attached program that causes more infected e-mail to be sent. These viruses place such heavy demands on e-mail server computer resources that they are unable to handle the volume, thus the denial of service. Some viruses attack the hardware and have been known to throw the mechanical components of a computer system, such as disk-access arms, into costly spasms. Many companies warn their PC users to back up all software prior to every Friday the thirteenth, a favorite date of those who write virus programs.

Some viruses are relatively benign, but can be annoying. For example, an error message might pop up that says, "This one's for you, Bosco." Another might insert the word "WAZZU" in the middle of your text. The Cookie Monster virus displays "I want a cookie" then locks up the system until you key in "Fig Newton."

TYPES OF COMPUTER VIRUSES

Two types of viruses—macro viruses and worms—have become alarmingly popular during the last few years. A **macro virus** is a program or portion of a program that is written in the macro language of a particular application, such as Microsoft Word or Microsoft Outlook. One well-publicized and hugely destructive macro virus was *Melissa,* which was distributed as an e-mail attachment. When opened, the macro program caused the virus to be sent to the first 50 people in the Outlook contact list. Melissa so overwhelmed millions of e-mail servers to the point they could no longer perform their function.

A **worm** is a computer program or portion of a program that makes copies of itself. Typically, the worm will interfere with the normal operation of a program or a computer. Worms exist as separate entities and do not attach themselves to files, programs, or documents. One of the most devastating incarnations of the worm was the *Love.bug* or *I Love You* worm that invaded millions of computers through e-mail and Internet Relay Chat (IRC) channels.

Though not officially a virus because it does not replicate itself, the **Trojan horse** can be equally damaging. Named after the wooden horse the Greeks used to capture Troy, the Trojan horse needs someone to e-mail it to you for it does not e-mail itself. Fortunately, most Trojan horses take the form of a practical joke, but some can be harmful. In a classic Trojan horse scenario, one claims to rid your PC of viruses but, instead, plants viruses in your system.

Most people who write and circulate virus programs fall into two groups. The first group, mostly young males from around the world, create viruses to impress each other with their cleverness. The second, and far more dangerous group, creates viruses with malicious intent. Some do not know the harm they do, but some do. These people are just plain mean and want their viruses to result in property damage and cause human suffering. Sadly, terrorists have embraced the virus as a weapon of war.

SOURCES OF COMPUTER VIRUSES

In the PC environment, there are three primary sources of computer viruses (see Figure 5-20).

- *The Internet.* The most common source of viral infection is the very public Internet, on which people download and exchange software and send e-mail. All too often, a user logs on to the Internet and downloads a game, a utility program, or some other enticing piece of freeware from an unsecured site, but gets the software with an embedded virus instead. Sometimes viruses are attached to e-mails. A good rule is to know the sender before opening anything sent with an e-mail.

- *Diskettes and DVDs/CD-ROMs.* Viruses also are spread from one system to another via common interchangeable disks. For example, a student with an infected application disk might unknow-

THE CRYSTAL BALL:

Cyber War We now live in a world in which we must be ever vigilant—there are those who want to harm us because of the color of our skin, our religious beliefs, our nationality, or for no particular reason at all. Traditionally, the efforts of terrorists have focused on the destruction of property and physical harm; however, terrorists now are researching ways to destroy one of our most valuable personal and commercial assets—the contents of our disks. They do this by seeking points of vulnerability in PCs and servers and by planting destructive viruses. Terrorists will also continue their denial-of-service attacks in an attempt to cripple server computers worldwide. Sadly, cyber terror is now part of the terrorist's arsenal of evil.

ingly infect several other laboratory computers with a virus, which, in turn, infects the applications software of other students. Software companies have unknowingly distributed viruses with their proprietary software products. Ouch!

- *Computer networks.* Viruses can spread from one computer network to another.

How serious a problem are viruses? They have the potential of affecting an individual's career and even destroying companies. For example, a financial adviser who inadvertently forwards a virus to his clients may lose credibility and clients. A company that loses its accounts receivables records—records of what the company is owed—could be a candidate for bankruptcy.

FIGURE 5–20   **HOW VIRUSES ARE SPREAD**

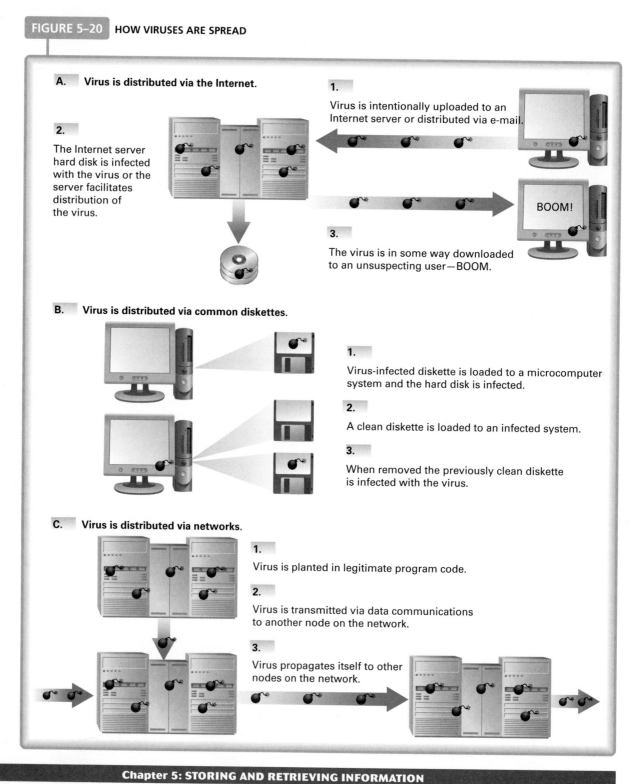

A.   **Virus is distributed via the Internet.**

1.
Virus is intentionally uploaded to an Internet server or distributed via e-mail.

2.
The Internet server hard disk is infected with the virus or the server facilitates distribution of the virus.

BOOM!

3.
The virus is in some way downloaded to an unsuspecting user—BOOM.

B.   **Virus is distributed via common diskettes.**

1.
Virus-infected diskette is loaded to a microcomputer system and the hard disk is infected.

2.
A clean diskette is loaded to an infected system.

3.
When removed the previously clean diskette is infected with the virus.

C.   **Virus is distributed via networks.**

1.
Virus is planted in legitimate program code.

2.
Virus is transmitted via data communications to another node on the network.

3.
Virus propagates itself to other nodes on the network.

VIRUS PROTECTION

The software package distributed with new PCs usually includes an **antivirus program** and a short-term subscription to a virus update service. The best way to cope with viruses is to recognize their existence and use an antivirus program. Your chances of living virus free are greatly improved if you periodically use this program to check for viruses and are careful about what you load to your system's hard disk. Computer viruses are introduced continuously into the cyberworld, so antivirus vendors, such as Symantec and McAfee, offer a subscription service that lets you download protection for new viruses.

Here are some tips that will help minimize your vulnerability to viruses.

- Delete e-mails from unknown, suspicious, or untrustworthy sources, especially those with files attached to an e-mail.

- Never open a file attached to an e-mail unless you know what it is, even if it appears to come from a friend.

- Download files from the Internet only from legitimate and reputable sources. If you feel comfortable with the source but want an extra level of protection, download the file to a floppy disk and test it with your own antivirus software.

- Update your antivirus software at least once a week as over 200 viruses are discovered each month.

- Back up your files periodically. If you catch a virus, your chances of surviving are pretty good if you maintain current backups of important data and programs.

Traditionally, virus protection has been at the PC or client level. However, this may change as companies look to network and Internet service providers for more services. New tools are being developed that can check for viruses at the server level before files reach the PC. An ISP's prescan of all files will protect subscribers from all known viruses at the time. This service is inviting for companies concerned about keeping current with protection from the never-ending stream of viruses circulating the Internet.

PERSONAL COMPUTING:
Virus Protection Don't leave home without protection from viruses and hackers. There is too much at stake, possibly your almost-completed term paper, your family photo album, the use of your PC for days or weeks, and so on. Typically, a new computer will have one of the popular virus protection programs installed; however, for continued protection from new viruses you will need to subscribe to the software vendor's online update service. Having antivirus software provides only partial protection (legacy viruses), so it is important to continually update the virus definitions database.

5-4.1	A computer virus is a computer-generated program that causes an unpleasant event on a computer. (T/F)
5-4.2	The number of computer viruses is in which range: (a) 25–50, (b) 100–500, (c) 20,000–30,000, or (d) 50,000 and up.
5-4.3	A denial of service virus place high demands on: (a) backup capabilities, (b) hackers, (c) server resources, or (d) vaccine research.
5-4.4	One way to fight computer viruses is to use what type of software: (a) antibug, (b) antivirus, (c) redo, or (d) backup?

SECTION SELF-CHECK

5-5 Backing Up Files: Better Safe Than Sorry

Safeguarding the content of your disks may be more important than safeguarding hardware. After all, you can always replace your computer, but you often cannot replace your lost files.

BACKUP FOR PERSONAL COMPUTING

The first commandment in computing, at any level, is *back up your files!*

The backup process serves two important functions.

- *Protection against loss of valuable files.* When you create a document, a spreadsheet, or a graph and you want to recall it at a later time, you *store* the file on disk. You can, of course, store many files on a single disk. If the disk is in some way destroyed (hard disk crash, demagnetized, burned, and so on), stolen, or lost, your files are gone unless you have a backup.

- *Archiving files.* Important files no longer needed for active processing can be archived to a backup medium. For example, banks archive old transactions (checks and deposits) for a number of years. PC users periodically archive their e-mail.

Backup Media

PC users employ a variety of backup media.

- *Rewritable optical media.* Rewritable optical discs—CD-RW or DVD+RW—have emerged as the backup medium of choice for the active PC user, offering 650-MB and 4.7 GB-capacities, respectively.

WHY THIS SECTION IS IMPORTANT TO YOU

At one time or another, just about everyone who works with computers loses work for which there is no backup. It's never a pleasant experience. This section helps you take that first step toward regularly backing up your valuable personal information and avoiding one of life's traumas.

- *Diskettes.* Backing up a complete hard disk to 1.44-MB floppies is impractical because it would require hundreds, perhaps thousands, of diskettes. However, if this is your only option, you should back up critical files to diskette.

- *High-capacity diskettes.* The Zip disk, SuperDisk, or HiFD disk drive provide a good backup medium for the casual PC user, offering disk backup capacities in the 100- to 750-MB range.

- *Backup to portable hard disks.* The cost of a portable hard disk continues to drop, making it an increasingly viable alternative for backup.

Backup Methods

You can choose from three common backup methods.

- *Full backup.* A full backup copies all files on a hard disk to backup media.

- *Selective backup.* Only user-selected files are backed up.

- *Incremental backup.* Only those files that have been modified since the last backup are backed up.

The frequency with which files are backed up depends on their *volatility,* or how often you update the files on the disk. If you spend time every day working with files, you should back them up each day. Others should be backed up no more often than they are used. Figure 5-21 illustrates a six-CD-RW or DVD+RW backup rotation.

Figure 5-22 illustrates and explains a backup procedure for only those critical files that are used daily. In the figure, two *generations* of backup are maintained on Backup Sets A and B. Critical disk

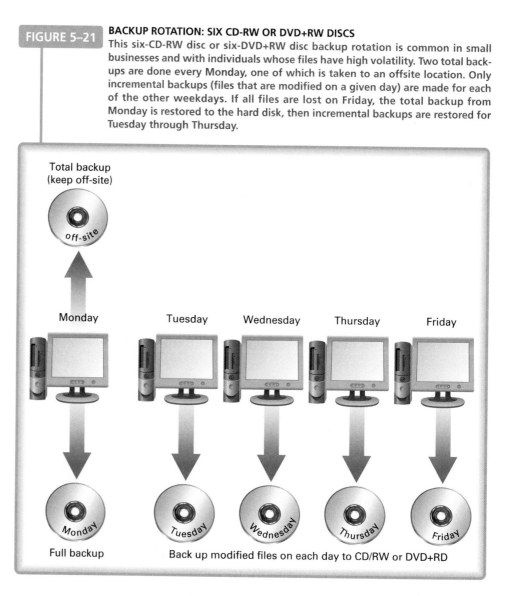

FIGURE 5–21 — **BACKUP ROTATION: SIX CD-RW OR DVD+RW DISCS**
This six-CD-RW disc or six-DVD+RW disc backup rotation is common in small businesses and with individuals whose files have high volatility. Two total backups are done every Monday, one of which is taken to an offsite location. Only incremental backups (files that are modified on a given day) are made for each of the other weekdays. If all files are lost on Friday, the total backup from Monday is restored to the hard disk, then incremental backups are restored for Tuesday through Thursday.

Total backup
(keep off-site)

off-site

Monday   Tuesday   Wednesday   Thursday   Friday

Monday   Tuesday   Wednesday   Thursday   Friday

Full backup   Back up modified files on each day to CD/RW or DVD+RD

FIGURE 5–22

DISK/DISC BACKUP ROTATION: TWO BACKUP SETS
After each day's processing, critical disk files are copied alternately to Backup Sets A and B. In this manner, one backup set (possibly several interchangeable disks or a CD-RW or a DVD+RW) is always current within a day's processing. If the critical work files and the most recent backup are accidentally destroyed, a third backup is current within two days' processing. Backup Sets A and B are alternated as the most current backup.

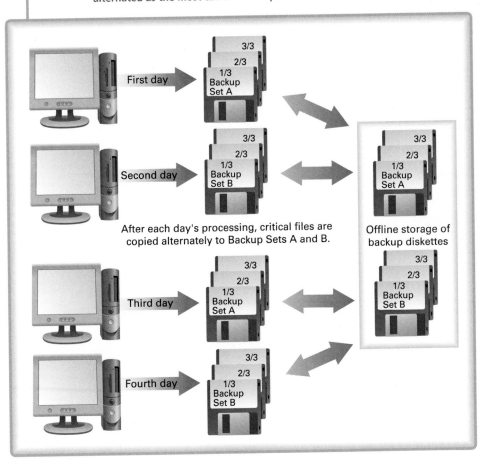

files are copied alternately to Backup Sets A and B each day. This technique is popular with individual users whose main concern is the backup of their currently active files.

Restoring Files

If you lose your data or programs, you will need to restore the backed-up file to disk. If you use a backup system similar to the one shown in Figure 5-21, then some updating will occur between total backup runs. To re-create your files, you need to use the last total backup and then incorporate all subsequent incremental backups. For example, assume a virus wiped your hard drive clean at the end of the day on Thursday. To restore the backup files, you would restore the full backup from Monday, then the modified backup from Tuesday, and finally the modified backup tape from Wednesday. Then you would need to redo any processing that was done on Thursday prior to the virus striking.

Other Backup Options

In practice, the type of backup you employ depends on circumstances and available hardware. Here are a few more commonly used approaches to backup.

- *Backup to a server computer.* Users on a local area network can periodically upload user files to the server computer, whose files normally are backed up daily.
- *Backup to another PC on a home network.* Users on a home network can periodically upload their files to another PC on the network.

FIGURE 5–23 Automatic Retrieval Tape Storage
This robotic tape storage and retrieval unit holds hundreds of high-density tape cartridges, each with a capacity of 25 GB (gigabytes). The tape cartridges are automatically loaded and unloaded to a tape drive as they are needed for processing. Companies use tape storage and retrieval systems to back up massive master files on magnetic disk storage.

- *Backup to a notebook/desktop PC.* Many people have both a desktop and a notebook PC, linking the PCs via USB or some other connector to transfer user files to whichever PC is in use. One system serves as backup to the other.

- *Magnetic tape.* The cost of rewritable optical disc drives has dropped so dramatically that the use of magnetic tape drives, called **tape backup units** (**TBUs**), is all but eliminated for personal computing. TBUs, which are not applicable for routine information processing because they are sequential only, use a $1/4$-inch cartridge (QIC), also called a **data cartridge.** The self-contained data cartridge is inserted into and removed from the tape drive in much the same way you would load or remove a videotape from a VCR. TBUs are still common in the business environment. Some businesses use automatic retrieval tape storage (see Figure 5-23).

BACKUP FOR INTERNET AND NETWORK SERVERS

At the Skalny Basket Company in Springfield, Ohio, Cheryl Hart insisted on daily backups of the small family-owned company's accounts receivables files. The backups were inconvenient and took 30 minutes each day. Cheryl took the backup home each day in her briefcase, just in case. On December 23, she packed her briefcase and left for the Christmas holidays. Five days later, Skalny Basket Company burned to the ground, wiping out all inventory and its computer system. The company was up in smoke, all except for tape cartridges that contained records of its accounts receivables. Cheryl said, "We thought we were out of business. Without the tape, we couldn't have rebuilt."

Small companies like the Skalny Basket Company can use backup methods like those used in personal computers. However, larger companies that depend on online transaction processing and a shared database must be up and running at all times. When the system goes down, the company goes down. When downtime is simply unacceptable, the network server must be made **fault-tolerant.** That is, the network server must be designed to permit continuous operation even if important components of the network fail. To accomplish this goal, parts of the system must be redundant (for example, disk storage).

To minimize the impact of catastrophic disk failure, companies use **RAID** (**Redundant Array of Independent Disks**) to provide fault-tolerant backup of disk systems. RAID spreads data across several integrated disk drives such that a duplicate copy is maintained on a separate disk system at all times. When an online transaction is completed and logged on one disk, an exact entry is made to a duplicate disk. The disk system is considered fault-tolerant because it is highly unlikely that two disks will fail at the same time.

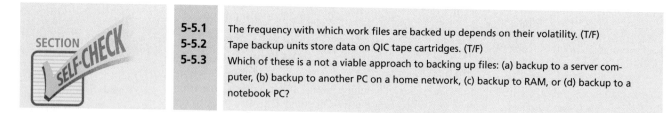

SECTION SELF-CHECK

5-5.1 The frequency with which work files are backed up depends on their volatility. (T/F)

5-5.2 Tape backup units store data on QIC tape cartridges. (T/F)

5-5.3 Which of these is a not a viable approach to backing up files: (a) backup to a server computer, (b) backup to another PC on a home network, (c) backup to RAM, or (d) backup to a notebook PC?

5-1 MASS STORAGE, FILES, AND FILE MANAGEMENT

Data and programs are stored in **mass storage** for permanent storage. **Magnetic disk drives** and **magnetic tape drives** are popular devices for mass storage. Tape is used mostly for backup capability and archival storage. **Optical laser disc** technology continues to emerge as a mass storage medium.

The file is the foundation of permanent storage on a computer system. Filenames in the Windows environment can include spaces, but some special characters are not permitted. An optional three-character extension identifies the type of file (for example, *myphoto.gif* is a graphics file). Popular file types include the **ASCII file** (txt), **data file** (mdb for Access), **document file** (doc for Word), **spreadsheet file** (xls for Excel), **Web page file** (htm), **source program file** (vbp for Visual Basic), **executable program file** (exe), **graphics file** (gif, bmp, jpg, tif, and pcx), **audio file** (wav), and **video file** (mov). Most popular applications programs have at least one **native file format.**

Everything we do on a computer has to do with a file and, therefore, mass storage. We can create, name, save, copy, move, delete, retrieve, update, display, print, play, execute, download, upload, export, import, compress, and protect files. **File compression** is used to economize on storage space. PC users routinely compress file to **zip files** for download/upload on the Net and unzip the compressed or "zipped" files for use in applications. The executable **self-extracting zip file** must be executed to unzip the file(s).

The Windows Explorer is a utility program that lets you view and manage folders/files. Folders are created for specific disk drives. You must give the operating system the **path** to follow to store or retrieve a particular file. Common file management activities include save/save as, open, copy, move, delete, and rename.

5-2 MAGNETIC DISKS

Data are retrieved and manipulated either sequentially or randomly. There are two types of magnetic disks: **interchangeable magnetic disks** and **fixed magnetic disks**. Magnetic disk drives enable random- and sequential-processing capabilities.

Popular types of interchangeable magnetic disks include the 3.5-inch diskette, also called a floppy disk, the 120-MB **SuperDisk**, the 200-MB **HiFD disk**, and the 100-, 250-, or 750-MB **Zip disk**, which is inserted into a **Zip drive**. The floppy disk, SuperDisk, and HiFD disk are the same size but have different **disk densities.**

There are three types of hard disks—those that are permanently installed, those that are portable, and those that are interchangeable between like systems. Hard disks contain at least one platter and usually several disk platters stacked on a single rotating spindle. The rotation of a magnetic disk passes all data under or over **read/write heads,** which are mounted on **access arms.** The **portable hard disk** is an external device that is easily connected to any personal computer via a USB port or FireWire port.

The way in which data and programs are stored and accessed is similar for both hard and interchangeable disks. Data are stored via serial representation in concentric **tracks** on each recording surface. The spacing of tracks is measured in **tracks per inch** (TPI). In **sector organization,** the recording surface is divided into pie-shaped **sectors,** and each sector is assigned a number. Adjacent sectors are combined to form **clusters.**

Each disk cluster is numbered, and the number of the first cluster in a file comprises the **disk address** on a particular file. The disk address designates a file's physical location on a disk. A particular **cylinder** refers to every track with the same number on all recording surfaces.

Some high-performance disk manufacturers employ **zoned recording** where zones contain a greater number of sectors per track as you move from the innermost zone to the outermost zone.

Each disk used in the Windows environment has a **Virtual File Allocation Table** (**VFAT**) in which information about the clusters is stored. Clusters are *chained* together to store file information larger than the capacity of a single cluster. The **ScanDisk** utility lets you return lost clusters to the available pool of usable clusters.

The **defragmentation** process rewrites fragmented files into contiguous clusters. A Windows utility program called **Disk Defragmenter** consolidates files into contiguous clusters.

Before a disk can be used, it must be **formatted.** Formatting creates *sectors* and *tracks* into which data are stored and establishes an area for the VFAT.

The **access time** for a magnetic disk is the interval between the instant a computer makes a request for transfer of data from a disk-storage device to RAM and the instant this operation is completed. The **data transfer rate** is the rate at which data are read from (written to) mass storage to (from) RAM. **Disk caching** improves system speed.

Apply the dictates of common sense to the care of diskettes (avoid excessive dust, avoid extremes in temperature and humidity, and so on).

5-3 OPTICAL LASER DISCS

Optical laser disc storage is capable of storing vast amounts of data. The main categories of optical laser discs are *CD, CD-ROM, CD-R, CD-RW, DVD, DVD-ROM, DVD-R, DVD+RW, DVD-RW, DVD-RAM,* and *FMD-ROM.*

A CD-ROM is inserted into the CD-ROM drive for processing. Most of the commercially produced read-only CD-ROM discs contain reference material or support multimedia applications. Multidisk player/changers are called **jukeboxes.**

A blank **compact disc-recordable** (**CD-R**) disc looks like a CD-ROM and once information is recorded on it, it works like a CD-ROM. **CD-RW** (**CD-ReWritable**) allows users to rewrite to the same CD media and "burn" discs, such as audio CDs.

The DVD (digital video disc) looks like the CD and the CD-ROM, but it can store up to about 17 GB. DVD drives can play CD-ROMs and CDs. **DVD-R** is like CD-R but with the recording density of DVD-ROM. **DVD-RAM, DVD+RW,** and **DVD-RW** are like CD-RW, giving us rewritable capabilities for high-capacity DVD technology. **FMD-ROM,** a very high density, multilayer disc, holds up to 140 GB of data.

The typical PC will have at least a DVD-ROM drive and possibly another read/write disc drive. Most people who want to burn discs and use optical media for backup and transfer purposes are installing a DVD-ROM/CD-RW combination drive or a DVD+RW/CD-RW combination drive.

The choice of which technologies to choose for a system or an application is often a trade-off between storage capacity, cost (dollars per megabyte), and speed (access time).

Each year, improvements are made in existing mass storage devices as the storage industry strives to meet our craving for more storage.

5-4 VIRUSES AND VIRUS PROTECTION

A **computer virus** is a program that "infects" other programs and databases upon contact. A **macro virus** is a program that is written in the macro language of a particular application. A **worm** is a computer program that exists as a separate entity and invades computers via e-mail and IRC. The **Trojan horse** does not replicate itself but depends on the cooperation of unsuspecting users to spread itself.

The primary sources of computer viruses are the Internet (e-mail and downloads), common interchangeable disks, and computer networks. **Antivirus programs** exist to help fight viruses.

5-5 BACKING UP FILES: BETTER SAFE THAN SORRY

You can replace your computer, but you often cannot replace your lost files, so back up your files. The backup process provides protection against loss of valuable files and enables archiving of files. Popular PC backup media includes rewritable optical media, diskettes/floppies, high-capacity diskettes, and portable hard disks.

Three common backup methods are full backup, selective backup of files, or incremental backup. When backing up only critical daily-use files, use at least two generations of backup.

Beside backup to a local disk/disc, you can also backup to a server computer, to another PC on a home network, to a notebook/desktop PC, or to magnetic tape drives, called **tape backup units** (**TBUs**), that use **data cartridges**. When downtime is unacceptable, the network server must be made **fault-tolerant**. **RAID** (**Redundant Array of Independent Disks**) minimizes the impact of catastrophic disk failure by spreading data across several integrated disk drives.

KEY TERMS

access arm (p. 217)
access time (p. 220)
antivirus program (p. 229)
ASCII file (p. 208)
audio file (p. 210)
CD-R (compact disc-recordable) (p. 225)
CD-RW (CD-ReWritable) (p. 225)
cluster (p. 218)
computer virus (p. 227)
cylinder (p. 219)
data cartridge (p. 232)
data file (p. 208)
data transfer rate (p. 220)
defragmentation (p. 221)
disk address (p. 218)
disk caching (p. 220)
Disk Defragmenter (p. 220)
disk density (p. 215)
document file (p. 208)
DVD+RW (p. 225)
DVD-R (p. 225)
DVD-RAM (p. 225)

DVD-RW (p. 225)
executable program file (p. 210)
fault-tolerant (p. 232)
file compression (p. 211)
fixed magnetic disk (p. 214)
FMD-ROM (p. 225)
formatted (p. 220)
graphics file (p. 210)
HiFD disk (p. 215)
interchangeable magnetic disk (p. 214)
jukebox (p. 224)
macro virus (p. 227)
magnetic disk drive (p. 208)
magnetic tape drive (p. 208)
mass storage (p. 208)
native file format (p. 210)
optical laser disc (p. 208)
path (p. 213)
portable hard disk (p. 217)
RAID (Redundant Array of Independent Disks) (p. 232)
read/write head (p. 217)

ScanDisk (p. 220)
sector (p. 218)
sector organization (p. 218)
self-extracting zip file (p. 211)
source program file (p. 210)
spreadsheet file (p. 208)
SuperDisk (p. 215)
tape backup unit (TBU) (p. 232)
track (p. 218)
tracks per inch (TPI) (p. 218)
Trojan horse (p. 227)
video file (p. 210)
Virtual File Allocation Table (VFAT) (p. 219)
Web page file (p. 208)
worm (p. 227)
Zip® disk (p. 215)
Zip® drive (p. 215)
zip file (p. 211)
zoned recording (p. 219)

MATCHING

1. fault-tolerant system
2. fixed disk
3. simgame.exe
4. TBU
5. zoned recording
6. virus type
7. disk clusters
8. DVD+RW
9. native file format
10. video file type
11. path
12. edit menu
13. zip file
14. cylinder
15. disk access time

a. chained together
b. tape backup
c. rewritable optical disc
d. hard disk
e. uses disk space efficiently
f. depends on read/write head movement
g. permits continuous server operation
h. worm
i. has multiple tracks
j. reference to file location
k. mov
l. associated with a program
m. compressed file
n. copy/cut/paste
o. executable file

5-1.1 An ASCII file is a text-only file that can be read or created by any word processing program or text editor. (T/F)

5-1.2 WINTER.SALES and .ADD are valid filenames in the Windows environment. (T/F)

5-1.3 The Windows Explorer is an integrated Web browser and file management tool. (T/F)

5-1.4 A move file operation results in two copies of the same file. (T/F)

5-1.5 We do all of the following to files except: (a) create files, (b) update files, (c) throw files, or (d) execute files.

5-1.6 Which of the following is not a type of file: (a) audio, (b) spreadsheet, (c) source program, or (d) book?

5-1.7 What must you give the operating system to retrieve a particular file: (a) its hierarchical position, (b) the file's path, (c) the outbound corridor, or (d) its directory name?

5-1.8 Which is not a path separator symbol in UNIX, Windows, or Mac OS X: (a) /, (b) \, (c) :, or (d) ;?

5-2.1 Magnetic disks have sequential-access capabilities only. (T/F)

5-2.2 Hard disks and fixed disks are one and the same. (T/F)

5-2.3 Both the diskette and the HiFD disk are the same size but have different disk densities. (T/F)

5-2.4 Information on interchangeable disks cannot be stored offline. (T/F)

5-2.5 The highest-capacity Zip disk has a greater capacity for storage than the HiFD disk. (T/F)

5-2.6 TPI stands for tracks per inch. (T/F)

5-2.7 The capacity of clusters is based on a multiple of 521 bytes. (T/F)

5-2.8 In a disk drive, the read/write heads are mounted on an access arm. (T/F)

5-2.9 Before a disk can be used, it must be formatted. (T/F)

5-2.10 The innermost zone has fewer sectors than the outermost zone in zoned recording. (T/F)

5-2.11 Which of these statements is *not* true: (a) the rotation of a magnetic disk passes all data under or over a read/write head; (b) the heads are mounted on access arms; (c) the standard size for PC hard disks (diameter) is 8 inches; (d) a hard disk contains several disk platters stacked on a single rotating spindle?

5-2.12 The standard size for common diskettes is: (a) 3.25 inches, (b) 3.5 inches, (c) 3.75 inches, or (d) 5.25 inches.

5-2.13 The VFAT is searched by the operating system to find the physical address of the (a) first cluster of the file, (b) read/write head, (c) microprocessor, (d) midsector of the file.

5-2.14 What denotes the physical location of a particular file or set of data on a magnetic disk: (a) cylinder, (b) data compression index, (c) CD-R, or (d) disk address?

5-2.15 TPI refers to: (a) sector density, (b) cylinder overload, (c) track density, or (d) bps thickness.

5-2.16 The disk caching area is: (a) on a floppy disk, (b) in RAM, (c) on a hard disk, or (d) on the monitor's expansion board.

5-2.17 In zoned recording, tracks are grouped into: (a) sectors, (b) regions, (c) zones, or (d) partitions.

5-3.1 CD-ROM is a spinoff of audio CD technology. (T/F)

5-3.2 A CD-ROM stores data in spiraling tracks. (T/F)

5-3.3 Jukebox refers to a player/changer that can handle multiple CD-ROMs. (T/F)

5-3.4 DVD+RW is like rewritable storage technology. (T/F)

5-3.5 The CD-ROM drive specifications 32X, 40X, or 75X refer to its: (a) speed, (b) diameter, (c) number of platters, or (d) sector groupings.

5-3.6 The data transfer rate for a 40X CD-ROM is how many MB per second: (a) 3, (b) 6, (c) 11.25, or (d) 12.

5-3.7 Which optical laser disc has the greatest storage capacity: (a) double-sided DVD-ROM, (b) FMD-ROM, (c) 75X CD-ROM, or (d) CD-RW?

5-4.1 Worms exist as separate entities and do not attach themselves to files. (T/F)

5-4.2 The Trojan horse e-mails itself. (T/F)

5-4.3 All downloaded files on the Internet are checked for viruses at the ISP level, eliminating the need for antivirus software at the PC level. (T/F)

5-4.4 The profile of one who writes viruses is an older female from southeast Asia. (T/F)

5-4.5 It is recommended to delete e-mails from unknown, suspicious, or untrustworthy sources. (T/F)

5-4.6 What can hide and duplicate itself within legitimate programs: (a) computer virus, (b) PC bug, (c) program germ, or (d) Trojan horse?

5-4.7 Which of these is not a virus: (a) Wooden Horse, (b) Melissa, (c) The Cookie Monster, or (d) Love.bug?

5-4.8 Which of these is not a source for computer viruses: (a) interchangeable disks, (b) the Net, (c) computer networks, or (d) antivirus programs?

5-4.9 Sometimes viruses are attached to: (a) e-mails, (b) chat notes, (c) hypertext, or (d) disk labels.

5-5.1 Any system with a weekly backup requirement from 100 MB to 1 GB is a candidate to use floppies as a backup medium. (T/F)

5-5.2 A fault-tolerant network is one designed to have continuous operation. (T/F)

5-5.3 Incremental backups play no role in restoring files. (T/F)

5-5.4 The backup process serves two important functions—protection against loss of valuable files and cache storage. (T/F)

5-5.5 Which of these would not be considered a backup medium: (a) CD-RW, (b) Zip disk, (c) DVD-ROM, or (d) portable hard disk?

5-5.6 Which of the following generally is not an application for magnetic tape storage: (a) routine information processing, (b) backup for disk storage, (c) archival storage, or (d) medium for transfer between computers?

5-5.7 In the full backup method: (a) only user-selected files are backed up, (b) only those files that have been modified since the last backup are backed up, (c) only volatile files are backed up, or (d) all files are backed up.

5-5.8 When performing critical files backup using interchangeable disks it is best to maintain at least: (a) one generation, (b) two generations, (c) four generations, or (d) eight generations.

ACCESSIBILITY TO E-MAIL ARCHIVES

E-mail may be the corporate Achilles heel when it comes to lawsuits. Attorneys can subpoena e-mail archives on disk or tape relative to pending lawsuits. Among the thousands of e-mail messages sent each day in a typical medium-sized company, attorneys are likely to find statements that support their cause. People tend to be conversational when writing e-mail messages. People don't write e-mail with the thought that it might be shown as evidence in a court of law. To avoid the potential for litigation, many companies routinely purge e-mail archives. Had the people at Microsoft Corporation been more diligent about purging their e-mail, U.S. government prosecutors would not have been able to subpoena the company's e-mail. The e-mail they eventually found was critical to the government's antitrust suit against Microsoft.

Discussion: *Should companies save e-mail? If so, for how long?*

Discussion: *Should attorneys be allowed to subpoena e-mail archives? Why or why not?*

MP3 FILE SHARING

MP3 is an abbreviation for a method of compressing audio files, usually music, into a digital format that can be downloaded easily and played on your PC or an MP3 player. Some MP3 players are as small as a watch and can hold several hours of music in their solid-state memory. The music industry, which has relied almost exclusively on CD and cassette tape media to market and distribute its products in recent years, is now confronted with millions of music-hungry people who routinely share MP3 files (via the Internet and diskettes), both commercially and noncommercially. In the same vein, netizens have begun to share movies, as well (over a half-million a day).

Discussion: *In the eyes of the music industry, if you receive an MP3 file containing copyrighted music, then you are receiving stolen goods. Do listeners share this view? Why or why not?*

Discussion: *Sometimes people attend concerts and tape parts of the concerts, make MP3 files of the music, then send these MP3 files to friends. Is this practice unethical or illegal, or both? Explain.*

Discussion: *People routinely use digital cameras and illegally tape first-run movies at theaters. They then post the movie file to the Internet. Would you download and view an illegal movie video? Why or why not?*

Discussion: *Violating copyright laws is punishable by up to five years in prison and a $250,000 fine. Describe what someone would have to do to get the maximum sentence for copyright violations.*

Discussion: *The upside to MP3 file sharing is that an aspiring artist can place his or her music on the Internet and make it available at little or no charge. Would it be ethical for an artist to change his or her mind and ask users to pay a fee for music that was previously offered for free?*

DISCUSSION AND PROBLEM SOLVING

5-1.1 Describe seven personal activities that might result in information being read from or written to magnetic disk (for example, buying a candy bar at Wal-Mart).

5-1.2 Name and briefly describe applications for four different types of files.

5-1.3 Describe file compression and why and how it might be used.

5-2.1 Traditionally, personal computers have had a floppy disk drive. However, some personal computers no longer come with a floppy drive. Is the floppy drive needed anymore? Explain.

5-2.2 A program issues a "read" command for data to be retrieved from hard disk. Describe the resulting mechanical movement and the movement of data.

5-2.3 What happens during formatting? Why must hard disks and diskettes be formatted?

5-2.4 A floppy disk does not move until a read or write command is issued. Once it is issued, the floppy begins to spin. It stops spinning after the command is executed. Why is a hard disk not set in motion in the same manner? Why is a floppy not made to spin continuously?

5-2.5 The SuperDisk and Zip disk serve similar purposes on a computer system. The SuperDisk drive is compatible with the traditional floppy diskette, but the Zip disk reads and writes data more rapidly. Costs are comparable. Which one would you choose and why?

5-2.6 What would determine the frequency with which you would need to defragment your hard drive? Explain.

5-3.1 List six content areas that are distributed commercially on CD-ROM (for example, electronic encyclopedias).

5-3.2 Describe the potential impact of optical laser disc technology on public and university libraries. On home libraries.

5-3.3 Describe at least two applications where CD-RW or DVD+RW would be preferred over a hard disk for storage.

5-3.4 The DVD+RW drive also has the capabilities of the CD-RW drive, the "CD burner." Currently the DVD+RW drive is more expensive than the CD-RW drive, but prices are converging. Speculate on when or if DVD+RW will replace CD-RW.

5-3.5 With the capability to store digital music, the audio CD has revolutionized the way we play and listen to recorded music. Now music can be downloaded over the Internet and played on PCs, solid-state MP3 players, and other electronic devices. Does this signal the beginning of the end of the audio CD? Explain.

5-3.6 The only internal mechanical movement in a typical notebook PC is associated with the disk and optical drives. Someday soon both may be replaced with solid-state non-volatile memory. Speculate on how this might change the appearance of notebook PCs and on how we use and what we do with them.

5-4.1 What name is given to programs intended to damage the computer system of an unsuspecting victim? Describe three sources of these.

5-4.2 What would be appropriate punishment for the originator of a virus that destroyed the user files of thousands of people?

5-4.3 Several years ago, antivirus companies let owners of authorized copies of their software download updated virus protection at no cost. Now they charge an annual subscription of around $5. Is it worth it? Explain.

5-5.1 Describe a backup method, including backup medium, that might be used in a small company with a local area network serving 28 users.

5-5.2 Every Friday night a company makes backup copies of all master files and programs (over 30 GB). Why is this necessary? The company has a TBU (50-GB cartridges), a DVD+RW drive, and two 120-MB portable hard disk drives. Which storage medium would you suggest for the backup? Why?

5-5.3 How many 3.5-inch diskettes would you need to do a daily backup of the files (2 MB total) you created for a college course?

FOCUS ON PERSONAL COMPUTING

1. The typical PC user is somewhat lax when it comes to organizing folders and naming files; therefore, the typical PC's folder/file structure could use some cleanup. Set up a hierarchical file structure that includes specific folder categories within general areas of usage. For example, one major folder might be "State University" with subfolders for each semester. Each semester subfolder would have subfolders for your various classes and perhaps a miscellaneous folder with subfolders for your extracurricular activities. Rename folders/files as needed.

2. Set up a backup procedure within the context of available hardware that meets your ongoing backup needs. Label all interchangeable media, if applicable, and write up the backup procedure, including diagrams as needed. Backup your user files.

3. If you are an active user and have not defragmented your hard disk, use a disk defragmenter utility and "defrag" your hard disk. Defragmenting the hard disk can substantially improve system performance.

INTERNET EXERCISES @ www.prenhall.com/long

1. The Online Study Guide (multiple choice, true/false, matching, and essay questions)
2. Internet Learning Activities
  • Magnetic Disk
  • Optical Storage
3. Serendipitous Internet Activities
  • Travel

chapter

6

Learning Objectives

Once you have read and studied this chapter, you will have learned:

- **The operation and application of common input devices (Section 6-1).**

- **The operation and application of common output devices (Section 6-2).**

- **The scope of and technology for multimedia applications (Section 6-3).**

- **The breadth of assistive input/output technology for disabled people (Section 6-4).**

INFORMATION INPUT AND OUTPUT

Why this chapter is important to you

When PCs arrived as a viable consumer product in the late 1970s, choices for input were limited. Input was mostly via the standard QWERTY keyboard. Output was a small low-resolution monitor, a really slow printer, and a tinny little speaker that made annoying sounds when you tapped the wrong key. Now we have ergonomic keyboards, or, if you prefer, speech-recognition software that lets you talk to your PC. Monitors come in many different shapes, sizes, and qualities. All-in-one devices offer fast photo-quality color printing, along with copying, scanning, and faxing capabilities.

There is an endless array of input/output devices you can connect to a PC for what seems to be an infinite number of applications. You can scan in photographs. You can capture real-time video images from your camcorder. You can enter the TV signal directly to your PC for recording or viewing. An innovative input device can even give PCs a sense of smell. New and exciting I/O devices are being announced every month.

Today, you are the person who makes the decisions about which input/output devices you hang on your PC. If you have a good grasp of available input/output devices, you can take full advantage of your PC system. Did you know the mouse is but one of many options for point-and-draw devices? Did you know you could enjoy videophone conversations with your friends across town or around the world? Did you know that you could use your scanner to scan in text from printed documents? Did you know that carefully selected I/O options, such as ergonomic keyboards and speech-recognition software, could reduce neuromuscular problems associated with entering data to a computer? The knowledge you gain from this chapter should prove helpful when it comes time to configure and purchase a PC.

When it comes to buying a PC or related hardware, you are generally on your own. Realistically, you cannot depend on salespeople or friends to make these important monetary decisions for you. It takes personal knowledge and research. This and the previous two chapters should help you get the biggest bang for your PC buck.

6-1 Input Devices

We routinely communicate directly or indirectly with a computer. Even people who have never sat in front of a PC communicate with computers. Perhaps you have had one of these experiences.

● Have you ever been hungry and short of cash? No problem. Just stop at an automatic teller machine (ATM) and ask for some "lunch money." The ATM's keyboard and monitor enable you to hold an interactive conversation with the bank's computer. The ATM's printer provides you with a hard copy of your transactions when you leave. Some ATMs talk to you as well.

● Have you ever called a mail-order merchandiser and been greeted by a message like this: "Thank you for calling BrassCo Enterprises Customer Service. If you wish to place an order, press one. If you wish to inquire about the status of an order, press two. To speak to a particular person, enter that person's four-digit extension or hold, and an operator will process your call momentarily." The message is produced by a computer-based voice-response system, which responds to the buttons you press on your telephone keypad.

We communicate with these computers through input/output devices. *Input devices* translate our data and communications into a form that the computer can understand. The computer then processes these data, and an *output device* translates them back into a form we can understand. In our two examples, the ATM's keypad, touch screen monitor, and the telephone keypad serve as input devices, and the ATM's monitor, printer, and the voice-response system serve as output devices (see Figure 6-1).

Input/output devices are quietly playing an increasingly significant role in our lives. The number and variety of I/O devices are expanding even as you read this, and some of these devices are fairly exotic (see Figure 6-2). For example, there is an electronic nose that can measure and digitally record smells. It's used to analyze aroma in the food, drink, and perfume industries. Commuters enjoy another benefit of I/O as they drive through toll plazas at highway speeds. For each passing car, toll road computers grab the customer number from a credit card-sized transmitter mounted on the car windshield, then process the transaction and flash a "Thank You" message.

This chapter is about I/O devices. This first section is on input devices, and we will begin with the *keyboard* and the *mouse*, the most popular input devices.

FIGURE 6–1

TERMINALS FOR BANKING CUSTOMERS: AUTOMATIC TELLER MACHINES
The widely used automatic teller machine (ATM) supports a variety of input/output methods. The magnetic stripe on the ATM card contains identification and security information that, when read, is sent to the bank's computer system. The ATM responds with instructions via its monitor. The customer enters an identification number and data via a keypad. In the figure, the computer processes the customer's request and then provides instructions for the customer via the monitor and verbally with a voice-response unit.

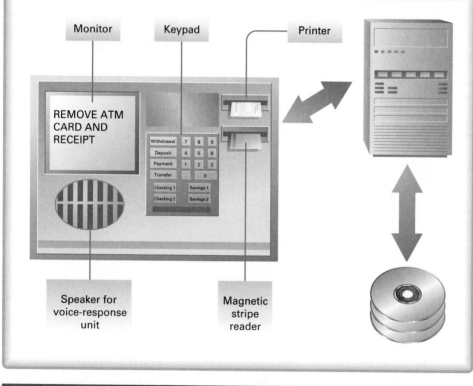

FIGURE 6–2 The Tablet PC
Innovations in input/output are happening all the time. This Acer PC is evolutionary in its approach to user interaction. The PC provides a variety of I/O options and easily converts from a tablet PC to a notebook PC by simply twisting the screen, which is closed with the screen on top when used as a tablet PC. The tablet PC offers full desktop PC functionality with the simplicity of a pen and paper.

Photo courtesy of Intel Corporation

THE KEYBOARD

Every notebook and desktop PC comes with a keyboard. There are two basic types of keyboards: alphanumeric keyboards and special-function keyboards.

Traditional Alphanumeric Keyboards

The typical keyboard has 101 keys with the traditional *QWERTY* (the first six letters on the third row) key layout, 12 function keys, a numeric keypad, a variety of special-function keys, and dedicated cursor-control keys (see Figure 6-3). PC, workstation, and terminal keyboards vary considerably in

FIGURE 6–3   **A REPRESENTATIVE PC KEYBOARD**

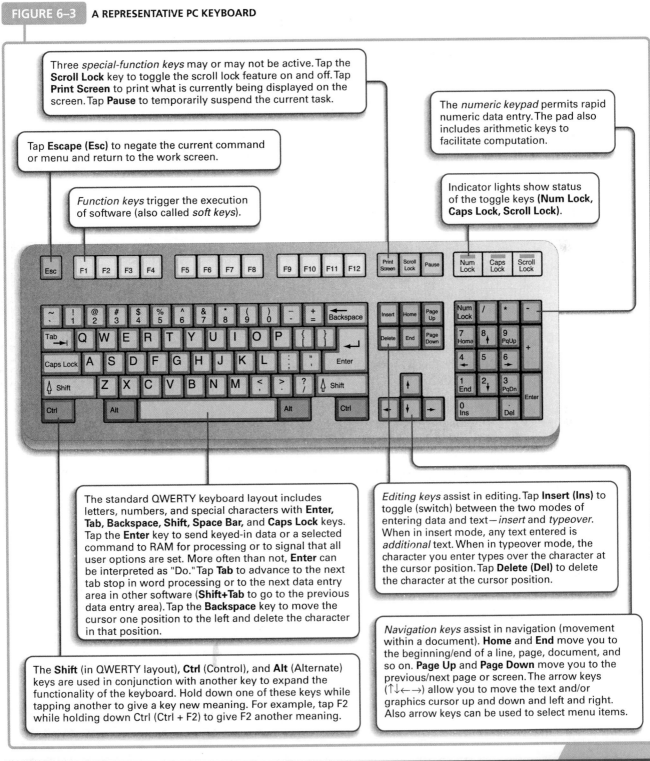

Three *special-function keys* may or may not be active. Tap the **Scroll Lock** key to toggle the scroll lock feature on and off. Tap **Print Screen** to print what is currently being displayed on the screen. Tap **Pause** to temporarily suspend the current task.

The *numeric keypad* permits rapid numeric data entry. The pad also includes arithmetic keys to facilitate computation.

Tap **Escape (Esc)** to negate the current command or menu and return to the work screen.

Function keys trigger the execution of software (also called *soft keys*).

Indicator lights show status of the toggle keys (**Num Lock, Caps Lock, Scroll Lock**).

The standard QWERTY keyboard layout includes letters, numbers, and special characters with **Enter, Tab, Backspace, Shift, Space Bar,** and **Caps Lock** keys. Tap the **Enter** key to send keyed-in data or a selected command to RAM for processing or to signal that all user options are set. More often than not, **Enter** can be interpreted as "Do." Tap **Tab** to advance to the next tab stop in word processing or to the next data entry area in other software (**Shift+Tab** to go to the previous data entry area). Tap the **Backspace** key to move the cursor one position to the left and delete the character in that position.

Editing keys assist in editing. Tap **Insert (Ins)** to toggle (switch) between the two modes of entering data and text—*insert* and *typeover*. When in insert mode, any text entered is *additional* text. When in typeover mode, the character you enter types over the character at the cursor position. Tap **Delete (Del)** to delete the character at the cursor position.

Navigation keys assist in navigation (movement within a document). **Home** and **End** move you to the beginning/end of a line, page, document, and so on. **Page Up** and **Page Down** move you to the previous/next page or screen. The arrow keys (↑↓←→) allow you to move the text and/or graphics cursor up and down and left and right. Also arrow keys can be used to select menu items.

The **Shift** (in QWERTY layout), **Ctrl** (Control), and **Alt** (Alternate) keys are used in conjunction with another key to expand the functionality of the keyboard. Hold down one of these keys while tapping another to give a key new meaning. For example, tap F2 while holding down Ctrl (Ctrl + F2) to give F2 another meaning.

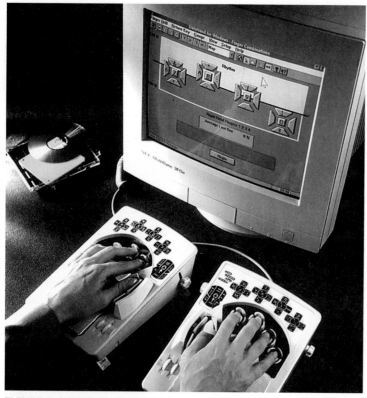

FIGURE 6–4 Keyboard Alternative
The DataHand System is ergonomically designed as two independent units molded to fit the shape of the human hand. The operator-friendly design incorporates the traditional key placement found on standard keyboards, allowing both beginners and experienced keyboard users to learn the DataHand System easily.

appearance (see Figure 6-4). Some may have a few more special function keys (for example, retrieve mail or Windows "Start" buttons). Portable computers have a simple QWERTY keyboard with a minimum number of special-function keys. When tapped, the keyboard's **function keys** trigger the execution of some type of software activity. For example, HELP (context-sensitive user assistance) often is assigned to F1 (Function Key 1). Function keys are numbered and assigned different functions in different software packages.

The cursor-control keys, or arrow keys, can be used to select options from a menu. These keys also allow you to move the **text cursor** *up* (↑) and *down* (↓), usually a line at a time, and *left* (←) and *right* (→), usually a character at a time. The text cursor always shows the location of where the next keyed-in character will appear on the screen. The text cursor can appear as several shapes depending on the application, but frequently you will encounter a blinking vertical line (|). Other important keys common to most keyboards are illustrated and described in Figure 6-3.

Special-Function Keyboards

Some keyboards are designed for specific applications. For example, the cash-register-like terminals at most fast-food restaurants have special-purpose keyboards. Rather than key in the name and price of an order of French fries, attendants need only press the key marked "French fries" to record the sale. Such keyboards help shop supervisors, airline ticket agents, retail salesclerks, and many others interact more quickly with their computer systems.

POINT-AND-DRAW DEVICES

The keyboard is too cumbersome for some applications, especially those that rely on a *graphical user interface* (GUI) or require the user to point or draw. Of course, interaction with all Windows operating systems is via a GUI. The GUI lets you *point and click* with the mouse to navigate between and within programs and to issue commands. The effectiveness of GUIs depends on the user's ability to make a rapid selection from a screen full of menus or graphic icons (each of which represents a program or user option). In these instances, a point-and-draw device, such as a mouse, can be used to *point* to and select (click) a particular user option quickly and efficiently. Also, such devices can be used to *draw*. For example, computer artists use mice to create images.

The handheld mouse, or something like it, is a must-have item on any PC or workstation. When the mouse is moved across a desktop, the **mouse pointer** on the display moves accordingly. The mouse pointer can be positioned anywhere on the screen. It is displayed as an arrow, a crosshair, or a variety of other symbols, depending on the current application and its position on the screen. Figure 6-5 illustrates several of the many mouse pointer schemes available to users. The text cursor and mouse pointer may be displayed on the screen at the same time in some programs, such as word processing. The mouse is either attached to the computer by a cable (the mouse's "tail") or linked via a wireless connection (either infrared or radio wave as shown in Figure 6-6).

Mice and other point-and-draw devices have one or two buttons. Mice used with Wintel PCs typically will have a left and right button plus a wheel between the buttons to facilitate scrolling. Mouse operations are introduced in Chapter 2.

For the moment, the mouse remains the most popular point-and-draw device. However, a variety of devices are available that move the mouse pointer to point and draw, and each has its advantages and disadvantages. Here are a few of the more popular ones (see Figure 6-7).

● *Trackball.* The **trackball** is a ball inset in a small external box or adjacent to and in the same unit as the keyboard. The ball is rolled with the fingers to move the mouse pointer. Some people find it helpful to think of a trackball as an upside-down mouse with a bigger ball on the top.

- *Trackpad.* The **trackpad** has no moving parts and is common on notebook PCs. Simply move your finger about a small touch-sensitive pad to move the mouse pointer.
- *Joystick.* The **joystick** is a vertical stick that moves the mouse pointer in the direction the stick is pushed. Video arcade wizards are no doubt familiar with the joystick, which is used mostly for gaming.
- *Trackpoint.* A **trackpoint** is usually positioned in or near a notebook's keyboard. Trackpoints function like miniature joysticks but are operated with the tip of the finger.
- *Digitizer tablet and pen.* The **digitizer tablet and pen** is a pen and a pressure-sensitive tablet whose *X-Y* coordinates correspond with those on the computer's display screen. Some digitizing tablets also use a crosshair device instead of a pen. Digitizer tablets are used to enable drawing or sketching of images, such as X-rays, and for many other drawing and engineering applications.

SCANNERS

A variety of **scanners** read and interpret information on printed matter and convert it to a format that can be stored and/or interpreted by a computer (see Figure 6-8).

OCR and Bar Code Scanners

In **source-data automation,** data are entered directly to a computer system at the source without the need for key entry transcription. For example, scanners read preprinted **bar codes** on consumer products, eliminating the need for most key entry at checkout counters. **Bar code scanners** use laser technology to scan and interpret an image, printed text, or some kind of code, enabling source-data automation in many applications. Transactions at Wal-Mart stores throughout the world are recorded *automatically* at the *source* of the transaction (the cash register), keeping sales and inventory information up to the second.

Bar code scanners use **OCR (optical character recognition)** technology to read coded information and text information into a computer system. This ability includes reading your handwriting, as well. More commonly, scanners read bar codes. Bar codes represent alphanumeric data by varying the size of adjacent vertical lines. There is a variety of bar-coding systems. Compare the POSTNET bar codes on metered mail with those on packing labels and with those on consumer products. One of the most visible bar-coding systems is the Universal Product Code (UPC). The UPC, originally used for supermarket items, is now being printed on other consumer goods.

The United States Postal Service relies on both OCR and bar code scanning to sort most mail. At the Postal Service, light-sensitive scanners read and interpret the ZIP code and POSTNET bar code on billions of envelopes each day. The ZIP information is then sent to computer-based sorting machines that route the envelopes to appropriate bins for distribution.

Are there advantages to using OCR over bar codes or bar codes over OCR? The advantage of bar codes over OCR is that the position or orientation of the code being read is not as critical to the scanner. In a supermarket, for example, the UPC can be recorded even when a bottle of ketchup is rolled over the laser scanner.

Two types of OCR and bar code scanners—*contact* and *laser*—read information on labels and various types of documents. Both bounce a beam of light off an image, and then measure the reflected light to interpret the

FIGURE 6-5 | **MOUSE POINTER SCHEMES**
This figure shows three of many predefined mouse pointer schemes available to Windows users. From left to right the schemes are the Windows system default scheme, ocean, and nature. Each mouse pointer shape provides a visual clue showing what Windows is doing or what you can do in various situations. The "normal select" pointer is highlighted in blue at the top of the figure.

Normal Select			
Help Select			
Working In Background			
Busy			
Precision Select			
Text Select			
Handwriting			
Unavailable			
Vertical Resize			
Horizontal Resize			
Diagonal Resize 1			
Diagonal Resize 2			
Move			
Alternate Select			
Link Select			

FIGURE 6-6 Wireless PC
This Intel concept PC gives us some insight as to what we might see in future PCs. Notice that the PC is wireless—the mouse, keyboard, and monitor are no longer tethered to the system unit by wires.

FIGURE 6–7 POINT-AND-DRAW DEVICES

TRACKPAD

This Dell Inspiron 8100 notebook PC is equipped with a trackpad that allows you to move the mouse pointer with the tip of your finger.

Photo courtesy of Dell Computer Corp.

PEN WITH TOUCH-SENSITIVE DISPLAY

These students are using a pen with a tablet PC's touch-sensitive display to interact remotely via a wireless link to the school's server computer and the Internet.

Courtesy of Xybernaut

JOYSTICK AND GAME PAD

This Microsoft Sidewinder Force Feedback Pro (joystick) and the Gravis Stinger (game pad) are designed specifically for PC action games and flight simulation programs. They move airplanes, aliens, and monsters, as well as the mouse pointers. The Sidewinder is both an input and output device. It provides tactile output in the form of force feedback (vibration and pressure) to add realism to the gaming experience.

Courtesy of Advanced Gravis Computer Technology Ltd.

DIGITIZER TABLET AND PEN

Infrared technology enables handwritten notes and drawings to be transferred to Palm organizers, such as the Palm VII shown here. As users write on the notepad with the SmartPen™, their notes and drawings are instantly transferred to the Palm. This digitizer tablet and pen gives users the best of both worlds.

Courtesy of Seiko Instruments USA Inc.

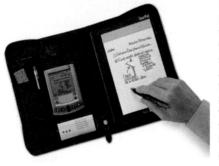

TRACKPOINT

The trackpoint is conveniently located within the keyboard of this IBM ThinkPad i series notebook PC.

Courtesy of International Business Machines Corporation

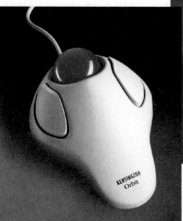

TRACKBALL

This Kensington Orbit Trackball is a mouse alternative that reduces wrist and elbow fatigue and, therefore, the risk of carpal tunnel syndrome.

Courtesy of Kensington Technology Group

CROSSHAIR AND DIGITIZER

This ALTEK digitizer uses a crosshair for medical imaging. The backlighting system enables the digitizing of x-rays for such applications as radiation treatment planning.

Courtesy of ALTEK Corporation

FIGURE 6–8 | SCANNERS AND SCANNER APPLICATIONS

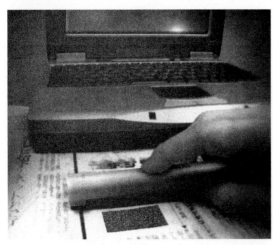

THE INTACTA.CODE™
The bar-code has taken on a new meaning with the recent invention of the INTACTA.CODE™. This print bar code is capable of storing photo images, MP3 music files, gaming software demos, or anything else that can be digitized. When newspaper or magazine readers scan the printed INTACTA.CODE™ into their computers, special software, working with standard scanners, decodes the dot pattern to the original electronic file.

Courtesy of Intacta Technologies

BAR CODES IN MANUFACTURING
Here at the Dell Computer Corporation manufacturing facility in Austin, Texas, bar codes on boxed parts are scanned as they are moved throughout the warehouse to ensure efficient inventory management, a goal of every manufacturing company.

Courtesy of Dell Computer Corp.

PERSONAL SCANNERS
Consumers are now using bar code scanners small enough to hang on a keychain to make purchases or gather information with one scan of a bar code. The tiny scanner allows consumers to scan products and services anywhere, anytime. Transactions such as purchases, inquiries, and payments can be made while commuting on a train or anywhere else. To retrieve the data contained in the scanner, the unit synchs up (synchronizes) with a PC, and uploads the data stored in its memory, enabling consumers to complete online transactions or locate additional information about the product or services of interest.

Courtesy of Symbol Technology, Inc.

FIGURE 6–8 continued

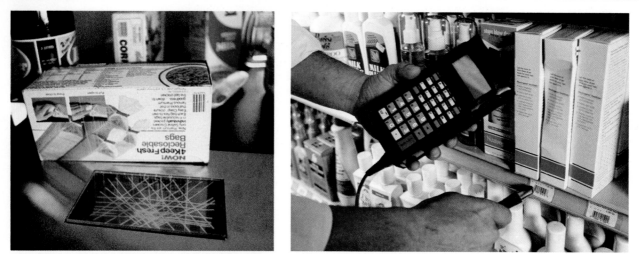

SCANNERS IN THE SUPERMARKET: STATIONARY AND HANDHELD
Supermarket checkout systems are now an established cost-saving technology. The automated systems use stationary laser scanners to read the bar codes that identify each item (left). Price and product descriptions are retrieved from a database and recorded on the sales slip. Stockers use handheld scanners to order products and update the database (right).

Courtesy of International Business Machines Corporation

EXPEDITING THE 2000 U.S. CENSUS
One of the reasons the 2000 U.S. census went smoothly is that the millions of completed mark-sense census forms were read by page scanners enabling the data to be entered directly to the system for processing.

Courtesy of Lockheed Martin Corporation

image. Handheld contact scanners make contact as they are brushed over the printed matter to be read. Laser-based scanners are more versatile and can read data passed near the scanning area. Scanners of both technologies can recognize printed characters and various types of bar codes. Scanners used for OCR or bar code applications can be classified into three basic categories.

- *Handheld label scanners.* These devices read data on price tags, shipping labels, inventory part numbers, book ISBNs, and the like. Handheld label scanners, sometimes called **wand scanners,** use either contact or laser technology. You have probably seen both types used in libraries and various retail stores. Hoping to add value to its magazine, *Forbes* has distributed almost a million handheld scanners to its subscribers for free. Readers use the scanners to scan "cues" that take them directly to related Web sites for more information.

- *Stationary label scanners.* These devices, which rely exclusively on laser technology, are used in the same types of applications as wand scanners. Stationary scanners are common in grocery stores and discount stores.

- *Document scanners.* Document scanners are capable of scanning documents of varying sizes. Document scanners read envelopes at the U.S. Postal Service, and they also read turnaround documents for utility companies. A **turnaround document** is computer-produced output that we can read and is ultimately returned as computer-readable input to a computer system. For example, when you pay your utility bills, you return a check and a stub for the invoice (the turnaround document). The stub is scanned, and payment information is entered automatically to the utility company's system.

Most retail stores and distribution warehouses, and all overnight couriers, are seasoned users of scanner technology. Salespeople, inventory management personnel, and couriers would much prefer to wave their "magic" wands than enter data one character at a time.

Optical Mark Recognition

You are probably familiar with one of the oldest scanner technologies, *optical mark recognition* (OMR). One of the most popular applications for these scanners is grading tests. All of us at one time or another has marked answers on a preprinted multiple-choice test answer form. The marked forms are scanned and corrected, comparing the position of the "sense marks" with those on a master to grade the test. The results of surveys and questionnaires often are tabulated with OMR technology.

Optical Scanners

Optical scanners can read written text and hard copy images then translate the information into an electronic format that can be interpreted by and stored on computers. The image to be scanned can be a photograph, a drawing, an insurance form, a medical record—anything that can be digitized. Once an image has been digitized and entered to the computer system, it can be retrieved, displayed, modified, merged with text, stored, sent via data communications to one or several remote computers, and even faxed. Manipulating and managing scanned images, known as **image processing,** is becoming increasingly important, especially with recent advances in optical storage technologies (for example, rewritable CD-ROM and DVD-RAM). Organizations everywhere are replacing space-consuming metal filing cabinets and millions of hard copy documents, from tax returns to warrantee cards, with their electronic equivalents. Image processing's space-saving incentive, along with its ease of document retrieval, is making the image scanner a must-have peripheral in most offices. The same is true of the home as people begin converting their family photo albums and other archives to electronic format.

Page and Hand Image Scanners

Image scanners are of two types: *page* and *hand.* Virtually all modern scanners can scan in both black and white images and color images. *Page image scanners* work like copy machines. That is, the image to be scanned is placed face down on the scanning surface, covered, then scanned. The result is a high-resolution digitized image. Inexpensive sheet-fed page scanners weighing less than two pounds accept the document to be scanned in a slot. The *hand image scanner* is rolled manually over the image to be scanned. About five inches in width, hand image scanners are appropriate for capturing small images or portions of large images.

In addition to scanning photos and other graphic images, image scanners can also scan and interpret the alphanumeric characters on regular printed pages. People use page scanners to translate printed hard copy to computer-readable format. For applications that demand this type of translation, page scanners can minimize or eliminate the need for key entry. Today's image scanners and the accompanying OCR software are very sophisticated. Together they can read and interpret the characters from most printed material, such as a printed letter or a page from this book.

Image Processing: Eliminating the Paper Pile

Companies and even individuals are becoming buried in paper, literally. In some organizations, paper files take up most of the floor space. Moreover, finding what you want may take several minutes to hours. Or, you may never find what you want. Image processing applications scan and index thousands, even millions, of documents (see Figure 6-9). Once these scanned documents are on the computer system, they can be easily retrieved and manipulated. For example, banks use image processing to archive canceled checks and to archive documents associated with mortgage loan servicing. Insurance companies use image processing in claims processing applications.

Images are scanned into a digital format that can be stored on disk, often optical laser disc because of its huge capacity. For example, a decade's worth of hospital medical records can be scanned and stored on a handful of optical laser discs that fit easily on a single shelf. The images are organized so they can be retrieved in seconds rather than minutes or hours. Medical personnel who need a hard copy can simply print one out in a matter of seconds.

The State of Louisiana Department of Public Safety routinely supplies driver information to other state agencies and to outside organizations, such as insurance companies, and is a perfect example of how image processing can reduce the need for paper while making records more accessible. The department has the dual problem of keeping up with thousands of documents received each week and with servicing thousands of requests for driver information, mostly for problem drivers. The amount of paperwork involved could be staggering. However, because this department has gone to image processing for driver information, other state agencies have direct access to the image bank over communication lines, and the department has no trouble handling outside requests for information. The department's long-range plan calls for using image processing to minimize or eliminate paper and microfilm in as many applications as possible.

The real beauty of image processing is that the digitized material can be easily manipulated. For example, any image can be easily faxed to another location (without being printed). A fax is sent and received as an image. The content on the fax or any electronic image can be manipulated in many ways. OCR software can be used to translate any printed text on the stored image to an electronic format (see Figure 6-9). For example, a doctor might wish to pull selected printed text from various patient images into a word processing document to compile a summary of a patient's condition. The doctor can even select specific graphic images (X-rays, photos, or drawings) from the patient's record for inclusion in the summary report.

MAGNETIC STRIPES AND SMART CARDS

The magnetic stripes on the back of charge cards and badges offer another means of data entry at the source. The magnetic stripes are encoded with data appropriate for specific applications. For example, your account number and personal identification number are encoded on a card for automatic teller machines.

Magnetic stripes contain much more data per unit of space than do printed characters or bar codes. Plus, because they cannot be read visually, they are perfect for storing confidential data, such as a personal identification number. Employee cards, security badges, and library cards (see Figure 6-10) often contain authorization data for access to physically secured areas, such as a computer center, or to protected resources, such as e-books in a library. To gain access, an employee or patron inserts a card or badge into a **badge reader.** This device reads and checks the authorization code before permitting the individual to enter a secured area. When badge readers are linked to a central computer, that computer can maintain a chronological log of people entering or leaving secured areas.

The **smart card** looks like any garden-variety charge card, but with a twist. It has an embedded microprocessor with up to 32 KB of nonvolatile memory (see Figure 6-11). Because the smart card can hold more information, has processing capability, and is almost impossible to duplicate, smart cards may soon replace cards with magnetic stripes. Already, smart cards are gaining widespread acceptance in Europe and in the United States, especially smart cards with *stored value*. The dual-function stored-value smart card serves as a credit card and as a replacement for cash. Customers with these cards can go to automatic teller machines to transfer electronic cash from their checking or savings account to the card's memory. They are used like cash at the growing number of stores that accept stored-value cards. Each time the card is used, the purchase amount is deducted from the card's stored value. To reload the card with more electronic cash, the card's owner must return to an automatic teller machine. The stored-value smart card is another big step toward the inevitable elimination of cash.

SPEECH RECOGNITION

Speech recognition was possible over 20 years ago, but only when the words were spoken in discrete speech (slowly, one word at a time) to an expensive, room-sized mainframe computer. The power of

THE CRYSTAL BALL:
Talking with Computers Although successful for many people, speech recognition remains a novelty with most PC users. Speech recognition has become a mature killer app and will begin to expand into new applications. For example, it is likely that you will be able to record the text of a telephone conversation in your cellular phone's memory, should you so desire. You will be able to walk into your room, speak "Poseidon," or some other system wake-up command, and then begin your "conversation" with your computer, speaking commands and entering text. Our PCs and other electronic devices and appliances will be constantly listening for our wake-up command.

FIGURE 6–9 IMAGE PROCESSING

PAGE SCANNER
Inexpensive image scanners have given rise to a variety of image processing applications. Here, a graphic artist scans an image into the system on a page scanner.

Photo courtesy of Hewlett-Packard Company

HAND SCANNER
A manager uses a hand scanner to convert text in a magazine into electronic text that can be inserted into a word processing document.

Courtesy of Caere Corporation

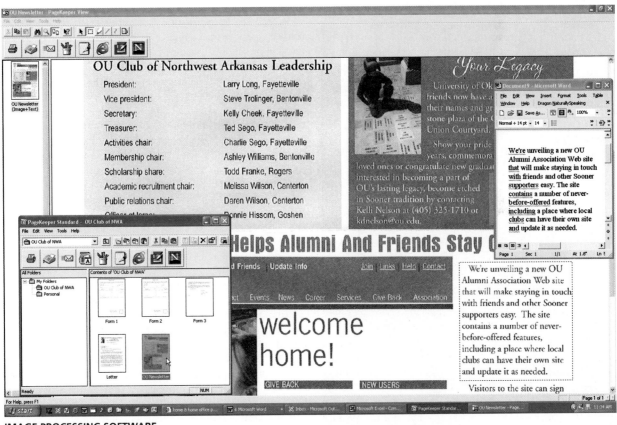

IMAGE PROCESSING SOFTWARE
PageKeeper image processor software helps you organize documents in your computer. The software lets you scan documents, such as this newsletter, into a folder system (bottom left). Once in the system, documents are retrieved and viewed easily (background). You also can make annotations on documents and copy contents to other documents (see the Word document on the right).

FIGURE 6-10 Intelligent Plastic
Smart cards and magnetic stripe cards have a variety of applications, including banking, medical records, security, and more. In the photo, a girl uses her card to gain access to the library's automated resources via a thin client workstation.

PCs has finally caught up with speech-recognition technology. With the modern speech-recognition software and a quality microphone, the typical off-the-shelf PC is able to accept spoken words in continuous speech (as you would normally talk) at speeds of up to 125 words a minute. Speech recognition has made hands-free interaction possible for surgeons during operations and for quality control personnel who use their hands to describe defects as they are detected. Many executives now dictate, rather than keyboard, their e-mail messages. Also, speech recognition is a tremendous enabling technology for the physically challenged.

Speech recognition has emerged as the newest *killer application*. In the PC world, a killer application has a profound impact on personal computing. The "killer app" handle places speech-recognition systems alongside some pretty good company: word processing, spreadsheet, database, and Internet browser applications. Speech recognition capability is now built into modern versions of the Microsoft Office suite. Software companies offer more sophisticated and/or application-specific speech recognition software (law, medicine, engineering, and so on).

Speaker-Dependent Speech Recognition

If you were to purchase a **speech-recognition system** for your PC, you would receive software, a generic vocabulary database, and a high-quality microphone with noise-canceling capabilities. Successful speech recognition depends on a strong, clear signal from the microphone. The microphone, which is mounted

on a headset, filters out general office noise, including ringing phones and slamming doors. The size of the vocabulary database ranges from 30,000 words for general dictation to more than 300,000 words for technical, legal, or medical dictation.

Once you have installed the hardware and software, you are ready to speak to the computer. The basic steps involved in speech recognition are illustrated in Figure 6-12. The system will accept most of your spoken words (see Figure 6-13). However, you can *train* the system to accept virtually all of your words. It helps to train the system to recognize your unique speech patterns. We all sound different, even to a computer. To train the system, simply read to it for about an hour—the longer the better. Even if a word is said twice in succession, it will probably have a different inflection or nasal quality. The system uses artificial intelligence techniques to learn our speech patterns and update the vocabulary database accordingly. The typical speech-recognition system never stops learning, for it is always fine-tuning the vocabulary so it can recognize words with greater speed and accuracy. Each user on a given PC would need to customize his or her own vocabulary database. To further customize our personal vocabulary database, we can add words that are unique to our working environment, such as acronyms or product names (for example, QRCV or Xbox).

It is only a matter of time before we all will be communicating with our PCs in spoken English rather than through time-consuming keystrokes. Already, thousands of attorneys, doctors, journalists, and others who routinely rely on dictation and writing are enjoying the benefits of speech recognition.

Bill Gates of Microsoft has said that we will soon be able to operate our computers by verbally conversing with them. He also indicated that one of the options available to us, as users, would be to give our PCs a personality. What kind of personality would you give your computer: somber, serious, happy-go-lucky, polite, rude, frivolous, Valley girl, punk? The possibilities are endless.

Speaker-Independent Speech Recognition

Some speech-recognition systems are speaker-independent; that is, they can accept words spoken by anyone. Such systems are restricted to accepting only a limited number of words and tasks.

FIGURE 6-11 Smart Card Production
Each smart card has embedded nonvolatile memory and a processor (shown here) that can be loaded with information and programmed for a wide variety of applications.

However, speaker-independent speech-recognition systems are becoming more sophisticated, able to interpret more vocabulary from a wider audience with improved accuracy.

Today, speech-enabled applications are being implemented in all types of industries. For example, thousands of salespeople in the field can enter an order simply by calling in to the company's computer and stating the customer number, item number, and quantity. Several airline companies offer a speech-enabled airline reservation system. Telephone companies have introduced speech-enabled directory service. Modern speech-enabled systems speak to the users more like a human operator might. For example, rather than saying, "Would you like me to repeat the menu options?" it might say, "I did not understand you. Would you mind repeating that?" The system also allows people who are experienced with the system to "barge in" in the middle of a speech-response statement so that calls can be completed more quickly.

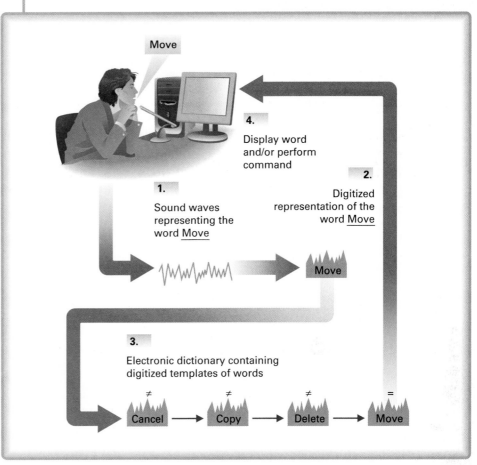

FIGURE 6–12

SPEECH RECOGNITION
The sound waves created by the spoken word *Move* are digitized by the computer. The digitized template is matched against templates of other words in the electronic dictionary. When the computer finds a match, it displays a written version of the word.

Move

4.
Display word and/or perform command

1.
Sound waves representing the word Move

2.
Digitized representation of the word Move

Move

3.
Electronic dictionary containing digitized templates of words

Cancel → Copy → Delete → Move

PATTERN RECOGNITION: "VISION" SYSTEMS

Some data are best entered and processed visually. However, the simulation of human senses, especially vision, is extremely complex. A computer does not actually see and interpret an image the way a human being does. Computers need cameras for their "eyesight." To create a visual database, a **pattern recognition system,** via a camera, digitizes the images of all objects to be identified, and then stores the digitized form of each image in the database. When the system is placed in operation, the camera enters each newly "seen" image into a digitizer. The system then compares the digitized image to be interpreted with the prerecorded digitized images in the computer's database, much like a speech-recognition system does with speech input. The computer identifies the image by matching the structure of the input image with those images in the database. This process is illustrated by the digital vision-inspection system in Figure 6-14.

As you can imagine, pattern recognition systems are best suited to very specialized tasks in which only a few images will be encountered. These tasks are usually simple, monotonous ones, such as inspection. For example, in Figure 6-14, a digital vision-inspection system on an assembly line rejects those parts that do not meet certain quality control specifications. The vision system performs rudimentary gauging inspections, and then signals the computer to take appropriate action. Security using biometric identification is another popular application for pattern recognition (see Figure 6-15).

Vision input offers great promise for the future. Can you imagine traveling by car from your hometown to Charleston, South Carolina, without the burden of actually driving? Sound far-fetched? Not really. DaimlerChrysler, the automobile maker, is actively developing a system that will allow you to do just that. The copilot system is a step up from cruise control, freeing the driver from both the accelerator pedal and the steering wheel. Like cruise control, the driver would remain behind the wheel, even when the system is operational. The foundation technology is vision input. When traveling down the German Autobahn, the system "sees" the lines on either side of the lane and makes minor adjustments in direction to keep the automobile centered in the lane. This part of the system works well; however,

FIGURE 6-13 TALKING TO COMPUTERS

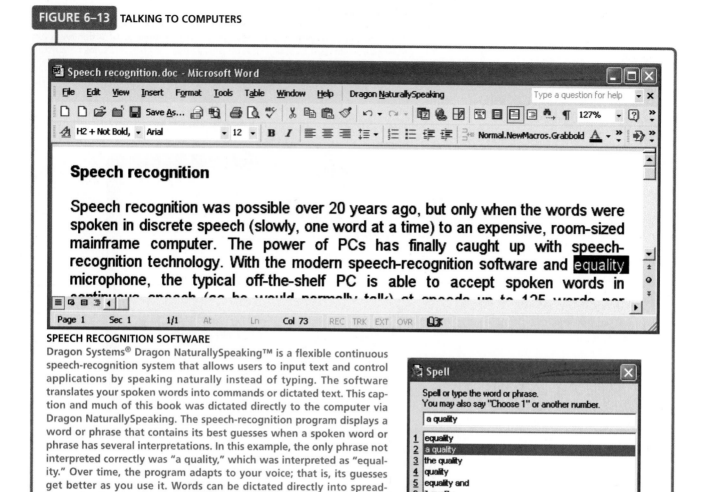

SPEECH RECOGNITION SOFTWARE
Dragon Systems® Dragon NaturallySpeaking™ is a flexible continuous speech-recognition system that allows users to input text and control applications by speaking naturally instead of typing. The software translates your spoken words into commands or dictated text. This caption and much of this book was dictated directly to the computer via Dragon NaturallySpeaking. The speech-recognition program displays a word or phrase that contains its best guesses when a spoken word or phrase has several interpretations. In this example, the only phrase not interpreted correctly was "a quality," which was interpreted as "equality." Over time, the program adapts to your voice; that is, its guesses get better as you use it. Words can be dictated directly into spreadsheet, database, presentation graphics, and any other type of software that accepts text.

SPEECH RECOGNITION IN A MEDICAL CLINIC
This radiologist (right) is dictating his findings directly to the computer. He can also issue commands, such as "move left," "paste that," or "give me help."

Courtesy of Dragon Systems, Inc.

DaimlerChrysler engineers have many hurdles to overcome (exit ramps, pedestrians, and so on) before you see this feature in showroom automobiles. Someday the safest drivers on the road will not be driving at all.

DIGITAL CAMERAS: DIGICAMS

We all know that a picture is worth 1000 words, whether at home or the office. We now have the tools to capture still and video imagery, easily and economically. Personal computing and the Net have made it easy to share these images and video with our neighbors or with friends around the world.

Capturing Still Images

Most people still take photographs in the traditional manner—with a camera and film. We drop off our rolls of film for developing, and then we enjoy

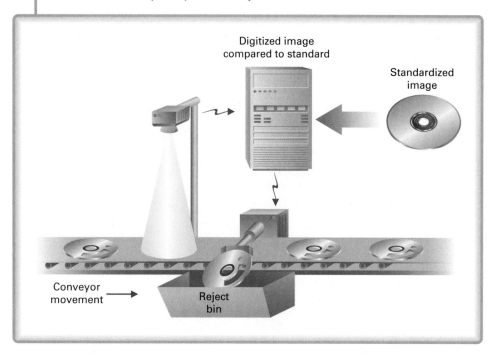

FIGURE 6–14 **DIGITAL VISION-INSPECTION SYSTEM**
In this digital vision-inspection system, the system examines parts for defects. If the digitized image of the part does not match a standard digital image, the defective part is placed in a reject bin.

the results in the form of prints and slides. Some people use image scanners to digitize photos for use in newsletters, magazines, and so on. This process may change forever as the price of **digital cameras** continues to plummet. You can get a good digital camera for as little as $200 and a very good one for less than $500. Those used by professional photographers are considerably more expensive. When you take a picture with a modern **digicam**, a digitized image goes straight to onboard flash memory in the form of a memory stick. Once in the interchangeable memory cards or "stick," it can be uploaded to a PC and manipulated (viewed, printed, modified, and so on) as you would other graphic images (see Figure 6-16).

There are many applications for digital cameras. Customers from all over the world make special requests to a designer jewelry store. Store personnel take photos of available merchandise from various angles, and then they e-mail the photos to the customer. An automobile repair center takes photos of all major repair jobs to show customers exactly what the problem was and for training purposes. To help them to adjust braces better, orthodontists use digital cameras to track the migration of patients' teeth. Online retailers use digital cameras when preparing product Web pages, thereby skipping the film developing and scanning process altogether. One of the most popular applications is expanding the family photo album. Typically, photos are stored permanently on hard disk, optical laser discs, or high-density interchangeable disks, such as the Zip disk.

Photo images are an effective way to communicate. Now that the digital camera has become a popular consumer item, images are streaming through the Internet by the millions to grandmothers, parents, old friends, business colleagues, customers, clients, and just about everyone else. Most images are sent as attachments to e-mail. Here is a hint. To minimize upload/download time, send images in an efficient file format, such as JPG (or JPEG), and at a resolution that fits how the images are to be viewed/used. Choose high resolution only if the image is to be printed. The smaller the file, the more quickly it downloads.

Once you own a digital camera, the cost of photography plummets because the costly, time-consuming developing processing is

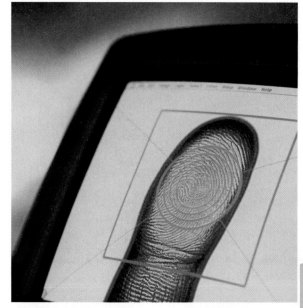

FIGURE 6–15 Pattern Recognition Applications
Security is an emerging application for pattern recognition, including fingerprint and facial identification.

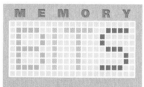
FIGURE 6–16

DIGITAL PHOTOGRAPHY
We may be entering an era of filmless photography. This image of Niagara Falls was taken with a digital camera, the one in the inset. You can capture, view, print, store, and transmit almost any image. Images are stored on interchangeable memory cards (see inset) or diskettes, then uploaded to a PC and used in countless applications, from the family photo album to training software.

Photo courtesy of Intel Corporation

Long and Associates

eliminated. With digital cameras, you can take all the photos you want and just keep the really good ones. With the cost of high-resolution digital cameras about that of a quality 35-mm camera, a lot more people are going digital for photography.

Desktop Video Cameras

Already the relative inexpensive digital video camera (around $70) is standard on some PCs. The desktop **digital video camera** lets you capture motion video in the area of the PC. Two popular uses for these cameras are to capture video for real-time Internet-based videophone conversations and as Webcams. If you have a PC, videophone software, an Internet connection, and a digital video camera, you are set to have videophone conversations, whereby you both see and hear the other party. Your digital video camera lets the other person see you and his or hers lets him or her see you. **Webcams** are digital video cameras that are continuously linked to the Internet, providing still and video imagery from thousands of sites, usually 24 hours a day. Webcams are located in zoos, classrooms, offices, living rooms, forests, on top of tall buildings, and just about any other place you can imagine beaming stills or video of whatever is happening into cyberspace.

Digital video cameras have many applications. They are used to create video content for Web pages. People use them to capture low-resolution still images. More and more companies are opting to save the airfare and have videoconferences instead. The emergence of low-cost rewritable optical disc storage means that you can use digital video cameras for the family video, too. Digital video imagery can really eat up the megabytes on a hard disk, so people often move captured video to optical laser discs. A CD-R will hold about 15 minutes of video.

FIGURE 6–17 Digital Moviemaker
This RCA digital camcorder can capture favorite scenes that can be shared with your friends and relatives. The digital video can be viewed via TV or PC. Within a few years, most new camcorders will be digital.

Photo courtesy of RCA

Digital Camcorders

Handheld **digital camcorders** offer another way to capture video (see Figure 6-17). Digital camcorders offer greater portability and the quality of the video is higher than that of desktop cameras, but so is the price ($500 to $1000). Video is stored on digital tape, but it can be uploaded to a PC for digital video editing. Digital video is edited easily, that is, parts can be deleted, moved, or copied to meet application needs.

Another way to capture video is to use a standard analog camcorder or VCR in conjunction with a **video capture card.** Simply plug the cable from the camera or VCR into the expansion card and hit the record or play button. The analog signal is sent to the video capture card where it is digitized for viewing, editing, and storage.

HANDHELD AND WEARABLE DATA ENTRY DEVICES

Some close-to-the-source data entry tasks still require the use of some keystrokes and are best performed on handheld data entry devices. The typical *handheld data entry device,* which is actually a small computer, has the following:

- A limited external keyboard or a soft keyboard (displayed on a touch-sensitive screen)
- A small display that may be touch sensitive
- Some kind of storage capability for the data, usually solid-state nonvolatile flash memory
- A scanning device, capable of optical character recognition

After the data have been entered, the portable data entry device is linked with a central computer, and data are *uploaded* (transmitted from the data entry device to a central computer) for processing.

Stock clerks in department stores routinely use handheld devices to collect and enter reorder data. As clerks visually check the inventory level, they identify the items that need to be restocked. They first scan the price tag (which identifies the item), and then enter the number to be ordered on the keyboard.

Handheld and wearable computers, introduced in Chapter 1, frequently are used as data entry devices (see Figure 6-18). Some PCs have pressure-sensitive writing pads that recognize hand-printed alphanumeric characters. Also, they permit the entering of graphic information. For example, police officers use handheld PCs to document accidents, including recording the handwritten signatures of the participants.

FIGURE 6–18 Wearable Information Retrieval and Data Entry Hardware
This wearable PC is worn around the head and on the waist. This U.S. Army mechanic enters data and retrieves information in a hands-free environment, eliminating the need to carry maintenance manuals during field maneuvers.

Courtesy of Xybernaut

TOUCH SCREEN MONITORS

We usually think of monitors as output devices, but some enable input, as well. **Touch screen monitors** have pressure-sensitive overlays that can detect pressure and the exact location of that pressure. Users simply touch the desired icon or menu item with their finger. Educators realize that we are born with an ability to point and touch, and are beginning to use touch screen technology in the classroom to teach everything from reading to geography. Interactive touch screen systems are installed in shopping centers, zoos, airports, grocery stores, post offices, and many other public locations.

6-1.1	Input devices translate data into a form that can be interpreted by a computer. (T/F)
6-1.2	The wheel on the wheel mouse makes it easier to drag icons. (T/F)
6-1.3	The Universal Product Code (UPC) was originally used by which industry: (a) supermarket, (b) hardware, (c) mail-order merchandising, or (d) steel?
6-1.4	Which is not generally considered a source-data automation technology: (a) keyboard, (b) OCR, (c) speech recognition, or (d) UPC?
6-1.5	Memory on smart cards is: (a) volatile, (b) nonvolatile, (c) inert, or (d) never more than 1024 bits.
6-1.6	The Webcam is associated with all but which of the following: (a) digital video, (b) the World Wide Web, (c) touchpad input, or (d) The Internet?

SECTION SELF-CHECK

WHY THIS SECTION IS IMPORTANT TO YOU

There are hundreds of output devices that provide hard copy output, video, and audio, all with different features and price tags. It's up to you to determine how big, clear, fast, or loud you want these devices to be. Familiarizing yourself with the options should help you stretch your PC dollar and get exactly those devices that meet your personal computing output needs.

6-2 | Output Devices

Output devices translate bits and bytes into a form we can understand. There are many output devices, including monitors, printers, plotters, multimedia projectors, and voice-response systems, all presented in this section.

MONITORS AND GRAPHICS ADAPTERS

The output device we are most familiar with is the monitor, which displays system output. Monitors come in all shapes and sizes to meet a variety of application needs (see Figure 6-19). We describe monitors and their capabilities in terms of the following:

- Technology
- Graphics adapter (the electronic link between the processor and the monitor)
- Size (diagonal dimension of the display screen)
- Resolution (detail of the display)
- Refresh rate

Technology: CRT and Flat-Panel

The basic technology employed in the bulky, boxy **CRT monitors** that you see used with most desktop personal computers has been around since the 1940s. These monitors offer excellent resolution at a very competitive price. However, their footprint, the amount of space they take up on a desk, remains a user concern. The alternative, the **flat-panel monitor,** which is found on all notebook PCs, has a much smaller footprint. Some of the space-saving flat-panel monitors are less than 1/4-inch thick. The more expensive flat-panel monitor is becoming an increasingly viable option for the PC user as the price continues to drop toward that of the CRT. You must still pay a premium to save desk space and energy, as much as two to three times the cost per unit of viewing area. It is inevitable that the space-saving, energy-saving flat-panel displays will eventually displace the traditional CRT-type monitors for desktop PCs.

Flat-panel monitors use a variety of technologies, the most common being *LCD* (liquid crystal display). LCD monitors are *active matrix* or *passive matrix*. Active matrix monitors have higher refresh rates and better contrast, making for a more brilliant display. Active matrix LCD monitors are also known as TFT (thin film transistor) LCD monitors. Millions of transistors are needed for TFT LCD monitors. Color monitors need three transistors for each pixel: one each for red, green, and blue. Active matrix LCD displays are more expensive than passive matrix displays; therefore, active matrix LCD displays are usually associated with the better notebook PCs.

Graphics Adapters

The **graphics adapter** is the device controller for the monitor (see Figure 6-20). Some are built into the motherboard. On desktop PCs, graphics adapters usually are inserted into an *AGP bus* expansion slot on the motherboard. The monitor cable is plugged into the graphics adapter board to link the monitor with the processor. All display signals en route to the monitor pass through the graphics adapter, where the digital signals are converted to signals compatible with the monitor's display capabilities.

Most existing graphics adapters have their own RAM, called **video RAM** or **VRAM,** whereby they prepare monitor-bound images for display. The size of the video RAM is important in that it determines the number of possible colors and resolution of the display, as well as the speed at which signals can be sent to the monitor. Gamers, those who do video editing, and others who place extreme demands on graphics adapters will want to upgrade the standard graphics adapter to one with enough VRAM to handle heavy video demands. The newer AGP graphics adapters enjoy much better performance by using the PC system's RAM directly.

Monitor Size

Display screens vary in size from 5 to 60 inches (measured diagonally). The monitor size for newly purchased desktop PCs has inched up from 14 inches to 17 inches over the past 10 years and is now moving toward 19 inches. If your applications involve the heavy use of graphics, such as computer-aided design or commercial art, or you routinely switch between a variety of open programs, you might want to consider a 20-plus inch monitor. The larger displays, 30 inches and up, usually are designed for viewing by two or more people.

PERSONAL COMPUTING:
Sharing Peripheral Devices Modern operating systems make it easy for us to set up a network in our home or in a dormitory suite. There is no reason for every PC to be configured with a dedicated printer, scanner, and/or DVD burner. Printers can be shared and files are transferred easily between networked computers; so, if you do not mind walking to another room to pick up your printout or scan a photo, consider the economics of peripheral sharing.

FIGURE 6–19 MONITORS

46-INCH TFT LCD PANEL DISPLAY
This 46-inch TFT LCD panel offers 1280 by 720 resolution and a 170° viewing angle in all directions.

Courtesy of Samsung Electronics Co., Ltd.

DURABLE MONITORS
In video arcades, the action takes place on large, durable monitors.

Photo courtesy of Intel Corporation

FLAT PANEL MONITORS
Flat-panel LCD monitors may be the wave of the future for desktop PCs.

Photo courtesy of Intel Corporation

MULTIPLE MONITOR ENVIRONMENTS
Monitors are an integral component of virtually all computer-based applications, including video editing. This one-person studio employs a variety of high-resolution CRT and flat panel monitors.

Photo courtesy of Hewlett-Packard Company

TOUCH SCREEN MONITORS
A growing number of ATMs (shown here) and public information kiosks use touch screen monitors with input/output capabilities.

Courtesy of Diebold, Incorporated

WORLD'S SMALLEST MONITOR
Kopin Corporation's CyberDisplay™ is the world's smallest high-performance, high-resolution, full-function information display. The microdisplays are especially designed for portable products, such as with cellular phone applications (videophone, e-mail, and so on), shown here, and also with wearable computers.

Courtesy of Kopin Corporation

FIGURE 6–20 High-Performance Graphics Adapter
This Sun Microsystems Elite3D graphics system enables real-time interactive 3D visualization, which is necessary for such applications as 3D design and modeling, dynamic simulation, and video effects.

Courtesy of Sun Microsystems, Inc.

Monitor Resolution

Monitors vary in their quality of output, or *resolution*. Resolution depends on the *number of pixels that can be displayed,* the *number of bits used to represent each pixel,* and the *dot pitch of the monitor.* A **pixel** is an addressable point on the screen, a point to which light can be directed under program control. The typical monitor is set to operate with a *screen area* of 786,432 addressable points in 1024 columns by 768 rows; however, most can have screen area settings ranging from 640 by 480 to 2000 by 1600. The 2000 by 1600 setting has over three million addressable points. The higher the number of pixels, the more information you can display on your screen.

Each pixel, short for *picture element* (see Figure 6-21), can be assigned a color or, for monochrome monitors, a shade of gray. **Gray scales** refer to the number of shades of a color that can be shown on a monochrome monitor's screen. Most color monitors mix red, green, and blue to achieve a spectrum of colors, and are called **RGB monitors.** One of the user options is the number of bits used to display each pixel, sometimes referred to as **color depth.** In 8-bit color mode, 256 colors are possible (2^8 = 256). The 16-bit mode *high-color* mode yields 65,536 colors. *True color* options, either 24-bit or 32-bit mode, provide photo-quality viewing with over 16 million to over 4 billion colors. There is a trade-off between resolution and system performance. Differences in color depth are illustrated in Figure 6-22. Greater resolutions demand more of the processor, leaving less capacity for other processing tasks.

Its **dot pitch,** or the distance between the centers of adjacent pixels, also affects a monitor's resolution—the lower the dot pitch number, the greater the number of pixels in the display. Any dot pitch equal to or less than .28 mm (millimeters) provides a sharp image. A dot pitch of .25 is even better. When you have an opportunity, use a magnifying glass to examine the pixels and observe the dot pitch on your computer's monitor.

Refresh Rate

The monitor's *refresh rate* also affects the quality of the display. The phosphor coating on a monitor's CRT (cathode-ray tube) must be repainted or refreshed 50 to over 100 times each second (Hz) to maintain clarity of the image. Generally, monitors with faster refresh rates have fewer flickers and are easier on the eyes.

FIGURE 6–21 Pixels
This photo of children enjoying a snow day off from school illustrates how computers use picture elements, or pixels, to portray digital images. Thousands (even millions) of pixels, each a single point on a graphics image, are arranged in rows and columns to create the image. In the inset image, the pixels are so close together they portray continuous color. The blowup highlights the individual pixels.

LCD PROJECTORS

Businesspeople have found that sophisticated and colorful graphics add an aura of professionalism to any report or presentation (see Figure 6-23). This demand for *presentation graphics* has created a need for corresponding output devices. Graphic images can be displayed on a monitor or they can be projected onto a large screen to be viewed by a group of people or an audience with the aid of a **multimedia projector.**

The need for overhead transparencies and 35-mm slides is beginning to fade as presenters discover the ease with which they can create dynamic multimedia presentations, then present them with multimedia projectors. These output devices fall into two categories: *LCD panels* and *LCD projectors.* The LCD panels, which are about the size of a notebook PC, are used with overhead projectors. The LCD panels are placed directly on the overhead projector as you would position a transparency acetate. The light from the overhead projector is directed through an LCD panel and whatever image is on its display is shown on a large screen for all to see. The LCD projectors use their own built-in lens and light source to project the image on the screen.

WEARABLE DISPLAYS

For those knowledge workers who are constantly in motion yet need access to critical information, there is the **wearable display.** Usually the wearable display is worn on a wireless headset, thus untethering us from our personal computer. Of course, the wearable display is standard with wearable PCs. A variety of technologies is emerging for wearable displays, one of which, RSD, eliminates any screen outside of the eye and addresses the retina with a stream of pixels.

There are many uses for wearable displays. For example, privacy-minded people use these displays in crowded areas, such as on an airplane. Mobile workers enjoy the convenience of being able to view needed information as they go about their jobs. For example, airplane quality control inspectors use wearable displays.

PRINTERS

Printers produce hard copy output, such as college term papers, management reports, cash register receipts, labels, memos, and payroll checks. Dozens of manufacturers produce hundreds of printers. There is a printer manufactured to meet the hard copy output requirements of any individual or company, and almost any combination of features can be obtained (see Figure 6-24). You can specify its size (some weigh less than a pound), speed, quality of output, color requirements, and even noise level. PC printers sell for as little as a pair of shoes or for as much as a wardrobe full of clothes. High-speed, high-volume enterprise printers that produce utility bills, credit-card charge summaries, and the like can cost as much as a house.

Any person or company about to purchase a printer must consider:

- What's the budget?
- Is color needed or will black and white do?
- What will be the volume of output (pages per hour, day, or week)?
- How important is the quality of the output?
- What special features are needed (ability to print envelopes, on legal size paper, on multipart forms, on both sides of the paper, and so on)?
- Can printing needs be met with an all-in-one printer/copier/scanner/fax device?
- If the printer is to be shared on a network, what do the other users want?

Think about these considerations as you read about various printer options. Keep in mind that color, additional features, and each increment in speed and quality of output add to the cost of the printer.

Printer technology is ever changing. Three basic technologies dominate the PC printer arena: page (laser), ink-jet, and dot-matrix. The advantages and disadvantages of these technologies are summarized in Figure 6-25. All PC printers have the capability of printing graphs and charts and offer considerable flexibility in the size and style of print. All printers also can print in portrait or landscape format. **Portrait** and **landscape** refer to the orientation of the print on the page. Portrait format is like the page of this book—the lines run parallel to the shorter sides of the page. In contrast, landscape output runs parallel to the longer sides of the page. Landscape is frequently the orientation of choice for spreadsheet outputs with many columns (see Figure 6-26).

FIGURE 6–22   **COLOR DEPTH** The same Niagara Falls image is shown at three levels of color depth: 8 bit with 256 (2^8) possible colors, 16-bit *high color* with 65,536 (2^{16}) possible colors, and 32-bit *true color* with over 4 billion (2^{32}) possible colors.

8-bit

16-bit high color

32-bit true color

FIGURE 6–23 LCD Projectors
LCD projectors are used in conjunction with presentation software, such as Microsoft PowerPoint, and notebook PCs.

Photo courtesy of Hewlett-Packard Company

Page Printers

Nonimpact **page printers** use laser, LED (*light-emitting diode*), LCS (*liquid crystal shutter*), and other laser-like technologies to achieve high-speed hard copy output by printing *a page at a time*. Page printers are also referred to simply as **laser printers.** The operation of a laser-based page printer is illustrated in Figure 6-27. Most of the laser printers in use print shades of gray; however, color laser printers are becoming increasingly popular as their price continues to drop.

Economically priced desktop page printers have become the standard for office printing. These printers, which print at speeds of 4 to 32 pages per minute (ppm) for text-only printing, can run through up to six feet of paper during a business day. Printing in color (when available) and/or printing graphic images may slow down output to about 25% the rated monochrome text-only output speed. Most page printers print on standard letter and legal paper.

FIGURE 6–24 PRINTERS

COLOR PRINTERS
Color printers let users add color to their everyday business (memos, reports, spreadsheets, graphs) and home (banners, invitations, photos) printing needs. The Hewlett-Packard color ink-jet (left) and color laser (right) printers provide high-quality color output. The ink-jet printer can print photo-quality images directly from a digital camera or via a PC.

Photos courtesy of Hewlett-Packard Company

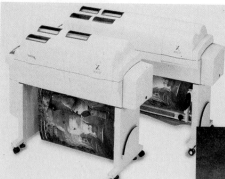

LARGE-FORMAT PRINTERS
Typical applications for this large-format ink-jet printer include point-of-sale displays, billboards, banners, backlit signs, backdrops for photography or video, and trade show graphics. Large-format prints are typically 22 inches and larger.

Courtesy of Xerox Corporation

IT'S A FAX, A PRINTER, A COPIER, AND A SCANNER
This compact and lightweight four-in-one RCA Docuport lets road warriors take the office with them.

Photo courtesy of RCA

SPECIAL-FUNCTION PRINTERS
There is a printer for every job. This printer prints wristbands for hospital patients. The wristbands include bar-coded patient information that can be read with wand scanners.

Courtesy of Diebold, Incorporated

ENTERPRISE PRINTERS
Enterprise printers are designed for high-volume printing (telephone bills, financial statements, insurance coverage summaries, and so on). This IBM printer can print over 400 miles of cut sheet paper per month at 600 dpi resolution.

Courtesy of International Business Machines Corporation. Unauthorized use not permitted.

FIGURE 6–25 PRINTER SUMMARY

	Pros	Cons	Outlook
Page/laser printers	• High-resolution output • Fast (up to 32 ppm) • Quiet • Low cost per page	• High purchase price • Cut sheet only	• High-speed, high-quality page printers will remain the mainstay of office printing for the foreseeable future.
Ink-jet printers	• High-resolution output (but less than that of page) • Quiet • Small footprint • Energy-efficient	• Higher cost per page than laser • Slower than laser (up to 20 ppm) • Cut sheet only • High cost of print cartridges	• Ink-jet printers will remain the choice for any environment, home or office, with low-volume printing needs.
Dot-matrix printers	• Inexpensive • Can print multipart paper • Can print on fanfold paper • Low cost per page • Energy efficient	• Noisy • Low resolution • Poor quality graphics output • Limited font selection	• Dot-matrix printers are used only in those situations that require printing on multipart forms and/or fan-fold paper.
All-in-one (multifunction) printers	• Can function as a printer, a scanner, a copier, and a fax machine • Get four functions for the price of 1 or 2 • Functional specifications close to separate devices (output quality, speed, and so on)	• Can handle only one function at a time • Larger footprint than a comparable printer	• The all-in-one printer has emerged as the choice in the home or home office with copier, scanner, and fax needs, too

FIGURE 6–26

PORTRAIT AND LANDSCAPE ORIENTATION
Shown here are print previews—for a word processing document to be printed in portrait orientation, and a spreadsheet document to be printed in landscape orientation.

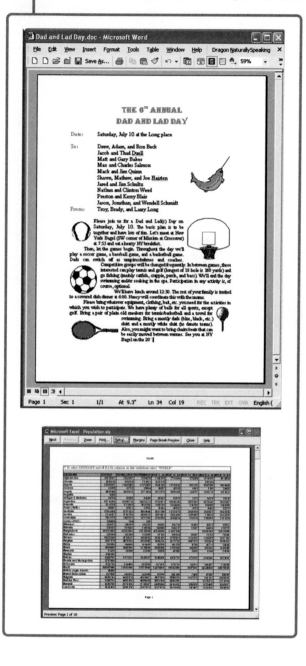

All desktop page printers are capable of producing *near-typeset-quality* (*NTQ*) text and graphics. The resolution (quality of output) of the low-end desktop page printer is 600 *dpi* (dots per inch). High-end desktop page printers are capable of at least 1200 dpi. The dpi qualifier refers to the number of dots that can be printed per linear inch, horizontally or vertically. That is, a 600-dpi printer is capable of printing 360,000 (600 times 600) dots per square inch. Commercial typesetting quality is a minimum of 1200 dpi and is usually in excess of 2000 dpi. Desktop page printers are also quiet (an important consideration in an office setting). Other pros and cons of page printers are summarized in Figure 6-25.

Ink-Jet Printers

To the naked eye, there is little difference between the print quality of nonimpact **ink-jet printers** and page printers. Although the output quality of ink-jet printers is more in line with page printers, their mechanical operation is more like that of the dot-matrix printer because they have a print head that moves back and forth across the paper to write text and create the image (see Figure 6-28). Several independently controlled injection chambers squirt ink droplets on the paper. The droplets, which dry instantly as dots, form the letters and images. Resolutions for the typical ink-jet printer are about that of page printers, 1200 dpi for regular black and white printing and up to 4800 dpi for color printing on premium photo paper. Print speeds for high-quality color output (photos) range from 1 to 2 ppm and print speeds for normal black-and white-only printing are 4 to 8 ppm. Print speeds for draft (low-resolution) output are significantly higher, up to 15 ppm for draft color output and 20 ppm for draft black and white output.

The color ink-jet printer is emerging as the choice for budget-minded consumers. SOHO (small office/home office) buyers also are opting for color ink-jet printers by the millions. The cost of color ink-jet printers ranges from about $100 to about $500. The pros and cons of home/office ink-jet printers are summarized in Figure 6-25.

Large-Format Ink-Jet Printers

Page, ink-jet, and dot-matrix printers are capable of producing page-size graphic output, but are limited in their ability to generate large-scale, high-quality, perfectly proportioned graphic output. For example, on a blueprint, the sides of a 12-foot-square room must be exactly the same length. Architects, engineers, graphics artists, city planners, and others who routinely generate high-precision, hard copy graphic output of widely varying sizes use another hard copy alternative—**large-format ink-jet printers**, also called **plotters.** Plotters use ink-jet technology to print on roll-feed paper up to 4 feet wide and 50 feet in length. Plotters can be used for large printing needs, such as commercial posters or blueprints, or they can be used to produce continuous output, such as plotting earthquake activity or a five-year project activity chart.

Dot-Matrix Printers

The **dot-matrix printer** forms images *one character at a time* as the print head moves across the paper. The dot-matrix printer is an *impact printer;* that is, it uses from 9 to 24 tiny *pins* to hit an ink ribbon and the paper. The dot-matrix printer arranges printed dots to form characters and all kinds of images in much the same way as lights display time and temperature on bank signs. Dot-matrix printers print up to 450 cps (characters per second).

Most dot-matrix printers can accommodate both *cut-sheet paper* and *fanfold paper* (a continuous length of paper that is folded at perforations). The *tractor-feed* that handles fanfold paper is standard with most dot-matrix printers. Impact printers, as opposed to nonimpact printers, touch the paper and can produce carbon copies along with the original. Other pros and cons of dot-matrix printers are summarized in Figure 6-25.

The All-in-One: Print, Fax, Scan, and Copy

Traditionally, businesses have purchased separate machines to handle these paper-related tasks: computer-based printing, facsimile (fax), scanning, and copying (duplicating). The considerable overlap in the technologies used in these machines has enabled manufacturers to create **all-in-one peripheral devices**. These multifunction devices are popular in the small office/home office environments and in other settings where the volume for any of their functions is relatively low. The laser all-in-one peripheral is more expensive than the ink-jet all-in-one.

You can easily pay in excess of $1000 for a printer, a scanner, a copier, and a fax machine. Many people with low volume needs are choosing the all-in-one device for 20 to 40% of the cost of separate peripherals. It's an easy choice when you consider that there is relatively little loss of functionality when compared to separate devices. The popularity of the all-in-one device has exploded since the print/scan/copy quality and the speeds of the all-in-one are now comparable to that of the separate devices.

FIGURE 6–27

LASER-BASED PAGE PRINTER OPERATION
The enclosure of a desktop page printer is removed to expose its inner workings. (A) Prior to printing, an electrostatic charge is applied to a drum. Then laser beam paths to the drum are altered by a spinning multisided mirror. The reflected beams selectively remove the electrostatic charge from the drum. (B) Toner is deposited on those portions of the drum that were affected by the laser beams. The drum is rotated and the toner is fused to the paper to create the image.

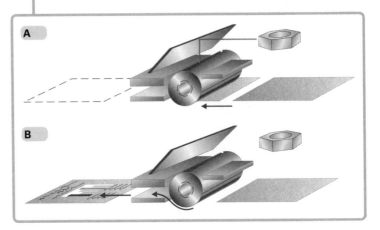

FIGURE 6–28

INK-JET PRINTERS
Ink-jet printers are miniature technological marvels. Tiny droplets of ink, about one millionth the volume of a drop of water, in either blue, red, yellow, or black, are positioned with great precision on the paper to form characters and images. The droplets, which are mixed to form a wide range of possible colors, are squirted from a nozzle less than the width of a human hair. Ink-jet printers use interchangeable cartridges with up to 100 nozzles for each of the four colors. Frequently, black has its own cartridge, whereas the other colors share a separate cartridge. Movement of the print heads and paper are coordinated under program control to squirt the dots to form the text and images. Several methods are used to squirt the droplets onto the paper. One method involves superheating ink in a tiny chamber such that it boils and the pressure forces droplets out the nozzle. The chamber cools, ink flows into the chamber, and a process is repeated every few millionths of a second. The dots of color are overlapped to increase the density and, therefore, the quality of the image.

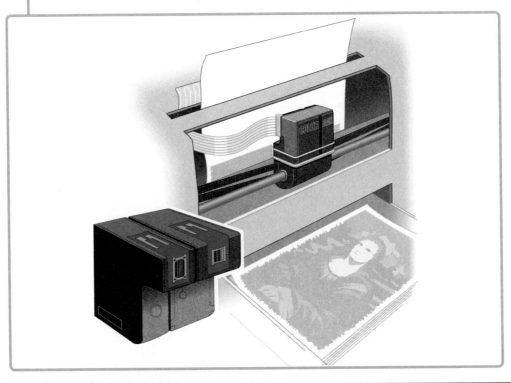

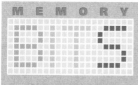

Output Devices

- Monitors
  - CRT
  - Flat-panel
  - Touch screen (input and output)
  - Wearable display
- Printers
  - Page (laser) printers (color option)
  - Ink-jet printers
  - Large-format ink-jet printers (color option)
  - Dot-matrix printers
  - All-in-one multifunction peripherals (print, fax, scan, and copy)
- Multimedia projectors (screen image projection for groups)
- Sound systems
- Voice-response systems
  - Recorded voice
  - Speech synthesis

SOUND SYSTEMS

For the first decade of personal computing small, tinny-sounding speakers came with PCs, primarily to "beep" users when an operation was completed or interaction was needed. PC sound systems have come a long way since then. Today we watch surround sound DVD movies and we listen to CDs and MP3 music recordings on our PCs. We also use our PCs for gaming and multimedia presentations. Simple speakers can no longer meet today's audio output requirements for PCs.

PC sound systems vary from a couple of small speakers embedded in notebook PCs to sophisticated sound systems that provide surround sound with subwoofers, thunderous Dolby Digital audio, and up to 100 watts of power. As with any quality sound system, audio can be adjusted to fit the user's tastes.

VOICE-RESPONSE SYSTEMS

Anyone who has used a telephone has heard "If you're dialing from a touch-tone phone, press 1." You may have driven a car that advised you to "fasten your seat belt." These are examples of talking computers that use output from a voice-response system. There are two types of **voice-response systems:** One uses a *reproduction* of a human voice and other sounds, and the other uses **speech synthesis.** Like monitors, voice-response systems provide temporary, soft-copy output.

The first type of voice-response system selects output from a digitized audio recording of words, phrases, music, alarms, or anything you might record, just as a printer would select characters. In these recorded voice-response systems, the actual analog recordings of sounds are converted into digital data, then permanently stored on disk or in a memory chip. When output occurs, a particular sound is routed to a speaker. Sound chips are mass-produced for specific applications, such as output for automatic teller machines, microwave ovens, smoke detectors, elevators, alarm clocks, automobile warning systems, video games, and vending machines, to mention only a few. When sounds are stored on disk, the user has the flexibility to update them to meet changing application needs.

Speech synthesis systems, which convert raw data into electronically produced speech, are popular in the PC environment. All you need to produce speech on a PC are a sound expansion card, speakers (or headset), and appropriate software. Such **text-to-speech software** often is packaged with speech recognition software. Text-to-speech technology produces speech by combining phonemes (from 50 to 60 basic sound units) to create and output words.

The existing technology produces synthesized speech with only limited vocal inflections and phrasing, however. Despite the limitations, the number of speech synthesizer applications is growing. For example, a visually impaired person can use the speech synthesizer to translate printed words into spoken words. Some people use their notebook PCs to "read" their e-books to them. Translation systems offer one of the most interesting applications for speech synthesizers and speech-recognition devices. Researchers are making progress toward enabling conversations among people who are speaking different languages. A prototype system has already demonstrated that three people, each speaking a different language (English, German, and Japanese), can carry on a computer-aided conversation. Each person speaks in and listens to his or her native language.

SECTION SELF-CHECK

6-2.1	Ink-jet printers are nonimpact printers. (T/F)
6-2.2	You would be more likely to print a spreadsheet in landscape format than in portrait format. (T/F)
6-2.3	The tractor-feed on dot-matrix printers enables printing on what kind of paper: (a) cut-sheet paper, (b) fanfold paper, (c) landscape paper, or (d) portrait paper?
6-2.4	What technology converts raw data into electronically produced speech: (a) voice response, (b) reproduction analysis, (c) speech synthesis, or (d) sound duping?
6-2.5	All other things being equal on a monitor, which dot pitch would yield the best resolution: (a) .24 dot pitch, (b) .26 dot pitch, (c) .28 dot pitch, or (d) .31 dot pitch?

6-3   The Multimedia Experience

The quality, sophistication, and diversity of input/output devices continue to grow. Dolby sound, colorful digital imagery, tactile feedback, and many other devices that tickle our senses have transformed personal computing into a multimedia experience. That experience could be anything from colorful illustrations for a cyber greeting card to full multimedia class presentations involving sound, animation, and motion video.

MULTIMEDIA: SHOW TIME

Multimedia is an umbrella term that refers to the capability that enables the integration of computer-based text, still graphics, motion visuals, animation, and sound. In the mid-1990s, multimedia was relatively new and multimedia PCs, still a bit pricey, were atypical. Today, all PCs are multimedia-ready; that is, they have peripheral devices, including storage, and software that can deliver the multimedia experience. Most software packages and the Net take advantage of a PC's multimedia capabilities. Consider the *show biz* appeal of the applications in Figure 6-29 and in these examples.

- *The Internet*. You can go on the Web and listen to live broadcasts from hundreds of radio stations, view animated visuals of how things work, visit pages for vacation spots and view videos of the local attractions, and much more.

- *Video Editing*. **Video editing** is the process of manipulating ***video*** images. Not too long ago, video editing was the exclusive purview of video editing specialists working with hardware that cost in excess of $100,000. Now, you can do sophisticated video editing on your home PC. The hardware and software needed over and above a typical PC—a video capture card and video editing software—can be purchased for under $100. Video editing software lets you pick the video segments you want, sequence the clips, add background music, add scene transitions, place text over video, and employ many other special effects. You can even do fast and slow motion to create exciting "movie" sequences.

- *Presentations*. Knowledge workers prepare convincing presentations by blending colorful charts with animation and attention-getting audio.

- *Kiosks*. Interactive kiosks with touch-sensitive screens provide public users with detailed information about a city, a company, a product, events, and so on.

- *Tutorials*. Multimedia is rapidly becoming the foundation of computer-based training. For example, companies prepare interactive tutorials to introduce newcomers to company procedures. Thousands of workers are now learning Word, Excel, and other popular applications via interactive multimedia tutorials that are enlivened with music, graphics, and motion. A Department of Defense study concluded that such tutorials take about a third less time, cost about a third less, and are more effective than traditional training methods.

- *Online reference*. CD-ROM-based and Web-based multimedia alternatives are beginning to replace encyclopedias, technical reference manuals, product information booklets, and the like. Electronic versions of reference materials are easier to use and much, much lighter to carry.

- *Interactive publications*. Books, magazines, and newspapers are already being distributed as multimedia publications on CD-ROM and online via the Internet. The printed page will never be able to share moving visuals and sounds.

- *The family photo album*. The PC has emerged as the modern photo album. We use digital cameras to take pictures, then, if needed, we do touch-ups with photo illustration software. Photos in an electronic photo album are easily accessible and viewed. CD and DVD burners have made it possible for us to select video clips and images from the family archives and burn custom CDs and DVDs.

- *Entertainment center*. Our notebooks are portable movie theaters, capable of showing DVD movies or streaming video over the Internet. They can play any of millions of songs now available for download over the Internet or they can play the music from thousands of Internet radio stations from around the world. With a video capture card, your PC is easily transformed into a television with a remote channel changer.

With multimedia, the combined use of text, sound, images, motion video, and animation transforms a PC into an exciting center for learning, work, or play.

Growing with Multimedia

The next stage of multimedia growth comes when you decide to *develop* sophisticated multimedia applications—either your own multimedia title on CD-ROM or DVD, an interactive tutorial, a Web site, or an information kiosk. At this point, you or your company may need to invest in some or all of the following hardware and software.

- *Video camera, videocassette recorder/player, audiocassette player, and television*. These electronic devices are emerging as staples in many households and companies. The video camera (digital or analog) lets you capture motion video source material that can be integrated with multimedia applications. The videocassette recorder/player and audiocassette player are handy, but not a requirement. The television provides an alternative output device.

FIGURE 6–29 MULTIMEDIA APPLICATIONS

3-D IMAGES THAT INCLUDE YOU

Virtual reality may be the ultimate multimedia experience. The virtual reality (VR) theater at Iowa State University lets you interact with 3D images, including a tornado. The VR theater presents computer-generated images on the walls, floor, and ceiling and the view changes based on the viewer's perspective.

Courtesy of Iowa State University Photo Service

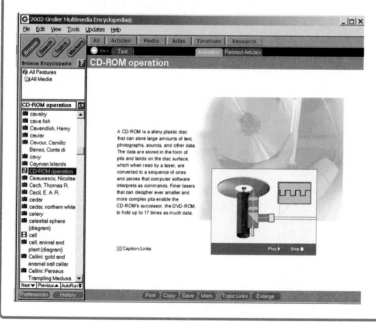

THE MULTIMEDIA ENCYCLOPEDIA

Far more people are choosing multimedia encyclopedias, such as the *2001 Grolier Multimedia Encyclopedia* shown here, than traditional print encyclopedias. They cost considerably less, are about 100 pounds lighter, and offer the advantages of multimedia. With electronic encyclopedias you can enjoy animation presentations, such as the audio-supported animation of how a CD-ROM works (shown here), and video that are not possible in print encyclopedias.

Grolier Multimedia Encyclopedia © 2001 by Grolier Interactive Inc.

FIGURE 6–29 continued

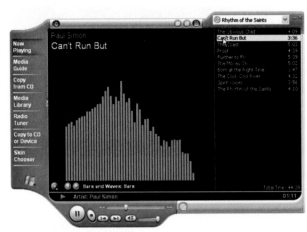

WINDOWS MEDIA PLAYER
The Windows Media Player software that comes with any Windows operating system lets you play your digital media, including music, videos, DVDs, Internet radio, and audio CDs. The software lets you hear and "see" the music on Paul Simon's classic CD, *Rhythm of the Saints*.

SIMULATION IN EDUCATION
People retain 10% of the information they see; 20% of what they hear; 50% of what they see and hear; and 80% of what they see, hear, and do. These facts make a good case for increased use of computer-based simulation in education and training. Commercial airline pilots use flight simulators, such as this one, to learn normal flight operations and to practice emergency procedures.

Courtesy of Lockheed Martin Corporation

MULTIMEDIA IN THE HOME AND OFFICE
Multimedia capability opens the door for a broad range of applications. This telecommuter uses his PC to do video editing for a film production studio.

Courtesy of Autodesk, Inc.

INFORMATIVE KIOSKS
The manner in which we obtain information is changing rapidly. Virgin Entertainment Group provides kiosks that enable customers to preview hundreds of thousands of CDs, DVDs, and Console Games.

Courtesy of International Business Machines Corporation. Unauthorized use not permitted.

FIGURE 6–29 continued

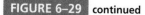

LCD PROJECTORS
Dr. C. Everett Koop, former U.S. Surgeon General, uses an LCD projector and multimedia displays during his speeches to make his points and illustrate concepts.

Photo courtesy of Intel Corporation

PERSONAL COMPUTING AND PHOTOGRAPHY
Miss America photographer Bruce Boyajian prints a photo on a high-resolution ink jet printer for Miss Texas, Stacy James, along the runway between rehearsals during the 81st annual Miss America Pageant being held in Atlantic City, N.J. Digital photos can be easily enhanced with special effects or lightened/darkened as needed.

Courtesy of Epson America, Inc. Photo by Thomas P. Costello.

- *Synthesizer.* A good keyboard synthesizer can reproduce a variety of special effects and sounds, including those of almost any musical instrument. A synthesizer can be played to create original source music for inclusion in a multimedia application.

- *Video capture card.* This expansion card lets you capture and digitize full-motion color video with audio. The digitized motion video can then be used as source material for a CD-ROM-based multimedia application.

- *Scanner.* A scanner lets you capture black/white and color images from hard copy source material.

- *Digital camera.* A digital camera captures high-resolution digital images that can be integrated into multimedia applications.

- *CD-RW or DVD+RW.* Optical laser rewritable technology lets you write and rewrite to high-capacity optical media. Multimedia applications generally have huge storage requirements and usually are distributed on CD-ROM or DVD.

- *Applications development software.* If you plan to develop sophisticated multimedia applications, you will need to upgrade to application development tools and authoring systems. **Authoring systems** let you create multimedia applications that integrate sound, motion, text, animation, and images.

- *PC source library.* The source library contains digitized "clips" of art, video, and audio that you can use as needed to complement a multimedia application.

Multimedia File Resources

Multimedia applications draw content material from a number of sources, such as text and database files, sound files, image files, animation files, and motion video files.

Text and Database Files

A little over a decade ago, most computer-based applications were designed strictly around text and numbers. However, this has changed. An animation of how the human heart works is far more effective than is a textual description of how it works.

Many CD-ROM titles and Web sites involve the use of databases. For example, one CD-ROM title contains information on every city in the United States (name, population, major industries, and so

THE CRYSTAL BALL:
The E-Book Books haven't changed much since Johann Gutenberg invented the printing press. The printed page is limited for any book or document that contains an index, including all varieties of reference books, encyclopedias, "how to" books, and, of course, textbooks. By 2010, virtually all of these books will be electronic books. Many are now. E-books will continue to evolve with greater flexibility in that they can be formatted for any device with a display and memory, even cell phones and automobile dashboard displays. E-books offer many advantages over traditional books: animation, motion video, drill-down capability, "active words" (for related information), hyperlinks, and margin notes.

on) stored and sorted in a database. Retail Web sites maintain databases of the products they sell in their online stores.

Sound Files

Sound files are of two types: *waveform* and *nonwaveform*. The waveform files, or **wave files**, contain the digital information needed to reconstruct the analog waveform of the sound so it can be played through speakers. The primary Windows waveform files are identified with the WAV extension (for example, SOUNDFIL.WAV).

Another popular sound file format is MP3, which enables CD-quality music to be compressed to about 8% of its original size while retaining CD sound quality. For example, a three-minute song on CD takes 33 MB of disk space, but it can be compressed to 3 MB in MP3 format. That is a compression ratio of 11 to 1. The compression to MP3 format causes no noticeable loss of the quality of the sound because the compression process simply removes sounds outside of the audible range of the human ear, both low and high.

The nonwaveform file contains instructions as to how to create the sound, rather than a digitized version of the actual sound. For example, an instruction might tell the computer the pitch, duration, and sound quality of a particular musical note. The most common nonwaveform file, which is primarily for recording and playing music, is known as the **MIDI file**. MIDI files are identified with the MID extension (for example, MUSICFIL.MID). MIDI stands for Musical Instrument Digital Interface. MIDI provides an interface between PCs and electronic musical instruments, such as the synthesizer. A typical application involving MIDI files has the PC recording notes played by a musician on a synthesizer. The musician then adds additional instruments to the original track (layering) to create a full orchestral sound (see Figure 6-30). MIDI files occupy much less file space than comparable waveform audio files.

Image Files

Multimedia is visual, so it involves plenty of images. These are the most common sources of images.

- *You.* You can create your own images using the graphics software and techniques discussed in Chapter 2, "Software," and in this chapter.

- *Clip art.* Anyone serious about creating multimedia material will have a hefty clip art library of up to 100,000 images. Copyright-free clip art is readily available on the Web.

- *Scanned images.* If you have a scanner, you can scan and digitize any hard copy image (photographs, drawings, and so on).

- *Photo images.* Commercial photo image libraries make vast photo image resources available to the public, for a fee. Photo illustration software is often packaged with a variety of copyright-free images. Also, you can create your own images with a digital camera and/or a scanner.

Photo illustration software enables you to create original images as well as to dress up existing digitized images, such as photographs, scanned images, and electronic paintings. Images can be retouched with special effects to alter dramatically the way they appear (see Figure 6-31). Photo illustration software is to an image as word processing software is to text. A word processing package allows you to edit, sort, copy, and generally do whatever can be done to electronic text. Photo illustration software allows you to do just about anything imaginable to digitized photos or drawings. The result of a photo illustrator's effort is a composite image with stunning special effects.

FIGURE 6–30

DIGITAL AUDIO SEQUENCER AND MIDI
Digital Orchestrator Pro™ (a software product from Voyetra Turtle Beach, Inc.) is one of the most popular digital audio sequencers. The program lets you create multitrack recordings from external audio sources, such as the output from a keyboard synthesizer or an audio CD. Digital audio and MIDI tracks exist side by side in perfect sync, making song editing a snap. This image is one of the many views in the intuitive user interface that allows users to edit virtually any facet of a song.

FIGURE 6-31

PHOTO ILLUSTRATION SOFTWARE
Photo illustration software, such as *Microsoft® PhotoDraw®* (shown here), lets you work with digital images, such as those resulting from a digital photograph and scan of an image. With photo illustration software you can touch up your photographs and apply a wide variety of special effects to all or portions of your images. Once you're satisfied with your artistic work, you can post them to the Internet or print them on greeting cards, T-shirts, calendars, and so on.

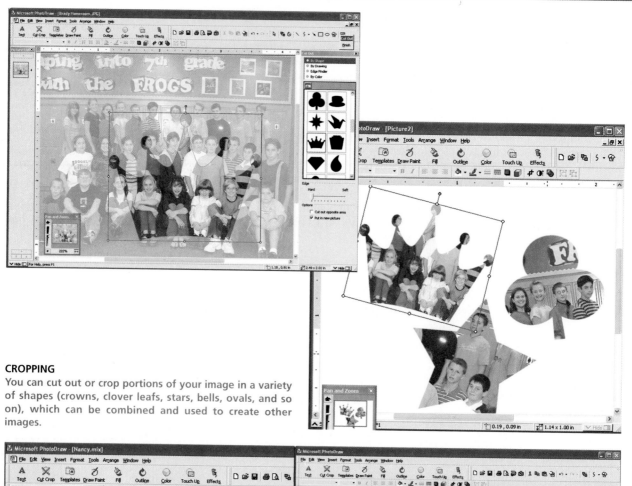

CROPPING
You can cut out or crop portions of your image in a variety of shapes (crowns, clover leafs, stars, bells, ovals, and so on), which can be combined and used to create other images.

CONTRAST AND BRIGHTNESS
The contrast and brightness feature can be used to save photographs that may otherwise be too dark (or light) in spots. Here, the contrast and brightness are adjusted to enhance the quality of the photo.

SPECIAL EFFECTS
The special effects shown here are but a few of the many that can be applied to give your digital images an artistic touch. Clockwise from the original image at the top left, they are the mosaic (image is flipped horizontally), *glowing edges, neon glow,* and *grayscale* effects.

For example, you can show the changes that take place as one image is modified to become an entirely different image. This process is called **morphing**, a term derived from the word *metamorphosis*. You also can feather images to blend with their surroundings, enter artistic text over the image, change colors, include freehand drawings, isolate objects for special treatment, distort specific objects (for example, *glass blocking*), and much more.

An interesting application of what photo illustration software can do is the electronic aging of missing children. Artists combine a child's snapshot with a database of measurements showing how human facial dimensions change in a fairly predictable way over time. Such retouched snapshots have helped find hundreds of children since the mid-1980s.

Animation Files

The next step up from a static display of images is a dynamic display—that is, one that features movement within the display. **Animation,** or movement, is accomplished by the rapid repositioning (moving) of objects on the display screen. For example, animation techniques give life to video-game characters. You can create your own animation using software, such as Macromedia® Director®, or you can purchase a commercial animation library. The latter contains animation templates that can be applied to different presentation needs.

Animation involves the rapid movement of an object, perhaps the image of a dollar sign, from one part of the screen to another (see Figure 6-32). The animation is accomplished by moving the object in small increments in rapid succession, giving the illusion of movement. The object may gradually change shape, as well. Most presentation software packages, which are discussed in Chapter 2, have several built-in animation features that help you include simple animation in the slides used in a presentation. For example, the *animated bullet build* feature can be applied to a simple text chart to integrate animation into the presentation of the bullet points on the chart. Also, the *animated charting* feature can be applied to bar and pie graphs to animate the presentation of the important aspects of the graph.

The judicious use of animation can enliven any presentation. Some of the most important presentations take place in courtrooms. How can a lawyer best present evidence to help the judge and jury understand the case? An increasing number of lawyers are illustrating expert testimony with animated computer graphics. In re-creating a plane crash, for example, data from the plane's data recorder can be used to prepare an animated graphic showing the exact flight path, while the cockpit voice recorder plays in the background.

Motion Video Files

Obtaining relevant motion video for a particular multimedia application can be a challenge. You will need a video camera and a video capture board to produce original motion video for inclusion in a multimedia application. Depending on your presentation, you may need actors, props, and a set, as well. For example, you will frequently see video clips of on-screen narrators in multimedia presentations and tutorials. Videos are produced as you would any video product (set, actor, and so on), then digitized for storage on optical media or hard disk.

Motion video files are disk hogs; that is, they take up lots of space, up to a gigabyte per minute of video unless files are compressed. Just as we can compress text (zip files) and audio (MP3 and MIDI files), we can also compress video files. Digital video is functionally like motion picture film, whereby still images are displayed rapidly, from 15 to 60 frames per second, to create the illusion of motion. Video can be compressed up to 20 to 1 by recording and storing that portion of the image that changes from

FIGURE 6–32

ANIMATION
Macromedia®, a software company, practices what it preaches. Here, the movie feature found in *Director*® is used to create an animated example that demonstrates the software's "Ink Effects" (window in lower right corner).

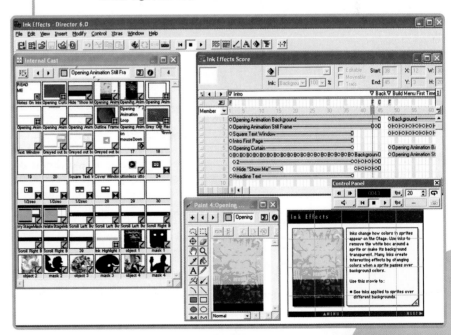

Multimedia Resources
- Text files
- Database files
- Sound files
  - Waveform
  - Nonwaveform
- Image files
- Animation files
- Motion video files
  - Video for Windows (avi)
  - QuickTime (mov)
  - MPEG (mpg)

frame to frame. Video compression is greater when motion is minimal (for example, a talking head). These are popular video compression formats in use today (filename extensions are in parentheses).

- **Video for Windows** (avi) from Microsoft Corporation
- **QuickTime** (mov) from Apple Computer Company
- **MPEG** (mpg) is an ISO (International Standards Organization) standard developed by MPEG (Moving Picture Experts Group)

Each of these formats is being continually redefined and upgraded to new standards to take advantage of continually improving technologies (computing capacity, Internet bandwidth, monitor resolution, and so on). Once video is encoded and compressed, the resulting files can be stored locally or at Internet server sites for playback.

CREATING A MULTIMEDIA APPLICATION: PUTTING THE RESOURCES TOGETHER

Once you have prepared and/or identified the desired sight and sound resource material, you are ready to put it together. A variety of software packages is available to help you accomplish this task.

- *Presentation software.* As we have already seen in Chapter 2, presentation software such as PowerPoint can help you prepare and create stimulating multimedia presentations.
- *Authoring systems.* To create interactive multimedia tutorials and titles, you will need an authoring system, such as ToolBook or Macromedia Director.
- *Multimedia programming.* The creation of sophisticated commercial multimedia titles, such as the multimedia encyclopedia, may require the use of several multimedia development tools, including high-end authoring systems and programming languages, such as Visual Basic and C++.

Multimedia possibilities stretch the human imagination to its limits. Already we see that multimedia will change the face of publishing. Many feel that interactive e-books based on multimedia technology have the potential to be more accessible and effective than traditional books, especially as learning tools. Early indications are that passive entertainment, such as TV and movies, may have to move aside to make way for interactive multimedia entertainment that involves the viewer in the action.

SECTION SELF-CHECK

6-3.1 Animation is accomplished by the slow, but gradual, repositioning of objects on the display screen. (T/F)

6-3.2 Video can be compressed up to 20 to 1 by recording and storing that portion of the image that changes from frame to frame. (T/F)

6-3.3 What photo illustration process takes place as one image is modified to become an entirely different image: (a) morphing, (b) transforming, (c) morphic, or (d) transformer?

6-3.4 The process of manipulating *video* images is: (a) movie handling, (b) video capturing, (c) tape processing, or (d) video editing.

6-4 Technology for the Disabled

The Americans with Disabilities Act of 1990 prohibits discrimination that might limit employment or access to public buildings and facilities. Under the law, employers cannot discriminate against any employee who can perform a job's "essential" responsibilities with "reasonable accommodations." Increasingly, these "accommodations" take the form of a personal computer with special input/output peripherals and software, called **assistive technology.** Almost 20,000 assistive technology-based products are available for the disabled (see Figure 6-33). Assistive technology in its many forms has enabled people with disabilities greater freedom to work and live independently.

For example, getting a complete impression of the contents of a computer screen is a problem for the visually impaired, as is the ability to maneuver around such features as pull-down windows and click-on icons. The partially sighted can benefit from adaptive software packages that create magnified screen displays, while voice synthesizers can let the blind "read" memos, books, and computer screens.

For the hearing impaired, voice mail and a computer's beeps can be translated into visual cues, such as a screen display of text or flashing icons. Advances in communications and video technologies have made it possible for users to sit in front of their respective computer screens and have sign language conversations.

FIGURE 6–33 ASSISTIVE TECHNOLOGY FOR DISABLED PEOPLE

KEYBOARD INPUT AND BRAILLE OUTPUT
This personal computer is configured with a traditional keyboard for input and an electronic Braille display, enabling this blind man real-time two-way interaction with his PC. Electronic Braille displays have from 20 to 80 cells, the Braille equivalent to a character. The electronic Braille display processes eight dots per cell, rather than the six used for Braille embossing. The dots convey certain attributes, such as capitalization, cursor location, and so on.

MAGNIFIER UTILITY PROGRAM
This visually impaired person uses a seeing eye dog for navigation around town and a magnifier utility program for navigation around Windows and applications programs.

SIGN LANGUAGE TO TEXT CONVERSION
At 18, Ryan Patterson won the Intel Science Talent Search and a $100,000 prize. His winning entry was a glove that converts American Sign Language to text. Those people with speech can use speech recognition software for rapid text entry and, now, those without speech can enjoy rapid text entry, too. To do so, they use their sign language while wearing Ryan's invention, a device that is sure to improve the quality of life for many people.

Virtually any type of physical movement can be used to input commands and data to a computer. This is good news for people with limited use of their arms and hands. Alternative input devices can range from a standard trackball (instead of a mouse) to the relatively slow sip-and-puff devices to speech-recognition systems. There are even software programs that allow keystroke combinations to be entered one key at a time.

Surveys show that employers who provide "assistive technologies" to their employees gain highly motivated and productive workers.

SECTION SELF-CHECK

6-4.1 The Americans with Disadvantages Act of 2002 prohibits discrimination that might limit employment or access to public buildings and facilities. (T/F)

6-4.2 Under the law, employers must make what kind of accommodation for disabled people: (a) reasonable, (b) sensible, (c) rational, or (d) logical?

6-1 INPUT DEVICES

A variety of input/output (I/O) peripheral devices provides the interface between the computer and us. There are two basic types of keyboards: traditional alphanumeric keyboards and special-function keyboards. A widely used keyboard layout is the 101-key keyboard with the traditional *QWERTY* key layout, 12 **function keys,** a numeric keypad, a variety of special-function keys, and dedicated cursor-control keys. The cursor-control keys can be used to select menu options or to move the **text cursor.** Some special-function keyboards are designed for specific applications. The mouse and its cousins enable interaction with the operating system's graphical user interface (GUI) and they help us to draw. These include the **trackball, trackpad, joystick, trackpoint,** and **digitizer tablet and pen.** When these point-and-draw devices are moved, the **mouse pointer** on the display moves accordingly. Along with buttons, the wheel mouse also has a wheel for scrolling.

The trend in data entry has been toward **source-data automation.** A variety of **scanners** read and interpret information on printed matter and convert it to a format that can be interpreted directly by a computer. **OCR (optical character recognition)** is the ability to read printed information into a computer system. **Bar codes** represent alphanumeric data by varying the size of adjacent vertical lines. Two types of OCR or **bar code scanners**—*contact* and *laser*—read information on labels and various types of documents. Scanners used for OCR or bar code applications can be classified into three basic categories—handheld label scanners (called **wand scanners**), stationary label scanners, and document scanners (which are often used with **turnaround documents**).

The most popular application for *optical mark recognition* (*OMR*) is for grading sense-mark tests.

An **optical scanner** uses laser technology to scan and digitize an image. Image scanners provide input for **image processing.** Image scanners are of two types: *page* and *hand.*

Magnetic stripes, **smart cards,** and badges provide input to **badge readers.**

Speech-recognition systems can be used to enter spoken words in continuous speech at speeds of up to 125 words a minute by comparing digitized representations of words to similarly formed templates in the computer system's electronic dictionary. Some speech-recognition systems are speaker-independent; that is, they can accept words spoken by anyone.

Pattern recognition systems are best suited to very specialized tasks in which only a few images will be encountered.

Digital cameras (digicams) are used to take photos that are represented digitally (already digitized). The desktop **digital video camera** lets you capture motion video in the area of the PC. The **Webcam** is a popular application for these cameras. Handheld **digital camcorders** offer another way to capture video. Use a **video capture card** to capture video from a standard analog video camera or VCR.

Handheld and wearable data entry devices have a limited external keyboard or a soft keyboard, a small display that may be touch-sensitive, nonvolatile RAM, and often a scanning device.

Touch screen monitors permit input as well as output. They have pressure-sensitive overlays that can detect pressure and the exact location of that pressure.

6-2 OUTPUT DEVICES

Output devices translate bits and bytes into a form we can understand. The most common "output only" devices include monitors, printers, plotters, **multimedia projectors,** sound systems, and voice-response systems.

Monitors are defined in terms of their technology (**CRT monitor** or **flat-panel monitor**), **graphics adapter** (which has **video RAM** or **VRAM**), size, resolution (number of **pixels,** number of bits used to represent each pixel, and **dot pitch**), and *refresh rate.*

Gray scales are used to refer to the number of shades of a color that can be shown on a monochrome monitor's screen. **RGB monitors** mix red, green, and blue to achieve a spectrum of colors. One user option is the number of bits used to display each pixel, sometimes referred to as **color depth.**

Flat-panel monitors are used with notebook PCs and some desktop PCs, many of which use LCD technology. **Wearable displays** give us freedom of movement.

Three basic PC printer technologies include page, ink-jet, and dot-matrix. Printers can print in **portrait** or **landscape** format. Nonimpact **page printers (laser printers)** use several technologies to achieve high-speed hard copy output by printing a page at a time. The color option is available for laser and ink-jet printers.

Nonimpact **ink-jet printers** have print heads that move back and forth across the paper, squirting ink droplets to write text and create images. The color ink-jet printer is emerging as the choice for home and small office consumers.

Large-format ink-jet printers, also called **plotters,** use ink-jet technology to print on roll-feed paper up to four feet wide.

The **dot-matrix printer,** an impact printer, forms images one character at a time as the print head moves across the paper.

Multifunction **all-in-one peripheral devices** are available that handle several paper-related tasks: computer-based printing, facsimile (fax), scanning, and copying.

PC sound systems vary from a couple of small speakers embedded in notebook PCs to sophisticated sound systems that provide surround sound.

Voice-response systems provide recorded or synthesized audio output (via **speech synthesis**). **Text-to-speech software** enables you to produce speech on a PC.

6-3 THE MULTIMEDIA EXPERIENCE

Multimedia refers to the capability that enables the integration of computer-based text, still graphics, motion visuals, animation, and sound. A good example of multimedia is **video editing,** the process of manipulating *video* images. Three elements in particular distinguish multimedia: sound, motion, and the opportunity for interaction.

The next stage of multimedia growth would include some or all of the following hardware and software: a video camera, a videocassette recorder/player, an audiocassette player, a television, a synthesizer, a video capture card, a scanner, a digital camera, CD-RW or DVD+RW, professional applications development software, and a source library.

Multimedia applications draw content material from a number of sources, including text files, database files, sound files, image files, animation files, and motion video files. Sound files are of two types: *waveform* (or **wave file**) and *nonwaveform* (or

MIDI file). Sources for image files include those the user creates, clip art, scanned images, and photo images.

Photo illustration software enables you to create original images as well as to dress up existing digitized images. Images can be retouched with special effects, such as **morphing**. **Animation** is accomplished by the rapid repositioning of objects on the display screen.

Motion video files can be compressed up to 20 to 1. The most popular video compression formats in use today are **Video for Windows** (avi), **QuickTime** (mov), and **MPEG** (mpg).

Popular tools for creating multimedia applications include presentation software, **authoring systems**, and multimedia programming (for example, Visual Basic and C++).

6-4 TECHNOLOGY FOR THE DISABLED

Personal computers with special input/output peripherals and software, called **assistive technology**, have enabled people with disabilities greater freedom to work and live independently. These include magnified screen displays and voice synthesizers for people with visual impairment. Some paraplegics use sip-and-puff devices. Hiring disabled people and equipping them with assistive technologies has proven to be a good business strategy.

KEY TERMS

all-in-one peripheral device (p. 263)
animation (p. 271)
assistive technology (p. 272)
authoring system (p. 268)
badge reader (p. 248)
bar code (p. 243)
bar code scanner (p. 243)
color depth (p. 258)
CRT monitor (p. 256)
digital camcorder (p. 254)
digital camera (digicam) (p. 253)
digital video camera (p. 254)
digitizer tablet and pen (p. 243)
dot pitch (p. 258)
dot-matrix printer (p. 262)
flat-panel monitor (p. 256)
function key (p. 242)
graphics adapter (p. 256)
gray scales (p. 258)
image processing (p. 247)
ink-jet printer (p. 262)

joystick (p. 243)
landscape (p. 259)
large-format ink-jet printer (p. 262)
laser printer (p. 260)
MIDI file (p. 269)
morphing (p. 271)
mouse pointer (p. 242)
MPEG (p. 272)
multimedia (p. 265)
multimedia projector (p. 258)
OCR (optical character recognition) (p. 243)
optical scanner (p. 247)
page printer (p. 260)
pattern recognition system (p. 251)
photo illustration software (p. 269)
pixel (p. 258)
plotter (p. 262)
portrait (p. 259)
QuickTime (p. 272)
RGB monitor (p. 258)

scanner (p. 243)
smart card (p. 248)
source-data automation (p. 243)
speech-recognition system (p. 250)
speech synthesis (p. 264)
text cursor (p. 242)
text-to-speech software (p. 264)
touch screen monitor (p. 255)
trackball (p. 242)
trackpad (p. 243)
trackpoint (p. 243)
turnaround document (p. 247)
video capture card (p. 255)
video editing (p. 265)
Video for Windows (p. 272)
video RAM (VRAM) (p. 256)
voice-response system (p. 264)
wand scanner (p. 247)
wave file (p. 269)
wearable display (p. 259)
Webcam (p. 254)

MATCHING

1. smart card
2. assistive technology
3. MPEG
4. color depth
5. landscape
6. photo illustration software
7. all-in-one peripheral device
8. video RAM
9. dot-matrix printer
10. animation
11. pattern recognition system
12. mouse pointer
13. multimedia projector
14. video editing
15. joystick

a. page orientation for spreadsheets
b. moved with a point-and-draw device
c. rapid repositioning of objects
d. gives freedom to disabled people
e. fax, copy, print, and scan
f. video format
g. printing multipart forms
h. gaming control
i. "vision" capability
j. number of colors
k. morphing
l. VRAM
m. provides screen image display for groups
n. embedded processor
o. sequencing video clips

6-1.1 The primary function of I/O peripherals is to facilitate computer-to-computer data transmission. (T/F)

6-1.2 An ATM's input/output capabilities are: (a) input only, (b) output only, (c) both input and output, or (d) customer input only.

6-1.3 Use the keyboard's numeric keypad for rapid numeric data entry. (T/F)

6-1.4 Only those keyboards configured for notebook PCs have function keys. (T/F)

6-1.5 Which of the following is not a point-and-draw device: (a) joystick, (b) document scanner, (c) trackpad, or (c) trackpoint?

6-1.6 User interaction with the Windows XP operating systems is via a(n): (a) GUI, (b) Gooie, (c) mouse interface, or (d) user-friendly menu.

6-1.7 Pattern recognition systems are best suited to generalized tasks in which a wide variety of images will be encountered. (T/F)

6-1.8 Optical character recognition is a means of source-data automation. (T/F)

6-1.9 The preprinted bar codes on consumer products have actually increased the number of keystrokes at supermarket checkout counters. (T/F)

6-1.10 The United States Postal Service uses OCR to sort mail. (T/F)

6-1.11 Speech-recognition systems can be trained to accept words not in the system's original dictionary. (T/F)

6-1.12 The enhanced version of cards with a magnetic stripe is a(n): (a) badge card, (b) intelligent badge, (c) smart card, or (d) debit card.

6-1.13 Which of these is not a type of scanner: (a) document scanner, (b) stationary label scanner, (c) wand scanner, or (d) magnetic scanner?

6-1.14 Manipulating and managing scanned images would be considered: (a) image processing, (b) parallel processing, (c) scanner management, or (d) image administration.

6-1.15 Which of the following is not true of digital cameras: (a) uses the same film as 35-mm cameras, (b) digitized images are uploaded from the camera, (c) uses flash memory to store photos, or (d) can be purchased for as little as $200?

6-2.1 Dot-matrix printers generate graphs with greater precision than plotters. (T/F)

6-2.2 The graphics adapter is the device controller for a high-resolution speech synthesizer. (T/F)

6-2.3 The passive matrix LCD monitor provides a more brilliant display than those with active matrix technology. (T/F)

6-2.4 What type of printer would you be most likely to find in a busy office: (a) laser printer, (b) ink-jet printer, (c) multifunction duplicator system, or (d) glove box printer?

6-2.5 Which of these is not one of the capabilities of all-in-one multifunction peripheral devices: (a) duplicating, (b) faxing, (c) scanning, or (d) vision input?

6-2.6 Which of these does not play a part in determining a monitor's resolution: (a) number of colors mixed within a pixel, (b) number of pixels, (c) number of bits that represent a pixel, or (d) dot pitch?

6-2.7 Which of these would not be a pixel density option for monitors: (a) 1024 by 768, (b) 640 by 480, (c) 123 by 84, or (d) 1600 by 1200?

6-2.8 Most flat-panel monitors are used in conjunction with: (a) server computers, (b) tower PCs, (c) notebook PCs, or (d) desktop PCs.

6-2.9 Which of these I/O devices produces hard copy output: (a) monitor, (b) printer, (c) multimedia projector, or (d) voice-response system?

6-2.10 Which kind of printer is used to print originals with carbon copies: (a) ink-jet, (b) large-format ink-jet, (c) dot-matrix, or (d) laser?

6-2.11 In text-to-speech technology, speech is produced by combining: (a) firmware, (b) synonyms, (c) phonemes, or (d) digitized templates.

6-2.12 Gamers looking to purchase a new PC would pay special attention to the amount of what: (a) gray scales, (b) VRAM, (c) image RAM, or (d) ppm of output.

6-3.1 Books and newspapers are not yet available as multimedia publications. (T/F)

6-3.2 Which is the following would not normally be associated with multimedia hardware: (a) scanner, (b) digital camera, (c) modem, or (d) video capture card?

6-3.3 Which of the following would not be considered one of the major elements of multimedia: (a) sound, (b) sequential access, (c) the opportunity for interaction, or (d) animation?

6-3.4 What type of program lets you create multimedia applications that integrate sound, motion, text, animation, and images: (a) authoring, (b) writer, (c) integrator, or (d) direction?

6-3.5 MIDI files are: (a) waveform files, (b) nonwaveform files, (c) minidigital files, or (d) minifiles.

6-3.6 Which of these is out of place: (a) avi, (b) gif, (c) mpeg, or (d) mov?

6-4.1 One input device used by disabled people is the sip-and-puff device. (T/F)

6-4.2 Assistive technology for the disabled includes what piece of electronically-wired clothing that converts sign language to text: (a) a set of rings, (b) two bracelets, (c) a pair of shoes, or (d) a glove?

IS WHAT WE SEE AND HEAR REAL OR NOT?

There was a time when photographs could be used as evidence in a court of law. Powerful computers and photo illustration software have changed that. Most image professionals now deal with digital images that can be electronically modified to achieve the desired result. Magazines routinely alter fashion covers to hide the "flaws" of supermodels. For example, a graphics artist might take a little off the thigh or add a little shadow to highlight the cheekbone. Advertisers "fix" deficiencies in product presentations and, generally, enhance the image whenever possible. It is impossible to distinguish the reality from "special effects" in TV commercials and at the movies. All commercial music is digitally recorded and, if needed, digitally enhanced to remove mistakes or to get the right sound.

Discussion: Has information technology taken away our ability to perceive what is artificial and what is natural? Explain.

Discussion: Is it ethical to present a digitally enhanced still image, video, or song without warning those who might otherwise assume that what they see and hear is real?

PREDICTING ELECTION RETURNS

Prior to 1951, people had to wait until the votes were counted to find out who won an election. That changed when a "giant brain," the Univac I computer, predicted Dwight Eisenhower the winner over Adlai Stevenson in the 1951 presidential election with only 5% of the votes counted. Today, computers are as much a part of Election Day as political rhetoric and flag waving. In presidential elections, the major television networks predict the state results for most states shortly after polls are closed. In the 2000 election, all major television networks gave Florida to Democratic candidate Al Gore early in the evening, only to withdraw their prediction later. Then several major networks predicted Republican candidate George W. Bush the Florida winner in the middle of the night. The Vice President conceded the election because Florida gave Bush a majority of the electoral votes. Again, the networks admitted they were premature, so Gore

withdrew his concession. During all the television hoopla of the 2000 election, the Internet pollsters were using exit interviews to predict races and post results online before the polls closed.

Critics contend that these computer predictions may not be accurate and can keep people who have not voted away from the polls. Voters confess, "Why vote when the winner is already known?" The news media contend that it's the public's right to know.

Discussion: Should the media be allowed to report predicted election results on the day of the election before all polls across the various time zones are closed?

Discussion: Would you go to the polls and vote if you knew that several major news services have already picked your candidate to win? How about if they predicted your candidate's opponent to win?

Discussion: The major TV networks have agreed to wait until the polls close in a particular state before predicting the winner for the state. The Internet media have no such agreement. Should they?

THE SPYCAM

Wireless technology for peripheral devices and the proliferation of small, inexpensive, wireless video cameras has created many new applications for personal computing—some good and many bad. The video cameras can be placed within 100 feet of the host unit and can send back clear streaming video images. Moreover, the camera is tiny and is hidden easily from view. You can imagine where pranksters and the lower elements of our society might have placed these cameras. Restrooms, college communal showers, conference rooms, the doctor's office, every room in the house, and so on, are now vulnerable to the spycam.

Discussion: Should those who purchase wireless video cameras be warned of the legal consequences of using this technology to "spy" on people, perhaps by a cigarette-like label? Explain why or why not.

Discussion: What would you do if you had a wireless video camera that could be placed discretely anywhere within 100 feet of your PC?

DISCUSSION AND PROBLEM SOLVING

6-1.1   Describe two instances during the past 24 hours in which you had indirect communication with a computer; that is, something you did resulted in computer activity.

6-1.2   Describe an automated telephone system with which you are familiar that asks you to select options from a series of menus. Discuss the advantages and disadvantages of this system.

6-1.3   Name four types of point-and-draw devices. Which one do you think you would prefer? Explain your reasoning.

6-1.4   What is the relationship between a trackpad and a mouse pointer? Between a trackpad and a text cursor?

6-1.5   The QWERTY keyboard, which has been the standard on typewriters and keyboards for decades, was actually designed to keep people from typing so rapidly. Speculate on why built-in inefficiency was a design objective.

6-1.6   Today's continuous speech-recognition systems are able to interpret spoken words more accurately when the user talks in phrases. Why would this approach be more accurate than discrete speech where the user speaks one word at a time with a slight separation between words?

6-1.7   In the next generation of credit cards, the familiar magnetic stripe probably will be replaced by embedded microprocessors in smart cards. Suggest applications for this capability.

6-1.8   Some department stores use handheld label scanners, and others use stationary label scanners to interpret the bar codes printed on the price tags of merchandise. What advantages does one scanner have over the other?

6-1.9   Compare today's pattern recognition systems with the vision capability portrayed in such films as 2001 and 2010. Do you believe we will have a comparable vision technology by the year 2010?

6-1.10   Today, literally billions of pages of documentation are maintained in government and corporate file cabinets. Next year, the contents of millions of file cabinets will be digitized via image processing. Briefly describe at least one situation with which you are familiar that is a candidate for image processing. Explain how image processing can improve efficiency at this organization.

6-1.11   Describe how your photographic habits might change (or have changed) if you owned a digital camera.

6-2.1 Four PCs at a police precinct are networked and currently share a 5 ppm ink-jet printer. The captain has budgeted enough money to purchase one page printer (20 ppm) or two more 5 ppm ink-jet printers. Which option would you suggest the precinct choose and why?

6-2.2 Describe the input/output characteristics of a workstation/PC that would be desirable for engineers doing computer-aided design (CAD).

6-2.3 By purchasing 17-inch low-quality monitors rather than 19-inch high-quality monitors, a large company can save up to $200 per employee on the cost of new PCs. In the long run, however, health and overall efficiency implications of this decision may result in costs that far exceed any savings. Explain.

6-2.4 In five years, forecasters are predicting flat-panel monitors less than .25-inch thick may be placed everywhere around the home and office. Speculate on how these ultrathin monitors might be used in the home. In the office.

6-2.5 Would an all-in-one multifunction peripheral be appropriate in your home or would you prefer purchasing separate devices for the various document-handling functions (duplicating, faxing, printing, and scanning)? Explain your reasoning.

6-2.6 Describe the benefits of using a notebook PC in conjunction with a multimedia projector during a formal business presentation as opposed to the traditional alternative (transparency acetates and an overhead projector).

6-2.7 People are calling PC-based speech-recognition software a "killer app." Why?

6-3.1 Multimedia was the buzzword of the mid-1990s, but its glitter is wearing off. Why?

6-3.2 Describe two scenarios for which information kiosks would be applicable.

6-3.3 Identify and briefly describe at least three situations where you have witnessed the use of computer animation.

6-3.4 Would a music composer work with a wave file or a MIDI file? Explain.

6-4.1 Employers can easily spend from $20,000 to $50,000 on assistive technology for a single disabled employee. What is the payback to the employer?

6-4.2 Discuss possible applications for an assistive device (the electronic glove) that enables conversion of American Sign Language to text.

FOCUS ON PERSONAL COMPUTING

1. It seems as if we are always in a hurry to do something specific when we do personal computing and we don't take time to assess and, if needed, adjust I/O features to meet our needs more effectively. Take time to explore these features. Open your Control Panel and open the settings for any I/O device. Familiarize yourself with the device's features and settings and customize them as you see fit. For example, you might prefer the "nature" scheme for the mouse pointer or you might opt for a higher resolution on your display. Examine and customize all input/output devices on your system, including sound and audio devices.

2. Modern operating systems provide a minimum level of functionality for people with disabilities. For example, one utility provides visual warnings for system-produced sounds. Another enables the keyboard to perform mouse functions. Search for "accessibility" in the Windows Help and Support Center and learn more about these capabilities. Open and experiment with the Magnifier utility and/or use your system's text-to-speech capabilities. These may not be available with all operating systems or they may need to be installed.

INTERNET EXERCISES @ www.prenhall.com/long

1. The Online Study Guide (multiple choice, true/false, matching, and essay questions)

2. Internet Learning Activities
- Input
- Output
- Printers
- Multimedia

Chapter

7

Learning Objectives

Once you have read and studied this chapter, you will have learned:

- How the application of the concept of connectivity is affecting your life (Section 7-1).

- Alternatives and sources of data transmission services that have enabled the networking of our world (Section 7-2).

- The function and operation of data communications hardware (Section 7-3).

- The various kinds of network topologies, essential local area network concepts and terminology, and the scope and potential of home networking (Section 7-4).

NETWORKS AND NETWORKING

Why this chapter is important to you

Ten years ago, the number-one reason people purchased a PC was for word processing. Now people buy PCs for many reasons, but frequently they do so to get on the Internet. Everyone wants to logon and travel through cyberspace, soaking up all it has to offer. Each day our world is becoming increasingly connected—electronically. If you are not already online, you, too, will eventually want to be connected. When you are, you can save yourself both time and money by knowing the basics of data communications and networking.

Data communications was relatively new in the mid-1960s. During the first 25 years of the communications era, data communications experts purchased, installed, and maintained multimillion-dollar communications hardware and channels. Now, most of the connected computer systems are personal computers owned by people like you. Relatively few of us are blessed with a technical support staff at our beck-and-call, so we, the users, are the people who purchase, install, and maintain our own communications hardware and channels—not the experts. Usually the hardware is no more involved than a modem and a telephone line. However, this is beginning to change as homes and small offices begin to network multiple PCs and upgrade to broadband (high-speed) Internet connections.

This chapter introduces you to data communications and networking concepts that will prove helpful at home and make you a more informed employee at work. You'll learn about communications-related hardware and be introduced to various delivery alternatives, including transmission options over traditional voice-grade telephone lines, cable TV lines, and wireless alternatives. Many people have literally thrown up their hands in frustration when dealing with communications tasks and issues. Hopefully, what you learn from this chapter will help eliminate some of that frustration.

WHY THIS SECTION
IS IMPORTANT
TO YOU

People who understand information technology trends, such as
digital convergence and global
connectivity, are better prepared
to cope with our increasingly
wired society.

7-1   Our Wired World

Millions of people are knowledge workers by day and Internet surfers by night. As knowledge workers, we need ready access to information. In the present competitive environment, we cannot rely
solely on verbal communication to get that information. Corporate presidents cannot wait until the
Monday morning staff meeting to find out whether production is meeting demand. Field sales representatives can no longer afford to play telephone tag with headquarters personnel to get answers for
impatient customers. The president, the field rep, and the rest of us now rely on *computer networks* to
retrieve and share information quickly. Of course, we will continue to interact with our coworkers,
but computer networks simply enhance the efficiency and effectiveness of that interaction.

As surfers, we surf the Internet, America Online, CompuServe, or other commercial information
services. Once logged on to one of these networks, cybersurfers can chat with friends, strangers, and
even celebrities. We can go shopping, peruse electronic magazines, download interesting photos and
songs, plan a vacation, play games, buy and sell stock, send e-mail, and generally hang out. It's official:
We now live in a weird, wild, wired world where computer networks are networked to one another
and we are never far from a computer network (see Figure 7-1). This chapter is devoted to concepts
relating to computer networks and communications technology. Once you have a grasp of this technology, you will find it easier to understand the different uses and applications of networks.

DIGITAL CONVERGENCE

We are going through a period of **digital convergence.** That is, TVs, PCs, telephones, movies, college
textbooks, newspapers, and much, much more are converging toward digital compatibility. For example, movies that are now frames of cellulose are in the process of digital convergence. The 200,000

FIGURE 7–1

YESTERDAY AND TODAY
When you contrast businesses of today with those of yesterday, one thing sticks out—
communications and networking. The main links between filling stations of the 1950s
and their suppliers were the telephone and the postal service. Today, customers can pay
at the pump via credit card or via a wireless "billfold." Point-of-sale terminals inside the
convenience stores record each sale and change inventory directly on corporate server
computers.

Photo courtesy of Phillips Petroleum Company

frames required for a full-length movie will converge to 16 billion bits. Major components of this book's learning system are on CD-ROM and the Internet. Future editions will follow the trend toward digital convergence with an increasing portion of the material being distributed digitally. You can even go online and purchase the digital equivalent of United States Postal Service postage stamps. Millions of printed pages in the file cabinets of thousands of companies are being converted to more easily accessible digital images via image processing.

Digital convergence, combined with an ever-expanding worldwide network of computers, is enabling our society to take one giant leap into the future. Already the TV, PC, video game, stereo system, answering device, and telephone are on a collision course that will meld them into communications/information centers. We'll have video-on-demand such that we can view all or any part of any movie ever produced at any time, even in a window on our office PC. Instead of carrying a billfold, we might carry a credit-card-sized device that would contain all the typical billfold items such as money, credit cards, pictures, driver's license, and other forms of identification. These items will all be digital. When we buy a pizza in the future, we might simply enter a code into our electronic billfold to order and pay for the pizza automatically. The possibilities are endless.

Digital convergence is more than a convergence of technologies. Information technology is the enabling technology for the convergence of industries, as well. For example, the financial industries—banking, insurance, and securities—are rapidly converging. Health care establishments—clinics, hospitals, medical insurers, medical schools—are converging. Government agencies, including the air traffic control agencies (see Figure 7-2), are consolidating their efforts through digital convergence.

With half the industrial world (and many governments) racing toward digital convergence, there is no question that we are going digital over the next few years. Our photo album will be digital. Our money will be digital. Already, digitized movies are being transmitted to theaters where they are shown via high-definition projection units.

CONNECTIVITY

All of this convergence is happening so that information will be more easily accessible to more people. To realize the potential of a universe of digital information, the business and computer communities are continually seeking ways to interface, or connect, a diverse set of hardware, software, and databases. This increased level of **connectivity** brings people from as close as the next room and as far as the other side of the world closer together.

- Connectivity means that a marketing manager can use a PC to access information in the finance department's database.
- Connectivity means that a network of PCs can route output to a shared page printer.
- Connectivity means that a manufacturer's server computer can communicate with a supplier's server computer.
- Connectivity means that you can send your holiday newsletter via e-mail.
- Connectivity means that the appliances, including PCs, in your home can be networked.

Connectivity is implemented in degrees. We can expect to become increasingly connected to computers and information both at work and at home during the coming years. Thirty years ago, there were tens of thousands of computers. Today, there are hundreds of *millions* of them! Plus, we have the Internet! Computers and information are everywhere. Our challenge is to connect them.

THE ERA OF COOPERATIVE PROCESSING

We are living in an era of *cooperative processing*. Companies have recognized that they must cooperate internally to take full advantage of company resources, and that they must cooperate externally with one another to compete effectively in a world market. To promote internal cooperation, businesses are setting up **intracompany networking** (see Figure 7-3). These networks allow people in, say, the sales department to know the latest information from the production department. Companies cooperate externally (with customers and other companies) via **intercompany networking** (see Figure 7-3) or, more specifically, via **business-to-business (B2B)** e-commerce. **E-commerce,** electronic commerce, is the term used to describe business conducted online. B2B relies on computer networks and the Internet to transmit data electronically between companies.

FIGURE 7–2 Air-to-Ground Connectivity
At any given time, thousands of commercial airplanes are airborne. Each, however, is connected to the ground in that it is continuously updating the database for Air Route Traffic Control Centers around the country, such as this one in Seattle, Washington.

Courtesy of Lockheed Martin Corporation

FIGURE 7–3   INTRACOMPANY AND INTERCOMPANY NETWORKING

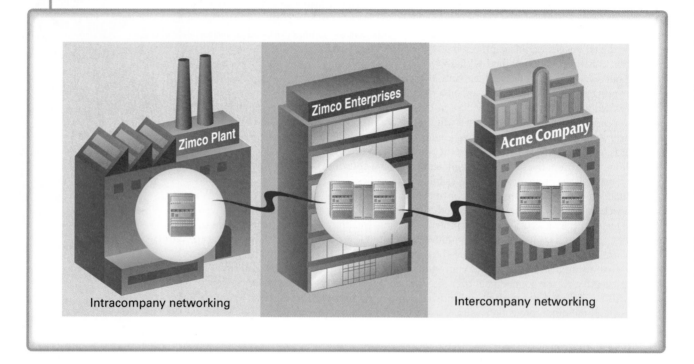

Zimco Plant

Zimco Enterprises

Acme Company

Intracompany networking

Intercompany networking

Increasingly, business between companies is being moved to the Internet. More specifically, it will be moved to a company's *intranet* with actual B2B interactions taking place over their *extranets*. An **intranet** is essentially a closed or private version of the Internet that is based on TCP/IP protocols (see Figure 7-4). Employees use the same browser that they use for the Internet, so an intranet looks and feels like the Internet. In fact, employees can browse seamlessly between their intranet and the Internet. However, it is accessible only by those people within the company. For most organizations, building an intranet is relatively easy because the typical organization provides Internet service and, therefore, has everything in place for the intranet—servers, support for TCP/IP, browser software, local area networks (LANs), and so on. A wealth of company information is made available on intranets, including daily announcements, the sales/marketing database, the menu for the company cafeteria, human resources information (benefits, job openings, and so on), corporate policies, and so on.

FIGURE 7–4   **THE INTERNET, INTRANETS, EXTRANETS, AND VPNS** This figure illustrates how VPNs use tunneling technology and the Internet. The graphical communications overview also shows the relationships between TCP/IP-based intranets and extranets, both with and without Internet access.

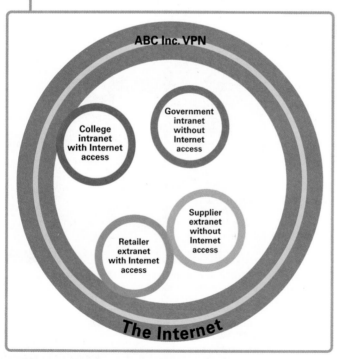

ABC Inc. VPN

College intranet with Internet access

Government intranet without Internet access

Retailer extranet with Internet access

Supplier extranet without Internet access

The Internet

An **extranet** is simply an extension of an intranet such that it is partially accessible to authorized outsiders, such as customers and suppliers (see Figure 7-4). In practice, an extranet is two or more overlapping intranets. Invoices, orders, and many other intercompany transactions can be transmitted via an extranet. For example, at major retail chains, such as Wal-Mart, over 90% of all orders are processed directly—business to business—often via an extranet.

For decades, companies have leased communications lines from telecommunications companies to create their own private networks that link offices in remote locations, suppliers, and, sometimes, customers. This type of private network, however, is an expensive proposition, primarily because of the line cost. An alternative is the **virtual private network,** or **VPN,** which has evolved as a less expensive alternative to the private network. The cost savings for VPNs is realized because its channels for communications are over a public infrastructure—the Internet (see Figure 7-4). The VPN employs encryption and other security measures to ensure that communications are not intercepted and that only authorized users are

FIGURE 7-5

BUSINESS-TO-BUSINESS E-COMMERCE
In the figure, the traditional interaction between a customer company and a supplier company are contrasted with similar interactions via business-to-business (B2B) e-commerce. Enabling technologies for B2B include extranets and VPNs.

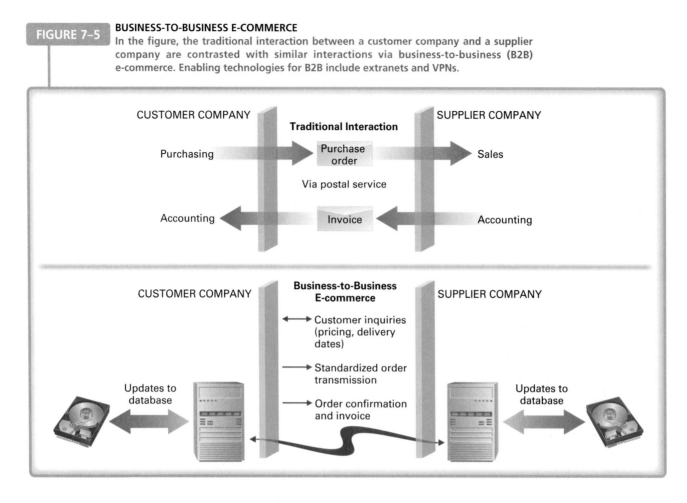

allowed access to the network. VPN uses **tunneling** technology. In tunneling, one network uses the channels of another network to send its data. In the case of VPNs, transmissions are "tunneled" through the Internet. VPNs have been a boon to companies whose policies encourage telecommuting and want knowledge workers on the go to stay connected.

In time, B2B e-commerce will be entirely over the Internet, an extranet, or a VPN. Figure 7-5 contrasts the traditional interactions between a customer and supplier company with interactions via B2B and extranets. Business-to-business commerce is expected to grow to a whopping $1.6 trillion by 2005, almost 10% of all U.S. business trade!

The phenomenal growth of the use of PCs in the home is causing companies to expand their information system capabilities to allow linkages with home and portable PCs, primarily via the Internet. This form of cooperative processing increases system efficiency while lowering costs. For example, in many banks, services have been extended to home PC owners in the form of home banking systems. Subscribers to a home banking service use their personal computers as terminals linked to the bank's server computer system, either directly or via the Internet, to pay bills, transfer funds, and ask about account status.

7-1.1	We are going through a period of digital convergence. (T/F)
7-1.2	B2B is the same as intracompany networking. (T/F)
7-1.3	VPN uses what type of technology for its channels: (a) conduit, (b) tunneling, (c) canals, or (d) subway?
7-1.4	One approach to using computers to transmit data electronically between companies is called: (a) 3CPO, (b) 2B or -2B, (c) B2B, or (d) DIT.

SECTION SELF-CHECK

7-2 The Data Communications Channel

A **communications channel** is the medium through which digital information must pass to get from one location in a computer network to the next. People often use slang terms for communications channel, such as *line, link,* or *pipe.* Communications channels link PCs, servers, and other devices in a network. They provide links between networks, whether between rooms at home or between remote offices. And, they enable you, other individuals, and companies to access the Internet, which, itself, is made up of a variety of communications links.

TRANSMISSION MEDIA

Some communication channels involve a physical link (wire or cable) and others are wireless. Channels are rated by their capacity to transmit information, which is cited in terms of *bits per second (bps).*

Twisted-Pair Wire

Twisted-pair wire is just what we think of as regular telephone wire. Each twisted-pair wire is actually two insulated copper wires twisted around each other. At least one twisted-pair line provides **POTS** (plain old telephone services) to just about every home and business in the United States. Telephone companies offer two different levels of twisted-pair service. All companies offer voice-grade service. The other service may or may not be available in your area.

- *POTS.* When you call the telephone company and request a telephone line, it installs POTS. This analog line permits voice conversations and digital transmissions with the aid of a modem. Traditional modem technology permits data transmission up to 56 K bps.

- *DSL. Digital Subscriber Line* (DSL) is delivered over a POTS line. Data can stream along the same line while you talk. DSL, one of the broadband options, is introduced in Getting Started and discussed further in Chapter 1.

Coaxial Cable

Most people know coaxial cable as the cable in "cable television." **Coaxial cable,** or "coax," contains electrical wire (usually copper wire) and is constructed to permit high-speed data transmission with a minimum of signal distortion. It is laid along the ocean floor for intercontinental voice and data transmission; it's used to connect terminals and computers in a "local" area (from a few feet to a few miles); and it delivers TV signals to close to 100 million homes in America alone. Coaxial cable has a very "wide pipe." That is, it is a high-capacity channel that can carry digital data at up to 10 M bps, as well as more than 100 analog TV signals. Internet access via cable TV coax cable is hundreds of times faster than POTS. Cable modem broadband access, introduced in Getting Started and Chapter 1, is comparable to DSL.

Wireless Communication

High-speed communications channels do not have to be wires or fibers. Data can also be transmitted via **microwave signals** or **radio signals** in much the same way that signals travel from a remote control to a TV or VCR or between a cellular telephone tower and a cell phone. Transmission of these signals is line-of-sight; that is, the signal travels in a straight line from source to destination.

Microwave signals are transmitted between transceivers. Because microwave signals do not bend around the curvature of the earth, signals may need to be relayed several times by microwave repeater stations before reaching their destination. Repeater stations are placed on the tops of mountains, tall buildings, and towers, usually about 30 miles apart.

PERSONAL COMPUTING:
Justifying the Cost of Broadband Internet Access Always-on Internet access at broadband speeds is a different experience than dialup access at 56 K bps. Without the waiting, you are more willing to explore the resources of the cyberworld. Simply, you go more places and do more things, and many of these activities save both time and money. The enhanced experience can easily justify the added cost. In most urban markets, cable modem or DSL broadband access is available for about $50 a month. That amount is roughly the subscription costs for dialup Internet access plus the cost of an extra telephone line. The majority of Internet-active families have a "data line" for Internet activities, which is not needed for always-on broadband.

Satellites: Sky High Repeater Stations

Satellites eliminate the line-of-sight limitation because microwave signals are bounced off satellites, avoiding buildings, mountains, and other signal obstructions. One of the advantages of satellites is that data can be transmitted from one location to any number of other locations anywhere on (or near) our planet. Satellites are routinely launched into orbit for the sole purpose of relaying data communications signals to and from earth stations (see Figure 7-6). A satellite, which uses microwave signals and is essentially a repeater station, is launched and set in a **geosynchronous orbit** 22,300 miles above the earth. A geosynchronous orbit permits the communications satellite to maintain a fixed position relative to the earth's surface. Each satellite can receive and retransmit signals to slightly less than half of the earth's surface; therefore, three satellites are required to cover the earth effectively (see Figure 7-7). Internet access via satellite is available to companies and to individuals at speeds up to 48 M bps. Broadband digital satellite Internet access, which is introduced in Getting Started and Chapter 1, is comparable to cable modem and DSL access speeds.

PCs Communicating without Wires

PCs in the office and on the road can be linked via wireless connections often using *Wi-Fi* (the *IEEE 802.11b* standard) technology introduced in Chapter 3. One of the greatest challenges and biggest

FIGURE 7–6   WIRELESS COMMUNICATION

INTERNET ACCESS VIA DIGITAL SATELLITE
This digital satellite dish enables two-way high-speed access to the Internet. All that is needed for this type of wireless link is a southern exposure to the satellite, a satellite modem, a dish, and a coaxial cable to transmit the signal to the PC.

Long and Associates

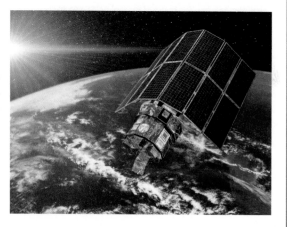

SATELLITE COMMUNICATIONS
Common carriers rely heavily on communications satellites and a network of earth stations to help them offer high-speed data communications to customers. This Orbital Seastar satellite enables wireless data transmissions via satellite.

Courtesy of Lockheed Martin Corporation

Courtesy of Orbital Sciences Corporation

expenses in a computer network is the installation of the physical links between its components. The **wireless transceiver** provides an alternative to running a permanent physical line (twisted-pair wire, coaxial cable, or fiber optic cable). A wireless LAN PC card about the size of a thick credit card replaces a physical line to the data source. For example, wireless communication is routinely used to link these devices:

- Desktop PC and notebook PC
- PC (desktop, laptop, or palm/pocket) and local area network (LAN)
- PC and server computer
- PCs in a home network

The wireless LAN PC card hooks into a USB, PCI, or PCMCIA slot. Transceivers, which have a limited range (about 50 feet), link computers via omnidirectional (traveling in all directions at once) radio waves. Access points, which are hardwired to a central server computer, are positioned throughout a building, a neighborhood, or a college campus to extend the reach of the wireless LAN. When using transceivers, the source computer transmits digital signals to its transceiver, which, in turn, retransmits the signals over radio waves to the other transceiver. Transceivers provide users with

FIGURE 7–7

SATELLITE DATA TRANSMISSION
Three satellites in geosynchronous orbit (staying over the same point on earth) provide worldwide data transmission service.

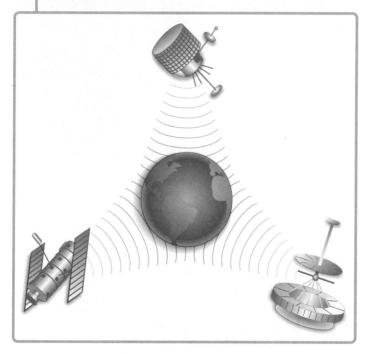

tremendous flexibility in the location of PCs and terminals in a network.

The 2002 Winter Olympics in Salt Lake City, USA, was the perfect venue for widespread use of wireless networks. Many sites at the games were temporary or difficult to wire and were thus made-to-order situations for wireless networks. Wireless networks allowed judges, statisticians, and journalists to move with the action within and between venues.

The Future of Wireless

Very high speed wireless Internet service may be headed to our doorstep. Line-of-sight wireless technologies **MMDS** (Multichannel Multipoint Distribution Service) and **LMDS** (Local Multipoint Distribution Service) provide for network access at fiber optic-level speeds. Industry forecasters are predicting that MMDS will provide Internet services at 1 G bps (gigabits per second) for 70% of the residential and small office market within 5 years. That is about 1000 times faster than current domestic broadband options. ISPs are very interested in MMDS because it can offer high-speed Internet service within a 35-mile radius with minimal investment in equipment. LMDS is a wireless solution to bringing very high bandwidth to homes and offices on the last mile of connectivity.

Fiber Optic Cable: Light Pulse

Twisted-pair wire and coaxial cable carry data as electrical signals. **Fiber optic cable** carries data as laser-generated pulses of light (see Figure 7-8). Made up of bundles of very thin, transparent, almost hair-like fibers, fiber optic cables transmit data more inexpensively and much more quickly than do copper wire transmission media. The Internet backbone, the primary channels for Internet transmissions, is mostly fiber optic cable. In the time it takes to transmit a single page of *Webster's Unabridged Dictionary* over twisted-pair copper wire (about 3 seconds) over a regular modem, the entire dictionary could be transmitted over a single optic fiber! Businesses that demand very high-speed B2B communications have fiber optic cable linked directly to their server computers.

Each time a communications company lays a new fiber optic cable, the world is made a little smaller. In 1956, the first transatlantic cable carried 50 voice circuits. Then, talking to someone in Europe was a rare and expensive experience. Today, a single fiber can carry over 32,000 voice and data transmissions, the equivalent of 2.5 billion bits per second. Nowadays, people call colleagues in other countries or link up with international computers as readily as they call home.

Another of the many advantages of fiber optic cable is its contribution to data security. It is much more difficult for a computer criminal to intercept a signal sent over fiber optic cable (via a beam of light) than it is over copper wire (an electrical signal).

Fiber optic technology is taking giant leaps. Already scientists are able to transmit data over a special fiber optic cable at 3.28 terabits per second (trillion bps), but only over a distance of a city block. At that rate, the new high-tech fiber can transmit the equivalent of three days' worth of Internet traffic (worldwide) in a single second! This technology is still in the laboratory, but this new technology may give us a very big "pipe" through which to receive information in the near future.

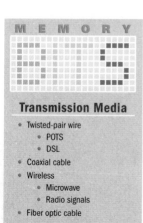

Transmission Media

- Twisted-pair wire
  - POTS
  - DSL
- Coaxial cable
- Wireless
  - Microwave
  - Radio signals
- Fiber optic cable

COMMON CARRIERS

It is impractical for individuals and companies to string their own fiber optic cable between distant locations, such as Hong Kong and New York City. It is also impractical for them to set their own satellites in orbit, although some companies have. Therefore, most people and companies turn to communications **common carriers,** such as AT&T, MCI, and Sprint, to provide communications channels for data transmission. Organizations pay communications common carriers, which are regulated by the Federal Communications Commission (FCC), for *private* or *switched* data communications service.

A **private line** (or **leased line**) provides a dedicated data communications channel between any two points in a computer network. The charge for a private line is based on channel capacity (bps) and distance. Some companies have private lines that link remote offices, primarily with fiber optic cable.

FIGURE 7–8

FIBER OPTIC CABLE
For the better part of the 20th century, our country was being laced with the twisted-pair copper wire extending between telephone poles. Today, wherever possible, telephone poles and twisted-pair wire are being replaced by the more versatile fiber optic cable. More than 90% of long-distance telephone and Internet traffic in the United States is carried over 15 million miles of optical fiber, the hair-thin strands of glass that make up fiber optic cable. Fiber optic cable is capable of transmitting voice, video, and computer data as laser-generated pulses of light. Two optical fibers can handle the equivalent of 625,000 telephone calls or Internet dialup connections at once.

Courtesy of International Business Machines Corporation. Unauthorized use not permitted.

Courtesy of Corning, Inc.

A **switched line** (or **dialup line**) is available strictly on a time-and-distance charge, similar to a long-distance telephone call. You (or your computer) make a connection by "dialing up" a computer, then a modem sends and receives data. Switched lines offer greater flexibility than do private lines because they allow you to link up with any communications-ready computer. A regular POTS telephone line is a switched line.

The number and variety of common carriers is expanding. For decades, it was just the telephone companies. Now cable TV and satellite companies provide common carrier services. Data rates offered by common carriers range from voice-grade POTS (up to about 56 K bps with a modem) to the widest of all pipes, the massive 622 M bps channel.

The emergence of Internet-connected intranets, extranets, and VPNs has changed the way companies link with remote locations and other companies. Although the leased line is still the corporate choice when very high-speed communication is required, most companies opt for cost-saving Internet-based alternatives for all other communication needs.

CONTROLLING TRANSMISSIONS OVER COMMUNICATIONS CHANNELS

Computers must adhere to strict rules when transmitting information between computers.

Communications Protocols

Communications protocols are rules established to govern the way data are transmitted in a computer network. A protocol describes how these data are transmitted. Communications protocols are defined in *layers,* the first of which is the physical layer. The physical layer defines the manner in which nodes in a network are connected to one another. Subsequent layers, the number of which vary between protocols, describe how messages are packaged for transmission, how messages are routed through the network, security procedures, and the manner in which messages are displayed. A number of different protocols are in common use. The protocol you hear about most often is TCP/IP (Transmission Control Protocol/Internet Protocol), which actually is a collective reference to the protocols that link computers on the Internet (TCP and IP). These protocols are discussed in Chapter 3, "Going Online."

Asynchronous and Synchronous Transmission

Protocols fall into two general classifications: *asynchronous* and *synchronous* (see Figure 7-9). In **asynchronous transmission,** data are transmitted at irregular intervals on an as-needed basis. Most communication between computers and devices is asynchronous, occurring as needed at irregular intervals. Internet interaction is asynchronous. *Start/stop bits* are appended to the beginning and end of each message. The start/stop bits signal the receiving terminal/computer at the beginning and end of the message. In PC data communications, the message is a single byte or character. Asynchronous transmission, sometimes called *start/stop transmission,* is best suited for low-speed data communications, such as that between the Internet and a PC with a standard 56 K bps modem.

In **synchronous transmission,** the source and destination operate in timed synchronization to enable high-speed data transfer. Start/stop bits are not required in synchronous transmission. Data transmission between computers and hardware that facilitates high-speed data communications is normally synchronous.

DATA TRANSMISSION IN PRACTICE

A communications channel from Computer A in Seattle, Washington, to Computer B in Orlando, Florida (see Figure 7-10), usually would consist of several different transmission media and, perhaps, multiple protocols. The connection between Computer A and a terminal in the same building is probably coaxial cable or twisted-pair wire. The Seattle company might use a common carrier company such as AT&T to transmit the data via a leased line. AT&T would then send the data through a combination of transmission facilities that might include copper wire, microwave signals, radio signals, and fiber optic cable.

FIGURE 7–9 **ASYNCHRONOUS AND SYNCHRONOUS TRANSMISSION OF DATA**
Asynchronous data transmission takes place at irregular intervals. In asynchronous transmission, the message is typically a single character with parity bits added to ensure transmission accuracy. Synchronous data transmission requires timed synchronization between sending and receiving devices. The message is typically a block of characters.

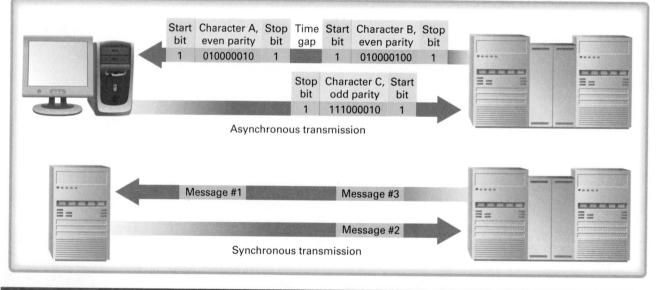

FIGURE 7–10

DATA TRANSMISSION PATH
It's more the rule than the exception that data are carried over several transmission media between source and destination.

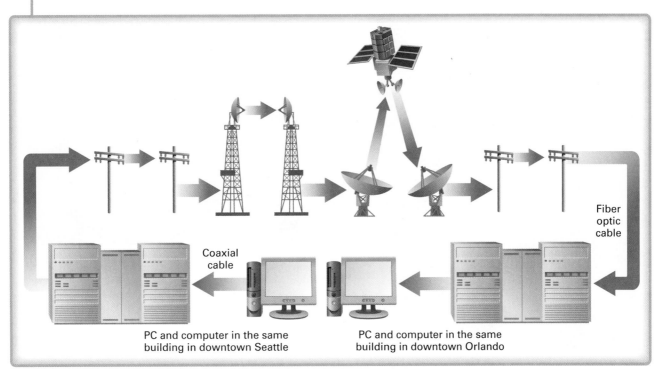

PC and computer in the same building in downtown Seattle

PC and computer in the same building in downtown Orlando

Coaxial cable

Fiber optic cable

7-2.1 It is more difficult for a computer criminal to tap into a fiber optic cable than a copper telephone line. (T/F)

7-2.2 The wireless transceiver will never replace the physical link between the source and the destination in a network. (T/F)

7-2.3 Synchronous transmission is best suited for data communications involving low-speed I/O devices. (T/F)

7-2.4 Communications satellites in geosynchronous orbit are how many miles above the earth: (a) 200, (b) 2,200, (c) 22,300, or (d) 100,000?

SECTION SELF-CHECK

7-3 Data Communications Hardware

WHY THIS SECTION IS IMPORTANT TO YOU

Data may be entered in St. Paul, processed in St. Petersburg, and the results displayed in St. Croix, but how? Read on to learn about the hardware that makes data communications possible, as you will surely use these capabilities in the home and at the office.

Data communications, or **telecommunications,** is the electronic collection and distribution of information between two points. Information can appear in a variety of formats—numeric data, text, voice, still pictures, graphics, and video. As we have already seen, raw information must be digitized before we can input it into a computer. For example, numerical data and text might be translated into their corresponding ASCII codes. Once the digitized information has been entered into a computer, that computer can then transfer the information to other computers connected over a network. Ultimately, all forms of digitized information are transmitted over the transmission media (for example, fiber optic cable) as a series of binary bits (1s and 0s).

Data communications hardware is used to transmit digital information between terminals and computers or between computers and other computers. There is a vast array of communications and networking hardware. Figure 7-11, which shows the integration of some of these devices with terminals and computer systems, is a representative computer network. With so much networking hardware, networks are a lot like snowflakes—no two are alike. Unlike snowflakes, however, networks never melt. Once created, networks seem to have a life of their own, growing with the changing needs of the organization.

With the trend toward digital convergence, the number and variety of network hardware components that enable data communications continue to evolve, with new devices being introduced almost monthly. There are *concentrators, switching hubs, bridges, routers, brouters* (combination bridges and routers), *network interface cards, front-end processors, multiplexors,* various types of *modems,* and

FIGURE 7–11 THE EVOLUTION OF TERMINALS

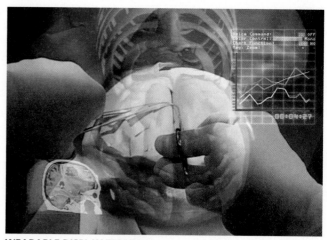

WEARABLE DISPLAY TERMINAL
The terminal is the visual link to a computer system for many knowledge workers; however, it is being redefined with recent technological innovations. This Microvision wearable display is integrated into eyeglasses, goggles, or helmets. The system enables the display of an image that doesn't block the user's (a surgeon in this example) view but will, instead, superimpose a color image on top of it.

Photo courtesy of Microvision Incorporated

AIRLINE CHECK-IN KIOSK
For decades, the terminal has been behind the airline check-in counter. Now, many airlines are making a terminal available to their customers in the form of a self-service check-in kiosk. This airline check-in kiosk has a touch screen monitor, allowing the passenger to interact with the airline's central computer system.

Courtesy of International Business Machines Corporation. Unauthorized use not permitted.

many more special-function devices that route, pass along, convert, package and repackage, and format and reformat bits and bytes traveling along communications links. Most of these are beyond the scope of an introductory study of IT. We will, however, talk about a couple of the more personal devices: the modem, a device that comes with most new PCs, and the network interface card, a device found on most corporate PCs and an increasing percentage of home PCs. Also, we will talk about a few other devices to help you better understand the fundamental terminology of data communications.

THE STANDARD TELEPHONE-LINK MODEM

Even if your PC is not connected to a corporate local area network with a digital line to cyberspace, you can establish a communications link between it and any remote computer system in the world, assuming you have the authorization to do so. However, you must first have ready access to a *telephone line,* and your PC must be equipped with a *modem*.

Telephone lines were designed to carry *analog signals* for voice communication, not the binary *digital signals* (1s and 0s) needed for computer-based data communication. The modem (modulator-demodulator) converts *digital* signals into *analog* signals so data can be transmitted over telephone lines (see Figure 7-12). The digital electrical signals are modulated to make sounds similar to those you hear on a touch-tone telephone. Upon reaching their destination, these analog tone signals are demodulated into computer-compatible digital signals for processing. A modem is always required for two computers to communicate over a telephone line. It is not needed when the PC is wired directly to a computer network (for example, cabling between embedded network interface cards) or another PC (for example, via USB cables).

FIGURE 7–12

HARDWARE COMPONENTS IN DATA COMMUNICATIONS
Devices that handle the movement of data in a computer network are the modem, the multiplexor, the front-end processor, the router, network interface cards (expansion cards in the local area network-based PCs), and the host computer. Also in the figure, electrical digital signals are modulated (via a modem) into analog signals for transmission over telephone lines and then demodulated for processing at the destination. The lightning bolts indicate transmission between remote locations.

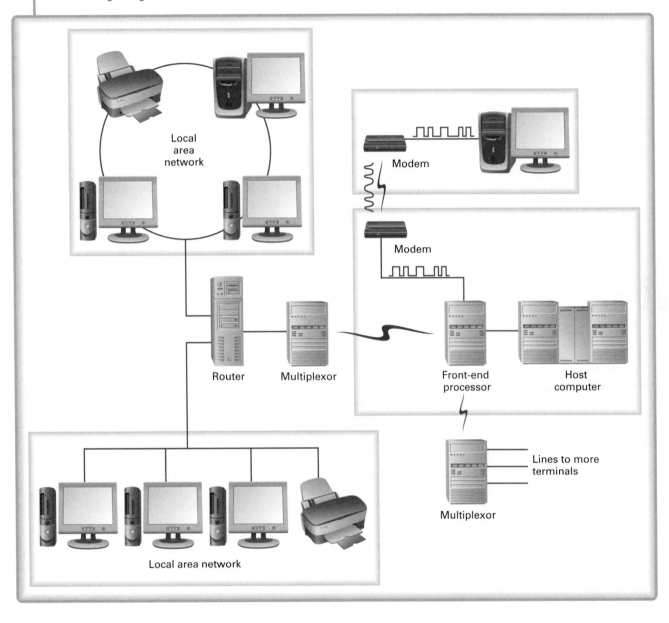

Modems for PCs and terminals are *internal* and *external*. Most PCs have internal modems; that is, the modem is on an optional add-on circuit board that is simply plugged into an empty expansion PCI slot in the PC's motherboard. On notebooks, modems are on interchangeable PC cards or built into the motherboard. The external modem is a separate component, as illustrated in Figure 7-12, and is connected via a serial interface or USB port. To make the connection with a telephone line and either type of modem, you simply plug the telephone line into the modem just as you would when connecting the line to a telephone.

The typical modem is a voice/data/fax modem. Besides the data communications capabilities, it allows you to make telephone calls through your PC and modem hookup (using a microphone, speakers, and/or a headset). The fax feature enables a PC to simulate a *fax* machine. Instead of sending a document to a printer, you simply send it to the fax modem along with a destination fax number. With people routinely using e-mail (with attachments as needed) you might think that the fax machine might be gathering dust, but this is not the case. A survey indicated that the number of faxes sent in large companies almost doubled in the first year of this millennium to about 2000 per day.

OTHER MODEMS

Traditional modems are largely unused by those people with broadband Internet access. Instead, they use a cable modem, a DSL modem, or a satellite modem. Typically, these broadband modems are external and connect to the PC via a USB port; however, they may be installed in an expansion slot or linked via a network interface card, too.

The *cable modem* that supports cable Internet access (over cable TV lines) is similar to the telephone modem, but instead of modulating the PC's digital signals to analog tone signals, it modulates the digital signals to RF (radio frequency) carrier signals. The RF carrier signals are demodulated by another cable modem to digital information upon arrival at their destination.

The *DSL modem* isn't actually a modem. It is a DSL transceiver, but tradition calls for the "modem" moniker. Regardless of what it is called, it provides the connection between the user's computer or network and the DSL line. All DSL signals are routed to a telephone company's **DSLAM (Digital Subscriber Line Access Multiplexor)**, where they are combined into a very-high speed Internet connection, usually a fiber-optic cable.

The modem name tag also is attached to the device that enables uplink and downlink from satellite—the *satellite modem*. The satellite modem is actually two modems, one for the uplink signal conversion and one for the downlink signal conversion.

NETWORK INTERFACE CARDS

The *network interface card (NIC)*, which we introduced in Chapter 4, "Inside the Computer," is an add-on board or PC card (for notebooks) that enables and controls the exchange of data between the PCs in a LAN. Each PC in the LANs in Figure 7-12 must be equipped with an NIC. The cables or wireless transceivers that link the PCs are connected physically to the NICs. Whether as an add-on board or a PC card, the NIC is connected directly to the PC's internal bus. With the Ethernet standard for LAN architecture a de facto standard, the NIC is often called an **Ethernet Card.**

ROUTERS

Computer networks are everywhere—in banks, in law offices, in the classroom, and in the home. In keeping with the trend toward greater connectivity, computer networks are themselves being networked and interconnected to give users access to a greater variety of applications and to more information. For example, the typical medium-to-large company links several PC-based networks to the company's enterprise-wide network. This enables end users on all networks to share information and resources.

Because networks use a variety of communications protocols and operating systems, incompatible networks cannot "talk" directly to one another. The primary hardware/software technology used to alleviate the problems of linking incompatible computer networks is the **router.** Routers help to bridge the gap between incompatible networks by performing the necessary protocol conversions to route messages to their proper destinations.

Organizations that are set up to interconnect computer networks do so over a **backbone.** The backbone is a collective term that refers to a system of routers and other communications hardware and the associated transmission media (cables, wires, and wireless links) that link the computers in an organization.

Routers, once limited to the business environment, are becoming popular in the home, too. Broadband ISPs often sell routers to their customers to enable sharing of the Internet signal on a home network. If you wish to share an Internet signal among several PCs in your home network, ask your ISP if you will need a router or if you can share the Internet through your PCs peer-to-peer networking capability.

TERMINALS

A variety of terminals enables both *input to* and *output from* a remote computer system. Interactions via a terminal form the foundation for a wide variety of applications, from airline reservations to point-of-sale systems in retail outlets.

Dumb and Smart Terminals

Terminals come in all shapes and sizes and have a variety of input/output capabilities (see Figure 7-11). The most popular general-purpose terminal is the traditional **video display terminal (VDT)** that you

THE CRYSTAL BALL:
Fax on the Brink of Extinction
Facsimile or fax was invented in 1842, by the Scotsman Alexander Bain; however, the first wire photo was sent from Cleveland to New York in 1924. By the mid-1950s, the fax had become a mainstream business tool and its use has increased steadily until now. Everything the fax does can be done more quickly, more efficiently, and at less cost within the context of online systems, image processing, networking, and the Internet. As people familiarize themselves with the alternatives, look for fax machines to take their place alongside the typewriter and other obsolete off line business equipment.

see in hospitals and airports. The primary input mechanism on the *VDT,* or simply the *terminal,* is a *keyboard.* Output is displayed on a *monitor.* Most of these terminals are dumb; that is, they have little or no intelligence (processing capability).

Some terminals, called **Windows terminals,** have some processing capabilities and RAM; however, they are not designed for stand-alone operation. The Windows terminal is so named because the user interacts with a Windows graphical user interface (GUI). All Windows terminals are configured with some type of point-and-draw device, such as a mouse, to permit efficient interaction with the GUI.

Telephone Terminals and Telephony

The telephone's widespread availability is causing greater use of it as a terminal. You can enter alphanumeric data on the touch-tone keypad of a telephone or by speaking into the receiver (voice input via speech recognition). You would then receive computer-generated voice output from a voice-response system. Salespeople use telephones as terminals for entering orders and inquiries about the availability of certain products into their company's server computer. Brokerage firms allow their clients to tap into the firm's computers via telephone.

The telephone by itself has little built-in intelligence; however, when linked to a computer, potential applications abound. **Telephony** is the integration of computers and telephones, the two most essential instruments of business. In telephony, the computer, often a PC, acts in concert with the telephone. For example, a PC can analyze incoming telephone calls and take appropriate action (take a message, route the call to the appropriate extension, and so on).

Special-Function Terminals: ATMs and POSs

The number and variety of special-function terminals are growing rapidly. Special-function terminals are designed for a specific application, such as convenience banking. You probably are familiar with the *automatic teller machine* (*ATM*) and its input/output capabilities.

The ATM idea has caught on for other applications. A consortium of companies is installing thousands of ATM-like terminals that will let you order and receive a wide variety of documents on the spot. For example, you can now obtain an airline ticket, your college transcript, and an IRS form electronically, and many more applications are on the way.

Another widely used special-function terminal is the *point-of-sale* (*POS*) terminal. Clerks and salespeople in retail stores, restaurants, and other establishments that sell goods and services use POS terminals. POS terminals have a keypad for input, at least one small monitor, and a printer to print the receipt. Some have other input/output devices, such as a badge reader for credit cards, a wand or stationary scanner to read price and inventory data, and/or a printer to preprint checks for customers.

SPECIAL-FUNCTION COMMUNICATIONS DEVICES IN THE BUSINESS COMMUNITY

In Figure 7-12, there is a *host computer,* or server computer, that is responsible for the overall control of the network and for the execution of applications (for example, a hotel reservation system). To improve the efficiency of a business computer system, the *processing load* is sometimes *distributed* among several other special-function processors. The two communications-related processors in the network of Figure 7-12, the front-end processor and the multiplexor, are under the control of and subordinate to the host. In Figure 7-12, the host computer is a large server computer; however, the host could just as well be a PC or a supercomputer, depending on the size and complexity of the network.

The terminal or computer sending a **message** is the *source.* The terminal or computer receiving the message is the *destination.* The **front-end processor** establishes the link between the source and destination in a process called **handshaking.** The term *front-end processor* has evolved to a generic reference for a computer-based device that relieves the host computer of a variety of communications-related processing duties. These duties include the transmission of data to and from remote terminals and other computers. The host can instead concentrate on overall system control and the execution of applications software.

If you think of messages as mail to be delivered to various points in a computer network, the front-end processor is the post office. Each computer system and terminal/PC in a computer network is assigned a **network address.** The front-end processor uses these addresses to route messages to their destinations. The content of a message could be a prompt to the user, a user inquiry, a program instruction, an "electronic memo," or any type of information that can be transmitted electronically—even the image of a handwritten report.

The **multiplexor** is an extension of the front-end processor. It is located down line from the host computer—at or near a remote site. The multiplexor collects data from several low-speed devices, such as terminals and printers. It then "concentrates" the data and sends them over a single communications channel (see Figure 7-13) to the front-end processor. The multiplexor also receives and

FIGURE 7–13 **CONCENTRATING DATA FOR REMOTE TRANSMISSION**
The multiplexor concentrates the data from several low-speed devices for transmission over a single high-speed line. At the host site, the front-end processor separates the data for processing. Data received from a front-end processor are interpreted by the multiplexor processor and routed to the appropriate device.

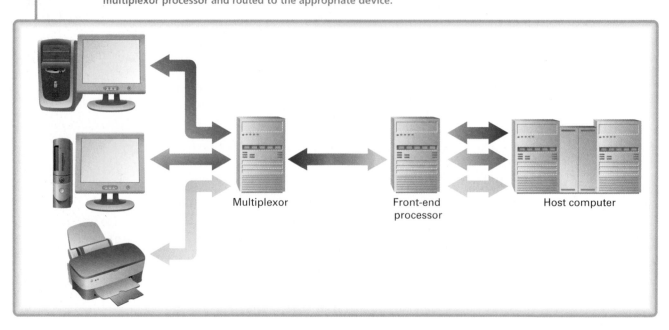

Multiplexor   Front-end   Host computer
                     processor

distributes host output to the appropriate remote terminals. Using one high-speed line to connect the multiplexor to the host is considerably less expensive than is using several low-speed lines to connect each terminal to the host. For example, an airline reservation counter might have 10 terminals, and it would be very slow and very expensive to connect each directly to the host computer. Instead, each terminal would be connected to a common multiplexor, which in turn would be connected to the central host computer.

7-4 Networks

Networks are about sharing and communication. Networks facilitate the sharing of hardware (from printers to backup disk storage to server computers), software, data, and Internet access. They also make it easier for us to share ideas and communicate all kinds of information, from meeting schedules to product design data. The telephone system is the world's largest computer network, so you have been sharing and communicating on a network for most of your life. A telephone is an endpoint, or a **node**, connected to a network of computers that routes your voice signals to any one of the 500 million telephones (other nodes) in the world.

In a computer network the node can be a terminal, a computer, or any destination/source device (for example, a printer, an automatic teller machine, or even a telephone). Within an organization, computer networks are set up to meet the specific requirements of that organization. Some have 5 nodes; others have 10,000 nodes. Each network is one of a kind (see Figure 7-14). We have already seen the hardware and transmission media used to link nodes in a network. In this section, we intro-

FIGURE 7–14 NETWORKS IN PRACTICE

VISUAL AREA NETWORKING

Using a wireless tablet PC, Dr. Eng Lim Goh of SGI demonstrates Visual Area Networking. Visual Area Networking allows users to interact with visualization supercomputers anywhere they are, with any client device. It removes the requirement to have either the data or the advanced visualization capability local to the user.

Courtesy of SGI. Tablet image courtesy of SONICblue, Inc. Screen images courtesy of Landmark Graphics Corporation.

NETWORK CONTROL CENTER

This Global Network Control Center controls the entire ORBCOMM satellite constellation. ORBCOMM's mission is to revolutionize the way companies and individuals use wireless data communications. The satellites envelop the earth in low-altitude orbits, which allows messages to be sent and received by small, low-power access devices.

Courtesy of Orbital Sciences Corporation

HOSPITALS LINK UP

The workstations and PCs at this hospital are on a network and linked to a server computer. A computerized patient records system allows physicians to easily access up-to-date patient chart information from workstations throughout the hospital.

Courtesy of Harris Corporation

WIRELESS LOCAL AREA NETWORK

From anywhere within the hospital, this doctor can insert a wireless local area network PC Card into his notebook to enable a link to the hospital's LAN. Wireless links permit mobile users to create networks in minutes, without restrictive, conventional wire connections.

Courtesy of Raytheon Company

duce network topologies and the various types of networks. LANs, the most popular type of network, are discussed in more detail.

NETWORK TOPOLOGIES

A **network topology** is a description of the possible physical connections within a network. The topology is the configuration of the hardware and shows which pairs of nodes can communicate. The basic computer network topologies—star, ring, and bus—are illustrated in Figure 7-15. However, a pure form of any of these three basic topologies is rare in practice. Most computer networks are *hybrids*—combinations of these topologies.

Star Topology

The **star topology** involves a centralized host computer connected to several other computer systems, which are usually smaller than the host. The smaller computer systems communicate with one another through the host and usually share the host computer's database. The host could be anything from a PC to a supercomputer. Any computer can communicate with any other computer in the network. Banks often have a large home-office computer system with a star network of smaller server computer systems in the branch banks.

Ring Topology

The **ring topology** involves computer systems of approximately the same size, with no one computer system as the focal point of the network. When one system routes a message to another system, it is passed around the ring until it reaches its destination address.

Bus Topology

The **bus topology** permits the connection of terminals, peripheral devices, and PCs along a common cable called a **network bus**. The term *bus* is used because people on a bus can get off at any stop along the route. In a bus topology a signal is broadcast to all nodes, but only the destination node responds to the signal. It is easy to add devices or delete them from the network, as devices are simply daisy-chained along the network bus. Bus topologies are most appropriate when the linked devices are physically close to one another.

TYPES OF NETWORKS

Networks tend to be classified by the proximity of their nodes.

- *The LAN.* The *local area network* (*LAN*), or **local net**, connects nodes in close proximity, such as in a suite of offices or a building. The local net, including all data communications channels, is owned by the organization using it. Because of the proximity of nodes in local nets, a company can install its own communications channels (such as coaxial cable, twisted

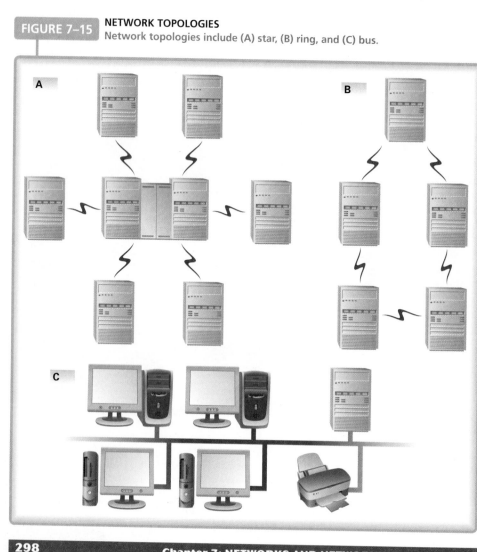

FIGURE 7–15

NETWORK TOPOLOGIES
Network topologies include (A) star, (B) ring, and (C) bus.

pair wire, fiber optic cable, wireless transceivers, and so on). Therefore, LANs do not need common carriers. LANs, the most popular type of network, are more fully explained later in this section.

- *The WAN.* A **WAN**, or **wide area network**, connects nodes, usually local area networks (LANs), in widely dispersed geographic areas, such as cities, states, and even countries. Wal-Mart, the largest retailer in the world, links the LANs in over 2000 stores and warehouses. The WAN often depends on the transmission services of a common carrier to transmit signals between nodes in the network. The emergence of virtual private networks (VPNs) and the potential for cost savings has resulted in many WANs being setup as VPNs over the world's grandest WAN, the Internet.

- *The MAN.* The **MAN**, or **metropolitan area network**, is a network designed for a city. MANs are more encompassing than local area networks (LANs) but smaller than wide area networks (WANs).

When we refer to LANs, WANs, and MANs, we refer to all hardware, software, and communications channels associated with them.

The focus of this section is the LAN, the most common network. Strictly speaking, any type of computer can be part of a LAN, but, in practice, PCs, thin clients, and workstations provide the foundation for local area networks. PCs in a typical LAN are linked to each other and share resources such as printers and disk storage. The distance separating devices in the local net may vary from a few feet to a few miles. As few as two and as many as several hundred PCs can be linked on a single local area network.

Most corporate PCs are linked to a LAN to aid in communication among knowledge workers. LANs make good business sense because these and other valuable resources can be shared.

- *Applications software.* The cost of a LAN-based word processing program (for example, Microsoft Word) is far less than the cost of a word processing program for each PC in the LAN.

- *Links to other LAN servers.* Other LANs become an accessible resource. It is easier to link one or more LANs to a single LAN than to many individual PCs.

- *Communications capabilities.* Many users can share a dedicated communications line or broadband Internet access.

- *I/O devices.* With a little planning, a single page printer, plotter, or scanner can support many users on a LAN with little loss of office efficiency. In a normal office setting, a single page printer can service the printing needs of up to 20 LAN users.

- *Storage devices.* Databases on a LAN can be shared. For example, some offices make a national telephone directory available to all LAN users.

- *Add-on boards.* Add-on boards, such as video capture boards, can be shared by many PCs.

Like computers, automobiles, and just about everything else, local nets can be built at various levels of sophistication. At the most basic level, they permit the interconnection of PCs in a department so that users can send messages to one another and share files and printers. The more sophisticated local nets permit the interconnection of server computers, PCs, and the spectrum of peripheral devices throughout a large but geographically constrained area, such as a cluster of buildings.

In some offices, you plug a terminal or PC into a network just as you would plug a telephone line into a telephone jack. This type of data communications capability is being installed in the new "smart" office buildings.

LAN OVERVIEW

Local nets, or LANs, are found in just about any office building. The basic hardware components in a PC-based LAN are the network interface cards, or NICs, in the PCs; the transmission media that connect the nodes in the network; and the servers. LANs may also have routers, modems, and other previously mentioned network hardware.

LAN Access Methods

Only one node on a LAN can send information at any given time. The other nodes must wait their turn. The transfer of data and programs between nodes is controlled by the access method embedded in the network interface card's ROM. The two most popular access methods are *token* and *Ethernet*.

Token Access Method

When a LAN with a *ring* topology uses the **token access method,** an electronic *token* travels around a ring of nodes in the form of a header. Figure 7-16 demonstrates the token-passing process for this type

FIGURE 7–16 THE TOKEN ACCESS METHOD IN A LAN WITH A RING TOPOLOGY

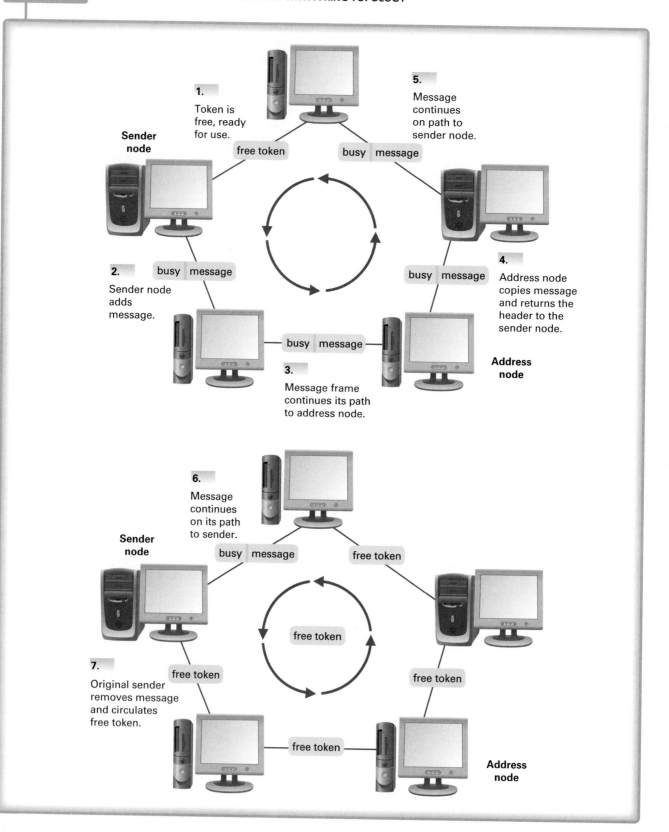

1.
Token is free, ready for use.

Sender node

free token

busy message

5.
Message continues on path to sender node.

2.
Sender node adds message.

busy message

busy message

4.
Address node copies message and returns the header to the sender node.

busy message

3.
Message frame continues its path to address node.

Address node

6.
Message continues on its path to sender.

Sender node

busy message

free token

free token

7.
Original sender removes message and circulates free token.

free token

free token

free token

Address node

of LAN. The header contains control signals, including one specifying whether the token is "free" or carrying a message. A sender node captures a free token as it travels from node to node, changes it to "busy," and adds the message. The resulting *message frame* travels around the ring to the addressee's NIC, which copies the message and returns the message frame to the sender. The sender's NIC removes the message frame from the ring and circulates a new free token. When a LAN with a *bus* topology uses the token access method, the token is broadcast to the nodes along the network bus. Think of the token as a benevolent dictator who, when captured, bestows the privilege of sending a transmission.

Ethernet

In the popular **Ethernet** access method, nodes on the LAN must contend for the right to send a message. To gain access to the network, a node with a message to be sent automatically requests network service from the network software. The request might result in a "line busy" signal. In this case the node waits a fraction of a second and tries again, and again, until the line is free. Upon assuming control of the line, the node sends the message and then relinquishes control of the line to another node. Ethernet LANs operate like a conversation between polite people. When two people begin talking at the same time, one must wait until the other is finished. This all happens very quickly as Ethernet LANs can transmit information at up to 1 GB (one billion bits) per second.

LAN Transmission Media and Servers

Three kinds of transmission media can be connected to the network interface cards: twisted-pair wire, coaxial cable, and fiber optic cable. In wireless transmission, the cable runs from the transceiver to the NIC. Figure 7-17 illustrates how nodes in a LAN are connected in a bus topology with a wiring hub at the end that allows several more nodes to be connected to the bus.

In a LAN, a *server* is a component that can be shared by users on the LAN. The three most popular servers are the file server, the print server, and the communications server.

- *File server.* The **file server** normally is a dedicated computer, sometimes a high-performance PC or a workstation, with a high-capacity hard disk for storing the data and programs shared by the network users. For example, the master customer file, word processing software, spreadsheet software, and so on would be stored on the server disk. When a user wants to begin a spreadsheet session, the spreadsheet software is downloaded from the file server to the user's RAM.

- *Print server.* The **print server** typically is housed in the same dedicated PC as the file server. The print server handles user print jobs and controls at least one printer. If needed, the server *spools* print jobs; that is, it saves print jobs to disk until the requested printer is available, then routes the print file to the printer.

- *Communications server.* The **communications server** provides communication links external to the LAN—that is, links to other networks. To accomplish this service, the communications server controls one or more modems, or perhaps access to a DSL line.

These server functions may reside in a single PC or can be distributed among the PCs that make up the LAN. When the server functions are consolidated, the server PC usually is *dedicated* to servicing the LAN. Some PCs are designed specifically to be dedicated **LAN servers.** Until recently, you would purchase a traditional single-user PC and make it a dedicated server. Using a single-user PC continues to be an option with small- to medium-sized LANs, but not in large LANs with 100 or more users. Now, PC vendors manufacture powerful computers designed, often with multiple processors, specifically as LAN servers. LAN servers are configured with enough RAM, storage capacity, and backup capability to handle the resource needs of hundreds of PCs.

LAN SOFTWARE

In this section, we explore LAN-based software, including LAN operating systems alternatives and a variety of applications software.

Network Operating Systems

LAN operating systems, the nucleus of a local net, come in two formats: *peer-to-peer,* sometimes called *P2P,* and *dedicated server.* In both cases, the LAN operating system is actually several pieces of software. Each processing component in the LAN has a piece of the LAN operating system resident in its RAM. The pieces interact with one another to enable the nodes to share resources and communication.

The individual user in a LAN might appear to be interacting with an operating system, such as Windows XP. However, the RAM-resident LAN software *redirects* certain requests to the appropriate LAN component. For example, a print request would be redirected to the print server.

FIGURE 7-17

LAN LINKS
In this figure, nodes in a LAN are linked via a bus topology. One of the nodes is linked to a wiring hub that enables several PCs to be connected to the network bus. The wiring hub acts like a multiplexor, concentrating transmissions from several nodes. The LAN is linked to other LANs with fiber optic cable.

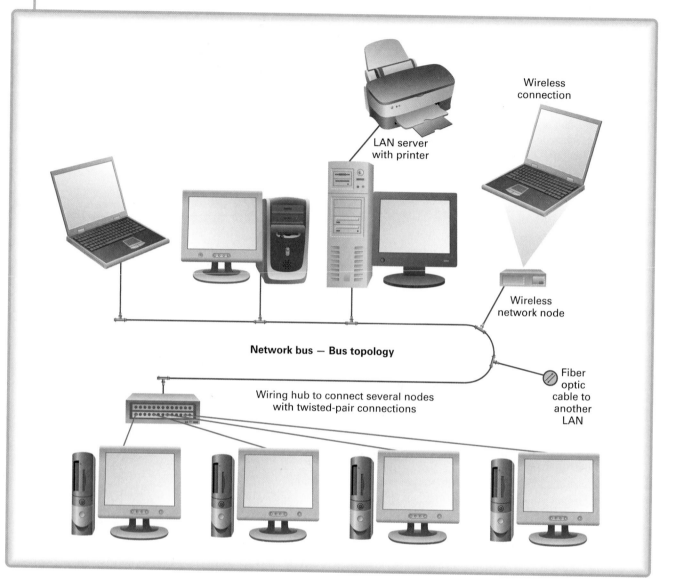

Peer-to-Peer LANs

In a **peer-to-peer LAN,** all PCs are peers, or equals. Any PC can be a client to another peer PC or any PC can share its resources with its peers. Peer-to-peer LANs are less sophisticated than those that have one or more dedicated servers in support of client/server networking. Because they are relatively easy to install and maintain, peer-to-peer LANs are popular when small numbers of PCs are involved (for example, from 2 to 20). PCs running the Windows operating system can be linked together in a peer-to-peer LAN.

Client/Server LANs

In LANs with dedicated servers, the controlling software resides in the file server's RAM. LANs with dedicated servers can link hundreds of clients (PCs and thin clients) in a LAN while providing a level of system security that is not possible in a peer-to-peer LAN. Control is distributed among the clients in the LAN. Novell, IBM, and Microsoft are major providers of LAN software. Each offers a family of LAN operating system, or "server," software to meet a variety of networking and Internet-based processing needs.

Applications Software for LANs

LAN-based PCs can run all applications that stand-alone PCs can run, plus those that involve electronic interaction with groups of people.

Shared Applications Software

LANs enable the sharing of general-purpose software, such as CBT (computer-based training), word processing, spreadsheet, and so on. LAN-based applications software is licensed for sharing. The PCs on the LAN with a dedicated central server interact with a file server to load various applications programs. When a LAN-based PC is booted, software that enables the use of the network interface card, communication with the file server, and interaction with the operating system are loaded from the PC's hard disk to RAM. Depending on how the LAN system administrator configured the LAN, you may see a graphical user interface that lists software options or you may see a prompt from the operating system. When you select a software package, it is downloaded from the LAN's file server to your PC's RAM for processing. You can then work with shared files on the file server or with your own local files (those stored on your PC).

Groupware: Software for the Group

LANs have opened the door to applications that are not possible in the one-person, one-computer environment. For example, users linked together via a LAN can send electronic mail to one another. Scheduling meetings with other users on the LAN is a snap. This type of multi-user software designed to benefit a group of people is called *groupware*. Local area networks and groupware provide the foundation for *workgroup computing*. The breadth of workgroup computing encompasses any application that involves groups of people linked by a computer network. The following is a sampling of workgroup computing applications.

- *Electronic mail (e-mail)*. E-mail enables people on a LAN to route messages to one another's electronic mailbox.

- *Instant messaging*. Instant messaging allows messages to be sent and displayed in real-time.

- *Calendar and scheduling*. People can keep online calendars and schedule meetings automatically. The scheduling software automatically checks appropriate users' electronic calendars for possible meeting times, schedules the meeting, and informs the participants via electronic mail.

- *Brainstorming and problem solving*. A LAN enables collaborative brainstorming and problem solving.

- *Shared whiteboarding*. Shared whiteboards permit a document or image to be viewed simultaneously by several people on the network. All people involved can draw or make text annotations directly on the shared whiteboard. The annotations appear in the color associated with a particular participant.

- *Setting priorities*. Groupware is available that enables LAN users to establish priorities for projects through collective reasoning.

- *Electronic conferencing*. Conferencing groupware lets LAN users meet electronically.

- *Electronic forms*. American businesses and government spend over $400 billion each year to distribute, store, and update paper forms. Electronic forms groupware lets LAN users create forms for gathering information from other LAN users.

Networks on the Fly

The number and variety of workgroup computing applications can only increase. Already, notebook PC users are creating networks on the fly. That is, they bring their computers to the meeting and attach them to a common cable or activate their wireless transceivers to create a peer-to-peer LAN. In effect, we have progressed from the *portable computer* to the *portable network*. Once part of a LAN, users can enjoy the advantages of networking and groupware. Many colleges now have classes in which students bring notebook PCs to class, then create a wireless LAN with each other and with the professor's PC.

THE HOME NETWORK

A few years ago it was unthinkable to maintain a local area network in a home. The cost of hardware, software, and professional technical support was simply prohibitive. Today, people routinely link their computers in a *home network* (see Figure 7-18). The home network is a term coined to refer to small LANs in the home—perhaps two, three, or four nodes.

FIGURE 7–18 Wireless Home Network
This notebook PC is link to the Internet via a wireless home network.
Courtesy of International Business Machines Corporation. Unauthorized use not permitted.

Homes with one or more kids' PCs, a parents' PC, and perhaps a parent's notebook PC from the office are becoming more the norm than the exception in the United States. Most families subscribing to broadband Internet access are multiple PC homes and over 80% of them have opted to set up a home network. About 20 million American families have home networks. And, why not? They are inexpensive, easy to install, and provide tremendous value to the family. Enabling broadband access to all PCs in the household is a tremendous value. Plus, the home network permits the sharing of all kinds of resources—the printer, the scanner, the DVD burner, files, and more. Not to be overlooked is the gaming aspect of home networking: at home, the whole family can join in a multiplayer game.

Most home networks are built around the **HPNA** networking standard developed by the Home Phoneline Networking Alliance. HPNA, also called **HomePNA**, allows the elements of the network to communicate over the home's existing telephone wiring. A home's phonelines can support voice/fax/data, broadband internet access, and HPNA networking—simultaneously. This is possible because each service occupies a different frequency band. Most home networks use phone lines, but they can be set up as wireless LANs, as well. The wireless option is slightly more expensive; however, wireless offers the ultimate mobility to the notebook user, who can work as easily in the backyard under a shade tree as in the home office.

Networking

- Network topologies
  - Star
  - Ring
  - Bus
  - Hybrid
- Types of networks
  - Local area network (LAN or local net)
  - Wide area network (WAN)
  - Metropolitan area network (MAN)
- LAN operating systems
  - Peer-to-peer
  - Client/server
- LAN applications software
  - Shared
  - Groupware for workgroup computing
- The home network
  - HPNA networking standard
  - Peripheral and file sharing
  - Internet connection sharing
  - Multiplayer gaming

To set up a home network you will need to purchase and install HPNA network interface cards (adapters) in all PCs planned for the network. The HPNA adapters are installed in an expansion slot in desktop PCs or inserted in a PC card slot in notebook PCs. HPNA USB external adapters can be used, as well. The relatively inexpensive HPNA cards (about $30 to $50 per PC) may be all you need for the home network. However, the type of broadband service (DSL, cable modem, or satellite) and/or ISP selected may require the use of specific software or hardware (for example, a router or Ethernet card).

The Windows environment makes it easy for you to set up a peer-to-peer local area network for Internet, peripheral, and file sharing. When you turn on the PCs for the first time, the Windows network wizard leads you through the setup procedure. For example, you will be given the option to share your files and/or printer with others.

Internet sharing can be accomplished via software or hardware. When using the software approach, one of the PCs is designated as a "gateway" to the Internet. The gateway and all other PCs on the network run Internet connection sharing (ICS) software. In this method, the broadband Internet access signal is fed into the gateway PC and the ICS software coordinates Internet access among the networked PCs. The downside of the ICS approach is that the gateway computer must be turned on for the other computers to access the Internet.

The hardware approach to Internet sharing involves the use of a router. The router was price prohibitive for home networking until recently, but the explosion of home networks has resulted in a dramatic reduction in router prices, to the point that it is a viable option for home networking. The router, which connects to a broadband modem, is the gateway to the Internet and shares access directly with the other PCs on the network. The router handles all Internet sharing processing duties, so a PC need not be dedicated to these tasks.

SECTION SELF-CHECK

7-4.1 An endpoint in a network of computers is called a: (a) break point, (b) stop bit, (c) node, or (d) PC.

7-4.2 Twisted-pair wire, coaxial cable, and fiber optic cable can be used to connect nodes on a LAN via network interface cards. (T/F)

7-4.3 Which of the following doesn't fit: (a) WAN, (b) LAN, (c) DAN, or (d) MAN?

7-4.4 Which would not be a type of LAN server: (a) communications server, (b) file server, (c) print server, or (d) scan server?

7-4.5 Which of the following devices would be an unlikely component in a home network: (a) router, (b) notebook PC, (c) dedicated Internet server, or (d) NIC?

7-1 OUR WIRED WORLD

We rely on *computer networks* to retrieve and share information quickly; thus the current direction of **digital convergence. Connectivity** facilitates the electronic communication between companies and the free flow of information within an enterprise.

This is the era of cooperative processing. To obtain meaningful, accurate, and timely information, businesses have decided that they must cooperate internally and externally to take full advantage of available information. To promote internal cooperation, businesses are promoting both **intracompany** and **intercompany networking.** Intercompany networking can also be called **business-to-business (B2B) e-commerce.** More business between companies is being moved to the Internet. More specifically, it will be moved to a company's *intranet* with actual B2B interactions taking place over their *extranets.* An **extranet** is an extension of an **intranet,** a closed or private version of the Internet.

A **virtual private network** uses **tunneling** technology to enable a private network over the Internet. A **VPN** employs encryption and other security measures to ensure that communications are not intercepted.

7-2 THE DATA COMMUNICATIONS CHANNEL

A **communications channel** is the facility through which digital information must pass to get from one location in a computer network to the next.

A channel may be composed of one or more of the following transmission media: telephone lines of copper **twisted-pair wire, coaxial cable, microwave signals, radio signals, fiber optic cable,** and **wireless transceivers.** Satellites are essentially microwave repeater stations that maintain a **geosynchronous orbit** around the earth. Two services are made available over twisted-pair wire: **POTS** (plain old telephone services) and Digital Subscriber Line (DSL). Some cable television systems offer high-speed Internet access over coaxial cable (cable modem). Line-of-sight wireless technologies **MMDS** (Multichannel Multipoint Distribution Service) and **LMDS** (Local Multipoint Distribution Service) provide for network access at fiber optic-level speeds.

Communications **common carriers** provide communications channels to the public, and lines can be arranged to suit the application. A **private** or **leased line** provides a dedicated communications channel. A **switched** or **dialup line** is available on a time-and-distance charge basis.

Communications protocols are rules established to govern the way data are transmitted in a computer network. The protocol you hear about most often is **TCP/IP (Transmission Control Protocol/Internet Protocol),** the foundation protocol for the Internet.

Asynchronous transmission begins and ends each message with start/stop bits and is used primarily for low-speed data transmission. **Synchronous transmission** permits the source and destination to communicate in timed synchronization for high-speed data transmission.

7-3 DATA COMMUNICATIONS HARDWARE

Data communications (also called **telecommunications**) is the electronic collection and distribution of information from and to remote facilities. Data communications hardware is used to transmit digital information between terminals and computers or between computers. These hardware components include the modem, the *network interface card* (*NIC*), the **front-end processor,** the **multiplexor,** and the **router.** The NIC often is called an **Ethernet Card.**

Voice/data/fax modems, both internal and external, modulate and demodulate signals so that data can be transmitted over telephone lines. Besides the data communications capabilities, they let you make telephone calls via your PC and simulate a fax machine. The cable modem, a DSL modem, or a satellite modem enables broadband Internet access. The **DSLAM (Digital Subscriber Line Access Multiplexor)** routes DSL signals to telephone companies for processing.

The front-end processor establishes the link between the source and destination in a process called **handshaking,** then sends the **message** to a **network address.** The front-end processor relieves the host computer of communications-related tasks. The multiplexor concentrates data from several sources and sends them over a single communications channel.

The primary hardware/software technology used to enable the interconnection of incompatible computer networks is the **router.** A **backbone** is composed of one or more routers and the associated transmission media.

Terminals enable interaction with a remote computer system. The general-purpose terminals are the **video display terminal (VDT)** and the *telephone.* Terminals come in all shapes and sizes and have a variety of input/output capabilities.

Windows terminals with processing capabilities enable the user to interact via a graphical user interface. **Telephony** is the integration of computers and telephones.

An assortment of special-function terminals, such as automatic teller machines (ATMs) and point-of-sale (POS) terminals, are designed for a specific application.

7-4 NETWORKS

Computer systems are linked together to form a computer network. In a computer network, the **node** can be a terminal, a computer, or any other destination/source device. The basic patterns for configuring computer systems within a computer network are **star topology, ring topology,** and **bus topology.** The bus topology permits the connection of nodes along a **network bus.** In practice, most networks are actually hybrids of these **network topologies.**

The local area network (LAN), or **local net,** connects nodes in close proximity and does not need a common carrier. A **WAN,** or **wide area network,** connects nodes, usually LANs, in widely dispersed geographic areas. The **MAN,** or **metropolitan area network,** is a network designed for a city.

The physical transfer of data and programs between LAN nodes is controlled by the access method embedded in the network interface card's ROM, usually the **token access method** or **Ethernet.** The three most popular servers are the **file server,** the **print server,** and the **communications server.** These server functions may reside in a dedicated **LAN server.**

The **LAN operating system** is actually several pieces of software, a part of which resides in each LAN component's RAM. In a **peer-to-peer LAN,** all PCs are equals. Any PC can share its resources with its peers. In LANs with dedicated servers, the controlling software resides in the file server's RAM.

LANs and *groupware* provide the foundation for *workgroup computing.* The breadth of workgroup computing encompasses any application that involves groups of people linked by a computer network. Workgroup computing applications include electronic mail, instant messaging, calendar and scheduling, brainstorming and problem solving, shared whiteboarding, and others.

The home network is a term coined to refer to small LANs in the home. Home networks enables Internet connection sharing, peripherals sharing, and multiplayer gaming. Most home networks are built around the **HPNA (HomePNA)** networking standard. Internet sharing can be accomplished via software where one of the PCs is designated as a "gateway" to the Internet, or it can be done via hardware with a router handling the Internet sharing duties.

KEY TERMS

asynchronous transmission (p. 290)
backbone (p. 294)
bus topology (p. 298)
business-to-business (B2B) (p. 283)
coaxial cable (p. 286)
common carrier (p. 288)
communications channel (p. 285)
communications protocol (p. 290)
communications server (p. 301)
connectivity (p. 283)
data communications (p. 291)
digital convergence (p. 282)
DSLAM (Digital Subscriber Line Access Multiplexor) (p. 294)
e-commerce (p. 283)
Ethernet (p. 301)
Ethernet Card (p. 294)
extranet (p. 284)
fiber optic cable (p. 288)
file server (p. 301)
front-end processor (p. 295)

geosynchronous orbit (p. 286)
handshaking (p. 295)
HPNA (HomePNA) (p. 304)
intercompany networking (p. 283)
intracompany networking (p. 283)
intranet (p. 284)
LAN operating system (p. 301)
LAN server (p. 301)
LMDS (p. 288)
local net (LAN) (p. 298)
MAN (metropolitan area network) (p. 299)
message (p. 295)
microwave signal (p. 286)
MMDS (p. 288)
multiplexor (p. 295)
network address (p. 295)
network bus (p. 298)
network topology (p. 298)
node (p. 296)

peer-to-peer LAN (p. 302)
POTS (p. 286)
print server (p. 301)
private line (leased line) (p. 288)
radio signal (p. 286)
ring topology (p. 298)
router (p. 294)
star topology (p. 298)
switched line (dialup line) (p. 289)
synchronous transmission (p. 290)
telecommunications (p. 291)
telephony (p. 295)
token access method (p. 299)
tunneling (p. 285)
twisted-pair wire (p. 286)
video display terminal (VDT) (p. 294)
virtual private network (VPN) (p. 284)
WAN (wide area network) (p. 299)
Windows terminal (p. 295)
wireless transceiver (p. 287)

MATCHING

1. VPN
2. node
3. digital convergence
4. B2B
5. WAN
6. intranet
7. fiber optic cable
8. twisted-pair wire
9. front-end processor
10. Ethernet
11. MAN
12. asynchronous transmission
13. POS system
14. switched line
15. DSLAM

a. combines DSL signals
b. network access method
c. e-commerce
d. transmitted at irregular intervals
e. PC in a home network
f. network in metropolitan area
g. POTS media
h. dialup line
i. retail store terminals
j. relieves host of communications duties
k. more encompassing than a LAN
l. pulses of light
m. tunnels on Net
n. internal Internet
o. moving toward digital compatibility

CHAPTER SELF-CHECK

7-1.1 Either a company has connectivity or it does not, with no in-between. (T/F)

7-1.2 Electronic commerce is the term used to describe business conducted online. (T/F)

7-1.3 An intranet uses the TCP/IP protocol. (T/F)

7-1.4 Connectivity is implemented: (a) all at once, (b) after the Internet option has failed, (c) in degrees, or (d) to thwart B2B.

7-1.5 VPN stands for: (a) virtual private network, (b) very personal network, (c) virtual POTS net, or (d) vat pat nat.

7-1.6 A closed or private version of the Internet is called: (a) a fishnet, (b) an intranet, (c) an overnet, or (d) an addnet.

7-2.1 The two basic types of service offered by common carriers are a private line and a switched line. (T/F)

7-2.2 Microwave relay stations are located approximately 500 miles apart. (T/F)

7-2.3 The channel capacity for DSL service is about 10 times that of cable TV digital service. (T/F)

7-2.4 Communications protocols describe how data are transmitted in a computer network. (T/F)

7-2.5 The unit of measure for the capacity of a data communications channel is: (a) bps, (b) bytes per second, (c) RAM units, or (d) megabits.

7-2.6 Which of these terms is not used to refer to a communications channel: (a) link, (b) pipe, (c) passageway, or (d) line?

7-2.7 DSL service is delivered to homes over what kind of line: (a) POTS, (b) satellite, (c) cable, or (d) fiber?

7-2.8 Which transmission media offers the greatest capacity: (a) fiber optic cable, (b) twisted-pair wire, (c) coax, or (d) microwave signal?

7-3.1 The typical modem is a voice/data/fax modem. (T/F)

7-3.2 The DSLAM facilitates satellite broadband communications. (T/F)

7-3.3 A communications device establishes the link between the source and destination in a process called: (a) handshaking, (b) greeting, (c) hello good-bye, or (d) messaging.

7-3.4 What device converts digital signals into analog signals for transmission over telephone lines: (a) router, (b) brouter, (c) modem, or (d) client/server?

7-3.5 Which of these is not used for broadband communications: (a) cable modem, (b) DSL modem, (c) twisted-pair modem, or (d) satellite modem?

7-3.6 Special-function terminals can be found in most department stores. (T/F)

7-3.7 ATMs are now available in some areas of the country that will let you order and receive Internal Revenue Service (IRS) forms and airline tickets. (T/F)

7-3.8 The telephone is considered a terminal. (T/F)

7-3.9 Which terminal permits system interaction via a GUI: (a) a dumb terminal, (b) a Windows terminal, (c) a text-based terminal, or (d) a traditional VDT?

7-3.10 The primary input/output on the VDT is: (a) the mouse and microphone, (b) the keyboard and speaker, (c) a hard disk and monitor, or (d) the keyboard and monitor.

7-4.1 In a LAN with a dedicated server, the operating system for the entire LAN resides in the server processor's RAM. (T/F)

7-4.2 In a peer-to-peer LAN, the less powerful PCs are clients to the more powerful PCs. (T/F)

7-4.3 A router is required for any home network doing Internet sharing. (T/F)

7-4.4 A LAN is designed for "long-haul" data communications. (T/F)

7-4.5 The central cable called a network bus is most closely associated with which network topology: (a) ring, (b) star, (c) bus, or (d) train?

7-4.6 Which LAN access method passes a token from node to node: (a) token, (b) Ethernet, (c) contention, or (d) parity checking?

7-4.7 Which of these applications permits a document or image to be viewed simultaneously by several people on the network: (a) scheduling, (b) whiteboarding, (c) electronic forms, or (d) brainstorming?

7-4.8 Most home networks are built around what networking standard: (a) phoneline PD, (b) HPNA, (c) home networking, or (d) Ethernet?

IT ETHICS AND ISSUES

THE DIGITAL DIVIDE: IS IT RACIAL OR ECONOMIC?

Much has been made in the news about an ever-growing digital divide that heretofore has been described primarily along racial lines. The divide refers to the disparity between groups of people who have computers and access to the Internet and those who do not. Politicians have presented the digital divide as a disparity between races, generally white and African American. A comprehensive study, however, reveals that the digital divide is not so much an issue of race, but of economics. A very high percentage of those with the money to buy PCs and be online make the cyber investment. Those without funds do not have that option.

Discussion: *What can be done about the digital divide?*

Discussion: *Universal access to the Internet is a stated goal of many U.S. politicians. Discuss approaches to achieving this universal access given that only 70% of the population can afford PCs or Internet appliances in their homes.*

THE INTERNET'S IMPACT ON THE FAMILY UNIT

According to the results of an Internet usage survey at Stanford University's Institute for the Quantitative Study in Society, Americans report they spend less time with friends and family, shopping in stores, and watching television. Also, Americans spend more time working for their employers at home—without cutting back their hours in the office. Another result indicated that time on the Internet increased with Internet experience (number of years using the Internet).

Discussion: *Is the Internet having a negative impact on the family unit? Explain.*

Discussion: *The survey showed that regular Internet users (5 or more hours per week) choose to work more at home than others in the general population. Why do you think they do this?*

Discussion: *A key finding of the study was that "the more hours people use the Internet, the less time they spend in contact with real human beings." Should society make an effort to educate people to this trend? Why or why not?*

SHARING INTERNET ACCESS VIA WI-FI

The price structure for broadband Internet service, such as cable modem and GSL, is based on the statistical reality that the average consumer will use less than 1% of the line's potential capacity to carry information. Many consumers have picked up on the fact that they have a lot of excess capacity and are willingly to share this capacity through wireless "home networking," which, in fact, may involve PCs in a dozen apartments and a dozen families. Broadband providers claim that their fee structure is designed for single-family usage. Broadband consumers claim that they are paying for always-on Internet access and how they use it is up to them.

Discussion: *Businesses pay significantly more for broadband capacity, primarily because businesses can be expected to use a signifi-* cantly *higher percentage of the lines capacity than a family. Should individuals be allowed to share Internet capacity, even if they do it for free?*

Discussion: *In many cases, a broadband line is installed and billed to a particular address, but users in nearby apartments on a wireless LAN share the Internet and the bill. Discuss the legal ramifications of this arrangement from the account owner's perspective. From the perspective of those who share the line. From the Internet provider's perspective.*

DISCUSSION AND PROBLEM SOLVING

7-1.1   Discuss ways that the trend toward digital conversion has changed your life over the last two years. Speculate on ways that it might change your life during the next five years.

7-1.2   Select a type of company and give an example of what information the company might make available over its Internet, its intranet, and its extranet.

7-2.1   It's getting crowded in space with so many companies and countries launching communications satellites into geosynchronous orbit. Is there a danger of having too many satellites hovering above the earth? If so, what can be done about it?

7-2.2   Describe circumstances in which a leased line would be preferred to a dialup line.

7-2.3   The cost of a normal 56 K bps dialup connection with unlimited access to the Internet costs anywhere from $15 to $25. How much more would you pay to get Internet access via cable TV, satellite, or DSL that is 10 to 50 times faster than that provided by a 56 K modem? Explain.

7-2.4   Speculate on the different types of transmission media that might be used to transmit data for a one-hour Internet session.

7-3.1   Explain why you must use a modem to send data over a plain old telephone line.

7-3.2   Describe how a multiplexor can be used to save money.

7-3.3   Over the years, Internet access speeds have moved gradually higher. Do you expect to see a significant jump in consumer-oriented Internet access speeds, perhaps a doubling of capacity, over the next few years? Why or why not?

7-4.1   Identify the type and location of at least five different types of nodes in your college's network.

7-4.2   A variety of communications hardware, including a router, is needed to link local area networks that use different communications protocols. Why are not all LANs designed to use the same standards for communication so that communications hardware tasks can be simplified?

7-4.3   Describe how information can be made readily accessible to many people in a company, but only on a need-to-know basis.

7-4.4   The five PCs in the purchasing department of a large consumer-goods manufacturer are used primarily for word processing and database applications. What would be the benefits associated with connecting the PCs in a local area network?

7-4.5   The mere fact that PCs on a LAN are networked poses a threat to security. Why?

7-4.6   Some metropolitan area networks are completely private; that is, communications common carrier services are not used. Network nodes can be distributed throughout large cities. How do companies link the nodes on the network without common carrier data communications facilities?

7-4.7   Describe at least one situation in academia or the business world where creating a portable network would be inappropriate. That is, a situation where people with notebook PCs link them in a network by attaching them to a common cable or by using wireless transceivers. Briefly describe what the network might do.

7-4.8   Do you have a home network? If so, describe it in detail, listing all related communications hardware and software. If not, speculate on when and why you might consider installing a home network.

FOCUS ON PERSONAL COMPUTING

1. On your Windows desktop, click *Start* on the taskbar, then choose *Help and Support*. Enter "home networking" and then open appropriate descriptions in the results list and learn more about home networking in the Windows environment. Click on hypertext links to expand your knowledge of the topic, as needed. Now, do the same for "HPNA," the technology used in most home networks, and "ICS," the type of software that enables Internet connection sharing. Briefly describe at least one newfound piece of knowledge for each topic that you feel will help you in the creation of a home network.

2. Do the preliminary design for a phone-line-based home or small office network, preferably for a home or office with which you are familiar. Draw a diagram of the house or office including the location of each PC, shared resource (printer, scanner, DVD burner, and so on), and telephone jack. Create a table and label the columns "PCs," "Modems," "Network adapters," "Peripherals," and "To be purchased," then fill in the table. The last column would list the extra hardware you will need to implement your home/small office network (HPNA adapters, ethernet cards, router, and so on). Go online and price out the hardware needed to create the network.

1. The Online Study Guide (multiple choice, true/false, matching, and essay questions)
2. Internet Learning Activities
   - Online Books
   - Transmission Media
   - Terminals
   - Networks
3. Serendipitous Activities
   - Government

PERSONAL COMPUTING BUYER'S GUIDE

From the time you purchase and plug in your first PC, you are committed to a lifetime of buying newer and better PCs, PC upgrades, PC peripherals, and PC software. Also, you subscribe to PC services and are caught up in an endless loop of PC supplies and accessories. The personal computing adventure is great fun, but it isn't cheap. But neither is Disneyworld.

The emphasis in this buyer's guide is on the actual buying and decision processes. Other sections of the book cover hardware, software, and Internet concepts.

BEFORE YOU BUY: ANSWER THESE QUESTIONS

A sleek new PC is like a shiny new car; it invites impulse buying. Resist this urge and get a system that fits your budget and meets your personal computing needs. Before you purchase anything, answer these important questions.

How Much to Spend?

You can purchase a new personal computer for under $500. However, if you choose an array of performance features and opt for the latest technology in peripheral and storage devices, the cost of a personal computer could easily exceed $5000. Ultimately, the amount you spend on a personal computer depends on your financial circumstances and your spending priorities. If personal computing is one of your priorities, here is a good rule to follow: *purchase as much power and functionality in a personal computer system as your budget will permit.* You'll need it more quickly than you think.

Desktop PC or Notebook PC?

The choice between a *desktop PC* and a *notebook PC* (see Figure 7-19) usually hinges on two considerations: *need for portability* and *cost.*

- *Portability.* If your lifestyle demands portability in personal computing and you are willing to pay considerably more for approximately the same computing capability as a comparable desktop PC, then you should seriously consider a notebook PC.
- *Cost.* If cost is a concern and portability isn't, the desktop PC is for you.

Notebook PC owners sacrifice some conveniences to achieve portability. For instance, input devices, such as the keyboard and point-and-draw devices, are given less space in portable PCs and may be more cumbersome to use. These inconveniences, however, are offset by the convenience of having your PC and its capabilities with you wherever you are.

Desktop PCs outsell notebook PCs two to one; however, each year notebooks are gaining significant ground and should surpass desktops in sales in the near future.

Figure 7–19 — DESKTOP OR NOTEBOOK PC?
The desktop PC offers more power for your personal computing dollar, but the notebook PC offers portability.

Which Platform?

The Wintel PC (Windows o.perating system, Intel or equivalent processor) represents the dominant PC platform with over 90% of the PC pie. The Apple Computer Company line of personal computers represent about 5% of the PC market, and the remainder of the market is comprised mostly of Linux-based systems and those with legacy Microsoft operating systems.

When making the platform decision, consider compatibility with the other PCs in your life: your existing PC (if you have one), the one at work/home, and/or the one in your college lab. Also, consider your career interests. Apple computers have it all and do it all; some would argue that they do it better than Wintel machines. Nevertheless, the Apple line of computers, especially at the high end, have been tabbed as niche machines because they are so pervasive in certain types of industries, including publishing, video/film editing, graphics, animation, illustration, and music.

Companies, whether software or automobile, tend to build products for the largest markets, in the case of software—Wintel. Therefore, Wintel PCs have a substantial advantage in the range of available software and, because of volume sales, software prices. Apple computer users also have access to a wide range of software; however, the Apple selection pales when you compare it to available Wintel software.

Who Will Use the PC and How Will It be Used?

Plan not only for yourself, but also for others in your home that might use the system. Get their input and consider their needs along with yours. The typical off-the-shelf entry-level notebook or desktop personal computer has amazing capabilities and will do most anything within the boundaries of the digital world. Nevertheless, depending on how you plan to use the system (for example, video editing, gaming, multimedia viewing), you may need to supplement the basic system with additional hardware and software.

What Input/Output Peripheral Devices Do You Need?

A good mix of input/output peripheral devices can spice up your computing experience. I/O devices come in a variety of speeds, capacities, and qualities. Generally, the more you pay the more you get. However, there is no reason to pay for extra speed, capacity, or quality if you do not need it.

Several suggestions for I/O devices are listed below for the "typical" user. *Priority suggestions are listed first.* Of course, priorities will vary, but these should give you a benchmark for decision making. Normally, the printer (or possibly an all-in-one peripheral: print, scan, fax, and copy) is the only additional peripheral input/output device that you would get at or near the time of purchase; however, you should consider upgrading the monitor, mouse, and keyboard. All other optional I/O devices you might want can be purchased as the need arises at the best prices.

1. Printer or All-in-One Peripheral
No PC system is complete without access to a printer. The keyword here is "access." If you already have a PC system in your home with an acceptable printer, you probably don't need two printers. This resource is easily shared via walk-net or a home network. Walk-net is just transferring print files via interchangeable discs or diskettes.

The ink-jet printer has emerged as the overwhelming choice of budget-minded people buying home/home office PC systems. The quality of any of today's mainline ink-jet printers is remarkable, so your decision boils down to how much you are willing to pay for additional print quality, faster print speeds, and special features (for example, printing on both sides of the paper).

You might wish to consider getting an all-in-one multifunction peripheral, that is, a device that prints, faxes, scans, and copies (duplicates). The considerable overlap in the technologies used in these machines has enabled manufacturers to create a reasonably priced machine that does it all.

2. PC Headset
Desktop PCs are sold with a basic microphone and speakers. You'll need to purchase a quality headset with a mike (from $25 to $50) if you wish to take advantage of the speech recognition capability made available with the newer Microsoft Office suites (see Figure 7-20). If you purchase speech recognition software separately, the headset comes with the product.

Figure 7–20 — THE PC HEADSET
If you plan to use speech recognition technology, you will need a high-quality headset with a directional microphone that picks up the user's voice, but not the ever-present noises around the office and home.

3. Scanner
If you choose an all-in-one peripheral (see priority peripheral #1), you will not need a stand-alone scanner. The scanner is a good investment in your personal computing adventure. With a scanner, you can convert any color hardcopy document and even small 3D images (jewelry, heirlooms, and so on) to an electronic image that can be integrated into anything from a newsletter to a greeting card. The scanner can read text and speak the words with the help of text-to-speech software. The scanner doubles as a copy machine for small volume copying (scanner to printer) and as a fax machine (used in conjunction with the fax software that comes with all PCs and a dial-up modem). Any name-brand flatbed scanner with an 8.5-inch by 11.7-inch scanning area that scans at 1200 X 2400 dpi (dots per inch) or better should be all you need unless you are doing professional image editing.

4. Internet or Web Camera
The Internet or Web camera certainly is not a PC system necessity, but for as little as $50, it can add some serious spice to your personal computing experience. These versatile little cameras, which can capture both still and video images, plug into your computer like any other peripheral. You can use them for many tasks, including videophone conversations, setting up a Webcam (streaming images over the Internet), maintaining security, or for monitoring your baby.

5. Game Controllers

If you have gamers in the house, game controllers are must-have items. The game controller is very much a matter of personal preference, so be sure and invite input from your gamers before buying. Many computer games are multi-player games, so you may wish to purchase two of these relatively inexpensive devices.

6. Digital Camera/Digital Camcorder

If you enjoy taking and sharing pictures, then you will want to consider owning a digital camera. With a digital camera, the cost of photography plummets because the costly, time-consuming developing processing is eliminated. With digital cameras, you can take all the photos you want and just keep the good ones. Once the images are downloaded to your PC, you can enhance, edit, send, or view them at your leisure.

If you are in the market for a *digital camcorder*, you may not need to spend the extra money for a separate digital camera for still photography. Most modern digital camcorders let you take excellent megapixel still images, as well as digital video.

7. USB Multiport Hub

The most popular way to connect input/output devices to a PC is via a USB port. Typically, a personal computer will have two or six USB ports. Those ports, however, can be filled quickly. Fortunately, USB technology allows you to daisy-chain multiple devices to a single port. It's quite possible that you'll need more ports than are made available on the system unit, and, if you do, you will need to purchase a USB 2.0 multiport hub.

ENTRY LEVEL, SWEET SPOT, AND PERFORMANCE PERSONAL COMPUTERS

New desktop or notebook PCs can be grouped into three general categories based on cost and performance—*entry-level systems, sweet spot systems,* and *performance systems.* Soon after their introduction, these systems begin their slow slide into a lower category or obsolescence—for example, the performance system moves into the sweet spot category and, eventually, into the entry-level category.

Technological innovation continues its relentless march toward defining a new level of across-the-board performance each year. This means that what was a performance system a couple of years ago can look very much like today's entry-level system.

Buying an Entry-Level Personal Computer

If your financial circumstances and spending priorities dictate that you purchase an entry-level system, you have no choice but to go with a minimal system or, perhaps, a used PC system. In most circumstances, this system will do the job. Today's entry-level PCs can be five times as fast as a performance PC that was purchased five years ago for $5000. All modern PCs are amazingly capable machines.

Entry-level or "affordable" personal computers offer good value, but, typically, they do not give the buyer as much flexibility to customize the PC at the time of the sale. For example, you may have only one or two choices for the monitor. Often, affordable personal computers are sold off-the-shelf, as is.

Generally, fewer, slower, less, and older are terms used to describe the system components for entry-level PCs. For example, an affordable PC system might have fewer USB ports, a slower CD-RW disc drive, less RAM, and a processor with older technology. But you have to put these descriptors into perspective. An affordable PC may have a processor that is 40% slower than a performance machine processor, but it still is very, very fast.

The downside of purchasing an entry-level system is that a new affordable PC may be at least one year, and as much as two years, closer to technological obsolescence than one of the more expensive intermediate or high-end PCs. To be sure, if you purchase an entry-level PC you will lose out on technology bragging rights, but you can always brag about saving enough money to purchase a big-screen TV.

Hitting the Sweet Spot PC

In sports, the "sweet spot" is the area on a baseball bat, a tennis racket, or head of a golf club that is the most effective part with which to hit a ball. Every consumer market has a sweet spot, too. The PC market's sweet spot offers the greatest value. When you purchase a sweet spot PC, you're not paying a premium for state-of-the-art technology, but you still are getting near leading-edge performance. Most people looking to buy their first PC or another PC will want a good, solid PC that will run virtually all current and future applications over the next two or three years. For these people, a good place to look is the sweet spot in the personal computing market.

Typically, the PC sweet spot is a desktop PC that is about 6 to 12 months off the technology; that is, the major components in the system, such as the processor and hard disk, were introduced up to a year earlier. State-of-the-art performance systems might be 30% faster and capable of storing twice the information, but they may cost twice, even three times, as much as a sweet spot PC.

Finding the Sweet Spot PC

Generally, the sweet spot is relatively easy to find. To find it, go to the Web site for any major PC vendor that markets directly to the public (for example, Dell, Hewlett Packard, IBM, or Gateway), then navigate to the page that features their home/small office desktop PC options. The system in the middle represents the current "sweet spot." Once you have perused the system specifications at several vendor Web sites, you should have a good read on the current PC sweet spot. Be advised, however, that the sweet spot is continuously changing and what you see today as the high-end system may be featured as a sweet spot system in a few days.

If you don't have access to the Internet, the sweet spot is fairly obvious at any major PC retailer, such as Best Buy, Office Depot, and so on. The sweet spot is represented by those similarly priced PC systems in the middle price range.

Customizing the PC Sweet Spot System

You may not have the flexibility to customize a sweet spot system. Those sold in retail outlets and, sometimes, online via direct marketers may be offered as a package deal—what you see is what you get. However, most vendors that market directly to customers, via the Internet or telephone sales, give the consumer plenty of flexibility to customize their orders.

It is likely that the come-on price of a sweet spot system will not include some needed and important upgrades. Depending on your budget and personal computing needs, consider the following recommendations. *The recommendations are listed by value, with the biggest payout for your PC dollar listed first.*

- *Buy a surge suppressor.* Inexpensive surge protectors provide essential protection from lightning hits and other electrical aberrations. An uninterruptible power source (UPS) offers superior protection to a surge suppressor but adds $60 to $80 to the system price.
- *Upgrade memory.* The easiest and most effective way to improve performance of a personal computer is to increase RAM. Modern PCs operate reasonably well at 256 MB; however, increasing RAM to 512 MB or more has a tremendous impact on overall performance, as much as 50%, depending on your mix of applications.
- *Buy the three-year warranty.* This is the best deal of all the manufacturers' options at the time of purchase, especially for notebooks. It gives you piece of mind that you have somewhere to go when something goes wrong or you need some answers—and, there is a good chance that it will and you will.
- *Upgrade the size/type of the monitor.* The standard off-the-shelf PC system normally comes with a manufacturers-grade CRT monitor (15 to 17 inches). These are of acceptable quality for home use and should outlast the other PC components. However, with so much of what we do being presented as multimedia, a 19-inch or bigger monitor will enhance your personal computing adventure. Expect to pay about $100 per extra inch for a CRT-style monitor. An alternative to the CRT monitor is the space-saving, flat-panel LCD monitor. Although the price of flat-panel LCD monitors is dropping, you can expect to pay a premium for LCD monitors— especially the larger ones (19 inches and up).
- *Upgrade the speaker system.* For $30 to $90 extra, you can have a speaker system with surround sound and a floor-shaking subwoofer that will make those DVD movies, MP3 downloads, and games come alive with sound. If you choose top-of-the-line speakers, you may need to upgrade the *sound card,* as well.
- *Upgrade the keyboard and mouse.* For about $30 to $60 extra, you can get an enhanced keyboard and an ergonomically designed mouse that will last the useful life of the system (which may not be the case with the standard devices). Wireless versions of these devices let you interact with your computer from anywhere near the PC.
- *Upgrade the hard disk capacity.* You can never have enough hard disk space, especially if you have gamers in the house and/or you plan to store digital images and videos on the PC. Generally, choose a hard disk that is at least one step above the hard disk bundled with the standard sweet spot system.
- *Choose the de facto standard office suite.* Given a choice between Microsoft Office and some other office suite, choose the home or small business version of Microsoft Office. The applications in the Microsoft Office suite are taught in virtually all schools at all levels and this suite is the de facto standard in business and government. If you work at home, consider the professional version.
- *Upgrade the CD-ROM/DVD option.* If the sweet spot system is not configured with a rewritable option, CD-RW and/or DVD+RW, you should consider choosing a combination drive (DVD/CD-RW) or choosing one of the rewritable options for the second drive bay, which is normally empty. If you plan on creating and copying custom CDs, having a CD-ROM drive and a separate drive for rewritable media is handy. Also, having a rewritable disc drive facilitates important backup duties.
- *Upgrade the video card.* The interface between the processor and the monitor is the video card. Any modern video card will handle the display tasks for a typical user; however, if you expect to be involved with sophisticated multimedia applications and/or serious gaming, you should consider upgrading to a high-quality video card with at least 64 MB of VRAM.
- *All-in-one multifunction peripheral: print, scan, fax, and copy.* An all-in-one multifunction peripheral (see Figure 7-21) capable of handling all print, scan, fax, and copy functions rounds out any PC system. Purchasing individual devices to achieve this level of functionality could cost up to $1000. A quality multifunction peripheral can be purchased for 25% of that amount. You can live a long and healthy life without sending/receiving another fax, but we now live in a multimedia world where printing and scanning high-resolution images is commonplace. Plus, the duplication capability comes in handy.
- *HPNA adapter.* For an extra $20 or so, you can add a home networking HPNA adapter PCI card to your system. This relatively inexpensive upgrade makes your new PC ready for phoneline home networking if and when you need it.

Figure 7–21 — THE ALL-IN-ONE MULTIFUNCTION PERIPHERAL
This telecommuter configured his tower PC with a multifunction peripheral that is a printer, fax machine, a copier, and a scanner—all in one device. Multifunction printers are ideal for the home or small offices where volume for any single function is low.

Photo courtesy of Hewlett-Packard Company

These are the essential upgrades and/or choices you might wish to consider. Everything else, such as game pads, digital cameras, extra USB ports, software, and so on can be purchased later as your personal computing needs come into focus.

The Performance PC

If you are in the market for a performance PC, you are flushed with a surplus of discretionary funds or you are a power user with special processing needs. Those special needs might include, but are not limited to, video editing, computer-aided design (CAD), Web design, software development, IT writing/publishing, and graphics/illustration.

The performance PC represents leading-edge technology and, in contrast to the entry-level system, the key descriptors are more, faster, greater, and newer. The performance PC will have every kind of port, and plenty of them. It will have a DVD+RW drive and, perhaps, 1 to 2 GB of RAM. It will have at least one state-of-the-art processor. The performance PC is feature rich, with high-end video and sound cards that could add as much as $700 to the price of the system. The system might be configured with a video editing package that would include a video capture card and related software. The system unit would include an enhanced power unit and extra fans for cooling the many heat-producing components.

People who buy performance PCs are veteran PC users who have collaborated on the purchase of many PCs in the past. They already are aware of the considerations presented in this buyer's guide.

WHAT SPECIAL HARDWARE DO YOU NEED FOR INTERNET ACCESS AND HOME NETWORKING?

Your personal computer can be linked to the rest of the world through the Internet or to the other PCs at your house via home networking.

Internet Access

Internet access falls into two categories, *dialup access* and *broadband access*. You pay a little more for broadband, which can be up to 50 times faster than the traditional dialup access.

Dialup Internet Access
The dialup, 56 K bps data/voice/fax modem is installed in virtually all new PCs. Keep this relatively inexpensive (about $20) option because, eventually, you may need it for data, voice, or fax communications.

Broadband Internet Access
The difference between dialup and broadband access is stark: dial-up is a lot of click and wait where broadband displays Web pages in seconds or fractions of seconds. *Cable* (via cable modems), *DSL*, and *satellite* are the leading broadband technologies for home Internet access.

Depending on which service you choose, you will need a cable modem, a DSL modem, or a satellite modem, but, normally, you purchase the broadband modem when you subscribe to the service, not when you purchase your PC. Sometimes the modem is included with the subscription fee and, sometimes, you must buy it. In any case, it's always a good idea to use the modem suggested by the broadband service provider.

Home Networking

The spread of PCs throughout the house has prompted the growth of home networking (see Figure 7-22). Two special types of network interface cards (NICs) allow families to link all their PCs using ordinary phone lines or wireless communications for simultaneous Internet access, printer and file sharing, and multiplayer gaming.

Figure 7–22 — HOME NETWORKING
These two teenager PCs are on a phone-line home network with mom's PC, which has the printer, and dad's PC, which has the scanner. The router (on top of the system unit in the inset) enables sharing of the DSL broadband signal via the phone-line network. All PCs have HPNA phone-line adapters, two external (to the left of the monitor) and two internal.

To set up a home network you need the software, which is built into all Windows operating systems, and you need a home networking NIC, an *HPNA adapter*, installed on each PC on the network (about $20 each). The adapter can be installed internally or be connected via USB externally. HPNA adapters can be selected as an option at the time you purchase your PC or they can be purchased and easily installed at a later date.

FACTORS TO CONSIDER WHEN BUYING A PC

It's easy to overlook important considerations that could influence your decisions. This summary offers insight that can help you avoid some of the problems incurred by other PC buyers.

What Software is Preinstalled on the PC?

Arguably, the most challenging aspect of choosing between alternative PCs is appraising the worth of the software preinstalled with the system and integrating that assessment into the overall evaluation of the PC system. And, that's the way PC vendors meant it to be. They want the quality or variety of their software bundle(s) to either confuse the buyer or be the difference maker, depending on the quality of their offerings.

If the PC purchase decision was based solely on hardware, we could compare oranges with oranges—but it's not. When you bundle software into the PC purchase price, and all vendors do this, it's more like comparing oranges to grapefruit.

The bundled software frequently is the biggest variable in the PC purchase decision process. What software PC vendors choose to offer with their systems can be substantially different between competitors and even within their own line of PCs.

The Operating System

Every new PC is sold with an operating system, typically the latest version of *Microsoft Windows,* either the *Home Edition* or the *Professional Edition.* The Home Edition is sufficient for 95% of the home computers. The Professional Edition has a few security and networking features that might be reason enough for the telecommuter to pay extra for this advanced version of Windows.

The Software Suite

A software suite is bundled with all but the very low-end PCs and some promotional PCs. Most new personal computers are bundled with *Microsoft Office XP Standard* (also called *Office XP Small Business*), *Microsoft Office XP Professional,* or *Microsoft Works Suite.* Occasionally, a vendor will offer an alternative suite, such as the *WordPerfect Suite,* which continues to be popular in the legal field.

If Microsoft Works is the default software bundle for a particular system, you can expect to pay about $100 to upgrade to the industry standard Microsoft Office suite. If you are buying an off-the-shelf PC with Works already installed, the upgrade to Office XP may not be an option.

These software suites may or may not be accompanied by other software or service incentives. For example, additional software preinstalled with Microsoft Office XP might include antivirus software, a personal finance package, or perhaps an online encyclopedia.

Optional Software Bundles

When you purchase a PC online or via mail order, major direct marketer manufacturers will give you an opportunity to order additional software. These offerings are in two main categories: *individual software packages* and *optional bundles* (topical groups of three or four software packages).

Generally, any of the individual software packages can be purchased online or at retail outlets at the PC vendor's offering price or for a few dollars less. Don't feel as if you need to make a decision now on these individual software packages, unless antivirus software is not included with the price of the PC. If this is the case and the vendor offers a quality antivirus package, you should purchase it with the system.

Quality of Hardware/Software Support Services

PC hardware is very reliable and routinely operates continuously without incident for years. Even with a history of reliability, the possibility exists that one or several of the components eventually will fail and have to be repaired. Most retailers or direct-marketer vendors will offer a variety of hardware service contracts from same-day, on-site repairs that cover all parts and service to a carry-in (or mail-in) service that does not include parts and can take several weeks.

Since hardware support services vary within and between vendors, you should look over the options carefully and choose the one right for your circumstances. It's important that you understand *exactly* what you must do to get your system repaired. As a rule of thumb, choose at least some level of repair service for the effective life of your system (about 3 years).

WHERE TO BUY HARDWARE/SOFTWARE?

PCs and associated hardware and software can be purchased at thousands of convenient bricks-and-mortar locations and from hundreds of retail sites on the Internet.

Bricks-and-Mortar Computer Retailers with Authorized Service Centers

Several national retail chains and many regional chains specialize in the sale of PC hardware and/or software. Also, there are thousands of computer stores with no chain affiliation. Most market and service a variety of PC systems. Some make their own line of computers and are happy to custom-build one for you. Find these dealers under "Computer and Equipment Dealers" in the Yellow Pages.

Bricks-and-Mortar Computer Retailers without Authorized Service Centers

Computer/electronics departments of most department stores, discount warehouse stores, and office supply stores sell PCs and PC software. For the most part, these stores treat computers as they would any consumer item. When you walk out the door, you are covered by the manufacturer's warranty. For this category of retailers, what you see on the shelf is what you get. Any further technical support comes from the hardware and software manufacturers within the limits of their warranties. These are prepackaged systems and the retailer has relatively little flexibility in system configuration because they do not have a service center.

Direct Marketers

Most major manufacturers of PC hardware (Dell, Gateway, Hewlett-Packard, IBM, and so on) and most major software companies (Microsoft, Symantec, Broderbund, and so on) are direct marketers; that is, they sell directly to the customer. The direct marketer's "store window" is a site on the Internet (see Figure 7-23). Orders can be entered via the Internet, telephone, fax, or mail. The trend is toward entering orders interactively via the Internet. The direct marketer makes and sends the requested product(s) to the customer within a few days. Direct marketers offer an array of popular PC software and accessories.

The strength of the direct marketer's sales program is online sales via the Internet. Once you decide which PC system you want, you can *customize*, or *configure*, it to pick exactly the options you want on your PC system.

Buying directly from the manufacturer via the Internet has many advantages. The manufacturers' Web sites are comprehensive in that they present all conceivable options, plus they provide enough information to answer any questions you might have.

Retailers of Preowned and Refurbished Computers

The used-computer retailer was as inevitable as the used-car dealer was. A computer that is no longer powerful enough for one user may have more than enough power for

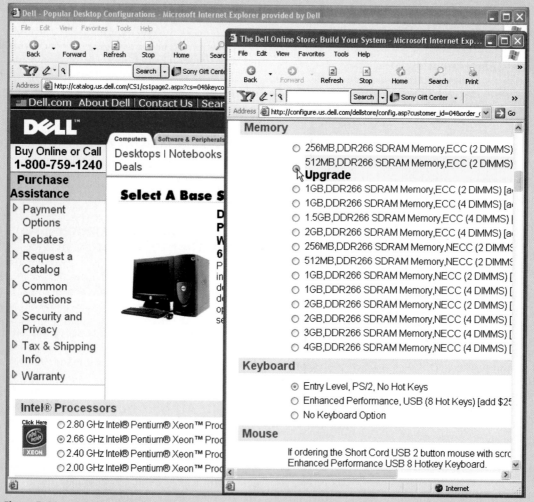

Figure 7–23 — BUYING DIRECT
Dell Computer Corporation is a direct marketer with a Web site that provides detailed information about any available system. The customer can go to the Dell Web site to customize and purchase a system entirely online. In this example, the customer is given an opportunity to choose from 14 RAM options up to 4 GB and from two keyboards.

another. Used-computer retailers are easy to find: just look under "Computer and Equipment Dealers—Used" in the Yellow Pages.

Most major computer manufacturers also sell used computers, called *refurbished* or *remanufactured computers* . Typically, such systems are current models and were used only for a few days or weeks. For whatever reason, these systems were returned to the manufacturer. The problem components were replaced, probably with refurbished components, and the system was offered for sale via the company's Web site at a 10 to 15% discount off the price of the new system. The warranty remains the same.

Online Auctions

A great source for anything used is an online auction. PCs and electronics are among the most popular items up for auction on the Internet. Online auctions go on 24 hours a day with people all over the world registering bids on millions of items. The typical PC system put up for auction on eBay at *www.ebay.com* is 3 to 5 years off the technology and goes for $50 to $250. Avoid bidding on any system that is deinstalled because it offers no software.

WHICH PC MANUFACTURER IS BEST FOR YOU?

All big-name manufacturers, such as Dell, Hewlett-Packard, Compaq (now part of Hewlett-Packard), Gateway, IBM, and Apple, produce quality personal computers that can be expected to last well beyond their useful life. Surprisingly, however, these big-name manufacturers account for a less than half of personal computer sales.

The bulk of PC sales are by small "white box" PC vendors. Many small PC companies have emerged that custom-build and sell "no-name" PCs to school districts, city governments, small companies, and individuals. Some of these small players are excellent and have a solid record of providing good service, price, and flexibility. White box vendors typically sell for less than mainstream manufacturers. To do so, however, they may use components of lesser quality, reduced motherboard features, and/or components that may be off the technology.

Ultimately, the answer to the question "Which PC manufacturer is best for you?" is the manufacturer that offers systems that provide the best match for your personal computing needs and your personal bank account.

THE TOTAL COST OF OWNERSHIP

The spending on personal computing continues once you have paid for and installed the hardware and software. As soon as you get your PC system, you will want to stock up on supplies, subscribe to vital services, and purchase important accessories. Invariably, you will want to build your software portfolio (see Figure 7-24). Most personal computing consumables are associated with the printer and interchangeable disk drives (Zip disks, CD-R, DVD+RW discs, and other storage media). These considerations bring us to an important concept in personal computing—the *total cost of ownership*.

Figure 7–24 — THE SOFTWARE PORTFOLIO This mix of software, which includes a smattering of utility, applications, and games software, might be considered typical for a home office software portfolio. The retail cost of the software shown here is over $2000.

The amount shown on the price tag for a PC system is in no way representative of what you must pay to get into the personal computing business. That price tag doesn't include a printer. The cost of a printer seldom includes a cable, another expense. Of course, you will want paper on which to print, probably two or three different qualities and in several shades. Printer cartridges can cost $40 or more.

It's easy for a teenager to spend $500 a year on gaming hardware and software. You'll need a place to put the PC and a comfortable chair. Access to the Internet will cost you from $20 to $60 a month. And the costs go on and on. If you have a spending limit, consider the estimated incidental costs shown in Figure 7-25.

FIGURE 7–25

ONE-TIME AND ANNUAL INCIDENTAL EXPENSES FOR PERSONAL COMPUTING
The personal computing cost ranges listed are for a first-time user. The low end of the ranges is representative for casual home users and the high end of the ranges is applicable to sophisticated users with home offices.

	One-Time Cost	Annual Cost
Software	$100–$1500	$100–$800
Cables	$0–$50	
Supplies (printer cartridges, plain paper, photo paper, diskettes, Zip disks, CD-RW and/or DVD+RW discs, and DVD/CD-R blanks, and so on)	$100–$200	$100–$500
Internet service provider (ISP) and/or Information service	$0–$500 (one-time ISP costs are setup and installation fees plus equipment cost [modem, router, satellite dish, and so on] for broadband service)	$250–$800 (includes basic Internet service; the high-side expense is for broadband service)
Subscriptions (technology magazines, virus protection service, online databases, and so on)		$0–$200
UPS (uninterruptible power source) or Surge Protector	$40–$300	$0–$100 (UPS battery replacement)
Additional data telephone line (optional)	$0–$50	$0–$350
Furniture and Accessories (desk, chair, lights, mouse pad, and so on)	$30–$500	$50–$150
System Maintenance (this amount is nothing until the warranty runs out)		$0–$300
Insurance		$0–$100
Miscellaneous, including accessories (USB 2.0 hub, new game pad, and so on)		$0–$300
TOTAL ESTIMATED INCIDENTAL EXPENSES	$270–$3100	$500–$3600

1. As a rule, you should purchase as much power and functionality in a PC system as your budget will permit. (T/F)
2. The choice between a desktop PC and a notebook PC usually hinges between the need for portability and styling. (T/F)
3. An entry-level PC has components that are no more than six months off the technology. (T/F)
4. The surge protector is designed to provide protection from lightning hits. (T/F)
5. Hardware upgrades are not advised for sweet spot PC systems. (T/F)
6. As a rule of thumb, choose at least some level of repair service for the effective life of your new PC system. (T/F)
7. The all-in-one peripheral device does all but which of the following document tasks: (a) fax, (b) print, (c) scan, or (d) shred?
8. Which device would you expect to be the most costly: (a) game pad, (b) scanner, (c) Web camera, or (d) headset with a mike?
9. Which of these devices is required for phoneline home networking: (a) multifunction peripheral device, (b) 1394 ports, (c) surge protector, or (d) HPNA adapters?
10. Although direct marketers offer customers a variety of ways to enter their PC orders, the trend is toward entering orders via: (a) telephone, (b) the Internet, (c) fax, or (d) snail mail.
11. The total cost of ownership of a PC encompasses all but which of the following: (a) opportunity costs, (b) PC purchase price, (c) ISP charges, or (d) printer supplies?

SECTION SELF-CHECK

chapter 8

Learning Objectives

Once you have read and studied this chapter, you will have learned:

- To place society's dependence on computers in its proper perspective (Section 8-1).

- Key ergonomic and environmental concerns that should be considered in the design of your workplace (Section 8-2).

- Considerations critical to evaluating important ethical questions in the use of information technology (Section 8-3).

- The types and scope of computer and IT crime (Section 8-4).

- The points of security vulnerability for a computer center, an information system, and a PC (Section 8-5).

IT ETHICS AND HEALTHY COMPUTING

Why this chapter is important to you

Information technology is not all bits, bytes, and procedures. The IT revolution continually raises difficult questions that beg for answers and serious issues that must be resolved.

How we fare as a society depends on how we cope with a continuous stream of information technology issues. Just about any IT issue is fuzzy, and there are few historical individual, corporate, or national perspectives from which to derive a solution. Frequently, we must address these issues as they surface to determine what course of action to take. This chapter should help you make better decisions on the critical IT issues of the day and make you more sensitive to ethical concerns.

Eventually, we probably will wear our computer systems, but until then, you will spend much of your day an arm's length from your PC. Reading this chapter will give you a better understanding of the ergonomics (human-machine interaction) of computing and help you build a healthy workplace and avoid some of the health problems associated with the computing environment.

Trillions of bytes of information travel over millions of miles of wires and through the air from computer to computer. This information, which often is sensitive in nature, eventually resides on magnetic storage devices. Whether traveling at the speed of light or spinning on a disk, this information is vulnerable to theft and/or abuse. This chapter will help you to understand better what can be done to minimize the exposure of information and computer systems to the criminal elements of our society.

WHY THIS SECTION
IS IMPORTANT
TO YOU

This section will help you to better comprehend information technology within our society by making you aware of our society's readiness to accept IT and of our society's level of dependency on IT.

8-1 | The Information Technology Paradox

We as a society are caught in an information technology paradox: Information technology is thriving in a society that may not be ready for it.

ARE WE READY FOR INFORMATION TECHNOLOGY?

One in every seven VCRs blinks "12:00" because its owner is unable to set the clock. Less than 20% of the working population can claim information technology competency. Many college curricula do not require courses on computers or IT. Corporate executives are seriously concerned that the skill level of workers is not keeping pace with the technology. Worse, millions of workers may not have the foundational skills needed for retraining. Executives throughout the country are concerned about spending money on remedial training just to get their employees to the point that they can give them information technology-related job training. To better prepare the workforce for the explosion of information technology applications (see Figure 8-1), we may need to revise curricula and raise standards at all levels of education.

DO WE REALLY WANT INFORMATION TECHNOLOGY?

Some of us want to wrap ourselves in information technology. Some of us want nothing to do with it. Most of us want it, but in moderation. This reluctant acceptance of information technology has resulted in many IT-based opportunities being overlooked or ignored. For whatever reasons, business, government, and education have elected not to implement computer applications that are well within the state of the art of computer technology. Literally thousands of money-saving IT-based systems are working in the laboratory and, on a small scale, in practice. However, society's pace of IT acceptance has placed such applications on the back burner. A few examples follow.

Smart houses feature computer-controlled lighting, temperature, and security systems. Such systems start the coffeemaker so we can awaken to the aroma of freshly brewed coffee. They even help with paying the utility bills and provide perimeter security. This technology is available today and is relatively inexpensive if properly designed and installed during construction. In any case, such a system would pay for itself in a few years through energy savings alone. Generally, neither those in the construction industry nor potential buyers are ready for smart houses, even though they offer tremendous benefits and are cost effective.

Although sophisticated computer-controlled medical equipment is used routinely in health care, relatively few physicians take advantage of the information-producing potential of the computer to improve patient care. There are expert systems that can help them diagnose diseases, drug-interaction databases that can help them prescribe the right drug, computer-assisted searches that can call up literature pertinent to a particular patient's illness, and online forums through which they can solve health problems and share ideas. Large groups of physicians are not ready for the age of information, even though these applications have the potential for saving lives.

On a larger scale, society continues to rebuke the concept of a cashless society. A cashless society is technologically and economically possible. In a cashless society, the amount of a purchase is transferred automatically from the purchaser's bank account to the vendor's bank account. Thus, billing, payment, and collection problems are eliminated, along with the need to write checks and to remember to mail them. Properly implemented, a cashless society will result in substantial savings for all concerned—government, business, and individuals. We are on a journey to a cashless society and already are 90% there. The remainder of the journey will take a few years because too many of us still like the jingle in our pockets.

Why have these cost-effective and potentially beneficial computer applications not been implemented? Among the reasons are historical momentum, resistance to change, limited education, and lack of available resources. In the case of domestic-control systems, it is probably a matter of education, both of the builder and the homeowner. In the case of computer diagnosis of illness, some physicians are reluctant to admit that the computer is a valuable diagnostic aid, and IT is a void in medical school curricula. In the case of the cashless society, concerns about invasion of privacy are yet to be resolved.

These and thousands of other "oversights" will not be implemented until enough people have enough knowledge to appreciate their potential. This is where you come in!

REACHING THE POINT OF NO RETURN

Albert Einstein said that "concern for man himself and his fate must always form the chief interest of all technical endeavors." Some people believe that a rapidly advancing information technology exhibits little regard for "man himself and his fate." They contend that computers are overused, mis-

THE CRYSTAL BALL:
Centralized Online Placement Services for College Graduates For decades, face-to-face on-campus interviews have defined the student recruitment process. Many students still find jobs through this traditional approach to placement services; however, within a few years we can expect a single, mature one-stop Web site to emerge that will be sensitive to the privacy of student information. Today, students may send hundreds of printed resumes only to be filtered by employers with a one-criterion glance. The one-stop site offers a more efficient approach. It will allow students to post comprehensive resumes that would allow interested employers to drill down for more information. Employers would have a new level of filter options.

FIGURE 8–1   OUR DEPENDENCE ON COMPUTERS

HERTZ'S NEVERLOST® SYSTEM

Many travelers are beginning to depend on Hertz's NeverLost® onboard navigation system. The system gives drivers turn-by-turn driving directions to almost any destination via an in-car, video screen and/or voice prompts. At the heart of the NeverLost system is a GPS receiver, used to calculate the exact location of the car based upon signals from orbiting satellites, a computer map, and a database that directs the traveler to his or her designated destination.

©2000 Hertz System, Inc. Hertz is a registered service mark and trademark of Hertz Systems, Inc.

PERSONAL COMPUTING AND HOME NETWORKING

The spread of personal computing and home networking has prompted further dependence on our computers for many of life's little chores, including help with homework, real-time stock quotes, personal finances, shopping, personal interactions around town and around the world, and a thousand other tasks.

Photo courtesy of Intel Corporation

CRUISE SHIP SYSTEMS

Professionals in all endeavors continue to include greater use of technology in their jobs. Crew members on-board the "Radiance of the Seas" of the Royal Caribbean Cruise Lines have in-cabin access on to the Internet and productivity applications, including the CrewNection service which links the ship's crew and integrates the services database and processing.

Courtesy of International Business Machines Corporation. Unauthorized use not permitted.

used, and generally detrimental to society. This group argues that the computer is dehumanizing and is slowly forcing society into a pattern of mass conformity. To be sure, the age of information is presenting society with difficult and complex problems; but they can be overcome.

Information technology (IT) has enhanced our lifestyles to the point that most of us take it for granted. There is nothing wrong with this attitude, but we must recognize that society has made a real commitment to computers. Whether it is good or bad, society has reached the point of no return in its dependence on IT, including a growing dependence on the Internet. Competition demands a continued and growing use of IT. On the more personal level, we are reluctant to forfeit the everyday conveniences made possible by IT. For example, our PCs and the conveniences of the Internet are now an integral part of our daily activities.

Society's dependence on computers is not always apparent. For example, today's automobile assembly line is as computer dependent as it is people dependent: An inventory-management system makes sure that parts are delivered to the right assembly point at the right time; computer-controlled robots do the welding and painting; and a process-control computer controls the movement of the assembly line.

Turn off the computer system for a day in almost any company and observe the consequences. Most companies would cease to function. Within minutes, we would be without gas, electricity, water, radio, TV, or any modern means of communication. The world's financial institutions would fall into disarray.

Turn off a computer system in a business for several days and there is a good chance that the company would cease to exist. It is estimated that a large bank would be out of business in two days if its computer systems were down. A distribution company would last three days, a manufacturing company would last five days, and an insurance company would last six days. In fact, the probability of a victim company's long-term survival would be low if it were unable to recover critical operations within 30 hours. Recognizing their dependence on computers, most companies have made their systems fault-tolerant or have made contingency plans to follow in case of disaster.

Dependence on IT is not necessarily bad as long as we keep it in perspective. However, we can't passively assume that information technology will continue to enhance the quality of our lives. It is our obligation to learn to understand computers so that we can better direct their application for society's benefit. Only through understanding can we control the misuse of information technology. As a society we have a responsibility to weigh the benefits, burdens, and consequences of each successive level of automation.

SECTION SELF-CHECK

8-1.1 We, as a society, are still at least a decade away from dependence on computers. (T/F)
8-1.2 Approximately 75% of the working population can claim information technology competency. (T/F)
8-1.3 A smart house might have all of these computer-controlled features except: (a) lighting, (b) temperature, (c) fertilizing, or (d) security.

WHY THIS SECTION IS IMPORTANT TO YOU

The information in this section should help you to be comfortable in and to remain healthy at your workplace.

8-2 The Workplace

Our workplace is changing because we are attuned more to considerations involving human safety and comfort, and we are more sensitive to the growing importance of *green computing*.

ERGONOMICS AND WORKPLACE DESIGN

For close to a hundred years, the design of automobiles was driven by two basic considerations: appearance and functionality. Engineers were asked to design cars that were visually appealing and could go from point A to point B. Surprisingly little attention was given to the human factor. That is, no one considered the connection between the driver and passengers and the automobile. About 25 years ago, automobile executives discovered that they could boost sales and enhance functionality by improving this human connection. Thus began the era of ergonomically designed automobiles. Today, human factors engineers apply the principles of ergonomic design to ensure that the interface between people and cars is *safe, comfortable, effective,* and *efficient.*

Ergonomics is the study of the relationships between people and the things we use. The emergence of ergonomics is beginning to have an impact on the relationship between knowledge workers and their workplaces. Computers are still relatively new in the workplace, and ergonomics has only recently emerged as an important consideration in fitting computers into workplace design (see Figure 8-2).

FIGURE 8–2   HARDWARE FOR THE ERGONOMICALLY DESIGNED WORKPLACE

THE IN-AIR MOUSE

Ultra Mouse is a wireless mouse that employs gyroscopic, motion-sensing technology such that it can be used on and away from the desktop. The Ultra Mouse's gyroscope lets you use intuitive in-air gestures to control the movement of the mouse pointer. With the in-air mouse, you can have frequent changes in postures, thus reducing some of the uncomfortable symptoms associated with repetitive motion.

Courtesy of Gyration, Inc.

HANDS FREE MOUSE

NaturalPoint™ Smart-Nav™ mouse alternative products give you hands free control of a computer cursor. The ergonomic Smart-Nav™ provides precise cursor control through simple head movement allowing your hands to remain on your keyboard, or at your side. The user positions a reflective dot on his/her forehead, glasses, or microphone and an infrared camera tracks its motion to move the cursor.

Courtesy of Natural Point

FACTORY MICE

This ITAC Systems Mouse-Track is a mouse alternative, ergonomically designed for use in extremely harsh environments. The dust-resistant dome encoder lets you point with your index finger, not your elbow or thumb, thus reducing the risk of carpal tunnel syndrome.

Courtesy of ITAC Systems, Inc.

STRESS RELIEVER

The repetitive-stress injuries (RSIs) associated with the keyboard may be eliminated at some time in the future as more people move to speech-recognition technology to interact with their PCs. This executive dictates directly to a computer system using speech-recognition software.

Courtesy of International Business Machines Corporation. Unauthorized use not permitted.

USING THE FEET FOR INPUT

Give your hands a rest with a programmable Foot Switch. This Foot Switch adds input versatility with a three-button keyboard for your feet.

Use Courtesy Kinesis® Corporation, Bothell, WA

CONTOURED KEYBOARD

This contoured keyboard is designed to fit the shape and movements of the human body. The design puts less stress and strain on muscles, reducing the user's risk for fatigue in hands, wrists, and arms.

Courtesy of Kinesis Corporation

REASONS FOR CONCERN

During the 1980s, the knowledge worker's workplace gained attention when workers began to blame headaches, depression, anxiety, nausea, fatigue, and irritability on prolonged interaction with a terminal or PC. These and other problems often associated with extended use of a terminal or PC are called **video operator's distress syndrome**, or **VODS**. Although there was little evidence to link these problems directly with using terminals or PCs (the same problems occurred in other work environments), VODS caused people to take a closer look at the workplace and the types of injuries being reported. As the number of *repetitive-stress injuries* (*RSIs*) increased for knowledge workers, workstation ergonomics became an increasingly important issue for corporate productivity.

A poorly designed workplace has the potential to cause **cumulative trauma disorder** (**CTD**), a condition that can lead to a permanent disability of motor skills. CTD now accounts for more than half of all work-related problems. It typically occurs when people ignore human factors considerations while spending significant time at the keyboard. Other workstation-related injuries include mental stress, eyestrain, headaches, muscular injuries, and skeletal injuries. Hand and wrist problems associated with keyboarding have always been the main complaint, with the repetitive-stress injury called **carpal tunnel syndrome** (**CTS**) being the most common. A few years ago, the options for reducing keystrokes were few. Today, we speak to our computers via speech-recognition software with accuracy rates in excess of 95%, thus substantially reducing keystrokes and, in some situations, eliminating keystrokes altogether.

Talk about the radiation emitted by CRT-type monitors has unduly frightened office workers. A controversial, and apparently flawed, study in the late 1980s concluded that women who are exposed to the radiation emitted from terminals and PCs may have a higher rate of miscarriage than those who are not. A comprehensive four-year federal government study concluded that women who work with terminals and PCs and those who do not have the same rate of miscarriage.

WORKPLACE DESIGN

Proper workplace design, whether on the factory floor or in the office, is good business. Any good manager knows that a healthy, happy worker is a more productive worker. A good manager also knows that the leading causes of lost work time are back/shoulder/neck pain and CTD.

The key to designing a proper workplace for the knowledge worker is *flexibility*. The knowledge worker's workplace should be designed with enough flexibility to enable it to be custom-fitted to its worker. Figure 8-3 highlights important considerations in workplace design. Ergonomic problems in the workplace are being addressed in legislation and in proposed regulations from the Occupational Safety and Health Administration (OSHA).

Attention to the overall environment can reduce stress and increase worker performance. For example, indirect lighting can reduce glare. Proper ventilation eliminates health concerns caused by the ozone emitted by laser printers. Excessive exposure to ozone can cause headaches and nausea.

One of the most important factors in ergonomic programs is employee training. Workers should be shown how to analyze their workstations and make necessary adjustments (such as lowering monitor contrast and brightness or increasing chair lumbar support). Each knowledge worker can then contribute to the quality of his or her workplace by following a couple of simple rules. First, make the adjustments necessary to custom-fit your workplace. Second, take periodic minibreaks. These minibreaks should involve looking away from your monitor and/or generally altering your body orientation for a few seconds (make a fist, turn your head from side to side, roll your shoulders, walk around your desk, wiggle your toes, wrinkle your nose, twirl your arms, and so on).

WORKING SMART

Information technology has proven many times over that it can play a role in improving personal productivity and overall office efficiency. If abused, however, information technology, especially relating to the PC and the Internet, can have the opposite effect. These are common abuses that, if eliminated, can make a positive contribution to workplace efficiency.

- *Sending and receiving frivolous e-mail.* Most organizations tolerate an appropriate amount of personal e-mail, just as they do personal telephone calls. But, there is a limit. Nonessential e-mail, live chat, and instant messaging cause breaks in work momentum resulting in reductions in efficiency of as much as 50%. Of course, knowledge workers should resist the urge to subscribe to nonbusiness-related mailing lists (joke of the day, bizarre news, and so on).

FIGURE 8–3

ERGONOMIC CONSIDERATIONS IN WORKPLACE DESIGN
Knowledge workers often spend four or more hours each day at a PC or terminal. Today workers are more sensitive to the impact of workplace design on their health and effectiveness, so they are paying more attention to the ergonomics (efficiency of the person-machine interface) of the hardware, including chairs and desks.

The Hardware
Monitor location (A). The monitor should be located directly in front of you at arm's length with the top at forehand level. Outside windows should be to the side of the monitor to reduce glare. *Monitor features.* The monitor should be high-resolution with anti-glare screens. *Monitor maintenance.* The monitor should be free from smudges or dust buildup. *Keyboard location (B).* The keyboard should be located such that the upper arm and forearms are at a 90-degree angle. *Keyboard features.* The keyboard should be ergonomically designed to accommodate better the movements of the fingers, hands, and arms.

The Chair
The chair should be fully adjustable to the size and contour of the body. Features should include: *Pneumatic seat height adjustment (C); Seat and back angle adjustment (D); Back-rest height adjustment (E); Recessed armrests with height adjustment (F); Lumbar support adjustment (for lower back support) (G); Five-leg pedestal on casters (H).*

The Desk
The swing space. Use wraparound workspace to keep the PC, important office materials, and files within 18 inches of the chair. *Adjustable tray for keyboard and mouse (I):* The tray should have height and swivel adjustments.

The Room
Freedom of movement. The work area should permit freedom of movement and ample leg room. *Lighting.* Lighting should be positioned to minimize glare on the monitor and printed materials.

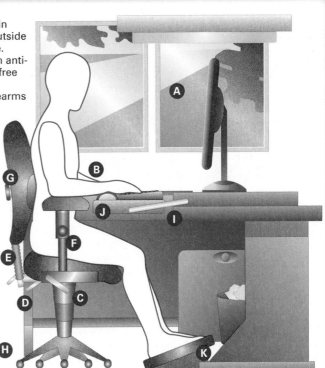

Other Equipment
Wrist rest (J). The wrist rest is used in conjunction with adjustable armrests to keep arms in a neutral straight position at the keyboard. *Footrest (K).* The adjustable footrest takes pressure off the lower back while encouraging proper posture.

- *Engaging in nonbusiness Internet browsing.* With all the resources of the Internet at our fingertips it is easy to seek out reviews of the latest movies, determine the book value of your old car, or check out the statistics from last night's game. Some companies have adopted zero-tolerance policies while others are struggling with ways to control nonbusiness cybersurfing.

- *Gaming on company time.* Personal computing offers plenty of opportunities to play games. Operating systems are even distributed with games. Hundreds of games are available for download. It is easy to join a multiplayer game on the Internet. You can play games of chance. Most corporations frown on employees doing gaming on company time.

- *Toying with the technology.* The typical user exploits less than 20% of a software package's features. Some people view software as a toy and are carried away with all of the interesting features. They learn about and integrate sophisticated features into their projects even though all of the extra effort does little or nothing to enhance the end result. This type of technological overkill wastes time.

The PC can be an invaluable tool in the workplace or it can be a serious diversion. Those who make good use of IT and do not abuse information technology tend to realize career goals more quickly.

GREEN COMPUTING

The dawning of the age of green computing is upon us. **Green computing** is merely environmentally sensible computing. Computers drain critical resources such as electricity and paper. They also produce unwanted electrical, chemical, and bulk-waste side effects. As a society, we finally are adopting a more environmentally sound position with respect to the use and manufacture of computing hardware.

Saving Energy and Trees

United States government agencies and many businesses have adopted policies that require that all new PCs, monitors, and printers must comply with the Environmental Protection Agency's *Energy Star* guidelines. To comply with Energy Star requirements, monitors and processors in standby mode (not in use) can consume no more than 30 watts of power. Printers are permitted a range of 30 to 45 watts. Computer manufacturers have been moving toward more energy-efficient products in hopes of reducing manufacturing costs and increasing product competitiveness.

It costs about $250 a year to keep a PC and laser page printer running 24 hours a day. We could save a lot of money and fossil fuel if we turn off our PCs and peripheral devices or place them in energy-saving standby mode when not in use. Judicious computing can even save trees— why print a letter or send a fax when e-mail is faster and better for the environment? Green computing means printing only what needs to be printed, saving the paper for more meaningful applications.

Other recommendations by green computing proponents include buying equipment from vendors who are manufacturing environmentally safe products, purchasing recycled paper, recycling paper and toner printer cartridges (which would probably end up in landfills), buying reconditioned components rather than new ones, recycling old PCs and printers, shopping electronically to save gas, and telecommuting at least once or twice a week.

What to Do with Old PCs?

Eventually every PC wears out or simply becomes obsolete. No level of maintenance, upgrading, or troubleshooting can save them. Within the next year, over 300 million computers will outlive their usefulness and have no market value. If these PCs were simply thrown out with the trash, they would contribute over 8 million tons of very unfriendly waste to landfills. A typical PC and its peripherals will contain mercury, cadmium, lead, and other toxic and bioaccumulative compounds. Any environmentalist can tell you that these elements and compounds can have a dramatic impact on ground, water, and air quality.

The average useful life is about three years for a business PC and about four years for a home PC. Currently, only about 20% of PCs and peripherals are recycled (see Figure 8-4), compared to 70% for major appliances, such as dishwashers and refrigerators. Clearly, we need to act more responsibly with PCs at the end of their lives.

At present, there is little or no economic incentive to recycle hardware. For most companies, it is less expensive and easier to throw old hardware in the dumpster (but only where it is legal to do so). Adopting a **product stewardship policy** is often the difference between practicing environmentally responsible recycling and having a dumpster full of potentially harmful electrical components. Consider this: a CRT monitor contains 2-plus pounds of lead to protect users from radiation.

The throwaway option, however, may disappear over the next few years as more states place PCs and their peripheral devices on their lists of hazardous materials. In some states, dumping old hardware already is illegal. Many states are requiring or will be requiring consumers to pay a disposal fee in advance when they purchase their PC systems. It is only a matter of time before each of us will have "cradle-to-grave" responsibility for PCs and computer hardware.

If you feel your system still has some useful life, consider giving it to an individual or to an organization, such as a nursery school, that needs it. However, keep this in mind: about 70% of all hardware donations are discarded. Literally, millions of people are looking for individuals and organizations that might want their old PCs and peripherals, so only give away systems that are no more than four or five years off the technology, fully functional, have a good mix of software, and are Internet ready. Realistically, the rest have little or no value.

A number of recycling companies and several major computer vendors, such as Intel and IBM, provide PC recycling services both to consumers and to businesses of all sizes. If your old PC system is a candidate for recycling, send your old system away for proper disposal. Expect to pay between $30 and $40 (including shipping) for this service.

FIGURE 8–4 Recycling Obsolete PCs
Most of the components in obsolete PCs can be recycled, including these plastic cases from old computers.

Courtesy of International Business Machines Corporation.

Unauthorized use not permitted.

8-2.1	Attention to the overall workplace design can reduce stress and increase worker performance. (T/F)
8-2.2	Hardware manufacturers that comply with the Environmental Protection Agency's Energy Star guidelines sell only recycled PCs. (T/F)
8-2.3	Problems associated with extended use of a PC are collectively called: (a) VODS, (b) CTS, (c) CTD, or (d) SOV.
8-2.4	Environmentally sensible computing is called: (a) blue computing, (b) green computing, (c) yellow computing, or (d) red computing.
8-2.5	A typical PC contains all but which of the following: (a) potassium hydroxide, (b) cadmium, (c) mercury, or (d) lead?

SECTION SELF-CHECK

8-3 | Ethics in Information Technology

The computer revolution has generated intense controversy about IT ethics. Society continues to raise questions about what is and is not ethical with regard to IT activities. These ethics issues are so important to our society that IT ethics are being integrated into college curricula. Educators believe that if people are made aware of the consequences of their actions, then fewer people will be motivated to plant dangerous computer viruses, contaminate information systems with false information, post pornographic material to the Internet, or abuse the sanctity of intellectual property. Educators warn us of dire consequences should we fail to instill a sense of ethics in future generations. If ethical abuses are left unabated, all roads on the information superhighway will be toll roads for encrypted data; that is, only those who pay for the key to the encrypted information can view it. If this were to happen, we would become a more secretive society, far less willing to share accumulated knowledge.

AN IT CODE OF ETHICS

Most major IT professional societies have adopted a code of ethics. Their codes warn the members, who are mostly professionals in the information technology fields, that they can be expelled or censured if they violate them. Rarely, however, has any action been taken against delinquent members. Does this mean there are no violations? Of course not. A carefully drafted code of ethics provides some guidelines for conduct, but professional societies cannot be expected to police the misdeeds of their members. In many instances, however, a code violation is also a violation of the law.

A code of ethics provides direction for IT professionals and users so that they act responsibly in their application of information technology. The recently updated Association for Computing Machinery (ACM) Code of Conduct summarized in Figure 8-5 provides excellent guidelines for both knowledge workers and for computing and IT professionals. ACM is the largest professional society for computing and IT professionals.

If you follow the ACM code shown in Figure 8-5, it is unlikely that anyone will question your ethics. Nevertheless, well-meaning people routinely violate this simple code because they are unaware of the tremendous detrimental impact of their actions. With the speed and power of computers, a minor code infraction easily can be magnified to a costly catastrophe. For this reason, the use of computers in this electronic age is raising new ethical questions, the most visible of which are discussed in the following sections (see Figure 8-6).

THE PRIVACY OF PERSONAL INFORMATION

The issue with the greatest ethical overtones is the privacy of personal information. Some people fear that computer-based record keeping offers too much of an opportunity for the invasion of an individual's privacy.

Who Knows What about You?

Each day your name and personal information are passed from computer to computer. Depending on your level of activity, this could happen 100 or more times a day. Thousands of public- and private-sector organizations maintain data on individuals. The data collection begins before you are born and does not end until all your affairs are settled and those maintaining records on you are informed of your parting. Much of this personal data is collected without your consent and then is passed freely between organizations, again, without your consent.

WHY THIS SECTION IS IMPORTANT TO YOU

IT ethics-conscientious people are more likely to protect personal privacy, honor copyright laws, report unethical activity, and generally do what is right when confronted with controversial situations relating to technology. The material in this section will prepare you to make good decisions regarding IT ethics and issues.

THE CRYSTAL BALL:
Online Voting on the Horizon After the Florida election debacle, we are acutely aware that United States voting machines are antiquated. Similar punched-card technology was used in 1890 for taking the national census. It is now apparent that U.S. cities, counties, states, and the nation need a better way to elect candidates. Several major companies and consortiums claim that the U.S. could implement a standardized, federally supported online voting system that would be easier to use, more accessible, more accurate, far more reliable, verifiable, and more secure. Plus, the results would be posted internationally in real time. Other countries, including Brazil, and even states, including Arizona, have conducted online elections. You should be able to vote from your PC within this decade.

FIGURE 8–5

A CODE OF CONDUCT FOR KNOWLEDGE WORKERS AND IT PROFESSIONALS
The first two sections (shown here) of the Association for Computing Machinery (ACM) Code of Conduct are applicable to all knowledge workers and IT professionals. The full code and detailed explanations can be found at the ACM Web site at <http://acm.org>. The last two sections (not shown) deal with organizational leadership and code compliance.

1. General Moral Imperatives

1.1 Contribute to society and human well-being

1.2 Avoid harm to others

1.3 Be honest and trustworthy

1.4 Be fair and take action not to discriminate

1.5 Honor property rights including copyrights and patents

1.6 Give proper credit for intellectual property

1.7 Respect the privacy of others

1.8 Honor confidentiality

2. More Specific Professional Responsibilities

2.1 Strive to achieve the highest quality, effectiveness, and dignity in both the process and products of professional work

2.2 Acquire and maintain professional competence

2.3 Know and respect existing laws pertaining to professional work

2.4 Accept and provide appropriate professional review

2.5 Give comprehensive and thorough evaluations of computer systems and their impacts, including analysis of possible risks

2.6 Honor contracts, agreements, and assigned responsibilities

2.7 Improve public understanding of computing and its consequences

2.8 Access computing and communication resources only when authorized to do so

- *Tax data.* The Internal Revenue Service maintains the most visible stockpile of personal information. It, of course, keeps records of our whereabouts, earnings, taxes, deductions, employment, and so on. Now the IRS is supplementing basic tax information with external information to create personal profiles to tell if a person's tax return is consistent with his or her lifestyle. By law, all IRS data must be made available to about 40 different government agencies.

- *Education data.* What you have accomplished during your years in school, such as grades and awards, is recorded in computer-based databases. Included in these databases is a variety of information such as your scores on college entrance exams, data on loan applications that include details of your family's financial status, roommate preferences, disciplinary actions, and so on. In one instance, a Chicago woman was turned down for several government jobs because of a note her third-grade teacher had entered in her file. In the note, the teacher stated that in her view the girl's mother was crazy.

- *Medical data.* Medical files, which contain a mountain of sensitive personal data, are not always treated with the respect they deserve. In many hospitals, hundreds of employees, most of whom do not have a need-to-know, have ready access to patient information. Your medical records list all your visits to clinics and hospitals, your medical history (and often that of your family), allergies, and diseases you (and often members of your extended family) have or have had. They also may include assessments of your mental and physical health.

- *Driver and crime data.* State motor vehicle bureaus maintain detailed records on over 150 million licensed drivers. This information includes personal descriptive data (sex, age, height, weight, color of eyes and hair) as well as records of arrests, fines, traffic offenses, and whether your license has been revoked. Some states sell descriptive information to retailers on the open market. The FBI's National Crime Information Center (NCIC) and local police forces maintain databases that contain rap sheet information on 20 million people. This information is readily available to hundreds of thousands of law-enforcement personnel.

- *Census data.* With the 2000 census still fresh in our minds, we are reminded that the U.S. Bureau of the Census maintains some very personal data: names, racial heritage, income, the number of bathrooms in our home, and persons of the opposite sex who share our living quarters. Individual files are confidential. Statistics, however, are released without names.

- *Insurance data.* Insurance companies have formed a cooperative to maintain a single database containing medical information on millions of people. This revealing database includes claims, doc-

FIGURE 8–6 IT ISSUES

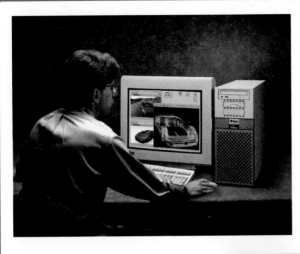

ETHICS AND COMPUTERS
We all have an obligation to adopt a code of ethics when working with computers. The focus of this CAD designer's work is a closely held corporate secret until the first newly designed automobile hits the showroom.

Courtesy of Sun Microsystems, Inc.

PERSONAL INFORMATION
Many times each day, even as you sleep, businesses, government agencies, or other institutions are creating or updating your personal information on their databases. Here, the Municipal Services Department uses image processing to maintain records on parking violations. Anymore, most of the events in our lives become a matter of someone's record (purchases at a department store, electronic payment of a highway toll, the results of a test, surfing to a particular Web page, a cell phone call, a traffic violation, and so on).

Courtesy of Lockheed Martin Corporation

tors' reports, whether you have been refused insurance, how risky you would be as an insuree, and so on.

- *Lifestyle data.* A number of cities are installing two-way cable TV that allows the accumulation of information on people's personal viewing habits. When you watch an X-rated movie, or any other movie, your choice is recorded in the family's viewing database. As interactive cable TV matures, you will be able to use it to pay bills, respond to opinion polls, and make dinner reservations. This, of course, will add a greater variety of information to your personal file.

- *Credit data.* Credit bureaus routinely release intimate details of our financial well-being. About one third of those who ask to review their records (you have the right to do this at any time) challenge their accuracy. Credit bureaus are bound by law to correct inaccuracies within two weeks of being notified of them.

- *World Wide Web data.* When you visit a Web site, your e-mail address may be recorded in a user database on the Web site's server computer. If you interact with a site, your selections and preferences may be noted and placed on the database. Any personal information you enter goes in the database, too. Some Web sites share information for the same e-mail address enabling them to build a more comprehensive personal profile of their visitors/customers. Frequent cybersurfers may have records in hundreds or even thousands of Web site databases.

- *Employment data.* Even before you report to work, your employer has gathered a significant body of data on you. Job-related information is maintained at current and past employers, including the results of performance reports, disciplinary actions, and other sensitive data.

- *Financial institutions.* Banks and various financial institutions not only keep track of your money, they also monitor the volume and type of transactions you make. Their records include how much money you have or owe and how you choose to invest your money.

- *Miscellaneous data.* Every time you make a long-distance telephone call, the number is recorded. Many Web sites not only record your visit but they also record your activities at the site, as well. When you make a credit card purchase, your location at the time and the type of item you buy are recorded. Local and state governments maintain records of property transactions that involve homes, automobiles, boats, guns, and so on.

The social security number, now assigned to all U.S. citizens, is the link that ties all our personal information together. It doubles as a military serial number, and in many states, it serves as your driver's license number. It is the one item, along with your name, that appears on almost all personal forms. For example, your social security number is a permanent entry in hospital, tax, insurance, bank, employment, school, and scores of other types of records.

The few organizations discussed here represent the tip of the personal information iceberg. Political organizations, magazines, telemarketers, charities, and hundreds of other organizations maintain and often share personal information. For the most part, these and thousands of other organizations are making a genuine attempt to handle personal data in a responsible manner. However, instances of abuse are widespread and give us cause for concern.

Information technology is now the basis for processing and storing personal information, and the storage of personal information will increase in the future. However, it's not IT or computers that abuse the privacy of our personal information; it's the people who manage them. We as a society must be prepared to meet the challenge with a system of laws that deals realistically with the problem. At present, Federal laws give individuals little protection. We are not told when data are being gathered about us. We are not allowed to choose who sees this information. In most cases, we are not allowed to view, remove, or correct personal information contained on some database. The good news is that laws are being put in place that will, though slowly, provide better protection for our personal information. For example, a new law limits what data-gathering companies can do with "personally identifiable financial information." The law dictates that these companies must get your permission before they can sell your credit report data, including your name, address, telephone number, and social security number. This means that those in the data gathering business and direct marketers will need to work harder and spend more money to get targeted personal information.

Sources of Personal Data

There is indeed reason for concern regarding the privacy of personal information. For example, credit card users unknowingly leave a "trail" of activities and interests that, when examined and evaluated, can provide a surprisingly comprehensive personal profile.

The date and location of all credit card transactions are recorded. In effect, when you charge lunch, gasoline, or clothing, you are creating a chronological record of where you have been and your spending habits. From this information, a good analyst could compile a very accurate profile of your lifestyle. For example, the analyst could predict how you dress by knowing the type of clothing stores you patronize. On a more personal level, records are kept that detail the duration, time, and numbers of all your telephone calls. With computers, these numbers easily can be matched to people, businesses, institutions, and telephone services. So each time you make a phone call, you also leave a record of whom or where you call. The IRS, colleges, employers, creditors, hospitals, insurance companies, brokers, and so on maintain enormous amounts of personal data on everyone. A person with access to this information could create quite a detailed profile of almost anyone, including you. The profile could be fine-tuned further by examining your Internet activity, such as what messages you posted to the Internet, what sites you visited, and the kinds of software you downloaded.

We, of course, hope that the information about us is up-to-date and accurate. However, this is not always the case. You can't just write to the federal government and ask to see your files. To be completely sure you examine all your federal records for completeness and accuracy, you would have to write and probably visit more than 5000 agencies, each of which maintains databases on individuals. The same is true of personal data maintained in the private sector.

Computer experts feel that, whatever the source, the integrity of personal data can be more secure in computer databases than it is in file cabinets. They contend that we can continue to be masters and not victims if we implement proper safeguards for the maintenance and release of this information and enact effective legislation to cope with the abuse of it.

Violating the Privacy of Personal Information

Now you know that a lot of your personal information exists on computers, but is this information being misused? Some say yes, and most will agree that the potential exists for abuse. Consider the states that sell lists of the addresses and data on their licensed drivers. At the request of a manager of several petite women's clothing stores, a state provided the manager with a list of all its licensed drivers who were women between the ages of 21 and 40, less than 5 feet 3 inches tall, and under 120 pounds. Is the sale of such a list an abuse of personal information? Does the state cross the line of what is considered ethical practice? You be the judge.

When you visit a Web site, the server may gather and store information about you, both on its system and on your system. Frequently, Web sites will leave a cookie on your hard disk. The **cookie** is a message given to your Web browser by the Web server being accessed. The information in the cookie, which is in the form of a text file, then is sent back to the server each time the browser requests a page from the server. The cookie may contain information about you, including your name, e-mail address, interests, and personal preferences. Anytime you enter personal information at a Web site, chances are your browser is storing it in a cookie. The main purpose of the cookie is to personalize your interaction with the Web site and to enable the server to present you with a customized Web page, perhaps with your name at the top of the page. A cookie is not necessarily bad because it contains your personal preferences and basic personal information. A good cookie can make your interaction with an often-visited Web site more efficient and effective.

A recent study found that none of the 100 most popular shopping Web sites was in compliance with Fair Information Practices, a set of principles that provides basic privacy protection. Personal information has become the product of a growing industry. Companies have been formed that do nothing but sell information about people, including their e-mail addresses. Not only are the people involved not asked for permission to use their data, they seldom are told that their personal information is being sold! A great deal of personal data can be extracted from public records, both manual and computer-based. For example, one company sends people to county courthouses all over the United States to gather publicly accessible data about people who have recently filed papers to purchase a home. Computer-based databases then are sold to insurance companies, landscape companies, members of Congress seeking new votes, lawyers seeking new clients, and so on. Such information even is sold and distributed over the Net. Those placed on these electronic databases eventually become targets of commerce and special-interest groups.

The use of personal information for profit and other purposes is growing so rapidly that the government has not been able to keep up with abuses. Antiquated laws, combined with judicial unfamiliarity with information technology, make policing and prosecuting abuses of the privacy of personal information difficult and, in many cases, impossible.

Computer Matching

In **computer matching**, separate databases are examined and individuals common to both are identified. The focus of most computer-matching applications is to identify people engaged in wrongdoing. For example, federal employees are being matched with those having delinquent student loans. Then, wages are garnished to repay the loans. In another computer-matching case, a $30-million fraud was uncovered when questionable financial transactions were traced to common participants.

The Internal Revenue Service also uses computer matching to identify tax cheaters. The IRS gathers descriptive data, such as neighborhood and automobile type, then uses sophisticated models to create lifestyle profiles. These profiles are matched against reported income on tax returns to predict whether people seem to be underpaying taxes. When the income and projected lifestyle do not match, the return is audited.

Proponents of computer matching cite the potential to reduce criminal activity. Opponents of computer matching consider it an unethical invasion of privacy.

Creating New Applications for Personal Information

The mere fact that personal information is so readily available has opened the door for many new applications of information technology. Some people will praise their merits and others will adamantly oppose them. For example, one Federal proposal is to have computer-based background checks done on all airline passengers. The results of the checks would be used to identify which passengers' luggage to search. The proposed system would examine names, addresses, telephone numbers, travel histories, and billing records to search for irregularities that might indicate possible terrorist or smuggler activity. This application, like many others that involve the use of personal information, has the potential to have a positive impact on society. Protectors of the rights of individuals will argue that the benefits derived may not be great enough to offset this invasion into personal information.

Each new application involving the use of personal information will be scrutinized carefully; but it is inevitable that our personal information will be used for a variety of applications. These may include systems that locate compatible mates, assign schoolchildren to classes, track sex offenders, identify employees who do not meet company character standards, target sales to likely customers, and so on.

No Easy Answers to the Privacy Question

The ethical questions surrounding the privacy of personal information are extremely complex and difficult to resolve. For example, consider the position of the American Civil Liberties Union. On one hand, the ACLU is fighting to curb abuses of personal information and on the other, it is lobbying the government for greater access to government information, which may include personal information. Are these goals in conflict?

On one side of the fence, consumer organizations and privacy advocates are lobbying for privacy legislation that can protect the interests and rights of online users. The e-commerce sector is pulling legislatures in the other direction. Online businesses want voluntary controls and industry self-regulation instead of new privacy legislation. New laws probably will reflect a compromise between the two views on the privacy of personal information.

As automation continues to enrich our lives, it also opens the door for abuses of personal information. Research is currently being done that may show that people with certain genetic and/or personality makeups have a statistical predisposition to a physical problem or a mental disorder, such as early heart failure or depression. Will employers use such information to screen potential employees?

By now, it should be apparent to you that we may never resolve all of the ethical questions associated with the privacy of personal information. Just as the answer to one question becomes clearer, a growing number of applications that deal with personal information raises another.

COMPUTER MONITORING

One of the most controversial applications of information technology is **computer monitoring**. In computer monitoring, computers continuously gather and assimilate data on job activities to measure worker performance, often without the workers' knowledge (see Figure 8-7). Today, computers monitor the job performance of millions of American workers and millions more worldwide. Most of these workers are online and routinely interact with a server computer system via a terminal or PC. Others work with electronic or mechanical equipment linked to a computer system.

Many clerical workers are evaluated by the number of documents they process per unit of time. At insurance companies, computer-monitoring systems provide supervisors with information on the rate at which clerks process claims. Supervisors can request other information, such as time spent at the PC or terminal and the keying-error rate.

Computers also monitor the activities of many jobs that demand frequent use of the telephone. A computer logs the number of inquiries handled by directory-assistance operators. Some companies employ computers to monitor the use of telephones by all employees.

Although most computer monitoring is done at the clerical level, it also is being applied to persons in higher-level positions, such as commodities brokers, programmers, loan officers, and plant managers. For example, CIM (computer-integrated manufacturing) enables corporate executives to monitor the effectiveness of a plant manager on a real-time basis. At any given time, executives can tap the system for productivity information, such as the rate of production for a particular assembly.

Not all computer monitoring is aimed at assessing ongoing job performance. About two-thirds of all U.S. companies monitor employee Internet browsing activities, too. Companies would prefer that their employees not view pornography, play games, gamble, or engage in nonwork browsing while at work. In fact, one in every four companies has fired at least one employee based on the results of Web monitoring information.

Many organizations encourage management scrutiny of employee electronic mail. In this form of monitoring, a robotic scanner "reads" employee e-mail searching for key words and phrases ("party," "skiing," "have a drink," and so on). Questionable e-mail messages are sent to management for review. The purpose of this type of monitoring is to ensure that internal communications are work-related and of a certain level of quality. Companies justify e-mail monitoring by citing their need to protect intellectual property and to provide documentation that can protect the company in case of litigation. Many organized worker groups have complained that this form of monitoring is an unnecessary invasion of privacy and can actually be counterproductive.

Workers complain that being constantly observed and analyzed by a computer adds unnecessary stress to their jobs. However, management is reluctant to give up computer monitoring because it has proved itself to be a tool for increasing worker productivity. In general, affected workers are opposing any further intrusion into their professional privacy. Conversely, management is equally vigilant in its quest for better information on worker performance and Internet activities.

FIGURE 8–7 COMPUTER MONITORING

MONITORING MOBILE WORKERS
With a portable terminal, this trucker is expected to communicate with headquarters. He can send sales information, transaction records, and progress reports quickly, accurately, and wirelessly to the host computer. The host computer can also dispatch instructions, updates, and work orders back out to its workforce. Anyone who records transactions on a computer system is a candidate for computer monitoring.

Courtesy of Symbol Technologies, Inc.

MONITORING OFFICE KNOWLEDGE WORKERS
The scope and extent of computer monitoring is on the rise in companies throughout the world, especially among knowledge workers who perform transactions. Companies that do not use computer monitoring are the exception.

Courtesy of Sun Microsystems, Inc.

8-3.1 Personal information has become the product of a growing industry. (T/F)

8-3.2 Your personal data cannot be passed from one organization to another without your consent. (T/F)

8-3.3 A message given to your Web browser by the Web server being accessed is a: (a) cake, (b) pie, (c) cookie, or (d) tart.

8-3.4 The term used to describe the computer-based collection of data on worker activities is called: (a) computer matching, (b) computer monitoring, (c) footprinting, or (d) pilferage.

8-4 Computer and IT Crime

The ethical spectrum for computer issues runs from that which is ethical, to that which is unethical, to that which is against the law—a computer crime. There are many types of computer and IT crimes, ranging from the use of an unauthorized password by a student in a college computer lab to a billion-dollar insurance fraud. The first case of computer crime was reported in 1958. Since then, all types of computer-related crimes have been reported: fraud, theft, larceny, embezzlement, burglary, sabotage, espionage, and forgery. We know computer crime is a serious problem, but we don't know how serious. Some studies estimate that each year the total money lost from computer crime is greater than the sum total of that taken in all other robberies. In fact, no one really knows the extent of computer crime because much of it is either undetected or unreported. In those cases involving banks, officers may elect to write off the loss rather than announce the crime and risk losing the goodwill of their customers. Computer crimes involving the greatest amount of money have to do with banking, insurance, product inventories, and securities.

A record number of computer crime cases are being reported each year; however, the federal government is opting not to prosecute many of them. The increase in computer crime combined with the

WHY THIS SECTION IS IMPORTANT TO YOU

Everything associated with computers is growing rapidly—the number of computer professionals, robotics, the Internet, and *computer crime*. Understanding the material in this section will reduce the chances of you becoming a victim of a computer-related crime and will help you understand what you can do to prevent it.

reluctance to prosecute gives us some insight into the progress of the government's war on computer crime. In recent years, prosecutors filed charges in only 25% of the hundreds of computer crime cases given to federal prosecutors. This percentage of referrals being prosecuted is considerably lower than the average of all referrals. The FBI has noted that computer crime is very difficult to prove. Also, prosecutors may be ill-prepared from a technical perspective to prosecute such cases. Most of those who are convicted receive relatively light sentences or are released on probation with no jail time.

Fortunately, only a small percentage of the people with an inclination toward crime are capable of committing high-tech crimes. Unfortunately, the criminal element in our society, like everyone else, is moving toward information technology competency. Thanks to the improved controls made possible through automation, though, business-related crime, in general, is decreasing. Computers have simply made it more difficult for people to commit business crimes. For the most part, stereotypical criminals and undesirables do not commit computer crimes. Instead, trusted computer users commit them with authorized access to sensitive information.

COMPUTERS AND THE LAW

Companies try to employ information technology within the boundaries of any applicable laws. Unfortunately, the laws are not always clear because many legal questions involving the use of information technology are being debated for the first time. For example, is e-mail like a letter or a memo, subject to freedom-of-information laws? Or, is it private, like telephone calls? This question is yet to be resolved. To no one's surprise, IT law is the fastest growing type of law practice.

Laws governing information technology are beginning to take shape (see Figure 8-8). Prior to 1994, federal laws that addressed computer crime were limited because they applied only to those computer systems that in some way reflected a "federal interest." The Computer Abuse Amendments Act of 1994 expanded the scope of computer crimes to computers "used in interstate commerce." Effectively, this applies to any computer, including home PCs, with a link to the Internet. These laws make it a felony to gain unauthorized access to a computer system with the intent to obtain anything of value, to defraud the system, or to cause more than $1000 in damage. Although most states have adopted computer crime laws, current laws are only the skeleton of what is needed to direct an orderly and controlled growth of information technology applications.

The Children's Online Privacy Protection Act (COPPA) went into effect in 2000. There was a two-year transition period giving Internet organizations an opportunity to gear up for conforming to the new law. It is the first law governing online privacy. The new law requires that Internet Web sites obtain verifiable consent from parents before collecting, using, or disclosing personal information from children under the age of 13. The law offers a variety of methods for parental consent, including e-mail, snail mail, fax, and so on. Parents are overwhelmingly in favor of this law; however, critics say that it may limit the variety of activities that children will have on the Internet.

Existing federal and state laws concerning the privacy of personal information are being updated every year. At the same time, new laws are being written. Current federal laws outline the handling of credit information, restrict what information the IRS can obtain, restrict government access to financial information, permit individuals to view records maintained by federal agencies, restrict the use of education-related data, and regulate the matching of computer files. States have or are considering laws to deal with the

FIGURE 8–8

IT LEGISLATION

Information technology-related legislation is being revised in the House of Representatives as quickly as it is being proposed. The background screen shows the most recent version of a proposed bill—the Networking and Information Technology Research Advancement Act. The House and Senate Web sites make the full text of proposed legislation and other pertinent information available online, including pages dedicated to providing current information for the press (see inset).

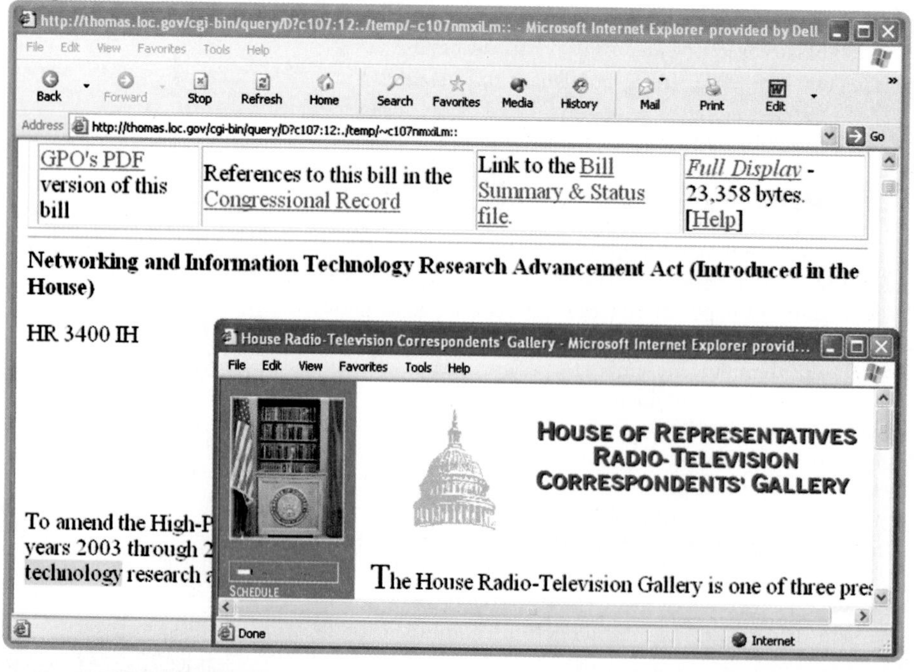

handling of social security numbers, criminal records, telephone numbers, financial information, medical records, and other sensitive personal information.

Computer crime is a relatively recent phenomenon. As a result, legislation, the criminal justice system, and industry are not yet adequately prepared to cope with it. Only a handful of police and FBI agents in the entire country have been trained to handle cases involving computer crime. And when a case comes to court, few judges and even fewer jurors have the background necessary to understand the testimony.

AREAS OF COMPUTER AND IT CRIMINAL ACTIVITY

Computer and IT crimes can be grouped into several categories, described in the following sections.

Crimes That Create Havoc Inside a Computer

Computer viruses and *Trojan horses* (discussed in Chapter 5) fall into this category. A computer virus is a program that takes control of the victim's system, with results that range from exasperating (the display of a harmless political message) to tragic (the loss of all programs and data). Furthermore, computer viruses can copy themselves from system to system when unsuspecting users exchange infected disks. A Trojan horse is any seemingly useful program that hides a computer virus or a logic bomb. A **logic bomb,** in contrast, is a set of instructions that is executed when a certain set of conditions are met. For example, a disgruntled employee might plant a logic bomb to be "exploded" on the first Friday the thirteenth after his or her record is deleted from the personnel database.

Crimes That Involve Fraud and Embezzlement

Most computer crimes fall under the umbrella of fraud and embezzlement. Fraud involves obtaining illegal access to a computer system for the purpose of personal gain. Embezzlement concerns the misappropriation of funds.

- A 17-year old high school student tapped into an AT&T computer and stole more than $1 million worth of software. (Fraud)

- One person hacked his way into a system and illegally transferred $10,200,000 from a U.S. bank to a Swiss bank. He probably would have gotten away with this electronic heist if he had not felt compelled to brag about it. (Fraud)

- A U.S. Customs official modified a program to print $160,000 worth of unauthorized federal payroll checks payable to himself and his co-conspirators. (Embezzlement)

- Three data entry clerks in a large metropolitan city conspired with welfare recipients to write over $2 million of fraudulent checks. (Embezzlement)

Computers can be both an invitation to fraud and a tool to thwart fraud. For example, at one time, the automated system in place in the pits at the Chicago Board of Trade and the Chicago Mercantile Exchange made it possible for traders to fill personal orders either simultaneously or ahead of their customers to get better prices. A system, involving handheld computer trading devices, could be implemented that would electronically record every trade in sequence, preventing such abuses.

The *salami technique* for embezzlement requires that a Trojan horse (unauthorized code hidden in a legitimate program) be planted in the program code of a financial system that processes a large number of accounts. These covert instructions cause a small amount of money, usually less than a penny, to be debited periodically from each account and credited to one or more dummy accounts. A number of less sophisticated computer-manipulation crimes are the result of data diddling. *Data diddling* is changing the data, perhaps the "ship to" address, on manually prepared source documents or during online entry to the system.

Attempts to defraud a computer system require the cooperation of an experienced IT specialist. A common street thug does not have the knowledge or the opportunity to be successful at this type of computer crime. Over 50% of all computer frauds are internal, that is, employees of the organization being defrauded commit them. About 30% of those defrauding employees are IT specialists.

Crimes That Involve Negligence or Incompetence

Not all computer crime is premeditated. Negligence or incompetence can be just as bad for an organization as a premeditated crime. Such crimes usually are a result of poor input/output control. For example, after she paid in full, a woman was sent follow-up notices continually and was visited by collection agencies for not making payments on her automobile. Although the records and procedures were in error, the company forcibly repossessed the automobile without thoroughly checking its procedures and the legal implications. The woman had to sue the company for the return of her automobile. The court ordered the automobile returned and the company to pay her a substantial sum as a penalty.

Companies that employ computers to process data must do so in a responsible manner. Irresponsible actions that result in the deletion of a bank account or the premature discontinuation of electrical service would fall into this category. Lax controls and the availability of sensitive information invite scavenging. *Scavenging* is searching for discarded information that may be of some value on the black market, such as a printout containing credit card numbers.

Crimes That Involve Unauthorized Access to the Internet and Networking

Security on the Internet and computer networks is an ongoing problem. Internet-related intrusions number in the thousands each month. The Internet is so vulnerable that computer science professors have been known to ask their students to break into files at a particular site on the Internet. Successful students bring back proof of system penetration to show they understand the protocols involved.

Any computer enthusiast who enjoys the lawful excesses of personal computing (programming, building PCs, and so on) would qualify as a **hacker.** Hackers created the term **cracker** to distinguish themselves from overzealous hackers, who "crack" through network/Internet security and tap into everything from local credit agencies to top-secret defense systems. These "electronic vandals" often leave evidence of unlawful entry, perhaps a revised record or access during nonoperating hours, called a **footprint.**

Many of the millions of Internet sites are vulnerable to attacks by vandals. Vandals have substituted images on home pages with ones that are embarrassing to the organization. Others have bombarded sites with thousands of randomly generated requests for service to preclude their use by legitimate users. These are called *denial of service* attacks. Each day hackers and crackers are finding new ways to wreak havoc on the Internet.

One of the major motivators for unauthorized access is **industrial espionage.** Companies representing most of the world's countries have attempted a shortcut to success and have attempted to steal product design specifications, product development schedules, trade secrets, software code, strategic plans, sales strategies, customer information, or anything else that would give them a competitive advantage. The typical corporate computer has everything corporate spies would want, so their objective is to circumvent security measures and gain access to a target company's system, look around, and extract whatever pertinent information they can.

The Computer Abuse Amendments Act of 1994 changed the standard for criminal prosecution from "intent" to "reckless disregard," thus increasing the chances of successful prosecution of crackers. Two computer crackers were sentenced to federal prison for their roles in defrauding long-distance carriers of more than $28 million. The crackers stole credit card numbers from MCI. The cracker who worked at MCI was sentenced to three years and two months, and the other cracker was sentenced to a one-year prison term. Countries throughout the world are struggling to define just punishment for cybercrimes. Some countries have adopted a zero tolerance policy in their cyber laws. For example, two brothers in China were executed for a $30,000 electronic heist. There is a concern that the media glorifies criminally oriented hackers, creating heroes for a new generation of computer criminals. This glorification may begin to fade as we read about more and more crackers serving hard time.

The Internet's cybercops on the Computer Emergency Response Team (CERT) often work around the clock to thwart electronic vandalism and crime on the Internet. CERT concentrates its efforts on battling major threats to the global Internet. Lesser problems are left to the Internet service providers and to police. A few years ago, the cybercops tracked hackers who were out to prove their ingenuity by breaking into systems just to prove they could. These hackers were mostly harmless, more out to prove their hacking abilities than to act maliciously. Now cyberthiefs are after more than self-esteem: They want to steal something. They intercept credit card numbers, reroute valuable inventory, download copyrighted software, or make illegal monetary transactions. Fortunately, CERT has found that security incidents generally are decreasing relative to the size of the Internet. Unfortunately, as soon as CERT people plug a hole in the Internet, another is found. The problem will not go away and may become more difficult to cope with as perpetrators gain sophistication.

Security experts say that the best way to deal effectively with crime on the Internet is the universal adoption and use of an international encryption standard. At present, some people and companies are reluctant to adopt such a standard because it would effectively end open worldwide communication. However, if abuse continues, universal encryption may be the only solution.

Unauthorized entry to a computer network is achieved in a variety of ways. The most common approach is *masquerading*. People acquire passwords and personal information that will enable them to masquerade as an authorized user. The *tailgating* technique is used by company outsiders to gain access to sensitive information. The perpetrator simply begins using the terminal or computer of an authorized user who has left the room without terminating his or her session. The more sophisticated user might prefer building a trap door, scanning, or superzapping. A *trap door* is a Trojan horse that permits unauthorized and undetected access to a computer system. Trap doors usually are implemented by an insider during system development, usually a programmer. *Scanning* involves the use of a computer to test different combinations of access information until access is permitted (for example, by stepping through a four-digit access code from 0000 to 9999). *Superzapping* involves using a program that enables someone to bypass the security controls.

Crimes in Which the Internet Becomes a Tool for Crime

To thousands of con artists, the Internet offers a quicker, more efficient vehicle for dozens of old-fashioned scams: pyramid schemes, chain letters, offers of free government money, debt-elimination schemes, rip and tear (the big prize—for a fee), and a wealth of get-rich-quick rip-offs. The Internet, also, has opened the door for more sophisticated, technology-based scams, such as **pumping and dumping,** which is illegal. In this scam, seemingly legitimate sources flood the Internet with bogus information about the successes of a particular company. The Internet blitz travels via e-mail, newsgroups, instant messaging, and other means of Internet communication. If the fraud works, the net effect is to artificially "pump" up the price of the company's stock. The con artists then "dump" their stock at peak value to realize big gains.

Online auction sites, such as eBay, expand the con artist's reach to millions of people. Scammers are delighted to have this opportunity to sell things they do not have and will never deliver. With over 100,000 bids being posted every hour on millions of items up for auction, this type of scam is difficult to prevent.

Cyberstalking has emerging as one of the fastest-growing areas of Internet crime. Cyberstalking is technology-based stalking where the Internet becomes a vehicle by which the stalker directs threatening behavior and unwanted advances to another netizen (citizen of the Internet). Cyberstalkers find their victims in chat rooms, in newsgroups, in discussion forums, and through e-mail. Most cyberstalkers are men and target women and children. Cyberstalking can be in the form of a threatening or obscene communication (real-time or e-mail), flaming (verbal abuse), mountains of junk e-mail, sexually explicit images, inappropriate messages left at various online locations, viruses, and identity theft. When cyberstalking goes offline, it can become a terrifying experience that elevates electronic harassment to the potential for physical harm.

Crimes That Involve the Abuse of Personal Information

With so much personal information floating around cyberspace, **identity theft** has emerged as one of the fastest growing criminal activities. Identity theft occurs when someone is able to gather enough personal information on you (without your knowledge) to assume your identity. The objective of identity theft is fraud or theft. Identity thieves open new credit card accounts using your name, address, date of birth, and social security numbers. Then, they spend away, sticking you with the bill. Identity thieves have become very imaginative, setting up cellular phone accounts and bank accounts in your name.

Any willful release or distribution of inaccurate personal information would fall into this category, as well. For example, it is a crime to post false information about an individual to the Internet with intent to defame.

Crimes That Support Criminal Enterprises

Money laundering and databases that support drug distribution would fall into this category. Technology has tremendous potential to improve the plight of humanity. Sadly, it has just as much potential for evil. The criminal elements of our society have ingeniously used information technology to support hundreds of criminal ventures from illegal gambling to complex multi-country money laundering schemes.

Crimes That Involve the Theft of Software or Intellectual Property

Federal copyright law automatically protects software from the moment of its creation. This law is the same one that protects other intellectual property (books, audio recordings, films, and so on). The Copyright Law of 1974 gives the owner of the copyright "the exclusive rights" to "reproduce the copyrighted word." Unless specifically stated in the license agreement, the purchasers can install the software to only one computer. The general rule is: one software package per computer. Any other duplication, whether for sale or for the owner's personal use, is an infringement of copyright law.

It is copyright infringement to allow simultaneous use of a single-user version on a LAN by more than one person. LAN versions of software packages are sold with a *site license* that permits use by a specific number of users. Also, the Software Rental Amendments Act of 1990 prohibits the rental, leasing, or lending of copyright software.

The unlawful duplication of proprietary software, called **software piracy,** is making companies vulnerable to legal action by the affected vendors (see Figure 8-9). The term **pilferage** is used to

FIGURE 8–9 PROTECTION FOR INTELLECTUAL PROPERTY

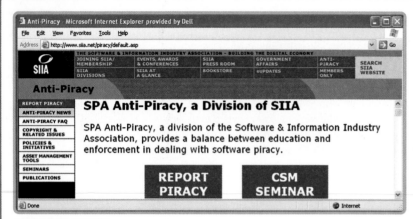

SOFTWARE PIRACY

The Software & Information Industry Association (SIIA) sponsors a vigorous ongoing anti-piracy campaign to protect copyrighted software. Anti-piracy information and support are available from its Web site at http://www.siia.net. The task of catching pirates who sell illegal copies of popular computer programs has become more challenging with the advent of the Internet. The site makes it easy for people to report copyright abuses. Almost 1 million Web sites offer illegal software, resulting in a loss of revenue to software vendors of about $15 billion per year.

COPYRIGHT LAW

Copyright laws protect literature, music, the design of a silicon chip, and software, to name a few. The law protects Intel's innovative bumpless technology chip design.

Photo courtesy of Intel Corporation

describe the situation in which a company purchases a software product without a site-usage license agreement, then copies and distributes the software throughout the company. If such piracy is done "willfully and for the purpose of commercial advantage or private financial gain," perpetrators are subject to fines up to $250,000 and 5 years in jail. Software piracy doesn't pay. Two pirates in Canada were forced to walk the plank with a $22,500 fine. This and similar rulings have sent the message loud and clear: Software piracy will not be tolerated.

Vendors of software for personal computers estimate that for every software product sold, two more are illegally copied. Software piracy is a serious problem, and software vendors are acting vigorously to prosecute people and companies who violate their copyrights. Worldwide, the software industry loses billions of dollars a year to software piracy. According to figures compiled by the Business Software Alliance (BSA), virtually all of the software in Vietnam (97%) is illegal (without a license). China is close behind at 94%, followed by Indonesia (89%) and Russia (88%). It is estimated that the software industry loses about $11 billion a year through software piracy.

The Net poses big problems for software vendors, especially with the widespread use of broadband access, which permits downloads in minutes rather than hours. How do you keep people from distributing copies of software over the Internet? In all likelihood, software eventually will be encrypted such that the purchaser receives a cryptographic key to decode the program and data files. The key would exist in the program, identifying the owner and the buyer. If the buyer illegally distributes the program over an electronic highway, cybercops will be able to trace the action back to the source of the crime.

Some company managers confront the issue head-on and state bluntly that software piracy is a crime and offenders will be dismissed. This method has proven effective. Some, who are actually accomplices, look the other way as subordinates copy software for office and personal use.

Intellectual property rights issues have been front-page news since recording companies began actively suing file sharing enterprises to get them to stop promoting the sharing of copyrighted MP3 songs. The sharing of songs has been attractive to netizens, even to those with slow dialup Internet access. Now, with the rapid expansion of broadband access, netizens are beginning to share pirated versions of feature length movie files. Industry analysts are estimating that up to 400,000 first-run movies are downloaded illegally each day. Films on DVD-ROM are copied and posted to the Net. Digital camcorders are taken to movie theaters where they are used to capture films illegally for Net distribution. The abuse of intellectual property rights in the film industry is nowhere near that of the music recording industry, however, we can look for aggressive litigation as movie moguls move to protect their intellectual property rights.

The penalties for copyright infringements are now more severe. In the United States, crimes involving copyright and identity theft violations result in increased punishment. The creation of counterfeit intellectual material, such as software, music, and books, can result in prison sentences up to 16 months, no matter what the motivation of the perpetrator. The greater the market value of the counterfeit copies is, the stiffer the punishment.

8-4.1	Many legal questions involving computers and information processing are yet to be incorporated into the federal laws. (T/F)
8-4.2	What law is violated when an organization duplicates proprietary software without permission: (a) civil rights, (b) antitrust, (c) copyright, or (d) patent?
8-4.3	The first law governing online privacy is: (a) COPPA, (b) Cabana, (c) adult-oriented, or (d) temporary.
8-4.4	A set of instructions that is executed when a certain set of conditions are met is called a: (a) logic virus, (b) scavenger, (c) data diddler, or (d) logic bomb.

SECTION SELF-CHECK

8-5 | Computer, Internet, and System Security

Computer security has been breached and financial losses were incurred in about 80% of the organizations responding to a recent survey, almost half of them within the past year. Losses often are in the millions. The problem is serious and will not go away anytime soon. To minimize unethical abuses of information technology and computer crime, individuals and organizations must build an envelope of security around hardware and embed safeguards into the information systems. Security concerns take on added importance now that millions of businesses have a presence on the Internet and/or are actively involved in e-commerce. In either case, their computer systems are connected via the Internet and, therefore, are vulnerable. Their link to the Net is just one of many points of vulnerability, and too much is at stake to overlook the threats to the security of any computer system. These threats take many forms—white-collar crime, computer viruses, natural disasters (such as earthquakes and floods), vandalism, and carelessness.

In this section, we discuss commonly applied measures that can help to neutralize security threats to a computer center, an information system, and a PC.

COMPUTER-CENTER SECURITY

Enterprise-wide information systems provide information and processing capabilities to workers throughout a given organization. Some systems extend to customers, suppliers, and others outside the organization. Generally, network server computers located in centralized computer centers handle such systems. The center can be anything from a secure room for the LAN server to an entire building for the organization's server computers and the information services staff. Whether a room or a building, the computer center has a number of points of vulnerability: *hardware, software, files/databases, data communications (including the Internet),* and *personnel.* We discuss each separately in this section and illustrate them in Figure 8-10.

Hardware

If the hardware fails, the information system fails. The threat of failure can be minimized by implementing security precautions that prevent access by unauthorized personnel and by taking steps to keep all hardware operational.

Common approaches to securing the premises from unauthorized entry include the use of closed-circuit TV and monitors, alarm systems, as well as computer-controlled devices that check employee badges, fingerprints, or voice prints before unlocking doors at access points. Computer centers also should be isolated from pedestrian traffic. Computer-room fires should be extinguished by a special chemical that douses the fire but does not destroy the files or equipment.

Any complex system is subject to failure. However, for many organizations, network failure is simply unacceptable. For example, if the network supporting the Hilton Hotel reservation system went down for a couple of hours, thousands of reservations and, perhaps, millions of dollars would be lost. Such systems must be made *fault-tolerant.* Fault-tolerant networks are designed to permit continuous operation even if important components of the network fail. To accomplish this goal, parts of the system, such as the server computer or hard disks, must be duplicated. For example, a LAN might have an alternate LAN server. RAID systems, discussed in Chapter 5, "Storing and Retrieving Information," provide fault-tolerant backup of disk systems. Fault-tolerant networks are designed to enable alternate routing of messages. Of course, no network can be made totally fault-tolerant. The degree to which a network is made fault-tolerant depends on the amount of money an organization is willing to spend.

FIGURE 8–10

SECURITY PRECAUTIONS
Some or all of the security measures noted in the figure are in force in most organizations. Each precaution helps minimize the risk of a computer center's, an information system's, or a PC's vulnerability to crime, disasters, and failure.

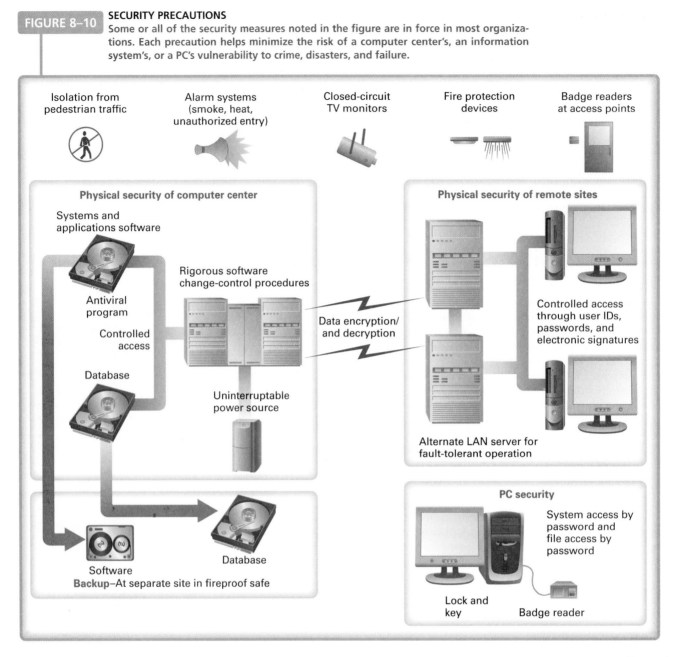

Isolation from pedestrian traffic

Alarm systems (smoke, heat, unauthorized entry)

Closed-circuit TV monitors

Fire protection devices

Badge readers at access points

Physical security of computer center

Systems and applications software

Rigorous software change-control procedures

Antiviral program

Controlled access

Database

Data encryption/ and decryption

Uninterruptable power source

Physical security of remote sites

Controlled access through user IDs, passwords, and electronic signatures

Alternate LAN server for fault-tolerant operation

Software
Backup–At separate site in fireproof safe

Database

PC security

System access by password and file access by password

Lock and key

Badge reader

Computers must have a "clean," continuous source of power. To minimize the effects of "dirty" power or power outages, each critical computer should draw its power from an **uninterruptible power source** (**UPS**). Dirty power, with sags and surges in power output or brownouts (low power), causes data transmission errors and program execution errors. A UPS system serves as a buffer between the external power source and the computer system. In a UPS system, batteries deliver clean power to the computer and are regenerated continuously by an external power source. If the external power source fails, the UPS system permits operation to continue for a period of time after an outage. This time cushion allows operators to either "power down" normally or switch to a backup power source, usually a diesel-powered generator. UPS systems are considered essential equipment in the business world where server computers must be operational 24/7. Each year, the UPS system is becoming more widely accepted as a critical component of a home or small office PC.

Software

Unless properly controlled, the software for an information system can either be modified for personal gain or vandalized and rendered useless. Close control of software development and the documentation of an information system are needed to minimize the opportunity for computer crime and vandalism.

Unlawful Modification of Software

Bank programmers certainly have opportunities to modify software for personal gain. In one case, a couple of programmers used the salami embezzlement technique and modified a savings system to make small deposits from other accounts to their own accounts. Here's how it worked: The interest for each savings account was compounded and credited daily, with the calculated interest rounded to the nearest penny before being credited to the savings account. Programs were modified to round down all interest calculations and put the "extra" penny in one of the programmers' savings accounts. It may not seem like much, but a penny a day from thousands of accounts adds up to a lot of money. The "beauty" of the system was that the books balanced and depositors did not miss the 15 cents (an average of 1/2 cent per day for 30 days) that judiciously was taken from each account each month. Even auditors had difficulty detecting this crime because the total interest paid on all accounts was correct. However, the culprits got greedy and were apprehended when someone noticed that they repeatedly withdrew inordinately large sums of money from their own accounts. Unfortunately, other enterprising programmers in other industries have been equally imaginative.

Operational control procedures built into the design of an information system will constantly monitor processing accuracy. Unfortunately, cagey programmers have been known to get around some of them. Perhaps the best way to safeguard programs from unlawful tampering is to use rigorous change-control procedures. Such procedures require programmers to obtain authorization before modifying an operational program. Change-control procedures make it difficult to modify a program for purposes of personal gain.

Viruses

Melissa, Chernobyl, Michelangelo, Friday the 13th, Stoned, Jerusalem, and *Love Bug* are phrases that strike fear in PC users. They're names of computer viruses. The infamous *Michelangelo* virus hits on March 6, the artist's birthday, destroying stored data. *Friday the 13th* causes its damage on those days. Even though computer viruses have no metabolism of their own, some people are convinced that they fit the definition of a living system because they use the metabolism of a host computer for their parasitic existence.

The growing threat of viruses has resulted in tightening software controls. *Virus software,* which has been found at all levels of computing, "infects" other programs and databases. The virus is so named because it can spread from one system to another like a biological virus. Viruses are written by outlaw programmers to cause harm to the computer systems of unsuspecting victims. Left undetected a virus can result in loss of data and/or programs and even physical damage to the hardware. Viruses are discussed in detail in Chapter 5, "Storing and Retrieving Information."

Individuals and companies routinely run antivirus programs on both client and server computers, to search for and destroy viruses before they can do their dirty work. Many organizations encourage employees to run antivirus programs prior to March 6th and any Friday the 13th. IBM researchers are working on an electronic *immune system* that would automatically detect viruses and neutralize them with digital antibodies. The immune system would inoculate other computers on the network, stopping the spread of the virus.

Files/Databases

A database contains the raw material for information. Often the files/databases of a company are its lifeblood. For example, how many companies can afford to lose their accounts receivable file, which documents who owes what? Having several *generations of backups* (backups to backups) to all files is not sufficient insurance against loss of files/databases. The backup and master files should be stored in fireproof safes in separate rooms, preferably in separate buildings. Approaches to system backup are covered in Chapter 5.

Data Communications

The mere existence of data communications/Internet capabilities poses a threat to security. A knowledgeable criminal can tap into the system from a remote location and use it for personal gain. In a well-designed system, such hacking is not an easy task. The typical company experiences over 30 hacker attacks each week, but rarely is an attack successful. But it can be and has been done! When one criminal broke a company's security code and tapped into the network of computers, he was able to order certain products without being billed. He filled a warehouse before he eventually was caught. Another tapped into an international banking exchange system to reroute funds to an account of his own in a Swiss bank. In another case, an oil company consistently was able to outbid a competitor by "listening in" on the latter's data transmissions. On several occasions, overzealous hackers have tapped into sensitive defense computer systems. Fortunately, no harm was done.

How do companies protect themselves from these criminal activities? Most companies use the science of **cryptography** to scramble sensitive communications sent over computer networks or the Internet. Cryptography is analogous to the code book used by intelligence people during the "cloak-and-dagger" days of the post-World War II era. Instead of a code book, however, a key is used in conjunction with **encryption/decryption** techniques to unscramble the message. Here is how it works. Before a message is sent, it is *encrypted* such that the bit structure of the message is rearranged according to some mathematical algorithm. Both sender and receiver (people and/or computers) must have the *key*, which may be a number or phrase. The key is the basis for both encryption and decryption. Once encrypted according to an algorithm and its key, the message becomes a meaningless string of bits to anyone who might unlawfully intercept it. The receiver, a person or a computer, uses a key to decrypt and read the message.

Two types of encryption systems are in common use, symmetric-key encryption and public-key encryption. **Symmetric-key encryption** requires that each computer in a communications loop have the key needed to encrypt/decrypt the message. **Public-key encryption** requires both a private key, known only to a particular person/computer, and a public key.

With the rapid growth of e-commerce, Internet security is beginning to mature. A few years ago, people were reluctant to send their credit card number over the Internet. Today, people routinely purchase items with their credit cards. The difference is that Web site security has been beefed up with protocols for transmitting data securely over the World Wide Web. One protocol, **Secure Sockets Layer** (SSL) uses public-key encryption technology to encrypt data that are transferred over the SSL link. Many Web sites use this protocol to transmit sensitive information, such as credit card numbers, between Web client and Web server. There are a couple of ways to tell if you are using a secure Internet protocol. The "http" in the browser's URL bar becomes "https" and/or a padlock icon appears in the status bar at the bottom of the browser.

Most personal transmissions over the Internet are e-mail. Some who send sensitive information are opting to use a digital ID. The **digital ID** serves as an electronic substitute for a sealed envelope. The digital ID becomes part of the browser or e-mail software and allows you to encrypt your e-mail. The digital ID ensures that messages and attachments are protected from tampering, impersonation, and eavesdropping.

Recently a new federal law legalized online signatures. In effect, the **e-signature** has the same legal status as a personalized signature on many documents. However, it does not apply to family law documents, such as wills, trusts, adoptions, or divorce. It is not legal for several other situations, including cancellation of utility services or insurance, rental agreements, or product recall notifications. An e-signature is the ability to e-sign an electronic document. The e-signature has one or more electronic symbol(s) and an embedded security procedure that verifies that the e-signature is from a specific individual and any changes to the electronic document must be detectable. The legalization of the e-signature should have a positive impact on e-commerce. It is expected to reduce administrative costs and it should expedite online transactions.

Personnel

Possibly the biggest threat to a company's security system is the dishonesty and/or negligence of its own employees. Managers should pay close attention to who is hired for positions with access to computer-based information systems and sensitive data. Many companies flash a message on each networked PC or terminal such as: "All information on this system is confidential and proprietary." It's not very user-friendly, but it gets the message across to employees that they may be fired if they abuse the system. Someone who is grossly negligent can cause just as much harm as someone who is inherently dishonest.

INFORMATION SYSTEMS SECURITY

Information systems security is classified as physical or logical. **Physical security** refers to hardware, facilities, magnetic disks, and other items that could be illegally accessed, stolen, or destroyed. For example, restricted access to the server computer room is a form of physical security (see Figure 8-11).

Logical security is built into the software by permitting only authorized persons to access and use the system. Logical security for online systems, including Internet-based systems, is achieved primarily by using *user IDs* and *passwords*. Only those people with a need to know are given user IDs and told the password. On occasion, however, these security codes fall into the wrong hands. When this happens, an unauthorized person can gain access to programs and sensitive files simply by dialing up the computer and entering the codes.

User IDs and passwords remain the foundation of logical security. Users of LAN-based PCs must enter IDs and passwords before being allowed access to LAN resources. The user ID is your electronic

FIGURE 8–11 COMPUTER AND IT SECURITY

LOCK IT UP

The Kensington MemoryLock™ effectively blocks access to the inside of your computer. The hard drive, memory, and all your important information are protected when you lock it up.

Courtesy of Kensington
Technology Group

HIGH-TECH SECURITY SYSTEMS

Physical security is serious business in many companies, especially in areas that house sensitive information and access to computer systems. Shown here is the security control center where computers monitor access to secure areas throughout the company. In the inset, an employee swipes a smart card to gain access to a controlled area. The security system generates an ongoing log of personnel movement in and out of secure areas. Also, the system can monitor the whereabouts of individual employees.

Courtesy of Diebold, Incorporated

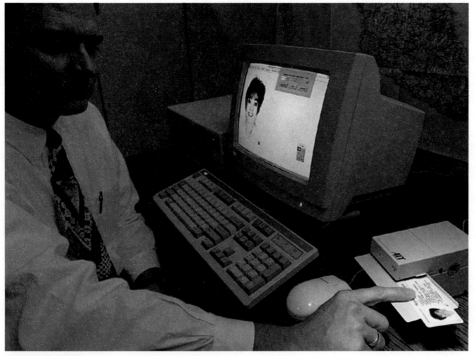

THE PC ID CARD

This Secure ID Document System provides instant access to sensitive real-time information for such applications as border monitoring, health care, and voter registration. A virtually tamper-proof identification card includes information on the bearer that can easily be verified using scanner technology.

Courtesy of E-Systems, Inc.

identifier and may be known by your friends and colleagues. The password, however, is yours alone to protect and use.

- Never tell anyone your password.
- Never write down your password.
- Change your password frequently.

Keeping user IDs and passwords from the computer criminal is not easy. One approach companies use is to educate employees about techniques used to obtain user IDs and passwords, such as tailgating. The tailgater simply continues a session begun by an authorized user when the user leaves the room. Some companies have added another layer of security with the *electronic signature*. The electronic signature, which is built into hardware or software, can be a number or even a digitized signature of an individual. The host or server computer checks the electronic signature against an approved list before permitting access to the system. This measure thwarts the tailgater who attempts to use illegally obtained passwords on unauthorized PCs or software.

Biometric identification systems, once considered revolutionary, are now in common use all around us. With biometric identification systems, we don't need to enter a user ID and password. Biometric identification systems detect unique personal characteristics that can be matched against a database containing the characteristics of authorized users. Several biometric methods are illustrated in Figure 8-12, including fingerprint, palm print (hand geometry), iris scans, and facial recognition. The voiceprint is another common means of biometric identification. Biometric devices are considered superior to traditional methods because they detect personal characteristics that can't be duplicated. All of these biometric technologies are being used for IT security and for other types of security, as well.

In the aftermath of the September 11, 2001, terrorist attack on America, it has become apparent that Americans may be willing to make greater personal privacy sacrifices than in the past in return for safety. **Face recognition technology,** which has been implemented at a number of major airports, enables the identification of known criminals and terrorists. The system creates a digital map of a person's face, called a *faceprint,* which is matched against a database of digital maps to see if there is a match. The system can scan faces in the crowd or a line at an airport ticket counter. In all likelihood, your face will be matched against a database of criminals and terrorists at some time in the future at airports and other public venues that might be vulnerable to attack.

PC SECURITY

Twenty-five years ago, the security problem was solved by wrapping the mainframe-based computer center in an envelope of physical security. Today the security issue is far more complex. PCs more powerful than the mainframes of 25 years ago pepper the corporate landscape. We even carry them with us. It's impractical to apply mainframe standards of security to PCs. If we did, we would all be working in concrete buildings under heavy security, and mobile computing would end.

Server computer security is planned and controlled carefully by security professionals. In contrast, PC security frequently is the responsibility of the individual users who may or may not have security training. As PC users, we have an ongoing obligation to be ever aware of security concerns. Generally, our PCs are readily accessible to other people in the area.

The conscientious PC user has several physical and logical security measures that can be used to safeguard valuable and/or sensitive information. The most frequently used physical tools include the *lock and key* and the *badge reader.* The lock and key, which come standard on most modern PCs, work like an automobile ignition switch. That is, the PC functions only when the lock is turned to the enable position. The badge reader is an optional peripheral device that reads magnetic stripes on badges, such as credit cards. The PC is disabled until an authorized card is inserted and read by the badge reader.

Often the content of your PC's screen bares your soul or perhaps sensitive corporate data. Some people place a special filter over the screen that permits only straight-on viewing. People use it in the office, airplane, or wherever they need to feel secure about their display.

Individual files on a PC can be secured by assigning them unique passwords. For example, if you were using a word processing package to prepare personnel performance evaluations, you could secure these files by assigning each a password. To recall a file at a later session, you or any other user would have to enter the name of the file and the associated password to gain access to it.

LEVEL OF RISK

No combination of security measures will completely remove the vulnerability of a computer center, an information system, a PC, or a file. Security systems are implemented in degrees. That is, an information system can be made marginally secure or very secure, but never totally secure. Each company

FIGURE 8–12

BIOMETRIC ACCESS METHODS
Biometrics is a method of measuring unique physical traits or behavioral characteristics. Shown here are four techniques. Your fingerprint, palm print, retina, or face can be used to verify your identity. The security industry has looked to biometric identification technologies to help consumers protect themselves against theft and fraud. Soon we may no longer have passwords or user IDs that can be stolen or forgotten.

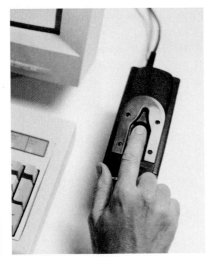

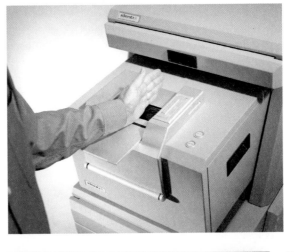

FULL HAND PALM SCANNER

The full hand palm scanner captures a digital image of the entire hand from the carpal crease to the fingertips. Over 30% of the latent prints at a crime scene are from the palm, not the fingers, so forensic examiners have more information they can use to find criminals.

Courtesy of Identix Corporation

FINGERPRINT SCANNER

In a fraction of a second, this biometric sensor can verify, compare, and store a user's fingerprint template. This fingerprint recognition system can be used to secure a computer system from unauthorized use and/or limit access to specific data or files.

Courtesy of Identix Corporation

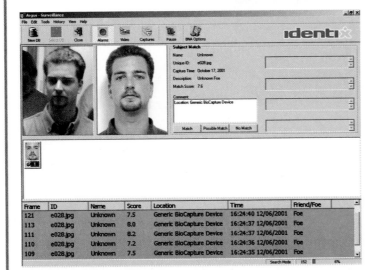

IRIS SCANNER

Biometric iris scanning technology, which scans the eye's retina through the pupil, provides a quick security access system in businesses and public facilities around the world.

Courtesy of International Business Machines Corporation. Unauthorized use not permitted.

FACE RECOGNITION SYSTEM

Face recognition software (left) uses a neural-based pattern-recognition technology that can extract local features unique to each face to eliminate the need for passwords or user IDs. Although face recognition systems do their job automatically, security control room operators have the flexibility to home in on specific subjects and do manual scans, as well (right).

Courtesy of Identix Corporation

must determine the level of risk that it is willing to accept. Unfortunately, some corporations are willing to accept an enormous risk and hope that those rare instances of crime and disaster do not occur. Some of them have found out too late that *rarely* is not the same as *never*!

SECTION SELF-CHECK

8-5.1 Virusology is the study of the assignment of security codes. (T/F)

8-5.2 Public-key encryption requires both a private key and a public key. (T/F)

8-5.3 Logical security for online systems is achieved primarily by user IDs and: (a) passwords, (b) secret codes, (c) numerical IDs, or (d) social security numbers.

8-5.4 What letter is added to "http" in the URL bar to indicate a secure Internet protocol: (a) i, (b) p, (c) s, or (d) t?

8-5.5 Data can be transmitted securely over the World Wide Web with which protocol: (a) Secure Sockets Layer, (b) ATM, (c) ASCII, or (d) security sheet protocol?

8-1 THE INFORMATION TECHNOLOGY PARADOX

We as a society are caught in an information technology paradox: Information technology is thriving in a society that may not be ready for it.

A reluctant acceptance of information technology has resulted in many information technology-based opportunities being overlooked or ignored. Among the reasons they are not implemented are historical momentum, resistance to change, limited education, and lack of available resources.

Society has reached a point of no return with regard to dependence on computers. Only through understanding can we control the misuse or abuse of computer technology.

8-2 THE WORKPLACE

Human factors engineers are applying the principles of **ergonomic** design to ensure that the interface between knowledge worker and workplace is safe, comfortable, effective, and efficient. The knowledge worker's workplace should be designed with enough flexibility to enable it to be custom-fitted to its worker. Attention to the overall environment (lighting, noise, and ventilation) can reduce stress and increase worker performance.

Problems associated with extended use of a terminal or PC are referred to as **video operator's distress syndrome**, or **VODS**. As the number of **repetitive-stress injuries** (**RSIs**) increased for knowledge workers, workstation ergonomics became an increasingly important issue for corporate productivity. A poorly designed workplace has the potential to cause **cumulative trauma disorder** (**CTD**), a condition that can lead to a permanent disability of motor skills.

The PC can be an invaluable tool in the workplace or it can be a serious diversion. These diversions may include sending and receiving frivolous e-mail, engaging in nonbusiness Internet browsing, gaming on company time, and toying with the technology.

Green computing adopts a more environmentally sound position with respect to the use and manufacture of computing hardware. The EPA's *Energy Star* guidelines are being used to standardize energy usage for monitors and processors. Good green computing includes sending e-mail (rather than paper), purchasing recycled paper, buying reconditioned components, and telecommuting once or twice a week.

Individuals and companies should adopt a **product stewardship policy** that encourages recycling and the proper handling of obsolete PCs and computer hardware.

8-3 ETHICS IN INFORMATION TECHNOLOGY

A code of ethics provides direction for IT professionals and users so they can apply computer technology responsibly.

Thousands of public- and private-sector organizations maintain data on individuals, including tax, education, medical, driver and crime, census, insurance, lifestyle, credit, Web, employment, financial, and other data.

The dominant ethical issue is the privacy of personal information. As automation continues to enrich our lives, it also opens the door for abuses of personal information. Personal information has become the product of a growing industry. Not only are the people involved not asked for permission to use their data, they seldom are told that their personal information is being sold. The mere fact that personal information is so readily available has opened the door for many new applications of information technology. For example, **cookies** containing personal information are passed freely around the Internet. **Computer matching** involves the examination of separate databases to identify individuals common to both. **Computer monitoring** is used to measure worker performance.

8-4 COMPUTER AND IT CRIME

Computer and IT crime is a relatively recent phenomenon. Therefore, laws governing information technology are few, and those that do exist are subject to a variety of interpretations.

Crimes that create havoc inside a computer include computer viruses and Trojan horses. A **logic bomb** is a set of instructions that is executed when a certain set of conditions are met.

Most computer crimes fall under the umbrella of fraud and embezzlement. Fraud involves obtaining illegal access to a computer system for the purpose of personal gain. Embezzlement concerns the misappropriation of funds. The salami technique and data diddling are used for fraud and embezzlement.

Negligence or incompetence can be just as bad for an organization as a premeditated crime. Such crimes usually are a result of poor input/output control.

Many computer and IT crimes involve unauthorized access to the Internet and networking. Overzealous **hackers** and **crackers** often leave evidence of unlawful entry called a **footprint**. One of the major motivators for unauthorized access is **industrial espionage**. The Internet's cybercops on the Computer Emergency Response Team are ever vigilant in the fight against Internet crimes. Unauthorized entry to a computer network is achieved in several ways, including masquerading, tailgating, a trap door, scanning, and superzapping.

The Internet has become a tool for crime where con artists have updated traditional scams for use in the cyberworld and have created new technology-based crimes such as **pumping and dumping** and **cyberstalking**.

Identity theft, one of the fastest growing criminal activities, is a crime that involves the abuse of personal information.

Computers and IT are used in support of many criminal enterprises, including money laundering.

Crimes that involve the theft of software or intellectual property often leave evidence of the unlawful duplication of proprietary software, called **software piracy**, and **pilferage**. The sharing of copyrighted MP3 and movie files over the Internet is a crime.

8-5 COMPUTER, INTERNET, AND SYSTEM SECURITY

The threats to the security of computer centers and information systems call for precautionary measures. A computer center can be vulnerable in its hardware, software, files/databases, data communications (including the Internet), and personnel.

Organizations use a variety of approaches to secure the computer center, including the installation of an **uninterruptible power source** (**UPS**) and the use of **cryptography** to scramble messages sent over data communications channels. A key is used in conjunction with **encryption/decryption** techniques to scramble/unscramble the message. Two types of encryption systems are in common use, **symmetric-key encryption** and **public-key encryption**.

The **Secure Sockets Layer (SSL)** protocol enables the transmission of data securely over the World Wide Web. The **digital ID** is the equivalent of a sealed envelope for our e-mail.

A new federal law legalized **e-signatures**, giving them the same legal status as a personalized signature on many documents.

The growing threat of viruses has resulted in the tightening of software controls. Virus software "infects" other programs and databases. Antivirus programs search for and destroy viruses.

To protect your work, maintain several generations of backups, storing them in fireproof safes in separate rooms or buildings.

Information systems security is classified as **physical security** or **logical security.** Logical security for online systems is achieved primarily by using user IDs and passwords. Another security measure is the electronic signature.

In the PC environment, people use several methods to control accessibility, including the *lock and key* and the *badge reader.* Properly equipped PCs can add an extra layer of security by incorporating biometric security methods, such as fingerprints, voice prints, retinal scans, and so on.

Security systems are implemented in degrees, and no computer center, LAN server, PC, or system can be made totally secure.

KEY TERMS

biometric identification system (p. 346)
carpal tunnel syndrome (CTS) (p. 326)
computer matching (p. 333)
computer monitoring (p. 334)
cookie (p. 333)
cracker (p. 338)
cryptography (p. 344)
cumulative trauma disorder (CTD) (p. 326)
cyberstalking (p. 339)
digital ID (p. 344)

encryption/decryption (p. 344)
ergonomics (p. 324)
e-signature (p. 344)
face recognition technology (p. 346)
footprint (p. 338)
green computing (p. 327)
hacker (p. 338)
identity theft (p. 339)
industrial espionage (p. 338)
logic bomb (p. 337)
logical security (p. 344)

physical security (p. 344)
pilferage (p. 339)
product stewardship policy (p. 328)
public-key encryption (p. 344)
pumping and dumping (p. 339)
Secure Sockets Layer (SSL) (p. 344)
software piracy (p. 339)
symmetric-key encryption (p. 344)
uninterruptible power source (UPS) (p. 342)
video operator's distress syndrome (VODS) (p. 326)

MATCHING

1. pilferage
2. green computing
3. public-key encryption
4. ergonomics
5. scavenging
6. https
7. logic bomb
8. cracker
9. computer monitoring
10. cyberstalking
11. CTD
12. ACM
13. cookie
14. pumping and dumping
15. COPPA

a. contains information sent to a Web site
b. can result in motor skill disability
c. overzealous hacker
d. has IT code of conduct
e. stock scam
f. indicates a secure Net link
g. causes damage to computers
h. measurement of worker performance
i. online privacy law
j. low-tech way to get sensitive information
k. engineering for humans
l. environmentally sensible computing
m. requires private and public key
n. corporate theft of copyright software
o. targets women and children

CHAPTER SELF-CHECK

8-1.1 The expert diagnosis system is as much a part of the doctor's medical kit as the stethoscope. (T/F)

8-1.2 Society now embraces the concept of a cashless society. (T/F)

8-1.3 Which of these is not a reason potentially beneficial computer applications have not been implemented: (a) historical momentum, (b) resistance to change, (c) too much education, or (d) lack of available resources?

8-1.4 Which of these is not an emphasis in medical school curricula: (a) the use of IT, (b) internal medicine, (c) SDTs, or (d) human anatomy?

8-2.1 A monitor emits radiation. (T/F)

8-2.2 The typical user takes advantage of 95% of a software package's features. (T/F)

8-2.3 Personal e-mail is never tolerated in a business environment. (T/F)

8-2.4 A greater percentage of home appliances are recycled than PCs. (T/F)

8-2.5 All states now require that PCs be recycled. (T/F)

8-2.6 What is the approximate cost of running a PC and a laser printer 24 hours a day for a year: (a) $10, (b) $50, (c) $250, or (d) $2250?

8-2.7 The study of the relationships between people and their machines is called: (a) humanology, (b) human economics, (c) ergology, or (d) ergonomics.

8-2.8 Hand and wrist problems are associated with: (a) ACL, (b) carpal tunnel syndrome, (c) CLA, or (d) SC syndrome.

8-2.9 Laser printers can emit: (a) lead, (b) a harmless water-based compound, (c) sulfur dioxin, or (d) ozone.

8-3.1 The ACM Code of Conduct was recently adopted by the U.S. Senate and is now the law of the land. (T/F)

8-3.2 Over 90% of all knowledge workers embrace new technology and seek to incorporate it in their jobs. (T/F)

8-3.3 Credit bureaus are bound by law to correct inaccuracies in their personal data. (T/F)

8-3.4 All Internet Web sites must be in compliance with Fair Information Practices. (T/F)

8-3.5 About what percentage of all U.S. companies monitor employee Internet browsing activities: (a) 1%, (b) 15%, (c) 67%, or (d) 100%?

8-3.6 When separate databases are examined and individuals common to both are identified, this is: (a) computer matching, (b) footprinting, (c) computer monitoring, or (d) pilferage.

8-3.7 The number of federal government agencies that maintain computer-based files on individuals is between: (a) 50 and 100, (b) 500 and 1000, (c) 5000 and 10,000, or (d) 50,000 and 100,000.

8-4.1 Over 50% of all computer frauds are internal. (T/F)

8-4.2 Crackers created the term hacker to distinguish themselves from overzealous crackers. (T/F)

8-4.3 A trap door is a Trojan horse that permits unauthorized and undetected access to a computer system. (T/F)

8-4.4 In the United States, gaining unauthorized access to any computer system with the intent of defrauding the system is a: (a) violation of public ethics, (b) misdemeanor, (c) high crime, or (d) felony.

8-4.5 Which term is used to describe the situation in which a company copies and distributes software without a site-usage license agreement: (a) pilferage, (b) thieving, (c) pinching, or (d) filching?

8-4.6 The evidence of unlawful entry to a computer system is called a: (a) bitprint, (b) footprint, (c) handprint, or (d) fingerprint.

8-5.1 Although expensive, some companies implement the security measures needed to be totally secure. (T/F)

8-5.2 Normal ceiling-mounted water sprays are installed in all computer centers for fire protection. (T/F)

8-5.3 What name is given to a program intended to damage the computer system of an unsuspecting victim: (a) virus, (b) bug, (c) germ, or (d) fever?

8-5.4 When network downtime is unacceptable, the network must be made: (a) earthquake ready, (b) faultless, (c) uptime tolerant, or (d) fault-tolerant.

8-5.5 What can be used to scramble messages sent over data communications channels: (a) public keys, (b) encoding, (c) cryptography, or (d) ASCII plus?

8-5.6 An e-signature is the ability to e-sign: (a) an encrypted SSL Layer 1 packet, (b) an OCR label, (c) a system unit, or (d) an electronic document.

IT ETHICS AND ISSUES

RECYCLING OLD COMPUTERS

They say a dog year is equal to 7 human years. One computer year is about the same as 20 human years, so computers get "old" very quickly. Old cars of ages 20 or older still get people from point A to point B and some become desirable antiques. But what do you do with an old computer whose components are worth virtually nothing? About 80% of those computers, about 300 million worldwide, are sent to landfills and only 20% are recycled. Electronic components in computers are generally not biodegradable and they can contain many toxic substances.

Discussion: Should the government regulate the disposal of obsolete computers? Justify your response.

Discussion: What did you do with your obsolete computer? What will you do with your current PC once it becomes obsolete?

Discussion: Should corporations police themselves and adopt a PC product stewardship policy? If not, why? If so, write a proposed policy.

COOKIES AND PERSONAL PRIVACY

Some Internet Web sites create and store a file on the user's PC called a *cookie*. Each time the user accesses that Web site the personal information in the cookie is sent to the Web server. The cookie may contain your name and other personal information, perhaps your password to access that Web site, and personal preferences. Most Web sites use cookies to personalize the user's interaction with the Web site. For example, some online retailers have "one-click" ordering where all the personal information needed to complete an order is extracted from your cookie. Over 95% of the top e-commerce sites use cookies.

Discussion: Discuss the advantages and disadvantages of cookies from the perspective of the Web site sponsor. From the perspective of the user.

Discussion: E-commerce companies are using the information in cookies to give preferential services, performance, and pricing to high-priority customers. Is it ethical for companies to treat visitors to their Web site differently? Explain.

Discussion: Would you be for or against legislation that would require all telecommunications companies, including online information services and companies with a presence on the Web, to tell people what information is being collected on them and how it's being used?

VIOLATING THE COPYRIGHT OF INTELLECTUAL PROPERTY

Educators report that they are having difficulty instilling respect for the copyrights on intellectual property. The statistics confirm their concerns. It is estimated that for every legitimate copy of a software package there are two pirated versions installed on other PCs. In some countries, virtually all software is counterfeit. The original developers receive no royalties for sales.

Discussion: The capabilities for copying CDs, CD-ROMs, and DVDs are now commonplace in the home and office. People routinely use these capabilities to duplicate copyrighted music and software for friends and, occasionally, for corporate use. If you knew of someone who routinely violated copyright laws, would you report him or her? Why or why not?

Discussion: *Your boss asked you to install your graphics program on three other PCs in the office. The license permits only one installation. What would be your response to your boss's request?*

Discussion: *A neighbor of yours who lives paycheck to paycheck has asked if he can borrow your copy of Quicken (financial management software). He installs the software on his computer and returns the Quicken CD-ROM to you within an hour. Was anyone guilty of violating copyright laws? Explain.*

Discussion: *How would you respond to a teenager arrested for shoplifting who downplayed the crime saying, "Everybody does it and nobody ever gets caught"? How would you respond to a manager charged with duplicating copyrighted software who downplayed the incident saying, "Everybody does it and nobody ever gets caught"?*

Discussion: *What can each of us do to help guard against the pirating of copyrighted software?*

SCANNING FOR SHOPLIFTERS

A high-tech surveillance technology that has been used in the past to trap pedophiles, terrorists, and, at European soccer games, hooligans, is being employed by some retailers to identify shoplifters. The face-recognition technology matches a digital facial scan against a database of known shoplifters. The technology can scan people's faces within a crowd using 80 facial features and identify people with 99% accuracy. There are, of course, concerns about invasion of personal privacy; however, individual scans are deleted after they had been matched against the database. Also, this technology offers great promise for apprehending criminals; the governments of many countries are using it or evaluating it.

Discussion: *Do you consider this application of face-recognition technology an invasion of privacy? If so, do the benefits justify the means?*

Discussion: *Identify and describe at least two other applications (not mention above) for face-recognition technology.*

DISCUSSION AND PROBLEM SOLVING

8-1.1 Describe what yesterday would have been like if you had not used the capabilities of computers. Keep in mind that businesses with which you deal rely on computers and that many of your appliances are computer-based.

8-1.2 Two lawyers used the Internet to broadcast thousands of e-mail messages advertising their services. They were subsequently flamed (sent angry e-mail messages) and vilified by Internet users for what they believed to be an inappropriate use of the Net. The attorneys broke no laws. Was the reaction of the Internet users justified? Explain.

8-2.1 Why is green computing important to society?

8-2.2 Expand these abbreviations and briefly describe what they mean: VODS, RSI, and CTD.

8-2.3 Evaluate your workplace at home, school, or work from an ergonomic perspective. Consider the concepts presented in Section 8-2 and the guidelines illustrated in Figure 8-3.

8-2.4 What can you do, which you are not doing now, that would be a move toward green computing?

8-3.1 Give an example of how computer monitoring might be applied at the clerical level of activity. Give another example for the operational, tactical, or strategic level.

8-3.2 The Internal Revenue Service also uses computer matching to identify those who might be underpaying taxes. Is this an invasion of privacy or a legitimate approach to tax collection?

8-3.3 In the past, bank officers have been reluctant to report computer crimes. If you were a customer of a bank that made such a decision, how would you react?

8-3.4 Who knows what about you? List as many nongovernment organizations (specific names or generic) as you can that collect and maintain personal information about you. Do the same for government organizations.

8-3.5 Discuss the kinds of personal information that can be obtained by analyzing a person's credit card transactions during the past year.

8-4.1 Why would a judge sentence one person to 10 years in jail for an unarmed robbery of $25 from a convenience store and another to 18 months for computer fraud involving millions of dollars?

8-4.2 Discuss what you can do at your college or place of employment to minimize the possibility of computer crime.

8-4.3 Generally, society has an erroneous perception of hackers. What is this perception and why is it erroneous?

8-4.4 Internet cybercops at CERT are no longer concerned with minor intrusions to Net security. Why is this?

8-5.1 What should be done at your college to improve computer security?

8-5.2 What should be done at your place of work to improve computer security?

8-5.3 Which scenario offers the greatest security for your credit card: paying for a meal at a restaurant, buying a pair of shoes over the Internet, or purchasing a PC via telephone mail order? Explain.

8-5.4 What precautions can be taken to minimize the effects of hardware failure?

8-5.5 The use of a digital ID provides secure passage for your e-mail and its attachments. How much would you pay for the use of a digital ID per e-mail?

8-5.6 The e-signature does not apply to family law documents, such as wills, trusts, adoptions, or divorce. Should it? Explain.

FOCUS ON PERSONAL COMPUTING

1. With green computing now a societal imperative, if not law, we have cradle-to-grave responsibility for our PCs. Survey five people who have discarded obsolete PCs. Assess each with regard to proper product stewardship. Find an organization that will accept and probably dispose of computer hardware. Describe the process by which you transfer your obsolete hardware to the organization and note the cost to you.

2. Write a personal computing code of ethics that relates to your specific computing environment and can serve as your guide during personal computing activities, including your interaction with the cyberworld.

3. Assess your workplace. Describe what you can do to make it more ergonomically compatible with personal computing, that is, minimize health concerns and maximize effective interaction.

INTERNET EXERCISES @ www.prenhall.com/long

1. The Online Study Guide (multiple choice, true/false, matching, and essay questions)

2. Internet Learning Activities
- Ergonomics
- Ethics in Computing

3. Serendipitous Internet Activities
- Music

ANSWERS TO THE SECTION, CHAPTER, AND IT ILLUSTRATED SELF-CHECKS

CHAPTER 1

Section Self-Check
1-1.1 A
1-1.2 B
1-1.3 C

1-2.1 F
1-2.2 A
1-2.3 T

1-3.1 T
1-3.2 B
1-3.3 A

1-4.1 T
1-4.2 B
1-4.3 C

1-5.1 F
1-5.2 F
1-5.3 A
1-5.4 D
1-5.5 D
1-5.6 B

1-6.1 T
1-6.2 T
1-6.3 A

1-7.1 T
1-7.2 F
1-7.3 A
1-7.4 D

Matching
1 N
2 O
3 C
4 M
5 L
6 K
7 H
8 F
9 G
10 A
11 J
12 D
13 B
14 I
15 E

Chapter Self-Check
1-1.1 A
1-1.2 C
1-1.3 F

1-2.1 A
1-2.2 C
1-2.3 D

1-3.1 F
1-3.2 C
1-3.3 B

1-4.1 T
1-4.2 F
1-4.3 F
1-4.4 B
1-4.5 F

1-5.1 F
1-5.2 T
1-5.3 B
1-5.4 C
1-5.5 B

1-6.1 F
1-6.2 T
1-6.3 A
1-6.4 C
1-6.5 F

1-7.1 T
1-7.2 B
1-7.3 D
1-7.4 D
1-7.5 T
1-7.6 A
1-7.7 T

IT Illustrated
1 T
2 T
3 F
4 T
5 T
6 B
7 C
8 A
9 B
10 D

CHAPTER 2

Section Self-Check
2-1.1 T
2-1.2 B
2-1.3 D
2-1.4 T
2-1.5 A
2-1.6 B
2-1.7 T
2-1.8 B

2-2.1 F
2-2.2 F
2-2.3 D
2-2.4 D
2-2.5 C
2-2.6 T

2-3.1 F
2-3.2 A
2-3.3 T
2-3.4 T
2-3.5 C
2-3.6 A
2-3.7 T
2-3.8 B
2-3.9 B
2-3.10 F
2-3.11 A
2-3.12 B
2-3.13 B

2-4.1 A
2-4.2 C
2-4.3 A
2-4.4 T
2-4.5 T

Matching
1 D
2 K
3 F
4 L
5 E
6 C
7 I
8 N
9 M
10 O
11 A
12 H

13 G
14 J
15 B

Chapter Self-Check
2-1.1 F
2-1.2 F
2-1.3 B
2-1.4 F
2-1.5 C
2-1.6 F
2-1.7 C
2-1.8 C
2-1.9 B
2-1.10 T
2-1.11 F
2-1.12 F
2-1.13 D
2-1.14 D

2-2.1 T
2-2.2 F
2-2.3 F
2-2.4 C
2-2.5 D
2-2.6 T
2-2.7 D
2-2.8 F

2-3.1 T
2-3.2 T
2-3.3 D
2-3.4 C
2-3.5 B
2-3.6 T
2-3.7 T
2-3.8 T
2-3.9 T
2-3.10 C
2-3.11 A
2-3.12 F
2-3.13 T
2-3.14 F
2-3.15 T
2-3.16 C
2-3.17 C
2-3.18 D
2-3.19 F
2-3.20 F
2-3.21 T
2-3.22 D

2-3.23 A
2-3.24 D
2-3.25 D
2-3.26 T
2-3.27 B
2-3.28 T

2-4.1 C
2-4.2 B
2-4.3 A
2-4.4 C
2-4.5 B
2-4.6 C
2-4.7 B
2-4.8 D
2-4.9 D
2-4.10 T

CHAPTER 3

Section Self-Check
3-1.1 F
3-1.2 T
3-1.3 A
3-1.4 A
3-1.5 B
3-1.6 D
3-1.7 F

3-2.1 T
3-2.2 B
3-2.3 D
3-2.4 A
3-2.5 F

3-3.1 T
3-3.2 F
3-3.3 C
3-3.4 D
3-3.5 B
3-3.6 C

Matching
1 F
2 H
3 B
4 A
5 L
6 K
7 O
8 D
9 C
10 N
11 M
12 J
13 G
14 I
15 E

Chapter Self-Check
3-1.1 T
3-1.2 T
3-1.3 F
3-1.4 F
3-1.5 F
3-1.6 A
3-1.7 C
3-1.8 B
3-1.8 A
3-1.10 B
3-1.11 B
3-1.12 A
3-1.13 B
3-1.14 B
3-1.15 F
3-1.16 B
3-1.17 D
3-1.18 F

3-2.1 F
3-2.2 F
3-2.3 C
3-2.4 B
3-2.5 D
3-2.6 D

3-3.1 T
3-3.2 T
3-3.3 T
3-3.4 B
3-3.5 C
3-3.6 C
3-3.7 B
3-3.8 B

CHAPTER 4

Section Self-Check
4-1.1 T
4-1.2 T
4-1.3 A
4-1.4 D
4-1.5 B

4-2.1 F
4-2.2 T
4-2.3 B
4-2.4 A
4-2.5 B

4-3.1 T
4-3.2 F
4-3.3 B
4-3.4 A
4-3.5 B

4-4.1 T
4-4.2 F
4-4.3 B
4-4.4 C

Matching
1 N
2 J
3 O
4 K
5 M
6 I
7 A
8 C
9 L
10 E
11 D
12 G
13 F
14 H
15 B

Chapter Self-Check
4-1.1 F
4-1.2 F
4-1.3 F
4-1.4 A
4-1.5 B
4-1.6 C
4-1.7 A

4-2.1 T
4-2.2 T
4-2.3 F
4-2.4 D
4-2.5 A
4-2.6 C
4-2.7 B
4-2.8 A

4-3.1 F
4-3.2 F
4-3.3 T
4-3.4 D
4-3.5 A
4-3.6 C

4-4.1 F
4-4.2 F
4-4.3 F
4-4.4 C
4-4.5 C
4-4.6 D
4-4.7 C

IT Illustrated
1 T
2 F
3 T
4 C
5 A
6 D

CHAPTER 5

Section Self-Check
5-1.1 F
5-1.2 T
5-1.3 F
5-1.4 B
5-1.5 A

5-2.1 F
5-2.2 F
5-2.3 B
5-2.4 A
5-2.5 C

5-3.1 T
5-3.2 A
5-3.3 D
5-3.4 T
5-3.5 A

5-4.1 T
5-4.2 D
5-4.3 C
5-4.4 B
5-5.1 T
5-5.2 T
5-5.3 C

Matching
1 G
2 D
3 O
4 B
5 E
6 H
7 A
8 C
9 L
10 K
11 J
12 N
13 M
14 I
15 F

Chapter Self-Check

5-1.1 T
5-1.2 F
5-1.3 T
5-1.4 F
5-1.5 C
5-1.6 D
5-1.7 B
5-1.8 D

5-2.1 F
5-2.2 T
5-2.3 T
5-2.4 F
5-2.5 T
5-2.6 T
5-2.7 F
5-2.8 T
5-2.9 T
5-2.10 T
5-2.11 C
5-2.12 B
5-2.13 A
5-2.14 D
5-2.15 C
5-2.16 B
5-2.17 C

5-3.1 T
5-3.2 T
5-3.3 T
5-3.5 T
5-3.5 A
5-3.6 B
5-3.7 B

5-4.1 F
5-4.2 F
5-4.3 F
5-4.4 F
5-4.5 T
5-4.6 A
5-4.7 A
5-4.8 D
5-4.9 A

5-5.1 F
5-5.2 T
5-5.3 F
5-5.4 F
5-5.5 C
5-5.6 A
5-5.7 D
5-5.8 B

CHAPTER 6

Section Self-Check

6-1.1 T
6-1.2 F
6-1.3 A
6-1.4 A
6-1.5 B
6-1.6 C

6-2.1 T
6-2.2 T
6-2.3 B
6-2.4 C
6-2.5 A

6-3.1 F
6-3.2 T
6-3.3 A
6-3.4 D

6-4.1 T
6-4.2 A

Matching

1 N
2 D
3 F
4 J
5 A
6 K
7 E
8 L
9 G
10 C
11 I
12 B
13 M
14 O
15 H

Chapter Self-Check

6-1.1 F
6-1.2 C
6-1.3 T
6-1.4 F
6-1.5 B
6-1.6 A
6-1.7 F
6-1.8 T
6-1.9 F
6-1.10 T
6-1.11 T
6-1.12 C
6-1.13 D
6-1.14 A
6-1.15 A

6-2.1 F
6-2.2 F
6-2.3 F
6-2.4 A
6-2.5 D
6-2.6 A
6-2.7 C
6-2.8 C
6-2.9 B
6-2.10 C
6-1.11 C
6-2.12 B

6-3.1 F
6-3.2 C
6-3.2 B
6-3.4 A
6-3.5 B
6-3.6 B

6-4.1 T
6-4.2 D

CHAPTER 7

Section Self-Check

7-1.1 T
7-1.2 F
7-1.3 B
7-1.4 C

7-2.1 T
7-2.2 F
7-2.3 F
7-2.4 C

7-3.1 T
7-3.2 F
7-3.3 D
7-3.4 A
7-3.5 B

7-4.1 C
7-4.2 T
7-4.3 C
7-4.4 D
7-4.5 C

Matching

1 M
2 E
3 O
4 C
5 K
6 N
7 L
8 G

9 J
10 B
11 F
12 D
13 I
14 H
15 A

Chapter Self-Check

7-1.1 F
7-1.2 T
7-1.3 T
7-1.4 C
7-1.5 A
7-1.6 B

7-2.1 T
7-2.2 F
7-2.3 F
7-2.4 T
7-2.5 A
7-2.6 C
7-2.7 A
7-2.8 A

7-3.1 T
7-3.2 F
7-3.3 A
7-3.4 C
7-3.5 C
7-3.6 T
7-3.7 T
7-3.8 T
7-3.9 B
7-3.10 D

7-4.1 F
7-4.2 F
7-4.3 F
7-4.4 F
7-4.5 C
7-4.6 A
7-4.7 B
7-4.8 B

IT Illustrated

1 T
2 F
3 F
4 T
5 F
6 T
7 D
8 B
9 D
10 B
11 A

CHAPTER 8

Section Self-Check

8-1.1 F
8-1.2 F
8-1.3 C

8-2.1 T
8-2.2 F
8-2.3 A
8-2.4 B
8-2.5 A

8-3.1 T
8-3.2 F
8-3.3 C
8-3.4 B

8-4.1 T
8-4.2 C
8-4.3 A
8-4.4 D

8-5.1 F
8-5.2 T
8-5.3 A
8-5.4 C
8-5.5 A

Matching

1 N
2 L
3 M
4 K
5 J
6 F
7 G
8 C
9 H
10 O
11 B
12 D
13 A
14 E
15 I

Chapter Self-Check

8-1.1 F
8-1.2 F
8-1.3 C
8-1.4 A

8-2.1 T
8-2.2 F
8-2.3 F
8-2.4 T
8-2.5 F
8-2.6 C
8-2.7 D
8-2.8 B
8-2.9 D

8-3.1 F
8-3.2 F
8-3.3 T
8-3.4 F
8-3.5 C
8-3.6 A
8-3.7 C

8-4.1 T
8-4.2 F
8-4.3 T
8-4.4 D
8-4.5 A
8-4.6 B

8-5.1 F
8-5.2 F
8-5.3 A
8-5.4 D
8-5.5 C
8-5.6 D

GLOSSARY

1394 bus A recent bus standard that supports data transfer rates of up to 400 M bps, over 30 times faster that the USB bus. (See also *FireWire*.)

1394 port Enables connection to the 1394 (FireWire) bus.

Absolute cell address A cell address in a spreadsheet that always refers to the same cell.

Access arm The disk drive mechanism used to position the read/write heads over the appropriate track.

Access point A communications hub that enables a link to a LAN via short-range radio waves.

Access time The time between the instant a computer makes a request for a transfer of data from disk storage and the instant this operation is completed.

Accumulator The computer register in which the result of an arithmetic or logic operation is formed. (Related to *arithmetic and logic unit*.)

Active window The window in Microsoft Windows® with which the user may interact.

ActiveX controls A program that uses Microsoft's ActiveX technology that can be downloaded and executed by a browser to enable multimedia in Web pages. (See also *applet*.)

Address (1) A name, numeral, or label that designates a particular location in RAM or disk storage. (2) A location identifier for nodes in a computer network.

Address bus Pathway through which source and destination addresses are transmitted between RAM, cache memory, and the processor. (See also *data bus*.)

AGP (Accelerated Graphics Port) board A graphics adapter that permits interfacing with video monitors.

AGP bus A special-function bus designed to handle high-resolution 3-D graphics.

All-in-one peripheral device A peripheral device that handles several paper-related tasks: computer-based printing, facsimile (fax), scanning, and copying.

Alpha A reference to the letters of the alphabet. (Compare with *numeric* and *alphanumeric*.)

Alphanumeric Pertaining to a character set that contains letters, digits, punctuation, and special symbols. (Related to *alpha* and *numeric*.)

America Online (AOL) An online information service.

Analog signal A continuous waveform signal that can be used to represent such things as sound, temperature, and velocity. (See also *digital signal*.)

Animation The rapid repositioning of objects on a display to create movement.

Anonymous FTP site An Internet site that permits FTP (file transfer protocol) file transfers without prior permission.

ANSI The American National Standards Institute is a non-government standards-setting organization that develops and publishes standards for "voluntary" use in the United States.

Antivirus program A utility program that periodically checks a PC's hard disk for computer viruses then removes any that are found.

Applet A small program sent over the Internet or an intranet that is interpreted and executed by Internet browser software. (See also *ActiveX controls*.)

Application generator A system development tool used to actually generate the system programming code based on design specifications.

Application icon A miniature visual representation of a software application on a display.

Application window A rectangular window containing an open, or running, application in Microsoft Windows.

Applications programmer A programmer who translates analyst-prepared system and input/output specifications into programs. Programmers design the logic, then code, debug, test, and document the programs.

Applications service provider (ASP) An ASP is a company that provides software-based services and solutions to customers via the Internet from a central server computer.

Applications software Software designed and written to address a specific personal, business, or processing task.

Argument That portion of a function that identifies the data to be operated on.

Arithmetic and logic unit That portion of the computer that performs arithmetic and logic operations. (Related to *accumulator*.)

Arithmetic operators Mathematical operators (add [+], subtract [-], multiply [*], divide [/], and exponentiation [^]) used in programming and in spreadsheet and database software for computations.

Artificial intelligence (AI) The ability of a computer to reason, to learn, to strive for self-improvement, and to simulate human sensory capabilities.

ASCII [American Standard Code for Information Interchange] A 7-bit or 8-bit encoding system.

ASCII file A generic text file that is stripped of program-specific control characters.

Assembler language A programming language that uses easily recognized symbols, called mnemonics, to represent instructions.

Assistant system This knowledge-based system helps users make relatively straightforward decisions. (See also *expert system*.)

Assistive technology Enabling input/output peripherals and software for people with disabilities.

Asynchronous transmission A protocol in which data are transmitted at irregular intervals on an as-needed basis. (See also *synchronous transmission*.)

Attached file A file that is attached and sent with an e-mail message.

Audio file A file that contains digitized sound.

Audio mail An electronic mail capability that lets you speak your message instead of typing it.

Authoring system Software that lets you create multimedia applications that integrate sound, motion, text, animation, and images.

Automatic teller machine (ATM) An automated deposit/withdrawal device used in banking.

B2B (business-to-business) An e-commerce concept that encourages intercompany processing and data exchange via computer networks and the Internet. (Contrast with *B2C*.)

B2C (business-to-consumer) An e-commerce concept that encourages electronic interactions between businesses and consumers via Internet server computers. (Contrast with *B2B*.)

Backbone A system of routers and the associated transmission media that facilitates the interconnection of computer networks.

Back-end applications software This software on the server computer performs processing tasks in support of its clients, such as tasks associated with storage and maintenance of a centralized corporate database. (See also *front-end applications software*.)

Background (1) That part of RAM that contains the lowest priority programs. (2) In Windows, the area of the display over which the foreground is superimposed. (Contrast with *foreground*.)

Backup file Duplicate of an existing file.

Backup Pertaining to equipment, procedures, or databases that can be used to restart the system in the event of system failure.

Backward compatible Reference to a modern platform's ability to run programs written for legacy platforms.

Badge reader An input device that reads data on badges and cards.

Bandwidth Generally the range of frequencies in a communications channel or, specifically, the number of bits the channel can transmit per second.

Banner ad Horizontal Internet advertisement that entices users to click on them to link to the site being promoted.

Bar code A graphic encoding technique in which printed vertical bars of varying widths are used to represent data.

Bar code scanner A device that scans and interprets text and codes.

Bar graph A graph that contains bars that represent specified numeric values.

Batch processing A technique in which transactions and/or jobs are collected into groups (batched) and processed together.

Baud (1) A measure of the maximum number of electronic signals that can be transmitted via a communications channel. (2) Bits per second (common-use definition).

Binary A base-2 numbering system.

BIOS (Basic Input Output System) Flash memory-based software that contains the instructions needed to boot a PC and load the operating system.

Bit A *binary digit* (0 or 1).

Bit-mapped graphics Referring to an image that has been projected, or mapped, to a screen based on binary bits. (See also *raster graphics*.)

Bits per second (bps) The number of bits that can be transmitted per second over a communications channel.

BMP A popular format for bit-mapped files.

Boilerplate Existing text in a word processing file that can in some way be customized for use in a variety of word processing applications.

Bold A font presentation attribute that thickens the lines of a character.

Boot The procedure for loading the operating system to RAM and readying a computer system for use.

Bots See *intelligent agent*.

Broadband access Generic term for high-speed Internet access.

Broadband connection Typically, a reference to a high-speed Internet link via cable, satellite, or DSL.

Browsers Programs that let you navigate to and view the various Internet resources.

Bug A logic or syntax error in a program, a logic error in the design of a computer system, or a hardware fault. (See also *debug*.)

Bus An electrical pathway through which the processor sends data and commands to RAM and all peripheral devices.

Bus topology A computer network that permits the connection of terminals, peripheral devices, and microcomputers along an open-ended central cable.

Business-to-business See *B2B*.

Business-to-consumer See *B2C*.

Button bar A software option that contains a group of pictographs that represent a menu option or a command.

Byte A group of adjacent bits configured to represent a character or symbol.

C A transportable programming language that can be used to develop software.

C++ An object-oriented version of the C programming language.

Cache memory High-speed solid-state memory for program instructions and data.

CAD See *computer-aided design*.

Carpal tunnel syndrome (CTS) A repetitive-stress injury.

Carrier Standard-sized pin connectors that permit chips to be attached to a circuit board.

Cascading menu A pop-up menu that is displayed when a command from the active menu is chosen.

Cascading windows Two or more windows that are displayed on a computer screen in an overlapping manner.

Cathode-ray tube See *CRT*.

CBT See *computer-based training*.

CD production station A device used to duplicate locally produced CD-ROMs.

CD-R [Compact Disc-Recordable] The medium on which CD writers create CDs and CD-ROMs.

CD-ReWritable (CD-RW) This technology allows users to rewrite to the same CD media.

CD-ROM disc [CompactDisk Read-Only Memory disc] A type of optical laser storage media.

CD-ROM drive A storage device into which an interchangeable CD-ROM disc is inserted for processing.

CD-RW See *CD-ReWritable*.

Celeron A line of Intel® microprocessors designed for low-cost PCs.

Cell The intersection of a particular row and column in a spreadsheet.

Cell address The location—column and row—of a cell in a spreadsheet.

Central processing unit (CPU) See *processor*.

Centronics connector A 36-pin connector that is used for the electronic interconnection of computers, modems, and other peripheral devices.

CGM A popular vector graphics file format.

Channel The facility by which data are transmitted between locations in a computer network (e.g., terminal to host, host to printer).

Channel capacity The number of bits that can be transmitted over a communications channel per second.

Chat An Internet application that allows people on the Internet to converse in real time via text or audio.

Chief information officer (CIO) The individual responsible for all the information services activity in a company.

Chip See *integrated circuit*.

Chipset A motherboard's intelligence that controls the flow of information between system components connected to the board.

Choose To pick a menu item or icon in such a manner as to initiate processing activity.

CISC [Complex Instruction Set Computer] A computer design architecture that offers machine language programmers a wide variety of instructions. (Contrast with *RISC*.)

Click A single tap on a mouse's button.

Client application (1) An application running on a networked workstation or PC that works in tandem with a server application. (See also *server application*.) (2) In object linking and embedding, the application containing the destination document. (See also *OLE*.)

Client computer Typically a PC or a workstation that requests processing support or another type of service from one or more server computers. (See also *server computer*.)

Client program A software program that runs on a PC and works in conjunction with a companion server program that runs on a server computer. (See also *server program*.)

Client/server computing A computing environment in which processing capabilities are distributed throughout a network such that a client computer requests processing or some other type of service from a server computer.

Clip art Prepackaged electronic images that are stored on disk to be used as needed in computer-based documents.

Clipboard An intermediate holding area in internal storage for information en route to another application.

Clone A hardware device or a software package that emulates a product with an established reputation and market acceptance.

Cluster The smallest unit of disk space that can be allocated to a file.

Coaxial cable A shielded wire used as a medium to transmit data between computers and between computers and peripheral devices.

COBOL [*Common Business Oriented Language*] A third-generation programming language designed to handle business problems.

Code (1) The rules used to translate a bit configuration into alphanumeric characters and symbols. (2) The process of compiling computer instructions into the form of a computer program. (3) The actual computer program.

Color depth The number of bits used to display each pixel on a display.

Command An instruction to a computer that invokes the execution of a preprogrammed sequence of instructions.

Common carrier A company that provides channels for data transmission.

Communications channel The facility by which data are transmitted between locations in a computer network.

Communications protocols Rules established to govern the way data in a computer network are transmitted.

Communications server The LAN component that provides external communications links.

Communications software (1) Software that enables a microcomputer to emulate a terminal and to transfer files between a micro and another computer. (2) Software that enables communication between remote devices in a computer network.

Compact disc-recordable See *CD-R*.

Compatibility Pertaining to the ability of computers and computer components (hardware and software) to work together.

Compile To translate a high-level programming language into machine language in preparation for execution.

Compiler A program that translates the instructions of a high-level language to machine language instructions that the computer can interpret and execute.

Compound document A document, such as a word processing document, that contains one or more linked objects from other applications.

CompuServe An online information service.

Computer An electronic device capable of interpreting and executing programmed commands for input, output, computation, and logic operations.

Computer-aided design (CAD) Use of computer graphics in design, drafting, and documentation in product and manufacturing engineering.

Computer-aided software engineering (CASE) An approach to software development that combines automation and the rigors of the engineering discipline.

Computer-based training (CBT) Using computer technologies for training and education.

Computer competency A fundamental understanding of the technology, operation, applications, and issues surrounding computers.

Computer literacy See *computer competency*.

Computer matching The procedure whereby separate databases are examined and individuals common to both are identified.

Computer monitoring Observing and regulating employee activities and job performance through the use of computers.

Computer network An integration of computer systems, terminals, and communications links.

Computer operator One who performs those hardware-based activities needed to keep production information systems operational in the server computer environment.

Computer system A collective reference to all interconnected computing hardware, including processors, storage devices, input/output devices, and communications equipment.

Computer virus See *virus*.

Computerese A colloquial reference to the language of computers and information technology.

Configuration The computer and its peripheral devices.

Connectivity Pertains to the degree to which hardware devices, software, and databases can be functionally linked to one another.

Context-sensitive Referring to an on-screen explanation that relates to a user's current software activity.

Control unit The portion of the processor that interprets program instructions, directs internal operations, and directs the flow of input/output to or from RAM.

Cookie A message given to your Web browser by the Web server being accessed. The cookie is a text file containing user preference information.

Cooperative processing An environment in which organizations cooperate internally and externally to take full advantage of available information and to obtain meaningful, accurate, and timely information. (See also *intracompany networking*.)

Coprocessor An auxiliary processor that handles a narrow range of tasks, usually those associated with arithmetic operations.

CPU See *processor*.

Cracker An overzealous hacker who "cracks" through network security to gain unauthorized access to the network. (Contrast with *hacker*.)

Cross-platform technologies Enabling technologies that allow communication and the sharing of resources between different platforms.

CRT [*Cathode-Ray Tube*] The video monitor component of a terminal.

Cryptography A communications crime-prevention technology that uses methods of data encryption and decryption to scramble codes sent over communications channels.

CSMA/CD access method [*Carrier Sense Multiple Access/Collision Detection*] A network access method in which nodes on the LAN must contend for the right to send a message.

Cumulative trauma disorder (CTD) Repetitive motion disorders of the musculoskeletal and nervous systems that, often, are a result of poor workplace design.

Current window The window in a GUI in which the user can manipulate text, data, or graphics.

Cursor-control keys   The arrow keys on the keyboard that move the cursor vertically and horizontally.

Cursor, graphics   Typically an arrow or a crosshair that can be moved about a monitor's screen by a point-and-draw device to create a graphic image or select an item from a menu. (See also *cursor, text.*)

Cursor, text   A blinking character that indicates the location of the next keyed-in character on the display screen. (See also *cursor, graphics.*)

Custom programming   Program development to create software for situations unique to a particular processing environment.

Cyberphobia   The irrational fear of, and aversion to, computers.

Cyberstalking   Technology-based stalking where the Internet becomes a vehicle by which the stalker directs threatening behavior and unwanted advances to another person.

Cylinder   A disk-storage concept. A cylinder is that portion of the disk that can be read in any given position of the access arm. (Contrast with *sector.*)

Data bits   A data communications parameter that refers to a timing unit.

Data bus   A common pathway between RAM, cache memory, and the processor through which data and instructions are transferred. (See also *address bus.*)

Data cartridge   Magnetic tape storage in cassette format.

Data communications   The collection and distribution of the electronic representation of information between two locations.

Data compression   A method of reducing disk-storage requirements for computer files.

Data entry   The transcription of source data into a machine-readable format.

Data file   This file contains data organized into records.

Data flow diagram   A design technique that permits documentation of a system or program at several levels of generality.

Data mining   An analytical technique that involves the analysis of large databases, such as data warehouses, to identify possible trends and problems.

Data path   The electronic channel through which data flows within a computer system.

Data processing (DP)   Using the computer to perform operations on data.

Data processing (DP) system   Systems concerned with transaction handling and record-keeping, usually for a particular functional area.

Data transfer rate   The rate at which data are read/written from/to disk storage to RAM.

Data warehouse   A relational database created from existing operational files and databases specifically to help managers get the information they need to make informed decisions.

Data warehousing   An approach to database management that involves moving existing operational files and databases from multiple applications to a data warehouse.

Data/voice/fax/modem   A modem that permits data communication with remote computers via a telephone-line link and enables telephone calls and fax machine simulation via a PC.

Data   Representations of facts. Raw material for information. (Plural of *datum.*)

Database   The integrated data resource for a computer-based information system.

Database administrator (DBA)   The individual responsible for the physical and logical maintenance of the database.

Database software   Software that permits users to create and maintain a database and to extract information from the database.

DDR SDRAM   A "double data rate" SDRAM. (See also *SDRAM.*)

Debug   To eliminate bugs in a program or system. (See also *bug.*)

Decision support system (DSS)   An interactive information system that relies on an integrated set of user-friendly hardware and software tools to produce and present information targeted to support management in the decision-making process. (Contrast with *management information system* and *executive information system.*)

Decode   To reverse the encoding process. (Contrast with *encode.*)

Decoder   That portion of a processor's control unit that interprets instructions.

Dedicated keyboard port   A port built into the system board specifically for the keyboard.

Dedicated mouse port   A port built into the system board specifically for the mouse or other similar device.

Default options   Preset software options that are assumed valid unless specified otherwise by the user.

Defragmentation   Using utility software to reorganize files on a hard disk such that files are stored in contiguous clusters.

Density   The number of bytes per linear length or unit area of a recording medium.

Desktop   The screen in Windows upon which icons, windows, a background, and so on are displayed.

Desktop PC   A nonportable personal computer that is designed to rest on the top of a desk. (Contrast with *laptop PC* and *tower PC.*)

Desktop publishing software (DTP)   Software that allows users to produce near-typeset-quality copy for newsletters, advertisements, and many other printing needs, all from the confines of a desktop.

Destination application, Clipboard   The software application into which the Clipboard contents are to be pasted. (Contrast with *source application.*)

Detailed system design   That portion of the systems development process in which the target system is defined in detail.

Device controller   Microprocessors that control the operation of peripheral devices.

Device driver software   Software that contains instructions needed by the operating system to communicate with the peripheral device.

Dialog box   A window that is displayed when the user must choose parameters or enter further information before the chosen menu option can be executed.

Dialup connection   Temporary modem-based communications link with another computer.

Dialup line   See *switched line.*

Digicam   See *digital camera.*

Digital   A reference to any system based on discrete data, such as the binary nature of computers.

Digital camcorder   Portable digital video camera.

Digital camera   A camera that records images digitally rather than on film.

Digital certificate   An attachment to an electronic message that verifies that the sender is who he/she claims to be.

Digital convergence   The integration of computers, communications, and consumer electronics, with all having digital compatibility.

Digital ID   A digital code that can be attached to an electronic message that uniquely identifies the sender.

Digital jukebox   An Internet-based software application that enables the selection, management, and playing of Internet-based music.

Digital signal   Electronic signals that are transmitted as in strings of 1s and 0s. (See also *analog signal.*)

Digital Subscriber Line   See *DSL.*

Digital video camera A camera that enables the capture of motion video directly into a PC system (used for Webcam applications).

Digital video disc See *DVD*.

Digital video disc plus RW See *DVD+RW*.

Digitize To translate data or an image into a discrete format that can be interpreted by computers.

Digitizer tablet and pen A pressure-sensitive tablet with the same *x*-*y* coordinates as a computer-generated screen. The outline of an image drawn on a tablet with a stylus (pen) or puck is reproduced on the display.

DIMM [*Dual In-line Memory Module*] A small circuit board, capable of holding several memory chips, that has a 64-bit data path and can be easily connected to a PC's system board. (Contrast with *SIMM*.)

Dimmed A menu option, which is usually gray, that is disabled or unavailable.

Direct access See *random access*.

Direct-access storage device (DASD) A random-access disk storage.

Direct conversion An approach to system conversion whereby operational support by the new system is begun when the existing system is terminated.

Disc, optical A storage medium which uses lasers for the data read/write operations.

Disk address The physical location of a particular set of data or a program on a magnetic disk.

Disk caching A hardware/software technique in which frequently referenced disk-based data are placed in an area of RAM that simulates disk storage. (See also *RAM disk*.)

Disk defragmenter A utility program that consolidates files into contiguous clusters on a hard disk.

Disk density The number of bits that can be stored per unit of area on the disk-face surface.

Disk drive icon Graphical representation of a disk.

Disk drive, magnetic A magnetic storage device that records data on flat rotating disks. (Compare with *tape drive, magnetic*.)

Disk optimizer A program that reorganizes files on a hard disk to eliminate file fragmentation.

Disk, magnetic A storage medium for random-access data storage available in permanently installed or interchangeable formats.

Diskette A thin interchangeable disk for secondary random-access data storage (same as *floppy disk*).

Docking station A device into which a notebook PC is inserted to give the notebook PC expanded capabilities, such as a high-capacity disk, interchangeable disk options, a tape backup unit, a large monitor, and so on.

Document A generic reference to whatever is currently displayed in a software package's work area or to a permanent file containing document contents.

Document file The result when work with an applications program, such as word processing, is saved to disk storage.

Document icon A pictograph used by Windows within an application to represent a minimized document window.

Document window Window within an application window that is used to display a separate document created or used by that application.

Domain expert An expert in a particular field who provides the factual knowledge and the heuristic rules for input to a knowledge base.

Domain name That portion of the Internet URL following the double forward slashes (*//*) that identifies an Internet host site.

DOS [*Disk Operating System*] See *MS-DOS*.

Dot-matrix printer A printer that arranges printed dots to form characters and images.

Dot pitch The distance between the centers of adjacent pixels on a display.

Double-click Tapping a button on a point-and-draw device twice in rapid succession.

Download The transmission of data from a remote computer to a local computer.

Downsizing Used to describe the trend toward increased reliance on smaller computers for personal as well as enterprise-wide processing tasks.

Downstream rate The data communications rate from server computer to client computer.

Downtime The time during which a computer system is not operational.

DP See *data processing*.

Drag A point-and-draw device procedure by which an object is moved or a contiguous area on the display is marked for processing.

Drag-and-drop software Software that lets users drag ready-made shapes from application-specific stencils to the desired position on the drawing area to do drawings for flowcharting, landscaping, business graphics, and other applications.

Draw software Software that enables users to create electronic images. Resultant images are stored as vector graphics images.

Driver The software that enables interaction between the operating system and a specific peripheral device.

Driver module The program module that calls other subordinate program modules to be executed as they are needed (also called a *main program*).

DSL (Digital Subscriber Line) A digital telecommunications standard for data delivery over twisted-pair lines with downstream transmission speeds up to 9 M bps.

DSLAM (Digital Subscriber Line Access Multiplexor) A device that communications companies use to multiplex DSL signals to/from the Internet.

DTP See *desktop publishing*.

Dual in-line memory module See *DIMM*.

DVD (Digital video disc) The successor technology to the CD-ROM that can store up to about 8.5 gigabytes per side.

DVD+RW (Digital video disc plus RW) One of the rewritable standards for high-capacity DVD. (Contrast with *DVD-RAM* and *CD-RW*.)

DVD-R The capability to record data to a DVD disc. (Contrast with *CD-R*.)

DVD-RAM One of the rewritable standards for high-capacity DVD. (Contrast with *CD-RW* and *CD+RW*.)

DVD-ROM High-density read-only optical laser storage media.

DVD-RW One of the rewritable standards for high-capacity DVD. (Contrast with *DVD-RAM* and *DVD+RW*.)

DVD-Video DVD format for playing movies.

Dynamic IP address A temporary Internet address assigned to a user by an ISP.

EBCDIC [*Extended Binary Coded Decimal Interchange Code*] An 8-bit encoding system.

Echo A host computer's retransmission of characters back to the sending device.

ECML (electronic-commerce modeling language) A standard that will enable people to make online purchases via an electronic wallet.

E-commerce (electronic commerce) Business conducted online, primarily over the Internet.

E-commerce hosting service A company that creates and maintains e-commerce Web sites for a fee.

EDI See *electronic data interchange.*

Edutainment software Software that combines *education* and enter*tainment.*

Electronic book An electronic version of a book (also called *e-book*).

Electronic commerce See *e-commerce.*

Electronic data interchange (EDI) The use of computers and data communications to transmit data electronically between companies.

Electronic dictionary A disk-based dictionary used in conjunction with a spelling-checker program to verify the spelling of words in a word processing document.

Electronic document See *online document.*

Electronic mail A computer application whereby messages are transmitted via data communications to "electronic mailboxes" (also called *e-mail*). (Contrast with *voice message switching.*)

Electronic messaging A workgroup computing application that enables electronic mail to be associated with other workgroup applications.

Electronic money (e-money) A payment system in which all monetary transactions are handled electronically.

Electronic publishing (e-publishing) The creation of electronic documents that are designed to be retrieved from disk storage and viewed.

Electronic ticket (e-ticket) An electronic alternative to the traditional paper ticket for airlines, movies, and so on.

Electronic trading (e-trading) Making online investments electronically through an online brokerage service.

Electronic wallet An electronic version of a wallet/purse, which can be used to make online purchases.

E-mail See *electronic mail.*

E-mail server A host or network that services e-mail.

E-money See *electronic money.*

Emoticons Keyboard emotion icons used to speed written interaction and convey emotions in online communications.

Encode To apply the rules of a code. (Contrast with *decode.*)

Encoding system A system that permits alphanumeric characters and symbols to be coded in terms of bits.

Encryption/decryption The encoding of data for security purposes. Encoded data must be decoded or deciphered to be used.

Enhanced television A TV presentation combining video and general programming from broadcast, satellite, and cable networks.

Enterprise computing Comprises all computing activities designed to support any type of organization.

Enterprise-wide information system Information systems that provide information and processing capabilities to workers throughout a given organization.

Entity relationship diagram A business modeling tool used for defining the information needs of a business, including the attributes of the entities and the relationship between them.

EPS (Encapsulated PostScript) A vector graphics file format used by the PostScript language.

Ergonomics The study of the relationships between people and machines.

E-signature An electronic method of placing a legal signature on an electronic document.

E-tailing Online retailing.

Ethernet A local-area-net protocol in which the nodes must contend for the right to send a message. (See also *token access methods.*)

Ethernet card An Ethernet-standard network interface card.

E-ticket See *electronic ticket.*

E-time See *execution time.*

E-trading See *electronic trading.*

Exception report A report that has been filtered to highlight critical information.

Executable program file A file that contains programs that can be executed and run on a computer.

Execution time The elapsed time it takes to execute a computer instruction and store the results (also called *E-time*).

Executive information system (EIS) A system designed specifically to support decision making at the executive levels of management, primarily the tactical and strategic levels.

Exit routine A software procedure that returns you to a GUI, an operating system prompt, or a higher-level applications program.

Expansion board These add-on circuit boards contain the electronic circuitry for many supplemental capabilities, such as a fax modem, and are made to fit a particular type of bus (also called *expansion cards*).

Expansion bus An extension of the common electrical bus that accepts the expansion boards that control the video display, disks, and other peripherals. (See also *bus.*)

Expansion card See *expansion board.*

Expansion slots Slots within the processing component of a microcomputer into which optional add-on circuit boards may be inserted.

Expert system An interactive knowledge-based system that responds to questions, asks for clarification, makes recommendations, and generally helps users make complex decisions. (See also *assistant system.*)

Explorer Windows software that enables the user to do file management tasks.

Export The process of converting a file in the format of the current program to a format that can be used by another program. (Contrast with *import.*)

Extranet An extension of an intranet such that it is partially accessible to authorized outsiders, such as customers and suppliers. (See also *intranet.*)

E-zine An online magazine.

Facsimile (fax) The transferring of images, usually of hard-copy documents, via telephone lines to another device that can receive and interpret the images.

FAQ A frequently asked question.

Fault-tolerant Referring to a computer system or network that is resistant to software errors and hardware problems.

Fax See *facsimile.*

Fax modem A modem that enables a PC to emulate a facsimile machine. (See also *modem.*)

Feedback loop A closed loop in which a computer-controlled process generates data that become input to the computer.

Fetch instruction That part of the instruction cycle in which the control unit retrieves a program instruction from RAM and loads it to the processor.

Fiber optic cable A data transmission medium that carries data in the form of light in very thin transparent fibers.

Field The smallest logical unit of data. Examples are employee number, first name, and price.

File (1) A collection of related records. (2) A named area on a disk-storage device that contains a program or digitized information (text, image, sound, and so on).

File allocation table (FAT) MS-DOS's method of storing and keeping track of files on a disk.

File compression A technique by which file size can be reduced. Compressed files are decompressed for use.

File format The manner in which a file is stored on disk storage.

File server   A dedicated computer system with high-capacity disk for storing the data and programs shared by the users on a local area network.

File Transfer Protocol (FTP)   A communications protocol that is used to transmit files over the Internet.

Filtering   The process of selecting and presenting only that information appropriate to support a particular decision.

Filtering program   A program that denies Internet access to specified content.

Firewall   Software that is designed to restrict access to an organization's network or its Intranet.

FireWire   The Apple Computer Company name for the 1394 bus standard.

Fixed disk   See *hard disk.*

Flaming   A barrage of scathing messages from irate Internet users sent to someone who posts messages out of phase with the societal norms.

Flash memory   A type of nonvolatile memory that can be altered easily by the user.

Flat files   A file that does not point to or physically link with another file.

Flat-panel monitor   A monitor, thin from front to back, that uses liquid crystal and gas plasma technology.

Floating ad   Internet advertisement that "floats" over the requested page for a few seconds.

Floating menu   A special-function menu that can be positioned anywhere on the work area until you no longer need it.

Floppy disk   See *diskette.*

Floppy disk drive   A disk drive that accepts either the 3.5-inch or 5.25-inch diskette.

FLOPS   [*Floating point operations per second*] A measure of speed for supercomputers.

Flowchart   A diagram that illustrates data, information, and work flow via specialized symbols which, when connected by flow lines, portray the logic of a system or program.

Flowcharting   The act of creating a flowchart.

FMD-ROM   Very high density, multilayer disc that holds up to 140 GB of data. (Contrast with *DVD-ROM.*)

Folder   An object in a Windows® graphical user interface that contains a logical grouping of related files and subordinate folders.

Font   A typeface that is described by its letter style, its height in points, and its presentation attribute.

Footprint   (1) The evidence of unlawful entry or use of a computer system. (2) The floor or desktop space required for a hardware component.

Foreground   (1) That part of RAM that contains the highest priority program. (2) In Windows, the area of the display containing the active window. (Contrast with *background.*)

Form factor   Refers to a computer's physical shape and size.

Formatted disk   A disk that has been initialized with the recording format for a specific operating system.

FORTRAN   [*FORmula TRANslator*] A high-level programming language designed primarily for scientific applications.

Fourth-generation language (4GL)   A programming language that uses high-level English-like instructions to retrieve and format data for inquiries and reporting.

Frame   A rectangular area in a desktop publishing-produced document into which elements, such as text and images, are placed.

Frames (Web page)   The display of more than one independently controllable sections on a single Web page.

Freeware   Copyright software that can be downloaded and used free of charge.

Front-end applications software   Client software that performs processing associated with the user interface and applications processing that can be done locally. (See also *back-end applications software.*)

Front-end processor   A processor used to offload certain data communications tasks from the host processor.

Full-duplex line   A communications channel that transmits data in both directions at the same time. (Contrast with *half-duplex line.*)

Function   A predefined operation that performs mathematical, logical, statistical, financial, and character-string operations on data in a spreadsheet or a database.

Function key   A special-function key on the keyboard that can be used to instruct the computer to perform a specific operation.

Functional specifications   Specifications that describe the logic of an information system from the user's perspective.

Function-based information system   An information system designed for the exclusive support of a specific application area, such as inventory management or accounting.

Gb   See *gigabit.*

GB   See *gigabyte.*

General-purpose computer   Computer systems that are designed with the flexibility to do a variety of tasks, such as CAD, payroll processing, climate control, and so on.

General system design   That portion of the system development process in which the target system is defined in general.

Geosynchronous orbit   An orbit that permits a communications satellite to maintain a fixed position relative to the surface of the earth.

GFLOPS   A billion FLOPS. (See *FLOPS.*)

GIF   A popular format for bit-mapped files.

Gigabit (Gb)   One billion bits.

Gigabyte (GB)   One billion bytes.

Gigahertz (GHz)   Billions of clock cycles per second

GIGO   Garbage in, Garbage out.

GPS (global positioning system)   A system that uses satellites to provide location information.

Grammar and style checker   An add-on program to word processing software that highlights grammatical concerns and deviations from effective writing style in a word processing document.

Graphical user interface (GUI)   A user-friendly interface that lets users interact with the system by pointing to processing options with a point-and-draw device.

Graphics adapter   A device controller that provides the electronic link between the motherboard and the monitor.

Graphics conversion program   Software that enables files containing graphic images to be passed between programs.

Graphics file   A file that contains digitized images.

Graphics software   Software that enables you to create line drawings, art, and presentation graphics.

Gray scales   The number of shades of a color that can be presented on a monochrome monitor's screen or on a monochrome printer's output.

Green computing   Environmentally sensible computing.

Grid computing   Using available computing resources more effectively by tapping the unused processing capabilities of many PCs via a network and/or the Internet.

Groupware   Software whose application is designed to benefit a group of people. (Related to *workgroup computing.*)

Hacker   A computer enthusiast who uses the computer as a source of recreation. (Contrast with *cracker.*)

Half-duplex line A communications channel that transmits data in one direction at the same time. (Contrast with *full-duplex line*.)

Half-size expansion board An expansion board that fits in half an expansion slot.

Handheld PC Any personal computer than can be held comfortably in a person's hand (usually weighs less than a pound). (See also *personal digital assistant*.)

Handshaking The process by which both sending and receiving devices in a computer network maintain and coordinate data communications.

Hard copy A readable printed copy of computer output. (Contrast with *soft copy*.)

Hard disk A permanently installed, continuously spinning magnetic storage medium made up of one or more rigid disk platters. (Same as *fixed disk*; contrast with *interchangeable magnetic disk*.).

Hard disk drive See *hard disk*.

Hardware The physical devices that comprise a computer system. (Contrast with *software*.)

Help command A software feature that provides an online explanation of or instruction on how to proceed.

Help desk A centralized location (either within an organization or outside of it) where computer-related questions about product usage, installation, problems, or services are answered.

Hexadecimal A base-16 numbering system.

HiFD disk A storage technology that supports very high-density diskettes up to 200 MB. (Contrast with *Zip disk* and *SuperDisk*.)

High-level language A language with instructions that combine several machine-level instructions into one instruction. (Compare with *machine language* or *low-level language*.)

Hit When a Web page is retrieved for viewing or is listed in results of a search.

Home network A network of PCs in a home or small office.

Home page The Web page that is the starting point for accessing information at a site or in a particular area.

Horizontal scroll bar A narrow screen object located along the bottom edge of a window that is used to navigate side to side through a document.

Host computer The processor responsible for the overall control of a computer system.

Hot plug A universal serial bus (USB) feature that allows peripheral devices to be connected to or removed from the USB port while the PC is running.

Hoteling Providing on-site office space that is a shared by mobile workers.

Hotkey A seldom used key combination that, when activated, causes the computer to perform the function associated with the key combination.

HPNA (HomePNA) A Home Phoneline Networking Alliance standard that allows the elements of the network to communicate over a home's existing telephone wiring or via wireless links.

HTML (HyperText Markup Language) The language used to compose and format most of the content found on the Internet.

HTTP (HyperText Transfer Protocol) The primary access method for interacting with the Internet.

Hub A common point of connection for computers and devices in a network.

Hyperlinks Clickable images or text phrase that let you link to other parts of a document or to different documents together within a computer system or on the Internet.

I/O [Input/Output] Input or output or both.

IBM Personal Computer (IBM PC) IBM's first personal computer (1981). This PC was the basis for PC-compatible computers.

Icons Pictographs used in place of words or phrases on screen displays.

Identity theft When a person gathers personal information to assume the identity of another person for illicit reasons.

IEEE 802.11a A wireless communications standard capable of 11 M bps up to about 300 feet from an access point.

IEEE 802.11b (Wi-Fi) A wireless communications standard capable of 54 M bps up to about 50 feet from an access point.

iMac An Apple Computer personal computer.

Image processing A reference to computer applications in which digitized images are retrieved, displayed, altered, merged with text, stored, and sent via data communications to one or several remote locations.

Image scanner A device that can scan and digitize an image so that it can be stored on a disk and manipulated by a computer.

Impact printer A printer that uses pins or hammers that hit a ribbon to transfer images to the paper.

Import The process of converting data in one format to a format that is compatible with the calling program. (Contrast with *export*.)

Inactive window A Windows window that displays an application that is running but not being used by the user. (Contrast with *active window*.)

Industrial espionage Theft of proprietary business information.

Industrial robot Computer-controlled robots used in industrial applications.

Information Data that have been collected and processed into a meaningful form.

Information-based decision A decision that involves an ill-defined and unstructured problem.

Information repository A central computer-based database for all system design information.

Information resource management (IRM) A concept advocating that information be treated as a corporate resource.

Information service A commercial network that provides remote users with access to a variety of information services.

Information society A society in which the generation and dissemination of information becomes the central focus of commerce.

Information superhighway A metaphor for a network of high-speed data communication links that will eventually connect virtually every facet of our society.

Information system A computer-based system that provides both data processing capability and information for managerial decision making.

Information technology (IT) A collective reference to the integration of computing technology and information processing.

Information technology competency (IT competency) Being able to interact with and use computers and having an understanding of IT issues.

Infrared port See *IrDA port*.

Ink-jet printer A nonimpact printer in which the print head contains independently controlled injection chambers that squirt ink droplets on the paper to form letters and images.

Input Data entered to a computer system for processing.

Input/output (I/O) A generic reference to input and/or output to a computer.

Input/output-bound application An IT application in which the amount of work that can be performed by the computer system is limited primarily by the speeds of the I/O devices.

Instant messaging   Internet application in which personal communications are sent and displayed in real-time.

Instruction   A programming language statement that specifies a particular computer operation to be performed.

Instruction cycle   Defines the process by which computer instructions are interpreted and executed.

Instruction register   The register that contains the instruction being executed.

Instruction time   The elapsed time it takes to fetch and decode a computer instruction (also called *I-time*).

Integrated circuit (IC)   Thousands of electronic components that are etched into a tiny silicon chip in the form of a special-function electronic circuit.

Integrated information system   An information system that services two or more functional areas, all of which share a common database.

Integrated Services Digital Network (ISDN)   A digital telecommunications standard for data delivery over twisted-pair lines with transmission speeds up to 128 K bps.

Intelligent agent   Artificial intelligence-based software that has the authority to act on a person or thing's behalf. (Also called *bot*.)

Interactive   Pertaining to online and immediate communication between the user and the computer.

Interchangeable magnetic disk   A magnetic disk that can be stored offline and loaded to the computer system as needed. (Contrast with *hard disk* or *fixed disk*.)

Intercompany networking   Companies cooperating with customers and other companies via electronic data interchange and extranets. (Contrast with *intracompany networking*.)

Internet (the Net)   A global network that connects more than tens of thousands of networks, millions of large multiuser computers, and tens of millions of users in more than one hundred countries.

Internet appliance   An inexpensive communications device for Internet applications.

Internet Protocol address   See *IP address*.

Internet Relay Chat (IRC)   An Internet protocol that allows users to join and participate in group chat sessions.

Internet service provider (ISP)   Any company that provides individuals and organizations with access to or presence on the Internet.

Internet site specialist   A person responsible for creating and maintaining one or more Internet sites.

Interoperability   The ability to run software and exchange information in a multiplatform environment.

Intracompany networking   Computer networking within an organization. (Contrast with *intercompany networking*.)

Intranet   An Internet-like network whose scope is restricted to the networks within a particular organization. (See also *extranet*.)

Invoke   Execute a command or a macro.

IP address (Internet Protocol address)   A four-number point-of-presence (POP) Internet address (for example, 206.28.104.10).

IRC   See *Internet Relay Chat*.

IrDA port   Enables wireless transmission of data via infrared light waves between PCs, printers, and other devices (also called *infrared port*).

ISP   See *Internet service provider*.

Itanium®   High-end Intel processor.

I-time   See *instruction time*.

Java   Platform-independent language used for Web-based applications.

Joystick   A vertical stick that moves the mouse pointer on a screen in the direction in which the stick is pushed.

JPEG   A bit-mapped file format that compresses image size.

JPG   The Windows-based extension for JPEG files, a bit-mapped file format that compresses image size.

Jukebox   A storage device for multiple sets of CD-ROMs, tape cartridges, or disk modules enabling ready access to vast amounts of online data.

Kb   See *kilobit*.

KB   See *kilobyte*.

Kernel   An operating system program that loads other operating system programs and applications programs to RAM as they are needed.

Key field   The field in a record that is used as an identifier for accessing, sorting, and collating records.

Keyboard   A device used for key data entry.

Keypad   That portion of a keyboard that permits rapid numeric data entry.

Kilobit (Kb)   1024, or about 1000, bits.

Kilobyte (KB)   1024, or about 1000, bytes.

Knowledge base   The foundation of a knowledge-based system that contains facts, rules, inferences, and procedures.

Knowledge-based system   A computer-based system, often associated with artificial intelligence, that helps users make decisions by enabling them to interact with a knowledge base.

Knowledge engineer   Someone trained in the use of expert system shells and in the interview techniques needed to extract information from a domain expert.

Knowledge worker   Someone whose job function revolves around the use, manipulation, and dissemination of information.

LAN operating system   The operating system for a local area network.

LAN server   A high-end PC on a local area network whose resources are shared by other users on the LAN.

Landscape   Referring to the orientation of the print on the page. Printed lines run parallel to the longer side of the page. (Contrast with *portrait*.)

Laptop PC   Portable PC that can operate without an external power source. (Contrast with *desktop PC* and *tower PC*; see also *pocket PC*.)

Large-format ink-jet printer   See *plotter*.

Laser printer   A page printer that uses laser technology to produce the image.

Layout   A reference to the positioning of the visual elements on a display or page.

Leased line   See *private line*.

LindowsOS   A Linux-based operating system for PCs that has a Windows-like interface.

Linux   An open source spin off of the UNIX operating system that runs on a number of hardware platforms and is made available for free over the Internet.

Listserv   A reference to an Internet mailing list.

LMDS   A fixed line-of-sight wireless technology designed to enable high-bandwidth "last mile" connectivity.

Load   To transfer programs or data from disk to RAM.

Local area network (LAN or local net)   A system of hardware, software, and communications channels that connects devices on the local premises. (Contrast with *wide area network*.)

Local bus   A bus that links expansion boards directly to the computer system's common bus.

Local net   See *local area network*.

Log off   The procedure by which a user terminates a communications link with a remote computer. (Contrast with *logon*.)

Logic bomb   A harmful set of instructions that are executed when a certain set of conditions are met.

Logic error A programming error that causes an erroneous result when the program is executed.

Logical operators AND, OR, and NOT operators can be used to combine relational expressions logically in spreadsheet, database, and other programs. (See also *relational operators*.)

Logical security That aspect of computer-center security that deals with user access to systems and data.

Logon The procedure by which a user establishes a communications link with a remote computer. (Contrast with *log off*.)

Loop A sequence of program instructions executed repeatedly until a particular condition is met.

Low-level language A language comprising the fundamental instruction set of a particular computer. (Compare with *high-level language*.)

Mac OS X The operating system for the Apple family of microcomputers.

Machine cycle The cycle of operations performed by the processor to process a single program instruction: fetch, decode, execute, and place result in memory.

Machine language The programming language that is interpreted and executed directly by the computer.

Macintosh An Apple Computer personal computer.

Macro A sequence of frequently used operations or keystrokes that can be invoked to help speed user interaction with microcomputer productivity software.

Macro language Programming languages whose instructions relate specifically to the functionality of the parent software.

Macro virus A program written in the macro language of a particular application.

Magnetic disk See *disk, magnetic*.

Magnetic disk drive See *disk drive, magnetic*.

Magnetic-ink character recognition (MICR) A data entry technique used primarily in banking. Magnetic characters are imprinted on checks and deposits, then scanned to retrieve the data.

Magnetic stripe A magnetic storage medium for low-volume storage of data on badges and cards. (Related to *badge reader*.)

Magnetic tape See *tape, magnetic*.

Magnetic tape cartridge Cartridge-based magnetic tape storage media.

Magnetic tape drive See *tape drive, magnetic*.

Mail merge A computer application in which text generated by word processing is merged with data from a database (e.g., a form letter with an address).

Mailing list An Internet-based capability that lets people discuss issues of common interest via common e-mail.

Main menu The highest-level menu in a menu tree. (See also *menu*.)

Main program See *driver module*.

Mainframe computer A large computer that can service many users simultaneously in support of enterprise-wide applications.

MAN See *Metropolitan Area Network*.

Management information system (MIS) A computer-based system that optimizes the collection, transfer, and presentation of information throughout an organization, through an integrated structure of databases and information flow. (Contrast with *decision support system* and *executive information system*.)

Mass storage Various techniques and devices used to hold and retain electronic data.

Massively parallel processing (MPP) An approach to the design of computer systems that involves the integration of thousands of microprocessors within a single computer.

Master file The permanent source of data for a particular computer application area.

Mb See *megabit*.

MB See *megabyte*.

Megabit (Mb) 1,048,576, or about one million, bits.

Megabyte (MB) 1,048,576, or about one million, bytes.

Megahertz (MHZ) One million hertz (cycles per second).

Memory See *RAM*.

Menu A display with a list of processing choices from which a user may select.

Menu bar A menu in which the options are displayed across the screen.

Menu tree A hierarchy of menus.

Message A series of bits sent from a terminal to a computer, or vice versa.

Metafile (WMF) A class of graphics that combines the components of raster and vector graphics formats.

Metropolitan Area Network (MAN) A data network designed for use within the confines of a town or city.

MHZ See *megahertz*.

MICR See *magnetic-ink character recognition*.

Microcomputer (or micro) A small computer (See also *PC*.)

Micropayment Electronic payment for goods and services in very small amounts.

Microprocessor A computer on a single chip. The processing component of a microcomputer.

Microsecond One millionth of a second.

Microsoft Network (MSN) An information service provider sponsored by Microsoft Corporation.

Microwave signal A high-frequency line-of-sight electromagnetic wave used in wireless communications.

MIDI [Musical Instrument Digital Interface] An interface between PCs and electronic musical instruments, like the synthesizer.

MIDI file A nonwaveform file result for MIDI applications.

Millisecond One thousandth of a second.

Minicomputer (or mini) A midsized computer.

Minimize Reducing a window on the display screen to an icon.

MIPS Millions of instructions per second.

MMDS A fixed line-of-sight wireless technology designed to deliver network access at fiber-optic speeds.

Mnemonics A memory aid often made up from the initials of the words in a term or process.

Modem [MOdulator-DEModulator] A device used to convert computer-compatible signals to signals that can be transmitted over the telephone lines, then back again to computer signals at the other end of the line.

Monitor A television-like display for soft-copy output in a computer system.

Moore's Law The density of transistors on a chip doubles every 18 months.

Morphing Using graphics software to transform one image into an entirely different image. The term is derived from the word *metamorphosis*.

Motherboard See *system board*.

Mouse A point-and-draw device that, when moved across a desktop a particular distance and direction, causes the same movement of the pointer on a screen.

Mouse pointer A symbol that indicates the positioning of the point-and-draw device pointer on the screen.

MP3 A sound file format that enables CD-quality music to be compressed to about 8% of its original size while retaining CD sound quality.

MPEG A video file format with the extension MPG or MPEG.

MPP See *massively parallel processing.*

MS-DOS [*MicroSoft-Disk Operating System*] The pre-Windows PC operating system.

Multifunction expansion board An add-on circuit board that contains the electronic circuitry for two or more supplemental capabilities (for example, a serial port and a fax modem).

Multifunction printer Multifunction machines that can handle several paper-related tasks such as computer-based printing, facsimile, scanning, and copying.

Multimedia Computer application that involves the integration of text, sound, graphics, motion video, and animation.

Multimedia projector An output peripheral device that can project the screen image (display) onto a large screen for group viewing.

Multiplatform environment A computing environment that supports more than one platform. (See also *platform.*)

Multiplexor A communications device that collects data from a number of low-speed devices, then transmits the combined data over a single communications channel. At the destination, it separates the signals for processing.

Multitasking The concurrent execution of more than one program at a time.

Multiuser PC A microcomputer that can serve more than one user at any given time.

Nanosecond One billionth of a second.

National Information Infrastructure (NII) Refers to a futuristic network of high-speed data communications links that eventually will connect virtually every facet of our society. (See also *information superhighway.*)

Native file format The file format normally associated with a particular application.

Natural language A programming language in which the programmer writes specifications without regard to the computer's instruction format or syntax—essentially, using everyday human language to program.

Navigation Movement within and between a software application's work areas.

Net PC Same as *network computer* (*NC*).

Netiquette Etiquette on the Internet.

Network address An electronic identifier assigned to each computer system and terminal/PC in a computer network.

Network administrator A data communications specialist who designs and maintains local area networks (LANs) and wide area networks (WANs).

Network bus A common cable in a bus topology that permits the connection of terminals, peripheral devices, and microcomputers to create a computer network.

Network computer (NC) A single-user computer, usually diskless, that is designed to work with a server computer to obtain programs and data (also called *Net PC*).

Network interface card (NIC) A PC expansion card or PCMCIA card that facilitates and controls the exchange of data between the PC and its network.

Network topology The configuration of the interconnections between the nodes in a communications network.

Network, computer See *computer network.*

Neural network A field of artificial intelligence in which millions of chips (processing elements) are interconnected to enable computers to imitate the way the human brain works.

Newbie A new user on the Internet.

Newsgroup The electronic counterpart of a wall-mounted bulletin board that enables Internet users to exchange ideas and information via a centralized message database.

Node An endpoint in a computer network.

Nondestructive read A read operation in which the program and/or data that are loaded to RAM from disk storage reside in both RAM (temporarily) and disk storage (permanently).

Nonimpact printer A printer that uses chemicals, lasers, or heat to form the images on the paper.

Nonvolatile memory Solid-state RAM that retains its contents after an electrical interruption. (Contrast with *volatile memory.*)

Non-Windows application A computer application that will run under Windows but does not conform to the Windows standards for software.

Notebook PC A notebook-size laptop PC.

Numeric A reference to any of the digits 0-9. (Compare with *alpha* and *alphanumeric.*)

Object A result of any Windows application, such as a block of text, all or part of a graphic image, or a sound clip.

Object linking and embedding See *OLE.*

Object-oriented language A programming language structured to enable the interaction between user-defined concepts that contain data and operations to be performed on the data.

Object-oriented programming (OOP) A form of software development in which programs are built with entities called objects, which model any physical or conceptual item. Objects are linked together in a top-down hierarchy.

Object program A machine-level program that results from the compilation of a source program. (Compare with *source program.*)

OCR See *optical character recognition.*

Offline Pertaining to data that are not accessible by, or hardware devices that are not connected to, a computer system. (Contrast with *online.*)

OLE [*Object Linking and Embedding*] The software capability that enables the creation of a compound document that contains one or more objects from other applications. Objects can be linked or embedded.

Online Pertaining to data and/or hardware devices accessible to and under the control of a computer system. (Contrast with *offline.*)

Online document Documents that are designed to be retrieved from disk storage (locally or over a network) and viewed on a monitor. (Same as *electronic document.*)

Online thesaurus Software that enables a user to request synonyms interactively during a word processing session.

Open application A running application.

Open source software Referring to software for which the actual source programming code is made available to users for review and modification.

Operating system The software that controls the execution of all applications and system software programs.

Optical character recognition (OCR) A data entry technique that permits original source data entry. Coded symbols or characters are scanned to retrieve the data.

Optical disc See *disc, optical.*

Optical laser disc A storage medium that uses laser technology to score the surface of a disc to represent a bit.

Optical scanner A peripheral device that can read written text and hard-copy images, then translate the information into an electronic format that can be interpreted by and stored on computers.

Option buttons Circle bullets in front of user options that when selected include a dot in the middle of the circle.

Output The presentation of the results of processing.

Packet Strings of bits that contain information and a network address that are routed over different paths on the Internet according to a specific communications protocol.

Page (Web) The area in which information is presented on the World Wide Web.

Page printer   A printer that prints a page at a time.

Paint software   Software that enables users to "paint" electronic images. Resultant images are stored as raster graphics images.

Palmtop PC   See *pocket PC*.

Parallel conversion   An approach to system conversion whereby the existing system and the new system operate simultaneously prior to conversion.

Parallel port   A direct link with the microcomputer's bus that facilitates the parallel transmission of data, usually one byte at a time.

Parallel processing   A processing procedure in which one main processor examines the programming problem and determines what portions, if any, of the problem can be solved in pieces by other subordinate processors.

Parallel transmission   Pertaining to the transmission of data in groups of bits versus one bit at a time. (Contrast with *serial transmission*.)

Parameter   A descriptor that can take on different values.

Parity checking   A built-in checking procedure in a computer system to help ensure that the transmission of data is complete and accurate. (Related to *parity error*.)

Parity error   Occurs when a bit is dropped in the transmission of data from one hardware device to another. (Related to *parity checking*.)

Password   A word or phrase known only to the user. When entered, it permits the user to gain access to the system.

Patch   A modification of a program or an information system.

Path   The hierarchy of folders that lead to the location of a particular file.

Pattern recognition system   A device that enables limited visual input to a computer system.

PC   [*Personal Computer*] A small computer designed for use by an individual. (See also *microcomputer*.)

PC card   Same as *PCMCIA card*.

PC specialist   A person trained in the function and operation of PCs and related hardware and software.

PCI local bus   [*Peripheral Component Interconnect*] Intel's local bus. (See also *local bus*.)

PCMCIA card   A credit-card-sized module that is inserted into a PCMCIA-compliant interface to offer add-on capabilities such as expanded memory, fax modem, and so on (also called *PC card*).

PCX   A bit-mapped file format.

PDF   See *portable document format*.

Peer-to-peer computing   A type of computing in which people allow their stored data to be shared.

Peer-to-peer LAN   A local area network in which all PCs on the network are functionally equal.

Pen-based computing   Computer applications that rely on the pen-based PCs for processing capability.

Pen-based PC   A portable personal computer that enables input via an electronic pen in conjunction with a pressure-sensitive monitor/drawing surface.

Pentium®   An Intel microprocessor.

Pentium® II   Successor to the Intel® Pentium Pro microprocessor.

Pentium® III   Successor to the Intel® Pentium II microprocessor.

Pentium® 4   Successor to the Intel® Pentium III microprocessor.

Pentium® Pro   Successor to the Intel® Pentium microprocessor.

Peripheral device   Any hardware device other than the processor.

Personal computer (PC)   See *PC*.

Personal computing   A computing environment in which individuals use personal computers for domestic and/or business applications.

Personal digital assistant (PDA)   Handheld personal computers that support a variety of personal information systems.

Personal home page   A Web site for an individual.

Personal identification number (PIN)   A code or number that is used in conjunction with a password to permit the user to gain access to a computer system.

Personal information management (PIM) system   Software application designed to help users organize random bits of information and to provide communications capabilities, such as e-mail and fax.

Phased conversion   An approach to system conversion whereby an information system is implemented one module at a time.

Photo illustration software   Software that enables the creation of original images and the modification of existing digitized images.

Physical security   That aspect of computer-center security that deals with access to computers and peripheral devices.

Picosecond   One trillionth of a second.

Picture element   See *pixel*.

Pie graph   A circular graph that illustrates each "piece" of datum in its proper relationship to the whole "pie."

Pilferage   A special case of software piracy whereby a company purchases a software product without a site-usage license agreement, then copies and distributes it throughout the company.

Pilot conversion   An approach to system conversion whereby the new system is implemented first in only one of the several areas for which it is targeted.

Pipelining   When a processor begins executing another instruction before the current instruction is completed, thus improving system throughput.

Pixel   [*Picture element*] An addressable point on a display screen to which light can be directed under program control.

Platform   A definition of the standards by which software is developed and hardware is designed.

Plotter   A device that produces high-precision hard-copy graphic output (also called *large-format ink-jet printer*).

Plug-and-play   Refers to making a peripheral device or an expansion board immediately operational by simply plugging it into a port or an expansion slot.

Plugin   A complementary application to an Internet browser.

PNG   A license-free bit-mapped file format, similar to GIF.

Pocket PC   A handheld personal computer (also called *palmtop PC*).

Point-and-draw device   An input device, such as a mouse or trackpad, used to *point* to and select a particular user option and to *draw*.

Pointer   The highlighted area in a spreadsheet display that indicates the current cell.

Polling   A line-control procedure in which each terminal is "polled" in rotation to determine whether a message is ready to be sent.

POP (point-of-presence)   An access point to the Internet.

Pop-out menu   A menu displayed next to the menu option selected in a higher-level pull-down or pop-up menu.

Pop-under ad   Internet advertisement that opens in a separate browser window "under" the requested page.

Pop-up menu   A menu that is superimposed in a window over whatever is currently being displayed on the monitor.

Port   An access point in a computer system that permits communication between the computer and a peripheral device.

Port replicator A device to which a notebook PC can be readily connected to give the PC access to whatever external peripheral devices are connected to its common ports (keyboard, monitor, mouse, network, printer, and so on).

Portable document An electronic document that can be passed around the electronic world as you would a print document in the physical world.

Portable Document Format (PDF) A standard, created by Adobe Corporation, creating portable documents.

Portable hard disk External hard disk device that is easily connected to any PC.

Portal A Web site or service that offers a broad array of Internet-based resources and services.

Portrait Referring to the orientation of the print on the page. Printed lines run parallel to the shorter side of the page. (Contrast with *landscape.*)

Post Office Protocol (POP) Refers to the way an e-mail client software gets e-mail from its server.

POTS Short for *plain old telephone* service, the standard voice-grade telephone service common in homes and business.

Power up To turn on the electrical power to a computer system.

PowerPC processor A RISC-based processor used in Apple iMac and other computers.

PPP (Point-to-Point Protocol) A method by which a dialup link is connected to an ISP's local POP.

Presentation software Software used to prepare information for multimedia presentations in meetings, reports, and oral presentations.

Prespecification An approach to system development in which users relate their information processing needs to the project team during the early stages of the project.

Print server A LAN-based PC that handles LAN user print jobs and controls at least one printer.

Printer A device used to prepare hard-copy output.

Private line A dedicated communications channel provided by a common carrier between any two points in a computer network. (Same as *leased line.*)

Procedure-oriented language A high-level language whose general-purpose instruction set can be used to produce a sequence of instructions to model scientific and business procedures.

Process/device control Referring to a computer-based system that controls processes and/or devices.

Processor The logical component of a computer system that interprets and executes program instructions.

Processor-bound application The amount of work that can be performed by the computer system is limited primarily by the speed of the computer.

Product stewardship policy A policy that encourages responsible consideration of products.

Program (1) Computer instructions structured and ordered in a manner that, when executed, causes a computer to perform a particular function. (2) The act of producing computer software. (Related to *software.*)

Program register The register that contains the address of the next instruction to be executed.

Programmed decision Decisions that address well-defined problems with easily identifiable solutions.

Programmer One who writes computer programs.

Programmer/analyst The title of one who performs both the programming and systems analysis function.

Programming language A language programmers use to communicate instructions to a computer.

Programming The act of writing a computer program.

PROM [*Programmable Read-Only Memory*] ROM in which the user can load read-only programs and data.

Prompt A program-generated message describing what should be entered.

Proprietary software package Vendor-developed software that is marketed to the public.

Protocols See *communications protocols.*

Prototype system A model of a full-scale system.

Prototyping An approach to systems development that results in a prototype system.

Proxy server computer A computer between the client PC and a actual server that handles many client requests before they reach the actual server.

Pseudocode Nonexecutable program code used as an aid to develop and document structured programs.

Public-domain software Software that is not copyrighted and can be used without restriction.

Public-key encryption Communications-based encryption that requires a private key and a public key.

Pull-down menu A menu that is "pulled down" from an option in a higher-level menu.

Pull technology Technology where data are requested from another program or computer, such as with an Internet browser. (Contrast with *push technology.*)

Pumping and dumping A scam where someone floods the Internet with bogus information about a particular company.

Push technology Technology where data are sent automatically to an Internet user. (Contrast with *pull technology.*)

Query by example A method of database inquiry in which the user sets conditions for the selection of records by composing one or more example relational expressions.

Query language A user-friendly programming language for requesting information from a database.

QuickTime Software that lets you view videos, listen to music, and view panoramas.

Radio signals Signals that enable data communication between radio transmitters and receivers.

RAID (Redundant Array of Independent Disks) An integrated system of disks that enables fault-tolerant hard disk operation.

RAM [*Random-Access Memory*] The memory area in which all programs and data must reside before programs can be executed or data manipulated.

RAM disk That area of RAM that facilitates disk caching. (See also *disk caching.*)

Rambus DRAM See *RDRAM.*

Rambus in-line memory module See *RIMM.*

Random access Direct access to records, regardless of their physical location on the storage medium. (Contrast with *sequential access.*)

Random-access memory See *RAM.*

Random processing Processing data and records randomly. (Contrast with *sequential processing.*)

Range A cell or a rectangular group of adjacent cells in a spreadsheet.

Rapid application development (RAD) Using sophisticated development tools to create a prototype or a functional information system.

Raster graphics A method for maintaining a screen image as patterns of dots. (See also *bit-mapped graphics.*)

RDRAM (Rambus DRAM) A new RAM technology capable of very high-speed transfer of data (600 MHz) to/from the processor.

Read The process by which a record or a portion of a record is accessed from the disk storage medium and transferred to RAM for processing. (Contrast with *write*.)

Read-only memory (ROM) A memory chip with contents permanently loaded by the manufacturer for read-only applications.

Read/write head That component of a disk drive or tape drive that reads from and writes to its respective storage medium.

Record A collection of related fields (such as an employee record) describing an event or an item.

Register A small high-speed storage area in which data pertaining to the execution of a particular instruction are stored.

Relational database A database, made up of logically linked tables, in which data are accessed by content rather than by address.

Relational operators Used in formulas to show the equality relationship between two expressions (= [equal to], < [less than], > [greater than], <= [less than or equal to], >= [greater than or equal to], <> [not equal to]). (See also *logical operators*.)

Relative cell address Refers to a cell's position in a spreadsheet in relation to the cell containing the formula in which the address is used.

Resolution Referring to the number of addressable points on a monitor's screen or the number of dots per unit area on printed output.

RGB monitor Color monitors that mix red, green, and blue to achieve a spectrum of colors.

RIMM [*Rambus In-line Memory Module*] The circuit board designed to hold rambus in-line memory module memory chips.

Ring topology A computer network that involves computer systems connected in a closed loop, with no one computer system the focal point of the network.

RISC [*Reduced Instruction Set Computer*] A computer design architecture based on a limited instruction set machine language. (Contrast with *CISC*.)

Robot A computer-controlled manipulator capable of locomotion and/or moving items through a variety of spatial motions.

Robotics The integration of computers and industrial robots.

ROM [*Read-Only Memory*] RAM that can be read only, not written to.

Root directory The directory at the highest level of a hierarchy of directories.

Routers Communications hardware that enables communications links between LANs and WANs by performing the necessary protocol conversions.

RS-232C connector A 9-pin or 25-pin plug that is used for the electronic interconnection of computers, modems, and other peripheral devices.

Ruler bar In the document window, a line that shows appropriate document measurements.

Run To open and execute a program.

Scalable system A system whose design permits expansion to handle any size database or any number of users.

Scalable typeface An outline-based typeface from which fonts of any point size can be created. (See also *typeface*.)

ScanDisk A Windows utility program that enables the repair of lost clusters on a hard disk.

Scanner A device that scans hard copy and digitizes the text and/or images to a format that can be interpreted by a computer.

Scheduler Someone who schedules the use of hardware resources to optimize system efficiency.

Screen-capture programs Memory-resident programs that enable users to transfer all or part of the current screen image to a disk file.

Screen name Another name for user ID at logon.

Screen saver A utility program used to change static screens on idle monitors to interesting dynamic displays.

Script A small scripting language program downloaded with a Web page and run on the client PC.

Scripting language A programming language for creating scripts.

Scroll arrow Small box containing an arrow at each end of a scroll bar that is used to navigate in small increments within a document or list.

Scroll box A square object that is that is dragged along a scroll bar to navigate within a document or list.

Scrolling Using the cursor keys to view parts of a document that extend past the bottom or top or sides of the screen.

SCSI bus [*Small Computer System Interface*] This hardware interface allows the connection of several peripheral devices to a single SCSI expansion board (or adapter).

SCSI controller The add-on circuitry needed for a SCSI port.

SCSI port A device interface to which up to 15 peripheral devices can be daisy-chained to a single USB port. (Contrast with *USB port*.)

SDRAM (Synchronous Dynamic RAM) RAM that is able to synchronize itself with the processor enabling high-speed transfer of data (600 MHz) to/from the processor.

Search engine An Internet resource discovery tool that lets people find information by keyword(s) searches.

Sector A disk-storage concept of a pie-shaped portion of a disk or diskette in which records are stored and subsequently retrieved. (Contrast with *cylinder*.)

Sector organization Magnetic disk organization in which the recording surface is divided into pie-shaped sectors.

Secure Sockets Layer (SSL) A protocol developed by Netscape for transmitting private documents via the Internet.

Select Highlighting an object on a windows screen or a menu option.

Self-extracting zip file An executable zip file that, when executed, unzips itself.

Sequential access Accessing records in the order in which they are stored. (Contrast with *random access*.)

Sequential files Files containing records that are ordered according to a key field.

Sequential processing Processing of files that are ordered numerically or alphabetically by a key field. (Contrast with *random processing*.)

Serial port A direct link with the microcomputer's bus that facilitates the serial transmission of data.

Serial representation The storing of bits, one after another, on a storage medium.

Serial transmission Pertaining to processing data one bit at a time. (Contrast with *parallel transmission*.)

Server A LAN component that can be shared by users on a LAN.

Server application (1) An application running on a network server that works in tandem with a client workstation or PC application. (See also *client application*.) (2) In object linking and embedding, the application in which the linked object originates.

Server computer Any type of computer, from a PC to a supercomputer, which performs a variety of functions for its client computers, including the storage of data and applications software. (See also *client computer*.)

Server program A software program on the server computer that manages resources and can work in conjunction with a client program. (See also *client program*.)

Shareware Copyrighted software that can be downloaded for free, with its use based on an honor pay system.

Shortcut icon A graphic icon that represents an application or document that when chosen causes the application to be run or the document to be opened.

Shortcut key A key combination that chooses a menu option without the need to display a menu.

Shut down The processes of exiting all applications and shutting off the power to a computer system.

SIMM [*Single In-line Memory Module*] A small circuit board, capable of holding several memory chips, that has a 32-bit data path and can be easily connected to a PC's system board. (Contrast with *DIMM.*)

Simultaneous click Tapping both buttons on a point-and-draw device at the same time.

Skyscraper ad Vertical Internet advertisement that entices users to click on them to link to the site being promoted.

Slides One of the images to be displayed in presentation software.

Smalltalk An object-oriented language.

Smart card A card or badge with an embedded microprocessor.

Soft copy Temporary output that can be interpreted visually, as on a monitor. (Contrast with *hard copy.*)

Soft font An electronic description of a font that is retrieved from disk storage and downloaded to the printer's memory.

Soft keyboard A keyboard displayed on a touch-sensitive screen such that when a displayed key is touched with a finger or stylus, the character or command is sent to memory for processing.

Software The programs used to direct the functions of a computer system. (Contrast with *hardware*; related to *program.*)

Software engineer A person who develops software products to bridge the gap between design and executable program code.

Software engineering A term coined to emphasize an approach to software development that embodies the rigors of the engineering discipline.

Software installation The process of copying the program and data files from a vendor-supplied master disk(s) to a PC's hard disk.

Software package One or more programs designed to perform a particular processing task.

Software piracy The unlawful duplication of proprietary software. (Related to *pilferage.*)

Software portfolio The mix of software on a PC.

Software suite An integrated collection of software tools that may include a variety of business applications packages.

Sort The rearrangement of fields or records in an ordered sequence by a key field.

Source application, Clipboard The software application from which the Clipboard contents originated. (Contrast with *destination application.*)

Source data Original data that usually involve the recording of a transaction or the documenting of an event or an item.

Source-data automation Entering data directly to a computer system at the source without the need for key entry transcription.

Source document The original hard copy from which data are entered.

Source program file This file contains high-level instructions to the computer that must be compiled prior to program execution.

Source program The code of the original program (also called *source code*). (Compare with *object program.*)

Spam Unsolicited junk e-mail.

Spammer A person who distributes spam.

Speech-recognition system A device that permits voice input to a computer system.

Speech synthesis Converting raw data into electronically produced speech.

Speech synthesizers Devices that convert raw data into electronically produced speech.

Spelling checker A software feature that checks the spelling of every word in a document against an electronic dictionary.

Spreadsheet file A file containing data and formulas in tabular format.

Spreadsheet software Refers to software that permits users to work with rows and columns of data.

SQL A type of query language.

Star topology A computer network that involves a centralized host computer connected to a number of smaller computer systems.

Start button Permanent button on the Windows® task bar.

Stop bits A data communications parameter that refers to the number of bits in the character or byte.

Streaming audio Internet-based audio that is received and played in a steady, continuous stream.

Streaming video Internet-based video that is received and played in a steady, continuous stream.

Structure chart A chart that graphically illustrates the conceptualization of an information system as a hierarchy of modules.

Structured system design A systems design technique that encourages top-down design.

Stylus A pen-like point-and-draw device.

Subroutine A group or sequence of instructions for a specific programming task that is called by another program.

Supercomputer The category that includes the largest and most powerful computers.

SuperDisk A disk-storage technology that supports very high-density diskettes.

Switched line A telephone line used as a regular data communications channel (also called *dialup line*).

Switching hub A type of hub that accepts packets of information sent within a network, then forwards them to the appropriate port for routing to their network destination, based on the network address contained in the packet.

Symmetric-key encryption Communications-based encryption that requires each computer in a loop to have the key.

Synchronous dynamic RAM (SDRAM) RAM that is able to synchronize itself with the processor enabling faster throughput.

Synchronous transmission A communications protocol in which the source and destination points operate in timed alignment to enable high-speed data transfer. (See also *asynchronous transmission.*)

Syntax The rules that govern the formulation of the instructions in a computer program.

Syntax error An invalid format for a program instruction.

System Any group of components (functions, people, activities, events, and so on) that interface with and complement one another to achieve one or more predefined goals.

System board A microcomputer circuit board that contains the microprocessor, electronic circuitry for handling such tasks as input/output signals from peripheral devices, and memory chips (same as *motherboard*).

System check An internal verification of the operational capabilities of a computer's electronic components.

System life cycle A reference to the four stages of a computer-based information system—birth, development, production, and end-of-life.

System maintenance The process of modifying an information system to meet changing needs.

System programmer A programmer who develops and maintains system programs and software.

System prompt A visual prompt to the user to enter a system command.

System software Software that is independent of any specific applications area.

System specifications (specs) Information system details that include everything from the functionality of the system to the format of the system's output screens and reports.

System unit An enclosure containing the computer system's electronic circuitry and various storage devices.

Systems analysis The examination of an existing system to determine input, processing, and output requirements for the target system.

Systems analyst A person who does systems analysis.

Systems testing A phase of testing where all programs in a system are tested together.

T-1 line A high-speed digital link to the Internet (1.544 M bps).

T-3 line A high-speed digital link to the Internet (44.736 M bps).

TAN See *tiny area network*.

Tape backup unit (TBU) A magnetic tape drive designed to provide backup for data and programs.

Tape drive, magnetic The hardware device that contains the read/write mechanism for the magnetic tape storage medium. (Compare with *disk drive, magnetic*.)

Tape, magnetic A storage medium for sequential data storage and backup.

Target system A proposed information system that is the object of a systems development effort.

Task The basic unit of work for a processor.

Taskbar In a Windows session, the bar shows what programs are running and available for use.

TCP/IP [Transmission Control Protocol/Internet Protocol] A set of communications protocols developed by the Department of Defense to link dissimilar computers across many kinds of networks.

Telecommunications The collection and distribution of the electronic representation of information between two points.

Telecommuting "Commuting" via a communications link between home and office.

Telemedicine Describes any type of health care administered remotely over communication links.

Telephony The integration of computers and telephones.

Template A model for a particular microcomputer software application.

Terabyte (TB) About one trillion bytes.

Terminal Any device capable of sending and receiving data over a communications channel.

Terminal emulation mode The software transformation of a PC so that its keyboard, monitor, and data interface emulate that of a terminal.

Text cursor A symbol controlled by the arrow keys that shows the location of where the next keyed-in character will appear on the screen.

Text-to-speech software Software that reads text and produces speech.

TFLOPS A trillion FLOPS. (See *FLOPS*.)

Thesaurus, online See *online thesaurus*.

Thin client A networked workstation that depends on a server computer for much of its processing and for permanent storage.

Third-generation language (3GL) A procedure-oriented programming language that can be used to model almost any scientific or business procedure. (Related to *procedure-oriented language*.)

Thread (newsgroup) An original Internet newsgroup message and any posted replies to that message.

Throughput A measure of computer system efficiency; the rate at which work can be performed by a computer system.

Throwaway system An information system developed to support information for a one-time decision, then discarded.

Thumbnail A miniature display of an image or a page to be viewed or printed.

TIF The Windows-based extension for TIFF files, a bit-mapped file format often used in print publishing.

TIFF A bit-mapped file format often used in print publishing.

Tiled windows Two or more windows displayed on the screen in a nonoverlapping manner.

Tiny area network (TAN) A term coined to refer to very small local area networks, typically installed in the home or small office.

Title bar A narrow Windows screen object at the top of each window that runs the width of the window.

Toggle The action of pressing a single key on a keyboard to switch between two or more modes of operation, such as insert and replace.

Token access method A local-area-net protocol in which an electronic token travels around a network giving priority transmission rights to nodes. (See also *Ethernet*.)

Toolbar A group of rectangular graphics in a software packages user interface that represent a frequently used menu option or a command.

Top-level domain (TLD) The highest level in the Internet URL (com, org, edu, and so on).

Touch-screen monitors Monitors with touch-sensitive screens that enable users to choose from available options simply by touching the desired icon or menu item with their finger.

Tower PC A PC that includes a system unit that is designed to rest vertically. (Contrast with *laptop PC* and *desktop PC*.)

Track, disk That portion of a magnetic disk-face surface that can be accessed in any given setting of a single read/write head. Tracks are configured in concentric circles.

Track, tape That portion of a magnetic tape that can be accessed by any one of the tape drive's read/write heads. A track runs the length of the tape.

Trackball A ball mounted in a box that, when moved, results in a similar movement of the mouse pointer on a display screen.

Trackpad A point-and-draw device with no moving parts that includes a touch-sensitive pad to move the mouse pointer or cursor.

Trackpoint A point-and-draw device that functions like a miniature joystick, but is operated with the tip of the finger.

Tracks per inch (TPI) A measure of the recording density, or spacing, of tracks on a magnetic disk.

Transaction A procedural event in a system that prompts manual or computer-based activity.

Transaction file A file containing records of data activity (transactions); used to update the master file.

Transmission medium The central cable along which terminals, peripheral devices, and microcomputers are connected in a bus topology.

Transaction-oriented processing Transactions are recorded and entered as they occur.

Transparent A reference to a procedure or activity that occurs automatically and does not have to be considered by the user.

Trojan horse A virus that masquerades as a legitimate program.

TSR [Terminate-and-Stay-Resident] Programs that remain in memory so they can be instantly popped up over the current application by pressing a hotkey.

Tunneling The technology where one network uses the channels of another network to send its data.

Turnaround document A computer-produced output that is ultimately returned to a computer system as a machine-readable input.

Twisted-pair wire A pair of insulated copper wires twisted around each other for use in transmission of telephone conversations and for cabling in local area networks.

Typeface A set of characters that are of the same type style.

Unicode A 16-bit encoding system.

Uniform Resource Locator (URL) An Internet address for locating Internet elements, such as server sites, documents, files, bulletin boards (newsgroups), and so on.

Uninterruptible power source (UPS) A buffer between an external power source and a computer system that supplies clean, continuous power.

Unit testing That phase of testing in which the programs that make up an information system are tested individually.

Universal product code (UPC) A 10-digit machine-readable bar code placed on consumer products.

Universal Serial Bus (USB) A bus standard that permits up to 127 peripheral devices to be connected to an external bus.

UNIX A multiuser operating system.

Upload The transmission of data from a local computer to a remote computer.

Upstream rate The data communications rate from client computer to server computer.

Uptime That time when the computer system is in operation.

URL See *uniform resource locator*.

USB 2.0 A second generation USB standard that is 40 times faster than the original.

USB hub A device that expands the number of available USB ports.

USB port (Universal Serial Bus port) A high-speed device interface to which up to 127 peripheral devices can be daisy-chained to a single USB port. (Contrast with *SCSI port*.)

USENET A worldwide network of servers, often hosting newsgroups that can be accessed over the Internet.

User The individual providing input to the computer or using computer output.

User-friendly Pertaining to an online system that permits a person with relatively little experience to interact successfully with the system.

User ID A unique character string that is entered at logon to a network to identify the user during personal communications and to the server computer. (See also *screen name*.)

User interface A reference to the software, method, or displays that enable interaction between the user and the software being used.

User liaison A person who serves as the technical interface between the information services department and the user group.

User Location Service (ULS) Internet-based listing of Internet users who are currently online and ready to receive Internet telephone calls.

User name Same as *user ID*.

Utility software System software programs that can assist with the day-to-day chores associated with computing and maintaining a computer system.

Vaccine An antiviral program.

VDT [Video Display Terminal] A terminal on which printed and graphic information are displayed on a television-like monitor and into which data are entered on a typewriter-like keyboard.

Vector graphics A method for maintaining a screen image as patterns of lines, points, and other geometric shapes.

Vertical scroll bar A narrow screen object located along the right edge of a window that is used to navigate up and down through a document or list.

VGA [Video Graphics Array] A circuit board that enables the interfacing of very high-resolution monitors to microcomputers.

Video capture card An expansion card that enables full-motion color video with audio to be captured and played on a monitor or stored on disk.

Video display terminal See *VDT*.

Video editing The process of manipulating video images.

Video file This file contains digitized video frames that when played rapidly produce motion video.

Video for Windows Software that lets you view videos and listen to music.

Video mail (V-mail) Mail that is sent as video rather than as an electronic document.

Video operator's distress syndrome (VODS) Headaches, depression, anxiety, nausea, fatigue, and irritability that result from prolonged interaction with a terminal or PC.

Video RAM (VRAM) RAM on the graphics adapter.

Videophone An Internet-based capability that permits two parties to both see and hear one another during a conversation.

Virtual file allocation table (VFAT) Windows® method for storing and keeping track of files on a disk.

Virtual machine The processing capabilities of one computer system created through software (and sometimes hardware) in a different computer system.

Virtual marketplace A generic reference to the whole of Internet-based retailing.

Virtual private network (VPN) A private network over the Internet.

Virtual reality An artificial environment made possible by hardware and software.

Virtual world An environment that is simulated by hardware and software.

Virus A program written with malicious intent and loaded to the computer system of an unsuspecting victim. Ultimately, the program destroys or introduces errors in programs and databases.

Visual Basic A visual programming language.

Visual C++ A visual programming language.

Visual programming An approach to program development that relies more on visual association with tools and menus than with syntax-based instructions.

V-mail See *video mail*.

Voice message switching Using computers, the telephone system, and other electronic means to store and forward voice messages. (Contrast with *electronic mail*.)

Voice-response system A device that enables output from a computer system in the form of user-recorded words, phrases, music, alarms, and so on.

Volatile memory Solid-state semiconductor RAM in which the data are lost when the electrical current is turned off or interrupted. (Contrast with *nonvolatile memory*.)

VPN See *virtual private network*.

WAN See *wide area network*.

Wand scanner A handheld OCR scanner.

Wave file A Windows sound file.

Wearable display A display that is worn on a wireless headset.

Wearable PC   A small personal computer that is worn.

Web   See *World Wide Web*.

Web hosting company   A company which maintains a network of interconnected Web servers for the Web sites.

Web page   A document on the Web that is identified by a unique URL.

Web page design software   A Web site authoring system.

Web presence providers   A company that hosts individual and corporate Web site on their Internet server for a fee.

Webcam   A digital video camera that sends still and video imagery over the Internet.

Webcast   The broadcasting of real-time audio and/or video streams over the Internet.

Webmaster   An individual who manages a Web site.

Wheel mouse   A mouse with a "wheel" to facilitate scrolling.

Whiteboarding   An area on a display screen that permits a document or image to be viewed and worked on simultaneously by several users on the network.

Wide area network (WAN)   A computer network that connects nodes in widely dispersed geographic areas. (Contrast with *local area network*.)

Wi-Fi   See *IEEE 802.11b*.

Window   A rectangular section of a display screen that is dedicated to a specific document, activity, or application.

Windows®   A generic reference to all Microsoft Windows operating system products.

Windows .Net Server   A server-side Microsoft operating system.

Windows® 2000   A 32-bit operating system by Microsoft Corporation (successor to Windows NT).

Windows® 2000 Server   The server-side portion of the Windows 2000 operating system.

Windows® 95   An operating system by Microsoft Corporation.

Windows® 98   An operating system by Microsoft Corporation (the successor to Windows 95).

Windows® application   An application that conforms to the Windows standards for software and operates under the Microsoft Windows platform.

Windows® CE   A Microsoft operating system whose GUI is similar to that for Windows 9x operating systems, designed to run on handheld PCs, PDAs, and other small computers.

Windows Me (Millennium Edition)   A consumer-oriented operating system by Microsoft Corporation (the successor to Windows 98).

Windows® NT   A 32-bit operating system by Microsoft Corporation.

Windows® terminal   An intelligent terminal that can run Windows operating systems, but is not designed for stand-alone operation.

Windows XP   An 32-bit operating system by Microsoft Corporation (successor to Windows 2000).

Windows XP 64-Bit Edition   A 64-bit version of Windows XP.

Windows XP Home Edition   The client-side operating system for home and small business.

Windows XP Professional Edition   The client-side operating system for businesses.

Wintel PC   A personal computer using a Microsoft Windows® operating system in conjunction with an Intel® or Intel-compatible processor.

Wireless LAN PC card   A device to enable a wireless link between a PC and a LAN.

Wireless transceiver   Short for *transmitter-receiver*, a device that both transmits and receives data via high-frequency radio waves.

Wizard   A utility within an application that helps you use the application to perform a particular task.

WMF (Windows metafile)   A popular format for metafiles.

Word   (1) For a given computer, an established number of bits that are handled as a unit. (2) Word processing component of Microsoft Office.

Word processing software   Software that uses the computer to enter, store, manipulate, and print text.

Workgroup computing   Computer applications that involve cooperation among people linked by a computer network. (Related to *groupware*.)

Workspace   The area in a window below the title bar or menu bar containing everything that relates to the application noted in the title bar.

Workstation   A high-performance single-user computer system with sophisticated input/output devices that can be easily networked with other workstations or computers.

World Wide Web (the Web, WWW, W3)   An Internet server that offers multimedia and hypertext links.

Worm   A virus that invades computers via e-mail and IRC.

WORM disk   [Write-Once Read-Many disk] An optical laser disc that can be read many times after the data are written to it, but the data cannot be changed or erased.

WORM disk cartridge   The medium for WORM disk drives.

Write   To record data on the output medium of a particular I/O device (tape, hard copy, PC display). (Contrast with *read*.)

WYSIWYG   [What You See Is What You Get] A software package in which what is displayed on the screen is very similar in appearance to what you get when the document is printed.

X terminal   A terminal that enables the user to interact via a graphical user interface (GUI).

XHTML   The new standard for Web page development, replacing HTML.

Yahoo   An Internet portal.

Year 2000 problem (Y2K)   An information systems problem brought on by the fact that many legacy information systems still treat the year field as two digits (98) rather than four (1998).

Zip disk   The storage medium for Zip drives. (Contrast with *HiFD disk* and *SuperDisk*.)

Zip drive   A storage device that uses optical technology together with magnetic technology to read and write to an interchangeable floppy-size 100, 250, or 750 MB Zip disks.

Zip file   A popular file compression format.

Zoned recording   Disk recording scheme where zones contain a greater number of sectors per track as you move from the innermost zone to the outermost zone.

Zoom   An integrated software command that expands a window to fill the entire screen.

INDEX

Discourse and Context in Language Teaching

A Guide for Language Teachers

Marianne Celce-Murcia

Elite Olshtain

CAMBRIDGE
UNIVERSITY PRESS

PUBLISHED BY THE PRESS SYNDICATE OF THE UNIVERSITY OF CAMBRIDGE
The Pitt Building, Trumpington Street, Cambridge, United Kingdom

CAMBRIDGE UNIVERSITY PRESS
The Edinburgh Building, Cambridge CB2 2RU, United Kingdom
40 West 20th Street, New York, NY 10011-4211, USA
10 Stamford Road, Oakleigh, VIC 3166, Australia
Ruiz de Alarcón 13, 28014 Madrid, Spain
Dock House, The Waterfront, Cape Town 8001, South Africa

http://www.cambridge.org

First published 2000

Printed in the United States of America

Typeface Times 10/12 pt.   *System* QuarkXPress®

Library of Congress Cataloging-in-Publication Data

Celce-Murcia, Marianne.
Discourse and context in language teaching / by Marianne Celce-Murcia
and Elite Olshtain.
p. cm.
Includes bibliographical references and index.
ISBN 0-521-64055-5 (hb) – ISBN 0-521-64837-8 (pb)
1. Language and languages – Study and teaching. 2. Discourse analysis. 3. Pragmatics.
I. Olshtain, Elite. II. Title.
P53 .C38 2000
418'.0071–dc21
                                                          00-031155
                                                          CIP

A catalogue record for this book is available from the British Library

ISBN 0-521-64055-5   hardback
ISBN 0-521-64837-8   paperback

Book design: Edward Smith Design, Inc.
Text composition: Dewey Publishing Services
Illustrations: Suffolk Technical Illustrators, Inc., V. G. Myers

TABLE OF CONTENTS

ACKNOWLEDGMENTS

This book began as a collaborative project at the TESOL Conference held in San Antonio, Texas, in 1989. It was there that we decided to begin working together toward the completion of a teachers' handbook that focused on the role of discourse in language teaching. We both had several other projects in progress, so the present text unfolded slowly and in many ways has benefited from our evolving thoughts on the topic over time.

We owe an enormous debt to our colleague Elana Shohamy, who had faith in our project and drafted Chapter 11 (Assessment) at our invitation. We asked Elana to do this because we know that she has far greater expertise than we do on the role of discourse in assessment. Many, many thanks, Elana.

We are deeply indebted to Carleen Curley and Joe Plummer for their expert assistance with the word processing of the manuscript. We also thank Sun Young (Sunny) Oh for her capable work on the glossary and Namhee Han and Amy Seo for their dedicated assistance with compiling the references.

Thanks are also due to our graduate students, who served as "guinea pigs" when these materials were piloted at UCLA in Spring 1997 and Fall 1999 and at Hebrew University in Spring 1998. Professor Sung-Ock Sohn audited the Spring 1997 class at UCLA and gave us many insightful comments.

To Miriam Eisenstein-Ebsworth and Henry Widdowson – as well as several anonymous reviewers of the manuscript who gave us feedback and comments at various stages of its development – we offer sincere thanks. We have not incorporated all of their suggestions and we are certain they disagree with aspects of the final version; nonetheless, we wish to express genuine gratitude for their feedback since we have found it invaluable in our revision process. Thanks also to Evelyn Hatch, who read and gave us feedback on portions of the manuscript. Needless to say, we are solely responsible for any errors and omissions remaining in the text.

This handbook is our collaborative work; however, we have benefited from previous collaborations with other colleagues who have influenced this work. In this regard, Marianne Celce-Murcia would like to acknowledge by name Diane Larsen-Freeman, Sharon Hilles, Donna Brinton, and Janet Goodwin.

We also thank the fine professionals in the New York office of Cambridge University Press who helped us with this project from acquisition through production: Mary Vaughn, Debbie Goldblatt, and Mary Carson, as well as Tünde A. Dewey of Dewey Publishing Services.

Last but not least, we lovingly acknowledge our husbands, Daniel and Zeev, who have supported our efforts on this project and have unselfishly given us the time we needed to complete it.

CREDITS

PART I

BACKGROUND

CHAPTER 1

Introduction to Discourse Analysis

"The analysis of discourse is, necessarily, the analysis of language in use. As such, it cannot be restricted to the description of linguistic forms independent of the purposes or functions which those forms are designed to serve in human affairs."

(Brown and Yule, 1983:1)

" . . . one must learn more than just the pronunciation, the lexical items, the appropriate word order, . . . one must also learn the appropriate way to use those words and sentences in the second language."

(Gass and Selinker, 1994:182)

INTRODUCTION

This chapter and the next one provide a foundation for the framework we present in this book – a framework in which both discourse and context are crucial to effective language teaching. Chapter 1 deals with **discourse,** which refers primarily to the language forms that are produced and interpreted as people communicate with each other. Chapter 2 deals with **pragmatics** (i.e., context and its various features), which deals primarily with the social, cultural, and physical aspects of the situations that shape how people communicate with each other. Another way of looking at this distinction is to say that Chapter 1 deals primarily with textual aspects of messages whereas Chapter 2 deals primarily with the situational aspects of messages.

Sometimes it is hard to draw the line between text and context since the same forms may be used to signal important information in either domain. A good example of this is the referential use of demonstratives in English (e.g., *this, that*). Consider the following examples:

1. Child (pointing at food on the plate in front of him): *What's this?*
2. *Claude thinks we should postpone the picnic. What do you think of this?*

In the first example, the referent of *this* is the food on the child's plate. The referent is clear because the child is physically pointing to what he is talking about. We call this situational (or deictic) reference, which is part of context. In the second example, the referent of *this* is an idea previously mentioned in the ongoing discourse "we should postpone the picnic." We refer to this type of reference as textual (or anaphoric) reference because we find the referent in the prior text.

In addition, pragmatic analysis would take language variation in use into account. For instance, in the first example the speaker is a child talking at home, a circumstance under which the question "What's this?" is appropriate. An adult guest invited to dinner would not ask the question this way since it might be insulting to the host, so the guest might instead say something like: "What's this new dish you're serving?" In addition to interlocutor-related factors such as age and social relationship, communicative factors such as politeness and appropriacy are also relevant to pragmatic analysis and need to be part of one's overall communicative competence. Language teaching, therefore, must be concerned with how both the discourse itself and the overall context contribute to communication.

HUMAN COMMUNICATION

Human communication fulfills many different goals at the personal and social levels. We communicate information, ideas, beliefs, emotions, and attitudes to one another in our daily interactions, and we construct and maintain our positions within various social contexts by employing appropriate language forms and performing speech activities to ensure solidarity, harmony, and cooperation – or to express disagreement or displeasure, when called for. The acquisition of communication skills in one's first language is a lifelong process, but the basic skills are acquired quite early in life. When learning another language, we have to add to, change, and readjust our native language strategies to fit the new language and culture.

Whether we teach "language for communication" or "language as communication" (Widdowson, 1984:215), it is imperative that we combine knowledge of the target language with skills and strategies that enable us to use the language effectively and appropriately in various social and cultural contexts. This book is intended to help teachers develop frameworks of knowledge and decision-making processes that take recent thinking in discourse analysis into account (from both the linguistic and sociocultural perspectives).

We have written this book to provide language teachers with a discourse perspective on the language areas they are traditionally prepared to teach: pronunciation, grammar, and vocabulary. These areas are indeed the resources of any language and must be part of a language teacher's knowledge. However, when language is used for communication, these areas are resources for creating and interpreting discourse in context, not language systems to be taught or learned out of context for their own sake.

When language is used for communication, the coparticipants typically employ one or more skills simultaneously: listening, reading, speaking, or writing. They often switch quickly from one role and skill to another (e.g., from listening to speaking and back to listening again), or they are engaged in a task that involves carrying out several skills simultaneously (e.g., listening and note taking/writing). The language produced interactively by such coparticipants is discourse (i.e., language in use). We thus agree with Cook (1989), who claims that discourse analysis is useful for drawing attention to the language skills (i.e., listening, reading, speaking, writing), which put users' knowledge of phonological, grammatical, and lexical resources into action whenever language users achieve successful communication.

WHAT IS DISCOURSE?

There are two types of definitions traditionally given for the term "discourse." Formal definitions typically characterize discourse as a unit of coherent language consisting of more than one sentence; functional definitions characterize discourse as language in use (Schiffrin, 1994). Taken alone, both of these definitions are deficient. A piece of discourse in context can consist of as little as one or two words, as in "Stop" or "No Smoking." Alternatively, a piece of discourse can consist of hundreds of thousands of words as in the case of a very long novel. Usually, a piece of discourse falls somewhere in between these two extremes. The notion of "sentence" is not always relevant – especially when we consider spoken discourse. Likewise, the phrase "language in use" is so general that it can be almost meaningless. It presupposes that we know what "language" consists of and that a piece of discourse is an instance of putting elements of language to use.

The most satisfying definition of discourse is one that combines these two perspectives: A piece of discourse is an instance of spoken or written language that has describable internal relationships of form and meaning (e.g., words, structures, cohesion) that relate coherently to an external communicative function or purpose and a given audience/interlocutor. Furthermore, the external function or purpose can only be properly determined if one takes into account the context and participants (i.e., all the relevant situational, social, and cultural factors) in which the piece of discourse occurs. Using a language entails the ability to both interpret and produce discourse in context in spoken and written communicative interaction, which is why we assign such a central role to discourse in our discussion of frameworks that should inform language teaching.

WHAT IS DISCOURSE ANALYSIS?

Discourse analysis is minimally the study of language in use that extends beyond sentence boundaries. It started to attract attention from a variety of disciplines in the late 1960s and through the 1970s. At least two terms came to be used in parallel fashion: **text linguistics**, which focused on written texts from a variety of fields and genres, and **discourse analysis**, which entailed a more cognitive and social perspective on language use and communication exchanges and which included spoken as well as written discourse.

Although today discourse analysis can be considered a well-defined discipline on its own, it is closely linked with a number of other disciplines and could, in fact, serve as an umbrella term for a variety of approaches. Ethnography of communication, from the sociological or anthropological point of view, for instance, is language analysis of communicative behavior and of its role within given social contexts. Within linguistics, discourse analysis has taken at least two different paths: one is the extension of grammatical analysis to include functional objectives and the other is the study of institutionalized language use within specific cultural settings (Bhatia, 1993:3–4). The former, which is theoretical in nature, can often be related to a particular school of linguistic analysis such as formal linguistics (e.g., van Dijk's text linguistics) or systemic linguistics (e.g., Bhatia's genre analysis); the latter is more concerned with describing actual communication within institutionalized contexts (e.g., doctor-patient interaction, legal contracts).[1] More general discourse analysis investigates everyday conversation, written discourse of all types, narrative, and other kinds of written or spoken texts. In this book, we have adopted Östman and Virtanen's (1995) position on discourse analysis, which is to regard it "as an umbrella-term for all issues that have been dealt with in the linguistic study of text and discourse."[2]

Another important aspect of discourse analysis is that of application. Thus, many discourse studies have been motivated by concern with language teaching, with speech analysis, with the writing or reading process, and with genre and register analyses. It is these different types of **applied discourse analysis** that are most relevant to the aims of this book and will therefore be addressed in subsequent chapters. It is also these different types of applied discourse analysis that have led to a general movement within language pedagogy, which moves from focus on **grammar** to concern with **discourse** and also moves away from language analysis, as the goal of language teaching, to the goal of teaching language for communication. The present book is designed to help the teacher make this transition.

It is not our purpose here to survey comprehensively all the various approaches to discourse analysis; however, the number of different approaches that scholars are currently pursuing explains in part the amorphous nature of discourse analysis today. This makes it difficult for us to define discourse analysis with precision. However, we will illustrate and make reference to different types of discourse analysis in the chapters that follow. These examples and our discussions of them will give the reader an evolving sense of what discourse analysis is. We see no problem with this approach, given that discourse analysis is currently a developing area in linguistics and related disciplines (anthropology, sociology, psychology, and philosophy). This is why we believe we should work with a fluid and contingent definition of discourse analysis.

TYPES OF DISCOURSE

There are many different ways to classify discourse. One dimension is the written/spoken distinction resulting in *written* or *spoken* texts. Both types of text can be further distinguished according to **register** (level of formality) or **genre** (communicative purpose, audience, and conventionalized style and format). Also, some discourse is largely *monologic* (where one speaker or writer produces an entire discourse with little or no interaction) while other discourse is *dialogic* or *multiparty* in nature (where two or more participants interact and – to varying degrees – construct the discourse together).

The distinction made between speech and writing is often referred to as **channel** (Hymes, 1968) or **medium**, due to the fact that a different physiological process is involved in each. Yet it is clear that we can have written language that is intended to be spoken and spoken language that is designed to be read (or which was first spoken and then written down). These distinctions further interact with register and genre as can be seen in Table 1.

Table1. The Oral-literacy Continuum		
CHANNEL / LITERACY	SPOKEN	WRITTEN
orate	e.g., conversation	e.g., informal letters, drama, poetry
literate	e.g., lectures, sermons, speeches	e.g., expository essays, articles

Discourse can also be either *planned* or *unplanned* (Ochs, 1979). Unplanned discourse includes most conversations and some written texts such as informal notes and letters. Planned discourse includes prepared speeches or sermons in oral discourse and carefully edited or published written work. The dimension of discourse planning could be added to the features of Table 1.

Most everyday interactions, whether written (e.g., notes, shopping lists, ads, etc.) or spoken, take place in familiar situations. The interlocutors rely heavily on social convention and contextual information. This type of discourse is considered context-embedded and is probably most relevant to the orate/spoken and some orate/written types of discourse. On the other hand, most instances of written discourse and some examples of spoken discourse are removed from the immediate physical context and handle their topic(s) at a more abstract and conceptual level. This type of discourse is context-reduced, and users of such discourse need to rely more heavily on their knowledge of the language code and genre types because the context is partly unfamiliar, less immediate, and less accessible. This type of discourse is characteristic of literate spoken and written texts. Often planned discourse is context-reduced while unplanned discourse is context-embedded. Educated, proficient language users are able to use with flexibility and appropriacy both planned and unplanned and context-embedded and context-reduced discourse.

Discourse has also been described as **transactional** versus **interactional** (Brown and Yule, 1983), where transactional discourse involves primarily the transmission of information or the exchange of goods and services, and interactional discourse is those instances of language use that shape and maintain social relations and identities and express the speaker's/writer's attitude toward the topic or toward the interlocutor(s). In this book we treat both transactional discourse, where the management of new and old information is often salient, and interactional discourse, where the turn-taking system of the target language and the realization patterns of its speech acts and stance markers can be crucial.

With the exception of spoken versus written discourse, most of these different discourse types represent continua rather than hard and fast dichotomies. For example, a conversation where one speaker dominates can be somewhat monologic, and a letter to a friend can exhibit both interactional and transactional features. A proficient language user develops the knowledge and the skill to manipulate the different types and purposes of discourse according to his/her needs. This entails knowledge of language, of discourse, of writing and speaking conventions, of sociocultural norms as well as other more specific areas of knowledge. The various chapters in this book address many of these knowledge types.

REGISTER AND GENRE IN DISCOURSE ANALYSIS

Discourse is frequently studied from the perspective of register or genre. Discourse registers usually reflect the level of formality or informality of an instance of discourse or its degree of technical specificity versus general usage. A genre, on the other hand, is a culturally and linguistically distinct form of discourse such as narrative (e.g., a story), exposition (e.g., a research report), procedural discourse (e.g., a recipe), and so on.[3]

According to Swales (1981, 1985, 1990) and Bhatia (1993), "a genre is a recognizable communicative event characterized by a set of communicative purpose(s) identified and mutually understood by the members of the professional or academic community in which it regularly occurs" (Bhatia, 1993:13). Both authors emphasize the communicative purpose of the text as the most important feature related to genre. It is this communicative purpose that shapes the genre and gives it internal structure.

Register, as already mentioned, reflects the degree of formality of the particular text by using a characteristic set of lexical and grammatical features that are compatible with the particular register. A lower register is represented by the use of more colloquial (orate) and everyday-type vocabulary and fewer complex grammatical forms while a higher register requires the use of lexical items that are professional or academic in nature along with denser grammatical structures, resulting in a more literate spoken or written text.

FIELDS OF STUDY WITHIN DISCOURSE ANALYSIS

A number of research areas within discourse analysis have received particular attention and have become significant areas of investigation in their own right. With respect to considerations relevant to language teaching, we will briefly discuss five such areas: cohesion, coherence, information structure and conversation analysis (with focus on turn-taking), and critical discourse analysis.

COHESION

The use of various cohesive ties to explicitly link together all the propositions in a text results in **cohesion** of that text. The most obvious structural features of such connected discourse are the cohesive ties identified and discussed by Halliday and Hasan (1976, 1989). There are four types of grammatical ties (reference, ellipsis, substitution, and conjunction) as well as a variety of lexical ties, which we discuss in greater detail in Chapters 4 and 5. The following brief text exhibits synonymous repetition as one textual feature of cohesion that creates *lexical ties*:

> Natural beauty plays a starring role in Santa Monica, and seaside is the perfect vantage from which to watch the performance. Early risers will notice that the show begins just after sunrise.
>
> (*Santa Monica Official Visitors Guide,* 1998:18)

In this text the same event is referred to with three different noun phrases: "a starring role" (first mention; new information; use of an indefinite article); "the performance" (the use of the definite article indicates anaphoric reference to an earlier mention, and the semantic information relates this lexical item to "starring role"); and "the show" (the third reference made to the same event, which functions here as a synonym for "the performance"). This example may seem to display a complicated system of lexical ties and reference, but such lexical connections are very common in English writing.

In the following excerpt from a letter written by a mother asking for advice on dealing with pre-teens, there are some examples of *grammatical cohesive ties*:

> I am a working mother with two pre-teens. After dropping them off at school, I have to get right to work. But my children are disorganized and always late. A few times, I have had to turn around and go back home because one or the other forgot something.
>
> (*Children-LA's Best Calendar of Family Events,* July 1998:12)

The use of the pronoun *them* in the first line is an anaphoric reference to "two pre-teens." The conjunction *but,* which begins the second sentence, expresses the counter-expectation arising from the second and third sentences. The phrase "always late" is an elliptical form of the clause "they are always late" and the phrase *one or the other* is a good example of ellipsis at the noun phrase level meaning "one child or the other child." Had the writer produced *the other one* instead of *the other* we would also have had an example of substitution in this text, *one* would have substituted for *child* (somewhat awkwardly in this context). Of course, there is also lexical cohesion in this text, most obviously in the repetition of *working* and *work* in lines 1 and 2; *children* refers back to *pre-teens* and also relates more indirectly to *mother*. The words *school* and *home* are semantically related items as are *disorganized* and *forgot something*. The cohesion of the text is a result of all these cohesive ties, which link together the words and propositions occurring in the text.

COHERENCE

In addition to cohesion, which is expressed via language resources, or **bottom-up** connections in text, effective discourse also requires **coherence**, which can be viewed as part of **top-down** planning and organization. Coherence contributes to the unity of a piece of discourse such that the individual sentences or utterances hang together and relate to each other. This unity and relatedness is partially a result of a recognizable organizational pattern for the propositions and ideas in the passage, but it also depends on the presence of linguistic devices that strengthen global unity and create local connectedness. Recognizable patterns may include those based on temporal or spatial relations or those based on semantically associated relations such as problem-solution or cause-effect. Coherence may also depend in part on patterns and strategies of text development that are very culture specific.

While the overall coherence of a longer passage depends on the presence of a conventional scheme or organization that is recognizable as generic or specific to a particular communicative purpose and discourse community, the overall coherence of such a passage also depends on the degree of coherence within each paragraph or section of the text. Each sentence or utterance is related both to the previous and following sentences in ways that lead the reader toward an easier and more effective interpretation of the text.

The notion of coherence applies to all four chapters in Part III of this handbook since the ability to use top-down information and strategies to interpret discourse (when listening or reading) or to produce discourse (when writing or speaking) assumes an understanding of the discourse community's assumptions – as well as a degree of control over its language conventions. These are some of the things that constitute coherence in the target discourse community. We shall be discussing more factors contributing to coherence later in Chapters 7 (Reading) and 8 (Writing).

INFORMATION STRUCTURE

The major concern of the area of discourse analysis referred to as **information structure** is the presentation of "old" (known) information versus "new" (unknown) information. Languages use grammatical and discourse features in order to indicate which bits of information are known and which are new. European researchers often use the terms **theme** and **rheme**, while in North America **topic** and **comment** are more common. It seems that the basic principle for information structure is that *themes/topics* (*old information*) generally precede *rhemes/comments* (*new information*) in order of presentation.

In spoken discourse, old or given information is frequently recoverable from the situation. In written discourse, grammatical and discourse features play an important role in making this distinction (the use of determiners, pronouns, word order in the sentence). Propositions within a larger piece of discourse also involve more local considerations of "well formedness." According to Bardovi-Harlig (1990), a sentence within a passage functions at three levels: the syntactic, the semantic, and the pragmatic. In order to understand her definitions, we need to better understand the terms "topic" and "comment."

A topic is a discourse entity that connects one part of the discourse to other parts through continuity in given information (i.e., old or known information) that runs through the entire discourse and helps us understand what is being discussed. Thus, if there is a main character in the passage and most of the sentences are about that person, the identification of the main character will be known information and various grammatical and lexical devices will be used to connect the sentences through references to the main character, such as in the following text about Rona:

> Rona was the youngest of three sisters. <u>She</u> liked music and literature.
> Being <u>the youngest sister</u> was in some ways a blessing and in others
> a curse. . . .

In this example all noninitial references to Rona point back to her initial mention and link the topic of subsequent sentences in the discourse back to the initial mention.

The comment, on the other hand, is what is said about the topic and that is generally new or added information. In each sentence of the example some additional information is added in the comment, developing the discourse according to the writer's intention. In the text "being the youngest of three sisters" and "liking music and literature" are comments about Rona. The terms "topic" and "comment" relate to the textual function of managing new information (comments) and old information (topics). Ties of grammatical and lexical cohesion often provide the glue needed for such information management.

In the example about Rona, the topic of the text is also the subject of the first sentence, so its initial position is part of the normal (or unmarked) rules of English grammar. However, as we shall discuss in more detail in Chapters 4 (Grammar) and 8 (Writing), special grammatical constructions may be used to bring forward elements that would not be found in initial position in the usual discourse sequence. The passage might have continued as follows:

> For example, there was less responsibility involved in being the
> youngest. The most important tasks were assigned to Rona's
> older sisters.

Here the grammatical subject "there" follows an introductory conjunctive tie ("for example") and allows new information ("less responsibility") to function as the marked topic of the first new sentence while the noun phrase "the most important tasks" is both the subject and topic of the next sentence, amplifying on "less responsibility." "Rona" has temporarily become part of the two comments (involved in being the youngest/were assigned to Rona's sisters) for a stretch of discourse before she once again has the potential to become the topic.

Thus understanding how information is managed at the local level can help contribute to coherence at the global level. The three subfields of discourse analysis presented here were chosen to illustrate textual features of discourse that are relevant to language teaching. The next subfield to be discussed here is relevant to conversational exchanges, and the last describes a special subfield dedicated to exposing social inequality in language.

TURN-TAKING IN CONVERSATION ANALYSIS

In conversation, in addition to managing new and old information in a coherent way, the interlocutors also have to take stock of and constantly monitor each other to control the **turn-taking** system of the target language in question since this is another feature of discourse in oral interaction. The conversational turn-taking system (Sacks, Schegloff, and Jefferson, 1974) of any language includes conventions governing matters such as the following: how conversations open and close, who speaks when and for how long, who can interrupt (and how this is done), how topics get changed, how much time can elapse between turns or between speakers, whether or not speakers can overlap, and whether or not speakers can complete or repair each other's utterances. There are often important cultural (and subcultural) differences in the way discourse communities do turn-taking. A lack of understanding of these differences can cause problems in cross-cultural communication.

One important source of organization in the turn-taking system is the "adjacency pair," where the first speaker says something that conventionally requires of the interlocutor a response that is often partly predictable. Thus a typical adjacency pair for a conventional greeting to open a conversation in English might be:

    1: Hello, how are you?
    2: Fine, thanks.

Other adjacency pairs often have at least two conventional options. If the first part of the pair is an invitation, the second part can be an acceptance or a refusal. If the first part of the pair is a request for confirmation, the second part can confirm or disconfirm:

    1: You're from Manchester?
    2: Yes. / No, Liverpool.

In any given speech community such adjacency pairs can have highly conventionalized and formulaic phrases associated with them. Needless to say, mastering these conventions and phrases in a second language will contribute greatly to oral fluency and communicative competence. We shall have more to say about this in Chapter 9 (Speaking).

CRITICAL DISCOURSE ANALYSIS

The primary interest of **critical discourse analysis** is to deconstruct and expose social inequality as expressed, constituted, and legitimized through language use – notably in the public media such as newspapers, radio, television, films, cartoons, and the like, but also in settings such as classrooms, courtrooms, news interviews, doctor-patient interactions, as well as in everyday talk. Critical discourse analysts believe that discourse tends to become normative with repeated use and thus appears to be neutral; however, in actual fact, discourse is never neutral. It must thus be analyzed in terms of the political ideology, social history, and power structures that it embodies and expresses, explicitly or indirectly. The research of critical discourse analysts often takes on a problem-posing/problem-solving quality and addresses discriminatory use of language directed at women, lower socioeconomic classes, members of ethnic, racial, religious, and linguistic minorities, and others. Critical discourse analysts also may suggest remedies in the form of nondiscriminatory behaviors and language practices that could replace the problematic discourse. Some critical discourse analysts who are well known to language educators are Fairclough (1995), Pennycook (1995), and Phillipson (1992).

Many critical discourse analysts believe that education in general and foreign and second language education in particular are ideological and political, but that most language teachers are unaware of this. They argue that discourse in the language classroom as well as the discourse of language textbooks and teaching materials are all in need of critical examination to ensure that discourse that is discriminatory and that reinforces social inequality be avoided to the extent that this is possible, or – at the very least – explicitly and critically discussed if it comes up.

In our experience, language teachers who are exposed to the writings and ideas of critical discourse analysts tend either to relate strongly to this theoretical and analytical approach or to be quite put off by it since it represents a sociopolitical (or ideological) perspective on language and education. We believe it is important that teachers understand what critical discourse analysis is and that they are at the very least sensitized to the potentially discriminatory and demeaning discourse that may arise in the classroom and in teaching materials and be prepared to deal with it constructively (i.e., to use such instances of discourse as opportunities for discussions and activities that can make the language classroom a more democratic and open discourse community). Above all, language teachers should be sensitive to and aware of potential reactions to what they say in class – potential reactions from the whole group or from individual students – as well as reactions to what they write on student papers. It may be useful for teachers to ask themselves if a critical discourse analyst might find anything they have said or written to be problematic or offensive.

WHAT IS CONTEXT?

The term **context** in discourse analysis refers to all the factors and elements that are nonlinguistic and nontextual but which affect spoken or written communicative interaction. Halliday (1991:5) describes context as "the events that are going on around when people speak (and write)." As mentioned previously, discourse may depend primarily on contextual features found in the immediate environment and be referred to as **context-embedded**; or it may be relatively independent of context (**context-reduced** or **decontextualized**) and depend more on the features of the linguistic code and the forms of the discourse itself.

Context entails the situation within which the communicative interaction takes place. Discourse analysis of context entails the linguistic and cognitive choices made relevant to the interaction at hand. In contrast, pragmatic analysis of context and contextual description relates to the participants taking part in the interaction, the sociocultural background that is relevant, and any physical-situational elements that may have some bearing on the exchange. Human communication relies quite heavily on context and on the *shared knowledge* that the interactants have with respect to a variety of contextual features. These issues are dealt with in Chapter 2.

SHARED KNOWLEDGE

In a communicative exchange both interactants rely on their prior knowledge, which may or may not be shared. Shared knowledge is perhaps most important for everyday communicative exchanges. When such exchanges take place between participants who are familiar with each other, they rely on their shared knowledge. Thus, in the following exchange between husband and wife the discourse is meaningful to both because they share knowledge on which the exchange is based:

> **Wife:** The reception is in the garden. (implies that it will be cool)
> **Husband:** I'm wearing the brown jacket. (implies that he has taken
> the proper precautions)

An outsider may not necessarily get the implied meanings from simply listening to the exchange. When a communicative exchange occurs among strangers, the physical environment often supplies the contextual factors that may be necessary, such as in the following exchange at an airport:

> **Traveler:** I am looking for my bags; I just got off this flight.
> **Attendant:** Baggage Claim is one flight down. You can take the elevator.

For discourse where context is not readily available (written text or formal speeches), those interpreting the discourse have to rely more heavily on the text itself and on their prior knowledge. Relevant prior knowledge can create the appropriate context within which it is possible to understand and properly interpret the discourse.

In the language classroom, context-reduced discourse is not always presented to students along with the background they need to be able to interpret it. Thus, let us imagine that in an English-as-a-foreign-language classroom, somewhere in a non-English-speaking country, the teacher introduces the "Gettysburg Address" as a reading passage. If the students are not familiar with the history of the United States and with the background of the Civil War, and the conditions under which President Lincoln delivered this speech, they will have a difficult time understanding the text. A great deal of background knowledge is needed in order to create the global context within which the text can be understood. Some sections of this book will address the need to create a meaningful context within the language classroom so that (a) difficult texts can be properly interpreted and (b) students can learn and become enriched by the content and information that they encounter, thus enabling real communication to take place.

Contextualized and interactive uses of language can be acquired relatively quickly (two to three years) given the right type of language instruction and/or the right learning environment; however, mastering decontextualized and impersonal forms of language along with related literacy skills requires a much higher level of proficiency in the target language and normally takes at least five to seven years even under the best of conditions (Cummins, 1979; Collier, 1989). School literacy requires learners to use language in such decontextualized situations, and second language learners often encounter difficulties in general scholastic performance due to a lack of the appropriate type of linguistic proficiency. For more advanced language learners, it is often necessary to develop strategies for dealing with even less contextualized genres of language such as published articles, legal documents, research reports, and technical manuals.

TYPES OF CONTEXT

Duranti and Goodwin (1992) propose four types of context:

a. setting (physical and interactional)
b. behavioral environment (nonverbal and kinetic)
c. language (co-text and reflexive use of language)
d. extrasituational (social, political, cultural, and the like)

For our specific purposes, two of these types of context are particularly important, corresponding roughly to Duranti and Goodwin's (a) and (c) respectively: (1) the situational context – i.e., the purpose, the participants, and the physical and temporal setting where communication is taking place (i.e., analyzed as pragmatics) and (2) the discourse context (or co-text), the stream of prior and subsequent language in which a language segment or an exchange occurs (i.e., analyzed as discourse). For example, if someone encounters a friend and says "Hello," the person expects some sort of oral response. Or, if one hears an utterance such as "Who else was there?" one looks to prior discourse about the people present at some event in order to interpret the utterance.

In written texts we can often make sense of the message and understand the meaning thanks to the **co-text**, the language material in any particular piece of discourse. In the following passage, excerpted from the middle of an article in *Time* magazine on the National Cherry Festival in the United States, it becomes clear how important co-text is in the process of interpreting the written text:

Indeed, the victory for vendors and consumers could well be the festival's loss. The 6,000 Sara Lee slices typically sold at the festival are donated by the company, with proceeds funneled back to the festival organization.

(*Time*, July 1998:4)

In this piece of discourse, in order to understand what "victory" the writer is talking about, we need to have read the earlier sections of the article. To understand why this is the "festival's loss" we need to read on and find out that there used to be a donation (which will no longer exist) that everyone attending made to the festival organization. And if the reader does not know (from prior knowledge) who or what Sara Lee is, s/he may find out via cataphoric reference when "the company" is mentioned. All the cohesive devices and the coherence organization elements work within the wider co-text and need to be properly identified by anyone trying to interpret the meaning of the text.

THE ORGANIZATION OF THIS BOOK

In Part 1 of this book we present theoretical background information. Chapter 1 provides an introduction to discourse and discourse analysis, whereas Chapter 2 (Pragmatics in Discourse Analysis) provides further background on the importance of context and shared knowledge for appropriate production and adequate interpretation of discourse.

There are two basic frameworks that underlie the approach proposed in this book and guide its organization (i.e., *a language knowledge framework* and *a discourse processing framework*). We are using the term "knowledge" to refer to what cognitive psychologists (Anderson, 1985) call **declarative knowledge**, which refers to things such as facts, rules, and images that one is able to describe explicitly. In terms of learning a language, this type of knowledge refers to things such as knowing the grammar rules and word meanings explicitly and being able to state them. We are using the term "processing" to refer to what the same cognitive psychologists call **procedural knowledge**, which is the ability to apply complex cognitive skills automatically in appropriate ways without even thinking about them. This ability enables language users to produce and interpret written and spoken discourse effectively.

In Part 2 of this book we consider the three language resources (phonology, grammar, and vocabulary) that are part of the language knowledge framework, which we present in Figure 1.1 on the next page, and will discuss in greater detail later.

This diagram illustrates how pragmatic knowledge (see Chapter 2) overlays and influences language knowledge and how discourse draws on both language knowledge (phonology, grammar, vocabulary) and pragmatics when language users communicate, both as receivers and producers.

Depending on the type and extent of knowledge and experience a learner has, different processing strategies for interpreting and producing discourse will be activated or developed. Nonnative language users often lack the proficiency that would allow them to process easily the spoken and written discourse to which they are exposed in a second language. An important way in which they can compensate for their lack of knowledge is for them to rely heavily on contextual features and prior knowledge to process new information. This is referred to as **top-down** or **knowledge-driven** interpretation. For example, when reading a difficult article, the reader might consider where the article appeared, who wrote it, and what the title is in order to facilitate interpretation of a linguistically difficult text.

In contrast, language processing that relies heavily on linguistic features such as spelling patterns, grammatical inflections, and word choices is referred to as **bottom-up** or **data-driven** interpretation, which in some cases is facilitated by nonverbal cues

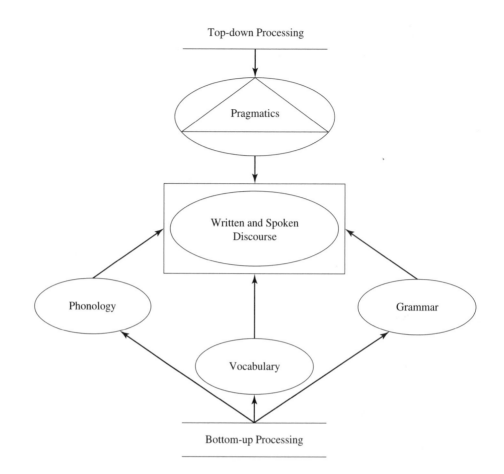

Figure 1.1 Language Knowledge Framework

such as gestures, illustrations, and so on. Effective language users are able to combine top-down and bottom-up processing in arriving at a reasonable interpretation of what the speaker/writer intended.

Figure 1.2 presents an integrated picture of the discourse processing framework. When top-down processing is activated, language users combine their **prior knowledge** (content schemata) and **sociocultural and discourse knowledge** (formal schemata) with their assessment of pragmatic and contextual features relevant to the task at hand. All these elements are channeled through pragmatic considerations in order to produce and interpret discourse. When bottom-up processing occurs, language users combine language knowledge with specific and local communication features in order to produce or interpret discourse. Sometimes top-down processing takes priority; at other times bottom-up concerns require more attention, but ideally there is purposeful integration of both types of processing. Successful discourse processing also requires **metacognitive awareness**, which enables language users to fine-tune their production/interpretation process. Ideally, discourse processing involves automatic procedural knowledge; however, in some cases, it is useful and necessary to activate nonautomatic declarative knowledge to correct errors and to resolve ambiguities or contradictions in the production or interpretation of discourse.

In Figures 1.1 and 1.2, knowledge components appear inside ovals: content knowledge, discourse knowledge, and language knowledge. Processing elements appear inside triangles: assessment of contextual features, consideration of pragmatic features, and processing strategies; metacognition is inside a diamond, and spoken or written discourse

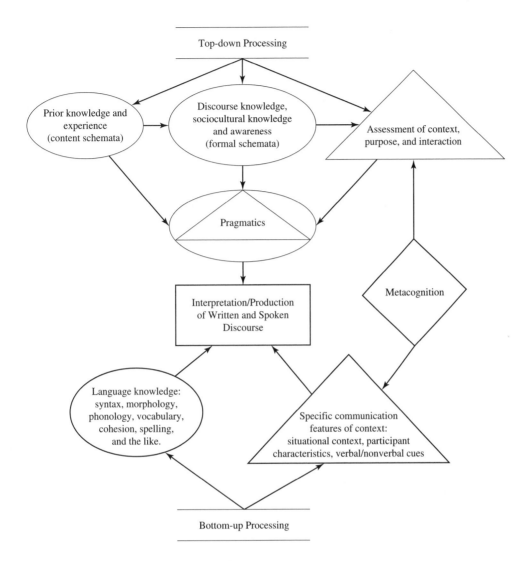

Figure 1.2 Discourse Processing Framework

(product or text) is always represented inside the central rectangular box. Discourse and pragmatics are sometimes represented with two shapes simultaneously since these two areas can reflect both knowledge and processing. Thus the term "discourse" may occur in a rectangle and/or an oval, and the term "pragmatics" may occur inside a triangle or inside an oval and a triangle simultaneously. These visual shapes will be used consistently in the specific adaptations of these two figures that we present in each chapter throughout the book.

Effective language users shift easily from one discourse processing mode to the other, depending on the requirements of the production/interpretation task. For example, the reader encountering an unfamiliar word in a text will use the word's syntactic position and morphological endings (i.e., bottom-up processing) to facilitate interpretation of the unfamiliar lexical item but will also use clues in the preceding and subsequent discourse (co-text) and the situational context (i.e., top-down processing) to arrive at an interpretation.

In Part 3 of this book we treat the four language skills (listening, reading, writing, and speaking) in terms of our discourse processing framework, which we will discuss in greater detail later.

In addition to elaborating on both the language knowledge framework and the discourse processing framework that we have introduced here, we will endeavor to make our approach to language teaching practical by suggesting throughout the text pedagogical applications that we believe are consistent with a discourse perspective on language and language teaching. The discussion questions and activities at the end of each chapter are designed to facilitate understanding and application of the approach we are proposing. The suggestions for further reading are intended to stimulate additional thinking of the topics and issues we raise.

A PEDAGOGICAL PERSPECTIVE ON COMMUNICATIVE COMPETENCE

The major goal of taking a language course is to enable students to develop **communicative competence**. The term "communicative competence" was first coined by Dell Hymes (1967, 1972) and his colleagues (anthropological linguists, sociolinguists, and functional linguists), who argued that language competence consists not only of Chomsky's (1957, 1965) grammatical competence but also of sociolinguistic or pragmatic competence, which covers all situated aspects of language use and related issues of appropriacy: the speaker (and, if different, the original author), the addressee(s), the message, the setting or event, the activity, the register, and so forth.

Hymes' term "communicative competence" was taken up by those language methodologists who contributed to the development of Communicative Language Teaching (e.g., Wilkins, 1976; Widdowson, 1978). However, a pedagogical framework based explicitly on the notion of communicative competence was first proposed by Canale and Swain (1980) and Canale (1983),[4] who argued that communicative competence could be described as consisting of at least four components:

1. Linguistic or grammatical competence, which consists of the basic elements of communication: sentence patterns, morphological inflections, lexical resources, and phonological or orthographic systems.

2. Sociolinguistic competence, which consists of the social and cultural knowledge required to use language appropriately with reference to formality, politeness, and other contextually defined choices.

3. Discourse competence, which involves the selection, sequencing, and arrangement of words, structures, and sentences/utterances to achieve a unified spoken or written whole with reference to a particular message and context.

4. Strategic competence, which includes the strategies and procedures relevant to language learning, language processing, and language production. It activates knowledge of the other competencies and helps language users compensate for gaps or deficiencies in knowledge when they communicate.

In our opinion, the core or central competency in the Canale and Swain framework is discourse competence since this is where everything else comes together: It is in discourse and through discourse that all of the other competencies are realized. And it is in discourse and through discourse that the manifestation of the other competencies can best be observed, researched, and assessed.

THE DISCOURSE APPROACH TO LANGUAGE TEACHING: NEW ROLES FOR TEACHERS, LEARNERS, AND MATERIALS

In the modern school setting and the changing learning environment with high-tech accessibility to libraries, computer networks, and other resources, the roles of teachers, learners, and materials is constantly changing. A discourse perspective on language teaching and language learning can be helpful in redefining such roles.

Teachers in the new learning settings are expected to become reflective researchers who evaluate and rethink their approaches, attitudes, and methods of presenting new subject matter to students, at every stage in the teaching/learning process. They are no longer the only decision maker in this process since learners share and become partners in the process; teachers, however, have a new and very important role to play by becoming personal mentors for individual students, coaching and guiding them to become autonomous learners.

Learners are no longer passive recipients of the teaching process. They are expected to be more independent, to make choices, and to initiate learning activities. They are expected to take responsibility for their own learning and become aware of their own strategies and tactics, using metacognition to assist them in improving their own learning endeavors. They are also often encouraged to carry out self-evaluation in order to further their learning and to develop metacognitive awareness in order to plan and regulate their language learning and language using skills. Discourse elements and routines are very important tools in helping autonomous learners to become successful.

Materials used in the learning/teaching process must allow the autonomous learner and the facilitating teacher to make choices, consider alternatives, and plan for specific needs. Only materials that are flexible enough to allow for and encourage such tactics can ensure the personal growth of both teachers and learners.

Chapter 12 addresses many of the issues we have raised here regarding the new roles of teachers, learners, and materials.

CONCLUSION

Two important influences in language teaching methodology over the past two decades have been (1) the arguments for making formal language learning as "natural" as possible (Krashen and Terrell, 1983) and (2) the importance of using "authentic" materials in the language classroom (Ur, 1984). The approach we present in this book allows for a principled response to these concerns in that language resources and discourse processing are presented in an interactive and integrated manner that encourages both principled use of authentic discourse samples and simulation of natural language processing.

In Part 1 we present the theoretical background for subsequent chapters. This chapter provides an introduction to discourse analysis, whereas Chapter 2 (Pragmatics in Discourse Analysis) provides background on the importance of context for the appropriate production and the adequate interpretation of discourse. We discuss the language resources underlying discourse knowledge in Part 2 and the language skills involved in discourse processing in Part 3. In Part 4 we treat important issues in implementation with respect to teaching language through discourse: Chapter 10 deals with curriculum development, Chapter 11 explores language assessment, and Chapter 12 treats the training of teachers and learners.

AUDIENCE AND GOALS

The audience for this book is language teachers who are interested in incorporating insights from relevant work in discourse analysis and pragmatics (i.e., how language is used in context to achieve different purposes) into their teaching. Understanding discourse should help language teachers to make decisions for classroom activities and to facilitate the learning process in the classroom. To this end, we give background and examples from many interrelated areas without claiming to be exhaustive in our coverage of discourse. The selection of the items we present is based on their suitability for demonstration purposes and pedagogical application.

The assumption underlying this book is that the communicative functions and uses of language can be best understood by focusing on and gaining an appreciation for the discourse level of language, i.e., language in use, without neglecting the linguistic resources that are used to create discourse and the language skills that are used to process discourse.

QUESTIONS FOR DISCUSSION

1. Why are both discourse analysis and pragmatics important in teaching language for communication?

2. How do top-down and bottom-up processing complement each other in interpreting and producing communicative discourse?

3. In what ways might language teachers be empowered by understanding and employing discourse as a major focus in their language teaching?

4. Why does "shared knowledge" play such a vital role in communication?

Suggestions for Further Reading

Brown, G., & Yule, G. (1983). *Discourse analysis.* Cambridge: Cambridge University Press.

Cook, G. (1989). *Discourse.* Oxford: Oxford University Press.

Nunan, D. (1993). *An introduction to discourse analysis.* Harmondsworth, England: Penguin.

Paltridge, B. (2000). *Making sense of discourse analysis.* Gold Coast, Australia: Antipodean Educational Enterprises.

Endnotes

[1] See Schiffrin (1994) for a detailed overview of various approaches to discourse analysis.

[2] Other terms that occur in the literature are *discourse linguistics, discourse studies,* or simply *discourse.*

[3] In literature reference is often made to different genres such as poetry, drama, and prose. Genres typically have subgenres (e.g., in literature, prose can be fiction or nonfiction; exposition can be divided into essays, articles, reports, briefs, and so on).

[4] Subsequent models of communicative competence have been proposed (e.g., Bachman, 1990 and Bachman and Palmer, 1996), but these are hierarchical models with discrete competencies that have been developed for doing research in language assessment rather than for pedagogical application. In terms of pedagogical applications, the Canale and Swain model has had the greatest influence. Celce-Murcia, Dörnyei, and Thurrell (1995) provide a pedagogically motivated elaboration of the Canale and Swain model.

CHAPTER 2

Pragmatics in Discourse Analysis

"Pragmatics is the study of how language is used in communication."

(Ellis, 1995:719)

"The pragmatics of language is concerned with audience-directed intention – how the speaker or writer intends the utterance to be taken."

(Olson, 1994:119)

INTRODUCTION

Traditional language analysis contrasts pragmatics with syntax and semantics (see Widdowson,1996, for a general introduction to linguistics). **Syntax** is the area of language analysis that describes relationships between linguistic forms, how they are arranged in sequence, and which sequences are well formed and therefore grammatically acceptable. Chapter 4 focuses on this type of linguistic knowledge and its relation to discourse.

Semantics is the area of language analysis that describes how meaning is encoded in the language and is therefore concerned mainly with the meaning of lexical items. Semantics is also concerned with the study of relationships between language forms and entities in real or imaginary worlds (Yule, 1996). Chapter 5 focuses on vocabulary and thus deals with some areas of semantics in relation to discourse.

Whereas formal analyses of syntax and semantics do not consider the users of the linguistic forms that they describe and analyze, **pragmatics** deals very explicitly with the study of relationships holding between linguistic forms and the human beings who use these forms. As such, pragmatics is concerned with people's intentions, assumptions, beliefs, goals, and the kinds of actions they perform while using language. Pragmatics is also concerned with contexts, situations, and settings within which such language uses occur.

A language user's **lexicogrammatical competence** is his/her knowledge of syntax and lexical semantics in the target language. In describing such competence we need to present the rules that account for the learner's **implicit formal knowledge** of grammar and vocabulary. **Pragmatic competence**, on the other hand, is a set of internalized rules of

how to use language in socioculturally appropriate ways, taking into account the participants in a communicative interaction and features of the context within which the interaction takes place.

While lexicogrammatical competence can be described in formal terms, pragmatic
competence is at present a much less formalized and structured area of inquiry. Since
pragmatics deals with human elements, it is less objective and more difficult to describe;
thus formal language analysis tends to exclude pragmatics. In recent years, however, more
attention has been directed toward pragmatic competence and even interlanguage
pragmatics for L2 learners (Blum-Kulka, et al., 1989; Kasper and Blum-Kulka, 1993),
which is the learner's developing pragmatic competence in the target language.

WHAT DOES PRAGMATICS ENTAIL?

According to Yule (1996), the area of pragmatics deals with **speaker meaning** and
contextual meaning. Speaker meaning is concerned with the analysis of what people
mean by their utterances rather than what the words and phrases in those utterances might
mean in and of themselves. Thus when a speaker says "I am hungry," the semantic meaning of this utterance is that the speaker feels pangs of hunger. Pragmatically viewed, if the
sentence is produced by a youngster who has come back from school at noon speaking to
his mother in the kitchen, it probably functions as a request for lunch. Alternatively, if it
is produced by the same youngster after having completed lunch, it could function as
a complaint expressing the opinion that there hasn't been enough food to eat for lunch, or
perhaps the child intends it as a request for a dessert. Speaker meaning, rather than sentence meaning, can only begin to be understood when context is taken into consideration.
Any utterance, therefore, can take on various meanings depending on who produced it and
under what circumstances.

Pragmatics studies the context within which an interaction occurs as well as the
intention of the language user. Who are the addressees, what is the relation between
speakers/writers and hearers/readers, when and where does the speech event occur? and
so on. Thus, the same utterance "I am hungry" when produced by a street beggar and
addressed to a passerby would be generally perceived as a request for money rather than
for food since shared knowledge – in this case – leads to this interpretation.

Pragmatics also explores how listeners and readers can make inferences about what
is said or written in order to arrive at an interpretation of the user's intended meaning.
Obviously, the emphasis in this kind of exploration must be placed not only on what is
actually said but also on what is not being said explicitly but recognized implicitly as part
of the communicative exchange, such as presupposition, implication, shared knowledge,
and circumstantial evidence.

From the above description of pragmatics, it may seem to the reader that this is
an impossible area of communicative interaction to analyze since it seems so difficult to
predict what different people might be intending. What makes human communication
possible, however, is the fact that pragmatic competence relies very heavily on conventional, culturally appropriate, and socially acceptable ways of interacting. These rules of
appropriacy result in regular and expected behaviors in language use. It is generally
understood that within a given social and cultural group, people usually know what is
expected and what is considered appropriate behavior, and this knowledge enables them
to interpret the language uses they encounter.

Furthermore, language forms are selected or preferred by interactants so as to accommodate and strengthen some of the shared and mutually perceived situational phenomena.
Two areas of language analysis that have looked at what allows the listener or reader to
make inferences based on what is said or written are **presupposition** and **implication**.

When a proposition is presupposed, it cannot be denied or called into question. For example:

> A: Isn't it odd that John didn't come?
> B: No, it's not odd at all.

In this brief exchange both speaker A and speaker B share the presupposition "John didn't come." The interlocutors in this exchange chose linguistic forms that enable them to share the presupposition. Notice that not all verbs or predicate adjectives have this property. If we change "odd" to "true," there would be no constant presupposition since the truth value of "John didn't come" changes from one syntactic environment to the next when the proposition is denied or questioned:

1. It is true that John didn't come.

2. It isn't true that John didn't come.

3. Isn't it true that John didn't come?

It is a combined knowledge of pragmatics and linguistics that enables interlocutors to be effective users of presupposition.

In the case of implication, the hearer/listener is able to make certain inferences based on what is said or written. These inferences go beyond the words themselves, yet are generally predictable from the linguistic forms chosen. For example, if someone says "Jane will support Bob. After all, she is his sister," we know that the speaker is not only giving a reason in the second clause for Jane's behavior, which is described in the first clause; through his use of the connector "after all," the speaker is also indicating that he believes both he and the listener share some obvious prior knowledge (i.e., Jane is Bob's sister). Here again we see how the choice of linguistic forms reflects the knowledge shared by the interlocutors.

From the examples given above, it seems obvious that a very important factor facilitating both spoken and written communication is shared knowledge. As we have seen, language users make linguistic decisions and choices based on certain presuppositions with respect to the situation and the participants in the communicative interaction. Such decisions are based primarily on what is perceived as shared knowledge.

Obviously, when we misjudge shared knowledge or the perceptions of the other participants in the interaction we might create an instance of miscommunication. This can happen among speakers of the same language and within the same sociocultural setting, as will become obvious from the following exchange between a university student and a clerk in a departmental office at a university in the United States; both were native speakers of English:

Woman (student):	Excuse me, where can I make some Xerox copies?
Clerk:	For?
Woman:	(silence)
Clerk:	Are you an instructor?
Woman:	No, a student.
Clerk:	We can only make Xerox copies for instructors.
Woman:	Well, I . . . OK. But where can I find a [pay] Xerox machine? (the original intention)
Clerk:	Oh, I see. Up the stairs, past the bookstore.

In the above exchange[1] there was obviously a breakdown in communication since the first utterance, which was an information question, was misunderstood by the clerk as a request; the clerk then applied to this situation nonrelevant prior knowledge that was unshared by the student.

In exchanges that take place between language users from different social or cultural groups or different linguistic groups, miscommunication can result from lack of shared knowledge of the world and of the appropriate target behavior. In our attempt to lead the L2 learner to communicative competence, which goes far beyond linguistic competence, pragmatics must be taken into account. While developing knowledge and understanding of how the new language works, the learner must also develop awareness and sensitivity to sociocultural patterns of behavior. It is only skillfully combined linguistic and pragmatic knowledge that can lead to communicative competence in the second language.

COOPERATION AND IMPLICATURE

Human communication is based on the fact that, as a rule, human beings want to communicate with one another successfully and want to maintain social harmony while doing so. It stands to reason, therefore, that during routine communication the participants involved in the interaction are willing and perhaps even eager to cooperate so as to ensure successful communication. It seems that most exchanges are characteristically, to some extent, cooperative efforts, and each participant tends to recognize some common purpose. On this premise, Grice (1975) developed the **cooperative principle** for conversation. This rather general principle maintains the following: "Make your conversational contribution such as is required, at the stage at which it occurs, by the accepted purpose or direction of the talk exchange in which you are engaged." It seems that interactants base their expectations on the cooperative principle and on other relevant contextual features. Grice's cooperative principle consists of four maxims:

1. **THE MAXIM OF QUANTITY**

   Make your contribution as informative as required.
   Do not make your contribution more informative than required.

   > *The mutual expectation of the interactants is that quantitatively the speaker's contribution is just right for the interaction at hand. More would be too much and less would be too little for successful communication to take place.*

2. **THE MAXIM OF QUALITY**

   Try to make your contribution one that is true.
   a. Do not say what you believe to be false.
   b. Do not say that for which you lack adequate evidence.

   > *The mutual expectation of the interactants is that the speaker makes propositions or provides information that s/he believes to be true.*

3. **THE MAXIM OF RELATION**

   Be relevant.

   > *The mutual expectation of the interactants is that the speaker makes a contribution to the communicative exchange that is relevant to the topic and the situation of this exchange.*

4. **THE MAXIM OF MANNER**

   a. avoid obscurity
   b. avoid ambiguity
   c. be brief
   d. be orderly

The mutual expectation of the interactants is that the speaker makes
his/her contribution as clear and as comprehensible as possible,
and that while doing so, s/he takes all precautions to ensure such
clarity in terms of performance and delivery.

These maxims can be considered basic assumptions that people follow in their communicative interactions; however, it must be acknowledged that they assume Anglo-American culture. We believe the maxims get reinterpreted when applied to other cultures. In most cultures, it is generally the case that people provide just the appropriate amount of information for the other party to be able to interpret the intention. We can usually assume that people tell the truth (or the truth as best known to them), that their contributions are relevant to the discussion at hand, and that they try to be as clear as they can. Whenever a speaker is aware of having unintentionally violated a maxim, s/he will immediately try to adjust and make corrections in order to restore adherence to the maxims. It is often the apologetic additions that make it obvious that a speaker is self-correcting violations of this kind. Thus, for instance, if a speaker told us a story with too many details (perhaps making the wrong assumptions about what the hearer already knows), s/he might apologize by saying: "You probably know all this, so let me get to the main point." Or in the opposite situation, where someone (at an information counter perhaps) may not have given us enough information about something, s/he may simply add supplementary information upon realizing the confused look on the hearer's face. It is quite clear that communicators are very aware of the need to cooperate in terms of quantity of information in order to allow the other party to make the proper inferences and to get to the intention of the language user.

Similarly, when one is not completely sure that one has proper evidence for the statements one makes, it is possible to use various hedges in order not to take full responsibility for the quality of an utterance. As speakers in this case, we may add qualifying openers such as: *As far as I know; I am not quite sure but I believe that . . . ; I think that . . . .* The addition of such openings to an utterance releases speakers from the need to adhere fully to the maxim of quality and allows them to state beliefs or opinions rather than facts.

The maxim of relation (or relevance) plays a very important role in maintaining the topic of a conversation. As soon as we want to change the topic, we can do so by using some introductory or opening phrase such as "On another matter altogether . . . ," but we can also do so by producing an utterance that is no longer relevant and thus move the conversation toward a new topic. The added information being conveyed here is that I would rather speak about something else. This can also be done explicitly, as it often is, by people like diplomats or politicians when they answer a problematic question with the phrase "No comment."

It is, therefore, generally assumed that communication is successful because interactants adhere to the cooperative maxims. When they don't, the assumption may be that they deliberately violate a maxim in order to convey additional (implicit) information or add some special meaning, i.e., implicature, beyond what is actually said. Thus, the politician who answers a reporter's question with "No comment" leaves deliberate room for implicature and interpretation on the part of the hearer. In some cases, the reporter might simply say later, "so and so was unwilling to comment," which is a way for the reporter to ignore the implicature. Alternatively, the reporter may present some speculation related to the fact that at this point the speaker did not disclose all the details.

Within each culture there are acceptable ways to "deliberately" violate maxims. For instance, when complimenting a person, one is not expected to adhere fully to the maxim of quality. Similarly, when thanking someone for an unusually nice gift, the receiver might deliberately violate the maxim of quantity and say more than necessary in order to express a deeper sense of gratitude. Since such a "violation" is usually recognized by both inter-actants, it has added communicative value.

When communication takes place between two interactants who do not share the same language or the same culture, unintended violations of the maxims can easily occur. Here we assume that the four maxims apply to all cultures but that their interpretation may be quite different. Being informative or relevant in some cultures may sound crude and inappropriate in others, but there would still be some mutual expectation with respect to the maxims that would make communication more or less successful. Furthermore, the value related to each maxim might be quite different in different cultures. Thus, *quantity* may be differently perceived by speakers of different cultures. One example of such differences is the amount of information perceived as appropriate when giving someone directions in response to a request. In some cultures the appropriate answer would be brief and informative. In others it would be lengthy and contain some digressions from the main point. If a speaker from the first culture directly translates the directions s/he gives into the language of the other culture, the speaker may sound somewhat disinterested or rudely terse. If, however, a speaker from the latter culture does the same thing when functioning in the former one, s/he may sound overly verbose and perhaps even annoying. In other words, such *pragmatic transfer* might result in the violation of a maxim in the new language and culture. When such cross-cultural violations take place, the speakers may not be aware of the need to carry out a correction and may therefore leave the impression of being impolite or even aggressive, when this was not at all the speaker's intention.

SPEECH ACTS SERVE SOCIAL FUNCTIONS

As we have seen, successful communication takes place when speakers share knowledge, beliefs, and assumptions and when they adhere to similar rules of cooperative interaction. Language, however, is not only a vehicle to exchange thoughts and ideas; we often use utterances in order to perform social actions or functions. If a teacher in a traditional classroom tells a student, "I will have to inform your parents about your behavior," it usually is not only a statement that imparts information since it may also have the power of a threat with dire consequences. By making this statement, the teacher may also have performed a threatening act.

Similarly, when one friend tells another, "You look great today," this utterance serves not only as a description but functions mainly as a "compliment" and as such fulfills a social function. Social actions performed via utterances are generally called *speech acts*. All cultures use speech acts in order to perform social functions and in most languages there are some **performative verbs** that directly represent the speech acts (Austin, 1975) such as: *apologize, complain, compliment, request, promise,* and so forth. Although these performative verbs carry the lexical meaning of the speech act they convey, they are not always the most common realization of the speech act in normal conversation. Thus, when apologizing in a spoken situation, English speakers tend to use the expression "I'm sorry" much more often than the more formal "I apologize."

A speech act is usually performed within a situation that provides contextual elements that help interpret the speaker's intention. Thus if a person says "It's really cold in here" in a room where there is an open window and the addressee is near the window, this utterance can easily be interpreted as a request for the interlocutor to close the window. Contextual and social information make it possible for interactants to interpret each other's intentions even when these intentions are not explicitly stated.

When a speech act is uttered, the utterance carries **locutionary meaning** based on the meaning of the linguistic expressions. Thus, our earlier example "I am hungry" is a basic description of the speaker's state. However, it takes on **illocutionary force** when it acts as a request and the illocutionary force has the intended meaning of "please give me some food." Furthermore, since a speech act is directed toward an addressee who "suffers the consequences" of the act, it also has **perlocutionary force**, which is the effect the act has on the addressee. Every realization of a speech act has therefore three dimensions: locutionary meaning, illocutionary force, and perlocutionary effect.

Speech acts can be classified according to how they affect the social interaction between speakers and hearers. The most basic categorization (Searle, 1969) consists of five different types of speech acts: declaratives, representatives, expressives, directives, and commissives.

Declaratives (also called **performatives**) are speech acts that "change the world" as a result of having been performed. Some good examples of such declarative speech acts are when the jury foreman announces, "We find the defendant not guilty!" and when the justice of the peace says, "I now pronounce you man and wife."

Representatives are speech acts that enable the speaker to express feelings, beliefs, assertions, illustrations, and the like. An example of such a representative speech act would be a statement made by a speaker at an agricultural convention such as "Today, tomatoes can be grown in the desert."

Expressives are among the most important speech acts for learners of a second or a foreign language. These speech acts express psychological states of the speaker or the hearer. Apologizing, complaining, complimenting, and congratulating are examples of expressives.

Directives are speech acts that enable speakers to impose some action on the hearer. Through directives the speaker can express what s/he wants and then expect the hearer to comply. Inherently, these are face-threatening acts toward the hearer since they usually impose on the hearer. Commands, orders, and requests are examples of directives.

Commissives are speech acts that enable speakers to commit themselves to future actions. Promises and refusals are commissives. By definition these are speech acts whereby the speaker takes on or refuses some responsibility or task and are, therefore, face-threatening to the speaker, or imposing on the speaker. The use of performative verbs makes such speech acts more explicit. In the case of a promise, the choice of the verb "promise" makes the statement a stronger commitment, which is more costly to the speaker but advantageous to the hearer. In the case of refusals, on the other hand, the use of the verb "refuse" strengthens the denial of compliance and can lead to conflict or to a clash between the interlocutors.

Although it seems that all languages share a similar inventory of speech acts, the realizations and the circumstances that are appropriate for each speech act may be quite different in different cultures, and a learner needs to acquire speech act knowledge as part of language acquisition. This is what Celce-Murcia, Dörnyei, and Thurrell (1995) refer to as *actional competence* in their model of communication competence, which – among other things – extends the model of Canale and Swain (1980) and Canale (1983) to include speech acts. Chapter 9, which deals with the speaking skill, makes suggestions for the teaching of speech acts.

POLITENESS

Since communication can be viewed as the primary and most inclusive social framework for language use, it is logical to expect all speech communities to develop rules and ways in which to improve and accommodate communicative acts in order to ensure and promote social harmony. The area of **politeness** deals with perceptions, expectations, and conventional realizations of communicative strategies which enhance social harmony. In acquiring one's first language, a person also acquires these rules of politeness as part of one's sociocultural and pragmatic competence. When learning a second language, one needs to acquire the new culture's politeness framework, which often is very different from that of one's own culture. Perhaps a good example of opposing cross-cultural perceptions of politeness is the following incident, which took place in the United States, where a Japanese-born daughter-in-law came by unexpectedly to visit her American-Jewish mother-in-law during lunchtime. The daughter-in-law had stopped earlier at a snack shop to buy a sandwich to eat while visiting her mother-in-law. The Japanese rules of politeness dictated both that she not impose on her mother-in-law in any way and that she should demonstrate that she stopped by only to enjoy her company. On the other hand, the Jewish mother-in-law was shocked and quite offended that her daughter-in-law did not feel that she could come over at any time and expect to get a sandwich or some simple lunch from her mother-in-law. In both cases, there are important cultural expectations of "what is polite," but these perceptions clash in terms of cultural presuppositions: in the Japanese case, it is most important to maintain respect for the freedom of choice of the other person and to avoid imposition at all costs. In the Jewish tradition, feelings of solidarity and hospitality override any question of imposition, and so it is expected that someone who is close to you will "impose" from time to time as a normal part of the social relationship.

This example is also a good illustration of **negative** versus **positive politeness** in Brown and Levinson's (1978) terms. Negative politeness avoids imposition whereas positive politeness expects imposition. The Japanese culture is more negative politeness oriented in that maintaining social distance is highly valued, whereas the American-Jewish culture places higher value on lack of social distance and focuses on group solidarity and positive politeness as more appropriate values for family interactions. In the example described here, positive politeness ranks group solidarity as having very high value in the one culture, whereas in the other culture negative politeness is primarily concerned with maintaining the other party's "freedom of action" and avoiding imposition at all costs. When one moves from one culture to another, it may take a long time to become fully sensitive to the subtleties of a new set of politeness rules.

Leech (1983) adds the **politeness principle (PP)** to Grice's (1975) more general cooperative principle (CP) in order to "minimize the expression of impolite beliefs . . . and [maximize the expression of polite beliefs]" (81). The essence of Leech's PP is to minimize unfavorable behavior towards the hearer or a third party while attempting to increase favorable consequences. Leech suggests a *cost-benefit scale* where the claim is that when the speaker is impolite, there is a higher cost for the hearer. Conversely, when the speaker is polite, there is greater benefit for the hearer. To be polite, therefore, means to minimize cost to the hearer and to be impolite is to maximize it. The following definitions and example may help clarify this:

> *Cost to Hearer* = *speaker is impolite, inconsiderate, and does not value hearer's well-being*
>
> *Benefit to Hearer* = *speaker is polite and considerate of the hearer even at his/her own expense*

> Example: *a situation where an insurance agent is asked to help the customer with an unusual claim, which turns out not to be covered by the policy, and the customer complains bitterly. If the agent chooses to be impolite, s/he might say something like, "If you don't like our policy, take your business elsewhere." But if s/he chooses to be polite, the agent might say, "We are very sorry that our policy doesn't cover your claim, but I am sure another agency might be more accommodating in future. Would you like me to recommend some other agencies?"*

In the first case, the agent who responds impolitely does not consider the customer's (hearer's) benefit, while in the second case, although the agent cannot offer direct assistance, s/he is still very considerate of the customer's needs (lowering the hearer's costs).

Each culture may have rather different norms with respect to the expected politeness considerations of "cost-benefit." As we have seen from the earlier example about the Japanese daughter-in-law and the Jewish-American mother-in-law, the Japanese perception of politeness and "benefit to the hearer" entailed the notion of "minimizing imposition," whereas the Jewish expectation was "to accept and appreciate family hospitality." Consequently, we see that rules of politeness cannot be translated directly from one culture to another.

Leech (1983) suggests that these politeness principles are inherent in the categorization of speech acts as well as in the realization of each speech act. Therefore, he classifies illocutionary functions in terms of how they interact with the goal of achieving social harmony:

competitive: the illocutionary goal competes with the social goal
(e.g., ordering, requesting, demanding, begging)
convivial: the illocutionary goal coincides with the social goal
(e.g., offering, inviting, greeting, thanking, congratulating)
neutral:[2] the illocutionary goal is indifferent to the social goal
(e.g., asserting, reporting, announcing, instructing)
conflictive: the illocutionary goal conflicts with the social goal
(e.g., threatening, accusing, cursing, reprimanding)

(Leech, 1983:104)

Considerations of politeness often relate to the degree of **directness** expressed in speech acts. When talking about Leech's **competitive** speech acts or Brown and Levinson's **face-threatening** speech acts, there is implied imposition on the hearer in the actual performance of the speech act. In order to lessen the force of the imposition, all languages seem to have conventionalized less direct (or **indirect**) realizations of such speech acts. Instead of saying to the hearer, "Close the door," we might prefer an indirect version, e.g., "It's cold in here." However, it should also be recognized that an indirect speech act is often harder to interpret and so speakers of languages often develop **conventionally indirect** realization patterns which enable us to make indirect requests that are nonetheless unambiguous such as "Could you close the door?" or "Do you want to open the door?" – the former is more polite and formal; the latter is more casual and familiar. Being conventionally recognized request forms, such questions should not be answered literally but according to their illocutionary force. However, this fact is not always obvious to second language learners, who have acquired different ways of expressing conventionalized indirect speech acts in their first language.

All cultures are concerned with maintaining social harmony, and therefore we find rules of politeness incorporated in the rules of speech that one has to acquire as part of language learning. Each language, accordingly, has developed a repertoire of speech act realizations that enable the language user to be a "polite" interactant and an accurate interpreter of discourse. In most cultures these rules of linguistic behavior are also accompanied by appropriate eye gaze, body language, and gestures. When learning a new language, the learner cannot possibly expect to acquire complete pragmatic competence, yet it is possible to incorporate the study of a manageable amount of pragmatic information into a language program and to include activities which make the learner aware of and sensitive to the major features of politeness and common variations on expressing politeness in the new language.

However, as Beebe (1996) has pointed out on several occasions, we do not recommend teaching second language learners always and only to be polite since there are occasions and circumstances in which users of the target language will behave rudely or offensively in their interactions with nonnative speakers. On such occasions, language learners should be able to recognize the rude or offensive behavior and to know that they may respond in ways that are less than polite. They should also be aware of expressions and resources they can use to convey their displeasure with interlocutors who are being rude to them.

CONCLUSION

This chapter has surveyed some of the most important factors affecting language users' choices of linguistic form. With reference to sociocultural appropriacy and presupposition, we have examined the context-embedded nature of speaker meaning and intention and how the hearer is able to determine these by relying on shared knowledge, context, and conventional expressions. Grice's Cooperative Principle, Leech's Politeness Principle, and Austin and Searle's Speech Act Theory have been examined cross-culturally to show that each speech community is pragmatically as well as grammatically unique. In terms of comprehending and producing discourse competently in the target language, it is as important to understand the pragmatics of the target culture as it is to understand the grammar and vocabulary of the target language.

QUESTIONS FOR DISCUSSION

1. What kind of context is needed to understand an utterance like (a) "Yes, he did," and one like (b) "Why don't you put the flowers over there?"
2. Comment on the following speech exchange with reference to Grice's maxims (it occurred between two native English speakers):
    A: Can you pass the salt?
    B: I can, but I won't.
3. Which of the three following requests is most polite, and why?

    a. Open the window.
    b. Could you open the window?
    c. I'd like you to open the window.

4. Come up with an example from your own experience that illustrates either negative face (emphasis on social distance) or positive face (emphasis on in-group solidarity) with reference to politeness.
5. When answering the telephone, it is customary for Italian speakers to pick up the receiver and say, "Pronto" (literally, "I'm ready"). What do you think might happen interactionally if an Italian – newly arrived in the United States and speaking fluent English – were to answer the phone in his/her hotel room and say, "I'm ready."?

Suggestions for Further Reading

Blakemore, D. (1992). *Understanding utterances: An introduction to pragmatics.* Oxford: Blackwell.
Leech, G. N. (1983). *Principles of pragmatics.* London: Longman.
Levinson, S. C. (1983). *Pragmatics.* Cambridge: Cambridge University Press.
Yule, G. (1996). *Pragmatics.* Oxford: Oxford University Press.

Endnotes

[1] Example presented by a student in a course on cross-cultural interaction, TESOL Summer Institute 1990, Michigan State University.
[2] Leech (1983) uses the term **collaborative** where we have substituted the term **neutral** since our students found Leech's term confusing and misleading, given his description of this category.

PART 2

LANGUAGE KNOWLEDGE

CHAPTER 3

Phonology

"A short term pronunciation course should focus first and foremost on suprasegmentals as they have the greatest impact on the comprehensibility of the learner's English. We have found that giving priority to the suprasegmental aspects of English not only improves learners' comprehensibility but is also less frustrating for students because greater change can be effected."

(McNerney and Mendelsohn, 1987:132)

INTRODUCTION

Phonology, the linguistic study of sound systems, gives us different types of information that is helpful for better understanding what spoken discourse sounds like, and this information will be our focus here. However, we will also say something about the relationship of phonology to the written language later in the chapter when we briefly discuss the relationship between punctuation and pronunciation. In this chapter, our focus is on the intelligibility of a speaker's oral discourse. A threshold-level ability is needed so that learners can comprehend speech and be comprehended.

Our treatment of English phonology is not comprehensive but rather is intended to sensitize the teacher to typical trouble spots. The norm presented is North American English; however, other major dialects have similar trouble spots, and users of those dialects can make the necessary adaptations. The notational system we use for marking intonation is the Fries-Pike system (see Pike, 1945), which superimposes intonation as a line drawn over the sentence or utterance: When the line is directly under the words, this signals mid-level pitch, whereas when the line is just above the words, it signals high pitch; when somewhat below the words, the line signals low pitch, and when the line is one space above the words, it signals extra high pitch.

Example: This is how the system looks. (mid → high → low)

Later we will see that a speaker can either glide or step from one pitch level to another. Other notational systems can be used instead to signal intonation if the teacher wishes.

The phonology of a language is often described by linguists in terms of **segmental** and **suprasegmental** systems, where "segmental" refers to the individual vowel and consonant sounds and their distribution, while "suprasegmental" refers to the patterns of *rhythm* (i.e., the timing of syllable length, syllable stress, and pauses) and the *intonation contours* (i.e., pitch patterns) that accompany sound sequences when language is used for oral communication. These suprasegmental features are collectively referred to as **prosody**. Prosody is extremely important in properly conveying the speaker's message and intention to the listener. In fact, there is evidence that children acquiring their first language master prosody before segmentals. For example, children can understand that they are being scolded or being asked to make a choice based on prosody before they can recognize words or produce sound segments. Different types of processing seem to be involved in the acquisition of prosody and of other aspects of the sound system: Gestalt or holistic processing is used in the acquisition of prosody; however, analytical processing occurs in the acquisition of segmentals (Bloom, 1970; Peters, 1977). For adults speaking a second language, ability to process and to approximate the target prosody contributes greatly to negotiation of a holistic signal that can guide the listener's understanding of what the speaker is trying to convey. For example, a tourist speaking very little of the target language can often understand the gist of an utterance related to a buying-selling transaction merely from the prosody: [╱⌢╱], meaning, "Is this okay?" uttered by the salesperson who has just wrapped a parcel.

In the past, pronunciation instruction has often overemphasized segmental distinctions (e.g., [Look at the] ship/sheep). Like McNerney and Mendelsohn (1987), whom we quoted at the start of this chapter, we take the position that effective oral communication requires control of prosody perhaps as much as (if not more than) control of the target language's vowel and consonant sounds. The acceptability of suprasegmental phonology in oral discourse may well influence the effectiveness of any interaction because it affects the speaker's conversational style and the listener's ability to make inferences. It colors the speaker's level of politeness, of cultural appropriacy, and compliance with social rules. In a speaker's conversational performance, matters such as relinquishing the floor to another speaker, taking a turn, interrupting, or asking a confirmation question as opposed to making a statement are all things that are often signaled by prosodic features rather than by sound segments or by syntactic or lexical elements (Dalton and Seidlhofer, 1994).

WHERE THINGS CAN GO WRONG

Inappropriate prosody can involve quite subtle types of miscommunication, types that are not as obvious as a confusion at the segmental level, which the listener is typically able to correct by using context or knowledge of the world (e.g., I had rice/lice for dinner). It is thus often difficult to detect prosodic problems as "errors," and they easily get misconstrued by the listener as unintended messages or inappropriate behaviors.

INTONATION

For example, one of the authors, while teaching in Nigeria, noticed that many native speakers of Yoruba tended to superimpose the vowel length and the falling-rising pattern for their word *beeni* (the equivalent of "yes") on the English word *yes*. This frequently occurred in interactions where, in response to a question in English such as "Are you coming to our supper party on Saturday?", the Yoruba speaker uttered a long drawn-out "Yes" utterance that began high, then fell, and then rose again:

Y\e͜s

Several native English speakers – both British and North American – who had no knowledge of Yoruba came to a similar conclusion: They told the co-author that they felt Yorubas were wishy-washy people, unable to respond with a decisive "yes" or "no" when asked a simple question.

Another striking example comes from the research of Argyres (1996), who studied the intonation of yes/no questions in the English produced by two native speakers of Greek in comparison with that of two native speakers of North American English. The native speakers of Greek, who were advanced level and highly fluent in English, tended nonetheless to superimpose the falling Greek intonation for yes/no questions onto the English yes/no questions they uttered:

Are you COMing?

This made the Greeks seem impatient and rude to the English speakers who evaluated the questions of all four speakers. The native English speakers' intonation, by contrast, tended to rise on such questions:

Are you COMing?

In Argyres' study, native English-speaking judges listened to many instances of these yes-no questions in randomized order on a tape recording; they rated the questions of the native Greek speakers as being significantly ruder and rated their questions as being more negative than those of the native English speakers.

Gumperz (1978) provides yet another example, this one involving Indian-English speakers working as food servers in a cafeteria in England. Their speech is perceived by their British interlocutors (i.e., the customers at the cafeteria) as "insulting" because of inappropriate intonation and pausing, the result of transfer from their regional dialect of Indian English.

Such miscommunication problems are extremely insidious and hard to explain to both those who produce them and those who miscomprehend them. The existence of such problems, however, underscores the urgency of getting language teachers to understand how intonation functions in oral discourse, as well as the necessity of helping them to develop some strategies for teaching appropriate intonation to nonnative speakers.

RHYTHM

When multisyllabic words are pronounced with an incorrect rhythm, some serious or humorous errors in comprehension may occur. The late Don Bowen told us (personal communication) about a native Spanish speaker who came to his office quite distraught because she knew she needed help with her pronunciation. She had been to an American drugstore, a large store with a food counter and other amenities in addition to a pharmacy. She had a bad headache, and when an elderly gentleman asked if he could help her, she asked for some "ahs pee REEN." A few moments later the gentleman returned with a dish of rice pudding, for this is what he had understood. The woman had wanted some aspirin.

In an interaction that one of the coauthors had with a nonnative speaker, the speaker was talking about an "ex e CU tor." This sounded like "executioner" to the coauthor, who was quite befuddled until substantial additional co-text made it clear that the speaker was talking about the "ex EC u tor" of a will.

Thus while intonation errors miscommunicate the speaker's stance, politeness, and intentions; errors in word stress and other aspects of rhythm often miscommunicate an important piece of information in the speaker's message. Both areas must be addressed in the language classroom.

BACKGROUND

The discussion of what can go wrong in terms of intonation has not so far considered the fact that most of the world's languages can be classified as either (a) **tone languages** or (b) **intonation languages**. Some tone languages are Asian languages such as Chinese, Thai, Vietnamese, or African languages such as Yoruba, Ibo, and Hausa. Many Indian languages of the Americas such as Navaho and Quechua are also tone languages. In tone languages, pitch applies lexically to distinguish words. Thus the segmental sequence /ma/ in Chinese can mean "horse," "mother," "numb," or "to scold" (among other things) – depending on the tonal pattern of the word; and the segmental sequence /ɔkɔ/ in Yoruba can mean "hoe," "vehicle," or "husband," again depending on the tonal pattern of the word.

In contrast to these tone languages, there are intonation languages such as Japanese, Korean, English, French, German, Spanish, Russian, Arabic, Hebrew, i.e., virtually all European and Middle Eastern languages. Intonation languages apply pitch patterns to entire utterances, not just to lexical items the way tone languages do. (To be fair, many tone languages also have some intonational features, and some intonation languages have some word-level pitch-accents; nonetheless, there seems to be a fundamental difference in the scope of pitch between these two types of languages.)

In general, if learners speak an intonation language as their first language, it is assumed they will learn the intonation of another language more easily than will someone who speaks a tone language as their first language, or vice versa. However, just because two languages happen to be intonation languages does not mean that their utterance-level pitch patterns will be the same. They rarely are. For example, while English uses up to four pitch levels, Spanish uses only two or at most three, with the result that Spanish speakers seem to have a somewhat flat intonation in English, which signals disinterest to English listeners. And even though Japanese uses rising-falling intonation on prominent syllables in declarative utterances as English does, pitch contours in Japanese are more compact and the fall and rise occur much more quickly than in English because Japanese does not distinguish stressed and unstressed syllables: As Todaka (1990) shows, prominence in Japanese does not involve stress, pitch, and syllable length the way it does in English. This perhaps indicates that teachers should not assume too much, given the fact that their students are native speakers of tone languages or intonation languages, when teaching intonation.

In order to illustrate the importance of rhythm and intonation in spoken English discourse, we first need to briefly discuss word-level stress patterns because any multi-syllabic English word has a distinct stress pattern that interacts with other prosodic features. *Word stress* is basic to prosody: With incorrect word stress, meaning is obscured (as we have previously shown with what can go wrong under "rhythm"). With incorrect word stress, the prosody of entire utterances can go awry, as we shall demonstrate.

If we assume at least two levels of stress for English syllables – *stressed* (strong) versus *unstressed* (weak) – words of two, three, or four syllables exhibit the following patterns, given that any English word of two or more syllables tends to have at least one strongly stressed syllable:

móther	abóut	grádual	offícial	understánd
séven	refér	símilar	audítion	apprehénd
círcumstances		extrémity		institútion
pércolator		invéterate		salutátion

Other similar patterns obtain for words with five or more syllables, some of which may have two stressed syllables (a *primary* and a s*econdary*).[1]

The main point is that new information, as noted in Chapter 1, typically occurs toward the end of an utterance and tends to receive the greatest prominence (i.e., it is the most important stressed element at the utterance level). The pitch or intonation contour of an utterance uses as a pivot the stressed syllable of the word that carries the new information and receives the prominence. Thus in answer to the question "Where have you been?" the person addressed might respond:[2]

(I've been) to the BOOKstore.

Here the new information is "bookstore," and it is the stressed syllable of this word that is spoken with prominence and serves as the focal point for stress and intonation in the utterance. Note that if the response had been "I've been to the store," the new information would be "store," a one-syllable word, which would carry both the rise and fall of the intonation contour, resulting in a glide intonation rather than the step intonation contour shown in the first example:

(I've been) to the STORE.

However, because of inherent word stress on "bookstore" in this context, it would always be inappropriate to say "I've been to the bookSTORE."

These utterances are examples of normal, unmarked declarative intonation in North American English, which begins with a mid-level pitch and ends in a rise-fall pattern. To describe English intonation properly, we need to refer to four levels of relative pitch: *low, medium, high,* and *extra high,* which is reserved for marked intensity of expression. The above utterances have a medium-high-low contour, where "high" indicates the new information and "low" indicates the end of the utterance.

Imagine now that the speaker who initiated the conversation (i.e., "Where have you been?") responds to the utterance "I've been to the bookstore" with the following yes/no question:

You've been to the BOOKstore?

This is not the most typical yes/no question. It has declarative word order, and with the exception of changing the subject pronoun to maintain reference to the same person (*I → you*), the question simply echoes the previous speaker's assertion. In this sequential context, the declarative word order with yes/no question intonation (medium-high-rise) does not mean "Have you been to the bookstore?" but rather "Have I understood you correctly?" If, for the same utterance, the speaker were to rise to extra high pitch instead of just high pitch on the first syllable of "bookstore," then the speaker's message would be one of surprise or disbelief (i.e., "I can't believe you went to the bookstore!"). In other words, speakers have the option of using different intonation contours on the same string of words to signal different meanings.

One final preliminary comment we need to make is that not every word is stressed in English speech. In unmarked utterances, only those words that convey the core *propositional information* (typically nouns, adjectives, and main verbs – sometimes adverbs) are *stressed.* Words that carry *grammatical information* (e.g., articles, prepositions, personal and relative pronouns, auxiliary verbs, conjunctions) tend to be *unstressed.* This helps account for the typical rhythm of English, which consists of a rhythm group – often referred to as a *"thought group"* – that tends to have one prominent syllable. Over a series of thought groups, stressed syllables tend to occur at regular intervals regardless of the number of syllables per thought group. The following three sentences illustrate this principle. In terms of rhythm, the sentences all have three strong stresses or beats and – in a relative sense – are spoken using the same amount of time even though the first sentence has only three syllables and the third one has seven:

JACK/ SELLS/ CARS.

JACK / has SOLD/ some CARS.

JACK/ has been SEL/ling some CARS.

This heavily stress-determined nature of English rhythm is different from the rhythm in many other languages in which the number of syllables in an utterance more closely determines its overall length. The challenge for the learner – as we show in the next section – is to put word stress, thought groups, utterance prominence, and intonation together properly.

PROSODY IN CONTEXT

In several of the previous examples we looked at how stress and intonation operate in a particular context. This is important because the linguistic and social context establishes whether any piece of information in an ongoing communication is old or new and whether or not it is relevant.

Sperber and Wilson (1986:11) provide us with a nice example of relevance: When a host uses normal stress and intonation and asks a guest "Do you know what time it is?" the host is explicitly asking for the time of day from the guest. Indirectly, the host could be suggesting that it is time for the guest to leave without being too obvious. However, if the host is fed up and is not too concerned about politeness, s/he might choose to give special prominence to the word *time*, thereby expressing some consternation at the fact that s/he and his/her guest are still sitting and chatting.

Such examples reveal prosodic variation and underscore the fact that speakers have different prosodic alternatives available to them. The choice made usually communicates the speaker's intention unless the speaker or listener is unaware of the range of possible target-language implications of using a given prosodic pattern and miscommunicates or misconstrues the point.

We believe the foregoing introduction and background make it clear why we are devoting a chapter to phonology (as part of language knowledge) in our discussion of discourse and context in language teaching. As shown in Figure 3.1 on page 36, all language resources are necessary for successful communicative interaction. This chapter focuses on phonology, which is knowledge that is especially relevant for both listening and speaking (see Chapters 6 and 9 respectively).

Phonology is the primary means through which oral language processing of semantic meaning and pragmatic functions takes place. Without sounds systems there would be no spoken language and no oral communication; thus language teachers – from the beginning level on – must ensure that their learners have every opportunity to develop an intelligible pronunciation and to comprehend a variety of speakers and dialects (Eisenstein, 1983) in the target language.

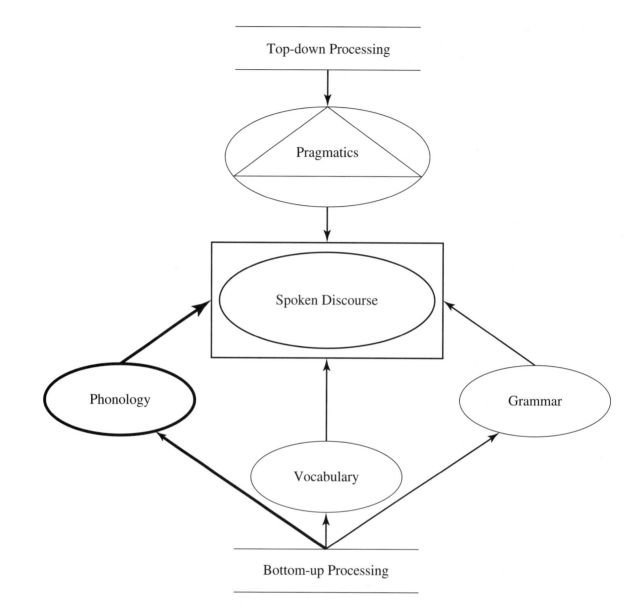

Figure 3.1 Phonology and Language Knowledge

INFORMATION MANAGEMENT FUNCTIONS OF PROSODY

Prosody performs two related information management functions in English and many other languages: first it allows the speaker to segment information into meaningful word groups (bottom-up processing in Figure 3.1), and second it helps the speaker signal new or important information versus old or less important information (top-down processing in Figure 3.1). The listener, of course, makes use of the same prosodic system to segment speech into thought groups and words and to distinguish new from given information. The following two sections discuss these functions in greater detail.

SEGMENTING INFORMATION INTO MEANINGFUL WORD GROUPS

In English, meaningful word groups typically end with a pause, a change in pitch, and a lengthening of the last stressed syllable (Gilbert, 1983). Such prosodic clues from the speaker help the speaker produce and the listener comprehend spoken English. Gumperz and Kaltman (1980:52, 62) describe the speaker's use of prosody in marking meaningful word groups as follows: "By tone grouping, or utterance chunking, a speaker organizes information into groups . . . Prosody therefore becomes an integral part of the linguistic processes by which we signal information about thematic cohesion, perspective, message prominence. . ."

This chunking function of prosody in grammar is nicely illustrated by paired examples such as the following where the same words with different prosody express very different meanings:

  a. "Father," said Mother, "is late."
  b. Father said, "Mother is late."

  c. Have you met my brother Fred?
  d. Have you met my brother, Fred?

In somewhat less extreme examples, we can observe that the organizing function of prosody helps speaker signal (and the listener hear) the difference in meaning between constructions such a restrictive and nonrestrictive relative clause:

  e. My sister who lives in Texas has three children.
  f. My sister, who lives in Texas, has three children.

or between a declarative utterance and an exhortation:

  g. Wolverines fight to win.
  h. Wolverines, fight to win!

At the discourse level a grammatically inappropriate prosodic segmentation can mislead the listener and cause confusion about, if not misinterpretation of, a longer stretch of discourse. To give a real example, in response to the question "How long does it generally take to produce a new textbook (from initial proposal to finished product)?" the speaker responded, "Four to five years," but was understood as saying "Forty-five years." In this case there was a temporary communication problem until the intended number of years was sorted out.

SIGNALING NEW VERSUS OLD INFORMATION

The other information management function of prosody, i.e., marking new versus old information, has been discussed by Chafe (1980), who points out that within a thought group, words expressing old or given information are generally spoken with weak stress and low pitch whereas words expressing new information are spoken with strong stress and high pitch.

Allen (1971:77) provides some excellent examples of the prosodic regularities that Chafe has pointed out:

X: I've lost an umBRELla.

Y: A LAdy's umbrella?

X: YES. One with STARS on it. GREEN stars.

In this exchange, the syllables in capital letters are stressed and signal that the word containing the stressed syllable conveys new information. Each contour – or intonation group – contains one main piece of new information, and this new information is uttered with prominence (strong stress, extra length, and high pitch). Whatever information is new tends to receive special prosodic attention (i.e., the word is stressed and the pitch changes) as indicated in this additional example:

A: Can I HELP you?

B: YES, please. I'm looking for a BLAzer.

A: Something CASual?

B: YES, something casual in WOOL.

Note once again that new information tends to come toward the end of the utterance.

SOME COMMUNICATIVE FUNCTIONS OF PROSODY

A salient type of interaction management is expressed in a contrast. A contrast is being signaled either because the interlocutor shifts the focus of attention or because there is now a contrast where there was none before. Consider, for example, the following exchange:

A: HeLLO. I'd like to buy some fresh PEPpers.

B: Would you like the GREEN ones or the RED ones?

A: The RED ones.

Here Speaker A makes a request for "peppers," but Speaker B needs clarification since both "green" and "red" peppers are available. Thus the interactional focus shifts from "peppers" to the variety (i.e., color) of peppers that A would prefer.

Contexts in which *contradictions* or *disagreements* arise are also good examples of interactional management where the shift in focus from one constituent to another is very clear:

A: It's COLD.

B: It's NOT cold.

A: It IS cold.

B: Come on, it's not THAT cold.

Here Speaker A begins by describing the weather or environment as cold and emphasizes the word *cold*; Speaker B disagrees by restating the same utterance in negative form and stressing the word *not*. Speaker A responds by reasserting the original proposition, this time by emphasizing the verb BE, which in its affirmative form contrasts with Speaker B's prior negation of the proposition. In the final turn, Speaker B tries to persuade Speaker A to downgrade the initial assessment by emphasizing the degree modifier *that*.

When one speaker corrects another (or if one immediately corrects oneself), we have another type of interactional management that conversation analysts call *repair*. Correction is often similar to disagreement from a prosodic point of view:

A: You're from LONdon, AREn't you?

B: Not LONdon, DOver.

Learners of English need ample opportunity to practice the prosodic characteristics of such interactional management strategies in realistic dialogue sequences.

In fact, we should briefly reconsider word stress in relation to prosody. Some multi-syllabic words have more than one stressed syllable. With such words, the prominence may well shift depending on where the new information or the contrast falls (e.g., forty-five):

A: Did you say forty-FIVE or forty-SIX?

B: Did you say FORty-five or FIFty-five?

In no context, however, would a native speaker give prominence to the unstressed syllable in this particular word and say "forTY-five."[3]

INTONATION AND SENTENCE TYPES

In order to deploy intonation effectively at the level of discourse, learners need first to become aware of, understand, and practice the relationships between intonation, syntax, and context in spoken English. For each of the six syntactic patterns that we will discuss, there is a *neutral* (or *unmarked*) intonation contour that can easily be altered by changes in context. Without a grasp of these patterns and possible changes, the learner will not be able to use intonation effectively at the more global discourse level when speaking or listening. It is important for the learner to understand that *grammatical sentence types* (e.g., declaratives) may differ from *functional utterance types* (e.g., statement/question) in prosodic signaling only. For a more detailed presentation, see Celce-Murcia, Brinton, and Goodwin (1996).

I. DECLARATIVES

Unmarked or neutral versions of most English declarative sentences have rising-falling intonation and fairly predictable prominence on the new information occurring toward the end of the utterance:

Max writes PLAYS.

However, in actual use, declaratives are sometimes marked such that one constituent occurring earlier in the utterance, for example the subject noun *Max,* is singled out for special focus or emphasis.

It would not, however, make sense to present the unmarked and marked versions of sentences like "Max writes plays" in isolation and out of context. Teachers and learners must understand that one version is appropriate in one context, whereas the other is appropriate in another. For example, consider the following conversational exchange:

A: What does your neighbor Max |MOR|ris do?

B: Max/He writes PLAYS.

Such a context is an environment in which the unmarked version of the statement would be used because "Max" is old information and his occupation is new information. On the other hand, given a context such as the following:

A: Is it true that Peter writes |PLAYS?

B: No, |MAX| writes plays.

the marked version of the rejoinder is appropriate since the false assumption (i.e., that Peter writes plays) can be corrected simply by emphasizing in the response the name of the person who actually does write plays, i.e., Max.

2. IMPERATIVES AND EXCLAMATIONS

Like declaratives, imperatives (often referred to as commands or directives when viewed pragmatically) generally take the rise–fall intonation contour, but they are often more forceful or affectively loaded than declarative sentences and thus may make use of level 4 (extra high pitch) more often. English imperatives are structurally simple: They tend to omit the subject noun (understood "you") and use uninflected verb forms:

Write more |PLAYS!

Buy me the |NEWS|paper.

Sometimes the verb receives prominence instead of the object noun, either because there is no object (i.e., the verb is intransitive):

COME!

or because the verb is signaling a contrast or new information:

di|RECT| plays! (instead of writing them)

Another sentence type that also tends to be potentially more affectively loaded and generally shorter than a declarative is an exclamation.

Good GRIEF!

|NICE| one!

Like declaratives and imperatives, exclamations also exhibit rising-falling intonation, but they sometimes give prominence to two constituents rather than one and regularly make use of extra high pitch.

WHAT a per|FOR|mance!

We mention exclamations briefly because the potential use of extra high pitch in exclamations seems to be superimposed on several of the following question types, which also can take on exclamatory qualities.

3. YES/NO QUESTIONS

The unmarked grammar for an English yes/no question involves the inversion of the subject and the auxiliary verb (or the addition of *do* as the auxiliary in sentences that have no lexical auxiliary verb). When this option conveys no special presuppositions, it is accompanied by rising intonation. However, since the intonation can rise on whichever constituent is in focus, this intonation pattern often has two or (if a bit longer and more complex) three possible realizations of the rising contour. For example:

a.   Does Max write PLAYS? (focus of the question is on "plays")

b.   Does MAX write plays? (focus of the question is on "Max")

However, it is also possible when using this same syntactic option that the speaker chooses a marked rising–falling intonation pattern. This pattern can signal an inference (or guess), or it may also indicate the speaker's impatience with the interlocutor. Again, different realizations of the contour are possible depending on which constituent is being emphasized.

b.   Does Max write PLAYS?

b'. Does MAX write plays?

As mentioned previously, in an even more highly marked version of this yes/no question, there is no inversion: in terms of its syntax, the sentence is a declarative, yet it still functions as a question because of the rising intonation. This uninverted yes/no question form can also take different intonation contours.

4. WH-QUESTIONS

Wh-questions are those questions where the constituent being questioned appears in the form of a wh-word (*what, who, when, where,* and the like). They follow the same rising-falling intonation as declaratives when they are unmarked. They are designed to elicit rather than to state specific information. As with declaratives, there are often two or more different realizations of the contour depending on whether the result of the action or the agent of the action is in focus:

a.   What does Max WRITE? (focus on result/product)

a'. What does MAX write? (focus on agent)

Such rising-falling intonation surprises some nonnative speakers, who assume that all questions – regardless of type – should be spoken with rising intonation. However, when wh-questions are spoken with rising intonation, the prosody is marked and signals "I didn't hear everything you said; clarify or repeat what comes *after* the constituent I have emphasized":

b.   What does Max WRITE? (problem word(s): after "write")

b'. What does MAX do? (problem word(s): after "Max")

Here (b) means "Tell me more clearly exactly what Max *writes*" while (b') means "Tell me again more clearly what *Max* in particular does." Using this marked prosody for the more routine elicitation of information that is signaled above in (a) or (a') would be highly inappropriate.

5. QUESTION TAGS

Question tags follow declaratives. The declaratives themselves have rising-falling intonation, and so do the question tags when they are used in what Brown (1981) has described as their two most frequent functions, i.e., seeking confirmation as in (a) or making a point rhetorically as in (b):

    a. It's a nice DAY, ISn't it?

    b. People are worried about the eCONomy, AREn't they?

Although in most other languages question tags tend to rise, in English question tags have rising intonation only on those occasions when they are used much like unmarked yes/no questions: to elicit a "yes" or "no" answer from the addressee, to challenge the addressee's information, or to seek further clarification because either the speaker is unsure of the addressee's claim or the speaker simply doesn't know the answer:

    c. The home-team WON, didn't they?

    d. You didn't finish the CANdy, did you?

Note that in examples (c) and (d) the statement preceding the tag tends not to fall as completely as it does in (a) and (b) because it anticipates the real question signalled by the rise in the tag's intonation.[4]

The rising-falling pattern illustrated in (a) and (b) is definitely the more frequent contour for question tags in English because tags are used most frequently to seek confirmation or to make a point. This is a problem for nonnative speakers since many of them speak native languages where all question tags have rising intonation regardless of discourse function. Such students must learn that in English the speaker has a choice between using a tag to confirm an assumption (using the rising-falling pattern) or to ask an informal type of yes/no question (using rising intonation).

6. ALTERNATIVE QUESTIONS

True alternative questions generally show a rise on the first part, a pause, and then a rise-fall on the second part:

    a. Would you like JUICE or COFfee?

They differ semantically, syntactically, and pragmatically from yes/no questions having objects conjoined by *or*. These have rising intonation and do not force a choice:

    b. Would you like JUICE or COFfee?

Here the true, *closed-choice* alternative question (a) means "make a choice and tell me whether you want juice or whether you want coffee. These are the two alternatives available." It has a more fully expanded counterpart (i.e., Would you like juice, or would you like coffee?). Many nonnative speakers answer questions like (a) with a "yes" or "no," which is not appropriate and indicates that the addressee has not understood the meaning of the speaker's intonation (and has not realized that only one of the alternatives should be selected). Even alternative questions that focus on the affirmative or negative value of a proposition (e.g., Are you coming or not?) do not typically elicit "yes" or "no" responses from native speakers, who tend to respond with a shortened or complete response:

I AM. / I'm COMing.   OR   I'm NOT. / I'm NOT coming.

Sentence (b) on page 42, in contrast to (a), means more or less "Would you like something to drink? (Incidentally, I can offer you juice or coffee.)" Such a question is not a true alternative question (however, it is sometimes called an *open-choice* question): There is no expanded question form, and the addressee typically answers with a "yes" or "no" and then expands the response as appropriate:

Yes, thanks. Some coffee would be nice.

No, thank you. (I'm not thirsty.)

When nonnative speakers make intonation errors with true alternative questions, sometimes a familiar context helps the listener disambiguate. This happened to one of the authors when a nonnative-English-speaking waitress offered the people at her table three choices for salad dressing with rising intonation:

Ranch, French, or ItaliAN? (also incorrect syllabification and word stress)

In this context a native-English-speaking waitress would normally say:

Ranch, French, or iTALian?

When people are conversing, the context is not always this explicit, and in instances where it is not, incorrect prosody often contributes to miscommunication. In this interaction, if the native-English-speaking listeners had taken the nonnative-speaking waitress literally, they might have said "yes" and expected to get a tray with all three dressings. Since the native speakers compensated for the inappropriate intonation, they all chose one of the three options.

Along with stress and intonation, we could also discuss common reductions in connected speech. We refer the reader to the section on teaching the comprehension of reduced speech in Chapter 6 (Listening). The information presented there could also be used to teach pronunciation.

APPLYING KNOWLEDGE OF SHORT EXCHANGES TO LONGER SAMPLES

Although we believe that learners need to develop a sense of target language prosody from the very beginning levels (and we also feel the best way to do this is with short, well-contextualized exchanges such as those illustrated above), teachers must also provide learners with opportunities to apply these patterns over longer stretches of discourse that resemble sustained authentic interaction.

One resource that we have used successfully for this purpose is excerpts from modern drama. Consider, for example, the following passage from Tennessee Williams' play, *The Glass Menagerie,* which incorporates most of the patterns we have presented. (Amanda is the mother of Tom and Laura; Laura is shy and somewhat physically handicapped):

Amanda:	You mean you have asked some nice young man to come over?
Tom:	Yep. I've asked him to dinner.
Amanda:	You really did?
Tom:	I did!
Amanda:	You did, and did he – accept?
Tom:	He did!
Amanda:	Well, well – well! That's – lovely!
Tom:	I thought you would be pleased.
Amanda:	It's definite, then?
Tom:	Very definite.
Amanda:	Soon?
Tom:	Very soon.
Amanda:	For heaven's sake, stop putting on and tell me some things, will you?
Tom:	What things do you want me to tell you?
Amanda:	*Naturally,* I would like to know when he's coming.
Tom:	He's coming tomorrow.
Amanda:	*Tomorrow?*
Tom:	Yep. Tomorrow.
Amanda:	But, Tom!
Tom:	Yes, Mother?
Amanda:	Tomorrow gives me no time.
Tom:	Time for what?
Amanda:	Preparations!

For practicing the oral interpretation of such a script, learners perform best when they can listen at will to a recording of professional actors reading the interaction. Before they do this, they should use their knowledge of short exchanges and sentence structure to predict (and subsequently confirm or revise) the stress and intonation that each utterance has in such an exchange. Learners can then practice in groups of three: someone to read Amanda, someone to read Tom, and someone to "coach" the readers. The instructor circulates to give feedback and serve as an extra drama coach. The three roles should alternate regularly so that each group member can practice each role. When learners can give convincing readings of well-selected dramatic excerpts like this one, they are well on the way to improving their control of prosody.

Despite our success with using such play-reading activities in the classroom, we know that some language teaching professionals claim that using excerpts from contemporary plays is not really "authentic" language practice. An alternative strategy would be to record native speakers conversing and then transcribe the conversation – again making the recording and the transcript available to the learners so that a pedagogical strategy similar to the above one can be used. It would, however, be important to select an excerpt that allowed for practice of many different stress and intonation patterns occurring with a variety of sentence types. Another useful activity is to have advanced learners record a natural conversation (or a TV or radio conversation) and then transcribe it focusing on stress, intonation, and reduced speech.

TEACHING YOUNGER LEARNERS

It can be especially challenging to work on pronunciation with younger learners. One useful technique is to use finger or hand puppets to present naturalistic exchanges that focus on pronunciation. Here is an example of a dialog that could be presented using two puppets speaking in turn:

P1:   Hi! How ARE you?
P2:   Fine. How are YOU?
P1:   Do you have rollerskates?
P2:   Yeah, sure!
P1:   (Do you) want to go skating outside?
P2:   Yes. Let's get our skates!

In this brief exchange, learners first hear the dialog and watch the puppets several times. Then by voicing for the puppets, they practice the typical stress and intonation for the "how are you" sequence and also the rising intonation for yes/no questions in contrast to the rising-falling intonation of the statements and exclamations

Another popular activity with younger learners is to use Carolyn Graham's (1978) jazz chants or other repetitive rhythm sequences that are adapted to help the learners practice exchanging relevant information while practicing word and utterance stress:

What's your name and how old are you?
What's your name and how old are you?
    My name is Sam and I'm eight years old.
    My name is Sam and I'm eight years old.

Teachers can get learners to clap out the rhythm as they practice such exchanges.

PROSODY AND PUNCTUATION

In certain cases, the punctuation found in written English reflects the intonation of spoken English. For example, a period (or full stop) at the end of a written sentence usually signals rising-falling intonation in the corresponding spoken utterance:

Writing   Ed is a teacher.

Spoken   [ɛdɪzəti:tʃər]

At the end of a clause or phrase, a comma often signals level intonation or a slight rise, followed by a pause, to signal that the speaker is not yet at the end of the utterance (hereafter we represent sound segments with conventional spelling rather than phonemic notation for ease of reading).

In the following examples the comma represents a slight rise from low to medium pitch, followed by a pause after the word preceding the comma:

a.   **Direct address**

Joan, we're WAITing for you.

b.   **Listing nonfinal members of a series**
(Who came?)

Bob, Sue, and BILL.

Likewise, there are written conventions for distinguishing nonrestrictive (commas) from restrictive (no commas) relative clauses, and two quite different prosodic patterns should also be used; in this case the commas signal pauses and a separate lower intonation contour for the nonrestrictive clause rather than a simple rise.

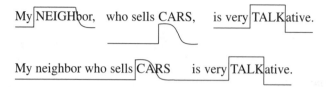

However, as Allen (1971) points out, there are also cases where a comma occurs in writing without signaling any rise or pause in the corresponding spoken utterance. Thus in the following examples, the comma does not equal a rise and pause (or a separate contour).

a. **Place-name divisions**

Joe lives in Springfield, Ohio.

b. **Time divisions**

Joe was born in August, 1951.

c. **Straightforward yes/no responses**

(Did you see it?) Yes, I did.

Strong emotion is often signaled by an exclamation point in writing and more extreme pitch changes in speech:

What a ball game!   (WHAT a BALL game!)

Likewise, in yes/no questions that reflect no special presuppositions, the question mark (?) may correspond to rising intonation:

Is Ed a TEAcher?

However, the question mark at the end of wh-question that elicits information most typically corresponds to rising-falling intonation in speech:

What's your NAME?

(Rising intonation on this question would mean, "Repeat your name; I didn't hear it.") Finally, as we have seen, English question tags may either rise or rise and fall, depending on their meaning. However, when they appear in written form, a question mark usually occurs at the end of both types regardless of intonation.

Thus students who are much more comfortable with written English than with spoken English will have to be warned, as Allen (1971) suggests, that punctuation is not a completely reliable guide to intonation. Instead, the structure, meaning, and purpose of the entire text and each utterance are what must guide the choice of a stress pattern, pauses – if any – and a pitch contour when a written text or script is read aloud – or when a speaker utters his own words!

SUMMARY OF TEACHING APPLICATIONS

The main point in this chapter concerning the interaction of phonology and oral discourse is that the phonology – specifically the prosodic or suprasegmental elements – provides us with all the possible rhythm and intonation combinations. The message and context (discourse and situation), on the other hand, is what determines the most appropriate choice of prosody in any given situated utterance. The general pragmatic strategy used by English speakers is to emphasize new or contrastive information and to de-emphasize given or noncontroversial information (what is already known or shared). English speakers utilize prosody for information management and interactional management. In other words, in any language class where oral skills are taught, the interaction of discourse and prosody must be highlighted and taught since contextually appropriate control of rhythm and intonation are an essential part of oral communicative competence.

While during the past two decades increased attention has been given recently to describing the interaction between intonation and discourse in English (e.g., Brazil, et al., 1980), some of the most accessible practical advice to date comes in a short article by Allen (1971); based on an understanding of student needs, she recommends that teachers do the following (p. 73):[5]

1. direct students' attention to a few major patterns (for example, the intonation contours discussed in this chapter)

2. alert students to differences between the punctuation system and the intonation system

3. distinguish between isolated sentences, which generally can take several intonation contours, and the intonation of ongoing discourse, in which case only one intonation contour is generally appropriate

4. teach students skills so they can make reasonable guesses about the speaker's intention in any given speech situation, based on the speaker's stress and intonation

To this list we would add (5) using the notion of management of (i) new and old information and of (ii) interactional moves involving contrast, correction/repair, and contradiction – to explain shifting focus in ongoing discourse – and (6) alerting students to similarities and differences in intonation between their native language and the target language – especially in classes where the students share the same native language since research shows that transfer of intonation patterns appears to be a common problem contributing to miscommunication.[6]

When practicing dialogs, reading discourse excerpts, and doing more realistic role plays and speech act simulations, the teacher must be sure to spend time on practicing rhythm and intonation and allowing the learners the opportunity both to (1) observe (ideally on videotape) and monitor their performance with respect to prosody and (2) to receive feedback on repeated performances in order to improve their speech production.

CONCLUSION

In this overview of phonology and discourse we have emphasized the information management functions of prosody in oral discourse. There are also obvious functions related to conversation management whereby a speaker lets the listener know if s/he wishes to continue or is ready to yield the floor. Much more difficult to describe and teach, however, are the social functions of intonation, which may reveal things such as the speaker's degree of interest or involvement, the speaker's reticence or assertiveness, the relationship between speaker and hearer, the speaker's expression of sarcasm, and so forth. In this section we have only touched on some of the more salient emotions such as surprise, disbelief, and impatience with respect to how they are signaled through prosody. Will we ever be able to fully understand and teach English prosody's more subtle social and emotional functions? This is unclear since some researchers (Crystal, 1969) feel that generalizable descriptions are not possible because there is too much variation in the expression of such subtleties even among individuals speaking the same dialect.

QUESTIONS FOR DISCUSSION

1. What are some social contexts or discourse contexts in which appropriate prosody is especially crucial?

2. Why is prosody such a difficult language area for nonnative speakers to master?

3. Have you ever observed or experienced a situation where someone has been misunderstood because of inappropriate prosody? If so, share your experience with others in your class/group.

4. What would be a good pedagogical sequence for introducing intermediate level EFL students to prosody (in any language)?

SUGGESTED ACTIVITIES

1. Find some dialog (e.g., some transcribed speech, a comic strip, an excerpt from a play) that lends itself to practice of prosody. Show how you might exploit this kind of material in the classroom.

2. Prepare to discuss the following example sentences (or word sequences) and show how differences in prosody could signal differences in meaning in each case:

   a. Mary teaches engineering.

   b. Jan is Polish, isn't he?

   c. Would you like to go see a movie or get something to eat?

   d. Mary said Cathy is late.

3. Make up your own example of a string of words that could signal two different meanings because of prosodic differences.

4. How would you tutor a student of English whose native language has a very staccato syllable-timed rhythm to better approximate the stress-determined rhythm of English?

5. Develop a mini-lesson using the following excerpt to teach prosody to nonnative speakers; you can assume they have read and discussed the short story "Hills Like White Elephants" by Ernest Hemingway, from which the dialog is taken:

   > "And we could have all this," she said. "And we could have everything and every day we make it more impossible."
   > "What did you say?"
   > "I said we could have everything."
   > "We can have everything."
   > "No, we can't."
   > "We can have the whole world."
   > "No, we can't."
   > "We can go everywhere."

"No, we can't. It isn't ours any more."

"It's ours."

"No, it isn't. And once they take it away, you never get it back."

"But they haven't taken it away."

"We'll wait and see."

"Come back in the shade," he said. "You mustn't feel that way."

"I don't feel any way," the girl said. "I just know things."

"I don't want you to do anything that you don't want to do—"

"Nor that isn't good for me," she said. "I know. Could we have another beer?"

"All right. But you've got to realize—"

"I realize," the girl said. "Can't we maybe stop talking?"

Suggestions for Further Reading

Allen, V. F. (1971). Teaching intonation: From theory to practice. *TESOL Quarterly,* 5(1), 73–81.

Celce-Murcia, M., Brinton, D., & Goodwin, J. (1996). In *Teaching pronunciation: A reference for teachers of English to speakers of other languages* (pp. 131–220). New York: Cambridge University Press.

Dalton, C., & Seidlhofer, B. (1994). *Pronunciation.* Oxford: Oxford University Press.

McCarthy, M. (1991). *Discourse analysis and phonology.* In *Discourse analysis for language teachers* (pp. 88–117). Cambridge: Cambridge University Press.

Wong, R. (1988). *Teaching pronunciation: Focus on rhythm and intonation.* Washington, DC: Center for Applied Linguistics.

Endnotes

[1] Pronunciation dictionaries of English, such as Jones (1991) for British English and Kenyon and Knott (1953) for American English, will indicate sound segments, syllable structure, and stress patterns for English words.

[2] As explained in the introduction, we use the Fries-Pike notation system for North American intonation (see Pike, 1945), where a line superimposed over the utterance indicates the intonation rises and falls as in the widely used textbook by Prator and Robinett (1985). We use solid capital letters to indicate prominent syllables.

[3] There are, however, certain situations such as the number contrasts involving multiples of ten versus teens where a speaker might stress an unstressed syllable to correct or clarify, e.g., "I said fifTY not fifTEEN." Perhaps a better strategy to teach nonnative speakers is to get them to say paraphrases like, "I said five-0 not one-five."

[4] The whole domain of question tags is complicated by the fact that grammar can be marked as well as intonation (They won, did they? I can't, can't I?). We don't go into this here because we are focusing on phonological resources in this chapter, not on all possible grammatical and phonological combinations. For further discussion of the grammar of tag questions, see Celce-Murcia and Larsen-Freeman (1999).

[5] To implement these suggestions teachers must of course be fully aware of the phonological resources of the target language.

[6] Recommendation (6) assumes that well-qualified teachers will be aware of major L1/L2 differences if they deal with a linguistically homogeneous group of learners.

CHAPTER 4

Grammar

"A discourse-oriented approach to grammar would suggest not only a greater emphasis on contexts larger than the sentence, but also a reassessment of priorities in terms of what is taught about such things as word order, articles, ellipsis, tense and aspect, and some of the other categories."

"...grammar is seen to have a direct role in welding clauses, turns and sentences into discourse ..."

(McCarthy, 1991:62)

INTRODUCTION

In the past many ESL/EFL teachers have viewed "grammar" from an exclusively sentence-level perspective. We hope to demonstrate in this chapter that such a perspective, when applied pedagogically, has had negative consequences for the way in which the grammar of second and foreign languages has been taught and tested. A sentence-based view of grammar is also inconsistent with the notion of communicative competence, which – as we have mentioned in Chapter 1 – includes at least four interacting competencies: linguistic (or "grammatical") competence, sociolinguistic (or pragmatic) competence, discourse competence, and strategic competence (Canale, 1983).[1] In this chapter we will be exploring in some detail the nature of the dynamic relationship between grammar and discourse as part of language knowledge, that is, the relationship between the morphological and syntactic aspects of language knowledge and some of the pragmatic aspects of language knowledge and discourse processing, both top-down and bottom-up (See Figure 4.1 on page 51). We will also suggest some new directions for the teaching and testing of grammar.

Whereas the interrelationships between phonology and discourse, which we discussed in the preceding chapter, applied primarily to spoken language, the interrelationships between grammar and discourse apply to written discourse as much as – if not more than – spoken discourse. Furthermore, in terms of our discourse processing framework, which was introduced in Chapter 1 and which will be elaborated in Part 3, we will see that grammatical knowledge is somewhat more critical for discourse production, i.e., for writing

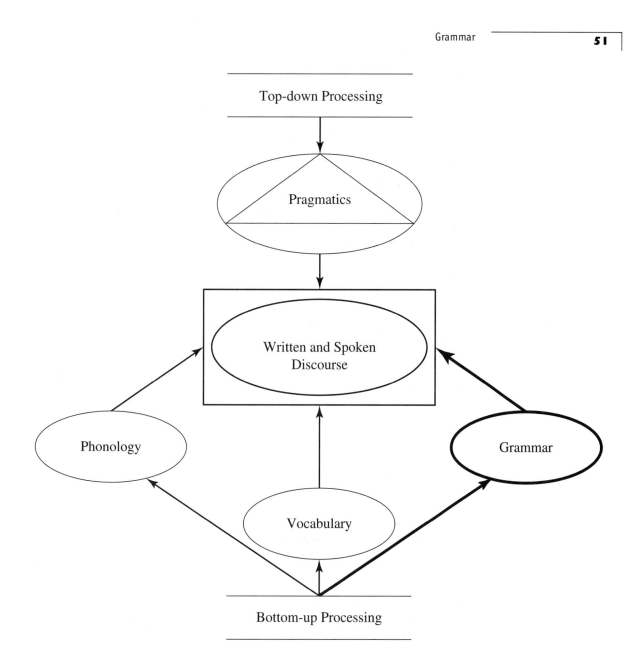

Figure 4.1 Grammar and Language Knowledge

(Chapter 8) and speaking (Chapter 9), than it is for discourse reception, i.e., listening (Chapter 6) and reading (Chapter 7). This is because listening and reading comprehension draw heavily and simultaneously on multiple sources for interpretation including meaning of vocabulary items, content, and formal schemata; situational/contextual information; and knowledge of the world. Grammar thus tends to have a subordinate role for the receptive skills and to be used on an "as needed" basis for resolving problems of interpretation rather than being deployed as a primary resource.

The study of grammar (or morphology and syntax) in formal linguistics tends to be restricted to the sentence level; moreover, many formal linguists have a preference for looking at grammar or syntax as an innate, autonomous, and context-free system. The problem with this perspective is that there are few grammar choices made by speakers or writers that are strictly sentence level and completely context-free. In English, for example, we propose the following list of context-free, sentence-based rules:

- determiner-noun agreement
- use of gerunds after prepositions
- reflexive pronominalization within the clause[2]
- *some–any* suppletion in the environment of negation[3]

These are the local agreement rules that operate within sentences in isolation as well as within sentences that occur in context. Gender and number agreement rules in languages such as French, Spanish, and German are also examples of such mechanical local operations.

In contrast to this small set of local agreement rules, the vast majority of grammatical choices that a speaker/writer makes depend on certain conditions being met in terms of meaning, situational context, and/or discourse context (i.e., co-text). Such grammatical choices are clearly not context-free. All languages have context-dependent options in grammar that enable speakers and writers to accomplish specific pragmatic and discourse-forming functions.

Using English as our example language, we propose that all of the following choices involving rules of English grammar are sensitive – at least in part – to discourse and context (the list is far from exhaustive):

- use of passive versus active voice
- indirect object alternation
- pronominalization (across clauses)
- article/determiner choice
- position of adverbials (phrases, clauses) in sentences
- use of existential *there* versus its non-use
- tense-aspect-modality choice
- right/left dislocation of constituents
- choice of logical connector
- use versus non-use of *it* clefts and *wh*-clefts

Similar lists of context-sensitive grammatical choices can be generated for any language. In all such cases, the speaker/writer's ability to produce the required form or construction in a grammatically accurate way is but part of a much larger process in which the semantic, pragmatic, and discourse appropriateness of the construction itself is also judged with respect to the context in which it is used. While phrase structure rules may account for all the possible grammatical forms that these structures have, it is pragmatic rules or rules of use) that determine which form works best in which context and why.

Another problem with traditional sentence-based approaches to analyzing and teaching grammar is that they have overlooked many frequent and important forms. For example, Bolinger (1977) pointed out that utterances like examples (a) and (b) are fundamentally different from each other in that (a) could conceivably be used to initiate an exchange among interlocutors who were aware that a party had been scheduled, whereas (b) could only be used noninitially by one of the interlocutors and then only if there is prior discourse establishing that one or more specific individuals had come to the party.

a. Did anyone come to the party?

b. Did anyone else come to the party?

Words such as "else," which typically require prior discourse for their interpretation, are generally ignored in sentence-level grammars, which treat the structure of sentences like example (a) but ignore those like example (b). Forms like "else" are, however, discussed in functional or discourse-based approaches to grammar such as Halliday (1994) and Halliday and Hasan (1976, 1989), where interclausal cohesive ties (i.e., semantic and syntactic ties that cross clause or sentence boundaries) are identified and described.

TREATMENTS OF GRAMMAR IN DISCOURSE

Halliday and Hasan (1976), who were among the first to describe the grammatical and lexical relations that hold across sentence or clause boundaries, discuss four types of *cohesive ties* in English that are related to the *grammar of texts*,[4] as previously mentioned in Chapter 1.

1. Ties of **Reference** (pronouns, possessive forms, demonstratives, and the like)

    Paul bought a pear. He ate it.

Here "Paul" and "he" and also "pear" and "it" are coreferential (i.e., both forms in each set refer to the same entity) and form cohesive ties in the text.

2. Ties of **Substitution** (e.g., nominal *one(s)*, verbal *do*, clausal *so*)

    A: Did Sally buy the blue jacket?
    B: No, she bought the red one.

Here "one" replaces "jacket," and they form a structural and lexical/semantic tie and are coclassificational (i.e., refer to the same class of entities) but not coreferential.

3. Ties of **Ellipsis** (or substitution by zero)

    A: Who wrote this article?
    B: Bill.

In this context "Bill" – standing alone without a predicate – functions elliptically to express the entire proposition, "Bill wrote the article."

4. Ties of **Conjunction**[5]

    Christmas is coming; however, the weather seems very un-Christmaslike.

Here the conjunctive adverb "however" signals a tie between the clause that follows and the clause that precedes it. In this case it means that the two events/states are somehow in conflict or signal a counter expectation – at least in the mind of the person who produced this short piece of text.

Let us now consider how all four types of ties would function simultaneously in a piece of authentic oral discourse from a conversation between two young men attending university in the United States.

Patrick:	Why would I want to beat up Eddie? He's one of the best roommates I've ever had.
John:	Oh, compared to what – to Darryl? Yeah, I'm sure he is.
Patrick:	No, compared to all the other ones too. He's one of the best.
John:	What about Carey?
Patrick:	Carey was the best, but I only had him for six weeks in summer.
John:	You didn't have him long enough for him to turn bad on you.
Patrick:	That's true, I guess.

(UCLA oral corpus, see endnote 11)

In this dialog, there is a cohesive referential tie in Patrick's first turn between "Eddie" and "He." In John's first turn, the referential and cohesive use of "he" referring to "Eddie" continues; encoded in turn-final "is" there is also ellipsis of "one of the best roommates you've ever had." In Patrick's second turn, not only does the referential and cohesive use of "he" persist, but the phrase "all the other ones too" contains two referential ties: "the" and "other." Patrick's use of "the" suggests that knowledge of Patrick's past roommates is information shared by John and Patrick; Patrick's use of "other" is a special type of comparative reference that forms a cohesive tie with respect to "Darryl" (other than Darryl). The same phrase contains the nominal substitute "ones," which forms a cohesive tie with "roommates" and which makes it possible for Patrick to avoid repeating "roommates" here. The use of "too" at the end of the first clause would be considered an additive cohesive connective by many analysts (paraphrasable with "also"). In the same turn by Patrick, we also see ellipsis in the phrase "one of the best," with omission of the noun "roommates" after "best," thus using another device to avoid repetition. There are no cohesive ties in John's second turn, but Patrick's third turn starts with "Carey was the best," which again is elliptical with cohesive omission of "roommate" after "best." The connective "but" – coming between the two clauses in this turn by Patrick – expresses a cohesive tie of contrast between the clauses. In the second clause of this turn "him" refers cohesively to "Carey." In his third and final turn John also uses "him" twice to refer cohesively to "Carey." Patrick, in his final turn, uses the referential demonstrative "that" to refer back cohesively to the entire preceding sentence uttered by John, a practice sometimes referred to as "text reference." Thus, while this text contained at least one example of each of the grammatical cohesive devices described by Halliday and Hasan (1976), there were many more examples of reference (personal, comparative, and demonstrative) than there were of substitution or conjunction. Several tokens of ellipsis also occurred and were in fact expected, given that the excerpt analyzed comes from an informal conversation between two peers.

All languages make use of cohesive ties: The way in which and the extent to which a particular type of tie is preferred or used, however, is language specific. For example, using contrastive analysis as well as making use of parallel written texts in English and Chinese, Wu (1982) shows that both languages have equally large inventories of logical connectors or conjunctives; however, in written discourse English makes significantly more frequent use of its stock of conjunction-marking words and phrases than does Chinese. Also, Meepoe (1997) reports that in parallel conversational data collected for English and Thai, Thai often prefers lexical repetition (i.e., lexical cohesion) in contexts where English prefers using ellipsis or referential forms to express such cohesive ties.

The typology of cohesive devices was extended in Halliday and Hasan (1989) to include other grammatical phenomena sensitive to discourse level patterning such as *structural parallelism, theme-rheme development,* and *adjacency pairs* (e.g., an invitation followed by an acceptance), discourse relationships that not only English but other languages also exhibit.

PERSPECTIVES IN ANALYZING GRAMMAR AND DISCOURSE

In investigating the relationship between grammar and discourse, one can take either a **macropragmatic approach** or a **microanalytic approach** (both are necessary and relate to each other). In a macropragmatic approach (e.g., Levinson, 1983; Stubbs, 1983), one starts with a definable speech event or a written or oral genre such as narration or argumentation and uses a relevant corpus to characterize the overall macrostructure in terms of steps, moves, or episodes and then relates features of the macrostructure to microstructure textual elements such as reference conventions, tense and aspect patterns, use of active versus passive voice, and so forth. This is the discourse analytic approach that one can most readily relate to top-down language processing.

In a microanalytic approach (e.g., Haiman and Thompson, 1989; Schiffrin, 1987) one begins with forms or constructions of interest such as tense-aspect forms or discourse markers and, based on analysis of a corpus, proceeds to show what the distribution and discourse functions of the target forms are. Most functional grammarians follow some version of the microanalytic approach and have uncovered much useful information that contributes to our understanding of the interaction of grammar and discourse. This approach can be related most readily to bottom-up language processing.

Many sentence-level grammatical rules that have been assumed to be "context-free" can in fact be stated more accurately if researchers take into account authentic discourse and communicative contexts. For example, pedagogical grammars typically present and teach subject-verb agreement in English as a sentence-level rule; however, Reid (1991) has argued compellingly against this position, and we thus did not include this rule in our list of context-free rules in the introduction to this chapter. Especially in the case of collective noun subjects, subject-verb agreement in English can often be flexible depending on the perspective of the speaker/writer, i.e., the speaker or writer has a choice (Celce-Murcia and Larsen-Freeman, 1999).

    a. The gang was plotting a takeover.

    b. The gang were plotting a takeover.

If the speaker/writer views the gang as a unit, then the singular verb form in (a) is selected. However, if the speaker views the gang as several individuals, then the plural verb form in (b) may well occur.[6]

Similarly, Lagunoff (1992, 1997) examines cases like the following where *they* (or some form of *they: them, themselves, their*) is used within the sentence as a pronoun referring back to a grammatically singular form where prescriptive grammar would require a singular pronoun (i.e., *he, him, himself, his*).

1. Everybody is ready now, aren't they?
2. Neither Fred nor Harry had to work late, did they?
3. Someone has deliberately made themselves homeless.
4. Anyone running a business should employ their spouse.

Lagunoff's explanation for the pervasiveness and naturalness of using *they* to refer to singular antecedents is, first of all, that some subject nouns are grammatically singular yet notionally plural, where the inherently plural sense encourages the use of *they* as an anaphoric pronoun as in (1) and (2). Secondly, other subject nouns are grammatically singular yet nonspecific and vague in their reference as in (3) and (4), and this also encourages the anaphoric use of *they*-related forms.[7]

Halliday and Hasan (1976, 1989) have provided us with comprehensive working descriptions of reference, substitution/ellipsis, and conjunction using English as the language of illustration. These are all discourse-sensitive areas of grammar which are commonly referred to under the rubric of "cohesion" and for which we have provided examples. In the next part of this chapter we discuss and exemplify three other areas representing some grammatical rules and constructions that we now understand much better because of discourse-based research:

1. Word-order choices
2. Tense, aspect, and modality
3. Marked constructions (i.e., constructions that do not follow the normal subject-verb-object pattern)

WORD-ORDER CHOICES

Thompson (1978) reminds us that some languages (e.g., Chinese, Czech, Latin) have a highly flexible word order; for such languages word-order differences have a pragmatic basis. Conversely, there are languages with a fairly rigid or fixed word order like English or French, and in such languages we say that word order is syntactically determined. However, even in a language like English where word order is quite predictable syntactically, there are many word-order variations that are pragmatically motivated and depend on context for their explanation and interpretation.

In this section we shall first discuss dative alternation in English sentences with indirect objects and then discuss verb particle movement in English sentences with separable phrasal verbs. Other languages also offer similar local word-order choices to speakers and writers.[8]

DATIVE ALTERNATION

In a *sentence-level* approach to grammar we learn that there are often two equivalent ways of expressing (in active voice) a proposition with a verb of transfer like *give* that takes three underlying arguments or participants (an agent, a recipient, and what is being transferred):

1. Sid gave the car to Jim.
2. Sid gave Jim the car.

In a pragmatic or *discourse-sensitive* approach to grammar examples (1) and (2) are viewed as *nonequivalent* because they occur in different discourse contexts.

In other words, if Gladys (Sid's wife and Jim's mother) comes home and says, "Where's Jim?," Sid can answer, "I gave him the car (and he's gone for the day)." but not "I gave the car to Jim." However, if Gladys comes home and says to Sid, "I don't see the car. Where is it?," Sid can respond, "I gave the car/it to Jim" but he is unlikely to say, "I gave Jim the car" unless he gives extra phonological prominence to "Jim" rather than "the car" when he says the latter sentence, thus using prosody to override syntax in ways that we discussed in Chapter 3. These preferences in word order show us that discourse is sensitive to the ordering of old and new information, and that new information generally occurs closer to the end of the clause. Thompson and Koide (1987) and Williams (1994), using data from natural language, have demonstrated that with verbs allowing for two objects and for flexible word order many if not most instances of dative alternation are in fact determined at the discourse level.[9]

WORD ORDER VARIATION WITH SEPARABLE PHRASAL VERBS

English language grammarians have long debated what difference, if any, exists between the two possible word orders in constructions composed of separable phrasal verbs and lexical (rather than pronominal) direct objects.

1. Edward gave up his reward.
2. Edward gave his reward up.

For sentence-level formalists these sentences are equivalent. Bolinger (1971) was among the first to suggest that such sentences were not equivalent since the degree of newness or importance of the direct object played a prominent role in determining the word order. The wording parallel to (1) would be preferred in contexts where the direct object (i.e., the reward) was truly new or specially emphasized information; the word order in (2) would be preferred where the direct object had already been mentioned but was not sufficiently recent or well established as old information to justify the use of the pronoun (as in *Edward gave it up*). With use of the pronoun both the word order and the pronominaliza-tion signal the givenness and topicality of the direct object. This suggests that with sepa-rable transitive phrasal verbs we have a three-way distinction rather than a binary choice:

1. Edward gave up his reward.   (new or emphasized info./obj.)
2. Edward gave his reward up.   (neither new nor old info./obj.)
3. Edward gave it up.   (old info./obj.)

Thus in the context of a question such as "What did Edward give up?" the preferred response is (1), or more likely (1'):

  (1') He gave up his reward.

In the context of an even more specific query such as "What did Edward do with his reward?" the preferred response is (3), or more likely (3'):

  (3') He gave it up.

This leaves a sentence like (2), or (2'), for contexts where "reward" has a somewhat less recent mention, e.g., "The reward – the whole situation – it's very embarrassing, isn't it? What did poor Edward decide to do?"

  (2') He gave the/his reward up.

    Chen (1986) was among the first to use analysis of discourse to demonstrate the validity of Bolinger's observations by testing them against a large corpus of spoken English data.
    Two text segments from *Newsweek* (August 26, 1996) illustrate Bolinger's rule-of-thumb in action:

1. Until now, Dole has faced not just a gender gap but a gender chasm. Can he woo back GOP women? (p. 28)
2. . . . He [FDR] was a realist who understood that the appearance of optimism was crucial for morale; Ronald Reagan understood that, too, and the purpose of this year's Republican convention was to rekindle that flame (and snatch the party back from the pinched hatemongers of Houston). (p. 29)

From a grammatical perspective the writer of the first text could have asked, "Can he woo GOP women back?" However, this word order would have de-emphasized the direct object "GOP women," and this writer is emphasizing "GOP women." Thus the final posi-tion of the direct object "GOP women" is rhetorically effective in this context.
    The writer of the second text could have put in the parentheses "(and snatch back the party...)." This wording, however, would emphasize "the [Republican] party" – which is already well established by the preceding mention of the "Republican convention" – rather than the action of "snatching back" that the writer wishes to emphasize. By putting the phrasal verb particle "back" in verb-phrase final position, the writer somewhat de-emphasizes "the party" and emphasizes the action of snatching back.

TENSE, ASPECT, AND MODALITY

As mentioned in Chapter 1, coherence refers to the unity in discourse through which individual sentences in discourse relate to each other logically. The use of the tense, aspect, and modality system as a source of coherence in discourse has become an increasingly prominent topic in applied linguistics because of the pioneering work of sociolinguists like Wolfson (1982) and discourse analysts like Schiffrin (1981), who examined the systematic use of the historical present tense and its variation with the simple past tense in oral narratives of native English speakers. In this section we shall discuss past habitual narrative discourse organized around the use of *used to* and *would/('d)* and future scenarios organized around the use of *be going to* and *will/('ll)*.

USED TO –WOULD('D)

Drawing on the work of Mann and Thompson (1988), Suh (1992) demonstrates with episodes such as the following that *used to* and *would* are often employed in past habitual oral narratives where *used to* typically initiates a rhetorical frame, and *would* (or its contracted form *'d*) is used to elaborate the discourse, as in this discourse produced by a young Chicano farm worker:

> The bad thing was they *used to* laugh at us, the Anglo kids. They *would* laugh because *we'd* bring tortillas and frijoles to lunch. They *would* have their nice little compact lunch boxes with cold milk in their thermos and *they'd* laugh at us because all we had was dried tortillas. Not only *would* they laugh at us, but the kids *would* pick fights.[10]

Suh proposed that the semantically more salient form tends to occur first to frame the discourse (*used to*), whereas the more ambiguous and contigent forms occur noninitially. Suh found many tokens like the one above where there would also be occasional use of the simple past tense by the speaker in the extended elaboration to interject an evaluation or some background information into the discourse. On the basis of the many past habitual episodes she found that conformed to this pattern, Suh posited the "framework-elaboration hypothesis" and proceeded to look for other discourse phenomena of a related nature.

BE GOING TO – WILL('LL)

Suh (1992) then also found many examples of episodes where English speakers narrated oral future scenarios that began with *be going to* and were then subsequently elaborated with *will* or its contracted form *'ll*. The following oral account by a medical intern of the gastric restriction procedure for the morbidly obese is one such example:

> They*'re going to* go in and have their gut slit open, their stomach exposed and have it stapled off so that there *will* be two pou-, an upper pouch in the stomach which *will* hold about two ounces of food, it's got a little hole right in the middle of that pouch where food when it's finally ground up *will* slowly go through.
>
> (from UCLA oral corpus)[11]

In these future scenarios the simple present tense is sometimes used alongside *will* to add some minor descriptive details within the elaboration phase of the episode. Thus with authentic examples like these we see that tense-aspect-modality sequences play an important role in creating coherence in oral narratives and that tendencies of the type identified by Suh (1992) and others should be presented to learners using authentic discourse and appropriate follow-up activities.

MARKED CONSTRUCTIONS

Sometimes languages develop special constructions to accommodate the flow of information in discourse or for special rhetorical effect in certain contexts. In English structures like *wh*-clefts, *it*-clefts, and sentences beginning with existential *there* are examples of such constructions. Most pedagogical treatments for language learners are problematic in that they treat such constructions at the sentence level only and never ground their instruction in authentic discourse.

In the section below we shall discuss *wh*-clefts and existential *there*.

WH–CLEFTS

Kim (1992) did an extensive analysis of the use of *wh*-clefts (also known as pseudo-clefts) in English conversation. He concluded that their general or overarching function is to mark a disjunction by the speaker with respect to the preceding discourse – a disjunction that allows the speaker to go back to some previous utterance and address it. Within this general view of *wh*-clefts, Kim distinguished those *wh*-clefts that are informational and mark the gist of the talk (i.e., that restate, sum up, or refocus the topic) from those that are interactional and respond to a problem (a challenge from the interlocutor or a perceived misunderstanding/miscommunication).

The first type of *wh*-cleft often occurs when a speaker begins to conclude a talk or lecture, e.g., "What I've tried to share with you this morning is ten important ideas that have changed the way I teach . . ." (David Nunan, Braztesol Conference, Goiania, Brazil, July, 1996). The following conversational excerpt is an example of the second type of *wh*-cleft (i.e., a response to a problem).

A: An' I was wondering if you'd let me use your gun.

B: My gun?

A: Yeah.

B: What gun? ◄─────────────────┐

A: Don't you have a beebee gun?   │

B: Yeah.   │

A: Oh it's –   │

B: Oh I have a lot of guns.   │

A: You do?   │

──► **B:** Yeah. What I meant was WHICH gun. ─┘

(Kim, 1992:64, from telephone data collected
and transcribed by Irene Daden)

In the last line of this episode Speaker B uses the *wh*-cleft to repair the ambiguous "what gun" that he had uttered six turns back. When Speaker B said "what gun," this phrase was misinterpreted by his interlocutor (Speaker A) as expressing a challenge (i.e., "I don't have any guns" rather than expressing the neutral information question that Speaker B had intended when he asked the question. Once Speaker B realized what the problem was, he repaired his earlier question using a *wh*-cleft and the determiner *which*.

EXISTENTIAL "THERE"

In an analysis of sentences with existential *there* subjects in spoken discourse, Sasaki (1991) addresses the role that this construction plays with regard to topic continuity in oral discourse. For example, in sentences like the following:

> "There are some special ways to cut the climbing roses."

Sasaki specifically looked at the discourse function of the logical subjects (e.g., "some special ways") and the postmodifying elements (e.g., "to cut the climbing roses"). She was able to demonstrate that sentences in her spoken corpus with initial nonreferential *there* functioned in the following discourse-sensitive ways:

- The logical subjects tend to express new information and to persist as the topics of subsequent clauses.

- The logical subjects tend to be entailed (i.e., they are related to something previously mentioned) and do not normally begin episodes.

- The postmodifying elements that follow and modify the logical subject have high topic continuity, i.e., their referents have previously been mentioned.

Keeping this in mind, let's examine the longer segment in which the above example utterance with *there* occurs as part of a radio talk show (GL="Garden Lady" and C="Caller").

  GL: Hi, you're on the air.

    C: Hi, I have a very old kind of a vine type rose I think that grows (.) it's actually my next door neighbor's vacant yard and uhm I don't really know how to prune that thing. It seems like a floribunda type,

  GL: uhhum

    C: and I'm not really sure where to cut or . . .

  GL: Yeah, there are some special ways to cut the climbing roses. Basically what you are going to do is pick out three or four of the biggest canes and you are going to leave those and then what you want to do is you cut back the side branches to about six inches. And that way you're ending with a nice scaffold a nice basic layout on your rose against the wall. Is it against a wall? Or just kind of rambling?

    C: It's coming around up over the top of a fence.

  GL: Yeah, well you can trim it back at will if it's getting out of control . . .

(UCLA oral corpus – see endnote 11)

In this episode the four opening turns establish that the caller wants to find out how she should prune a climbing rose. When the Garden Lady uses the existential *there* clause, she introduces the subtopic "some special ways (to cut)" and then continues to focus on the "special ways" for most of the remaining dialog with this caller. In other words, one important discourse function of the existential *there* construction is to introduce for subsequent development a specific subtopic of something more general than has already been established, along with the assumption that this subtopic will be further developed in subsequent discourse.

PEDAGOGY AND ASSESSMENT

At the present time few would disagree with the proposal that EFL/ESL learners must be made aware of and given opportunities to interpret and practice the use of cohesive devices that signal reference, substitution, ellipsis, and conjunction in English. There are also encouraging signs that leaders in the language teaching profession are beginning to acknowledge that the teaching of grammar to ESL/EFL learners should be carried out in context with discourse or text providing the appropriate pedagogical frame (cf. McCarthy, 1991; Widdowson, 1990). In other words, there is growing agreement that teaching grammar exclusively at the sentence level with decontextualized and unrelated sentences, which has long been the traditional way to teach grammar, is not likely to produce any real learning. Likewise, if we want to test a learner's proficiency level with respect to grammar, sentence-level, discrete point test items are not likely to be a good way to measure the grammar a learner can actually use when s/he speaks or writes, i.e., new testing formats must complement the changes now underway in teaching practice. (See Chapter 11 on assessment).

The biggest problem, however, is that there are very few materials currently available that show the teacher how to teach grammar using discourse-based and context-based activities and formats. In this section of the chapter we would like to make some concrete suggestions that classroom teachers can adapt and extend for their own purposes when teaching grammar.

TEACHING YOUNGER LEARNERS

It is generally accepted that younger learners do not benefit from formal grammar instruction, yet some focus on form can be helpful. To focus on form in a painless manner, we suggest using meaningful exchanges that highlight useful grammatical forms. For example if the grammar objective is yes/no questions ("Can you . . .?"), students could be exposed to a series of questions about themselves. After answering these questions, they can address them to peers:

a. Answer the following about yourself:
   Can you ride a bicycle?
   Can you eat ten cookies?
   Can you phone the principal?

b. Ask a friend:
   Can you ride a bicycle?
   Can you eat ten cookies?
   (make up your own questions)

If they can do the activity in a relatively error-free manner, they have probably internalized some grammar.

In order to make sure that young learners use language in meaningful ways we must remember to combine *form* and *context*. For example, students can tell about personal experiences in order to use verbs in the past tense. Students can talk about their plans to use future verb forms and future time expressions.

TEACHING BEGINNERS (OF ALL AGES)

It is most challenging to use discourse-based teaching techniques with beginners since their knowledge of the target language is so limited. The teacher often has to teach vocabulary and structures in preparation for the comprehension and generation of discourse. Certainly Asher's (1977) Total Physical Response technique, which requires the learner to listen and respond actively to commands, can be used at this level to present grammar and to practice the comprehension of grammar at the discourse level if a series of coherent related sentences is used for listening and responding. With just a few articles of clothing, for example, the teacher can use the TPR technique to introduce and practice two intransitive phrasal verbs (*stand up, sit down*) and two separable transitive phrasal verbs (*put on, take off*). This type of activity, given the continuity and flow of speech from the teacher, prepares the learner for the subsequent comprehension and production of related narrative discourse (e.g., The boy stood up and put on his hat).

I	II	III
Stand up	Stand up	Stand up
Come here	Come here	Come here
Put the hat on	Put the coat on	Put the scarf on
Take it off	Take it off	Take it off
Return to your desk	Return to your desk	Return to your desk
Sit down	Sit down	Sit down

Each scenario can be repeated several times, especially the first one. The teacher should help the first few students if they have difficulty and should repeat each scenario with several different students until the whole class is able to follow the instructions easily. When this happens, the teacher can introduce the next new scenario. Beginners would not yet be ready to produce the separable phrasal verbs with variable word order and with pronominal objects, but activities like these set the scene for later related production activities. Also, even though only one student carries out the commands at any given moment, the entire class is generally very attentive and is learning by listening and observing.

To involve the entire class in a listening activity that focuses on grammar, Celce-Murcia and Hilles (1988:44) suggest listen-and-color exercises. For example, each student would receive a picture of a boy and a girl wearing a tee shirt and pants and walking a dog. The teacher gives – as many times as needed – a set of connected instructions that requires the students to distinguish the possessive pronouns *his* and *her* (as well as recognizing vocabulary dealing with colors, articles of clothing, and body parts).

> Color her hair red, color his hair yellow, color his pants brown, color her pants green, and color his dog black, and so forth.

When moving on to beginning-level activities that include production of simple discourse, it is very important to spend time eliciting or learning the vocabulary related to a particular topic or task so that the wordstore can be used to practice structures and to perform activities relevant to the topic. For example, in a beginning-level ESL/EFL class each learner can generate a nuclear family tree in diagram form (following a model from the teacher, who presents first, thus building up the learners' receptive vocabulary and grammar). Then by learning a few kinship terms (in singular and plural form), the first-person singular possessive adjective *my,* and the three present-tense forms of the copula *be (am, is, are)*, learners should be able to present their family trees and introduce their families to the class in the form of a short discourse – not simply as a series of disjointed simple sentences:

> I am Antonio. My father is José and my mother is Ana. My brother is Jorge, and my two sisters are Maria and Anita.

Depending on the age and needs of individual students, it may be necessary to introduce a few more kinship terms so that they can introduce spouses, grandparents, or other relatives who form part of their immediate family unit. Such additional vocabulary can be introduced as the need arises. As individual students make oral presentations, the class should listen and draw the family tree described. The trees drawn by the students listening and the trees from which the speakers made their oral presentations can then be compared to check for consistency and accuracy.

Another productive activity has the whole class working together to generate master lists under three activity headings:

1. Things I like to do when I have time
2. Things I have to do every day
3. Things I do occasionally

The first heading elicits leisure activities, e.g., go to the beach, play football, watch TV. The second heading includes things like make my bed, study, do the dishes. The third will contain activities like visit my grandmother, go to the movies, write a letter to my cousin. The teacher can help generate the vocabulary for the lists, as needed, and can make sure that the short verb phrases written on the chalkboard or the overhead projector are grammatically and lexically accurate. At this point each learner will be ready to generate his/her own short list, selecting at least two items from each of the three master lists created in class but making it pertinent to his or her own reality. Working with a partner, the learner will write two conjoined sentences that describe what he and his partner do every day, using the information in the individually generated lists (and, of course, using the simple present tense):

> Every day I make my bed, study, and do the dishes, and Sergio walks his
> dog and practices the piano.

These short personalized texts will then be read aloud to the class for comprehension and retelling or summarization by others. Similar activities will be carried out using the information generated for the other two activity lists to further reinforce the simple present tense.

As a more challenging communicative activity, the learners can draw on all the materials they have generated for their family tree description and their activities to write a simple letter introducing themselves to a pen pal (ideally a real person who will respond), thus incorporating the target structures and vocabulary they have learned into a larger piece of discourse generated for purposes of communication.

This should not, however, be the end of the unit. As a final step the teacher should present to the class data that the learners themselves have generated, with the data grouped according to each structure being taught (copula *be*, simple present tense, personal pronouns). The teacher directs the learners to come to some kind of grammatical generalization in their own words about each structure. Finally, the teacher gives them the formal rule for each structure and gets them to compare it with the rule they have generated. If useful, the students can also work at correcting some of the errors they have produced while covering the material in the unit.

TEACHING INTERMEDIATE LEARNERS

For intermediate-level students, stories are often an engaging way to comprehend and practice grammar and discourse. The following fable about the fox and the crow, for example, can be used to present or to reinforce (or to test) one of the main conventions governing English article usage. Learners should be asked to use one article in lieu of each number; for first mention (or new information), they should use the indefinite article (*a/an*) with singular countable nouns; for second or subsequent mentions (i.e., old information), they should use the definite article (*the*).

> There was once (1) crow who stole (2) wedge of cheese from (3) kitchen window. She flew off with (4) cheese to (5) nearby tree. (6) fox saw what (7) crow had done, and he walked over to (8) tree.
> "Oh, Mistress Crow, you have such lovely black feathers, such slender feet, such (9) beautiful beak, and such fine black eyes! You must have (10) beautiful voice. Would you sing for me?"
> (11) crow felt very proud. She opened her beak and sang "CAW-CAW-CAW." Of course (12) cheese fell down and (13) fox snatched it up and ate every bite.[12]

When learners are able to use *a/an* and *the* appropriately, the rule can be extended to include use of the zero article before first mentions of plural countable nouns and mass nouns (these nouns also take *the* for second mention as is illustrated by the subsequent mentions of *cheese* in the fable).

Much like stories, the lyrics to songs can also be used to present and practice grammar in discourse. For example, Pete Seeger's antiwar song "Where Have All the Flowers Gone?" can be used as a warm-up activity to prepare students to participate in short exchanges that require *wh*-questions with the present perfect tense[13] since in this song each stanza repeats the frame (Where have all the _____ gone?). The construction practiced in the song could then be extended to talk about more concrete information familiar to class members. For example:

> **T:** Amir isn't in class today.
> **S1:** Where has he gone (instead of coming to class)?
> **S2:** I don't know. (Maybe) he's gone to the beach.
>
> **T:** Maria you're late today.
> **S1:** Where have you been?
> **M:** I've been to my son's school.

For intermediate-level students such use of the present perfect demonstrates how English speakers can talk about past events without ever leaving the extended present as the frame of reference, which is one of the most important functions of the present perfect tense.

Similarly, listening to and singing the lyrics of the well-known folk song "If I Had a Hammer" can be a warm-up activity for practicing the present hypothetical use of conditionals in drills such as the following:

> **T:** What do you wish you had (that you don't have)?
> **S1:** A million dollars.
> **S2:** A Harley Davidson.
> **S3:** A Rolls Royce.
> Etc.
> **T:** S1, tell us what you would do if you had a million dollars.
> **S1:** (If I had a million dollars,) I'd buy a house for my parents, for myself, and for all my brothers and sisters.
> Etc.

Sometimes low intermediate and intermediate-level learners need to develop their ability to process grammar and interpret discourse that they hear or read much more than they need to practice productive use of discourse-level grammar. These students need their foreign or second language to read textbooks and manuals or perhaps to listen to lectures or talks by experts or teachers. Such learners must be exposed to spoken or written discourse that trains them to recognize and comprehend the meaning and role of crucial structures. For example, consider the following passage, which highlights the passive voice:

American Film Classics: A Survey of 100 People
by Harold Smithers

One hundred Americans (fifty in New York and fifty in Los Angeles) were asked to identify their three favorite classic films. *Casablanca* was mentioned most frequently, then *Citizen Kane*, and the third choice was *Gone with the Wind*. Only four other movies were named more than five times each. They were *Ben Hur*, *The Birth of a Nation*, *Sunset Boulevard*, and *The Ten Commandments*. It is interesting to note that while both the male and female respondents mentioned *Casablanca* as a favorite classic, *Gone With the Wind* was suggested mainly by women and *Citizen Kane* mainly by men.

Such a passage can be taped and played back as a simulated radio broadcast segment beginning (in lieu of the title and byline) with "This is Harold Smithers reporting on a survey I carried out on American classic films." The class should listen once to get the general idea (What is the passage about?). Then they can be asked to listen again and jot down answers to the following questions:

1. How many people were surveyed and where?
2. Which three films were the favorites?
3. What other films where mentioned more than five times?
4. Did men and women like the same films?

If the above passage is presented in written form, the same comprehension questions can be asked but the analysis of grammar in discourse can be more rigorous. Assuming they are familiar with the necessary metalanguage, the learners can be asked to underline all passive verb phrases, circle all subject noun phrases, and put boxes around any explicit agents. In pairs or groups the learners can discuss their answers to questions such as these:

1. Why is the passive voice so frequent in this text?
2. Who is/are the agent(s) in sentences that have no expressed, explicit agent?
3. Could the passage have been written or spoken using only the active voice? If so,
   a. Would the tone of the reporter be the same?
   b. Would there be the same focus on the films?

Similar exercises designed primarily for building up recognition and comprehension skills can also be developed for other structures such as relative clauses, tense and aspect sequences, and pronouns and other referential words. It is best if authentic texts can serve as the basis for such activities. If necessary, they can be simplified or adapted for use with lower-level learners.

For high intermediate-level students another textual resource that can be used to present grammar in context is short poems. For example, teachers can use "The Night Will Never Stay" by Eleanor Farjeon (1951) to help contextualize the use of *will* + VERB, where *will* is epistemic and compatible with an interpretation of future inevitability rather than a simple specific future time. It can be pointed out that other words in the poem like *never, still,* and *though* help reinforce this interpretation of *will.*

The Night Will Never Stay

The night will never stay,
The night will still go by,
Though with a million stars
You pin it to the sky;

Though you bind it with the blowing wind
And buckle it with the moon,
The night will slip away
Like sorrow or a tune.

Eleanor Farjeon

After reading and discussing the poem (with all vocabulary clarified and with focus on the target *will* construction) the learners are ready individually or in groups to make up their own poem about other experiences that inevitably come to an end (the rainbow, the sunlight, the rain, first love, and so forth). Some students need to be reassured that if they cannot generate a perfect rhyme or if they use metric patterns that differ from the model, their poems will still be acceptable.

TEACHING ADVANCED LEARNERS

With advanced learners one way to proceed is to use an inductive-analytic approach to teaching grammar in discourse (see also Chapter 12, where we discuss the value of teaching learners to do discourse analysis). For example, one can give an advanced class three authentic texts using *used to* and *would (d)* such as the "young Chicano farm worker" text on page 58 and the following two:

Merchant Marine

I used to phone my wife three, four times every trip. In Calcutta I'd wait five hours to get a phone call through. If I didn't get it through one night, I'd call again and wait three, fours hours the next morning. Finally, just hearing her voice, I'd stand and actually choke up on the phone.[14]

Summers on the Farm

I used to spend the summer with my uncle Joe on his farm. I'd get up at the crack of dawn and I'd milk cows, bring in the hay, and feed the chickens. I'd complain like hell about all the work, but it really was a good experience.

(author data)

The teacher can then ask the students to give a description of the use of *used to* and *would('d)* in the three texts, all of which represent past habits and experiences. If the students need some help, give them guiding questions (such as the following) on the chalkboard or the overhead projector:

1. Where does *used to* occur in these texts?
2. Where does *would('d)* occur?
3. Which form establishes a frame or topic?
4. Which form introduces supporting details?
5. Which form expresses "past habits or states" most clearly?

As a follow-up practice, suggest some topics, for example:

- Describe some past habit or activity you did when you were younger.
- Describe someone else's past habits or activities.

Ask each student to give a brief oral presentation on one of the topics and then prepare a written version of his/her talk to reinforce at the discourse level the grammar they have practiced.

Learners who do such activities can remember and apply reasonably well the grammar they learn this way since they have discovered how grammar is a resource for telling a story or creating text rather than grammar simply existing as a set of abstract sentence-level rules.

TESTING GRAMMAR

Although discourse and language assessment are treated more comprehensively in Chapter 11, we would like to mention here that discourse-level testing formats need to be used systematically to test learners' ability to use grammar in context. To accomplish this, tests will very often look much like text-based practice activities. One discourse-based test format is the cloze procedure, which we illustrated for practicing use of articles via the fable about the fox and the crow. As a cloze test this passage can measure the extent to which learners are aware of the "first mention" versus "second/subsequent mention" principle in article usage. Other grammar points that one could test with cloze passages include prepositions, pronouns, demonstratives, and logical connectors. Using texts with "gaps" (i.e., texts with one to five words missing rather than only the one-word blanks used in a cloze-type test) one can help students practice using or can test their knowledge of several grammar points:

- choice of tense-aspect forms
- order of direct and indirect objects
- choice of infinitive versus gerund
- choice of active versus passive voice

One can also ask learners to complete short texts to test their knowledge of grammar and discourse. For example,

(1) I'm going to buy a boat so . . .
(2) Phil used to live in Dover, but . . .

are clauses that are completed in rather predictable ways by native English speakers (nonnative speakers should be able to complete such tasks with similar responses):

(1') [so] I can go fishing.
      [so] I can sail to Catalina.

(2') [but] he doesn't live there anymore.
      [but] now he lives in London.

The testing of grammar in context is an area where even less progress has been made than in teaching grammar through discourse; however, we expect to see major developments in the future in this area.

CONCLUSION

As we have demonstrated, many if not most of the choices we make among all the grammatical options open to us can usefully be re-examined in terms of their contextual or pragmatic motivations and discourse function(s). Once this is accomplished, the teaching of grammar can be better integrated with the teaching of the language skills (listening, speaking, reading, writing) and with the goal of teaching language as communication. Knowledge of grammar should include not only sentence-level ordering rules and options but also an awareness that phenomena such as word-order choices, tense-aspect choices, and use of special grammatical constructions are in fact pragmatic, discourse-level choices that speakers and writers make. It is important that we reconceptualize such constructions in relation to discourse and communication. For language teaching purposes it is counterproductive to view grammar as an autonomous sentence-level system, yet this has been the perspective not only of formal linguists but also of traditional language teaching methods such as grammar translation and audiolingualism.

Admittedly, there will always be a few local and fairly mechanical grammatical rules that learners need to practice, such as basic word order, making sure determiners and their nouns agree, selecting the correct reflexive pronoun object, and using gerunds after prepositions. Such rules must be learned and practiced at the sentence level and then extended to automatic use in discourse-level contexts. Mechanical rules like these are the exceptions, however. Most of the "rules" that we traditionally refer to as the core of "grammar" should be taught as grammatical choices made at the level of discourse. This is the level at which learners can best process, understand, and apply the conventions of grammar in their second or foreign language.

LANGUAGE VARIATION AT THE GRAMMATICAL LEVEL

As we have stated, much of what might be considered grammatical variation at the sentence level turns out to be a principled semantic or pragmatic choice at the discourse level, e.g., the way we use active and passive voice in written texts or the way we order direct and indirect objects in our speech. There is also variation in grammar between formal written discourse and informal spoken discourse. Thus, we formally write:

There are two letters on my desk.

This is the premise on which he based his argument.

But we informally may say:

There's two letters on my desk.

This is the premise he based his argument on.

However, there is also grammatical variation between dialects of a language. For example:

Geographical variation

Standard British: Have you a pencil?

Standard American: Do you have a pencil?

Social/ethnic variation

Black English vernacular: I didn't say nothing.

Standard English: I didn't say anything.

To the extent that each dialect consistently follows grammar rules that are different from the rules used in other dialects, we can describe this variation. It is useful for teachers and learners to be aware of such grammatical variation and to understand nonjudgmentally what it signals in terms of the user's probable nationality or ethnic identity. In most cases, language learners want to acquire the standard version of the geographical dialect most useful for their purposes.

The following chapter will discuss grammar's partner in language knowledge at the discourse level – vocabulary. Grammar needs vocabulary for meaning, and vocabulary needs grammar for structure. Some linguists (Halliday, 1985) talk about grammar and vocabulary as one entity: **lexicogrammar**. While this is a theoretically appealing notion, for pedagogical purposes we feel that it is still useful to maintain some distinction between these two areas of language knowledge, focusing on the relationship that each has to discourse.

DISCUSSION QUESTIONS

1. Some ESL teachers believe that well-selected comic strips offer good materials for teaching grammar in context. Do you agree? Why or why not? Are there other types of authentic materials that you think teachers should consider using for teaching grammar through discourse and in context?

2. Some researchers claim that experiments show that sentence-level instruction in grammar has no effect on an ESL/EFL learner's ability to use grammar for communicative purposes. Does this outcome surprise you? Why do you think this might be true? Do you think that discourse-based grammar instruction would yield different results? Why or why not?

3. You have a student who objects to your discourse-level approach to teaching grammar. He wants to study grammar at the sentence level as he has always done before. What will you say and do to persuade him of the validity and necessity of working with a discourse-based approach?

4. Many researchers feel that there is too much emphasis on production and testing of grammar rather than a focus on its comprehension and interpretation. Many would argue that recognition and comprehension should precede production. With a partner discuss ways of creating discourse-based activities geared toward developing the learner's recognition grammar.

SUGGESTED ACTIVITIES

1. Find a sentence-level grammar exercise in a language textbook. What is the objective of this exercise? Think of two different ways to teach this objective through discourse instead.

2. Consider the active voice/passive voice distinction (e.g., Leonardo da Vinci painted the Mona Lisa/The Mona Lisa was painted by Leonardo da Vinci). What are two possible sentence-level teaching activities? What are two possible discourse-based teaching activities? Discuss the strength and weaknesses of the sentence-level and the discourse-level activities. Which do you think would be better and why?

3. Consider the two following texts; then describe the interaction of the simple past tense and the underlined past perfect tense in the organization of these texts. Is this pattern consistent with Suh's frame-elaboration hypothesis or not?

    a. The students sat in the bleachers of Pauley Pavilion watching the faculty enter in their caps and gowns. Dignitaries continued to arrive while the band played a festive melody for the onlookers. To the cheers of the crowd, President Clinton came in and took his assigned seat on the podium. UCLA's 75th anniversary celebration had begun.

        (from the UCLA *Daily Bruin*, May 25, 1994)

    b. In the 1980s researchers at Stanford University were trying to teach American sign language to Koko, a gorilla. Koko was well cared for and was surrounded by interesting objects. Her caretakers continually exposed her to signs for the food items and toys in her environment. Koko particularly loved eating bananas and playing with kittens. One day she was hungry but couldn't find any bananas. She went to the researcher and made a good approximation of the sign for "banana." Koko was rewarded with a banana, but even more important, the research team knew that Koko had made the connection between a sign and the object it represented.

        (author data)

4. What follows is a paragraph from a book on cultural differences (Hall & Hall, 1990: 3–4). How might you exploit this bit of authentic discourse to teach grammar in context?

    > Culture can be likened to a giant, extraordinarily complex, and subtle computer. Its programs guide the activities and responses of human beings in every walk of life. This process requires attention to everything people do – to survive, to advance in the world, and to gain satisfaction from life. Furthermore, cultural programs will not work if crucial steps are omitted, which happens when people unconsciously apply their own rules to another system.

5. If you have younger learners, develop an activity involving meaningful exchange that will help them practice questions about habits and preferences (i.e., that will make use of the auxiliary verb *do*).

Suggestions for Further Reading

Batstone, R. (1994). *Grammar*. Oxford: Oxford University Press.

Celce-Murcia, M. (1991). Discourse analysis and grammar instruction. *Annual Review of Applied Linguistics, 11*, 135–151.

Celce-Murcia, M., & Hilles, S. (1988). Text-based exercises and activities. In *Techniques and resources in teaching grammar* (pp. 149–168). Oxford: Oxford University Press.

Celce-Murcia, M., & Larsen-Freeman, D. (1999). The tense-aspect-modality system in discourse. In *The grammar book: An ESL/EFL teachers course*, 2nd ed., (pp. 161–181). Boston: Heinle & Heinle.

Hatch, E. (1992). *Discourse and language education.* New York: Cambridge University Press. (See especially Chapters 6, 7, and 8, pp. 209–290.)

McCarthy, M. (1991). Discourse analysis and grammar. In *Discourse analysis for language teachers* (pp. 34–63). Cambridge: Cambridge University Press.

Endnotes

[1] Celce-Murcia, Dörnyei, and Thurrell (1995) further divide communicative competence into linguistic, sociolinguistic, discourse, strategic, and actional competencies, where "actional competence" refers to more formulaic aspects of language such as the oral speech acts or the written rhetorical moves that function as part of communicative competence.

[2] This rule seems to apply whether the reflexive pronoun is a true reflexive object (John shared himself.), an emphatic (John himself did it.), or an adverbial (John lives by himself.).

[3] R. Lakoff (1969) argues that the "some-any" rule does not exist and that the use of these two determiners is very semantically motivated.

[4] Halliday and Hasan (1976) also discuss "lexical cohesion," but that will be part of the following chapter on vocabulary, thus we do not take it up here.

[5] We note that Halliday and Hasan (1976) acknowledge that conjunction is a slippery area of cohesion given that conjunctions display both lexical and grammatical behavior; however, they decide to group it with the grammatical devices. We agree with this decision.

[6] Reid (1991) argues that all nouns – not just collective nouns – have similar potential flexibility of number. We feel that his extreme position raises some problems of its own.

[7] Some may argue that vagueness of gender as well as vagueness of reference is at work in examples such as (4); however, note that the existence of more gender-specific information in sentence (4) does not seem to rule out the use of *they* forms: *Anyone running a business should employ their wife.*

[8] For example, French offers a similar but not identical choice with regard to dative alternation when the indirect object is a personal pronoun: J'ai donné le livre á ELLE (pas a LUI). [contrastive use of *elle*] (I gave the book to her [not to him]) versus Je lui ai donné le livre. (I gave him/her the book/ I gave the book to him/her).

[9] There are some constraints on this choice. For example, when the pronoun *it* functions as the direct object, the indirect object never occurs before the direct object except for a very small number of frozen and reduced oral formulas (where the indirect object functions as a pronominal clitic that has attached to the verb) (cf. Gimme it / Give me it/*Give Mary it).

[10] Text from Terkel, 1977, p. 32.

[11] The UCLA oral corpus is an in-house informal and unedited data base of transcribed speech that Marianne Celce-Murcia and her students have assembled over the years; it was put on line by Fred Davidson.

[12] This exercise is adapted from Celce-Murcia and Hilles (1988:152). This version of the text-based exercise focuses on *a/an* versus *the*. It could also be used to practice the pronouns *he, she,* and *it* instead of the articles *a/an* and *the*.

[13] In North American English one could also say "Where did all the flowers go?" without a significant difference in meaning. The present perfect would be impossible if some specific past time had been mentioned ("Where did you go last night?").

[14] This text is adapted from Terkel, 1977, p. 267.

CHAPTER 5

Vocabulary

"Bringing a discourse dimension into language teaching does not by any means imply an abandonment of teaching vocabulary. Vocabulary will still be the largest single element in tackling a new language for the learner and it would be irresponsible to suggest that it will take care of itself in some ideal world where language teaching and learning are discourse driven."

(McCarthy, 1991:64)

"Strategies which learners can use independently of a teacher are the most important of all ways of learning vocabulary. For this reason it is worthwhile ensuring that learners are able to apply the strategies and that they get plenty of help and encouragement in doing so. By mastering a few strategies learners can cope with thousands of words."

(Nation, 1990:174)

INTRODUCTION

Language pedagogy has viewed and treated vocabulary in very different ways over the years. In the grammar-translation approach, which was codified by Karl Plötz in the 1880s (Kelly, 1969), and in the reading approach of the 1930s, word lists were a core element of the language curriculum. In contrast, the audiolingual approach, dominant from the 1940s through the 1960s, deliberately suppressed the teaching of vocabulary in favor of teaching grammar and pronunciation. In current naturalistic and communicative approaches, there is a widely shared assumption that vocabulary will be learned automatically and indirectly without any explicit formal instruction, merely through exposure to and practice with the target language. Research in second and foreign language vocabulary acquisition (for an overview see Coady, 1993) indicates that formal instruction is beneficial and suggests a mixed approach to vocabulary instruction in which basic or core vocabulary is explicitly taught along with strategies that will allow learners to deal effectively with less frequent vocabulary that they encounter in context so that such vocabulary can be learned when needed (see Chapter 7 for a discussion of guessing word meanings from context).

Formal linguists have tended to focus on syntax; they have long maintained that any human language is a rule-governed innate system and that those who have acquired a natural language apply its rules in original and creative ways by producing utterances they have never heard before (Chomsky, 1965). In contrast to this perspective, linguists who focus on vocabulary rather than grammar (e.g., Hoey, 1992; Nattinger and DeCarrico, 1992; Sinclair, 1966) believe that a significant proportion of social, professional, and everyday language use is formulaic, routine, and fairly predictable. How can such different views of language and language use coexist? The fact that formal linguists have focused on context-free aspects of syntax and that lexicographers have focused on words, which derive much of their meaning from context, is part of the explanation. The other part of the difference lies in the research methods that formal syntacticians and contemporary lexicographers have used. The syntacticians use largely introspective methods and contrived data arising from native-speaker intuition to support their hypotheses, whereas modern lexicographers use computer-assisted analyses of very large corpora – analyses in which meanings, frequencies, and co-occurrences of words and phrases can be analyzed on the basis of a large number of contextualized tokens for any given lexical item.

This new vision of vocabulary (or lexis), where word meanings are viewed as reflecting use in context, forms the basis of this chapter. In it we discuss the importance of discourse-grounded activities for learners who need to use L2 vocabulary productively in their speech and writing. We do not ignore the importance of receptive vocabulary for listening and reading purposes; in fact we discuss "lexical accessibility" and related issues in Chapter 7 on reading. However, here we give emphasis to productive use of vocabulary and ways of learning and using new vocabulary because we feel this area has been neglected and because this is where insights from discourse analysis are most important for supplementing what we already know about L2 vocabulary use and learning. (See Figure 5.1. on page 75.)

Like knowledge of phonology and grammar, vocabulary knowledge can be viewed in terms of both top-down and bottom-up strategies. The top-down pragmatically driven strategies include the speaker's background knowledge of the topic or speech situation at hand and the knowledge shared with the interlocutor. Vocabulary items tend to group or associate around topics (Halliday and Hasan, [1976] call this "lexical collocation" at the textual level). For example, if we know a reading passage or an oral discussion is dealing with the topic of "Art Museums," we can expect words like *painting(s), artist(s), sculpture/sculptors(s), curator, exhibit(s),* and the like to occur as part of the discourse. Likewise, in any language, speech acts and speech activities have describable **macrostructures** with typical steps or moves, often in a predictable sequence, with highly conventionalized words and phrases associated with each step or move (Nattinger and De Carrico, 1992). For example, when English speakers apologize, it is very common to hear something like, "I'm (really/very/terribly) sorry" from the person doing the apologizing. Knowing the vocabulary and set phrases associated with a topic or speech activity is thus a large part of being able to talk or write about the topic or perform the speech activity in the target language.

Bottom-up strategies related to vocabulary knowledge are used when learners don't know a word. From a speech production perspective, the L2 speaker can ask interlocutors for assistance ("What's the word for the thing that . . . ?") or use a circumlocution or a gesture to get the meaning of the target word across. L2 writers normally have more time than speakers, so they can look up the target word in their L1 in a bilingual dictionary and find possible equivalents in the L2. Here the tricky part involves selecting the best equivalent for the context. Learners can ask a native speaker – or a more experienced learner – for assistance, if such help is available. Some effective L2 writers simply generate as much text as they can in the target language and leave blanks for words they don't know or can't recall. They later fill in these missing words using bottom-up strategies.

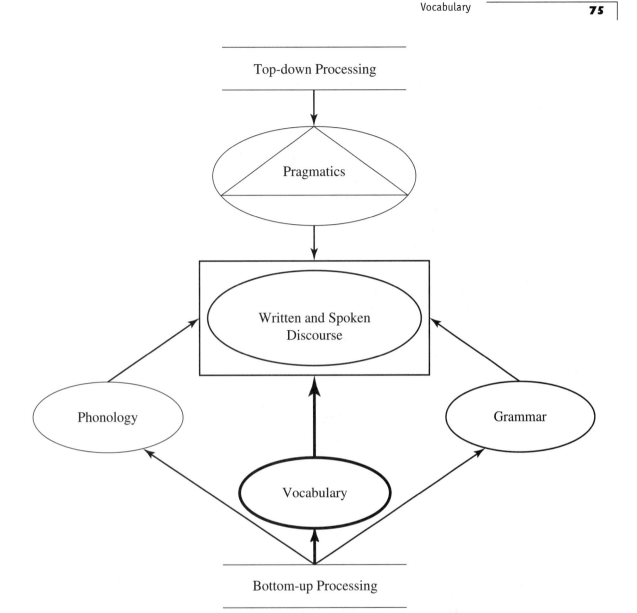

Figure 5.1 Vocabulary and Language Knowledge

BACKGROUND

There are several notions we need to explore before we can treat our topic in detail. These include a discussion of receptive versus productive vocabulary, content words versus function words, the differences among the language skills (listening, speaking, reading, writing) in terms of vocabulary requirements, the literal versus figurative vocabulary distinction, and the qualitative differences between vocabulary, on the one hand, and grammar and phonology on the other.

RECEPTIVE VERSUS PRODUCTIVE VOCABULARY

First, the notion of **receptive** versus **productive** vocabulary is very important. Users of any language, including both native and nonnative speakers, have much more receptive than productive vocabulary. English readers may understand – perhaps even subconsciously – many words like *adumbrate* and *anent* when they encounter them in a text, yet they may well be unlikely to use these words in their own speech or writing. This is because such readers have receptive but not productive control of these words; productive control implies receptive control, but the reverse is not necessarily true.

Some applied linguists feel that the major challenge in teaching vocabulary is to teach more receptive vocabulary so that L2 learners can become more efficient readers (see the volume on second language reading and vocabulary learning edited by Huckin, Haynes, and Coady, 1993). This is no doubt because there is an enormous discrepancy in the number of words one needs to know in English for engaging in everyday conversation versus the number of words needed for extensive academic reading. Some estimate that productive use of as few as three thousand words and phrases will suffice for informal conversation. In contrast, it is estimated that a receptive vocabulary of fewer than 10,000 words will prevent a reader from comprehending all but the most rudimentary written English texts. Estimates indicate that the best English L1 college and university students have a receptive vocabulary of at least 100,000 words – some claim that they can recognize as many as 200,000 words – and that this is necessary to ensure efficient reading of sophisticated texts .

There do seem to be ways of teaching large amounts of receptive vocabulary fairly quickly and efficiently by having learners simply associate words with meanings out of context using word lists, vocabulary cards, and so forth. (See Nation, 1990). Such strategies, even if they turn out to be effective for improving receptive knowledge and reading comprehension, are not necessarily effective for teaching productive use of lexis; however, it must be acknowledged that receptive knowledge of vocabulary is a first step toward achieving productive use, i.e., toward learners' becoming skillful speakers and writers in their second languages. Lack of productive vocabulary and lack of word-associated grammatical information are, in fact, major factors contributing to the poor writing skills of many university-level ESL students (Christine Holten, personal communication). In research related to Holten's observation, Santos (1988) found that subject-matter university instructors who were asked to respond to L2 student essays were more annoyed by lexical errors than grammatical errors in the L2 students' writing, indicating that language teachers should take care to evaluate – and to correct if needed – learners' lexical choices in their written work as well as their ability to use lexical items in grammatically appropriate ways, e.g., correct part of speech, correct inflections, correct article or preposition, correct collocation, and the like.

CONTENT WORDS VERSUS FUNCTION WORDS

The distinction between **content** words and **function** words is a useful one in analyzing vocabulary. Most vocabulary items are content words and belong to the large, open word classes (i.e., word classes that readily accept new words and discard old ones that are no longer useful: nouns, verbs, adjectives, and some adverbs). Function words are those vocabulary items that belong to closed words classes (i.e., word classes that do not readily admit new items or lose old ones: pronouns, auxiliary verbs, prepositions, determiners, and many adverbs). Conventional wisdom suggests that function words should be taught as part of grammar and content words as part of vocabulary, but this a somewhat spurious distinction since what is handled by the grammar of one language may be part of the vocabulary of another – hence we are attracted by Halliday's composite term "lexicogrammar," which we find quite useful for describing a language resource continuum:

| lexis | ————— (The lexicogrammatical continuum) ————— | grammar |

(words: N,V,Adj/Adv) (idioms) (phrasal forms) (function words) (inflections and syntax)

Along this continuum more stable aspects of meaning tend to be represented lexically whereas more fluid and complex messages require grammar in addition to lexicon for their expression.

HOW MUCH VOCABULARY FOR EACH SKILL?

With reference to the four language skills, the fewest vocabulary items are needed for speaking, while more words are needed for writing and for listening comprehension, with the largest number of words needed for reading. However, while listening and reading require receptive understanding of vocabulary, speaking and writing require productive use of vocabulary. In other words, in addition to knowing the general meaning of words and phrases in a text – which is often sufficient for the listener or reader to comprehend the gist of a message – the speaker or writer must know each word's pronunciation or spelling, its part of speech, its syntactic restrictions, any morphological irregularities, its common collocations (other words with which it is likely to co-occur), and its common contexts (texts in which it is likely to occur).

DIFFERENT MODALITY OR REGISTER, DIFFERENT VOCABULARY

The vocabulary used by skilled speakers and writers changes according to *modality* and *register*. For some languages such as Arabic, modality differences may be highly marked since the vocabulary of the local spoken variety and the vocabulary of the more classical written variety can be very different. This makes learning the literate skills (reading and writing) more of a challenge than in a language like English where there is significant overlap between the vocabulary of the spoken and the written variety – but where the vocabulary of the written language is nonetheless much more extensive. There is another type of challenge with a language like Chinese where the written characters have nothing to do with the sound segments or syllables of the spoken language but directly represent ideas. It takes learners years to learn the thousands of characters for words and phrases that are required for fluent reading and writing in such a language, where few associations can be made with the sound system.

Speakers and writers also make different lexical selections according to how *formal* or *informal* any act of communication is; (modality and register are not always totally independent factors in that spoken language tends to be more informal than written language). Moreover, in one's native language as well as in functionally active second or foreign languages, users develop and enrich their vocabulary throughout their lives as they are exposed to new concepts and new areas of interest. Educated native speakers of English have overlapping but different vocabularies for speaking and writing. They have different vocabularies for general versus professional or specialized communication. Advanced L2 users of English will also have some control of these different vocabularies. The main difference between L1 and L2 users seems to be that

> . . . words in the L2 are less well organized and less easily accessible
> than those of L1. However, these differences seem to diminish over
> time with increased proficiency. Semantic development in L2 seems
> to be a process of starting with a mapping of L1 meanings into L2 and
> then gradually developing L2 meanings and meaning structures. The
> final result is two separate systems which are still highly interrelated.

(Coady, 1993:15)

SOCIOCULTURAL VARIATION IN THE USE OF VOCABULARY

Vocabulary is an obvious area for language variation (Eisenstein, 1983). Hatch and Brown (1995:307ff) point out that one dimension along which vocabulary use tends to vary is gender. In English, women are said to use more elaborate color vocabulary than men, with women more frequently using highly selective color terms such as *mauve, ecru, aubergine,* and so forth. Similarly, in the United States, teenage girls – but less often boys – use *totally* as an intensifier. Gender-based choices are made in other languages too. To say "thank you" in Portuguese, women say *obrigada* and men say *obrigado.* In Japanese, women use the utterance-final particle *ne?* (which is a bit like a question tag in English) more frequently than men.

English speakers of both genders seem to agree that different terms should be used to describe the same quality, according to the gender of the person being described:

> *beautiful, pretty* (to describe women)
>
> *handsome, virile* (to describe men)

As Hatch and Brown observe, except for those gender-sensitive choices that are the same for speakers of both sexes, it is not always clear whether variation in lexical choice should be attributed to gender or to differences in status or power; however, the variations exist, and awareness of them must be part of vocabulary instruction – the exception being that academic and technical writing appear to be relatively free of gender-based preferences when compared with informal spoken language.

Geographical dialects often reflect vocabulary differences. British and American English are good examples in this regard, with each national group having developed some culturally distinctive vocabulary:

British	**American**
the cinema	*the movies*
a film	*a movie*
a lift	*an elevator*
a boot (of a car)	*a trunk*
a flat	*an apartment*
a lorry	*a truck*

Within each of these two countries, there may be further dialect distinctions among speakers by region such that in different parts of the United States, *skillet, frying pan,* and *spider* are words used to describe the same cooking implement.

Some vocabulary variation is due to the age of the speakers (Hatch and Brown, 1995: 309) such that expressions of positive assessment by the speaker have changed from generation to generation in the United States.

> 1940s and 1950s – *keen, in the groove*
> 1960s and 1970s – *cool, groovy*
> 1980s and 1990s – *rad, awesome*

Also, in many languages a special vocabulary gets used only with children or by children; this is known as "baby talk." For example:

English	**French**
go potty (use the toilet)	*faire dodo* (go to sleep)
dudu (feces)	*nounou* (Teddy bear)
an owie (something that hurts)	*un bobo* (something that hurts)

The selection of a **euphemism** (i.e., a word that is considered less direct and thus less distasteful or offensive) often reflects one or more of these factors. For example, when asking where *the toilet* is, there are many possible lexical items one can use as euphemisms in English:

British: *the loo, the W.C. (water closet)*
American: *the john* (informal), *the bathroom* (general)
Female/upper middle class: *the powder room*
Children: *the potty*
Public establishments: *the ladies' room, the men's room*

THE UNIQUENESS OF VOCABULARY

We must also recognize that while vocabulary does have many formulaic and routinized aspects (Nattinger and DeCarrico, 1992), it is also a unique area of L2 language learning. Whereas grammar and phonology/orthography are generally systematic competencies needed for all spoken or written communication – and thus are competencies which demonstrate patterns of acquisition across learners – vocabulary acquisition and use can be quite specific once learners have mastered the 2,000–3,000 words that constitute the basic everyday vocabulary, the main semantic categories of which follow:[1]

- cardinal and ordinal numbers (1 to 1,000) – with reference to addresses, phone numbers, dates, and common measurable concepts such as age, height, weight, time, distance, money, quantity, and so forth
- common foods
- words for days of the week, months, and seasons
- articles of clothing
- eating utensils
- body parts
- furniture
- family relationships
- colors
- shapes and sizes
- negative and positive evaluation
- cities, countries, and continents
- oceans, lakes, rivers, and mountains
- common animals
- common occupations
- common actions/activities/experiences

Beginning-level learners will probably not learn all their basic vocabulary through discourse-oriented activities, so it is a good idea for teachers of such students to keep in mind teaching techniques such as the use of pictures, picture dictionaries, word lists/cards, and the "key word" technique to assist students in acquiring the basic vocabulary they need to become effective at applying more general discourse-based strategies. Nation (1990:166–7) provides a good example of the key word technique: if English speakers wish to master the Thai phrase *khaaw saan,* meaning "uncooked rice," they should think of an English word that sounds similar to the Thai phrase like *council,* and then form a mental image of a council, a group of people, sitting around a table with a heap of uncooked rice on it. This image and the English word associated with it will help them remember the meaning of the Thai phrase.

Apart from the general basic vocabulary outlined above, vocabulary acquisition often becomes highly personal from a developmental perspective in a way that the acquisition of grammar and phonology do not. Learners interested in sports will learn a very different vocabulary from those interested in music, who in turn will learn a different vocabulary from those interested in politics. This has been noted even in child second language acquisition studies where two young children at the same stage of development in their second languages already exhibit noticeable differences in vocabulary development and specialization: Miki, the Japanese boy learning English (Yoshida, 1977), acquired many words for vehicles whereas Caroline, the American girl learning French (Celce-Murcia, 1977), acquired many words needed for playing house.

LITERAL VERSUS FIGURATIVE USE: A MATTER OF CONTEXT (OR CO-TEXT)

In addition, vocabulary can be **literal** or **figurative** (with figurative language including idiomatic and metaphorical use; Lakoff and Johnson, 1980). For example, a sentence such as "He got the axe" may mean literally that some male person went and fetched a tool for chopping wood, or it may mean figuratively that some male person was fired from his job, that is, terminated. The interpretation that one arrives at may depend on the co-text. If the discourse continues, "and he chopped down the tree," the literal interpretation takes hold. If the subsequent discourse is "so now he's looking for another job," the figurative interpretation is the coherent one. The physical context can, of course, also disambiguate. If the interlocutors are in a forest, the literal interpretation is favored, but if they are in an office, the figurative reading is.

Virtually all vocabulary has the possibility of being colored by the co-text and context in which it occurs. A noun like "stocking" might be defined in a dictionary as follows:

[n. a close-fitting covering, usually knitted, for the leg and foot]

However, as Carter and McCarthy (1988) point out, a word like "stocking" has quite different meanings and referents in different contexts:

- My mother still has silk stockings from World War II.
- The stockings were hung by the chimney with care, in hopes
  that Saint Nicholas soon would be there.

In the first context, silk stockings represent the hosiery once worn by well-dressed women, which are now made of nylon rather than silk. In contrast, the Christmas stockings referred to in the second example, an excerpt from Clement Clark Moore's poem "The Night Before Christmas," now tend to be large, decorative, stocking-shaped containers that children hang up on the chimney mantle (if their home has a fireplace and chimney) or elsewhere in the home on Christmas Eve so that Santa Claus – or his helpers – can fill them up with gifts. No one ever wears such a stylized Christmas stocking, which is typically made of felt.

We can therefore begin to appreciate that a great deal of the meaning of any word comes from the larger cultural context and/or the immediate co-text or situational context in which the word occurs as well as from the many associations for a word that most native speakers share.

CREATING VOCABULARY

Even though many lexical choices are very formulaic, words are also formed almost as creatively as sentences are formed by syntactic rules. In fact, new words that no one has used before (and perhaps no one will ever use again) can be invented for specific communicative purposes. An example of this comes in the following story related to us by Sandra Thompson (personal communication): Two busloads of college students were going back to their university after a football game. It was the weekend before Halloween, and several students wanted to stop at a farmer's stand on the way home to buy pumpkins to carve into jack-o'-lanterns; other students wanted to get home as quickly as possible to study and work on assignments. One student said, "OK, this is the pumpkin-bus. If you want to buy a pumpkin, ride on this bus. The other bus is the regular bus and will go right back to campus, so if you don't want a pumpkin, ride that bus." The instructions were understood by everyone present, and yet it is likely that the spontaneously formed noun compound *pumpkin-bus* was used uniquely on this occasion; it has not made its way into general English vocabulary. People do, however, make up new words all the time that catch on and survive. (For example, consider the word *nerd*, "a socially inept and physically unattractive but brainy person – typically male - who specializes in something scientific or technical." Example use: *He's a computer nerd.*).

Vocabulary changes faster than syntax or phonology. It is the part of language that can respond immediately to changes in environment, experience, or culture. If something new is discovered or invented, language users will create a new word, borrow a word, or extend the meaning of an existing word to express the new phenomenon. On the other hand, words expressing objects or ideas no longer in use will be discarded and fall out of use.

PRODUCTIVE PROCESSES OF WORD FORMATION

Every language has one major or several alternative ways of creating new words. Thus speakers of any language can create one-time coinages that do not last or new words that might be adopted and promoted by agents of change such as television or radio, the press, the entertainment industry, and the like. These agents of change can be instrumental in establishing and spreading the use of a new word or expression, especially if the new lexical item facilitates communication. In English, for example, there are three productive word formation processes. (See Adams [1973] for further discussion.)

- **compounding** (e.g., the *pumpkin-bus* example, where two nouns come together to form one). Established compounds illustrating some of the frequent productive patterns in English include *mailman, fifty-one, blackbird, and three-legged.*

- **affixation** (i.e., the addition of prefixes or suffixes to a stem to create derivative words – e.g., *re*wind, *un*cool, *anti*-Gingrich, wet*ness*, lobby*ist*, and sister*hood*.)

- **conversion** (i.e., typically the conversion of a noun or an adjective into a verb without the addition of other elements).

  For example:
  I'd rather *office* here. (from the noun "office")
  His grass has *green*ed. (from the adjective "green")

The second or foreign language learner eventually has to master these word production mechanisms in the target language in order to take full advantage of these processes as a strategy for comprehending and using vocabulary. In fact Olshtain (1987) found that the mastery of such word production processes are one index of second language acquisition development in that it indicates a gradual approximation of native-like productive lexical knowledge.[2] Certainly awareness of such productive processes is also helpful when applying bottom-up processing strategies to either productive use or receptive comprehension of vocabulary.

In many languages there are also less productive but nonetheless very frequent and useful patterns of use for stems or roots and affixes, knowledge of which is valuable to L2 learners who need to do academic reading and writing. For example, the affix *-ity*, although not productive in English, occurs in many abstract nouns: *serenity, opacity, reality,* and the like. Likewise; the stem *tele-,* which means "far, distant," occurs in many words such as *telegraph, telephone,* and *television.* There are useful sources (such as Green, 1990, for English) that the foreign or second language teacher can consult in developing materials to help the learner develop strategic awareness of useful roots and affixes for developing effective bottom-up word comprehension strategies and assist in better lexical selection for productive tasks.

LEXICAL BORROWING

Words are different from grammatical and phonological systems in one other very important way: native speakers of one language can readily borrow a word or expression from another language, but they are much less likely to borrow structures or sounds from other languages.[3] Thus English has words that reflect not only its native Germanic origins, it also has thousands of words borrowed from Norman French and later varieties of French, some words borrowed from Latin, some from Greek, and some from other languages.

The borrowing process works in reverse as well. Today languages as diverse as French, Hebrew, and Japanese are borrowing many words from the English language. However, when the speakers of these languages borrow words, they often change the meaning or limit the meaning in interesting ways. For example, in Hebrew a car, bus, or truck can have both a front "back axle" and a rear "back axle" since the term "back axle" was borrowed from English (pronounced "bekaks" in Hebrew) to mean the axle or rod to which the wheels are attached, independent of front or back position. Another example – in colloquial Hebrew the word "tape" is routinely used to mean "tape recorder" even though a Hebrew word "rashamkol" (literally "voice recorder") exists to express the notion.

Words are slippery: They are created, they die off, they are borrowed, they change meaning. Words constantly need to be interpreted and reinterpreted in terms of the cultural contexts and discourse contexts in which they are being used at any given point in time. For language learners, vocabulary is also less stable than grammatical or phonological systems. If grammatical or phonological systems have been reasonably well acquired, they can be retained over long periods of time and can be revived and fairly easily reactivated if they have fallen into disuse. Each word, however, once learned, then has the potential to be misused or even forgotten unless it is used and re-used on a regular basis.

VOCABULARY AND DISCOURSE ANALYSIS

Issues of vocabulary selection when generating discourse are ultimately tied up with shared knowledge about (1) what is being said/written (i.e., the topic), (2) how it is being said/written (i.e, modality and genre), and (3) who is saying or writing it to whom (i.e., register, speech community). These are some of the topics we explore in this section.

TYPES OF VOCABULARY IN FIELDS OF SPECIALIZATION

A specialized field such as biology or physics may well have three types of vocabulary: (1) a core vocabulary it shares with all sciences and technologies; (2) a specific vocabulary for its own branch of science; and (3) even more specific vocabulary known primarily to those in a specific subarea (e.g., microbiology, plasma physics). Discourse analysis and lexical concordance analysis (i.e., having access to all tokens of a word form in context for a given corpus) of appropriate written corpora can identify vocabulary items of each type, which in turn is useful information for the language teacher who is preparing learners specializing in a given academic or professional field (i.e., language learning for specific purposes). Such learners are often very eager to master the English vocabulary used in their discipline – presumably to have access to publications in English, to participate in international conferences, and so forth.[4]

LEXICAL COLLOCATION AND LEXICAL COHESION

At the level of the sentence, words come together to form **collocations**, i.e., they form semantic and structural bonds that become routines or chunks that native speakers can access for comprehension or production. Thus English L1 users say and write *tall building* rather than *high building* or *statistically significant* rather than *statistically important*, and so on. Or, if asked to provide words for completing a sentence like "John ____ money," native speakers will spontaneously produce verbs from a very small set: *earns, makes, saves, has, likes, wants, spends,* and *needs* (Seal, 1981). Such collocations reflect both local word-combining tendencies, which any language has, and also more general content schemata or information structures that all L1 English users share for a word like "money." This is the most common use of the term "lexical collocation," and it is different from Halliday and Hasan's (1976) use of the term to refer to vocabulary items that are likely to appear in the same text because of topic association, and so forth.

Ideally, we want L2 users to form the same word combinations (or lexical chunks) and utilize the same schemata as L1 users, but often this does not happen because of interference from the first language or because of insufficient exposure and attention to the pertinent collocations in the target language. For example, the nonnative English speaker who says or writes "bridging the hole" instead of "bridging the gap" may be understood by the interactants; however, if the interactants are native speakers of English or advanced users of English, they are likely to notice the collocation error that was made.

At the level of discourse, Hasan (1984; see also Halliday and Hasan 1976, 1989) has done much to shed light on lexical relationships in text. She examines different types of lexical relationships in discourse, which collectively constitute **lexical cohesion**, for example:

- repetition/reiteration:
    a. same word/stem minus inflections, part of speech: tooth-teeth
    b. synonym: tooth-dental
- antonym: good/bad; black/white
- part-whole: room-house; steering wheel-car
- general-specific (either direction) animal-dog; city-Reno
- member of same set: dog-cat; green-yellow

There are two further qualifications we should make to this list of lexical relationships. First, the whole notion of **repetition** or **reiteration** differs from one language and culture to another. In some languages it is considered good style to simply repeat the same word several times (e.g., Arabic, Japanese) whereas in other languages (e.g., English) it is necessary to vary repetitions and use different synonyms or appropriately related words in order to achieve good style. Second, all languages have a stock of general words (in English: *person, plant, animal, stuff, thing, idea, time, place,* and so forth.) that seem to be somewhere between pronouns and fully explicit lexical items in terms of marking cohesion. These general words are highly frequent and are the most general of words on the general-specific continuum for lexical meaning; they tend to occur more often in informal spoken discourse than elsewhere:

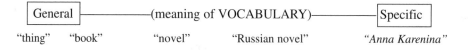

| General | ————————(meaning of VOCABULARY)———————— | Specific |

"thing"   "book"   "novel"   "Russian novel"   *"Anna Karenina"*

One can examine any given piece of discourse to see what lexical chains occur in order to determine which lexical relationships are obtained. Usually texts of several clauses have at least two interacting lexical chains. Consider the following text:[5]

> The town of Sonoma, California, launched the Salute to the Arts in 1986 as a one-day event held in a single quadrant of Sonoma Plaza with some thirty restaurants and wineries, a few art displays, and one mariachi trio. Today the festival is a wine country tradition consisting of an opening-night gala and two full days of food, wine, and art featuring more than 100 restaurants, wineries, and art galleries. It benefits seventeen nonprofit arts, cultural, and educational organizations.

In this short text there are several interrelated lexical chains:

- Salute to the Arts, festival, tradition, gala, benefit
- town, Sonoma, Sonoma Plaza, wine country, California
- 1986 (one-day event), today (two full days)

In addition, the "Salute to the Arts" chain has three subchains:

- food, restaurants
- wine, wineries
- art, art displays, art galleries

And "benefit(s)" is a set with three types of nonprofit beneficiaries: arts organizations, cultural organizations, and educational organizations. Without these cross-clausal lexical relationships the text would not be as cohesive and coherent as it is. Each lexical chain can be further analyzed in terms of the semantic relationships in the chain. For example, the lexical chain consisting of *town, Sonoma, Sonoma Plaza,* and *wine country, California* can be further analyzed in that *town* is more general than *Sonoma,* a specific town. *Sonoma Plaza* is one part of the whole town, which is turn is part of the *wine country,* which is in *California.* Language teachers and language learners need to be fully aware of the role that the lexicon plays in forming cohesive and coherent discourse.

RHETORICAL DEMANDS, DISCOURSE COMMUNITIES, AND INDIVIDUALS

It is also important that teachers and learners become aware of the fact that specific vocabulary items tend to be associated with certain rhetorical text patterns. For example, the problem-posing portion of an expository text is likely to contain words like *difficulty, hinder,* and *hamper* while the solution/result portion of the same text will contain words like *resolve, outcome,* and *address* (McCarthy, 1991:79). Learners who are strategically aware of such patterns will be more effective readers and writers than those who are not.

Sometimes vocabulary items used in a particular way reflect a specific discipline and the preferences of insiders of that discipline. In fact, the **specialized lexis** that develops as a part of **specialized genres** is one of the defining traits of any **discourse community**. With this in mind, Leech (1995) assembled sizable databases of articles from four different academic journals (*Memory and Cognition, Linguistic Inquiry, Human Organization,* and *Behaviour*) in an attempt to see if he could detect lexical-choice differences among the four discourse communities. Among the results he uncovered, Leech found that authors publishing in *Memory and Cognition* (M&C) and *Linguistic Inquiry* (LI) used different lexical phrases for what is seemingly the same semantic purpose; namely, Leech found that when making or rejecting knowledge claims either by citing previous research or by presenting one's own research in an article, M&C authors tended to use the verb "suggest" (*prior research would suggest . . .; the data we cite strongly suggest . . .*) whereas LI authors tended to use the verb "explain" (*X's account does/does not explain . . .; the rule presented above explains . . .*). Leech accounts for this lexical difference by referring to the distinct research traditions of the cognitive psychologists who submit manuscripts to M&C and the formal MIT-school linguists who submit manuscripts to LI. However, what Leech's research should signal to language teachers is that second language learners with an academic major or research specialization will have to master uses of seemingly nontechnical lexical items that are used in ways quite specific to their discipline and to the discourse genres of their discipline in order to read and write effectively as a member of the discourse community working in that discipline.

Sometimes certain low frequency words get associated with particular individuals who have a predisposition to use them with unusual frequency. In other words, the lexical items become features of an individual's speaking or writing style. For example, a well-known former professor of American history at the University of Illinois used the word "prodigious" several times in virtually every lecture he gave. It was thus impossible for students in this professor's classes to ignore this word, and, in fact, as an inside joke, some students kept track of the number of times the Professor said the word "prodigious" during each lecture. Needless to say, everyone in the class learned the meaning of the word.

More typically, such characteristic use of vocabulary develops in groups like the cognitive psychologists or formal linguists whose writings Leech studied and compared. Leech's examples are not a matter of personal style (which is something distinct that is nonetheless accessible to all or most language users). Instead, such examples are a matter of group membership, i.e., one must belong to the group to fully understand the use of the terms. Such groups may be constituted in different ways and are sometimes very small (e.g., in extreme cases, twins, siblings, or a small group of friends make up some of their own secret words as a sign of group solidarity and insider status).

VOCABULARY ITEMS THAT NEED DISCOURSE TO BE COMPREHENDED AND LEARNED

Words that serve a discourse function rather than expressing semantic content are much more dependent on context and co-text for their meaning and use. They have been largely ignored in language teaching approaches that treat grammar at the sentence level and vocabulary in word lists. We shall discuss two such cases (*else* and *well*) in some detail to illustrate this point.

Else

The English function word *else* is a useful and relatively frequent lexical item (570th in frequency, according to Francis and Kucera, 1982). Yet it is not well treated in ESL/EFL textbooks where sentence-level grammar and vocabulary exercises are the norm because like other reference words (e.g., personal pronouns, demonstratives, and the like) it requires some prior discourse for its interpretation.

Else occurs in five grammatically restricted environments:

1. after compound pronouns/adverbs:

$$\left\{ \begin{array}{ll} \text{some-} & \text{-one} \\ \text{any-} & \text{-body} \\ \text{every-} & \text{-thing} \\ \text{no-} & \text{-place/where} \end{array} \right\} \; else$$

2. after *wh*-interrogatives:

    (who/what/when/where/why/how) + (ever) *else*

3. after *or*:

    or *else*

4. in a determiner function (a) after certain quantifiers:

    all/little/(not) much *else*

    or (b) used alone like a pronoun (now rare):

    He cannot do else.

5. as a premodifier of "where" in the adverbial expression:

    "*else*where"

According to a data-based analysis by Yap (1994), in the position following the quantifiers *all/little/(not) much*, "else" occurs almost exclusively in written discourse. The adverbial form "elsewhere" occurs somewhat more frequently in written than in spoken discourse. The other patterns with *else*, however, are all more frequent in spoken than in written discourse.

For both spoken and written discourse "else" occurs most frequently after compound pronouns/adverbs, next after *wh*-words, and then in the "or else" combination. The combination form "elsewhere" is less frequent, and the determiner/pronominal uses of "else" represent the least frequently occurring functions.

In Yap's database, the most frequent meaning of "else" in discourse is "other" (81 percent or her spoken tokens and 87 percent of her written ones):

> . . . that would be as sensible as arguing that the price of crude oil remained unchanged through the 1970s while the value of everything else declined by about 75 percent.

> (Heyne, 1983:296)

(where "everything else" = "all commodities other than crude oil")

There were, however, three other minor readings of "else" that Yap identified (each of which is heavily context-dependent):

1. "more, additional"

    > They were better trained, better looking, better built, better disciplined, and something else – they were better dancers.

    > (Brown corpus–Hobbies 40 3 RB)

    ("something else" = "something more")

2. "alternative, otherwise"

    This stain often disrupts the normal cell activity or else colors
    only the outside.

    (Brown corpus – Hobbies 330 8 RB)

    ("or else" = "the other possibility")

3. "negative alternative, absence of other possibilities"

    There was nothing else I could do. . . .

    (Brown corpus – Belle Lettres 300 5 RB)

    ("nothing else" = "no other alternative")

Sentence-level exercises cannot possibly convey to nonnative speakers the importance of the word *else* and the ways in which it is used in English. What is needed
are many fully contextualized examples (taken or adapted from authentic materials) to
provide learners with the necessary exposure to and practice with "else," a function word
that is both semantically and grammatically complex. It must also be contrasted with
"more" and "(an)other," words with which it is easily confused by L2 learners.

Well

Schiffrin (1987) and Kinsler (1987) have looked at the discourse particle *well* (which is different from the adjective *well* in "I'm feeling well" or the adverb *well* in "He did it well").
The discourse marker *well* is interactionally very important in English conversation since
it is a marker speakers use to shift the orientation of talk in some way. Kinsler did a discourse analysis of almost 300 tokens of *well* occurring in spontaneous conversations, and
what follows are the six major "shifts" that people marked with *well* in her data.[6]

1. A shift in the next turn to a comment, opinion, evaluation, or explanation
    rather than facts, reports, descriptions (56 tokens)

    A: It's like one little group that always stays together.
    B: Well that's good.

2. A shift in the next turn to a disagreement, reservation (i.e., a dispreferred response)
    (48 tokens)

    A: If they see me with the cane, why don't they give me
    the so-called right of way?
    B: Well they probably do, once they see it.

3. A shift by one speaker from narration or description to reported (quoted)
    speech (41 tokens)

    – You know, they gave us a room and they said well during the day
    the room holds forty-eight people.

4. A modification, restart, or repair (39 tokens)

    – He w- he had- well he was twenty years old when he volunteered
    for the paratroopers.

5. A topic opener, introducer, shifter, resumer, response (33 tokens)

    A: That doesn't make sense as far as breeding goes.
    B: We:ll, first of all, I happen to not have an awful lotta faith in breeding.

6. A closing, preclosing (10 tokens)

– Well anyway listen. I gotta do a lot of studying.[7]

Slightly over 10 percent of Kinsler's data had tokens of *well* that co-occurred with other words in clusters: *well now, well then, oh well, well look/listen,* and *well thank you.* These collocates also need to be part of a complete description of *well.*

As part of her research Kinsler (1987) conducted a related experiment. She recorded two discussion groups – one with native speakers, the other with fluent nonnative speakers of different L1 backgrounds. Both groups addressed similar topics and spoke for about the same length of time. Only one of the nonnative speakers used the discourse particle *well.* He used it six times. All of the native speakers used the discourse particle *well,* and it occurred a total of sixty-eight times in their discussion. Since *well* is a lexical item that is pivotal for native speakers engaged in informal social interaction, it is important to make learners aware of its presence and of the appropriate discourse environments for using it.

TEACHING VOCABULARY THROUGH DISCOURSE

Several of the suggestions we made in Chapter 4 for teaching grammar could also be used to teach vocabulary. The difference would be one of focus. For example, when using the Family Tree diagram, the focus could be on the teaching of kinship terms. Likewise, when using the fable about the fox and the crow the focus could be on the vocabulary: *fox, cheese, kitchen window, tree, crow, feathers, eyes, mouth, voice,* and so forth. In fact, stories are powerful contexts for teaching vocabulary. If learners are interested in a story, they will learn the vocabulary that they need to know in order to understand and retell it. In the following we discuss some other discourse contexts for teaching vocabulary. Both children and adults seem to respond positively to learning vocabulary through stories and visuals (children – pictures; adults – charts / diagrams).

USING INFORMATIVE TEXTS

One way to present an item like *else* is to select excerpts from spoken or written texts where the target word is used in a particularly salient manner. Such texts are amenable to comprehension activities, discussion, and analysis to help raise learner awareness. The following paragraph is taken from an introductory economics textbook and would be especially appropriate for use with advanced learners who have at least some basic knowledge of economics:

> Of course, everything is finally relative to everything else. It's logically possible to insist that money has maintained a constant value in recent years and everything else has gone up. But that would be as sensible as arguing that the price of a barrel of crude oil remained unchanged through the 1970s while the value of everything else declined by about 75 percent. When we find oil prices moving relative to everything else, common sense tells us to look for the explanation in changes that have occurred in the conditions of supply or demand for oil – not for "everything else." When we see money prices moving relative to everything else, common sense ought to dictate the same course of inquiry.

(Heyne, 1983:296)

This text is very unusual in having six tokens of *everything else*. However, this unusual yet authentic text allows the teacher to focus on *else* in it most frequent and basic sense of "other" within the context of a meaningful analogy provided in an economics textbook. Certainly, if students read and comprehend this text, they will gain considerable exposure to, experience with, and understanding of *else*.

USING CARTOONS

The following dialog from a *Peanuts* cartoon[8] provides one example of how to teach a word like *well*. Scene: At the beach, Linus has built a small sand castle and Lucy has built a large life-sized throne, which we don't see until the sixth and final frame, at which point Lucy is sitting on the throne as she speaks; the cartoon's dialog is as follows:

Lucy: That's a nice looking castle.

Linus: This is more than a castle. This is the King's castle . . .

Lucy: Well, that's almost as good . . .

Linus: Almost? Almost as good as what?

Lucy: Almost as good as the Queen's throne!

In addition to the use of *well* in its highly frequent and useful disagreement function in Lucy's second turn, the cartoon contains four tokens of *almost*, which is another word like *else* or *well* in that it is also a frequent lexical item sensitive to grammar and discourse. This cartoon could thus be used to teach *almost,* too.

Once comprehended, such a comic strip can be used as a template to stimulate the creation of dialogs or role plays by students working in pairs or small groups. For example,

A: That's a nice looking car.

B: This is more than a car. This is a Mercedes . . .

A: Well, that's almost as good . . .

B: Almost? Almost as good as what?

A: Almost as good as a Rolls Royce!

USING INTERACTIVE ROLE PLAYS

Interactive role plays are an excellent vehicle for teaching and practicing the macrostructure and vocabulary of speech acts. Tamanaha (1998) asked native speakers of English and Japanese (all college students) to do the same role play:

> You borrowed a comic book (Japanese *manga*) from a friend, but your dog tore a few pages out of it. You were unable to find the same comic book at the bookstores to replace it. Now you are meeting your friend at the cafeteria to return it. Apologize to her.

(Tamanaha, 1998:7)

Tamanaha role-played the friend in both the English and Japanese role plays and found definite differences in the way that the English and Japanese speakers tended to carry out their apologies. Overall the English speakers demonstrated a greater variety of openings and of remedial behaviors. In addition to saying "I'm sorry," the English speakers made more offers of repair (e.g., "I'll still try to keep looking for it"), asked more often about what to do as a remedy (e.g., "What can I do to make it up to you?"), and offered more comments on the situation (e.g., "I shouldn't have left the book where my dog could get it."). In contrast, the Japanese speakers used more uniform account prefaces, opening most frequently with *jitsuwa* ("actually") and they tended to emphasize that they would not repeat a similar offense in future and to make pleas for a continued amicable relationship with the offended party.

After the offended party offers forgiveness, English speakers tend to accept the offer and end their apology, whereas the Japanese speakers continue to repeat their apology (*sumimasen* meaning "I'm sorry") several times before they feel they can accept the offended party's forgiveness.

Comparing interactive role plays in two languages as Tamanaha has done is an excellent way to discover linguistic and cultural differences in speech act behavior as well as identify the target language vocabulary needed to carry out the speech act in the L2. This descriptive information can then be applied pedagogically in second language instruction.

USING PROBLEM-SOLVING TASKS

Problem-solving tasks can also be used to introduce vocabulary for immediate use and practice as can values clarification exercises. The following is an example of a problem-solving activity used to practice vocabulary (Celce-Murcia and Rosensweig, 1979:250). Although the following exercise focuses on "Describing Americans," a similar task could be created to describe any national or ethnic group.

Describing Americans

Many adjective have been used to describe Americans. Some are complimentary and others are not. On the next page, there is a list of sixteen adjectives used by foreign students in the United States to describe Americans. Your task is to rank these adjectives placing the number 1 by the adjective that you feel best describes Americans, the number 2 by the adjective that you feel describes Americans second best, and so on through number 16, which is your estimate of the adjective that describes Americans least well. Remember that your ranking is from a foreign student's viewpoint, and it should be based on your general overall impressions of Americans, not on a few specific examples or exceptions.

Do this ranking individually at home. Then in class you will do it in small groups for twenty-five minutes. Do not forget that in the groups, you must reach a consensus on the rankings. Everyone must agree on the ranking that your group gives to each adjective.

Discussion questions and suggested topics for writing should follow this activity. In this unit, the lexical focus is on adjectives. In the course of the problem-solving activity, the students will use the adjectives frequently, thus reinforcing their understanding of them. Then by using the adjectives in follow-up discussions and essays productive use can be acquired.

A variety of text types such as essays, songs, poems, fables, plays, and short stories can be used first to practice decoding of vocabulary in context with subsequent follow-up activities such as retellings, preparing summaries, preparing alternative stories or plays, and so forth to ensure use and reuse of the most useful new vocabulary encountered. Language teachers must constantly look for tasks that will help their students review and reuse new vocabulary in meaningful and contextualized practice, e.g., writing letters to someone who will respond, or preparing a class publication of the essays, poems, and stories the students have produced.

RANKINGS		
INDIVIDUAL **AT HOME**	**GROUPS** **IN SCHOOL**	
		hurried
		talkative
		efficient
		hospitable
		outgoing
		showy
		devious
		traditional
		polite
		punctual
		tolerant
		pushy
		friendly
		frank
		reserved
		cosmopolitan

USE OF DICTIONARIES

For beginning level learners and young learners who do not yet have an extensive vocabulary in their first language, using pictures in general and using picture dictionaries in particular can be an excellent way to teach the semantically more concrete items of basic vocabulary. Research (Lotto and de Groot, 1998) shows, however, that more sophisticated adult learners master vocabulary faster and better by associating an L2 word with an equivalent word in the L1 rather than with a picture. Thus using pictures is not necessarily an appropriate strategy for all learners when teaching and learning vocabulary.

Many foreign language teachers hold strong opinions regarding the type of dictionaries their students should use, and they often favor monolingual dictionaries and try to discourage the use of bilingual dictionaries by learners. Traditional pedagogy has long dictated that learners should first use monolingual learner's dictionaries at the beginning stage and then standard L1 dictionaries for the intermediate and advanced stages. However, beginning level learners may not be proficient enough to use anything but a bilingual dictionary; also, the dictates of traditional pedagogy do not reflect what most proficient language learners seem to do.

In a comparative study of advanced learners' use of bilingual and monolingual dictionaries, Frolova (1993) had twenty-six Russian learners of English and twenty-one

American learners of Russian complete a questionnaire that probed the types of dictionaries they used in their foreign language and for what purposes. She also asked her consultants to tell her about those aspects of their dictionaries that left them dissatisfied.

All of Frolova's consultants were advanced university-level learners who were seriously trying to master the foreign language they were studying. All of them used both bilingual and monolingual dictionaries (i.e., they needed a set of several dictionaries to meet their purposes). Bilingual dictionaries had been most heavily used by these learners during their earlier periods of language study; however, they did not completely abandon their bilingual dictionaries as they became more proficient. For example, when they needed to find an unknown word in the foreign language for productive purposes, the bilingual dictionary was often where they had to start by looking up the equivalent word in their first language to find candidates for the word they needed in the foreign language. In fact the majority of Frolova's consultants preferred bilingual dictionaries to monolingual ones regardless of the task that they were performing in their foreign language. The Russian learners of English, however, tended to use monolingual English dictionaries more frequently than the Americans used monolingual Russian dictionaries. Frolova speculates that size may be one of the reasons because Russian monolingual dictionaries are enormous, bulky, multivolume affairs whereas many good single-volume monolingual dictionaries are available for English.

All of Frolova's consultants reported similar complaints regarding their dictionaries, specifically insufficient attention to idioms, inadequate word definitions, lack of information on collocations, and lack of authentic examples to demonstrate current usage. She concludes that language teachers should spend some time instructing their students on when and how to use both bilingual and monolingual dictionaries effectively to help them develop a sense of which type of dictionary (or what combination of dictionaries) is best suited for a specific language task.

Bilingual dictionaries, for example, are excellent resources for doing exercises like the following, which are designed to raise learner awareness of lexical differences signaled by derivations in a language like English.

ENGLISH	YOUR LANGUAGE
interesting	
interested	
dependent	
dependable	
discriminating	
discriminatory	

(Adapted from Feuerstein and Schcolnik, 1995:43)

A combination of monolingual and bilingual dictionaries could be used to complete exercises that raise awareness of how differences in part of speech relate to differences in meaning.

Nouns		Verbs	
ENGLISH	YOUR LANGUAGE	ENGLISH	YOUR LANGUAGE
fly		fly	
book		book	
mark		mark	

(Adapted from Feuerstein and Schcolnik, 1995:30)

Another newer option may be for learners to consult the electronic dictionaries that are part of word processing programs. Some teachers say that these dictionaries are not very good now but that they are constantly improving.

USING COGNATES AND AVOIDING FALSE COGNATES

Cognate vocabulary exists when vocabulary items in two languages can be recognized by most users as being the same word (Holmes and Ramos, 1993). When the target language has a significant amount of cognate vocabulary, Lotto and de Groot (1998) found that the task of vocabulary learning is made easier. Here are some common cognates:

> Hand (German)   hand (English)
> progresso (Spanish and Portuguese)   progress (English)
> restaurant (French)   restaurant (English)

Reading comprehension in particular is greatly enhanced, especially for beginning-level learners.

The other side of the coin is the existence of false cognates, which are words with the same etymological origin but with different meanings:

> Gift (German "poison")   gift (English "a present")
> marmelada (Portuguese "a quince   marmalade (English "an orange
>   desert")   preserve")
> librarie (French "bookstore")   library (English "a large
>   book collection – either
>   personal or institutional – or
>   the room or building in which
>   such a collection is stored")

Holmes and Ramos (1993) conclude from their study of English cognate recognition by low-level Portuguese L1 readers of English that cognate recognition is a well-used strategy that language teachers can exploit. However, there are two sources of error they tell teachers to watch out for: (1) grammatical transpositions occur whereby verbs are read as nouns, sometimes creating minor misreadings, and (2) reckless guessing is done with both cognates and false cognates, resulting in an inaccurate reading of the text. When more advanced and properly sensitized Portuguese learners of English were asked to write summaries in Portuguese of English texts and then asked to go over the drafts in small groups to produce a collaborative summary, the result was good use of cognate vocabulary and no semantic inaccuracies due to false cognates (Holmes and Ramos, 1993).

However, the false cognate problem reappears when intermediate and advanced L2 learners are speaking or writing spontaneously. For example, there is the English L1 speaker who, when speaking French, sometimes says "librarie" instead of "bibliotheque" for "library" – in spite of being fully aware of the false cognate and the appropriate equivalences. Likewise, there is the French speaker who, due to L1 interference, writes "Photography passionates me" instead of "Photography is my passion." In other words, because of direct transfer from French, he uses the wrong part of speech in English. Debra Friedman (personal communication) tells us of the Russian speaker who wrote "modern fabrics" in an essay when what he intended was "modern factories," i.e., another example of a false cognate causing an error. When L2 users are focusing on their message and the act of communication, false cognates and part-of-speech errors involving cognates are not infrequent in spoken and written production – especially if there is insufficient time to monitor production.

REMARKS ON ACQUISITION AND ATTRITION

ACQUISITION AND USE

One way that both children and adults have been observed to acquire a second language naturalistically is through an initial focus on words, formulaic language, routines, and lexicalized chunks, which can later be analyzed into smaller units so that grammar can evolve (i.e., patterns can be broken down and recombined with other patterns). This is often called "holistic learning." We could also call it a lexical approach to second language acquisition. In fact, Larsen-Freeman (1997:88) offers the following reinterpretation of Chomsky's position on first language acquisition, which puts a greater emphasis on lexicon than did his earlier work:

> Even Chomsky, while still maintaining the distinction between syntax and lexis in his minimalist position, asserts a much more prominent role for the lexicon and claims that knowledge of a language is universal grammar plus a language-specific lexicon; thus language acquisition is in essence a matter of determining lexical idiosyncrasies.

Many studies of L2 vocabulary learning are short-term experiments, not longitudinal in nature, so we still know very little about how people learn vocabulary in a second language and what works best pedagogically. Some of the results reported in such experiments are fairly self-evident:

> . . . cognates and high frequency words were easier to learn than noncognates and low frequency words.

> (Lotto and de Groot, 1998:32)

Perhaps studies dealing with more holistic and task-based language use will ultimately provide more revealing insights about vocabulary acquisition and use.

Burnett (1998), for example, found that the ability to effectively use idioms such as *jump on the bandwagon* in expository writing revealed a higher level of writing expertise and sophistication for both L1 and L2 writers than did simple grammatical accuracy. This was based on her analysis of many essays written by L1 and L2 writers taking the statewide University of California Subject A Examination, a reading and writing test that assesses the literacy skills of entering freshmen. The essays had been graded independently by composition experts before Burnett analyzed them. She found that the highly rated L1 writers used more idioms and used them with greater grammatical flexibility than the highly rated L2 writers. Both highly rated L1 and L2 writers used more idioms than low rated L1 and L2 writers, suggesting that idiom use may be a useful index of literacy development for both native speakers and advanced nonnative speakers. (Burnett notes that less advanced nonnatives who made grammatical errors did not use any idioms.)

ATTRITION

When lexical items in a first or second language are no longer used, this may lead to retrieval difficulties, which in turn might interfere with fluency in the spoken language in particular. This process of problematic retrieval, when it eventually leads to forgetting, is referred to as *language attrition*. It is especially pronounced in the area of vocabulary. For example, bilingual adults whose first and dominant language is English but who no longer live in an English-speaking environment were found to suffer from retrieval difficulties when trying to use less frequent, content-specific words in English (Olshtain and Barzilay, 1991).

In the Olshtain and Barzilay study, the native English-speaking consultants were asked to tell a story from picture cues using the children's book *Frog, Where Are You?*, which consists only of a series of pictures. There were a number of lexical items that caused retrieval difficulties for almost all the consultants: *cliff, antlers, pond,* among others. In their frustrated attempts to retrieve the word *pond*, these attriters followed a retrieval path starting with a more general concept, then replacing it with a more specific item – which was often not yet the correct choice – eventually getting to the intended word: (1) a body of water; (2) a small, shallow lake; (3) a "pond." This process closely mirrors the acquisition of specific vocabulary items by learners: The general concept comes first, and it then moves gradually toward the more specific item.

CONCLUSION

There is much more we could say about teaching vocabulary through discourse. This chapter is suggestive rather than exhaustive, and we encourage classroom teachers to continue to inform themselves about this topic and to involve their students in experiments and projects to discover what best encourages their learning, retention, and appropriate use of vocabulary. It is likely that there are some highly individual and idiosyncratic strategies related to this process.

We conclude this chapter with a checklist of questions/reminders for teachers to address before presenting any new lexical items to their students:

1. Does the target word have a close equivalent in the student's L1?

2. Is the use and distribution of the words similar in the L1 and L2?

3. Does the new word present specific morphosyntactic difficulties in usage (e.g., *news* is a singular noun but looks plural)?

4. Does the new word present problems in pronunciation (i.e., difficult sounds, problems with stress patterns or reduced vowels in words such as *comfortable*)?

5. Does the new word usually appear in a collocation with other words? For example, *lieu* is usually part of the fixed phrase *in lieu of* and the adjective *gradual* is often followed by abstract nouns that indicate some type of process: *change, development, growth,* and the like.

6. Is the word a noun compound or verb-particle combination? (If so, these may well need special attention.)

7. Are there idiomatic or metaphoric uses of the word that are common and useful?

8. What are some of the contexts and texts in which this word is most likely to occur?

The answers to these questions should help the teacher prepare more effective vocabulary lessons.

DISCUSSION QUESTIONS

1. Reflect on your own L2 learning experiences. What problems and successes have you had in learning vocabulary? What strategies have worked best for you?

2. What reasons does this chapter give to support the notion that learning vocabulary is different from learning grammar or pronunciation in a second language? Can you think of any other reasons?

3. What are the advantages and disadvantages of learning vocabulary in word lists versus learning vocabulary through spoken discourse or written texts? Could these approaches be complementary?

4. What do you use dictionaries for in your second or foreign language(s)? What kind of dictionary do you prefer and why (bilingual-monolingual; learner-L1)? Do you have any complaints about the dictionaries you use?

SUGGESTED ACTIVITIES

1. Find a newspaper article that you could use to teach vocabulary. Pick out the words that you feel are crucial for understanding the text and that have enough contextual support to allow the reader to guess the meaning. Now ask a target learner to read the text and then tell you (a) which words s/he does not know at all, and (b) which words s/he is not sure of regarding meaning. Finally, compare your own list with the information you elicited from the learner. What are the similarities and the differences? Which vocabulary items will you teach in conjunction with the text and why?

2. Develop an activity you could do with intermediate level language learners to increase their receptive vocabulary. Now develop another activity to teach the same learners some of the same words as productive vocabulary. What are the differences in these activities in terms of the language skills needed, the number of words you introduced, and the degree of communicative activity that takes place?

3. Examine a story or essay written by an intermediate level language learner. Are there any errors of lexical choice or grammatical errors associated with lexical restrictions? Describe what you find and suggest ways of dealing with any such errors you identify.

4. What vocabulary do you probably need to teach low intermediate EFL learners for them to be able to understand and retell the following story? How will you teach the vocabulary?

The Ant and the Dove (Adapted from a fable by Aesop)

A dove saw an ant fall into a brook. The ant struggled to reach the bank. In pity, the dove dropped a piece of straw into the brook beside the ant. Clinging to the straw, the ant floated safely to shore.

Soon after, the ant saw a man getting ready to kill the dove with a stone. But just as the man threw the stone, the ant stung him in the heel. The pain made the man miss the dove, and the startled bird flew to safety in a nearby tree.

A kindness is never wasted.

5. With younger learners, it can be useful to retell a well-known tale (one you are sure they are familiar with), e.g., "Little Red Riding Hood." Begin with a meaningful change such as "She lives in Chicago." Other changes will follow, "Her mother sends her to visit her grandmother on the other side of town. How will she go there? What should she be careful of? Who might help her if she gets lost?" The students can tell a modern version of the story working together in groups and looking up words that they need. If you were to do this activity with young learners, what familiar story would you use, and what kind of a modern context would you set it in?

Suggestions for Further Reading

For other discussions of vocabulary in discourse, see:

Carter, R., & McCarthy, M. (Eds.). (1988). *Vocabulary and language teaching.* London: Longman.

McCarthy, M. (1991). *Discourse analysis for language teachers* (Chapter 3). Cambridge: Cambridge University Press.

For useful teacher references/handbooks, see:

Gairns, R., & Redman, S. (1986). *Working with words.* Cambridge: Cambridge University Press.

Hatch, E., & Brown, C. (1995). *Vocabulary, semantics, and language education.* New York: Cambridge University Press.

Morgan, J., & Rinvolucri, M. (1986). *Vocabulary.* Oxford: Oxford University Press.

Nation, I. S. P. (1990). *Teaching and learning vocabulary.* New York: Newbury House.

For textbooks with many exercises that teach vocabulary through discourse, see:

McCarthy, M., & O'Dell, F., with Shaw, E. (1997). *English vocabulary in use: Upper intermediate reference and practice for students of North American English.* New York: Cambridge University Press. (There is also a 1999 British edition of this text by McCarthy and O'Dell, published by Cambridge University Press.)

Nation, I. S. P. (1994). *New ways in teaching vocabulary.* Alexandria, VA: TESOL.

Seal, B. D. (1990). *American vocabulary builder* (Vols. 1, 2). New York: Longman. (There is also a 1987 edition of the two volumes for British English published by Longman, London.)

For a useful learner resource, see:

Alexander, L. G. (1994). *Right word, wrong word: Words and structures confused and misused by learners of English.* London: Longman.

Endnotes

[1] We thank Marjorie Walsleben for her input into this list of lexical categories.

[2] Olshtain's findings were based on the examination of word formation knowledge exhibited by intermediate and advanced learners of Hebrew as a second language as compared with native Hebrew speakers.

[3] When languages borrow sounds or grammatical patterns, it takes centuries to consolidate, e.g., the borrowing of the sound /ʒ/ from French into English, in words such as *pleasure* or *beige*.

[4] Spoken language differs from written language in that it can be characterized by the frequent use of several very general words: *thing, person, stuff, time, place,* and so forth.

[5] This text is adapted from the information brochure for the 1995 Sonoma Salute to the Arts, p. 1.

[6] The examples are taken from Kinsler's data but edited somewhat for brevity and ease of reading (i.e., conversation analysis conventions are not used).

[7] Obviously, other words such as *anyway* and *listen* also signal that the conversation is about to close in this example.

[8] The *Peanuts* cartoon cited appeared in the *Los Angeles Times* comic section on July 8, 1990.

EPILOGUE TO PART 2: INTERRELATIONSHIPS AMONG LANGUAGE RESOURCES

In Part 2 we have discussed the resources of language (i.e., phonology, grammar, and vocabulary) in three separate chapters, which might suggest that these resources function discretely. This is definitely not the case. We have discussed each language resource separately for purposes of drawing attention to its special and typical features; however, in any true instance of communication, these resources overlap and interact in ways that manifest themselves through discourse (i.e., through an oral or written text that is situated in a given context and that satisfies pragmatic expectations). As previously illustrated in Chapters 3 through 5, we can visualize these integrated language resources as they function within the language knowledge framework (see Figures 3.1, 4.1, and 5.1).

Phonology and vocabulary can interact at the level of discourse in a variety of ways. Words that are hard to pronounce tend to be avoided by both first and second language learners while they are communicating, and words that are similar in sound tend to be confused. An example of the first strategy (i.e., avoidance) comes from the early speech of a young child who had been exposed to both English and French from birth and could comprehend both languages; however, she initially produced vocabulary items based on what was easiest for her to articulate regardless of the source language (Celce-Murcia, 1977). For example, at age two years and four months the child said:

French: fille [fiː] and never English girl, but

English: boy [bɔy] and never French garçon

An example of the second tendency (confusion based on similar sounds) is the fluent but inaccurate English speech of a tour guide in the Middle East, who consistently confused the pronunciation of the words lentil and lintel. The English-speaking tourists listening to him could generally figure out from context whether the guide was referring to a horizontal crosspiece above a door or window at an archeological site or to the soup of the day at the restaurant where the group would stop for lunch. However, the guide's inconsistent production caused initial momentary confusion and then later became a source of humor once the tourists figured out the guide's communication problem:

"Ah, he means 'lintel' not 'lentil'!"

"I'm HUNgry. I wish we WERE talking about 'lentils' instead of 'lintels'!"

Grammar and phonology interact and overlap in many ways, some of which were illustrated in Chapter 3, where we demonstrated, for example, that intonation could override syntax and make a formally declarative utterance function as a question for the speaker and listener. Another example of the interaction of grammar and phonology comes in the regular morphological endings that mark the simple past tense (-ed) and the simple present tense -(e)s that marks the third person singular only since there is no overt inflection elsewhere for verbs other than be. Many fluent but inaccurate nonnative speakers of English simply omit these morphological endings when producing connected speech. In most cases, the listener can disambiguate; however, the omission can cause confusion when it is important to contrast the use of the simple past tense to signal specific examples with the use of the simple present tense to signal a state or generalization. Consider, for example, the telegraphic interlanguage of a nonnative veterinary assistant:

Cats contract feline leukemia. Not inoculate. Cat recover.

Despite good contextual support, the above discourse is much harder to process unambiguously than the following:

> Cats contract feline leukemia if not inoculated, but this cat recovered
> well from the disease.

In this example, not only the verb tense markers but the connectors "if" and "but" play a role in disambiguating the meaning.

Certainly grammar and vocabulary also interact when users of English are communicating. The problem that many nonnative speakers have in distinguishing the -*ing* and -*en* participles that derive from emotive verbs (e.g., *surprise, annoy, amuse*) results in errors such as:

> *I am interesting in modern art.

The distinction between the two forms requires that users combine a casual/agentive subject with a progressive participle or an active verb:

> Modern art is interesting to me/interests me.

versus combining a patient/affected subject with a passive participle or passive verb:

> I am interested in modern art/by modern artists like Dali.

In such cases, the vocabulary item selected must occur within an appropriate grammatical frame and carry the appropriate morphological inflection or there can be confusion and miscommunication. For example, after a rather chaotic verbal exchange between a native and a nonnative speaker of English, the nonnative speaker comments:

> Sorry, I'm confusing. (intending to say "I'm confused")

To which the native speaker retorts:

> Yes, you certainly are!

In such cases, the context may help disambiguate the message by appeal to pragmatic information (as discussed in Chapter 2). In this particular example, pragmatic information contributes to the sarcasm in the native speaker's retort – sarcasm that may not necessarily have been fully understood by the nonnative speaker, who may nonetheless take offense from the tone of voice in which the retort was uttered.

In most instances of communication, all of the language resources are deployed simultaneously to create discourse. When language inaccuracies occur, the intended message may be comprehended because the contextual support is clear and unambiguous. However, there are many segments in ongoing discourse without adequate contextual support, which are not understood, or which are in fact misunderstood. Most commonly the source of such a problem is inaccurate or inappropriate deployment of one or more of the three language resources (phonology, grammar, vocabulary) that have contributed elements to the creation of the discourse segment in question.

Learners thus need ample opportunity both within and outside the classroom to use all their language resources to produce and interpret situated and purposeful discourse – all the while drawing on all the pragmatic information and strategies at their disposal to get their intended messages across or to figure out the speaker's or writer's intended message.

PART 3

LANGUAGE PROCESSING

CHAPTER 6

Listing[1]

"It is unlikely that we ever achieve an exact match between intention and interpretation, and we probably would not know it if we did. We arrive at the degree of convergence necessary to the purpose of interaction and no more. Comprehension is never complete: it is always only approximate, and relative to purpose."

(Widdowson, 1990:108)

"The underlying paradox in listening research is the routine unconscious ease of listening and the extreme difficulty of investigating it, particularly as the process itself is unseen and inaccessible."

(Lynch, 1998:6)

INTRODUCTION

When people listen – whether they are listening to a lecture, a news broadcast, or a joke, or are engaging in a conversation – they are listening to a stretch of discourse. In fact, listening is the most frequently used language skill in everyday life. Researchers (e.g., Morley, 1991; Rivers, 1981; Weaver, 1972) estimate that we listen to twice as much language as we speak, four times as much as we read, and five times as much as we write! It is thus remarkable that several of the otherwise excellent publications that have appeared over the past several years with the purpose of informing language teachers about discourse analysis and its pedagogical applications (e.g., Cook, 1989; McCarthy, 1991; Hatch, 1992) have had little to say about the listening process.

Both L1 and L2 models of the listening process (cf. Anderson and Lynch, 1988) acknowledge that listening has both top-down and bottom-up aspects. *Top-down listening processes* involve activation of schematic knowledge and contextual knowledge. **Schematic knowledge** is generally thought of as two types of prior knowledge (Carrell and Eisterhold, 1983): (1) **content schemata**, i.e., background information on the topic, and (2) **formal schemata**, which consist of knowledge about how discourse is organized with respect to different genres, different topics, or different purposes (e.g., transactional versus interactional), including relevant sociocultural knowledge. **Contextual knowledge** involves an understanding of the specific listening situation at hand (i.e., listeners assess who the participants are, what the setting is, what the topic and purpose are). All of this gets filtered through **pragmatic knowledge** to assist in the processing of oral discourse. In addition, good listeners make use of their understanding of the ongoing discourse or co-text (i.e., they attend to what has already been said and predict what is likely to be said next).

The *bottom-up level of the listening process* involves prior knowledge of the language system (i.e., phonology, grammar, vocabulary). Knowledge of the phonological system allows the listener to segment the acoustic signals as sounds that form words, words and/or phrases that form clauses or utterances unified by intonation contours having some key prominent element. Knowledge of vocabulary allows the listeners to recognize words within phrases, and knowledge of grammar allows for recognition of inflections on words as well as recognition of the phrases or clauses that function as parts of cohesive and coherent instances of text. Thus all types of language analysis can come into play at the level of discourse when listening is being done.

The bottom-up processing of oral discourse is where the physical signals or clues come from; however, it is generally acknowledged that this level cannot operate with any accuracy or efficiency on its own and that it requires the benefit of and interaction with top-down information to make discourse comprehensible to the listener. This interaction of top-down and bottom-up processing is crucial to our Speech Reception Framework presented in Figure 6.1 on the next page.

For native speakers and skilled L2 speakers, bottom-up processing is assumed to be automatic, whereas it is not automatic and can be the source of serious problems for beginning and less than expert L2 learners. For example, a university lecturer said "commonest" in one segment of her lecture, and one of the L2 listeners in the class wrote "Communist" in his notes, thus indicating that he had misunderstood in a fundamental way that segment of the lecture (Harada, 1998).

To help compensate for less than automatic bottom-up processing, learners need to make use of listening strategies and **metacognition** (two components in Figure 6.1 that we have not yet discussed but shall take up at this point). Examples of listening strategies include: (a) extract an important detail from ongoing speech; (b) identify the gist of a segment; (c) predict what will come next in a segment.

Mendelsohn (1995, 1998) outlines how to teach strategy-based L2 listening:

1. Raise learner awareness of the power and value of using strategies

2. Use pre-listening activities to activate learners' background knowledge

3. Make clear to learners what they are going to listen to and why

4. Provide guided listening activities designed to provide a lot of practice in using a particular strategy (e.g., listening for names or dates) using simplified data initially, if needed

5. Practice the strategy using real data with focus on content and meaning

6. Use what has been comprehended: take notes on a lecture to prepare a summary, fill in a form to gather data, and so forth

7. Allow for self-evaluation so that learners can assess how accurate and complete their listening has been (Vandergrift, in press)

Metacognition is also a type of strategy that learners can use to enhance L2 listening. Metacognition involves the *planning, regulating, monitoring,* and *management* of listening and thus is related to several of the listening strategies listed, in particular 1, 2, 3, and 7. Metacognitive strategies give learners an overview of the listening process. They allow for prediction, for monitoring of errors or breakdowns, and for evaluation (Vandergrift, 1997).

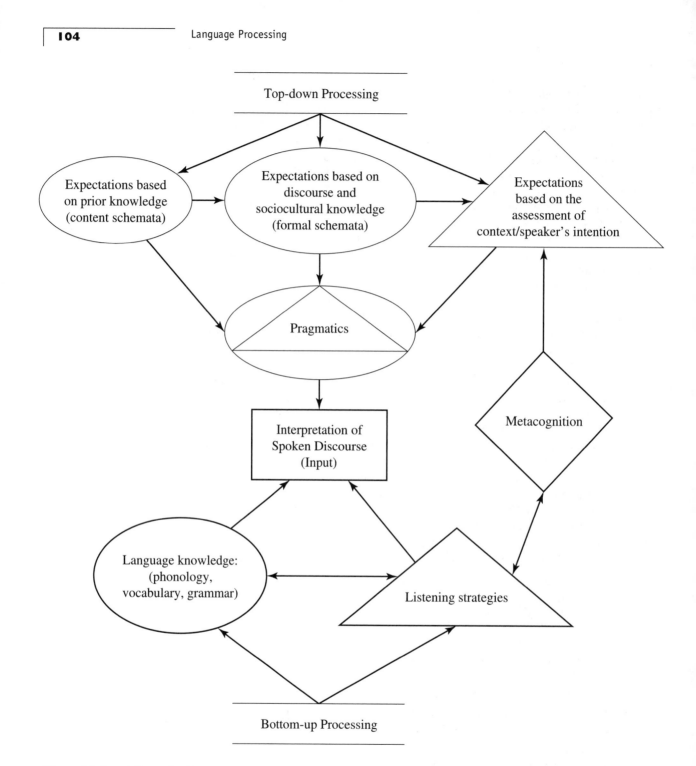

Figure 6.1 Speech Reception Framework

THE LISTENING PROCESS: RELEVANT BACKGROUND AND RESEARCH

BACKGROUND

In the early 1980s it was popular to assume that only top-down skills needed to be enhanced to improve L2 listening comprehension. However, it is now more generally acknowledged (cf. Peterson, 1991) that both top-down and bottom-up listening skills should be integrated and explicitly treated pedagogically to improve L2 listening comprehension. The discourse level is in fact where top-down and bottom-up listening intersect and where complex and simultaneous processing of background information, contextual information, and linguistic information permit comprehension and interpretation to take place.

Given the *interactive model* of the listening process that we describe in this chapter, we can see that many factors related to the L2 listener are relevant to his/her success or failure: among these are the learner's language learning experience, i.e., L2 proficiency in general and L2 listening ability in particular, including experiences with listening to a variety of speakers who have different accents and who speak different dialects while engaging in a variety of speech situations (lectures, movies, face-to-face conversations, telephone conversations, and so forth.) This exposes learners to the reality of language variation. Also relevant are factors such as the listener's prior knowledge (topic, content schemata, sociocultural information, and the like), the listener's memory and attention, and his/her general problem-solving ability (i.e., ability to come up with the best interpretation out of several possible ones in a given context as well as an ability to predict what might come next or later in a given instance of oral discourse.)

We must also consider the *compensatory strategies* (i.e., the listening strategies and metacognition we have discussed) and *communication strategies,* which good L2 listeners have and which weak ones lack: strategies such as asking questions of one's interlocutor, getting the other speaker to slow down, tape recording and relistening to a lecture, watching a movie a second or third time, and various other strategies. In ongoing conversations, good listeners are able to recognize a problem and to alert the interlocutor in some appropriate way if they have not processed the input well enough to make an interpretation; they are thus in a position to negotiate a repetition and/or clarification. Ability to implement such strategies helps the listener whose listening comprehension is not yet nativelike, and thus such strategies should be part of oral skills training.

There are of course also situation-specific factors external to the listener: the quality of the acoustic signal and the amount of background noise. Similarly, there are nonlinguistic situation-specific factors such as room temperature, distractions, or being in a test-taking situation, and listener-internal factors such as lack of interest in the speaker or topic, lack of attention, and so forth. In any given situation, these factors may impair listening comprehension, which is something complex, dynamic, and rather fragile to begin with because of the transitory nonpermanent nature of the speech signal. Our opening quote from Widdowson, which applies to reading as well as to listening, emphasizes the incomplete nature of and lack of precision inherent in the comprehension process.

As Lynch (1998) points out, all listening experiences can be placed along a continuum from *nonreciprocal* (e.g., listening to a radio news broadcast) to *reciprocal* (face-to-face conversation). At the reciprocal end of the continuum the L2 listener's oral communication strategies already mentioned, are very important; however, at the nonreciprocal end of the continuum, L2 listeners must use their own top-down and bottom-up processing skills without benefit of any interaction with, or feedback from, the speaker. L2 learners generally agree that nonreciprocal listening tasks are more difficult than reciprocal listening tasks.

Another very important factor in L2 listening is the learner's *task flexibility*. As the situation and the task demand, can listeners get the overall gist of an oral communication?

Can they accurately comprehend important details such as names, numbers, times, and dates? In other words, Nida's (1953) notions of *general versus selective listening* are still very relevant today. A good listener is able to do the type of listening needed. Either of both types of listening can be important depending on the situation or task. Teachers, therefore, must give learners realistic opportunities to engage in both types of listening.

RESEARCH

Based on the assumption that one can discover much about how a process works by examining cases of its malfunction, Garnes and Bond (1980) analyzed a corpus of 890 "mishearings" committed by native speakers of English while the speakers were engaging in everyday conversation. Based on their analysis of these hearing errors, Garnes and Bond proposed that listeners process incoming speech by employing the following four *microprocessing strategies* (holding the stream of speech in short-term memory would, of course, underlie all of these):

1. attending to stress and intonation and constructing a metrical template, or pattern, to fit the utterance
2. attending to stressed vowels
3. segmenting the speech stream into words that correspond to the stressed vowels and their adjacent consonants
4. seeking a phrase – with grammar and meaning – compatible with the metrical template identified in the first strategy and the words identified in the third

This is primarily a bottom-up model. However, when processing speech, it is possible that listeners use compensatory strategies to overcome deficiencies in any of these steps, which would bring in top-down processing too. If we consider that while the listener is doing the four steps, s/he is actively attending to context (situational and co-textual) and calling up all relevant content and formal schemata, then we can begin to see where things might easily break down for the L2 listener. Interference from the sound system of the native language, which may well favor a different processing procedure because of differences in rhythm and/or syllable structure, will make it hard to construct metrical templates and to identify stressed syllables and their vowel nuclei. Lack of a large audio-receptive lexicon and lack of knowledge about common collocations will impede segmentation of each intonation contour into words or chunks; likewise, imperfect knowledge of morphology and syntax will make it difficult to identify word, phrase, or clause boundaries and to assign meanings.

An examination of written transcriptions of audio-recorded speech that were prepared by advanced second language learners at UCLA indicates that verbs are commonly misheard (e.g., *thought* for *fraught*). Personal names are often not recognized as such (e.g., *down the reed* instead of *Donna Reed*), and idioms are often misheard (e.g., *more stuff and barrel* for *lock, stock, and barrel*); both proper names and idioms in fact are prime candidates for mishearing even among native speakers (Celce-Murcia, 1980). These are some of the errors that intermediate and advanced L2 learners make due to lack of lexical, grammatical, and cultural knowledge as much as to difficulties with the L2 sound system (See also Harada, 1998). In their attempts to process oral discourse, low-level learners can even misconstrue the hesitation phenomena produced by native speakers as words (cf. Voss, 1979; Griffiths, 1991):

uh heard as *a*

huh? heard as *up?*

hmm heard as *him*

Although some of these mishearings could conceivably be clarified by context and pragmatic support, there are many cases where such information is not accessible to nonnative speakers.

To see what problems low-intermediate L2 listeners have with aural comprehension of English, Martin (1982) asked five native speakers of Spanish to listen to short but complete radio broadcast segments and then give immediate paraphrases (in English or Spanish) of what they had heard. Martin also asked them to introspect and report back on their problems. Here are two samples of her data:

1. *Original radio segment*: New York. A presidential economic expert says
   the current recession will linger for at least a few more months. (p. 78)

1'. *Learner's report*: I understood something about one expert, economy
   in relation to the president. I didn't understand that very well. (p. 45)

2. *Original radio segment*: Poland. The Communist government denies
   that Solidarity leader Lech Walesa will soon be free. (p. 78)

2'. *Learner's report*: I missed the very beginning. I don't know what said
   that. Someone in Poland. (p. 42)

Noting that places where comprehension broke down seemed to yield the best information about the L2 learners' listening strategies, Martin followed the same procedure but with longer segments and then, in examining all her data, she found that her consultants had used two different strategies: (1) *bottom-up word level* strategies (which associate meanings with specific words) and (2) *top-down idea level* (which deal with establishment of a topic and help relate all subsequent meaning bits to the main idea). Her data indicated that three progressive stages seemed to underlie the listening process for these L2 learners:

1. An initial *orientation period* when the listener gets used to the physical features,
   i.e., the speaker's voice quality and pronunciation, rate of speech, and vocabulary;
   this varies in length but the listener cannot process the discourse effectively
   until s/he gets oriented to the speech signal.

2. A *search for a main idea* that begins with the listener taking in words, phrases,
   and/or clauses; these can then be decoded and pieced together to form a tentative
   message based on top-down strategies.

3. *New incoming information* is *matched against the perceived main idea* and/or the
   listener's previous knowledge; adjustments are made and problems of consistency
   are identified, reflecting the listener's effort to use both top-down and bottom-up
   strategies to interpret the message.

Martin speculated that the top-down and bottom-up strategies and the three stages interacted and probably were often used simultaneously by her consultants. Even though there were tendencies that all the listeners followed, there were also interesting differences. Each consultant approached listening using somewhat different combinations of the strategies identified.

From this review of research on listening, it seems that listeners make use of prosodic knowledge – specifically stress and intonation – in combination with top-down processing to identify main ideas, while they use knowledge of sound segments in ways that are more closely related to bottom-up processing, e.g., identifying words, phrases, or grammatical inflections. There is also experimental evidence indicating that listening practice is more important for oral skills development than speaking practice. Anderson and Lynch (l988:16) show that learners who have had sufficient and focused task-based experience as listeners are better able at some later time to perform a similar oral communication task than are other learners who had only been given prior speaking practice (i.e., giving learners practice only in listening was more effective than giving practice only in speaking). One can safely assume that giving practice with both skills – first listening and then speaking – would be the best possible preparation, but if the teacher doesn't have time to do both, then listening practice (with awareness raising and analysis) should take precedence.

TEACHING LISTENING FROM A DISCOURSE PERSPECTIVE

TEACHING BOTTOM-UP STRATEGIES

What can be done by teachers to encourage their students to engage in listening practice at the discourse level? In many instances where reduced speech or imperfect acoustic processing might obscure a message, an effective listener is able to use the situational context and/or the preceding and following discourse (co-text) to disambiguate or to decide on the best interpretation. For example, if the speaker says

"I'm lookin' fer Joe 'n' Barney. Have ya seen 'm?"

the effective listener will process the final unstressed syllable /ɪm/ as *them* rather than *him* given the prior mention of two people: *Joe* and *Barney*. Whether the speaker is native or nonnative, there must be sufficient information in the situation or co-text to process the acoustic signal properly. If, for example, the listener knows that Joe and Barney are typically together this could make the processing even easier for the listener.

In North American English the reduced form *whaddaya,* i.e., /wʌ́dəyə/, can represent either "what do you" or "what are you." Again, training the listener to attend to the discourse context and the local grammar can help disambiguate such a reduced form. Imagine, for example, a dialog between two students:

A: I dunno what classes to take.
   Whaddaya think I should take?

B: It all depends. *Whaddaya* gonna
   do after you finish school?

The first occurrence of the reduced form corresponds to "What do you" in the environment of the verb *think*. The second occurrence corresponds to "What are you" in the environment of the *gonna do* (i.e., *going to do*). Eisenstein (1983:26) in fact encourages teachers to expose learners to such reduced speech forms, which are generally not represented orthographically, to enhance their listening comprehension.

Sometimes the only difference between two possible interpretations is a hard-to-hear unstressed syllable. Once again the co-text, in this case what comes after the problematic sequence, can provide the information needed to choose correctly:

1. Maria (a. praised/b. appraised) the vase. She said it was gorgeous.
2. Jonathan (a. steamed/b. esteemed) it. He told me how valuable it was yesterday.

In the first example (a) is selected by effective listeners, while (b) is selected in the second. Good listeners can store the speech signal in memory long enough to use the information given in the subsequent intonation contour to help disambiguate the potentially problematic string.

Thus far we have discussed how problematic sounds or sequences of sounds can be segmented and comprehended if the listener makes effective use of context. The same is often true in cases where stress or intonation causes the difference.

In North American English the modal auxiliary *can* and its negative contracted form *can't* differ mainly with respect to stress when they occur in context. When spoken in isolation, the vowel sound is the same and the difference between a final /n/ and a final /n/ plus an unreleased [t˚] can be virtually imperceptible:[2]

can /kæn/

can't /kænt̚/

However, in context the difference is clearer because *can* is usually unstressed and its vowel reduced to schwa /kən/, while *can't* is stressed and retains its full vowel sound /kænt/. When we ask listeners to match what they hear with the best following clause, they should pick (b) if the speaker says (1) and pick (a) if the speaker says (2):

1. /àykəndúwɪt/   a. It's illegal.
2. /àykænt̚duwɪt/   b. It's easy.

For some compound words where more than one syllable is stressed, prominence can occur on different syllables in different contexts to convey different meanings. For example, we have the following contrasts as possibilities:

FIFty-one versus SIXty-one

fifty-ONE versus fifty-TWO

Given the context "Eisenhower was elected president in '52 not '51," the prominence should fall on the "two" and the "one" not the "fifty." However, in the context, "I can't remember whether Uncle Jack is 51 or 61," the prominence should fall on the "fifty" and the "sixty." This is not at all obvious to many second language learners, so practice in detecting prominence and explaining its function in discourse – i.e., signaling new information or contrast – should be part of instruction in listening.

Like stress, intonation can help listeners comprehend a speaker's meaning and intention if used alongside other cues (Rost, 1990). The direction of the speaker's pitch at the end of an utterance can be particularly crucial. With the same string of words, intonation can signal the certainty of a declarative (a) versus the uncertainty of an interrogative (b):

a. Marsha is feeling BETter.

b. Marsha is feeling BETter?

The terminal fall in (a) signals that the speaker's utterance is declarative while the terminal rise in (b) signals an interrogative that seeks confirmation. Any terminal pitch followed by a pause is an opening for the listener to respond, but the listener needs to comprehend the meaning of the words and the grammar as well as the intonation of an utterance in order to respond appropriately. Thus (a) could be responded to with (a') while for (b) the response in (b') would be more appropriate:

(a') I'm glad to hear that.

(b') Yes, it's a surprisingly quick recovery.

Using (b') as a response to (a) is possible only if the listener already knows the information in (a); however, (a') would be a somewhat odd response to (b). Tag questions and "or" questions are some of the other constructions in English where intonation can be especially crucial (see Chapter 3 for further discussion).

These examples are all fairly local. They make use of information in the immediately surrounding discourse to disambiguate or select a reasonable interpretation for a problematic segment. Even in these cases, we can still fairly confidently say that the co-text is helping the listener with bottom-up, data-driven processing. We emphasize this because for many practitioners the assumption has been that discourse-level information assists the listener only (or mainly) with top-down processing, and indeed, there are many convincing examples of discourse-level information being very helpful with top-down processing. Our point is that both types of processing are useful and necessary for effective listening comprehension and that they typically interact.

TEACHING TOP-DOWN AND INTEGRATED STRATEGIES

Moving on to top-down processing, we offer the example of a university-level history professor who begins his lecture with the following statement, thereby providing his listeners with a useful *organizer*:

> Today we're going to consider three forces that helped to shape the Carolingian Empire. We'll look at religion, we'll look at the prevailing social structure, and we'll consider economic factors.

With these opening words, the professor has verbally established the **topic** or **main idea** for his lecture:

> Three forces helped shape the Carolingian Empire.

The professor then lists the three forces on the board – each of which we now know will be discussed during the lecture:

1. religion
2. social structure
3. economic factors

The L2 listener who has comprehended the opening statement (i.e., the topic) and its relationship to the list (which is in effect an outline of subtopics) is in a much better position to understand and take notes on the lecture than the L2 listener who has missed the opening information about the overall topic. Second language learners in English-for-academic-purposes programs can be trained to process such material by listening to a variety of lecture openings and being told to write down the topic and to predict what the lecture will cover. Their written notes can then be checked, and feedback and clarification can be provided if necessary.

Learners can also benefit from listening to long segments extracted from authentic lectures and working at getting the *gist*, i.e., writing down the main points or topic(s). This global task can be complemented by subsequently relistening to the same segments and jotting down the *details* (the facts, dates, names, results, and so forth). Learners can also listen to a lecture while looking at a partial outline where they must fill in the missing information. Such listening-related tasks are done so that the learners can eventually become more effective at using both top-down and bottom-up listening strategies.

To integrate practice in listening comprehension more fully with other skills in communicative language teaching, Geddes and Sturtridge (1979) suggest the use of "jigsaw" listening activities, where several small groups of learners each listen to a different part of a larger piece of discourse (e.g., a story, a recipe, a mini-lecture, a news broadcast) and write down the important points. Later each group shares their information with another group and then another so that each group can piece together gradually the larger discourse segment and then report on their overall summary of the discourse. With such an activity there should then be an opportunity at the end for everyone to listen to the entire piece of discourse to decide whether the reports and each group's reconstruction has been accurate.

TEACHING USE OF THE TELEPHONE

VOICE MAIL AND ANSWERING MACHINES

With the proliferation of voice mail systems and telephone answering machines, second language listeners should be exposed to a variety of authentic voice-mail messages; after each message they should write down the essential information so that they would be able to respond appropriately to the message had the call been intended for them. For example:

> Hi, this is Judy. Uh. It's Tuesday afternoon and I'm calling to see if you have notes from the geography lecture today. I missed it because of a dental appointment; so if you have the notes, just bring them tomorrow so I can borrow them. Hmm. If not, call me back at 213-876-4201 tonight so I can call someone else. Okay, thanks. Bye.

The listeners (working individually or in small groups) should be asked to reconstruct two possible scenarios in terms of responding to this telephone message:

Scenario 1: (I have the notes for the geography lecture.)
       Judy wants them
       I'll bring them to class tomorrow
       No need to call Judy back

Scenario 2: (I don't have the notes for the geography lecture.)
       Judy wants them
       I should call Judy at 213-876-4201
       I'll tell her I don't have the notes

NONRECIPROCAL TELEPHONE LISTENING

Today many phone messages are prerecorded and the listener cannot ask questions or slow down the interlocutor. Getting the right information depends on being able to understand the range of options, the specific instructions, and how to respond by performing the proper action on the Touch-Tone telephone. For example:

- If you want to know the locations of Weight Watcher meeting places in your area, punch in your zip code now
- If you want to know meeting times before 3 P.M., press "one"
- If you want to know meeting times after 3 P.M., press "two"
- If you want to know all the weekly meeting times at this location, press "three."

This type of nonreciprocal telephone information message is now used for a variety of purposes such as activating credit cards, giving information about airplane flight arrival and departure times, and giving information about movies currently screening along with theaters and show times, and so forth. Often such messages are so complicated that even native speakers must dial the telephone number two or more times to understand all the desired information. In some cases, one must do this sort of telephone listening and punching in of appropriate numbers as a preliminary to actually talking to someone (e.g., when trying to follow up on a medical insurance claim). Such listening tasks can be quite daunting for L2 learners who have not been properly prepared.

TELEPHONE USE: EVERYDAY CONVERSATION

Inexperience in dealing with live interactive telephone conversation in the target language can also be a serious problem for some second language learners. They need opportunities to listen to, interpret, and sum up what they hear in a series of authentic recorded phone conversations. Their listening skills can be greatly facilitated if they are exposed to authentic telephone conversations and also taught the *conversational structures* and options as well as the formulaic expressions that the work of Sacks, Schegloff, and Jefferson (1974) have shown typically manifest themselves in informal telephone conversations among speakers of North American English. There are of course special conventions associated with telephone conversation such that even a native speaker unfamiliar with these conventions in his own language would have a difficult time managing a telephone conversation. Since these conventions vary from language to language and dialect to dialect, it is certain that nonnative speakers who have not had any special instruction will experience some difficulty.

The general conversational structure of an informal telephone conversation in North American English (Sacks et al., 1974) is as follows:[3]

Opening segment

Summons: phone rings
Answerer: Hello?

Caller: Hi, $\left\{ \begin{array}{l} can \\ may \end{array} \right\}$ I speak with _____?

Answerer: $\left\{ \begin{array}{l} \textit{This is} _____. \\ \textit{S/he's not here. Can I take a message?} \\ \textit{Wait a minute. I'll call him/her.} \end{array} \right\}$

Or the opening after the phone rings may be as follows:

(Addressee: Hello?)
  Caller: Hi, _____. This is _____.

The "How-Are-You" segment

Addressee: Hi, how ARE you?
  Caller: Fine thanks. And YOU?
Addressee: Pretty good./Just fine.

Topic establishment

$\left\{ \begin{array}{l} \text{(Direct)} \\ \quad \text{Caller: I'm calling because . . .} \\ \text{(Indirect)} \\ \quad \text{Caller: Are you free Friday night?} \end{array} \right\}$

(call proceeds; topics are established; topics change)

Preclosing

Addressee: You know, I'd like to talk a bit longer, but I've got a calculus exam at ten o'clock tomorrow. Can I call you back tomorrow afternoon?

Caller: Oh sure.

Closing

Addressee: Talk to you later then.

Caller: Yeah. Bye.

Addressee: Good-bye.

Listening to a number of phone conversations that more or less follow this pattern prepares second language learners not only for informal telephone conversation but will also assist them in being more effective in face-to-face conversation. This is important because L2 students have told us that they often don't know how to end a conversation or to decline an invitation politely, and so they end up talking much longer than they would like to, or (even worse) they accept invitations they would truly rather decline.

LISTENING TO SPEECH ACTIVITIES

The entire area of social functions or *speech activities* can be challenging in L2 listening as well as speaking (see Chapter 9). Olshtain and Cohen (1991), for example, have found for "apologies" that if L2 listeners hear sample *apologies* and get a sense of the overall structure of apologies in English, they can then comprehend and analyze subsequent instances of apologies to see how minimal or elaborate they are and to judge their overall appropriacy in terms of the context in which they occur.

To give learners a sense of the overall structure of a speech act like an apology, Olshtain and Cohen make use of the notion *speech act set,* which refers to the routinized ways in which a given speech act can pattern. Apologies differ according to culture with respect to what members of the culture will apologize for and how they will do this. In all cultures, however, the speaker's aim in uttering an apology is to provide support for and placate the addressee, who has been adversely affected by something that the speaker is at least partially responsible for.

Olshtain and Cohen report five strategies that have been observed cross-culturally in apologies:

General strategies minimally necessary for an apology

1. Explicit expression: *Excuse me./I'm sorry./I apologize.*

2. Admission of responsibility: *It's my fault./I didn't mean to do it.*

Situation-specific strategies; optional ways to elaborate an apology

3. An excuse/explanation: *The bus was late.*

4. An offer to make amends: *I'll buy you another vase.*

5. A promise of nonrecurrence: *It won't happen again.*

In English, for example, if someone forgets a meeting with his/her boss, a possible apology – with strategy numbers indicated – is:

I'm really very sorry. (1)

I completely forgot about the meeting. (2)

The alarm on my watch didn't go off. (3)

> Can we make another appointment or meet now? (4)
>
> This won't happen again, you can be sure. (5)
>
> > (from Olshtain and Cohen, 1991:156)

Compare this rather serious and elaborate apology with a more casual apology that one student might make to another after knocking over a cup of coffee:

> Sorry, Joe. (1)
>
> I didn't mean to knock your coffee over. (2)
>
> I'll buy you another one. Want cream and sugar? (4)

Other researchers (e.g., Hawkins, 1985) have found that learners can improve significantly in their ability to process and produce speech acts like apologies and complaints when they are thoroughly familiar with the speech act set and have been exposed to and have analyzed many authentic instances of the target speech act occurring in different contexts. In addition, Hawkins mentions that learners report genuinely enjoying the process of learning about the structures and options used in such social interactions (see Chapter 12 for a unit on teaching complaints).

PEDAGOGICAL STRATEGIES AND PRIORITIES

What are some of the most useful exercises and activities for L2 listeners? Many teachers have recorded short segments from radio or TV news broadcasts, which they then play several times in class for their students to give them an opportunity to experience multiple listenings and to carry out a variety of tasks:

- extract topic/gist (first listening)
- get details of news item (second listening)
  (who, what, when, where)
- evaluate emotional impact of news items (third listening)
  (this can vary but the listener should give reasons for the choice):
  - neutral report of the information
  - information makes me happy/sad
  - information worries/surprises me
  - information annoys me
  - other

It can also be useful for second language listeners to look at a faithful transcript of a lecture or a conversation with all the pauses, false starts, incomplete sentences, and so forth, represented. Access to such transcripts – along with appropriate guidance from the teacher – can make listeners aware of many things (including the fact that spontaneous or live speech is "messy" much of the time). More specifically, it helps learners see the discourse function of items such as the following:

- cue words and discourse markers that signal what the main points and minor points are (e.g., sequential organizers such as *first, second, finally*)
- lexical and structural cues including lexical routines and chunks that signal a new term and/or a definition or some other notional construct (see Nattinger and DeCarrico, 1992). For example, "in other words" signals that the speaker will be paraphrasing or further explaining what has immediately preceded.

- key text segments that serve as higher order organizers (like the opening segment from the history professor's lecture we quoted on page 110).

Also important for comprehending interactive reciprocal discourse are:

- words and phrases used to open or close a topic in conversation
- ways to ask a question or to interrupt the speaker
- ways to ask for clarification or elaboration

In order to help younger learners to develop good listening strategies, teachers need to design a variety of listening tasks that resemble games and at the same time focus on identification and recognition of spoken sequences. The easier tasks may require simply the identification of certain key words such as counting the number of times the word "king" appears in a story as the class listens. More complex activities may require matching of actions and personalities in the story (Who played the guitar?) or even finding reasons for actions (Why did they look for the leader of the group?). A final activity should involve a collaborative retelling of the story by the whole class, which means that the learners have to listen carefully to what their peers contribute as well as remember the story.

CONCLUSION

In this chapter we hope we have demonstrated that in addition to using acoustic information to perceive and segment the stream of speech (i.e., to do bottom-up processing) native listeners – and even more so, nonnative listeners – must actively use a variety of schemata and contextual clues, especially those clues that are available in the ongoing discourse, to accurately interpret oral messages (i.e., to do top-down processing). Phonological signals such as stress, pause, and intonation; lexico-grammatical signals such as discourse markers, lexical phrases, and word order; and higher-level organizing elements such as the adjacency pairs that we find in conversational structure are all critical in signaling information to the listener. Research findings have implications for language pedagogy in that they reinforce the notion that listening comprehension is indeed the primary skill in developing oral communicative competence. The findings are particularly relevant in settings where the target language is being used as a medium of instruction for academic purposes. They also have implications for materials development in terms of the type and range of practice materials needed to teach listening comprehension effectively.

It is appropriate that we have discussed listening first in this section dealing with how the four language skills relate to discourse processing and to each other. In fact, we shall see in the following chapter that reading makes use of many of the same top-down processing strategies and prior knowledge frameworks that listening does. In addition, listening, in those cases where it is interactive and reciprocal, also shares language knowledge and top-down strategies with speaking; effective reciprocal listening requires special strategies that directly involve speaking (e.g., back-channeling with "uh-huh" or some other marker to let the speaker know you are listening, asking for repetition or clarification). This relationship will come up again in Chapter 9, which deals with speaking.

DISCUSSION QUESTIONS

1. Why is context so important for the teaching and learning of listening comprehension?

2. Compare the listening strategies you use in your first language with those you use in a second or foreign language. What are the similarities and differences?

3. Give an example of a situation where learners would have to use both top-down and bottom-up listening strategies to achieve comprehension.

4. Can you recall an instance where you misheard something in your first language or a foreign language? What did you "hear"? What did the other speaker say? What may have caused this mishearing?

SUGGESTED ACTIVITIES

1. Record a short segment such as a news item from radio or TV. Design two listening tasks using this segment – one for native speakers and one for nonnative speakers. What did you do that was different?

2. Record someone telling an anecdote or a story that is completely new to the nonnative speakers you are teaching or tutoring. Then have the learners listen to this story one segment at a time. After each segment the class should retell (a) what they have heard and (b) what they think will be said in the next segment. Then have them listen to the next segment to check their predictions against what was actually said.

3. Prepare a listening task for an intermediate language class. In addition to the task itself, incorporate awareness-raising by asking the learners to reflect on what they have done to achieve comprehension and why there might be trouble spots or segments that are not fully comprehensible. If you are able to try out this activity, be sure to include time for the students to discuss in groups both what they comprehended and their strategies for achieving comprehension.

4. Prepare three different listening tasks that would help younger learners develop good listening strategies. Discuss the issues related to sound-meaning correspondences with your colleagues.

Suggestions for Further Reading

Anderson, A., & Lynch, T. (1988). *Listening.* Oxford: Oxford University Press.

Dunkel, P. (1991). Listening in the native and second/foreign language: Toward an integration of research and practice. *TESOL Quarterly, 25*(3), 431–457.

Mendelsohn, D. (l998). Teaching listening. *Annual Review of Applied Linguistics, 18*, 81–101.

Morley, J. (1991). Listening comprehension in second/foreign language instruction. In M. Celce-Murcia (Ed.), *Teaching English as a second or foreign language,* 2nd ed. (pp. 81–106). Boston: Heinle & Heinle.

Peterson, P. W. (1991). A synthesis of models for interactive listening. In Celce-Murcia, M. (Ed.), *Teaching English as a second or foreign language,* 2nd ed. (pp. 106–122). Boston: Heinle & Heinle.

Rost, M. (1990). *Listening in language learning.* London: Longman.

Endnotes

[1] Earlier versions of this chapter, or portions of it, were published as Celce-Murcia (1995a) and as Chapter 7 in Celce-Murcia, Brinton, and Goodwin (1996).

[2] There is less of a comprehension problem in British English, where *can* is pronounced /kæn/ and *can't* is pronounced /kant/.

[3] Henry Widdowson (personal communication) suggests that the conversational conventions for informal phone calls among British English speakers would be quite different from what we present here for North American English. If a corpus of informal British English phone calls is available, a similar template could be prepared for British English that reflects the macrostructure of informal phone conversations in that dialect.

CHAPTER 7

Reading

"Texts, I would suggest, do not communicate: people communicate by using texts as a device for mediating a discourse process. It is the process which is the communicative occurrence."

(Widdowson, 1984:125)

"In our classrooms and on our campuses, we should assist students to draw from their past strategies and experiences and to develop new approaches to texts and tasks. Our classrooms should encourage student research into their own literacy and text histories, into current approaches to literate practices, and into strategies that work in a variety of contexts."

(Johns, 1997:19)

INTRODUCTION

Even in this modern age of multimedia and high-tech environments, it is still the case that most of us rely on our reading ability in order to gain information or expand our knowledge. Whether it is the sports fan who rushes to the sports page of the newspaper, the investor who checks the financial page, or the tennis instructor who needs to know the weather forecast, information is available to all of them in print and it has to be processed via reading. In a literate society, skill in reading is imperative since so much of what one needs to know is communicated via written text: instructions on how to get out of an underground parking area, instructions on how to operate the pump in a self-service gas station, or the precautions one needs to take when trying out a new drug or ointment. We could not function in modern society without reading. Yet for some people this is not an easily accessible skill.

In a second or foreign language, reading carries even greater potential importance than in the first language since it is often the only readily available exposure to the target language. A learner of another language will be able to retain some of the knowledge gained in a course of study by continuing to read in that language for many years after graduating from the course. For anyone learning the language of a remote country, reading opens up a world of literature and culture representing that country in a manner that would not otherwise be possible.

When we think of English as a world language or language of wider communication, reading takes on a very significant role in most professions. Scientists keep abreast of the developments in their fields of study by reading scientific journals in English, lovers of art subscribe to art magazines in English, and lovers of nature subscribe to nature magazines in English. For those who are keen on using the Internet, reading is a basic skill that makes access to computers and the Internet possible. This chapter deals with the development of the reading skill in a second or foreign language and places particular emphasis on the difficulties that the nonnative speaker encounters when reading in the new language.

READING FOR COMMUNICATION

THE INTERACTIVE NATURE OF THE READING PROCESS

In the process of trying to understand a written text the reader has to perform a number of simultaneous tasks: *decode* the message by recognizing the written signs, *interpret* the message by assigning meaning to the string of words, and finally, *understand* what the author's intention was. In this process there are at least three participants: *the writer, the text,* and *the reader.* The writer may be distant in time and space from the particular reader of the text and from the act of reading; nonetheless, it was at the time of writing that the author produced the text with the intention of transmitting a message to a potential reader, and therefore, the dialog between reader and writer via the text can take place at any time after that. Reading is, therefore, inherently interactive, involving the three participants.

The *psycholinguistic-cognitive* approach to reading (Barnett, 1989) is learner-centered and places cognitive development and text processing at the core of its view on reading. Prior knowledge that individuals bring to the reading or writing situation is central in this approach. An important term employed by the psycholinguistic-cognitive group is **schema** (**schemata** in the plural) to refer to prior knowledge. Many of the theorists belonging to this approach have been instrumental in changing teaching methodologies from the traditional focus on isolated features of texts to the interactive and collaborative view of the composing process (Silva, 1990), which develops as part of reader-text interaction.

Historically, two separate approaches to reading developed in the literature and research: bottom-up approaches and top-down approaches. Bottom-up approaches view reading as "a series of stages that proceed in a fixed order from sensory input to compre-hension" (Hudson, 1998:46). Gough (1972) is one of the proponents of this approach. On the other hand, top-down approaches view the interpretation process as a continuum of changing hypotheses about the incoming information. Smith (1971, 1988, 1994) and Goodman (1968, 1976) are major proponents of such an approach. More recently, approaches that take an interactive view of reading require an integration and combina-tion of both top-down and bottom-up approaches to describe the reading process.

The interactive nature of the reading process has been described and studied for the past two decades by many researchers in this field (Rumelhart 1977, 1980, 1984; Rumelhart and McClelland, 1982; Stanovich 1980, 1981, 1986). Some of the studies have focused on the writer, rather than on the features of the text; others have focused on the strategies of interpretation employed by the reader. Figure 7.1 on page 120, presents our discourse processing model, first presented in Chapter 1, as it applies to reading.

Since top-down and bottom-up processing take place simultaneously – the reader needs to recruit his or her prior knowledge and prior reading experience, apply knowledge of writing conventions, and consider the purpose of reading in order to engage in top-down processing. In Figure 7.1 the knowledge components are in ovals, and the purpose

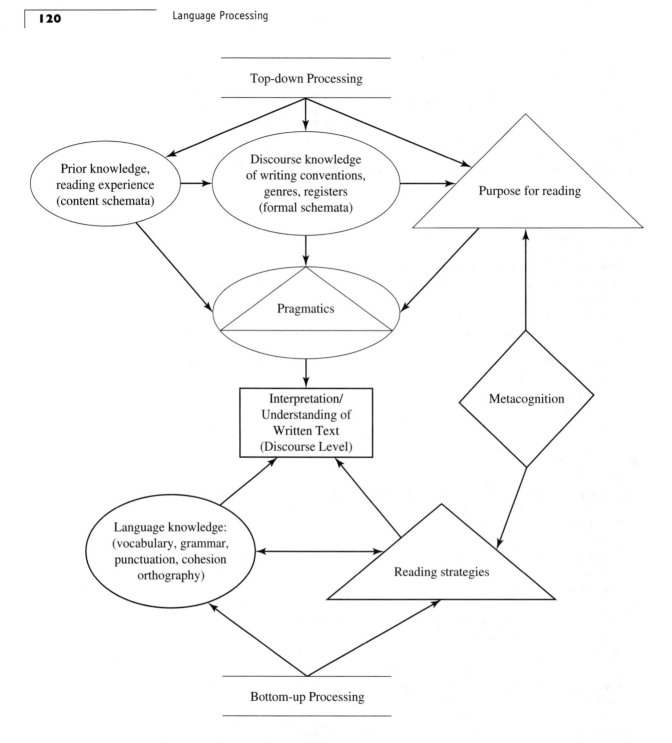

Figure 7.1 Reading: Written Text Reception Framework

of reading is in a triangle as part of the pragmatic considerations. At the same time, the reader needs to recruit his/her linguistic knowledge and various reading strategies in order to decode the written text through bottom-up processing. It is the effective integration of these processes that leads to the appropriate interpretation and understanding of the written text and creates the interactive reading process. Prior knowledge (the first oval on the top left) related to reading includes content knowledge as well as experience in reading. The second cluster of knowledge (the second oval) refers to knowledge of writing conventions, including genre and registers as well as knowledge of sociocultural and contextual background, which can be important in facilitating the reading process. The purpose of reading, on the other hand, is more closely related to the individual needs of the reader and to the personal expectations that s/he has with respect to the given text. Different texts may require different combinations of the elements presented in Figure 7.1, for the same reader. A less familiar text, for instance, may require more top-down evaluation, whereas a linguistically more difficult text may require more bottom-up considerations (such as the meanings of difficult words). Similarly, the same text may be processed differently by different readers, depending on their prior knowledge and their knowledge of the target language.

Figure 7.1 is in many respects similar to Figure 6.1 (see Chapter 6, Listening) since in both chapters we are concerned with interpretation of discourse. In the context of listening the assessment of the situation within which the spoken interaction occurs plays a crucial role, and it is filtered through pragmatic considerations. In the context of reading, the knowledge of written conventions and the purpose of reading will determine the approach and attitude the reader will have toward the written text. Linguistic knowledge combined with reading or listening strategies will enable the interpreter to do bottom-up processing in order to complement the top-down processing.

The reading task requires readers to choose and apply some of what they know to each new text. It seems that "good" readers do this very effectively while poorer readers encounter a multitude of difficulties. This chapter is concerned with discourse features of texts that might enhance the reading and interpretation of a text if the reader can use them as facilitating clues, while the same discourse features might interfere with the interpretation process if unfamiliar to the reader.

Top-down processing is often referred to as the knowledge-driven or concept-driven approach to a text, and it consolidates all the elements that the reader brings to the reading process. It is, in fact, a *reader bound* approach that relies heavily on the reader's global interpretation process. Let us imagine that a person comes across a scrap of paper on which the following section of a text is printed without a title, without graphics or any other indication as to where the text might have appeared originally, by whom it may have been written, and for what purpose:

> On August 2, 1939, Albert Einstein told the president of the United States
> that his scientific colleagues had evidence to show that an atomic bomb
> might be made.

Any reader coming across this piece of text might recruit all his/her knowledge concerning the atomic bomb, the tragic history of Hiroshima and Nagasaki, the fight against nuclear weapons, or any other potentially related topic that seems relevant. On the basis of such "background" or "prior knowledge," the reader might construct some initial hypotheses about the text and accordingly have expectations as to what might come next. The next sentence in the given text is the following:

> Six years later, in February 1945, Klaus Fuchs met a Russian agent
> whom he knew by the code name "Raymond" and passed on to him
> what he knew about making the bomb.

Our imaginary reader can now narrow down and focus attention more specifically on the initial development of the atomic bomb in the United States and the transmission of this secret information to Russia. Yet, the reader still has too little information about the text in order to anticipate the aim or message of the text. The next bit of text might do the trick for most readers:

> Was one of these men right to disclose his terrible knowledge, and was the other wrong? Or were they both wrong? Do scientists have a sense of right and wrong?

At this stage most readers would realize that the text is concerned with questions of ethics and the responsible conduct of scientists. Had the reader seen the title, "A Moral for an Age of Plenty" (Bronowski, 1977:196) or had s/he known the name of the author, s/he might have narrowed down the expectations and hypotheses based on the content of the title and/or the knowledge the person might have about Bronowski as an author of articles related to philosophic, scientific, and moral issues.

The top-down processing of a text, therefore, recruits the reader's background knowledge of both content and text genre, and his/her expectations and experiences (see Figure 7.1), and applies them to the interpretation of the text, as the reader moves along from one section to the next, within the text. This type of processing is easier and more effective when readers are familiar with the subject matter of the text and it becomes more difficult when such preparatory information is not available.

Simultaneous with the top-down processing, readers utilize a bottom-up approach, also known as data-driven processing, which is *text bound* and which relies heavily on linguistic information (both semantic and syntactic in nature) available in the text. It is the *complementary* utilization of the two types of processing that make text interpretation possible.

During the 1980s a strongly communicative view of reading assigned more attention to top-down processing, which at the time was new and less familiar to teachers and learners than bottom-up techniques, which had long been commonly practiced in the language classroom. In the late 1980s and the beginning of the 1990s we see increasing arguments for viewing the two types of processing as complementary and interactive in nature. Grabe (1988) emphasizes the need to allow for all subskills to be available to the reader, and he speaks in favor of the Interactive Parallel Processing models described by Griffin and Vaughn (1984) and Waltz and Pollack (1985). Furthermore, it has been shown that good readers have excellent decoding skills and can decode letters and words rapidly in a bottom-up fashion (van Dijk and Kintsch, 1983). For ESL/EFL readers it seems necessary to develop and promote awareness of and skill in both types of processing so that the individual reader can find individual compensatory techniques to overcome linguistic and content deficiencies.

In the following paragraph, for instance, taken from a passage by Asimov (1985) entitled "Back to Basics," the ESL/EFL reader must be able to recognize some of the key words and their exact meanings (*brittle, chipped, tough*) in order to understand the point being made by the author:

> But then about 5000 years ago, people began using metal. It had advantages. Whereas rock was brittle and had to be chipped into shape, metal was tough and could be beaten and bent into shape.
>
> (Asimov, 1985:5)

If the readers of this paragraph do not know the three key words and their meanings, they will have to depend more heavily on top-down strategies and make use of their knowledge about materials in order to understand the paragraph. The problem in doing so, however, is that rock can be both hard and brittle, and metal can be both tough and flexible, and a reader who does not know the accurate meanings of these words might reach wrong conclusions about the message of the text.

Good and effective reading must, therefore, be viewed as combining both rapid and accurate recognition and decoding of letters, words, collocations, and other structural cues with sensible, global predictions related to the text as a whole. In other words, good readers constantly *integrate* top-down and bottom-up processing techniques. In order to do so, readers bring their prior knowledge and experience to the reading process and at the same time interact effectively with the text by using their linguistic knowledge and individual reading strategies (see Figure 7.1). This is the interactive nature of the interpretation process.

During the last decade new literacy approaches have evolved. These can be viewed within the socioliterate school of thought, which views reading as a social and cultural event involving written language. Bloome (1993), for instance, proposes viewing reading as a social process focusing on author-reader interaction. According to this approach to reading, the individual constructs the meaning of the text within a culture. This approach further emphasizes the context of the literacy event and thus has affected classroom pedagogy through what has become known as the *whole language approach*. In philosophy, the whole language approach seems quite compatible with the communicative approach in language teaching since it places the learner and his/her needs in the center but within a social context where communication takes place and personal choices are made in accordance with cultural and social perspectives. Taken to the extreme, this approach might inadvertently diminish the significance of the knowledge components. It is our position in this book that language knowledge and discourse processing should interact in any communicative event, especially when second or foreign language learning contexts are considered. Figure 7.1 presents, therefore, a practical realization of the reading process, encompassing the various approaches to reading we have discussed while slightly simplifying the picture.

THE EFFECTIVE READER

What do we know about "good" or effective readers? Perhaps the first important study done in this area was the extensive research carried out by Gibson and Levin (1975) with adults reading in their native language. The most significant finding indicated that good readers adjust to the materials at hand and quickly fit their "attack" skills to the type of text they are reading and to their personal objective for reading. Furthermore, when mismatches occur (e.g., between title and text, between expectations and text, between extratextual knowledge and text, between linguistic competence and text) good readers know how to abandon nonsuccessful strategies and select new ones, how to re-deploy old strategies, and how to combine those that seem to work best in the particular interpretation process at hand.

A reader faced with a written text usually goes through a quick sequence of mental questions: Should I read this text? What do I expect to get out of it? What do I expect it to tell me? What do I know about the writer of the text and the purpose for which it was written? In most cases readers have good reasons for reading a certain text: curiosity, relevance to personal concerns, pleasure, academic or professional purposes, and so forth. The reason or purpose for reading the text will guide readers in the intensity with which they want to read the text and in the selection of appropriate reading strategies.

During the reading process itself the ongoing questions might be: Do I understand the author's point? How carefully do I need to read this? Do I understand all the important words? Do I see where the argument seems to be going? Is this worth the time and effort that I am devoting to it? How can I read this faster and better? It is obvious that these questions relate to both top-down and bottom-up processing of the text, and that they are also related to the reader's purpose and choice in reading. Furthermore, these questions concern issues related to both the reader and the text in question.

During the reader's processing of the text, the reader moves along a decision-making continuum that is basically seeking answers to such questions. When reading comprehension is effective, there is probably a close match between the reader's expectations and the actual text; however, there are often serious mismatches that may lead to difficulty in processing. The effective reader makes constant adjustments to the text by recruiting background knowledge for top-down processing and by changing strategies to fit bottom-up decoding of the particular text. Such a reader thus combines top-down and bottom-up techniques in the most efficient and most expedient way in order to understand the text.

Good readers are not only effective strategy users, they are also effective decoders (van Dijk and Kintsch, 1983) who successfully employ accurate and automatic bottom-up techniques. They are capable of recognizing words, expressions, and phrases quickly and effectively, even without reliance on context and therefore consciously use bottom-up strategies mostly for compensation when top-down strategies indicate a mismatch. Reading speed in a second language can also be a problem. In English, research shows that readers should process at least two hundred words per minute to read effectively. Thus, in some cases it may be necessary to help learners measure and increase their reading rates in order for them to improve their comprehension. See Fry (1975) for suggestions on how to increase reading rates.

Good readers also make efficient use of co-text – the information available in the text at the local level. But perhaps most important, good readers readjust constantly. They continuously match old and new information and experience, both at the global and local level, very much like good listeners do, as described in Chapter 6. Furthermore, as Grabe (1991:381) states in his summary of research on good readers, "They appear to make better use of text organization . . . [and] write better recalls by recognizing and using the same organizational structure as the text studied."

While the effective reader in the first language may be an efficient intuitive user of the various processing techniques, the ESL/EFL reader may have to be made aware of these strategies in order to be able to use them consciously whenever linguistic or content deficiencies create difficulties in reading. It is, therefore, important to encourage the reader to develop **metacognitive** awareness of the interpretation process and of individual processing strategies. Such metacognitive awareness connects top-down with bottom-up processing, as indicated by the lines connecting metacognition (the diamond) with other elements in Figure 7.1.

A study carried out by Schoonen, Hulstijn, and Bossers (1998) shows that metacognitive knowledge plays an important role for advanced readers in both the first language (Dutch) and the foreign language (English). According to this study, weaker students in grades six and eight have not yet acquired metacognitive knowledge and could benefit from special instruction in this area, while older good readers exhibit metacognitive knowledge. The most significant finding in terms of foreign language teaching in this study is that strong metacognitive knowledge, reading goals, and text characteristics cannot compensate for language-specific knowledge if the latter remains below a certain threshold level. It emphasizes, therefore, the need for the effective reader to have both language knowledge for bottom-up processing and prior knowledge for top-down processing with the metacognitive knowledge acting as mediator.

FEATURES OF A WELL-WRITTEN TEXT

COHERENCE

A well-written text exhibits two important features: it has **coherence**, and it has **cohesion**. These inherent features of a well-written text facilitate the interpretation of the text during the reading process. While creating the text, the writer invests time and effort to make the text coherent and cohesive; the effective reader takes advantage of these features. However, we must remember that not all texts are necessarily "well written" and therefore the interpretation process might be hindered.

Coherence is the quality that makes a text conform to a consistent world view based on one's experience and culture or convention, and it should be viewed as a feature related to all three participants in the interactive process: the writer, the written text, and the reader. The notion of coherence thus incorporates ways and means by which ideas and propositions in a text are presented conceptually. It is the result of the writer's plan and relates to the discourse world of written texts, to pragmatic features, and to a content area; it usually fits a conventionally and culturally acceptable rhetorical organization, sequence, and structure. Widdowson (1978) relates coherence to illocutionary development. According to Widdowson, coherence is perceived through the interpretation of the particular illocutionary act or acts and through the illocutionary development of the conversation (described in greater detail in Chapter 9) or the written text. In other words, Widdowson perceives the reading of a text as a dialog between reader and writer where the illocutionary intention of the writer (persuasion, declaration, suggestion, and so forth) needs to be understood by the reader. Yet, since the reader and writer are removed from each other in time and space, the interaction is very different from the type of interaction experienced in oral discourse. Widdowson (1984) describes reading as a nonreciprocal activity: "The writer is a participant in that he is enacting a discourse with an assumed and absent interlocutor but he is at the same time detached from immediate involvement . . ." (77), and similarly the reader is a nonreciprocal participant when trying to interpret the written text.

For schema theorists, the coherence of a text is central, and cohesion is a linguistic consequence of coherence. This is compatible with top-down or concept-driven theories of reading. For a while Halliday and Hasan (1976) were criticized by Carrell (l982) and others for taking the position that cohesion is the basis for coherence. But later Hasan (1984) clearly stated her position, which is that coherence is a feature of the text that indicates "the property of hanging together" (183). Halliday and Hasan are concerned with describing the language system, whereas schema theoreticians such as Carrell (1982) are primarily interested in human psychology and the reading process. They seem to be looking at the same process from two different perspectives. Hasan (1985:94) further asserts that ". . . cohesion is the foundation on which the edifice of coherence is built. Like all foundations, it is necessary but not sufficient by itself."

Culturally determined and socially accepted conventional discourse structures of written texts refer to types of texts such as narrative fiction, academic research reports, news columns in a daily newspaper, and so forth. One type of written genre that has a specific prescribed and conventional format is the business letter. The format supplies at least part of the coherence and as such creates a frame of reference for both writers and readers. The format of the business letter varies across cultures, while the functions of the business letter are universal and incorporate relevant illocutionary acts such as requesting information, placing orders, apologizing, and persuading. According to the culturally accepted format, the writer would present the information in a conventionally coherent fashion; for instance, whether the information about the company and the product should come first or whether the response and interest of the customer should come first would depend on the particular culture and its conventions.

In addition to the possibility of following some conventional format, a text needs to "make sense" to the reader in order to be fully coherent. This is very much in line with the interlocutionary perspective that speakers/writers have the responsibility to make their intentions clear through the text. In the interactive approach to reading, as we have seen, coherence is not only text-based it is also reader-centered. From the reader's point of view, coherence is the result of the interaction that takes place between text-presented knowledge and text-user's schemata or stored knowledge regarding information and text structures. Schemata can be viewed as frames of reference that readers possess, structures of the world and of reality in the readers' minds, which enable them to develop "scenarios" to be projected onto the events predicted as part of the interpretation process. When the reader's scenario or schema matches the text, interpretation is easier than when there are mismatches, and some kind of mediation strategies need to be applied. In other words, in order to process and understand a text, readers need to match the schemata of context and form presented by the writer in the text with their own schemata and their own view of the world and of the subject area or content presented in the text. Coherence, therefore, is created by the reader while reading and is partially intratextual and partially extratextual.

COHESION

Cohesion is an overt feature of the text, providing surface evidence for the text's unity and connectedness. Cohesion is realized linguistically by devices and ties that are elements or units of language used to form a larger text (spoken or written). Since cohesion relies heavily on grammatical and lexical devices (see Chapters 4 and 5), it relates to the reader's linguistic competence. Deficiencies in this area may cause the reader to miss important cohesive links and, as a result, to have difficulties in the interpretation process.

As a simple example of how some cohesive devices work, consider the following sequence of sentences taken from a narrative constructed by a young child:

> (1) There was a little boy who had a dog and a frog. (2) One day the frog got out of its jar and ran away. (3) The boy and the dog looked for the frog everywhere, but they could not find it.

The three main characters in the story are all introduced as new information with the indefinite article in sentence (1). *The frog* is referred to again in sentence (2) through lexical repetition and the use of the definite article to indicate old information [information from sentence (1)] and in sentence (3) through the use of a personal pronoun "it" to indicate old information with strong topic continuity. *The jar* is presented as information associated with *the frog* through the use of the possessive adjective *its* in sentence (2). *The boy* and *the frog* are signaled as old or known information through lexical repetition and the use of the definite article in sentence (3). The *but* introducing the last clause of sentence (3) signals an adverse result or outcome. The three sentences are also related to one another through the consistent use of the past tense verb forms: *was, had, got out, ran away, looked.* The child telling this brief story managed to present a well-connected, cohesive English text.

Elements in a text that have the same referent or classification form a "cohesive chain" (Halliday and Hasan, 1976), which ties together parts in the text and thus the text itself into a whole. Such cohesive chains can also be viewed as signals that a particular writer has chosen in order to structure the text in view of the communicative goal for producing the text. These chains facilitate the interpretation of the text by the reader since they help to segment the text (Enkvist, 1987). The most common discourse strategies involve temporal, locative, and/or participant/topic-oriented continuity. There are basically two types of reference that are important in constructing cohesion: endophoric reference, which relates to anaphoric (i.e., backward) and cataphoric (i.e., forward) reference within the text, and exophoric reference, which relates to context outside the text. In top-down processing exophoric reference plays an important role, whereas endophoric reference facilitates bottom-up processing.

Cohesion is not to be confused with coherence: A text may be ostensibly cohesive but make no sense (lacking coherence), and a text might lack overt cohesive devices yet be perfectly coherent if the ideas or information presented make logical connections with reality. In the following text taken from an example given by Halliday and Hasan (1989:83) we have a superficially cohesive text that makes no sense and is therefore not coherent:

> A cat is sitting on a fence. A fence is often made of wood. Carpenters work with wood. Wood planks can be bought from a lumber store.

In this text "the overt, linguistically signalled relationships between propositions" (Widdowson, 1978:31) are made evident, yet the propositions are not logically connected in terms of how we perceive the world. Carrell (1982:484), on the other hand, provides a good example of a short text that seemingly has no overt cohesion yet it makes perfect sense and enables the reader to perceive it as fully coherent:

> The picnic was ruined. No one remembered to bring a corkscrew.

Coherence in this text is created due to the fact that both the writer and the reader share knowledge and schemata that relates corkscrews to wine bottles and wine to picnics. The extratextual knowledge in this case is imperative for the perception of coherence in the text. In fact nonnative speakers of English who do not drink wine often find Carrell's short text to be incoherent.

Support for the reader-based view of coherence can be found in Hasan (1984), where she claims that speakers (or readers and writers) are sensitive to variation in coherence and therefore "textual coherence is a relative, not an absolute property" (Hasan, 1984:181). Hoey (1991:12) goes even further and defines cohesion as a "property of the text . . . which is objective, capable in principle of automatic recognition" and coherence as a feature of the reader's evaluation of the text which "is subjective and (thus) judgments concerning it may vary from reader to reader."

DIFFICULTIES ENCOUNTERED BY READERS WHILE READING

GLOBAL PROCESSING DIFFICULTIES

Readers often face a dilemma with respect to the plausibility of the message or the information presented in the text, when perceived from their own point of view. In cases like these, we say that there is a mismatch between the reader's view of the world and the view that seems to be presented in the text. When there is no such mismatch, the interaction between plausibility and context works well in advancing the interpretation of the text. When, however, a mismatch occurs, it greatly interferes with comprehension and demonstrates the disadvantages of relying too heavily on top-down processing. The following paragraph is taken from an article, "Accidental Drug Addiction," by Muriel Nellis (1978), which first appeared in a women's magazine. It is, therefore, addressed to women readers although it describes the problems of drug addiction in general terms. The reader who encounters the following paragraph and who is preoccupied with sex discrimination might misinterpret the article as a text with a bias against women and one in which the author treats women prejudicially:

> Prescriptions for mood-altering drugs are disproportionately high among women because they constitute the largest group of patients seeking medical advice. It is known that women will reach out for and accept help at critical points in their lives.
>
> (Nellis, 1978:7)

In fact, when the entire text is examined, it is clear that the article criticizes physicians who have a tendency to more readily prescribe anxiety-reducing drugs for women than for men. Here, there may not be a case of mismatch in the basic worldviews of the reader and the writer; however, a reader who approaches the text with preconceived expectations might misread the message. This situation is further aggravated for ESL/EFL readers who may not understand some of the key words such as "disproportionately," for example, or may not understand the subtle meaning of an expression such as "reach out for and accept."

Since at this intratextual level of processing there needs to be interaction between global coherence and local coherence, language teachers can help students look for and recognize some of the features related to these concepts by asking these questions: Where did the text appear and what do we know about the journal or the book where it appeared? Who is the author and what do we know about him/her? When was the article or text published and what were the issues of concern at that time? Strategies that combine top-down processing with scanning the text for key sentences can help the reader construct the overall coherence of the text. In a well-written passage the global coherence of the text meshes with the more local coherence of paragraphs and sentences. A short article by Alfred North Whitehead (1957) is a good example of how a close match between global and local coherence is maintained via the rhetorical structure of the text and cohesive elements that indicate relatedness of ideas within the text. The article has three distinct paragraphs, and each paragraph begins with a sentence that relates to the article's title, "Universities and Imagination." The title, by the way, might surprise the reader from the start, since universities and imagination are not two concepts that we would expect to appear together. The three opening sentences of each of the paragraphs in the essay (Whitehead, 1957:8) try to explain to the reader what the writer had in mind when he presented this title, thus enabling the reader to create the coherent picture.

1. The justification for a university is that it preserves the connection between knowledge and the zest for life by uniting the young and old in the imaginative consideration of learning.

2. Imagination is not to be divorced from the facts: It is a way of illuminating the facts.

3. Youth is imaginative, and if the imagination is strengthened by discipline, this energy of imagination can in great measure be preserved throughout life.

Most readers' personal schemata would connect universities with concepts such as knowledge, learning, research, facts, discipline, and the like, but not necessarily with imagination. The writer is trying to make this new connection in order to get his ideas across. He uses a combination of the expected concepts with the unexpected notion of imagination. In each of the opening sentences of the three paragraphs we find some of the expected terms and at least one mention of some form of the word "imagination." This forces the reader to connect his/her existing schema with a new view of the world as presented by the writer and thus create coherence both at the global level and the paragraph level.

Whitehead's article is obviously a good piece of writing and therefore facilitates the interpretation process. Often, however, such global and local connections are not this explicit and the reader has to exert considerable effort to make sense of the writer's intention.

Language classes need to make students aware of such difficulties and encourage them to develop individual strategies as well as to develop some tolerance for coping with complex or poorly written texts.

Another source of difficulty might be in the interaction between old and new information. This starts out with the writer making certain assumptions about prior or shared knowledge with the reader. There are linguistic, cohesive devices that separate new information from old information in the text, but the assumed background knowledge usually cannot be retrieved from the text since it is extratextual in nature. In these passages Whitehead assumes that all readers of his article have some basic knowledge about universities; without such background knowledge they could not make sense of the writer's particular message.

In order to be able to identify old and new information in the text and thus evaluate the writer's position and intention and recruit his/her own relevant schema, the reader must employ linguistic knowledge that grammatically signals such distinctions. The most important grammatical signals in English include reference markers, the sequence of tenses, conjunctions, the article system, and so forth. Linguistic competence is necessary in order for a reader to successfully recognize the internal connections within the text and be able to relate old to new information. General knowledge of the world, on the other hand, is necessary in order to connect one's background knowledge to the ideas presented in a written text. The main function of discourse features that relate to signalling the text's cohesion and coherence is to make text processing possible.

Carrell (1988) discusses two types of difficulties that learners may encounter when reading: too much reliance on text-based features via bottom-up processing resulting in text boundedness, or alternatively, too much reliance on knowledge-based processing, thereby allowing inappropriate schemata and irrelevant extratextual knowledge to interfere with proper text interpretation.

In the first case we find readers who get bogged down by linguistic complexity and miss the main point made in a paragraph or a whole text, and in the second case the reader ignores some of the information or ideas presented in the text because of adhering rigidly to preconceived expectations that may not in fact materialize. Both of these paths for misinterpreting a text stem from the fact that for the particular reader with the particular text the interaction between top-down and bottom-up processing is not optimal.

GRAMMATICAL FEATURES THAT CAUSE READING DIFFICULTIES

Every language has some linguistic features at the sentence level that can be perceived as difficult. In English, nominalization is a grammatical process that enables the writer to compact a great deal of information into one noun phrase. This density of information and the complexity of the resulting structure greatly affect the processing of the written text. The complexity of any given English noun phrase may be due to multiple modifiers such as one finds in complex compounds, relative clauses with deleted relative pronouns, and various other compound modifiers in prenominal position. These types of structures are extremely common in English exposition in general and in scientific writing in particular. The stringing together of multiple modifiers can make recognition of the head noun during bottom-up processing quite difficult. Thus, in examples such as the following, ESL/EFL readers might have a hard time recognizing the head noun of the compound:

1. common prescribed drugs
2. a recent government study
3. peak efficiency level
4. mood altering legally prescribed drugs

Since from the reader's point of view it is not at all clear that the head must be in final position (other languages do not necessarily have such a feature), any of the individual nouns might be perceived as potential heads of the phrase. In (1) it might be especially hard for the reader with a first language where modifiers follow the head noun to realize that in this case the head is the noun *drugs* because the two words that proceed *drugs* could be mistaken for a subject and a verb; in (2) the words *government* and *study* might compete in the reader's mind for the position of head noun if s/he has no restriction on head noun position in his/her language. Thus if the sentence is "A recent government study claims that . . ." the difference between "the government claims" or "the study claims" might be politically very significant. In (3) all three elements might compete for the position of head noun in the ESL/EFL reader's mind, and in (4) the sheer length of the noun phrase as well as the analysis of its constituents creates a slowdown in processing. Readers whose linguistic proficiency enables them to make quick and accurate identification of the head noun in these complex noun phrases will end up processing the text faster and more accurately. This bottom-up processing skill is facilitative when it works well, but damaging when the ESL/EFL reader misinterprets the position of the head noun. This particular grammatical difficulty might affect both speed and accuracy. Special tasks can be designed to help learners identify the head noun in such complex structures and practice the rule of final position in the phrase, which seems superficially easy but which proves to be most confusing for many second language learners

Adjectival clauses with deleted subjects potentially create a twofold difficulty. On one the one hand, they may interfere with the identification of the modifier and the head; on the other hand, the grammatical form of the participles may mislead readers into thinking that such a construction is a verb phrase. The following examples will illustrate these two problems:

1. Hundreds of species of plants and animals, hurt by dramatic environmental changes in the next century, will face extinction.
2. Science-based technology has been described as the principal tool . . .
3. Leaders selected democratically reflect voters' choices.

The above examples were given to a group of intermediate-level EFL students to translate into their native language in order to assess their ability to interpret adjectival modifiers in English. In all cases the students did not recognize the relative clauses as modifiers and perceived them as independent verb phrases. However, in (1), where the adjective clause is nonrestrictive, the misinterpretation was not so serious: "Hundreds of plants and animals will be hurt by . . . ." In (2), where the implied adjective clause "technology that is based on science" resulted in a prenominal adjective compound, students were less accurate in their interpretations: "Science has been based on . . ." since they mistook the word "science" for the head noun of the construction, falling into the twofold trap of such constructions. Perhaps the most problematic example in this set of sentences is example (3). Here it turned out that the translation supplied by most students meant something like "All leaders are elected democratically and reflect voters' choices." This is obviously an erroneous interpretation as the sentence really means "Leaders who are democratically elected (and not necessarily those who are not) reflect voters' choices." Students who did not make this connection showed a very different understanding of the point expressed in the text, a fact that could greatly mislead them when reading a passage containing such a construction.

DISCOURSE FEATURES THAT MIGHT CAUSE PROBLEMS

Reference needs to be maintained throughout a written message of any sort in order to ensure both cohesion and coherence. The reader relies on grammatical features that provide indications of reference such as the pronoun system, the article system, or demonstratives.

However, English often creates ambiguity in terms of such referential ties since redundant elements such as case and gender are not always available, or if available, still allow for multiple possible antecedents. For example, "Bob talked to Hans and then drove his car to Berlin." What does "his" refer to – Bob or Hans?

Let us consider some of the pronoun references in the following passage from *The Half-People* by Marya Mannes (1958):

> 1　People on horses look better than they are. People
> 　　in cars look worse than they are. On any of our
> 　　highways this last observation, unfortunate as it
> 　　may be, is inescapable. For the car, by bisecting
> 5　the human outline, diminishes it producing a race
> 　　of half-people in a motion not of their own making.
> 　　Automobiles can be handsome things, particularly if
> 　　they are foreign, but they bestow none of their
> 　　power and beauty on their passengers. It is not
> 10　only that the people in cars face in one direction,
> 　　like gulls in the wind or curious penguins, but that
> 　　the sleekness and brightness of the car exterior
> 　　makes them look shabby if not down-right sordid.
>
> (Mannes, 1958:38–39)

In the first two sentences in lines 1 and 2 the pronoun "they" is used to refer back to "people on horses" in the first sentence and to "people in cars" in the second. This seems to be the most common and immediate use of pronouns and should not create difficulties for the reader. In line 3, the expression "this last observation" refers only to the second sentence and the reader would have to recognize the fact that the scope of "observation" here is limited only to the previous statement. In line 5, the pronoun "it" is used to refer to the "human outline;" some ESL/EFL readers might have difficulty recognizing this link since in their own language they may have access to additional pronoun features such as gender to help them retrieve the antecedent more easily. But the most difficult case of reference in this passage is undoubtedly the use of "them" in line 13, referring to "the people in cars" mentioned in line 10, because of the distance between the referent and its antecedent and because the reader might think that the reference is to *cars*, or *gulls* and *penguins*. The ESL/EFL reader's text processing might be slowed down considerably by such instances of reference which require a second or even a third reading of the sentence in order to ensure comprehension.

Another important device of English discourse and grammar that creates intersentential cohesion within a written text is the use of tense and aspect markers. In narrative texts it is usually the simple past tense, or its historical present variant, that carries the plot forward and helps the reader focus on the main events and on the protagonist's main actions. The progressive aspect within the past time frame of reference, on the other hand, enables the writer to provide background for the main story and to set the scene. In the following two sequential excerpts from the article "A Moral for an Age of Plenty" by Bronowski (1977:204), we can clearly see how the progressive aspect is used to set the scene within which the main event is about to occur:

> . . . Slotin was again doing an experiment of this kind. He was
> nudging toward one another, by tiny movements, several pieces
> of plutonium . . .

The main event is presented later in the simple past tense:

> Slotin moved at once; he pulled the pieces of plutonium apart
> with his bare hands.

ESL/EFL reading courses should provide activities that enable learners to locate instances of obscure reference, giving them the opportunity to practice identification and utilization of such reference. They should also point out grammatical features such as tense and aspect that help readers distinguish between the main plot of a story and the background. A passage like the one above from Bronowski can help learners to focus on the thread of the story and to find time signals.[1]

LEXICAL ACCESSIBILITY

Psycholinguistic models of reading have placed special emphasis on the reader being able to combine personal knowledge (i.e., top-down processing) with textual information (i.e., bottom-up processing) in order to get at the meaning of written texts. Accordingly, textbook writers and reading specialists have often suggested that readers guess the meaning of unfamiliar words by using clues from the text, thus minimizing the use of dictionaries. This strategy is useful and generally very effective and provides readers with important short cuts and increases decoding speed. However, there are some serious pitfalls that readers need to watch out for. Haynes (1993) in her studies of the "perils of guessing" finds that ESL readers can be good guessers only when the context provides them with immediate clues for guessing, while insufficient context and a low proficiency level on the part of the learner may lead to mismatches in word analysis and recognition that can cause confusion and misinterpretation of the target text. She recommends that teachers make students aware of these difficulties, encouraging them to occasionally double-check their guesses by using the dictionary.

Dubin and Olshtain (1993) further emphasize the need for teachers to consider the extent to which a given text provides useful contextual clues. The authors arrived at a definition of the contextual support needed in the text for proper interpretation of unfamiliar lexical items, which includes thematic clues derived from the main idea of the text as well as semantic information at the paragraph and sentence level. Only when readers can combine their general knowledge with information drawn from the text is there a good chance that guessing word meanings from context will be successful. The optimal level of textual support, from the reader's point of view, for any particular lexical item in the text should be derived from a combination of five different sources:

1. The reader's general schemata or general knowledge structures extending beyond the text
2. The reader's familiarity with the overall content of the text
3. Semantic information provided in the paragraph within which the lexical item appears
4. Semantic information in the same sentence
5. Structural constraints in the sentence

The following paragraph from Dubin and Olshtain (1992:186) entitled "The Demise of the Dinosaurs" contains the word *succumb* in the fourth line, a word which will not be familiar to many ESL/EFL readers yet whose semantic elements can easily be reconstructed from the text since all five types of support occur:

1 In an age when our own species, Homo Sapiens,
2 ponders survival, it seems particularly important
3 to find out what happened to the reptiles that
4 dominated this planet for so long. Did they succumb
5 to a single catastrophe? If so, what?

To assign the proper meaning to the word *succumb,* the reader needs to use a combination of all the elements we have suggested. If the readers have general knowledge about dinosaurs and have understood the title, which focuses on the demise of dinosaurs, they possess knowledge about the first two points. It is obvious that the paragraph deals with the question of what happened to dinosaurs and within the sentence where the word *succumb* appears, there is a semantic clue – *catastrophe* – that can help the reader assign *succumb* compatible semantic features. Furthermore, there are structural clues indicating that the word *succumb* must be a verb. It can thus be said that in this particular context the difficult lexical item *succumb* has ample textual support, and most readers should be able to guess its meaning from context.

However, in line 2 of the same paragraph there is another word which might be unknown to many readers and for which it would be almost impossible to get the meaning from the text, i.e., the verb *ponders.* If the reader does not know the meaning of the item itself, there is no way of reconstructing it since the text provides no explicit support. This is a verb that has no obligatory semantic links with its direct object (i.e., *survival*); thus its immediate environment cannot make it more accessible to the reader. Furthermore, in this sentence the subject of *ponders* (i.e., *our own species*) could select almost any verb and certainly does not provide any particular information about the need to use a verb like *ponder.* Thematic or extratextual knowledge also does not help here. We thus conclude that there is little chance that readers would be able to infer the meaning of the verb *ponders* from context.

For teaching purposes it is necessary to analyze reading passages carefully before they are assigned to intermediate-level students. Words that have high textual support in a passage should be designated as words that students can guess from context (such as *succumb* in the preceding passage). Students should be encouraged to identify the clues that help them guess from context so that they become efficient guessers whenever sufficient clues are available. On the other hand, the teacher or textbook writer should identify the words that have no textual support in the passage and provide easily accessible glosses[2] for them. Students should be shown why the meaning of certain words cannot be guessed from the context (such as the verb *ponders*). If learners feel they need the meaning of such words in order to understand the passage, they will have to look them up in the dictionary if a gloss has not been provided. One of the most useful skills we can develop in ESL/EFL readers is the ability to distinguish between words that can be guessed from context and words that need to be looked up in the dictionary. Experience with appropriate activities at the intermediate level should enable advanced students to make such decisions on their own.

SUGGESTIONS FOR DEVELOPING A READING COURSE

DEFINING READING GOALS

A discourse-based approach to reading with its emphasis on the reader's awareness and full participation in the reading process leads toward a number of major goals to be attained and implemented in a reading course. Four such goals will be discussed in this section, the focus being that a reading course today should try to do the following: maximize independent reading opportunities, facilitate negotiated interaction with texts, foster metacognitive awareness and learner autonomy, and expand access to new content areas.

When planning a reading course, one of the major considerations should be giving learners ample time and opportunity to engage in independent reading. Silent reading in guided situations, shared reading in groups, and individual reading inside and outside the classroom should all be carefully planned as an integral part of the reading course. It is only when reading independently, according to self-defined needs and goals, that the learner can develop truly effective reading strategies.

Many reading courses provide learners with activities that are limiting and local in nature and do not enable true interaction with the text. A discourse-oriented reading course should allow learners to negotiate their interaction with text by constantly being involved in making choices and decisions with respect to the text. For example, learners can be told of different reading purposes for the same text and the consequences related to each. Accordingly, students can then make decisions about how they would prefer to process the text. The activities accompanying a text should provide the learners with a variety of ways to attack the text.

For readers to become effective and autonomous, they should be aware of the various considerations and strategies involved in successful processing. Metacognitive awareness (see Figure 7.1) helps readers make decisions and choices before, during, and after their reading of the text. This is particularly important for ESL/EFL readers who have to overcome many of the difficulties discussed in this chapter. Good strategies can often overcome linguistic deficiencies when dealing with complex texts.

Another important goal of a discourse-oriented course is to expose the learner to a variety of texts, genres, content areas, and styles of writing. While engaging in the processing of such different texts and in doing the accompanying activities, the learner can develop both the knowledge component and the processing skills that we have been emphasizing in this book.

READING ACTIVITIES THAT LEAD TO THE DEVELOPMENT OF STRATEGIC READING

The knowledge component necessary for reading effectively, as we have seen in Figure 7.1, consists of three subcomponents that need to be tackled in developing a reading course: *language knowledge,* which includes recognition of vocabulary and syntax as well as graphic representations; *discourse knowledge* and *sociocultural knowledge,* which include recognition and understanding of discourse features that are textual in nature (e.g., cohesion), discourse features that relate to writing conventions and genres and social and cultural knowledge related to writing; and *general (prior) knowledge* or knowledge of the world. Students participating in a reading course need strengthening and development in activating all three areas. Special activities need to be developed in order to provide learning experiences leading to improvement in their ability to function in all these areas.

In order to help learners become independent and strategic readers they need to engage in the processing of a large stock of multipurpose reading matter. The selection of the reading passages, stories, and articles is perhaps the most important feature of a good reading course. These selections should be interesting from the students' point of view, so that they will motivate reading as such, and they should be suitable and adaptable to the kinds of learning and reading activities that the course intends to promote.

Feuerstein and Schcolnik (1995) provide a full range of reading activities that are useful for the development of discourse-oriented reading courses. Dictionary skills and vocabulary work are strongly emphasized in their book since these skills help learners expand their receptive vocabulary. Features of text organization, of grammatical and logical connections within the text, are addressed as important topics in learning-to-read activities. Furthermore, strategies related to previewing a text and making predictions before and during the reading process and strategies related to focus on external and internal features of a text are all treated in this text.

It is the combination of intensive work on the knowledge component along with ample processing activities that makes for a successful reading course. However, in order to ensure the development of strategic reading skills the teacher must also devote attention to reader awareness and metacognition, as we have discussed.

For younger learners, reading activities can focus on (a) the purpose of reading; (b) the development of reading strategies; and (c) gaining information and knowledge. Such activities, when aimed at younger readers, need to be interesting and have an element of fun and enjoyment. For example, the teacher can scramble the sentences of an interesting anecdote and ask the learners to unscramble them. The task should help learners discern the coherent/logical organization of the text as well as the grammatical/cohesive connections. Such an activity can be done in small groups to facilitate interaction with a follow-up discussion session to resolve any questions or problems.

CONCLUSION

To conclude, this chapter presents the reading process as an interactive communicative activity in which the reader plays a crucial role in the interpretation process and in which the text as produced by the writer, includes both facilitating and complicating features that need to be utilized and tackled. Intermediate and advanced courses in ESL/EFL reading should enable students to experience, practice, and become efficient in coping with textual difficulties of the types discussed in this chapter. The ultimate aim is for readers to become self-sufficient and responsible for developing efficient reading strategies that suit their needs and interests.

DISCUSSION QUESTIONS

1. Discuss the misinterpretations that might result from overuse of (a) top-down processing, and (b) bottom-up processing.

2. Discuss the characteristic features of a "well-written text."

3. Describe the strategies that a reader needs to develop in order to become efficient.

4. Compare the reading strategies presented in this chapter with the listening strategies presented in Chapter 6.

5. In addition to deciding which words need to be glossed (because they are crucial but lack contextual support), should teachers also ask their students which words they do not know and cannot figure out?

SUGGESTED ACTIVITIES

1. If you teach younger learners, design one reading activity for guessing and hypothesis building and one for inferencing; use passages of appropriate length and content for such learners.

2. Examine the three texts that follow this list of activities and identify a grammatical feature of English that might create interpretation difficulties; exemplify the problem with excerpts from the relevant text(s).

3. Choose one of the three texts for an intermediate ESL or EFL class. Find five words that have high textual support and five words that have low textual support. For each of the ten items, explain which textual elements support or blur the meaning. Suggest ways of teaching the text.

4. Analyze one of the three texts to indicate (a) what specific message the text presents and (b) what cohesive elements were used by the writer of the text.

5. Prepare teaching activities for one of the three texts with special focus on the cohesive devices. In your activities draw students' attention to the significance of such devices.

1

The Green Banana

By Donald Batchelder

Although it might have happened anywhere, my encounter with the green banana started on a steep mountain road in the interior of Brazil. My ancient jeep was straining up through spectacular countryside when the radiator began to leak, ten miles from the nearest mechanic. The over-heated engine forced me to stop at the next village, which consisted of a small store and a scattering of houses. People gathered to look. Three fine streams of hot water spouted from holes in the jacket of the radiator. "That's easy to fix," a man said. He sent a boy running for some green bananas. He patted me on the shoulder, assuring me everything would work out. "Green bananas," he smiled. Everyone agreed.

We exchanged pleasantries while I mulled over the ramifications of the green banana. Asking questions would betray my ignorance, so I remarked on the beauty of the terrain. Huge rock formations, like Sugar Loaf in Rio, rose up all around us. "Do you see that tall one right over there?" asked my benefactor, pointing to a particular tall, slender pinnacle of dark rock. "That rock marks the center of the world."

I looked to see if he were teasing me, but his face was serious. He in turn inspected me carefully to be sure I grasped the significance of his statement. The occasion demanded some show of recognition on my part. "The center of the world?" I repeated, trying to convey interest if not complete acceptance. He nodded. "The absolute center. Everyone around here knows it."

At that moment the boy returned with my green bananas. The man sliced one in half and pressed the cut end against the radiator jacket. The banana melted into a glue against the hot metal, plugging the leaks instantly. Everyone laughed at my astonishment. They refilled my radiator and gave me extra bananas to take along. An hour later, after one more application of green banana, my radiator and I reached our destination. The local mechanic smiled, "Who taught you about the green banana?" I named the village. "Did they show you the rock marking the center of the world?" he asked. I assured him they had. "My grandfather came from there," he said. "The exact center. Everyone around here has always known about it."

As a product of American higher education, I had never paid the slightest attention to the green banana, except to regard it as a fruit whose time had not yet come. Suddenly on that mountain road, its time and my need had converged. But as I reflected on it further, I realized that the green banana had been there all along. Its time reached back to the very origins of the banana. The people in that village had known about it for years. My own time had come in relation to it. This chance encounter showed me the special genius of those people, and the special potential of the green banana. I had been wondering for some time about those episodes of clarity which educators like to call "learning moments," and knew I had just experienced two of them at once.

The importance of the rock marking the center of the world took a while to filter through. I had initially doubted their claim, knowing for a fact that the center was located somewhere in New England. After all, my grandfather had come from there. But gradually I realized they had a valid belief, a universal concept, and I agreed with them. We tend to define the center as that special place where we are known, where we know others, where things mean much to us, and where we ourselves have both identity and meaning: family, school, town, and local region.

The lesson which gradually filtered through was the simple concept that every place has special meanings for the people in it; every place represents the center of the world. The number of such centers is incalculable, and no one student or traveler can experience all of them, but once a conscious breakthrough to a second center is made, a life-long perspective and collection can begin.

The cultures of the world are full of unexpected green bananas with special values and meaning. They have been there for ages, ripening slowly, perhaps waiting patiently for people to come along to encounter them. In fact, a green banana is waiting for all of us who leave our own centers of the world in order to experience other places.

(From Batchelder, 1977)

2

We Should Cherish Our Children's Freedom to Think

By Kie Ho

Americans who remember "the good old days" are not alone in complaining about the educational system in this country. Immigrants, too, complain, and with more up-to-date comparisons. Lately I have heard a Polish refugee express dismay that his daughter's high school has not taught her the difference between Belgrade and Prague. A German friend was furious when he learned that the mathematics test given to his son on his first day as a freshman included multiplication and division. A Lebanese boasts that the average high-school graduate in his homeland can speak fluently in Arabic, French and English. Japanese businessmen in Los Angeles send their children to private schools staffed by teachers imported from Japan to learn mathematics at Japanese levels, generally considered at least a year more advanced than the level here.

But I wonder: If American education is so tragically inferior, why is it that this is still the country of innovation?

I think I found the answer on an excursion to the Laguna Beach Museum of Art, where the work of schoolchildren was on exhibit. Equipped only with colorful yarns, foil paper, felt pens and crayons, they had transformed simple paper lunch bags into, among other things, a waterfall with flying fish, Broom Hilda the witch and a house with a woman in a skimpy bikini hiding behind a swinging door. Their public school had provided these children with opportunities and direction to fulfill their creativity, something that people tend to dismiss or take for granted.

When I was 12 in Indonesia, where education followed the Dutch system, I had to memorize the names of all the world's major cities, from Kabul to Karachi. At the same age, my son, who was brought up a Californian, thought that Buenos Aires was Spanish for good food – a plate of tacos and burritos, perhaps. However, unlike his counterparts in Asia and Europe, my son had studied creative geography. When he was only 6, he drew a map of the route that he traveled to get to school, including the streets and their names, the buildings and traffic signs and the houses that he passed.

Disgruntled American parents forget that in this country their children are able to experiment freely with ideas; without this they will not really be able to think or to believe in themselves.

In my high school years, we were models of dedication and obedience; we sat to listen, to answer only when asked, and to give the only correct answer. Even when studying word forms, there were no alternatives. In similes, pretty lips were always as red as sliced pomegranates, and beautiful eyebrows were always like a parade of black clouds. Like children in many other countries in the world, I simply did not have a chance to choose, to make decisions. My son, on the other hand, told me that he got a good laugh – and an A – from his teacher for concocting "the man was as nervous as Richard Pryor at a Ku Klux Klan convention."

There's no doubt that American education does not meet high standards in such basic skills as mathematics and language. And we realize that our youngsters are ignorant of Latin, put Mussolini in the same category as Dostoevski, cannot recite the Periodic Table by heart. Would we, however, prefer to stuff the developing little heads of our children with hundreds of geometry problems, the names of rivers in Brazil and 50 lines from "The Canterbury Tales"? Do we really want to retard their impulses, frustrate their opportunities for self-expression?

When I was 18, I had to memorize Hamlet's "To be or not to be" soliloquy flawlessly. In his English class, my son was assigned to write a love letter to Juliet, either in Shakespearean jargon or in modern lingo. (He picked the latter, his Romeo would take Juliet to an arcade for a game of Donkey Kong.)

Where else but in America can a history student take the role of Lyndon Johnson in an open debate against another student playing Ho Chi Minh? It is unthinkable that a youngster in Japan would dare to do the same regarding the role of Hirohito in World War II.

Critics of American education cannot grasp one thing, something that they don't truly understand because they are never deprived of it: freedom. This most important measurement has been omitted in the studies of the quality of education in this country, the only one, I think, that extends even to children the license to freely speak, write and be creative. Our public education certainly is not perfect, but it is a great deal better than any other.

(From Dubin and Olshtain, 1987.
Reading on Purpose, pp. 133–34)

3

Back to Basics

By Isaac Asimov

In prehistoric times the chief toolmaking material was stone. In fact, that period is referred to as the Stone Age. There were advantages to stone: There was a lot of it. It could be had almost anywhere just for the picking up. And it lasted indefinitely. The pyramids still stand, and the rocks of Stonehenge are still there.

But then about 5,000 years ago, people began using metal. It had advantages. Whereas rock was brittle and had to be chipped into shape, metal was tough and could be beaten and bent into shape. Metal resisted a blow that would shatter rock, and metal held an edge when a stone edge would be blunted.

However, metal was much rarer than rock. Metal occasionally was found as nuggets, but generally it had to be extracted from certain not very common rocks (ores) by the use of heat. Finally, about 3,500 years ago, people found out how to extract iron from ores. Iron is a particularly common metal and is the cheapest metal even today. Iron properly treated becomes steel, which is particularly hard and tough. However, iron and steel have a tendency to rust.

About 100 years ago aluminum came into use. It is a light metal and can be made even stronger than iron, pound for pound. What's more, it is even more common than iron and won't rust. However, aluminum holds on so tightly to the other atoms in its ores that a great deal of energy must be used to isolate it, so it is more expensive than iron.

In the Twentieth Century plastics came into use. They are light materials that are organic (that is, built of the same atoms that are found in living organisms). Plastics can be as tough as metals, can be molded into shape, can be resistant to water and to deterioration such as rust, and can come in all sorts of compositions so as to have almost any kind of property desired.

However, plastics usually are derived from the molecules in oil and gas, and oil and gas aren't going to last forever. When oil is gone, plastics, for the most part, will be gone as well. Then, too, plastics are inflammable and liberate poisonous gases when burned.

Well, then, are there any other alternatives? How about getting back to basics, to the rocks that human beings used before they developed the sophisticated way of life called civilization. Rock remains far more common and cheaper than either metal or plastics. Unlike plastics, rock doesn't burn; and unlike metal, rock doesn't rust. Unfortunately, rock remains just as brittle now as it was during the Stone Age. What can be done about that?

It might be possible to treat rock so that it loses some of its brittle-ness. That will, of course, make it more expensive, but it would be infinitely more useful, and, as in the case of metals long ago, the usefulness might more than make up for the expense. This is all the more possible as the expense becomes more minimized.

For instance, different rocks can be combined and treated in such a way as to make the powdery substance called Portland cement. Water is added, and molecules of water adhere to the molecules in the powder, causing the powder to set into the hard, rocklike cement. As the cement dries, however, some of the water evaporates, leaving tiny holes behind. It is the presence of these holes that makes the cement brittle.

Scientists who work with cement have been developing ways of treating it during preparation in such a way as to make the holes formed by water evaporation much smaller than they would be ordinarily. The brittleness disappears, and the result is cement that can be bent, that is springy, and that won't shatter on impact.

It is important to search for a way of forming this tough cement that would involve as little labor and energy as possible. Scientists who work with materials are trying to find ways, for instance of converting rocks into glassy materials without using the high temperatures required to form glass in the old-fashioned way. They also are trying to form ceramics and refractories (rocky materials that can be heated to a very high temperature and then cooled again without being changed in the process) in ways that consume little energy.

If all this works out, the result may be relatively cheap stone that has all its own excellent properties plus some of those associated with metals and plastics. These developments could bring about a high-tech stone age that will mean a civilization far less wasteful of energy, far less concerned with preventing fire and rust, and far less subject to the disaster of dwindling resources.

(From Asimov, I., 1985. Back to Basics. *American Way* [in-flight magazine of American Airlines])

Suggestions for Further Reading

Carrell, P., Devine, J., & Eskey, D. (Eds.). (1988). *Interactive approaches to second language reading.* New York: Cambridge University Press.

Feuerstein, T., & Schcolnik, M. (1995). *Enhancing reading comprehension in the language learning classroom.* San Francisco: Alta Book Center.

Silberstein, S. (1994). *Techniques and resources in teaching reading.* New York: Oxford University Press.

Endnotes

[1] See Dubin and Olshtain, 1990, pp. 34–35 for examples of effective learner activities to use with this passage.

[2] Two types of glosses are possible: (1) for linguistically homogenous learners, a translation into their native language can be expedient; (2) for linguistically heterogeneous learners a definition in English with very clear examples would be needed.

CHAPTER 8

Writing

"What is particularly striking about these ESL teachers' responses . . . is that the teachers overwhelmingly view themselves as language teachers rather than writing teachers; they attend primarily to surface-level features of writing and seem to read and react to a text as a series of separate sentences or even clauses, rather than as a whole unit of discourse."

(Zamel, 1985:86)

"In most writing courses today, students are asked to revise and resubmit assignments after an opportunity to receive some kind of feedback from peers and/or the instructor . . . Students are encouraged to understand that the process of writing involves hard work and that improvement is often a result of a major investment of time."

(Kroll, 1998:231)

INTRODUCTION

Given the interactive reading model presented in Chapter 7, we understand better why an experienced writer has the responsibility to compose a written text that will be understood by an intended reader who is distant in time and place from the writing process, but who nevertheless will be able to comprehend the text. It is the responsibility of the writing teacher to help novice writers develop into experienced writers. This chapter is designed to help the writing teacher meet this responsibility.

A skilled writer, who writes often and for a variety of purposes, does not necessarily find the writing process easy. Many such writers report on the difficulties they encounter in sitting down to initiate a writing task or to carry out the final reformulation of something that has already been written in draft form. Personal writing strategies, preferences, and techniques characterize each individual writer. Some writers begin the composing process by drawing up outlines, others design flow charts or make lists of questions to be addressed, while some simply sit down, experience a natural flow of creativity, and start writing. Many writers report that they might use different strategies for different types of writing. Since variation from writer to writer seems to be the most outstanding feature of the composing process, how then can this skill be taught?

Here again, we are not really talking about teaching a person how to write but about creating the best context and the most suitable conditions to encourage a person to write, particularly in a second language. Becoming aware of the composing process, learning about oneself as a writer, and relating to written texts and potential audiences of such texts is, in fact, what novice writers need to experience in either their first or second language. Accordingly, language teachers and writing teachers need to become aware of the individual differences that their learners exhibit and of the variety of texts that can be created. When writing is viewed as a communicative act, producing a successful written text is a complex task that requires simultaneous control over a number of language systems. It also entails an ability to factor in considerations of the ways the discourse must be shaped for a particular audience and a particular purpose (Kroll, 1991:261).

WRITING AS COMMUNICATION

THE INTERACTIVE APPROACH

Writing, when viewed as a language skill used for communication, has much in common with both reading and speaking. Writing is the production of the written word that results in a text but the text must be read and comprehended in order for communication to take place. The writer, in other words, communicates his/her ideas in the form of a written text from which a known or unknown reader will eventually extract the ideas and their meanings. Sometimes writers write texts for themselves to read, such as shopping lists, personal diaries, or notes taken during a lecture. Here the initial intention is for the person who writes to be also the sole reader of these texts at a later time. But most of the time we *write* so that someone else can *read* and comprehend the message; the relationship that holds between reading and writing is quite obvious: it is the relationship between the production and reception ends of the continuum. The relationship of writing to the speaking skill, however, is quite different: Both speaking and writing are productive language skills that enable a language user to express ideas and communicate them to others – to listeners in the former setting and readers in the latter. Here, too, the relationship is quite clear, many rules of linguistic production are shared by these two skills in spite of the different modes of communication.

Various rationales have been suggested for the relationship between speech and writing, with two conflicting positions: (1) that writing is different from speech and (2) that writing is similar to speech. The former view reflects the observation that speaking is related to the "here" and "now" of a given speaker and is therefore strongly "context-bound." The real listener present in the communicative setting provides continuous feedback and interaction that becomes an integral part of speaking. Also, the speaker and listener can switch roles at any time and the interaction allows for clarification, negotiation, and co-construction of meaning.

In the first approach, writing is viewed as a much more decontextualized production process in which the writer needs to continually consider and accommodate an absent reader-audience to his or her ideas (Chafe, 1982; Flower, 1972; Olson, 1977; Ong, 1982). A writer cannot rely, therefore, on the context to provide support for interpretation. According to this view, writing competence develops as a gradual liberation from a dependence on context for meaning. This "liberation" is achieved through skillful mastery of the potential linguistic repertoire, matched with effective use of conventional rhetoric – with the subsequent revision process leading to the final written text. Successful adult academic writing is the result of the writer's autonomous and decontextualized production process which, in turn, results in texts that are self-contained and potentially communicative to readers who are removed in place and time from the writing process itself.

The second school of thought takes a more social view of the writing process and therefore perceives it as similar to speech. Such an approach often compares writing to speech events (Myers, 1987) that need to adhere to specific writing conventions. The social interactionist view (Nystrand, 1990) perceives conversational dialog to be as important for the development of writing competence as it is for the development of spoken discourse. Perhaps the strongest relation between speech and writing was expressed by Vygotsky (1962, 1973), who viewed writing as monologic speech based on socialized dialogic speech.

In this chapter, the writing perspectives presented are based on our basic model of discourse processing as first introduced in Chapter 1 and as adapted to writing in Figure 8.1 on the next page. Figure 8.1 has a lot in common with Figure 7.1 (see page 120), since both reading and writing deal with written text. In both processing frameworks the language user begins with prior knowledge and experience with written texts, combining this with discourse knowledge of writing conventions and with assessment of the purpose and intent related either to reading or writing, as the case may be. Language knowledge is important for bottom-up processing whether we are interpreting a written text or editing our written product. The main difference, of course, is that the reading process is receptive while the writing process is productive. Furthermore, metacognition plays a crucial role in both types of processing; in the writing process metacognition is most significant in revision and editing of the written product. Sasaki and Hirose (1996) found that among Japanese university students writing expository texts in English as a foreign language – L2 proficiency, L1 writing ability and metacognition (which they called "metaknowledge") – were all significant predictors of success in L2 writing. However, L2 proficiency explained the largest portion, L1 writing ability the second largest, and metacognition the smallest portion of success in L2 writing. It is probably the case that the user's actual proficiency in the target language outweighs any other factor. Yet, it also seems clear that, in general, metacognitive knowledge can help the user compensate for lack of knowledge in the language area.

Perhaps the most significant similarity between the writing process and speech production is a concern with bridging the gap between producer and receiver. While the speaker needs to take the listener's context into account, the writer has to consider the potential reader audience.

Bereiter and Scardamalia (1987) particularly emphasized the need to develop a "reader-based" approach to writing in order to ensure the communicative power of the text. It is such a reader-based approach that places special focus on the connection between reading and writing and views writing as aiming to produce a text that can be "read successfully." In such a view the writer has the responsibility of creating a text which accommodates to the potential reader(s). The writer needs to use language, content, and conventions of writing in a way that will enable the reader to extract the intended meaning effectively, even though the act of reading will be carried out at a time and place removed from and independent of the act of writing. The writer has to be fully "committed" both to the content and the form of the written text in order to ensure that the text communicates in a setting where interaction is decontextualized. In order to be successful in this enterprise, the writer must develop evaluation and reformulation strategies as part of the writing process, continually reassessing the potential reader's position.

The reader-based model of writing might be most typical of Western-oriented discourse communities. Within Western culture, however, there may be communities or specific writing contexts in which a writer-based style is preferred (for medical treatment or analysis, for instance).

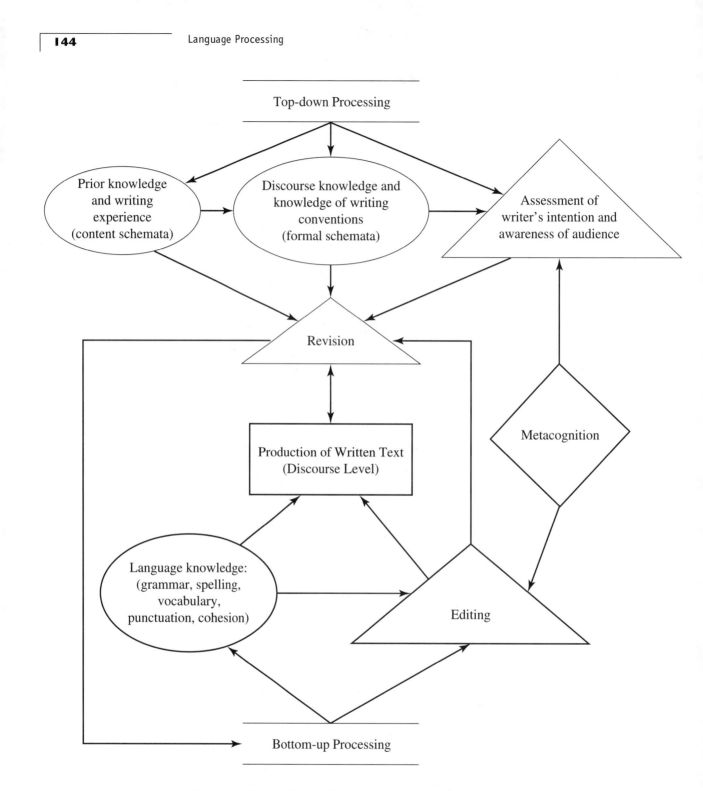

Figure 8.1 Writing: Written Text Production Framework

In this chapter we shall look at the writing process within an interactive and communicative model in much the same way as we looked at reading in Chapter 7. Here, too, we are concerned with three components: the writer, the reader, and the text, but the focus is now on the writer, and since writing is a productive skill we must concern ourselves with motivations and goals for writing. Why writers write and what they intend to achieve through the activity of writing are crucial questions for understanding the writing process. Furthermore, although our concern is with writing in the second language context, the starting point must be in first language writing theory and research, since much of the most important research has been done by observing people as they write in their first language. Much of this L1 research is relevant to our work in second and foreign language settings and serves as a basis for the research done in second language writing.

WRITING FOR A READER – MATCHING THE WRITER'S AND READER'S SCHEMATA

One normally becomes a literate writer in one's own language by being exposed to and reading a great variety of texts in one's first or dominant language and, of course, by writing in that language. A child often reaches school with some basic knowledge of the letters of the alphabet (or of some basic icons in other writing styles) and perhaps a very limited number of reading experiences and even fewer experiences in writing, if any. It is actually through schooling and personal development throughout our lifetime that we expand our use of the writing skill. Not all people have similar daily writing needs; in fact, many of us can go through life successfully without engaging in much writing. In other words, we can be avid consumers of written information without being in a situation where we need to impart information or feelings through writing. For many of us this is definitely a choice and a preference. Society tends to assume and require much greater language proficiency for writing than for any of the other language skills, and this special mixture of personal inclination and social expectations of proficiency accounts for the anxiety that is often attached to our perceptions of writing. All these facts bear upon writing instruction and need to be taken into account.

The school environment is usually the first and most dominant situation in which young people are expected to partake in writing tasks, and students often perceive the teacher as their only reader audience. Developing a more expanded notion of reader audience is part of becoming a "good communicator" in writing. Being able to anticipate the readers' needs when they read the text we are creating is perhaps the most important characteristic of a successful writer. Novice writers find it difficult to go through this process of reader-consideration since they have not, as yet, developed self-feedback techniques that can guide them. Even if they can easily adapt to an interlocutor in a conversation where the listener's feedback is available, they may find the task of generating "imaginary reader feedback" almost impossible. That is why novice writers often have trouble deciding how much has to be said on a particular topic or issue and how to stay on the same topic without boring the reader. Experienced writers, on the other hand, are sensitive to the reader, as well as to background knowledge and potential **content schemata** and thus are able to use elaboration skills to create a text that is comprehensible and communicative in nature. Hinds (1987), Eisterhold (1990), and Connor and Farmer (1990), further stressed the writer's responsibility for creating a communicative text.

Research in writing (Kinsler, 1990; Shaughnessy, 1977; Wallace and Hayes, 1991) has found that training in elaboration skills is important not only for young writers but also for college students in freshmen courses and basic writers of any age who lack the sense of an audience and fail to generate potential reader demands for elaboration. The triangle encompassing revision in Figure 8.1 exhibits the need for writers to revise their work in order to consider features of elaboration and reader-based awareness. School writing, from the student's point of view, is often based on "teacher as audience" with the result that students write incoherent, telegraphic texts aimed at showing the teacher that they "know the stuff" without bothering to properly develop the topic. Often, when such students are questioned about their incoherent style of writing, their answer is, "Well, I know the teacher already knows the material." Writing instruction needs to place special focus on developing this awareness of potential reader audiences in L1 and later on in L2. Sasaki and Hirose (1996), who looked at Japanese university students writing in English as a foreign language, found that while good and weaker writers had both carried out two basic writing activities in their first language in high school – *kansoubun* (personal impressions of materials read) and *shoronbun* (short expository papers) – the better writers had also done a considerable amount of summary writing and paraphrasing of materials that they read (154). There is good reason to believe that having a good foundation in writing in one's first language can help one eventually become a good writer in a second language.

Among the most recent approaches to writing theory and writing instruction, the four components of the model presented by Berlin (1982, 1987, 1988) are highly relevant: the writer (or "knower"), the audience (or "reader"), reality (or "context"), and the language of the written text. These four components were further developed in Johns (1990) and can serve as the basis for a theoretical as well as an instructional model. Since the focus of this section of the chapter is on the writer, it leads us to a consideration of the expressivist versus the cognitive movements. The expressivist approach views writing as an act which leads to and encourages "self-discovery" and is therefore crucial in the development of an educated person. Various leaders of this movement, particularly Elbow (1973, 1981a, 1981b), have emphasized fluency and power over the writing act as major aims in the writing class. As a result, Elbow contributed significantly to instructional approaches by encouraging writing activities such as personal journals and dialog journals both in English as a mother tongue and in other languages that adhere to Western conventions of writing.

The cognitivist approach, on the other hand, places great importance on "writing as a problem-solving activity" and therefore emphasizes *thinking* and *process* in writing. A significant contribution to writing theory from this school of thought comes from Flower's work (Hayes and Flower, 1983; Flower, 1985; 1989). According to this approach, writing requires the ability to work with higher-order thinking skills. The writer makes plans, considers the context, chooses and generates alternatives, presents arguments – giving them the proper support – and arrives at a well-supported conclusion. All of this is part of the problem-solving process that is then translated into writing. Such a *composing* process is complex and very individual in nature. Rather than following a linear progression of development, this composing process reflects recursivity: We write a first version, we make changes, and we rewrite and reformulate the whole passage. Each new version is a more carefully thought-out presentation of the message (revision). The revisions require careful interaction between top-down and bottom-up productions of the written text (i.e., at the top-down level it is the audience and the intent that are most important while at the bottom-up level attention needs to be given to language features and other conventions of the written text).

The expressivists and the cognitivists, as well as the interactionists, have had an impact on writing in second language contexts. The expressivists led to the development of the use of journals and individual rewriting in the ESL classroom (Urzua, 1986, 1987) and the cognitivists to the important work on the process of ESL writing, which includes responding to peer or teacher feedback (Zamel, 1985; Raimes, 1987; Kraples, 1990; Friedlander, 1990; and others). The interactionists have further developed interactive perspectives on the writing process. Another interactive view of writing that has also influenced second language teachers draws on Bakhtin's (1973) work. Bakhtin focuses on intertextuality, i.e., the relation of any text to other texts. Both the reader and the writer develop a deeper understanding of the process through shared experience with various texts. A cycle of activities that represents this approach consists of:

- a preparatory stage prior to the actual writing process
- the creation of a first draft
- the evaluative dialogs that can be done either with a peer or writing
  partner who provides feedback, or via self-questioning carried out by the writer
- a rewriting of the text
- an editing process which renders the text ready for use

Thus, the writer becomes fully aware of the complexity of the writing process and relates it to other experiences with reading or writing texts; but the most important aspect of this approach is the fact that a communicative text must be composed with an interactive perspective in mind. This is in fact a sociocultural perspective on writing.

Going back to the four components of Berlin's model, we have viewed the writer thus far as a creator, designer, and reformulator of the text. Such a process, if it is to adjust to a reader audience, has to take into account the given audience and what that audience brings to the reading process. If we agree to view the writer as responsible for the communicative potential of the text, the audience needs to be defined or "imagined" by the writer. Furthermore, the writer needs to take into consideration the reality in which a text is written and the imagined reality in which the text will be read. All of these could be viewed as "top-down" considerations that require global planning. It is Berlin's fourth component, the language of the text, which places additional responsibility on the writer to also make his/her text accessible to readers at the local level.

In the attempt to consider the various top-down and bottom-up strategies, one might recruit Grice's (1975) maxims here (quantity, quality, relevance, and manner – further discussed in Chapters 2 and 9). In any discourse production sequence these maxims can be of help during revision and editing. As mentioned in Chapter 2, the maxims are probably universal, although their realization are very different from culture to culture. The maxim of quantity, for instance, requires that the writer carefully consider the amount of information that should be imparted in the text or, in other words, what content elaboration might be necessary. The appropriate quantity depends on cultural norms. In some cultures the norm requires the writer to spell out many details, while in others brevity and focus are appreciated. Whatever the norms might be, considerations of quantity are important if we want to produce an effective written text.

The maxim of quality requires the writer to provide support and justification for his/her position in order to render the text accurate and give it truth-value. Here again cultural norms are the key to appropriacy. Within some cultures, anything that is written down, "black on white" so to speak, carries truth-value and does not require support. In other cultures, justification and evidence are important. In academic writing, for instance, citing references is an important means of supporting one's claim.

The maxim of relevance requires the writer to create a text that makes sense within the potential context in which it will be read. For example, in a Japanese business letter, it is customary and therefore relevant to begin a letter by reference to nature and weather. In such letters, the maxim of relevance renders weather descriptions as relevant. In a comparable business letter in English such descriptions might be deemed irrelevant. All of these are top-down considerations in the composing process and they relate to the writer's evaluation of the potential reader. It is primarily the maxim of manner that requires bottom-up techniques to make the text unambiguous, to make it clear in terms of its linguistic forms and sentence structure as well as clear in the physical shape or format in which it is presented, so that form and content are compatible and processing made possible. The structural and lexical choices made will depend on the language in which the text is written, but in each language and each culture some considerations of manner will be crucial and classroom activities need to prepare students in this area.

Pennycook (1996) provides a convincing example of intercultural differences in the attitude towards a written text when comparing Western notions of authorship to Chinese notions, as exhibited by students studying in Hong Kong. The particular example on which Pennycook focuses has to do with plagiarism in the Western sense of the word, which is perceived very differently by Chinese-speaking students. There are other cultures, of course, that also regard the written text with much more reverence than the modern Western tradition does. It would be wise for writing teachers to have an "open mind" to other cultures and carefully study such intercultural differences before penalizing students for actions that – although unacceptable by Western standards – might be acceptable behaviors in their own cultures. Teaching writing in a second language should also include appropriate discussion of cultural expectations regarding issues such as plagiarism.

WRITING AS PROCESS

CREATING COHERENCE IN A TEXT

A writer who undertakes the task of creating a written text for communication purposes is faced with the need to organize his/her thoughts into a sequence which makes sense. Some people may start writing by scribbling down ideas at random, and while doing that, the organization features of the text emerge. Others first plan the overall outline in varying degrees of detail and only then start writing, and yet others will write an introduction that then serves as an abstract, a basis for the whole text. These are just some of the different ways in which individual writers approach writing, since the writing process is a personally adapted creative process that varies from person to person.

Whatever the initial steps of writing are for the individual writer, they eventually lead to the process of organizing thoughts. Such planning can never take place in its entirety before the actual text is written, since often the organization of a text crystallizes only during the writing process. Therefore, an experienced writer goes through a number of revisions of the text. With computers at hand to do word processing, such revisions become easier, although some new constraints emerge, which will be discussed later. If the writer is experienced and proficient in these planning steps, there is a good chance that the resulting text will contain ideas, concepts, and propositions presented conceptually in a way that is consistent with the cultural conventions of writing in the target language, that is, writing that will result in a coherent text.

CONTRASTIVE RHETORIC

In teaching ESL/EFL we often come across the difficulty that students encounter when reading or writing expository texts if they come from a cultural background where coherence conventions are different from those in Western rhetorical tradition. Problems of this sort are dealt with systematically in the subfield of written discourse called **contrastive rhetoric**.

The impetus for contrastive rhetoric studies is generally attributed to Robert Kaplan. His seminal and controversial article (Kaplan, 1966) and subsequent work (e.g., Kaplan, 1972, 1982) renewed debate among applied linguists regarding the validity of the Whorfian

Hypothesis (Whorf, 1966), which proposes that the language a given people speak accounts in large part for the way they think; these thought patterns in turn are reflected in the way they speak and write.

Today researchers in contrastive rhetoric generally agree on a weak version of Whorf's hypothesis, i.e., that users of each language with a literate tradition may develop and codify over time culturally based and linguistically specific rhetorical patterns as follows:

- macrostructures for formal exposition and other genres
- specific conventions for achieving cohesion (e.g., reference, conjunction) at the microdiscourse level

Hartmann (1980) and others have emphasized the need for researchers in contrastive rhetoric to use parallel texts when carrying out any comparative analysis so that the genre, topic, and register of the texts are controlled. For example, one can compare – on many levels – personal essays on the same topic or news articles on the same topic in two or more languages. Some relevant contrastive rhetoric studies focusing on Japanese and English are described in the next paragraph.

Hinds (1980, 1983, 1986) compared English and Japanese expository writing and coherence features in particular and found that Japanese has a number of rhetorical organizational patterns that are quite different from those found in English expository writing. In some of these patterns, the main theme is not foregrounded as it is in English but rather hinted at. Some of the clarifications an English reader may need in order to process an expository text may not be there explicitly in the Japanese text and, as a result, an English-speaking reader of such a translated text might rate the text as incoherent and unacceptable. English teachers may view English essays written according to one of the Japanese organizational patterns as lacking in coherence and unity, and thus rate them lower than essays written with English organizational patterns. In Ricento's (1987) study it was made clear that some types of Japanese texts translated into English are more easily processed by native speakers of Japanese proficient in English than by native speakers of English, due to the differences in rhetorical organization. In a task requiring the reordering of scrambled paragraphs from a text translated from Japanese into English, Japanese speakers fluent in English performed the task better than native English speakers for certain rhetorical text types, probably because they were familiar with the relevant Japanese rhetorical tradition, a tradition that does not hold for English. Language teachers and writing teachers should be aware of such cultural differences that may cause their students difficulties in English writing. Thus Ricento suggests that teachers working with Japanese students should remember, for instance, that a Japanese writer may often begin an essay with an anecdote and postpone the introduction of the topic of the discourse for several paragraphs. If Japanese students follow this rhetorical strategy in English, they might subsequently be penalized for digression and lack of coherence.

STRATEGIES AND STEPS IN CREATING COHERENCE

We know from our discussion of reading in Chapter 7 how important coherence is for the proper interpretation of a text. Although the reader, while interpreting the text, creates his/her own coherent version of the text, this happens most easily if the text has been carefully planned by the writer. It is the responsibility of the writer to produce a text that will be coherent to the potential reader, and it is the responsibility of the writing teacher to help writers develop strategies to do so. These strategies involve considerations of extratextual features that relate to the background knowledge the reader is likely to bring to the reading of the text and intratextual features that the writer must build into the text in order to ensure coherence.

Many different activities can make students aware of the importance of coherence. The following are two such activities:

A. For the first activity, students are given a list of sentences that are the main statements of a paragraph. In order to create a "logical" paragraph they have to change the order of the sentences and add two or three additional sentences. This activity will require coherence considerations and some background knowledge.

   1. He liked to experiment with gases.
   2. He could not see the atoms but he imagined them.
   3. According to Dalton's theory the atoms of an element were all the same size and weight.
   4. He had an interesting hobby.
   5. He developed a new atomic theory.

In the same class, different students will come up with slightly different versions of the passage. The discussion of the similarities and differences among these versions will focus on questions of coherence.

B. The following activity is a "Guided Creative Writing Through Cloze." The following cloze task involves the provision of words that can easily be suited to the grammatical environment in the passage but for which there are *no semantic* clues. However, once the first blank is filled in, it will affect, to some extent, all the other blanks, so a variety of different possibilities exist for each blank. This is by no means an easy task since it is not the usual cloze, which leads to the reconstruction of the original passage or one similar to it. This is not a task of retrieval but a task of creation. The learner must concern him/herself mostly with the coherence of the whole text which s/he will develop. If the student chooses to fill the first blank with the word *cruise* then all the other blanks will depend on that first choice. If, on the other hand, the word *journey* is chosen the other fillers will be related to this key word. Thus, the second choice could be *upper-deck* or *train station* respectively.

As we go through the cloze, it becomes more difficult because of the other constraints that come with each new blank. It is therefore almost certain that no two students will end up with the same written passage, and all of the students will be fully involved in a creative activity of the type that requires a sequence of problem-solving steps. This is the strength of this activity since it will force learners to consider the coherence of the passage at every step of the way.

Fill in each blank with one word.

It is a great experience to go on a (1)_____. I went to the (2)_____ and sat down. For a while I looked at the (3)_____. Then, I listened to the (4)_____. It was very (5)_____.

   The lady next to me was (6)_____. Her eyes were (7)_____ and she had two (8)_____ and another small (9)_____. Later that day we almost became (10)_____. When we arrived at (11)_____, I felt very(12)_____. I knew that I would always (13)_____ the experience. I knew I would never (14)_____ it.

The different passages resulting from this activity can then be evaluated for coherence in a collaborative classroom activity. As can be seen from the cloze task given above, cohesion within the passage has been provided through local grammatical clues, but the content of the whole passage and its coherence will depend on the words that were chosen as fillers.

An important consideration in the creation of coherence in a text is the choice of genre and rhetorical format, which in turn is closely related to the purpose of writing. At the most general level we distinguish between the narrative genre and factual or expository writing. McCarthy and Carter (1994) refer to these as the two prototype genres. The narrative is structured around a chronological development of events and is centered around a person or hero. Consequently, a narrative is usually personalized or individualized and tells about the events related to the person or persons involved. An expository text, on the other hand, has no chronological organization but rather a logical one and is usually objective and factual in nature.

In writing a narrative one may simply want to tell a story, teach a lesson through analogy, render a complex emotionally loaded message in an accommodating form, or provide the reader with a sophisticated literary experience. Although in all of these cases the rhetorical format would be the narrative, different subgenres of narratives would present different conventions and constraints for fables, folktales, novels, personal biographies, and so forth. Furthermore, the expected readers for each of these written subgenres would be different, and so would be the place where the written text might appear. All of these are relevant facts to consider when a text is being written and coherence is being created. The writing classroom must provide learners with experience in writing various text types according to learners' interests and needs.

In writing an expository text the purpose and the intended audience become of crucial importance. A text that focuses on the latest developments in biology, for instance, might take a different form depending on whether it is intended for inclusion in a popular magazine, a biology textbook, or a scientific journal. Each of these text types adhere to certain writing conventions. In the first instance, the purpose is to impart information to the public at large; in the second case, the text is intended for students who are just being introduced to the subject area, whereas the third audience consists of scientists who know the field quite well. Obviously, coherence needs to be created somewhat differently for each of these audiences relating to the different background knowledge that each of them brings to the reading of the text.

Lautamatti (1990) makes an important distinction between *propositional coherence* and *interactional coherence*. Propositional coherence, the semantic property of texts described in Chapter 7, creates a logical progression within the text. On the basis of this progression, comprehension of the text can be established in the mind of the reader who perceives a connecting thread among the propositions presented in the text and relates it to his/her own knowledge of the world. Formally, this type of coherence is reflected in the cohesive features of the text such as appropriate use of referential ties, lexical chains, and conjunctions or transitional expressions.

Interactional coherence, on the other hand, is more prominent in spoken discourse (discussed in Chapter 9), yet it may also apply to more personal or intimate types of writing, such as in personal letters where the reader is known and shares a lot of information with the writer. The more academic and informative type of writing that most writers are involved in requires greater attention to propositional coherence in order to compensate for the lack of interactional coherence. Planning ahead, organizing the ideas and propositions, providing connections and support, and constantly revising the text to make it more "reader-based" are some of the ways in which a writer creates coherence in a written text. It is, therefore, always a conscious and carefully thought out process.

CREATING A WELL-WRITTEN TEXT

It is possible to view coherence as a feature of a text that is related to top-down planning and organization. A well-written text, however, also has to conform to more local and specific features of the text such as choosing proper lexical items and grammatical forms, appropriate use of cohesive devices, and using proper punctuation and other details of form. These relate to bottom-up strategies in creating a text. Most experienced writers report that they plan and think out the passage before they start writing, and they deal with the bottom-up strategies only after the first draft is complete. Others see the top-down and bottom-up approaches in writing as so intertwined that they cannot separate them.

One of the important features of a well-formed text is the unity and connectedness that make the individual sentences in the text "hang" together and relate to each other. This unity and relationship is partially a result of coherent organization of the propositions and ideas in the passage, but it also depends considerably on the painstaking process carried out by the writer to create formal and grammatical cohesion among paragraphs and among sentences in each paragraph. Thus, by employing various linguistic devices the writer can strengthen the coherence, create global and local unity, and render the passage in a manner that conforms with the expectations of experienced readers.

The overall coherence of a longer passage depends on the coherence within each paragraph or section of the text; this is especially relevant in expository writing. Each sentence in such a piece of writing is related both to the previous and the following sentences and creates, at the same time, the basis for the connection with the following one. Harris (1990) investigated the organizational functions fulfilled by opening sentences of paragraphs in scientific writing. The analysis of one hundred such opening sentences led the investigator to classify such sentences into five different groups: (1) sentences that announce or identify the topic, (2) sentences that state a fact or give a definition of the main topic, (3) sentences that show similarities or differences related to the main scientific element discussed (which could be considered part of a definition of that element), (4) sentences that identify an important natural or scientific event in the past, and (5) sentences that point out a false assumption or the lack of evidence for understanding some phenomenon. Whether we accept these as being five separate categories or types of opening sentences or whether we want to define the categories somewhat differently is not crucial. What is important here is the fact that all these types have an organizational function in the paragraph, and as Harris reports, some scientific paragraphs tend to have two organizing sentences – the opening one and another one. In rare cases, there are even three organizing sentences in a paragraph. This obviously illustrates the variation in style that exists among experienced writers, yet what is common to all types of opening sentences is the fact that they "lead the reader" toward an easier and more effective interpretation process. A skilled writer makes good use of such opening sentences in order to communicate better and to show consideration for the reader.

Bardovi-Harlig (1990) takes us one step further toward a more local consideration of "well-formedness" of a text by analyzing discourse pragmatics at the sentence level. According to Bardovi-Harlig (1990:45), a sentence within a passage has three levels: the syntactic, the semantic, and the pragmatic. In order to understand Bardovi-Harlig's definition we need to understand the terms *topic* and *comment*.[1] Topic is considered an entity of discourse that connects one part of the discourse to other parts through given information that runs through the whole discourse. Thus, if there is a main character in the passage most of the sentences are about that person, the identification of the main character will be known information, and various grammatical and lexical devices will be used to connect the sentences through references to the main character. This is shown in the following example about Rona, which appeared in Chapter 1:

Rona was the youngest of three sisters. *She* liked music and literature. Being *the youngest sister* was in some ways a blessing and in others a curse . . . .

In this example, all references to Rona are anaphoric since they link the topic of the subsequent sentences across the discourse back to the initial mention of Rona, the topic of the text. Comment, on the other hand, is what is said about the topic and that is new or added information. In each of the sentences some additional information is added, developing the process of advancing the discourse according to the writer's intention. In this text, Rona's being the youngest of three sisters and her liking music and literature are comments.[2] These terms relate to the pragmatic function of the sentence, in other words, its textual function, which is often realized via the semantic and grammatical ties of cohesion[3] (see Chapter 4, Grammar, for examples of relevant cohesive forms).

In the example about Rona the topic of the text is also the subject of the first sentence, so its initial position is part of the rules of grammar in English. However, fronting devices may bring forward elements that would not be found in this position in the usual discourse sequence. The following are three versions of a postcard written in English and presented in McCarthy (1991:53–54) to illustrate the use of fronting devices in English. The first version illustrates an exaggerated use of fronting, the second does not use any marked fronting, and the third represents what can be considered the most interesting and linguistically acceptable version of the three since it makes judicious and context-sensitive use of fronting.

Version (a) – Exaggerated fronting

Dear Joan,

Me, I'm sitting here at my desk writing to you. What's outside my window is a big lawn surrounded by trees and it's a flower bed that is in the middle of the lawn. When it was full of daffodils and tulips was in the spring. Here you'd love it. It's you who must come and stay sometime; what we've got is plenty of room.

Love,
Sally

Version (b) – No fronting devices

Dear Joan,

I'm sitting here at my desk writing to you. A big lawn surrounded by trees is outside my window and a flower bed is in the middle of the lawn. It was full of daffodils and tulips in the spring. You'd love it here. You must come and stay sometime; we've got plenty of room.

Love,
Sally

Version (c) – Discriminating use of fronting

Dear Joan,

I'm sitting here at my desk writing to you. Outside my window is a big lawn surrounded by trees, and in the middle of the lawn is a flower bed. It was full of daffodils and tulips in the spring. You'd love it here. You must come and stay sometime; we've got plenty of room.

Love,
Sally

In teaching writing it is important to expose students to such different stylistic versions of the same text so that they can understand what options the English language makes available to them and how some choices can render the message in a text in a more effective or convincing manner. Such activities can engage whole class reaction to given texts or might be organized as pair work to promote discussion of their textual differences.

In order to create the thread that holds the text together and creates unity and interest, an experienced writer will use the cohesive elements in the language in order to establish a clear sequence of anaphoric reference. Thus, the writer manages to maintain the reader's focus on the topic while distributing new information in consecutive portions that hold the reader's interest and create anticipation of what is to follow in the discourse. The skillful use of these elements develops over time, through considerable and varied writing experiences. The final result should be a reader-based type of writing. In the previous example of the brief beginning of a text about Rona we can see how anaphoric reference links the sentences into a continuing story thereby creating interest on the reader's part about what is coming next.

From what has been said thus far, it is clear that creating a well-written text is a process that requires many conscious decisions along the way, especially prior to writing. Many experienced writers need to plan the overall structure of a text in order to ensure global coherence; each paragraph needs to be structured so as to contribute to creating a coherent entity within the larger unit of several paragraphs; within each paragraph the opening sentence should be carefully composed to serve a major purpose in the logical development of the ideas presented. Also, within the paragraph and eventually within each sentence, cohesion should be properly exploited to ensure back reference and forward progression in the discourse. All this is the responsibility of a successful writer. Successful writing is usually achieved through revision and rewriting. Teasdale (1995) reports on research in the area of revision. The results of various studies on L1 revision have shown that especially for writers of less experience or lower proficiency, revision tends to be made at the word, phrase, and sentence level. More experienced or more proficient writers exhibit a greater variety of revision operations, and these writers are more likely to revise not only at the surface or local level, but at the global level as well.

WRITING INSTRUCTION

BREAKING THE INITIAL BARRIER

Writing, as we have seen, is a solitary creative task that not everybody feels comfortable with. One of the initial steps in writing instruction must, therefore, involve breaking the barrier and alleviating the anxiety which may accompany the writing task. Such anxiety usually stems from the student's fear of failure – not being able to think of what to write about, not knowing how to express it properly, not being able to compose successfully, and, as a result of all this, feeling incompetent. The teacher's first goal in writing instruction must be to convince students that everybody can write successfully for some purpose, even if the resulting writing products are quite different.

Perhaps the most important barrier to break is the feeling that "I have nothing to write about." Preparatory work prior to writing is crucial here – brainstorming activities, discussions, and oral interactions of various types such as role-play activities through which students can discover they have a lot to say about the subject can be most helpful. On the other hand, there is no better way to break the barriers to writing than through writing itself. That is why another good technique is to encourage students to write about anything at all. Personal writing may be a good starting point, even if there is an understanding that no one will read the product except the writer. This is a good time to start a self-awareness program with respect to writing:

- How do I feel about the writing experience that I have just had?
- What hindered my fluency in writing?
- What made it easier and what made it more difficult?

All of these self-directed questions help the student become more aware of the writing process and of him/herself as a writer.

These steps to breaking barriers to writing are relevant for all writers, especially for writers in their L1. With L2 writers we are often faced with the fact that second or foreign language writers may never have developed into independent writers in their first language, and therefore L2 difficulties are now added to general anxiety about writing. In such a case, the second or foreign language teacher must cope with two different problems: writing anxiety in general and the challenge of writing in a second or foreign language.

At the initial stage even students who are experienced writers in their first language may feel that they will never be able to reach fluency and ease in writing in another language, and therefore they have the additional "barrier" of language. These students need to find out that there is a lot of effective and practical writing that they can do in the new language quite easily. A sequence of easy writing tasks needs to be developed in the form of games, role-play activities, and other nonthreatening writing opportunities. For instance, there is the well-known party game where each person writes one sentence in reaction to the sentence that appears just before but where no one sees any of the previously written sentences. When the whole paper is unfolded and read in sequence, it results in a very funny noncoherent jumble, which can then be used in the writing class to point out why very local coherence alone cannot hold the whole passage together and how coherence cannot be achieved unless the writer has the global picture of the text in mind at all times. This is an activity that students are not afraid to participate in since they remain anonymous and everybody is treated in the same manner. Such a game can be an excellent technique for breaking down initial resistance to writing.

CHOOSING A TOPIC AND CHOOSING THE GENRE

In order to create a communicative written message the writer needs to be motivated to write and to impart information of some type. The major success of a writing teacher may stem from his/her ability to develop writing tasks that suit the students' needs and interests. Creating some kind of communication gap that requires a written message can be very helpful. Let us assume that someone has information about a trip or a party that most students would like to participate in; however, this information can only be received through a written request – this would lead to a practical writing task that would be well motivated, provided the students actually get the information. Just as we shall emphasize in Chapter 9 that speaking has to be communicative and relevant, we would like to make the point here that writing in a second or foreign language has to be motivated.

An even more natural and believable context for writing messages could be a "laryngitis" day in class, where the whole class (teacher and students) agree that they all have laryngitis and cannot talk and that all communication has to be carried out through writing. Communication can be done through notes, texts on the board or the overhead projector, or computer Internet messages. Such a special situation provides a challenge and the need to write becomes natural and relevant.

Choosing a topic or a theme for writing is an important initial step for classroom writing. Once the students as a group, or individuals on their own, have identified a topic on which they want to write, the next step would be to think of the reader or the audience to whom the written product would be addressed. The identification of the intended reader leads to a whole list of considerations that need to be thought out prior to the actual task of writing. A series of basic questions could be very helpful in this regard:

a. What is the reader likely to know about the subject?

b. What will the reader want to know about the subject?

c. How should I organize the information I have so that it is easily understood by the reader?

d. Can I use some special gimmick to make the written passage more interesting and more appealing to the reader?

Once these questions have been considered, there is often room for the choice of genre as well. Will the written product be a story? Will it be a factual description? Will it be in the form of a letter or perhaps an advertisement in a newspaper? Sometimes we are writing in a situation in which the genre is given and the audience is well defined. Other times we can make these decisions when we engage in the writing process. In most classrooms, writing is perceived as being addressed to the teacher. This can definitely be the case, for example, in a "dialog journal." But most of the time teachers assign writing as a learning activity without creating a specific communicative context, and students make the mistake of thinking that they are writing to the teacher. This often results in the kind of context-embedded, unelaborated writing that is not rated highly by the teacher herself since she expects decontextualized but coherent academic writing to be produced in response to the assignment.

TACTICS FOR PLANNING THE WRITING PROCESS

Silva (1993) reports on seventy-two different studies related to L2 writing and concludes that L2 writing is quite different from L1 writing, although the general composing process is quite similar. L2 writers seem to do less planning and have more difficulty setting up goals and organizing the written materials to meet these goals, in comparison to L1 writers. Silva emphasizes that L2 writers have special needs that are not always met in their writing classes. It is important to provide L2 learners with effective writing instruction. This section will offer some suggestions for training L2 writers in planning and carrying out communicative activities that result in written texts.

Many different ways of planning for the activity of writing have been suggested in the literature. One of the best known is that of preparing an outline for the text that one is going to write. Another common and more intricate planning technique is preparation of a flowchart. Both of these approaches provide the writer with a system for mapping out the main ideas to be presented in a logical way. Such a mapping can then serve as a basis for determining the rhetorical structure of the passage.

Let us assume that a brainstorming activity led to three major topics that students want to write about: (1) describe the town you live in; (2) consider the advantages and disadvantages of a new communication system within your school; and (3) personal perspectives in music – a social perspective. The whole class can now engage in working with possible flowcharts for each topic that will enable every student to make his/her final choice of topic. Alternatively, each student could make his/her own choice of one topic and work on his/her own flow chart. As an example, let us consider the first topic and develop a potential flowchart. The elements to consider might be the following: special features of the town, factual information, history, places of entertainment, transportation, specialization in industry or local crafts, and so forth.

Once the flowchart is agreed upon though brainstorming or class discussion, each student or group of students may choose their particular organization of the whole passage. Whether the writer/s decide to start with transportation or history of the real or imaginary town will be their own choice. Elements of cohesion and coherence can be discussed in the larger setting so that all students are aware of these considerations in their writing efforts. Depending on the town we are talking about and on the interests of the students in the class, a different focus could be given to the description. Students should discuss these things and search for the most interesting way to present them. If the town is known, for instance, as a tourist attraction, the writing could be aimed at the potential tourist and presented as a travel article or a brochure because the reader-audience can be well defined.

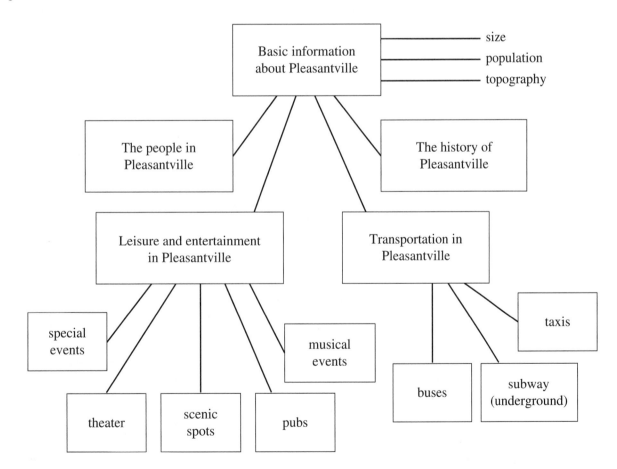

Figure 8.2 Flowchart on Pleasantville as a Prewriting Activity

The planning stage is also important in breaking the writing barrier since it helps writers realize that there is a lot they have to say about the topic. Since different writers prefer different types of planning, it is best to create an instructional procedure in which all students try out different ways and finally choose what they feel is most appropriate for them. Experimenting with different planning formats helps to develop the students' awareness of content schemata.

READING AS A MODEL FOR WRITING

Many writing courses and certainly most autodidactic strategies in writing involve using well-written passages from literature, or passages written by others, as models for one's own writing. At the least such passages serve as stimuli for writing by providing content people want to react to. Thus, many writing classes begin with reading texts, analyzing them, looking at them from both the reader's and writer's perspective, and finally using them as models for writing or using them as a piece of communication to respond to.

If we were going to use the example from the flowchart "Describe your hometown," we could bring to class brochures intended for tourists and other descriptions of towns throughout the world, which would provide a variety of models or sample writings for learners. Later they would choose which approach(es) from the models to follow. This kind of activity alerts students to the reading audience since they themselves act as readers and can be critical of the way in which the sample information is being presented. The analysis of models has the potential of making them much better writers once they start writing about their own town.

Wu (1994) reports on a study that focused on a reading-to-write task carried out with both native and nonnative speakers with different writing abilities. The aim of the study was to find out to what extent such a task might have different effects on native versus nonnative writers – of both high and low writing ability – in terms of their use of lexical items as well as propositions, which appeared in the given reading text (the prompt). Wu's findings indicate that the two nonnative groups (both the high and low ability groups), although exhibiting strategically different patterns of borrowing from the prompt, differed greatly from the native speakers with high writing ability in terms of the much larger quantity of vocabulary they borrowed directly from the source text. On the other hand, the lower proficiency native group differed from the other three groups since they paid too little attention to what was provided in the prompt and took no advantage of it.

In academic work, an important writing task is summarizing. This is typically a reading-writing activity and in many ways resembles part of the task given to the writers in Wu's study. In many cases a summary is done for the writer's own use. We read an article or a book, and we summarize it for ourselves so that we will have the main facts and information available for future use without having to read the article again. Individuals who are good readers, good learners, and experienced writers develop effective personal ways of summarizing. However, summarizing is also an assignment that is often required as part of an academic course. Summaries may have at least two types of audiences: (1) the instructor who uses them to find out if the students have understood the material or (2) fellow students who share their readings through summaries of the articles they have read. The second goal in summary writing is much more motivating and communicative since students can tell themselves the following: "I read the article and understood it. My friends did not read this particular article, and I want to share what I learned with them. I have to write the kind of summary that will give them all the important information they need from this article in a manner in which they can understand it without having to read the whole article themselves." It is this type of motivation that turns this activity into a meaningful communicative writing task.

From what has been said, summarizing can be best perceived as a writing activity within a content class. The reading of any article or chapter in a book is never out of context in a content course since the course provides the metastructure for the subject at hand. The content schemata therefore develop within the course of study. Furthermore, the formal schemata are also greatly dictated by the subject matter and the type of readings assigned in the particular course so that students can be much more familiar with what is expected than if they are simply writing "summaries" in an English writing course.

In the academic world summarizing is a study aid, an aid to research, a way to retain information, and a way to communicate ideas with others. It is therefore easy to motivate and engage students in the development of the metacognitive skills needed for summarizing. Eventually they overcome some of the constraints and difficulties discussed by Kirkland and Saunders (1991). Some of these difficulties relate to properly understanding the original article in order to be able to report the gist of it and evaluate it by critiquing it. However, understanding it is only the first step. Usually the article cannot serve as a good model for summary writing. Summarizing requires mastery of writing conventions and a sound grasp of the content and objective of the text that is being summarized. This then needs to be paired up with the purpose for writing the summary in order to help the writer decide how detailed or how concise the summary is to be. Such summaries might be written in a history class, in a biology class, or in any other subject area. It is obvious that the style and genre in which each subject is usually written in textbooks will affect the summaries. In fact, biology is a good example of an area where the summary needs to be compatible with the scientific style in which biology topics are usually described. Overall, summary writing can be viewed as excellent writing practice to do in various subject areas.

THE PORTFOLIO

The portfolio, which is usually an ongoing collection of different writing assignments kept by the student in a folder or workbook, has become an important concept in developing writing skills and in giving teachers a fairer and more perceptive way to evaluate. Each student writes and rewrites assignments, personal messages, essays, letters, summaries, and any other kind of writing done for a class. All drafts and versions of these are kept in the portfolio. Once in a while, individual students meet with the teacher to discuss certain writing activities. For a final evaluation the students can select a preset number of items they consider best or most representative, and the evaluation can be done on those items only, i.e., on the portfolio. Kroll (1998) discusses the value and the techniques employed in such evaluations and the advantages that this has over the evaluation of one instance of writing.

A portfolio is also useful in preparing a longer writing project that involves collecting information and a variety of data on a topic before the actual writing is done. Thus, students have an opportunity to go through various types of writing tasks within the larger project: They write down notes, they prepare summaries in the library, they access the internet, they make lists and plans of action, they write letters to authorities or key people in the community, and so forth. All these activities need guidance and advice from the teacher or an older and more experienced tutor, but they are all authentic writing tasks that lead in the end to a larger and more complete writing project. The students spend time coordinating all the various bits of information and creating a coherent presentation ensuring cohesion and unity within the final presentation. The various individual tasks are kept in the portfolio and become an integral part of the writing project.

WRITING AND REWRITING

One of the most important things a writing class should aim at is bringing the students to the point where they are willing to revise and feel comfortable about revising what they have written. Two major techniques are helpful in this context: peer review/feedback and self-questioning. Various approaches to peer review use an adapted role-play technique where the reader (a peer) takes the written text and tries to understand it. S/he then reacts to the text and asks questions about it. The writer of the text copes orally while further clarifying the written text, answering the questions, considering the problems of interpretation that arose, and then rewrites the passage to make it more "reader-based." Since students act both as writers and as readers, there is a very useful interaction between reading-writing development here for all students involved. However, this approach to revising requires very careful preparation on the part of the students: They must learn to respect each other's work, they need to learn how to offer and accept constructive criticism, they have to learn how to identify problematic features of the text. Very often working in pairs or groups of three can help students prepare themselves for such peer evaluations. The teacher, on the other hand, has to be willing to relinquish her own total control of the process and allow students to interact freely and take advantage of each other's suggestions and feedback.

It is still the case, however, that the teacher is the one who reacts to students' writing by responding to the textual and content features of the writing. Zamel (1985) claims that most ESL teachers react to every student assignment as if it were a final draft. Furthermore, their comments are usually vague and prescriptive and do not encourage or motivate the students to carry out a reformulation of the text. They give students a very limited view of the writing process and the expected outcome. It is very important for teachers, whether they work with a portfolio or not, to consider their students' writing as work in progress.

Conferencing with students seems to be a much more appealing way to respond to students' work. This is gradually becoming a more acceptable way of working on revision in writing classes, perhaps thanks to the use of portfolios. Such conferencing does not always have to take place between teacher and student, it can also be done by two students, each of them playing the role of the writer once and then the role of the "evaluator," who is perceived more as a potential reader. Such a reader will have been trained to ask relevant questions and will focus on what is clear and makes sense to the reader and what needs to be elaborated on since it is not clear enough. Such feedback can be most helpful to students engaged in rewriting and reformulating.

Leki (1995) reports on a study of writing tasks across the curriculum. This study involved five foreign students at a university in the United States who develop writing strategies as part of the subject matter for the classes they take in English. An important feature in improving their writing was the positive and constructive feedback these students received on their writing tasks in their disciplinary courses. This feedback allowed the students to shift strategies when necessary. In the ESL class Leki suggests we make use of such successful experiences with useful feedback on writing. Students can also be directed to recall past experiences and become aware of their own writing strengths and weaknesses.

Computers have enabled teachers of writing to develop new ways of training students in writing tasks and have allowed ESL students to practice and develop better writing skills. Using texts as models of writing is one technique that can easily be adapted to computer activities: a short (either a well-written or alternatively a poorly written) text is given and students are asked to alter, expand, shorten, or elaborate on this text. The results can then be compared to a peer's product. The computer enables the students to choose from a bank of texts, work on any given text directly by making editorial changes in the original text, and retain the possibility of comparing new versions with the original one.

Another technique that can easily be used in computer courseware is a "self-questioning" technique whereby a student-writer tries to answer the questions a potential audience might raise as well as getting the learners to engage in a self-evaluation sequence. Thus the students may have to answer question such as: Will an audience be able to understand what I meant? Did I provide enough support for my claims? Do I need to add a few examples? Such a self-questioning device can lead to useful rewriting and careful reconsideration of the text. The main advantage of the computer is that students can work on their texts individually or in pairs, and rewrite or readjust the texts easily. Use of the computer also facilitates ongoing feedback and evaluation by the teacher, who can monitor the progress of students on-line and provide constant feedback.

A TOP-DOWN OR BOTTOM-UP APPROACH?

In this section of the chapter we have taken a top-down approach to writing by placing more emphasis on the content, the organization, and the structure of the written passage rather than its linguistic form. However, we maintain that in the long run, in order to ensure that the written passage has communicative power and long-lasting effect, it also needs to be well written in terms of the proper choice of words and use of cohesive devices, grammatical structures, spelling, and punctuation. It is our contention that these bottom-up features should be focused on later in the writing process, when the initial barriers have been removed and the student is willing to engage in the creative process of communication through writing. In other words, we may need to encourage students to just start writing in order to "liberate" them from basic writing inhibitions, with the understanding that these initial writing efforts do not have to be perfect. Gradually, as students feel more comfortable with writing, they can be made aware of the need to use proper morphology and grammar, make appropriate vocabulary choices and pay attention to the way in which the text is presented. Students will eventually learn to choose the proper register and organize their ideas in a way that can easily be understood by their readers. It is a combination of work done in an alternating fashion – text generation and revision in response to feedback – that can lead to better writing skills.

CONCLUSION

This chapter has presented the composing process as an interactive communicative activity, in much the same way that reading was presented in Chapter 7. Here, however, the focus is on the writer's decision-making processes and on the ongoing evaluation process, both of which are integral parts of the composing act. The evolving written product is viewed as discourse constantly changing to suit the writer's goals as well as the writer's need to accommodate potential readers.

The writing skill is often perceived as the most difficult language skill since it requires a higher level of productive language control than the other skills. Additionally, writing requires careful planning and revision, processes which in themselves worry students and create anxiety. This chapter highlights both the difficulties involved in any kind of writing, particularly writing in a second or foreign language, and offers practical ways in which to create useful writing opportunities in the language classroom.

The ultimate aim of teaching writing in a second language program is to encourage students to develop techniques and self-evaluation strategies that will enable them to write according to their personal needs. Language classrooms should provide students with a variety of writing opportunities, as illustrated in this chapter. Teamwork and collaborative writing projects can be particularly effective activities in the second language classroom.

DISCUSSION QUESTIONS

1. Consider how the top-down/bottom-up metaphor applies to the writing process. What are the top-down aspects? What are the bottom-up aspects?

2. How is it possible that "coherence" in written language can be different from one language community to another?

3. Which connection do you feel is most important for fostering effective writing: the connection between speaking and writing or the connection between reading and writing? Give reasons for your choice.

4. We have discussed very briefly potential uses of computers in the teaching of writing. Try to suggest at least one additional possibility and then share your ideas on this topic with someone else.

SUGGESTED ACTIVITIES

1. Consider the following opening paragraph of an L2 student essay entitled "Our Town" (see flowchart for Pleasantville in the section on "Tactics for Planning the Writing Process"). What would help this student to improve in terms of coherence and cohesion in this paragraph?

    > Our town is big and beautiful. Many people want to come here in summer. We are all very happy here. People can choose place to make sport or place of nature. The nature is beautiful here. There are many good buses we can use. Mountains are around the town so we have good, fresh air and good place for picnic. My family can to spend time in mountains on weekend.

2. Collect and analyze writing samples from four or five L2 learners with the same native language (one that you are familiar with, if possible). What common writing problems can you identify? Are some problems unique to only one of the writers? What is the best explanation for your findings?

3. Ask a native speaker and a nonnative speaker to write an essay on some common topic (e.g., Why human rights are/are not important). What are the similarities and differences between the two essays?

4. Develop three different writing activities for young learners in a context that is familiar to you. One writing activity should be in the form of a narrative or story, the second should be descriptive (based on a picture or place), and the third should be something procedural such as road instructions or a recipe. It is important that young learners begin to write texts other than narratives from the start.

Suggestions for Further Reading

Cumming, A. (1998). Theoretical perspectives on writing. *Annual Review of Applied Linguistics, 18*, 61–78.

Kroll, B. (Ed.). (1990). *Second language writing: Research insights for the classroom.* New York: Cambridge University Press.

Leki, I. (1995). Coping strategies of ESL students in writing tasks across the curriculum. *TESOL Quarterly, 29,*(2), 235–260.

Raimes, A. (1983). *Techniques in teaching writing.* New York: Oxford University Press.

Tribble, C. (1996). *Writing.* Oxford: Oxford University Press.

Endnotes

[1] Topics and comments are discussed in Chapter 1 under the subtitle "Information Structure." (See pages 8 and 9.)

[2] *Focus* and *background* are different terms used for related phenomena; *background* refers to the preceding discourse while *focus* advances the interactive act of communication.

[3] In some European traditions of discourse analysis, the terms *theme* and *rheme* are more common: *theme* is another term for *topic* as is *rheme* for *comment*.

CHAPTER 9

Speaking

"Spoken language, as has often been pointed out, happens in time, and must therefore be produced and processed 'on line.' There is no going back and changing or restructuring our words as there is in writing; there is often no time to pause and think, and while we are talking or listening, we cannot stand back and view the discourse in spatial or diagrammatic terms . . . ."

(Cook, 1989:115)

"For each occasion on which we speak, there are certain requirements we must seek to satisfy. It is our perception of these requirements that lies behind our purposeful utterances: we pursue a purpose that is in some sense imposed upon us by our reading of the present situation vis-à-vis our listener; and our listener's perception of that situation provides a framework within which to interpret what we say."

(Brazil, 1995:31)

INTRODUCTION

Immigrants recently arrived to a new country need to do their shopping in the supermarket, talk to the drugstore clerk in order to identify the right type of shampoo or soap for the baby, see the doctor about any unusual health symptoms, and in general take care of daily routines. To do this in a foreign language and a new culture requires both some knowledge of the language and of the culture and some experience as a participant in such interactions. In general, new immigrants are in a difficult and very frustrating situation since they have to cope with a whole world of new and unfamiliar elements.

Tourists traveling to another country need to get information about hotels, transportation, entertainment, traffic rules, and many other unexpected features of vacationing. However, usually tourists are less concerned with survival issues and are more focused on how to make their vacation pleasant and personally amenable. Their successful – or unsuccessful – achievement of a pleasant vacation may depend on how well they can communicate with the local people.

Foreign students, upon first arriving in another country, need to communicate on a survival level like the new immigrant, on the one hand, and like a university student, on the other. Perhaps they have the hardest job of all. While taking care of all their daily routines, foreign students have to register at the university; speak to clerks, advisors, professors, and classmates; and function efficiently in an academic environment.

All of these people, whether in a temporary or more permanent transition to a new culture, need to make themselves understood in another language. They need to be able to speak that language. Learning to speak a new language is the focus of this chapter.

In some ways speaking can be considered the most difficult skill to acquire since it requires command of both listening comprehension and speech production subskills (e.g., vocabulary retrieval, pronunciation, choice of a grammatical pattern, and so forth) in unpredictable, unplanned situations. On the other hand, speaking can be viewed as the easiest skill since one can use body language, demonstration, repetition, and various other strategies to make oneself understood. This chapter will deal with the linguistic, the sociocultural, the contextual, and the personal features of speaking in another language.

MAKING ONESELF UNDERSTOOD IN A SECOND LANGUAGE

MESSAGE AND MEDIUM IN ORAL COMMUNICATION

The simple statement "I am hungry" has a literal meaning that can easily be interpreted by anyone who knows the meaning of the words of this statement and something about the syntax and the sound system of English. As noted in Chapter 2, this is the locutionary meaning of this sentence, but we can easily imagine any number of situations in which this statement takes on various illocutionary forces. In Chapter 2 we saw that this utterance, when pronounced by a youngster back from school and addressed to the mother, can be used with the illocutionary force of a request such as "I am ready for lunch" or "I'd like a snack," depending upon the time of day and the customs in the particular household. The mother has no problem understanding the message since she and her son or daughter share knowledge that makes the message accessible. The same statement when pronounced by a homeless person on the street probably means "Could you give me some money." When the same statement is produced just before dinner by a guest of long acquaintance who has been invited to dinner, it can mean "I look forward to this meal because I know that you cook well," in which case it can be interpreted as a compliment to the host. These few examples stress the point that in order to interpret any spoken message we need to have a wealth of information beyond the linguistic elements appearing in any statement produced in the oral medium or channel (see Chapter 1). Sometimes this distinction between speaking and writing is also referred to as modality.

Mismatches and misunderstanding in oral communication can be the result of any of the following problems or conditions:

a. The speaker does not have full command of the target linguistic knowledge and produces an unacceptable or even unintelligible form (it could be unacceptable or unintelligible in terms of phonology, grammar, or lexical choice).

b. The necessary background knowledge (content, propositions) is not shared by the speaker and the hearer, and they bring a different set of expectations to the spoken interaction.

c. The speaker and the hearer don't share sociocultural rules of appropriacy, and therefore the speaker may have violated such a rule from the hearer's point of view due to pragmatic transfer from the first language.

The basic assumption in any oral interaction is that the speaker wants to communicate ideas, feelings, attitudes, and information to the hearer or wants to employ speech that relates to the situation. The objective of the speaker is to be understood and for the message to be properly interpreted by the hearer(s). It is the speaker's intention that needs to be communicated to the hearer. However, a "faulty" production in any of the above three areas (see previous page) might create a piece of spoken discourse that gets misunderstood.

In an attempt to ensure proper interpretation by the hearer, the speaker has to be concerned with factors of form (specific to the oral medium), which are linguistically controlled, as well as factors of appropriacy, which are pragmatically controlled by the speech situation and by the prevailing cultural and social norms. Factors of form or medium relate to the speaker's linguistic competence as well as to the possibility of faulty delivery of the spoken utterance. Condition (a) may cause a misinterpretation at the propositional level created by factors of medium. In the following example, a taxi driver who has fluent but ungrammatical English tries to find out over the phone from a customer whether he should deliver a package to the customer's home: "Here taxi driver, you want come to home?" It takes the customer quite a few minutes to understand the message simply because it is hard to process, although the context and the situation are known to both parties. Here, the propositional meaning is not immediately accessible: Who is supposed to come to the home? Obviously the driver – but this can be deduced only from logical and situated interpretation, not from the linguistic delivery, which should have been, "Do you want me to bring the package to your home?"

In the following example the delivery and the grammar reflect perfectly good English, yet the message is unclear since the utterance does not conform to rules of social appropriacy. In an American home a foreign guest is offered a cup of coffee:

> **Host:** [holding a pot of coffee] Would you like a cup of coffee?
> **Guest:** I don't care. (It could mean "Don't mind if I do," which is positive, or it could mean "Please don't bother on account of me," which might be negative or at least polite declination)

The host, in this case, is baffled and does not know whether the answer means "yes" or "no." In exasperation she puts the pot of coffee on the table without pouring it into the cups. Both the host and the guest are uncomfortable until eventually a third person joins the group and cheerfully says: "Oh, a pot of fresh coffee. I'd love some. Does anyone else want coffee?" at which point the foreign guest quickly reformulates his response: "Yes, I want coffee."

For the speaker to be able to produce utterances that communicate his intended message, all three conditions need to be met at least partially: The linguistic form should enable the hearer to make propositional identification; in addition, the physical context, shared world knowledge, and sociocultural norms should enable the hearer to come up with an interpretation of the intended message.

THE INTERACTIVE PERSPECTIVE OF ORAL COMMUNICATION

In this chapter we shall look at speech production within the interactive and communicative discourse processing model presented in Chapters 1, 6, 7, and 8. The speaker, as shown in Figure 9.1, brings to the interpersonal communicative act a set of presuppositions about the situation, the participants in the exchange, and the expected outcome of the exchange (first oval in the figure). Knowledge of the sociocultural rules of appropriacy (second oval) and the focus on the intended message with respect to the listener's situation (see the opening quote from Brazil) guide the speaker in making choices that form the spoken product. Thus, the speaker initiates the interaction with a communicative intention that is to be realized through verbal utterances that make use of the speaker's language knowledge and repertoire of speaking skills and communication strategies. The hearer, on the other hand, brings his or her own set of presuppositions and expectations to the interaction in order to interpret the speaker's message, and later react to it by changing roles and becoming the speaker.

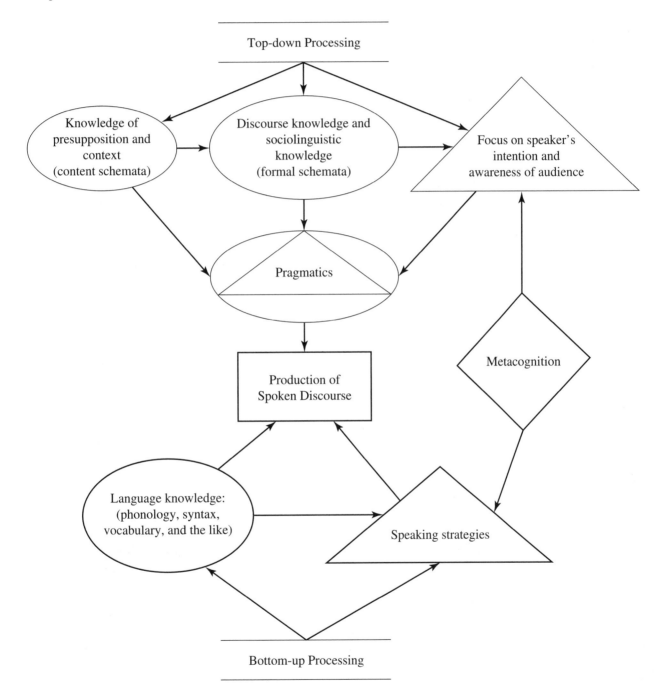

Figure 9.1 Speaking: Speech Production Framework

In many ways Figure 9.1 is similar to Figure 8.1 since both speaking and writing are concerned with the production of discourse. Hatch (1992) recognized the similarities between these two skills but identified three parameters that can differentiate between the production of spoken and written discourse: *planning, contextualization,* and *formality.* Although speech production relies on presuppositions, sociocultural rules, and speaker intention (see Figure 9.1), it is usually less planned than writing, more contextualized, and more informal. Perhaps the main reasons for these differences is that speech is produced *on-line* and that it is prototypically reciprocal in nature. The reciprocity develops during the ongoing negotiation of meaning between the speaker and listener, thus producing a joint construction of communication (in discourse analysis this process is often referred to as co-construction). This is definitely the case in interactions in the first language, but many second language researchers also see oral production as an opportunity for learners to establish collaborative co-construction of discourse (Swain and Lapkin, 1997) and thus formulate meanings mutually understood while developing their interlanguage interactively.

Although the communication model in Figure 9.1 works for both spoken and written interaction, the distinctions we have made play an important role in acquiring and activating the two modalities (see also the opening quote from Cook). As noted, spoken communication is frequently unplanned and usually develops through sequential steps in oral interaction, as hearers and speakers interact and take turns at talk. Furthermore, much spoken communication occurs when the interactants see each other (except when speaking on the telephone, for instance); thus they share time and space during the interaction and can rely on *contextual* and *situational* clues. Spoken communication tends to rely heavily on the immediate context and on information shared by the speaker and the hearer and thus is generally much more context-embedded than written discourse.

In real life situations there is a continuum of oral communication that ranges from the immediate and most familiar environment to more formal and decontextualized situations. Thus, all conversations taking place at home, in situations with close friends, and in other familiar settings are contextually supported. When we give a formal lecture, a presentation, or an address, the oral communication is much more uni-directional, and it relies more heavily on linguistic and conventional rhetorical codes. In these situations, formal speaking shares many features with written communication. Often, in preparation for such formal speaking tasks we produce a written draft or outline. Planning, decontextualization, and use of more formal language thus account for the similarity between such spoken discourse and much written discourse.

CHOOSING THE LINGUISTIC FEATURES

In producing spoken discourse speakers use their grammatical competence in order to produce linguistically acceptable utterances in the target language. The ability to choose lexical items and use them in their proper morphological form, the ability to arrange the lexical items in an acceptable word order, and the ability to pronounce the words in an intelligible fashion all contribute to the linguistic realization of the utterance. In order for this verbal product to become a meaningful piece of discourse, it must relate to the context in which the interaction is carried out through use of clues that reflect cohesion and coherence. In other words, a speaker moves from conceptualization of a message to the capacity for performance by going through the various steps presented in Figure 9.1. At any point the level of knowledge and processing skill might facilitate or interfere with the production of the spoken discourse, but ultimately it is the contextual features that affect the efficacy of communication.

Levelt (1978) identified three important contextual factors in speech production: *demand, arousal,* and *feedback. Demand* refers to the amount of processing required by a task. Ideally, the response to the task matches the demand of the task but in many situations the demand is either too high or too low, creating some kind of malfunction and miscommunication. This is particularly evident in foreign or second language interaction where the speaker may have a hard time adjusting to the demands of the task. An example of such a situation is the following exchange taking place between a Japanese man selling tickets at the railway station in Tokyo and a foreign tourist:

Tourist:	Two tickets for Kyoto, please.
Clerk:	(*hands over the tickets and points in the direction of the tracks*) Track three!
Tourist:	What time is the next train?
Clerk:	Ten o'clock.
Tourist:	And the one after that?
Clerk:	Hmm . . . Track three, please!

In this exchange the clerk was reacting well to the demands of the task as long as they were within his capacity. When the sequence became more complex, he simply repeated the basic information and made it clear that he could not cope with anything more than that.

Levelt's second contextual factor is arousal, which refers to the speaker's emotional and cognitive response to a task and relates to the importance that the individual attaches to the communicative interaction. In the example it is obvious that the Japanese-speaking clerk felt that he had completed his task in giving all the relevant information, and he made no additional effort to understand anything beyond that. In longer and more involved exchanges, it may be necessary for the speaker to invest in the role relationship for a specific discourse (Angelil-Carter, 1997) and reach a deeper understanding of what the mutual expectations are and how the communicative exchange could be improved.

Levelt's third factor is feedback, which the speaker receives from the listener(s) or the wider environment affecting the performance. In a second language context it is especially important for learners and language users to be attentive to feedback and back-channeling during conversation. The speaking and communication strategies of learners need to take into account the value of feedback, and when such feedback is lacking, students should be able to elicit it. For example, in the example with the Japanese railway clerk, had the clerk wanted to continue the interaction, he could have said something like: "Excuse me, I don't understand," and the tourist would have tried to make the meaning of the question clearer.

The linguistic features, or the code complexity (Skehan, 1996), may have a serious impact on successful production of spoken discourse. Mastering question formation, using appropriate word order, placing proper stress on multisyllabic words, and so forth might facilitate conversation greatly or hinder it when these features are lacking. Yet, it seems, that sociocultural norms, as noted in Chapter 2, may play an even more significant role in successful interaction. Thus, considerations of politeness and ways to save face are often realized through specific choices made by speakers using their linguistic repertoires. In English, for instance, it is normally not considered polite to express disagreement in a direct manner. We don't use forms of disagreement such as "You're wrong; this is not right/acceptable; you can't do this" unless we are in a position to reproach the hearer, e.g., parent to child, teacher to student. When we prefer to maintain a more harmonious social interaction with a professional colleague or someone in authority, we look for indirect representations of disagreement such as "Well, you could look at it differently." However, in order to produce such an utterance, the speaker needs to have reached a certain level of language knowledge. In the process of speech production, language ability needs to be combined with sociocultural considerations.[1]

An added difficulty, especially for foreign language learners who acquire the target language only in instructional settings, is the fact that normal, colloquial speech has some unique language features. Thus, the spoken language, as McCarthy and Carter (1995) demonstrate, has many grammatical features that function quite differently from those found in written language, which is what most current descriptive grammars use as their standard. Based on their work with the Nottingham Corpus of Spoken English, McCarthy and Carter have identified several grammatical features of spoken English. From among the many they have identified, we emphasize the following (the examples are theirs):

- pervasive ellipsis of subjects, predicates, and auxiliary verbs
  (such ellipsis occurs in any highly interactive dialog excerpt)

- an initial slot to frame or introduce topics: "That house on the corner,
  is that where you live?" (211)

- tails (or final slots) for amplification or extension: "And he's quite
  a comic, that fellow, you know." (211)

- reporting verbs with past continuous tense: ". . . Pauline and Tony
  were telling me you have to get a taxi." (211)

In order to be able to make such choices in spoken discourse the learner needs to have acquired a threshold repertoire of language resources and to have developed some sensitivity to differences between the spoken and the written language.

Different speech production tasks require language users to recruit their various types of knowledge together with their performance skills and communication strategies. An excellent opportunity for the overall process of speech production is story retelling. Upshur and Turner (1995) use story retelling as an evaluation technique for oral production ability and show how evaluation scales could be developed for this process. The communicative effectiveness of this speech production task requires at least the following subtasks: coherent organization of the story and inclusion of all the important propositions, cohesion created by using appropriate connectors, and appropriate choice of lexical items. All of these relate to knowledge in Figure 9.1, which is presented in oval shapes. An evaluation of the production of the natural flow of speech, however, also requires the consideration of the degree of hesitation and overall fluency, which relate to the processing features of speaking. This type of activity, however, does not assess pragmatic knowledge or contextualization, which will be discussed in the subsequent sections of this chapter.

ADHERING TO RULES OF APPROPRIACY

Sociocultural rules of appropriacy are viewed today as an integral part of a person's communicative competence. The field of pragmatics, as presented in Chapter 2, can be viewed as the study of the relations holding between the use and meaning of linguistic utterances and the social situations within which they are produced. Leech (1983:11) perceives general pragmatics as consisting of two subfields: **pragmalinguistics**, which is related to use of language in context (i.e., linguistics); and **sociopragmatics**, which is related to societal rules of behavior (i.e., sociology). Sociolinguistic competence, as identified by Canale and Swain (1980), Canale (1983), and Bachman (1990), consists of both the pragmalinguistic and sociopragmatic rules of the target language that need to be acquired, and this competence enables the speaker to produce utterances that are both linguistically and pragmatically appropriate.

The pragmalinguistic and sociopragmatic rules of any language are concerned with (1) characteristics of the individuals who take part in the communicative exchange, (2) features of the situation in which this exchange takes place, (3) the goal of the exchange, and (4) features of the communicative medium through which the exchange is carried out.

Any language variation that occurs in the utterances actually produced may be related in one way or another to any of these sets of features.

Individual characteristics related to sex, age, social status, social distance, and the specific roles the participants play within the interaction may have a significant effect on the realization of any instance of spoken discourse. Learners of a second language have to adjust to the rules of speaking in their new language, rules that may be quite different from the ones functioning in their first language. In some cultures age may be a significant factor in choosing certain formulaic or politeness features of address; in other cultures status or social distance may affect spoken discourse. Such sociocultural norms need to become part of the speaker's knowledge. Furthermore, speakers will have to make choices with respect to register. In any language, speakers use more than one register on a regular basis – a more intimate and casual register is used in immediate and familiar contexts while a more formal register is used in occupational or everyday situations with interactants that the speaker does not know well (see also Eisenstein, 1983).

The social and contextual factors, as we have seen thus far, play a much more significant role in spoken interaction than in written communication since most of the oral exchanges we normally engage in are not preplanned. Decisions and choices need to be made under the pressure of trying to communicate messages. This is one of the reasons why speaking is often perceived as the hardest skill to master in another language.

MAXIMS OF ORAL INTERACTION

The relationship between utterances and their function in social interaction is the concern of Speech Act Theory (Searle, 1969). A speech act is realized when a verbal utterance functions as a social act. "Please close the door!" is an utterance that functions as a request by the speaker to the hearer in the hope that the hearer will comply and carry out the request. "Your paper is excellent" is a statement that functions as a compliment; it is an expression of solidarity when produced by a friend or colleague but an evaluation when it is uttered by the professor. These are once again examples of speech acts where the utterance – in addition to its propositional meaning – also has **illocutionary force** (see Chapter 2 for relevant definitions).

In normal spoken communication, people use talk as a social tool. The **cooperative principle** proposed by Grice (1975) is particularly strong in maintaining the flow of exchange between speaker and hearer. As mentioned in Chapters 2 and 8, Grice suggests a set of four maxims that apply when natural conversation functions efficiently.

a. the maxim of *quantity*, which relates to the provision of information by the speaker for the hearer's benefit. In other words, we are concerned here with the speaker's evaluation of what the hearer knows (old information) as opposed to what the hearer needs to find out (new information) about the content of the communicative interaction in order to interpret the message. The maxim of quantity refers to the effective speaker making the right decision with respect to the amount of information imparted – not too much and not too little.

b. the maxim of *quality* refers to the speaker's conviction and belief that s/he is stating the truth. The cooperative assumption between speaker and hearer is such that the hearer accepts the utterances made by the speaker as statements of "the way things are" from the speaker's point of view.

c. the maxim of *relevance* refers to the fact that the speaker needs to make sure that the hearer sees the relevance of what is being said to what s/he knows about the situation and the goal of the interaction. If for some reason the speaker suddenly decides to change the topic or interrupt the normal flow of the conversation, it will be expected that s/he explains the reason for this change.

d. the maxim of *manner* refers to the delivery of the message. The speaker is expected to produce a coherent, well-presented utterance that does not make it difficult for the hearer to carry out the interpretation process. It is the speaker's responsibility, therefore, in case of a faulty start or an ambiguous outcome to clarify and adjust the utterance so that it abides by the maxim of manner and is accessible for interpretation.

The assumption underlying the cooperative principle is that speakers want to be understood and interpreted correctly and hearers want to be effective decoders of the messages they receive. They are perceived as constructing meaning cooperatively during communicative interaction. In other words, both parties make an effort to cooperate in this exchange of ideas, feelings, beliefs, and so forth. A nonnative speaker, however, is someone who does not have full command of the target language, is often very concerned with his/her linguistic performance, and thus cannot always concern him/herself with these maxims. Furthermore, although such maxims probably exist in every human language, they can function quite differently from language to language with respect to the value of any given maxim, as the following example will show.

The maxim of quantity functions differentially across cultures. A group of students taking a class in discourse analysis at Tel Aviv University several years ago went out into the streets of a suburb where many speakers of Hebrew, speakers of American English, and speakers of South African English live. The students wanted to find out how the various residents would respond to a request for information regarding directions. The students asked, "Is this the right way to the main bank?" They expected a confirmation. Hebrew speakers reacted to this with an affirmative utterance consisting invariably of one single word translatable as: "Right," "Correct!," or "True!" The American speakers consistently had two moves such as: "Yes, you will see the bank after you cross the intersection." The South Africans usually had three or more moves: "Yes, you're right. You should cross the next intersection first and then walk for another 300 meters. The bank will be on your right." It is obvious that in answering this simple request for confirmation, the three different cultural groups perceive quantity as being important in expressing a confirmation, but they perceive quantity in ways that are very different from one another. At one end of the continuum Hebrew speakers prefer to be brief and direct, while at the other end, South African English speakers feel more elaboration is required, with American English speakers in the middle. When speaking in another language or dialect, one has to be aware of the norms and the expectations of the speakers of that culture (or subculture) when applying Grice's four maxims.

PARTICIPATING IN ORAL INTERACTION

MAINTAINING THE FLOW OF SPEECH

When observing the flow of speech taking place between a speaker and a hearer in the normal sequence of events, one feels amazed at the smooth way in which the roles are switched between the two and at the way ideas keep being transferred from one interactant to the other as if they had carefully rehearsed the sequence, although what one is observing is a one-time, unique interaction.

Turn-taking rules, which exist in every language, make it possible for the speaker and hearer to change roles constantly and construct shared meaning by maintaining the flow of talk with relatively little overlap between the two and very brief pauses between turns.

Members of a **speech community** know how to participate in this type of exchange by adhering to turn-taking rules that are appropriate in their community, by allowing overlap (if acceptable) to occur between utterances, and by using pause lengths that are compatible with their particular sociocultural norms.

Conversation Analysis (Sacks, et al., 1974; Schiffrin, 1994: 232–279; Levinson, 1983: 284–370) attempts to describe the sequences that are developed and the sequential constraints that are characteristic of the natural flow of conversation. A native speaker knows how to function at the transition points – both by reacting appropriately when there is a pause in the flow and by using a variety of signals to "get the floor" or to "close a conversation." Most important, speakers know how the two parts of an *adjacency pair* fit together, such as a question and its answer, a greeting and the response to it, or any other two-part exchanges in the conversation. The compatibility that is required within adjacency pairs (i.e., interlocutor exchanges that occur in sequence and are directly related to each other) is linguistically, semantically, and pragmatically conditioned.

Since the rules applying to conversation can be somewhat different in different cultures, the learner of a new language often has to recognize and develop new rules of behavior. Thus, there are differences in the length of pauses that are "tolerable" within the conversational flow (i.e., in one culture these may be extremely short and when conversation stops for any reason, the interactants feel that they must quickly "find something to say" – in another culture pauses of some length may be expected, and perhaps even considered polite, in that they allow for reflection and avoid overlaps with other speakers). In order to be an effective communicator, the learner should have the linguistic, semantic, and pragmatic knowledge to function successfully and appropriately in terms of the conversational turn-taking system of the new language.

ACCOMMODATING THE HEARER(S)

The initiating speaker in a communicative interaction has, in many instances, controlling power over the flow, content, and manner of the interaction. Based on the cooperative principle, the speaker needs to accommodate the hearer and facilitate the interpretation of the spoken message. But beyond adhering to the four maxims and the rules of sociocultural appropriacy, the speaker also needs to maintain (or in some cultures learn to avoid) eye contact and to pay careful attention to the hearer's body language and overall reaction in order to be prepared to carry out repair in case anything goes wrong in the exchange. This places special responsibility on those speakers who in the natural course of events need to attend to unexpected mishaps in the exchange, but even more so on the initiator of a conversation, especially if that initiator also holds a special position or status in the interaction (salesperson to customer, interviewer to interviewee, and the like).

The situation is, however, different for the nonnative speaker who needs to expend much greater effort and exert more attention in order to maintain the flow of the interaction. Nonnative speakers often deliberately turn some of these tasks over to the native speaker/hearer who becomes more active and responsible. As mentioned before, the nonnative speaker needs to have some command of the rules of speaking in the new language in addition to his/her linguistic and sociolinguistic competence and an awareness of the discourse differences between his/her L1 and the new language in the various areas mentioned.

The learner of a second or foreign language needs to develop **strategies** in the new language that will enable him/her to recruit the help of interlocutors in an evaluation process regarding whether the two interactants understand each other. Let us consider the following exchange between a native and nonnative speaker overheard in a hotel registration area; the tourist is a nonnative speaker while the hotel employee is a native speaker:

> **NN:** I can use phone here?
>
> **N:** Oh, you would like to make a telephone call? No, this is the hotel phone, but there is a pay phone around the corner.
>
> **NN:** Excuse me – I do not understand. Where I can make phone?
>
> **N:** Just a minute, let me show you. Do you have a quarter on you?
>
> **NN:** Yes, yes.
>
> **N:** OK, there is the public telephone.
>
> **NN:** Thank you, thank you.

In this conversation we see a typical situation, in which although the nonnative speaker initiated the conversation, it was soon controlled by the native speaker, perhaps for two reasons – the native speaker in this case had both more information as well as linguistic ability not shared by the nonnative participant. As a result the native speaker produced a flow of linguistic input, which was not always clear to the nonnative participant and which turned the latter more often into a listener rather than a speaker.

A similar conversation took place at another hotel (in a non-English-speaking country) where the reception clerk was not a native speaker and the American tourist was the initiator of the conversation.

> **N:** Excuse me, can I use this phone to make a call?
>
> **NN:** No, sorry. This is the house phone. Where do you want to call?
>
> *(The tourist is somewhat taken aback by the direct question.)*
>
> **N:** I need to call a friend in town. (spoken somewhat reluctantly)
>
> **NN:** In the city you can use the phone on that desk. Dial zero first and the operator will pass you to the outside line.
>
> **N:** Thank you.

In this case the clerk is in control of the information, and she has the language ability to impart this information although there is a problem both with her sociolinguistic norms and her linguistic delivery. In this type of an exchange among native English speakers the question "Where do you want to call?" would probably not appear since it can be perceived as an invasion of one's privacy. Instead, the clerk would probably ask: "Are you calling inside the city or is it a long-distance call?" Initially, the clerk's direct question might have created pragmatic failure – the tourist could have felt insulted and gotten angry. Soon however, the tourist understood that the receptionist was simply asking for information which she needed in order to give the answer. Furthermore, although the verb "pass" is used inappropriately in the clerk's final instructions, the English-speaking tourist understood the message. In this conversation we find that the nonnative speaker, although she does not have full mastery of the needed linguistic and sociolinguistic rules, she does possess the relevant knowledge as well as having an official function, which enables her to maintain a strong position in the interaction. The native speaker, on the other hand, accommodates her since from his point of view, the goal of the interaction is to get the relevant information and to make the phone call.

Interacting as a speaker in a new language requires self-awareness and self-evaluation and a considerable amount of tolerance and accommodation, both for one's limitations in production and for the reactions of interlocutors. Learners of a second or foreign language need to be exposed to a variety of situations in which such exchanges take place, but above all, nonnative speakers need to possess communication strategies that can facilitate and make adjustments in incomplete or failing interactions.

Bongaerts and Poulisse (1989) found similarities in the use of communication strategies in L1 and L2 when they were defined in terms of conceptual strategies rather than *compensatory strategies,* which are more typical of nonnative speakers. Nonnative speakers' communication strategies differed from native speakers' strategies in terms of frequency and formulation types rather than in mental processes.

An important pedagogical question relating to speaking and communication strategies is whether *strategy-based instruction* can improve speaking ability in a second or foreign language. Cohen (1998) reports on a study of such strategy-based instruction and discusses the pedagogical implications (151) of the findings. According to Cohen, the study was carried out at the University of Minnesota, where fifty-five students of French and Norwegian as foreign languages made up an experimental and control group with the experimental group getting strategy-based instruction. The results indicate that such instruction is worthwhile and suggest that an integration of strategy training with the regular language instruction taking place in the classroom can improve learners' ability to communicate through spoken discourse. Learners' awareness of strategies and the choices they make before and during speaking may lower anxiety, increase self-confidence, and provide learners with ways in which to evaluate their own performance. There is no doubt that the discourse processing features of the speaking skill and the resulting spoken discourse (i.e., product) require the language user's focus on special communication strategies, which are found in the triangle in the lower half of Figure 9.1 but which often require the user to combine all areas of knowledge and processing skills in order to interact successfully.

SOME PREREQUISITES FOR SPEAKING IN ANOTHER LANGUAGE

In order to be able to speak in another language and make oneself understood, it is usually not necessary to reach a perfect level of competence and control. In fact, people can communicate orally with very little linguistic knowledge when they make good use of pragmatic and sociocultural factors. But in order to become a truly effective oral communicator in another language, there are a number of prerequisites.

The linguistic, sociocultural, and discourse competencies needed to ensure better oral communication include the following areas, all of which are part of discourse knowledge:

a. knowing the vocabulary relevant to the situation

b. ability to use discourse connectors such as *well; oh; I see; okay*

c. ability to use suitable "opening phrases" and "closing phrases" such as *Excuse me* or *Thank you for your help*

d. ability to comprehend and use reduced forms (reducing vowel sounds is particularly important in English)

e. knowing the syntax for producing basic clauses in the language

f. ability to use the basic intonation – or tone – patterns of the language

g. ability to use proper rhythm and stress in the language and to make proper pauses

h. awareness of how to apply Grice's maxims in the new language

i. knowing how to use the interlocutor's reactions and input

j. awareness of the various conversational rules that facilitate the flow of talk

In a study of the production of speech acts by EFL learners in which participants were videotaped and then asked to self-report while watching a replay, Cohen and Olshtain (1993) found that learners are fully aware of their linguistic difficulties while engaged in communicative interaction. In verbal reports they can actually explain what coping strategies they employed at certain points of difficulty. Sometimes learners decide to abandon the message or omit an utterance that they would have liked to say because they are not sure of some grammatical feature; at other times they realize that they have to be satisfied with only a partial delivery of a thought. In some cases, learners even opt to deliver a different thought from the one they originally intended because they can't remember a word or an expression.

Therefore, beyond the linguistic competence that learners or nonnative speakers need to have in a second or foreign language, they also have to develop compensatory strategies in order to overcome deficiencies in any of these areas. Such compensation-communication strategies should be included within a more general strategy-based type of instruction as was described earlier. The compensation strategies would consist of paraphrasing when vocabulary items are missing, appealing for help when a concept or notion cannot easily be communicated, using examples and explanations to clarify one's intention, and so forth. These strategies can best be developed by ample exposure to authentic speech in the classroom and by participating in a large variety of oral practice activities. Such activities should include both spontaneous conversations, which are usually not preplanned, and brief preplanned oral presentations that suit the learner's interests. Oxford (1990) defines "compensation strategies" (91) in detail and focuses on how learners can overcome their limitations in speaking. Such instances of strategy use (adjusting or approximating the message, coining words or using circumlocution, paraphrasing, getting help from the native speaker) need to be encountered in class via communicative activities. Crookall and Oxford (1990) provide a wealth of simulations and games for such classroom activities, such as using packs of ninety-six cards with photographs of faces representing young, old, plain, attractive, sad, happy, tired, and animated people of all ages, occupations, ethnicities, and so forth. The learners' descriptions of these faces can focus on compensation strategies such as guessing intelligently, using a circumlocution or synonyms, or generating a reasonable topic (Crookall and Oxford:114–115). Such activities are needed in addition to the more global speaking activities such as story-telling, descriptions, self-reports, and the like. In the following section we will further expand our discussion of speaking activities in the language classroom.

When planning speaking classes or speaking programs for second language learners, we are often faced with the need to define the goals of the program. In order to answer this need appropriately, it would be advisable to look at what advanced learners in second language acquisition tend to do when involved in the production of spoken discourse. Young (1995) reports on a study focused on conversational style in proficiency interviews where advanced learners were found to speak faster and with fewer pauses or hesitations, persist on the topic longer, and take more initiative with respect to their participation in the conversation. These are some of the features that a speaking course can encourage learners to develop while being engaged in useful communicative activities in the language classroom.

SPEAKING IN THE LANGUAGE CLASSROOM

Speaking activities and speaking practice in the classroom should enable students to gain experience using all the "prerequisites" for effective oral communication that have been mentioned. Klippel (1984) provides ample ideas for fluency activities, and Ur (1981) offers a variety of group task-centered activities to promote the use of the spoken language in contexts that are suitable for the typical foreign language classroom.

What makes a classroom activity useful for speaking practice? The most important feature of a classroom speaking activity is to provide an authentic opportunity for the students to get individual meanings across and utilize every area of knowledge they have in the second or foreign language. They should have the opportunity and be encouraged to become flexible users of their knowledge, always keeping the communicative goal in mind. Speaking activities, like listening activities, can be presented on a continuum from easier to more difficult tasks. For young or beginning-level learners, the teacher may begin with guessing games that require only one-word answers and gradually increase the complexity so that the learners have the opportunity to express themselves using longer discourse units as soon as possible.

Role play is an excellent way in which to simulate, in the classroom, real communication that is relevant to experiences outside the classroom (Crookall and Oxford, 1990; Jones, 1982; Bygate, 1987; Shoemaker and Shoemaker, 1991; Shrum and Glisan, 1994). In role play students can have an opportunity to use their knowledge of vocabulary, of narration, of speech acts, of discourse fillers, of turn taking, of pauses, and so forth. However, role play can be a very difficult or unnatural task if the students do not have sufficient language for or information about the participants, the situation, and the background for the simulated interaction. Care must be taken that all these are available to students so that the activity can be both meaningful and challenging.

Group discussions are an effective speaking activity in large classrooms (Ur, 1981). Students in the second or foreign language classroom should have ample opportunity to participate in group discussions, doing brainstorming, and in many other speaking activities where they need to participate by producing a word, a term, an expression, or a clause and not necessarily maintain a long stretch of conversation. In fact, a considerable amount of classroom time should be devoted to such group activities in order to facilitate the spoken production of individual students, thereby preparing them for more autonomous speaking activities.

Using the target language outside the classroom can be a very useful requirement in homework assignments in those cases where the target language is spoken in the environment (second language contexts). Students can be given tasks that require them to collect meaningful information from stores, restaurants, museums, offices, and other public establishments and then report back in class. Thus, we have a multipurpose activity: Natural interaction in the spoken language serves as a speech initiator outside the classroom for data collection; then the student gives a report as a planned oral presentation in class.

Using the learner's input to create meaningful speaking activities helps make the activity relevant to the learner and authentic in the real sense of the word. Making and choosing friends is a very real concern for teenagers anywhere. An activity based on this topic can start by some self-reporting on the characteristics that the individual students look for in their friends and can then continue on to a pair discussion or a class discussion on the issue (Olshtain, et al., 1993:27).

Feedback, as an integral part of spoken practice, is particularly important in order to encourage learners to develop a variety of communication skills needed for successful oral communication. It is important that teachers have ample opportunity to provide learners with personal feedback on spoken performance that can point out not only individual difficulties, but also strengths on which the learner may capitalize such as a rich vocabulary, good stress and rhythm, or a pleasant personality. Such feedback must be conveyed in a manner that supports the learners rather than embarrasses them.

Looking at *authentic speech* in the form of *written transcripts* can be a useful instruction technique for learners to think about features of oral discourse that they may not be aware of. Such transcripts might provide examples of useful expressions, connectors, feedback techniques, and many other details that would stand out more clearly in the written form than if the same learners were just listening to these bits of discourse. The best presentation of this technique that we have seen is in Riggenbach (1999), who recommends that learners become mini-discourse analysts, i.e., become careful observers who engage in the collection, transcription, analysis, and subsequent generation of spoken discourse.

With emphasis on performance and delivery that ensures successful transmission of the message, peer feedback can also be used very effectively. This can be done in pairs, in groups, or in planned deliveries in front of the whole class. It is important to develop a positive and encouraging atmosphere so that such feedback is helpful and constructive and not damaging. Checklists can help learners with the process of self-evaluation.

Self-evaluation and self-analysis can be another helpful means of improving one's spoken delivery in a foreign or second language, with a range of points to watch out for from basic intelligibility at the one end of the continuum, to effective and persuasive talk at the other end. Students can be recorded or can record themselves using videotaping with playback for analysis. While watching themselves and others on a playback of their participation in spoken interaction, learners can perform self-analyses that will enable them to greatly improve their oral deliveries.

Burns (1998) provides some important elements needed to develop useful spoken interactions in the classroom. She presents typologies of such interactions that combine interpersonal intent with pragmatic considerations. Special emphasis is placed on a variety of spoken genres to which learners can be exposed in a variety of forms accompanied by analysis and discussions. For example, a casual conversation of a confirming nature might involve two long-term friends talking to each other at a book club meeting; in contrast, a more formal conversation might be a lecturer and an undergraduate student talking to each other at an end-of-course party. The opportunity to be exposed to and to discuss the key features in such different types of authentic interaction can be an important part of developing the learner's pragmatic and interactional competence (Burns, 1998:109).

An important new development in language teaching is computer conferencing. Lappanen and Kalaja (1995) describe experimenting with such techniques for a content-area course where Finnish students used their second language by participating in a discussion followed by an instructed writing activity. In comparison to more traditional settings, students in this study were initiating much more "talk;" even though they were typing instead of speaking, they were interacting and using a variety of speech acts such as disagreeing and challenging, among others. Perhaps most important, students were exposed to each other's feedback much more than they would in any other context.

The above are just a few ways in which the teacher can give proper attention to the speaking skill in the foreign or second language classroom beyond the communicative activities that involve all the language skills, with the speaking skill included. This is compatible with our basic belief that in order to help learners become good communicators we need to create opportunities to focus on each skill individually as well as creating many opportunities to integrate two, three, or all four skills.

CONCLUSION

The teaching of spoken language in the language classroom is often perceived as a very difficult task for both the teacher and the students. Most of the teaching materials based on the communicative approach claim to present "real communication in authentic situations" but are in fact still heavily based on descriptions of written English (Yule, 1995). The teaching of speaking from a discourse perspective implies taking a pedagogical shift from focusing on linguistic performance to focusing on a more pragmatic perspective. Contextual and situational features of spoken interaction must become an integral part of classroom activities and personal considerations, and choices have to be offered to students practicing speech production. This chapter has raised the various issues related to teaching speech production from a discourse perspective and offers the teacher a range of appropriate activity types and resources (see the Suggestions for Further Reading at the end of the chapter) for implementing such an approach.

DISCUSSION QUESTIONS

1. How are listening and speaking interdependent in communication strategies?
2. Why are context and background knowledge important for effective speaking activities in the classroom?
3. What are some things language teachers can do to create opportunities for genuine oral communication in the classroom?
4. Describe the most important characteristics of planned versus unplanned oral discourse.

SUGGESTED ACTIVITIES

1. Choose a topic used in a subject matter textbook and design three different speaking activities that would involve both individual learner input and information collected outside the classroom.
2. Prepare a role-play activity that provides full information on context, language, participants, and situational communicative goals, so that students can enact the role play in class with a complete feeling of involvement.
3. Develop a self-evaluation checklist for students to use when they listen individually to their own oral performance on an audio- or videotape.
4. If you teach younger learners, prepare a sequence of five speaking activities related to personal hobbies, starting with less demanding ones and moving on to more complex and expressive tasks.

Suggestions for Further Reading

Brown, G., & Yule, G. (1983). *Teaching the spoken language.* Cambridge: Cambridge University Press.

Brown, H. D. (1994). Teaching oral communication skills. In *Teaching by Principles* (pp. 253–281). Englewood Cliffs, NJ: Prentice Hall Regents.

Bygate, M. (1987). *Speaking.* Oxford: Oxford University Press.

Bygate, M. (1998). Theoretical perspectives on speaking. *Annual Review of Applied Linguistics, 18,* 20–43.

Nolasco, R., & Arthur, L. (1987). *Conversation.* Oxford: Oxford University Press.

Nunan, D. (1989). *Designing tasks for the communicative classroom.* Oxford: Oxford University Press.

Riggenbach, H. (1999). *Discourse analysis in the language classroom:* Vol. 1. *The spoken language.* Ann Arbor, MI: University of Michigan Press.

Schiffrin, D. (1994). *Approaches to discourse.* Oxford: Blackwell.

Shoemaker, C. L., & Shoemaker, F. F. (1991). *Interactive techniques for the ESL classroom.* Boston: Heinle & Heinle.

Shrum, J. L., & Glisan, E. W. (1994). *Teachers handbook: Contextualized language.* Boston: Heinle & Heinle.

Endnote

[1] See, for example, the analysis of and the examples showing the uses of the discourse marker *well* in Chapter 4.

EPILOGUE TO PART 3: INTEGRATION OF LANGUAGE SKILLS AND DISCOURSE PROCESSING

In this section of the book we treated each of the four language skills separately. However, in real-life communication there is very rarely a separate and independent use of any of these skills. The exceptions occur when people simply listen or read without doing anything else for a period of time. While speaking, it is in fact necessary to listen; and while writing, it is necessary to read – in order to monitor one's own language production at the very least. In real-life communication, skill use is typically simultaneous or overlapping and integrated. For example, in academic settings students often write down notes while listening to lectures, or they make summaries or jot down references while reading. In a group discussion, students might switch rapidly from talking, to listening, to writing down ideas, or to reading (or re-reading) any relevant text(s) they have at hand. If one person reads aloud for the group, he is reading and speaking simultaneously while the others are listening.

In the language classroom it is important that the teacher create situations and activities that encourage the type of simultaneous and integrated use of language skills that the learners will be expected to use for communicative purposes outside the classroom. One way that teachers can guide their preparation and thinking is to combine the language knowledge framework and the discourse processing framework (see Figures 1.1 and 1.2 in Chapter 1). When using language for communication, we combine the language knowledge areas with the discourse processing strategies as shown in Figure A on page 181.

Language classroom activities that reflect the same integration of language resources and language processing strategies will allow for the teaching of language through discourse.

For example, a class project for low-intermediate students might involve carrying out a survey of eating habits in the community, with focus on health and environmental considerations. Such a project would begin with a brainstorming activity that involves the entire class – a speaking activity – during which the students would decide how to go about carrying out the survey, who the audience will be, and what resources they will need to consult. Let us assume that the class has decided to work in groups and that each group would work with a different age group of consultants and would make use of different written sources. This would lead to a *writing* activity in order to summarize the procedures and a *reading* task to get information from the written sources. In the following session, each group would present their information via a *planned speaking* activity while the other groups would be involved in *listening* and note taking. Finally, each group would develop a questionnaire, go out and collect the data, analyze the data, write a report, and deliver an oral presentation. This type of project involves the use of all language skills in an integrated fashion, with a logical sequence of activities leading to a common educational goal. All students participating in this project would have an opportunity to use the language resources at their disposal and the four language skills in meaningful and communicative ways. For further discussion of such project work, see Fried-Booth (1986).

With advanced language learners, content-based language teaching offers a wealth of opportunities for the integration of skills. Thus, if such learners are using the content of introductory psychology to further develop their target language resources and language skills, they will be listening to psychology lectures and reading related textbook materials. They will participate in small group oral discussions and write reports (and write papers and take written quizzes and examinations). The focus of all these activities in such a content-based curriculum will be the psychology content. However, ideally, a language teacher is also present to assist with problems in pronunciation, grammar, vocabulary, and discourse that interfere with the appropriacy and accuracy of learners' interpretations of discourse while listening to lectures or discussions or while reading their textbook.

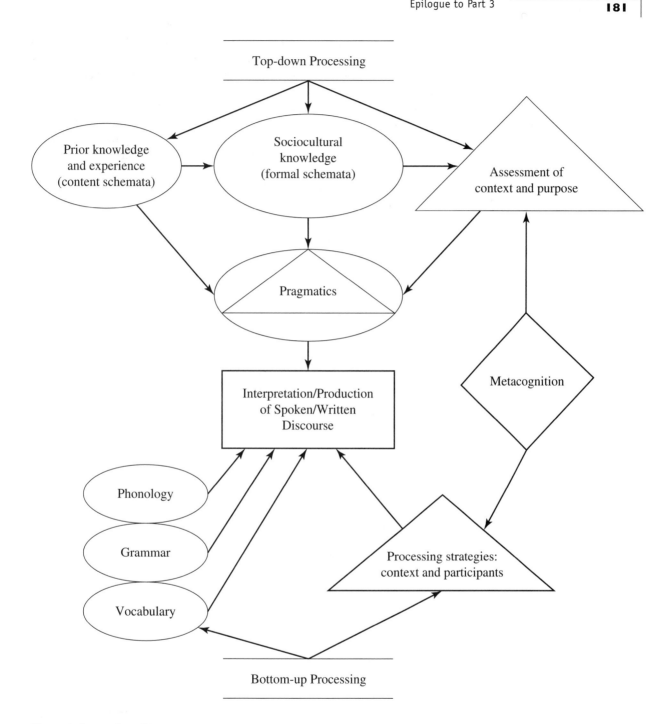

Figure A Integration of Language Knowledge and Discourse Processing

Attention should also be given to content and form of the learners' various productions of discourse while they are speaking and writing. Both group and individual feedback and correction, which will be discussed in Chapter 12, are important for the language development of such learners.

The language the learners produce or interpret will all be instances of discourse: lectures, textbook chapters, quizzes, papers, class discussions, and so forth. The learners will need to draw upon both their language resources and their discourse processing strategies when they interpret and produce such content-based discourse. Thus, without careful attention to language per se, content-based instruction will not necessarily facilitate language development; it may simply teach content. For further discussion of content-based language learning, see Brinton et al. (1989).

PART 4

IMPLEMENTATION

CHAPTER 10

Curriculum Design
and Materials Development

"It should be useful to examine patterns of participation and the language functions and forms
needed and used within them – useful not only for conducting classroom research . . . , but
for developing teaching goals as well, especially goals for content-linked [language] teaching."

(Cazden, 1995:386)

"Negotiating the curriculum means deliberately planning to invite students to contribute to,
and to modify, the educational curriculum, so that they will have a real investment both
in the learning journey and in the outcomes."

(Boomer, et al., 1992:14)

INTRODUCTION

A language curriculum can be viewed as a document that provides guidelines for textbook
writers, teacher trainers, language teachers, developers of computerized and high-tech
teaching aids, language testers, and many other populations that might function as stakeholders in the language teaching context. As such, a curriculum should express the cultural,
social, and political perspectives of the society within which it is to be implemented. It
combines past and present ideologies, experiences, philosophies, and innovations with
aspirations and expectations for the future. It serves as the major framework within which
educational decision making is carried out with respect to goal specification and teaching
methodology, teacher training and textbook selection.

Discourse analysis has had a very important impact on language curriculum design in
the 1980s and 1990s, as it has had with respect to other areas of language teaching.
Specifically, a discourse approach underlies a view of curriculum design that places the
social context of learning and language use at the center. Decisions related to content,
product, and process in the curriculum draw heavily on the state of the art in discourse
analysis. In spite of the fact that there is no one simple definition of discourse analysis,
and although discourse analysis comprises at least six different approaches – speech act
theory, interactional sociolinguistics, ethnography of communication, pragmatics, conversation analysis, and variation analysis (Schiffrin, 1994) – it serves to define a large part of
the research agenda for applied linguistics in general, and language teaching in particular.

A discourse-oriented curriculum places special emphasis on three areas: *context, text types,* and *communicative goals.* As a result, the definition of goals, tasks, and procedures always takes contextual features into account. In this respect such a curriculum is different from a linguistically oriented curriculum, where contextual features might be viewed as external to the curriculum. Furthermore, in a discourse-oriented curriculum the selection of materials and of written or spoken texts is guided by discourse features and levels of complexity. Teaching methodology and learning activities are guided by communicative goals at the general as well as at the specific level. Thus, a discourse perspective ideally permeates the language curriculum at all levels and in all aspects.

ASPECTS OF LANGUAGE CURRICULUM DESIGN

SYLLABUS OR CURRICULUM?

In an attempt to give workable definitions to the terms "curriculum" and "syllabus," we shall follow the position presented in Dubin and Olshtain (1986:3) and assume the following:

a. A **curriculum** is a document of an official nature, published by a leading or central educational authority in order to serve as a framework or a set of guidelines for the teaching of a subject area – in our case a language – in a broad and varied context. Thus, a state at the national level, a board of education at the district level, a community at the municipal level or a university or college at the local academic level may choose to issue a document stating the scope and goals of its program for teaching a second or foreign language. Accordingly, such a curriculum will present overall broad perspectives that can apply to a large number of different programs within the specified context. At the state level, the document will be concerned with goals that apply to all types of schools and segments of the population. At the district level it will apply to all schools within that district and at a given university to all the language courses – even though they might be taught in different departments.

b. A **syllabus**, in contrast to the curriculum, is a more particularized document that addresses a specific audience of learners and teachers, a particular course of study or a particular series of textbooks. Ideally, in this sense, a curriculum should be implemented through a variety of syllabuses and each of these syllabuses should be compatible with the overall curriculum. At the state level this would mean that the curriculum provides general guidelines for all educational planners and policy makers and all material and courseware developers. All textbooks, supplementary materials, tests, and courseware would be designed so as to fit the goals specified in the general curriculum.

According to the distinction made here between curriculum and syllabus, it follows that the curriculum should state the following: the goals, the rationale, and the guiding principles for language teaching, in a broad sense. The syllabus, on the other hand, should translate these guiding principles into specific goals, content, and activities to be carried out in a particular, and well-defined context. Obviously, the general principles apply to both the curriculum and the syllabus; it is mostly the degree and type of specification that differ.

Graves (1996) makes a similar distinction between curriculum and syllabus with the added perspective of different roles for teachers. According to Graves, the syllabus has a narrow role of specification and ordering of course content with teachers acting as implementers rather than developers. In our view, teachers can also act as developers both within the broader curriculum and the narrower syllabus, depending on the basic approach to curriculum or syllabus design.

WHO IS THE "CUSTOMER" AND WHO ARE THE "STAKEHOLDERS"?

When a group of experts and practitioners sit down to develop a curriculum, the first question that needs to be considered is the audience for whom the curriculum is relevant. In most cases the first audience that comes to mind is the teachers. It is often assumed that well-informed teachers, who carefully plan their teaching and who feel responsible and accountable for their work, need to have a good understanding of the curriculum. In fact, however, it is very seldom that the practicing classroom teacher would need to consult the curriculum – from her point of view the realization of the curriculum is the textbook and the courseware, and in some cases the course syllabus. Language teachers are usually not the actual "customers" of the curriculum, but they certainly are consumers of the products based on the curriculum. We could compare the situation here to food products intended for babies: the customers in this case are the mothers who have to decide what is good, nutritious, and safe for their babies to eat, but the real consumers of the baby food are the babies themselves.

In the case of the language curriculum, the consumers are first and foremost the learners and second the teachers. The learners are greatly affected by the curriculum and their needs have to be taken into account when planning the curriculum; the teachers are also affected by the curriculum in a major way since their teaching is related to the curriculum specifications as it is presented in the more specific course syllabus or particular textbook that they happen to be using. But neither of these two groups are the actual customers. Who then is the major customer of the language curriculum, given the way we have defined it here? Probably the textbook writers or the course and materials developers, test developers, and program evaluators are the major customers of the curriculum.

Once we have defined materials and test developers or program evaluators as the major customers of the curriculum, we can define the main purpose of the curriculum itself: to provide these material and test developers with clear and unambiguous guidelines for developing materials, courses, and assessment instruments that are capable of realizing the goals and the philosophy presented in the curriculum. This leads us to the understanding that a language curriculum needs to specify the general educational philosophy, the linguistic, social, and cultural goals, and the overall societal expectations of the program. The field of discourse analysis plays a key role in the definition of such goals by placing emphasis on the learners' communicative needs, which entail social and cultural perspectives in addition to the linguistic elements of the curriculum. Pragmatics and sociolinguistics become a part of the theoretical basis for curriculum design. Furthermore, the curriculum needs to specify the pedagogical approach to language teaching and language learning and the scope of the program (time and resources). All of this information is crucial for materials and test developers in order to ensure that the materials and tests will be compatible with the curriculum. This information is also relevant to teacher trainers in both pre-service and in-service institutions, and often they too can be perceived as customers of the curriculum.

In a true marketing situation the needs and wants of the customers, their perceptions, beliefs, and preferences would dictate the nature of the product – which in our case is the curriculum. In an educational context, however, the stakeholders need to be carefully defined since they are the ones that dictate the educational philosophy and approach. The curriculum is therefore both a political and an educational document.

Who might the stakeholders be? If we are considering curriculum design at the national level, it is obvious that the highest policy agency in the specific country or state, such as the Ministry of Education or the Board of Education, is a major stakeholder and will play a significant role in defining the curriculum components. If we are talking about a democratic system, some of these components might be affected by the political party in power at the time the curriculum is drawn up and on the general educational and linguistic policies that are followed. It is easy to imagine how different political positions might affect bilingual policies, considerations of first versus second language issues, and so forth. The situation might be even more prominent in a context where there is a fixed regime, and a given ideology that guides the overall educational situation.

If we are thinking of the school district or regional educational system, then the parents might constitute a major group of stakeholders. The parents have very definite vested interests in their children's education, and if they are involved in the educational policy of the district, they might have a very strong influence on the curriculum. A good example of such parental influence is the pressure from parents in many countries to teach English as a foreign language at an earlier age than was planned by the experts who worked on the curriculum. Such pressure might eventually result in changes in the curriculum.

At the university level stakeholders could be other department heads, employment agencies, and the government. If, at a given university, languages are taught by a special "service" unit, and if a certain language is required by all departments for access to critical library materials and research, then the various departments are important stakeholders. Employment agencies, on the other hand, recruit university graduates and may therefore have vested interests in the level of language proficiency attained by graduates. Whatever the particular context, stakeholders need to be considered and taken into account when the curriculum is developed.

THREE MAJOR LANGUAGE-CURRICULUM APPROACHES AND OTHER ORGANIZING PRINCIPLES

Language curriculum design is a constantly changing and expanding subfield of applied linguistics, as pointed out by Yalden (1987) and further focused on in Olshtain (1989). From an educational perspective, language curriculum design has drawn upon the general field of curriculum development; from applied linguistics it has drawn upon relevant fields such as language teaching methodology, second language acquisition research, language planning and policy making, language assessment, and, of course, language analysis, within which discourse analysis is of central importance.

The changing trends and approaches in each of these fields have had their impact on language curriculum design, and as a result several major curriculum types have evolved. We will discuss three major views of language curricula – each encompassing several possible approaches: a *content-based* curriculum, a *process-based* curriculum, and a *product-based* curriculum. We will present a very broad definition of these three types and show how the changing trends in language education and discourse analysis have been incorporated into the three types. More specific curriculum organizing principles such as *task-based, needs-based,* and *learner-based* types of instruction will be discussed within the three major approaches. Each of these trends has had its impact on course design and instructional practices as well as teacher education.

A **content-based** curriculum is by definition focused on the content perspective of the course. The term "content" can relate to at least three different areas of content: *linguistic* content, *thematic* or *situational* content, and *subject-matter* content. What has become known in language teaching as the grammar translation method, the structural syllabus, and the notional-functional syllabus can all be viewed as different approaches to the design of programs focused on *language* content. The grammar translation approach places grammatical rules and translation from one language to the other at the center of curriculum design. The structural approach views structural/formal language features and patterns (phonological, morphological, and syntactic) as central, and the notional/functional approach singles out semantic notions (concepts) and (social) functions as the key elements in identifying language content for curriculum design. What all of these have in common is that they rely heavily on linguistic theory, although we are talking about different schools of thought: traditional grammar, structural-descriptive linguistics, and sociolinguistics or functional grammar and discourse analysis respectively.

The thematic and situational approach to content became central in the communicative approach since the emphasis here is on contextualization and meaningful and relevant use of the target language during the learning process. There are two main objectives in this approach: first, themes and topics included in the curriculum should provide appropriate cultural background for the language material and the activities carried out; second, themes and topics should motivate interest and be relevant and appealing to the learner audience. When a curriculum is designed around a thematic approach, the focal element is the theme that controls the selection of structures, functions, and vocabulary to be taught. It is this type of content-based curriculum that is closely connected to the various subfields of discourse analysis. In particular, speech act theory and text analysis are relevant to carrying out text selection for each dominant theme.

The subject matter content is focal in what is known today as "content-based instruction" (Mohan, 1986; Krahnke, 1987; Brinton, Snow, and Wesche, 1989; Corson, 1990; Snow, 1998). This approach is based on the notion that second language learning can be very effective when the focus is on acquisition of knowledge and information via the target language. In other words, the learner uses the target language in order to acquire knowledge and learns a great deal of language as a natural by-product of such use. Programs based on this approach might differ considerably in the degree to which linguistic and content issues are separated or integrated, but they all view language use as serving the subject-matter dimension, and language instruction as accompanying and facilitating subject-matter development. This type of content-based curriculum leans heavily on discourse analysis with respect to text analysis within the particular subject matter.

Snow (1998) presents an updated description of the present scope of content-based instruction. In the United States "content-ESL" programs are implemented in about 15 percent of the public schools. Throughout the world content-based instruction is often found in university or college contexts or in various other programs entitled "English for Specific Purposes." Furthermore, content-based instruction has also impacted teacher training models, as can be seen from the work of Kaufman (1997), who describes a teacher training program where ESL trainees collaborate with teachers of English, science, and social studies in order to prepare the trainees to understand the unique needs of ESL learners in mainstream classrooms.

A **process-based** curriculum is concerned with the process of language learning and language teaching. It may be focused on one or all of the following: a *task-based* curriculum, a *needs-based* curriculum, and a *learner-based* curriculum. The task-based syllabus design evolved from the gradual shift that took place in the early 1980s from emphasis on *product* in language learning to emphasis on *process*. This shift started with notions such as "Language learning may be seen as a process which grows out of the interaction between learners, texts and activities" (Breen and Candlin, 1980:95). Towards the end of the 1980s the process-based syllabus (Breen, 1987) became a working reality in many learning contexts, with special focus being placed on the language learning tasks and activities that learners were expected to carry out as part of their learning process.

The basic characteristic of a task-based program is that it uses activities that the learners have to do for "noninstructional" purposes outside of the classroom, turning them into opportunities for language learning inside the classroom. Tasks, in this sense, are viewed as a way of bringing the real world into the classroom.

Long (1985, 1989) and Long and Crookes (1989) view *tasks* as a potentially unifying unit of analysis in course design, and they distinguish between *pedagogic tasks* and *target tasks*. Pedagogic tasks are designed in the form of problem-solving activities for classroom work constituting approximations of the target tasks and gradually leading learners towards the target tasks. Target tasks are activity types in which the learners will eventually engage long after the course of study, matching real-life situations. Long and Crookes maintain that the choice of target tasks in the curriculum should be made according to a task-based needs analysis of the learners. Tasks are perceived as potentially being a suitable unit of analysis that is compatible with findings from second language acquisition research.

The definition of a task is particularly important. According to Skehan (1998) a task is an activity that satisfies the following criteria: *meaning* is primary, there is a *goal* that needs to be worked toward, the activity is *outcome-evaluated* and there is a *real-world* relationship. The syllabus designer, the teacher, or the students can choose tasks for the language classroom. Whoever it is, the decision maker needs to have information about the nature of the task, the requirements made by the task, and the potential outcomes of the task.

Yule (1997) argues that communicative effectiveness is the key element in tasks since tasks provide the need to focus on *discourse*-embedded meanings to be communicated and much less on sentence-based syntax. It is, therefore, discourse analysis that can provide the basis for task definition in terms of communicative goals, situational features, and social and cultural perspectives.

In contrast to all of the researchers mentioned above, who view a task-based syllabus as one way of doing a process-oriented curriculum, Markee (1997:35) uses the term "task-based" language teaching as an umbrella term for process-oriented approaches to language teaching.

The *learner-based* curriculum places the learner and his/her needs at the center of planning. As a result, relatively little planning can be done prior to the onset of the course of study. The syllabus will develop gradually from loosely planned guidelines based on learners' needs, and it will change throughout the course to further accommodate the changing needs of the learners and teachers. As Nunan (1988) explains, "A crucial distinction between traditional and learner-centered curriculum development is that, in the latter, no decision is binding. This is particularly true of the content selection and gradation" (5). Learners are viewed not only as the focus of the curriculum, they are also full participants in its development.

Nunan's approach to curriculum design gave teachers a central role in the decision-making process. His use of course documentation and retrospection, which could capture classroom activities and their complexities, became the basis for making teachers resourceful and competent in learner-centered course design. There is no doubt that this approach affected curriculum development in general and teacher and learner roles in particular.

Strategy-based instruction is a more recent approach to course planning. According to Cohen (1998:65) this approach can be viewed as relying on the notion that language learning can be facilitated by learners' becoming aware of various strategies, which they may consciously employ during learning and language-using experiences. Teachers and materials can provide strategies-based instruction to students as part of their language curriculum. The advantage of the strategy-based approach to teaching in general, and to course design in particular, is that strategies introduced during the course of study can usually be used long after the course has been completed.

A **product-based** curriculum places emphasis on the outcomes of the course of study or in other words on "what the learners should know and be able to produce in the L2" upon course completion. This knowledge will most likely be specified in the curriculum for two types of components: *language resources* and *language skills*. Since today a holistic view must guide curriculum development, we need to concern ourselves with the comprehensive, overall knowledge that the learner is supposed to achieve as a result of the program. A skill-oriented focus in the curriculum document allows for the integration of language areas with skill ability, very much in line with the approach taken in this book. Thus, the curriculum might specify that graduates of the program will be able to express themselves in spoken language on topics of an everyday nature and on topics related to certain areas of personal interest. Such an ability requires a certain level of language proficiency in syntax and lexicon and a level of ability to pronounce English intelligibly. Similarly, the curriculum would specify the type of reading and writing ability and the type of texts that students are supposed to be able to read and understand, and the type of writing they should be able to produce by the end of the course. Basically, a product-based curriculum looks at the end result of the program and provides the type of specification that is compatible with the general approach to teaching outlined in the curriculum.

In a discourse-oriented, product-based curriculum, attention is given to text types on the one hand, and to contextual features on the other. When specifying what students are expected to be able to do at the end of the course, such a discourse-oriented curriculum would emphasize what texts students should be able to process and under what contextual circumstances. Thus, a foreign language university course for Ph.D. students might specify the requirement that students be able to understand a scientific article in their area of interest and to translate its essence into their native language.

The product-based curriculum also takes another important perspective into account: What levels of *fluency* and *accuracy* are students expected to reach at the end of the course of study? Fluency usually relates to the ease and speed with which students carry out communicative activities whereas accuracy refers to form features of the output. If the graduates are expected to be able to interact in everyday communicative situations, fluency might be perceived as more important than accuracy. For professionals such as physicians, lawyers, and others who need to express themselves accurately to achieve full credibility, accuracy would also seem to play a significant role. Thus, form-focused instruction may have to be considered in addition to the various other approaches. Ellis (1998), among others, argues in favor of not excluding form-focused instruction from communicative language programs until more research is carried out in this area.

From what has been said in this section, it is becoming obvious that up-to-date curriculum design with a discourse perspective might integrate various approaches that have been presented here. Such a curriculum can be content-based, task-based, and strategy-based, as well as product oriented, if these issues are all relevant to the needs of the particular student audience. Any curriculum taking a discourse perspective is, however, sure to have two important features: focus on authentic texts and interactional communicative events in language use, and focus on the social and cultural environment within which language processing and interaction take place. Its goals would need to combine the various areas of knowledge specified in the previous chapters: language knowledge, sociocultural knowledge, and pragmatic knowledge together with processing skills leading to an interactionist perspective of language use. Learners, in other words, would be expected to be able to use language in specified interactional contexts.

THE LEARNING CONTEXT: DEFINING SPECIFIC NEEDS AND GOALS

THE FACT-FINDING STAGE

Before any general language curriculum can be designed (at the state, district, or school level), whether content, process, or product oriented, it is necessary to carry out a careful analysis of the language needs and the linguistic context in which the curriculum is to be implemented. In other words, many of the decisions that need to be made and the choices that will be implemented (as described in the previous section) have to be based on the particular learning context. As outlined in Dubin and Olshtain (1986, Chapter 1), a number of basic questions need to be answered as background information for the development of the language curriculum:

- who are the learners? (age, sex, interests, background, context)
- who are the teachers? (target language proficiency, professional training)
- where is the program going to be implemented? (within the school system, within private settings, or other places)
- how will the program be implemented and evaluated? (who will develop syllabuses, textbooks, and other materials; what tests will be used?)

Information concerning these questions can be collected from official documents, by interviewing students and teachers, by interviewing graduates of existing programs, and by talking to leaders in the educational community such as governmental officials, teacher trainers, and so forth.

Program planners also need to understand the language setting within which the new curriculum will be implemented, where language setting refers to the "totality of communication roles" (Gumperz, 1968) in the discourse community. What is particularly important is the role of the target language in that discourse community. If we are talking about English as the target language, English usually functions as the *language of wider communication,* which enables speakers of different languages to communicate with one another. As such, English is the language of academic, technological, and commercial communication at the international level. The definition of curriculum goals has to relate to the role that English plays in the particular community. The following might be the broad definition of the major goals for teaching English in one of the South-Asian countries now gaining rapid access to the Western world:

> English is taught in the school system from Grade X to Grade Y, and is viewed as a language of wider communication that enables speakers of different languages to communicate with one another. Students completing Grade Y should be able to use English as a means of:
> - achieving personal, intellectual, and professional development
> - gaining access to modern science, technology, and general information
> - gaining access to other cultures and international contacts
> - contributing to the improvement of society and life in the country

These general goals for teaching English in the particular context should be further translated into more specific goals. In order to be able to define the latter properly, a series of careful discourse analyses might have to be carried out in order to establish the needs of the graduates of the program in academic institutions, at workplaces, in society in general, and so forth. In other words, curriculum planners need to have a good under-standing of the language use within relevant discourse communities since such areas and levels of use is what the graduates of the program aspire to reach.

GOAL DEFINITIONS: CASES EXEMPLIFYING CURRICULUM DEVELOPMENT FROM A DISCOURSE PERSPECTIVE

In this section we present some practical cases of curriculum or syllabus development, viewing them from the discourse perspective. These are examples of how curriculum con-siderations can be translated into practical routes for application. Celce-Murcia (1995b), while arguing for a discourse analysis perspective in curriculum development, presents three cases where discourse analysis plays very different roles:

1. an EFL course for chemical engineering students where discourse analysis plays a peripheral role in the careful analysis and selection of articles to be used in the course. A discourse perspective also influences the reading methodology used to teach such texts.

2. an intermediate ESL writing course where discourse analysis plays an enlarged role by getting teachers and learners to compare and analyze parallel compositions on similar topics from the ESL students and a control group of native speakers.

3. a nonspecialist Egyptian EFL teacher training course, where discourse analysis plays a central role by providing a detailed description of the discourse features of both the target language textbooks in use and videotapes and transcripts of native and nonnative EFL teachers in action in the classroom. These data provide optimal content for the language development and pedagogical training of the nonspecialist teachers.

In all three cases discussed by Celce-Murcia, discourse-based tasks were designed on the basis of the prior discourse analysis of the relevant target language use.

The three cases are, in the terminology presented in this chapter, syllabus types devel-oped for specific courses with well-identified audiences. In all of these cases there is no general curriculum to which the syllabuses need to adhere, and the programs can be devel-oped in response to the immediate needs of a particular group of learners. In addition to the overall discourse considerations specified, these syllabuses or courses could also have made informed choices with respect to task-based, form-focused or strategy-based approaches.

Another case concerns the development of a trilingual curriculum for a Jewish day school in a Spanish-speaking country. The particular school in question decided to open a trilingual setting for children, beginning in kindergarten and leading all the way to the twelfth grade (K through 12 context) with the following general emphases: Hebrew is to be taught as the language of heritage, Spanish as the first language of the students and the dominant language in society, and English as a language for wider communication and especially future academic work since many of the graduates may continue their higher education in an English-speaking university.

A careful needs analysis with a discourse focus established the following facts about the target population: The students will continue to function in the Spanish-speaking community for all their daily routines, social interactions, and work experiences; there-fore, they need to develop an educated proficiency in their L1; they will visit the United States almost every summer and will be active consumers of the American culture during their years of schooling, and most will eventually attend academic institutions in the United States for their college and university education; therefore, they need English. The students will also be active participants in their local Jewish community and in the religious services where Hebrew is used, and they will go on frequent trips to Israel and use the Hebrew language for daily interaction with relatives and friends there.

The curriculum goals resulting from this analysis were specified as follows: The overall school program will be divided into three parallel tracks – the humanities and social science track, the science and technology track, and the religious-cultural track. All the humanities and social science classes will be carried out in Spanish; science and technology will be done in English throughout the program; religion and heritage studies will be conducted in Hebrew. In order to create a meaningful trilingual learning context, the school designated special areas of work for each of the languages, especially for the younger children ages four through eight. Thus, children may arrive at school on Monday to start with two to three hours in the heritage program, which is all in Hebrew. This takes place in the "Hebrew Wing," where, once you enter, everything is in Hebrew – games, books, songs, labels, signs, and decorations, and of course the spoken language and the language of instruction is Hebrew. Later in the day the same group of children move to a "young science class" in the "English Wing," where everything is in English, and where the major content areas relate to computer games, scientific experiments, films; other aids all relate to the world of science, inventions, and discoveries. This group may end the day by moving to the "Spanish Wing," where everything is in Spanish, to do a storytelling activity. The following day they may have a different routine perhaps starting with a writing class in Spanish, continuing to an English mathematics class, and finishing with Bible stories in Hebrew.

What is unique about the situation described here is the fact that from a very young age the students begin to recognize the three parallel "worlds" of English, Hebrew, and Spanish, gaining a high level of proficiency in all but with different emphases on the content and discourse features in each. For each of these three "worlds," students will be able to develop communicative competence by developing language knowledge, relevant sociocultural knowledge, and processing skills that are compatible with the content and context of the particular "world" or "wing." In Spanish they have many opportunities to focus on all types of interaction, as native speakers usually do. In English they are more focused on scientific and technological texts and some conversational interactions relevant to their experiences in the language learning context. In Hebrew they develop knowledge of the language and of the sociocultural norms in order to be able to communicate in familiar contexts as well as comprehend more literary and religious subject matter. This particular school curriculum, which divides the students' educational world into "three separate language worlds," was found to be most appropriate for the needs expressed by the school and the community, and it enabled the planners to develop a discourse perspective for each of these language worlds.

In the context of the trilingual school the school curriculum specifies the goals for each of the three languages with a somewhat different focus in each. It also sets up the beginning of reading and writing – initially Spanish in the first grade, English in the second grade, and Hebrew in the third. Thus, youngsters can first establish their reading skills in their native language, next in another Western Indo-European language with a Roman alphabet, and finally in the more difficult Semitic language, Hebrew, with its very different writing system. Beyond these general principles, each language group has its own syllabus to follow, a syllabus relevant to the uses of that particular language that is compatible with the overall curriculum.

The cases presented in this section served to demonstrate some of the varieties of learning contexts in which language curricula and syllabuses need to be developed. In each case the discourse perspectives are matched to a very careful analysis of the learners' needs.

MAJOR COMPONENTS OF AN INTEGRATED CURRICULUM AND KEY PRINCIPLES FOR IMPLEMENTATION

INTEGRATING CONTENT, PROCESS, PRODUCT AND CONTEXT IN A DISCOURSE-BASED CURRICULUM

A discourse-based curriculum that takes into account the findings of research done in applied linguistics, second language acquisition, curriculum development, and sociolinguistics needs to combine the different dimensions discussed earlier: content (*what* is to be included in the course), process (*how* learning and teaching are to be implemented), and product (*what* should be achieved) with the context in which learning takes place (*where* the curriculum is to get implemented). We suggest, therefore, that in an integrated curriculum the general goals of the program be followed by a specification of these four domains, which will be discussed in detail subsequently. For each domain, the curriculum should present a statement of intent and a list of guiding principles, which will facilitate effective implementation of the curriculum and which will help the potential customers.

The content domain in an integrated discourse-based curriculum or syllabus will consist of at least four types of content: *thematic content, linguistic content, cultural content, and subject-matter content.*

Generally speaking, the thematic content should expose students to situations, texts, or discourse types that are relevant to the interest and experiences of the learners and that match their future expectations of language use. A discourse approach is crucial here since the pragmatic and ethnographic perspective would provide planners with the sociocultural framework within which the target language is to be used, and speech act theory and conversational analysis would provide guidance in the selection of relevant contexts. Furthermore, discourse analysis of written and spoken texts is significant in both oral and written text and task selection.

Among the various principles that should underlie the development of a discourse-based *content domain* we need to emphasize the following: *contextualization, authenticity,* and *integration* (see Figure 10.1).

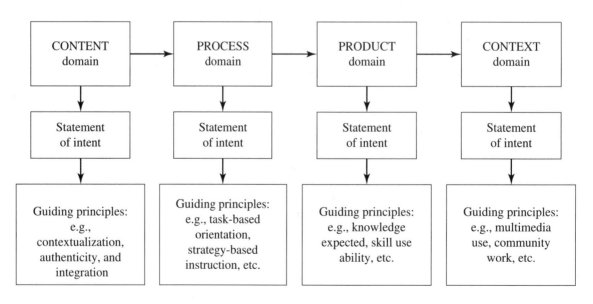

Figure 10.1 A Discourse-Oriented Language Curriculum: An Integrated Approach

Contextualization refers to the need to present linguistic content within thematic and situational contexts that reflect the natural use of language. Thus, when teaching a grammatical topic such as the tense-aspect system or relative clauses, or any other linguistic element, the presentation of the grammatical point as well as its practice and use should be a very close simulation of how native speakers might use that form in actual communication. The English past tense, for example, can be learned and taught most effectively within a real or a "fictional" narrative where the simple past form is central to the development of the main plot and the present tense or progressive aspect typically describes the background. Relative clauses, on the other hand, can best be learned and taught within a context that requires identification and specification of nouns (defining characteristics): the need to single out individuals within a group or to select items with special characteristics. The contextualization principle relies heavily on discourse and contextual analysis (Celce-Murcia, 1990) in an attempt to pair up grammatical form with meaningful sociocultural context.

Authenticity has been discussed in great detail with respect to the communicative approach to language teaching and has addressed at least two perspectives: the type of language used in the classroom or during the learning process, and the tasks employed while learning the language. The main issue raised by authenticity advocates has been a struggle against the contrived and unnatural use of language that was so typical of textbooks produced in the fifties and sixties, when the emphasis was on grammatical form at the expense of meaning and context. However, as is to be expected, the new focus was also accompanied by certain risks – curriculum developers and textbook writers sometimes carried the authenticity principle too far, ignoring the needs and proficiency level of the learners while adhering to "authentic" language and texts intended for native speakers of the target language. Here again, discourse analysis has played a very important role in redefining authenticity within the learning context.

A useful redefinition of authenticity is provided by Ur (1984), who distinguishes between "genuine authentic" as opposed to "imitation authentic," the former being unadapted, natural interaction among native speakers and the latter an approximation of real speech that takes into account the learners' level of ability.

Ur claims that learners learn best "from listening to speech which, while not entirely authentic, is an approximation of the real thing, and is planned to take into account the learners' level of ability and particular difficulties" (1984:23). Furthermore, the context within which learners function is never identical to a similar situation in the real world and activities, and tasks must pass the "classroom authenticity test" in order to be suitable for learning purposes. Perhaps the most important characteristic of this "classroom authenticity" is to ensure that the particular task is relevant and appropriate to the learning situation.

At the very earliest stage of language acquisition, while the learner's proficiency is still limited, it is already possible to recruit the learner's input for language learning activities. In the first two or three weeks of the English course (even in a limited EFL course) students can be asked to fill in "What is true for you?" where the statements which they need to react to are written next to a picture that provides the context. They may not yet know all the words in the statements and certainly do not know how to use the present simple with action verbs in English, but they can make simple choices:

I read comics.

I eat hot dogs.

I play ping-pong.

(Adapted from Olshtain, et al., 1996:11–23)

Such an activity makes the English lesson relevant and interesting and therefore authentic for each learner in the group. At a more advanced level we could have personal questionnaires where students provide true answers about themselves such as the following:

> What is you attitude toward knowledge? Write *yes* or *no*.
>
> Do you like quizzes? ___
>
> Do you solve puzzles? ___
>
> Do you try to discover new facts? _____
>
> Count the number of times you used *yes* to score yourself.

> (Adapted from Olshtain, et al., 1991:176)

A further development of the *input principle* should stress that teachers and learners must realize that in authentic, natural language use there isn't "one right answer," and students should be encouraged to give "real answers." Thus when asking questions that test students' comprehension of a passage, we should develop grids that have "things we know for sure from reading the passage as opposed to things we don't know" or "things that happened, things that didn't happen, and things I am not sure about." Such extension of classroom work to natural, true-to-life situations contributes to making the learning process more authentic. The *feedback principle,* on the other hand, relates to the purpose of carrying out a learning task and therefore belongs in the *process domain,* where it will be further discussed.

The *integration principle* calls for consolidation of knowledge and skill use. For learning activities to become relevant and interesting, they need to involve the various language skills in an appropriate manner. Thus if students were asked to solve a problem related to the theme presented in the language class (in a unit on space exploration, personal equipment that is needed, for example) they should be encouraged to use their background knowledge and their language skills in order to find all the factual information that is relevant. They might listen to audiotapes or a video, they might look up facts in an encyclopedia or a computerized database, or consult appropriate Web sites on the Internet, they may interview experts, and so on. Such activities integrate general learning with linguistic knowledge and ensure both authenticity and contextualization while combining the activities with proper focus on the appropriate processing skills.

The *process domain* refers to the establishment of principles related to the learning/acquisition process from the learners' perspective and the teaching process from the teacher's perspective. Therefore, the process domain in the curriculum should specify the principles relevant to these two processes. Concerning the learners, the principles should be based on second language acquisition research. These principles should include statements such as the following (see Figure 10.1: Statement of intent):

- Language learners are most successful when they are encouraged to experiment with language in use and to "take risks."

- Language learners learn best when they are given attainable goals, on the one hand, and challenging tasks, on the other.

- Language learners become effective acquirers when they are aware of their learning strategies and make individual choices of tasks to do from the many tasks they are given as options.

We believe these three principles are basic to the position we have taken in this book, but any given curriculum would probably contain a more detailed list. The principles specified in the curriculum will ultimately depend on the conviction and beliefs of the members of the curriculum committee or authority that issues the curriculum document.

With respect to teachers, the principles should be based on classroom-oriented research specifying the best teaching techniques that facilitate language learning and turn the classroom environment into a useful language learning environment. Such principles might state:

- In order to provide learners with the most conducive learning environment, within school-centered situations, teachers should be aware of the students' needs and interests.

- Teachers should try to maximize opportunities for meaningful language use in the classroom by using pair/group work and other techniques that involve learners in authentic tasks.
  (see Figure 10.1; Process domain – Guiding principles)

The process domain in the curriculum lays out some of the most important principles for developing an effective learning and acquisition process. Considerations of the approach to language instruction will be central to this domain, and therefore task-based, strategy-based, form-focused instruction types will be specified in this part of the curriculum, again in tandem with the particular beliefs and convictions held by the curriculum designers. Two important and more general principles belong to this domain: a *metacognitive orientation* (aimed at student autonomy and responsibility) and a *feedback-focused approach.*

The metacognitive orientation has played a central role in Chapters 6, 7, 8, and 9, which deal with the processing perspective of language use. The feedback-focused approach needs some additional elaboration. It is our position that the term "feedback" applies to language learning in two different realizations: *linguistic feedback* and *performance feedback.*

Linguistic feedback relates to input that is in fact a reaction to a learner's production of language (either by repetition, correction, or incorporation/ reformulation). This is the kind of feedback a hearer provides for the speaker when the speech produced was consistent or inconsistent with linguistic norms (positive feedback reinforces what was said while negative feedback tells the speaker that there is some discrepancy that needs to be corrected). Such linguistic feedback play a very important role in language acquisition (Ellis, 1998).

Performance feedback is the *evaluation* a learner receives while using the language. This kind of feedback is how teachers react to students' work in general and how the students themselves evaluate their success in carrying out an activity in the second or foreign language. In most cases, both language and content will be evaluated. Performance feedback can play a significant role in enhancing the learner's motivation to improve.

The *product domain* specifies the actual goals which should be attained by students who successfully complete the course of study (see Figure 10.1). These goals can be specified in terms of integrating types of knowledge and types of processing ability relating to language use and language skill application. An example of such a goal can be the following:

At the end of the course students should be able read and understand authentic text intended for popular reading and related to their personal interests, such as newspaper articles, magazines, brochures, and the like. Students should be able to carry out simple writing activities involving personal communication such as letters to friends, descriptions, notes, and so forth.

The principles in this domain relate to the acquisition of phonology, grammar, and lexis, and the development of proficiency in the four language skills. Perhaps the most important function of the product domain is to provide course or program evaluators with clear definitions of the expected outcomes of a course of study.

With respect to language processing skills, each skill should be addressed separately followed by a series of guidelines for the integration of skills. Such specifications of skill-use is important in the product domain since they can be valuable information for testing and evaluation purposes. The following are some examples of such principles for skill and subskill use:

With respect to the listening skill (see Chapter 6)

- Students should have adequate opportunities to develop useful recognition and interpretation strategies such as distinguishing between new and old information, identifying key words and expressions, guessing from context, predicting and making inferences based on a careful consideration of the various features of the context.

With respect to the reading skill (see Chapter 7)

- *Pre-reading* activities should emphasize top-down strategies such as making predictions from what we know, making hypotheses, deciding on the purpose for reading. Students should be able to use all these when reading for comprehension.

- *While-reading* activities should focus on textual features, hypotheses testing and strategy adaptation, bottom-up strategies in order to verify accurate interpretation, skimming and scanning for specific information, guessing meanings from context. Students should be able to use these when reading for comprehension.

- *Post-reading* activities should enable learners to use the information received from the passage for other personal and enriching purposes. Students should be able to carry out library work, projects, further reading, and other activities that link the content of a reading text with their personal world (useful for alternative evaluation approaches).

These are just a few examples of the kind of principles the product domain of a curriculum could specify. The experts responsible for curriculum development will need to decide the nature and extent of such statements depending on the particular situation for which the curriculum is created.

The *context domain* should list recommendations with respect to the learning situation such as having learning centers, using computers and multimedia, facilitating interaction with the wider social and cultural environment, and so forth. Such recommendations are important for policy planners, who need to concern themselves with human and financial resources in order to accommodate the goals of the curriculum and in order to take advantage of beyond the classroom resources.

CONCLUSION

The discourse-based curriculum, as we have seen so far, is an official document developed by experts on the basis of consideration of social, cultural, and linguistic needs, including research in applied linguistics, with special emphasis on learning and teaching and methodological principles. Such a document defines goals, populations of students and teachers, and contexts in which learning is to take place. It also presents principles related to the four domains discussed in this chapter and summarized in the flowchart in Figure 10.1. Textbook writers, material developers, language testers, teacher trainers, program evaluators, and policy makers will find this information very helpful in their work. The actual realization of the curriculum will be carried out through the development of compatible syllabuses for specific learners and specific courses of study.

As was argued early on in this chapter, the true and most direct customers of the curriculum are the materials and course developers who will attempt to implement the guidelines presented in the curriculum. The process of materials development is the best test to which the curriculum can be put. A number of steps need to be followed by such developers, however:

1. The needs and goals of specific learner populations must be defined according to age level, school grade, professional needs, and so forth.

2. A general syllabus for the specified population needs to be developed and made compatible with the general curriculum.

3. The principles specified in the curriculum need to be translated into:
   a. a detailed mapping of what needs to be taught
   b. a checklist for the evaluation of materials

4. Policy and procedures with respect to evaluation processes need to be specified.

5. Curriculum field testing and plans for revision need to be specified.

While these "planning" processes are being carried out, a language tester or language testing team should also be consulted so that assessment tools can be developed that are fully compatible with the specifications of the general curriculum and the specific syllabus.
A language curriculum is a document that reflects the state of the art of language teaching at a given point in time. In order to be relevant it needs to be updated periodically (every five to ten years) so that it keeps abreast of changes and new approaches to language teaching and to education in general. A language curriculum designed during or after the 1990s for the new millennium can be viewed as a reflection of the postmethod and postcommunicative era, as a document where form and function need to be reconciled with communication needs and social contexts.

DISCUSSION QUESTIONS

1. Take a course syllabus that is handy and discuss it in terms of the four dimensions described in this chapter: content, process, product, and context.

2. Discuss the notions "customers" and "consumers" of a curriculum or syllabus with respect to an educational situation that is familiar to you.

3. Discuss some of Kumaravadivelu's (1994) macrostrategies with a partner and try to translate the ideas into principles that can guide curriculum development:
   - maximize learning opportunities
   - minimize perceptual mismatches
   - facilitate negotiated interaction
   - activate intuitive heuristics (i.e., strategies)
   - foster language awareness
   - contextualize linguistic input
   - integrate language skills
   - promote learner autonomy
   - raise cultural consciousness
   - ensure social relevance

4. Eisenstein (1983), among others, argues that it is important to include language variation as part of content and process in the language curriculum. With a partner, discuss some activities for learners that would illustrate how language variation could be incorporated into a discourse-based curriculum.

SUGGESTED ACTIVITIES

1. Choose an audience of language learners and define their linguistic and social needs for a given second or foreign language. Specify their needs with respect to one of the language skills and draw up a list of relevant principles.
2. Choose a language textbook that you are familiar with and analyze the curriculum principles that are reflected in the textbook in terms of four dimensions: content, process, product, and context.
3. Use the learner audience that you defined in Suggestion 1 and write up a set of principles to ensure an integration of language skills in the suggested curriculum.
4. Interview educators and teachers in your area to find out how much they know about the language curriculum in their school.

Suggestions for Further Reading

Brinton, D., Snow, A., & Wesche, M. (1989). *Content-based second language Instruction.* Boston: Heinle & Heinle.

Burton, J. (1998). Current developments in language curriculum design: An Australian perspective. *Annual Review of Applied Linguistics, 18,* 287–303.

Dubin, F., & Olshtain, E. (1986). *Course design.* Cambridge: Cambridge University Press.

Markee, N. (1997). *Managing curricular innovation.* Cambridge: Cambridge University Press.

Mohan, B. (1986). *Language and content.* Reading, MA: Addison Wesley.

Nunan, D. (1988). *The learner-centered curriculum.* Cambridge: Cambridge University Press.

Olshtain, E. (1989). Changing directions in language curriculum design. *Annual Review of Applied Linguistics, 10,* 135–144.

Yalden, J. (1987). *Principles of course design for language teaching.* Cambridge: Cambridge University Press.

CHAPTER 11

Assessment

by Elana Shohamy (guest author)

> "A weakness of current [oral proficiency assessment] models is that they focus too much on the individual candidate rather than on the candidate in interaction. Given the interactional nature of performance assessment . . . , we should be looking to those in our field who are studying talk in interaction."
>
> (McNamara, 1996:85)

> "No assessment device is good or bad in itself but only in context. Only when we know what we are seeking to discover can we claim that a particular kind of assessment is appropriate or not."
>
> (White, 1995:34)

INTRODUCTION

Just as linguists have lagged behind in describing discourse (in comparison to descriptions of grammar, phonology, or lexicon), so language testers have also been remiss in attending to the assessment of discourse in language learners. We feel that this is a critical deficit since learners' performance in the four skills (listening, reading, speaking, and writing) is largely dependent on their discourse knowledge. Their ability to interpret language and to make themselves understood cannot be assessed directly via tests consisting of multiple-choice grammar items and/or vocabulary items. This chapter is addressed to language teachers who wish to be in a better position to assess the discourse competence of their students.

The chapter begins by reviewing some of the currently most influential communicative competence models as well as the status of discourse in models of communicative competence. The chapter also reviews research relevant to a discourse perspective on language assessment. The second major part of the chapter deals with findings from research that teachers can adapt and apply to the assessment they do in their own classrooms. Also included is a consideration of *alternative assessment* strategies that take performance at the discourse level into account. Finally, the chapter concludes that experts in language assessment will need to work collaboratively with discourse analysts and classroom teachers to design better language testing approaches and instruments.

THEORY OF DISCOURSE AND LANGUAGE TESTING

While specific elicitation tests and tasks have been developed for assessing discourse, there have been a number of debates about the role of discourse in language testing. The rationale for these debates among language testers is that if there can be clear identification of the structure of language, including discourse, it will be possible to design tests to match such descriptions. Yet, it should be noted that the data used in these discussions have come exclusively from tests, whereas the structure of language remains a much broader construct than what is measured on language tests.

The first and most important proposal for describing the structure of language that included a specific focus on discourse was the one developed by Canale and Swain (1980) and Canale (1983). Their framework widened the scope of language testing theory by examining the various components of language within a framework of communicative competence. In this framework they identified three components that interact in communication: (1) linguistic competence, (2) sociolinguistic competence, and (3) strategic competence. Canale (1983) subsequently added a fourth discourse component, which referred specifically to the user's ability to process and produce language at a level beyond the sentence, e.g., ability to participate in conversations and to process and produce written texts of some size.

From a theoretical point of view the main question about Canale and Swain's proposal has been whether the discourse component could be considered an independent component. The relationship between the discourse component and the other components, and the specific role of discourse within this framework, was not entirely clear, nor was it clear how all the components were to be integrated into an overall communicative competence model and how communicative competence would be translated into communicative performance.

Some studies have attempted to validate the Canale and Swain framework. Harley, Cummins, Swain, and Allen (1990) examined whether grammatical, discourse, and sociolinguistic competence could be distinguished empirically. Factor analysis failed to confirm the hypothesized three-trait structure (i.e., grammar, discourse, and sociolinguistic appropriacy) for language proficiency. In other studies, there has been some support for separation of the grammar and discourse components; however, the evidence was not as strong for the separate existence of sociolinguistic competence (Milanovic, 1988; Swain, 1985).[1]

Schachter (1990) in her reaction to the Harley et al. (1990) study claims that the discourse trait was not well defined, and she argues that the *discourse-level knowledge* of text that the researchers assumed seemed to be *micro-sociolinguistic knowledge* rather than discourse knowledge, which would include areas better known as cohesion and coherence. She argued that discourse should be defined more clearly as pragmatic knowledge, since discourse knowledge involves both cultural conventions and appropriate grammatical choices. According to Schachter, the study by Harley et al. tested a very limited concept of pragmatic knowledge. Therefore, it is difficult to determine whether the small number of items chosen to test the discourse trait truly tested what the researchers had assumed. Schachter concludes that whether or not discourse competence constitutes a separate kind of knowledge will come not from tests where researchers attempt empirical validation, but rather from more clearly delineated theoretical models.

A more recent model of language ability that also includes discourse is the one proposed by Bachman (1990) and Bachman and Palmer (1996). In this model, language ability consists of *organizational* and *pragmatic competencies*. Organizational competence consists of *grammatical* and *textual* subcompetencies while pragmatic competence consists of *illocutionary* and *sociolinguistic* competencies. They claim that textual competence is separate from grammatical competence and includes knowledge of the conventions for joining utterances together to form a text, which for them is essentially a unit of language – spoken or written – that consists of two or more utterances or sentences that are structured according to rules of cohesion and rhetorical organization. According to Bachman (1990), the model consists of both the language knowledge and the procedural capacity to implement or execute that knowledge in appropriate acts of communication. An attempt is also made in this model to characterize the process by which various components interact with each other as well as with the context in which language use occurs. However, the model has not been validated to date so that information on whether or not these components are independent is not available, although the model is based on previous empirical work (Bachman and Palmer, 1982), which suggested that textual (i.e., discourse) competence is closer to grammatical competence in contrast to sociolinguistic competence, which is rather independent.

Regarding the role of the discourse component in language testing, there has been no further clarification of the matter in recent discussions among language testers. There seems to have been little incorporation of theory and research from discourse analysis to the development of theoretical models. Furthermore, the fact that most of the testing models have not been examined empirically suggests they are hypotheses in need of empirical support rather than "models" since relatively little is known about the role of discourse within the other components that make up language knowledge in testing contexts. Thus, at present, the questions about the relationship between the discourse component and the other components making up the structure of language ability have not been resolved.

RESEARCH ON DISCOURSE AND LANGUAGE TESTING

This section will report on the effects of discourse considerations on research in language testing. As will become obvious, there have been some direct applications of the research results to discourse testing practices.

There have been extensive studies in language testing where the focus has been on discourse. Studies that have focused on quantitative analyses have examined mainly the effect of different discourse elements on test takers' scores. The main question being asked is the extent to which different features identified as being in the domain of discourse analysis affect test takers' scores on language tests. Thus, the issue is not the validity of the discourse elements within communicative language competence, but rather the extent to which these features manifest themselves in testing situations and their effect on test takers' scores. A number of studies investigate how elements such as subject matter or discourse type and style manifest themselves in language tests and tasks, with special attention given to the effect of these features on the scores that test takers obtain on language tests. The other direction in research has been the examination, using a variety of *qualitative procedures*, of the type of discourse that is obtained on oral proficiency tests and whether that elicited language resembles the type of language occurring in nontesting situations. A selective sampling of relevant studies follows.

THE EFFECT OF TEST FEATURES ON TEST TAKERS' SCORES

READING COMPREHENSION TESTS

Numerous language testing studies have examined how specific discourse features such as *discourse topics/content, discourse domains,* and *discourse types/styles* manifest themselves in testing situations. We will first look at studies concerned with the role of subject matter content on reading comprehension test takers' scores. (Recall that reading comprehension was discussed in detail in Chapter 7).

EFFECT OF SUBJECT MATTER OR CONTENT

The examination of the effect of subject matter on reading test takers' scores has yielded largely controversial results. Douglas and Selinker (1985; 1990) in an investigation of the effect of subject matter on test takers' scores on reading tests demonstrated how performance can vary when different topics are covered (e.g., professional specialization versus everyday subjects). They found that familiarity with the content of what the text communicates affects the respective roles of language proficiency and cognition. As a result, the nature and fluency of communication are also affected. They concluded that generalizing language ability from one type of subject matter or content to another on language tests may not be justified.

Hock (1990) showed that both language proficiency and prior knowledge predicted test takers' scores on a cloze test (i.e., a reading passage where every nth word is deleted and the test taker fills in the missing words); however, even in cases favoring prior knowledge, language proficiency appeared to be a more important predictor of scores.

In the IELTS test (International English Language Testing System), texts are selected to be relevant to the various academic specializations of the test takers. Yet, Clapham (1994) examined the effect of background knowledge in relation to test performance in reading for academic purposes on the IELTS test with a large sample (n=842) and found no such effect. She therefore recommends that EAP proficiency tests should NOT have subject matter-specific reading modules. The reading passages should come from authentic texts in different academic fields, but should be equally comprehensible to students in all subject areas.

EFFECT OF TITLES

With regard to the effect of the title of a passage on reading comprehension, Brown (1989) investigated tasks calling on one test taker to explain in writing to another test taker the content of a short video. When the test taker writing the explanation is given a title for the video, both the writer's explanation and the reader's understanding are better.

EFFECT OF CLEAR RHETORICAL STRUCTURE

Jonz (1989) showed that subjects did better on a cloze test that had a clear rhetorical structure than on one that did not, and Lee and Riley (1990) demonstrated that students did better on a free recall task when there was a clear rhetorical structure to the information they were asked to recall.

EFFECT OF MISSING COHESIVE TIES

Research on *discourse processing* is reported by Jonz (1987, 1989, 1991), who experimented with a *discourse-type cloze test* and found that scores on a *cohesion-based test* show that nonnatives are far less capable of coping with the loss of redundant cohesive information than are native speakers. When cohesive ties are available, nonnatives employ them in comprehension to a greater extent than native speakers do. On cloze tests, nonnative speakers appear to be far more reliant on text in comprehension processes than are natives. Such a study also provides support for the notion that cohesion-based cloze tests can be used to assess text processing skills.

EFFECT OF DIFFERENT QUESTION TYPES AND TEST TYPES

Shohamy (1984) and Gordon (1987) examined the processing of texts in second language reading comprehension tests using different question types – *multiple-choice* in the L1 and L2, *open-ended* questions in the L1 or L2 – and found significant differences in the scores that subjects received on the tests. It was shown that strategies that test takers utilize in processing discourse are heavily dependent on the discourse type of the question. Specifically, the multiple-choice format – which consists of a statement plus a number of additional statements (i.e., the alternatives) – represents a special text type that readers processed differently from other types of texts.

In a related study that examined discourse processing on reading comprehension tests, Fillmore (1981) showed that the discourse genre appearing in reading comprehension tests represents a genre that is used only on standardized tests, and that the procedures for processing such discourse differs from those which learners normally use in nontesting reading situations. For example, on reading comprehension tests readers refer to the test questions, which guide them to focus on specific information in the text, thereby creating different discourse processing strategies in the reader.

Summing up all of these problems with reading comprehension tests, Spolsky (1994) points to the complexity in measuring text comprehension on tests, given all the possible sources of miscomprehension present in different discourse types and genres. The specific potential sources of discourse-level miscomprehension that Spolsky identifies are (1) the texts used for the test, (2) the test questions, (3) the answers produced in response to the test questions, and (4) the interpretation of the answers produced and the assignment of scores.

Another significant problem with the traditional multiple-choice reading comprehension test has been discussed by Perkins (1998:213), who says, "research has shown that readers bring different networks of knowledge structures to the reading task and very well may build different propositional networks for texts. This finding has caused researchers to abandon the one-text, one-meaning interpretation of a text . . . ; such a position spells doom for our favorite question: 'What is the main idea of the essay/paragraph/text?'" The solution to the problem, according to Perkins, is to allow for open-ended essay responses to questions dealing with reading comprehension and to have learners keep journals on their readings, which can be assessed in much the same way that portfolios are now used to assess writing skills. (See Chapter 8 as well as the last section of this chapter for a discussion of portfolios in writing assessment.)

ORAL PROFICIENCY TESTS (SPEAKING AND LISTENING COMPREHENSION)

With regard to *discourse styles*, Shohamy (1983) found significant differences in the scores on oral tests that represented different discourse styles and genres (e.g., an interview versus a reporting task). In another study, Shohamy, Reves, and Bejarano (1986) found that a test taker's performance on the *interview*, which represents a specific oral discourse style, could not be used to make a valid prediction of test taker performance on other oral discourse styles such as *discussions* and *oral reports,* or of a variety of *speech acts*, as exemplified in *role-play* situations. Only moderate correlations were obtained between scores of test takers who were tested on a variety of different discourse types and genres. It therefore seems necessary to test oral proficiency more comprehensively by including a number of different oral discourse types in the assessment.

Shohamy and Inbar (1991) investigated the effect of different genres along the oral-literate continuum (Ong 1982) on test takers' scores on a listening comprehension test, controlling for topic across genres. In this case the test takers were Hebrew-speaking high school students in Israel. The three types of discourse selected for the research project were an interview, a lecturette (i.e., a mini-lecture), and a news broadcast – each varying in their degree of oral versus literate elements. The results revealed significant differences among test takers' scores for each of the discourse types, despite the fact that the content across the three genres was identical. The interview resulted in the highest listening comprehension scores, followed by the lecturette, with the news broadcast resulting in the lowest scores.

DISCOURSE PRODUCTION TESTS: TRANSFER OF DISCOURSE COMPETENCE FROM L1 TO L2

Some studies have examined the transfer of discourse competence and features from first language (L1) to second language (L2) tests. Vignola and Wesche (1991) looked at the transfer of discourse organizational features in writing from L1 to L2 and found that organizational structure did transfer. A similar finding was obtained by Cumming (1990).

Similarly, Harley et al. (1990) report that in their validation study on the discourse tasks in their instrument, unlike in the other parts of the test, the coherence scores of the immersion students were close or equivalent to those of the native speakers, and there were relatively few significant between-group differences. The strong performance of second language learners in the area of discourse coherence can be explained via transfer of the proficiency they have in this area in their first language.

The use of cohesion markers in scoring language samples was examined by Anderson (1989), who investigated the usefulness of cohesion frequency analysis in differentiating proficiency in the oral and written production of learners of English as a second language. The data from written compositions and oral stories were analyzed via holistic evaluation (i.e., a single score reflecting overall quality), type of cohesion, and frequency counts. The results indicated that the frequency with which cohesion was used related inconsistently to the holistic evaluation results. A similar conclusion was reached by Lindsay (1984), who found, however, that the linguistic accuracy and appropriacy of cohesive markers – rather than simply the number of cohesive ties used – needed to be considered when assessing writing samples. Good writers did not necessarily use more cohesive ties; however, they did tend to use them correctly and appropriately whereas poor writers did not.

Collectively, this research on language processing and language tests suggests that top-down discourse features of test texts and tasks (e.g., coherence, rhetorical structure, titles, text types) as well as certain bottom-up discourse features (e.g., cohesion, test question types) interact with the learner's language proficiency to affect test scores. Both the discourse (texts and tasks) of language tests and the discourse that these tests elicit from test takers must be better understood for language assessment to make progress in measuring discourse competence.

A QUALITATIVE EXAMINATION OF THE LANGUAGE ELICITED ON ORAL PROFICIENCY TESTS

With the growing interest in conversation analysis, a number of recent studies have examined the type of discourse elicited and produced on different types of language tests, specifically on oral proficiency tests with an interview format. These studies have analyzed the type of oral discourse elicited, the tester and test taker's interactional styles, and the context in which the discourse and the topics are evaluated, utilizing a variety of qualitative and quantitative procedures. This research brings together a number of subfields such as conversation analysis, discourse analysis, cross-cultural pragmatics, and language-variation studies. Such an *interdisciplinary approach* can provide a better understanding of the language elicited during oral interaction tests; it also has practical implications for designing more effective means of assessment. The main advantage of these studies is that they examine the type of discourse that is, in fact, produced on tests and compares it to what the expectations of text designers are, thus contributing to (or calling into question) the validity of the tests.

USE OF HUMANS VERSUS MACHINES TO ELICIT ORAL SAMPLES

Shohamy (1994) researched various aspects of *direct* (human to human) versus *semidirect* (human to machine) tests using both qualitative and quantitative procedures. The direct test was the Oral Proficiency Interview (OPI); the semidirect test (SOPI) was a test developed by the Center for Applied Linguistics (Stansfield and Kenyon, 1988; Shohamy and Stansfield, 1991). In the SOPI a test taker responds in the L2 to an oral stimulus heard on a tape in the L1. The tasks include giving directions, describing, narrating, discussing topics, and simulating speech acts. In a number of concurrent validation studies, which correlated the scores obtained from tests takers who took both tests, the correlations were very high. Yet qualitative analyses of the discourse obtained from the two tests revealed that different speech genres emerged from the two types of tests and different discourse strategies and features were utilized by the test takers despite the high correlations obtained between the overall scores on the two tests. For example, there was more paraphrasing and more error correction on the taped test and more switches to the L1 on the direct test. A discourse analysis of the data elicited by the two tests revealed that they differed in terms of the communicative properties they exhibited, i.e., they differed in terms of discourse strategies, prosodic paralinguistic features, speech functions, and discourse markers. The main contribution of this study in terms of discourse is that it shows that qualitative discourse analysis is needed in order to examine the validity of the tests since quantitative-correlational analysis tends to block out many discourse-level features. Thus while quantitative analysis may be necessary, it is certainly not sufficient.

Shohamy, Donitze-Schmidt, and Waizer (1993) examined the type of discourse obtained from five different elicitation procedures using identical tasks for all procedures. Some of the procedures required interactions with humans, others with different types of machines (telephone, video recorder, and audio recorder). Results of the analyses using a coding scheme showed that the discourse obtained from the different procedures, despite using identical tasks, was different in a number of ways. The language obtained from the video-recorded and audio-recorded procedures was more direct and did not involve much use of pragmatic devices; the language elicited from the test takers interacting directly with testers (i.e., face-to-face or on the phone) was more elaborated and indirect and involved a large number of pragmatic and social devices. The discourse that was most elaborated and also included the highest number of pragmatic devices was that obtained from the telephone task.[2]

CONVERSATION ANALYSIS OF ORAL INTERVIEWS

Van Lier (1989), called for examination of the type of discourse features produced on oral tests, especially on the oral interview, by considering the criterion of conversational "naturalness" in the oral interview. In particular he examined the extent to which the interview resembles conversation in terms of degree of planning, predictability of sequence of outcomes, equal distribution of rights and duties to talk, and other conversational principles. He focused on issues of interview turn-taking, symmetry of topic nomination and maintenance, and characteristics of the interviewing process that thwart the purpose of the interview as a test that simulates communication, and which may be responsible for pragmatic failure during oral testing interactions.

Lazaraton (1991) and Young and Milanovic (1992) examined the *discourse features* and *rhetorical styles* exemplified on oral interview tests. Lazaraton (1994) conducted a number of qualitative studies on various aspects of the Cambridge Assessment of Spoken English (CASE). In one study she monitored the conduct of the examiners in the CASE test. She described the language used by native speakers in communicative situations, the ways that native speakers accommodate to various situations, and the ways they accommodate to their less than proficient interlocutors. She focused on the role that questions play in this accommodation process, relating to the interactional and pragmatic features, focusing specifically on native-speaker question behaviors in the language proficiency interview. She showed that interviewers routinely modify their question prompts in response to some perceived trouble from the nonnative interlocutors. Using conversation analysis, she describes a variety of data samples and shows that the question modifications differed in a variety of testing situations as well as in ordinary conversations. She suggests that the systematic and recurrent patterns of question design that emerge are best accounted for by approaching them from an interactional perspective such as that employed in conversation analysis.

Examination of differences in conversational styles between two groups of test takers at different oral proficiency levels was conducted by Young (1995). In his study, which compared the conversational styles of intermediate and advanced learners of ESL on oral proficiency interviews, the interviewers did not vary in their interviewing style with the two groups of learners. Young found differences in the amount of talk and rate of speaking (advanced learners talked more and faster than intermediate learners). He also found differences in the extent of context dependence (advanced learners elaborated more in answers to questions), and in the ability to construct and sustain narratives (advanced learners were able to do so; intermediate learners could not). There were no differences between the two groups in the frequency of initiation of new topics, nor in the reaction to topics introduced by the interviewers. This lack of difference in Young's data is contrary to the findings of other studies and contradicts the claim that there are proficiency-related differences in topic initiation and reaction to topics on language proficiency interviews.

Variations in questions posed by interviewers at key junctures in the interview process was examined by Ross (1994). By analyzing the discourse of full length oral proficiency interviews, he found that perceptions of oral proficiency are reflected in the extent of accommodation in interviewer questioning, i.e., the extent of accommodation provides a strong indicator in determining the test taker's oral proficiency. He also noticed that, at the upper end of the proficiency continuum, where accommodation diminishes, issues of register, style, and rhetorical skill become more important. At the lower end of the continuum, where the majority of second language learners are located, the degree of interviewer accommodation can provide a useful metric for assessment.

ANALYZING ORAL INTERVIEWS AS PROCEDURES OR SCRIPTS

In another study, Ross (1994) analyzed twelve Foreign Service Institute (FSI) interviews in order to examine systematic interviewer procedures or scripts for conducting the interview. Results suggest that the interviews are conducted according to a procedural script that provides an underlying structural schema for the interviewer and that formulaic speech, which was discussed in Chapter 5, plays a crucial role in helping the interviewer frame new topics in major portions of the interview. A further finding was that interviewers may resort to time-sharing procedures in order to dedicate some of their limited attentional resources to the task of monitoring and evaluating the interviewee's speech – i.e., language interviews are not subject to the same recipient-design constraints that are characteristic of ordinary conversations. Ross also concluded that the oral interview is co-constructed discourse, in that both the test taker and interviewer contribute to the sketching of the proficiency picture, which has been traditionally viewed as the product of only the test taker's effort and ability. Also, in terms of discourse, if there are insufficient instances of accommodation owing to insufficient interviewer practice in providing effective repairs for interactional troubles, or if the interviewer has difficulty in crafting appropriately framed questions in probes, the performance of the test takers could be adversely affected.

CONCLUSIONS FROM QUALITATIVE RESEARCH

Virtually all of these studies conclude that the language interview is an interactive practice. According to He and Young (1998:5–6), "Interactive practices are co-constructed by participants, each of whom contributes linguistic and pragmatic resources to the practice. Participants bring the following resources, among others, to a given practice: a knowledge of rhetorical scripts, a knowledge of certain lexis and syntactic patterns specific to the practice, a knowledge of how turns are managed, a knowledge of topical organization, and a knowledge of the means for signaling boundaries between practices and transitions within the practice itself." Here in fact we have an agenda laid out for ongoing research on the oral interview procedure, which begins to be satisfied by some of the studies included in Young and He (1998). The extent to which test takers share in the knowledge resources of the testers, the more likely they are to be successful performers on the tests.

CRITERIA FOR DETERMINING THE QUALITY OF THE LANGUAGE ELICITED

Another important question that relates to the discourse elicited by a test is the issue of what scorers should consider as the "appropriate criteria" for determining the quality of the elicited discourse. Among the major points of discussion in this area over the past few years have been (1) the selection of the *"appropriate" target discourse*, (2) *native* versus *nonnative* criteria, and (3) the notion of an *appropriate discourse community*. With the growing recognition of language variation in discourse types and discourse communities (see Eisenstein, 1983), there is little agreement nowadays as to what should be considered "correct" or "appropriate" discourse. Traditionally native speaker proficiency was accepted as the "correct" or appropriate criterion, which was operationalized as rating scales that defined native proficiency. However, current debates question whether the native speaker should be considered as a criterion for appropriate language use given that there are many variations in discourse even among native speakers representing different varieties and dialects. Since English is the world's current lingua franca, this makes it more difficult to determine what "correct" English is. It is therefore debatable whether the native speaker can be used as the criterion for top-level performance.

A series of studies conducted by Hamilton, Lopes, McNamara, and Sheridan (1993) found great variability in the performance of native speakers on the IELTS test. Specifically, they found that performance by native speakers was related to educational level and work experience, leading the researchers to conclude that the native speaker should not be considered as the criterion for appropriacy. Similarly, a study by Marisi (1994) found that the Oral Interview Proficiency test (OPI) administered in French discriminated against French Canadian speakers and did not rate them as native speakers. Thus, the test is not sensitive to the issue of regional variation. The recommendation is that there should be a larger range of acceptable levels of appropriate language and that these should include regional differences.

This relates directly to the issue of discourse communities (Baynham, 1995), given that different communities use different types of discourse. Thus the issue of determining the quality and level of appropriate discourse must be seriously considered.

WHAT RESEARCH CAN TELL TESTERS AND TEACHERS

A number of conclusions on the assessment of discourse can be reached based on the above review of research.

I. THE NEED TO ELICIT A VARIETY OF DISCOURSE TYPES

First, given the variety of discourse types, domains, and genres, and given the findings that these differences tend to affect test takers' scores, it is essential to include a variety of discourse types on tests since it is not possible to draw the same conclusions about language proficiency across discourse types. This relates to processing in listening or reading tasks as well as to production in writing and speaking tasks since it is not possible to generalize from performance in one discourse type or modality to another. This suggests that if a test taker does well on one test type, it cannot be deduced that s/he will do equally well on another. There is a need, therefore, to include as many different discourse types as possible in order to arrive at a valid assessment of an individual test taker. This is parallel to the position taken in this book, which is that for comprehension purposes learners should be exposed to a variety of discourse types and genres – including the language variation inherent in these genres – and that learners should also be encouraged to produce a variety of text types and genres.

2. THE NEED TO USE A VARIETY OF DISCOURSE FEATURES
AND CRITERIA IN EVALUATION

Second, in evaluating elicited discourse, it is essential to include specific features of the language sample, either through a rating scale or through different types of coding schemes. The decision as to which elements to include in the rating scales or coding systems depends on the purpose of the assessment and on the specific elements that a test is designed to assess. Testers thus need to create their own scales based on features and criteria that they consider to be important and that reflect specific teaching and testing goals. Chun (1988a, b), for example, claims that intonation is a powerful tool for negotiating meaning, managing interaction, and achieving discourse coherence. Thus intonation needs to be assessed, and for oral discourse rating, scales should be constructed that address different degrees of intonation control. (The importance of intonation was discussed in Chapter 3.) Also, features of connected discourse that have been identified by discourse analysts need to be applied to the evaluation of real proficiency in a second language. In the area of semantics, a speaker's control of the cause-result relationship involves, among other things, the ability to produce the different grammatical and lexical manifestations of this relationship. Other testable discourse features may be the ability to make inferences while listening to a lecture or the ability to place stress on the proper elements according to the preceding context when speaking. Examples of cohesive devices that can be evaluated in discourse include pronominalization and the classification of lexical items within a hierarchy. Such competencies should be evaluated using a variety of procedures such as having test takers respond to comprehension questions or give paraphrases in context.

Language testing textbooks (e.g., Cohen, 1995; Alderson, Clapham, and Wall, 1994) provide guidance on how rating scales can be developed. Language testers could collaborate with teachers in developing rating scales or coding sheets that address a variety of discourse features. One practical procedure is to elicit appropriate samples and then group them into a number of levels according to language proficiency. Based on the specific discourse features that are being evaluated, one level represents texts that include "good" control of discourse features, another level represents "average" control, and the third level "weak" control. Then a team of testers or teachers can try to determine the reasons why certain samples were included in each of the levels; these reasons will provide a basis for constructing explicit rating scales. Special consideration should also be given to a variety of social contextual criteria that may be relevant such as native or advanced nonnative as the target expectation, as well as the discourse communities and the region the language assessment is tapping (e.g., men/women; young/old; native/immigrants; British/North American, and so forth).

3. DEVELOPING ALTERNATIVE AND COMPLEMENTARY EVALUATION PROCEDURES

Most language tests follow traditional patterns of data collection, usually using the type of tests that are prepared by large testing corporations. Thus, even many classroom teachers who can easily use a variety of different data collection procedures have adopted more or less the types of tests that are used by external testers, usually multiple choice. However, we recommend that teachers use different types of elicitation techniques, rather than simply using standard test formats, in order to better assess discourse. The wide range of alternative assessment procedures available implies that any use of language, whether produced on a test, in a portfolio, or in natural use in the classroom, provides a legitimate and valid language sample. It allows for the elicitation of discourse in a more natural way, free of testing effect.

Even multiple-choice reading comprehension tests can be made more authentic if the test designer starts by collecting complete answers to open-ended test questions from appropriate test takers. The answers thus obtained can help the test designer formulate the correct answers and the distractors for the multiple-choice questions.

However, the emphasis should be on other procedures and sources for sampling language proficiency such as self assessment, observations, peer assessments, use of narratives, portfolios, interviews, dialog journals, diaries, "think aloud" protocols, checklists, exhibits, dramatic performances, oral debates, and performance on a variety of role-play tasks, done with human beings or with machines (e.g., video, audio, telephones). These are often referred to as alternative or complementary assessment.

The data collection procedures developed by Olshtain and Blum-Kulka (1985) for both ethnographic and quantitative data collection on speech-act behavior and sociocultural preferences, can also serve as testing procedures aimed at assessing discourse competence. The authors suggest that both researchers and testers work with a variety of instruments that represent varying degrees of authenticity in terms of an actual communicative exchange between speakers. Thus, the most authentic data collection or performance evaluation can be done when spontaneous speech is recorded ethnographically. When such natural data are unavailable, the next best thing is a simulation or role-play activity of a potentially natural encounter.

The situational and the contextual clues need to be provided in detail whether one is working with a research consultant or a test taker in order to enable them to perform as naturally as possible. Both the testing and the data collection situation require some control of the variables involved in speech behavior such as features relating to the participants (power, age, social distance, status) or features relating to the event (an offense that deserves an apology, a social gathering that presents certain expected verbal behavior such as a birthday party, and so on). Such features must be provided to the research consultant or the test taker. When adequate control of variables is achieved, Olshtain and Blum-Kulka (1985) claim that a written discourse completion task can function quite effectively in eliciting or testing appropriate speech act behavior, as the following example demonstrates:

At the University
Ann and Judith are friends attending the same class. Ann missed
a class the day before and would like to borrow Judith's notes.

Ann: _____

Judith: Sure, let me have them back before class next week.

In this example it is obvious that Ann made a request to get the lecture notes from Judith. Both the research consultant and the test taker have a chance to demonstrate what they think Ann could have said. Similarly, judgement tests can be used to evaluate the range of acceptability of responses from either native speakers who act as research consultants on their language or of learners who have a chance to exhibit the degree to which their second language ability resembles the native speakers' norm. Thus, for the example cited, the respondent might be shown a number of possible requests and be asked to choose the best or to rate the level of acceptability for each possibility:

"Can I borrow your notes from yesterday, please?"

"I missed yesterday's class. Give me your notes, okay?"

"Do you think I could borrow your notes?"

By using a variety of assessment instruments, it is possible to create an authenticity continuum that makes the testing of discourse more accessible.

FEATURES OF NEW ASSESSMENT TYPES

There are certain characteristics of the new assessment types suggested here that we need to address briefly for these features can assess a larger domain of language. First, teachers and students are more involved in developing and designing the assessment procedures. Also, the assessment instruments are tailor-made according to the students' or the program's needs. Assessment conferences are held where the learner obtains feedback that leads to improvement through individual diagnostic profiles that clearly indicate the learner's strengths and weaknesses. There should be ongoing formative assessment, with regular conferences where the teacher, the student, and often a parent and other relevant individuals are present.

The teacher or tester prepares a careful description of and recommendations regarding learner performance that then leads to some sort of feedback and judgement. The interpretation of the results is fully contextualized with a focus on understanding the whole in light of the parts. A variety of assessment instruments are used, and these provide information about different aspects of language knowledge from various perspectives and contexts. Putting all the information together provides the best insight into the person's language proficiency. In these assessment conferences a dialog among the participants is held where each participant brings a different perspective, and together they arrive at important insights.

ILLUSTRATION OF AN ALTERNATIVE ASSESSMENT BATTERY

In order to better assess various aspects of the acquisition of Hebrew as a second language by immigrant children, a team of language testers in Israel developed a battery of assessment instruments. The main purpose of the battery was to diagnose language problems so that recommendations could be made regarding appropriate strategies for subsequent teaching and learning of Hebrew by these children. The rationale for using alternative procedures in this context was that the language proficiency of immigrant children manifests itself in different contexts, in and out of the classroom, in a dynamic way, and that in order to arrive at meaningful insights into language proficiency a variety of these contexts need to be sampled. Thus, multiple instruments that could tap different aspects of the learners' language were used, each instrument contributing unique and new information with regard to understanding and gaining deeper insight into the language knowledge of these learners. Through the use of multiple instruments a comprehensive and ongoing picture of achievement and proficiency of each immigrant child could be obtained.

The assessment model developed based on the above principles included instruments to assess the following domains of language:

a. *basic threshold language* (mastering elementary features
    of the target language)

b. *academic language* (the language needed for each school subject)

c. *life* (the language needed for settings outside school)

d. *learning aids* (ability to use learning resources that are heavily
    language dependent such as the dictionary, the library, and so forth)

These four target domains for language use were arrived at through discussions with educational experts such as subject-matter teachers, second language teachers, and curriculum planners.

These domains were then converted into tables of specifications for each of the four age levels assessed (elementary low, grades 2–4; elementary high, grades 5–6; middle school, grades 7–9; and senior high, grades 10–12).

Four procedures were selected for the assessment of the above language domains: (1) a *test* that included multiple-choice items, open-ended items, and completion items, all of which were based on authentic texts with pictures; (2) a *self-assessment* procedure; (3) an *observation* instrument used by two teachers (one a humanities teacher, one a science teacher); and (4) a *portfolio* for which students selected additional language samples representing their reading and writing activities from a set list.

Once all the information had been assembled, it was rated via a number of scales, including one for discourse. Then an assessment conference was held in which the Hebrew as a second language teacher, the homeroom teacher, and often a parent, met with the student to discuss and interpret the results of the four instruments. Such conferences led to conclusions, recommendations, and the development of appropriate pedagogical strategies for the learner concerned. The use of multiple procedures enabled the assessors to capture different aspects and domains of language knowledge as exemplified in different situations in and out of the classroom since the different instruments were capable of "seeing" different things.

CONCLUSION

I have argued elsewhere (Shohamy, 1991; 1998) that language testers can no longer overlook discourse since it is an integral part of communicative competence. There is a pressing need for language testers to develop a variety of procedures to elicit and assess discourse skills. The best solution is probably a team approach, with discourse analysts providing the what and language testers providing the how. By working together in consultation with language teachers and language learners, they will be able to develop assessment procedures and tests that will evaluate the language of the learner more comprehensively.

QUESTIONS FOR DISCUSSION

1. How might you assess discourse informally without using formal assessment procedures?

2. What tasks would you include in a portfolio designed to demonstrate discourse competence? How would you rate the portfolio?

3. Why is it important to assess performance in discourse (in addition to performance in grammar and vocabulary – and, for oral skills, pronunciation)?

SUGGESTED ACTIVITIES

1. Select four objectives (one each for writing, speaking, listening, and reading) that you expect your students to master, each involving some aspect of discourse. Select specific genres for each (e.g., a story, a speech). Design tasks which will assess these objectives in each of the skills. Decide on the evaluation criteria, all of which should be related to discourse quality.

2. Use authentic ads for jobs from your local newspaper (or any target-language newspaper) and develop reading and writing tasks for students (e.g., Which of the jobs listed are you best/least qualified for and why?).

3. Design a self-assessment instrument that assesses discourse (or some aspects of discourse). Make sure it addresses all four language skills.

4. Design a rating scale to assess discourse that includes five levels, from no discourse competence to nativelike discourse competence.

Suggestions for Further Reading

Alderson, C., Clapham, C., & Wall, D. (1995). *Language test construction and evaluation.* Cambridge: Cambridge University Press.

Bachman, L., & Cohen, A. (Eds.). (1998). *Interfaces between second language acquisition and language testing research.* Cambridge: Cambridge University Press.

Cohen, A. D. (1994). *Assessing language ability in the classroom.* Boston: Heinle & Heinle.

McNamara, T. F. (1996). *Measuring second language performance.* London: Longman.

Young, R., & He, A. W. (Eds.). (1998). *Talking and testing: Discourse approaches to the assessment of oral proficiency.* Amsterdam: John Benjamins.

Endnotes

[1] There is evidence suggesting that the degree of independence of sociolinguistic competence from grammatical competence is language-specific. Koo's (1995) research indicates that grammatical and sociolinguistic competence are highly interrelated and virtually inseparable in a language like Korean, which encodes honorifics grammatically, whereas the two competencies may be much more independent in a language like English, which has few socially conditioned grammatical forms. Koo's study did not specifically address the status of the discourse component.

2 In a related study currently in progress, Connor-Linton and Shohamy are applying six of Biber's (1988) dimensions of language variation for identifying registers in spoken and written English – i.e., (1) informal versus involved production; (2) narrative versus non-narrative; (3) explicit reference versus situation dependent reference; (4) objective expression versus persuasion; (5) abstract versus nonabstract information; (6) linear information versus elaboration. These dimensions are being used to analyze the spoken texts collected by Shohamy, Donitze-Schmidt, and Waizer (1993) by coding the linguistic characteristics of the spoken samples to determine whether different elicitation procedures have elicited different registers and thus different types of discourse.

CHAPTER 12

Discourse Training for Teachers and Learners

"Discourse analytic techniques can help language learners become conscious of the processes that operate to produce the language that they hear and use. At the "macro" level, for example, the examination of an authentic "thanking" sequence by native speakers may help learners begin to see how, in English, this particular speech act is structured. At a finer "micro" level, learners may analyze the strategies which speakers use to maintain discourse (e.g., stalling mechanisms and repair phenomena). Or they may notice that different rules of grammar seem to be operating in spoken English than in written English . . . students can [also] use such techniques to evaluate their own language performance."

(Riggenbach, 1991:153–4)

"Teachers have their own constructs about teaching which influence their reaction to theoretical perspectives on learning and models of practice. . . . How teachers respond to formal theory and the extent to which it leads practice in large part depends on their constructs."

(Schoonmaker and Ryan, 1996:146)

INTRODUCTION

The opening quote from Riggenbach, which we very much support, must apply to language teachers before it can apply to their students. If teachers are not properly acquainted with a variety of approaches to discourse analysis, they will not be able to implement the pedagogical approach we propose. As Schoonmaker and Ryan's quote further emphasizes, the teacher's own constructs about teaching can be very important in influencing their instructional work. Can we help teachers develop constructs that are based on a discourse approach to learning and teaching? In this final chapter we focus on what language teachers and language learners should know about discourse analysis in order to take advantage of the teaching and learning approach suggested in this volume.

First we look at teachers and review what they need to know about discourse before we examine three additional areas of discourse analysis that apply to teaching: (1) teacher feedback and correction strategies, (2) the self-examination by teachers of their own classroom discourse, and (3) reflective teaching as a process that ideally should involve discourse analysis. Then we move on to demonstrate, with three sample language units and a discussion of learner strategies, the type of discourse analytic techniques that language students can profit from, provided their teachers have grounding in discourse analysis and know how to approach language instruction through discourse.

TEACHER AWARENESS

In order for language teachers to implement the type of classroom teaching, syllabus design, and assessment procedures proposed in this text, they need to become familiar with the basic notions underlying discourse analysis and gain some experience with various approaches to discourse and with doing different types of discourse analysis for different purposes. This is a natural extension of the language training that well-prepared language teachers now receive in phonetics for teaching pronunciation and in lexico-grammar for teaching a variety of skills. Both phonetics and lexico-grammar must interact with the discourse level for full realization and adequate description. Features of the sound system such as prominence and intonation make little sense without appealing to language at the level of discourse (see Chapter 3). Likewise, the lexico-grammar needed for speaking or writing is inextricably linked with discourse if one wishes to fully understand the semantic and pragmatic functions that are expressed in discourse via lexico-grammatical resources (see Chapters 4 and 5).

Fortunately, there are now a number of texts that introduce language teachers to discourse. These range from basic introductions (Kramsch, 1981; Cook, 1989; Nunan, 1993; Paltridge, 2000) to more sophisticated treatments (Hatch, 1992; McCarthy, 1991; McCarthy and Carter, 1994; Riggenbach, 1999). There are also some introductions to discourse analysis that are not directed exclusively toward language teachers, but which can be usefully adapted to serve the needs of language teachers (Brown and Yule, 1983; Stubbs, 1983; Schiffrin, 1994).

Language teachers need to be aware of how oral discourse, especially conversation, is structured and how it differs from written discourse. They need to be aware of the various genres and text types that occur in speech and writing. They need to be aware of both the macro or top-down features that make discourse genres cohere (Enkvist, 1987) and the micro or bottom-up elements that make any piece of discourse cohesive (Halliday and Hasan, 1976). They need to understand that there are connections between the topics of discourse, the formats of texts, the sociocultural context in which texts occur, and the linguistic forms through which given pieces of discourse are realized. They need to understand that all discourse is interactive – but that dialogic oral discourse is more inter-active than monologic oral discourse, which in turn is generally more interactive than written discourse. Finally, teachers need to realize that the roles of all the participants in any act of spoken or written communication are crucial. Chapters 1 and 2 of this book presented the reader with the most fundamental issues in discourse analysis and with the study of pragmatics as related to human communication, background that can help teachers incorporate relevant concepts into their teaching perspectives.

Language teachers with an understanding of discourse analysis and pragmatics are in a position to apply this knowledge to their teaching of spoken and written language and to the teaching of the language elements needed for the realization of communication through speech or writing: pronunciation/orthography, grammar, and vocabulary. Teacher knowledge of discourse applies critically to classroom presentation and practice activities, as we have demonstrated in Chapters 3 through 9. It also applies in important ways to curriculum design, materials development, and language assessment as demonstrated in Chapters 10 and 11.

DISCOURSE-SENSITIVE FEEDBACK AND CORRECTION

There are many occasions when a language teacher might ask learners to make judgments about grammaticality, lexical choice, or overall organization of a piece of discourse. This might be particularly important in form-focused instruction within a communicative perspective. Chaudron's research (1983) suggests that learners gain skill in doing such tasks as they become more proficient users of the target language. Beginners are rather weak at making such judgments, but given proper grounding, they can become quite good when they reach the intermediate or advanced level. Learning how to recognize, locate, and describe an error can begin with the teacher posing problems based on common but local student errors. For example:

> You say, "I enjoy to go to the movies," and I say,
>
> "I enjoy going to the movies." What's the difference?

The critical segments – in this case sentences – can be written on the board if necessary to raise learner awareness and stimulate self-correction.

The shorter the segment, the easier – and more artificial – it is for learners to detect and correct errors. Thus it is important that error detection and correction exercises involve more challenging and realistic discourse-level activities as soon as possible so that learners can begin to detect and correct errors at the discourse level as well as in shorter, more controlled segments. For example, learners working in pairs or small groups can be asked to judge each clause in a connected text produced by a high intermediate EFL learner as grammatical or ungrammatical. If they are sufficiently advanced, they should also be asked to correct any errors they detect.

	Grammatical	Ungrammatical	Correction
1. I have experience of financial management procedures.			
2. I took two accounting classes as part of my diploma in data processing.			
3. In my present position I develop workload trend that serve as baseline for the company's budget.			
4. In my past position I developed a new accounting system to ensure efficient billing.			

A lexical awareness-raising exercise at the discourse level might involve presenting a nonnative text with italicized words that high intermediate or advanced learners, working in pairs or small groups, would judge as appropriate or inappropriate and then suggest better choices for the words they felt were inappropriate:

> The following are some of my *successful* projects:

> (i) I developed a drug accounting system for the pharmacy, which was *appreciated* at the national level, (ii) I worked with Dietetics to improve the *manufacturing* of meals, and (iii) I *redesigned* the hospital classroom, *doing* a better learning *space* for all hospital *employees*.

Such an activity is very difficult, and the learners should be directed to make use of resources such as dictionaries, thesauruses, native speakers, and the teacher so that they can ask and answer relevant questions:

> What kinds of things do we "appreciate"?

> What verbs can be used to describe the preparation of meals?

> What can be "manufactured"?

> Does the verb *do* normally express a result?

The learners might also want to try completely blocking out the italicized words to see what lexical items they (or their consultants) would select, given the context of the entire passage.

Borg (1998) reports on a language teacher's approach to the teaching of grammar, which makes use of the students' errors in building classroom activities. Similar to Chaudron (1983), the teacher's position here is that using students' errors is a good way of creating a student-centered approach and of eliciting feedback and reactions to this data from the students. Furthermore, Borg's main message is that researchers should pay more attention to "teachers' pedagogical systems" and the beliefs and constructs that guide them, in order to better understand what grammar teaching in the second language classroom really entails.

As learners become adept at making targeted judgments and corrections, they can be asked to correct errors in their own language production whenever the teacher feels that they are consciously aware of the correct target form(s). Rather than marking up a learner's work, the teacher or tutor can ask questions to cue reorganization or refocusing of ideas and to suggest rewordings for sentences or phrases that contain grammatical or lexical errors. For example, consider this unedited opening paragraph from a low-intermediate ESL writer.[1]

College Life

> As term begins, students are busy to choose the right classes for themselves. Right classes are which they can get a good grade from by the end of the term. The most concern issue of a college student is how he can do well on the examinations and receive a good transcript.

As part of comprehensive feedback, a sheet attached to the essay can guide content reconsiderations and suggest rewordings that the learner can refer to when writing a second draft:

Organization and content suggestions
- make it clear at the outset that you refer to college/university education
- consider contrasting a concern for learning with the concern for simply getting good grades
- do all students share the same concerns?

Suggested rewordings

the term

busy choosing

The right classes are those in which

a good grade by the end of the term.

The greatest concern of a college student

a transcript with good grades.

Finally, there are two discourse-based approaches to error correction that are quite promising: (1) interview analysis for correction of oral discourse, and (2) reformulation for correction of written discourse. They are intended for learners at the intermediate and advanced level rather than for beginners.

In interview analysis (Wechsler, 1987) the teacher-tutor records an extended conversation with the learner and transcribes exactly what the learner has said (or gets the learner to do this if s/he is sufficiently advanced, with subsequent verification of the faithfulness of the transcript by the teacher or tutor). The transcription then becomes the material used for error correction. The learner reads over the transcription, which represents his/her own oral discourse, and with the teacher-tutor's help, learns to correct the errors with a colored pen or pencil. The focus of correction is ideally on inaccuracies that detract from the meaning the learner is trying to express. The learner repeats each form after making an agreed-upon correction and then rereads aloud longer segments several times after all the targeted errors have been corrected.

In reformulation (Cohen, 1983; 1985) the teacher-tutor takes a paragraph or longer text written by the learner and rewrites it in his/her own words (i.e., the teacher-tutor can change the overall organization, the grammar, the spelling, the words, and so forth to make it sound more natural and accurate but should strive to retain the original message). The learner then compares the reformulated version to the original to see if the message has been preserved. If not, meaning is negotiated and further changes are made in the reformulation until the learner agrees that the message is the same. Then the learner tries to understand why certain changes were made: Was the organization unclear? Were there grammatical or lexical errors? If so, what? Were there unidiomatic expressions?

Once language learners become expert in learning how to benefit from reformulations, they do not need to use teachers or skilled tutors each time for feedback. On occasion they can simply ask one or more good writers who are native or near-native users of the target language to reformulate a passage for them, and they can then analyze the similarities and differences between the original and the reformulation(s) to become better aware of their errors and problems within relevant authentic discourse contexts.

Both interview analysis and reformulation can be very time-consuming. They are probably more appropriate as individual tutoring strategies rather than as classroom activities. However, teachers can make certain adaptations such as getting students to tape-record a memorable story. Then the students can transcribe the story exactly as they told it on the tape – errors and all. After the teacher checks the accuracy of each student's transcription, the learners rewrite the story, trying to correct any errors they notice. In this type of approach teachers can supervise the work instead of doing it all themselves and students become more aware of their own learning problems within the context of their own discourse.

Discourse-grounded feedback and correction in the language classroom must fulfill two requirements:

    a. they should provide students with a better understanding of how language areas and discourse and pragmatic considerations may interact in their classroom activities

    b. they should provide students with the experience of employing both top-down and bottom-up processing strategies

This section has presented a few examples of such feedback and correction techniques, but obviously the list of possibilities is endless. It will ultimately depend on the language teacher's creativity to ensure that the learners are exposed to a variety of feedback and correction strategies.

TEACHER SELF-EXAMINATION OF PEDAGOGICAL DISCOURSE

Another application of discourse analysis to classroom teaching is suggested by Dobbs (1995), who advises teachers to first get the students' permission and then record their own tutorial sessions or one-on-one conferences with individual students. The teachers can later record classroom sessions once they are experienced in doing this activity, which should enable them to answer several questions. The questions stimulate awareness-raising and self-examination, and may lead to changes in the discourse patterns that the teacher chooses to use when tutoring or when teaching in the classroom.

Dobbs's checklist includes the following questions for language teachers regarding the instructional sessions they record:

1. What is the percentage of teacher versus student talking time?

2. What are the types and percentages of questions you asked – display versus referential? (Display questions are questions to which the teacher already knows the answers whereas referential questions are true questions asked by the teacher because s/he doesn't know the answer).[2]

3. What is the rate at which you spoke – too fast/slow?

4. How much student response time did you allow before speaking again?

5. How did you check for student understanding?

6. What did you do when the student(s) did not seem to understand?

7. How often did you give positive reinforcement – too often/not often enough?

8. Did you allow/encourage self-correction? When you did corrections, of what? how often? at what point?

9. Did the student(s) ever interrupt, sustain his/her talk, or initiate a topic?

10. Did you hear any anger, boredom, condescension, or frustration in your own voice?

The most general or overarching question that Dobbs wants teachers to address after doing this activity is to state explicitly what features of their own discourse or of their students' discourse they are now more aware. Acknowledging that there is no single "right" or "wrong" way for teachers to talk to students, Dobbs concludes:

> Whatever our students' ages, if we want to facilitate rather than dictate, we should try to increase our awareness of how patterns of discourse work. We should be aware that traditional patterns such as asking

> numerous display questions or the use or overuse of certain types of
> caregiver language tends to centralize authority in the teacher and to
> infantilize and even alienate the students. We should also be aware that
> asking referential questions, encouraging students not only to learn
> new information but to teach it . . . [are approaches that] give students
> more opportunity to use their second language, more control over their
> language learning experience and increased practice with analytical
> and critical thinking skills . . . .
>
> (Dobbs, 1995:26)

Dobbs here seems to take the currently popular pedagogical position, i.e., that display questions are not useful for the learner's language development whereas referential questions are. However, Koshik (1998) in a careful turn-by-turn analysis of talk in ESL writing conferences, concludes that effective pedagogical discourse will make use of display questions when the teacher is reminding the student of concepts related to grammar or rhetoric or when the teacher is doing consciousness-raising activities with the learner. Thus not all uses of so-called display questions are ineffective.

Cullen (1998) addresses teacher talk in the classroom by looking more closely at what actually happens in the classroom. Cullen's main point is that the criteria for assessing communicative use of classroom language needs to be based on ". . . what it takes to be communicative in the context of the classroom itself, rather than in some outside context" (186). Cullen further draws our attention to the fact that the primary function of teacher talk is to support and enhance learning. Subsequently, he mentions the need to recognize the importance of the pedagogical function of teacher talk within the classroom context and to view it as genuine communication. Like Koshik (1998) he argues that display questions are often pedagogically necessary, and when they are, they constitute legitimate classroom communication. Cullen's position is compatible with the approach we have taken in this book, where the classroom should be viewed as a discourse context within which language learning occurs and the members of the class viewed as a discourse community.

REFLECTIVE LANGUAGE TEACHING

The language teacher, like other contemporary school teachers, is faced with the need to develop professional knowledge and expertise through reflection and self-analysis. Reflective language teachers pay special attention to various events that take place in the classroom and then reflect on their actions, decisions, and overall performance in the classroom. On the basis of such reflection as well as previous experience, teachers can develop personal and professional convictions that will guide their work in the future and provide them with theoretical constructs as well as practical techniques that work.

In recent years attempts have been made to establish a connection between professional knowledge that is shaped by experience and its verbal manifestation in spoken or written narrative (Britton and Pellegrini, 1990; Bruner, 1986; 1990). This type of investigation into teacher knowledge is very much in line with one of the goals of discourse analysis (van Dijk, 1990), and narrative discourse is a particularly useful instrument for verbalization and reflection. The narrative-knowledge connection has come to occupy an important place in educational research (Carter, 1993; 1994; Connelly and Clandinin, 1988). By telling professional, interpretive stories about their experiences, teachers can impose order and coherence on that experience and develop their own practical knowledge.

A case study by Olshtain and Kupferberg (1993) of an expert foreign language teacher revealed a very powerful *professional knowledge* component that had been developed by the teacher based on reflection. The study was based on the analysis of data collected via a number of different techniques: classroom observation, oral interviews of the expert teacher, and the teacher's verbal report during her viewing of a lesson videotaped in her classroom. The findings pointed to the fact that this particular expert teacher had a clear and well-defined set of principles that guided her work, and she was able to verbalize these principles and relate them to professional experience. One such principle had to do with providing every student in her class the opportunity to produce meaningful speech during the lesson. She felt very strongly about the need for "meaningful speech" and thus often volunteered to take her class on field trips during which only English was spoken. When she watched the videotapes of her lesson, she was able to explain how important this feature was to her and how she was pleased to see the implementation of it during the lesson. Upon further reflection, she emphasized the need to expand these experiences to field trips.

In a continuation of this case study, a larger study was carried out with three groups of language teachers (Olshtain and Kupferberg, 1998): novice teachers, teachers with limited experience, and expert teachers. The instrument used for data collection was a *discourse questionnaire*, which consisted of a list of problem-solving items related to language teaching. For each item on the list the teachers were asked to react with a brief written narrative. Participants were instructed to tell a story relevant to the particular problem presented. Thus, for instance, a problem could present a hypothetical classroom situation in which the weaker students in the class were unable to participate in a communicative activity designed by the teacher because of their lack of proficiency, while stronger students were not challenged enough. The expert teachers tended to use *realis* descriptions in their personal reports, usually taken from their own classroom experience and life history. Present and past tense forms with active and highly transitive statements (e.g., I introduced the concept of debate teams; debates continued throughout the year; I make sure that each student gets an opportunity to speak in class) were predominant in their discourse. The novices, on the other hand, presented hypothetical, *irrealis* comments typically involving the use of modal verbs (e.g., I will answer this question hypothetically; I think I would talk to the students; One could develop a questionnaire for students to work with in pairs, and so forth). The inexperienced teachers had to fall back on ideas presented in their methodology courses during their preservice training.

It was obvious in this study that the experienced, expert teachers had appropriated and personalized important professional experiences and had reached a level of empowerment, which was reflected in their discourse via the use of realis statements. The novices, on the other hand, were still suffering from professional insecurity that was reflected in their discourse through the use of irrealis forms.

Professional narratives can serve language teachers in developing their practical knowledge component through the verbalization of real classroom experience. This technique can be used not only for research but first and foremost for teacher development and reflection and as a sound basis for team-teaching.

Ho (1995) suggests the use of lesson planning as a means of reflection to help inexperienced or preservice teachers make use of their limited experience to bring about self-development and professional growth. The procedure suggested by Ho operates within a series of lessons during which teachers have the opportunity to reflect, plan, act, and observe, thus constantly improving their teaching. Ho's procedure also combines the micro approach (directly observable behavior) with the macro approach (generalizations and inferences beyond the observed phenomena). There are, of course, other means of encouraging reflection such as teaching journals, lesson reports, audio and video recordings of lessons, peer observation, and many others. What all of these means have in common is the fact that teachers are encouraged to take a close, reflective look at their own work and consider it within the broader scope of language teaching.

We have seen how teachers can use knowledge of discourse to expose students to prototypical language routines and texts and to provide them with discourse-based learning activities. Teachers can also use the discourse produced by their learners in order to encourage elaboration or to provide feedback and correction. In addition to these possibilities, teachers can use discourse analysis to look at their own patterns of one-on-one interaction and classroom interaction and then reflect on what they have observed and make changes as needed. They can also record and analyze their own professional narratives, or critically examine their own lesson plans, as additional exercises in professional development.

ENGAGING LANGUAGE LEARNERS IN DISCOURSE ANALYSIS[3]

To support our belief that it is beneficial for language learners to do some discourse analysis as a part of their learning, we present three rather different instructional units designed to have students do discourse analysis as part of the language learning process: (1) a speech act (i.e., complaining), (2) a discourse-level grammatical distinction (*be going to* versus *will*), and (3) a writing task (the comparison/contrast essay). We also briefly discuss learner strategies and how they can impact on learner awareness of discourse.

A SPEECH ACT: COMPLAINING

Hawkins (1985) documents her use of discourse analysis to teach the complaint "script," i.e., the macrostructure of a speech activity, to high-intermediate level ESL students in an oral communication skills class.[4] The basic complaint script in English, according to Hawkins, involves two goals: to call attention to behavior the speaker finds objectionable and then to change that behavior. The two goals present the learner with a dilemma since s/he must strike a delicate balance and be polite yet assertive in calling attention to the objectionable behavior while at the same time achieving the goal of getting the person responsible to change his/her behavior.

Hawkins pretested the twenty-three students in her class by having them respond in writing to six prompts they heard orally that described situations designed to elicit complaints. For example:

> You take a morning off from work to go to the doctor because of
> a serious medical problem that is causing you pain. For two hours you
> sit in the waiting room. During your wait, you periodically check with
> the woman at the desk to find out why you haven't been called to the
> examination room. She keeps telling you that the doctor will be with you
> "in a few minutes" and she looks up and says, "Don't worry, the doctor
> will be with you in just a few more minutes. I'll call your name when
> it's your turn."

The prompts were taken from a study by Schaefer (1982), based on research to which a number of Evelyn Hatch's graduate students at UCLA had contributed. The prompts covered a variety of relationships between the complainer and the addressee, including social status, sex, and physical appearance.

Hawkins then carried out, as part of a variety of classroom activities, a four-step unit on complaints over the next three weeks. First, each student had to record and transcribe one native speaker responding to the same six oral prompts that Hawkins had used on the pretest. Second, the students were introduced to a discourse framework, which was based on the seven complaint components listed in Schaefer (1982) for analyzing the data they had collected:

Seven typical complaint components

(Some components may be missing or reordered in any given complaint.)

1. opener (O) – utterance that initiates the complaint
2. orientation (OR) – utterance that provides the addressee with information about the complainer's identity and/or intent in initiating the complaint
3. act statement (AS) – utterance that states the trouble source
4. justification
   a. of the speaker (Js) – an utterance by the complainer that explains why s/he is personally making the complaint
   b. of the addressee (Ja) – an utterance by the complainer that offers a reason for the addressee's having committed the wrong (e.g. "Maybe you didn't have time, but . . .")
5. remedy (R) – utterance that calls for an action to correct the wrong
   a. threat (T) – a type of remedy in which the complainer states an action s/he will execute depending on what the addressee does (e.g. "or I'll take my business elsewhere")
6. closing (C) – an utterance made by the complainer at the end of the complaint to conclude his/her turn.
7. valuation (V) – an utterance by the complainer that expresses his/her feelings about either the addressee or the wrong that's been committed. (Usually this part is found with other components such as act statements, e.g., "This pizza is terrible!")

As part of step two, Hawkins showed the students how this framework could help them not only to understand but to segment and classify the native-speaker data they had collected. She used several examples like the following one, which is a native speaker's response to the sample prompt on page 224, along with an analysis, to show her students how to analyze complaints:

Sample complaint along with sample analysis

        O: Well,
     AS: I've been waiting two hours.
Ja and V: I know the doctor might have gotten tied up, and that it's not your fault, but this is ridiculous.
Js and V: I've already taken three hours off from work, and I really have to be back at noon.
      R: Could you please see what you can do?
R and T: If I can't get in to see the doctor in the next ten minutes, I'll have to leave and simply schedule another appointment or find another doctor.
      C: Thanks.

In the third step of the unit Hawkins had her students work in small groups to analyze the data they had collected from native speakers. They then recorded the information on tally sheets provided by the instructor so that they could clearly indicate the similarities and the differences between the complaints produced by the native speakers and their own pretest complaints.

In the fourth and final step the groups came together as a whole class to combine the results of each small group. There was a class discussion about what native speakers do when they complain and what nonnative speakers do when they complain in the same situations, how their verbal behaviors differ, and what is – and is not – likely to be an effective complaint in English.

Hawkins subsequently gave her students a post-test in which they responded in writing to the same six original complaint prompts, which were again presented orally. Approximately three and one-half weeks had passed between the pretest and the post-test.

The pre- and post-test complaint data were ordered randomly and then were rated for effectiveness by a native speaker who owns a business and has to deal with complaints on a daily basis. Hawkins' statistical analysis of the pre- and post-test ratings indicated that there was a significant positive change in the effectiveness of student complaints after using the instructional procedure outline above, which consisted in large part of having the students learn about the structure of the complaints they had elicited from native speakers.[5]

A natural extension of Hawkins' work would be to focus on reactions to complaints. Language learners could deal with the more complete communicative interaction within which the person who is the addressee of the complaint has to react, and there is a continued exchange within which apologies, promises, or excuses might come up. It is important, however, to make sure that students are given sufficient choices of speech act realization to take into account the various pragmatic and situational features of the exchange. Boxer and Pickering (1995), who also happen to discuss the speech act of complaining, alert materials developers and textbook writers to the fact that real choices in natural communication also include indirect strategies for speech acts (an indirect complaint in our case) that are extremely important, especially when the speech act is likely to create conflict or antagonism. We would add that, especially when we focus on complaining, opting out of the speech act may also be a common – or even preferred strategy.

A DISCOURSE-LEVEL GRAMMATICAL CONTRAST: "WILL" VERSUS "BE GOING TO"

A very frequent and persistent question from ESL/EFL teachers and students is "What is the difference between *going to* and *will*?" Previous accounts, based on the work of Binnick (1972) and McCarthy and Carter (l995), among others, have offered something like this: *be going to* is more informal, immediate, and interactive than *will*, which is more neutral or formal; *be going to* primarily refers to the immediate future or plans in future time, but *will* has several other meanings that are modal in nature, such as promising, predicting with certainty, and so forth.

These accounts are certainly not wrong, but they are only partially useful to teachers and learners unless accompanied by relevant and fully contextualized data samples. The research of Suh (l989) suggests a complementary account of the two forms based on the discourse organizing functions of *be going to* and *will* in essentially monologic oral narrations dealing with future scenarios, something already briefly suggested in Chapter 4; namely, that *be going to* is used to frame and initiate a discourse episode while *will* is used for the subsequent details and elaborations. To teach this notion inductively to learners, we would expose them to several authentic texts such as the one on the gastric restriction procedure found in Chapter 4 on page 58 along with the following three example texts:

1. Finally, tonight on to the weather forecast for the South. The night's going to be rather cloudy, but most places will remain dry. The temperature will fall around 4 degrees Celsius near the coast, but a few degrees lower than this inland with some ground frost in some valleys and a few fog patches . . . and the winds, they'll be southeast . . . and moderate . . . tomorrow.[6]

2. Now today I'm going to do my lecture but . . . I'm sure they'll be curious about you and . . . if you'd be willing to come back and talk about some of these things I think it would be great. Maybe we'll just do . . . an interview hour where they ask questions.[7]

3. D: I think what is going to happen on the civil case is that the judge is going to dismiss the complaint that is down there right now. They will then file a new complaint which comes back to Ritchie again. That will probably happen the twentieth, twenty-first, and twenty-second. Then twenty days will run before any answers have to be filed and the depositions will be commenced so we are eating up an awful lot of time.[8]

Then the learners are asked to work in pairs or groups, first reading the texts for comprehension and then answering questions such as the following, which will help lead them to an understanding of the text-organizing functions of the two target forms:

1. Where does *be going to* occur in these texts?
2. Where does *will* occur in the these texts?
3. Which form seems to establish a frame or topic?
4. Which form seems to introduce supporting details or elaborations?
5. Which form seems to be more of a bridge with the present?
6. Which form seems to indicate a more distant future?
7. Do other forms intervene? If so, what is their role?

If the learners are very advanced and sufficiently sophisticated in analyzing discourse, it might be possible simply to instruct them to look for *be going to* and *will* in the texts and to come up with a generalization about their discourse functions. By suggesting some questions, we assume that most students need some guidance to complete such a task.

After each group answers these questions, the whole class can then regroup to compare results. The teacher mediates as needed. As a final step, the students can apply the text-organizing structure they have discovered to communicate brief narrative episodes that deal with the future by either speaking or writing informally on topics such as these: What are your plans for this coming weekend? What are your plans for the upcoming summer vacation? (We tested these topic questions informally with several native English speakers, all of whom followed the predicted pattern of use.)

THE COMPARISON/CONTRAST ESSAY

To test the efficacy of proposals that Celce-Murcia (1989) had made regarding the usefulness of having language learners do discourse analysis to enhance acquisition of the rhetorical skills needed for academic writing, Holten (1991) carried out a classroom experiment involving two sections of the same EFL/ESL writing course at UCLA (ESL 35: Developmental Composition). All students in both sections had taken a composition placement examination that included writing an essay in which they were asked to compare two different views of what the true measure of a knowledgeable person is (years of formal education or an ability to understand people and society and to behave appropriately).

Holten then administered an experimental treatment to one English 35 class of eighteen students, while another experienced instructor with a class of sixteen students followed the same syllabus outline but used her own process-oriented writing activities during the three weeks that the comparison-contrast essay unit was taught in English 35.[9] At the end of the unit an in-class essay was required of all the students; it was a comparison-contrast essay based on two readings dealing with the issue of homelessness by Kozol (1988) and Main (1988), essays that presented rather different points of view and that had been read and discussed quite thoroughly in both classes.

For the first step of the experimental treatment Holten had her class read an eight-para-graph essay from the *Los Angeles Times* entitled "Small Boats, Big Boats, Boys and Men" by Lloyd M. Krieger. She directed the students to fill out a form asking them to identify the sections of the essay that were developed using comparison-contrast as the focus; then they studied the article's organization and specified the linguistic and discourse devices used to develop the comparisons and contrasts. The results of each student's reading and analysis were discussed first in small groups and then by the entire class.

The second text-based activity that Holten had her students do was to read and analyze two short compositions written by native English-speaking UCLA students (not profes-sional writers) comparing and contrasting the transportation systems in Los Angeles and some other large city. The learners' instructions were to read the two texts about trans-portation and to look for the comparison-contrast organizational patterns used. Then they were told to study each text and fill out a grid to explain (1) why each writer had chosen the organizational pattern s/he did and (2) what linguistic and discourse-level devices s/he had used to develop the essay.

Here is one of the two native-English, student-generated texts the ESL 35 class analyzed:

Transportation in L.A. and Dublin

The cities of Los Angeles and Dublin have very different transportation needs. Consequently, the modes of transportation, both public and private, are very different as well. These differences can be explained when one examines the differences in the size of the cities, the different patterns of residence and the importance of private property.

Los Angeles is a huge city of over three million residents, and it encompasses an incredible land area. Dublin, on the other hand, is a very compact city. When one lives over ten miles from the city center, he is considered to live in the surrounding countryside. The result of these spatial differences is that Dublin is able to design a public transportation system that adequately covers its city territory. Los Angeles, on the other hand, covers such a huge sprawl that it is difficult to provide transportation to all areas of the city.

The residents of Dublin generally live in a more urban environment, often in multi-family dwellings located close to the town center. Los Angeles, however, does not really have a single town center. Also, there is a tendency for Angelenos to prefer single-family dwellings, often located in distant suburbs. The result of this is that L.A. residents must have their own car to get them from distant homes to their work in one of the many possible business districts. Dubliners, on the other hand, generally work in the downtown area. All the bus and train lines terminate at the central point along the river in the city center.

The most important difference which explains the reliance on private transportation in L.A. is California's love affair with the automobile. The ability to have one's own car gives one the freedom to pursue one's own individual goals, without relying on the arbitrary time schedules of public transportation. This desire for independence and private ownership is very much a part of American culture, particularly in the West. Ireland, however, gives less emphasis to these values. The transportation system of Dublin exemplifies an older, more traditional concept of city living and a more cooperative life style.

These activities, including the reading and discussion of the Kozol (1988) and Main (1988) articles on homelessness took place over a three-week period. On the final day of this unit the students in both classes wrote an essay in class expressing their own comparison-contrast interpretation of the two essays dealing with homelessness. When the comparison-contrast essay written for the placement test and the unit-final essays were compared for the eighteen students in the experimental class and the sixteen students in the control class, results indicated that eight of the experimental students (44 percent) made striking improvements in their ability to produce a coherent comparison-contrast essay whereas only four of the control students (25 percent) exhibited comparable progress. These results would seem to support the notion that teaching ESL students to do discourse analysis of authentic texts of the kind that they themselves will be expected to produce can have positive benefits for many of the learners.[10]

LANGUAGE LEARNING STRATEGIES

The humanistic approach to learning in general and to language learning in particular has placed the learner at the center of the learning process. As a result, the learner is viewed as an active and responsible partner. Accordingly, learners have to become more aware of the learning process, make choices and decisions, and self-assess their progress.

In the skills section of this book (Chapters 6 through 9) learner strategies were mentioned with reference to the various language skills. Although nonnative speakers may never be in full command of the target language, good reading or listening strategies may help them overcome various difficulties encountered during the interpretation process, and certain speaking and writing strategies may be useful in helping them avoid confusing errors that result in miscommunication. But in order to benefit fully from the use of strategies, learners have to become aware of their learning styles, listening and reading preferences, more successful individual strategies, and other choices available to them. Learners should ideally become well-informed decision makers and partners in the language learning process.

Scarcella and Oxford (1992) defined language learning strategies as ". . . specific actions, behaviors, steps, or techniques . . . used by students to enhance their own learning" (63). A discourse approach to language learning is compatible with an emphasis on individual learning strategies since it allows for the varied ways in which learners interpret meaning in context and build upon such experiences for use in future communications. Oxford (1990), mentioned in Chapter 9 on speaking, has suggested that there are six general types of language learning strategies: three direct strategies – memory strategies, cognitive strategies, and compensation strategies, and three indirect strategies – metacognitive strategies, affective strategies, and social strategies. In general, memory strategies help learners develop semantic mappings, use imagery and associations, and employ various mechanical techniques. Cognitive strategies focus on reasoning and analysis, and compensation strategies enable learners to overcome various limitations such as lack of vocabulary while speaking or inability to process an incoming utterance while listening. Metacognitive strategies help learners become aware of their learning strategies so that they can make choices, plan, organize, self-monitor, and self-evaluate by being mindful of their learning processes. Affective strategies help learners overcome various sources of anxiety and inadequacy, and social strategies lead learners to take advantage of social contacts and environments. It is obvious that a good language learner makes use of all or most of these strategies as appropriate.

The use of appropriate learning strategies often results in increased language proficiency and greater self-confidence (Cohen, 1990; 1998); it is often suggested that we help learners become aware of learning strategies so they can take full advantage of them.

Wenden (1991) emphasizes the importance of developing autonomous learners by encouraging students to become "successful" or "expert" learners by means of teaching them how to learn more effectively. It is often necessary to provide learners with some "learner training" in order to help them become successful learners, and part of this training is getting them to attend to discourse and context.

Learners who are aware of their learning strategies and preferences can become involved in deciding for themselves to what extent grammatical accuracy, for instance, is important to them or how they want to work on vocabulary enrichment. If learners decide that grammatical accuracy is important, they can spend individual time on practicing difficult forms by using various self-teaching materials such as computerized courseware or self-correcting workbooks. Similarly, if they are aware of the individual strategies for remembering new words or coping with the meaning of unfamiliar words within a text, they can consciously employ such strategies.

In the earlier sections of this chapter error correction was discussed. During error correction sessions in class, learners could be made aware that some grammar errors do not interfere with communication but simply sound nonnative or carry a social stigma. It will then be the learner's choice and decision to correct such errors once they have been pointed out. The teacher will help and guide the process, but the major responsibility for the correction will be the learner's.

Conclusion

Swales (1990) has pointed out several benefits of carrying out consciousness-raising activities with language learners that focus on the macro- and micro-structure of written discourse. Given the previous discussion, we feel his arguments can be expanded to include spoken as well as written discourse, and we have adapted his proposals accordingly so that benefits include the following: (1) learners improve both their receptive and productive language skills when teachers give attention to the structure and process of discourse; (2) learners examine general discourse features (i.e., top-down) before specific text features (i.e., bottom-up), and the general features help provide a context and an explanation for use of specific forms; and (3) learners develop metalinguistic awareness that is useful in critiquing their own speech and writing as well as that of others.

McCarthy and Carter (1995) have noted that focusing on discourse entails important changes for the way language is taught. In other words, traditional language teaching methodology (which includes presentation, practice, and production) may well need to be modified to include activities that involve learners in developing greater awareness of the nature of spoken and written discourse (and the differences between these modes). Instead of the traditional present-practice-produce sequence, they propose the following: illustration, interaction, and induction. By "illustration" they mean using real data wherever possible, presented in terms of choices that depend on context and use. By "interaction" they mean discourse-sensitive activities that focus on uses of language and negotiation of meanings, designed to raise learners' conscious awareness of critical features through observation and class discussion. By "induction" they mean getting learners to draw conclusions about the functions of different lexico-grammatical options, thereby developing a skill for noticing critical features of form. They conclude that such a teaching approach has "considerable potential for a more rapid acquisition by learners of fluent, accurate, and naturalistic . . . communicative skills" (1995:217).

Given all that we have said in this chapter and the preceding ones, we concur with McCarthy and Carter (1995). We would also like to add that language teachers who have used discourse-based approaches and materials in their classrooms (e.g., Hawkins, 1985; Holten, 1991) have reported that their students' reaction was very positive. The students volunteered that they had genuinely enjoyed the naturalistic data, the challenge of working with language at the discourse level, and learning from these activities. However, we must emphasize once more in this concluding chapter that language teachers must be knowledgeable about language in general and the discourse level of the target language in particular before their students can benefit from instruction that approaches learning language through discourse.

In addition to knowledge of discourse and ability to do discourse analysis, the pedagogical approach implemented in Chapters 10 though 12 also suggests new roles for language teachers, language learners, and instructional materials. The language classroom becomes a special type of discourse community in which teachers ideally become reflective classroom researchers who evaluate and rethink their approach, their attitudes, and their methods of presentation. The teacher is no longer simply the central authority figure and decision maker in the classroom but someone who embodies the role of a knowledgeable mentor, coach, or guide. Language learners cannot be passive recipients in such an approach. They must become more independent and learn to make choices and to initiate learning activities. They should be actively responsible for their own learning and aware of strategies and tactics that will help them improve. In particular, they should be able to use metacognitive strategies and self-evaluation to improve their language performance. In a discourse and context-based approach to language teaching, instructional materials should ideally offer choices to teachers and learners; they should be flexible and allow for adaptation to specific learner needs and contexts. They should be designed to facilitate the personal growth of both teacher and learners. The new roles may seem daunting to many, but they are highly desirable in that the approach we propose here encourages the positive development of both learners and teachers.

DISCUSSION QUESTIONS

1. What are some of the authors' arguments for teaching language through discourse? Can you think of any others?

2. What can a language teacher who has had no formal instruction or preparation in discourse analysis do to prepare for teaching language through discourse?

3. Do you feel that training in discourse is as important for language teachers as training in grammar or vocabulary? Why or why not?

4. At what proficiency level and what age can learners begin to benefit from learning language through discourse? Give your reasons.

SUGGESTED ACTIVITIES

1. Record a segment of your own classroom discourse (if you are currently teaching) or get the permission of another language teacher so you can record a session of his/her class. Then use the questions from Dobbs listed in this chapter (or an adaptation thereof) to analyze the classroom discourse.

2. Find a language learner who is willing to let you reformulate a piece of his/her writing. Read the text, ask questions about anything that is unclear, and then write a reformulation (restate the message in your own words). Then have a conference with the learner so that s/he can compare your reformulation with the original text and ask questions or let you know if the reformulation changes the meaning. Reflect on this experience. What did you learn from it? What did the learner get out of it?

3. Find a decontextualized language exercise (on vocabulary, pronunciation, grammar, listening, and so forth) in a textbook you have used or might use to teach language. Develop a better contextualized and discourse-based activity for teaching the same material.

4. If you teach younger learners, outline a unit that teaches language and content through context and discourse.

Suggestions for Further Reading

For insights into classroom language, see:

Cazden, C. (1998). *Classroom discourse: The language of teaching and learning.* Portsmouth, NH: Heinemann.

For discussions of discourse analysis that are addressed to language teachers, see:

Hatch, E. (1992). *Discourse and language education.* New York: Cambridge University Press.

McCarthy, M., & Carter, R. (1994). *Language as discourse: Perspectives for language teaching.* London: Longman.

On techniques teachers can use to study their own classroom discourse, see:

Fanselow, J. F. (1987). *Breaking rules: Generating and exploring alternatives in language teaching.* New York: Longman.

On the explicit use of discourse analytic techniques with language learners, see:

McCarthy, M., & Carter, R. (1995). Spoken grammar: What is it and how can we teach it? *ELT Journal, 49*(3), 207–218.

Riggenbach, H. (1991). Discourse analysis and spoken language instruction. *Annual Review of Applied Linguistics, 11*, 152–163.

Riggenbach, H. (1999). *Discourse analysis in the language classroom:* Vol. 1. *The spoken language.* Ann Arbor, MI: University of Michigan Press.

Swales, J. (1990). *Genre analysis: English in academic and research setting.* Cambridge: Cambridge University Press.

Endnotes

[1] The paragraph and suggested rewordings are adapted from Celce-Murcia and Hilles, 1988, pp. 166–167.

[2] Dobbs (1995) claims that both display and referential questions can serve as comprehension checks but that referential questions have been demonstrated to contribute more to the learner's language development. Many classroom researchers share this view. However, using transcripts of ESL writing conferences as her data, Koshik (1998) demonstrates that so-called display questions often do important pedagogical work with respect to raising the consciousness of learners about problems in discourse. Given Koshik's data and arguments, it appears that assumptions about "display" questions and "referential" questions will need to be reexamined.

[3] The research of Barbara Hawkins (1985), Kyung-Hee Suh (1989), and Christine Holten (1991) respectively form the basis for the first three sample units described in this part of the chapter.

[4] This is the ESL 34 class (Oral Communication for ESL Students) at the University of California, Los Angeles. Several of the enrolled students were foreign teaching assistants.

[5] Hawkins admits that she could have done several things to improve both her research design and her instruction such as making the pre- and post-test complaint prompts different but comparable, introducing and focusing on syntactic correlates of complaints (e.g., not every students noticed that *would* and *could* are more polite forms than *will* and *can*), and having the students give their complaints orally instead of in written form (this would be easy to do in the language laboratory). However, despite these reservations, we agree with Hawkins that her approach to teaching a useful speech activity such as complaining is on the right track.

[6] This passage is from the *Nationwide BBC*, February 20, 1975.

[7] This passage is from the UCLA oral corpus, a small in-house oral corpus used as a database for pilot studies. Note that the conditional "if" utterance is an evaluative aside and not part of the main oral narrative that is the future scenario.

[8] This passage is from the Whitehouse transcripts, 1974, p. 68.

[9] The class meets four hours per week: two meetings lasting two hours each.

[10] Swales (1990) has also had encouraging results using similar techniques to introduce rhetorical structure of written texts to foreign graduate students studying in the United States who need to master the scientific research article genre.

Glossary

applied discourse analysis (see *discourse analysis*)

appropriacy

> suitableness of the language used for the particular situation.
>
> > cf., **acceptable:** said of any situated usage that native speakers feel is linguistically and socially possible in their language. The term (*un*)*acceptable* covers a wider range of linguistic units/situations than (*un*)*grammatical*, and it is preferred to expressions such as (*in*)*correct* or *right/wrong*, since it does not have prescriptive overtones.

authenticity

> the degree to which the type of language and/or tasks that are used for teaching and learning a language have the qualities of natural – as opposed to contrived – speech or writing.

bottom-up/data-driven processing

> 1. interpreting the lowest-level units first, then proceeding to an interpretation of the rank above, and so on upward.
> 2. A way of language processing that makes use principally of information on the linguistic features that are already present in the data (e.g., spelling patterns, word order, grammatical inflections, word choices, and so forth).

channel

> the way in which a message is conveyed from one person to another (e.g., speech, writing). Further subcategories are possible (speech: face-to-face, telephone; writing: letter, newspaper, E-mail, and so forth).

co-construction

> joint construction of discourse during the ongoing negotiation of meaning between the speaker and the listener(s).

coherence

> the unity of a piece of discourse such that the individual sentences or utterances are connected to each other and form a meaningful whole with respect to the context of a situation, even when the connections are not explicitly made.

cohesion

> the grammatical and/or lexical relationships between the different elements of a text, which hold across sentences or clauses. Cohesion results from the use of various cohesive devices (e.g., reference, repetition, substitution) to explicitly link together all the propositions in a text.

collocation

> 1. the way in which lexical items co-occur regularly (e.g., a *tall* – rather than a *high* – building).

2. the restrictions on how words can be used together, for example, which prepositions are used with particular verbs, or which verbs and nouns are used together.

comment (see *topic*)

commissives

speech acts that speakers use to commit themselves to some future action, such as promises, threats, and refusals. For example:

If you don't stop fighting, I'll call the police. (threat)
I'll take you to the movies tomorrow. (promise)

content schema

one of the two types of schematic (or prior) knowledge; *content schema* refers to background information on the topic (see also ***formal schema***).

context

1. all the factors and elements that are nonlinguistic and nontextual, but which affect spoken or written communicative interaction.

2. the social, psychological, and physical setting in which language use takes place. The context often helps in understanding the particular meaning of the word, phrase, and so forth.

3. **discourse context** (see *co-text*)

contrastive rhetoric

the study of how written discourse differs across two or more different languages; often done by controlling genre and register.

cooperative principle

1. the general principle that Grice (1975) developed for conversation, which maintains, "Make your conversational contribution as is required, at the stage at which it occurs, by the accepted purpose of direction of the talk exchange in which you are engaged." This principle consists of four maxims – the maxim of quantity (be brief), quality (be true), relation (be relevant), and manner (be clear) – that can be considered basic assumptions that people follow in their communicative interactions.

2. a basic assumption in conversation that each participant will follow the same set of conventions ("maxims") when communicating and attempt to contribute appropriately, at the required time, to the current exchange of talk.

co-text

prior and subsequent textual forms and information that may have a bearing on interpreting some item in or portion of a text.

critical discourse analysis

a type of discourse analysis, which, assuming that discourse is not neutral, attempts to deconstruct and expose social inequality as expressed, constituted, and legitimized, explicitly or indirectly, through language use.

curriculum

a document of an official nature, published by a leading or central educational authority in order to serve as a framework or a set of guidelines for the teaching of a subject area (e.g., a language) in broad and varied contexts.

cf., **syllabus:** a more particularized document, which addresses content for a specific audience of learners and teachers, a particular course of study, or a particular series of textbooks.

declarative knowledge (in cognitive psychology)

information consisting of facts, concepts, rules, and images that are consciously known and thus can be described explicitly.

declaratives (in speech act theory)

speech acts that change the state of affairs in the world by being uttered. For example:

> Clergyman: *I now pronounce you man and wife.*
> Jury foreman: *We find the defendant not guilty.*

directives

speech acts that speakers use to get the listener to do something, such as commands, orders, requests, and suggestions. For example:

> *Please sit down.*
> *Don't do that.*

discourse

1. language forms that are produced and interpreted as people communicate with each other.

2. a continuous stretch of language – oral or written – which has been produced as the result of an act of communication and perceived to be meaningful, unified, and purposive.

discourse analysis

the study of language in use that extends beyond sentence boundaries.

cf., **applied discourse analysis:** a type of discourse analysis that is concerned with language teaching, speech analysis, the writing/reading process, genre/register analyses, and so forth.

discourse community

a group of speakers or writers who share a set of communicative purposes and use commonly agreed verbal conventions to achieve these purposes.

expressives

speech acts that express the feelings or attitudes of the speaker, such as apologies, complaints, compliments, and congratulations. For example:

> *I'm really sorry!*
> *The meal was very delicious.*

formal schema

a type of schematic knowledge that consists of knowledge of discourse organization or macrostructure with respect to different genres, different topics, or different purposes (see also ***content schema***).

genre

> a recognizable communicative event that uses verbal conventions in predictable ways to achieve communicative purpose(s) agreed upon by the members of the speech community in which it regularly occurs. Examples of genre are narrative (e.g., a story), exposition (e.g., a research report), and procedural discourse (e.g., a recipe).

grammar

> the inflections (morphology), word orders (syntax), and function words that serve as systematic resources for creating discourse and that also shape coherent discourse into formally acceptable phrases, clauses, and sequences.

illocutionary force

> the communicative force of an utterance. For example, the utterance "I am hungry" basically describes the speaker's physical state (**locutionary meaning**), but it takes on **illocutionary force** when it acts as a request, having the intended meaning of "please give me some food."

implication

> the hearer/reader is able to make certain inferences based on what is said or written that go beyond what is said; an implication is often but not necessarily true.

indirect speech acts (see *politeness*)

interactional discourse (see *transactional discourse*)

interlocutors

> people who are actively engaged in a communicative interaction.

language variation

> differences in choice of linguistic form (sounds, words, structures, and so forth) that indicate the geographical, social, ethnic, or historical origin, the gender, the register, the professional training, or affiliation of the user. Variation occurs at all levels of language use:

- Sound – *pen* pronounced as [pin] (rural and Southwestern United States) versus [pen] (general American)

- Word – *elevator* (American) versus *lift* (British)

- Structure – *Do you know John?* (modern English)
  Knowest thou John? (Elizabethan English)

- Registers

  – *There's several people waiting outside.*   Informal/spoken
  – *There are several people waiting outside.*   Formal/written:

- Speech Act ("suggesting")

  – *I suggest . . . .*   (direct, speaker has some authority or experience)
  – *You might try . . . .*   (formal, less direct, speaker has less authority)
  – *Why don't you . . . .*   (less direct, more informal)
  – *How about . . . .*   (very informal)

- Gender

  – *He's such a dear!*   (feminine register)
  – *He's a damn good guy!*   (masculine register)

lexicon (or **vocabulary**)

1. the words and collocations that serve as resources for creating discourse in conjunction with **grammar** (see also *collocation*).

2. often thought of as "receptive" lexicon (words a learner can understand) versus "productive" lexicon (words a learner can use).

literate/literacy

1. the ability to read and write a language.

2. styles and genres of discourse – whether written or spoken – that reflect a tradition of study and learning: essays, sermons, research articles, legal briefs, memoirs, and so forth.

locutionary meaning (see *illocutionary force*)

macropragmatics

an approach to the study of the relationship between grammar and discourse, in which one starts with a particular type of speech event or genre and uses a relevant corpus to characterize the overall macrostructure and then relates features of the macrostructure to microstructure textual elements.

cf., **microanalytic approach:** one begins with microstructure and, based on analysis of a corpus, proceeds to show the distribution and discourse functions of target forms (e.g., specific structures, inflections, words).

macrostructure

the underlying high-level structure that accounts for the overall organization of a text or discourse (see also *microstructure*).

metacognition

1. knowledge of the mental processes that are involved in different kinds of learning (e.g., recognizing which kinds of learning tasks cause difficulty, which approaches to a given task work better than others, and how to solve different kinds of problems, and so forth). Metacognitive knowledge is thought to influence the kinds of learning strategies learners choose.

2. a type of learner strategy used to enhance L2 language processing, which involves the planning, regulating, monitoring, and management of a language skill (listening, speaking, reading, or writing).

microstructure

low-level textual elements found in a piece of discourse, i.e., forms or constructions such as reference conventions, tense and aspect patterns, use of active versus passive voice, and so forth.

oral/orate

discourse styles and genres – whether written or spoken – typical of spoken language (conversation/dialog, nursery rhymes, story-telling, diary entries).

orthography

1. the systematic graphic resources that allow discourse to be visually represented. Such discourse is encoded through writing and decoded through reading.

2. Orthographic systems. Vary from language to language with some systems being alphabetic (e.g., English), some ideographic (e.g., Chinese), and some syllable-based (e.g., Korean).

performative verbs

> verbs that explicitly name the speech acts they perform, such as *apologize, complain, compliment, request, promise,* and the like.

perlocutionary force

> the effect on the addressee of an utterance used to perform a speech act (see also *illocutionary force*).

phonology

> 1. the systematic resources of sound, pitch, and rhythm that allow spoken discourse to be encoded and decoded in a given language.
> 2. The way these resources of sound, pitch, and rhythm may be sequenced or organized in a given language.

politeness*

> Showing awareness of another person's public self-image or face.
>
> **Positive politeness:** showing solidarity with another person.
>
> **Negative politeness:** awareness of another's right not to be imposed on.
>
> *Considerations of politeness often relate to the degree of **directness** expressed in speech acts. Since **indirect** speech acts, while they help lessen the force of the imposition on the hearer, are often harder to interpret, **conventionally indirect** speech acts are often used to make polite yet conventionally explicit requests such as "Could you close the door?" or "Do you wanna close the door?"

politeness principle

> the principle proposed by Leech (1983), the essence of which is to minimize unfavorable behavior toward the hearer or a third party while attempting to increase favorable consequences. This principle makes use of the notion of a cost-benefit scale, where the speaker's politeness or impoliteness relates to the hearer's benefit or cost, respectively.

pragmalinguistics

> one of the two subfields of general pragmatics; it is related to linguistics. Since pragmalinguistics concerns the pragmatic force of a linguistic token, pragmalinguistic failure is basically a linguistic problem, caused by differences in the linguistic encoding of pragmatic meaning (see also *sociopragmatics*).

pragmatics

> 1. the study of the relationships between the use and meaning of linguistic utterances and the social situations within which they are produced.
> 2. the study of how the meaning of discourse is created – or co-constructed – in particular contexts for particular interlocutors.
> 3. the study of the use of language in communication, particularly the relationships between linguistic forms and the contexts and situations in which they are used.

presupposition

> a proposition that cannot be denied or called into question, what interlocutors accept as given information.

procedural knowledge (in cognitive psychology)

1. knowledge concerning things we know how to do but which are not consciously known, such as "how to ride a bicycle," or "how to speak French."

2. the ability to apply complex cognitive skills automatically in appropriate ways without even thinking about them.

pronunciation (see *phonology*)

register

1. a socially defined variety of speech or writing (e.g., scientific, religious, legal, and so forth), which is distinguished from other registers by a distinctive set of lexical and grammatical features.

2. the level of formality or informality of an instance of discourse or its degree of technical specificity versus general usage.

representatives

speech acts that state what the speaker believes or knows, such as assertions, conclusions, and descriptions. For example:

> *This is a German dog.*
>
> *It was a very chilly, rainy day.*

schema (plural: **schemata**)

a pre-existing knowledge structure in memory, which typically involves the normal expected patterns of things and is essential to discourse processing. There are at least two types of schema (see *content schema* and *formal schema*.)

segmental phonology

the study that deals with the individual sound segments (e.g., vowel and consonant sounds) and their distribution and positional variants in a given language.

semantics

how meaning is encoded in language; deals largely with the meanings of lexical items (i.e., words).

sociopragmatics

a subfield of pragmatics related to sociology and societal rules of behavior. Sociopragmatics concerns the size of imposition, cost/benefit, social distance, and relative rights and obligations; sociopragmatic failure often results from cross-culturally different perceptions of what constitutes appropriate communicative behavior in a given context.

speech community

a group of people, identified regionally or socially, who have at least one language or speech variety in common.

strategies

procedures used in learning, thinking, communicating, and so forth that serve as a means of reaching a goal. In relation to language learning, strategies refer to those conscious or unconscious processes that language learners make use of in learning and using a language.

suprasegmental phonology

1. the study of how pitch patterns and rhythm units combine with sequences of sounds to express meanings and sociopragmatic functions.

2. in **tone** languages (like Chinese and Thai) pitch conveys meaning at the word level; in **intonation** languages (like English and Japanese) pitch conveys meaning at the phrasal or clausal level.

syllabus (see *curriculum*)

syntax

relationships between linguistic forms, how they are arranged in sequence, and which sequences are well formed or not.

text linguistics

a branch of linguistics, especially popular in Europe, that focuses on the analysis of written texts from a variety of fields and genres. Contextual information is often secondary to linguistic analysis.

top-down/knowledge-driven processing

1. interpreting discourse by reference to the high-level units first, then moving downward through the ranks below.

2. the type of processing strategy for interpreting and producing discourse that makes use of contextual features and prior knowledge to process new information.

topic

1. what is talked about or written about. In describing the information structure of sentences, a term for that part of a sentence that names the person, thing, or idea about which something is said (sometimes called *theme*).

2. a discourse entity that connects one part of the discourse to other parts through continuity in given information. The notion of topic runs through the entire discourse, helping people to understand what is being discussed. The topic may shift as the discourse progresses.

cf., **comment:** what is said about the topic (generally new or additional information sometimes called *rheme*).

transactional discourse

those instances of language use that involve primarily the transmission of information or the exchange of goods and services.

cf., **interactional discourse** primarily shapes and maintains social relations and identifies and expresses the speaker's/writer's attitude toward the topic or the interlocutor(s).

Vocabulary (see *lexicon*)

References

Adams, V. (1973). *An introduction to modern English word formation.* London: Longman.

Alderson, C.; Clapham, C.; & Wall, D. (1995). *Language test construction and evaluation.* Cambridge: Cambridge University Press.

Alexander, L. G. (1994). *Right word, wrong word: Words and structures confused and misused by learners of English.* London: Longman.

Allen, V. F. (1971). Teaching intonation: From theory to practice. *TESOL Quarterly, 5*(1), 73–81.

Anderson, A., & Lynch, T. (1988). *Listening.* Oxford: Oxford University Press.

Anderson, J. R. (l985). *Cognitive psychology and its implications,* 2nd ed. New York: Freeman.

Anderson, P. (l989, November). *Cohesion as an index for written and oral composition of ESL learners.* Paper presented at the annual meeting of the Midwest Modern Language Association. Minneapolis, MN, [ED 198529].

Angelil-Carter, S. (1997). Second language acquisition of spoken and written English: Acquiring the spectrum. *TESOL Quarterly, 31,* 263–287.

Argyres, Z. J. (1996). *The cross-cultural pragmatics of intonation: The case of Greek-English.* Unpublished master's thesis in TESL, UCLA.

Asher, J. (1977). *Learning another language through actions: The complete teachers guidebook.* Los Gatos, CA: Sky Oak Productions.

Asimov, I. (1985). Back to basics. *The American Way* [the magazine of American Airlines].

Austin, J. L. (1975). *How to do things with words,* 2nd ed. Oxford: Clarendon Press.

Bachman, L. (1990). *Fundamental considerations in language testing.* Oxford: Oxford University Press.

Bachman, L., & Cohen, A. (Eds.). (1998). *Interfaces between second language acquisition and language testing research.* Cambridge: Cambridge University Press.

Bachman, L., & Palmer, A. (l982). The construct validation of some components of communicative proficiency. *TESOL Quarterly, 16*(4), 449–465.

Bachman, L., & Palmer, A. (1996). *Language testing in practice: Designing and developing useful language tests.* Oxford: Oxford University Press.

Backmann, N. (1977). Learner intonation: A pilot study. In C. A. Henning (Ed.), *Proceedings of the first second language research forum* (pp. 30–37). Los Angeles: Department of English, ESL section, UCLA.

Bakhtin, M. (1981). *The dialogic imagination.* Austin: University of Texas Press.

Bardovi-Harlig, K. (1990). Pragmatic word order in English composition. In V. Connor & A. M. Johns (Eds.), *Coherence in writing: Research and pedagogical perspectives* (pp. 44–65). Alexandria, VA: TESOL.

Barnett, M. (1989). *More than meets the eye: Foreign language learner reading theory and practice.* Englewood Cliffs, NJ: Prentice-Hall Regents.

Batchelder, D. (1977). In D. Batchelder & E. G. Warner (Eds.), *Beyond experience.* Brattleboro, VT: The Experiment Press (The Experiment in International Living).

Batstone, R. (1994). *Grammar.* Oxford: Oxford University Press.

Baynham, M. (1995). *Literacy practices: Investigating literacy in social contexts.* New York: Longman.

Beebe, L. (1996, November). *Loose language: Pragmatic strategies for responding to rudeness.* Paper presented at the New York State TESOL Conference.

Bereiter, C., & Scardamalia, M. (1987). *The psychology of written composition.* Hillsdale, NJ: Erlbaum.

Berlin, J. A. (1982). Contemporary composition: The major pedagogical theories. *College English, 44,* 765–777.

Berlin, J. A. (1987). *Rhetoric and reality: Writing instruction in American colleges, 1900–1985.* Carbondale: Southern Illinois University Press.

Berlin, J. A. (1988). Rhetoric and ideology in the writing class. *College English, 50,* 477–494.

Bhatia, V. K. (1993). *Analyzing genre: Language use in professional settings.* London: Longman.

Biber, D. (1988). *Variation across speech and writing.* New York: Cambridge University Press.

Binnick, R. (1972). *Will* and *be going to.* In *Papers from the seventh regional meeting* (pp. 40–52). Chicago: Chicago Linguistic Society.

Blakemore, D. (1992). *Understanding utterances: An introduction to pragmatics.* Oxford: Blackwell.

Bloom, L. (1970). *Language development: Form and function in emerging grammars.* Cambridge, MA: MIT Press.

Bloome, D. (1993). Necessary indeterminacy and the microethnographic instruction. In M. Singer (Ed.), *Competent reader, disabled reader: Research and applications* (pp. 119–140). Hillsdale, NJ: Erlbaum.

Blum-Kulka, S.; House, J.; & Kasper, G. (Eds.). (1989). *Cross-cultural pragmatics: Requests and apologies.* Norwood, NJ: Ablex.

Bolinger, D. (1971). *The phrasal verb in English.* Cambridge, MA: Harvard University Press.

Bolinger, D. (1977). *Meaning and form.* London: Longman.

Bongaerts, T., & Poulisse, N. (1989). Communication skills in L1 and L2: Same or different? *Applied Linguistics, 10,* 253–268.

Boomer, G., et al. (1992). *Negotiating the curriculum.* London: The Falmer Press.

Borg, S. (1998). Teachers' pedagogical systems and grammar teaching: A qualitative study. *TESOL Quarterly, 32*(1), 9–38.

Bowen, J. D. (1975). *Patterns of English pronunciation.* New York: Newbury House.

Boxer, D., & Pickering, L. (1995). Problems in the presentation of speech acts in ELT materials: The case of complaints. *ELT Journal, 49*(1), 44–58.

Brazil, D. (1995). *A grammar of speech.* Oxford: Oxford University Press.

Brazil, D.; Coulthard, M.; & Johns, C. (1980). *Discourse intonation and language teaching.* London: Longman.

Breen, M. P. (1985). The social context for language learning: A neglected situation? *Studies in Second Language Acquisition, 7*(1), 135–158.

Breen, M. P. (1987). Contemporary paradigms in syllabus design. (2 parts.) *Language Teaching, 20*(2), 81–92, and *20*(3), 157–174.

Breen, M. P.; & Candlin, C. N. (1980). The essentials of a communicative curriculum in language teaching. *Applied Linguistics, 1*(2), 89–112.

Brinton, D.; Snow, A.; & Wesche, M. (1989). *Content-based second language instruction.* Boston: Heinle & Heinle.

Britton, B. K., & Pellegrini, A. D. (Eds.). (1990). *Narrative thought and narrative language.* Hillsdale, NJ: Erlbaum.

Bronowski, J. (1977). A moral for an age of plenty. In *A sense of the future: Essays in natural philosophy* (pp. 196–205). Cambridge, MA: The MIT Press.

Brown, C. (1981, March). *What discourse analysis reveals about tag questions.* Paper presented at the annual TESOL Conference. Detroit.

Brown, G. (1989). Making sense: The interaction of linguistic expression and contextual information. *Applied Linguistics, 10,* 97–108.

Brown, G., & Yule, G. (1983). *Discourse analysis.* Cambridge: Cambridge University Press.

Brown, G., & Yule, G. (1983). *Teaching the spoken language: An approach based on the analysis of conversational English.* Cambridge: Cambridge University Press.

Brown, H. D. (1994). *Teaching by principles.* Englewood Cliffs, NJ: Prentice Hall Regents.

Brown, P., & Levinson, S. (1978). Universals in language usage: Politeness phenomena. In E. Goody (Ed.), *Questions and politeness: Strategies in social interaction* (pp. 56–130). Cambridge: Cambridge University Press.

Bruner, J. (1986). *Actual minds, possible worlds.* Cambridge, MA: Harvard University Press.

Bruner, J. (1990). *Acts of meaning.* Cambridge, MA: Harvard University Press.

Bublitz, W. (1988). *Supportive fellow-speakers and cooperative conversations: Discourse topics and topical actions, participant roles and "recipient action" in a particular type of everyday conversation.* Amsterdam: John Benjamins.

Burnett, A. (1998). *The use of idioms in written discourse: A comparison of native and nonnative speakers of English.* Unpublished master's thesis in TESL, UCLA.

Burns, A. (1998). Teaching speaking. *Annual Review of Applied Linguistics, 18,* 102–123.

Burton, J. (1998). Current developments in language curriculum design: An Australian perspective. *Annual Review of Applied Linguistics, 18,* 287–303.

Bygate, M. (1987). *Speaking.* Oxford: Oxford University Press.

Bygate, M. (1998). Theoretical perspectives on speaking. *Annual Review of Applied Linguistics, 18,* 20–43.

Canale, M. (1983). From communicative competence to communicative language pedagogy. In J. Richards & R. Schmidt (Eds.), *Language and communication* (pp. 2–27). London: Longman.

Canale, M., & Swain, M. (1980). Theoretical bases of communicative approaches to second language teaching and testing. *Applied Linguistics, 1*(1), 1–48.

Carrell, P. L. (1982). Cohesion is not coherence. *TESOL Quarterly, 16*(4), 479–488.

Carrell, P. L. (1988). Interactive text processing: Implication for ESL/second language reading classrooms. In P. Carrell, J. Devine, & D. Eskey (Eds.), *Interactive approaches to second language reading* (pp. 239–259). New York: Cambridge University Press.

Carrell, P. L.; Devine, J.; & Eskey, D. (Eds.). (1988). *Interactive approaches to second language reading.* New York: Cambridge University Press.

Carrell, P. L. & Eisterhold, J. C. (1983). Schema theory and ESL reading pedagogy. *TESOL Quarterly, 17*(4), 553–574.

Carter, K. (1993). The place of story in the study of teaching and teacher education. *Educational Researcher, 22,* 5–12.

Carter, K. (1994). Preservice teachers' well-remembered events and the acquisition of event-structured knowledge. *Journal of Curriculum Studies, 26,* 235–257.

Carter, R., & McCarthy, M. (Eds.). (1988). *Vocabulary and language teaching.* London: Longman.

Cazden, C. (1995). New ideas for research on classroom discourse. *TESOL Quarterly, 29*(2), 384–387.

Cazden, C. (1998). *Classroom discourse: The language of teaching and learning.* Portsmouth, NH: Heinemann.

Celce-Murcia, M. (1977). Phonological factors in vocabulary acquisition: A case study of a two-year-old English-French bilingual. *Working Papers in Bilingualism, 13,* 27–41.

Celce-Murcia, M. (1980). On Meringer's corpus of "slips of the ear." In V. A. Fromkin, (Ed.), *Errors in linguistic performance: Slips of the tongue, ear, pen, and hand* (pp. 199–214). New York: Academic Press.

Celce-Murcia, M. (1989). On the need for discourse analysis in curriculum development. Paper presented at the annual TESOL convention, San Antonio, TX.

Celce-Murcia, M. (1990). Data-based language analysis and TESL. In J. E. Alatis (Ed.), *Proceedings from the Georgetown round table on languages and linguistics* (pp. 245–259). Washington, DC: Georgetown University Press.

Celce-Murcia, M. (Ed.) (1991a). *Teaching English as a second or foreign language.* Boston: Heinle & Heinle.

Celce-Murcia, M. (1991b). Discourse analysis and grammar instruction. *Annual Review of Applied Linguistics, 11,* 135–151.

Celce-Murcia, M. (1995a). Discourse analysis and the teaching of listening. In G. Cook & B. Seidlhofer (Eds.), *Principle and practice in applied linguistics: Studies in honor of H. G. Widdowson* (pp. 363–377). Oxford: Oxford University Press.

Celce-Murcia, M. (1995b). On the need for discourse analysis in curriculum development. In *Studies in language learning and Spanish linguistics, a festschrift for Tracy Terrell* (pp. 200–213). San Francisco: McGraw Hill.

Celce-Murcia, M.; Brinton, D.; & Goodwin, J. (1996). *Teaching pronunciation: A reference for teachers of English to speakers of other languages.* New York: Cambridge University Press.

Celce-Murcia, M.; Dörnyei, Z.; & Thurrell, S. (1995). A pedagogical framework for communicative competence: A pedagogically motivated model with content specifications. *Issues in Applied Linguistics, 6*(2), 5–35.

Celce-Murcia, M., & Hilles, S. (1988). *Techniques and resources in teaching grammar.* Oxford: Oxford University Press.

Celce-Murcia, M., & Larsen-Freeman, D. (1999). *The grammar book: An ESL/EFL teachers course,* 2nd ed. Boston: Heinle & Heinle.

Celce-Murcia, M., & Rosensweig, F. (l979). Teaching vocabulary in the ESL classroom. In Celce-Murcia, M. & L. McIntosh (Eds.), *Teaching English as a second or foreign language* (pp. 241–257). Rowley, MA: Newbury House.

Chafe, W. (1980). *The pear stories III: Advances in discourse processes.* Norwood, NJ: Ablex.

Chafe, W. (1982). Integration and involvement in speaking, writing, and oral literature. In D. Tannen (Ed.), *Spoken and written language* (pp. 35–53). Norwood, NJ: Ablex.

Chaudron, C. (l983). Research on metalinguistic judgments: A review of theory, methods, and results. *Language Learning, 33*(3), 343–377.

Chen, P. (1986). Discourse and particle movement in English. *Studies in Language, 10*(1), 79–95.

Chomsky, N. (1957). *Syntactic structures.* The Hague: Mouton.

Chomsky, N. (1965). *Aspects of the theory of syntax.* Cambridge, MA: MIT Press.

Chun, D. M. (1988a). The neglected role of intonation in communicative competence and proficiency. *Modern Language Journal, 72*(3) , 295–303.

Chun, D. M. (1988b). Teaching intonation as part of communicative competence: Suggestions for the classroom. *Die Unterrichtspraxis, 21,* 81–88.

Clapham, C. (l994). The effect of background knowledge on EAP reading test performance. Unpublished doctoral dissertation, Lancaster University.

Coady, J. (l993). Research on ESL/EFL vocabulary acquisition: Putting it in context. In T. Huckin; M. Haynes; & J. Coady (Eds.), *Second language reading and vocabulary learning* (pp. 3–23). Norwood, NJ: Ablex.

Cohen, A. D. (1983). Reformulating compositions. *TESOL Newsletter, 17*(6), 1, 4–5.

Cohen, A. D. (1985). Reformulation: Another way to get feedback. *The Writing Lab Newsletter, 10*(2), 6–10.

Cohen, A. D. (1990). *Language learning: Insights for learners, teachers, and researchers.* New York: Newbury House.

Cohen, A. D. (1994). *Assessing language ability in the classroom.* Boston: Heinle & Heinle.

Cohen, A. D. (1998). *Strategies in learning and using a second language.* London: Longman.

Cohen, A. D., & Olshtain, E. (1993). The production of speech acts by EFL learners. *TESOL Quarterly, 27*(1), 33–56.

Collier, V. (1989). How long? A synthesis of research on academic achievement in a second language. *TESOL Quarterly, 23*(3), 509–531.

Connelly, F. M., & Clandinin, D. J. (1988). *Teachers as curriculum planners: Narratives of experience.* Toronto: Ontario Institute for Studies in Education.

Connor, U., & Johns, A. M. (Eds.). (1990). *Coherence in writing: Research and pedagogical perspectives.* Alexandria, VA: TESOL.

Cook, G. (1989). *Discourse.* Oxford: Oxford University Press.

Corson, D. (1990). *Language policy across the curriculum.* Clevedon, England: Multilingual Matters.

Crookall, D., & Oxford, L. R. (1990). *Simulation, gaming, and language learning.* New York: Newbury House.

Crystal, D. (1969). *Prosodic systems and intonation in English.* Cambridge: Cambridge University Press.

Cullen, R. (1998). Teacher talk and the classroom context. *ELT Journal, 52*(3), 179–187.

Cumming, A. (1990). Expertise in evaluating second language compositions. *Language Testing, 7*(1), 21–29.

Cumming, A. (1998). Theoretical perspectives on writing. *Annual Review of Applied Linguistics, 18,* 61–78.

Cummins, J. (1979). Linguistic interdependence and the educational development of bilingual children. *Review of Educational Research, 49*(2), 222–251.

Dalton, C., & Seidlhofer, B. (1994). *Pronunciation.* Oxford: Oxford University Press.

Dobbs, J. (1995). Assessing our own patterns of discourse. *TESOL Journal, 4*(3), 24–26.

Douglas, D., & Selinker, L. (1985). Principles for language tests with the "discourse domains" theory of interlanguage: Research, test construction and interpretation. *Language Testing, 2*(2), 205–226.

Douglas, D., & Selinker, L. (1990). *Performance on a general versus a field-specific test of speaking proficiency by international teaching assistants.* Paper presented at the 12th Language Testing Research Colloquium, San Francisco, CA.

Dubin, F., & Olshtain, E. (1986). *Course design.* Cambridge: Cambridge University Press.

Dubin, F., & Olshtain, E. (1987). *Reading on purpose.* Reading, MA: Addison Wesley.

Dubin, F., & Olshtain, E. (1990). *Reading by all means.* Reading, MA: Addison Wesley.

Dubin, F., & Olshtain, E. (1993). Predicting word meanings from contextual clues: Evidence from L1 readers. In T. Huckin, M. Haynes, & J. Coady (Eds.), *Second language reading and vocabulary learning* (pp. 181–202). Norwood, NJ: Ablex.

Dunkel, P. (1991). Listening in the native and second/foreign language: Toward an integration of research and practice. *TESOL Quarterly, 25*(3), 431–457.

Duranti, A., & Goodwin, C. (Eds.). (1992). *Rethinking context: Language as an interactive phenomena.* Cambridge: Cambridge University Press.

Eisenstein, M. (1983). *Language variation and the ESL curriculum.* (No. 51, Language in education: Theory and practice series.) Washington, DC: Center for Applied Linguistics.

Eisterhold, J. C. (1990). Reading-writing connections: Toward a description for second language learners. In B. Kroll (Ed.), *Second language writing: Research insights for the classroom* (pp. 88-101). Cambridge: Cambridge University Press.

Elbow, P. (1973). *Writing without teachers.* New York: Oxford University Press.

Elbow, P. (1981a). *Embracing contraries: Explorations in learning and teaching.* New York: Oxford University Press.

Elbow, P. (1981b). *Writing with power: Techniques for mastering the writing process.* New York: Oxford University Press.

Ellis, R. (1998). Teaching and research: Options in grammar teaching. *TESOL Quarterly, 32,* 139–60.

Enkvist, N. E. (1987). Text linguistics for the applier: An orientation. In U. Connor & R. B. Kaplan (Eds.), *Writing across languages; Analysis of L2 text* (pp. 23–44). Reading, MA: Addison Wesley.

Fairclough, N. (1995). *Critical discourse analysis: The critical study of language.* London: Longman.

Fanselow, J. F. (1987). *Breaking rules: Generating and exploring alternatives in language teaching.* New York: Longman.

Farjeon, E. (1951). *Eleanor Farjeon's poems for children.* New York: Harper and Row.

Feuerstein, T., & Schcolnik, M. (1995). *Enhancing reading comprehension in the language learning classroom.* San Francisco: Alta Book Center.

Fillmore, C. (1981). Ideal readers and real readers. In D. Tannen (Ed.), *Analyzing discourse: Text and Talk* (pp 248-270). Washington, DC: Georgetown University Press. [Proceedings of the Georgetown University Round Table on Languages and Linguistics, 1981].

Flick, W. (1980). Rhetorical difficulty in scientific English: A study in reading comprehension. *TESOL Quarterly, 14*(3), 345–351.

Flower, L. S. (1979). Reader-based prose: A cognitive basis for problems in writing. *College English, 41*(1), 19–37.

Flower, L. S. (1985). *Problem-solving strategies for writing,* 2nd ed. San Diego: Harcourt Brace Jovanovich.

Flower, L. S. (1989). *Problem-solving strategies for writing,* 3rd ed. San Diego: Harcourt Brace Jovanovich.

Ford, C., & Thompson, S. (1996). Interactional units in conversation: Syntactic, intonational, and pragmatic resources for the management of forms. In E. Ochs, E. A. Schegloff, & S. A. Thompson (Eds.), *Interaction and grammar* (pp. 134–184). Cambridge: Cambridge University Press.

Francis, W. N., & Kucera, H. (1982). *Frequency analysis of English usage: Lexicon and grammar.* Boston: Houghton-Mifflin.

Fried-Booth, D. (1986). *Project work.* Oxford: Oxford University Press.

Friedlander, A. (1990). Composing in English: Effects of a first language on writing in English as a second language. In B. Kroll (Ed.), *Second language writing: Research insights for the classroom* (pp. 109–125). Cambridge: Cambridge University Press.

Frolova, E. (1993). *A comparative students of learners' use of bilingual dictionaries.* Unpublished master's thesis in TESL, UCLA.

Fromkin, V. A. (Ed.). (1980). *Errors in linguistic performance: Slips of the tongue, ear, pen, and hand.* New York: Academic Press.

Fry, E. (1975). *Reading drills for speed and comprehension,* 2nd ed. Providence, RI: Jamestown.

Gairus, R. & Redman, S. (1986). *Working with words.* Cambridge: Cambridge University Press.

Garnes, S., & Bond, Z. S. (1980). A slip of the ear: A snip of the ear? A slip of the year? In V. A. Fromkin (Ed.), *Errors in linguistic performance: Slips of the tongue, ear, pen, and hand* (pp. 231–240). New York: Academic Press.

Geddes, M., & Sturtridge, G. (1979). *Listening links.* London: Heinemann.

Gibson, E. J., & Levin, H. (1975). *The psychology of reading.* Cambridge, MA: MIT Press.

Gilbert, J. B. (1983). Pronunciation and listening comprehension. *Cross Currents, 10*(1), 53–61.

Givón, T. (Ed.). (1979). *Syntax and semantics, Volume 12: Discourse and syntax.* New York: Academic Press.

Goodman, K. S. (1968). The psycholinguistic nature of the reading process. In K. S. Goodman (Ed.), *The psycholinguistic nature of the reading process* (pp. 15–26). Detroit: Wayne State University Press.

Goodman, K. S. (1976). Behind the eye: What happens in reading. In H. Singer & R. B. Ruddell (Eds.), *Theoretical models and processes of reading.* Newark, DE: International Reading Association.

Gordon, C. (1987). *The effect of testing method on achievement in reading comprehension tests in English as a Foreign Language.* Unpublished master's thesis. Tel Aviv University, Israel.

Gough, P. B. (1972). One second of reading. In J. F. Kavanaugh & I. G. Mattingly (Eds.), *Language by ear and eye: The relationship between speech and writing* (pp. 331–358). Cambridge, MA: MIT Press.

Grabe, W. (1988). Reassessing the term "interactive." In P. Carrell, J. Devine, & D. Eskey (Eds.), *Interactive approaches to second language reading* (pp. 56–70). New York: Cambridge University Press.

Grabe, W. (1991). Current developments in second language reading research. *TESOL Quarterly, 25*(3), 375–406.

Graham, C. (1978). *Jazz chants.* New York: Oxford University Press.

Graves, K. (Ed.). (1996). *Teachers as course developers.* New York: Cambridge University Press.

Green, T.M. (1990). *The Greek and Latin roots of English.* New York: Ardsley House.

Grice, H. P. (1975). Logic and Conversation. In P. Cole & J. Morgan (Eds.), *Syntax and semantics 3: Speech acts* (pp. 41–58). New York: Academic Press.

Griffin, P., & Vaughn, B. (1984). *The nature of the interactive model of reading.* Paper presented at the 18th annual TESOL convention, Houston, TX.

Griffiths, R. (1991). The paradox of comprehensible input: Hesitation phenomena in L2 teacher talk. *JALT Journal, 13*(1), 23–41.

Gumperz, J. J. (1968). Types of linguistic communities. In *Language and social groups* (pp. 97–113). Stanford: Stanford University Press.

Gumperz, J. (1978). The conversational analysis of interethnic communication. In E. Lamar Ross (Ed.), *Interethnic communication.* Athens, GA: University of Georgia Press.

Gumperz, J. (1982). *Discourse strategies.* Cambridge: Cambridge University Press.

Gumperz, J., & Kaltman, H. (1980). Prosody, linguistic diffusion, and conversational inference. *Proceedings of the annual meeting of the Berkeley Linguistic Society, 6,* 44–65.

Haiman, J., & Thompson, S. (Eds.). (1989). *Clause combining in grammar and discourse.* Amsterdam: John Benjamins.

Hall, E. T., & Hall, M. R. (1990). *Understanding cultural differences: German, French, and American.* Yarmouth, ME: Intercultural Press.

Halliday, M. A. K. (1991). The notion of "context" in language education. In T. Le & M. McCausland (Eds.), *Language education: International developments* (pp. 4–26). Proceedings of the international conference, Ho Chi Minh City, Vietnam.

Halliday, M. A. K. (1994). *An introduction to functional grammar.* 2nd ed. London: Edward Arnold.

Halliday, M. A. K., & Hasan, R. (1976). *Cohesion in English.* London: Longman.

Halliday, M. A. K., & Hasan, R. (1989). *Language, context, and text: Aspects of language in a socio-semiotic perspective.* Oxford: Oxford University Press.

Hamilton, J.; Lopes, M.; McNamara, T.; & Sheridan, E. (1993). Rating scales and native speaker performance on a communicatively oriented EAP test. *Language Testing, 10*(3), 337–354.

Harada, T. (1998). Mishearings of content words by ESL learners. *CATESOL Journal, 10*(1), 51–70.

Harley, B.; Cummins, J.; Swain, M.; & Allen, P. (1990). The nature of language proficiency. In B. Harley, et al. (Eds.), *The development of second language proficiency* (pp. 7–25). Cambridge: Cambridge University Press.

Harris, D. P. (1990). The use of "organizing sentences" in the structure of paragraphs in science textbooks. In U. Connor, & A. M. Johns (Eds.), *Coherence in writing: Research and pedagogical perspectives*, (pp. 196–205). Alexandria, VA: TESOL.

Hartmann, R. R. K. (1980). *Contrastive textology: Comparative discourse analysis in applied linguistics.* Heidelberg, Germany: Julius Groos Verlag.

Hasan, R. (1984). Coherence and cohesive harmony. In J. Flood (Ed.), *Understanding reading comprehension* (pp. 181–219). Newark, DL: International Reading Association.

Hatch, E. (1992). *Discourse and language education.* New York: Cambridge University Press.

Hatch, E., & Brown, C. (1995). *Vocabulary, semantics, and language education.* New York: Cambridge University Press.

Hawkins, B. (1985, February). *Learning to complain through experience.* Paper presented at the Second Language Research Forum, UCLA.

Hayes, J. R., & Flower, L. (1983). Uncovering cognitive processes in writing: An introduction to protocol analysis. In P. Mosenthal, L. Tamar, & S. A. Walmsley (Eds.), *Research in writing* (pp. 206–220). New York: Longman.

Haynes, M. (1993). Patterns and perils of guessing in second language reading. In T. Huckin, M. Haynes, & J. Coady (Eds.), *Second language reading and vocabulary learning* (pp. 46–64). Norwood, NJ: Ablex.

He, A. W. (1994, March). *Elicited vs. volunteered elaboration: Talk and task in language proficiency interviews.* Paper presented at the meeting of the American Association for Applied Linguistics, Baltimore, MD.

He, A. W., & Young, R. (1998). Language proficiency interviews: A discourse approach. In R. Young & A.W. He (Eds.), *Talking and testing* (pp. 1–24). Amsterdam: John Benjamins.

Henning, G. (1992). Dimensionality in construct validity of language tests. *Language Testing, 9*(1), 1–11.

Heyne, P. (1983). *The economic way of thinking.* Chicago: Science Research Associates.

Hinds, J. (1980). Japanese expository prose. *Papers in Linguistics, 13,* 117–158.

Hinds, J. (1983). Contrastive rhetoric: Japanese and English. *Text, 3*(2), 183–195.

Hinds, J. (1986, March). *Coherence in Japanese expository prose.* Paper presented at the international TESOL convention in Anaheim, CA.

Ho, B. (1995). Using lesson plans as a means of reflection. *ELT Journal, 49*(1), 66–71.

Hock, T. S. (1990). The role of prior knowledge and language proficiency as predictors of reading comprehension among undergraduates. In J. de Jong & D. Stevenson (Eds.), *Individualizing the assessment of language abilities* (pp. 214–224). Clevedon, England: Multilingual Matters.

Hoey, M. (1991). *Patterns of lexis in text.* Oxford: Oxford University Press.

Holmes, J., & R. G. Ramos (1993). False friends and reckless guessers: Observing cognate recognition strategies. In T. Huckin, M. Haynes, & J. Coady (Eds.), *Second language reading and vocabulary learning* (pp. 86–108). Norwood, NJ: Ablex.

Holten, C. (1991, March). *Discourse analysis: A tool for students writing comparison/contrast essays.* Paper presented at the annual TESOL conference as part of the colloquium titled "Discourse Analysis and the Teaching of Writing," organized by Cynthia Holliday, New York.

Hopper, P. (1982). *Tense-aspect: Between semantics and pragmatics.* Amsterdam: John Benjamins.

Huckin, T.; Haynes, M.; & J. Coady (Eds.). (1993). *Second language reading and vocabulary learning.* Norwood, NJ: Ablex.

Hymes, D. (1967). Models of the interaction of language and social setting. *Journal of Social Issues, 23*(2), 8–38.

Hymes, D. (1972). On communicative competence. In J. B. Pride & J. Holmes (Eds.), *Sociolinguistics: Selected readings* (pp. 269–293). Harmondsworth, England: Penguin.

Johns, A. M. (1990). L1 composition theories: Implications for developing theories of L2 composition. In B. Kroll (Ed.), *Second language writing: Research insights for the classroom* (pp. 24–36). Cambridge: Cambridge University Press.

Johns, A. M. (1997). *Text, role, and context: Developing academic literacies.* Cambridge: Cambridge University Press.

Jones, D. (1991). *English pronouncing dictionary,* 14th ed. Cambridge: Cambridge University Press.

Jones, K. (1982). *Simulation in language teaching.* Cambridge: Cambridge University Press.

Jonz, J. (1987). Textual cohesion and second-language comprehension. *Language Learning, 37*(3), 409–438.

Jonz, J. (1989). Textual sequence and second language comprehension. *Language Learning, 39,* 209–249.

Jonz, J. (1991). Cloze item types and second language comprehension. *Language Testing, 8*(1), 1–22.

Kaplan, R. B. (1966). Cultural thought patterns in intercultural education. *Language Learning, 16,* 1–20.

Kaplan, R. B. (1972). *The anatomy of rhetoric: Prolegomena to a functional theory of rhetoric.* Philadelphia: Center for Curriculum Development.

Kaplan, R. B. (1982). An introduction to the study of written texts: The "discourse compact." *Annual Review of Applied Linguistics,* 138–152.

Kasper, G., & Blum-Kulka, S. (1993). *Interlanguage pragmatics.* New York: Oxford University Press.

Kaufman, D. (1997). Collaborative approaches in preparing teachers for content-based and language-enhanced settings. In M. A. Snow & D. M. Brinton (Eds.), *The content-based classroom: Perspectives on integrating language and content* (pp. 175–186). New York: Longman.

Kelly, L. G. (1969). *Twenty-five centuries of language teaching.* Rowley, MA: Newbury House.

Kenyon, J. S., & Knott, T. A. (1953). *A pronouncing dictionary of American English.* Springfield, MA: G. & C. Merriam Company.

Kim, K-H. (1992). *Wh-clefts and left dislocation in English conversation with reference to topicality in Korean.* Unpublished doctoral dissertation in applied linguistics, UCLA.

Kinsler, R. (1987). *A discourse analysis of "well."* Unpublished master's thesis in TESL, UCLA.

Kinsler, K. (1990). Structured peer collaboration: Teaching essay revision to college students needing remediation. *Cognition and Instruction, 7,* 303–321.

Kirkland, M., & Saunders, M. A. P. (1991). Maximizing student performance in summary writing: Managing the cognitive load. *TESOL Quarterly, 25*(1), 105–121.

Klippel, F. (1984). *Keep talking: Communicative fluency activities for language teaching.* New York: Cambridge University Press.

Knowles, P. L., & Sasaki, R. A. (1980). *Story squares: Fluency in English as a second language.* Cambridge, MA: Winthrop.

Koo, D-H. (1995). *An empirical study to test the distinctiveness of two hypothesized traits of language competence by designing and administering Korean tests.* Unpublished master's thesis in Teaching English as a Second Language, UCLA.

Koshik, I. (1998). *Reinvestigating the categories of display and referential questions in second language pedagogical discourse.* Ph.D. qualifying paper in applied linguistics, UCLA.

Kozol, J. (1988, Winter). Distancing the homeless. *Yale Review.*

Krahnke, K. (1987). *Approaches to syllabus design for foreign language teaching.* Englewood Cliffs, NJ: Prentice-Hall.

Kramsch, C. (1981). *Discourse analysis and second language teaching.* Washington, DC: Center for Applied Linguistics.

Krapels, A. R. (1990). An overview of second language writing process research. In B. Kroll, (Ed.), *Second language writing: Research insights for the classroom* (pp. 37–56). New York: Cambridge University Press.

Krashen, S., & Terrell, T. (1983). *The natural approach.* Hayward, CA: Alemany Press.

Kroll, B., (Ed.). (1990a). *Second language writing: Research insights for the classroom.* New York: Cambridge University Press.

Kroll, B. (1990b). What does time buy? ESL student performance on home versus class compositions. In B. Kroll (Ed.), *Second language writing: Research insights for the classroom* (pp. 140–154). New York: Cambridge University Press.

Kroll, B. (1991). Teaching writing in the ESL context. In M. Celce-Murcia (Ed.), *Teaching English as a second or foreign language* (pp. 245–263). Rowley, MA: Newbury House.

Kroll, B. (1998). Assessing writing abilities. *Annual Review of Applied Linguistics, 18,* 219–240.

Kumaravadivelu, B. (1994). The postmethod condition: (E)merging strategies for second/foreign language teaching. *TESOL Quarterly, 28*(1), 27–48.

Lagunoff, R. (1992). *A description of "they" as a singular pronoun.* Unpublished master's thesis in TESL, UCLA.

Lagunoff, R. (1997). *Singular "they."* Unpublished doctoral dissertation in applied linguistics, UCLA.

Lakoff, R. (1969). Some reasons why there can't be any "some-any" rule. *Language, 45*(3), 608–615.

Lakoff, G., & Johnson, M. (1980). *Metaphors we live by.* Chicago: University of Chicago Press.

Larsen-Freeman, D. (1997). Impressions of AILA 1996. In A. Mauranen & K. Sajavaara (Eds.), *Applied linguistics across disciplines* (pp. 87–92). Milton Keynes, UK: AILA.

Lautamatti, L. (1990). Coherence in spoken and written discourse. In U. Connor & A. M. Johns, (Eds.), *Coherence in writing* (pp. 29–40). Alexandria, VA: TESOL.

Lazaraton, A. (1991). *A conversation analysis of structure and interaction in the language interview.* Unpublished doctoral dissertation in applied linguistics, UCLA.

Lazaraton, A. (1994, March). *Question turn modification in language proficiency interviews.* Paper presented at the meeting of the American Association for Applied Linguistics, Baltimore, MD.

Lee, J. F., & Riley, G. L. (1990). The effect of pre-reading, rhetorically oriented frameworks on the recall of two structurally different expository texts. *Studies in Second Language Acquisition, 12*(1), 25–41.

Leech, D. (1995). *Characterizing formulaic expressions of knowledge claims in scientific English: An exploratory analysis using multiple linguistic approaches.* Unpublished doctoral dissertation in applied linguistics, UCLA.

Leech, G. N. (1983). *Principles of pragmatics.* London: Longman.

Leki, I. (1991). Twenty-five years of contrastive rhetoric: Text analysis and writing pedagogies. *TESOL Quarterly, 25*(1), 123–143.

Leki, I. (1995). Coping strategies of ESL students in writing tasks across the curriculum. *TESOL Quarterly, 29*(2), 235–260.

Leppänen, S., & Kalaja, P. (1995). Experimenting with computer conferencing in English for academic purposes. *ELT Journal, 49*(1), 26–36.

Levelt, W. J. M. (1978). Skill theory and language teaching. *Studies in Second Language Acquisition, 1,* 53–70.

Levinson, S. C. (1983). *Pragmatics.* Cambridge: Cambridge University Press.

Lindsay, D. B. (1984). *Cohesion in the compositions of ESL and English students.* Unpublished master's thesis in TESL, UCLA.

Long, M. H. (1985). A role for instruction in second language acquisition: Task-based language teaching. In K. Hyltenstam & M. Pienemann (Eds.), *Modeling and assessing second language acquisition* (pp. 77–99). Clevedon, England: Multilingual Matters.

Long, M. H. (1989). Task, group, and task-group interactions. *University of Hawaii Working Papers in ESL, 8*(2), 1–26.

Long, M. H., & Crookes, G. (1987). Intervention points in second language classroom processes. In B. K. Das (Ed.), *Patterns in classroom interaction in southeast Asia.* Singapore: Singapore University Press/RELC.

Lotto, L., & de Groot, A. (1998). Effects of method and word type on acquiring vocabulary in an unfamiliar language. *Language Learning, 48*(1), 31–69.

Lynch, T. (1998). Theoretical perspectives on listening. *Annual Review of Applied Linguistics, 18,* 3–19.

Main, T. (1988, May). What we know about the homeless. *Commentary.*

Mann, W., & Thompson, S. (1988). Rhetorical structure theory: A framework for the analysis of texts. *Text, 8*(3), 243–281.

Mannes, M. (1958). The half-people. In *More in anger* (pp. 38–39). New York: J. B. Lippincott.

Marisi, P. (1994). Questions of regionalism in native speaker OPI performance: The French-Canadian experience. *Foreign Language Annals, 25*(4), 501–521.

Markee, N. (1997). *Managing curricular innovation.* Cambridge: Cambridge University Press.

Martin, T. (1982). *Introspection and the listening process.* Unpublished master's thesis in TESL, UCLA.

McCarthy, M. (1991). *Discourse analysis for language teachers.* Cambridge: Cambridge University Press.

McCarthy, M., & Carter, R. (1994). *Language as discourse: Perspectives for language teaching.* London: Longman.

McCarthy, M., & Carter, R. (1995). Spoken grammar: What is it and how can we teach it? *ELT Journal, 49*(3), 207–218.

McCarthy, M., & O'Dell, F., with E. Shaw (1997). *Vocabulary in use: Upper-intermediate reference and practice for students of North American English.* New York: Cambridge University Press.

McNamara, T. F. (1996). *Measuring second language performance.* London and New York: Addison Wesley Longman.

McNerney, M., & Mendelsohn, D. (1987). Putting suprasegmentals in their place. In P. Avery & S. Ehrlich (Eds.), *TESL talk: The teaching of pronunciation* (pp. 132–140). Ontario, Canada: Ministry of Citizenship and Culture.

Meepoe, A. T. (1997, February). *How Thai ties: A discourse analysis of tying techniques in Thai.* Paper presented at the 23rd meeting of the Berkeley Linguistics Society, University of California, Berkeley.

Mendelsohn, D. (1995). Applying listening strategies in the second/foreign language listening comprehension lesson. In D. Mendelsohn & J. Rubin (Eds.), *A guide for the teaching of second language listening* (pp. 132–150). San Diego, CA: Dominie Press.

Mendelsohn, D. (1998). Teaching listening. *Annual Review of Applied Linguistics, 18,* 81–101.

Milanovic, M. (1988). *The construction and validation of a performance-based battery of English language progress tests.* Unpublished doctoral dissertation, University of London.

Mohan, B. (1986). *Language and content.* Reading, MA: Addison Wesley.

Morgan, J. & Rinvolucri, M. (1986). *Vocabulary.* Oxford: Oxford University Press.

Morley, J. (1991). Listening comprehension in second/foreign language instruction. In M. Celce-Murcia (Ed.), *Teaching English as a second or foreign language* (pp. 81–106). Boston: Heinle & Heinle.

Myers, M. (1987). The shared structure of oral and written language and the implications for teaching writing, reading and literature. In J. R. Squire (Ed.), *The dynamics of language learning* (pp. 121–146). Urbana, IL: ERIC.

Nation, I. S. P. (1990). *Teaching and learning vocabulary.* New York: Newbury House.

Nattinger, J. R., & DeCarrico, J. S. (1992). *Lexical phrases and language teaching.* Oxford: Oxford University Press.

Nellis, M. (1978, August). Accidental drug addiction. *Harper's Bazaar,* 34–150.

Nida, E. (1953). Selective listening. *Language Learning, 4*(3–4), 92–101.

Nolasco, R., & Arthur, L. (1987). *Conversation.* Oxford: Oxford University Press.

Nunan, D. (1988). *The learner-centered curriculum.* Cambridge: Cambridge University Press

Nunan, D. (1989). *Designing tasks for the communicative classroom.* Oxford: Oxford University Press.

Nunan, D. (1993). *An introduction to discourse analysis.* Harmondsworth, England: Penguin.

Nystrand, M. (1982). Rhetoric's "audience" and linguistics' "speech community:" Implications for understanding writing, reading and text. In M. Nystrand (Ed.), *What writers know* (pp. 1–28). New York: Academic Press.

Ochs, E. (1979). Planned and unplanned discourse. In T. Givon (Ed.), *Syntax and semantics: Discourse and syntax* (Vol. 12., pp. 51–80). New York: Academic Press.

Olshtain, E. (1987). The acquisition of new word formation processes. *Studies in Second Language Acquisition, 9,* 221– 232.

Olshtain, E. (1989). Changing directions in language curriculum design. *Annual Review of Applied Linguistics, 10,* 135–144.

Olshtain, E., & Barzilay, M. (1991). Lexical retrieval difficulties in adult language attrition. In H. W. Seliger & R. M. Vago (Eds.), *First language attrition: Structural and theoretical perspectives* (pp. 139–150). Cambridge: Cambridge University Press.

Olshtain, E., & Blum-Kulka, S. (1985). Crosscultural pragmatics and the testing of communicative competence. *Language Testing, 2*(1), 16–30.

Olshtain, E., & Cohen, A. D. (1991). Teaching speech act behavior to nonnative speakers. In M. Celce-Murcia (Ed.), *Teaching English as a second or foreign language* (pp. 154–165). Boston: Heinle & Heinle.

Olshtain, E.; Feuerstein, T.; Schcolnik, M.; & Zerach, B. (1993). *The junior files: File 2, English for tomorrow.* San Francisco: Alta Book Center.

Olshtain, E.; Feuerstein, T.; Schcolnik, M.; & Zerach, B. (1996). *Beginners' files: File one).* Tel Aviv, Israel: University Publishing Projects.

Olshtain, E., & Kupferberg, I. (1993). *Feedback as linguistic input in foreign language teaching: An expert case study.* Paper presented at the fifth conference of the European Association for Research on Learning and Instruction. Aix en Provence, France.

Olshtain, E., & Kupferberg, I. (1998). Teachers' professional knowledge as reflected in their domain-specific discourse. *Language Teaching Research (2/3),* 185–202.

Olson, D. R. (1977). From utterance to text. *Harvard Educational Review, 47,* 257–281.

Ong, W. (1982). *Orality and Literacy.* London: Methuen.

Östman, J-O., & Virtanen, T. (1995). Discourse analysis. In J. Verschueren, J-O. Östman, & J. Blommaert (Eds.), *Handbook of pragmatics.* Amsterdam: John Benjamins.

Oxford, R. L. (1990). *Language learning strategies: What every teacher should know.* New York: Newbury House.

Paltridge, B. (2000). *Making sense of discourse analysis.* Gold Coast, Australia: Antipodean Educational Enterprises.

Pennycook, A. (1995). *Cultural politics of English as an international language.* London: Longman.

Pennycook, A. (1996). Borrowing others' words: Text, ownership, memory, and plagiarism. *TESOL Quarterly, 30,* 201–230.

Perkins, K. (1998). Assessing reading. *Annual Review of Applied Linguistics, 18,* 208–218.

Peters, A. M. (1977). Language learning strategies: Does the whole equal the sum of the parts? *Language, 53*(3), 560–573.

Peterson, P. W. (1991). A synthesis of models for interactive listening. In M. Celce-Murcia (Ed.), *Teaching English as a second or foreign language* (pp. 106–122). Boston: Heinle & Heinle.

Phillipson, R. (1992). *Linguistic imperialism.* Oxford: Oxford University Press.

Pike, K. (1945). *The intonation of American English.* Ann Arbor: University of Michigan Press.

Prator, C. H., & Robinett, B. J. (1985). *A manual of American English pronunciation,* 4th ed. New York: Holt, Rinehart, & Winston.

Raimes, A. (1983). *Techniques in teaching writing.* New York: Oxford University Press.

Raimes, A. (1987). Why write? From purpose to pedagogy. *English Teaching Forum 25(4),* 36–41.

Reid, W. (1991). *Verb and noun number in English: A functional explanation.* London: Longman.

Ricento, T. K. (1987). *Aspects of coherence in English and Japanese expository prose.* Unpublished doctoral dissertation in applied linguistics, UCLA.

Riggenbach, H. (1991). Discourse analysis and spoken language instruction. *Annual Review of Applied Linguistics, 11,* 152–163.

Riggenbach, H. (1999). *Discourse analysis in the language classroom:* Vol. 1. *The spoken language.* Ann Arbor, MI: University of Michigan Press.

Rivers, W. (1981). *Teaching foreign language skills.* 2nd ed. Chicago: University of Chicago Press.

Ross, S. (1994, March). *Formulae and inter-interviewer variation in oral proficiency interview discourse.* Paper presented at the meeting of the American Association for Applied Linguistics, Baltimore, MD.

Rost, M. (1990). *Listening in language learning.* London: Longman.

Rubin, D. (1982). Adapting syntax in writing to varying audiences as a function of age and social cognitive ability. *Journal of Child Language, 9*(2), 497–510.

Rubin, D.; Goodrum, R.; & Hall, B. (1990). Orality, oral based culture, and the academic writing of ESL learners. *Issues in Applied Linguistics, 1*(1), 56–76.

Rumelhart, D. E. (1977). Toward an interactive model of reading. In S. Dornic (Ed.), *Attention and performance,* (Vol. 6., pp. 573–603). New York: Academic Press.

Rumelhart, D. E. (1980). Schemata: The building blocks of cognition. In R. J. Spiro, B. C. Bruce, & W. F. Brewer (Eds.), *Theoretical issues in reading comprehension* (pp. 33–58). Hillsdale, NJ: Erlbaum.

Rumelhart, D. E. (1984). Understanding understanding. In J. Flood (Ed.), *Understanding reading comprehension* (pp. 1–20). Newark, DE.: International Reading Association.

Rumelhart, D. E., & McClelland, J. L. (1982). An interactive activation model of the effects of context in perception. *Psychological Review, 89,* 60–94.

Rutherford, W. (1983). Language typology and language transfer. In S. Gass & L. Selinker (Eds.), *Language transfer in language learning* (pp. 368–370). New York: Newbury House.

Sacks, H.; Schegloff, E.; & Jefferson, G. (1974). A simplest systematics for the organization of turn-taking for conversation. *Language, 50*(4), 696–753.

Santos, T. (1988). Professors' reactions to the writing of non-native speaking students. *TESOL Quarterly, 22*(1), 69–90.

Sasaki, M. (1991). An analysis of sentences with nonreferential "there" in spoken American English. *Word, 42*(2), 157–178.

Sasaki, M., & Hirose, K. (1996). Explanatory variables for EFL students' expository writing. *Language Learning, 46,* 137–174.

Scarcella, R. C., & Oxford, R. L. (1992). *The tapestry of language learning.* Boston: Heinle & Heinle.

Scardamalia, M., & Bereiter, C. (1983). The development of evaluative, diagnostic, and remedial capabilities in children's composing. In M. Martlew (Ed.), *The psychology of written language* (pp. 67–95). Chichester, England: Wiley.

Schachter, J. (1990). Communicative competence revisited. In B. Harley et al. (Eds.), *The development of second language proficiency* (pp. 39–49). Cambridge: Cambridge University Press.

Schaefer, E. (1982). *An analysis of the discourse and syntax of oral complaints in English.* Unpublished master's thesis in Teaching English as a Second Language, UCLA.

Schank, R. C., & Abelson, R. P. (1977). *Scripts, plans, goals, and understanding: An inquiring into human knowledge.* Hillsdale, NJ: Erlbaum.

Schiffrin, D. (1981). Tense variation in narrative. *Language, 57*(1), 45–62.

Schiffrin, D. (1987). *Discourse markers.* Cambridge: Cambridge University Press.

Schiffrin, D. (1994). *Approaches to discourse.* Oxford: Basil Blackwell.

Schoonmaker, R., & Ryan, S. (1996). Does theory lead practice? Teacher's constructs about teaching: Top-down perspectives. *Advances in Early Education and Day Care, 8*, 117–151.

Seal, B. D. (1981). *In search of significant collocations.* Unpublished master's thesis in TESL, UCLA.

Seal, B. D. (1990). *American vocabulary builder* (Vols. 1, 2). New York: Longman.

Searle, J. R. (1969). *Speech acts.* Cambridge: Cambridge University Press.

Shaughnessy, M. (1977). *Errors and expectations: A guide for the teacher of basic writing.* New York: Oxford University Press.

Shoemaker, C. L., & Shoemaker, F. F. (1991). *Interactive techniques for the ESL classroom.* Boston: Heinle & Heinle.

Shohamy, E. (1984). Input and output in language testing. In T. Culhane, C. Klein-Braley, & D. Stevenson (Eds.), *Occasional paper – practice and problems in language testing,* (pp. 159–166). Essex, England: University of Essex, Department of Languages and Linguistics.

Shohamy, E. (1991). Discourse analysis in language testing. In W. Grabe (Ed.), *Annual Review of Applied Linguistics, 11,* 115–131.

Shohamy, E. (1994). The validity of direct versus semi-direct oral tests. *Language Testing, 11,* 99–124.

Shohamy, E. (1998). How can language testing and SLA benefit from each other? The case of discourse analysis. In L. Bachman & A. Cohen (Eds.), *Interfaces between second language acquisition and language testing research* (pp. 156–176). Cambridge: Cambridge University Press.

Shohamy, E.; Donitze-Schmidt, S.; & Waizer, R. (1993). *The effect of the elicitation method on the language samples obtained on oral tests.* Paper presented at the annual Language Testing Research Colloquium, Cambridge, England.

Shohamy, E., & Inbar. O. (1991). *The effect of the text and question type on test takers' scores on a listening comprehension test.* Paper presented at the tenth Language Testing Research Colloquium. Urbana, IL.

Shohamy, E.; Reves, T.; & Bejarano, Y. (1986). Introducing a new comprehensive test of language proficiency. *English Language Teaching Journal, 40,* 212–220.

Shohamy, E., & Stansfield, C. (1991). The Hebrew oral test: An example of international cooperation. *AILA Bulletin, 7.*

Shrum, J. L., & Glisan, E. W. (1994). *Teachers handbook: Contextualized language.* Boston: Heinle & Heinle.

Silberstein, S. (1994). *Techniques and resources in teaching reading.* New York: Oxford University Press.

Silva, T. (1990). Second language composition instruction: Developments, issues, and directions in ESL. In B. Kroll (Ed.), *Second language writing: Research insights for the classroom* (pp. 11–23). Cambridge: Cambridge University Press.

Silva, T. (1993). Toward an understanding of the distinct nature of L2 writing: The ESL research and its implications. *TESOL Quarterly, 27,* 657–677.

Sinclair, J. M. (1966). Beginning the study of lexis. In C. E. Bazell, J. C. Catford, M. A. K. Halliday, & R. H. Robins (Eds.), *In Memory of J. R. Firth* (pp. 410–430). London: Longman.

Skehan, P. (1996). A framework for the implementation of task-based instruction. *Applied Linguistics, 17*(1), 53–70.

Skehan, P. (1998). Task-based instruction. *Annual Review of Applied Linguistics, 18,* 267–286.

Smith, F. (1988). *Understanding reading: A psycholinguistic analysis of reading and learning to read,* 4th ed. New York: Holt, Rinehart, and Winston.

Smith, F. (1988). *Joining the literacy club.* Portsmouth, NH: Heinemann Educational Books.

Snow, M.A. (1998). Trends and issues in content-based instruction. *Annual Review of Applied Linguistics, 18,* 243–267.

Sperber, D., & Wilson, D. (1986). *Relevance.* London: Basil Blackwell.

Spolsky, B. (1994). Comprehension testing, or can understanding be measured? In G. Brown, K. Malmkjaer, A. Pollitt, & J. Williams (Eds.), *Language and understanding* (pp. 139–152). Oxford: Oxford University Press.

Stanovich, K. E. (1980). Toward an interactive – compensatory model of individual differences in the development of reading fluency. *Reading Research Quarterly, 16*(1), 32–71.

Stanovich, K. E. (1981). Attentional and automatic context effects in reading. In A. Lesgold & C. Perfetti (Eds.), *Interactive processes in reading* (pp. 241–267). Hillsdale, NJ: Erlbaum.

Stanovich, K. E. (1986). Matthew effects in reading: Some consequences of individual differences in the acquisition of literacy. *Reading Research Quarterly, 21*(4), 360–407.

Stansfield, C.; & Kenyon, D. (1988). *Development of the Portuguese speaking test: Final report to the U.S. Department of Education.* Washington, DC: Center for Applied Linguistics. [ED 296 586].

Stubbs, M. (1983). *Discourse analysis: The sociolinguistic analysis of natural language.* Chicago: University of Chicago Press.

Suh, K-H. (1989). *A discourse analysis of "be going to" and "will" in spoken American English.* Unpublished paper. Department of TESL and Applied Linguistics, UCLA.

Suh, K-H. (1992). *A discourse analysis of the English tense-aspect-modality system.* Unpublished doctoral dissertation in applied linguistics, UCLA.

Swain, M. (1985). Large-scale communicative language testing: A case study. In Y. Lee et al. (Eds.), *New Directions in Language Testing* (pp. 35–46). Oxford: Pergamon Press.

Swain, M., & Lapkin, S. (1997, March). *Task-based collaborative dialogue: Two adolescent French immersion students interacting and learning.* Paper presented at the annual American Association of Applied Linguistics meeting, Orlando, FL.

Swales, J. (1990). *Genre analysis: English in academic and research settings.* Cambridge: Cambridge University Press.

Tamanaha, M. (1998). *Interlanguage apologies by American learners of Japanese: A comparison with native speakers of Japanese.* Unpublished doctoral qualifying paper in applied linguistics, UCLA.

Teasdale, J. L. (1995). *The rhetorical effects of revision: Illustrations from students drafts.* Unpublished master's thesis in Teaching English as a Second Language, UCLA.

Terkel, S. (1977). *Working.* New York: Ballantine Books.

Thompson, S. A. (1978). Modern English from a typological point of view: Some implications for the function of word order. *Linguistische Berichte, 54,* 19–35.

Thompson, S. A., & Koide, Y. (1987). Iconicity and indirect objects in English. *Journal of Pragmatics, 11,* 399–406.

Todaka, Y. (1990). *An error analysis of Japanese students' intonation and its pedagogical application.* Unpublished master's thesis, UCLA.

Tribble, C. (1996). *Writing.* Oxford: Oxford University Press.

Upshur, J. A.; & Turner, C. E. (1995). Constructing rating scales for second language tests. *ELT Journal, 49*(1), 3–12.

Ur, P. (1981). *Discussions that work: Task-centered fluency practice.* New York: Cambridge University Press.

Ur, P. (1984). *Listening and language learning.* Cambridge: Cambridge University Press.

Urzua, C. (1986). A child's story. In P. Rigg & D. S. Enright (Eds.), *Children and ESL: Integrated perspectives* (pp. 93–112). Washington, DC: TESOL.

Vandergrift, L. (1997). The Cinderella of communication strategies: Reception strategies in interactive listening. *Modern Language Journal, 81*(4), 494–505.

van Dijk, T. A. (1990). The future of the field: Discourse analysis in the 1990s. *Text, 10,* 133–156.

van Dijk, T. A.; & Kintsch, W. (1983). *Strategies of discourse comprehension.* New York: Academic Press.

van Lier, L. (1989). Reeling, writhing, drawling, stretching, and fainting in coils: Oral proficiency interviews as conversations. *TESOL Quarterly, 23*(3), 480–508.

Vignola, M., & Wesche, M. (l991, April–June). L'ecriture en langue maternelle et en langue seconde chez les diplomes d'immersion francaise. *Etudes de Linguistique Applique, 94–115.*

Voss, B. (1979). Hesitation phenomena as sources of perceptual errors for non-native speakers. *Language and Speech, 22,* 129–144.

Vygotsky, L. S. (1962). *Thought and language.* Cambridge, MA: MIT Press.

Vygotsky, L. S. (1978). *Mind in society.* Cambridge, MA: Harvard University Press.

Wallace, D. L., & Hayes, J. R. (1991). Redefining revision for freshmen. *Research in the Teaching of English, 25,* 54–66.

Waltz, D., & Pollack, J. (1985). Massive parallel parsing: A strong interactive model of natural language interpretation. *Cognitive Science, 9,* 51–74.

Waugh, L. R., & Monville-Burston, M. (1986). Aspect and discourse function: The French simple past in newspaper usage. *Language, 62*(4), 846–77.

Weaver, C. (1972). *Human listening: Processes and behavior.* New York: Bobbs-Merrill.

Wenden, A. (1991). *Learner strategies for learner autonomy.* Englewood Cliffs, NJ: Prentice Hall.

Weschler, R. (l987). *An inquiry into interview analysis as a fine- tuning technique.* Unpublished master's thesis in Teaching English as a Second Language, UCLA.

White, E. M. (1995). An apologia for the timed impromptu essay test. *College Composition and Communication, 46*(1), 30–45.

White House Transcripts (1974). New York: Bantam Books.

Whitehead, A. N. (1975). *The aims of education and other essays.* New York: Macmillan.

Whorf, B. L. (1956). *Language, thought, and reality.* In J. B. Carroll (Ed.). Cambridge, MA: MIT Press.

Widdowson, H. G. (1978). *Teaching language as communication.* Oxford: Oxford University Press.

Widdowson, H. G. (1984). *Explorations in applied linguistics 2.* Oxford: Oxford University Press.

Widdowson, H. G. (1990). *Aspects of language teaching.* Oxford: Oxford University Press.

Widdowson, H. G. (1996). *Linguistics.* Oxford: Oxford University Press.

Wilkins, D. (1976). *Notional syllabuses.* Oxford: Oxford University Press.

Williams, R. S. (1994). A statistical analysis of English double object alternation. *Issues in Applied Linguistics, 5*(1), 39–58.

Wolfson, N. (1982). *The conversational historical present in American English narratives.* Dordrecht: Foris.

Wong, R. (1988). *Teaching pronunciation: Focus on rhythm and intonation.* Washington, DC: Center for Applied Linguistics.

Wu, R-J. (1994). *The effects of a prompt and background reading text on students' essays in a writing assessment context: Differences between ESL and English speakers.* Unpublished doctoral qualifying paper in applied linguistics, UCLA.

Yalden, J. (1987). *Principles of course design for language teaching.* Cambridge: Cambridge University Press

Yap, F-H. (1994, Fall). *A look at "else" in native discourse: Implications for ESL/EFL instruction.* Unpublished paper in applied linguistics and TESL, UCLA.

Yoshida, M. (1977). *A Japanese child's acquisition of English vocabulary.* Unpublished master's thesis in TESL, UCLA.

Young, R. (1995). Conversational styles in language proficiency interviews. *Language Learning, 45*(1), 3–42.

Young, R., & He, A. W. (Eds.). (1998). *Talking and testing: Discourse approaches to the assessment of oral proficiency.* Amsterdam: John Benjamins.

Young, R., & Milanovic, M. (1992). Discourse variation in oral proficiency interviews. *Studies in Second Language Acquisition, 14,* 403–424.

Yule, G. (1995). The paralinguistics of reference: Representation in reported discourse. In G. Cook & B. Seidlhofer (Eds.), *Principles and practice in applied linguistics: Studies in honor of H. G. Widdowson* (pp. 184–196). Oxford: Oxford University Press.

Yule, G. (1996). *Pragmatics.* Oxford: Oxford University Press.

Yule, G. (1997). *Referential communication tasks.* Mahwah, NJ: Erlbaum.

Zamel, V. (1985). Responding to student writing. *TESOL Quarterly, 19*(1), 79–101.

Author Index

Subject Index

academic world, summarizing in, 158–159

accommodating the hearer(s), 173–175

accuracy, product-based curriculum focus on, 190

actional competence, 25, 71*n*

adjacency pair, 10, 54
   flow of speech and, 173

adjectival clauses with deleted subjects, difficulties with, 130

advanced learners
   class project for, 180–181
   conversational styles of, on oral proficiency interviews, 208
   dictionary use by, 91–92
   teaching grammar to, 66–67

adverbial expression, *else* as premodifier of *where* in, 86

affective strategies, 229

affixation, word formation by, 81

affixes, patterns of use of, 82

age
   rules of appropriacy regarding, 171
   vocabulary variation due to, 78

alternative assessment battery
   developing, 211–212
   illustration of, 212–213

alternative questions, intonation of, 42–43

anaphoric (textual) reference, 3, 153, 154

answering machines, using, 111

antonym, 83

anxiety about writing, 145
   breaking initial barrier and, 154–155

apologies, structure of, 113–114

appealing for help, 176

applied discourse analysis, 5

appropriacy, rules of, 20
   adhering to, 170–171
   misunderstanding due to violation of, 165, 166

arousal, 169

article usage, teaching intermediate learners, 64

aspect markers, intersentential cohesion within written text using, 131
   See also tense, aspect, and modality sequences

assessment, 201–215

of ability to use grammar in context, 67–68

alternative procedures, developing, 211–212

criteria for determining quality of language elicited, 209

effect of test features on test takers' scores, 203–206

features of new types of, 212–213

oral proficiency tests, qualitative analysis of language elicited on, 206–209

rating scales and coding systems, 210–211

research on discourse and language, 203–209

theory of discourse and language, 202–203

assessment conferences, 212, 213

attrition, language, 95

audience
   curriculum design and identification of, 186
   of expository text, creating coherence for, 151
   of summaries, 158

audiolingual approach to vocabulary, 73

authenticity
   content domain and, 195–196
   genuine vs. imitation authentic, 195
   using variety of assessment instruments for, 212

authentic speech, learning from, 177

"baby talk," 78

background, 163*n*

background knowledge, misunderstanding due to lack of shared, 165, 166

barrier to writing, breaking initial, 154–155

beginners (of all ages)
   dictionary use by, 91
   teaching grammar to, 61–63

be going to
   future scenarios organized around, 58–59
   will vs., 226–227

bilingual dictionaries, 91–92

Board of Education, as stakeholder in curriculum, 187

body language, paying attention to hearer's, 173

borrowing, lexical, 82

bottom-up approach(es)
   to reading, 119–123
   in writing instruction, 161

bottom-up (data-driven) interpretation, 13–14, 15

bottom-up listening processes, 103, 104, 107–108
   teaching bottom-up strategies, 108–110

bottom-up processing
   prosody and, 36
   recognition of head noun during, 129–130
   text boundedness due to excess reliance on, 129
   of written text, interaction between top-down and, 146

bottom-up strategies, 8
   for listening, teaching, 108–110
   vocabulary knowledge and, 74–75
   in writing, 147–148, 152

business letter, coherence and format of, 125

Cambridge Assessment of Spoken English (CASE), 207–208

cartoons, teaching vocabulary with, 89

channel (medium), 5
   in oral communication, 165–166

children, vocabulary used only by, 78
   See also younger learners

Chinese, cohesive ties in, 54

chunking function of prosody, 37

chunks, lexical, 83

classroom
   integration of language skills and discourse processing strategies in, 180–182
   speaking in language, 176–178
   using target language outside, 177

classroom authenticity test, 195

closed-choice alternative question, 42–43

closed word classes, 76

closing phrases, ability to use, 175